Intellectual Property Law
in Ireland

Third Edition

To Kevin Boyle, mentor and friend   (B.C.)

To my dear Máire   (S.S.)

To my parents Noel and Bernie and to Peter   (N.H.)

INTELLECTUAL PROPERTY LAW IN IRELAND

Third Edition

by

Robert Clark

BA, LLM, Ph D, Barrister-at-law (King's Inns)
Professor Emeritus, School of Law, University College Dublin
Consultant, Technology and Life Sciences Group, Arthur Cox

Shane Smyth

BCL, BSc (Comp Sc), Solicitor, Partner, FRKelly

and

Niamh Hall

LLB (Dubl), Dip Comm Lit, Solicitor, FRKelly

Bloomsbury Professional

Published by
Bloomsbury Professional
Maxwelton House
41–43 Boltro Road
Haywards Heath
West Sussex
RH16 1BJ

Bloomsbury Professional
The Fitzwilliam Business Centre
26 Upper Pembroke Street
Dublin 2

978 184766 366 5
© R Clark, S Smyth & N Hall 2010

British Library Cataloguing-in-Publication Data
A catalogue record for this book is available from the British Library

Typeset by Marlex Editorial Services Ltd., Dublin, Ireland
Printed and bound in Great Britain by
CPI Antony Rowe, Chippenham, Wiltshire

Foreword to the First Edition

The law in relation to intellectual property has changed radically in the last few years. The Patents Act 1992, the Trade Marks Act 1996 and the implementation of a number of European Community directives in relation to copyright has brought Ireland into line with Europe in many respects. In addition, the whole scope of intellectual property has widened enormously with developments in technology, and perhaps it can also be said that the concept of intellectual property has changed. It now embraces a much more inclusive philosophy with a more equitable outlook, taking into account both the rights of the owner of the intellectual property to be fairly remunerated for his or her endeavour, and the rights or needs of the public to have access to and the benefit of the subject matter of such property.

It is, accordingly, fitting that two people from different backgrounds should come together to produce the first Irish textbook to deal with intellectual property in its entirety. Bob Clarke has a vast academic knowledge of intellectual property law and combines it with an enquiring mind which is very necessary to understand a changing concept. Shane Smyth, as well as being a lawyer, has all the practical experience gained over many years as a partner in the largest patent and trade mark agents in the country. In this book the union of the academic and the practitioner has given birth to an off spring which has the best of both, well researched and learned on the one hand and practical and all-embracing on the other.

I am particularly glad to see that the authors have dealt with intellectual property in a wide sense and have not restricted themselves to a commentary on various sections of legislation. They have considered in detail the large number of international conventions, treaties and agreements which now exist, and have placed our national provisions fairly and squarely in the context of European Community law and of international law generally. The traditional, somewhat insular, view of the subject in Ireland has thankfully been abandoned, and there is a serious attempt to foresee the world-wide problems which the 21st century will bring in this field.

It is not for a foreword to consider the details of a work such as this, that is for the critics and the commentators. Suffice it to say that it is an invaluable contribution which fills a huge void in Irish legal literature. In my view there would be a *prima facie* case of professional negligence against any solicitor, barrister, trade mark or patent agent - and perhaps even any judge, if such a cause of action could arise against a judge - who does not have this book in their library.

Mr Justice Brian McCracken
The High Court
Dublin 7
25 June 1997

Preface

Since the second edition of the book came out in 2004, the law relating to intellectual property has undergone extensive change and development. National legislation on patents, trade marks, copyright and designs has been amended by the Patents (Amendment) Act 2006, the Trade Marks (Amendment) Rules 2010 and the Copyright and Related Rights (Amendment) Act 2007. Innovations have been introduced such as the European Communities (Enforcement of Intellectual Property Rights) Regulations 2006 and the Consumer Protection Act 2007. The Commercial Court has revolutionised intellectual property litigation in Ireland. The exemptions and reliefs from tax for intellectual property expenditure have been revised. Meanwhile, European law has also moved on, with the EPC being replaced by the EPC 2000, the regulations on Community trade marks being amended and codified and the provisions on counterfeit goods and competition law being revised. Perhaps the greatest development has been as a result of the huge quantity of case law from Europe and, to a lesser but increasing extent, from Ireland. We have tried to show how this case law integrates with Irish and European legislation in order to make intellectual property law more accessible to all. In this regard, particular attention has been paid to try to make good use of recent judicial decisions to illustrate points of law that may be otherwise difficult to understand when couched in the dry language of a statute, or, even worse, the generalities that are favored in international treaties, or in the outpourings of the Community legislator.

Shane and Niamh would like to extend their gratitude to the partners, associates and staff of FRKelly for their invaluable assistance and contribution. Bob is grateful for the assistance afforded by the library staff within University College Dublin and the Institute of Advanced Legal Studies, London, and the library personnel (especially Therese) and his Practice Group colleagues, in Arthur Cox. The authors would also like to thank the personnel of Bloomsbury Professional and, in particular, Amy Hayes, for their guidance, expertise and endless patience.

Bob Clark
Shane Smyth
Niamh Hall

Dublin, 27 October 2010

Contents

Chapter 5   Patents Act 1992 – Maintenance and Dealings in Patents

Chapter 6   Patents Act 1992 – Infringements and Remedies

Chapter 7   Patents Act 1992 – Revocation and Proceedings before the Controller and Courts

Chapter 8   Patents Act 1992: Voluntary and Compulsory Licences

Chapter 9   Introduction to Copyright

Chapter 10   The Copyright Term

Chapter 11   Protected Works – Literary and Artistic Works

Chapter 12   Protected Works – Non-Berne Works

Chapter 18   Remedies for Copyright Infringement

Chapter 19   Moral Rights and the Droit de Suite

Chapter 20   Rights in Performances

Chapter 31   Trade Marks Act 1996: Relative Grounds for Refusal of Registration

Chapter 32   Trade Marks Act 1996: Infringement and Remedies

Chapter 33   Trade Marks Act 1996: Limitations On Rights Conferred

Chapter 34   Trade Marks Act 1996: Registration Procedure and Ownership

Appendices

Abbreviations

ADNDRC	Asian Domain Name Dispute Resolution Centre
BCI	Broadcasting Commission of Ireland
Berne Convention	Berne Convention for the Protection of Literary and Artistic Works 1971
BHB	British Horseracing Board
Brussels Convention	Brussels Convention on Jurisdiction and the Enforcement of Judgments in Civil and Commercial Matters
CA 1911	Copyright Act 1911
CA 1963	Copyright Act 1963
CDPA 1988	Copyright, Designs and Patents Act 1988 (UK)
CLÉ	Irish Book Publishers Association
Computer Programs Regulations 1993	European Communities (Legal Protection of Computer Programs) Regulations 1993
Comreg	Commission for Communications Regulation
COPAC	Common Patent Appeal Court
CPC	Community Patent Convention
CPR	Institute for Dispute Resolution (formerly known as Centre for Public Resources
CRRA 2000	Copyright and Related Rights Act 2000
CTM	Community Trade Mark
DBS	Direct Broadcast Satellite
DRP	Dispute Resolution Policy
EBU	European Broadcasting Union
EC Treaty	Treaty Establishing the European Community
ECHR	European Convention on Human Rights
ECJ	European Court of Justice
EEA	European Economic Area
EEC Treaty	Treaty Establishing the European Economic Community
EPC	European Patent Convention

EPO	European Patent Office
FSU	File swapping utility
GATT	General Agreement on Tariffs and Trade
HRA 1998	Human Rights Act 1998 (UK)
IB	International Bureau
ICANN	Internet Corporation for Assigned Names and Numbers
ICLA	Irish Copyright Licensing Agency
ICPPA 1927	Industrial and Commercial Property (Protection) Act 1927
IDA 2001	Industrial Designs Act 2001
IEDR	.ie Domain Registry
IMRO	Irish Music Rights Organisation
INFACT	Irish National Federation Against Copyright Theft
IPEA	the International Preliminary Examining Authority
IPIC	Treaty Treaty on Intellectual Property in respect of Integrated Circuits
IPRP	International Preliminary Report on Patentability
ISA	International Searching Authority
ISR	international search report
Lisbon Agreement	Lisbon Agreement for the Protection of Appellations of Origin and their International Registration 1958
Madrid Agreement	Madrid Agreement for the Representation of False or Deceptive Indications of Source of Goods 1891
Madrid Protocol	Protocol Relating to the Madrid Agreement Concerning the International Registration of Marks 1989
MCPS Mechanical	Copyright Protection Society
MCPSI Mechanical	Copyright Protection Society Ireland
NAF	National Arbitration Forum
OHIM	Office for Harmonisation in the Internal Market
PA 1964	Patents Act 1964
PA 1992	Patents Act 1992
Paris Convention	Paris Convention for the Protection of Industrial Property 1893

PCT	Patent Co-operation Treaty
PDO	Protected Designations of Origin
PGI	Protected Geographical Indications
pma	post mortem auctoris
PPA	Performers Protection Act 1968
PPI	Phonographic Performance Ireland
PRS	Performing Right Society and Performers Ltd
Rome Convention	Rome Convention for the Protection of Performers, Producers of Phonograms and Broadcasting Organisations (1961)
RTE	Radio Telefís Éireann
SPC	Supplementary Protection Certificate
TEU	Treaty on European Union
TLD	Top Level Domain
TLT	Trademark Law Treaty
TMA 1963	Trade Marks Act 1963
TMA 1996	Trade Marks Act 1996
TRIPS	Trade-Related Aspects of Intellectual Property Rights
UDRP	Uniform Domain Name Dispute Resolution Policy
UPOV	Convention Convention for the Protection of New Varieties of Plants – (UPOV: *Union Pour La Protection Des Obtentions Végétales*)
Washington Treaty	Treaty on Intellectual Property in respect of Integrated Circuits
WCT	World Intellectual Property Organisation Copyright Treaty
WIPO	World Intellectual Property Organisation
WPPT	World Intellectual Property Organisation's Phonograms and Performances Treaty
WTO	World Trade Organisation

Table of Cases

B

C

D

E

F

G

H

I

M

O

P

T

X

Y

Z

Decisions of the European Court are listed below numerically – these decisions are also included in the preceding alphabetical list

Tables of Statutes

Other Jurisdictions

Table of Statutory Instruments

Table of EU and International Legislation

Regulations

Treaties and Conventions

Chapter 1

Patents: A Brief History and Introduction

INTRODUCTION

[1.01] The level of use of the patent system by Irish nationals and Irish entities has been relatively low. This could be put down to a lack of inventiveness, but it could equally be attributed to a lack of awareness of the importance of a system which rewards even a low level of inventiveness with monopoly rights and which can often be the only effective way of protecting innovation.

The early laws of Ireland, the Brehon laws, recognised copyright[1] but not the concept of a protective right for inventions. As far back as 1474, the Venetians established a form of patent law which granted protection for a 10-year term. During the reign of James I (1566–1625), the Brehon laws were abolished and the common law of England became legally established in Ireland. The Statute of Monopolies 1623[2] was the first English statute which specifically referred to patents for inventions and many analogies can be drawn between this statute and modern patent legislation. Under s 6 of the Statute of Monopolies 1623, a 14-year patent monopoly was granted to 'any manner of new manufactures'[3] and 'to the true and first inventor and inventors of such manufactures'.[4] There were, of course, limitations imposed on this monopoly right including that it could not be used in a manner 'contrary to the law nor mischievous to the State by raising prices of commodities at home or hurt of trade, or generally inconvenient'. Again, these are concepts very similar to those found in modern legislation which provides that inventions are not patentable where their commercial exploitation would be contrary to public order or morality,[5] and which also provides for compulsory licences in a broad range of circumstances.[6]

[1.02] An example of the early grant of a monopoly right in Ireland was that given to William Wood on 12 July 1722[7] relating to the manufacture of copper coins for Ireland.

---

1   See Ch 9.
2   The statute was actually passed on 25 May 1624.
3   See Patents Act 1964 (PA 1964), s 2 and definition of invention.
4   See PA 1964, s 6(1)(a).
5   Patents Act 1992 (PA 1992), s 10(1)(a) as amended by the Patents (Amendment) Act 2006, but the section goes on to say that the exploitation shall not be deemed to be so contrary only because it is prohibited by law.
6   PA 1992, s 70 as amended by the Patents (Amendment) Act 2006.
7   Tomkins, 'A Short Historical Revision of the Law on the Protection of Industrial Property in Ireland' (Transactions of the Chartered Institute of Patent Agents) (1968–9) 87 CIPA cii).

This patent was later to be rescinded but not before Mr Wood received substantial compensation.[8] Prior to 1852, the cost, delay and cumbersome procedure for obtaining the grant of letters patent (the original term for the document granting the registration of a patent) were considered to be prohibitive. By modern day standards, the delay, for example of six months in 1850, would now be considered as insignificant. The relative cost was, however, sizeable.[9]

[1.03] The Patent Law Amendment Act 1853 established a single Patent Office for England, Scotland and Ireland, from which a single granted patent gave protection for Great Britain, Ireland, the Channel Islands and the Isle of Man. The effect of this Act was to dramatically increase the number of patents, applicants no doubt encouraged by the significant decrease in the cost of obtaining a patent. The Act did, however, introduce the concept of renewal fees to keep a patent in force. Renewal fees are now a feature of the patent laws of most jurisdictions.

[1.04] Although not repealing s 6 of the Statute of Monopolies,[10] the Patents, Designs and Trade Marks Act 1883 radically reformed patent law. The Board of Trade was empowered to order a compulsory licence on grounds very similar to those contained in s 70(2)(a), (b), and (d) of the Patents Act 1992 (PA 1992) and the preceding statute, the Patents Act 1964 (PA 1964). Importantly, the 1883 Act introduced the examination of patent applications by specially trained Examiners in the Patent Office, whose duties included examination of the sufficiency of disclosure in the patent specification. Another feature which has filtered through to modern legislation is provision for pre-application disclosure at certain exhibitions.[11] The Industrial Exhibitions Act 1865 allowed for the filing of a patent application subsequent to disclosure at a duly certified industrial exhibition.

[1.05] Certain grounds of opposition were allowed under the Patents, Designs and Trade Marks Act 1883, namely, 'obtaining', 'prior patenting', 'interference' and conflict with a pending, and hence unpublished, patent application. The ground of opposition based on a pending application imposed a duty on an Examiner to report to the Comptroller if a second application comprising the same invention was filed during the pendency of an earlier application. This duty was abolished by the Patents, Designs and Trade Marks Act 1888.

[1.06] Modern Irish legislation contains detailed provisions regarding the registration of patent agents, eligibility to act as a patent agent and the maintenance and control of the Register of Patent Agents.[12] The origins of this lie in the Patents, Designs and Trade Marks Act 1888 and the Register of Patent Agents Rules 1889.

---

8   Murdoch, *Invention and the Irish Patent System* (University of Dublin – Administrative Research Bureau, 1971).
9   Davenport, *The United Kingdom Patent System* (Kenneth Mason, 1979).
10 See para **[1.01]** above.
11 PA 1992, s 12(1)(b).
12 PA 1992, Pt X.

[1.07] A feature of the Patents Act 1902 was the introduction of examination as to the novelty of an invention. This involved a search that was restricted to British patent specifications of the preceding 50 years. Such novelty searches did not actually commence until 1905.

[1.08] It is common for a patent infringement action to be met with a counterclaim of invalidity of the patent. Until the Patents and Designs Act 1907, any such claim had to be made by a separate petition for revocation. Under the 1907 Act, invalidity could be counterclaimed by way of defence to the infringement proceedings.[13] Because patent protection confers rights, even against an innocent infringer, the 1907 Act provided a limitation on liability for damages for patent infringement in the case of parties who could prove that they had no reason to know of the existence of the patent. This provision, together with a statement that such knowledge could not be inferred from the use of the words 'patent' or 'patented' without the number of the patent on the product, is still part of modern Irish legislation.[14]

[1.09] The last piece of patent legislation to be passed before the foundation of the State was the Patents and Designs Act 1919 which increased the normal term of a patent from 14 years to 16 years and it was not until the PA 1992 that this became 20 years. The 1919 Act also provided that a patentee could offer a licence as of right and, to encourage this, a patent so endorsed paid only half of the normal renewal fees.

[1.10] The establishment of the Irish Free State (Saorstát Éireann) in 1921 left the position regarding patents in a vacuum. No mention was made of patents in the Irish Free State Constitution 1922 or in the Treaty forming part of the Constitution. Provided there was no inconsistency with the Constitution, the laws in force in the Irish Free State at the time of the coming into operation of the Constitution continued to be of full force and effect until repeal or amendment by enactment of the Oireachtas.[15] This repeal took place in 1927 and since the foundation of the Irish Free State there have been four major statutes dealing with the patent system:

(a) the Industrial and Commercial Property (Protection) Act 1927;[16]
(b) the PA 1964;
(c) the PA 1992,
(d) the Patents (Amendment) Act 2006.

The Industrial and Commercial Property (Protection) Act 1927 also dealt with trade marks, designs and copyright. Part II of that Act, which deals with patents, came into operation on 1 October 1927, repealing the existing UK legislation as it applied in the Irish Free State and setting up an independent Irish Patents Office.

[1.11] Unlike the PA 1992, the Industrial and Commercial Property (Protection) Act 1927 included a definition of 'invention',[17] namely:

---

13 PA 1992, s 61(1)(a).
14 PA 1992, s 49(1).
15 Constitution of the Irish Free State (Saorstát Éireann) Act 1927.
16 Art 73.
17 Industrial and Commercial Property (Protection) Act 1927, s 3.

any new and useful art, process, machine, manufacture or composition of matter, or any new and useful improvement in any art, process, machine, manufacture or composition of matter, and includes an alleged invention.

This definition was repeated in the PA 1964[18] but with the addition of the words 'and also any new method or process of testing applicable to the improvement or control of manufacture'. Under the Industrial and Commercial Property (Protection) Act 1927, if the invention was published or made available to the public before the date of application in any document published in the State or, prior to the establishment of the State, in the UK, then this was a ground of opposition[19] to a patent and also a ground of revocation.[20] This is to be contrasted with the position under modern patent law, where universal (or worldwide) novelty is required.

[1.12] Because of the provisions in the Industrial and Commercial Property (Protection) Act 1927 limiting the definition of 'publication' to publication within Ireland, it was possible for inventions which had already been patented in other jurisdictions to be validly patented in Ireland by 'the first party to introduce or import the invention into the Irish Free State'.[21]

The PA 1964 contained an anomaly whereby publication in Ireland was a ground of opposition[22] but in revocation proceedings the definition of publication was not limited to publication within Ireland.[23] There was also a broad definition of 'published' as being made available to the public by the written or spoken word or by public use, or in any other way.[24]

[1.13] Although the Industrial and Commercial Property (Protection) Act 1927 established the Irish Patents Office with Examiners to whom every application for patent was referred,[25] there was still an onus on an applicant to furnish what became known as evidence of novelty. The Examiners considered the application in a number of ways, including whether the invention was fairly described in the application and whether the complete specification was substantially the same as that described in the provisional specification.[26] In addition, an 'investigation' was carried out to ascertain whether the invention was claimed or described in a prior application made in Ireland.[27] The obligation imposed on an applicant to provide evidence of novelty was to show that the invention was not claimed or described in any earlier UK patent specification published in Ireland pursuant to an application for a UK patent made during the period commencing 50 years before the date of the application for a patent in Ireland and

---

[18] PA 1964, s 2.
[19] Industrial and Commercial Property (Protection) Act 1927, s 24.
[20] Industrial and Commercial Property (Protection) Act 1927, ss 41, 42.
[21] See Lysaght, *Patents, Designs and Trade Marks in the Irish Free State* (1931).
[22] PA 1964, s 19(1)(b).
[23] PA 1964, s 34(1)(e).
[24] PA 1964, s 2.
[25] Industrial and Commercial Property (Protection) Act 1927, s 14.
[26] Industrial and Commercial Property (Protection) Act 1927, s 17.
[27] Industrial and Commercial Property (Protection) Act 1927, ss 20, 21.

ending on 1 October 1927.[28] The evidence of novelty could take the form of a copy of an accepted equivalent UK patent application or a statutory declaration from an Irish or UK registered patent agent stating that, having carried out the required search and investigation, the invention was not wholly or in part claimed or described in an earlier British patent specification. Since disclosure of an invention prior to filing of the application was grounds for refusal, opposition or revocation of a patent, a procedure arose for the filing of a so-called provisional patent application. This was a relatively simple procedure that provided a date, ie the filing date, from which disclosure could take place without prejudice to the outcome or validity of a patent. The complete specification had to be lodged within nine months from the date of filing of the provisional specification.[29]

[1.14] The Industrial and Commercial Property (Protection) Act 1927 Act was amended in 1929 and 1957. The Industrial and Commercial Property (Protection) (Amendment) Act 1929 allowed for an assignment of patent rights to a Minister[30] and the Industrial and Commercial Property (Protection) (Amendment) Act 1957 included provisions for the inventor 'to be mentioned' in the patent.[31] There was not, however, a complete review of patent legislation until the PA 1964, which commenced on 1 July 1966. The PA 1964 was very similar to the UK Patents Act 1949 and hence case law under the corresponding sections of the UK Act were of persuasive authority. It is not true, however, to state that the PA 1964 is a mirror image of the UK 1949 Act. By way of example, s 32(1)(e) of the UK Patents Act 1949 provided for revocation of a patent on the ground that the invention was 'not new having regard to what was known or used in the United Kingdom' whereas s 34(1)(e) of the PA 1964 used the words 'is not new having regard to what was published', without putting any limitation on the need for such disclosure to take place in Ireland, ie universal novelty. In this regard the Irish legislation, by its definition of publication, conformed to art 4(2) of the Strasbourg Convention on the Unification of Certain Points of Substantive Law on Patents for Invention,[32] and, it could be said, was more like modern patent law on this issue than the UK legislation of that time. A report presented to the UK Parliament in 1970 concluded that the novelty criteria should be universal.[33]

[1.15] The definition of what was patentable had to take into account not just the definition of 'invention'[34] but also whether or not:

    (a)   the invention claimed was anything obviously contrary to well-established natural laws;

---

[28] Industrial and Commercial Property (Protection) Act 1927, s 19.

[29] Industrial and Commercial Property (Protection) Act 1927, s 16.

[30] Industrial and Commercial Property (Protection) (Amendment) Act 1929, s 6.

[31] Industrial and Commercial Property (Protection) (Amendment) Act 1957, s 2.

[32] Concluded on 27 November 1963 and entered into force on 1 August 1980. See para **[2.25]** *et seq.*

[33] Banks (Chairman), 'Report of the Committee to Examine the Patent System and Patent Law' (1970) Cmnd 4407.

[34] PA 1964, s 2.

(b)   the use of the invention would be contrary to public order or morality; or

(c)   the invention was a substance capable of being used as food or medicine which was a mixture of known ingredients possessing only the aggregate of the known properties of the ingredients, or a process producing such a substance by mere admixture.[35]

Section 8 of the PA 1964 provided for the filing of a provisional specification to be completed within 12 months with a possible extension to 15 months. An applicant had to file the results of an investigation, ie a novelty search, to show that the invention claimed in the complete specification was novel.[36] There were strict requirements as to the form that this evidence of novelty could take.[37] In addition, the Examiner searched for publication in Ireland before the date of filing of the applicant's complete specification in any other document.[38]

[1.16] The term of a patent under the PA 1964 was 16 years from the date of filing of the complete specification, subject to payment of renewal fees. Most High Court proceedings under the PA 1964 were applications under s 27 to extend the term of a patent. Most of these applications were heard by Costello J and related to pharmaceutical patents where, because of the strict regulatory requirements, there was a long delay in launching the drug. The principles upon which the High Court exercised its discretion to extend the term of a patent were stated in *Fleming's Patent*[39]:

(a)   was the invention one of more than ordinary utility?

(b)   had the patentee been adequately remunerated? and

(c)   was the absence of remuneration due to no fault of the patentee?

[1.17] These principles were applied in *JR Geigy AG*[40] and Costello J gave a 10-year extension. This was unusual, however, and most extensions granted were for a period of five years.[41] In *Fison's Petition*[42] an extension of term was refused by the High Court and this decision was upheld by the Supreme Court. The basis for the refusal was that 'the figures for the worldwide sales of this product, which have been very extensive, show that the patentee has been adequately, even handsomely, remunerated'. The courts recognised that it was correct to offset against profits in Ireland a portion of the research and development costs. In considering remuneration, the primary concern was the position in the Irish market; nevertheless, the worldwide remuneration could be taken

---

[35]   PA 1964, s 15.

[36]   PA 1964, s 8(6).

[37]   Patents Rules 1965 (SI 268/1965), r 27; Patents (Amendment) Rules 1970 (SI 159/1970), r 6; Patents (Amendment) (No 2) Rules 1978 (SI 110/1978); Patents (Amendment) Rules 1979 (SI 52/1979), r 2.

[38]   PA 1964, s 12(2).

[39]   *Fleming's Patent* (1918) 35 RPC 55.

[40]   *JR Geigy AG* [1982] FSR 278.

[41]   *Science Union Patent* (14 May 1987, unreported), HC, Costello J; *John Wyeth & Brother's Patent* [1985] RPC 545, Costello J.

[42]   *Fison's Petition* [1984] FSR 59.

into account.[43] Under the Patent Rules 1965, it was also possible to present the petition to the Controller,[44] but this was rarely done in practice.

[1.18] Although the PA 1992 contains extensive provisions regarding compulsory licences,[45] it did not include a special provision in respect of patents relating to food, medicine or to medical, surgical or other remedial devices as was contained in s 42 of the PA 1964. Under this (now repealed) special provision, the Controller was obliged to grant a licence of such patents unless, having regard to the desirability of encouraging inventors and the growth and development of industry and to such other matters as he considered relevant, there were good reasons for refusing the application. It could, of course, be argued that the very existence of this section encouraged the voluntary licensing of pharmaceutical patents but, for whatever reason, the section was not utilised in practice. Several applications were made under the corresponding section of the UK Patents Act 1949 (s 41) where it was established, *inter alia*, that a licence to supply a market by importation should not be granted[46] but the situation might be different if the patentee is supplying the home market by importation.[47] The UK courts have also given guidelines as to how to calculate an appropriate royalty based on the criterion that the product should be available to the public at the lowest price consistent with patentees deriving a reasonable advantage from their patent rights.[48]

[1.19] Shortly before the introduction of the PA 1992, an Irish-based generic pharmaceutical manufacturer, Clonmel Healthcare Ltd, made applications for licences under s 42 of the PA 1964 in respect of a number of patents. Since there is no corresponding section in the PA 1992, the applicant sought to avail of the transitional provisions of the PA 1992 which state that any application for a licence under s 42 of the PA 1964 which was pending at the commencement of the PA 1992 shall be decided under the provisions of the PA 1964.[49] The Controller did order a compulsory licence in respect of two patents on 2 June 1995 but on appeal to the High Court the orders were rescinded.[50] Carroll J held that the Agreement on the Trade-Related Aspects of Intellectual Property Rights (TRIPS)[51] annexed to the Agreement establishing the World Trade Organisation (WTO)[52] obliged the Controller to refuse to grant compulsory licences pursuant to s 42 of the PA 1964. Although the Controller had heard the

---

43 *Minerals & Chemical Corpn's Patent Extension* (2 February 1982, unreported), HC, Costello J.
44 Patents Rules 1965, rr 65–68.
45 PA 1992, ss 70, 71, as amended by the Patents (Amendment) Act 2006.
46 *Farmers Marketing Patent* [1966] RPC 546.
47 *Hoffmann-La Roche's Patent* [1969] RPC 504, [1971] 1 FSR 522.
48 *Geigy's Patent* [1964] RPC 391 and *Farbwerke Hoecht's Patent* [1973] RPC 253.
49 PA 1964, Sch 1, s 13.
50 *Allen & Hanburys Ltd and Glaxo Group Ltd v Controller and Clonmel Healthcare Ltd* [1997] FSR 1.
51 See para **[2.122]**.
52 Now formally incorporated into Irish legislation by the Patents (Amendment) Act 2006.

applications[53] prior to the entry into force of TRIPS,[54] his decision was rendered subsequently.[55]

[1.20] In November 1999 the government published a Patents (Amendment) Bill 1999. The stated main objective of the Bill was to bring patent law into accord with the provisions of TRIPS, which is part of the WTO Agreement, which in turn was formally signed by Ireland on 15 April 1994 and ratified on 15 November 1994. Following Council Decision No 94/900/EEC on 30 December 1994, the EU, Ireland and other EU Member States deposited instruments of ratification. The WTO Agreement, including TRIPS, entered into force on 1 January 1995 although art 65(1) of TRIPS includes a one-year transitional grace period. The Patents (Amendment) Bill 1999 did not find parliamentary time and lapsed with the dissolution of the Dáil in May 2002. It was revived in 2005 and was enacted as the Patents (Amendment) Act 2006.

---

[53] July/September 1994.
[54] 1 January 1995.
[55] June 1995.

Chapter 2

The Irish Patent System and International Conventions

INTRODUCTION

[2.01] As stated in the explanatory memorandum to the Patents Bill 1991, the principal objectives of that piece of legislation included the updating of the law so as to bring it into line with the laws applying generally in other European countries and to enable ratification of two international agreements concerning patents, namely, the European Patent Convention (Munich, 5 October 1973) and the Patent Co-operation Treaty (Washington, 19 June 1970). These agreements are designed to facilitate an applicant who wishes to file patent applications in a number of jurisdictions. The first real attempt at this, which still survives, is the International Convention for the Protection of Industrial Property (1883) (the Paris Convention).

PARIS CONVENTION

[2.02] The Paris Convention was signed in Paris on 20 March 1883 by 11 countries.[1] The UK was not amongst them but it acceded to the Paris Convention on 17 March 1884 and ratified it on 6 June 1884. Since UK patent legislation was at that time applicable in Ireland, it could be said that the provisions of the Paris Convention had effect in Ireland from its infancy. The Paris Convention was revised at Brussels (1900), Washington (1911), The Hague (1925), London (1934), Lisbon (1958) and Stockholm (1967) and it was amended on 28 September 1979.

[2.03] Although the Irish Free State was established on 6 December 1921, it was not until 4 December 1925 that Ireland formally acceded to the Paris Convention[2] and it is bound by the Stockholm revision.[3] The countries to which the Paris Convention applies are said to constitute a Union for the Protection of Industrial Property (known as the 'Paris Union'). Article 1(2) includes patents at the top of the list of the forms of industrial property to which the Paris Convention applies. The Paris Convention also applies to various kinds of 'industrial patents' recognised by contracting states. Hence,

---

[1] Belgium, Brazil, France, Guatemala, Italy, the Netherlands, Portugal, El Salvador, Serbia, Spain and Switzerland.

[2] For the circumstances surrounding accession, see Murdoch, *Invention and the Irish Patent System* (University of Dublin – Administrative Research Bureau, 1971) pp 37–39.

[3] Paris Convention, arts 1–12 came into force on 19 May 1970 and arts 13–30 on 26 April 1970.

there can be no doubt that short-term patents also fall within the provisions of the Paris Convention.

[2.04] The fundamental principle of the Paris Convention is that nationals of a contracting state enjoy the same protection as that afforded to nationals of the particular State where protection is being sought and no requirement as to domicile or establishment may be imposed as a prerequisite 'for the enjoyment of any industrial property rights'. Irish patent law provides that, in proceedings under the legislation, the Controller must be provided with an address for service in the EU;[4] such a provision is permitted under the Paris Convention.[5] Non-EU residents must be represented by a duly authorised patent attorney[6] and so cannot represent themselves. Again this is permitted under the Paris Convention.[7] Nationals of non-contracting states enjoy the same protection as nationals of contracting states if they are domiciled, or have a real and effective industrial or commercial establishment, in the territory of any one of the contracting states.[8] Article 4 of the Paris Convention has important practical application in that it provides for priority rights. In relation to patents, a person who has filed a first patent application (a 'priority application') in one contracting state is entitled, when filing in another contracting state, to claim the priority date of the first application, provided that the subsequent application is filed within 12 months of the priority application.

[2.05] In calculating the 12-month period, the actual day of filing is not included. Therefore, the period expires on the 12-month anniversary of the date of filing. If, in a country where priority is claimed, the 12-month period falls on an official holiday or a day upon which that national Patent Office is closed, the period is extended until the next working day.[9] This 12-month period enables an applicant to file a single patent application in a contracting state and delay the filing of further patent applications (known as 'Convention Applications') in other contracting states for up to 12 months without risking refusal or revocation on the grounds, for example, of prior publication.[10] Since the later applications are regarded as if they had been filed on the same day as the first application, rights are preserved in the countries where the later applications are filed against third parties who may, for example, file a patent application in respect of the same invention in that contracting state between the priority date and the expiry of the 12-month period.

[2.06] Section 25 of the Patents Act 1992[11] (PA 1992) (which deals with priority rights) does not state the period to be 12 months but allows for the period to be prescribed.

---

4   Patents Rules 1992 (SI 179/1992), r 92 as amended by the Patents (Amendment) Rules 2006 (SI 142/2006).
5   Paris Convention, art 2(3).
6   Patents Rules 1992, r 93 as amended by the Patents (Amendment) Rules 2006.
7   Paris Convention, art 2(3).
8   Paris Convention, art 3.
9   Paris Convention, art 4(C)(3).
10   PA 1992, s 27(2).
11   As amended by the Patents (Amendment) Act 2006.

This is sensible since priority periods have changed in the past.[12] Rule 21(1) of the Patents Rules 1992 (SI 179/1992) prescribes a priority period of 12 months. The Patents (Amendment) Act 2006 amended s 25 by extending the priority provisions to World Trade Organisation (WTO) member states that are not party to the Paris Convention. Under s 25(5) of the PA 1992,[13] a filing in a country not party to either the Paris Convention or the WTO can also give rise to priority if the Minister makes an order to that effect consequent upon bilateral or multilateral agreements.[14]

[2.07] If one (or more) priority dates are claimed, this must be declared when filing the Convention Application, indicating the date(s) and the country or countries in which the priority application(s) were made.[15] Rule 22 of the Patents Rules 1992[16] states that this information must be provided on the prescribed Form No 1 which is scheduled to the Rules and headed 'Request for the Grant of a Patent'. The filing number of each priority application must also be indicated but this can be done after the filing date.

[2.08] A certified copy of each priority application must also be filed together, where appropriate, with an English-language translation of such document.[17] The priority application is generally certified by the relevant national patent office. This certified priority document must be filed by the end of the sixteenth month from the earliest priority date with a maximum of a one month extension available. A longer period of 21 months after the priority date is allowed for filing an English-language translation of the priority document.[18] If the formalities for claiming the priority date are not complied with, it does not mean the loss of the application (which is then known as a 'non-Convention application') but it does mean the loss of the right of priority.[19] However, this can have significant consequences as any application for the same invention filed after the priority application anywhere in the world which does not claim priority from the priority application is likely to be refused or liable to be revoked if the invention contained in the priority application is publicly disclosed before the filing date of the non-Convention application.

[2.09] Section 26(2) of the PA 1992 allows for the claiming of multiple priority dates as provided in art 4(F) of the Paris Convention. Priority dates may arise from applications filed in different countries. Time limits run from the earliest priority date. It is also possible for multiple priorities to be claimed for any one claim. A priority date is not lost simply because an application contains one or more elements that were not included in the application from which priority is claimed. There must, however, be what is termed in the Paris Convention as

---

12 Previously seven months, Patents, Designs and Trade Mark 1883, s 103.
13 As amended by the Patents (Amendment) Act 2006.
14 Patents (International Arrangements) Order 1996 (SI 38/1996); Patents Act 1964 (Section 93) (Declaration Order) 1976 (SI 314/1976).
15 Paris Convention, art 4(D)(1).
16 As amended by the Patents (Amendment) Rules 2009 (SI 194/2009).
17 PA 1992, s 26(1); Patent Rules 1992 (SI 179/1992), r 22(2).
18 Patent Rules 1992 (SI 179/1992), r 22(3).
19 Paris Convention, art 4D(4).

'unity of invention within the meaning of the law of the country'.[20] The right of priority will only extend to those elements which have been included in the priority application(s).[21]

[2.10] Irish law provides that:

> if certain elements of the invention for which priority is claimed do not appear among the claims formulated in the previous application, priority may nonetheless be granted if the documents of the previous application as a whole specifically disclosed such elements.[22]

Article 4G of the Paris Convention provides that where an application is shown to contain more than one invention, it may be divided into one or more divisional applications as appropriate and the benefit of any priority will apply to the divisional application(s). This is reflected in s 24 of the PA 1992 which also provides that, to benefit from a priority right, the subject matter must not extend beyond the content of the earlier application as filed.

[2.11] Certain countries, but not Ireland, operate a system which allows for what is termed an 'inventor's certificate'. Such a certificate means that, where the government of that country utilises the invention, the inventor is rewarded if, for example, there were resultant savings to that government. As would be expected, these certificates were attractive in countries where most industry was in State control. Thus, for example, in the former Soviet Union, most applications by Soviet nationals were for inventors' certificates.[23] A priority right can be claimed from an inventor's certificate.

[2.12] The Paris Convention does not prescribe a uniform duration for patent rights and leaves this to national laws. What is provided, however, is that the benefit of priority should not affect the duration.[24] Section 36 of the PA 1992 states the duration to be 20 years from 'the date of filing of the patent application' and not from the priority date. This is one of the reasons for the tendency to file applications claiming priority very close to the 12-month anniversary date.

[2.13] The right of an inventor to be mentioned as such in a patent, although enshrined in the Paris Convention,[25] is not a provision which is used very much in practice either under former[26] or current legislation.[27]

---

[20] PA 1992, s 21 defines 'unity of invention' as relating to 'one invention only or to a group of inventions so linked as to form a single general inventive concept'.

[21] PA 1992, s 26(3).

[22] PA 1992, s 26(4); Paris Convention, art 4H.

[23] In 1968, 106,620 applications were made for inventors' certificates in the former Soviet Union, only 158 of which were by foreign nationals. In the same year, there were only 3,808 patent applications.

[24] Paris Convention, art 4*bis*.

[25] Paris Convention, art 4*ter*.

[26] Patents Act 1964 (PA 1964), s 21.

[27] PA 1992, s 17.

[2.14] Although the grant of a patent may be refused in cases where the commercial exploitation of the patent would be contrary to public order or morality,[28] there are limitations on how broadly this can be construed. The Paris Convention states that refusal, or revocation, of a patent cannot occur 'on the ground that the sale of the patented product or of a product obtained by means of a patented process is subject to restrictions or limitations resulting from the domestic law'.[29] This is reflected in the PA 1992 by the proviso that exploitation shall not be deemed to be contrary to public order or morality only because it is prohibited by law. The former legislation did not contain such a proviso and, under that legislation, the Irish Patents Office refused applications for inventions which were described as abortifacients for human use. In fact, s 15 of the Patents Act 1964 (PA 1964) empowered the Controller with a discretion in this regard and, as an alternative to refusal, an insertion could be made in the patent specification of a disclaimer in respect of use which would be in any manner contrary to law. No such discretion exists under s 10 of the PA 1992[30] and it remains to be seen as to what circumstances would lead to refusal of a patent on the ground of being contrary to public order or morality.[31]

[2.15] The Paris Convention allows contracting states to legislate for the granting of compulsory licences[32] and, in limited cases, the forfeiture of the patent in circumstances designed to prevent 'abuses' of patent rights. Apart from references[33] to a failure to work (or possibly, sufficiently work) the patent, there is no indication as to what might constitute such an abuse. It is left to contracting states to define such abuse.[34] Section 39 of the PA 1964 specifically set out 'the grounds deemed to constitute an abuse of monopoly rights'. These grounds are repeated in s 70 of the PA 1992[35] but a statement that they are deemed to constitute an abuse is notably absent. Although the Paris Convention does allow contracting states to provide for the forfeiture of a patent in cases where the grant of a compulsory licence would not be sufficient to prevent an abuse of the patent right, this provision is not part of Irish patent law. It is therefore necessary to consider compulsory licences in the context of EU law and art 31 of the Agreement on the Trade-Related Aspects of Intellectual Property Rights (TRIPS).

[2.16] The earliest time at which application for a compulsory licence can be made is three years from the publication of notice of grant,[36] which in order to comply with the Paris Convention must not be before the date of the grant of the patent, or prior to a date four years from the date of filing of the patent application. The

---

28 PA 1992, s 10(a) as amended by the Patents (Amendment) Act 2006.
29 Paris Convention, art 4*quater*.
30 As amended by the Patents (Amendment) Act 2006.
31 PA 1992, s 58(a).
32 Paris Convention, art 5.
33 Paris Convention, art 5.
34 Paris Convention, art 5A(2).
35 As amended by the Patents (Amendment) Act 2006.
36 PA 1992, s 70(1) as amended by the Patents (Amendment) Act 2006.

proprietor of a patent may oppose the grant of a compulsory licence[37] and the Paris Convention provides that the application 'shall be refused if the patentee justifies his inaction by legitimate reasons'.[38]

[2.17] Any compulsory licence which is granted must be non-exclusive and can only be assigned with the prior authorisation of the Controller and with the relevant part of the enterprise or goodwill.[39] The Paris Convention also specifically disallows the granting of a sub-licence, except with that part of the enterprise or goodwill which exploits such licence.[40] The PA 1992 does not contain this limitation, although, as the Controller can set the terms of the licence,[41] he or she would have a discretion to impose such a restriction in any particular case.

[2.18] There is no requirement to mark goods with a patent number in order to enforce patent rights[42] but the failure to do so will mean that damages or an account of profits will not be awarded against an innocent infringer.[43]

[2.19] Another important time period provided for in the Paris Convention is a grace period of not less than six months within which to pay outstanding renewal fees.[44] Section 36(3) of the PA 1992 allows a maximum six-month extension with additional fees payable for each month of extension.[45] Within two years from the date on which a patent lapses, application can be made to restore a patent where the failure to pay the renewal fee is shown to have been *prima facie* unintentional.[46]

[2.20] Section 42(d) and (e)[47] of the PA 1992 provides that the rights conferred by a patent do not extend to visiting aircraft or land vessels. Reciprocal treatment must be given to Irish registered vessels, aircraft or land vehicles temporarily in another contracting state.[48]

[2.21] The importation of a product obtained directly by a process which is the subject matter of a patent is an infringement.[49]

[2.22] Article 11 of the Paris Convention imposes an obligation on contracting states to grant temporary protection to patentable inventions exhibited at official or officially recognised international exhibitions. Since disclosure of an invention prior to

---

[37] PA 1992, s 73(3).
[38] Paris Convention, art 5A(4).
[39] PA 1992, s 70(3) as amended by the Patents (Amendment) Act 2006; Paris Convention, art 5A(4).
[40] Paris Convention, art 5A(4).
[41] PA 1992, s 70(3) as amended by the Patents (Amendment) Act 2006.
[42] Paris Convention, art 5D.
[43] PA 1992, s 49(1).
[44] Paris Convention, art 5bis.
[45] Patents Rules 1992, Sch I, Item No 15.
[46] PA 1992, s 37 as amended by the Patents (Amendment) Act 2006.
[47] As amended by the Patents (Amendment) Act 2006.
[48] Paris Convention, art 5ter.
[49] PA 1992, s 40(c); Paris Convention, art 5*quater*.

filing destroys the novelty in what might otherwise be a patentable invention, this provision allows for disclosure at certain exhibitions without prejudicing novelty.[50] Ireland is not a party to the Paris Convention on International Exhibitions signed at Paris on 22 November 1928[51] but recognises a disclosure at exhibitions under the auspices of that Convention as a non-prejudicial disclosure.[52]

[2.23] Each contracting state of the Paris Convention must provide a Central Office to enable the public to obtain details of patents and must regularly publish an official periodical paper. However, in relation to patents, the only information which the Paris Convention specifically states must be included in such a publication is the name of the owner of each patent granted together with a short designation of each patented invention.[53] The Patents Office Journal is published fortnightly. Prior to publication under s 28 of the PA 1992, the only information obtainable from the Journal is the name of the applicant, the title of the invention, the date of application, the priority date claimed and the number assigned to the application by the Irish Patents Office. An indication is also provided, by use of the letter 'S', that an application is for a short-term patent which has a lifespan of not more than 10 years compared with 20 years for the so-called 'long term' patent.

[2.24] Although the Paris Convention does not deal with many substantive matters of patent law such as criteria for patentability, it has remained in place, with most countries concluding separate and further agreements which supplement and do not contravene the Paris Convention.[54] Contracting states include all of the major industrial countries of the world.

STRASBOURG CONVENTION

[2.25] Ireland was the first country to ratify the Strasbourg Convention on the Unification of Certain Points of Substantive Law on Patents For Inventions (the Strasbourg Convention)[55] which came into force on 1 August 1980. There are 13 contracting states[56] and the Strasbourg Convention is only open for signature by Member States of the Council of Europe. The principal aim of the Strasbourg Convention is to create common criteria as to the patentability of inventions on issues such as novelty, inventive step and resolution of conflicts concerning concurrent applications.

---

[50] Patents Rules 1992, r 5; PA 1992, s 12.
[51] Amended and supplemented by Protocols of 10 May 1948, 16 November 1966 and 30 November 1972.
[52] PA 1992, s 12(1)(b).
[53] Paris Convention, art 12.
[54] Paris Convention, art 19.
[55] 27 November 1963.
[56] Belgium, France, Denmark, Germany, Ireland, Italy, Liechtenstein, Luxembourg, the Former Yugoslav Republic of Macedonia, the Netherlands, Sweden, Switzerland and the United Kingdom.

[2.26] Article 1 of the Strasbourg Convention states:

> patents shall be granted for any inventions which are susceptible of industrial application, which are new and which involve an inventive step. An invention which does not comply with these conditions shall not be the subject of a valid patent.

The criteria for patentability are set out in s 9 of the PA 1992[57] and art 52 of the European Patent Convention. However, the criteria in relation to a short-term patent under s 63(4) of the PA 1992 are different, namely:

> an invention shall be patentable ... if it is new and susceptible of industrial application provided it is not clearly lacking an inventive step.

Thus there is a conflict between the provisions relating to short-term patents as regards inventive step and art 1 of the Strasbourg Convention. The conflict could have been even more pronounced. In the Patents Bill 1991, as initiated, there was no requirement for an inventive step in respect of a short-term patent. This would have meant that valid short-term patents could have existed for an invention which was clearly obvious. Germany also operates a petty patent system which allows for a different standard of inventive step but these are identified as utility models and not patents so there is not the same level of conflict.

[2.27] The exceptions to patentability in s 10 of the PA 1992,[58] namely, inventions contrary to public order or morality and plant or animal varieties, are provided for in art 2 of the Strasbourg Convention. The Strasbourg Convention provides no definition of an invention but in art 3 there is a broad interpretation of the words 'susceptible of industrial application', namely, if the invention 'can be made or used in any kind of industry including agriculture'.[59]

[2.28] Under the Strasbourg Convention, the term used to refer to the knowledge against which novelty and inventive step must be considered is 'the state of the art',[60] which is broadly defined[61] and is not limited to the state of the art in Ireland. Thus, so-called 'universal novelty' is required. Contracting states may also provide that the state of the art includes prior concurrent patent applications which are unpublished. This option has been exercised under s 11(3) of the PA 1992 for consideration of novelty only and it is not applicable to the examination of inventive step.

[2.29] Article 11(2) of the Paris Convention does not allow the exhibiting of an invention at an officially recognised international exhibition to extend the 12-month priority period which may be claimed. However, the Strasbourg Convention provides that such exhibiting may not be considered as disclosure, provided the patent application is filed within six months of such disclosure.[62]

---

[57] As amended by the Patents (Amendment) Act 2006.

[58] As amended by the Patents (Amendment) Act 2006.

[59] PA 1992, s 14.

[60] Strasbourg Convention, art 4; PA 1992, s 11 as amended by the Patents (Amendment) Act 2006.

[61] Strasbourg Convention, art 4(2); PA 1992, s 11(2).

[62] Strasbourg Convention, art 4(4)(b); PA 1992, s 12(1)(b).

Another form of non-prejudicial disclosure, and subject to the same six-month time constraint, is where there has been 'an evident abuse in relation to the applicant or his legal predecessor'.[63] Section 12(1)(a) of the PA 1992 does not use these words and, as a consequence, could possibly be considered as unnecessarily limited. However, the words used, namely 'a breach of confidence or agreement in relation to, or the unlawful obtaining of the matter constituting, the invention'[64] would presumably be considered as evident abuse. The further and quite separate requirement that a patentable invention must also involve an inventive step[65] is judged by what is not obvious having regard to the state of the art.[66] However, as allowed for in the Strasbourg Convention, s 13 of the PA 1992 does not include unpublished prior concurrent applications as part of the state of the art in deciding whether or not there is an inventive step.

[2.30] In return for the monopoly rights granted by a State, the descriptive part of the specification 'must disclose the invention in a manner sufficiently clear and complete for it to be carried out by a person skilled in the art'.[67] The extent of the protection conferred by a patent shall be determined by the terms of the claims, but the Strasbourg Convention requires that a patent application contain a description of the invention with the necessary drawings referred to therein and one or more claims defining the protection sought.[68]

AGREEMENT CONCERNING INTERNATIONAL PATENT CLASSIFICATION

[2.31] The European Convention on the International Classification of Patents for Inventions (to which Ireland was a party) was signed in Paris in 1954 and came into force in August 1955.[69] Its objective was the adoption of a uniform system of classification for patents, inventors' certificates, utility models and utility certificates. This was later effectively replaced by the Agreement concerning International Patent Classification[70] (the IPC Agreement) which entered into force on 7 October 1975. Ireland became a party to the IPC Agreement with effect from 7 October 1975. The latest edition of the classification under the IPC Agreement is the eighth edition which became operative on 1 January 2006.

[2.32] The foreword to the IPC Agreement states that the classification has as its primary purpose the establishment of an effective search tool for the retrieval of patent documents by Patent Offices and other users in order to establish the novelty and evaluate the inventive step of patent applications (including the assessment of technical advance and useful results or utility). The classification contains eight

---

63 Strasbourg Convention, art 4(4)(a).
64 PA 1992, s 12(1)(a).
65 Different criteria apply to a short-term patent: PA 1992, s 63(4).
66 Strasbourg Convention, art 5; PA 1992, s 13.
67 Strasbourg Convention, art 8(2); PA 1992, s 19(1).
68 Strasbourg Convention, art 8(1); PA 1992, s 18(2).
69 Paris, 19 December 1954.
70 Strasbourg, 24 March 1971.

sections indicated by the letters A–H and these sections are divided into classes which are themselves further divided into sub-classes and grouped.[71] Along with the UK and a number of other countries, Ireland has declared that it does not undertake to include certain classification symbols on documents laid open for public inspection and in notices relating thereto.[72] Parties to the IPC Agreement include Japan, the US and Australia.

VIENNA CONVENTION

[2.33] The Vienna Convention on the Law of Treaties,[73] which deals with the rules of international law, is often used by the European Patent Office as an interpretation aid even though the European Patent Convention is not strictly speaking covered by the Vienna Convention.[74] The more important principles of the Vienna Convention include that:

(a) Treaty provisions must be construed according to the ordinary meaning of the terms in their context and in light of their object and purpose, so a judge is not entitled to depart from clear provisions of law. This relates to the requirement to interpret in good faith.

(b) Preparatory documents can be used to confirm a meaning or determine a meaning if the first and ordinary means of construction would lead to ambiguity or an absurd result.[75]

EUROPEAN PATENT CONVENTION

[2.34] The European Patent Convention 1973 (EPC) was signed by Ireland and 14 other European countries in Munich on 5 October 1973. It was ratified by Ireland on 1 May 1992 pursuant to the PA 1992 and the effective date of the EPC in Ireland is 1 August 1992. There are now 37 contracting states of the EPC as of 1 July 2010. These are Albania, Austria, Belgium, Bulgaria, Cyprus, Czech Republic, Germany, Denmark, Estonia, Spain, Finland, France, United Kingdom, Greece, Croatia, Hungary, Ireland, Iceland, Italy, Liechtenstein, Lithuania, Luxembourg, Latvia, Monaco, Former Yugoslav Republic of Macedonia, Malta, the Netherlands, Norway, Poland, Portugal, Romania, Sweden, Switzerland, Slovenia, Slovakia, San Marino and Turkey.

There are also so-called 'extension states' to the EPC which may still be designated by virtue of extension agreements. These countries are Bosnia and Herzegovina, Montenegro and Serbia. The effect of such designation is to extend the protection conferred by a European patent to these countries.

---

[71] See Guide, *Survey of Classes and Summary of Main Groups* (WIPO).
[72] Strasbourg Agreement, art 4(4)(i)
[73] 23 May 1969; entered into force on 27 January 1980.
[74] See, for example, Decision G5/83 *Second Medical Indication/Eisai* OJ EPO 3/1985 64.
[75] See, for example, G2/08 *Dosage Regimes/Abbott Respiratory* (19 February 2010, not yet reported).

[2.35] The principal objective of the EPC is to enable a patent applicant to secure patent rights in a number of European countries by way of a single application and prosecution before a centralised office, the European Patent Office (EPO). Prior to the EPC, a separate application had to be made and prosecuted before the national Patent Office of each country in which patent protection was required. If protection was required in a large number of countries, the procedure was both expensive and cumbersome.

[2.36] Instead of many separate applications, the EPC enables the filing of a single application that, by way of designation, can cover all contracting states and the extension states. The national patent laws of contracting states remain in place. The EPC can be utilised by applicants from non-contracting states and, in fact, among the major users are US and Japanese corporations. Prior to 1 August 1992, an Irish individual or entity could file an application at the EPO, but any person wishing to secure patent protection in Ireland had to file a separate patent application at the Irish Patents Office. Now there is a choice of filing either at the Irish Patents Office or before the EPO, designating Ireland.

[2.37] Although the EPC enables the filing and prosecution to grant of a single application, ultimately the grant of what is called a European patent[76] does not result in one unitary patent having a federal effect but a bundle of patents. The effect of s 119 of the PA 1992[77] is that a European patent designating Ireland is treated in the same way as if it were an Irish patent granted directly by the Irish Patents Office. There are also instances where an EPC application designating Ireland can (on compliance with certain conditions) be converted into what is effectively an Irish patent application.[78]

[2.38] After publication of the mention of grant, and subject to compliance with national requirements (known as validation), a European patent has the same rights as those conferred by a national patent granted in a designated State.[79] Infringement of a European patent is dealt with under national law.

EPC 2000 changes

[2.39] Concerns arose that EPC 1973 did not provide sufficient protection in all fields of technology as required by TRIPS. In addition, the EPO had decided that it could not interpret European patents in light of TRIPS as the EPO is not a member of TRIPS. Furthermore, not all contracting states of the EPC are signatories of TRIPS and so the Vienna Convention on the Law of Treaties which deals with the rules of international law does not require consideration of TRIPS in EPC matters.[80] Nevertheless, the EPO considered that it could take TRIPS into consideration as an indication of current trends. Further, certain procedural rules were included in EPC 1973 which made them difficult

---

[76] EPC, art 2(1).
[77] As amended by the Patents (Amendment) Act 2006.
[78] PA 1992, s 122 as amended by the Patents (Amendment) Act 2006.
[79] PA 1992, s 119 as amended by the Patents (Amendment) Act 2006.
[80] T1173/97 *Computer Program Product/IBM*, OJ EPO 1999 609.

to change. The Patent Law Treaty also came into force in 2000 and set out harmonised standards for filing, which were less rigorous than EPC 1973. On a more basic level, technology had moved on since 1973, in particular in the areas of software and biotechnology. For these reasons, changes were proposed for EPC 1973 which were agreed in 2000. [81] The changed version is known as the 'EPC 2000'.

[2.40] The EPC 2000 came into force on 13 December, 2007. It introduced a number of substantive changes to the European patent procedure to harmonise the EPC with new developments in international law such as TRIPS and the Patent Law Treaty. It also simplified the procedure for future changes by transferring some subject matter from the articles of the EPC to the rules.[82] The changes required a substantial renumbering of the EPC Rules but not the EPC Articles, which maintain their original numbering.

[2.41] The main changes introduced by the EPC 2000 are set out below. In summary, they include procedural changes to the filing requirements; extension of priority claims to WTO countries; acceptance of priority claims added up to 16 months after the priority date; and the abolition of the requirement for translations of the priority documents unless they are needed to verify the priority claim.

Procedure before the EPO

[2.42] The EPO has its seat in Munich with branch offices in Berlin and The Hague. European patent applications can be filed at The Hague or Munich or at the national Patent Office of a contracting state. There is also a sub-office in Vienna but applications cannot be filed through that office. All European patent applications, except divisional patent applications,[83] can be filed at the Irish Patents Office.[84]

[2.43] A European patent application can be filed in any of the three official working languages of the EPO (English, French or German)[85] and is first considered by the Receiving Section in The Hague. The Receiving Section initially examines whether or not the filing requirements have been met.[86]

Filing date

[2.44] Article 80 of EPC 1973 which dealt with the requirement to obtain a filing date has been replaced by Rule 40 of the EPC which allows for more flexibility regarding changes in the required form and content of applications. This also brings the EPC in line with the Patent Law Treaty. In particular, claims are no longer needed to establish a

---

[81] Act revising the Convention on the Grant of European Patents (European Patent Convention) signed on 29 November 2000.

[82] Contained in the Implementing Regulations to the Convention on the Grant of European Patents of 5 October 1973 as adopted by decision of the Administrative Council of the European Patent Organisation of 7 December 2006.

[83] A divisional application can result where a Patent Office decides that an application covers more than one invention or inventive concept.

[84] PA 1992, s 120(7) as amended by the Patents (Amendment) Act 2006.

[85] EPC, art 14.

[86] EPC, art 90 and Rule 40.

filing date and can be added within two months of filing, along with corrections of any other deficiencies such as missing parts.[87] However, there are strict requirements forbidding the introduction of any new subject matter after filing, which will apply to late-filed claims.[88]

Reference to previous application

[2.45] EPC 2000 provides that the applicant can omit the description and any drawings from the initial documents filed and instead submit a reference to a previously filed application.[89] The applicant may also, in its discretion, omit the claims in favour of a declaration that the previously filed application also replaces the claims.[90] To take advantage of this provision, the applicant must:

(a) state the filing date and number of the previous application and the Office with which it was filed;[91]

(b) indicate that the previous application replaces the description and any drawings, and optionally, the claims;[92]

(c) file a certified copy of the previous application within two months of the filing date and file a translation of the previous application (if in another language) into English, French or German within the same two-month period.[93]

Search

[2.46] A novelty search relating to the state of the known art is carried out after filing and an Extended European Search Report (EESR) is issued.[94] The EESR contains a classification in accordance with the IPC Agreement.[95] The EESR is transmitted to the applicant together with copies of any cited documents. The EESR provides a commentary from the Examiner as to, *inter alia*, the novelty and inventive step of the claims. Since the EPC 2000 came into force, searches can now legitimately be conducted in the EPO offices in Munich as well as in The Hague which was originally the only place authorised for searching under EPC 1973.[96]

[2.47] For applications filed after 1 January 2011, European patent applicants and Euro-PCT applicants must file with the EPO a copy of the search results received on the priority application.[97] If the search results have not been filed by the commencement of

---

87 Rule 56(2) EPC.
88 EPC, art 100(3).
89 Rule 40(1)(c) EPC.
90 Rule 57(c) EPC.
91 Rule 40(2) EPC.
92 Rule 40(2) EPC.
93 Rule 40(3) EPC.
94 EPC, art 92(1) and Rule 65.
95 Paras **[2.31]** and **[2.32]** above.
96 EPC 1973, art 17.
97 Rule 141 EPC as amended by Decision of the Administrative Council of 28 October 2009 amending the Implementing Regulations to the European Patent Convention (CA/D 18/09).

the examination, the EPO will give the applicant a two-month period to do so, failing which the application will be deemed withdrawn.[98] Before this, the EPO could invite the applicant to file a copy of all foreign search results[99] but this was not usually enforced.

[2.48] Under art 82 of EPC 2000, a European patent application must relate to one invention only or to a group of inventions so linked as to form a single general inventive concept, the so-called 'unity of invention'. If it is found that this requirement has not been met, an EESR will be drawn up only for the invention (or group) first claimed. The patent application can only proceed in respect of the searched subject matter. Any other invention can be the subject of another application known as a 'divisional application'.[100]

[2.49] It is possible to obtain an early search report from the EPO if an accelerated search is requested in writing.[101]

Publication

[2.50] Publication of a European patent application takes place as soon as possible after 18 months from filing or from the earliest priority date if priority is claimed.[102] This publication contains the description, the claims, the abstract and any drawings as filed. Also published in an annex is the EESR (if available) but not the Examiner's commentary which is available via the EPO website.[103]

[2.51] Details of the States designated are specified in the published application. Earlier publication can be requested (for example, if speed of registration is paramount because of an infringement issue) but there cannot be a postponement. To prevent publication, it is necessary to formally withdraw the application before termination of the technical preparations for publication. Upon publication, any third party may submit written observations concerning the patentability of the invention. The third party has no right of audience and is not officially informed as to the effect of the observations. However, by inspecting the file, the third party can determine the effect of any observations and submit further observations for as long as the application is pending.

[2.52] Under s 56 of the PA 1992, damages can be recovered for infringement from the date of publication,[104] subject to translation requirements where appropriate.

Fees and relationship to claims

[2.53] The EPO charges fees on filing and for examination, searches, designations, long specifications and on grant. In 2008, the EPO introduced further fees for each claim

---

[98] Rule 70b as inserted into the EPC by Decision CA/D 18/09.

[99] EPC, art 124(1).

[100] See para **[4.27]** *et seq.*

[101] Under the programme for accelerated prosecution of European patent applications (PACE) (see the Notice from the EPO, Special edition No 3, OJ EPO 2007, F1).

[102] EPC, art 93, which is similar to the corresponding provision for Irish patents, PA 1992, s 28(1).

[103] Rule 68(1) EPC.

[104] EPC, arts 64, 67.

beyond the fifteenth claim in each application.[105] On 1 April 2009, an additional fee was imposed for claims beyond the fiftieth claim in each application.[106] The effect of these changes is to encourage applicants to reduce the number of claims as much as possible, including by use of techniques such as combining alternatives, using multiple dependencies and transferring claim subject matter into the description where appropriate. While this could be viewed as draconian, in practice the EPO generally requires that all claims except one independent product claim and one independent process claim be deleted from the application in any event. Therefore, many applicants tend to limit their claims to a small number to save time and costs in dealing with inevitable objections. This practice has been incorporated into a new Rule 62a,[107] which only allows for one independent claim to be searched for each category, except in certain limited circumstances.

[2.54] At the time of filing the application, examination is automatically requested. However, examination cannot commence until the examination fee and the designation fee have been paid. The examination fee must be paid within six months of the date on which the publication of the search report is mentioned in the European Patent Bulletin.

Examination

[2.55] During examination, the Examiner will consider whether or not the invention meets the requirements of the EPC[108] including, but not limited to, novelty and inventive step[109] The applicant is invited to make 'observations' and amendments can be made to the description, claims and drawings. Accelerated examination can be requested in writing.[110]

Grant

[2.56] The Examiner is part of a team of three people referred to as the 'Examining Division' for that case. If the Examining Division decides to grant a patent, it informs the applicant of the text on which the grant will be based and the applicant must indicate approval or otherwise of the text within a specified period. Grant and printing fees must be paid and a translation of the claims into the two other official languages must also be filed. Grant is not effective until the date on which the mention of grant is

---

[105] Decision of the Administrative Council of 6 March 2008 amending the Implementing Regulations to the European Patent Convention (CA/D 2/08), increased to €210 from 1 April 2010.

[106] Decision of the Administrative Council of 14 December 2007 amending the Rules relating to Fees (CA/D 15/07), increased to €525 from 1 April 2010.

[107] As inserted with effect from 1 April 2010 by Decision of the Administrative Council of 25 March 2009 amending the Implementing Regulations to the European Patent Convention (CA/D 3/09).

[108] EPC, art 94.

[109] EPC, art 52(1).

[110] Programme for accelerated prosecution of European patent applications (PACE), Notice from the EPO, Special edition No 3, OJ EPO 2007, *ibid.*

published in the European Patent Bulletin.[111] Within a period of three months from the grant date (or six months in the case of Ireland), the patent must be validated in those States (selected from the available list of contracting states) where protection is desired. From the grant date, there follows a nine-month period within which any person may file notice of opposition. The opposition applies to the European patent in all of the contracting states in which the patent has effect.[112]

Opposition

[2.57] The grounds of opposition are stated in art 100 of the EPC and are as follows:

    (a)   the invention is not susceptible of industrial application, is not new and/or does not involve an inventive step;

    (b)   the invention is not patentable subject matter;[113]

    (c)   the publication or exploitation of the invention would be contrary to public order or morality;[114]

    (d)   insufficient disclosure of the invention;

    (e)   the subject matter of the European patent extends beyond the content of the application as filed or, if the patent was granted on a divisional application, goes beyond the contents of the parent patent application as filed.

The Opposition Division of the EPO considers the opposition and again invites observations from the parties 'as often as necessary'.[115]

[2.58] During opposition, the patentee may be invited to amend the description, claims and drawings. The claims of the patent may not be amended in such a way as to extend the protection conferred. A third party may intervene in opposition proceedings if it can prove that infringement proceedings relating to the opposed European patent have been instituted against that party, or that the owner of the opposed European patent has requested that the third party cease the alleged infringement of the patent and that proceedings have been instituted for a ruling that there is no infringement.[116] The Opposition Division may revoke the patent, reject the opposition or maintain the patent in amended form following oral proceedings (if requested by the patentee or opponent).

Appeal

[2.59] Appeal structures are in place in respect of refusal of the application at first instance as well as opposition proceedings. The appeal is to an EPO Board of Appeal and must be filed within two months of the date of notification of the decision appealed.[117] There is no possibility of an appeal to the Court of Justice of the European

---

[111] EPC, art 97(4).

[112] EPC, art 99(2).

[113] EPC, arts 52(2), 53(b).

[114] EPC, art 53(a).

[115] EPC, art 101(2).

[116] EPC, art 105.

[117] EPC, art 108.

Union (ECJ) as there are no provisions in the EPC permitting a referral by any instance of the EPO of questions of law to the ECJ.[118]

Alternatives to appeal: petition for review

[2.60] A further avenue of appeal has been introduced by the EPC 2000, namely a petition for review to the Enlarged Board of Appeal (EBA) of the EPO.[119] The EBA was previously only used for questions of principle referred by the Boards of Appeal but this has been expanded to cover fundamental procedural defects (eg omitting to hold a requested hearing) or criminal acts influencing a decision of a Board of Appeal. Each review commences with a preliminary assessment to see if it is clearly inadmissible.[120] It then enters a series of written exchanges between the petitioner and the EBA, without involvement of any third parties such as opponents.[121] A hearing may be held.[122] A decision is then made to reject or accept the petition and, if accepted, the proceedings before the Board of Appeal will be reopened.[123] The petition does not suspend the decision of the Board of Appeal so it continues to apply.[124] This may have consequences for third parties who start to use otherwise infringing products or processes pending the decision on the petition.

Alternatives to appeal: further processing

[2.61] EPC 1973 introduced further processing to permit the circumvention of the effects of missed deadlines. It initially covered failure to file documents so it only applied in limited circumstances. EPC 2000 expanded this to cover failure to pay fees. It also removed the requirement to wait until the application is withdrawn or abandoned before applying for further processing. Further processing requires only a simple request and a fee payment within two months of notification of the loss of rights[125] and there is no need to explain why the deadline was missed.

[2.62] Under EPC 2000, further processing has become the standard remedy for missed deadlines. Further processing will still be ruled out in respect of a small number of situations, including the time limits in respect of:

(a) requesting further processing or re-establishment of rights;
(b) the 12-month priority deadline;
(c) paying renewal fees under an extension;
(d) filing the declaration of priority;
(e) filing an appeal;
(f) filing a petition for review by the EBA;

---

[118] G2/06 *Stem Cells/Warf* [2009] EPOR 15.
[119] EPC, art 112a.
[120] Rule 108 EPC.
[121] Rule 109(1), (3) EPC.
[122] Rule 117 EPC.
[123] Rule 108(3) EPC.
[124] EPC, art 112a(3).
[125] Rule 135(1) EPC.

(g)   filing translations; and

(h)   filing divisional applications.[126]

Further processing is still not applicable in cases of a failure to pay renewal fees on time. Restitutio is the only option in such cases.

Alternatives to appeal: restitutio

[2.63] EPC 1973 introduced another procedure to assist in the circumvention of the effects of missed deadlines in special cases. This is known as 're-establishment of rights'[127] and is often called 'restitutio' (short for *'restitutio in integrum'*). EPC 1973 introduced restitutio for failures in correcting deficiencies and paying renewal fees. The EPC 2000 expanded restitutio to other areas, such as the period for filing a priority claim, which the further processing provisions would not cover. Indeed, restitutio cannot be sought where further processing is available instead.[128]

[2.64] The conditions for restitutio are strict. One must prove that the deadline was missed despite 'all due care' having been taken,[129] making it a much more burdensome option than further processing. The application for restitutio must generally be made within two months of the cause of non-compliance being removed (ie the failure being rectified) and not more than one year after the original time limit expired. An absolute deadline of two months applies for restitutio in relation to a priority claim or petition for review by the EBA.[130]

Translations

[2.65] A European patent is regarded as a bundle of national patents and therefore must comply with national requirements as to translations. This could involve significant translation costs of several thousand euro *per* patent. If the patent is the subject of an infringement action, the authentic text used by the court is the one granted by the EPO in one of the official EPO languages. Thus, the translations are rarely consulted in practice. Nonetheless, until 2008, most countries designated in a European patent required the filing of a translation of the patent specification into one of its official languages in a process known as 'validation'. The period for validation in all countries other than Ireland is three months. Rule 83 of the Irish Patents Rules 1992[131] provides for a six-month period. Where a translation was not filed by the due date, the European patent was deemed to be void *ab initio* in that country from the date of grant of the patent.[132] However, with the coming into force of the London Agreement on 1 May 2008, changes to the validation procedures were effected.

---

[126] EPC, art 121(4) and Rule 135(2).

[127] EPC, art 122.

[128] Rule 136(3) EPC.

[129] EPC, art 122(1).

[130] Rule 136(1) EPC.

[131] As replaced by the Patents (Amendment) Rules 2008.

[132] EPC, art 65(3); PA 1992, s 119(7).

London Agreement

[2.66] Countries[133] which have a national language which is one of the EPO official languages (English, French or German) will dispense entirely with translation requirements after accession to the London Agreement. Other countries have agreed only to require translation of the patent claims (not the full patent) into one specified EPO official language. Croatia, Denmark, Iceland, the Netherlands and Sweden have agreed to only require translation of the patent claims (not the entire patent specification) into their national languages provided that the text of the granted European patent specification is in the English language. Ireland has not yet acceded to the London Agreement, as of 1 July 2010. Regardless of accession to the London Agreement, when an application is allowed, it is still necessary to file a translation of the claims into the other two EPO official languages prior to grant.[134]

The effect of the London Agreement on Irish entities is that they will incur lower costs in seeking protection under the European patent system but that they may have to consider patents of third parties which are in French or German.

Duration

[2.67] Under art 63 of the EPC, the term of a European patent is 20 years from the date of filing of the application. A contracting state can extend the term of a European patent under the same conditions as those applying to its national patents in order to take into account a state of war or similar emergency conditions affecting that country. This article has been revised by an Act of 17 December 1991[135] and allows for the possibility of an extended term of duration of European patents whose subject matter is a product or a process of manufacturing a product or a use of a product which has to undergo an administrative authorisation procedure required by law before it can be put on the market.[136]

[2.68] Under EC Regulation No 1768/92 of 18 June 1992, concerning the Creation of a Supplementary Protection Certificate (SPC) for Medicinal Products, which has an effective date of 2 January 1993, EU Member States must allow for the duration of patents for medicinal products to be extended for a period equal to that which has elapsed between the date of filing the patent application and the date of grant of the first marketing authorisation in the EU, less five years. The maximum period for which this supplementary protection certificate can be granted is five years.[137] On 23 July 1996, the Council of Ministers adopted Regulation EC/1610/96 concerning the creation of a similar supplementary protection certificate (SPC) for plant protection products, eg herbicides, fungicides and insecticides.

---

[133] The UK, France, Germany and Switzerland plus Ireland if or when it accedes.

[134] If filed in English, the patent claims will have to be translated into French and German.

[135] OJ EPO 1997, p 313: entered into force on 4 July 1997.

[136] OJ EPO 1–2/1992, p 7.

[137] Plus a possible additional six months for a medicinal product for paediatric use. See para **[5.07]** *et seq.*

[2.69] In order to maintain a European patent application in force, it is necessary to pay annual renewal fees to the EPO. Under art 86 of the EPC, these fees are due in respect of the third year and each subsequent year, calculated from the date of filing of the application. The obligation to pay renewal fees to the EPO terminates on grant of the European patent. After grant, a European patent is subject to payment of national annuities in those countries in which the patent has been validated and in which it is desired to maintain protection.

Entitlement to file

[2.70] A European patent application may be filed by any national or legal person or any body equivalent to a legal person by virtue of the national law of the applicant's country.[138] There is no requirement for nationality of, or residence in, a contracting state. The right to a European patent belongs to the inventor or his successor in title.[139] If the inventor is an employee, the right to a European patent is determined by the law of the country in which the employee is mainly employed. If this cannot be established, the applicable law is that of the country in which the employer has its place of business to which the employee is attached. The inventor(s) must be identified (which is different to the position for Irish patents) and if the applicant is not the inventor or is not the sole inventor, there must be a statement indicating how the right to apply arose.[140]

Assignment and licences

[2.71] A European patent application can be assigned for one or more contracting states and such an assignment must be in writing.[141] In order to be effective, an assignment of a European patent application must be recorded in the EPO. After grant, assignment and recordal of the patent are governed by national laws.[142] A European patent application may be licensed in whole or in part for the whole or part of the territories of the designated contracting states.[143]

Unpatentable subject matter

[2.72] It is specifically stated in art 53[144] of the EPC that European patents shall not be granted in respect of:

(a)   inventions the publication or exploitation of which would be contrary to '*ordre public*' or morality, provided that the exploitation shall not be deemed to be so contrary merely because it is prohibited by law or regulation in some or all of the contracting states;

---

138 EPC, art 58.
139 EPC, art 60.
140 EPC, art 81.
141 EPC, art 72.
142 PA 1992, s 85; see also para [5.33] *et seq.*
143 EPC, art 73.
144 PA 1992, s 10.

(b)   plant or animal varieties or essentially biological processes for the production of plants or animals; this provision does not apply to microbiological processes or the products thereof; and

(c)   methods for treatment of the human or animal body by surgery or therapy and diagnostic methods practised on the human or animal body; this provision shall not apply to products, in particular substances or compositions, for use in any of these methods.

Article 52(4) of EPC 1973 had denied patentability to methods for treatment of the human or animal body by surgery or therapy and diagnostic methods practised on the human or animal body. This was achieved by means of a 'legal fiction' whereby such methods were not considered to be susceptible of industrial application. The EPC 2000 moved these methods to the exceptions to patentability in art 53(c) which was considered more intellectually honest as these are policy-based grounds founded on socio-ethical and public health considerations rather than a lack of susceptibility to industrial application.[145] However, regardless of the basis for refusal of these methods, products for use in any of these methods have always been patentable, sometimes even if these products were already known *per se* for use in a different method.

Criteria for patentability

[2.73] European patents are granted for any inventions which are susceptible of industrial application, which are new and which involve an inventive step.[146] The following are not regarded as inventions:[147]

(a)   discoveries, scientific theories and mathematical methods;

(b)   aesthetic creations;

(c)   schemes, rules and methods for performing mental acts, playing games or doing business, and programs for computers;

(d)   presentations of information.

These exclusions only apply to the extent to which a European patent application or patent relates to such subject matter or activities as such.[148]

Computer programs

[2.74] Originally, it was considered that an invention would be unpatentable if the novelty and inventive step lay completely in the computer program involved. Revised EPO guidelines[149] now adopt a more liberal approach. Thus, a computer program claimed as such or as a record on a carrier is unpatentable, irrespective of its content. The situation is normally unchanged when the computer program is loaded into a known computer. However, program controlled machines and program controlled

---

[145] G1/04 *Diagnostic methods*, OJ EPO 2006 334.

[146] EPC, art 52(1); PA 1992, s 9(1) as amended by the Patents (Amendment) Act 2006.

[147] EPC, art 52(2); PA 1992, s 9(2).

[148] EPC, art 52(3); PA 1992, s 9(3).

[149] EPO guidelines, C-IV, 2.3.

manufacturing and control processes are provided as examples of normally patentable subject matter. The combination of a known computer and a new program loaded into it could be patentable if the program causes the computer to operate in a new way from a technical point of view. What is required is a technical contribution to the known art; the essential ingredient in decisions of the EPO has been 'technical effect'. In the *Vicom* decision[150] in 1986, the EPO Technical Board of Appeal considered an application relating to a method and apparatus for improving the quality and speeding up of the processing of picture information. There was no novel end product but rather a process for manipulating electrical signals representing the picture in accordance with steps expressed mathematically. The Board decided that:

(a) even if the idea underlying an invention may be considered to reside in a mathematical method, a claim directed to a technical process in which the method is used does not seek protection for the mathematical method as such; and

(b) an invention which would be patentable in accordance with conventional patentable criteria should not be excluded from protection by the mere fact that for its implementation, modern technical means in the form of a computer program are used.

The technical contribution that the invention, as a whole, made to the known art was decisive. It was also regarded as illogical to grant protection for a technical process controlled by a suitably programmed computer but not for the computer itself when set up to execute the control. A distinction between embodiments of the same invention carried out in hardware or in software was held to be inappropriate as the choice between those two possibilities was not of an essential nature but was based on technical and economical considerations which bore no relationship to the inventive concept as such. The *Vicom* application was accepted with claims directed to a 'method of digitally filtering data'.

[2.75] In *Koch & Sterzel Application,*[151] the EPO Technical Board of Appeal considered the patentability of an x-ray apparatus controlled by a computer program to ensure optimum exposure with sufficient protection against overloading of the x-ray tube within a given routine. It was held that it was not necessary 'to weigh up the technical and non-technical features of a claim'. A mix of such features may be patentable if they interact so as to solve a technical problem.

The position of the EPO is reflected in two further decisions, involving IBM, which held that computer programs can be patentable if there are ' further technical effects going beyond the normal physical interactions between the program and the computer when the program runs or is loaded on a computer'.[152] However, a number of other IBM applications have been refused because they related to non-technical subject matter,

---

[150] T 208/84 *Vicom* [1987] EPOR 66.

[151] T 26/86 *Koch & Sterzel Application* [1988] EPOR 72.

[152] T 1173/97 *IBM and IBM II* [2000] EPOR 219; see para **[3.18]** *et seq.*

namely, document abstracting and retrieving,[153] linguistic expression processing[154] and spell checking.[155]

Micro-biological processes

[2.76] Article 53(b) of the EPC, which excludes patentability for plant or animal varieties or essentially biological processes for the production of plants or animals but permits patenting of microbiological processes or the products thereof, is almost identical to the wording in art 2(b) of the Strasbourg Convention.[156] Micro-organisms as such may be patented by a European patent. The words 'microbiological processes' include traditional processes using micro-organisms (but not essentially biological processes) and techniques of genetic engineering. Among patentable inventions are genetically engineered micro-organisms such as bacteria and viruses. Essentially, biological processes would include processes such as sexual reproduction. If the invention concerns a microbiological process or the product thereof and involves the use of a micro-organism which is not available to the public and which cannot be described in the European patent application in such a manner as to enable the invention to be carried out by a person skilled in the art, a culture of the micro-organism must be deposited with a recognised depositary institute. The institute must hold the status of international depositary authority under the Budapest Treaty on the International Recognition of the Deposit of Micro-organisms for the purpose of Patent Procedure (1977).[157]

Plant a n d animal varieties

[2.77] The unpatentability of plant varieties is due essentially to the existence of an alternative form of protection under the Convention for the Protection of New Varieties of Plants (UPOV – *Union Pour La Protection Des Obtentions Végétales*) 1961, as revised.[158] The practice of the EPO is to construe exclusions from patentability narrowly. Under the UPOV Convention,[159] a new variety must be distinct, uniform and stable. Hence, samples within the variety must be clearly distinguishable from previously known varieties, different samples within the variety must be similar and the variety must breed true over a number of generations. If these conditions are not complied with, then the EPO is inclined to consider that it is not a plant variety

---

[153] T22/85 *IBM/System for Abstracting Document* [1990] EPOR 98.
[154] T52/85 *IBM/Linguistic Expression Processing* [1989] EPOR 454.
[155] T121/85 *IBM/System for Spell Checking*, unreported, Supplement OJ EPO 6/1990, p 17.
[156] Strasbourg Convention on the Unification of Certain Points of Substantive Law on Patents for Invention, 27 November 1963; see para [2.25] *et seq.*
[157] Patents Rules 1992, r 14 as replaced by the Patents (Amendment) Rules 2009.
[158] Plant Varieties (Proprietary Rights) Act 1980 (Commencement) Order 1981 (SI 221/1981). See para [3.33] *et seq.*
[159] See para [3.33].

and hence is patentable, because only plants in the genetically fixed form of a plant variety are excluded from patentability.[160]

[2.78] Animal varieties are not patentable but this does not imply that a European patent cannot be granted for an animal. In the US, a patent was granted to Harvard University in relation to mice in which a particular gene had been introduced in order that the mice would develop a tumour. These were sold to laboratories as an aid to cancer research. The Examining Division in the EPO rejected the corresponding European application[161] on the grounds that animals are not patentable. The Technical Board of Appeal reversed the decision and sent the case back to the Examining Division to reconsider whether the application fell within the specific art 53 EPC exceptions including as to whether or not the invention was contrary to public order or morality. The Examining Division decided that the invention did not fall within any of the specific exclusions and, at the same time, decided that the invention assisted the research into cancer, posed no real threat to the environment and would reduce the overall level of animal suffering by reducing the number of animals required in conventional laboratory testing. The patent was granted. It was stressed that in other cases of transgenic animals, a different decision might be reached.

Novelty

[2.79] Article 52 of the EPC repeats art 1 of the Strasbourg Convention and states that European patents shall be granted for any inventions which are susceptible of industrial application, which are new and which involve an inventive step. Since EPC 2000 came into force, the definition of patentable inventions in art 52(1) now refers to 'all fields of technology' in line with TRIPS.

An invention is considered new if it does not form part of the state of the art.[162] The state of the art is everything made available to the public on a universal basis prior to the filing/priority date.[163] This involves the possibility that an invention may not be novel because of prior European patent applications which were not available to the public at the time of the later invention. Those earlier applications could destroy novelty but would not be taken into account for the purposes of assessing inventive step. They are often termed 'novelty only' prior art.[164] EPC 1973 applied a complicated system to such matters, where such applications would be deemed to form part of the state of the art only in overlapping designated countries.[165]

The EPC 2000 simplifies this system as it provides that all new European patent applications automatically cover all contracting states when filed. Therefore, any European patent application can act as 'novelty only' prior art against any later

---

[160] *Propagating Material/Ciba Geigy* [1984] OJEPO 112; *Hybrid Plants/Lubrizol* [1990] EPOR 173.
[161] *Harvard/Onco Mouse* [1990] EPOR 501.
[162] EPC, art 54(1).
[163] EPC, art 54(2).
[164] EPC, art 54(3).
[165] EPC 1973, art 54(3).

European patent applications. This does not change as regards any designation fees that might be paid. The EPO introduced a single designation fee of €525 on 1 April 2010. This means that applicants can defer making a decision to pursue protection in a particular country until after grant. This replaced the old system whereby designations were charged on a country-by-country basis with a maximum designation fee equivalent to the fee for seven designations. In this regard, EPC 1973 continues to apply for applications filed before 13 December 2007.

Non-prejudicial disclosures

[2.80] In a similar fashion to the Strasbourg Convention, the EPC allows for certain 'non-prejudicial disclosure' provided such disclosure does not occur more than six months prior to the filing of the European patent application.[166] These are as a consequence of:

(a)   an evident abuse in relation to the applicant or his legal predecessor, or

(b)   the fact that the applicant or his legal predecessor displayed the invention at an official, or officially recognised, international exhibition falling within the terms of the Convention of Paris on International Exhibitions of 22 November 1928, as revised on 30 November 1972.

In relation to (b), the applicant must, at the time of application, state that there has been such a display and, within four months of application, produce a certificate from the authority responsible for the protection of industrial property at that exhibition.

Priority rights

[2.81] In keeping with the Paris Convention, a European patent application may claim priority[167] by means of a declaration of priority. It is possible to correct or add a priority claim after filing, provided that it is done within 16 months from the priority date.[168] The date and country of the basic application must be identified. Priority may also be claimed from an earlier European patent application. This is called internal priority. It is also now possible to file a European patent application claiming priority from an application filed in a WTO country which is not party to the Paris Convention.[169]

Privilege and immunities of the EPO

[2.82] Under the European Patent Organisation (Designation and Immunities) Order 1996[170] the privileges and immunities of the European Patent Organisation under the EPC and the Protocol on the privileges and immunities of the European Patent Organisation have been implemented pursuant to the Diplomatic Relations and Immunities Acts 1967 and 1976.

---

[166] EPC, art 55; PA 1992, s 12(1).

[167] EPC, art 87; PA 1992, s 25(1) as amended by the Patents (Amendment) Act 2006.

[168] Rule 52(2) EPC.

[169] PA 1992, s 25(1) as amended by the Patents (Amendment) Act 2006.

[170] SI 392/1996.

PATENT CO-OPERATION TREATY

[2.83] The Patent Co-operation Treaty (PCT) was concluded in Washington on 19 June 1970 and ratified by Ireland with effect from 1 August 1992. Under art 1 of the PCT which is entitled 'Establishment of a Union', it is stated that the Union is created for the purpose of co-operation in the filing, searching and examination of applications, for the protection of inventions and for rendering special technical services. The Union is called the 'International Patent Co-operation Union'. There are 142 members (as of 1 July 2010) including all EU countries. The PCT is administered by the World Intellectual Property Organisation (WIPO) based in Geneva. The PCT, which does not result in any international patent, is divided into two 'chapters' and enables the filing of a single application designating as many contracting states as desired. It is also possible to designate the EPO in a PCT application.

[2.84] As significant changes were made to the PCT in respect of applications filed on or after 1 January 2004, the international phase will be dealt with under two sub-headings:

  (a)   applications filed before 1 January 2004;
  (b)   applications filed on or after 1 January 2004.

Applications filed before 1 January 2004

(I) PCT – Chapter I

[2.85] The 'international application' only needs to be filed in a single language and at a single Patent Office which is called the receiving office.[171] Irish applicants can file at the Irish Patents Office, the EPO or the International Bureau of WIPO.

[2.86] Priority can be claimed under the Paris Convention.[172] Subject to compliance with certain formalities, the receiving office accords as the international filing date, the date of receipt of the international application.[173] The receiving office then transmits a copy of the application to the International Bureau of WIPO and a further copy to the International Searching Authority (ISA).[174] The objective of the ISA is to discover any relevant prior art[175] and the search is made on the basis of the claims, with due regard to the description and any drawings. An International Search Report (ISR) is drawn up listing all of the documents that have any bearing on the patentability of the invention. The ISR is sent to the applicant and the International Bureau of WIPO. In the light of the search report, an applicant has a single opportunity to amend the claims voluntarily.[176]

---

[171] PCT, art 10.
[172] PCT, art 8.
[173] PCT, art 11.
[174] PCT, art 12.
[175] PCT, art 15(2).
[176] PCT, art 19.

[2.87] Approximately 18 months after the priority date, the International Bureau publishes the specification as filed together with the ISR (if available), and forwards the application and the ISR to the national Patent Offices of each contracting state designated, unless that requirement has been waived. The applicant is subsequently required to 'enter the national phase' in each country, at which point, the application becomes, in effect, a number of separate patent applications, one in each designated country, and these are prosecuted before the national Patent Offices or the EPO. Most applicants proceed with a limited number of countries selected from the list of designated countries and the application lapses for those countries in which national phase entry is not effected in due time.

[2.88] National phase entry entails, in most countries, filing a local language translation of the patent specification, appointing a local agent, and paying various national patent office fees. The deadline for national phase entry is 30 months (for some Patent Offices, most notably the EPO, 31 months) from the earliest priority date or, if no priority is claimed, from the filing date. Prior to 1 April 2002, a deadline of 20 months applied in some countries and Luxembourg, Uganda and the United Republic of Tanzania have[177] maintained this 20-month time limit pending revision of their national legislation.

(II) PCT – Chapter II

[2.89] If desired, the Chapter II (demand) phase must be requested within 19 months of the priority date, or the filing date of the PCT application, whichever is the earlier. The effect of filing a request under Chapter II is to postpone the deadline date for entry into the national phase from 20 months to 30 months from the priority date.

[2.90] Chapter II provides a system that allows patent applicants to request preliminary examination by an International Preliminary Examining Authority. This examination, which is stated to be non-binding, is as to novelty, inventive step and whether the claimed invention is industrially applicable.[178]

[2.91] The applicant will receive at least one Written Opinion listing any objections and is given a time period within which a response and any appropriate amendments may be filed. Within the prescribed time period, the Examination Report is drawn up.

[2.92] The Examination Report is transmitted to the applicant and to the International Bureau. This leads to the main current benefit of Chapter II applications: that the Written Opinion can be passed to national patent offices and it can assist the Examiner in that country examining the application and may enable granting of the patent with the minimum of costs and communication. In addition, having elected for Chapter II, an applicant can enter the national/regional phase within 30 months of the priority date for those countries which had retained the old 20-month deadline, although this is less important these days as the number of 20-month countries dwindles.

---

[177] As of 1 July 2010.
[178] PCT, art 33.

[2.93] The advantages of the PCT system are that, at a relatively low cost, it can delay the considerable expense of filing national or regional applications. This is important in many cases where cashflow problems arise in the early stages of a new product's life cycle. Translation costs do not arise until the national and/or regional filings.[179]

[2.94] It is also the experience of many patent practitioners that applicants may decide on foreign patent applications towards the very end of the 12-month priority period. In some cases, the decision to file is so late that translation(s) within the time scale allowed would not be possible. In these cases, the PCT system is a valuable tool. Ultimately, if applications are pursued, the PCT system does create an additional expenditure but there has been a deferral of patenting expenses, ie up to 30 months (Chapter II) as opposed to the normal 12-month priority period. Enterprise Ireland, which is the Irish State body responsible for funding certain patenting programs, often utilises the PCT system.

[2.95] Amendments to the PCT Regulations came into effect on 1 April 2007 and introduced changes which allow applicants to:

1. late-file missing elements and parts of the PCT application;
2. restore priority rights when cases are filed outside the normal 12-month priority period; and
3. rectify obvious mistakes more easily than before.

For the period from 1 April 2007 until 13 December 2007 when EPC 2000 came into force, the EPO had declared that the EPC was incompatible with the rule changes concerning (1) the missing elements and parts of the PCT application; and (2) the restoration of the right of priority. For applications filed on or after 13 December 2007, Rule 39a(3) of EPC 2000 provides essentially the same remedy as the corresponding PCT rule change. A related point to note is that EPC 2000 provides that the inclusion of one or more claims will no longer be a prerequisite for the accordance of a filing date. Therefore, once EPC 2000 came into force, missing elements were no longer an issue for obtaining a filing date in Europe.

[2.96] Rule 91 of the PCT has been substantially revised to make it easier to rectify obvious mistakes, but in practice, the revised rule makes little change to the type of rectifications that can be made. The most notable change is that now the mistake must be obvious to 'the competent authority' rather than to 'anyone'. There is also a new time limit which requires that a request for rectification must be submitted within 26 months from the earliest priority date, instead of the current 17-month deadline from the earliest priority date.

Rule 91(d) provides that, in case of a mistake in the description, claims or drawings, the competent authority shall only take into account the contents of the description, claims and drawings as originally filed. Mistakes which are not rectifiable include missing pages and parts, a mistake in the abstract, mistakes in amendments of the claims and mistakes in priority claims. The EPO has not submitted any reservation with respect to this rule change.

---

[179] PCT, art 39.

Designation

[2.97] Under art 45(2) of the PCT, it is stated that:

> the national law of the said designated or elected State may provide that any designation or election of such State in the International application shall have the effect of an indication of the wish to obtain a regional patent under the regional patent treaty.

One such regional patent treaty is the EPC. Ireland, together with Belgium, Cyprus, France, Greece, Italy, Latvia,[180] Malta, Monaco, the Netherlands, Slovenia, Swaziland and the African Intellectual Property Organisation (OAPI) countries have opted for this provision and so have excluded the grant of national patents directly from PCT applications. If patent protection in Ireland, for example, is desired via the PCT route, this can only be done by designating the EPO in the PCT application, and subsequently entering the European regional phase (in other words filing a European patent application) in which, at least, Ireland is a designated State. It is not possible to apply for a national Irish patent directly from an international patent application under the PCT.[181]

Applications filed on or after 1 January 2004

(I) Procedure under Chapter I

[2.98] In addition to the ISR, a Written Opinion will also be issued under PCT Chapter I. The main features of the Written Opinion are:

(a) it will be a preliminary non-binding opinion on the issues of novelty, inventive step and industrial applicability, similar in content and roughly equivalent to the current Written Opinion of the International Preliminary Examining Authority (IPEA);

(b) it will be transmitted by the ISA to the International Bureau (IB) and to the applicant, together with the ISR;

(c) unlike the ISR, the Written Opinion will not be published together with the international application;

(d) the IB and the ISA will not, unless requested or authorised by the applicant, allow access to it by any person or authority before the expiration of 30 months from the earliest priority date.

[2.99] Unlike the procedure under Chapter II, the applicant will not be given the opportunity to file amendments or arguments with the ISA prior to the ISA issuing the Written Opinion.

[2.100] After the Written Opinion is issued by the ISA, there is no express provision for it in the PCT Regulations but if the applicant so desires, it is possible to submit written comments to the IB on an 'informal' basis. This will be the only chance that the applicant will have to rebut the Written Opinion of the ISA in the international

---

[180] Which ceased granting national patents via the PCT in 2007.
[181] PA 1992, s 127(1).

phase if a demand (Chapter II) is not filed. Although any such informal comments will be forwarded to designated Offices together with the report mentioned below, they will not be transmitted to the ISA or indeed to the IPEA if a demand is filed later.[182] It will then be up to the designated offices to decide whether, and to what extent, to take the informal comments into account in the national phase.

[2.101] In addition, it will, of course, continue to be possible to submit amendments to the claims under art 19 of the PCT following the establishment of the ISR.

[2.102] If no demand has been filed, the Written Opinion issued by the ISA will be subsequently converted by the IB into an 'International Preliminary Report on Patentability (Chapter I of the Patent Co-operation Treaty)' (IPRP (Chapter I)), with essentially the same content as the Written Opinion of the ISA. The IPRP (Chapter I) will be:

(a) communicated to the designated Offices by the IB, but not before the expiration of 30 months from the priority date (although the Written Opinion of the ISA, as opposed to the IPRP (Chapter 1), may be communicated to a particular designated Office earlier than this in a case where the applicant has requested early national processing under art 23(2) before that Office);

(b) made available by the IB for public inspection but not before the expiration of 30 months from the earliest priority date.[183]

(II) Procedure under Chapter II

[2.103] If desired, the Chapter II (demand) phase must be requested within three months from the date of transmittal by the ISA of the ISR and the Written Opinion, or 22 months from the earliest priority date (or the international filing date if priority has not been claimed), whichever expires later.

[2.104] The Written Opinion which has been issued by the ISA will, in general, be used by the IPEA as its own first opinion, unless the IPEA notifies the IB to the contrary.

[2.105] Unlike the procedure under Chapter I, the applicant will be given the opportunity to file amendments to the description, claims and drawings (under art 34(2)(b) of the PCT) and arguments concerning the Written Opinion which will be taken into account by the IPEA. The IPEA may, at its discretion, issue further Written Opinions, provided that sufficient time is available, the applicant makes an effort to meet the Examiner's objections and the IPEA has sufficient resources to provide such services.

[2.106] An International Preliminary Examination Report will generally be issued by the IPEA around 28 months from the earliest priority date and will bear the title

---

[182] In which case any response to the Written Opinion would need to be submitted to the IPEA under PCT, art 34 as part of the international preliminary examination procedure.

[183] PCT, rr 44ter and 94.1(b).

'International Preliminary Report on Patentability (Chapter ll of the Patent Co-operation Treaty)' (IPRP (Chapter ll)). This report will be:

(a) transmitted by the IB to each elected Office, but, unless the applicant has made an express request to an elected Office under Article 40(2) of the PCT, not before the expiration of 30 months from the earliest priority date. Any arguments submitted by the applicant to the IPEA will also be accessible, upon request, to elected Offices as part of the file of the IPEA;

(b) made publicly available by the IB, provided than an elected Office has requested that this service be provided on its behalf, but not before the expiration of 30 months from the priority date unless so requested by the applicant.

Factors in deciding whether to file a demand under Chapter II

[2.107] The decision as to whether to file a demand or not may depend, to a large extent, on the results of the international search and the contents of the Written Opinion of the ISA. Where the Written Opinion of the ISA is not entirely positive, the applicant may wish to use the international preliminary examination procedure with a view to obtaining a positive IPRP (Chapter ll), either by presenting arguments to the IPEA Examiner (either in writing or orally) or by filing amendments to the description, claims and drawings. A positive IPRP (Chapter ll) could have considerable influence on the further prosecution of the application before the national Offices, in particular before those which do not require, or do not have the resources themselves to conduct, substantive examination of all international applications before granting a patent.

[2.108] It is important to note, however, that a demand should still be filed prior to the expiration of 19 months from the priority date if the applicant wishes to postpone entry into the national phase before those elected Offices which have not withdrawn their notifications of the incompatibility of the time limit under art 22(1) PCT with the applicable national law. The only countries which now apply a 20-month deadline are Luxembourg, Uganda and the United Republic of Tanzania.

COMMUNITY PATENT CONVENTION/EUROPEAN UNION PATENT

[2.109] By way of amendment to Article 29 of the Irish Constitution and following a Referendum,[184] the Eleventh Amendment of the Constitution Act 1992 introduced as Article 29.4.6° a provision that:[185]

> The State may ratify the Agreement relating to Community Patents drawn up between the Member States of the Communities and done at Luxembourg on the 15th day of December, 1989.

[2.110] The Community Patent Convention (CPC) was signed by all Member States of the EU. The CPC has not come into force and it requires ratification by all Member

---

[184] Held on 18 June 1992.
[185] 89/695/EEC, OJ L 401, 30 December 1989, p 1–27.

States, which is unlikely to occur at present. Under art 142 of the EPC, it is provided that any group of contracting states, which has provided by a special agreement that a European patent granted for those States has a unitary character throughout their territories, may provide that a European patent may only be granted jointly in respect of all of those States.

[2.111] The entry into force of the CPC has been identified by the European Commission of European Communities as necessary for the completion of the internal market under the Treaty on the Functioning of the European Union (the Treaty).[186] The objective is to remove the distortion of competition which may result from the territorial aspect of national patent rights. Under the CPC, this was to be achieved by establishing a Community patent system whereby a European patent granted by the EPO would have a unitary and autonomous character throughout the EU. As stated in the White Paper on the Treaty on European Union, the introduction of a Community patent system as envisaged by the Agreement would have a number of consequences:

(a)   Community patents would be granted on the basis of a single application for each such patent made to the EPO;

(b)   annual renewal fees would be payable in a single payment to the EPO;

(c)   a single patent licence agreement for a Community patent could be established for the internal market under the Treaty; and

(d)   Community patents would be subject to the common system of law set down in the Agreement.

[2.112] The unitary effect of a Community patent means that it could be granted, transferred, revoked or allowed to lapse only in respect of the whole of the EU.[187] Infringement is a matter to be tried in national courts[188] although application for revocation of a Community patent could be filed before the EPO.[189]

[2.113] There have been a number of Resolutions to the CPC, two of which have recognised the inconsistencies that can result from issues of infringement of a Community patent being decided in national courts. The Resolution on the centralisation in each contracting state of jurisdiction in actions for infringement of Community patents calls for judges experienced in such actions in all contracting states and centralisation of first instance jurisdiction to guarantee that actions will be dealt with by judges experienced in this field. An example of the problems which can arise can be seen in the *Epilady* case[190] where the English Patents Court refused an interlocutory injunction because of the absence of an arguable case that there was an infringement, and in an identical action in Germany, infringement was held to exist. The English Court of Appeal reversed the decision and granted the injunction taking cognisance of the German decision when deciding as to whether or not there was an

---

[186] [2010] OJ C 83 of 30 March 2010.

[187] CPC, art 2(2).

[188] CPC, art 69.

[189] CPC, art 56.

[190] *Improver Corpn v Remington Consumer Products Ltd* [1989] RPC 69.

arguable case. The German courts on appeal removed the injunction. Then at the full hearing, the English Patents Court held there was no infringement but the German court took the opposite view. In opposition proceedings before the EPO, the patent was revoked.

[2.114] At a diplomatic conference in Brussels in 1985, agreement was reached to provide for appeals from 'Community Patent Courts' at first instance, such as the Irish High Court, to be taken to a Common Patent Appeal Court (COPAC).[191] A further diplomatic conference in Luxembourg in December 1989 concluded a package of documents concerning COPAC and the protocol on the settlement of litigation concerning the infringement and validity of Community patents. These form the Agreement relating to Community patents and which is identified in Article 29.4.6° of the Irish Constitution.

[2.115] The creation of a centralised litigation procedure at this appellate level caused constitutional problems because effectively, decisions relating to property rights in Ireland would be dealt with by a court not established, and judges not appointed, in a manner provided for under the Constitution.[192] Article 29.4.5° of the Constitution provides that:

> No provision of this Constitution invalidates laws enacted, acts done or measures adopted by the State which are necessitated by the obligations of membership of the European Union or of the Communities or prevents laws enacted, acts done or measures adopted by the European Union or the Communities or by institutions thereof, or by bodies competent under the Treaties establishing the Communities, from having the force of law in the State.

[2.116] However, the CPC is an inter-governmental agreement outside the legal framework of the European Community treaties and would not fall within the ambit of this Article. Hence the need for the Referendum and the Eleventh Amendment of the Constitution Act 1992.

[2.117] Various initiatives have been taken to try to have the CPC ratified by all Member States. The biggest obstacle has been the refusal of some Member States to waive the requirement that the granted patent specification be translated into all of the EU's official languages. The perceived cost of this translation regime has made the Community Patent unattractive to industry. In 1997, the European Commission published a green paper proposing that the Community Patent be introduced by means of a Regulation, but despite intensive efforts to obtain agreement on the proposed Regulation since then, the language issue has defeated all attempts to find an acceptable compromise. Despite a proposal for a Community Patent Regulation and political agreement on the principle, the proposal foundered in 2004 when wording could not be agreed by the Ministers.

---

[191] Protocol on the Settlement of Litigation Concerning the Infringement and Validity of Community Patents (Brussels, 1985).

[192] Constitution of Ireland, Article 34.

[2.118] The subject was revived in 2006 when the European Commission launched a public consultation, followed by a White Paper in 2007. Agreement in principle on the renamed 'EU patent' was announced in December 2009 after a proposal to overcome the translation issues using machine translations. There is much to be decided and a finalised piece of legislation is some time away. However, now that the impasse has been resolved, other proposals have been progressed. For example a European and EU Patents Court has been proposed that will have exclusive jurisdiction over infringement and validity of European patents and EU patents.

BUDAPEST TREATY

[2.119] Ireland is a contracting state of the Budapest Treaty on the International Recognition of the Deposit of Micro-Organisms for the Purposes of Patent Procedure (1977) (Budapest Treaty). The Treaty entered into force for the first five countries, ie Bulgaria, France, Hungary, Japan and the US on 19 August 1980 and is now in force in 73 countries as of 1 July 2010, including the US and the UK. The basis of the Budapest Treaty is that contracting states are bound to recognise the deposit of a micro-organism with any depositary institution which has the status of international depositary authority under the Budapest Treaty. Such recognition includes the recognition of the fact and date of the deposit as indicated by the international depositary authority as well as the recognition of the fact that what is furnished as a sample is a sample of the deposited micro-organism.

[2.120] On 26 August 1980, the EPO filed the declaration specified in art 9 of the Budapest Treaty. This declaration states that the EPO accepts the obligation of recognition provided for in art 3(1)(a) of the Budapest Treaty, the obligations concerning the requirements in art 3(2) and all the effects of the provisions of the Budapest Treaty and the Regulations applicable to inter-governmental industrial property organisations.

[2.121] The Budapest Treaty is referred to in r 14 of the Patents Rules 1992, which also refers to certain forms provided for by the Regulations under the Budapest Treaty. Rule 14 provides for the depositing of a culture of a micro-organism with a depositary institution and the recognition of such. The definition of a depositary institute under r 14(21) means Ireland will almost certainly recognise the status of all international depositary authorities established under the Budapest Treaty because these authorities would:

    (a)   carry out the function of receiving, accepting and storing micro-organisms and the furnishing of samples thereof; and

    (b)   conduct its affairs in so far as they relate to the carrying out of those functions in an objective and impartial manner.

The Irish government approved accession to the Budapest Treaty and it came into force in Ireland on 15 December 1999.

TRIPS

[2.122] TRIPS is the acronym used to refer to the Agreement on Trade-Related Aspects of Intellectual Property Rights. TRIPS is part of the World Trade Organisation Agreement (WTO Agreement) which was formally signed by Ireland on 15 April 1994 and ratified on 15 November 1994. Following Council Decision No 94/800/EEC on 30 December 1994, the EU, Ireland and other EU Member States deposited instruments of ratification. The WTO Agreement including TRIPS entered into force on 1 January 1995, although art 65(1) of TRIPS does contain a one-year transitional grace period.

[2.123] The objective of TRIPS, as part of the negotiations to revise the General Agreement on Tariffs and Trade (GATT) and as stated in the preamble, is to reduce distortions and impediments to international trade by promoting effective and adequate protection of intellectual property rights and by ensuring that measures and procedures to enforce intellectual property rights do not themselves become barriers to legitimate trade. This is achieved in the main by identifying minimum standards to which each State must adhere. The provisions dealing with patents are contained in TRIPS, Pt II, s 5 (arts 27–34).

[2.124] In general, the PA 1992 is in compliance with the minimum thresholds imposed by TRIPS except in respect of the working requirements (requirements to manufacture the product within Ireland within a certain period of time) and compulsory licensing provisions. Article 27(1) of TRIPS states that 'patents shall be available and patent rights enjoyable without discrimination as to the place of invention, the field of technology and whether products are imported or locally produced'. This was considered by the Irish High Court in *Allen and Hanburys Ltd and Glaxo Group Ltd v Controller and Clonmel Healthcare Ltd*[193] and it was conceded that s 42 of the PA 1964 which allowed for a compulsory licence in respect of certain categories of invention[194] was indeed discriminatory. Section 70(3)(f) of the PA 1992 (now deleted by the Patents (Amendment) Act 2006) was an equivalent provision which was specific to patents relating to food and medicine in identifying that, in settling the terms of a compulsory licence for such:

> the Controller shall endeavour to secure that food and medicine shall be available to the public at the lowest prices consistent with the proprietors of patents deriving reasonable remuneration having regard to the nature of the invention.

Article 31 of TRIPS does allow for a compulsory licence, ie use without authorisation of the right holder but with certain in-built safeguards. Under art 31(b), except in the case of a national emergency, other circumstances of extreme urgency or public non-commercial use, it is necessary for a licence to be sought from the right holder on reasonable commercial terms and conditions and that such efforts have not been successful within a reasonable period of time. Although art 31(k) does allow the provision in art 31(b) to be negated where use is required to remedy a practice

---

[193] *Allen and Hanburys Ltd and Glaxo Group Ltd v Controller and Clonmel Healthcare Ltd* [1997] FSR 1.
[194] Namely foodstuffs and medicines.

which has been determined as anti-competitive, it is readily apparent that the provisions allowing for a compulsory licence in s 70 of the PA 1992[195] are broader than those allowed for under TRIPS.

[2.125] Article 34 of TRIPS deals with the burden of proof in the case of process patents for new products and is already reflected in s 46 of the PA 1992 in providing that the same product when produced without the consent of the patent owner shall, in the absence of proof to the contrary, be deemed to have been obtained by the patented process. In art 34, this can arise in circumstances where either:

(a)   the product obtained by the patented process is new; or

(b)   there is a substantial likelihood that the identical product was made by the process and the owner of the patent has been unable, through reasonable efforts, to determine the process actually used.

[2.126] Patentable subject matter is identified in art 27 of TRIPS as requiring inventions to be new, involve an inventive step and be capable of industrial application.[196] The rights which must be conferred by a patent in art 28 are already in place in Irish law by virtue of s 40 of the PA 1992.

---

[195] As amended by the Patents (Amendment) Act 2006.
[196] PA 1992, s 9(1).

Chapter 3

Patents Act 1992 – Patentability

INTRODUCTION

[3.01] The Patents Act 1992 (PA 1992) came into operation on 1 August 1992.[1] The PA 1992 enabled ratification of the European Patent Convention (EPC) and Patent Co-operation Treaty (PCT) and subject to the transitional provisions, repealed the Patents Act 1964 (PA 1964) and the Patents (Amendment) Act 1966. Unlike the PA 1964, there is no definition of 'invention'. There are, however, new criteria as to what is patentable. There is no longer an opposition procedure and the patent term under the PA 1992 is 20 years[2] with no provision for an extended term other than the limited ability to obtain a Supplementary Protection Certificate in appropriate circumstances.[3] The PA 1992 also introduces the completely new concept of a short-term patent. Also new to Irish law is the payment of annual maintenance fees on patent applications and a broader definition of infringement which embraces indirect use of an invention. From a practical point of view, the PA 1992 also streamlined the system for examination, and reduced the backlog of patent applications, which on 1 August 1992 was approximately five to six years. This backlog has also been reduced because of the greatly reduced number of Irish national patent applications as a consequence of ratification of the EPC.[4] In addition, the PA 1992 imposes a minimal obligation on the Irish Patents Office as regards examination.

[3.02] It should be noted that the Irish draftsmen did not copy or even mimic closely the UK Patents Act 1977. The UK Patents Act 1977 in s 130(7) provides that many sections of the Act are framed so as to have, as nearly as practicable, the same effect in the UK as the corresponding provisions of the EPC and the PCT in the territories to which those conventions apply. The effect of this is that in interpreting those sections identified, due weight must be given to the relevant provisions of the EPC and PCT and to their *travaux préparatoires*, such as official minutes of the conferences which led to the wording which was adopted.[5] This was deemed necessary because the UK draftsmen added their own gloss to the provisions which originated in the EPC and PCT and altered the wording to put them into UK statute format. No similar catch-all

---

[1]   Patents Act 1992 (Commencement) Order 1992 (SI 181/1992).

[2]   Previously 16 years under the PA 1964.

[3]   See para **[5.07]** *et seq*.

[4]   In 1991, there were 4,580 patent applications filed in the Irish Patents Office. In 1995 there were only 990 applications filed, of which 628 applications were for short-term patents. In 2008 there were 1,007 applications filed, of which 550 were for short-term patents.

[5]   *Fothergill v Monarch Airlines* [1980] 2 All ER 696.

provision is contained in the PA 1992 as the Irish draftsmen closely followed the wording of the EPC.[6] The Irish courts have also been willing to examine parliamentary history as an interpretation aid. In *Wavin Pipes Ltd v Hepworth Iron Co Ltd*,[7] Costello J observed that 'it had obviously been found helpful to base a great deal of Irish patent law on the law as it had evolved in England both as a result of judicial decisions and statutory enactment' but was prepared to find that differences did exist in the revocation sections of the old UK Patents Act 1949 and the Irish Patents Act 1964 (PA 1964). In addition, Costello J obtained assistance in the interpretation of the PA 1964 from an examination of its parliamentary history. In doing so, he followed the Supreme Court decision in *Bourke v A-G and Wymes*[8] which examined the *travaux préparatoires* of the European Convention on Extradition (1957) and formed the view that:

> if the Courts can properly look at the history of the adoption of an International Convention for the purpose of ascertaining the meaning of the words used in it, there would appear to be no reason in principle why in appropriate cases, they should not be free when construing the words of a statute to obtain assistance from the history of its enactment by Parliament.

[3.03] Section 129 of the PA 1992 specifically provides that judicial notice and notice by the Controller shall be taken of the EPC, PCT and, if or when ratified, the CPC. This includes decisions or opinions of 'a competent authority' under the EPC. In *Genentech Inc's Patent*,[9] Mustill LJ gave this term a restrictive interpretation by stating that this provision is directed to evidentiary matters, ie the proof of matters that might otherwise have to be proven as foreign law. It does not give any greater status to rulings of other courts than they would otherwise have possessed. The Enlarged Board of Appeal (EBA) of the EPO would be considered a competent authority and under the corresponding UK section, judicial notice has been taken of its decisions.[10]

[3.04] The Patents (Amendment) Act 2006 amended s 9(5) of the PA 1992 pursuant to which the criteria as to what is patentable and the requirements of novelty can be modified by the Minister following any amendment of the EPC.

WHAT INVENTIONS ARE PATENTABLE?

[3.05] Chapter II of the PA 1992 deals with patentability and conforms to arts 52 to 57 of the EPC and arts 1 to 5 of the Strasbourg Convention 1963. The PA 1964 included a definition of an invention as:

> any new and useful art, process, machine, manufacture or composition of matter, or any new and useful improvement in any art, process, machine, manufacture or

---

[6] Limited interpretation provisions were included in the PA 1992, s 38(7) (inserted by the Patents (Amendment) Act 2006) (amendments after grant) and s 45(3) (extent of protection) referring to the EPC.

[7] *Wavin Pipes Ltd v Hepworth Iron Co Ltd* [1982] FSR 32.

[8] *Bourke v A-G and Wymes* [1972] EPC 36.

[9] *Genentech Inc's Patent* [1989] RPC 147 at 266.

[10] *John Wyeth's and Schering's Applications* [1985] RPC 545.

composition of matter, and includes an alleged invention and also any new method or process of testing applicable to the improvement or control of manufacture.

The PA 1992 has no such definition and it simply states in s 9(1)[11] that an invention shall be patentable if it is susceptible of industrial application, is new and involves an inventive step. The PA 1992 specifically identifies in ss 9(2), (3) and 10[12] what is not considered to be an invention and what are unpatentable inventions. These are:

(a)   a discovery, scientific theory or a mathematical method;

(b)   an aesthetic creation;

(c)   a scheme, rule or method for performing a mental act, playing a game or doing business, or a program for a computer;

(d)   the presentation of information;

(e)   a method for treatment of the human or animal body by surgery or therapy;

(f)   a diagnostic method practised on the human or animal body;

(g)   a plant or animal variety or an essentially biological process for the production of plants or animals other than a microbiological process or the products thereof; and

(h)   an invention whose publication or exploitation would be contrary to public order or morality.

The subject matter or activities in (a) to (d) are excluded from patentability 'only to the extent to which a patent application or patent relates to such subject matter or activities as such'.[13]

Discovery, scientific theory or mathematical method

[3.06] In *Reynolds v Herbert Smith & Co Ltd*,[14] Buckley J drew the following distinction between discovery and invention:

> discovery adds to the amount of human knowledge, but it does so only by lifting the veil and disclosing something which before had been unseen or dimly seen. Invention also adds to human knowledge, but not merely by disclosing something. Invention necessarily involves also the suggestion of an act to be done, and it must be an act which results in a new product, or a new result, or a new process, or a new combination for producing an old product or an old result.

Thus a discovery is not patentable but a product or process making use of such could be patentable. The term 'mere discovery' is used to describe the discovery of a new advantage for an old article or process. A mere discovery is also unpatentable. In *Adhesive Dry Mounting Co Ltd v Trapp & Co*,[15] it was held that the idea of using an old material for an entirely new purpose, not being analogous to a purpose for which it had

---

[11]   As amended by the Patents (Amendment) Act 2006.

[12]   As amended by the Patents (Amendment) Act 2006.

[13]   PA 1992, s 9(3).

[14]   *Reynolds v Herbert Smith & Co Ltd* (1902) 20 RPC 123 at 126.

[15]   *Adhesive Dry Mounting Co Ltd v Trapp & Co* (1910) 27 RPC 341.

previously been used, may be good subject matter for a patent, but such an idea, however ingenious, can hardly justify a claim to a patent for the material itself.

New use of known article or substance

[3.07] A new use of a known article or substance may be patentable despite the fact that it already forms part of the state of the art for the known use. The leading case in this area is G2/88 *Friction Reducing Additive/MOBIL OIL III*.[16] Its main findings were:

(a) a new use of an old thing for a new purpose can be patentable;

(b) an old use of an old thing for a new purpose is not patentable as the only novelty is in the mind of the actor which is subjective;

(c) if there is no technical feature which reflects the new use, then there is no novel technical feature as all of the technical features are known;

(d) a new use in itself can be a technical feature if there is a new technical effect which underlies the new use.

In summary, a new use may reflect a newly discovered technical effect which is then regarded as a functional technical feature, ie the achievement in a particular context of that technical effect. If that technical feature had not previously been made available, then it is novel even though that technical effect may have inherently taken place in the state of the art.

[3.08] Even without the specific exclusion which is contained in the PA 1992, mathematical methods have long been held to be unpatentable. In *Young v Rosenthal*,[17] it was succinctly described by Grove J who gave the example: 'supposing a person discovered that three angles of a triangle are equal to two right angles, that is an abstract discovery and would not be the subject of a patent'. In *LIPS' Application*,[18] a claim for a ship's propeller was refused because it differed from the prior art only by the process of calculation by which its profile was determined and the only novelty alleged was the mental process by which the propeller blade thickness at different radical positions was determined.

Aesthetic creations

[3.09] The term 'aesthetic creations' is used in art 52(2)(b) of the EPC. In the UK Patents Act 1977, the words used are 'a literary, dramatic, musical or artistic work or any other aesthetic creation whatsoever'. The Copyright and Related Rights Act 2000 in Ireland does not define 'aesthetic' and in fact copyright can subsist in, for example, an artistic work irrespective of its artistic quality.[19] It is possible for patent and copyright

---

[16] G2/88 *Friction Reducing Additive/MOBIL OIL III* OJ EPO 1990 93, [1990] EPOR 73; [1990] OJ EPO 93.

[17] *Young v Rosenthal* (1884) 1 RPC 29 at 31.

[18] *LIPS' Application* [1959] RPC 35.

[19] Copyright and Related Rights Act 2000, s 2.

protection to exist in the same product. An object of aesthetic creation may be registrable as a design under the Industrial Designs Act 2001.

Schemes, rules or methods of performing a mental act, playing a game or doing business

[3.10] The exclusion from patentability of a scheme, rule or method for performing a mental act, playing a game or doing business is attributable to the view that these are most appropriate, if anything, to copyright law. Again, the boundaries between patent and copyright law can and do overlap and so, for example, the rules for a board game can enjoy copyright protection as a literary work and simultaneously patent protection can exist for the game apparatus, that is the pieces and the board, to be played in accordance with the rules.[20] The game of *Monopoly* was patented as are a multiplicity of other board games. In *Cobianchi's Application*,[21] a patent was allowed for a special pack of cards designed for playing canasta, the main novelty being that the symbols shown in two colours on an ordinary pack of cards were replaced by pips or other markings in two colours, ie a new pack of cards for playing an old game. Although this decision hinged on the old definition of an invention as a 'manner of new manufacture', the proviso in s 9(3) of the PA 1992 is likely to have brought about the same result since it is not the rules *per se* which were being patented and the rules were in any event known. The distinction is sometimes very narrow since the rules, although not patentable *per se*, are taken into account when deciding on novelty. A patent for a new arrangement of markings on the playing surface of a roulette game was refused.[22] Ingenuity or usefulness does not make a scheme or plan patentable[23] nor does the implementation of new workforce practices or the better use of manpower.[24] In refusing the grant of a patent for an invention entitled 'method of notation in writing music for pianos, organs and other musical instruments',[25] it was recognised that it is impossible to lay down a guiding principle but it appears that this case was decided on the basis of a lack of any technical aspect (ie susceptibility to industrial application). This decision was distinguished in *Pitman's Application*[26] where a patent was allowed for a method and means of teaching the pronunciation of a language since its recommended use in a speaking machine meant that a definite mechanical purpose was apparent. The position in the US on business methods has been more favourable than in Europe.[27]

---

[20] Notes of official rulings (1926) 43 RPC Appendix i.

[21] *Cobianchi's Application* (1953) 70 RPC 199.

[22] *Kent & Thanet Casinos Ltd v Baileys School of Dancing Ltd* [1968] RPC 318.

[23] *Ward's Application* (1911) 29 RPC 79 refusing a patent for a system of indexing.

[24] *Quigley's Application* [1977] FSR 373 (Australian decision).

[25] *C's Application* (1919) 37 RPC 247.

[26] *Pitman's Application* [1969] RPC 646.

[27] *Bilski v Kappos* (No 08-964, 28 June 2010), SC.

Presentation of information

[3.11] In relation to the issue of the presentation of information, in *Johnson's Application*,[28] a patent was refused because the different colouring of fertilisers used to distinguish one from another was considered as adding nothing to the efficiency of the fertiliser. This can be contrasted with *ITS Rubber Ltd's Application*,[29] which related to a squash ball characterised by being blue in colour, which aided vision. It was held that the colouring added a desirable characteristic and could be considered a manner of new manufacture. The subject matter was not the presentation of information as such, since the objective of the colouring achieved more than the mere purpose of differentiating different categories of squash ball.

Computer programs

[3.12] The exclusion of computer programs as such from patentability is taken from art 52(2)(c) and 52(3) of the EPC.[30] Similar wording is used in the UK Patents Act 1977.[31] It has long been acknowledged that computer programs enjoy copyright protection as a literary work. Notwithstanding this, in the UK and other countries, a large number of patents have been granted for inventions in which the computer program is an integral part, and in some cases, the only novel feature. The pursuit of patent protection for software-related inventions is attributable to a bid for the broader scope of protection than that existing under copyright law. The UK courts have also considered these provisions in detail. In *Merrill Lynch Inc's Application*,[32] Falconer J in the Patents Court considered an application in respect of a data processing system for implementing an automated trading market for securities. Also at issue was whether or not the application should be refused on the basis that it merely related to a method of doing business. A narrow and restrictive approach was taken in holding that there was no patentable subject matter because of lack of novelty in anything other than the computer program. This decision flew in the face of the *Vicom* decision of the EPO.[33] In *Genentech Inc's Patent*,[34] Dillon LJ in the Court of Appeal did not accept the reasoning of Falconer J and described it as 'a drastic change from English law as previously understood' quoting with approval the statement of Whitford J in the UK Patents Court, namely 'it is trite law that you cannot patent a discovery, but if on the basis of that discovery, you can tell people how it can be usefully employed, then a patentable invention may result'.[35] While critical of Falconer J's reasoning, the Court of Appeal made it clear that they were not voicing disagreement with the decision in the *Merrill Lynch* case, stating that:

---

[28] *Johnson's Application* (1930) 47 RPC 361.
[29] *ITS Rubber Ltd's Application* [1979] RPC 318.
[30] See para [2.74].
[31] UK Patents Act 1977, s 1 (2)(c).
[32] *Merrill Lynch Inc's Application* [1988] RPC 1.
[33] *Vicom* [1987] EPOR 66; see para [2.74].
[34] *Genentech Inc's Patent* [1989] RPC 147 at 240.
[35] *Genentech Inc's Patent* [1987] RPC 553 at 566, Patents Court (Whitford J).

it would be nonsense for the Act to forbid the patenting of a computer program, and yet permit the patenting of a floppy disc containing a computer program, or an ordinary computer when programmed with the program.

[3.13] In the Court of Appeal in *Merrill Lynch's Application*[36] Fox LJ quoted with approval the statement in *Vicom* that 'decisive is what technical contribution the invention makes to the known art', going on to say 'there must ... be some technical advance on the prior art in the form of a new result (eg a substantial increase in processing speed as in *Vicom*)'. The Court of Appeal dismissed the appeal, agreeing that there was no patentable invention.

[3.14] In *Gale's Application*,[37] the applicant had discovered an improved method of calculating the square root of a number with the aid of a computer. The Court of Appeal rejected the claim holding that it was:

> in substance a claim to a computer program, being the particular instructions embodied in a conventional type of ROM circuitry, and those instructions do not represent a technical process outside the computer or a solution to a technical problem within the computer.

The Court of Appeal also rejected the proposition that the prohibition against the patenting of computer programs as such could be circumvented by incorporating a program in a floppy disk.

[3.15] In *Fujitsu Ltd*[38] Laddie J reviewed the existing law in the context of software which assisted chemists to design new chemical compounds by enabling a computer operator to depict on his screen the crystal structure of two known chemicals. The two images could be rotated and their scales adjusted, so as to align the face of one with a complementary face of the other. It was possible to use the resulting picture as a blueprint for a new hybrid 'designer' chemical. Essentially the invention was the software which enabled the computer to be used as a tool to assist in the designing of new chemicals. Laddie J set out guiding principles and stated that the exclusion from patentability applied regardless of whether the subject matter was technical or non-technical. Focus was not to be directed to the control of the computer by the program, but to what the computer, so controlled, was doing. Laddie J held that the software left the operator to decide what data to work on, how to assess the results and which, if any, results should be used. The invention was held to be abstract and its effect determined by the personal skill and assessment of the operator. In substance, it was a scheme or method of performing a mental act and as such was unpatentable.

[3.16] A summary of the UK cases shows a movement towards the views of the EPO, ie the claimed invention must be viewed in its entirety to ascertain whether or not it addresses a technical problem as opposed to being simply an improvement in programming by the creation of new algorithms. The question is whether the software is essential to the achievement of a technical effect. The technical effect test is *a priori*, ie it is determined from general principles and it is not to be determined by comparison

---

[36] *Merrill Lynch's Application* [1989] RPC 561 at 569.
[37] *Gale's Application* [1991] RPC 305 at 328.
[38] *Fujitsu Ltd* [1996] RPC 511.

with the prior art. In relation to computer implemented inventions, the EPO Boards of Appeal[39] have specified that there must be a 'further technical effect', *ie* one going beyond the normal physical effects seen when programs are run. The term 'technical' is not defined but examples from the EPO include processing physical data[40] or processing that has an effect on the way in which a computer operates.[41]

[3.17] A proposal for a Directive on the patentability of computer implemented inventions was adopted by the European Commission in February 2002.[42] The proposed Directive retained the standard tests for patentability but stated that in order for there to be an inventive step, there had to be a technical contribution. The draft Directive sent to the European Parliament by the European Commission underwent many amendments, many of which introduced a special regime for computer-related inventions. Its proponents, such as IBM, Microsoft, Hewlett-Packard and the EPO supported it because they believed the Directive to be a confirmation of the existing practice relating to software patents. However, opponents of the directive objected to the vaguely defined phrase 'technical effect', arguing that the implementation of the harmonisation Directive would lead to abuse of the software patent system, suppressing innovation and eliminating competition by introducing a system that would allow almost unlimited patentability of software. The opponents carried the day and the final draft of the Directive was rejected by the European Parliament on 6 July 2005.

As a result, EU national patent laws and practices are not altered. The EPO continues to grant patents for software implemented inventions, which are widely defined as an invention whose implementation involves the use of a computer, computer network or other programmable apparatus, where the invention has one or more features which are realisable wholly or partly by means of a computer program, and which solves a technical problem. This position of the EPO has been reached through seminal decisions involving IBM and Hitachi. The EBA took the opportunity in G-3/08[43] to confirm the position reached in this case law.

T 1173/97 Computer Program Product/IBM[44]

[3.18] The EPO held that a computer program is not excluded from patentability under art 52(2) and (3) of EPC if, when it is run on a computer, it produces a further technical effect which goes beyond the 'normal' physical interactions between program (software) and computer (hardware). In reaching this conclusion, the EPO set out the following principles:

---

[39] T1173/97 *Computer Program Product/IBM*, OJ EPO 1999 609.

[40] T208/84 *Vicom* [1987] EPOR 74; T 26/86 *Koch & Sterzel Application* [1988] EPOR 72.

[41] T6/83 *IBM/Data Processor* [1990] EPOR 91; T59/93 *IBM/Method for interactive rotation of displayed graphic objects*, unreported, OJ EPO Special Edition 1995, 20 April 1994, p 14.

[42] COM (2002) 92.

[43] Opinion of the Enlarged Board of Appeal in relation to a point of law referred by the President of the EPO pursuant to art 112(1)(b) of the EPC, 12 May 2010.

[44] T1173/97 *Computer Program Product/IBM*, OJ EPO 1999 609; see also the identical decision in T0935/97 *IBM's Application* [1999] RPC 861, [1999] EPOR 301.

(a)   The EPO guidelines are not binding on the Board of Appeal, which can only interpret patents according to the EPC.

(b)   Technical character is an essential requirement under the EPC. Therefore, the term 'as such' means a mere abstract creation, lacking in technical character. Thus, a computer program or related product can be patentable if it has technical character.

(c)   Physical modifications of hardware, eg causing electrical currents, deriving from execution of the instructions given by programs do not create technical character. They are common features of all programs suitable for use on computers.

(d)   Where further effects deriving from the execution by the hardware of the instructions given by the program have a technical character or cause software to solve a technical problem, the invention can be patentable.

(e)   Examples of patentable software-implemented inventions include a program which manages an industrial process or the working of a piece of machinery and a program which is the only means or one of the necessary means of obtaining a technical effect achieved by the internal functioning of the computer.

(f)   Any specific further use of the system as a whole is irrelevant.

(g)   There is no reason to distinguish between a direct technical effect and the potential to produce technical effect (the indirect technical effect), ie a computer program.

(h)   The Board of Appeal overruled its own earlier case law which held that a computer program can be patentable where the basic idea underlying the invention resides in the program itself but distinguished these cases on the basis that none considered this type of program.

(i)   It is illogical to grant a patent for a method and not for the apparatus adapted for carrying out the same method, so it does not matter if the program itself is claimed or a recording of it on a carrier.

In summary, a computer program claimed by itself is not excluded from patentability if the program, when running on a computer or loaded into a computer, brings about, or is capable of bringing about, a technical effect which goes beyond the 'normal' physical interactions between the program and the computer hardware on which it is run.

T258/03 Auction Method/HITACHI[45]

[3.19] This decision involved an application for an automatic Dutch auction method executed in a server computer.[46] The main points of note from the decision are:

(a)   An apparatus is an invention since it comprises clearly technical features such as a 'server computer', 'client computers' and a 'network'. This reasoning is

---

[45] T258/03 *Auction Method/HITACHI* OJ EPO 2004 575 (in this case the invention was held to be obvious).
[46] Similar to the eBay system.

independent of the category of claim, so a claim to a method relating to a software-implemented invention is also not excluded from patentability.

(b)   The relevance of the technical aspects of the method claim should not need to be further qualified to determine technical character. If an invention is assessed based on the degree of banality of the technical features, this would have remnants of the German 'contribution to the state of the art' approach which has been held to be inapplicable to the registrability of European patents.

(c)   A method using technical means for a purely non-technical purpose is an invention. The presence of technical character may be implied by physical features or the nature of an activity or conferred on a non-technical activity by the use of technical means.

(d)   A non-invention as such would typically be a pure abstract concept devoid of any technical implications.

(e)   Method steps aimed at circumventing a technical problem rather than solving it by technical means cannot contribute to the technical character.

(f)   If a step in a method is particularly suited for being performed on a computer, it may be patentable.

Medical treatments

[3.20] Section 10(1)(c)[47] of the PA 1992 deals with methods for treatment of the human or animal body by surgery or therapy and diagnostic methods practised on the human body. These inventions were formerly the subject of a legal fiction, under which they were regarded as not susceptible of industrial application and therefore unpatentable under s 9(1). This was changed by the Patents (Amendment) Act 2006 which altered the treatment of these inventions so that they are now included in the exceptions to patentability.[48] These inventions are treated similarly under the EPC 2000. Short-term patents for such inventions would also appear to be precluded,[49] and if obtained, can be revoked.[50] This exclusion does not apply to a product, in particular a substance or composition, for use in any such method. The *Banks Report*[51] considered the possibility of patentability of known compounds in a known form that could be used against a disease for which it was not previously thought to be effective. It was considered that the extension of patent protection in this way would result, in effect, in patents for the treatment of human beings, since a claim for such an invention would have to specify the condition against which the compound was effective and include instructions for its use. This was considered to be undesirable. However, attitudes to such inventions have softened and second medical uses of known medicaments are now patentable under s 11(4).

---

[47]   Formerly PA 1992, s 9(4).
[48]   See para **[2.72]**.
[49]   PA 1992, s 63(4).
[50]   PA 1992, s 58 as amended by the Patents (Amendment) Act 2006, s 67.
[51]   Banks (Chairman), 'Report of the Committee to Examine the Patent System and Patent Law' (1970) Cmnd 4407.

[3.21] Under the PA 1964, methods for the medical treatment of human beings were considered unpatentable because they fell outside the definition of an invention by virtue of not being a 'manufacture'. In *C & W's Application*,[52] a patent was refused for a process of extracting lead from persons suffering from lead poisoning. It was considered that the question to be asked is whether the process is something to be used in the making of an object that is or may be of commercial value or is a process adapted to that end. In *Neva Corpn's Application*,[53] the principle that a process for the treatment of the human body could not be a manner of manufacture was confirmed by the refusal of an application in respect of a method of inducing loss of pain sensibility by sound recording.

[3.22] The courts have focussed on the word 'medical' and consider this as being limited to treatments of a curative nature. A patent was allowed for a method of contraception[54] and a method of defence against a human assailant by the injection of a painful non-lethal chemical irritant.[55] In the Australian case of *Joos v Comr of Patents*,[56] Barwick CJ allowed a patent for a process of improving the strength and elasticity of human hair observing that 'the process here is clearly cosmetic, in high contradistinction to a separate prophylactic or therapeutic medical process'. In *Bio-Digital Sciences Inc's Application*,[57] a patent was allowed for a method of testing cells and it was confirmed that medical treatment must be regarded as a narrow term which should be confined to the cure or prevention of disease. In *Puharich and Lawrence's Application*,[58] a patent was allowed for a hearing aid even though an operation was required for the insertion of the receiving device. Patents have also been granted which relate to animal husbandry such as treatments for tenderising meat[59] or improving growth.[60] The previous case law was recast by the EBA in two decisions on the patentability of methods of treatment.

G1/04 Diagnostic methods[61]

[3.23] It was held that a diagnostic method requires three elements to fall into the exclusion from patentability:

1. Diagnosis for curative purposes *stricto sensu*[62] representing the deductive medical or veterinary decision phase as a purely intellectual exercise. This

---

52 *C & W's Application* (1914) 31 RPC 235.
53 *Neva Corpn's Application* [1968] RPC 481.
54 *Organon Laboratories' Application* [1970] RPC 574.
55 *Palmer's Application* [1970] RPC 597.
56 *Joos v Comr of Patents* [1973] RPC 59.
57 *Bio-Digital Sciences Inc's Application* [1973] RPC 668.
58 *Puharich and Lawrence's Application* [1965] RPC 395.
59 *Swift's Application* [1962] RPC 37.
60 'Examination Guidelines for Patent Applications relating to Medical Inventions in the UK Intellectual Property Office' August 2008, para 42.
61 G1/04 *Diagnostic methods* OJ EPO 2006 334.
62 In the strictest sense.

means that a device which performs the deductive step may not fall within the exclusion.

2. Preceding steps which are constitutive for making that diagnosis, namely examination, data gathering and comparison. A full description of all four steps is (i) the examination phase involving collection of data, (ii) comparison of data with standard values, (iii) finding of any significant deviation (ie symptom) during comparison, and (iv) the attribution of deviation to a particular clinical picture, ie the deductive medical or veterinary decision phases.

3. Specific interactions with the human or animal body when carrying out the preceding steps which are of a technical nature. Not all steps must be technical in nature, eg the comparison and deductive decision phase are predominantly non-technical so they do not need to be practised on the body.

The other significant points from the decision are:

(a) The status of an activity as being a diagnostic method or not does not depend on a medical or veterinary practitioner being present or bearing responsibility, or that all method steps can be or are practised by medical or technical support staff, the patient or an automated system.

(b) It does not require a specific type or intensity of interaction to be a diagnostic method; it is sufficient if its performance implies any interaction with the human or animal body, necessitating the presence of that body. It does not require invasive treatment and, for example, it can include measurements of exhalations. It can involve direct physical contact or be practised from a certain distance.

(c) If some or all steps of a technical nature are carried out by a device without implying interaction with the body, eg using specific software, this is not excluded from patentability as it is not practised on the body. The same applies to *in vitro* method steps including DNA microarrays.

(d) Diagnosis is the determination of the nature of a medical or veterinary medical condition intended to identify or uncover a pathology. It includes a negative finding that a particular condition cannot be ruled out.

(e) Diagnosis is an intellectual exercise (at least until technology develops) and therefore a non-technical step, so the deductive decision phase is not regarded as an invention, but a method for conducting this step might be.

(f) The claim can include technical and non-technical features if they interact to bring about a technical effect.

(g) A narrow interpretation was adopted, which only excludes patentability if all constitutive steps are performed on the body. This has been criticised because it appears to allow patents where the deductive phase is carried out separately from the human body, eg by technological means.

(h) If one of preceding steps which are constitutive is missing, it is not a diagnostic method; at best it is a method of data acquisition or data processing.

(i) Intermediate findings of diagnostic relevance are not excluded from patentability, nor are methods for obtaining them.

(j)   If the applicant omits a feature to try to circumvent the exclusion, it may fall foul of art 84 of the EPC, which requires that all essential features necessary for clearly and completely defining a particular invention be included. A non-technical feature is essential if its essentialness is unambiguously inferable from the patent as a whole, eg if it discloses the method for obtaining findings of diagnostic relevance which allow the diagnosis.,

G1/07 Treatment by Surgery/Medi-Physics[63]

[3.24] This decision dealt with the exclusion of surgical methods. The issue concerned an imaging method in which a radioactive compound was 'delivered' to a patient. The imaging allowed blood flow to be seen, which was useful in various contexts including during surgery and drug delivery. Delivery of the compound could be either by inhalation (which is a non-surgical process) or by injection, for example, directly to the heart (which is surgical in nature). The claim language relating to 'delivery' was broad enough to cover both options. The EBA was asked whether claims of this type were excluded from patentability if they encompassed the surgical option (question 1); whether various strategies to get around this by disclaimer or limitation were valid (question 2); and whether an imaging method which allowed the surgeon to immediately decide on a course of action was a 'method for treatment of the human or animal body by surgery' (question 3).

The answers can be summarised as follows, using the same numbering:

1.   A claimed imaging method in which, when carried out, maintaining the life and health of the subject is important and which comprises or encompasses an invasive step representing a substantial physical intervention on the body which requires professional medical expertise to be carried out and which entails a substantial health risk even when carried out with the required professional care and expertise, is excluded from patentability as a method for treatment of the human or animal body by surgery.[64]

2   (a)   A claim which comprises a step encompassing an embodiment which is a 'method for treatment of the human or animal body by surgery' cannot be interpreted as encompassing that embodiment.

2   (b)   This exclusion from patentability can be avoided by disclaiming the embodiment, provided that the disclaimer fulfils all the requirements of the EPC and, where applicable, the requirements for a disclaimer to be allowable.[65]

2   (c)   Whether or not the wording of the claim can be amended so as to omit the surgical step without offending against the EPC must be assessed on the basis of the overall circumstances of the individual case under consideration.

---

[63]   G1/07 *Treatment by Surgery/Medi-physics* (15 February 2010, not yet reported).

[64]   EPC, art 53(c).

[65]   As defined in decisions G1/03 *Disclaimer/PPG* and G2/03/*Disclaimer/Genetic Systems* of the Enlarged Board of Appeal [2004] EPOR 33.

3.   A claimed imaging method is not to be considered as being a 'treatment of the human or animal body by surgery' merely because during a surgical intervention the data obtained by the use of the method immediately allows a surgeon to decide on the course of action to be taken during a surgical intervention.

[3.25] In reaching these conclusions, a number of interesting points were raised by the EBA:

(a)   It summarised the case law on the meaning of treatment by surgery. The jurisprudence is not consistent: some cases focused on the nature of the physical intervention and others on its purpose. A focus on purpose could give different conclusions for the same process, eg an injection for treating disease versus cosmetic purposes. There could be other approaches, eg the medical risk involved, whether a medical or veterinary practitioner should be responsible for carrying out the treatment, the degree of invasiveness or operative complexity, etc.

(b)   There is no principle of narrow interpretation of exclusions.

(c)   The aim of protection of the physician is better solved by national infringement law.

(d)   An invention is not patentable if at least one feature defines a physical activity or action that constitutes a method step for treatment of a human or animal body by surgery or therapy.

(e)   The terms 'surgery' and 'therapy' are not meant to be interpreted identically as they are included separately in the EPC.

(f)   The definition in G1/04[66] is non-exhaustive as it includes any physical intervention where maintaining the life and health are of paramount importance. This does not mean that it is limited to therapeutic surgery, but it does not include destructive treatments, ie where the conscious end, deliberate or incidental, is death.

(g)   To limit 'surgery' to therapeutic purposes would not give full effect to the purpose of the exclusion. The freedom of practitioners is important for serious and risky interventions like cosmetic surgery, organ transplants, embryo transfers, sex changes, castration and sterilisation too.

(h)   It could be defensible to allow such matters to be patentable for animals, but after long discussion it was decided that such activities should also be excluded from patentability for reasons of public health.

(i)   Surgery can include maintaining or restoring mental health.

(j)   Advances in safety and the now routine character of certain invasive techniques on non-critical parts of body mean that many such techniques are carried out in non-medical, commercial environments such as beauty salons, eg tattooing, body hair removal by optical radiation and micro abrasion. There are also many devices which must be connected to the patient such as for retrieving data by invasive steps to get better results. Excluding all such methods where safe

---

[66]   See para **[3.23]**.

routine techniques are used, even though they are invasive, goes beyond the purpose of public health.

(k) The EBA cannot give a definition which will delimit the exact boundaries of the new concept for all technical situations, which is the job of the first instance bodies and boards of appeal. The required medical expertise and health risk may not be the only criteria.

(l) This is not an authoritative, once and for all, definition, as the concept of surgery is an ever-changing technical medical reality. There is no general common concept and to a large extent it is a matter of convention.

(m) It is not necessary that the activity be invasive or tissues penetrated – repositioning limbs or manipulating body parts are traditionally regarded as surgical. Mere catheterisation or insertion of components of devices into the body can be surgical even if there is no penetration of tissues.

(n) There is a risk in omitting the surgical step as the specification needs to include all essential steps. It must be decided on a case-by-case basis whether the invention is fully and completely defined by the features without the step. It is also possible that the invention can no longer be carried out over the whole breadth of the claim or the problem is not solved if the step is omitted.

(o) It is well-accepted that methods for operation of a device without any functional link between the method and the effect are not a method for treatment. Such methods are teachings in which the performance is not required of a physical activity or action that constitutes a method step for surgical treatment or therapy in order for the teaching of the claimed invention to be complete. Therefore, even if use of the device requires a surgical step or is therapeutic treatment, this does not apply to the claimed method for operating the device.

(p) The imaging method here is a complete teaching *per se*, so the fact that it can be used in particularly advantageous ways in surgical intervention does not preclude patentability. Use in the course of a surgical intervention does not alter the character of the imaging method as not being a surgical step. The fact that a surgeon can use the imaging method to decide on a course of action by taking note of immediately produced image data does not make it a method for treatment of the human or animal body by surgery.

In relation to veterinary treatment, again there is a narrow interpretation. Thus, in *Swift's Application*,[67] a patent for injecting animals with a meat tenderising enzyme was allowed.

[3.26] The word 'therapy' embraces both curative and prophylactic treatments such as immunisation. In *Unilever Ltd (Davis's) Application*,[68] Falconer J also refused to draw any distinction between the prophylactic treatment of diseases in human beings and animals. This interpretation of the word 'therapy' has also been applied by the EPO.[69]

---

[67] *Swift's Application* [1962] RPC 37.
[68] *Unilever Ltd (Davis's) Application* [1983] RPC 219.
[69] *Pigs II/Duphar* [1988] 1 EPOR 10.

In *Pigs 1/Wellcome*,[70] the EPO refused to grant a patent for a method of curing mange mites in pigs even though the treatment could be carried out by farmers in general and did not require the services of a veterinary surgeon. This would be in line with the later decisions of the EPO on treatment by surgery which stated that the involvement of medical or veterinary practitioners was not decisive.[71]

[3.27] In another pig-related decision in the area,[72] *Salminen – Pigs III*, the EPO Technical Board of Appeal further clarified the meaning of the word 'therapy', which it regarded as requiring an exact meaning to allow consistent application of the exclusion. They held that therapy included 'any non-surgical treatment which is designed to cure, alleviate, remove or lessen the symptom of, or prevent or reduce the possibility of contracting any malfunction in the human body' and that it relates to 'the treatment of a disease in general or to a curative treatment in the narrow sense, as well as the alleviation of the symptoms of pain and suffering'.

That case involved a sensor that detects when a dam stands up and blows hot air at the piglets to make it uncomfortable for them to suckle, thus preventing them suffocating under the dam if she lies down again. It was held that this behaviour of newborn piglets is not a malfunction of piglets whose instinct is not adequately developed. Rather, it was concerned with preventing accidents and it was analogous to a method of preventing a worker trapping a hand in machinery. Therefore, the invention was a method for protection against disadvantageous consequences, so it could not reasonably be called a treatment by therapy practised on the bodies of the piglets.

[3.28] Although s 10(1)(c)[73] of the PA 1992 states that surgical, therapeutic or diagnostic methods practised on the human body are not patentable, it also indicates that this does not apply to products, particularly substances or compositions, for use in such methods.[74] For example, in the case of a substance or composition which is already known but has no known pharmacological activity, a patent may be obtained for the substance or composition for use as a medicament or for use in a specified medical treatment. This is known as first medical use and can be protected by way of purpose-limited product claims of the general format:

> Substance/composition X for use as a medicament / for use in treating a disease.

A new medical indication of a known drug, ie a second or subsequent medical indication, can also be patented. Protection is available by way of purpose-limited process claims, also known as 'Swiss-type claims', of the following format:

> Use of substance/composition X for the manufacture of a medicament for the treatment/prophylaxis of disease Y.

---

[70] *Pigs 1/Wellcome* [1988] 1 EPOR 1.
[71] G1/04 *Diagnostic methods* OJ EPO 2006 334.
[72] T58/87 *Salminen – Pigs III* [1989] EPOR 125.
[73] Formerly s 9(4).
[74] Section 10(2) inserted by the Patents (Amendment) Act 2006.

Such claims have been allowed by the EPO following a decision of the EBA, Decision G 5/83.[75]

[3.29] Since the EPC 2000 came into force, direct claims for second and subsequent medical uses of a substance are permitted. Thus, 'Swiss-type' claims are no longer necessary. This applies to pending applications filed before 13 December 2007 as well as new applications filed thereafter. This development has significant advantages aside from simplification, as the conventional 'Swiss-type' claim arguably required 'the manufacture of a medicament' for infringement to occur, which was not always the case.

When art 54(5) of the EPC 2000 came into force, many practitioners held the view that it could be advisable to include the new form of claim and the 'Swiss-type' claim in any new applications until the courts and the EPO had explored any distinctions. This appears to have been overtaken by events, in that the EBA decided, in Decision G 2/08, that the 'Swiss-type' should no longer be used and that the new form of claim is in any event wider than the 'Swiss-type' claim.

G2/08 Dosage Regime / Abbott Respiratory[76]

[3.30] In this decision, the EBA held that the Swiss-type claim is no longer an appropriate or acceptable claim format for future applications. There is no retroactive effect to this part of the decision, so that applications and patents with a priority date or filing date before three months after date of publication of decision using the Swiss-type claim wording will not be prejudiced.

The EBA admitted that the Swiss-type claim was a legal construct designed to exploit a loophole and indicated that, while such claims were valid and remain valid in pre-existing, pending applications and granted patents, the EPO should not in the future grant such claims. Instead, the EPO now grants second / subsequent medical use claims in the form:

Compound/Composition X for use in treating disease Y.

This change in practice at the EPO does not affect the substantive issue of what is patentable in relation to medical inventions, only the claim format that can be used. Indeed the part of the decision dealing with dosage regimes makes it clear that the effect of the decision is to give broader coverage for therapeutic use inventions.

It was also held that there was no reason to restrict the intention of the legislator to enshrine the case law which evolved from G5/83 into the interpretation of the new EPC 2000 provision. Therefore, under the pre-existing law it was well-established that a second medical use for the same illness was patentable if it was new and inventive, so this principle still holds true.

It held that art 54(4) and (5) contained a legal fiction in that there was notional novelty of a medicament even if it was already in the state of the art, provided that there was a new use. The notional novelty and non-obviousness are derived from the purpose of substance, ie its intended therapeutic use.

---

[75] Known as claims in 'Swiss form' or 'Swiss-type claims' as they were first accepted in Switzerland: *Second Medical Indication/Eisai* OJ EPO 3/1985 64.

[76] G2/08 *Dosage Regime/Abbott Respiratory* (19 February 2010, not yet reported).

Dosage Regimes Generally

[3.31] The traditional view on the patentability of dosage regimes was outlined in *Procter & Gamble/Gastrointestinal Compositions*.[77] In that case, there was prior art for the use of two compounds to be administered separately, one half an hour before the last meal and the other one at bedtime. The patent application was for the same two chemicals but administered within five minutes of each other. It was held that investigating the optimum regimen and the best individual treatment schedule to prescribe and modify drug regimes were all part of typical activities and duties of a doctor in exercising his professional skills of curing, preventing or alleviating symptoms of suffering or illness. It was held that there was no inventive step as it was obvious to make this adjustment to improve patient compliance, so a skilled person would have a strong incentive to solve this by administering the chemicals concurrently and preferably simultaneously.

[3.32] The decision in G2/08 *Dosage Regime/Abbott Respiratory* broke new ground in that it held that there is no prohibition against obtaining a patent for the use of a known medicament to treat an illness where the only novel feature of the treatment is a new and inventive dosage regime. The original referral to the EBA concerned a patent application for the use of nicotinic acid and a group of related compounds for the manufacture of a sustained release medicament, for use in the treatment of hyperlipidaemia by oral administration once *per* day prior to sleep. The only novel feature of the claimed invention was the dosage regime, ie the administration once *per* day prior to sleep. The prior art disclosed the same compounds in sustained release oral formulation to treat hyperlipidaemia. The provision of the EPC 2000 on second medical uses[78] states that where a substance or composition is known in a first medical use, the novelty provisions of the EPC shall not exclude the patentability of that substance or composition for any specific use in a therapeutic method provided that such use is not comprised in the state of the art. The EBA had to decide if the term 'specific use' was restricted to use for a new disease which was not yet known to be treatable by that substance, or if any new and inventive treatment regime was patentable, even if this involved treating the same disease with the same substance.

The EBA held that there was no legislative basis for the narrower interpretation and that the 'specific use' may include something other than the treatment of a different illness such as, for example, a new dosage regime to treat the same illness. The EBA warned that, even if novelty is found in the dosage regime, the claim as a whole must still involve an inventive step. Thus, for example, where the broad parameters of a dosage regime are known from the prior art and the claim is directed to specific selections within the known regime, this will be treated like any other selection invention. Thus, the applicant will be required to show an inventive step for the particular parameters chosen. It also held that the claimed definition of the dosage regime must not only be verbally different but also reflect a different technical teaching.

---

[77] T317/95 *Procter & Gamble/Gastrointestinal Compositions* [1999] EPOR 528.
[78] EPC, art 54(5).

Plant variety protection

[3.33] Apart from broadening the prospect of patent protection availability for new strains of plant material produced by way of genetic engineering, the international community has sponsored a number of attempts to secure agreements that are intended to source intellectual property rights for the producers of 'new' varieties of plants, when the reproduction of those plants is a further intended use of these plants. The most important international instrument is the International Convention for the Protection of New Varieties of Plants (the UPOV Convention),[79] which was first agreed in 1961 and revised in 1972, 1978 and 1991. It is this document, specifically the 1978 revision, signed by Ireland on 27 September 1979, that forms the basis of existing Irish statute law in the form of the Plant Varieties (Proprietary Rights) Act 1980. Certain aspects of the 1991 Revision[80] and the introduction of a EU Regulation on Community Plant Variety Rights[81] made a review and revision of the 1980 Act something of an inevitability and led to the Plant Varieties (Proprietary Rights) (Amendment) Act 1998. It should be noted that TRIPS allows WTO members to address biological process protection via patents or a *sui generis* system.[82]

The Plant Varieties (Proprietary Rights) Act 1980 and The Plant Varieties (Proprietary Rights) (Amendment) Act 1998

[3.34] In introducing the Plant Varieties (Proprietary Rights) Bill 1979 to Dáil Éireann,[83] the Minister for Agriculture, Thomas Hussey, explained that the production of a new plant variety was the result of a substantial investment in terms of time, skill and financial expenditure. Some strains took about 15 years to create. This effort was not always compensated for via the sale of the resultant propagating material alone, for upon such sale others could replicate the work of the originator and market that reproductive material; it was this realisation that caused the UPOV Convention to emerge at international level. The Minister asserted the need for Ireland to ratify the Convention and, in particular, the central principle that the propagating material of new plant varieties may be produced or marketed by the breeder of that variety, or by others, only with the breeder's prior authorisation and in accordance with the conditions set by the breeder.[84] The Minister conceded that governmental interest in such a scheme was the result of pressure from both the EEC[85] (only Luxembourg and Ireland had no such system in place) and by pressure from the agricultural sector who feared that if a system of remuneration were not in place, foreign breeders might decide to blacklist exports to Ireland. The Minister also indicated that a national law system would

---

[79] UPOV being the acronym for the International Union for the Protection of New Varieties of Plants (*Union Pour La Protection Des Obtentions Végétales*).

[80] The UPOV Convention 1991 Revision, art 3 directs existing Member States to apply the 1991 rules.

[81] Council Regulation 2100/94/EC ([1994] OJ L 227/1).

[82] TRIPS, art 27.3(b); *sui generis* meaning constituting a class of its own.

[83] 318, *Dáil Debates*, Cols 373–376.

[84] See UPOV Convention 1991 Revision, art 14.

[85] The predecessor to the European Union.

make domestic production of strains of plant more likely in a regulated legal environment. The Plant Varieties (Proprietary Rights) Act 1980 replaced a number of bilateral agreements (eg between Irish producers and groups like the Holland Producers Association) that had worked satisfactorily, albeit as instruments of private law.

[3.35] The breeder's right is a sole right to produce, for marketing purposes, and to export or import any reproductive material[86] of the variety for which rights are granted and the exclusive right to licence others to do so.[87] It is a proprietary right[88] in relation to any variety of any plant genus or species which has been independently bred or discovered and developed. This right is, however, controlled by the prospect of a compulsory licensing mechanism,[89] which can be used to prevent the breeder from unreasonably restricting the distribution of the said reproductive material.[90] The right is related to the distribution of reproductive material and does not apply, for example, to plant varieties to be utilised for making foodstuffs or the composting of vegetable material.

[3.36] Application for the grant of plant breeders' rights is made to the Controller and, if approved, is published and a certificate granted. The minimum period for protection is set at 25 years and the maximum is 30 years under the Plant Varieties (Proprietary Rights) (Amendment) Act 1998. In the same Act the minimum period for trees, vines and potatoes is set at 30 years and the maximum is 35 years.[91] Initially, protection was only available for varieties of wheat, oats, barley, potatoes, ryegrass and white clover,[92] but recent schemes have been put in place to cover certain trees and flowering plants such as Norway Maple, whitebeam, sunflower, paper daisy, as well as soft core fruits such as raspberry and other *rubus* plants.[93]

[3.37] The criteria for protection are that the variety must be new, distinct, uniform and stable.[94] These factors have a precise meaning and are not to be confused with the criteria for patent protection. The variety is new if at the date of filing the application, propagating or harvested material of the variety has not been sold or otherwise disposed of to others, by or with the consent of the breeder, for exploitation purposes, within the previous year in the country of filing, or within four years of that filing in any

86 Defined in Plant Varieties (Proprietary Rights) Act 1980, s 1.
87 Plant Varieties (Proprietary Rights) Act 1980, s 4(5) and (6).
88 Plant Varieties (Proprietary Rights) Act 1980, s 4(1) and (5).
89 Plant Varieties (Proprietary Rights) Act 1980, s 8.
90 Plant Varieties (Proprietary Rights) Act 1980, s 8(1).
91 Plant Varieties (Proprietary Rights) (Amendment) Act 1998, s 15.
92 See Plant Varieties (Proprietary Rights) Regulations 1981 (SI 23/1981), the Principal Regulations, which have been substantially amended and added to since then.
93 Plant Varieties (Proprietary Rights) Regulations 1992 (SI 369/1992); Plant Varieties (Proprietary Rights) (Amendment) (No 2) Regulations 1993 (SI 332/1993); Plant Varieties (Proprietary Rights) (Amendment) Regulations 1994 (SI 393/1994); Plant Varieties (Proprietary Rights) (Amendment) Regulations 2000 (SI 490/2000).
94 UPOV Convention, art 5; Plant Varieties (Proprietary Rights) Act 1980, s 5 and Sch 1.

other territory.[95] Thus, a 'new' variety can include existing or newly discovered plant varieties, as long as the person who files this kind of 'discovery' application can lodge a requisite amount of propagating material.[96]

[3.38] The distinctiveness criterion is set by art 7 of the UPOV Convention and this requires that the variety be 'clearly distinguishable from any other variety whose existence is a matter of common knowledge at the time of filing the application'.[97] The distinguishing characteristic of the variety must be recognisable and capable of description and recognition. This may be shown by one or more important morphological, physiological or other characteristic from any other variety and this can be satisfied, for example, by showing that the variety is highly resistant to mildew while apparently having no other distinctive feature vis-à-vis other plants of this variety.[98] The distinctions must be 'important' and the fact that other UPOV countries have granted applications will not assist in a determination.[99]

The question of the uniformity of the variety is tested in the light of the variations that may be expected from the particular features of its propagation,[100] while art 9 of the UPOV Convention requires that the variety will be deemed to be stable if its relevant characteristics remain unchanged after each repeated propagation, or in the case of a particular cycle of propagation, after each cycle.[101]

[3.39] The testing of applications is the function of the Department of Agriculture, Fisheries and Food. The Plant Varieties (Proprietary Rights) Act 1980 sets up the post of Controller of Plant Breeders' Rights who has specific powers and functions under the Act. It is the role of the Controller of Plant Breeders' Rights to process applications made for plant breeders' rights under the Plant Varieties (Proprietary Rights) Act 1980 whenever a species has been specified for those purposes by the Minister,[102] and it is the Controller who investigates and tests the legal[103] and botanical[104] merits of the application.

Once a species has been specified by the Minister, a breeder can register a variety within that species as long as the criteria set out above can be met. A name for the variety is registered and exclusivity is given for that name, but if a name is proposed which is likely to cause confusion, including confusion with a trade mark or trade

---

[95] UPOV Convention, art 6 (six years in the case of vines or trees); Plant Varieties (Proprietary Rights) Act 1980, Sch 1. On the meaning of sale, see *Re Sunworld Inc & Registrar* (1995) 33 IPR 106.

[96] 320 *Dáil Debates*, Cols 452–463.

[97] Plant Varieties (Proprietary Rights) Act 1980, Sch 1, para 1.

[98] *Maris-Druid Spring Barley* [1968] FSR 559.

[99] *L Daehnfelt Ltd v Controller* [1976] FSR 95.

[100] UPOV Convention, art 8; Plant Varieties (Proprietary Rights) Act 1980, Sch 1, para 3.

[101] Plant Varieties (Proprietary Rights) Act 1980, Sch 1, para 4.

[102] Plant Varieties (Proprietary Rights) Act 1980, s 4.

[103] Plant Varieties (Proprietary Rights) Act 1980, s 5.

[104] Plant Varieties (Proprietary Rights) Act 1980, ss 3(13) and 5.

name, the name of the variety may be denied registration.[105] Once registered, however, infringement of rights in that name can be actionable by the breeder.[106]

[3.40] There are grounds upon which a plant right may be revoked.[107] These include prior commercialisation, lack of distinctiveness, failure to supply reproductive material when so required, providing incorrect information at the time of application and failure to pay the necessary fees.[108] These matters are for the Controller to decide upon. A third party has no general right to challenge or seek revocation, for example, on the ground of an alleged lack of distinctiveness.

[3.41] Notices concerning the schemes in place are publicised in the form of a government publication, *The Official Journal of Plant Varieties*.[109] Assignments and other dealings in the right are to be notified to the Controller who registers such dealings in accordance with s 17 of the Plant Varieties (Proprietary Rights) Act 1980.

[3.42] The area of plant breeders' rights, which is essentially technical and specialist, can provoke substantial debate. The fact that plant discoveries may become the subject of protection causes much political resentment in the developing world, which fears that loss of species, increasing concentration of propagation technology into the hands of western multinational companies, and general strengthening of the breeders' monopoly, will impoverish farming communities in the developing world. Some attempts at balance are maintained by permitting reverse engineering[110] and by allowing the farmers an exemption whereby farmers may reserve seed from produce raised on their own lands for a successive sowing of the crop.[111] Loss of species and the dangers associated with monoculture are legitimate concerns for world farming, particularly when indigenous genetic diversity is lost, but it is argued by some supporters of legal protection that these serious dangers are not the result of plant breeding laws, for many countries in the developing world simply do not grant protection to plant varieties.[112]

[3.43] It seems that what is often in dispute is the right of research establishments in the developed world to regulate the agricultural and trading patterns of other countries and the fear that genetic uniformity may not be in anyone's long-term interest, least of all those farming in the developing world. These issues are complex and transcend the narrow focus of plant breeders' rights via *sui generis* protection methods.

---

[105] Plant Varieties (Proprietary Rights) Act 1980, s 12.

[106] Plant Varieties (Proprietary Rights) Amendment Act 1998, s 21(1).

[107] As well as limited grounds on which the grant can be refused: Plant Varieties (Proprietary Rights) Act 1980, s 5.

[108] Plant Varieties (Proprietary Rights) Act 1980, s 11.

[109] Plant Varieties (Proprietary Rights) Act 1980, s 19.

[110] UPOV Convention, art 15(1) (compulsory).

[111] UPOV Convention, art 15(2) (optional), not taken up by the Plant Varieties (Proprietary Rights) Act 1980; however, see the Plant Varieties (Proprietary Rights) (Amendment) Act 1998, s 19(2); Plant Varieties (Farm Saved Seed) Regulations 2000 (SI 493/2000) and Plant Varieties (Proprietary Rights) (Amendment) Act 1998 (Section 19(2)) Order 2000 (SI 491/2000).

[112] For example *Dworkin* [1983] EIPR 270.

The EU Council Regulation 1994[113]

[3.44] Regulation No 2100/94 of 27 July 1994 on Community Plant Variety Rights is closely modelled on the UPOV Convention and introduced a parallel system of EU law that co-exists with national law regimes but allows for the grant of industrial property rights which are valid throughout the EU. The Regulation introduced an EU-wide protection system for varieties of all botanical genera and species that are distinct, uniform, stable, new and designated by a denomination in accordance with certain rules.[114] The duration of the rights is 25 years, except for vine or tree varieties for which the duration is 30 years.[115] While the principle of Community exhaustion applies in this field, the Regulation gives a limited field of application[116] to art 101[117] of the Treaty on the Functioning of the European Union (the Treaty).[118] The intent behind this Regulation is to provide a high level of EU-wide protection that will ultimately mean that the Community Plant Variety Office (CPVO), which has its seat in Angers, France, will displace national systems.

The CPVO has a wide discretion to decide on complex scientific and technical matters and although there is an appeal to the General Court,[119] that court has a limited scope for judicial review of such matters.[120] For example, the General Court's discretion to require supplementary information does not enable facts to be submitted which were not raised before the CPVO. The further appeal to the Court of Justice of the European Union (ECJ) is on a point of law only. Thus it is particularly important to introduce and fully argue all scientific and technical issues before the CPVO and its Board of Appeal, as they are unlikely to be capable of introduction on further appeal.

G1/98 Transgenic Plant/Novartis[121]

[3.45] This is the leading case on plant varieties. It explained the background of the prohibition on patentability, in that it originated in the prohibition on dual protection in the UPOV Convention, which prohibition was abolished in 1991. The decision favoured a literal approach to patent construction so an invention would be patentable if the words 'plant variety' do not appear in the specification. This is in part because the exclusion in the processes section of the EPC only refers to plant, not plant variety, so it must mean something different.

---

[113] Council Regulation 2100/94/EC ([1994] OJ L 227/1) entered into force on 1 September 1994 –.

[114] Council Regulation 2100/94/EC, art 6.

[115] Council Regulation 2100/94/EC, art 19.

[116] Council Regulation 2100/94/EC, art 16.

[117] Formerly art 81 of the Treaty establishing the European Community (the EC Treaty).

[118] 30 March 2010 [2010] OJ C 83.

[119] Formerly known as the Court of First Instance.

[120] *Ralf Schräder v CPVO* Case C-38/09 (15 April 2010); see Würtenberger, 'Review of Community plant varieties decisions: the ECJ speaks' (2010) JIPLP 5(9), 627–30; doi:10.1093/jiplp/jpq088.

[121] G1/98 *Transgenic Plant/Novartis* [2000] EPOR 303, 309.

It also set out the following principles:

(a)　There is no conflict between patents and plant breeders' rights – once an invention is used, plant breeders' rights can protect the propagation of varieties.

(b)　An invention is not patentable if the subject matter is directed to plant varieties. If no plant variety is identified or several specific varieties are identified, it is patentable.

(c)　Article 64(2) of the EPC which relates to products of process claims is not relevant if the product produced by the process is a plant variety.

(d)　Microbiological processes mean processes using micro-organisms and are not the same as parts of living things used for generic modification. There is no difference in how the variety was obtained – genetic engineers have no privileged position.

Biotechnological inventions

[3.46] As discussed above, plant variety rights arise under the Plant Varieties (Proprietary Rights) Act 1980. The exception to patentability for plant and animal varieties and essentially biological processes for the production thereof which arises under Section 10(1)(b)[122] of the PA 1992 is taken from art 53(b) of the EPC.[123] This specific exception was not contained in the PA 1964 but both animals and plants were not considered to be a manufacture or composition of matter within the definition of an invention.[124] This exception to patentability applies to varieties only and, for example, a plant or animal treated by a patentable process can be patentable.[125] Many countries have separate patents and plant breeders' rights legislation and it is the existence of such which allows for the exclusion from patentability. Similar to the position in other countries, protection under the Plant Varieties (Proprietary Rights) Act 1980 imposes strict requirements when claiming a new variety. Consequently there was a tendency to grant a patent unless the subject matter was deemed a variety under the UPOV Convention.

[3.47] In *Plant Genetic Systems/Glutamine Synthetase Inhibitors*[126] the patent under opposition was a method of making plants resistant to a herbicide by inserting a transgene. The technical board of appeal of the EPO stated that a plant variety is a plant grouping within a single botanical taxon of the lowest known rank which, irrespective of whether it is protectable under the UPOV Convention, is characterised by at least one single transmissible character distinguishing it from other plant groupings and which is sufficiently homogeneous and stable in its own characteristics. The claimed subject matter applied to genetically altered plants which remain stable with regard to their altered, and thus characterising, characteristics, since this character is transmitted from generation to generation in the plants and their seeds. The starting material was derived from known plant varieties and the genetically

---

[122] Formerly s 10(b) until amended by the Patents (Amendment) Act 2006.

[123] See para **[2.76]**.

[124] *Rank Hovis McDougal v Controller* [1978] FSR 588, see para **[3.49]** below.

[125] *Hybrid Plants/Lubrizol* [1990] EPOR 173.

[126] T356/93 *Plant Genetic Systems/Glutamine Synthetase Inhibitors* [1995] EPOR 357.

altered plants were essentially derived varieties and fell within the definition of a plant variety under the UPOV Convention. The claimed plants were held to fall within the exclusion from patentability under art 53(b) of the EPC and the resulting plants were also held not to be the product of a microbiological process.

[3.48] Processes for treating plants are patentable. In *Lenard's Application*,[127] a patent was refused in respect of an improved pruning method for meeting or offsetting the advance of disease in clove trees even though Lloyd-Jacob J described such as unfortunate given the great advance in the culture of clove trees and the ingenuity involved. However, this decision was under the old UK Patents Act 1949 and hence there was a requirement that the method be a manner of manufacture. This requirement no longer exists under the PA 1992. This case was distinguished in the Australian decision *NRDC's Application*[128] where a patent was allowed for a selective herbicide on the ground that the process in question was only one for altering the conditions of growth, so that the contemplated end result would not be a result of the process but would be the inevitable result of that which was inherent in the plant. Where micro-organisms are employed, it is seen as analogous to a chemical process, in that, given the micro-organisms and the appropriate conditions, the desired result inevitably follows from the working of the process.

[3.49] In the High Court in the case of *Rank Hovis McDougall Ltd v Controller*,[129] McWilliam J considered an application for a patent for a naturally occurring micro-organism and for methods for its production. The matter fell for consideration under the PA 1964 and thus the definition of invention in s 9(7) of the PA 1964 which stated that 'where a Complete Specification claims a new substance, the claim shall be construed as not extending to that substance when found in nature'. The particular micro-organism under consideration provided edible protein and it was accepted that the strain of micro-organism was produced by an elaborate process which did not occur naturally. However, the micro-organism was viewed as a form of life. Even though a British patent had been granted in respect of the same organism, McWilliam J upheld the decision of the Controller and refused the application. It was held that the words 'manufacture' and 'composition' appearing in the definition of invention had to be distinguished from 'grow' or 'cause to grow' and since micro-organisms were composed of living cells which had been grown, they did not fall within the definition of invention. It was also held to be an unaltered substance occurring in nature and fell within the s 9(7) exclusion.

Article 2(b) of the Strasbourg Convention[130] specifically provides that the exclusion from patentability does not extend to micro-biological processes and the products thereof. In *Wavin Pipes Ltd v Hepworth Iron Co Ltd*,[131] Costello J pointed out that it was clear from the Dáil Debates that one of the objectives of the PA 1964 was to adhere to

---

127 *Lenard's Application* (1954) 71 RPC 190.
128 *NRDC's Application* [1961] RPC 134 at 147.
129 *Rank Hovis McDougall Ltd v Controller* [1978] FSR 588.
130 See paras **[2.25]–[2.30]**.
131 *Wavin Pipes Ltd v Hepworth Iron Co Ltd* [1982] FSR 32 at 38.

the Strasbourg Convention. It was clear that there was an inconsistency and, even before the PA 1992, the Irish Patents Office had relaxed its practice of prohibiting claims to living micro-organisms *per se*. In particular, following the US Supreme Court case of *Diamond v Chackarbarty*,[132] the Irish Patents Office recognised a distinction between unaltered micro-organisms occurring in nature and micro-organisms altered by human intervention. Section 10(b) of the PA 1992 accords with the provisions of art 2(b) of the Strasbourg Convention and art 53(b) of the EPC and thus, the exclusion relating to plant or animal varieties does not extend to microbiological processes or the products thereof.

[3.50] At EU level, there is Directive 98/44/EC of 6 July 1998 on the legal protection of biotechnological inventions which has been given statutory effect by the European Communities (Legal Protection of Biotechnological Inventions) Regulations 2000.[133] The Regulations contain a non-exclusive list of subject matter that is considered patentable and non-patentable. Inventions which concern plants or animals are specifically stated to be patentable if the technical feasibility of the invention is not confined to a particular plant or animal variety, the purpose of this provision being to confirm that transgenic plants are patentable.[134] Certain biotechnological inventions are regarded as not being patentable on the grounds of public order or morality.[135]

The European Communities (Legal Protection of Biotechnological Inventions) Regulations 2000 include provisions concerning the scope of protection of a patent for self-replicable material or material containing genetic information which permits its multiplication or propagation. The protection conferred by such a patent extends to all material obtained from the multiplication or propagation. Thus the scope of protection is achieved by extending the acts and materials which are considered as infringements rather than permitting broader claims.

[3.51] An exemption is made for farmers by way of an implied right to use the seed obtained from their harvest for further propagation on their own farm. This is often referred to as the 'Farmers' Privilege' derogation and corresponds to provisions in the Community Plant Variety Rights Regulation 1994.[136] There is a further derogation in relation to patented livestock and reproductive material. This derogation provides that the sale or any other form of commercialisation of breeding stock or other animal reproductive material to a farmer by the holder of the patent or with his consent implies authorisation for the farmer to use the protected livestock for an agricultural purpose, which includes making the animal or reproductive material available for the purposes of pursuing the agricultural activity of the farmer but not as a commercial reproduction activity.[137]

---

[132] *Diamond v Chackarbarty* 206 USPQ 193 (1980).

[133] SI 247/2000.

[134] G1/98 *Transgenic Plant/Novartis* [2000] EPOR 303, 309 OJ EPO 2000 111 and T356/93 *Plant Genetic System/Plant Cells* [1995] EPOR 357.

[135] Para **[3.53]**.

[136] Council Regulation 2100/94/EC.

[137] European Communities (Legal Protection of Biotechnological Inventions) Regulations 2000 (SI 247/2000), reg 10(2).

In the first ECJ decision on the infringement provisions of Directive 98/44/EC, *Monsanto Technology LLC v Cefetra BV and others*,[138] it was held that patent protection under the Directive does not extend to an end product (soy meal) which contains the patented product (a DNA sequence of soy beans which are resistant to certain herbicides), where the patented product does not perform the function for which it is patented in the end product. This was the case even though the patented product could perform the function for which it was patented if it was extracted from the end product and inserted into a cell of a living organism.

[3.52] In *Biogen Inc v Medeva plc*[139] the House of Lords considered the validity of a patent for products of genetic engineering or 'recombinant DNA technology', which consisted of altering the DNA of suitable cells to produce a protein, which in nature occurs in another organism. The patent was held to be invalid on grounds that included the excessive breadth of the claimed invention due to the fact that the same results could have been produced by different means. The House of Lords cautioned on the need not to stifle research and competition by allowing an inventor who had discovered a way of achieving an obviously desirable goal to monopolise every other way of doing so.

Public order and morality

[3.53] Section 10(a) of the PA 1992,[140] which excludes from patentability inventions the commercial exploitation of which are contrary to public order or morality, repeats the wording in art 53(a) of the EPC except that '*ordre public*' is not translated as public order in the EPC. The EPO guidelines[141] explain that the purpose of the exclusion is to prevent the patenting of inventions likely to induce riot or public disorder or to lead to criminal or other generally offensive behaviour. It is to be invoked only in rare and extreme cases and the obvious example of a letter bomb is given. The EPO guidelines suggest applying the test of whether it is probable that the public in general would regard the invention as so abhorrent that the grant of patent rights would be inconceivable.

Because exploitation of an invention is contrary to Irish law does not mean the invention is contrary to public order or morality. The Patents (Amendment) Act 2006 amended s 10(b) of the PA 1992 by substitution of the words 'publication or exploitation' with the words 'commercial exploitation' in order to comply with art 27(2) of TRIPS. This amendment makes what might or might not be capable of publication under general law irrelevant to this issue. A patented product could be manufactured in Ireland for export to other countries in which use of the invention is allowed. The PA 1964 contained a similar exclusion[142] and previously, claims for contraceptives were refused. If the exclusion was based on breach of Irish law, there could be anomalies.

---

[138] *Monsanto Technology LLC v Cefetra BV and others* Case C-428/08 (decision of 6 July 2010).
[139] *Biogen Inc v Medeva plc* [1997] RPC 1.
[140] As amended by the Patents (Amendment) Act 2006.
[141] EPO guidelines, C-IV, 3.1–3.3.
[142] PA 1964, s 15(1)(b).

Take the example of a refusal by the Irish Patents Office for an invention that is described as an abortifacient for human use. Since the EPO does not refuse such applications, there could be valid patents in Ireland which may have been refused if an applicant had attempted to proceed by way of a national patent application.

Section 34(1)(k) of the PA 1964 contained a provision that a patent could be revoked on the ground that the primary or intended use or exercise of the invention was contrary to public order or morality. However, even under broader wording, a patent in the UK was allowed for a game which could be used for unlawful gambling on the grounds that there was a degree of skill involved and hence the game was not necessarily used for gambling.[143]

[3.54] Article 53(a) of the EPC has been considered in the context of the patenting of a genetically engineered mouse[144] and whether such was immoral or contrary to *ordre public*. The mouse was intended for use in relation to research on treating cancer in humans and would reduce the number of animals normally needed in such research. Given the EPO guidelines, it is not surprising that the EPO decided that since the advantages were considerable, they outweighed any possible disadvantage, and the invention was not so abhorrent that the grant of a patent would be inconceivable. Therefore, the invention survived the 'careful weighing up of the suffering of animals and the possible risks to the environment with the inventions' usefulness to mankind'. Thus the refusal of the application was overturned. Once the patent was granted, it was opposed by various parties but was maintained in amended form. That decision was appealed, which led to a second important decision on the issue in T 315/03 *Harvard Oncomouse*.[145]

T315/03 Harvard Oncomouse

[3.55] This decision dealt in particular with the exclusion in Rule 23d(d) of the EPC 1973 (now Rule 28(d) EPC 2000), which states that biotechnical inventions that are unpatentable include processes for modifying the genetic identity of animals that are likely to cause them suffering without any substantial medical benefit to man or animal, and also animals resulting from such processes. It contained some important points of principle, as follows.

If this exclusion applies, the application must be refused and there is no need to consider further the issue of public order or morality under art 53(1). Rule 23d(d) is either an alternative or addition to art 53(a) depending on the facts. The assessment of rule 23d(d) or art 53(a) is at the effective date, namely the filing or priority date, but evidence arising thereafter can be taken into account provided it is directed to the position at the effective date. Otherwise, only a patentee is likely to have information before filing and some information is bound to emerge after filing. Rule 23d(d) requires necessary correspondence between the animal suffering and the medical benefit, ie that the animals which undergo the suffering are the ones which lead to the medical benefit. A likelihood of substantial medical benefit can at the very least be inferred from the

---

[143] *Pessers and Moody v Hayden & Co* (1908) 26 RPC 58.
[144] *Harvard/Onco-Mouse* [1991] EPOR 501.
[145] T315/03 *Harvard/Transgenic Animal* [2005] EPOR 31.

patent as the purpose is to further cancer research. There was also evidence on file showing actual medical benefits achieved using such mice. The main claim related to rodents and this was narrowed to mice in the appeal; they were closely related so it was credible that any member of the genus could be used as a model system. There was no evidence that there was any medical benefit from all rodents and there was no necessary correspondence for rodents *per se*. There was no evidence that rodents were so different that each would provide a contribution to cancer studies, eg each being specifically suited to studying a specific type of cancer. There was no doubt that it would cause suffering. The degree of suffering is not relevant for Rule 23d(d) as it implies there is an acceptable level, which is not only distasteful but unworkable; it would effectively be impossible to make findings on degrees of suffering. It was also held that Rule 23d(d) was not *ultra vires* the EPC and/or case law (if that is possible) as it is an interpretation of the pre-existing provision and the legislator can increase or reduce the number of exclusions or amend them by specifying a certain result if certain conditions are met.

[3.56] There is no single definition of morality which is an acceptable standard for European culture. Opinion poll evidence is of very little value. The 'careful weighing up' test in the earlier appeal against the refusal is appropriate for animal manipulation cases. This test allows for matters other than animal suffering and medical benefit to be taken into account, for example, availability of non-animal alternatives. The 'careful weighing up' test is broader than Rule 23d(d) as 'usefulness to mankind' includes substantial medical benefit but is wider. There was some evidence of public unease but it was only an extremely general truism. The furtherance of medical research is morally correct: the care of and concern for animals is an accepted tenet of European culture but it must be balanced against use of animals in medical and scientific research, which is also an established feature of European culture.

As regards public order, the environmental risks, eg escape or release of mice, were barely more than hypothetical in view of the secure conditions of lab mice and the level of regulation on the use and keeping of animals for experimental purposes. The EPO also rejected the arguments that the mice could cause damage (they could mate but might not survive long in the wild), that they are a threat to evolution and that there would be an increase in the number of transgenic mice that would encourage trade in animals (unlikely, as a temporary monopoly tends to reduce numbers compared to unfettered competition).

[3.57] Decision G1/98[146] on plant varieties was followed: a patent should not be granted for a single animal variety but could be granted if several varieties might fall within the scope of the claims. Article 53(b), which excludes plant or animal varieties or essentially biological processes for the reproduction of plants or animals (except microbiological processes or products thereof), does not apply, as there must be a claim to a taxonomic category at least as narrow as animal species. In this case, no new species is created. It is not an essentially biological process either, as genetic manipulation does not consist entirely of natural phenomena.

---

[146] See para **[3.45]**.

The decision also identified a potential area of controversy for the future in that each of the three authoritative language versions of the EPC use a different term: the English version uses 'variety', the German one 'species' in some places, 'race' in others and the French one 'race'. It was not decisive in this case.

[3.58] Another example of a patent which received a challenge on the basis of being contrary to morality is T 0080/05[147] which dealt with the gene *BRCA1*, mutations of which are connected to breast and ovarian cancer. The Opposition Division of the EPO revoked the patent at first instance. The Technical Board of Appeal of the EPO overruled this and maintained the patent, although in amended form. The key to this decision was the amendment by the patent application from the *BRCA1* gene or mutations thereof to methods for diagnosing a predisposition for breast and ovarian cancer caused by so-called frameshift mutations within the *BRCA1* gene.

[3.59] Under the European Communities (Legal Protection of Biotechnological Inventions) Regulations 2000[148] the commercial exploitation of the following biotechnological inventions are specifically stated to be contrary to public order or morality and therefore not patentable:

(a)   a process for cloning human beings;

(b)   a process for modifying the germ line genetic identity of human beings;

(c)   the use of human embryos for industrial or commercial purposes; and

(d)   a process for modifying the genetic identity of animals which is likely to cause them suffering without any substantial medical benefit to man or animal, and animals resulting from such a process.

G2/06 Stem Cells/Warf[149]

[3.60] On 25 November 2008, the long-awaited stem cells decision G 2/06 of the EBA was issued, which held that inventions concerning products which necessarily involve the destruction of human embryos are not patentable.

The application claimed a cell culture comprising primate embryonic stem cells and, at the time of filing, it was necessary to destroy a human embryo in order to obtain the stem cells. The EPC prohibits the grant of patents for inventions concerning 'uses of human embryos for industrial or commercial purposes'[150] and the application was refused on this basis. This refusal of the Examining Division was appealed to the Technical Board of Appeal[151] and the TBA referred specific questions to the EBA. The basis for the decision of the EBA was as follows:

(1)   The EPC forbids the patenting of claims directed to products that at the filing date could only be prepared exclusively by a method which necessarily involves

---

[147] See Ventose 'New developments in patent protection for the BRAC 1 gene at the European Patent Office' (2009) JIPLP 4(11), 771–3; doi:10.1093/jiplp/jpp152.

[148] SI 247/2000.

[149] G2/06 *Stem Cells/Warf* [2009] EPOR 15.

[150] Rule 23d(c) EPC 1973, now Rule 28(c) EPC 2000.

[151] T1374/04 *Stem Cells/Warf* [2009] EPOR 31.

the destruction of the human embryos from which said products are derived, even if said method is not part of the claim.

(2) It is irrelevant that after the filing date the same products could be obtained without having to use a method necessarily involving the destruction of human embryos, as technical developments after the filing date cannot be taken into consideration. A lack of disclosure allowing a person skilled in the art to carry out the invention in a way which complies with this Rule cannot be cured by subsequent technical developments.

The EBA stressed that 'this decision is not concerned with the patentability in general of inventions relating to human stem cells or human stem cell cultures'. Thus, this decision does not rule out grant of European patents relating to human embryonic stem cells, provided destruction of human embryos is not involved.

[3.61] The applicant had argued for a restrictive interpretation of embryo (14 days or older in accordance with usage in the medical field), but it was held that the legislators did not define the term so the EPO could only assume that it was not to be given a restrictive meaning. The only rule which can be discerned at this stage is that what an embryo is, is a question of fact in the context of any particular patent application.

The applicant also argued that use of human embryos must be claimed to be prohibited. This was rejected as it was not just the explicit wording of the claim that needed to be examined, it was also the technical teaching of the application as a whole as to how the invention was to be performed. Before human embryo stem cell cultures can be used, they have to be made. The only teaching involves use of human embryos involving their destruction. To restrict the application of the rule to explicit claims would have the undesirable consequences of making avoidance merely a matter of clever and skilful drafting of claims.

The applicant also argued that use of human embryos for making stem cell cultures was not use for industrial or commercial purposes. This was rejected as making a claimed new and inventive product is necessary for use and is the ordinary way of commercially exploiting the claimed invention, even where the intention is to use the product for further research. Use involving destruction is an integral and essential part of the industrial or commercial exploitation.

NOVELTY

[3.62] Section 11(1) of the PA 1992 states simply that an invention shall be considered to be new if it does not form part of the state of the art. An invention must be new in order to be patentable.[152] This simple statement repeats the words of art 54(1) of the EPC. The state of the art is broadly defined in the PA 1992, s 11(2). It includes everything made available to the public anywhere in the world, ie absolute novelty (sometimes called 'universal novelty'). It can be by means of written or oral description, by use, or in any other way. If the invention is made available to the public before the date of

---

[152] PA 1992, s 9(1) as amended by the Patents (Amendment) Act 2006.

filing[153] of the patent application the novelty is destroyed. In the PA 1964, the term 'state of the art' was not used but there was a broad definition of 'published' as made available to the public by the written or spoken word or by public use, or in any other way.[154] There was an anomaly in the PA 1964 whereby in revocation proceedings a patent could be revoked if the invention was published anywhere in the world prior to the priority date of the claim,[155] but in opposition proceedings account could only be taken of prior publication in Ireland, ie local novelty.[156]

[3.63] In *Wavin Pipes Ltd v Hepworth Iron Co Ltd*,[157] Costello J considered a revocation action in which one of the grounds was lack of novelty. The patentee argued that several of the patents which had been cited as part of the prior art were inadmissible because they were not published in the Republic of Ireland before the priority date. Costello J rejected this argument concluding that the omission of the words 'within the State' from the revocation provisions of s 34 of the PA 1964 must have been deliberate and accordingly, publication was not limited to what had been made available to the Irish public. Furthermore, regard was made to the parliamentary history of the Act and Ireland's intention to introduce the concept of absolute novelty in accordance with its international obligations, ie under the Strasbourg Convention.[158]

[3.64] The rationale behind the refusal to allow a patent in respect of an invention which forms part of the state of the art lies in the fact that if the invention has already been made available to the public, then a patent is of no advantage to the public, the disclosure having already taken place. As far back as 1885 and in *Humpherson v Syer*,[159] Bowen LJ held that there was prior publication where information had been communicated to any member of the public who was free in law or equity to use it as he pleased. In a similar vein, Fry LJ considered the relevant question to be whether it is the fair conclusion from the evidence that some English people, under no obligation to secrecy arising from confidence or good faith towards the patentee, knew of the invention at the date when the plaintiff took out his patent. In *Bristol-Myers Application*,[160] it was reiterated that communication even to a single member of the public without an inhibiting fetter was enough to amount to making available to the public.

[3.65] A further example of the courts' willingness to find that an invention has been made available to the public is the practice of attaching great significance to actual availability. Thus, in *Dalrymple's Application*,[161] a bulletin issued to members of a trade association which was marked 'Confidential – Not to be Published' and 'All Rights

---

[153] Defined in the PA 1992, s 2 to include a priority date.
[154] PA 1964, s 2.
[155] PA 1964, s 34(1)(e).
[156] PA 1964, s 19(1)(b), (c), (d).
[157] *Wavin Pipes Ltd v Hepworth Iron Co Ltd* [1982] FSR 32.
[158] See para **[2.25]**.
[159] *Humpherson v Syer* (1887) 4 RPC 407.
[160] *Bristol-Myers Application* [1969] RPC 146.
[161] *Dalrymple's Application* [1957] RPC 449.

Reserved – Private and Confidential. The bulletin is issued to you as a member, its contents are strictly confidential and must not be disclosed to non-members' was still held to be published and therefore formed part of the state of the art. The bulletin had been sent to 1,079 members and elsewhere.

[3.66] In *Monsanto Co (Brignac's) Application*,[162] a bulletin which was issued to the applicant's own salesmen was held to be published. On the facts, the salesmen were considered to be members of the public. There was no fetter upon the salesmen in respect of the information in the bulletin.

[3.67] Under the PA 1964, in deciding whether or not an invention was published in an earlier document, the High Court[163] applied the test of Sachs LJ in *General Tire and Rubber Co v Firestone Tyre and Rubber Co*, namely:[164]

> The earlier publication and the patentee's claim must each be construed as they would be at the respective relevant dates by a reader skilled in the art to which they relate having regard to the state of knowledge in such article at the relevant date. The construction of these documents is a function of the Court, being a matter of law, but, since documents of this nature are almost certain to contain technical material, the Court must, by evidence, be put in the position of a person of the kind to whom the document is addressed, that is to say, a person skilled in the relevant article at the relevant date ... when the prior inventor's publication and the patentee's claim have respectively been construed by the Court in the light of all properly admissible evidence as to technical matters, the meaning of words and expressions used in the art and so forth, the question whether the patentee's claim is new ... falls to be decided as a question of fact. If the prior inventor's publication contains a clear description of, or clear instructions to do or make, something that would infringe the patentee's claim if carried out after the grant of the patentee's patent, the patentee's claim will have been shown to lack the necessary novelty, that is to say, it will have been anticipated.

[3.68] In *Windsurfing International Inc v Tabur Marine (GB) Ltd*,[165] Oliver J stated the reasoning behind what is termed 'anticipation' (a lack of novelty), namely that it would be wrong to enable the patentee to prevent a man from doing what he has lawfully done before the patent was granted. In that case, the defendant's counterclaim to infringement cited as a ground for revocation a prior use of the invention some 10 years earlier. This use was a sailboard built and used by a then 12-year-old boy in close proximity and visible to people in a caravan site. It was held that such prior use even of a short duration was anticipation.

In *Quantel Ltd v Spaceward Microsystems Ltd*,[166] it was held that demonstrations of a prototype of the claimed invention at an exhibition were not disclosure because no one was allowed near the actual computer and no engineering description was provided. The public could see the computer in operation but its circuitry was concealed and the public had not been enabled to practice the actual invention for themselves.

---

[162] *Monsanto Co (Brignac's) Application* [1971] RPC 153.
[163] *Wavin Pipes Ltd v Hepworth Iron Co Ltd* [1982] FSR 32.
[164] *General Tire and Rubber Co v Firestone Tyre and Rubber Co* [1972] RPC 457 at 485.
[165] *Windsurfing International Inc v Tabur Marine (GB) Ltd* [1985] RPC 59 at 77.
[166] *Quantel Ltd v Spaceward Microsystems Ltd* [1990] RPC 83.

If prior art falls within the relevant claim, there is lack of novelty irrespective of whether or not the later application discloses advantages.[167]

[3.69] A test for anticipation which is often applied is what is termed the post-infringement or right to work test. Simply stated, this means that anything which would infringe a patent would also anticipate that patent if published before the priority date of the patent. This test was applied by Lord Diplock in *Bristol-Myers Co (Johnson's) Application*[168] where it was stated that:

> the right of a trader to go on dealing by way of trade in any man-made substance in which he had dealt before, without impediment by a monopoly in that substance granted to any other person, was not dependent upon his knowledge of its composition or how it could be made.

However, in *Asahi's Application*,[169] it was held that matter comprised in the state of the art had to be the subject of an enabling disclosure, ie a disclosure to the public of such type as would enable the working of the invention by a person skilled in the art.

[3.70] The UK House of Lords in *Synthon BV v SmithKline Beecham*[170] explored this concept of 'enabling disclosure'. This decision involved a class of compounds based on a formula with a number of variables. The Synthon patent had a preferred group which mentioned a particular compound PMS as illustration and provided an example of how to make it in crystalline form. The method described referred to a particular acid and seeding crystals. SmithKline Beecham's patent was confined to a particular form of crystalline PMS limited to particular measurements so as to avoid prior art. These measurements were different to the Synthon compound. This crystalline form was different to the Synthon patent so that a person skilled in the art would think that they identified different polymorphs. The SmithKline Beecham patent mentioned a variety of solvents and isolation by conventional means. Synthon argued that the SmithKline Beecham patent was invalid as theirs was a novelty-destroying unpublished application. It turned out that the Synthon method with seeding crystals did not work and the Synthon measurements were mistaken readings.

[3.71] The court held that there were two requirements, disclosure and enablement, namely that the ordinary skilled person would be able to perform the disclosed invention using the disclosed matter and common general knowledge. The court summarised the prior case law on disclosure as being that the prior art must disclose subject matter which if performed would infringe the patent, regardless of whether the user is aware of the infringement. The infringement must not be possible or even likely – it must be necessarily entailed by the performance. Enablement applies to prior art which has been made available and novelty-destroying unpublished applications.[171] Sufficiency of enablement can also be used in the revocation ground of insufficient disclosure to enable

[167] *EI Du Pont's (Witsiepe's) Application* [1982] FSR 303.
[168] *Bristol-Myers Co (Johnson's) Application* [1975] RPC 127 at 156.
[169] *Asahi's Application* [1991] RPC 485.
[170] *Synthon BV v SmithKline Beecham* [2005] UKHL 59, [2006] 1 All ER 685, [2006] RPC 10.
[171] EPC, art 54(3); see para **[3.74]**.

performance by a person skilled in the art. The House of Lords could not see any reason why the tests would be different depending on the context. However, there may be differences in the application of the test to the facts, eg someone testing for sufficiency of disclosure is trying to perform the invention and therefore has a goal in mind. The person skilled in the art will be assumed to be willing to make trial and error experiments to get the experiment to work for enablement. It was held that it does not matter that the measurements in the Synthon patent were wrong. If the compound is monomorphic, the measurements are superfluous. The person who made the compound from the Synthon teaching would be puzzled or disconcerted to find out the measurements were different from those contained in the patent but would have made the crystals and infringed the patent. As regards enablement, the question was would the person skilled in the art be able to get the compound to crystallise in light of the incorrect instructions in the patent. It was held that this was a question of fact. The skilled person would have tried other solvents from the range mentioned in the application or from their common knowledge and would have been able to make crystals in a reasonable time.

[3.72] In *Pall Corpn v Commercial Hydraulics (Bedford) Ltd*,[172] it was held that the supply prior to the priority date of test samples for customer evaluation had not made the invention available to the public because the nature of the samples had not been disclosed and this was not apparently ascertainable by examination.

In *C Van Der Lely NV v Bamfords Ltd*,[173] what was at issue was whether or not a photograph was clear enough to amount to a disclosure. The alleged invention related to a hay raking machine in which the rake wheels were driven by contact with the ground. It was argued that there could not be anticipation unless this was shown clearly and unmistakably. This was rejected by Lord Reid who saw no practical difference between a definite statement of fact and material from which the skilled person would clearly infer its existence. The question was whether the typical skilled person would infer that it was ground-driven from the photograph and it was held that the photograph amounted to anticipation even though the features were not explicitly disclosed in the photograph. This test in which the courts put themselves in the position of a skilled technician was also applied in *Dow Chemical AG v Spence Bryson & Co Ltd*[174] but the prior art must still contain clear and unmistakable directions to do what the patentee claims to have invented.[175]

[3.73] Sometimes at issue is the question of mosaics of documents in the context of assessing novelty. This is the piecing together of a number of prior documents in order to produce an anticipation of the invention.[176] The EPO guidelines make it quite clear that in considering novelty (as distinct from inventive step), it is not permissible to combine

---

172 *Pall Corpn v Commercial Hydraulics (Bedford) Ltd* [1990] FSR 329.

173 *C Van Der Lely NV v Bamfords Ltd* [1963] RPC 61.

174 *Dow Chemical AG v Spence Bryson & Co Ltd* [1984] RPC 359 at 399–400.

175 *General Tire and Rubber Co v Firestone Tyre and Rubber Co* [1972] RPC 457 at 486; *Ward's Applications* [1986] RPC 50.

176 *Von Heyden v Neustadt* (1880) 50 LJ Ch 126 at 128.

separate items of prior art together. However, if a primary document refers explicitly to another document as, for example, in providing more detailed information on certain features, the import of the latter may be regarded as incorporated into the document containing the reference.

[3.74] Also, when considering novelty, regard must be had to the possible effect of a prior concurrent application. Under s 11(3) of the PA 1992 which corresponds to art 54(3) of the EPC, the state of the art includes the content of an Irish patent application of earlier priority. This provision is designed to protect against double patenting and although limited to patent applications published under s 28 of the PA 1992, it is not limited to Irish national applications. Under s 120(1) and (2) of the PA 1992, patent applications published under s 28 include European patents designating Ireland. There is also an additional provision in s 127(5) that an international application designating Ireland (which is deemed to be an application for a European patent designating Ireland) which is published under the Patent Co-operation Treaty is only to be treated as published under s 11(3) when a copy has been supplied to the EPO in English, French or German and the relevant fee under the EPC has been paid. Section 127(5) of the PA 1992 was not in the Patents Bill as initiated. It was argued by Peter Barry TD that if this provision was not included, a PCT application would be part of the state of the art against an Irish application of later priority date even if the PCT application was published after the date of the Irish application in some language such as Japanese, Russian or Mongolian and even if the fees were never paid to the EPO to bring the PCT application into effect as a European application.[177]

The Dutch Patent Office, in considering their equivalent to s 11(3) of the PA 1992 held that account must be taken not only of the literal text of the earlier application but also of anything which an average person skilled in the art, interpreting what he had read, would have regarded as part of the earlier application.[178]

[3.75] The provisions of s 11(4)[179] of the PA 1992 allow for the patenting of a substance or composition used in the treatment of the human or animal body even if previously known for some other purpose as long as that purpose is not comprised in the state of the art. An area of contention in relation to this provision is that pertaining to what is called second or subsequent medical use, ie a patenting of a known drug in respect of a second or subsequent new medical use. The German courts have adopted a very liberal attitude and have held that there is no prohibition against claims for a second or subsequent medical use.[180] The Swiss Patent Office decided to allow claims in respect of the use of a known compound for the manufacture of a medicament for the treatment of a disease even though this compound had previously been used in the treatment of a different disease.[181] This approach has been followed by the EBA[182] and by the UK[183] and

---

[177] 413 *Dáil Debates*, Cols 1268–1270 and 414 *Dáil Debates*, Cols 176–177.
[178] [1981] FSR 356 (Netherlands Patent Office, Appeals Department Decision No 14, 633).
[179] As amended by the Patents (Amendment) Act 2006.
[180] Hydropyridine x 2B 4183 [1984] OJ EPO 26.
[181] Statement of the Swiss Federal Intellectual Property Office [1984] OJ EPO 581.
[182] *Eisai's Application* [1985] OJEPO 64.
[183] *John Wyeth and Brother Ltd's Application* [1985] RPC 545.

Swedish courts.[184] In *Bristol-Myers Squibb v Yew Tree*[185] a second medical use was described as 'an application of a substance for a different therapeutic purpose (for example to fight another illness or for prevention instead of cure)'. The novelty cannot lie in the method of use, but must lie in the new therapeutic purposes for which the substance is used.[186]

NON-PREJUDICIAL DISCLOSURES

[3.76] Non-prejudicial disclosures are limited to just two instances and these are identified in s 12 of the PA 1992. Both instances require that the disclosure at issue must have taken place not more than six months before the date of filing of the application. The first instance relates to circumstances in which there has been a breach of confidence, breach of an agreement or the unlawful obtaining of an applicant's invention. A somewhat similar provision in relation to unlawful obtaining existed under s 47 of the PA 1964. It is interesting to note that the wording used does not correspond to art 55(1)(a) of the EPC which refers to an evident abuse in relation to the applicant or his legal predecessor. In addition, the EPO Opposition Division has held that under art 55(1), the six-month grace period runs from the actual date of filing.[187]

[3.77] In *Gallay Ltd's Application*,[188] Lloyd-Jacob J considered a drawing sent to Rolls Royce who had approached the opponents with an insulation problem. The drawing was of an insulating component and there was no explicit request for confidential treatment. An order was subsequently placed for the component shown. It was held that even if it was not forwarded in confidence but in the ordinary course of business, this was not decisive. It was necessary to look further and in particular at the nature of the business and the circumstances surrounding the transaction. In that case, Rolls Royce were considered to be partners with the opponents in a design project and were therefore deemed to have had a duty of confidence. This case was followed in *James Industries Ltd's Patent*,[189] and thus it can be seen that if there is disclosure of confidential information for a specific purpose then this will normally be deemed to be imparted in confidence and the recipient is duty bound not to use the information for any other purpose. The disclosing party has a legal right to prevent use of the information for the recipient's own purposes.[190] In *Tecalemit Ltd's Application*,[191] it was alleged that a pamphlet kept in a company library where it was available to technical staff

---

[184] *Hydropyridine* (1988) 19 IIC 815.

[185] *Bristol-Myers Squibb v Yew Tree* [1999] RPC 253 at 278.

[186] *Bristol-Myers Squibb v Barker Norton Pharmaceuticals Inc* [2001] RPC 1.

[187] G3/98 *Six-month period/University Patents* [2001] EPOR 33 overturning *Passoni/Stand Structure* [1982] EPOR 79.

[188] *Gallay Ltd's Application* [1959] RPC 141.

[189] *James Industries Ltd's Patent* [1987] RPC 235. See also *Saltman Eng v Campbell* (1948) 65 RPC 203 and *Strachan & Henshaw Ltd v Pakcel* (1948) 66 RPC 49.

[190] *Humpherson v Syer* (1887) 4 RPC 407.

[191] *Tecalemit Ltd's Application* [1967] FSR 387.

amounted to disclosure. It was held that inspection by personnel of a technical department was not inspection by members of the public and there was consequently no disclosure.

[3.78] Lord Parker in *Bristol-Myers' Application*[192] followed a Court of Appeal decision in *Formento v Mentmore*[193] and rejected the contention that publication depends either upon anything in the nature of a dedication to the public or upon the degree of dissemination of the information alleged to have been published. On the contrary, if the information, whether in documentary form or in the form of the invention itself, has been communicated to a single member of the public without inhibiting fetter, that is enough to amount to a making available to the public. The mere receipt of information by an employee from a third party does not infer confidentiality in circumstances where the employer was free to publish the information or make use of it as it wished. There is an onus on the party relying on s 12(1)(a) of the PA 1992 to show there has been a breach of confidence.[194]

[3.79] The second instance of a non-prejudicial disclosure relates to display at certain exhibitions.[195] The exhibitor must file a supporting certificate issued by the authority responsible for the protection of industrial property at that exhibition[196] within four months of the date of filing of the patent application. The certificate must state the opening date of the exhibition and the date of first disclosure.

INVENTIVE STEP

[3.80] In most cases which are litigated, the invention has not been directly anticipated and hence is novel but what is at issue is whether or not prior art which can be inferred to be part of the state of the art can mean that the invention is obvious.[197] Under s 9 of the PA 1992,[198] in order for an invention to be patentable, it must involve an inventive step. The criterion used in relation to short-term patents is that the invention must not be clearly lacking an inventive step.[199] Although novelty and inventive step are separate criteria, they are interrelated. The question of whether or not there is inventive step only arises if there is novelty.[200] As in the case of novelty, regard must be had to the state of the art. The existence of an inventive step is judged by determining whether the invention as claimed would be obvious to a person skilled in the art at the priority/filing date of the application. The EPO guidelines define 'obvious' as that which does not go beyond the normal progress of technology but merely follows plainly

---

[192] *Bristol-Myers' Application* [1969] RPC 146 at 155.
[193] *Formento v Mentmore* [1956] RPC 87.
[194] *Microsonic's Application* [1984] RPC 29.
[195] Strasbourg Convention, art 4(4)(b).
[196] Patents Rules 1992 (SI 179/1992), r 5.
[197] PA 1992, s 13; *Molins v Industrial Machinery Co Ltd* (1938) 55 RPC 31.
[198] As amended by the Patents (Amendment) Act 2006.
[199] PA 1992, s 63(4).
[200] EPO guidelines, C-IV, 9.1.

or logically from the prior art, ie something which does not involve the exercise of any skill or ability beyond that to be expected of the person skilled in the art.[201] The guidelines then go on to indicate various ways in which a skilled person may arrive at an invention, namely:

(a) the formulation of an idea or of a problem to be solved (the solution being obvious once the problem is clearly stated);

   Example The problem of indicating to the driver of a motor vehicle at night the line of the road ahead by using the light from the vehicle itself. As soon as the problem is stated in this form the technical solution, ie the provision of reflective markings along the road surface, appears simple and obvious. The formulation of the problem points to the solution.

(b) the devising of a solution to a known problem;

   Example The problem of permanently marking farm animals such as cows without causing pain to the animals or damage to the hide has existed since farming began. The solution ('freeze-branding') consists of applying the discovery that the hide can be permanently depigmented by freezing.

(c) the arrival at an insight into the cause of an observed phenomenon (the practical use of this phenomenon then being obvious).

   Example The agreeable flavour of butter is found to be caused by minute quantities of a particular compound. As soon as this insight has been arrived at, the technical application comprising of the addition of this compound to margarine is obvious.

[3.81] The PA 1964 allowed for opposition on the ground that the invention 'is obvious and clearly does not involve an inventive step'.[202] Revocation was also provided on the same terms but the word 'clearly' was not used.[203] Since the question at issue was essentially one of obviousness, cases under the PA 1964 and the corresponding UK Patents Act 1977 are still important. However, the inclusion of the word 'clearly' in opposition proceedings meant that if there was any doubt, it had to be resolved in favour of the applicant.[204] The word 'clearly' appears in s 63(4) of the PA 1992 in relation to the consideration of the patentability of short-term patents only.

[3.82] In considering the British cases, Costello J in the High Court in *Beecham Group Ltd v Bristol-Myers* Co[205] held that the Controller's task was not that of adjudicating a dispute between two rival litigants but a statutory duty to decide whether or not monopoly rights which affect the public should be granted. In the same case, it was held that for the purpose of obviousness, regard should be taken of the whole contents of Irish patent applications bearing an earlier priority date even those which have not been published. Section 13 of the PA 1992 addressed this by making it clear that for the

---

[201] EPO guidelines, C-IV, 11.4.
[202] PA 1964, s 19(1)(e).
[203] PA 1964, s 34(1)(f).
[204] *Electric and Musical Industries (Clarke's) Application* [1970] RPC 5.
[205] *Beecham Group Ltd v Bristol-Myers Co* (13 March 1981, unreported), HC.

purposes of considering inventive step, no regard should be had of unpublished contents of a patent application.

Budd J in *Rawls v Irish Tyre and Rubber Services Ltd*[206] reviewed the British cases and from them summarised:

> the tests to be applied as to the characteristics and quality of ingenuity which distinguish invention from workshop improvement are these:– Has the improvement been a commercial success? Has it supplied a want? Has the problem awaited a solution for many years and is the device novel and superior to that which has gone before? Is it widely used and is it used in preference to alternative devices? It is apparent that the mere simplicity of the device is no objection and a very slight advance, something approaching to a scintilla, will suffice to support the invention. Moreover, an *ex post facto* approach and analysis of the invention is to be guarded against, because it is so easy to say after the event that the whole thing was perfectly obvious in the popular sense of the word.

[3.83] In *Windsurfing International Inc v Tabur Marine (GB) Ltd*[207] Oliver J identified four steps to be taken in the determination of any issue as to obviousness, namely:

(a) identifying the inventive concept embodied in the patent in suit;

(b) inputting to a normally skilled but unimaginative addressee what was common general knowledge in the art at the priority date;

(c) identifying the differences if any between the matter cited as being 'known or used' and the alleged invention;

(d) deciding whether those differences, viewed without any knowledge of the alleged invention, constituted steps which would have been obvious to the skilled person or whether they required any degree of invention.

This test was restated by Jacob LJ in *Pozzoli v BDMO SA*[208] as:

(1) (a) Identify the notional 'person skilled in the art';

(b) Identify the relevant common general knowledge of that person;

(2) Identify the inventive concept of the claim in question or if that cannot readily be done, construe it;

(3) Identify what, if any, differences exist between the matter cited as forming part of the 'state of the art' and the inventive concept of the claim or the claim as construed;

(4) Viewed without any knowledge of the alleged invention as claimed, do those differences constitute steps which would have been obvious to the person skilled in the art or do they require any degree of invention?

[3.84] The UK courts have adopted variations on what is called the *'Cripps* question'.[209] This question was originally formulated in *Sharpe & Dohme Inc v Boots Pure Drug Co Ltd*[210] and can be summarised as asking whether it was for all practical purposes

---

[206] *Rawls v Irish Tyre and Rubber Services Ltd* [1960] EPC 11 at 30.

[207] *Windsurfing International Inc v Tabur Marine (GB) Ltd* [1985] RPC 59 at 73–74.

[208] *Pozzoli v BDMO SA* [2007] EWCA Civ 588, [2007] FSR 37.

[209] Named after the counsel who put the question in *Sharpe & Dohme Inc v Boots Pure Drug Co Ltd* (1928) 45 RPC 153.

[210] *Sharpe & Dohme Inc v Boots Pure Drug Co Ltd* (1928) 45 RPC 153 at 173.

obvious to any skilled worker in the respective field given the state of knowledge existing at the date of the patent (which consists of the literature then available to that person and their general knowledge) that they could make the invention claimed. A variation of this question can be seen in *Olin Mathieson Chemical v Biorex*,[211] namely 'would the notional research group at the relevant date in the circumstances ... directly be led as a matter of course to try the invention in the expectation that it might produce a useful desired result'. In *Technograph Printed Circuits v Mills & Rockley (Electronics) Ltd*,[212] the *Cripps* question was essentially not *could* the skilled worker make the invention but *would* such a skilled person make the invention.

The EPO adopted what has been called the problem and solution approach as seen in *Metal Refining/BASF*[213] where the Appeal Board stated:

> When assessing inventive step, it is not a question of the subjective achievement of the inventor. It is rather the objective which has to be assessed. Objectivity in the assessment of inventive step is achieved by starting out from the objectively prevailing state of the art, in the light of which the problem is determined which the invention addresses and solves from an objective point of view and consideration is given to the question of the obviousness of the disclosed solution to this problem as seen by the man skilled in the art and having those capabilities which can be objectively expected of him. This also avoids the retrospective approach.

The 'problem and solution' approach as adopted by the EPO has been described as involving the following steps:

(i)   determination of the closest prior art;

(ii) determination of the distinguishing technical feature and its technical effect;

(iii) formulation of the objective technical problem; and

(iv) determination of whether the skilled person *would* have solved the above technical problem by the solution specified in the claim.

If the skilled person would have solved the problem, there is no inventive step. Conversely, if the skilled person would not have solved the problem, an inventive step is present.

The EPO maintains, in line with the English approach in the *Technograph Printed Circuits* case above, that it is not sufficient if the skilled person *could* solve the problem but there has not been any consensus to date on the procedure to be used in assessing whether the skilled person would or could solve the problem.[214]

[3.85] One of the criteria for assessing obviousness used by Costello J in *Wavin Pipes Ltd v Hepworth Iron Co Ltd*[215] was the alleged invention's commercial success. It was stressed, however, that this is not a determining factor but is of assistance on the question

---

[211] *Olin Mathieson Chemical v Biorex* [1970] RPC 157.

[212] *Technograph Printed Circuits v Mills & Rockley (Electronics) Ltd* [1969] RPC 395 at 404.

[213] *Metal Refining/BASF* [1983] OJEPO 133.

[214] Leber, 'The could/would-problem in the problem-solution approach: a proposal to solve this issue in a systematic manner' (2010) EIPR 32(5), 191–4.

[215] *Wavin Pipes Ltd v Hepworth Iron Co Ltd* [1982] FSR 32 at 48.

of obviousness. In *Samuel Parkes & Co Ltd v Cocker Bros Ltd*,[216] it was stated that when it has been found that the problem has awaited solution for many years and that the device is in fact novel and superior to what had gone before and has been widely used and, indeed, in preference to alternative devices, it is practically impossible to say that there is not that scintilla of invention necessary to support the patent. This question of the scintilla of invention also finds its way into Costello J's judgment in the *Wavin Pipes* case in an acceptance that even if a very slight advance on the prior art is found, there cannot be obviousness. What is important is whether the advance is technically or practically obvious and is not a question of being commercially obvious. The skilled person is not to be taken as applying their mind to the commercial consequences[217] and in particular, whether it would have appeared commercially worthwhile to exploit the invention.[218] It is important to guard against *ex post facto* analysis[219] as it is always easy to see how to arrive at an invention once it is known, using pieces of prior art selected with knowledge of the invention.[220] The question of obviousness must be answered without any knowledge of the alleged invention.[221]

[3.86] What is meant by a person skilled in the art is not defined in the PA 1992 and these words did not exist in the PA 1964. The EPO guidelines state that:[222]

> The 'person skilled in the art' should be presumed to be a skilled practitioner in the relevant field, who is possessed of average knowledge and ability and is aware of what was common general knowledge in the art at the relevant date … He should also be presumed to have had access to everything in the 'state of the art', in particular the documents cited in the search report, and to have had at his disposal the normal means and capacity for routine work and experimentation. If the problem prompts the person skilled in the art to seek its solution in another technical field, the specialist in that field is the person qualified to solve the problem.

In *Technograph Printed Circuits Ltd v Mills & Rockley (Electronics) Ltd*,[223] Lord Reid described this hypothetical person as:

> a skilled technician who is well acquainted with workshop technique and who has carefully read the relevant literature. He is supposed to have an unlimited capacity to assimilate the contents of, it may be, scores of specifications but to be incapable of a scintilla of invention. When dealing with obviousness, unlike novelty, it is permissible to make a mosaic out of relevant documents, but it must be a mosaic which can be put together by an unimaginative man with no inventive capacity.

---

[216] *Samuel Parkes & Co Ltd v Cocker Bros Ltd* (1929) 46 RPC 241.

[217] *Hallen Co v Brabantia* [1991] RPC 195.

[218] *Windsurfing International Inc v Tabur Marine (GB) Ltd* [1985] RPC 59.

[219] *Wavin Pipes Ltd v Hepworth Iron Co Ltd* [1982] FSR 32 at 48.

[220] *Southco v Dzus* [1990] RPC 587.

[221] *Shoketsu's Patent* [1992] FSR 184; *Windsurfing International Inc v Tabur Marine (GB) Ltd* [1985] RPC 59 at 73.

[222] EPO guidelines, C-IV, 11.3.

[223] *Technograph Printed Circuits Ltd v Mills & Rockley (Electronics) Ltd* [1972] RPC 346 at 355.

In certain areas of technology, it is permissible to view this notional person not as a single individual but as a group or team whose combination of multi-disciplinary skills would be employed.[224]

[3.87] An example of forming a mosaic of the state of the art in order to prove obviousness can be seen in *Allmänna Svenska v Burntisland*[225] where it was held that the substitution in a marine engine of an electrodynamic coupling described in one patent specification for a geared diesel drive described in another specification, although novel, was still obvious. The decision in this case is hard to reconcile with the court's reluctance to accept a mosaic of documents where at least one document is not within the general knowledge of a skilled person. This can be seen from the statement of Lord Reid[226] that 'it must be a mosaic which can be put together by an unimaginative man with no inventive capacity'. It is easier for a court to accept a mosaic if one document contains a reference to the other. The longer separate parts of an invention have been known from different documents but have not been combined, the more difficult it is to argue that the combination of the documents is obvious.[227]

[3.88] It is part of the state of the art if the information which has been disclosed enables the public to know the product under a description sufficient to work the invention. Products need not be known under their chemical description in order to be part of the state of the art. If a recipe which inevitably produces a substance is part of the state of the art, so is the substance as made by that recipe.[228]

[3.89] In *Glaxo Group Ltd*,[229] Glaxo's Irish patent for the asthma inhaler carrying a combination product sold as SERETIDE in Ireland was invalidated on the basis of lack of inventive step. In the course of the decision, Charleton J engaged in an assessment of the case law on inventive step. Glaxo had previously patented the two compounds contained in the product separately. In addition, Glaxo had sold a combination inhaler preparation containing similar products before the priority date of the patent in question. A third party applied for revocation on the basis of obviousness. The decision acknowledged the differences in approach to considering inventive step between the EPO and the English courts. The EPO Boards of Appeal generally adopt a 'problem and solution' approach. The courts in England use a four-step obviousness test from the *Windsurfing* decision[230] which had previously been approved in Ireland. Charleton J stated:

---

[224] *General Tire and Rubber Co v Firestone Tyre and Rubber Co* [1972] RPC 457; *Genentech's Patent* [1989] RPC 147.

[225] *Allmänna Svenska v Burntisland* (1951) 69 RPC 63.

[226] *Allmänna Svenska v Burntisland* (1951) 69 RPC 63 at 125.

[227] *Mitsubishi/Endless Power Transmission Belt* [1987] 3 EPOR 120.

[228] *Merrell Dow Pharmaceuticals Inc v HN Norton & Co Ltd* [1996] RPC 76.

[229] *Glaxo Group Ltd* [2009] IEHC 277, (26 June 2009, unreported), HC; the decision is under appeal to the Supreme Court. For a discussion of this case see Jennings, 'Glaxo's Seretide patent revoked by Irish High Court' (2010) JIPLP 5(2), 71–2.

[230] *Windsurfing International Inc v Tabur Marine (GB) Ltd* [1985] RPC 59.

I would prefer in future to use the European test but as the parties have agreed the English test, I regard it also as helpful as a point of reference. Neither test changes the result by its application.

This could indicate how the Irish courts will decide the correct test of obviousness in future. However, perhaps the difference is not as great as might appear at first glance because the *Windsurfing* test has been redefined and reordered in subsequent years in a different manner which is closer to the EPO 'problem and solution' approach.[231]

Charleton J applied the EPO 'problem and solution' approach to the facts, stating:

I have determined the closest prior art; it is difficult to see a technical problem to be solved other than choosing a particular drug, namely salmeterol instead of salbutamol or formoterol, and fluticasone propionate instead of beclomethasone dipropionate or another steroid; finally, the claimed inventive step would have been obvious to the skilled team.

He also stated that the result would be the same using the four-step English test.

INDUSTRIAL APPLICATION

[3.90] A patentable invention must be susceptible of industrial application and s 14 of the PA 1992 states that such susceptibility arises if the invention can be made or used in any kind of industry, including agriculture. This corresponds to art 57 of EPC and differs from the UK Patents Act 1977 which uses the words 'capable of' as opposed to 'susceptible of'. Although this is a new provision in Irish patent legislation, the PA 1964 did contain a definition of invention, but one which was almost certainly narrower since an invention could be susceptible of industrial application even if not an 'art, process, machine, manufacture or composition of matter'.[232]

[3.91] The word 'industry' should be given a broad meaning. As stated in the EPO guidelines,[233] it should be understood as including any physical activity of 'technical character', ie an activity which belongs to the useful or practical articles as distinct from the aesthetic articles; it does not necessarily imply the use of a machine or the manufacture of an article and could cover, for eg a process for dispersing fog, or a process for converting energy from one form to another.

There are very few inventions which would not be excluded under ss 9 and 10[234] of the PA 1992 and yet, would fail to fall under s 14. However, one such type of invention would be articles or processes alleged to operate in a manner clearly contrary to well established physical laws, eg a perpetual motion machine.

---

[231] Jacob LJ in *Pozzoli SpA v BDMO SA* [2007] FSR 37.
[232] PA 1964, s 2.
[233] EPO guidelines, C-IV, 5.1.
[234] As amended by the Patents (Amendment) Act 2006.

DISCLAIMERS

[3.92] In decisions G1/03[235] and G2/03,[236] the EBA clarified its position on the acceptance of disclaimers during patent examination or opposition. In those proceedings, the applicant had used disclaimers in order to overcome novelty objections. Previous case law had allowed for the use of disclaimers that are not based on the application as filed under certain circumstances (usually in order to overcome novelty objections). This practice had been called into question in decision T 323/97 of the Technical Board of Appeal, which held that negative features introduced into a claim could not contain subject matter that extends beyond that contained in the application as filed.[237]

The findings of the EBA were as follows:

1. An amendment to a claim by the introduction of a disclaimer may not be refused under art 123(2) EPC for the sole reason that neither the disclaimer nor the subject matter excluded by it from the scope of the claim has a basis in the application as filed. This allows applicants to limit claims to overcome novelty objections even where the disclaimer does not cover the subject matter of the application.

2. The following criteria are to be applied for assessing the acceptability of a disclaimer which is not included in the application as filed:

2.1 A disclaimer may be acceptable in order to:

(a) restore novelty by limiting a claim as regards the state of the art under art 54(3) and (4) EPC;[238]

(b) restore novelty by limiting a claim against an accidental anticipation under art 54(2) EPC[239] (where the subject matter turns out to be already known for an unrelated use, usually in chemistry and biotechnology); and

(c) disclaim subject matter which, under arts 52 to 57 EPC, is excluded from patentability for non-technical reasons.

2.2 A disclaimer should not remove more than is necessary either to restore novelty or to disclaim subject matter excluded from patentability for non-technical reasons.

2.3 A disclaimer which is or becomes relevant for the assessment of inventive step or sufficiency of disclosure adds to the subject matter of the application contrary to art 123(2) EPC and is therefore not acceptable.

2.4 A claim containing a disclaimer must meet the requirements of clarity and conciseness under art 84 EPC.

---

[235] G1/03 *Disclaimer/PPG*, OJ EPO 2004 413.

[236] G2/03 *Disclaimer/GENETIC SYSTEMS*, OJ EPO 2004 448.

[237] EPC, art 123(2).

[238] Article 54(4) was deleted by EPC 2000.

[239] An anticipation is accidental if it is so unrelated to and remote from the claimed invention that the person skilled in the art would never have taken it into consideration when making the invention.

[3.93] The decision also raised the following interesting points. It confirmed the definition of a disclaimer as 'an amendment to a claim resulting in the incorporation therein of a "negative" technical feature'. One can disclaim subject matter which is not patentable for non-technical reasons (ie there is nothing inherently wrong with the invention but it is excluded on policy grounds). Examples are inventions which are contrary to morality or which relate to therapy of human or animal bodies or which are incapable of industrial application. If a disclaimer makes a technical contribution, it is not permissible as one cannot exclude the possibility that a disclaimer might later turn out to be of technical relevance, eg because of prior art which comes to light later. It must be clear from specification that there is an undisclosed disclaimer and why it was introduced. It must not be hidden using undisclosed positive features between original claim and prior art. Excluded prior art must be indicated in the description and the relation between prior art and disclaimer shown. A disclaimer does not have a technical contribution so it does not change the identity of the invention. Therefore, it does not affect a priority claim.

For accidental anticipation, remoteness is not decisive as there are some situations where the skilled person would consult documents in a remote field. A lack of a common problem is even less decisive. The test is whether the disclosure is so unrelated and remote that the person skilled in the art would never have taken it into consideration when working on the invention. This principle is justified as the general concept does not disclose specific embodiments and general teaching does not directly and unambiguously disclose specific teaching. Conversely, one cannot amend a general concept with an undisclosed specific embodiment.

Chapter 4

Patents Act 1992 – Acquisition of Patent Rights

INTRODUCTION

[4.01] The Statute of Monopolies 1623 provided for the grant of a patent to the 'true and first inventor and inventors' of new manufactures and the Patents Act 1964 (PA 1964) stated that an applicant had to be the true and first inventor or their assignee[1] with an exception made in the case of a personal representative.[2] Section 15 of the Patents Act 1992 (PA 1992) contains no such limitation but this must be read in conjunction with s 16, which states that 'the right to a patent shall belong to the inventor or his successor in title' and which has a particular provision concerning employee inventions. There is no limitation on the number of co-applicants and there are special provisions relating to the co-ownership of patent applications[3] and the substitution of applicants.[4] Even though an applicant may not be the inventor, it is still necessary to identify the inventors within 16 months of the earliest priority date.[5] Where the applicant is not the inventor, it is also necessary to indicate the derivation of title.[6] The sometimes difficult task of determining the inventor is not greatly helped by the definition of an inventor,[7] stated to be 'the actual deviser of an invention'. The principal problem of identification lies in instances where there are large teams of individuals involved in research and development. In such cases, applicants should use their best endeavours to identify the actual devisers of the invention. Although s 17(2) of the PA 1992 states that the identification of the inventor in accordance with the belief of the applicant is what is important, presumably this belief must be reasonably held. Failure to provide details of the inventor and the derivation of title within 16 months from the priority date results in the patent application being deemed abandoned.[8] In *Nippon Piston Ring Co Ltd's Application*,[9] two applications were refused for failure adequately to identify the applicants' right to apply. It was, however, accepted that the requirement to identify the inventor had been satisfied by supplying a

---

[1] PA 1964, s 6(1).
[2] PA 1964, s 6(4).
[3] PA 1992, s 80.
[4] PA 1992, s 85.
[5] Patents Rules 1992 (SI 179/1992), r 6 as amended by the Patents (Amendment) Rules 2009 (SI 194/2009).
[6] PA 1992, s 17(2); Patents Rules 1992, r 6(1) as amended by the Patents (Amendment) Act 2006.
[7] PA 1992, s 2.
[8] PA 1992, s 17(2).
[9] *Nippon Piston Ring Co Ltd's Application* [1987] RPC 120.

certified copy of the priority document which did name the inventor, although this did not excuse the failure to identify the applicant's right to apply.

[4.02] Section 17(1) and (3) of the PA 1992 makes provision for one or more inventors to be mentioned and for the deletion of such a mention. A person alleging that they ought to have been mentioned or that an inventor is incorrectly mentioned must discharge the onus of proof by setting out fully the facts relied on.[10] The Controller sends a copy of that application and the evidence to the applicant or proprietor of the patent, the identified inventor(s) and to every other person whose interests the Controller considers may be affected by the application.[11] A counter statement may be filed within three months of the receipt of the documents.[12]

Under UK patent law there is provision for employee inventors to receive certain compensation in the case of a patent which is of outstanding benefit to the employer.[13] The identification of an employee as an inventor lends credence to any claim for such compensation. Irish patent law has no similar provision and judging from the experience under the PA 1964, there are likely to be very few applications for mention as an inventor.

[4.03] It is, of course, quite conceivable that several people could independently and simultaneously create the same invention. They may all be inventors but ownership resides in the person whose patent application has the earlier date of filing, provided that this application has been duly published.[14]

EMPLOYER/EMPLOYEE SITUATIONS

[4.04] If an inventor is an employee, the right to a patent is determined in accordance with the law of the State in which the employee is wholly or mainly employed or, if the identity of such State cannot be determined, in accordance with the law of the State in which the employer has his place of business to which the employee is attached.[15] The same provision exists in art 60(1) of the European Patent Convention (EPC) governing the right to a European patent. Unlike the situation in the UK Patents Act 1977, the Irish legislation does not set out any criteria for determining the ownership of employer/employee inventions. Although the situation in Ireland is governed by the common law, s 39 of the UK Patents Act 1977 is of some guidance in that it reflected the common law position of the time that an invention made by an employee belongs to an employer, where:

(a)　it was made in the course of the normal duties of the employee or in the course of duties falling outside his normal duties, but specifically assigned to him, and

---

[10]　Patents Rules 1992, r 7(1).
[11]　Patents Rules 1992, r 7(2).
[12]　Patents Rules 1992, r 7(1), (2) and (3).
[13]　PA 1977, s 40.
[14]　PA 1992, s 16(2).
[15]　PA 1992, s 16(1).

the circumstances in either case were such that an invention might reasonably be expected to result from the carrying out of his duties; or

(b)   the invention was made in the course of the duties of the employee and, at the time of making the invention, because of the nature of his duties and the particular responsibilities arising from the nature of his duties, he had a special obligation to further the interests of the employer's undertaking.

However, the UK case law should be treated with caution as it is accepted that UK law on the issue is now decided solely on the basis of the relevant provisions of the UK Patents Act 1977 rather than the pre-existing common law.[16]

[4.05] In the absence of an express provision to the contrary, the common law imposes an implied term that an employee is a trustee of his employer in relation to an invention made in the course of that person's duty as an employee. In *Patchett v Sterling Engineering Co Ltd*,[17] the inventor was employed as the appellant's chief designer. Lord Reid stated:

> It is, in my judgment, inherent in the legal relationship of master and servant that any product of the work which the servant is paid to do belongs to the master.

The implied term can only be displaced by a binding agreement to the contrary effect since, as stated by Lord Reid:

> of course, as the relationship of master and servant is constituted by contract, the parties can, if they choose, alter or vary the normal incidents of the relationship, but they can only do that by express agreement or by an agreement which can be implied from the facts of the case.

[4.06] Whether an invention was made by the inventor in the course of his duty as employee is often difficult to determine and is a question of fact in each case. In *Loewy's Application*,[18] the inventor, although described as a consulting engineer, was held to be an employee. The tests applied in reaching the conclusion were whether the inventor was or was not employed to make the invention or whether the invention was made in the course of employment in which it was part of the employee's duty to make such inventions.

[4.07] The UK Bank's Report into the patent system and patent law[19] quotes from the judgment of Danckwerts J in *Fine Industrial Commodities Ltd v Powling*[20] that:

> the mere existence of a contract of service does not in itself disqualify the officer or employee from taking out a patent for an invention made by him during his term of service, even though the invention may relate to subject matter germane to, and useful for, his employers in their business, and even though the employee may have made use of his employer's time and servants and materials in bringing his invention to completion, and

---

[16]   *LIFFE Administration & Management v Pinkava* [2006] EWHC 595, [2007] RPC 30.

[17]   *Patchett v Sterling Engineering Co Ltd* (1955) 72 RPC 50.

[18]   *Loewy's Application* (1951) 69 RPC 3.

[19]   Banks (Chairman), 'Report of the Committee to Examine the Patent System and Patent Law' (1970) Cmnd 4407, 132–133.

[20]   *Fine Industrial Commodities Ltd v Powling* (1954) 53 RPC 253 at 257.

may have allowed his employers to use the invention while he was in their employment. But all the circumstances must be considered in each case. It is very material to see what is the nature of the inventor's position in regard to the business.

It was pointed out that:

> in the Powling case, the employee was the managing director of the employing company and was held to be a trustee for the company of his interest in the invention. It seems to be generally true to say that directors of companies and managers of businesses to whom no specific duties are allocated have a general duty to forward the interests of the company or business and will accordingly hold any inventions made during their employment (at least so far as they relate to the relevant business) in trust for the employer.

[4.08] In *Electrolux Ltd v Hudson*,[21] the defendants were husband and wife and the husband was employed as a senior storekeeper. Outside working hours, the couple devised an adapter for use in vacuum cleaners without using the materials of their employer. The standard conditions of employment included a clause to the effect that the discovery of any process, invention or improvement relating to articles not only manufactured by the plaintiff but by any of its associated companies in the UK or elsewhere had to be fully disclosed to the plaintiff who had first option over such. It was held by Whitford J that it was doubtful whether such a provision was appropriate or reasonable even for a research worker employed by the plaintiff but that in any event, there was no implied term because the husband's duties were such that he was not employed to invent. While it was necessary to serve his employer with good faith and fidelity, this did not mean that he could not take part in activities that might be harmful to the business of the plaintiff.

In *Mellor v William Beardmore & Co Ltd*,[22] it was pointed out that notwithstanding that an inventor has used his employer's time and materials to aid him in completing the invention, the resulting patent could still belong to the employee. Where an employee is obliged by the terms of his employment to use his industry, skill, ingenuity and inventive ability to solve a technical problem, then the invention is held in trust for the employer because essentially that person has been employed to invent.[23] In *Harris's Patent*,[24] the employee/inventor was employed purely as a manager and salesman of a company engaged in the sale of valves under licence and there was no research and development carried out by the company. It was held that his duties were such that the invention was not made in circumstances where it might reasonably have been expected from his normal duties. This decision was made on the basis of the legislative provisions in the UK Patents Act 1977 and it was stated that this may not necessarily embody the position under the common law, which is used as the basis for the position in Irish law.

---

21 *Electrolux Ltd v Hudson* [1977] FSR 312.
22 *Mellor v William Beardmore & Co Ltd* (1927) 44 RPC 175.
23 *British Reinforced Concrete v Lind* (1917) 34 RPC 101; *Adamson v Kenworthy* (1931) 49 RPC 57.
24 *Harris's Patent* [1985] RPC 19.

[4.09] The distinction between the normal duties of an employee and those which are specifically assigned to him was explored in the UK case *LIFFE Administration & Management v Pinkava*,[25] where it was held that the court must consider more than the terms of the initial written contract of employment because any extra or different duties could initially be 'specifically assigned' but could over time become part of the 'normal' duties.

[4.10] Section 53 of the PA 1964 contained a specific provision which allowed the court or the Controller to determine disputes between an employer and employee and, in certain cases, apportion between them the benefit of the invention. There is no similar provision in the PA 1992. Section 81 of the PA 1992 allows the court to determine ownership and apportion it but this is limited to a two-year time period from the date of grant of the patent unless the patentee knew that he was not entitled to ownership of the patent; s 81 is not specific to the employer/employee situation.

[4.11] Section 41 of the UK Patents Act 1977 provides that compensation must be paid to an employee who invented a patent when the employer assigns the benefit of the patent to another person, provided that the benefit was to be assessed as if that person was not connected. There is no equivalent under Irish law.

FORM OF APPLICATION

[4.12] An Irish patent application must be filed at the Irish Patents Office. The request for the grant of a patent must be made on Form No 12 which is scheduled to the Patents Rules 1992[26] and must be accompanied by the requisite official fee.[27] The title of the invention appearing in the request for grant must be the same as the title in the specification.[28] The specification forming part of the patent application must commence with the title of the invention (which should be brief and indicate the matter to which the invention relates), continue with the description of the invention and be followed by the claim or claims and drawings, if any, in that order.[29]

[4.13] Since the title of the invention appears in the Official Journal shortly after the application is made, it may be important for an applicant to ensure that the title, while complying with the requirement of indicating the matter to which the invention relates, does not disclose information which the applicant does not wish to publish before the rest of the specification. The EPC states that the title should clearly and concisely state the technical designation of the invention and should exclude all fancy names.[30]

---

[25] *LIFFE Administration & Management v Pinkava* [2006] EWHC 595, [2007] RPC 30; for a critical analysis of this decision see Chandler, 'Ownership of employees' inventions: duties, expectations and variable objectivity' (2008) EIPR 30(4), 164–170.

[26] See Patents Rules 1992, Sch II; PA 1992, s 18; Patents Rules 1992, r 8.

[27] Patents, Trade Marks and Designs (Fees) Rules 2001 (SI 482/2001): the fee payable is €125.

[28] Patents Rules 1992, r 9.

[29] Patents Rules 1992, r 10.

[30] Rule 41(2)(b), EPC.

[4.14] The description of the invention, aided by drawings, must disclose the invention in a manner sufficiently clear and complete for it to be carried out by a person skilled in the art.[31] This fictional person is also used in deciding whether or not there is an inventive step.[32] In the Irish High Court decision in *Rawls v Irish Tyre and Rubber Services Ltd,*[33] Budd J approved the reasoning of Lord Shaw in *British Thomson-Houston Co Ltd v Corona Lamp Works Ltd*[34] that the reader of a specification must be taken to be:

> ordinarily intelligent and versed in the subject matter. Such a reader must be supposed to bring his stock of intelligence and knowledge to bear upon the document. If he is able to understand what the invention is and can produce the object and achieve the manufacture by the help of the written and drawn page, then the subject-matter of the invention does not fall because of vagueness.

[4.15] In addition, in construing a patent specification, its claims should be given a purposive construction rather than a literal one.[35]

The person skilled in the art and to whom the specification is addressed is to possess no more than average knowledge. As stated in *Edison and Swan v Holland,*[36] the relevant level of knowledge is that of:

> persons having a reasonably competent knowledge of what was known before on the subject to which this patent relates and having reasonably competent skill in the practical mode of doing what was then known.

Unlike the former position under the PA 1964, an applicant is not required to disclose the best known method of performing the invention except in the case of a short-term patent under s 63(7)(b)(i).

MICRO-ORGANISMS

[4.16] There are special conditions concerning applications relating to inventions which require for their performance the use of micro-organisms.[37] The conditions set out in r 14[38] of the Patent Rules 1992 apply where the micro-organisms used in the invention are not available to the public at the date of filing and cannot be described in the specification in such a manner as to enable the invention to be performed by a person skilled in the art. The conditions involve depositing a culture of the micro-organism in a depositary institution no later than the actual filing date of the application.[39] Details of

---

[31] PA 1992, s 19(1).

[32] PA 1992, s 13.

[33] *Rawls v Irish Tyre and Rubber Services Ltd* [1960] EPC 11 at 57.

[34] *British Thomson-Houston Co Ltd v Corona Lamp Works Ltd* [1921] 39 RPC 49 at 89.

[35] *Wavin Pipes Ltd v Hepworth Iron Co Ltd* [1982] FSR 32 at 53; *Catnic Components Ltd v Hill and Smith Ltd* [1981] FSR 60 at 65–66.

[36] *Edison and Swan v Holland* (1889) 6 RPC 243 at 280.

[37] PA 1992, s 19(2).

[38] As replaced by Patents (Amendment) Rules 2009.

[39] Patents Rules 1992, r 14(2) as replaced by Patents (Amendment) Rules 2009.

the name of the depositary institution, the date of the deposit and the accession number of the deposit must be given in the specification. The provision of this information constitutes an unreserved and irrevocable consent to the depositary institution to make the culture available on receipt of a certificate from the Controller.[40] Scheduled to the Patent Rules 1992 is the text of the prescribed request for the Controller's certificate authorising the release of the sample of the micro-organism. This form must be filed in duplicate, together with the form required under the regulations to the Budapest Treaty on the International Recognition of the Deposit of Micro-Organisms for the Purposes of Patent Procedure.[41] The request must include an undertaking not to make the culture, or any culture derived from it, available to any other person and secondly, not to use the culture otherwise than for experimental purposes relating to the subject matter of the invention. The undertakings can be varied by way of agreement.[42] They are not required of any Minister exercising the right to use an invention for the service of the State under s 77 of the PA 1992. The undertaking not to make the culture, or any culture derived from the micro-organism, available to the public, does not apply where it is necessary to give effect to a licence of right[43] or a compulsory licence.[44]

[4.17] Provided the preparations for publication of a patent application under s 28 of the PA 1992 have not been completed, an applicant can give notice that the sample of the micro-organism is only to be made available to an expert.[45] This preserves the confidentiality of the subject matter of the patent application but allows for experiments to be conducted thereon. In these circumstances, a request for the Controller's certificate authorising release to an expert must contain full particulars of the nominated expert[46] who must also provide the undertakings as regards non-release to other persons and non-use for other than experimental purposes relating to the subject matter of the invention.

[4.18] Rule 14(17)[47] of the Patent Rules 1992 also provides that an applicant or proprietor may make a new deposit or transfer the deposit to another institute in cases where the depositary institute can no longer satisfy a request for release and has notified the applicant accordingly. This must be done within three months of the receipt of such notification or of the depositary institution ceasing to perform the functions of a depositary institution or to conduct its activities as such in an objective and impartial manner and requires a declaration that the culture so deposited is of the same micro-organism as the culture originally deposited. There must also be an amendment to the specification to indicate the accession number of the transferred or new deposit and,

---

[40] Patents Rules 1992, r 14(4) as replaced by Patents (Amendment) Rules 2009.
[41] Patents Rules 1992, Sch II, Form No 6; see para **[2.119]** *et seq.*
[42] Patents Rules 1992, r 14(10) as replaced by the Patents (Amendment) Rules 2009.
[43] PA 1992, s 68 as amended by the Patents (Amendment) Act 2006; Patents Rules 1992, r 14(12) as replaced by the Patents (Amendment) Rules 2009.
[44] PA 1992, s 70 as amended by the Patents (Amendment) Act 2006; Patents Rules 1992, r 14(12) as replaced by the Patents (Amendment) Rules 2009.
[45] Patent Rules 1992, r 14(13) as replaced by the Patents (Amendment) Rules 2009.
[46] Patents Rules 1992, Form No 8, r 14(16)(a) as replaced by the Patents (Amendment) Rules 2009.
[47] As replaced by the Patents (Amendment) Rules 2009.

where applicable, the name of the depositary institution with which the deposit has been made.

THE CLAIMS

[4.19] A patent specification must contain one or more claims. Under s 20 of the PA 1992, the claims must define the matter for which protection is sought, be clear and concise and be supported by the description. The extent of the protection conferred by the patent/patent application is determined essentially by the terms of the claims.[48] Novelty and inventiveness are also determined by reference to the claims. When drafting claims, a patent agent strives to obtain the broadest possible protection for the invention, so that a patent cannot be avoided by making minor changes. In some instances, however, a claim must be very narrow in scope in order to distinguish the invention as claimed from what is already known. Since what is not claimed is disclaimed, the wording of a claim is extremely important.

[4.20] Claims essentially fall into two categories. Firstly, claims to a physical entity, which are often called product claims and, secondly, process claims, which are applicable to all kinds of activities in which the use of some material product for effecting the process is implied. The activity may be exercised upon material products, upon energy, upon other processes (as in control processes) or upon living things.[49]

Under s 34(1)(i) of the PA 1964, it was a ground for the revocation of a patent that the scope of any claim of the complete specification was not sufficiently and clearly defined or that any claim of the complete specification was not fairly based on the matter disclosed in the specification.

[4.21] The grounds for revocation in the PA 1992 are set out in s 58[50] and do not include failure to comply with s 20, ie that the claims shall define the matter for which protection is sought, be clear and concise and be supported by the description. Thus, a patent cannot be revoked on these grounds.[51] The onus is on the Irish Patents Office, during examination, to refuse the application if the claims are too wide or include matters not disclosed in the specification. This leads to the position that mistakes of the Irish Patents Office in allowing a claim that is too wide cannot later be put right. However, this seems to have been a deliberate decision of the parliamentary draftsman, who would have had the benefit of the Court of Appeal decision in *Genentech Inc's Patent* and Mustill LJ's regrets that, even as guardians of the public interest, their hands were tied. In addition, given the very limited examination undertaken by the Irish Patents Office and since, in most cases, a nationally filed Irish patent application is likely to conform to a granted European or UK patent, it would be extremely rare that an objection would arise under s 20 of the PA 1992, particularly as art 84 of the EPC and s 14(5) of the UK Patents Act 1977 have equivalent provisions.

---

48   PA 1992, s 45 as amended by the Patents (Amendment) Act 2006.
49   EPO guidelines, C-III, 3.1.
50   As amended by the Patents (Amendment) Act 2006.
51   *Genentech Inc's Patent* [1989] RPC 147.

Even though the claims must be supported by the description, it was made clear by Kenny J in the Irish High Court decision of *Farbwerke Hoechst AG v Intercontinental Pharmaceutical (Eire) Ltd*[52] that it is not permissible to supplement the claims by referring to the specification although it may be referred to as an indication of the sense in which words are used and as giving the technical background against which the claims have been formulated.

[4.22] Claims may be drafted in terms of the result to be achieved by the invention.[53] However, as *No-Fume Ltd v Pitchford*[54] made clear, the claim must mention those features that must be chosen to enable the result to be achieved, and the description must explain to a person skilled in the art how to conduct tests in order to find out how to achieve the result and to know that the result has been achieved. The EPO guidelines[55] state that claims which define the invention in terms of the result to be achieved may be allowed if the invention can only be defined in such terms and if the result is one which can be directly and positively verified by tests or procedures adequately specified in the description and involving nothing more than trial and error. The important question is what is clear and concise to a person skilled in the art. An imprecise term may still be clear to a skilled person.[56]

[4.23] The question of whether or not a claim is supported by the description was discussed in *Glatt's Application*.[57] The description referred to in s 20 of the PA 1992 is the description of the invention found in the specification which has been filed in support of the application and the claims must be within the contemplation of the inventor at the time of filing. The word 'support' requires the description to be the base which can fairly entitle the patentee to a monopoly of the width claimed.[58]

UNITY OF INVENTION

[4.24] A patent application must relate to one invention only or to a group of inventions so linked as to form a single general inventive concept which is referred to as 'unity of invention'.[59] Subject to this provision, a patent application may contain two or more independent claims in the same category (product, process, apparatus or use) where it is not appropriate to cover this subject matter by a single claim, having regard to the subject matter of the application.[60]

---

[52] *Farbwerke Hoechst AG v Intercontinental Pharmaceutical (Eire) Ltd* [1968] FSR 187 at 197.
[53] *Hughes Tool Co v Ingersoll Rand Co Ltd* [1977] FSR 406.
[54] *No-Fume Ltd v Pitchford* (1935) 52 RPC 231.
[55] EPO guidelines, C-111, 4.7.
[56] *British Thomson v Corona* (1921) 39 RPC 49.
[57] *Glatt's Application* [1983] RPC 122.
[58] *Schering Biotech's Application* [1993] RPC 249.
[59] PA 1992, s 21.
[60] Patents Rules 1992, r 11(1).

Any claim stating the essential features of an invention may be followed by one or more claims concerning particular embodiments (tangible forms of an abstract concept) of that invention.[61]

[4.25] Section 21(2) of the PA 1992 states that rules may be provided for treating two or more inventions as being so linked as to form a single inventive concept. Rule 17 of the Patents Rules 1992, allows for one and the same patent application to include:

(a) in addition to an independent claim for a product, an independent claim for a process specially adapted for the manufacture of the product, and an independent claim for a use of the product; or

(b) in addition to an independent claim for a process, an independent claim for an apparatus or means specifically designed for carrying out the process; or

(c) in addition to an independent claim for a product, an independent claim for a process specially adapted for the manufacture of the product and an independent claim for an apparatus or means specifically designed for carrying out the process.

The question of what is a single invention is a question of fact. In *Celanese Corpn Application*,[62] it was held that claims to intermediate and final chemical products did not relate to a single invention.

[4.26] The validity of a patent cannot be challenged on the ground that it relates to more than one invention. If, during examination, there is an objection that the application relates to more than one invention, the applicant can amend the specification and delete or amend the claims. The applicant may also file another patent application in respect of the additional invention, ie a divisional application.[63] This can also be done voluntarily.

DIVISIONAL APPLICATIONS

[4.27] It is extremely important that the subject matter of the divisional application does not extend beyond the content of the earlier (parent) application as filed because this is a ground for revocation under s 58(c) of the PA 1992. The divisional application may be filed within two months of amendment of the earlier (parent) application following:

(a) a search report;

(b) the grant of a patent that is being used as evidence in support of the earlier application, provided the grant fee has not been paid in either case; or

(c) at any time before grant under s 32 of the PA 1992.[64]

If there has been no amendment of the earlier application or the amendment of the earlier application does not fall within the above, then a divisional application may be filed at any time after filing of the earlier application except after refusal, withdrawal,

---

[61] Patents Rules 1992, r 11(2).
[62] *Celanese Corpn Application* (1952) 69 RPC 22.
[63] PA 1992, s 24; EPC equivalent is EPC, art 52.
[64] Patents Rules 1992, r 20(1) as amended by the Patents (Amendment) Rules 2009.

deemed withdrawal of the earlier application or after the applicant has paid the fee for the grant of a patent in respect of the invention to which that application relates.[65] A divisional patent application is deemed to have been filed on the date of filing of the earlier parent application and is entitled to any priority claimed, if appropriate. The result of this is that the novelty of the divisional application is not destroyed by the existence of the parent application. In all other respects, a divisional application proceeds as an independent substantive application. Since the reality of the Irish patent system is that there is little or no examination under the provisions of s 21 of the PA 1992, patents may be granted in respect of applications claiming more than one invention. Although a division of a corresponding EPC or UK application may have been required, the resulting patents may be used as combined evidence of the existence of a foreign patent application for the same invention under s 30 and an objection is unlikely to arise.

European divisional applications

[4.28] The same substantive principles apply to divisional applications of European patent applications as to Irish applications but there are some divergences as regards procedure.

Revised rules apply to requests for divisional applications after 1 April 2010. These more stringent rules were adopted because it was alleged that applicants were using the ability to file divisional applications at a late stage as a method of deferring costs and preserving their position regarding the inventions contained in the application. It was possible to file a divisional application at any time before the parent application was granted. From 1 April 2010, divisional applications must be filed within 24 months of the first communication[66] from the Examining Division or an objection regarding a lack of unity of invention.[67] This applies not only to the first divisional application but also to any subsequent divisional applications. Any new objections on lack of unity will start a new, separate 24-month period.[68] The parent application must still be in existence when the divisional application is filed.[69] Search reports and search opinions do not trigger the 24-month time limit.[70]

[4.29] This means that applicants will not be able to preserve their position by leaving the decision to divide until a late stage but must decide at a relatively early stage whether to incur the substantial additional costs in filing a divisional application or deleting one or more inventions from the application. Indeed, if a divisional application is filed and the EPO still maintains a lack of unity objection, the applicant may have little time to

---

[65] Patents Rules 1992, r 20(1) as amended by the Patents (Amendment) Rules 2009.

[66] See EPO guidelines, A–IV, 1.1,1.2.

[67] Rule 36(1)(a) and (b), EPC.

[68] Notice from the European Patent Office dated 20 August 2009 concerning amended Rule 36(1) and (2), EPC (European divisional applications) and consequential amendments to Rules 57(a) and 135(2), EPC.

[69] Rule 36(1), EPC: 'any pending European patent application...'

[70] Notice from the EPO dated 20 August 2009 *ibid.*

consider this before the 24-month deadline approaches. Any inventions which are deleted will lose novelty as they will be in the public domain and can therefore no longer be protected by patents. For these reasons, it is very important to progress the examination as quickly as possible in terms of replying to any objections quickly and requesting accelerated examination.[71]

The 24-month period will take place entirely in the European examination phase.[72] This means that the time limit will be tighter for a Euro-PCT application which is searched in the international phase compared to one which is not searched in the international phase or a direct European patent application. In addition, the deadline for a lack of unity objection runs from the first such objection.

Divisional applications after the 24-month period can be filed for existing independent applications up to 1 October 2010.[73]

G1/06 Sequence of Divisionals/Seiko[74] and G1/05 Divisional Exclusion and Objection (Interlocutory Decision)[75]

[4.30] These decisions of the EBA were the first major decisions concerning divisional applications and therefore deserve detailed examination. One query put by the referring EPO Technical Board of Appeal was whether a divisional application was invalid if it extended beyond an earlier application and whether this could be remedied. It was held that the divisional application was only invalid if the parent application does not comply with requirements for a filing date. There are no other grounds for invalidity based on, eg non-compliance with substantive requirements. If there is any non-compliance with substantive requirements, the divisional application is refused if the deficiency is incurable or if it is not removed.

The other key points of the decisions were as follows. Divisional applications are treated in the same manner as ordinary applications and have the same requirements. The question of compliance is decided on the text finally submitted or agreed after objections, comment and amendment. Also, the grounds for revocation in art 100 of the EPC do not include divisional applications where the subject matter extends beyond the parent application. Therefore, any deficiencies are an issue for the Examining Division, so the applicant has the opportunity to amend the application. The applicant can broaden the claims up to grant including directing claims at subject matter not encompassed in the claims as filed. Only after grant is the right to amend limited. It does not matter if the parent application is no longer pending while the divisional application is being examined as the divisional application is, in principle, independent. A divisional application can be directed, by amendment, to aspects of the parent application also

---

[71] Under the programme for accelerated prosecution of European patent applications (PACE), Notice from the EPO, Special edition No 3, OJ EPO 2007, F.1

[72] Programme for accelerated prosecution of European patent applications (PACE), Notice from the EPO, Special edition No 3, OJ EPO 2007, *ibid.*

[73] Notice from the EPO dated 20 August 2009 *ibid.*

[74] G1/06 *Sequence of Divisionals/Seiko*, OJ EPO 2008 307 (28 June 2007).

[75] G1/05 *Divisional Exclusion and Objection (Interlocutory Decision)*, OJ EPO 2008 271 (7 December 2006).

disclosed in the divisional application as filed but not encompassed by the claims of the divisional application.

[4.31] Sequences of divisional applications are not forbidden and are permitted by implication. In such cases, references to the parent application are construed as references to applications earlier in the sequence. Patentability is assessed in sequences as at the date of the original parent application, which is a necessary legal fiction. A divisional application cannot include subject matter added to the original parent application or a divisional application further up the sequence. The subject matter must be disclosed in each preceding application filed and still present, ie not unequivocally and definitively abandoned, in each such preceding application when the divisional application was filed. Content omitted or deleted from the original parent application or a divisional application further up the sequence cannot be introduced or re-introduced to that application or to a divisional application lower down the sequence.

The EPC allows for procedure and special conditions to be set out in the Implementing Regulations, so the EBA cannot include tighter conditions as this would trespass on the sphere reserved for the administrative council.

It was considered unsatisfactory that broad disclosures and unamended descriptions could be pending for up to 20 years. However, if necessary the legislator can deal with abuse and provide a remedy (which was effectively done when restrictions on divisional applications were introduced on 1 April 2010).

ABSTRACT

[4.32] The filing of an abstract was not a requirement under Irish patent legislation prior to the PA 1992. Under r 13 of the Patent Rules 1992, the abstract must commence with the title of the invention and contain a concise summary of the matter contained in the specification. The abstract must indicate the technical field to which the invention pertains and be drafted in such a way as to allow an understanding of the technical problem, the gist of the solution to that problem by means of the invention and the principal use or uses of the invention. Where appropriate, it should contain the chemical formula that, among those contained in the specification, best characterises the invention.[76] Statements on the alleged merits or value of the invention or on its speculative application must not be included.[77] The abstract should preferably contain fewer than 150 words.[78] The purpose of the abstract is that it should constitute an efficient instrument for the purposes of searching in the particular field by making it possible to assess whether there is a need to consult the patent application itself. The abstract is published under s 28 of the PA 1992.[79] Section 22 of the PA 1992 states that the abstract shall only serve for use as technical information.[80] It is not to be used for any other purpose and does not form part of the state of the art against a subsequently filed

---

[76] Patents Rules 1992, r 13(2).

[77] Patents Rules 1992, r 13(2).

[78] Patents Rules 1992, r 13(3).

[79] Patents Rules 1992, r 13(5).

[80] See also EPC, art 85.

co-pending application under s 11(3). It is important not to rely solely on the disclosure in an abstract when amending a specification. The EPO has refused to allow an abstract to be used as a basis for overcoming an objection that an amendment to an application constituted subject matter which extended beyond the content of the application as filed.[81] The Controller has power to reframe the abstract if he or she forms the view that it does not adequately fulfil its purpose. No appeal is available against this decision of the Controller.[82]

FILING DATES AND PRIORITY

[4.33] While s 18 of the PA 1992 lays down the requirements for an application for a patent under that Act, all of those requirements need not be complied with on the initial filing of the application. Section 23[83] of the PA 1992 lays down the minimum requirements to establish a filing date, namely the payment of the official filing fee and documentation containing: (a) an indication that a patent is sought; (b) information identifying the applicant or sufficient information to contact the applicant; and (c) a description of the invention even though it may not comply with the PA 1992 or the Patents Rules 1992. Section 8B of the Patents Rules 1992[84] provides that the filing fee must be paid within one month of the filing date but if this is not done, the Controller shall invite the applicant to pay the filing fee plus an additional fee[85] within one month of the date of the invitation. Like the revised provisions of Rule 40 of the EPC, a filing date can be established without the inclusion of any claims; this is similar to the position under the PA 1964 which did not require the inclusion of claims in a Provisional Patent Application. Under r 95[86] of Patents Rules 1992, it is necessary that documentation in a foreign language be accompanied by a translation, to include a translation of the description as filed.[87]

[4.34] Section 23(6) and (7)[88] of the PA 1992 deals with the question of drawings or parts of the description that are referred to in the application but which have been omitted from the documentation at the date of filing. Rule 18[89] of the Patents Rules 1992 provides for a two-month grace period from official notification and within which to make a request to treat the drawings as having been filed on the date of filing the application. If there is no request, any reference to the drawings or parts of the description is deemed to be deleted.

---

[81] See PA 1992, s 58(c); see *Identification System/Bull* [1989] 6 EPOR 344.
[82] PA 1992, s 96(1).
[83] As amended by the Patents (Amendment) Act 2006.
[84] As inserted by the Patents (Amendment) Rules 2009.
[85] The additional fee as introduced by the Patents (Amendment) Rules 2009 is €62.50.
[86] As amended by the Patents (Amendment) Rules 2009.
[87] Patents Rules 1992, s 10A as inserted by the Patents (Amendment) Rules 2009. See *Rohde and Schwarz's Application* [1980] RPC 155.
[88] As amended by the Patents (Amendment) Act 2006.
[89] As replaced by the Patents (Amendment) Rules 2009.

[4.35] Under r 19[90] of the Patents Rules 1992, the claims and the abstract can be filed within 12 months from the date of filing or, if priority has been claimed, from the date of priority. A divisional application is deemed to have the date of the parent application.[91]

There is also provision for the High Court to determine a question of entitlement to a granted patent. If it is found that a patent was granted to a person not entitled to it and revocation is ordered, then the party who had sought revocation can make a new application and that new application will be given the date of filing of the revoked patent.[92] In such a case and in any divisional application, after expiry of the period of 12 months allowed for in r 19,[93] the requirements must be met at the actual filing date of the new application or divisional application, as the case may be.

[4.36] The Paris Convention for the Protection of Industrial Property,[94] to which most countries adhere, allows for persons who have filed in a Convention country to claim this date when filing a corresponding patent application in further Convention countries. There is a 12-month priority period within which to file such further applications.[95] The effect of claiming priority is best illustrated by an example. If a patent application is filed in the UK on 2 January 2009 and a corresponding application in respect of the same invention is filed in Ireland in December 2009, then, provided the requisite formalities are complied with and priority claimed, the Irish application will be given the priority date of 2 January 2009. The importance and effect of such a provision is that there is a 12-month period from filing within which disclosure can take place without invalidating any subsequent patent, because novelty and inventiveness will be determined with reference to the priority date. If priority is claimed, publication of the invention will take place 18 months after the priority date, thus moving forward the date from which the contents of a patent specification are treated as being available to the public.[96]

[4.37] Section 25[97] of the PA 1992 provides that priority can also be claimed from an application in a Convention country for a utility model, a utility certificate or an inventor's certificate (which are all similar to a short-term patent in various foreign jurisdictions). The applicant claiming priority does not have to be the same applicant as that in the priority country but can be a successor in title.[98] There is also no requirement for a successful outcome to the application from which priority is claimed.[99]

[4.38] The 12-month priority period is prescribed in r 21(1) of Patents Rules 1992 and commences on the date following the date of filing of the previous application whose

---

[90] As replaced by the Patents (Amendment) Rules 2009.
[91] PA 1992, s 24.
[92] PA 1992, s 81.
[93] Patents Rules 1992 as replaced by the Patents (Amendment) Rules 2009.
[94] See paras **[2.02]–[2.24]**.
[95] Article 4C of the Paris Convention.
[96] PA 1992, s 28.
[97] As amended by the Patents (Amendment) Act 2006.
[98] Article 4A(1) of the Paris Convention.
[99] Article 4A(3) of the Paris Convention.

priority is claimed. Outside this period, the right of priority is normally lost. However, under r 21(2), if an applicant can show that, despite all due care, the application could not have been filed within the 12 months, an extended priority period of not later than 14 months from the date of filing the earlier application is prescribed.

It is possible to file and then withdraw, abandon or even have refused an application and then subsequently to re-file it and claim priority from this second application provided that the first application has not been published and that there are no rights outstanding. An applicant must be sure that there has been no public disclosure prior to filing the second application. Otherwise the invention would be considered to be part of the state of the art and not novel.[100]

[4.39] If priority is to be claimed, then an applicant must declare this[101] and Form No 1 relating to a request for the grant of a patent, which is scheduled to the Patents Rules, must indicate the date of the previous filing, the State in or for which it was made and the application number, if available.[102] It is also necessary to file a certified copy of the previous application, ie the priority document. This can be done within 16 months of the priority date with a possible further extension of one month. The certification must be by the authority (usually the national patent office) that received the previous application and includes a certificate stating the date of filing.[103] An English translation of the priority document is required within 16 months of the priority date when the basic application is in a language other than English or Irish.[104]

[4.40] It is also possible to claim priority from an application filed under the EPC even if Ireland has not been designated. In relation to an EPC application designating Ireland, the procedural requirements for claiming priority are deemed to have been complied with, provided the requirements of r 52(1) to (4) of the Patents Rules 1992 and Rule 53(1) and (3)[105] of the EPC have been met. It is possible to claim multiple priorities, even originating from different States. However, the 12-month period cannot be extended by making further applications and claiming priority from those applications. The time limit runs from the earliest date of priority.[106]

[4.41] The right of priority only extends to those elements of a patent application which are included in the application(s) whose priority is claimed.[107] This should be apparent from the claims but priority may still be allowed if the documents as a whole specifically disclose such elements.[108] Under the PA 1964 the same question was answered on the basis of whether the claim was fairly based on the matter disclosed in the specification.[109] The new criteria should probably be considered to be stricter and more

---

[100] PA 1992, s 11 as amended by the Patents (Amendment) Act 2006.
[101] PA 1992, s 26.
[102] Patents Rules 1992, r 22(1) as replaced by the Patents (Amendment) Rules 2009.
[103] Patents Rules 1992, r 22(5) as replaced by the Patents (Amendment) Rules 2009.
[104] Patents Rules 1992, r 22(7) as replaced by the Patents (Amendment) Rules 2009.
[105] Patents Rules 1992, r 22(10) as replaced by the Patents (Amendment) Rules 2009.
[106] PA 1992, s 26(2).
[107] PA 1992, s 26(3).
[108] PA 1992, s 26(4).
[109] PA 1964, s 10.

likely to equate to the test applied by the EPO under art 123(2) of the EPC dealing with amendment of a European patent application, which states that an amendment cannot contain subject matter which extends beyond the content of the application as filed. The test which is stated in EPO guidelines[110] is that:

> the subject-matter of the claim must be directly and unambiguously derivable from the disclosure of the invention in the priority document, also taking into account any features implicit to a person skilled in the art in what is expressly mentioned in the document.

[4.42] In *Stauffer Chemical Company's Application,*[111] Buckley LJ, in considering the matter under the 'fairly based' criteria of earlier legislation, observed that if a new feature was a development along the same line of thought which constitutes or underlies the invention described in the earlier document, then priority might be claimed. However if the additional feature involved a new inventive step or brought something new into the combination which represented a departure from the idea of the invention described in the earlier document, it could not form the basis of a priority claim.

PUBLICATION OF THE PATENT APPLICATION

[4.43] When an Irish patent application is filed at the Irish Patents Office, brief particulars are published in the fortnightly Patents Office Journal. The particulars are provided for in the Patents Rules 1992, r 65 and are as follows:

(a) the name of the applicant;

(b) the title of the invention;

(c) the date of filing;

(d) the date and country of any priority claimed;

(e) the number of the application given by the Irish Patents Office and the use of the letter 'S' to indicate if the application is in respect of a short-term patent.

The first four numerals indicate the year of filing. If an application is for a divisional application, the date of filing and any priority date of the parent application will also be indicated. This is the only information publicly available until publication of the application, which is as soon as practicable after the expiry of 18 months from the date of filing, or, if priority is claimed, from the date of priority. An applicant can, however, request earlier publication.[112]

[4.44] The information to be made publicly available is unclear in that r 23 of the Patents Rules 1992 simply states that it should include the description, claims, drawings (if any) and abstract as filed. If there has been an amendment of the claims prior to termination of the technical preparations for publication, both the original claims and the new or amended claims are published. If available, the statement of inventorship[113] and a copy of any priority document are also published together with all translations. A patent

---

[110] EPO guidelines, C-V, 2.2.

[111] *Stauffer Chemical Company's Application* [1977] RPC 33.

[112] PA 1992, s 28.

[113] Under the PA 1992, s 17(2).

application is not published if, before the termination of the technical preparations for publication, it has been finally refused or withdrawn or has been deemed to have been withdrawn.[114]

[4.45] Under r 23(3) of the Patents Rules 1992, it is for the Controller to determine when the technical preparations for publication of the application are to be treated as having been completed. However, in *Intera Corpn's Application*,[115] the Court of Appeal ordered an application not to be published and pointed out that each case had to be determined objectively on a case by case basis. In *Peabody International's Application*,[116] an application to stop publication was refused, it being held that preparations for publication were completed by the Patent Office on the day when the folio of documents for the application had been made ready for collection by the printer.

[4.46] Applications which are published under s 28 of the PA 1992 are advertised in the Patents Office Journal. The advertisement lists the applications becoming open to public inspection as from the date of issue of the Journal. Code marks showing the primary index under the International Patent Classification are also included for search purposes. The Controller can omit from the published patent application statements or other matter contrary to public order or morality.[117] Also, statements disparaging the products or processes of any particular person other than the applicant, or the merits or validity of applications or patents of any such person can be omitted.[118] Mere comparison with the prior art is not considered to be disparaging *per se*.[119] There is no appeal from the Controller's decision in relation to decisions to omit such statements.[120]

PROCEDURE UP TO GRANT

[4.47] The explanatory memorandum to the Patents Bill 1991 stated that:

> before the Bill was prepared, the procedure for examination and grant of patents under the present law was reviewed as there was concern about the large and growing backlog of applications awaiting examination in the Patents Office. It was clear that by continuing to follow present procedures, there was no prospect of either eliminating the present backlog in the foreseeable future or avoiding future backlogs. Accordingly, the present Bill now contains new provisions regarding examination which will both be adequate and speed up examination considerably.

In 1991, there were delays in the order of six years in the examination of applications. The new procedures under the PA 1992 were not dramatically different from those under

---

[114] PA 1992, s 28(2).
[115] *Intera Corpn's Application* [1986] RPC 459.
[116] *Peabody International's Application* [1986] RPC 521.
[117] PA 1992, s 28(5)(a).
[118] PA 1992, s 28(5)(b).
[119] PA 1992, s 28(5).
[120] PA 1992, s 96 as amended by the Patents (Amendment) Act 2006.

the PA 1964 but they streamlined the procedure to grant. However, the reduction in the backlog is more likely to be attributable to a substantial reduction in the number of nationally filed Irish patent applications following ratification of the EPC.

[4.48] The procedures leave open to an applicant a number of options. Under s 29 of the PA 1992 an applicant can prosecute the application by means of a search report requested from the Irish Patents Office on payment of the appropriate search fee. The request for such a search report and the fee must be submitted within 21 months from filing or, if claimed, the priority date. In the case of a divisional application filed on or after the 21 months from the filing date of the parent case, the request must be submitted on the actual filing date of the divisional application.[121] The search is not in fact carried out by the Irish Patents Office but with the approval of the Minister by the UK Patent Office.

[4.49] A patent application must include one or more claims and it is on the basis of such claim(s) that the search is undertaken. If it transpires in the course of the search that an application claims more than one invention, the search is conducted only in relation to the first invention specified in the claims. If the applicant wishes a search to be carried out in respect of any additional invention, then a request and further fee must be submitted within one month of the date of issue by the Controller to the applicant of the search report relating to the first invention.[122]

[4.50] The search report is sent to the applicant who has a two-month period from issuance to advise the Controller if the application is to be withdrawn.[123] The consequence of non-withdrawal is that the report is published. If the application is maintained (in the light of the search reports), the applicant has four months within which to submit amendments to the application or to advise the Controller that no amendment is considered necessary. If this is not done, the Controller may refuse the application.[124]

[4.51] An alternative to requesting a search report lies in s 30 of the PA 1992 and, if applicable, an applicant can avail of the option of submitting to the Controller a statement that an application for the same invention has been made in the UK, Germany, the EPO or under the PCT. This statement must be made within 21 months of the date of filing or priority date, if claimed. In addition to the statement, there must subsequently be filed evidence in the form of the search results issued on the relevant patent application or the grant of a patent from it. The form of evidence and the time limits for filing such, under r 27 of the Patents Rules 1992, are set out in Table 1.

---

[121] Patents Rules 1992, r 24(1).

[122] PA 1992, s 29(2); Patents Rules 1992, r 24(3).

[123] Patents Rules 1992, r 24(4).

[124] PA 1992, s 29(4).

Source	Form	Time Limit
(1) EPC	Copy of the published European patent application and related search report or a copy of the published specification of the granted European patent	Within two months of the publication of the search report or of the specification
(2) PCT	Copy of the published international application and related search report	Within two months of the publication of the search report
(3) UK Patent Office	Copy of the published application and related search report or a copy of the published specification of the granted patent	Within two months of the publication of the application or of receipt by the applicant of the search report (whichever is the later), or within two months of the publication of the specification
(4) German Patent Office (*Deutsches Patentamt*)	Copy of the published application and related search report or a copy of the published specification of the granted patent (*Patentschrift*)	Within two months of the publication of the search report or of the specification
(5) Countries where searches are carried out by the EPO	Copy of the published application and related search report of the EPO	Within two months of the publication of the search report

Table 1: Form of evidence and time limits for filing such under the Patents Rules 1992, r 27

The fifth source of evidence (EPO search countries) is provided for in r 27(1)(e) of the Patents Rules 1992, but there is an inconsistency because r 26,[125] which lists the prescribed sources, does not include this. This omission is likely to be regarded as an error and the inconsistency resolved in favour of an applicant relying on such a source. Belgium is an example of a country whose national patents office has its searches carried out under the auspices of the EPO. An extension of the time limit for filing the evidence under r 27 may be allowed by the Controller if a request for an extension is made and the official fee is paid within the extended period specified in the request.

[4.52] Section 30(2) of the PA 1992 also states that, if requested, an applicant must furnish details of foreign applications for the same invention. The time limit for furnishing such information is six months from the request and what is required is a list of all such applications and a copy of the report showing the result of any search made in relation to such applications.[126] The Controller can also specifically request a statement

---

[125] As replaced by the Patents (Amendment) Act 2006.
[126] Patents Rules 1992, r 25.

as to whether such applications are still pending, have been accepted, are withdrawn or deemed to have been withdrawn, or have been refused. It should be noted that the request for such information does not appear to be limited to instances where an applicant is relying on a foreign specification or search report under s 30(1).

[4.53] When the evidence under s 30(1) has been filed, there is a two-month time limit within which to notify the Controller of any withdrawal. Failure to withdraw means that the evidence will be published.[127] If there has been no withdrawal and the applicant is relying on the results of a search of a corresponding foreign application (s 30(1)(a) of PA 1992) then the Controller issues a notification that the applicant has an opportunity to amend the application in the light of that evidence. The applicant has four months from notification to submit either amendments or a statement that no amendment is considered necessary, failing which the application may be refused.[128] Similarly, if the evidence is based on the grant of a corresponding foreign patent (s 30(1)(b) of PA 1992) there is a four-month period from notification within which to submit amendments to the specification so that the subject matter claimed therein does not extend beyond that of the evidence.[129] Again, an applicant must make the required amendment or advise the Controller that the amendment is not considered necessary.

[4.54] Any amendment under ss 29(4) or 30(4) and (5) of the PA 1992 or statement that no amendment is considered necessary must be submitted by a patent agent.[130] There is no provision for this to be done by an applicant. The extremely limited examination that will be carried out by the Irish Patents Office is set out in s 31(1), which also contains the proviso that the Controller will not raise an objection because of non-compliance with s 9(1)[131] (unpatentability), s 11[132] (lack of novelty), s 13 (lacking inventive step), s 14 (no industrial application), s 19 (no clear and complete disclosure) or s 20 (unclear or lack of concise claims). The onus to ensure compliance with these substantive issues is with the applicant; failure to comply could lead to successful grounds for revocation under s 58.[133]

[4.55] It should be noted, however, that claims which do not define the matter in a clear and concise form and which are not supported by the description[134] are not included in the grounds for revocation, and therefore it may be extremely difficult for a third party to establish the scope of protection. There is provision for including in the Patents Rules 1992 examination of these substantive matters and objections for non-compliance[135] but this is only likely to arise if the current procedure leads to an abuse of the patent system.

---

127 PA 1992, s 30(3); Patents Rules 1992, r 28(1).
128 PA 1992, s 30(4); Patents Rules 1992, r 28(2).
129 PA 1992, s 30(5); Patents Rules 1992, r 28(2).
130 PA 1992, s 30(6).
131 PA 1992, as amended by the Patents (Amendment) Act 2006.
132 PA 1992, as amended by the Patents (Amendment) Act 2006.
133 PA 1992, as amended by the Patents (Amendment) Act 2006
134 PA 1992, s 20.
135 PA 1992, s 31(2).

[4.56] If, following the limited examination, the Controller requests compliance with requirements, then a time limit for dealing with the official action is indicated in the communication from the Controller. Failure to comply may lead to refusal of the application.[136] There is also a provision in s 31(5) of the PA 1992 that prohibits double patenting. In cases where there are two or more applications for the same invention with the same filing or priority date by the same applicant or his successor in title, the Controller may refuse to grant a patent in respect of more than one of the applications. This may arise, for example, in the case of a nationally filed application before the Irish Patents Office and a second EPO application designating Ireland. The words 'may refuse' suggest that the Controller has a discretion. However, in *IBM (Barclay & Bigar's) Application*,[137] the UK Patents Office held that the second application must be refused.

[4.57] If all formalities have been satisfied, the Controller will request payment of a grant fee. The fee must be paid within four months of the request with a possible three-month extension.[138] Failure to pay the fee means that the application is deemed to be withdrawn.[139] Once the grant fee and appropriate renewals have been paid, then a certificate of grant of a patent issues as per Form No. 3 annexed to the Rules. A notice of grant is published in the Patents Office Journal and the Controller also publishes a specification of the patent containing the description, claims and drawings (if any) and such matters that appear to the Controller at his or her discretion to be useful or important.[140] This, for example, could include information concerning foreign patent applications, which the Controller may have sought under s 30(2) of the PA 1992.

[4.58] In addition to amending an application under ss 29 or 30 of the PA 1992 following a search report or the grant of a corresponding foreign patent, an applicant is allowed to amend of its own volition.[141] Under s 32(3) the Controller may refuse to accept such amendment if it is considered that it should properly have been made under ss 29 or 30 and, presumably, within the time limits prescribed under these sections. The Patent Rules 1992 also impose restrictions on amendments made of an applicant's own volition and such amendments of the description, claims or drawings can only be made in accordance with the Rules.[142] If made prior to the time limits imposed under ss 29 and 30, then amendment of the description, claims and drawings can only take place once.[143] After making amendments under ss 29 and 30 or if there has been no such amendment and the time limit has expired, then amendment of the description, claims or drawings at an applicant's own volition can only be made with the consent of the Controller following

---

[136] PA 1992, s 31(1).
[137] *IBM (Barclay & Bigar's) Application* [1983] RPC 283.
[138] Patents Rules 1992, r 29.
[139] PA 1992, s 31(3); Patents Rules 1992, r 29.
[140] PA 1992, s 34.
[141] PA 1992, s 32(1).
[142] Patents Rules 1992, r 31(5).
[143] Patents Rules 1992, r 31(1).

the filing of an application for leave to amend,[144] which must give the reasons for desiring amendment.

[4.59] Any amendment of a patent application is invalid to the extent that it extends the subject matter disclosed in the application as filed.[145] This is a ground for revocation under s 58(c) of the PA 1992. The EPO guidelines[146] state that:

> an amendment should be regarded as introducing subject matter which extends beyond the content of the application as filed, and therefore is unallowable, if the overall change in the content of the application (whether by way of addition, alteration or exclusion) results in the skilled person being presented with information which is not directly and unambiguously derivable from that previously presented by the application, even when account is taken of matter which is implicit to a person skilled in the art.

In *Van Der Lely's Application*,[147] a divisional application was refused because the disclosure extended beyond that of the parent application. Falconer J accepted the Comptroller's view that the fundamental principle in determining additional subject matter is to decide whether one document presents the informed reader with information relevant to the invention which the other document does not. In *Ward's Application*,[148] it was held that matter must not be disclosed which extends, in the sense of enlarging upon, the original disclosure, ie which increases the specificity or particularisation of that disclosure. It would appear that unless an amended claim is supported by the unamended specification, the disclosure must have been extended.[149] Ambiguities are usually construed against an applicant. If a specification states, expressly or by implication, that a particular feature is essential, the applicant will normally be held to that.[150] In *Southco Inc v Dzus Fastener Europe Ltd*,[151] the Court of Appeal held that even though the main claim of the granted patent was worded differently from the application, it was allowable because it did not add fresh subject matter to the application even though there was a possible broadening of the claim.

[4.60] An application can be withdrawn at any time before grant. This must be a clear and unqualified statement of withdrawal if publication is to be avoided, and it is advisable to request official confirmation that the withdrawal is effective and to give sufficient time to ensure that preparations for publication have not been completed.[152] Once publication takes place, the contents of the application become part of the state of the art when considering novelty. Priority rights can still be claimed from an application

---

[144] Patents Rules 1992, r 31(2).

[145] PA 1992, s 32(2).

[146] EPO guidelines, C-VI, 5.3.1; EPC, art 123(2).

[147] *Van Der Lely's Application* [1987] RPC 61.

[148] *Ward's Application* [1986] RPC 50.

[149] *Raychem Ltd's Application* [1986] RPC 547.

[150] *Harding's Patent* [1988] RPC 515.

[151] *Southco Inc v Dzus Fastener Europe Ltd* [1992] RPC 299. See also *AC Edwards v Acme Signs & Displays Ltd* [1992] RPC 131.

[152] *Intera's Application* [1986] RPC 459.

which has been withdrawn or refused[153] but no other rights remain.[154] Under s 34(3) of the PA 1992, a lapsed patent application can be restored on the same grounds as those for restoring a patent under s 37.[155]

APPEAL

[4.61] The three-month deadline for appealing the Controller's decision to the High Court is calculated from the date when he makes his written statement of grounds available, rather than from the date of the decision, as previously was the case.[156] An appeal is a full rehearing on the merits.[157] There is also a further appeal to the Supreme Court on a point of law.[158]

SHORT-TERM PATENTS

[4.62] A short-term patent is a totally new concept under Irish law and it did not exist under the PA 1964 or the Industrial and Commercial Property (Protection) Act 1927. An explanation as to why such was introduced was given on the explanatory memorandum to the Patents Bill 1991 as follows:

> The provisions here are completely new to Irish law and were devised in the interests of the small inventor who may find that a full term patent is unnecessary for his particular invention. Experience has shown that small innovators and individual inventors find the task of obtaining a full patent costly and time consuming and, therefore, a disincentive to protecting inventions. Short-term patents will be capable of being obtained without undue official obstacles and lower official fees will apply. The period of protection will be 10 years which will particularly suit less technologically complex inventions which by their nature, will not have very long life cycles but which nevertheless have an important place in the whole process of industrial innovation and in encouraging the start-up of new projects.

[4.63] The concept of a system for securing a short-term patent (also known as a petty patent) to ensure that short-term monopoly protection can be obtained easily and inexpensively for small articles or simple inventions is not new and, for example, such exists under Australian law but with a different structure. Germany and some other countries have protection for what is termed a 'utility model', which again provides for a shorter term of protection in return for a simplified and speedier registration.[159]

---

[153] PA 1992, s 33(2)(b).
[154] PA 1992, s 33(2)(c).
[155] As amended by the Patents (Amendment) Act 2006.
[156] PA 1992, s 96 as amended by the Patents (Amendment) Act 2006.
[157] RSC, Ord 94, r 48.
[158] PA 1992, s 96(7).
[159] For a comparative European study, see the report produced for the European Commission in 2009: Van Eecke, Kelly, Bolger and Truyens, 'Monitoring and Analysis of Technology Transfer and Intellectual Property Regimes and their Use', available online at www.eutechnologytransfer.eu.

[4.64] Probably the best way of looking at the provisions governing a short-term patent is to look at how they differ from that of a regular or long term patent. Firstly, as the name suggests, it has a shorter duration, namely 10 years[160] as opposed to the usual 20-year term. Secondly, the criteria governing patentability are that the invention must be new, susceptible of industrial application and not clearly lacking an inventive step. In the Patents Bill 1991, as initiated, what was proposed was a short-term patent for an invention which did not involve an inventive step. This would have meant that valid patents could have existed for inventions which were clearly obvious. The proposal was not adopted. What exists in s 63(4) of the PA 1992 is simply a less onerous requirement for patentability, namely that the invention is not clearly obvious. There is, of course, a very fine line to be drawn between what is and what is not obvious, being a question of degree in each case. Many inventions seem in retrospect to be very simple but since the courts have long recognised that simplicity should not be confused with obviousness, it may well be that the difference will not in fact prove significant. However, in relation to a short-term patent, it is probably true to say there is no longer a requirement that in order to maintain a patent there must be a substantial exercise of the inventive power or inventive faculty.[161]

[4.65] Importantly, a short-term patent requires disclosure of the best method of performing the invention known to the applicant.[162] This differs considerably from the provisions relating to sufficiency of disclosure for a normal patent, which is that the invention as disclosed must be sufficiently clear and complete for it to be carried out by a person skilled in the art.[163] The words 'best method of performing' in fact appear in the revocation grounds under the PA 1964[164] and guidance as to interpretation can be obtained from this source. It is essentially a question of the good faith of the applicant. As stated by Pollock CB in *Tetley v Easton:*[165]

> A man has no right to patent a principle and then give to the public the humblest instrument that can be made from his principle and to reserve to himself all the better part of it.

[4.66] However, this is not restricted to cases of dishonest conduct in withholding information from the public. It covers any case in which the applicant has not disclosed the best method known to him of performing the invention, whatever the reason for the omission.[166] In the case of a body corporate, the relevant knowledge is that of the person who gave instruction for the application, and controlled it on the company's behalf, properly instructed so as to be in possession of the relevant information. The question of the date on which the determination of 'best method' is to be decided has not been dealt with by the Irish courts. In the UK there have been contrasting decisions. In *American*

---

160 PA 1992, s 63(1).
161 *Williams v NYE* (1890) 7 RPC 62.
162 PA 1992, s 63(7)(b)(i).
163 PA 1992, s 19(1).
164 PA 1964, s 34(1)(h).
165 *Tetley v Easton* (1833) 2 E & B 956.
166 *Du Pont De Nemours v Enka BV* [1988] FSR 69.

Cyanamid Co v Ethicon Ltd[167] it was held that there was no obligation on an applicant to incorporate in the complete specification improvements made after the filing of the priority application. In *Monsanto Co v Maxwell Hart (London) Ltd,*[168] the relevant date of knowledge of the best method was held to be the period shortly before the filing of the complete specification, ie usually some time after the filing date. In *American Cyanamid Co v Berk Pharmaceuticals Ltd,*[169] the patent was revoked because the specification was held not to describe the best method of performing the invention known to the patentee. Certain strains of micro-organisms were known by the patentee to produce higher yields and were not disclosed.

[4.67] A short-term patent may include a maximum of five claims.[170] The claims must be clear and supported by the description. Although s 20 of the PA 1992 dealing with claims pertaining to a full term patent also states that a claim should be 'concise', the absence of such a requirement for a short-term patent is unlikely to be of any consequence. There is, however, a requirement for an application for a short-term patent to be accompanied by any drawing referred to in the description.[171] It is not possible to hold both an ordinary patent and a short-term patent for the same invention.[172]

[4.68] A short-term patent is not examined against the existing state of the art and there is no requirement to submit any evidence of patentability by way of grant of an equivalent patent in other jurisdictions or search results in other jurisdictions.[173] In effect, this means that a short-term patent can be obtained in respect of an invention which is not novel or which is totally lacking in any inventive step. The *quid pro quo* of securing a short-term patent is that in order to enforce such against third parties by way of an action for infringement, it is at that stage necessary to carry out a prior art search.[174] This search is by way of a request accompanied by a fee to the Controller who in fact commissions the UK Patent Office to carry out the search as to the state of the art and prepare a report as to the results. The resulting search report is sent both to the proprietor of the short-term patent and the alleged infringer[175] and is also published.[176] Instead of requesting a search report, it is possible to submit the results of a search carried out in the UK or Germany or by the EPO or the World Intellectual Property Organisation (WIPO) in respect of the same invention.[177] A copy of a corresponding European, UK or German patent can also be used instead of a search report. Again, this evidence is published and a copy must be sent by the proprietor to the alleged

---

[167] *American Cyanamid Co v Ethicon Ltd* [1979] RPC 215.
[168] *Monsanto Co v Maxwell Hart (London) Ltd* [1981] RPC 201.
[169] *American Cyanamid Co v Berk Pharmaceuticals Ltd* [1976] RPC 231.
[170] PA 1992, s 63(7)(b)(ii).
[171] PA 1992, s 63(7)(b)(iii).
[172] PA 1992, s 64.
[173] PA 1992, s 65.
[174] PA 1992, s 66.
[175] PA 1992, s 66(1)(b).
[176] PA 1992, s 66(2).
[177] PA 1992, s 66(3).

infringer.[178] Essentially, these requirements are imposed so that alleged infringers will be able to consider the actual validity of the patent and counterclaim for revocation if appropriate. Because of the ease with which a short-term patent is granted as opposed to the rigours of securing a normal patent, it is entirely justified that the proprietor of a short-term patent be obliged to furnish the results of a state of the art search in respect of the invention before infringement proceedings can be instituted.

[4.69] It is also possible for a search to be requested by a person other than the proprietor of a short-term patent.[179] Such a person must show to the satisfaction of the Controller the following:

(a) there are grounds to suspect that the invention is not new or is clearly lacking an inventive step; and

(b) because of the person's legitimate business interests, it would, in all the circumstances, be reasonable that a search report be prepared.[180]

Aside from the usual High Court option, infringement proceedings on foot of a short-term patent can be brought before the Circuit Court irrespective of the amount of a claim.[181]

[4.70] The grounds for revocation of a short-term patent are the same as those for a normal patent but include an additional ground that the claims of the specification of the patent are not supported by the description.[182] Section 20 of the PA 1992 also imposes this requirement, but an objection under that provision can only be raised pre-grant and thus the onus lies with the Patents Office. In *Glatt's Application,*[183] a divisional application was rejected on the grounds that the claims were not supported by the description, the principle being that third parties should not have to face monopolies which were neither clearly sought nor founded by the inventor at the date of filing, but which were conceived later and claimed *post hoc*.[184] In *Protoned BV's Application,*[185] the claim referred to two types of spring, one of which was stated to be a 'mechanical compression spring'. The applicant sought to delete the word 'compression'. The deletion was not allowed because it had the effect of adding a whole range of springs not described in the body of the specification.

---

178 PA 1992, s 66(3).

179 PA 1992, s 66(6).

180 Patents Rules 1992, r 45(2).

181 PA 1992, s 66(4).

182 PA 1992, s 67.

183 *Glatt's Application* [1983] RPC 122.

184 Ie based on the fallacy that succession in terms of time implies a causal relationship.

185 *Protoned BV's Application* [1983] FSR 110.

Chapter 5

Patents Act 1992 – Maintenance and Dealings in Patents

RENEWAL FEES

[5.01] Under the Patents Act 1964 (PA 1964), there were no renewal fees payable during the pendency of an application. The Patents Rules 1965 provided for annual renewal fees at the expiration of the fourth year from the date of the patent.[1] Certainly, during the latter years of the PA 1964, it was rare that a patent would be granted within this period and the Rules allowed for payment of outstanding accumulated annuities at any time before the expiration of three months from the date of sealing the patent. The Patents Act 1992 (PA 1992) follows the European Patent Convention (EPC) model and for patent applications filed from 1 August 1992, annual renewal fees are payable on pending applications.

[5.02] Rules 33 and 34[2] of the Patents Rules 1992 prescribe that renewal fees are payable in respect of the third and each subsequent year calculated from the date of filing of the patent application. A renewal fee is payable on or before the last day of the month in which such year commences. Thus, for example, if a patent application was filed on 5 August 2003, the renewal fee for the third year would be payable on or before 31 August 2005 and annually thereafter.

[5.03] When a divisional application is filed after the expiry of the second year from the date of the parent application, accumulated renewal fees are paid at the time of filing the divisional application.

Renewal fees cannot be validly paid more than four months before the date on which they fall due.[3] When paid, the Controller issues a renewal certificate. The prescribed period for payment of a renewal fee can be extended, subject to a maximum extension of six months, provided the necessary extension fees are paid.[4] This extension is a requirement under art 5*bis* of the Paris International Convention for the Protection of Industrial Property. A court may refuse to award damages or make any order for infringement during any extended period and before the renewal fee is paid.[5]

---

[1] Patents Rules 1965 (SI 268/1965), r 61.
[2] Patents Rules 1992 (SI 179/1992).
[3] Patents Rules 1992, rr 33(2) and 34(3).
[4] PA 1992, ss 35(2) and 36(3).
[5] PA 1992, s 49(2).

[5.04] In the case of a European patent application designating Ireland, renewal fees from the third year are paid to the European Patent Office (EPO) under art 86(1) of the EPC. The renewal fees are only paid directly to the Irish Patents Office in respect of years that follow that in which the mention of the grant of the patent is published in the European Patent Bulletin. Where a renewal fee is due within two months of such publication, it may be paid within those two months.[6]

Where the period for paying a renewal fee has expired, r 34(5) of the Patents Rules 1992 imposes an obligation on the Controller to send a reminder to the proprietor or, if a representative has been appointed, to the address for service not later than six weeks after the last day for payment. The reminder must also advise of the consequence of non-payment, ie the lapsing of the patent.

DURATION OF A PATENT

[5.05] Under the PA 1964, an Irish patent remained in force for 16 years from the date of filing of the complete specification, provided renewal fees were paid. Section 27 of the PA 1964 allowed a patentee to petition either the High Court or the Controller for an extension of the term of a patent. If it appeared to the court or the Controller that the patentee had been inadequately remunerated by the patent, the term could be extended for a further term not exceeding five years, or, in exceptional cases, 10 years. In making a decision, regard was to be had to the nature and merits of the invention in relation to the public, to the profits made by the patentee as such, and to all the circumstances of the case. In *JR Geigy AG's Patent*,[7] the Irish High Court followed the principles in *Fleming's Patent*[8] and asked itself the following questions:

(a)   is the invention one of more than ordinary utility?

(b)   has the patentee been adequately remunerated?

(c)   is the absence of remuneration due to no fault of the patentee?

There were a number of petitions presented: mostly these were to the High Court. In almost all cases, the extensions sought were in relation to pharmaceutical or veterinary patents where there were delays in the introduction of the product onto the market because of delays in obtaining regulatory approval. While these cases are now of academic interest only, because the PA 1992 does not allow for an extended term, one must have regard to the transitional provisions of the PA 1992 and to the European Communities (Supplementary Protection Certificate) Regulations 2008.[9]

[5.06] Under s 36(1) of the PA 1992, a patent shall, subject to payment of renewal fees 'continue in force until the end of the period of 20 years beginning with the date of filing of the patent application'. This 20-year period is in keeping with that which exists in

---

6   Patents Rules 1992, r 34(2).

7   *JR Geigy AG's Patent* [1982] FSR 278.

8   *Fleming's Patent* (1918) 35 RPC 55.

9   SI 307/2008, which repealed the European Communities (Supplementary Protection Certificate) Regulations 1993 (SI 125/1993).

most countries and under the EPC. Article 33 of the Agreement on Trade-Related Aspects of Intellectual Property Rights (TRIPS) imposes a minimum duration of 20 years. The transitional provisions[10] effectively extended the term of a patent from 16 to 20 years for all patents granted under the PA 1964 and in force on 1 August 1992, subject to the payment of annual renewal fees for the additional term. If a patent had already been extended following a petition under the PA 1964, a patentee could not avail of the additional term under the PA 1992. After 1 August 1992, no petitions for an extension could be presented under the PA 1964. In cases where a patent expired prior to 1 August 1992 and a petition for extension under the PA 1964 had been presented prior to 1 August 1992, a patentee could elect to withdraw the petition and be granted four additional years as of right. However, this applied only in cases of an unopposed petition. If the petition was opposed, then the extension would be decided on its merits in accordance with s 27 of the PA 1964.

Supplementary Protection Certificate

[5.07] On 18 June 1992, Council Regulation 1768/92/EEC was adopted, the purpose of which was to provide for the creation of a Supplementary Protection Certificate (SPC) for medicinal products for human or animal use.[11] Regulations were later adopted to provide specific cover for plant protection products[12] and medicinal products for paediatric use.[13] These Regulations are implemented by the European Communities (Supplementary Protection Certificate) Regulations 2008[14] and are deemed to have come into operation on 25 July 2008.

[5.08] The problem for patentees with patents for medicinal products is stated in the preamble to Regulation 1768/92/EEC, namely:

> the period that elapses between the filing of an application for a patent for a new medicinal product and authorisation to place the medicinal product on the market makes the period of effective protection under the Patent insufficient to cover the investment put into the research.

The purpose of Regulation 1768/92/EEC is to compensate patentees for the period during which they could not exploit the invention, due to the need to obtain regulatory approval. This compensation takes the form of the grant of an SPC, which extends the patent term in respect of the product that is the subject of the SPC.

---

[10] PA 1992, Sch 1, para 2.

[11] Council Regulation 1768/92/EEC ([1990] OJ L182/1) of 18 June 1992.

[12] Regulation 1610/96/EC ([1996] OJ L198/30) of the European Parliament and of the Council of 23 July 1996 concerning the creation of a supplementary protection certificate for plant protection products.

[13] Regulation 1901/2006/EC ([2006] OJ L378/1) of the European Parliament and of the Council of 12 December 2006 on medicinal products for paediatric use.

[14] SI 307/2008 which repealed the European Communities (Supplementary Protection Certificate) Regulations 1993.

[5.09] Under Regulation 1768/92/EEC, an SPC can only be granted for a medicinal product for human or animal use. The term 'medicinal product' is defined in the Regulation as meaning:

> any substance or combination of substances presented for treating or preventing disease in human beings or animals and any substance or combination of substances which may be administered to human beings or animals with a view to making a medical diagnosis or to restoring, correcting or modifying physiological functions in humans or in animals.

A product can be an active ingredient or combination of active ingredients of a medicinal product and includes the product covered by the marketing authorisation and any use of the product as a medicinal product that was authorised before the expiry of the SPC, provided that these are covered by the basic patent.

[5.10] An SPC must be filed within six months of the date of the marketing authorisation in the relevant State or within six months of the date of grant of the patent, whichever is the later.

[5.11] An SPC takes effect when the patent expires and has a term equal to the period which elapsed between the date on which the application for the patent was lodged and the date of the first authorisation to place the product on the market in the EU, reduced by five years.[15] The maximum duration of an SPC is five years.[16] The maximum duration of a patent which has an SPC is 25 years.[17] It is necessary to pay annual renewal fees in Ireland during the term of the SPC. The date of the first marketing authorisation in the EU determines the SPC term in all Member States.

[5.12] The subject matter of SPC protection is identified in art 4 of Regulation 1768/92/EEC and extends only to the product covered by the authorisation to place the corresponding medicinal product on the market and for any use of the product as a medicinal product that has been authorised before the expiry of the SPC.

[5.13] An SPC is granted to the holder of the basic patent or his successor in title but there is no requirement that this entity must also be the holder of the marketing authorisation. For example, a licensee may be responsible for marketing and the securing of regulatory approval.

[5.14] A request for grant of an SPC on foot of an Irish patent is made before the Irish Patents Office in accordance with a form annexed to the statutory instrument.[18] The request must include a copy of the authorisation to place the product on the Irish market and in which the product is identified, containing in particular, the number and date of the authorisation and a summary of the product's characteristics. If this is not the first authorisation in the European Union, details of the country which granted the first authorisation, the authorisation

---

[15] Regulation 1768/92/EEC, art 13.
[16] 5.5 years in the case of medicinal product for paediatric use.
[17] 25.5 years in the case of medicinal product for paediatric use.
[18] SI 307/2008, Sch 1.

number, the authorisation date, the identity of the product thus authorised and the legal provision under which such authorisation took place must be indicated in the request.

[5.15] Obviously, third parties need to have knowledge of what is effectively an extension of the term of a patent. It is specifically provided that the Patents Office Journal will publish details of an application for an SPC and any grant, refusal or lapse or subsequent invalidity thereof. In addition, the Register must include the fact that a request for an SPC has been filed, any grant and its duration, rejection, withdrawal and invalidity. In relation to renewal fees, the Register should indicate payment or lapsing through non-payment and any restoration or invalidity. If market authorisation is withdrawn, an SPC shall lapse under art 14(d) of Regulation 1768/92/EEC but only for so long as the period of withdrawal. Any termination of the lapse is also published.

[5.16] An application for a declaration of invalidity of an SPC can be made to the Controller or the court.[19] A decision can be appealed in the same way as any other decision on a national Irish patent.[20] The grounds of invalidity are stated in art 15, namely:

(a)   the grant was contrary to the conditions for obtaining an SPC under art 3;

(b)   the basic patent has lapsed before its lawful term expires; and

(c)   the basic patent is revoked or limited to the extent that the product for which the SPC was granted would no longer be protected by the claims of the basic patent or, after the basic patent has expired, grounds for revocation exist which would have justified such revocation or limitation.

Under art 63 of the EPC, the term of a patent is fixed at 20 years from the date of filing of the application, the only exception being a possible extension to take into account a state of war or similar emergency conditions. A conference of the contracting states on the revision of art 63 was held in Munich on 16–17 December 1991, following which the EPC was revised to also allow for patent term extension. The revised art 63 permits contracting states to extend European patents in cases of national emergency or to compensate for marketing delays due to an administrative authorisation procedure required by law before a product can be marketed. This could, for example, include agricultural chemicals or aircraft and is not limited to Regulation 1768/92/EEC.

[5.17] On 23 July 1996, the Council of Ministers adopted Regulation 1610/96/EC concerning the creation of an SPC for plant protection products, eg herbicides, fungicides and insecticides. This Regulation was published on 8 August 1996 and consequently entered into force on 8 February 1997. The duration of the plant protection SPC is equal to the period which elapsed between the filing date of the basic patent and the date of the first authorisation to place the product on the market in the EU, reduced by five years. The maximum period allowable is five years from the end of the lawful term of the basic patent. Procedures under the Regulation are specifically stated to be

---

[19]   SI 307/2008, r 10.

[20]   Regulation 1768/92/EEC, art 17.

equally valid *mutatis mutandis* with the equivalent provisions in the medicinal products SPC Regulation 1768/92/EEC. Article 4 of the Regulation states:

> Within the limits of the protection conferred by the basic patent, the protection conferred by a certificate shall extend only to the product covered by the authorisations to place the corresponding plant protection product on the market and for any use of the product as a plant protection product that has been authorised before the expiry of the certificate.

RESTORATION OF A PATENT

[5.18] Section 29 of the PA 1964 provided that where a patent had lapsed by failure to pay a renewal fee, application could be made by the patentee, within three years of the date on which the patent ceased to have effect, for the restoration of the patent. If the Controller was satisfied that the failure to pay the renewal fee was unintentional and that no undue delay had occurred in the making or prosecution of the application for restoration, then an order for restoration was granted. Section 37 of the PA 1992 also allows for restoration of a lapsed patent and a patent application[21] but the time limit for such an application for restoration is two years from the date on which the patent lapsed.

[5.19] The application can be made by the person who was the proprietor of the patent or their personal representative. Where the patent is held by two or more persons jointly, the application may, with the leave of the Controller, be made by one of the joint owners without joining the others.[22] It was held in *Dynamics Research and Manufacturing Inc's Patent*[23] that the mere application for payment of a renewal fee cannot be regarded as an application for restoration. Rule 35 of the Patents Rules 1992 prescribes the information to be included in an application for restoration and the circumstances that led to the failure to pay the renewal fee must be identified. From the evidence, the Controller must satisfy himself that the failure to pay the renewal fee was *prima facie* unintentional, that reasonable care had been taken to ensure payment within the prescribed period and that there had been no undue delay in the making of the application for restoration. One of the most common reasons for failure to pay a renewal fee is lack of funds, but this is viewed as an intentional decision. Reasonable care means more than a normal system used to pay accounts, and a person:[24]

> must be prepared to set up a system containing safeguards more sufficient than those used to ensure that, for example, cheques to meet everyday accounts are sent when they should be.

Proper supervision is required and in *Tekdata Ltd's Application*,[25] the failure of a managing director to check that an accounts team was properly carrying out his

---

21 PA 1992, s 35(3).
22 PA 1992, s 37(2).
23 *Dynamics Research and Manufacturing Inc's Patent* [1980] RPC 179.
24 *Convex Ltd's Patent* [1980] RPC 423 at 432.
25 *Tekdata Ltd's Application* [1985] RPC 201.

instructions was held to be a lack of reasonable care. It is now common for patentees to rely on the services of specialist renewal agencies, and entrusting the payment of renewal fees to such an agency or to patent attorneys is the norm. However, such agencies and patent attorneys, unless they receive standing instructions to renew or unless instructed to the contrary, must look for renewal instructions on an annual basis. Patentees are obliged to have in place a system for dealing with requests and reminders for such instructions. A patentee can, however, rely on the services of a professional such as a patent attorney, solicitor[26] or a recognised renewal agency appropriately selected, qualified and experienced to carry out clear and unambiguous instructions.[27] In *Ling's Patent,*[28] it was held to be sufficient for a patentee to rely on the reminder from the Irish Patents Office provided there was no failure to take adequate care to notify the Irish Patents Office of a change of address.

[5.20] If upon assessing the evidence the Controller is not satisfied that a *prima facie* case has been made, he must inform the applicant, who has a one-month time period within which to request a hearing.[29] If the Controller finds that there is a *prima facie* case, the application is advertised in the Official Journal and there is a two-month period from advertisement within which opposition can be lodged.[30] The opposition procedure is set out in r 36 of the Patents Rules 1992. A formal notice of opposition is filed that must state the ground(s) of opposition to restoration and must be lodged in duplicate with the Controller, a copy of which is sent to the applicant for restoration. From receipt, the applicant must, within three months, file a counter-statement stating the grounds upon which the opposition is resisted. Again, this is filed in duplicate with the Controller who sends a copy to the opponent. Rule 36(6) goes on to state that the Controller may give such directions as he or she may think fit with regard to the subsequent procedure but this must include the right of a party to apply for and attend a hearing before the Controller.[31]

[5.21] If restoration is allowed, the unpaid renewal fees must be paid together with an additional penalty. However, more importantly, conditions are imposed which are designed to protect a third party who in good faith acted in the belief that a patent or patent application had lapsed and irrespective of whether or not that third party had opposed the application for restoration.[32]

[5.22] If these conditions are not complied with by the patentee, the Controller can revoke the order for restoration.[33] The imposition of these conditions arises in

---

[26] *Frazer's Patent* [1981] RPC 53.

[27] *Textron Inc's Patent* [1989] RPC 441.

[28] *Ling's Patent* [1981] RPC 85.

[29] Patents Rules 1992, r 35(2).

[30] PA 1992, s 37(4); Patents Rules 1992, r 36.

[31] Patents Rules 1992, Rule 67(1).

[32] PA 1992, s 37(8), as amended by the Patents (Amendment) Act 2006. Similar conditions were set out in the Patents Rules 1992, r 38 but these were repealed by the Patents (Amendment) Rules 2009.

[33] PA 1992, s 37(7) as amended by the Patents (Amendment) Act 2006.

circumstances where a person between the date of lapsing and the application for restoration 'began in good faith to do an act which would constitute an infringement' or 'made in good faith effective and serious preparations to do such an act'. The conditions are that such a person has a right to continue the act and therefore has a defence to an infringement action. The rights are personal and cannot be licensed.[34] If the act was done, or the preparations made, in the course of a business, such a person may authorise other partners in the business to continue, assign that right or transmit it on death (or, in the case of a body corporate, on dissolution) provided that this is done as part of the acquisition of that part of the business in the course of which the necessary act or the preparations therefor were done. These rights extend to any subsequent third party dealing with a product to which these rights apply.

[5.23] It might be thought that these safeguards were sufficient and that, consequently, the Controller should, when in doubt, decide in favour of an applicant for restoration. However, in the UK case of *Dynamics Research and Manufacturing Inc's Patent*,[35] the Assistant Comptroller had cause to consider similar sections of the UK Patents Act 1977 and observed that although they gave some protection, he was:

> not satisfied that they give full protection against a third party who has acted in some way or another in the thought that a patent is dead and gone forever without hope of resurrection. He might be wishing to expand into further developments of the invention, he might have arranged mergers, and so on, on the assumption that he would be able to work the patent and made all sorts of commercial arrangements. I am not a businessman, I cannot envisage the ramifications of them, but the possibilities are there.

[5.24] The worries expressed by the Assistant Comptroller were unlikely to be justified because of the words 'good faith' appearing in the s 37(8) of the PA 1992[36] since it is hard to envisage a set of circumstances in which a third party would be acting in bad faith as, presumably, it would be relying on the position as stated in the Register before acting, ie the lapsing of the patent. The problems are in the words 'continue' and 'began'. The word 'continue', if given a literal interpretation, could mean that the nature and extent of the act could not be varied. If a person has, for example, commissioned detailed, lengthy and expensive financial and marketing projections and reports, the position of such a person is uncertain. He has begun effective and serious preparations but what acts is he allowed to continue? Whitford J considered that the Assistant Comptroller was overly worried about the inadequacy of safeguards for third parties as applicants for restoration have a heavy onus to discharge.

---

[34] PA 1992, s 37(9) as amended by the Patents (Amendment) Act 2006.

[35] *Dynamics Research and Manufacturing Inc's Patent* [1980] RPC 179.

[36] Formerly included in the Patents Rules 1992, r 38, which was repealed by the Patents (Amendment) Rules 2009.

AMENDMENT OF PATENT SPECIFICATION AFTER GRANT

[5.25] Under s 38[37] of the PA 1992, the Controller possesses a discretionary power to allow the proprietor of a patent to amend the specification of a patent. This might be necessary to distinguish the claims of the patent from prior art which has come to light or in the event of a revocation action or threat of same. The amendment can include a change in the category of the invention (eg from a compound to the use of the compound in a composition for a particular purpose) to which the same criteria apply as any other amendment.[38]

A patent for a physical entity includes whatever its context, ie all uses known or unknown. A claim to a use is a claim to the physical entity only when being used in the course of a particular physical activity; it affords less protection than a claim to physical entity *per se*. Therefore, an amendment from a claim to physical entity to a physical activity involving use of that physical entity does not extend the protection sought and is admissible.[39] There are also special provisions which deal with the correction of an error in a patent specification.[40]

[5.26] Rule 39 of the Patents Rules 1992, which governs the procedure for requesting an amendment after grant, does not require an explanation of the reasons for seeking amendment. However, because the Controller's power is discretionary, it would appear that the Controller could call for such an explanation so as to determine whether or not to exercise his discretion in favour of an applicant. In the UK Patent Office decision in *Waddington Ltd's Application*,[41] an explanation was given that amendment was required because of prior art which had only recently come to the attention of the applicant. However, the applicant refused to disclose the prior art. It was held that it was necessary for the Controller to have particulars of that prior art so that he could take it into account in the exercise of his discretion.

If there are proceedings before the court or the Controller in which the validity of the patent has been or may be put at issue, amendment is not possible.[42] However, in such proceedings, the proprietor may, at the discretion of the court or Controller, be allowed to amend the patent specification with the added proviso of possible conditions being imposed. These include, but are not limited to, advertisement of the amendment[43] and payment of costs and expenses to the party challenging the validity.[44] In *Chevron's Patent*,[45] it was stated by Graham J that:

---

[37] As amended by the Patents (Amendment) Act 2006.
[38] G2/88 *Friction Reducing Additive/MOBIL OIL III* [1990] OJ EPO 93, [1990] EPOR 73.
[39] G2/88 *Friction Reducing Additive/MOBIL OIL III, ibid.*
[40] PA 1992, s 110 as amended by the Patents (Amendment) Act 2006.
[41] *Waddington Ltd's Application* [1986] RPC 158.
[42] PA 1992, s 38(1).
[43] Patents Rules 1992, r 39(1).
[44] PA 1992, s 38(2).
[45] *Chevron's Patent* [1970] RPC 580.

it is essential that those seeking amendment should realise that they have a heavy onus to discharge and can only expect to do so if they have full evidence to prove their case and put the whole story before the Court.

[5.27] It is dangerous for a patentee knowingly and deliberately to obtain claims of unjustified width because such could be viewed as 'covetous' claiming and could result in the refusal of an application for amendment.[46] Likewise, if a patentee's attention is drawn to the fact that a claim is unjustifiably wide and it does not take proper steps by amendment to remedy the position within a reasonable period of time, then an application for amendment may be refused. In *Autoliv Development Ab's Patent*,[47] there was a delay of four years before seeking amendment and after learning of the anticipating art. This was held to be a culpable delay and was such as to cause the discretion to be exercised against the applicant for amendment. In patent litigation, the court must examine the circumstances in detail before allowing amendment. If the evidence establishes that the patentee was aware of deficiencies in the specification but did not take any action to remedy such, it is improper for amendment to be allowed.[48] In *Bristol Myers Co v Manon Frères*,[49] amendment was allowed despite a long delay, as it was held that the lapse of time between the knowledge of a potentially damaging citation and the application to amend is only fatal if the patentee must always have known that his claim could not have been supported against the earlier citation.

It is possible that a patentee may be reluctant to proceed with an application for amendment because of the disclosure of privileged documents being used, for example, in other jurisdictions. Consequently, in *Bonzel v Intervention Ltd*,[50] the court allowed the hearing of certain evidence *in camera* and imposed an injunction against the use of certain documents other than in the amendment proceedings at issue.

[5.28] A summary of the tests applied are conveniently stated in *Smith, Kline & French Laboratories Ltd v Evans Medical Ltd*[51] *per* Aldous J:

> The discretion as to whether or not to allow amendment is a wide one and the cases illustrate some principles which are applicable to the present case. First, the onus to establish that amendment should be allowed is upon the patentee and full disclosure must be made of all relevant matters. If there is a failure to disclose all the relevant matters, amendment will be refused. Secondly, amendment will be allowed provided the amendments are permitted under the Act and no circumstances arise which would lead the Court to refuse the amendment. Thirdly, it is in the public interest that amendment is sought promptly. Thus, in cases where a patentee delays for an unreasonable period before seeking amendment, it will not be allowed unless the patentee shows reasonable grounds for his delay. Such includes cases where a patentee believed that amendment was not necessary and had reasonable grounds for that belief. Fourthly, a

---

[46] *Imperial Chemical Industries Ltd (Whyte's) Patent* [1978] RPC 11.

[47] *Autoliv Development Ab's Patent* [1988] RPC 425.

[48] *Chrome-Alloying Co Ltd v Metal Diffusions Ltd* [1962] RPC 33; *Western Electric v Racal-Milgo* [1981] RPC 253.

[49] *Bristol Myers Co v Manon Frères* [1973] RPC 836.

[50] *Bonzel v Intervention Ltd* [1991] RPC 553.

[51] *Smith, Kline & French Laboratories Ltd v Evans Medical Ltd* [1989] FSR 561 at 569.

patentee who seeks to obtain an unfair advantage from a patent, which he knows or should have known should be amended, will not be allowed to amend. Such a case is where a patentee threatens an infringer with his unamended patent after he knows or should have known of the need to amend. Fifthly, the Court is concerned with the conduct of the patentee and not with the merit of the invention.

This was approved in *Hsiung's Patent*[52] which also held that where the question of discretion has already been litigated and decided against a patentee seeking an amendment of his patent, that ground would apply to all future applications to permit amendments. A patentee should not be allowed an opportunity to formulate a different amendment.

[5.29] If an application for amendment is deemed acceptable, the court or the Controller requires advertisement of the proposed amendment[53] in the Patents Office Journal.[54] There is a three-month opposition period after advertisement.[55] If an application for amendment is made to the court, the applicant must notify the Controller who is entitled to appear and be heard.[56] The effective date of an amendment is the date of the grant of the patent[57] and the amendment is invalid to the extent that it extends the subject matter disclosed in the application as filed or the protection conferred by the patent.[58]

POST-GRANT AMENDMENTS TO EUROPEAN PATENTS

[5.30] One of the most important practical aspects of the EPC 2000 is that post-grant amendments (called 'limitations') are permitted centrally for the first time.[59] It is no longer necessary to apply separately to each patents office or court. The procedure is *ex parte* but third parties can file observations.[60] Limitation of the claims and amendments of the description and drawings are permitted. Limitations of claims can also be made during an opposition. If a limitation is still pending when an opposition is filed, the limitation procedure will be terminated and the limitation fee refunded.[61] If a limitation is accepted, new claims translations will be needed and further printing fees will be incurred. It may also be necessary to file amended translations with the national patents offices, according to the same procedures as apply to translation of the original documents.

The request for limitation is only examined for formalities to check whether what is requested is actually a limitation of the patent, whether the claims are still clear and

---

52 *Hsiung's Patent* [1992] RPC 497.
53 PA 1992, s 38(1), (2) and (5).
54 Patents Rules 1992, r 39(1).
55 Patents Rules 1992, r 39(2).
56 PA 1992, s 38(6).
57 PA 1992, s 38(4).
58 See PA 1992, s 38(3).
59 EPC, art 105a and Rule 90.
60 EPC, art 115.
61 Rule 93(2), EPC.

concise, and to ensure that there is no addition of subject matter or extension of protection.[62] The patentability of the amended claims is not considered. There is no limit to the number of times limitation may be requested.

SURRENDER OF A PATENT

[5.31] Section 39 of the PA 1992 includes a provision for the voluntary surrender of a patent by way of written notice to the Controller. The application is described as an 'offer' to surrender and the proprietor must declare the reasons for making such an offer.[63] In addition, the proprietor must furnish a declaration that no action for infringement or for the revocation of the patent is pending in any court.[64] The offer is advertised in the Patents Office Journal and within three months from advertisement; the surrender may be opposed 'by any person'. It appears that no *locus standi* is required, unlike the situation under s 36 of the PA 1964, which limited opposition to 'any person interested'. Rule 40(3)(c) of the Patents Rules 1992 requires the opponent to give reasons for opposing surrender but this could, for example, be the public interest. A bar to opposition would exist if the action was frivolous, vexatious or blackmailing.[65] The most likely opponent would be a licensee or a holder of a security interest.

[5.32] If the Controller is satisfied that a patent may be properly surrendered, he may accept the offer. Under s 39(5) of the PA 1992, the patent ceases to have effect from the date on which the notice of acceptance is published in the Patents Office Journal. However, no infringement action or compensation for State use arises for acts done earlier. The effect, however, is to make the surrender *ex tunc* (from then on) which means that a licensee cannot claim the return of royalties paid earlier.

Section 60(2) of the PA 1992 requires the Controller to revoke a patent in circumstances where there exists for the same invention a nationally filed Irish patent and a European patent designating Ireland. Because surrender does not amount to revocation, a surrender would technically not be sufficient to overcome an objection under s 60(2).[66]

PATENTS AS A PROPERTY RIGHT

[5.33] Other forms of intellectual property are specified in the relevant legislation as being personal property.[67] Although the PA 1992 does not specifically confirm that patents are personal property, it is implied in s 79 which states that the rules of law for ownership and devolution of personal property apply in relation to patents and patent

---

[62] Rule 95(2), EPC.
[63] Patents Rules 1992, r 40(1).
[64] Patents Rules 1992, r 40(1).
[65] *Braun's Application* [1981] RPC 355.
[66] *IBM (Barclay & Biger) Application* [1983] RPC 283.
[67] For example, registered designs under the Industrial Designs Act 2001, ss 22(1), 42(1) and 76(1); copyright under the Copyright and Related Rights Act 2000, ss 17(1) and 120(1) and trade marks under the Trade Marks Act 1996, s 26.

applications in the same way as choses in action (which are a particular type of personal property). This wording was first used in the former Irish PA 1964, which in turn mirrored a provision in the UK Patents Act 1949, s 54.[68] The nature of a patent as a personal property right, and more specifically one which is treated as a chose in action, was discussed by the House of Lords in *Allen & Hanburys Ltd v Generics (UK) Ltd and others:*[69]

> The legal nature of the right of property that vested in the grantee of a patent … [as] that of a chose in action was recognised, though inferentially only, in section 54(5) of the Act of 1949.

This decision also held that a patent licence is a contractual right, which is a defence to infringement, rather than a proprietary right (a right *in rem* which is exercisable against the world at large):

> A licence passes no proprietary interest in anything, it only makes an action lawful that would otherwise have been unlawful. In the context of the royal grant of patents for inventions it was a consent given by the proprietor of the patent to another person, the licensee, to do something that the patent entitled the proprietor of it to prevent anyone from doing except with his consent.

Whether a right is a proprietary right or merely a contractual right can affect the range of remedies which can be used against that right.[70] The nature of the right can also affect a lender's approach to taking a security interest over the right.[71]

[5.34] An exclusive licence is still a contractual right but the PA 1992 confers some rights on exclusive licensees which are similar to those which apply to proprietary rights.[72] For example, exclusive licensees are entitled to take an infringement action in their own name under s 51.

[5.35] The PA 1992 does not state that a licence is binding on the successor in title to the patent (other than in limited circumstances where a court orders the transfer of the patent)[73] so this is a particularly important point to cover in licence agreements when acting on behalf of the licensee. There is no requirement under the PA 1992 that a patent licence or assignment must be in writing to be binding but there would be significant difficulties in providing proof of the existence or terms of an oral agreement.[74]

[5.36] Section 85(1) of the PA 1992, by the use of the word 'shall', imposes a statutory obligation to record changes in ownership or an interest in a patent or a patent

---

68 Which has been replaced by clearer provisions in the Patents Act 1977, s 30.
69 *Allen & Hanburys Ltd v Generics (UK) Ltd and Gist-Brocades NV; Brocades (Great Britain) Ltd; Beecham Group Plc; The Comptroller General of Patents* [1986] RPC 203.
70 *Northern & Shell Plc v Condé Nast & National Magazine Distributors Ltd* [1995] RPC 117.
71 Henry, 'Mortgages of intellectual property in the United Kingdom' (1992) EIPR 14(5), 158–166.
72 In the English context, see *Terrell on the Law of Patents* (16th edn, 2006, Sweet & Maxwell) at 10–14.
73 PA 1992, s 82.
74 *Morton-Norwich Products Inc v Intercen* [1981] FSR 337; see also PA 1992, s 85(3).

application once published. The penalty for non-recordal is that a document in respect of which there has been no recordal will only be admitted in any court as evidence of title if the court so directs.[75] In the PA 1964, there were increased official fees for late recordal but this is no longer the position under the PA 1992. The statutory obligation appears to have little teeth and, for example, a patentee could simply record the change in ownership if and when the need arises. There are, however, delays in recordal before the Irish Patents Office and if an interlocutory or even interim injunction is necessary, and the court refuses to admit a document of title, the delays may prejudice the patentee. Similarly, the holder of an exclusive licence may also be delayed in instituting an infringement action under s 51 of the PA 1992. A licensee has an added incentive for recordal in order to be put on notice such as, for example, in a situation where the patentee makes application for an entry in respect of licences of right.[76] Recordal no longer requires the furnishing of the original assignment document, and a certified copy will suffice.[77] When recordal takes place, the Register identifies particulars of the instruments in respect of which recordal has been made.[78]

[5.37] Section 99 of the Companies Act 1963 as amended by s 122 of the Companies (Amendment) Act 1990, requires that a company must register with the Registrar of Companies certain specified charges within 21 days of their creation. Failure to comply means that the charge will be void as against the liquidator and any creditor of the company. The provision applies to a charge on a patent or a licence under a patent.

Co-ownership[79]

[5.38] Unless specifically agreed to the contrary, two or more persons who hold a patent application or to whom a patent has been granted, hold it as tenants in common in equal shares.[80] This means that there is no joint tenancy so no right of survivorship applies. Thus, the ownership of a deceased patentee's share in a patent devolves on his or her personal representative. If the existence of an agreement is not established, the patentees are entitled to equal shares in the patent no matter what their individual efforts amounted to in relation to the whole.[81] Every registered co-owner is entitled by himself or his agents to work the patented invention for his own benefit without accounting to the others unless there is an agreement to the contrary.[82] An agent does not include an independent contractor or the partner of a co-owner.[83] One co-

---

[75] PA 1992, s 85(7).

[76] PA 1992, s 68(1).

[77] Patents Rules 1992, r 58(1); PA 1992, s 85(6).

[78] PA 1992, s 85(3).

[79] For a comparative European study, see the report produced for the European Commission in 2009: Van Eecke, Kelly, Bolger and Truyens, 'Monitoring and Analysis of Technology Transfer and Intellectual Property Regimes and their Use' available online at www.eutechnologytransfer.eu.

[80] PA 1992, s 80(1).

[81] *Florey's Patent* [1962] RPC 186.

[82] PA 1992, s 80(2).

[83] *Howard and Bullough v Tweedales and Smalley* (1895) 12 RPC 519.

owner cannot licence the patent or assign any share in the patent without the consent of all other co-owners[84] unless there is an agreement to the contrary. The supplier to a co-owner who might otherwise be considered an indirect infringer under s 41(1) of the PA 1992 is deemed not to be an infringer.[85] Also exempt from infringement are persons acquiring a patented product from one co-owner only.[86] Such a person may deal with the product as if purchased from a sole patentee. One co-owner can sue for infringement joining the other co-owner(s) as party to the proceedings.[87] However, the joined co-owners are not liable for any costs or expenses unless they enter an appearance and take part in the proceedings.

Courts' authority to determine ownership

[5.39] Under s 16(1) of the PA 1992, the right to a patent belongs to the inventors, their successors in title or in certain cases, to their employer. An application to revoke a patent can be made on the grounds that there was a lack of entitlement of a claimant to be an owner of the patent.[88] If such an action is taken, it must be by a person who has referred the matter to the High Court and where entitlement in their favour has been determined.[89] The application to the High Court is made under s 81(1) of the PA 1992. There is a time limit of two years from grant unless it can be shown that the patentee knew at the date of grant that it was not entitled to be granted the patent.[90] A court will have to determine whether the test as to knowledge is subjective or objective. It is probably not sufficient that the referring party has previously simply alleged proprietorship to the patentee. No order can be made which affects the mutual rights and obligations of trustees or of personal representatives.[91]

[5.40] If a court finds that a patent was granted to a person not entitled in whole or in part, then the entitled party can make application[92] to revoke the patent or part of the patent. In such a case, the court may permit the person or persons making the revocation application to make a new application for a patent which will be treated as having been made on the same date as the original patent application.[93] A replacement application cannot proceed if it contains any additional matter over that contained in the original patent application.[94] An example where the referrer failed to establish entitlement in substitution of the original application is *Norris's Patent*.[95] However,

---

[84] PA 1992, s 80(3).
[85] PA 1992, s 80(4).
[86] PA 1992, s 80(5).
[87] PA 1992, s 48.
[88] PA 1992, s 58(e).
[89] PA 1992, s 57(2).
[90] PA 1992, s 81(2).
[91] PA 1992, s 81(3).
[92] PA 1992, s 57.
[93] PA 1992, s 81(4).
[94] PA 1992, s 81(5); *X Ltd's Application* [1982] FSR 143.
[95] *Norris's Patent* [1988] RPC 159.

it was held that there had been a contribution to a significant aspect of the invention and therefore an entitlement to become a joint proprietor of the granted patent.

[5.41] If a court order directs a change in ownership, then the position vis-à-vis a licensee or any other third-party rights is determined by whether or not there has been a complete change in ownership or if the new proprietors include some or all of the old proprietors.[96] In the latter instance, any existing licences or other rights appear to continue in force unless contractually otherwise provided. If there has been a complete change in ownership, then any licence or other rights in force prior to the transfer, lapse, as and from the date of registration of the new proprietors. In this event, previous proprietors or licensees who had acted in good faith and before the proceedings had used or made serious preparations to use the patent in Ireland, may continue to use as a non-exclusive licensee. A request for grant of this licence must be made by the previous proprietor within two months, and if by a licensee, within four months, of being notified by the Controller of the court order which transferred the patent.[97] Failing agreement between the parties, the terms of the licence can be settled by the Controller with the criterion that both the period and terms must be reasonable, presumably to both parties.[98]

THE REGISTER

[5.42] No details are entered on the Register until the patent application is published, which happens 18 months after the filing date or the earliest priority date, if earlier.[99] The Register details to be made publicly available are:[100]

(a) particulars of the applicants, their address for service and the inventors;

(b) the number and date of application;

(c) the details of the priority claims;

(d) the date of publication;

(e) the date on which an application is refused, withdrawn or has lapsed, if applicable;

(f) the date on which notice of the grant of the patent is published, if applicable;

(g) particulars of patentees and address for service, if different from applicants; and

(h) particulars of any interest or title in a patent, if applicable.

There is a prohibition in s 84(5) of the PA 1992 on entry in the Register of a notice of any trust whether express, implied or constructive, and the Controller is not affected by any such notice. However, there is a similar provision in the UK[101] but it was held in

---

[96] PA 1992, s 82(1).

[97] Patents Rules 1992, r 54.

[98] PA 1992, s 82(3).

[99] PA 1992, s 28.

[100] Patents Rules 1992, r 55.

[101] Patents Act 1977, s 32(3) as amended.

the UK case *Kakkar v Szelke*[102] that a document which affected the proprietorship of a patent, whether by creating trusts or otherwise, is not excluded from entry in the Register.

[5.43] Until a patent application is published, documents or information can only be secured with the consent of the applicant[103] unless it is to advise of withdrawal, bibliographic information or information required to be furnished to the EPO. Shortly after a patent application is filed, the following information is published in the Patents Office Journal namely:

   (a)   the name of the applicant;

   (b)   the title of the invention;

   (c)   the date of application;

   (d)   details of priority claimed, if any;

   (e)   whether or not the application is for a short-term patent; this is identified by the letter 'S';

   (f)   the number given to the application.

[5.44] Rule 64 of the Patents Rules 1992 prescribes information which the Controller is also obliged to furnish upon request. This includes whether or not a search report has been published, the form of evidence of novelty submitted and whether there has been an application for restoration.

[5.45] An aggrieved party may, at their option, apply either to the court or the Controller to amend the Register.[104] The cause of complaint by an applicant may be the non-insertion in or omission from the Register of any entry or any entry made in the Register without sufficient cause or wrongly remaining in the Register or an error or defect in the Register. The Controller may apply to the court of his or her own motion in the case of fraud in the registration or transmission of a patent application or a patent.[105] In *Beecham Group Ltd v Bristol Myers Co,*[106] the patentee failed to rectify the Register to delete a priority date claimed for the patent. It was held that the proprietor himself was not an aggrieved person. However, an aggrieved person may have some proprietary interest in the patent.[107]

[5.46] It is possible to apply to the Controller for a search[108] to be carried out as to novelty only or novelty and inventive step. A request for a search must be accompanied by a sufficiently full and detailed description (including drawings where appropriate) of the product, process or apparatus to be searched.[109] If possible, the sub-class or group units of the International Patent Classification should be identified.

---

[102] *Kakkar v Szelke* [1989] FSR 225.

[103] PA 1992, s 88(2).

[104] PA 1992, s 86(1) and (7).

[105] PA 1992, s 86(5).

[106] *Beecham Group Ltd v Bristol Myers Co* [1979] EPC 330.

[107] *Manning's Patent* (1902) 20 RPC 74.

[108] PA 1992, s 89.

[109] Patents Rules 1992, r 66.

Chapter 6

Patents Act 1992 – Infringements and Remedies

RIGHTS CONFERRED

[6.01] Under the Patents Act 1964 (PA 1964) it was an infringement of a patent for any person, without the licence of the patentee, to make, use, exercise or vend the invention in Ireland. Section 40 of the Patents Act 1992 (PA 1992) deals with the question of substantive or direct infringement, while s 41 introduces a new concept of contributory or indirect infringement.

[6.02] Under the transitional provisions,[1] a patent granted under the PA 1964 has the same effect as a patent granted under the PA 1992. Thus, any claim for infringement after 1 August 1992 is dealt with under the PA 1992 irrespective of the date of the patent. This is an important factor given that the PA 1992 displaces many of the concepts under the PA 1964 and, in particular, the large volume of UK cases which interpreted the corresponding provisions in the UK.[2] Claims for acts of infringement occurring prior to 1 August 1992 are now statute-barred.[3]

[6.03] The territorial scope is limited to infringement taking place in Ireland.[4] In the UK case of *Kalman v PCL Packaging,*[5] the Patents Court held that both an offer and the subsequent disposal needed to take place in the UK before infringement occurred. This, however, results from the wording 'offer to dispose' which is different from that in s 40. It appears from s 40 that a simple offer in Ireland can amount to an infringement and there is no reason why magazines which are printed abroad but which circulate in Ireland could not include advertisements which would amount to infringement in Ireland. If the advertisement specifically stated that the offer was not open to residents of Ireland, then a claim to infringement might be avoided. It is also quite permissible to serve proceedings outside Ireland against a party who is infringing in Ireland.[6] Council Regulation 1383/2003/EC enables the customs authorities to seize patent infringing goods at the point of entry.[7] In *Morton-Norwich Products Inc v*

---

1   PA 1992, Sch 1, para 1.
2   See *Genentech Inc's Patent* [1989] RPC 147.
3   Statute of Limitations 1957, s 11(2), setting a six year period to bring proceedings, except in cases of fraudulent concealment; see *Morton-Norwich Products Inc v Intercen* [1978] RPC 501.
4   PA 1992, s 40.
5   *Kalman v PCL Packaging* [1982] FSR 406.
6   *Electric Furnace Co v Selas Corpn of America* [1987] RPC 23.
7   Council Regulation 1383/2003/EC ([2003] OJ L196 7) of 2 August 2003.

Intercen[8] Graham J dealt with the question of joint tortfeasors and stated that it was clear that two persons who agree on common action, in the course of, and to the furtherance of which, one of them commits a tort in this country are joint tortfeasors.[9] The effect of this was that provided a tort was committed in the jurisdiction and it was proved that the defendants had a common design to commit it, then it does not matter that a person sued has not himself committed within the jurisdiction any act which, taken by itself, could be said to amount to an infringement.[10] In *Unilever plc v Gillette (UK) Ltd*,[11] a defendant's foreign parent company was joined as a co-defendant since the patentee was able to show a good arguable case that the two companies had acted in concert pursuant to a common design resulting in infringement. The mere fact of a parent and subsidiary relationship does not show a common design. It is the extent of the control actually exercised or the involvement that are the determining factors.[12] A plaintiff who has been injured by a number of joint tortfeasors (known as concurrent wrongdoers in Ireland) can choose whom to sue, including a defendant outside of the jurisdiction.[13]

[6.04] A third party does not infringe where it has consent from the proprietor. There is nothing to say that such consent needs to be in writing and thus it may be an implied consent. In *Betts v Willmott*,[14] it was established that an implied licence to use or re-sell a patented product arises in the case of an ordinary sale of the product. There is also an implied right to repair a patented product provided that such repairs do not amount to the manufacture of a new product[15]. In *Solar Thompson Engineering Co Ltd v Barton*,[16] it was made clear that the implied licence extends to a right to have the repairs carried out by a third party, such as a contractor, who can also use drawings even though protected under copyright. The repair must be a genuine one and not a replacement of the product disguised as a repair.[17] Also, the ambit of an implied licence for modifying a patented product is no wider than that for repairing it.[18] An implied licence can also arise by virtue of the failure of a proprietor to take earlier action against an infringement.[19] Conversely, a sufficiently prominent notice limiting permission to use the patented

---

[8] *Morton-Norwich Products Inc v Intercen* [1978] RPC 501.

[9] The concept of joint tortfeasors under Irish law has been replaced by the concept of concurrent wrongdoers under the Civil Liability Act 1961.

[10] See also *Puschner v Tom Palmer (Scotland) Ltd* [1989] RPC 430.

[11] *Unilever plc v Gillette (UK) Ltd* [1989] RPC 583.

[12] *Intel Corpn v General Instrument Corpn* [1991] RPC 235.

[13] *Molnlycke v Procter & Gamble* [1992] RPC 21; *Lubrizol Corpn v Esso Petroleum Co Ltd* [1992] RPC 467.

[14] *Betts v Willmott* (1871) 6 Ch App 239.

[15] See, for example, the UK House of Lords decision in *United Wire Ltd v Screen Repair (Scotland) Ltd* [2001] RPC 24.

[16] *Solar Thompson Engineering Co Ltd v Barton* [1977] RPC 537.

[17] *Sirdar Rubber v Wallington Weston* (1907) 24 RPC 539.

[18] *Delareed Ltd v Delkim Developments* [1988] FSR 329.

[19] *Habib Bank Ltd Zurich v Habib Bank AG* [1982] RPC 1.

invention in certain specified ways will be effective,[20] allowing the patentee to sue for infringement if the conditions of sale are breached.

Direct infringement

[6.05] Under s 40(a) of the PA 1992, direct infringement of a patent relating to a product can arise in a number of ways, namely, making, offering, putting on the market or using a product which is the subject matter of the patent, or importing or stocking the product for those purposes.

[6.06] In *Hoffmann-La Roche v Harris Pharmaceutical Ltd*,[21] Whitford J held that possession with the intention of using the products for trade purposes and for the securing of a profit amounts to an infringement, whether the dealing proposed is a dealing with a customer in the country or with an export customer. This was a decision on wording equivalent to that in the PA 1964, ie making, using, exercising or vending the invention, but would still appear to extend the scope of protection beyond that identified in the legislative provisions, and even Whitford J identified the need to protect the rights of a mere carrier against too broad an interpretation of his decision. In *Smith Kline Corpn v DDSA Pharmaceuticals Ltd*,[22] the defendant had imported a pharmaceutical product into the UK in bulk for tableting. It was intended to export it in its entirety to Nigeria. It was held that importing even with a view to subsequent export was an infringement and it was not incumbent on a plaintiff to show that it has suffered commercial loss.

[6.07] In *Upjohn Co v T Kerfoot & Co Ltd*,[23] the defendant had applied to the UK authorities (DHSS) for a product licence in respect of a pharmaceutical product. It was alleged that this included data obtained by tests on the product that may have been carried out abroad. It was held that while an application for a product licence and the submission of test data amounted to a step towards commercial use, it did not amount to an infringement.

[6.08] The New Zealand Court of Appeal distinguished the *Upjohn* case,[24] stating that while it supported the contention that the submission of data obtained from tests is not an infringement, it does not warrant a conclusion that the supply of a sample is not an infringement.[25] In reviewing the earlier decided cases, it was considered that they set the permissible use at the submission of an application and accompanying data to a regulatory authority. However, the sending of an embodiment of an invention to a government authority for approval was a use of the invention since by doing so the defendant acted for the commercial advantage or as a springboard, in order to be prepared to launch into the market when the patent expired.

---

[20] *National Phonograph v Menck* (1911) 28 RPC 229.
[21] *Hoffmann-La Roche v Harris Pharmaceutical Ltd* [1977] FSR 200.
[22] *Smith Kline Corpn v DDSA Pharmaceuticals Ltd* [1978] FSR 109.
[23] *Upjohn Co v T Kerfoot & Co Ltd* [1988] FSR 1.
[24] *Upjohn Co v T Kerfoot & Co Ltd* [1988] FSR 1.
[25] *Smith Kline & French Laboratories Ltd v Douglas Pharmaceuticals Ltd* [1991] FSR 522.

[6.09] It is, of course, sometimes difficult for a plaintiff to secure information on the identity of an infringer. In *Norwich Pharmacal v Customs and Excise Comrs*,[26] it was held that an action for discovery lies even against a non-infringer in order to identify infringers. Such an order would be made if the defendant was so mixed up in the transaction which *prima facie* constituted an infringement of the patent that he was under a duty to aid the patentee to prevent further loss to his intellectual property by disclosing the name of the supplier.[27] Information disclosure orders can also be sought under the European Communities (Enforcement of Intellectual Property Rights) Regulations 2006[28] against various people involved in the infringement or identified by such people as being involved.

[6.10] The Irish courts had occasion to consider discovery in a patent infringement action in *Ranbaxy Laboratories Ltd v Warner Lambert Company*.[29] The plaintiff argued that three letters from their patent agent to the EPO and one to the Danish Patents Office were not discoverable. It was held by McCracken J that these letters were not admissible as an aid for construction. The court approved the *obiter* comments on the status of correspondence with patent offices in *Rohm & Haas v Collag*[30] to the effect that a letter to the EPO does not have the same status as prior art but can contain objective information about and commentary on experiments conducted in response to official observations and therefore could be of assistance to resolve an issue of construction. These letters were not written from the point of view of an independent expert but written as part of submissions made on behalf of the patentee or inventor in relation to the invention itself. They did not deal with experiments, were not made in the course of the Irish patent application and took place after the priority date. Therefore the *Rohm & Hass* decision was not of assistance. The authors were not persons to whom the specification was addressed. In reality the letters were expressions of the opinion of the patentee as to the construction and were clearly inadmissible.

[6.11] Under s 40(b) of the PA 1992, the use of a process claimed in a patent is an infringement, as is offering the process for use in Ireland (the latter being only an infringement in circumstances where it as known or it should have been obvious to a reasonable person that such would infringe). It is only in the case of an act consisting of offering the process for use that knowledge or imputed knowledge is a requirement for a direct infringement. In *Kalman v PCL Packaging (UK) Ltd*,[31] it was held that an offer to sell equipment abroad for working a patented process in the UK was not in itself offering the process for use in the UK.

---

[26] *Norwich Pharmacal v Customs and Excise Comrs* [1974] RPC 101.

[27] See also *Smith Kline & French Laboratories Ltd v Global Pharmaceuticals* [1986] RPC 394 and *Société Romanaise v British Shoe Corpn* [1991] FSR 1.

[28] SI 360/2006.

[29] *Ranbaxy Laboratories Ltd v Warner Lambert Company* [2005] IESC 81, [2006] 1 ILRM 377.

[30] *Rohm & Haas v Collag* [2001] FSR 426.

[31] *Kalman v PCL Packaging (UK) Ltd* [1982] FSR 406.

[6.12] In *Furr v CD Truline (Building Products) Ltd*,[32] the defendants directed purchasers to use the articles in a way that was not the way stated in the method claim. It was held that the defendants could not be said to have offered a process for use since they clearly did not intend that the articles should be used in the claimed way.

[6.13] Article 64(2) of the European Patent Convention (EPC) states that if the subject matter of the European patent is a process, the protection conferred by the patent shall extend to the products directly obtained by such process. This is reflected in s 40(c) of the PA 1992, which classifies an infringing act to include offering, putting on the market, using or importing, or stocking for those purposes a product obtained by a patented process.

[6.14] Under s 46(1) in relation to a patent in respect of a process for obtaining a new product, if the same product is produced by an unauthorised party, it is deemed to have been obtained by the same process and is thus an infringement. The onus falls on a defendant to rebut this presumption. The effect of this provision is that if, for example, a product is treated by using a patented process, it would be extremely difficult for a third party to make the resultant new product without infringement occurring.

Indirect infringement

[6.15] The PA 1964 did not contain any specific provision concerning indirect or sometimes called contributory infringement, which is now found in s 41 of the PA 1992. Where there is a concerted design by two persons to infringe, both may be liable as joint tortfeasors.[33] However, in *Belegging v Witten Industrial Diamonds*,[34] the English Court of Appeal held that the selling of a commercial commodity to someone who, with the knowledge of the vendor, intended to use it in a patented product, was not in itself an infringement. Neither did supply for that sole purpose amount to procuring an infringement, Buckley LJ stating that 'facilitating the doing of an act is obviously different from procuring the doing of the act' but that if the defendants had procured, counselled and/or aided other persons to infringe, 'this may perhaps amount to an allegation of indirect infringement by the defendants themselves, but I am inclined to think that it is a claim in respect of a distinct, suggested tort of procuring infringement by others (based on the principle enunciated by Erle J in *Lumley v Gye)'*.[35] In *Dow Chemicals v Spence Bryson*,[36] it was held that where the second defendant persuaded and induced the first defendant to adopt the patented process in order to secure the first defendant's order for a supply of latex used in the process, and also provided the necessary technical assistance in establishing the process, this amounted to procuring an infringement.

---

[32] *Furr v CD Truline (Building Products) Ltd* [1985] FSR 553.
[33] *Morton-Norwich Products Ltd v Intercen Ltd* [1978] RPC 501.
[34] *Belegging v Witten Industrial Diamonds* [1979] FSR 59.
[35] *Lumley v Gye* (1853) 2 E & B 216 at 231.
[36] *Dow Chemicals v Spence Bryson* [1982] FSR 598.

[6.16] The wording in s 41(1) of the PA 1992 is taken from the CPC[37] and it enables a patentee to take action against any person who supplies or offers to supply any of the means, relating to an essential element of the invention, for putting the invention into effect. Thus, for example, the case of *Innes v Short and Beal*[38] would clearly fall within this provision. In that case the plaintiff was the patentee of an invention for using zinc powder to prevent corrosion in steam boilers. The defendant formerly sold the zinc powder under an agency agreement. The agency agreement terminated but the defendant continued to sell the zinc powder. Although an injunction was granted to restrain the defendant from selling powdered zinc with an invitation to the purchasers to use it so as to infringe the patent, this was based on an inducement to infringe. The provisions in s 41(1) do not require there to be such inducement although there must be knowledge that the 'means' in question are suitable for the infringing purpose. This knowledge can be inferred where it would be 'obvious in the circumstances to a reasonable person'. In *Furr v CD Truline (Building Products) Ltd*[39] an interlocutory injunction was refused, it being held that the defendant had not intended its articles to be used in the claimed manner and that it would not have been obvious to a reasonable person that the articles were intended to be used in that manner. An example of a case in which indirect infringement was held to occur is *Helitune Ltd v Stewart Hughes Ltd*,[40] where the patent in suit related to a method of detecting the degree of unbalance of helicopter rotor blades. The plaintiff asserted that there was a direct infringement by the defendant's blade tracker and an indirect infringement by the defendant's offer to supply a part of its tracker to another company. Aldous J in the Patents Court found that the defendant did know and any reasonable man would have known that its part would be used in a system which fell within the patent.

[6.17] The Malaysian High Court case of *Rhône Poulenc v Dikloride Herbicides*[41] related to a patent in respect of compositions for use in regulating plant growth. Certain claims also related to the 'treatment of rubber trees to stimulate the flow of latex'. The planters using the defendant's product were direct infringers and the defendants who provided their products to the planters were guilty of contributory infringement. It is necessary for the means to be an 'essential element of the invention' and this must be a question of fact in each case. The word 'essential' presumably means an element in relation to which an alternative would not suffice in order for the invention to be put into effect.

[6.18] Indirect or contributory infringement does not apply when the 'means' are 'staple commercial products' except where the supply or offer is made for the purpose of inducing the person supplied to do an act which constitutes a direct infringement.[42] The key words are 'staple commercial product' and there is no definition

---

[37] CPC, art 26; see para **[2.109]** *et seq.*
[38] *Innes v Short and Beal* (1898) 15 RPC 449.
[39] *Furr v CD Truline (Building Products) Ltd* [1985] FSR 553.
[40] *Helitune Ltd v Stewart Hughes Ltd* [1991] FSR 171.
[41] *Rhône Poulenc v Dikloride Herbicides* [1988] FSR 282.

of such. A similar provision exists in US patent law and guidelines may be obtained from this source[43] that suggest a meaning akin to raw materials of a type that are generally available or a commodity of commerce suitable for uses of which at least some would not amount to an infringement.

Under s 41(3) of the PA 1992, a person entitled to exploit an invention under these provisions does not include private users of the invention, those experimenting with the invention or pharmacists making up prescriptions. The issue of contributory infringement in relation to use for experimental purposes arose in *Monsanto Co v Stauffer Chemical Co Ltd*[44] and the UK Patents Court expressed the view that supply of the patented herbicide product known as 'Touchdown' was an infringement even if the activities of the person to whom the product was supplied was to use it for experimental purposes. The Court of Appeal went on to say that there was force in such an argument but did not rule on the issue. Therefore the issue has not yet been decided.

LIMITATIONS ON PATENT RIGHTS

[6.19] Sections 42[45] and 43 of the PA 1992 impose the following limitations on the extent of the rights granted.

Private and non-commercial purposes

[6.20] Under the PA 1992, s 42(a), 'acts done privately for non-commercial purposes' do not infringe. This provision was considered in *Smith Kline & French Laboratories v Evans Medical Ltd.*[46] The defendant had conducted in-house experiments to support evidence in opposition to an amendment of the patent sought by the plaintiff patentee. Aldous J, in the Patents Court, examined the word 'privately' even though it was accepted that the experiment was indeed carried out privately in this instance. It was stated that:

> as this subsection goes on to exclude acts done for commercial purposes, the word 'privately' includes commercial and non-commercial situations. This word is not, in my view, synonymous with secret or confidential and would include acts which were secret or confidential or were not. This word appears to me to be used as the opposite of publicly and to be used in the sense of denoting that the act was done for the person's own use. This construction of the word 'privately' is consistent with the rest of the subsection which provides that even if the acts are done privately in the sense of for the person's own use, there will be infringement if the acts are done for commercial purposes.

Since the act in this case was done privately, the dispute turned on whether it was done for purposes which were commercial. Although the stated sole purpose of the experiment was to produce evidence for the amendment proceedings, it was accepted

---

[42] PA 1992, s 41(2).

[43] Baillie, 'Contributory Infringement in the US' (1980–81) 10 CIPA 56.

[44] *Monsanto Co v Stauffer Chemical Co Ltd* [1985] RPC 515.

[45] As amended by the Patents (Amendment) Act 2006.

[46] *Smith Kline & French Laboratories v Evans Medical Ltd* [1989] FSR 513.

that in carrying out the experiment, the defendants acquired information which would be useful in commercial production. It was held that experiments done for the legal proceedings were not done for commercial purposes but if the experiment had a dual purpose which included the obtaining of commercial experience, then the exclusion did not apply. On the facts it was held that there was an issue to be tried. However, the test is subjective and if all the purposes are non-commercial, it is irrelevant that knowledge gained might be of commercial benefit.

Experimental purposes[47]

[6.21] Acts done for experimental purposes do not infringe if they relate to the subject matter of the patented invention. In *Monsanto Co v Stauffer Chemical Co*,[48] the Court of Appeal held that trials carried out in order to discover something unknown or to test a hypothesis or even in order to find out whether something which is known to work in specific conditions, eg of soil or weather, will work in different conditions, can fairly be regarded as experiments. However, trials carried out in order to demonstrate to a third party that a product works or, in order to amass information to satisfy a third party, whether a customer or a regulatory body, that the product works as its maker claims, are not to be regarded as acts done for experimental purposes. The section not only requires the act to be done for experimental purposes, but also that the purposes relate to the subject matter of the invention, ie an invention covered the patent in respect of which infringement is alleged. Thus experiments performed for the purpose of invalidating some other patent will not be exempt from infringement.[49]

Extemporaneous preparation of medicines

[6.22] No infringement arises where there is extemporaneous preparation of a medicine in a pharmacy for individual cases where such is in accordance with a medical prescription issued by a registered medical practitioner. Also excluded from infringement are acts concerning the medicine so prepared.[50] Unlike the situation under the equivalent UK provision,[51] there is no exclusion for prescriptions issuing from a dental practitioner. The exclusion does not extend to veterinary preparations. The provision is taken from art 27(c) of the CPC although the CPC does not require the prescription to be that of a registered medical practitioner. The word 'extemporaneous' means on the spur of the moment or without prior notice, so medicines which are prepared prior to a specific request are not exempt, such as, for example, bulk preparation of a

---

[47] For a comparative European study, see the report produced for the European Commission in 2009: Van Eecke, Kelly, Bolger and Truyens, 'Monitoring and Analysis of Technology Transfer and Intellectual Property Regimes and their Use' available online at www.eutechnologytransfer.eu.

[48] *Monsanto Co v Stauffer Chemical Co* [1985] RPC 515.

[49] *Smith Kline & French v Evans Medical Ltd* [1989] FSR 513.

[50] PA 1992, s 42(c).

[51] UK Patents Act 1977, s 60(5)(c).

common prescription. It is unclear whether or not the medical practitioner must be registered in this country.

Vessels, aircraft or land vehicles

[6.23] There are specific provisions exempting the use of patented inventions on certain vessels, aircraft or land vehicles temporarily or accidentally entering the State.[52] In the case of a vessel, this includes entry in the territorial waters of the State, the extent of such territorial protection also being identified in s 117 of the PA 1992. The exemption does not apply to vessels registered in the State. The wording corresponds to art 27(d) and (e) of the CPC. The vessel must be registered in a Member State of the Paris Convention.[53] The Patents (Amendment) Act 2006 [54] extended this to members of the World Trade Organisation as required under TRIPS. Certain 'Flag of Convenience' countries are not members such as, for example, Taiwan. It is also necessary that the invention be used exclusively for the needs of the vessel, which includes the vessel's machinery, tackle, gear and other accessories.

Limitations under EU law

[6.24] Article 29.4.10° of the Irish Constitution specifically states that:

> No provision of this Constitution invalidates laws enacted, acts done or measures adopted by the State necessitated by the obligations of membership of the European Union or of the Communities, or prevents laws enacted, acts done or measures adopted by the European Union or the Communities or by institutions thereof, or by bodies competent under the Treaties establishing the Communities, from having the force of law in the State.

Given the superiority of EU law over domestic legislation, it was not necessary for the PA 1992[55] to state as it does that the rights conferred by a patent do not extend to prevent acts which under the Treaty of Rome could not be prevented by the proprietor.

[6.25] Article 345[56] of the Treaty on the Functioning of the European Union (the Treaty)[57] states that the Treaty shall not in any way prejudice the rules in Member States governing the system of property ownership. However, while the Treaty does not affect the existence of patent and other intellectual property rights, there are situations in which the exercise of such rights must be restricted. The Court of Justice of the European Union (ECJ) has distinguished between the existence of intellectual property rights and their exercise.[58]

---

[52] PA 1992, s 42(d) and (e) as amended by the Patents (Amendment) Act 2006.

[53] Paris Convention for the Protection of Industrial Property 1893.

[54] In the amendments to s 42(d) and (e).

[55] PA 1992, s 43.

[56] Formerly EC Treaty, art 295.

[57] [2010] OJ C83 of 30 March 2010. (Formerly known as the EC Treaty until it was renamed following the commencement of the Treaty of Lisbon on 1 December 2009.)

[58] *Etablissements Consten SARL and Grundig-Verkaufs-GmbH v European Commission* Joined cases 56/64 and 58/64 [1966] ECR 299.

[6.26] Patent rights were considered in *Parke Davis & Co v Probel and Centrafarm*.[59] In that case, Parke Davis held a patent in the Netherlands. There was no corresponding patent in Italy where, at that time, it was not possible to secure a patent in respect of pharmaceutical products. The drug was produced in Italy and imported by Centrafarm into the Netherlands. Parke Davis sought an injunction to stop infringement in the Netherlands. It was argued by Centrafarm that the granting of an injunction would create an obstacle to free movement throughout the EU. It was nonetheless held that Parke Davis were not prevented under art 101 of the Treaty[60] from blocking the import of a competing drug manufactured in Italy where there was no patent protection and where Parke Davis had not marketed the drug. The important factor in this case was not the absence of a system for patent protection in one Member State but the fact that the imported product had not been put on the Italian market by the patentee or with its consent.

[6.27] Distinguishing between the existence of intellectual property rights and their exercise, it was considered that in the absence of some agreement, decision or concerted practice which prevented, restricted or distorted competition, the exercise of such rights did not fall within art 101(1) of the Treaty.[61] In relation to an abuse of a dominant position under art 102,[62] the charging of higher prices in one Member State as opposed to another does not necessarily show an abuse. Costs in marketing and patenting can vary from State to State and it is not unreasonable that an attempt be made to recoup such on a State-by-State basis.

[6.28] Article 34 of the Treaty[63] states that quantitative restrictions on imports and all measures having equivalent effect between Member States are not permitted. However, under art 36,[64] such prohibitions or restrictions are allowed on the grounds of the protection of industrial and commercial property where they are not 'a means of arbitrary discrimination or a disguised restriction on trade between Member States'. Thus, in the copyright case of *Deutsche Grammophon v Metro*,[65] the ECJ held that art 36[66] only permitted derogations from art 34[67] 'to the extent to which they are justified for the purpose of safeguarding rights which constitute the specific subject matter of such property'.

Doctrine of exhaustion

[6.29] In *Zino Davidoff SA v A&G Imports Ltd*,[68] Laddie J described the general principle of exhaustion of rights as follows:

---

[59] *Parke Davis & Co v Probel and Centrafarm* [1968] ECR 55.
[60] Formerly EC Treaty, art 81.
[61] Formerly EC Treaty, art 81.
[62] Formerly EC Treaty, art 82.
[63] Formerly EC Treaty, art 28.
[64] Formerly EC Treaty, art 30.
[65] *Deutsche Grammophon v Metro* [1971] ECR 487.
[66] Formerly EC Treaty, art 30.
[67] Formerly EC Treaty, art 28.
[68] *Zino Davidoff SA v A&G Imports Ltd* [1999] RPC 631, [1999] ETMR 700.

it is well established that a principle of exhaustion applies to all intellectual property rights. So if an article made in accordance with a patent is put upon the market in one member state by or with the consent of the owner of the patent rights, that owner cannot use those rights to prevent or hinder the importation of goods into a second member state or to prevent their sale there. The expression 'exhaustion of rights' accurately encapsulates the principle involved. The proprietary rights have been used up. The owner of them has nothing left to deploy against further exploitation of the goods. The principle applies not only to patents and copyright, but to trade marks as well. So, once the right holder has put protected products on the market or has consented to such marketing, he loses all rights to further exploitation.

This effect is indefeasible. The right owner cannot override it by contract. The member state cannot override it by national legislation.

[6.30] In *Centrafarm v Sterling Drug*,[69] the ECJ described the specific subject matter of a patent as:

> The guarantee that the patentee, to reward the creative effort of the inventor, has the exclusive right to use an invention with a view to manufacturing industrial products and putting them into circulation for the first time, either directly or by the grant of licences to third parties, as well as the right to oppose infringements.

The words 'for the first time' are a reference to the doctrine of the exhaustion of rights which was laid down in the *Deutsche Grammophon* case.[70] Simply put, this doctrine means that patent rights cannot be used to prevent the import of goods which have been marketed by the patentee or with his consent in another Member State. The application of this doctrine in the patent field can be found in the case of *Merck & Co Inc v Stephar BV*.[71] The plaintiff held a patent in the Netherlands for a pharmaceutical product which the plaintiff also sold in Italy. Similar to the situation in *Parke Davis v Probel*[72] no patent existed in Italy because Italian law did not allow for patents for pharmaceutical products. The defendant, attracted by the lower prices in Italy, acquired the product and sold it in the Netherlands. The ECJ held that the patentee's rights were exhausted when the goods were sold in Italy and stated:

> The substance of a patent right lies essentially in according the inventor an exclusive right of first placing the product on the market. That right of first placing a product on the market enables the inventor, by allowing him a monopoly in exploiting his product, to obtain the reward for his creative effort without, however, guaranteeing that he will obtain such a reward in all circumstances.

> It is for the proprietor of the patent to decide, in the light of all the circumstances, under what conditions he will market his product, including the possibility of marketing it in a Member State where the law does not provide patent protection for the product in question. If he decides to do so, he must then accept the

---

[69] *Centrafarm v Sterling Drug* [1974] ECR 1147.
[70] *Deutsche Grammophon v Metro* [1971] ECR 487.
[71] *Merck & Co Inc v Stephar BV* [1981] ECR 2063; see also *Merck & Co Inc v Primecrown Ltd* [1997] 1 CMLR 83.
[72] *Parke Davis v Probel* [1968] ECR 55.

consequences of his choice as regards the free movement of the product within the common market, which is a fundamental principal forming part of the legal and economic circumstances which must be taken into account by the proprietor of the patent in determining the manner in which his exclusive right will be exercised.

[6.31] In *Pharmon BV v Hoechst AG*,[73] the ECJ emphasised the importance of the need for a consent by the patentee before his rights are exhausted. In that case, Hoechst held patents for the drug 'frusemide' in both the UK and the Netherlands. In the UK, the drug was the subject of a compulsory licence. A UK company who had obtained such a licence produced and sold the drug to Pharmon who imported it into the Netherlands. The Court held that where a patented product was the subject of a compulsory licence, the patentee could not be said to have made a free choice about where the product should be first marketed in the EU. Therefore, the patentee was entitled to prevent importation into the Netherlands regardless of whether there was a prohibition against export in the terms of the compulsory licence.

[6.32] The issue of consent was further considered in *Allen & Hanbury v Generics (UK) Ltd.*[74] In that case, the patent for the drug 'salbutamol' was subject to licences of right in the UK under transitional provisions of the UK Patents Act 1977. Generics imported the drug from Italy where it was not patented and where it was being manufactured by a number of third parties as well as the plaintiff, arguing that they were entitled to do so under the UK licence of right. The UK patentee argued that the licence of right did not include a right to import. The effect of the licensing of right provisions is to remove the ability of a patentee to oppose third-party use but merely retain the right to a fair return by way of royalties. It was held that the patent right was not exhausted against foreign imports to the extent necessary to ensure the patentee the same rights as against domestic producers, ie the right to a fair return. Because UK law distinguished between domestic producers who could secure a licence as of right and importers who could be refused such a licence, it had to be considered whether or not such discrimination was justified under art 36.[75] The prohibition on imports could only be justified if it:

> is necessary in order to ensure that the proprietor of such a patent has, vis-à-vis importers, the same rights as he enjoys as against producers who manufacture the product in the national territory, that is to say the right to a fair return from his patent.

The Court found that no such prohibition was necessary for this purpose and the authorities could not prevent the licensee of right from importing products from other Member States. Effectively, therefore, the ECJ rejected the rights of the patent holder in favour of the rules of non-discrimination in the Treaty.

[6.33] Applying the doctrine of common origin by analogy from trade mark law, if patent rights of common origin are owned by different persons in particular Member

---

[73] *Pharmon BV v Hoechst AG* [1985] ECR 2281.
[74] *Allen & Hanbury v Generics (UK) Ltd* [1988] ECR 1245, [1988] FSR 312.
[75] Formerly EC Treaty, art 30.

States, a patentee cannot rely on a national patent to prevent the importation of goods lawfully marketed under a patent by a patentee in another Member State.[76] Much of the recent case law in the area of exhaustion of rights has been in relation to trade marks rather than patents but many of the principles could apply equally to all types of intellectual property rights.[77]

[6.34] Article 10 of the Directive on the Legal Protection of Biotechnological Inventions[78] applies the principle of exhaustion of rights to the results of propagation or multiplication where propagation or multiplication would necessarily occur following a disposal by the patent owner or their licensee.

Abuse of a dominant position

[6.35] Article 102 of the Treaty[79] prohibits an 'abuse of a dominant position'. Since a patent is a form of monopoly, it may inevitably put a patentee into a dominant position. However, it is only when it is abused that there is a prohibition. Examples of such an abuse are 'tie-ins', identified in art 102(d)[80] as:

> making the conclusion of contracts subject to acceptance by the other parties of supplementary obligations which, by their nature or according to commercial usage, have no connection with the subject of such contracts.

Thus, a patent licensee should not be compelled as part of the licence to buy unpatented goods. Also, any unfair commercial practice on the part of a dominant enterprise intended to eliminate, discipline or deter small companies is potentially an abuse of the monopoly right.[81]

[6.36] Contrasting views can be seen in the cases of *Volvo AB v Eric Veng (UK) Ltd*[82] and *Magill v ITP, BBC and RTE*.[83] In the first of these cases, the Court had to consider the issue of car body panels and whether or not car manufacturers could use intellectual property rights to prevent the manufacture of competing spare body panels. It was held that an abuse would arise only if the owner of the rights neither sold the goods itself nor licensed others to do so, as this would make obtaining a repair impossible. The charge of an excessive price would also amount to an abuse. The European Court stated:

> It must however be noted that the exercise of an exclusive right by the proprietor of a registered design in respect of car body panels may be prohibited by [art 102 of the Treaty] if it involves, on the part of an undertaking holding a dominant position, certain abusive conduct such as the arbitrary refusal to supply spare parts to

---

76 *Van Zuylen Frères v Hag AG* [1974] ECR 731; *Terrapin v Terranova* [1976] ECR 1039.
77 See **Ch 33**.
78 Council Directive 98/44/EC ([1998] OJ L213/13) of 6 July 1998, implemented by SI 247/2000.
79 Formerly EC Treaty, art 82.
80 Formerly EC Treaty, art 82(d).
81 *Engineering & Chemical Supplies v Akzo* [1986] 3 CMLR 273.
82 *Volvo AB v Eric Veng (UK) Ltd* [1988] ECR 6211.
83 *Magill v ITP, BBC and RTE* [1989] 4 CMLR 757.

independent repairers, the fixing of prices for spare parts at an unfair level or a decision no longer to produce spare parts for a particular model even though many cars of that model are still in circulation provided that such conduct is liable to affect trade between Member States.

This is hard to reconcile with the *Magill* case and the finding that broadcasters, in preventing publishers from meeting substantial potential demand for alternative listings, were abusing a dominant position which they held by virtue of copyright. It appears that the circumstances where an abuse of a dominant position can be held to exist may be broader for copyright holders compared to patentees.

[6.37] It is not always easy to establish whether a party is in a dominant position. In *Hugin v EC Commission*,[84] it was held that an approximate 12 per cent share of the EU market in respect of cash registers did not put Hugin in a dominant position. Again, spare parts were at issue. There was considered to be a dominant position in respect of recondition and repair of Hugin registers because, in the main, the spare parts for the Hugin registers were not interchangeable with spare parts for other registers.

[6.38] In *Eurofix and Bauco v Hilti AG*,[85] the defendant was fined by the European Commission for abuse of a dominant position by attempting to control the supply of unpatented nails for use with its patented fastening guns. Hilti's attempt to justify its behaviour on the grounds of safety and reliability failed. In addition, one of the many categories of conduct that were held to constitute a breach was the frustration and delay of legitimately available licences of right under the defendant's patents. The defendant had demanded excessive royalty payments.

[6.39] Another example of an abuse can be seen in *Elopak Italia Srl v Tetra Pak*.[86] The European Commission imposed a fine of 75 million ECU for activities aimed at eliminating competition by imposing unduly binding terms in sales and leasing contracts and discriminatory and predatory pricing. In *Pitney Bowes Inc v Francotyp-Postalia*,[87] the English High Court made it clear that a refusal to grant a licence on reasonable terms was not itself an abuse and, interestingly, Hoffmann J found some substance in the argument that patent rights may have to be considered differently because of the compulsory licensing provisions under UK law. In *Intel Corpn v Via Technologies Inc*[88] the Court of Appeal concluded that it is a defence to patent infringement that enforcement of the patent would enable the owner to act in breach of arts 101 and 102 of the Treaty. It was held that if the willingness to grant a licence was only on terms which involved a breach of art 101 and was part of the abusive conduct of which the complaint was made, then a defence could arise. Even if a defence is insufficient to avoid a claim to infringement, it may affect the remedies available.

---

[84] *Hugin v EC Commission* [1979] ECR 1869.
[85] *Eurofix and Bauco v Hilti AG* [1989] 4 CMLR 677.
[86] *Elopak Italia Srl v Tetra Pak* [1992] 4 CMLR 551; summary [1992] FSR 542.
[87] *Pitney Bowes Inc v Francotyp-Postalia* [1991] FSR 72.
[88] *Intel Corpn v Via Technologies Inc* [2002] All ER (D) 346: see also *British Leyland Motor Corpn v TI Silencers* [1981] FSR 213.

Block exemptions

[6.40] Provisions of a licence agreement which come within art 101[89] of the Treaty are potentially void on the basis of being contrary to competition law as being an anti-competitive agreement between undertakings or an abuse of a dominant position. Such agreements can also result in severe fines for the participants. Since intellectual property licence agreements often contain restrictions on competition in one form or another, the European Commission has, from an early date, issued specific regulations covering such agreements, referred to as 'block exemptions' as they set out rules for the types of these agreements that will not be regarded as anti-competitive.

If an agreement is not covered by a block exemption, it is potentially anti-competitive, and the parties must assess the potential effects of the agreement. Until May 2004, agreements which were not covered by a block exemption could be individually notified to the European Commission for a ruling on whether they were anti-competitive. Alternatively, any agreements to which the block exemption did not apply but which did not contain any prohibited clauses could be notified to the European Commission and deemed automatically exempt if the European Commission took no action within a specified four-month period. These notification systems were removed in May 2004.[90]

[6.41] The European Commission has issued a number of block exemption regulations for different types of licences including patent licence agreements. The Patent Exemption Regulation[91] was principally concerned with the licensing of patents with or without associated know-how and was originally due to expire on 31 December 1994 but was extended until the adoption of the Technology Transfer Block Exemption Regulation (772/2004/EC) on 1 April 1996.[92] A further Regulation, called the Know-How Block Exemption Regulation,[93] covered not only purely know-how agreements but also the majority of patent and know-how licences not covered by the Patent Exemption Regulation.[94]

[6.42] Commission Regulation 772/2004/EC is a block exemption regulation relating to technology transfer agreements. It became effective on 1 May 2004 and is due to expire on 30 April 2014. Its predecessor, Commission Regulation 240/96/EC, replaced both the Patent Licensing Block Exemption Regulation (2349/84/EEC) and the Know-How Licensing Block Exemption Regulation (556/89/EEC).[95] Regulation 772/2004/EC applies to:

---

[89] Formerly EC Treaty, art 81.
[90] Council Regulation 1/2003/EC on the implementation of the rules of competition laid down in Articles 81 and 82 of the Treaty, OJ L1, 4 January 2003, p 1–25.
[91] Commission Regulation 2349/84/EEC ([1984] OJ L219/15); [1985] FSR 191.
[92] Commission Regulation 772/2004/EC ([2004] OJ L123/15) which repealed and replaced Commission Regulation 240/96/EC ([1996] OJ L31/2).
[93] Commission Regulation 556/89/EEC ([1989] OJ L61/1) as amended by 151/93/EEC ([1993] OJ L21/8).
[94] Commission Regulation 556/89/EEC, preamble, para 2; art 1(6),(7).
[95] Which was not due to expire until December 1999.

(a)   pure patent licences, pure know-how licences or pure software copyright licensing, agreements, and mixed patent/know-how licences of any of the foregoing;

(b)   agreements for the sale and purchase of products where licences or assignments of intellectual property rights (i) are not the primary object of the agreement and (ii) are directly related to the production of the products produced with the licensed technology;

(c)   assignments of patents, know-how, software copyright or a combination thereof where an element of risk associated with the exploited technology remains with the assignor. Examples which are specifically mentioned are where the sum payable for the assignment is dependent on the turnover of the assignee of products produced with the assigned technology, the quantity of such products or the number of operations carried out employing the technology.

[6.43] The rationale behind Regulation 772/2004/EC, as with its predecessors, is that certain contractual provisions in licence agreements, although generally restrictive of competition, nevertheless have positive attributes which fall within the Treaty, art 101(3). In Regulation 772/2004/EC this is accomplished by a three-tier system:
Market share:

The following types of agreements are automatically covered by the block exemption and are not anti-competitive:[96]

Any agreements between competing undertakings[97] if the parties involved have a combined market share[98] that does not exceed 20 per cent of the relevant technology and product market.

Any agreement between parties who are not competing undertakings where they each have a market share of the relevant technology and product market which does not exceed 30 per cent.

Any other agreement to which the block exemption applies.

Regulation 772/2004/EC takes a different approach to its predecessors in this area. Previous Regulations included a list of clauses which were stated to be generally not restrictive of competition. This 'white list' of clauses was extensive and included, by way of example, an obligation on the licensee not to grant sub-licences or assign the licence, minimum quality standards and minimum royalty and production obligations. The white list allowed a licensor the right to terminate the agreement if the licensee contested the secret or substantial nature of the licensed know-how or challenged the validity of licensed patents within the EU belonging to the licensor or undertakings connected with the licensor. Regulation 772/2004/EC does not include a white list of permitted clauses. Effectively, anything which is not on the 'black list' is permitted unless in any particular case the agreement is deemed to have an anti-

---

[96] Regulation 772/2004/EC, art 3.
[97] As defined in Regulation 772/2004/EC, art 1(j).
[98] Regulation 772/2004/EC, art 8.

competitive effect, in which case the protection of the block exemption can be removed on a case-by-case basis.[99]

[6.44] Regulation 772/2004/EC identifies, by way of a 'black list', clauses which will remove the agreement from the benefit of the block exemption and potentially render it anti-competitive. This black list includes clauses whereby one party is restricted in the determination of prices, components of prices or discounts for the licensed products and non-compete restrictions. The black listed clauses under Regulation 772/2004/EC include:

Any obligations which directly or indirectly:[100]

(a) Require the licensee to grant an exclusive licence of or assign its own severable improvements[101] to or new applications of the licensed technology.

(b) Require the licensee not to challenge the validity of the intellectual property rights of the licensor in the EU (although this can be an event of termination in the licence agreement if the appropriate clause is included).

Where the parties are *not competing* undertakings:

(a) Any obligations that directly or indirectly limit the licensee's ability to exploit its own technology or limit the ability of any of the parties to carry out research and development, unless indispensible to prevent the disclosure of licensed know-how to third parties.[102]

(b) Any obligations which directly or indirectly, in isolation or in combination with other facts under the control of the parties, have as their object:[103]

(i) resale price maintenance, although the imposition of maximum sales prices or recommended sales prices is permitted so long as it does not amount to a fixed or minimum sales price as a result of pressure or incentives;

(ii) restrictions on passive sales to territories or customers except the following permitted clauses:

1 restrictions on passive sales into exclusive territories or customers reserved for the licensor;

2. restrictions on passive sales into exclusive territories or customers reserved for another licensee within the first two years of sales from that licensee to that territory or customer group;

3. obligations on the licensee to produce products only for its own use provided that the licensee if not prevented from selling the products as spare parts for its own products;

---

[99] Regulation 772/2004/EC, art 6.
[100] Regulation 772/2004/EC, art 5.
[101] Regulation 772/2004/EC, art 1(n).
[102] Regulation 772/2004/EC, art 5(2).
[103] Regulation 772/2004/EC, art 4(2).

4. obligations on the licensee to produce the products only for one customer, where the purpose of the licence is to create an alternative source of supply for that customer;

5. restrictions on sales to end-users by a licensee which is a wholesaler; or

6. restrictions on sales to unauthorised distributors by members of a selective distribution system;[104]

(iii) restrictions on active or passive sales to end-users by a licensee that is a retailer and a member of a selective distribution system, without prejudice to the possibility of preventing a member from operating out of an unauthorised place of establishment.

Where the parties are *competing* undertakings, any obligations which directly or indirectly, in isolation or in combination with other facts under the control of the parties, have as their object:[105]

(a) Resale price maintenance.

(b) Limitation of output except where imposed on a licensee in a non-reciprocal agreement[106] or only one licensee in a reciprocal agreement.[107]

(c) Allocation of markets or customers except the following permitted clauses:

(i) limitations on technical fields of use or product markets;

(ii) limitations on technical fields of use, product markets or exclusive territories reserved for the other party;[108]

(iii) obligations on the licensor not to licence the technology to another licensee in a territory (ie exclusivity obligations);

(iv) restrictions on active or passive sales into an exclusive territory or exclusive customer group of the other party or of another licensee which is not a competing undertaking of the licensor;[109]

(v) obligations on the licensee to produce products only for its own use provided that the licensee is not prevented from selling the products as spare parts for its own products;

(vi) obligations on the licensee to produce the products only for one customer, where the purpose of the licence was to create an alternative source of supply for that customer;[110] or

---

[104] Regulation 772/2004/EC, art 1(k), for example the distribution systems of luxury consumer brands that can only be sold through certain prestigious outlets and not through discount stores, etc.

[105] Regulation 772/2004/EC, art 4(1).

[106] A cross licence for competing technologies: Regulation 772/2004/EC, art 1(c).

[107] A licence or cross licence concerning non-competing technologies: Regulation 772/2004/EC, art 1(d).

[108] Applies to non-reciprocal agreements only.

[109] Applies to non-reciprocal agreements only.

[110] Applies to non-reciprocal agreements only.

    (vii)   restrictions on the licensee exploiting its own technology or restrictions on any of the parties carrying out research and development, unless this is indispensible to prevent the disclosure of licensed know-how.

Where the parties are not competing undertakings at the time the agreement was concluded but become competing undertakings afterwards, the rules applicable to non-competing undertakings will continue to apply to that agreement unless it is materially amended.[111]

[6.45] Under art 6 of Regulation 772/2004/EC, the European Commission may withdraw the benefit of the Regulation where it finds in a particular case that an agreement exempted by the Regulation nevertheless has certain effects which are incompatible with the conditions laid down in art 101(3) of the Treaty. Examples given include where the effect of the agreement is that the access of third parties' technologies or potential licensees to the markets is restricted or the parties do not exploit the licensed technology and have no validly objective reason therefor.[112]

[6.46] The other block exemption which may be relevant to patentees is Commission Regulation 2659/2000/EC of 29 November 2000 on the application of art 81(3) (now art 101(3)) of the Treaty to categories of research and development agreements. This block exemption deals, amongst other things, with the treatment of intellectual property rights in the results of research and development.

PATENT APPLICATIONS AND INFRINGEMENT

[6.47] Under s 26 of the PA 1964, it was specifically stated that no proceedings could be taken in respect of an infringement committed before the date of the publication of the complete specification, which occurred on acceptance. However, no infringement action could be taken until after grant.[113] Section 44 of the PA 1992 now provisionally provides protection from the date of first publication of the specification, ie 18 months from the earliest priority date or 18 months after the date of application where priority has not been claimed.[114] A patent application prior to publication cannot be used as a basis for an infringement action. Nor, when granted, can damages be secured for infringement during this period. From this date, there lies a claim for damages but, under s 56 of the PA 1992, a patent must be granted before proceedings for infringement can be taken.

[6.48] The words 'provisionally confer' in s 44 of the PA 1992 appear in art 67 of the EPC. It is a requirement under art 67 of the EPC that Ireland provide for an applicant, from the date of publication of the European patent application, the ability to claim reasonable compensation from any person who has used the invention in Ireland in circumstances where that person would be liable under national law for infringement of

---

[111] Regulation 772/2004/EC, art 4(3).

[112] Regulation 772/2004/EC, art 6(1).

[113] PA 1964, s 25.

[114] Bear in mind that the filing date, or priority date if any, establishes the relevant date for novelty.

a national patent. Under s 56(3) of the PA 1992, damages may be reduced if it would not have been reasonable to expect, from a consideration of the published application, that the ultimate patent would be infringed. With this in mind, an applicant should file a patent application with a set of claims of differing scope in order that the application contains at least a single claim that will be valid and liable to infringment.

[6.49] In the case of a European patent application designating Ireland and published by the EPO in French or German, relief under s 56 of the PA 1992 is dependant upon the filing and publication of an English translation of the claims. An exception arises in cases where an applicant has sent the translation to the person alleged to be infringing.[115] If a patent application is withdrawn, deemed to have been withdrawn or finally refused, then no claim of infringement can arise.[116]

Scope of protection

[6.50] The scope of protection conferred by a patent or a patent application is determined by the claims.[117] The description and drawings can be used to interpret the claims. This provision corresponds to art 69 of the EPC. Section 45(3) of the PA 1992 states that in interpreting this provision, a court must have regard to the directions contained in the Protocol on the interpretation of art 69 of the EPC. This Protocol is in fact scheduled to PA 1992 and, by way of directions to the interpretation of s 45, states:

> General Principles. Section 45 should not be interpreted in the sense that the extent of the protection conferred by a patent is to be understood as that defined by the strict, literal meaning of the wording used in the claims, the description and drawings being employed only for the purpose of resolving an ambiguity found in the claims. Neither should it be interpreted in the sense that the claims serve only as a guideline and that the actual protection conferred may extend to what, from a consideration of the description and drawings by a person skilled in the art, the patentee has contemplated. On the contrary, it is to be interpreted as defining a position between these extremes which combines a fair protection for the patentee with a reasonable degree of certainty for third parties.

The Protocol was intended to enter a middle ground between what was at least perceived as the extreme English literal approach and the equally extreme German guideline approach. In practice, however, the English courts have adopted the view that the pronouncement of Lord Diplock in *Catnic Components Ltd v Hill & Smith Ltd*[118] conforms to the Protocol. In the *Catnic* case, the patent related to steel lintels, and claim 1 required that a rear member of the lintel should 'extend vertically'. The lintel produced by the defendants differed from that claim, only in that the rear member, instead of being vertical, was inclined slightly to the vertical. The House of Lords held that, on the basis of a purposive rather than a literal construction, the patent was

---

[115] PA 1992, s 120(6).

[116] PA 1992, s 44(2).

[117] PA 1992, s 45(1) as amended by the Patents (Amendment) Act 2006.

[118] *Catnic Components Ltd v Hill & Smith Ltd* [1982] RPC 183.

infringed. Lord Diplock considered the 'pith and marrow' doctrine[119] under which a patent could be held to be infringed if a defendant takes the pith and marrow of the invention even if he does not meet all the requirements of the claims, and against this had to consider the principle expressed by Lord Upjohn in *Rodi & Weinberger AG v Henry Showell*[120] that 'the essential integers (of the claims) having been ascertained, the infringing article must be considered. To constitute infringement the article must take each and every one of the essential integers of the claim'. In *Catnic*, Lord Diplock stated the approach to be followed in these terms:[121]

> A patent specification is a unilateral statement by the patentee, in words of his own choosing, addressed to those likely to have a practical interest in the subject matter of his invention (ie skilled in the art), by which he informs them what he claims to be the essential features of the new product or process for which the letters patent grant him a monopoly. It is those novel features only that he claims to be essential that constitute the so-called 'Pith and Marrow' of the claim. A patent specification should be given a purposive construction rather than a purely literal one derived from applying to it the kind of meticulous verbal analysis in which lawyers are too often tempted by their training to indulge. The question in each case is: whether persons with practical knowledge and experience of the kind of work in which the invention was intended to be used, would understand that strict compliance with a particular descriptive word or phrase appearing in a claim was intended by the patentee to be an essential requirement of the invention so that any variant would fall outside the monopoly claimed, even though it could have no material effect upon the way the invention worked.

[6.51] In *Improver Corpn v Remington Consumer Products Ltd*,[122] the Court of Appeal held the statement of Lord Diplock correctly indicates the same approach to construction as is indicated in the Protocol on the interpretation of art 69 of the EPC. The UK Patents Court has suggested that the tests applied by Lord Diplock can be broken down into three questions:[123]

(1) Does the variant have a material effect upon the way the invention worked? If it does, then there is no infringement.

(2) If the variant has no material effect upon the way the invention worked, would that be obvious to the skilled addressee? If not, then there is no infringement.

(3) On the assumption that questions (1) and (2) are answered in the affirmative, does the specification make it obvious to the skilled addressee that the exclusion of the variant from the ambit of the claim could not have been intended? If so, there would be infringement.

---

[119] Lord Cairns in *Clark v Adie* (1877) 2 App Cas 315 at 320.

[120] *Rodi & Weinberger AG v Henry Showell* [1969] RPC 367 at 391.

[121] *Catnic Components Ltd v Hill & Smith Ltd* [1982] RPC 183 at 242–243.

[122] *Improver Corpn v Remington Consumer Products Ltd* [1989] RPC 69; see also *PLG Research v Ardon* [1993] FSR 197.

[123] *SouthCo Inc v Dzus Fastener Europe Ltd* [1990] RPC 587; *AC Edwards Ltd v Acme Signs* [1990] RPC 621.

These three questions are considered to be no more than aids to assist in arriving at the proper purposive construction.[124] In *Kirin-Amgen Inc v Transkaryotic Therapies Inc*[125] the Court of Appeal ruled that the answer to the first question depends on the level of generality used to describe the way the invention works. The wider the description, the easier it is to fit the variant into the description. The right approach was considered to be to describe the working of the invention at the level of generality with which it is described in the claim of the patent. The Court of Appeal further held that if the conclusion to the first question was that the skilled person would not have expected the variant to work at all, it could not have been obvious that it would work in the same way. Therefore, the answer to the second question must also be in the negative. The issue does arise as to whether the second question is really necessary since if the variant is not obvious to the skilled reader, there is a strong indication that the variant has a material effect on the way the invention works.

The EPO also holds the view that the wording of the claims is important in defining the scope of protection, as opposed to the German approach which focuses on the inventor's contribution to the art.[126]

Construction of claims

[6.52] The following two important cases have shed some light on how patent claims are likely to be construed in Ireland.

Kirin-Amgen Inc v Hoechst Marion Roussel Ltd[127]

[6.53] This House of Lords decision is the leading case on construction of claims. It involved a validity and infringement issue. Both parties succeeding in producing chemically-identical erythropoietin EPO, a protein which stimulates production of red blood cells by bone marrow, by different means. The method used by the defendant Hoechst Marion Roussel was not possible when the claimant Kirin-Amgen's patent was filed. This case set out a number of important principles, as follows.

[6.54] There are two options for construction: (1) the court can adhere to literalism and have a doctrine that supplements the claims by extending protection to equivalents (the US approach) which is precluded by art 69; or (2) the court can abandon literalism as happened in the UK in the *Catnic* decision per Lord Diplock (the principle of construction which actually gave effect to what the person skilled in the art would have understood the patentee to be claiming). The court held that the *Catnic* approach accords with the Protocol and there is no harm in a little explanation. General principles of legal document construction apply to the construction of claims. Words and grammar are given their natural and ordinary meaning, regardless of context or background unless ambiguous. If the language in the claim is ambiguous, the court can have regard to the context provided by the specification and drawings. If this is insufficient to resolve the

---

[124] *Wheatley v Drillsafe* [2001] RPC 133.

[125] *Kirin-Amgen Inc v Transkaryotic Therapies Inc* [2003] RPC 31.

[126] G2/88 *Friction Reducing Additive/MOBIL OIL III* [1990] OJ EPO 93, [1990] EPOR 73.

[127] *Kirin-Amgen Inc v Hoechst Marion Roussel Ltd* [2004] UKHL 46, [2005] RPC 169.

ambiguity, the court can have regard to background or extrinsic evidence of facts which the intended reader would reasonably have expected to have been within the knowledge of the author when they wrote the document. Unless the court can find an ambiguity, it cannot look beyond the natural and ordinary meaning so it may have to construe the claims in a way a reasonable reader would not have thought the author intended. This can cause injustice, though judges are adept at finding ambiguities to allow them to interpret the claims in a broader context. It is unusual that a court will conclude that the patentee must have meant something different from appearances and it will need some rational basis. However, there must necessarily be gaps in the court's knowledge of the background that led to the patentee expressing themselves that way so the court may not always understand why it did so. These general document construction principles have been refined in cases dealing with patents. Where the author is using language for a practical purpose and it would be liable to defeat the author's intentions if a rule of construction gives a meaning which is different from the way it would be understood by the person to whom it was addressed, the specification must be given a purposive construction rather than a purely literal one derived from lawyers' meticulous verbal analysis.[128] If a detailed semantic and syntactical analysis leads to a conclusion that flouts common sense, it must be made to yield to business common sense.[129] Construction is not directly concerned with what author meant to say. It is objective and focuses on what a reasonable person to whom the utterance is addressed would have understood the author to be using the words to mean. It is not the meaning of the words the author used, it is what the person would have understood the author to mean. This is highly sensitive to the context and background as it depends on the words chosen but also the identity of the audience. The notional addressee reads the specification on the assumption that its purpose is to describe and demarcate an invention, not to be a textbook or shopping list. This is the basis of purposive construction. Purposive construction does not mean that one can extend or go beyond the definition of the technical matter. The language chosen is usually of critical importance. Conventions of word meaning and syntax enable great accuracy and subtlety and the court will ordinarily assume that the patentee chose the language accordingly. It is a unilateral document and the words are usually chosen on skilled advice. However, the court must bear in mind that the patentee is trying to describe something which is new, has not existed before and for which there may not be any generally accepted definition. There will be occasions when it will be obvious to the skilled person that the patentee must have departed from conventional use of language or included an element which it did not mean to be essential, but these do not occur very often.

[6.55] The essential question is whether the person skilled in the art would understand the invention as operating at a level of generality that makes it irrelevant how the protein is made, ie whether the DNA which creates it is exogenous or not. This in turn depends on what is regarded as the invention. Is it the discovery of the EPO gene or of a method of making it? An invention is normally claimed at the same level of generality as defined in claims – it is unusual to claim a higher level of generality. A claim may cover products

---

[128] Per Lord Diplock in *Catnic* decision, *ibid*.

[129] Per Lord Diplock in *Antaois Compania Naviera SA v Salen. Rederierna AB* [1985] AC 191.

or processes involving use of technology which is unknown at the time the claim is drafted. The question is whether the person skilled in the art would understand the description in a way sufficiently general to include the new technology. It may be clear from the language, context and background that the patentee intended to refer in general terms to every way of achieving the result even though it used language which was in some respects inappropriate. In this case, the claims were not sufficiently general to include the other method of production.

[6.56] The patent office file should not be used to shed light on the construction of the claims, as the meaning should not change depending on whether one has sight of the file. In borderline cases, what seems fair and reasonable to one person can seem unfair to another – a degree of uncertainty is always inherent in construction of a document. This uncertainty can be alleviated by guidelines. Equivalence can be an important part of the background of facts which affect what one would understand the claims to mean. This is common sense and is contained in the EPC 2000.

[6.57] The *Improver* questions[130] are only guidelines and their limits were shown in this case. Once the question of infringement is decided, it would only cause confusion to answer the *Improver* or Protocol questions too. New technology gives rise to a situation where the *Improver* questions are unhelpful, in particular the second question: would it have been obvious to the person skilled in the art that the variant worked in the same way as the invention? When the technology is unknown, it is not obvious that it would work at all.

[6.58] The court approved with one exception the general principles proposed by Jacob LJ in *Technip France SA's Patent Application*.[131] Jacob LJ in a later case[132] summarised these principles as follows:

(a)   The first, overarching principle is that contained in Article 69 itself.

(b)   Article 69 says that the extent of protection is determined *by the terms of the claims*. It goes on to say that the description and drawings shall be used to interpret the claims. In short the claims are to be construed in context.

(c)   It follows that the claims are to be construed purposively – the inventor's purpose being ascertained from the description and drawings.

(d)   It further follows that the claims must not be construed as if they stood alone – the drawings and description only being used to resolve any ambiguity. Purpose is vital to the construction of claims. [Paragraph (e), which was not approved in *Kirin-Amgen*, is omitted].

(f)   Nonetheless purpose is not the be-all and end-all. One is still at the end of the day concerned with the meaning of the language used. Hence the other extreme of the Protocol – a mere guideline – is also ruled out by Article 69 itself. It is the terms of the claims which delineate the patentee's territory.

---

[130] See para **[6.51]**.

[131] Also known as *Rockwater Ltd v Technip France SA (formerly Coflexip SA)* [2004] EWCA Civ 381, [2004] RPC 46.

[132] *Mayne Pharma v Pharmacia Italia SpA* [2005] EWCA Civ 137

(g) It follows that if the patentee has included what is obviously a deliberate limitation in his claims, it must have a meaning. One cannot disregard obviously intentional elements.

(h) It also follows that where a patentee has used a word or phrase which, acontextually, might have a particular meaning (narrow or wide) it does not necessarily have that meaning in context.

(i) It further follows that there is no general 'doctrine of equivalents'.

(j) On the other hand purposive construction can lead to the conclusion that a technically trivial or minor difference between an element of a claim and the corresponding element of the alleged infringement nonetheless falls within the meaning of the element when read purposively. This is not because there is a doctrine of equivalents: it is because that is the fair way to read the claim in context.

(k) Finally purposive construction leads one to eschew what Lord Diplock in *Catnic* called (at p 243):

> the kind of meticulous verbal analysis in which lawyers are too often tempted by their training to indulge.

Ranbaxy Laboratories Ltd v Warner Lambert Company[133]

[6.59] This was the first significant judgment on claim construction by an Irish court in many years. The High Court approved the principles of the House of Lords in *Kirin-Amgen*. The decision involved a declaration of non-infringement. The last Irish decision on substantive patent infringement was decided in 1981,[134] before Ireland joined the EPC when the Protocol on interpreting claims came into effect. During that period, there had also been several landmark decisions in the UK on interpreting claims. Thus, the approach taken by the court in this decision was important as it indicated what principles of interpretation the Irish courts would use. The case concerned the famous anti-cholesterol drug Lipitor. More specifically, the court was asked to declare that a particular form of the drug produced by Ranbaxy did not infringe the patent. The patent related to a class of statin compounds, each of which has four possible forms (ie stereoisomers or enantiomers). The patent explicitly excluded two of the four stereoisomers by stating that the invention is concerned only with the *trans* isomers[135] of the compounds, not the *cis* isomers.

[6.60] Ranbaxy sought a declaration that if they were to make, import or sell a formulation containing only the *R-trans* isomer, and therefore not being a mixture of the *R-trans* and *S-trans* isomers, this would not infringe the patent. Warner-Lambert contended that the claims covered both the *R-trans* and the *S-trans* isomers, whether alone or when mixed in any ratio. Both parties agreed that the reaction sequences described in the patent's examples would give rise to a racemic (equal parts) mixture of

---

[133] *Ranbaxy Laboratories Ltd v Warner Lambert Company* [2007] IEHC 256 (10 July 2007, unreported) Clarke J; for a discussion of this case, see Brophy, 'Irish "Lipitor" litigation: High Court favours broad claim construction' (2008) JIPLP 3(3), 151–152.

[134] *Wavin Pipes Ltd v Hepworth Iron Co Ltd* [1982] FSR 82.

[135] *R-trans* and *S-trans*.

the *R-trans* and *S-trans* isomers, and these reaction sequences ended with a structural formula identical to that used in claim 1. The question thus arose whether this formula and reaction sequence implied that the claims were limited to the racemic mixture or whether they extended to cover the individual isomers alone and in mixtures of differing proportions.

[6.61] Clarke J considered the general principles of construction including the fact that the Protocol to EPC art 69 was a compromise between a strict literal interpretation of the claims and the use of the claims as a mere guideline. After approving the *Catnic* decision and the *Improver* questions, he acknowledged that, since *Kirin-Amgen*, the *Improver* questions 'no longer have quite the same status'. He endorsed the decision of the House of Lords in *Kirin-Amgen* as being the correct approach to claim construction: the claims are to be construed purposively, giving them the meaning which a reasonable person skilled in the art, reading the claims in context, would think the patentee had intended. Clarke J also held that the principle from *Kirin-Amgen* that commercial contracts must be construed in a way which agrees with 'business common-sense' was of broader application than purely technological questions. If, for whatever reason, the skilled addressee would take the view that no rational patentee would have meant to confine the claims in a particular manner, then the patent ought not to be construed in that way. However, the court does not rewrite what the parties agreed but rather simply interprets the words used in a manner which makes sense. Even if there is an obvious technical error, the court may be unable to correct it as may not be possible to tell what parties would have intended. If there is no stated or obvious reason why a limitation was added, it might be because of prior art or a mistake. If the limitation is clear and there is nothing in common general knowledge that could lead to a conclusion as to why the limitation was included, it will be difficult for the patentee to avoid the limitation.

[6.62] Business efficacy is only relevant where the court is faced with a choice between competing constructions one of which makes business sense and the other not or where there is clearly a technical error in drafting and it is clear from the remainder of the contract and general context what the correct provision should be. There is no reason why an analogous principle should not apply in patents. As regards the ranking of precedents, the court held that UK decisions require most attention, followed by non-UK common law authorities unless there is a material statutory difference or established variation in jurisprudence. Where there is foreign litigation on the same matters, the principle of comity of the courts means that the court in one jurisdiction should not lightly depart from the decision in the other country. The same applies to interpretation of claims.

[6.63] Experts for both sides agreed that the skilled person would have been aware that the potency of the compounds was to be found in the *R-trans* isomer and that the *S-trans* isomer would have been known at the priority date to have little or no potency. It was held that a conclusion that only the racemic mixture was covered would also have meant that the patentee had intended not to cover the active, potent *R-trans* isomer on its own, which a skilled addressee would not have seen as being in accordance with a rational patentee's intentions. The conclusion was that the skilled addressee would favour a claim construction which allowed for an effective monopoly of the *R-trans* isomer; it was not irrational that this claim construction would also include the *S-trans* isomer. The proper claim construction was therefore held to cover both individual isomers and any mixture of them. The judge therefore refused the declaration sought because Ranbaxy's product would infringe the patent.

[6.64] Costello J in the High Court, in the case of *Wavin Pipes Ltd v Hepworth Iron Co Ltd*,[136] adopted the *Improver* questions and also, in assistance, drew attention to words quoted with approval by Kenny J in *Farbwerke Hoechst Aktiengesellschaft v Intercontinental Pharmaceutical (Eire) Ltd*[137] to the effect that a patentee who describes an invention in the body of a specification obtains no monopoly unless it is claimed in the claim. A claim is a portion of the specification which fulfils a separate and distinct function. It alone defines the monopoly and the patentee is under a statutory obligation to state in the claims clearly and distinctly what is the invention which he desires to protect.[138]

[6.65] The *Farbwerke* case[139] is an example of the doctrine of equivalents occurring where a defendant replaces an inessential integer of a claim with an obvious equivalent. It was held by the Irish High Court that the defendant's starting material which was butylamine sulphate was chemically equivalent to the plaintiff's starting material, butylamine, in the process described in the specification, since any technician who failed to get a result with butylamine might be expected to try butylamine sulphate, even though not mentioned in the patent. This decision was made under the PA 1964 and the reasoning used was more in line with the 'pith and marrow' doctrine rather than the purposive construction. It is usual in many continental European countries to include obvious equivalents within the scope of protection but this would appear to be at variance with a strict interpretation s 45(1)[140] of the PA 1992 which specifically states that the extent of protection is to be defined by the claims. However, given s 45(3) and the second paragraph of the Protocol, it is conceivable that the same result would be reached today, but as a consequence of the claims being construed to properly cover butylamine sulphate as a starting material. An example of the German approach can be found in the *Formstein* case[141] where the German Supreme Court also considered the Protocol on art 69 and concluded that the decisive factor was the scope of the invention as it was appreciated by a person skilled in the art. The question asked by the German Supreme Court was:

> whether a person skilled in the art, has managed, on the basis of the invention protected by the claims, to solve the problem solved by the invention using methods which have the same effect, ie has achieved the desired result with other means which lead to the same

---

[136] *Wavin Pipes Ltd v Hepworth Iron Co Ltd* [1982] FSR 32.

[137] *Farbwerke Hoechst Aktiengesellschaft v Intercontinental Pharmaceutical (Eire) Ltd* [1968] FSR 187.

[138] *Electric and Musical Industries Ltd v Lisson Ltd* (1938) 56 RPC 23.

[139] *Farbwerke Hoechst Aktiengesellschaft v Intercontinental Pharmaceutical (Eire) Ltd* [1968] FSR 187.

[140] As amended by the Patents (Amendment) Act 2006.

[141] *Formstein case* [1991] RPC 599.

result. Solutions which a person of normal skill in the art, on the basis of the invention described in the claims, and the aid of his specialist knowledge, can discover to have the same effect, will ordinarily be within the protection of the patent.

In the UK Patents Court, Aldous J in *Bonzel v Intervention Ltd*[142] considered the word 'near' and construed it according to the perception of the skilled person in the light of the problem which the invention set out to solve. In *Willemijn Houdstermaatschappij v Madge Networks Ltd*,[143] there was held to be no infringement because the alleged infringement was considered to be outside the wording of the claim. The wording had a material effect on the manner of operation and this would have been obvious to a skilled addressee. In *Kastner v Rizla*[144] the Court of Appeal disregarded several features explicitly set out in the claims.

[6.66] In *Union Carbide v BP*,[145] the court substituted the language of a claim from 'said two-phase mixture' to encompass a two-phase mixture similar to the referenced mixture but with a substituted component. In *Wheatley v Drillsafe*,[146] Aldous LJ held that the words 'centre-less hole cutter', if read literally, meant a hole cutter without a centre, but in the context the words could be construed to encompass a cutter having a retractable probe. However, Aldous LJ was in the minority and the majority considered that the patentees' failure to claim a broader specification was the paramount consideration. In *Société Technique de Pulverisation v Emson Europe*[147] Lord Justice Hoffman stated the principle to be as follows:

> The well known principle that patent claims are given a purposive construction does not mean that an integer[148] can be treated as struck out if it does not appear to make any difference to the inventive concept. It may have some other purpose buried in the prior art and even if this is not discernible, the patentee may have had some reason of his own for introducing it.

[6.67] The Protocol on interpretation of art 69 of the EPC does not introduce into law a doctrine of infringement by equivalent effect by use of a different mechanism. The UK courts have been particularly careful not to use the term 'equivalents' when describing non-literal infringement and the doctrine of purposive construction is not a doctrine by which the natural language can be ignored and something else substituted in its place.

[6.68] During the Diplomatic Conference of November 2000, on a proposed amendment to the EPC, the conference adopted a proposal that for the purpose of determining the extent of protection of a European patent, due account shall be taken of any element which is equivalent to an element specified in the claims, thus opening up claim interpretation to encompass equivalents. This US practice of allowing references to

---

[142] *Bonzel v Intervention Ltd* [1991] RPC 553.

[143] *Willemijn Houdstermaatschappij v Madge Networks Ltd* [1992] RPC 386.

[144] *Kastner v Rizla* [1995] RPC 585.

[145] *Union Carbide v BP* [1999] RPC 409; see also *Pharmacia v Merck* [2002] RPC 41.

[146] *Wheatley v Drillsafe* [2001] RPC 133.

[147] *Société Technique de Pulverisation v Emson Europe* [1993] RPC 513 at 522.

[148] An integer is an element.

'equivalents' in applications (the 'doctrine of equivalents') came into force in the EU with the EPC 2000. Previously, the EPO guidelines had instructed Examiners to object to any statements referring to equivalents of claim features on the grounds of lack of clarity. The EPC 2000 now states in art 2 of the Protocol on interpretation of art 69 that due account must be taken in determining the scope of protection of the patent to any element which is equivalent to an element specified in the claims. The EPO states that this is not a binding definition of equivalents and does not state how they are to be taken into account so it will need further interpretation.

[6.69] The situation prior to grant is dealt with in s 45(2)[149] of the PA 1992. It is possible to secure claims which are wider in scope than the published claims at any time before the grant. Consequently, it is provided that the extent of protection prior to grant is determined by the claims published under s 28, ie publication which occurs within 18 months of filing or of the priority date. Any amended claims should not extend the scope of matter disclosed in the application; otherwise any subsequent patent is liable to revocation.[150]

[6.70] There is, of course, a difficult decision for a patent applicant to make on whether to secure widely worded claims that will provide a broader scope of protection but will increase the likelihood of a defendant being able to successfully argue invalidity on the grounds of anticipation as forming part of the state of the art or obviousness. The courts in the UK have applied the statement of Lord Moulton in *Gillette Safety Razor v Anglo-American Trading Co*:[151]

> I am of opinion that in this case, the defendant's right to succeed can be established without an examination of the terms of the specification of the plaintiff's letters patent. I am aware that such a mode of deciding a patent case is unusual, but from the point of view of the public, it is important that this method of viewing their rights should not be overlooked. In practical life, it is often the only safeguard to the manufacturer. It is impossible for an ordinary member of the public to keep watch on all the numerous patents which are taken out and to ascertain the validity and scope of their claims, but he is entitled to feel secure if he knows that that which he is doing differs from that which has been done of old only in non-patentable variations, such as the substitution of mechanical equivalents or changes of material shape or size. The defence that 'the alleged infringement was not novel at the date of the plaintiff's letters patent' is a good defence in law and it would sometimes obviate the great length and expense of the patent cases if the defendant could and would put forth his case in this form, and thus spare himself the trouble of demonstrating on which horn of the well-known dilemma the plaintiff had impaled himself, invalidity or non-infringement.

[6.71] This has become known as the *Gillette* defence. Since this mode of deciding a patent case is unusual, it must be strictly proved.[152] If a defendant can prove that the act complained of was merely what was disclosed in a publication which could be relied on

---

[149] As amended by the Patents (Amendment) Act 2006.
[150] PA 1992, s 58(c).
[151] *Gillette Safety Razor v Anglo-American Trading Co* (1913) 30 RPC 465.
[152] *Hickman v Andrews* [1983] RPC 147.

against the validity of the patent, without any substantial or patentable variation having been made, he has a good defence.[153]

Burden of proof

[6.72] The onus of proving infringement normally lies with the plaintiff, who can be either a patentee or an exclusive licensee.[154] Evidence of infringement must be obtained and exhibited in a form admissible under the general laws of evidence. Thus, an affidavit should be secured from a person who obtains the infringing product and who can verify the source, time and manner of purchase, exhibiting receipts, invoices or delivery notes. If the product is analysed, examined or experimented with, these facts should also be evidenced. Details of storage should be given if there is even only a slight possibility that the condition of the product may be affected.

[6.73] If the invention is a process for obtaining a new product, the burden of proof can shift to a defendant. If the same product is produced, there is an assumption that such a product is made by the patented process, unless the contrary is proved.[155] The onus is on a defendant to show non-infringement. Under s 40(c) of the PA 1992, it is an infringement to offer, put on the market, use, import, or stock a product obtained directly by a process protected by a patent.

[6.74] It is not clear what is meant by the same product. It could be argued that this means an identical product but if an analogy is drawn with trade mark law, it may extend, for example, to products of the same description under the Trade Marks Act 1963. The German Federal Supreme Court has already had to tackle this issue in relation to a chemical product which was not identical but which was held to be a product of the same composition.[156]

[6.75] In circumstances where a defendant must show non-infringement, there is, in some circumstances, a danger that a defendant would be forced to disclose manufacturing or business secrets in so doing. Indeed, a plaintiff might pursue an action with this very objective in mind. Hence, s 46(2) of the PA 1992 provides an important safeguard whereby the court can, at the court's discretion, hear the defendant's evidence in the absence of any other party to the proceedings. The factors to be considered by a court in deciding whether or not to exercise its discretion in favour of the defendant are stated in s 46(3) and the court must be satisfied as to the defendant's possession of a manufacturing or commercial secret, that the secret information would enable the burden of proof to be discharged and that it would be unreasonable to require disclosure. This would appear to be an exception to the natural justice principle of *audi alteram partem* (the right to know the case which is being made against you), which is a basic principle of fair procedures.

---

[153] *Terrell on the Law of Patents* (16th edn, 2006, Sweet & Maxwell), 8-76.
[154] PA 1992, s 51.
[155] PA 1992, s 46(1).
[156] *Re Alkylenediamine II* (1977) 8 IIC 350.

[6.76] Rather than exclude a plaintiff fully, a court could presumably exercise its discretion by limiting disclosure to, for example, the plaintiff's solicitor or counsel or to selected individuals upon terms aimed at securing that there will not be either use or further disclosure of the information in ways which might prejudice a defendant.[157] In *Centri-Spray Corpn v Cera International*,[158] an order was made permitting the plaintiff's employee to inspect drawings subject to an undertaking not to make use of information disclosed therein. The plaintiff was not allowed to take away the drawings or to take copies. In *Roussel Uclaf v ICI*,[159] the defendant was faced with the dilemma of protecting clearly valuable proprietary information and, at the same time, giving the plaintiff an opportunity to inspect materials which would have a considerable bearing on its case. In the circumstances, limited disclosure was ordered to a single nominee of the plaintiff and with undertakings incorporated in an order of the court.

REMEDIES

[6.77] The remedies which are available consequent on a finding of patent infringement are specifically identified in s 47 of the PA 1992. The proceedings must be brought by the proprietor of the patent or an exclusive licensee[160] and, except in the case of an infringement of a short-term patent,[161] the action must be taken in the High Court. An exclusive licence is defined in s 2 of the PA 1992 and means:

> A licence from a proprietor of or applicant for a patent which confers on the licensee or on the licensee and persons authorised by him, to the exclusion of all other persons (including the proprietor of or applicant for the patent), any right in respect of the invention.

The use of the words 'any right' would suggest an exclusive right could arise in a situation where, for example, the licence was in respect of manufacture only and not use or a licence limited to a particular part of the country. The language would permit several exclusive licensees to be created in respect of one patent.[162]

[6.78] The distinction must be drawn between a sole licence and an exclusive licence. A sole licence means that the licensor and the licensee have the right to use the subject matter but the licensor will not grant any other licences in respect of that subject matter. Sole licence is a term which is not defined in the legislation but this meaning is well-recognised and is in common use. Under a sole licence, there is no exclusion for the patent proprietor and thus such falls outside the definition. The holder of a sole licence as opposed to an exclusive licence has no right to take an infringement action. No particular form of grant is required to constitute an exclusive licence. The position is in each case a mixed question of law and fact as to whether a licence is in fact exclusive.

---

157 *Warner-Lambert v Glaxo Laboratories Ltd* [1975] RPC 354.
158 *Centri-Spray Corpn v Cera International* [1979] FSR 175.
159 *Roussel Uclaf v ICI* [1990] RPC 45.
160 PA 1992, s 51.
161 PA 1992, s 66(4), which permits such an action to be taken in the Circuit Court, as an alternative to the usual option of a High Court action.
162 *Courtauld's Application* [1956] RPC 208.

The fact that a party is appointed an agent to manufacture without others does not amount to an exclusive licence where an ability remains to appoint further agents.[163]

[6.79] A licence can be partly written and partly oral as in the case of *Morton-Norwich Products Inc v Intercen Ltd*.[164] In an exclusive licence, the licensee, in addition to an action for breach of contract, should be in a position to recover damages for infringement by a patent proprietor. In *PCUK v Diamond Shamrock Industrial Chemicals Ltd*,[165] Falconer J held that a sole licensee was clearly not in a position to take an action for patent infringement but may nevertheless have a claim under the tort of 'interference with business'.[166]

[6.80] An exclusive licensee is entitled to avail of the reliefs for infringement even in cases where there has been non-recordal of the interest on the register. There must, however, be evidence that, at the date of the writ, an exclusive licence is in place.[167] The patentee is entitled to the full set of reliefs even where an exclusive licensee has already obtained relief of its own.[168] The patentee must be a party to any proceedings taken by a licensee but if added as a defendant, a patentee has no liability for any costs unless they enter an appearance and take part in the proceedings.[169]

Injunctions

[6.81] Section 47(1)(a) of the PA 1992 does not identify the types of injunction of which a patentee can avail but does state that it should be by way of a restraint on the defendant 'from any apprehended act of such infringement'. This seems to rule out the possibility of a mandatory as opposed to a prohibitory injunction. However, in *Smithkline Beecham plc v Genthon BV*[170] Kelly J in the High Court ruled that the normal rules for interlocutory relief apply in applications for injunctions in patent infringement cases, which means that mandatory injunctions should be available. In this case the defendant accepted that it was infringing the plaintiff's patents but asserted that the patents were invalid. Consequently, in applying the principles in *Campus Oil v Minister for Energy*,[171] the plaintiff was able to fulfil the first criteria of demonstrating a serious issue for trial. On the issue as to whether damages would be an adequate remedy, Kelly J followed the Supreme Court ruling in *Westman Holdings Ltd v McCormack*[172] that if damages are found to be an adequate remedy for the plaintiff, the court should stop its enquiry there, and refuse the injunctive relief sought, without

---

[163] *Bondax Carpets Ltd v Advance Carpet Tiles* [1993] FSR 162.
[164] *Morton-Norwich Products Inc v Intercen Ltd* [1981] FSR 337.
[165] *PCUK v Diamond Shamrock Industrial Chemicals Ltd* [1981] FSR 427.
[166] See however *Lonrho v Shell* [1981] 2 All ER 456 at 461.
[167] *Procter & Gamble v Peaudouce (UK) Ltd* [1989] FSR 180.
[168] *Optical Coating Laboratory Inc v Pilkington PE Ltd* [1993] FSR 310.
[169] PA 1992, s 51(2).
[170] *Smithkline Beecham plc v Genthon BV* [2003] IEHC 623, (28 February 2003, unreported) Kelly J.
[171] *Campus Oil v Minister for Energy* [1983] EPC 88.
[172] *Westman Holdings Ltd v McCormack* [1992] 1 IR 151; [1992] 1 EPC 151.

going on to address the issue of the balance of convenience. The onus fell on the plaintiff to show that damages would not be an adequate remedy. The plaintiff had failed to discharge this onus and the interlocutory injunction was refused. While the judiciary are keen to point out that there is no inherent hostility[173] to interlocutory injunctions in patent infringement cases the reality is that a judge is more likely to grant an early trial and view damages as an adequate remedy.

[6.82] A permanent injunction is almost invariably granted at the conclusion of a trial to a patentee who succeeds in proving infringement of a valid patent. However, as an injunction is discretionary, the court may refuse to grant a permanent injunction where the defendant satisfies the court that no further infringement is likely.[174]

[6.83] Many patent infringement issues are effectively settled by an injunction. The Irish court considered the factors to be taken into account in determining the balance of convenience in *Smithkline Beecham plc v Genthon BV.*[175] The usual *Campus Oil* principles for interlocutory injunctions apply. The court held that the adequacy of damages is a separate question to the balance of convenience[176] and that the two issues should not be conflated. The court applied *Curust Financial Services Ltd v Loewe-Lack-Werk Otto Loewe GmbH & Co KG*[177] in terms of the examination as to whether the loss was clearly and exclusively a commercial loss, in a stable and well-established market, capable of being assessed in damages in terms of the loss actually suffered and probable future loss. Difficulty, as opposed to complete impossibility, in assessing damages should not mean it is an inadequate remedy. The court also held that patent infringement damages are compensatory for loss which is the natural and direct consequence of the defendant's act and is not excluded from recovery by public or social policy. Aside from being the market leader, the plaintiff also supplied the product to a third party in Ireland for sale under a different name and there was no information on the levels of sales of those products. The court held that where a defendant commences acts in full knowledge of the complaint, limited consideration will be given to the effect of the injunction in the balance of convenience. The defendant's product had been on the market for a year and while there was little or no information on market penetration, the market for new pharmaceutical products that are used exclusively by doctors or available only on prescription takes a long time to become established. The defendant undertook to keep records of all sales of product up to trial and the court was in a position to have a trial within five months. Therefore, unless the plaintiff could point to a particular feature giving rise to irreparable loss, damages would be an adequate compensation. The plaintiff was the brand leader, with a well-settled and growing market and would have had projections on anticipated growth in market share. If the defendant as the newcomer

---

173 *Unilever v Frisa NV* [2000] FSR 708.

174 *Per* Aldous J in *Coflexip SA v Stolt Comex Seaway MS Ltd* [2001] RPC 9..

175 *Smithkline Beecham plc v Genthon BV* [2003] IEHC 623, (28 February 2003, unreported) Kelly J.

176 *Westman Holdings v McCormack* [1992] 1 IR 151; [1992] 1 EPC 151.

177 *Curust Financial Services Ltd v Loewe-Lack-Werk Otto Loewe GmbH & Co KG* [1993] 2 CMLR 808.

to the market wrongfully made inroads into the plaintiff's market share, this would be easily discernable by a fall in the plaintiff's market share and the records of the defendant. The plaintiff alleged wilful and deliberate wrongdoing in the defendant's tactics in entering the market, lack of candour in correspondence and failure to clear an obstacle, but the court held that damages should also be recoverable for this loss. It is not clear whether these damages would be exemplary (punitive) in nature as they would not seem to be compensatory. The court also rejected arguments based on public health concerns (the fact was that both products had necessary authorisation from the Irish Medicines Board under different procedures), the effect on the third party licensee (for which no information was provided), the chance that the plaintiff might have to reduce prices (there was no evidence of irreparable loss or price structure collapse) and statistically insignificant reports of adverse side effects.

[6.84] Under the Brussels Convention on the Jurisdiction and Enforcement of Judgments in Civil and Commercial Matters 1968 and its EU replacement, the Brussels I Regulation,[178] the general rule is that the defendant must be sued in his home State but there is an exemption in matters relating to torts and a defendant may be sued in the country in which the patent infringement takes place. Therefore, an Irish domiciled defendant infringing a UK patent may be sued either in the UK or in Ireland. A split in proceedings may occur if the validity of a patent is being challenged since such must take place in the courts of the country having jurisdiction over the patent.[179]

Groundless threats

[6.85] A cease and desist letter claiming infringement should not issue lightly given the provisions governing 'groundless threats' contained in s 53[180] of the PA 1992. A practitioner alleging patent infringement on behalf of a client must be particularly cautious, as s 53[181] provides that such threats, if unjustified, could result in an injunction and damages actually being awarded against a patentee. The basis of this provision was well stated by Lindley LJ in *Skinner & Co v Perry*:[182]

> The legislature desires that threats of patent actions shall not hang over a man's head; that the sword of damages ... should either not be suspended, or should fall at once.

[6.86] The right to take an action for groundless threats as originally enacted was restricted so as to exclude any action in respect of alleged infringement relating to the manufacture or the importation of the patented product or the use of the patented process. The intention of this restriction was to limit the use of unjustified threats actions to secondary infringers, namely those who merely sold an infringing product

---

[178] Council Regulation 44/2001/EC ([2001] OJ L012/1) of 22 December 2000 on jurisdiction and the recognition and enforcement of judgments in civil and commercial matters.

[179] See O'Sullivan, 'Cross-Border Jurisdiction in Patent Proceedings in Europe' (1996) 12 EIPR 657.

[180] As amended by the Patents (Amendment) Act 2006.

[181] Remedies for groundless threats.

[182] *Skinner & Co v Perry* (1893) 10 RPC 1.

without having made or imported it, or those who bought the infringing product and subsequently used it. The philosophy underlying this restriction is that while a patentee can prevent such secondary infringements if ultimately successful in court, some means should exist to restrain patentees from making unjustified threats against those who know nothing about the manufacture or importation of an allegedly infringing product. Otherwise, such threats can have a severe commercial effect on the alleged infringer as they could encourage retailers or customers not to use or sell the product for fear of an action. If a patentee correctly identified the primary infringer, but worded the letter so that it included mention of the sale of a product (as well as its manufacture/importation), the primary infringer could initiate a court action for unjustified threats merely on account of this mention of the product's sale. The Patents (Amendment) Act 2006 closed this loophole by including in the exclusions 'a threat, made to a person who made or imported a product for disposal or used a process, to bring proceedings for an infringement alleged to consist of doing anything else in relation to that product or process'. In other words, if the party against whom the threat was made is a primary infringer, they no longer have recourse to the groundless threats action, irrespective of the wording of the letter.

[6.87] While there is no statutory requirement to put an infringer on notice before commencement of proceedings seeking injunctive relief, it is certainly normal to do so. If relief by way of an interlocutory injunction is to be sought, then it is necessary for prompt action. A normal cease and desist letter would identify the patent by number, the act alleged to be an infringement and the demands issued over and above cessation, such as damages and the handing over of infringing products. In practice, seven to ten days are usually given in any notice to an infringer. Given the complexity of patent litigation and the fact that the only defence is invalidity of a patent which invariably involves in-depth study as to the 'state of the art', it is quite normal for an alleged infringer to seek a further period of time. While this can often be reasonable, a patentee must be careful of time constraints which operate when seeking interlocutory relief. A patentee cannot risk entering into lengthy correspondence on invalidity in such circumstances. Acts which continue following a cease and desist letter provide a basis for inferring a deliberate intention to infringe and the likely repetition of such acts in the future.[183]

[6.88] In *Customagic Manufacturing Co Ltd v Headquarter & General Supplies Ltd*,[184] no notice was given and although Plowman J notes this as being very unusual, he felt the circumstances of the case in which the plaintiff had made two 'trap owners' justified the immediate issuance of proceedings. Moreover, if the plaintiff has reason to believe that there is a grave danger that the infringer, if put on notice in the usual way, will destroy evidence of infringement so as to defeat the ends of justice, an *Anton Piller*[185] order, which is usually obtained *ex parte*, may be granted in appropriately serious cases.

---

[183] *Steiner Products LD v Stevens* [1957] RPC 439.
[184] *Customagic Manufacturing Co Ltd v Headquarter & General Supplies Ltd* [1968] FSR 150.
[185] *Anton Piller KG v Manufacturing Processes Ltd* [1976] RPC 719.

[6.89] It is also no defence that the threats were made in good faith.[186] However, in the case of malicious threats, the common law remedies of malicious falsehood and trade libel are also available.[187]

[6.90] Although the threat must be to take proceedings for infringement, such a threat can take many forms, given the additional words 'or otherwise' that follow the stated examples of circulars or advertisements in s 53(1) of the PA 1992.[188] The question of whether or not a statement amounts to a threat is an objective one determined by whether or not the 'language used has been such as would convey to a reasonable man that there was an intention to bring proceedings'.[189] In *Luna Advertising Co Ltd v Burnham & Co*,[190] a threat was made by a representative of the defendant calling on a customer of the plaintiff and stating that a sign outside the customer's premises was an infringement and should be removed. Although there was no reference made to solicitors or court proceedings, the discussion had no real meaning except to the person threatened that the threatening party had legal rights and intended to enforce them unless the person threatened ceased the alleged infringing act.

[6.91] In *Bristol-Myers Co v Manon Frères Ltd*,[191] a retailer was verbally informed that the patentee would proceed against the defendant manufacturer for infringement. The retailer cancelled its orders. It was held that 'the defendant, though not directly threatened, could claim to be aggrieved by that threat'. Although the threat was held to be justifiable in that instance, it would otherwise have been actionable.

A general warning to the trade is not actionable since a court must be satisfied that a warning finger is pointed against some specific manufacturer, importer or vendor.[192] In *Olin Mathiesen Chemical Corpn v Biorex Ltd*,[193] a letter was sent to the Ministry of Health with the objective of trying to ensure that sales to hospitals would be prevented. It was held that such was an actionable threat. In *Bowden Controls v Acco Cable Controls Ltd*,[194] the plaintiff took an action on the basis of a letter written by the defendant to manufacturers in the UK, drawing attention to the result of proceedings in Germany and stating that the patentee had similar patents in all major European vehicle-manufacturing countries and intended to enforce its rights. An interlocutory injunction restraining such threats was granted: 'the fact that it (the letter) is not explicit that patent proceedings will be taken is in no way conclusive as a threat can be veiled or implied just as much as it can be explicit'.

---

[186] See discussion in Roberts, 'Threats: the next generation: the impact of the recent amendments to section 70 of the Patents Act 1977' (2005) EIPR 27(9), 334–338.

[187] *Wren v Weild* (1889) LR 4 QB 730; *Halsey v Brotherhood* (1881) 19 Ch D 386; *Farr v Weatherhead & Harding* (1932) 49 RPC 267.

[188] *Speedcranes Ltd v Thomson* [1978] RPC 221.

[189] *C & P Development Co (London) Ltd v Sisabro Novelty Co Ltd* (1953) 70 RPC 277.

[190] *Luna Advertising Co Ltd v Burnham & Co* (1928) 45 RPC 258.

[191] *Bristol-Myers Co v Manon Frères Ltd* [1973] RPC 836.

[192] *Alpi Pietro v John Wright & Sons* [1972] RPC 125.

[193] *Olin Mathiesen Chemical Corpn v Biorex Ltd* [1970] RPC 157 at 196.

[194] *Bowden Controls v Acco Cable Controls Ltd* [1990] RPC 427.

[6.92] It is important to note that while the heading to the section uses the words 'groundless threats', this does not appear in the section itself, which refers instead to 'unjustifiable' in the sense that infringement of a valid claim is not ultimately established. Thus, it is a defence to an action under s 53 for the patentee to prove that the patent was both valid and infringed, ie the threats were justified.

[6.93] The reliefs are stated in s 53(2) of the PA 1992 and are a declaration that the threats are unjustified, an injunction to restrain further threats, and damages. The use of the words 'shall be entitled' does not, however, remove the discretion of a court to refuse the relief. In *Benmax v Austin Motor Co*,[195] Evershed MR refused to grant any relief whatsoever, rejecting the suggestion of any obligation on the court and stating that the words mean nothing more than that the plaintiff shall be entitled *prima facie* to relief.[196] In *Cerosa Ltd v Poseidon Industries*,[197] an interlocutory injunction was granted even though infringement proceedings had already commenced.[198] This can be contrasted with the *Symonds Cider* case[199] in which it was held that the action was exhausted once the threat had been acted upon and an infringement action commenced.

[6.94] Under s 53(4) of the PA 1992, a mere notification of the existence of a patent or patent application does not constitute a threat. However, extra caution is necessary because the whole context of the notification is taken into account. In *Reymes-Cole v Elite Hosiery Co Ltd*,[200] a letter was not considered to be a mere notification of the existence of letters patent having regard to the inclusion of the allegation of infringement by a number of firms and the statement of impending proceedings against some of them. Under the corresponding UK legislation,[201] there is a broader right to provide 'factual information' regarding the patent, but there is no mention of patent applications.

Delivery up or destruction

[6.95] The purpose of an order under the PA 1992, s 47(1)(b), which requires that a defendant deliver up or destroy an infringing product, is to protect a patentee from further dealing in the infringing article, in particular in terms of use after expiry of the patent of products made while the patent was still in existence. However, the order cannot be granted except as part of an infringement action. It cannot be granted after the expiry of the patent.[202] The purpose of the order is to make the injunction more effective. Thus, in *Merganthaler Linotype Co v Intertype Ltd*,[203] Russell J stressed the

---

[195] *Benmax v Austin Motor Co* (1953) 70 RPC 143 at 284.
[196] See *Tudor Accessories v Somers Ltd* [1960] RPC 215.
[197] *Cerosa Ltd v Poseidon Industries* [1973] RPC 882.
[198] See also *HVE Electric Ltd v Cufflin Holdings Ltd* [1964] RPC 149.
[199] *Symonds Cider and English Wine Co Ltd v Showerings (Ireland) Ltd* [1997] ETMR 238. See **Ch 32**.
[200] *Reymes-Cole v Elite Hosiery Co Ltd* [1964] RPC 255.
[201] Patents Act 1977, s 70(5) as amended.
[202] *Monsanto Co v Stauffer Chemicals* [1987] FSR 57.
[203] *Merganthaler Linotype Co v Intertype Ltd* (1926) 43 RPC 381.

ancillary nature of the relief and that it ought not to go beyond what was necessary for the protection of the plaintiff. The order can be modified where an infringing article can be rendered non-infringing by some alteration or by the removal of some part. In *Electrical & Musical Industries Ltd v Lissen Ltd*,[204] Luxmoore J refused to order up delivery of a valve which could be used in a non-infringing manner as well as in an infringing manner. In *Codex Corpn v Racal-Milgo Ltd*,[205] Whitford J highlighted the care which should be given to the exact form of any order for delivery up or destruction that may be made. It was held to be sufficient to deliver up or destroy the elements in the apparatus which caused the act of infringement. Information disclosure orders can also be sought under the European Communities (Enforcement of Intellectual Property Rights) Regulations 2006[206] against people involved in the infringement or identified by such people as being involved.

Damages or an account of profits

[6.96] A plaintiff in patent infringement proceedings may claim damages in respect of such infringement[207] or an account of profits derived by the defendant[208] but cannot be awarded both.[209]

[6.97] In assessing a claim for damages, Lord Wilberforce in *General Tire & Rubber Co v Firestone Tyre & Rubber Co Ltd*[210] stated that there were two essential principles:

> first, that the plaintiffs have the burden of proving their loss; second, that the defendants being wrongdoers, damages should be liberally assessed but that the object is to compensate the plaintiffs and not punish the defendants.

[6.98] Damages are compensatory and not punitive. The measure of damages is to be, so far as possible, that sum of money which will put the injured party in the same position as he would have been in if he had not suffered the wrong. A way of calculating damages in patent infringement proceedings is on the basis of the loss of profits by the proprietor.[211] In cases where the effect of the infringement is to divert sales from the owner of the patent to the infringer, the measure of damages will then normally be the profit which would have been realised by the owner of the patent if the sales had been made by him.[212] However, the court must be satisfied that if infringement had not

---

[204] *Electrical & Musical Industries Ltd v Lissen Ltd* (1937) 45 RPC 5.

[205] *Codex Corpn v Racal-Milgo Ltd* [1984] FSR 87.

[206] SI 360/2006.

[207] PA 1992, s 47(1)(c).

[208] PA 1992, s 47(1)(d).

[209] PA 1992, s 47(2).

[210] *General Tire & Rubber Co Ltd v Firestone Tyre & Rubber Co Ltd (No 2)* [1976] RPC 197, [1975] FSR 273.

[211] *General Tire & Rubber Co Ltd v Firestone Tyre & Rubber Co Ltd (No 2)* [1975] FSR 273 (Lord Wilberforce), as approved by the High Court in Ireland in *Retail Systems Technology Ltd v McGuire* [2007] IEHC 13, [2007] ECDR 14.

[212] *United Horse-Shoe and Nail Co v Stewart* (1888) 13 App Cas 401, 5 RPC 260.

occurred the patentee would itself have had the business of the infringing acts.[213] If it is not possible to calculate damages on a loss of profit basis, then it should be possible to be compensated on a notional royalty basis, ie the measure of damages payable will be the sum which the defendant would have paid by way of royalty if, instead of acting illegally, he had acted legally and obtained a licence in advance.[214] This is somewhat illusory, as a patentee is unlikely to willingly give a licence of an important patent to a competitor. In *Smith, Kline & French Laboratories v Doncaster Pharmaceuticals,*[215] damages were assessed on the basis of the difference between the price a parallel importer of infringing products actually paid for the products and the price he would have had to pay in order to lawfully import the products.

It appears that a claim of exemplary damages is not available to a plaintiff except in very exceptional circumstances.[216]

[6.99] When an infringing article includes patented subject matter as an integral part, all damage caused by its sale will be compensated.[217] In *British Insulated Wire Co Ltd v Dublin United Tramway Co Ltd*[218] it was held that lost profits relating to articles sold with a patented article were not recoverable. However, more recently, Jacob J in the *Gerber Garment* case[219] compensated a plaintiff by way of ancillary damages once it was established that the entire loss, which included service contracts, was forseeably caused by the infringement. The Irish courts have not yet had to decide what level of allowance should be permitted for skill, expenditure and effort on the part of the infringer, although in the UK there have been some indications that this might be considered, at least where there has been no dishonesty.[220]

[6.100] The distinction between an account of profits and damages was well explained by Windeyer J in the Australian case of *Colbeam Palmer Ltd v Stock Affiliates Pty Ltd*:[221]

> by the former the infringer is required to give up his ill-gotten gains to the party whose rights he has infringed; by the latter he is required to compensate the party wronged for the loss he has suffered. The two computations can obviously yield different results, for a plaintiff's loss is not to be measured by the defendant's gain, nor a defendant's gain by the plaintiff's loss. Either may be greater, or less, than the other.

---

[213] *Catnic Components v Hill & Smith Ltd* [1983] FSR 512 at 521.

[214] *Meters Ltd v Metropolitan Gas Meters* (1911) 28 RPC 157.

[215] *Smith, Kline & French Laboratories v Doncaster Pharmaceuticals* [1989] FSR 401.

[216] *Morton-Norwich Products Inc v United Chemicals (London) Ltd* [1981] FSR 337.

[217] *Meters Ltd v Metropolitan Gas Meters Ltd* (1911) 28 RPC 157; *United Horse-Shoe and Nail Co Ltd v Stewart* (1888) 13 App Cas 401, 5 RPC 260.

[218] *British Insulated Wire Co Ltd v Dublin United Tramway Co Ltd* (1899) 17 RPC 14; *Clement Talbot Ltd v Wilson* (1909) 26 RPC 467.

[219] *Gerber Garment Technology Inc v Lectra Systems Ltd* [1997] RPC 443; see also *Coflexip SA v Stolt Offshore Ltd* [2003] FSR 41.

[220] *WWF-World Wide Fund for Nature v World Wrestling Federation Entertainment Inc* [2006] EWHC 184 (Ch), [2006] FSR 38.

[221] *Colbeam Palmer Ltd v Stock Affiliates Pty Ltd* [1972] RPC 303 at 308; see also *Celanese International v BP Chemicals* [1999] RPC 203.

There are, of course, difficulties in computation and it should be by reasonable approximation rather than by mathematical exactness and to ensure that neither party receives what justly belongs to the other.[222] Where there are a number of defendants, a plaintiff can elect between damages and an account for each defendant.[223] In order to assist in making an election between damages or an account of profits, a complainant is entitled to the disclosure of relevant information by a defendant, such as financial records.[224] A disclosure of information order can be obtained to assist in this under the European Communities (Enforcement of Intellectual Property Rights) Regulations 2006 (SI 360/2006). An account of profits was traditionally viewed as an equitable remedy, but in *AG v Blake*,[225] the House of Lords allowed for an account of profits for breach of contract in circumstances where normal remedies were inadequate.

[6.101] Under s 56(1) of the PA 1992, damages are recoverable from the date of publication of the application but no action can be brought until the patent is granted. Section 49(2) gives the court a discretion to refuse to award damages in respect of infringements committed during any period in which the patentee is in default of payment of renewal fees.

In the case of an innocent infringer under s 49(1), the court cannot award damages or an account of profits but can still grant an injunction and an award of costs. The onus lies on a defendant to show that it was unaware of the existence of the patent. This is often referred to as innocent infringement, but this defence does not arise because an infringer is unaware that its actions amount to an infringement but rather concerns its knowledge as to whether the patent existed.

[6.102] The onus is heavy, and this is illustrated by the case of *Lancer Boss Ltd v Henley Forklift Co Ltd*[226] where it was held that the defendant should at least have appreciated the probability of patents existing and have carried out investigations in this regard.

[6.103] Graham J, in considering the concluding words corresponding to s 49(2) of the PA 1992 that marking goods with the word 'patent' or 'patented' was not of itself conclusive of knowledge unless it was accompanied by the number of the relevant patent, held that an objective test was to be applied and gave the following example:

> Circumstances might however exist in which only a few examples of the plaintiffs' patented goods, though marked with a patent number, had been made and sold at the time of the infringement in question and the defendant might not have seen any of them. If so, it might well not be right to hold that at that time there had been sufficient notification to amount to the existence of reasonable grounds for supposing that a patent existed.[227]

---

222 *My Kinda Town Ltd v Soll* [1983] RPC 15.
223 *Electric Furnace Co v Selas Corpn of America* [1987] RPC 23.
224 *Island Records Ltd v Tring International plc* [1995] 3 All ER 444.
225 *AG v Blake* [2000] 4 All ER 385; see also *Experience Hendrix LLC v PPX Enterprises Inc* [2003] EMLR 515.
226 *Lancer Boss Ltd v Henley Forklift Co Ltd* [1975] RPC 307, [1974] FSR 14.
227 *Lancer Boss Ltd v Henley Forklift Co Ltd* [1975] RPC 307, [1974] FSR 14.

[6.104] A defendant who seeks to avail himself of the protection afforded by PA 1992, s 49(1) must plead and prove complete ignorance of the existence of the patent monopoly during the period in which the wrongful acts were being committed.[228] It is quite common for a patentee to draw a defendant's attention to a patent application (while not in terms which might constitute groundless threats) and by doing so rule out the possibility for a defendant to claim 'this special defence' since it is then 'inconceivable that any court could hold that they had any reasonable ground for supposing that this patent did not exist'.[229]

Innocent infringers

[6.105] The defence of innocent infringement was successfully raised in *Lux Traffic Controls Ltd v Pike Signals Ltd*[230] and it was even conceded by the patentee that it should also apply for a reasonable time period after finding out about the patents. Because of this concession, no argument was presented as to whether from the time of notice, a reasonable time period should be given to a defendant within which to investigate the assertions made by an alleged patentee and to cease infringement. However, a court is likely to allow such a period.

Specification drafting

[6.106] Section 49(3) of the PA 1992 provides that in a situation where a patent specification has been amended, no damages will be awarded for the period prior to the date of the decision allowing the amendment, unless the court is satisfied that the specification as originally published was framed in good faith and with reasonable skill and knowledge. Similar wording also appears in s 50(2) dealing with the relief available in respect of infringement of a partially valid patent.

[6.107] The question of good faith in framing a patent specification is basically an enquiry as to whether the patentee or his agent knew something detrimental to the patent as applied for in the form in which the specification was framed. In *General Tire & Rubber v Firestone Tyre & Rubber*, Russell LJ, in the Court of Appeal, commented that if a patent agent puts forward something of which he has no knowledge, which suffers from some fatal imperfection in the patent field, 'we do not consider that when the Patent Office accepts it without demur, it can be said that it was framed, otherwise than in good faith. It is, after all, the function of a patent agent to argue in honesty for the width of the application'.[231]

[6.108] In *Ronson Products Ltd v A Lewis & Co (Westminster) Ltd*,[232] a patent agent, in drafting a specification, departed in a material respect from the intention of the applicant despite having all relevant information in his possession. It was held that the admission

---

[228] *Benmax v Austin Motor Co Ltd* (1953) 70 RPC 143.
[229] *Wilbec Plastics Ltd v Wilson Dawes Ltd* [1966] RPC 513.
[230] *Lux Traffic Controls Ltd v Pike Signals Ltd* [1993] RPC 107.
[231] *General Tire & Rubber Co Ltd v Firestone Tyre & Rubber (No 2)* [1975] RPC 203.
[232] *Ronson Products Ltd v A Lewis & Co (Westminster) Ltd* [1963] RPC 103 at 138.

by the patent agent that the specification was wrong in view of the information in his possession must establish an absence of reasonable skill and knowledge. Accordingly, the onus that was on the patentee had not been discharged. Good faith and reasonable skill and knowledge may be assumed in the patentee's favour in the absence of internal or external evidence to the contrary.[233] The requisite knowledge is the law and practice relating to patent specifications. The fact that, with hindsight and following sustained argument and evidence from experts, it can be seen how the patent might have been more clearly drafted does not demonstrate a want of reasonable skill and knowledge.[234] In *Rediffusion Simulation Ltd v Link-Miles Ltd*,[235] Aldous J accepted that a distinction must be drawn between reasonable care and reasonable skill, and that the word 'skill' concerned skill in framing the specification as opposed to care in checking for errors. It was held that a patent agent, in altering a claim, was exercising skill and that it should have been a reasonable exercise of that skill to make such consequential amendments as were necessary. Failure to do so resulted in a refusal of damages.

[6.109] The restriction in s 49(3) of the PA 1992 only relates to damages and, therefore, a plaintiff is entitled to an account of profits in respect of infringing acts without being required to prove that the specification as originally published was framed in good faith and with reasonable skill and knowledge.[236]

[6.110] Although ss 40 and 41 of the PA 1992, which cover the rights relating to direct or indirect use of the invention, do not use the word 'infringe', relief by way of a declaration of infringement and validity under s 47(1)(e) follows as a matter of course in the event of a successful claim that a third party has committed any of the unauthorised acts.

[6.111] If the validity of a patent has been contested and it is found to be wholly or partially valid, then it is normal to request that the declaration contain a certificate of contested validity under s 52(1). The effect of such a declaration is that if, in subsequent proceedings for infringement or revocation of that patent, a final order or judgment is made in favour of the party relying on the patent (which can include an exclusive licensee), that party is entitled to his costs as between solicitor and own client, 'unless the court otherwise directs'.[237] The purpose is to discourage the duplication of proceedings contesting the validity of the patent and the incurring of unnecessary costs in fighting over matters that have already been decided in a previous action.

[6.112] In *Letraset International Ltd v Mecanorma Ltd*,[238] Graham J reviewed the large number of earlier cases on this provision and concluded that there was not very much

---

[233] *Molins & Molins v Industrial Machinery Co Ltd* (1938) 55 RPC 31.
[234] *Molnlycke & Peaudouce v Proctor & Gamble* [1992] FSR 549 at 606.
[235] *Rediffusion Simulation Ltd v Link-Miles Ltd* [1993] FSR 369 at 384.
[236] *Codex Corpn v Racal-Milgo Ltd* [1983] RPC 369.
[237] PA 1992, s 52(2).
[238] *Letraset International Ltd v Mecanorma Ltd* [1975] FSR 125.

assistance to be derived from them except to the extent that they make it clear that the court has a discretion as to whether it should grant the plaintiff solicitor-and-client costs or only party-and-party costs. *Prima facie*, a plaintiff, having obtained a certificate of validity in one action, is entitled in a subsequent action to his solicitor-and-client costs, unless the defendant can persuade the court to make an order to the contrary effect. The onus is clearly on the defendant who must show that there is something in the case which ought to persuade the judge that the normal rule should not apply. When there has effectively been no contest as to the validity of a patent, then it is not usual to grant a certificate. 'In a case where the matter has not been thoroughly gone into, the jurisdiction to grant certificates of validity should be exercised with great caution.'[239] However, in suitable cases, a court may depart from this general principle. In *New Inverted Incandescent Gas Lamp Co Ltd v Globe Light Ltd*,[240] the validity of the patent was disputed but only upon a certain construction of the specification and, accordingly, a certificate was refused. In *Edison & Swan Electric Light Co v Holland*,[241] the court refused the certificate on the grounds that a certificate had been granted in a previous action, and to give one in this action would have been to throw a doubt on the sufficiency of the former certificate. A new certificate may be granted in circumstances where the validity of a patent has been contested on new grounds.[242]

[6.113] The courts considered costs in a supplementary protection certificate case in *Sankyo Co Ltd*.[243] There was a judgment by consent for revocation but the proprietor objected to the award of costs against them. The basis for the objection was that no letter was sent by the petitioner before proceedings were initiated. They argued that a course of dealings led to the expectation that the order sought would have been agreed to if the appropriate letter was written, which the court considered fanciful. The court held that it might be prudent to send a warning letter prior to instituting proceedings but it was not necessary and not fatal in respect of costs if this was not done. There was no reason to depart from the normal practice on costs, so costs were awarded to the petitioner.

[6.114] The rights and limitations on the rights conferred on the proprietor of a patent also apply to a joint proprietor and include, under s 48(2) of the PA 1992, a statutory right to sue for infringement without the consent of any other joint proprietor. The other joint proprietors must be made party to the proceedings. If the others are joined as defendants, then they shall not be liable for any costs or expenses unless they enter an appearance and take part in the proceedings.[244] The purpose of such a provision is to ensure that all joint proprietors are on notice of an infringement action on foot of a patent in which they have such joint proprietorship. The provision should be read in conjunction with s 80 which defines the rights and obligations of co-ownership.

---

[239] *Gillette Industries v Bernstein* (1941) 58 RPC 271 at 285.

[240] *New Inverted Incandescent Gas Lamp Co Ltd v Globe Light Ltd* (1906) 23 RPC 157.

[241] *Edison & Swan Electric Light Co v Holland* (1889) 6 RPC 243.

[242] *Flour Oxidising Co Ltd v J & Rule Hutchinson* (1909) 26 RPC 597.

[243] *Sankyo Co Ltd* [2005] IEHC 114, [2006] 1 ILRM 161.

[244] PA 1992, s 48(2).

[6.115] If, in proceedings for infringement of a patent, some of the claims are held to be invalid but others are held to be valid, then an injunction may still be granted.[245] The claims can be considered separately and the invalidity of only some of the claims does not invalidate the whole patent and does not prevent the granting of relief in respect of the claims which are valid.[246] An injunction can be granted without any amendment of the patent, although such an amendment may be a condition for granting such relief.[247]

[6.116] The court also has a discretion to grant relief by way of damages or costs.[248] However, the onus is on the plaintiff to prove that the specification of the patent was framed in good faith and with reasonable skill and knowledge. In *Hallen Co v Brabantia (UK) Ltd,*[249] Aldous J considered this provision and held that it imposed upon a plaintiff a duty to prove on the balance of probabilities two things: firstly, that the specification was framed in good faith, which requires a plaintiff to prove that the specification was framed honestly with a view to obtaining a monopoly to which, on the material known to him, he believed he was entitled; and secondly, that the specification was framed with reasonable skill and knowledge. The words 'skill and knowledge' are a composite phrase relating to the competence employed in framing the specification and require the specification as framed to be in the form in which a person with reasonable skill in drafting patent specifications and a knowledge of the law and practice relating thereto would produce.

[6.117] Whether terms should be imposed allowing a patent to be amended, or some limitation ordered as to the date from which damages would be reckoned, is in the court's discretion, depending on the particular facts of each case. The defendant must establish the following:

(a)   that they received reasonable advice that the patent was not infringed or was invalid;

(b)   that they acted on this advice to their detriment; and

(c)   that the advice given was based in some way upon the defect to be cured by the amendment.

[6.118] The court should also consider, in the public interest, the possibility that the defect in the patent could have caused persons not before the court to act to their detriment. If so, it may be proper to allow the amendment only subject to conditions safeguarding the position of such persons. There is no apparent duty upon a patentee to tell the Patent Office of matters that could affect prosecution of a patent application.[250] It is, however, wise to do so because it could be relevant to the court's exercise of discretion on amendment.

---

[245] PA 1992, s 50(1).
[246] *C Van Der Lely NV v Bamfords Ltd* [1964] RPC 54 at 73.
[247] PA 1992, s 50(3).
[248] PA 1992, s 50(2).
[249] *Hallen Co v Brabantia (UK) Ltd* [1990] FSR 134.
[250] *Chiron Corpn v Organon Teknika* [1994] FSR 458 at 468.

Declaration of non-infringement

[6.119] It is possible for a person to secure from the court a declaration that their use of a process or the manufacture, use or sale of a product does not amount to an infringement. A declaration can also be sought in relation to proposed activities.[251] A declaration cannot be sought in respect of a patent application, only a granted patent. It is not necessary that the patentee or any exclusive licensee has asserted infringement. The person seeking a declaration from the court must first have written to the patentee or licensee seeking a written acknowledgment corresponding to that sought in the declaration.[252] They must provide full particulars of the process or product in question,[253] and there must be a failure by the patentee or licensee to give the acknowledgment sought.[254]

[6.120] This provision may be considered as a useful tool for establishing certainty before commencing activities which might be considered infringement. There are, however, two drawbacks. Firstly, and unless the court otherwise thinks fit, the party seeking the declaration must pay the costs of all parties.[255] Secondly, the validity of a patent cannot be challenged in that action. In both regards the PA 1992 differs from s 71 of the UK Patents Act 1977 where, unlike the Irish Act, it is also possible to seek a declaration before the Controller.

Right to continue use

[6.121] Similar to the position under trade mark law, there is a recognition that rights that are acquired subsequent to a third-party usage cannot be exercised against that party's continued usage. Section 55 of the PA 1992 gives a party certain specified rights of continuance. This arises where, in Ireland before the priority date, the third party was in good faith committing acts, or making effective and serious preparations to do such acts, that would have constituted infringement if the patent had been in force. This provision is necessary given that, if such usage is in secret, it is not a ground for revocation.[256] To form part of the state of the art, the information given by the user must have been made available to at least one member of the public who was free in law and equity to use it.[257]

[6.122] What is readily apparent is that s 55(1) of the PA 1992 discriminates in favour of persons whose activities have taken place in Ireland. This restriction may consequently be questionable under the Treaty. It is unclear as to whether or not the use must correspond exactly to the pre-patent usage and, for example, whether or not some

---

[251] PA 1992, s 54.

[252] PA 1992, s 54(1)(a).

[253] PA 1992, s 54(1)(a).

[254] PA 1992, s 54(1)(b).

[255] PA 1992, s 54(2).

[256] *PLG Research Ltd v Ardon International Ltd* [1993] FSR 197; *Merrell Dow Pharmaceuticals Inc v H N Norton & Co Ltd* [1996] RPC 76.

[257] Per Bowen LJ in *Humpherson v Syer* (1887) 4 RPC 407.

minor modifications can be made and still avoid infringement. In *Helitune Ltd v Stewart Hughes Ltd*,[258] Aldous J gave the example of an infringing process and suggested that this might be allowed to continue even though the product or process may subsequently be different to some degree and 'the fact that he alters that process after the priority date does not matter'. This can be contrasted with the view given in *Lubrizol Corpn v Esso Petroleum Co Ltd*[259] that the right was to the continued use of the specific act of commerce and was 'not meant to be a charter allowing him to expand into other products and other processes'.

[6.123] Section 55(2) of the PA 1992 allows an assignment of the right of continued use or transmission on death of an individual or dissolution of a body corporate. Authorisation is also given to business partners. A prior user cannot, however, licence a third party to exercise this right of continued use.[260] Any disposal of a patented product by virtue of the right of continued use carries with it an implied licence for further dealings in that product.[261] Section 37(7)[262] also provides for protection by way of continued use in circumstances where a patent lapsed but was subsequently restored.

LIMITATIONS ON EFFECTS OF PATENTS IN FINAL TWO YEARS

[6.124] Under the PA 1992, the term of patents granted under the PA 1964 was extended automatically from 16 to 20 years. As a balancing measure, the patentee's rights were limited during the final two years of this term, ostensibly preventing infringement action from being taken against a person who was making preparations to bring a product onto the market once the patent had actually expired, although this exemption was significantly weakened in the pharmaceutical field by a caveat stating that it did not apply to acts of importation. This measure has now been repealed entirely by s 34 of the Patents (Amendment) Act 2006, and this repeal is no doubt influenced by the earlier introduction of the so-called Bolar provisions, named after the US case *Roche Products Inc v Bolar Pharmaceuticals Corp Inc*[263] which were implemented in Ireland by the European Communities (Limitation of Effect of Patent) Regulations 2006.[264] The Bolar provisions provide a comprehensive, Europe-wide regime for allowing third parties to prepare for the expiry of a pharmaceutical patent by conducting the necessary trials and studies required to obtain marketing authorisation.

---

[258] *Helitune Ltd v Stewart Hughes Ltd* [1991] FSR 171.
[259] *Lubrizol Corpn v Esso Petroleum Co Ltd* [1992] RPC 281.
[260] PA 1992, s 52(3).
[261] PA 1992, s 52(4).
[262] As amended by the Patents (Amendment) Act 2006.
[263] *Roche Products Inc v Bolar Pharmaceuticals Corp Inc* 733 Fed 2d 858 (1984).
[264] SI 50/2006.

Chapter 7

Patents Act 1992 – Revocation and Proceedings before the Controller and Courts

REVOCATION OF A PATENT

[7.01] The grounds for seeking revocation of a patent are specifically stated in s 58[1] of the Patents Act 1992 (PA 1992). Unlike the Patents Act 1964 (PA 1964), there is no requirement that the party seeking revocation be an interested person. A revocation action can be taken either before the High Court or before the Controller. However, if there are already court proceedings pending in relation to the patent, then it is not possible to take revocation proceedings before the Controller without leave of the High Court.[2] This prohibition is not restricted to instances where the party seeking revocation is also a party to the court proceedings. A factor considered by the courts in deciding whether or not to put a stay on proceedings before the court and allow a revocation action to proceed before the Controller is the expense of court proceedings.[3] In *Gen Set SpA v Mosarc Ltd*,[4] a stay was refused where it was considered that both parties could afford court proceedings and that the issue in question was considered to be simple and straightforward and unlikely to be lengthy.

[7.02] Another instance where the High Court may be called upon to determine whether or not to grant a stay is an action for infringement of a European patent where there is also opposition at the European Patent Office (EPO) seeking revocation.[5] Under art 68 of the European Patent Convention (EPC), if the opposition proceedings are successful, the patent is deemed never to have been in force and, consequently, the High Court may be reluctant to waste time in deciding on an issue of infringement knowing that an EPO decision could make it a futile exercise. In *GD Searle & Co's and Monsanto Co's Patent*[6] McCracken J in the High Court granted a stay having regard to the costs of duplication and the undesirability of conflicting decisions but expressly allowed the petitioner liberty to apply to lift the stay in the event of some material alteration in the circumstances. The reasons advanced by McCracken J have in the

---

[1] As amended by the Patents (Amendment) Act 2006.

[2] PA 1992, s 57(5).

[3] *Hawker Siddeley Dynamics Engineering Ltd v Real Time Developments Ltd* [1983] RPC 395.

[4] *Gen Set SpA v Mosarc Ltd* [1985] FSR 302.

[5] *Amersham International plc v Corning Ltd* [1987] RPC 53; *Pal Corpn v Commercial Hydraulics* [1989] RPC 703.

[6] *GD Searle & Co's and Monsanto Co's Patent* [2002] FSR 381, also reported as *Merck & Co Inc v GD Searle & Co* [2001] IEHC 41, [2001] 2 ILRM 363.

intervening years fallen somewhat out of favour with the English courts, and it is notable that the judgment in *Searle* was heavily influenced by the English jurisprudence as it then stood. In *Glaxo Group Ltd v Genentech Inc*,[7] the Court of Appeal reviewed the case law and provided eight points of guidance as to the exercise of discretion when considering an application for a stay. Mummery LJ held that 'there are no grounds justifying the application by the Patents Court of a presumption that the duplication of legal proceedings in it and in the EPO is, without more, a ground for a stay'.

[7.03] If there are already revocation proceedings before the Controller, an application cannot be made to the court without the consent of the patentee or unless the Controller certifies in writing that the question of whether the patent should be revoked is one which would more properly be determined by the High Court.[8]

[7.04] The procedure governing revocation before the Controller is set out in r 41 of the Patents Rules 1992 and includes the payment of an official fee.[9] Before seeking revocation, it is normal to give a patentee an opportunity to voluntarily surrender their patent. Failure to do so can be held against the applicant for revocation when deciding on the issue of costs.[10]

[7.05] Section 61(1) of the PA 1992 identifies the circumstances in which the validity of a patent may be put in issue. In most instances of revocation, it would be by way of a defence to infringement proceedings.

[7.06] The first three grounds of revocation, under s 58(a), (b) and (c) of the PA 1992, have corresponding provisions in arts 100 and 138 of the EPC and are as follows:

The subject matter of the patent is not patentable under the Patents Act 1992

[7.07] A literal reading might suggest that this ground was limited to inventions within s 9(2) of the PA 1992 and that, because of their nature, were not appropriate to the patent system, ie non-patentable subject matter. This view could be said to be reinforced by s 9(3) where the words 'subject matter' appear when referring to inventions classified in s 9(3)(2). However, such an interpretation would be contrary to what must have been the legislative intention, namely to mirror art 138(1)(a) of the EPC, and, therefore, include as grounds for revocation not just excluded subject matter[11] but also lack of novelty,[12] lack of inventive step[13] and inventions not susceptible of

---

[7]   *Glaxo Group Ltd v Genentech Inc* [2008] EWCA Civ 23, [2008] FSR 18.
[8]   PA 1992, s 57(6).
[9]   €125 under the Patents, Trade Marks and Designs (Fees) Rules, 2001 (SI 482/2001).
[10] Patents Rules 1992 (SI 179/1992), r 42.
[11] PA 1992, s 9(2) and (3).
[12] PA 1992, s 11 as amended by the Patents (Amendment) Act 2006.
[13] PA 1992, s 13.

industrial application[14] or contrary to public order or morality, or plant or animal varieties,[15] or methods of treatment of the human body or diagnostic methods.[16]

The specification of the patent does not disclose the invention in a manner sufficiently clear and complete for it to be carried out by a person skilled in the art

[7.08] This is usually referred to as 'insufficiency' and adopts the wording used in s 19(1)[17] of the PA 1992. Revocation is limited to insufficiency of the specification and thus, for example, the fact that the claims under s 20 are not supported by the description is not a ground for revocation. In *Genentech Inc's Patent*,[18] it was held that the revocation provisions were a complete code and it was not open to a court to revoke a patent on the grounds that the claim was not supported by the description. The court cannot revoke a patent on the basis that the patent is not sufficiently clear or concise by any standard other than that of a person skilled in the art.[19] Even under the PA 1964, objections of ambiguity and lack of definiteness in the claims could not be raised under the guise of insufficiency.[20]

[7.09] It is not necessary that the applicant disclose the best method known to him of carrying the invention into effect[21] although the applicant should take care because a failure to disclose the best method may damage a claim to priority such as in the US.

Unlawful extension of disclosure

[7.10] An amendment to a specification cannot add new matter. In *Bonzel v Intervention Ltd*,[22] Aldous J held that the decision on whether or not there was extension of disclosure must be made on a comparison of the two documents read through the eyes of a skilled addressee. The task of a court was considered to be threefold:

- (i) to ascertain through the eyes of the skilled addressee what was disclosed, both explicitly and implicitly in the application;
- (ii) to do the same in respect of the patent as granted; and
- (iii) to compare the two disclosures and decide whether subject matter relevant to the invention had been added, whether by deletion or addition. The comparison is strict in the sense that subject matter will be added unless such matter is clearly and unambiguously disclosed in the application either explicitly or implicitly.

---

[14] PA 1992, s 14.

[15] PA 1992, s 10(b).

[16] PA 1992, s 10(c) as inserted by the Patents (Amendment) Act 2006; see **Ch 3**.

[17] See para **[4.14]**.

[18] *Genentech Inc's Patent* [1989] RPC 147.

[19] *Molnlycke AB v Proctor & Gamble* [1992] FSR 549.

[20] *Dual Manufacturing & Engineering Inc's Patent* [1977] RPC 189.

[21] This is only a requirement for short-term patents under PA 1992, s 63(7)(b)(i).

[22] *Bonzel v Intervention Ltd* [1991] RPC 553.

The EPO in its guidelines for examination[23] applies a novelty test. In that test, the EPO considers the application as filed and decides whether it would render the claim, as sought to be amended, invalid because it would not be new.

[7.11] The case of *Southco Inc v Dzus Fastener Europe Ltd*[24] concerned the pre-grant broadening of a claim and referred to a decision by the EPO Technical Board of Appeal where it was held that the replacement or removal of a feature from a claim would not be considered to extend the subject matter provided the skilled person would directly and unambiguously recognise that:

(a)   the feature was not explained as essential in the disclosure;

(b)   it is not, as such, indispensable for the function of the invention in the light of the technical problem it serves to solve; and

(c)   the replacement or removal requires no real modification of other features to compensate for the change.

The protection conferred by the patent has been extended by an amendment which should not have been allowed

[7.12] As originally enacted, this fourth ground of revocation[25] referred to 'an amendment of the application or the specification of the patent' which rendered any patent that was the subject of an extending amendment subject to revocation. This original provision was in direct conflict with s 32(2) which permitted widening of the claims of a patent application prior to grant, provided that the matter did not extend beyond that disclosed in the application.[26] Thus, patentees had a potentially serious problem that the legislature did not intend. This was rectified by the Patents (Amendment) Act 2006 which altered the wording to 'an amendment which should not have been allowed'.

[7.13] This provision brought Irish law closer to the provisions of the EPC whereby only two types of amendment are considered unacceptable:[27]

(1)   An amendment which extends the content of the application, ie adds new subject matter to the disclosure of the specification. Such an amendment is unacceptable both before and after grant. This is reflected in ss 32(2), 38(3) and 58(c) of the PA 1992.

(2)   An amendment which extends the protection conferred by the patent, which in effect broadens the scope of the claims of the granted patent. This type of amendment relates to a post-grant activity and is in accordance with s 38[28] of the PA 1992. Thus, the wording of s 58(d) does not correctly reflect this circumstance and is essentially a contradiction in terms.

---

[23]   EPO guidelines, C-VI, 5.4.

[24]   *Southco Inc v Dzus Fastener Europe Ltd* [1992] RPC 299.

[25]   PA 1992, s 58(d) as amended by the Patents (Amendment) Act 2006.

[26]   *Liversidge v British Telecommunications plc* [1991] RPC 229; PA 1992, s 38(3).

[27]   EPC, art 138(1)(d).

[28]   As amended by the Patents (Amendment) Act 2006.

[7.14] The effect of the original wording of s 58(d) on Irish patents that had been amended to bring them into conformity with a corresponding European patent application to satisfy the evidence of novelty requirement was that if the claims of the European specification had been broadened during the course of prosecution, potentially the corresponding Irish patent, which had been broadened to match it, could be revoked on the basis of s 58(d). It was also suggested that every national phase Irish patent derived from a European patent application in which the claims were broadened during prosecution was also vulnerable to a revocation action under s 58(d). The amendment to this section has resolved this conflict.

The proprietor of the patent is not entitled

[7.15] The final ground of revocation under s 58(e) of the PA 1992 corresponds to art 138(3)(e) of the EPC. The entitlement is by reference to s 16(1) and resides with the inventor, their successor in title or possibly an employer.[29] This particular ground of revocation is only open to a person who the court has determined to be the entitled party.[30] In addition, it is necessary that the attempt to establish the right was started within two years of grant unless it is shown that the patentee at the time of grant or when the patent was transferred to it knew it was not entitled to the patent.[31]

ONUS OF PROOF

[7.16] The onus of proof in revocation proceedings lies on an applicant for revocation but the evidential burden may shift according to the state of evidence during the course of the proceedings. The nature of the issue may affect the type and the cogency of the evidence necessary to bring the scales down on one side or the other. If something is inherently improbable, more weighty evidence is required to establish that it probably occurred than if it were inherently probable.[32] If the application for revocation is admissible, the court or Controller must consider whether the grounds for revocation prejudice the maintenance of the patent.[33] If so, the court or Controller may revoke the patent unconditionally.[34] It is also provided that if the patent is invalid to a limited extent, then the court or Controller may allow an amendment to the specification.[35] If a European patent designating Ireland is revoked, limited or amended under the EPC, it has the same effect as if this had occurred under the provisions of PA 1992.[36]

---

[29] See para **[4.01]**.
[30] PA 1992, s 57(2).
[31] PA 1992, s 81(2).
[32] *Dunlop Holdings Ltd* [1979] RPC 523.
[33] PA 1992, s 59(1).
[34] PA 1992, s 59(2).
[35] PA 1992, s 59(3) as amended by the Patents (Amendment) Act 2006.
[36] PA 1992, s 119(4).

WHEN CAN AN AMENDMENT BE MADE?

Re Irish Patent No 1121375 & 1499278 (Akzo Nobel NV/Norton Healthcare Ltd)[37]

[7.17] Norton Healthcare Ltd (Norton) applied for revocation of these patents and Akzo Nobel NV offered to amend the patents at trial if the registered form was revoked. Norton argued that this was a waste of time and money as even if they succeeded in the revocation action, no revocation would ensue. It was held that s 38 does not include a power to allow amendment instead of revocation but the court has a discretion to allow amendments of the specification on such terms as court thinks fit. This power can be exercised at any time while the court is seised of the action.

[7.18] The court approved the *Henderson v Henderson*[38] principles, which can be summarised as:

(a)   There should be finality in litigation and a party should not be twice vexed in the same matter.

(b)   The bringing of a claim or the raising of a defence in later proceedings may, without more, amount to abuse if the court is satisfied that the claim or defence should have been raised in the earlier proceedings if it was to be raised at all.

(c)   The onus of proof is on the party alleging abuse.

The court held that post-trial amendments are prohibited[39] but it is permissible to defend an allegation of invalidity while seeking to amend if unsuccessful. A patentee should not have to accept an allegation of invalidity to be allowed to amend the patent. The application to amend should be brought in a timely manner and will then be considered on its merits, with an appropriate costs order to address any inconvenience to the petitioner. The patentee must state in advance of trial whether it will contend that the claims prior to amendment are valid so that everyone knows where they stand.[40]

[7.19] The court also commented in *obiter dicta* that the principles set out by Aldous LJ in *Smithkline and French Laboratories Ltd v Evans Medical Ltd*[41] have much to recommend them in considering an application for amendment: essentially it is a wide discretion; the onus is on the patentee to establish that the amendments should be allowed; there must be full disclosure of all relevant matters; if there is a failure to disclose, the application to amend will be refused; the amendment will be granted if it is permitted under the Act and there are no circumstances which should lead to the court refusing the amendment; if there is a delay for an unreasonable period, the amendment

---

[37]   *Re Irish Patent No 1121375 & 1499278 (Akzo Nobel NV/Norton Healthcare Ltd)* [2005] IEHC 411, [2006] 3 EPC 321, [2006] 1 ILRM 209.

[38]   *Henderson v Henderson* [1843] 3 Hare 100; the most recent authoritative statement of the rule in *Henderson v Henderson* is by the House of Lords in *Johnson v Gore Wood & Co* [2000] UKHL 65, [2002] 2 AC 1.

[39]   *Nikken Kosakusho Works v Pioneer Trading Co* [2005] EWCA Civ 906, [2006] FSR 4.

[40]   *Nikken Kosakusho Works v Pioneer Trading Co* [2005] EWCA Civ 906, [2006] FSR 4.

[41]   *Smithkline and French Laboratories Ltd v Evans Medical Ltd* [1989] FSR 561.

will be refused unless reasonable grounds can be shown; reasonable grounds include where the patentee believed it was not necessary and had reasonable grounds for that belief; the amendment will be refused if the patentee is seeking an unfair advantage; and the court is concerned with the conduct of the patentee, not the merit of the invention. However, this view is not binding as the comments were *obiter*.

APPLICATION FOR REVOCATION BY THE CONTROLLER

[7.20] It is possible for the Controller to seek revocation on his or her own initiative[42] but the basis for such is limited to inventions forming part of the state of the art, being: (a) the content of a patent application with an earlier priority, and (b) double patenting:

(a)   Section 11(3) of the PA 1992 provides that the contents of a patent application with an earlier priority, although unpublished, may still be taken into account in determining novelty. Section 60(1), which allows for revocation on this ground at the initiative of the Controller, does require the Controller to show both that the prior patent or patent application is indeed part of the state of the art and that, as a consequence, the invention is lacking in novelty.

(b)   Double patenting arises in a situation where there has been both a national patent granted by the Irish Patents Office alongside a European patent designating Ireland for the same invention granted by the EPO and that, having designated Ireland, is treated as a national patent under the PA 1992.[43] It is possible for an applicant to proceed both nationally and through the European patent route but the applicant must ultimately make an election or risk revocation. A decision can be made at the end of the period for filing opposition to the European application designating Ireland or, if any opposition is lodged, the date when such opposition proceedings are finally disposed of. To avoid double patenting, the proprietor should take action before the grant of the patent in accordance with s 36(1), ie the date upon which notice of grant appears in the Official Journal.

[7.21] To decide whether or not an Irish patent and a European patent designating Ireland have been granted for the same invention, it is necessary to look at the claims of the patents, ascertain their scope and conclude whether they are the same. The word 'same' does not require that they be indentical but requires practical similarity.[44]

[7.22] If the Controller decides on a revocation action, the proprietor of the patent must be notified and afforded a period of three months to make observations and/or amend the specification.[45]

---

[42]   PA 1992, s 60.

[43]   PA 1992, s 119(1).

[44]   *Marley Roof Tile Co Ltd's Patent* [1992] FSR 614.

[45]   Patents Rules 1992, r 43.

VALIDITY AT ISSUE

[7.23] In addition to the grounds of revocation, the circumstances in which the validity of a patent may be put in issue are also expressly set out.[46] These are as follows:

- (a)   by way of defence to infringement proceedings;
- (b)   in proceedings relating to threats of infringement;[47]
- (c)   in proceedings relating to revocation;[48] and
- (d)   disputes as to the right to use the invention by the State.[49]

Where the Controller seeks revocation on his or her own initiative, it is not permitted to put the validity of the patent in issue.[50]

[7.24] The validity of a patent cannot be determined on the grounds of non-entitlement unless the issue has been resolved in 'entitlement proceedings' on the question of whether the patent was granted to a person entitled to such.[51]

[7.25] Proceedings in which validity is an issue on the grounds of non-entitlement must be commenced within two years of grant of the patent unless the proprietor of the patent knew at the time of grant or on transfer of the patent to them, that they were not entitled to the patent.

[7.26] The Controller must be given notice of any proceedings before the court where the validity of a patent is put at issue and of the decision of the court in respect of such proceedings.[52]

COSTS

[7.27] The Controller is empowered to award such costs as he or she may consider reasonable.[53] The amounts traditionally awarded have been nominal. Where a defendant seeks to amend a defence by alleging new grounds of revocation (eg because of prior art recently coming to the attention of the defendant) the plaintiff may seek to discontinue the action and recover costs by what is termed an '*Earth Closet*' order or '*See v Scott Paine*'[54] order. The costs recoverable by the plaintiff patentee are those between the time of service of the original particulars of objection and the time of the amended particulars. It is at the discretion of the courts whether or not to allow the amended claim of invalidity but in the past this tended to be automatic and thus a

---

46   PA 1992, s 61.
47   PA 1992, s 53.
48   PA 1992, s 57.
49   PA 1992, s 77.
50   PA 1992, s 61(4).
51   PA 1992, ss 61(2), (3), 81.
52   PA 1992, s 62.
53   PA 1992, s 91.
54   *See v Scott Paine* (1933) 50 RPC 56; see also *Baird v Moule's Patent Earth Closet Co* (1881) 17 Ch D 137 at 139.

defendant who is forced to carry out lengthy and expensive searches and who may only belatedly identify relevant prior art may find they are left with a large bill of costs. The injustice of such has recently been considered in *GEC Alsthom Ltd's Patent*[55] where Laddie J identified the following factors which the court should take into account when deciding what order to make:

(a) the timetable of the proceedings;

(b) the lateness of the amendment;

(c) the extent to which the patentee has been taken by surprise by the reliance on the new prior art;

(d) the extent to which the defendant has explained the lateness of the amendment.

Whether or not the defendant has been diligent in searching as to prior art is a major factor in determining whether or not to make a *See v Scott Paine* order.

[7.28] If a party to opposition, revocation or licence proceedings before the Controller does not reside or carry on business in Ireland or elsewhere in the EU,[56] the Controller may require that party to give security for costs. The same power resides in the High Court and also embraces matters relating to an appeal from any decision of the Controller.[57] In practice, security for costs is only an issue if raised by one of the parties. Non-compliance with a requirement for security can result in the proceedings or appeal being deemed abandoned.[58]

PROCEEDINGS BEFORE THE CONTROLLER OR THE COURT[59]

[7.29] The laws of natural justice require that a person has a right to be heard (the doctrine of *audi alteram partem)* and s 90 of the PA 1992 specifically provides that in the exercise of any discretionary powers by the Controller, any party that may be adversely affected has a right to be heard.[60] There is a 10-day period for application for a hearing from notice of that right by the Controller. Evidence before the Controller is by way of statutory declaration[61] which on appeal will be accepted by the courts in lieu of affidavit evidence. Rule 71 of the Patents Rules 1992 sets out the form which the statutory declaration should take and, if executed outside Ireland, it must be made and subscribed before a consular officer, a notary public, judge or magistrate.[62] Rule 73 dispenses with the need for authentication of the seal, signature or capacity of the person taking the declaration. Although the Controller may take evidence *viva*

---

[55] *GEC Alsthom Ltd's Patent* [1996] FSR 415; see also *Josiah Wedgwood & Sons Ltd v Stained Glass Systems Ltd* (16 October 1996, unreported), HC, Jacob J.

[56] Patents Rules 1992, r 70.

[57] PA 1992, s 91(2).

[58] PA 1992, s 91(2).

[59] PA 1992, Pt VIII.

[60] PA 1992, s 90; Patents Rules 1992, r 68.

[61] PA 1992, s 92(2).

[62] Patents Rules 1992, r 72.

voce[63] (by oral evidence) in lieu of, or in addition to, evidence by way of statutory declaration, this rarely occurs in practice. The Controller also has power to summon and examine witnesses, require production of documents and permit affidavit or other sworn testimony.[64] Non-compliance is an offence[65] and witnesses are entitled to the same immunities and privileges as before a court.[66]

[7.30] Section 94 of the PA 1992 extends privilege to communications with solicitors or patent agents or a third party instructed by them in relation to any matter concerning the protection of an invention, patent, design or technical information or any matter involving passing off. Although the wording is quite broad, it is limited to 'protection' thus leaving it questionable as to privilege in relation to issues such as compulsory licence applications. It also does not extend to any copyright advice which might be given by a patent agent. The extension of privilege to patent agents was deemed necessary, given that patent agents were not recognised as legal advisers and did not come within common law privilege.[67]

[7.31] The Rules of the Superior Courts provide for the discovery of documents which are or have been in a person's possession or power and relating to the proceedings and, if privilege is claimed, the court may inspect the document to decide on the validity of the claim of privilege. The existence of confidential information is not itself the basis of a claim to privilege[68] although a court may limit inspection of such information to legal or independent advisers.[69] The grounds of privilege are self-incrimination, public policy and legal professional privilege. In relation to the latter, documents within s 94 that are privileged are communications between a patent agent and a third party and that have come into existence for the purpose of obtaining or giving advice in relation to pending or contemplated proceedings. The proceedings must actually be in contemplation. In *Rockwell International Corpn v Serck Industries Ltd,*[70] Falconer J stated:

> As I understand the matter, it requires something more than the mere seeking of advice on the part of some party from the patent agent as to whether or not a particular course of action, whether it be making a product or using a process, would or would not infringe or might infringe a patent, or how he can avoid falling within the claims of a particular patent.

[7.32] Following *Re Duncan Garfield v Fay,*[71] there is authority for the proposition that a litigant's privilege arising in proceedings in a foreign court is also an answer to a

---

[63]   PA 1992, s 91(1).
[64]   PA 1992, s 92(3) as amended by the Patents (Amendment) Act 2006.
[65]   PA 1992, s 92(6).
[66]   PA 1992, s 92(5).
[67]   *Wilden Pump Engineering Co v Fusfield* [1985] FSR 159.
[68]   *Crompton (Alfred) v Customs and Excise Comrs* [1974] AC 405.
[69]   *Roussel-Uclaf v ICI* [1990] RPC 45.
[70]   *Rockwell International Corpn v Serck Industries Ltd* [1987] RPC 89.
[71]   *Re Duncan Garfield v Fay* [1968] 2 All ER 395; see also *Minnesota Mining Co v Rennicks (UK) Ltd* [1991] FSR 97.

claim for production of the document in proceedings before the Irish courts. In *Société Française Hoechst v Allied Colloids*,[72] an analysis report was prepared at the instigation of a UK patent agent in connection with French proceedings and was prepared for the conduct of those proceedings. It was held that privilege extended to that report. In *Sonic Tape plc's Patent*,[73] the personal recipient of letters from a patent agent was an employee of the applicant. After leaving that employment, the recipient sought to make use of copies of the letter in an inventorship dispute. It was held that he had received those letters both in a personal capacity and as a representative of his employer. On this basis, the employer could claim privilege for their contents as against third parties but not as against that person. The question of privilege has also been considered by the European Court of Justice, which recognised the confidentiality of written communications between a lawyer and client, provided that such communications are made for the purposes and in the interests of the client's right of defence and they emanate from independent lawyers, ie lawyers who are not bound to the client by a relationship of employment.[74]

---

[72] *Société Française Hoechst v Allied Colloids* [1992] FSR 66.

[73] *Sonic Tape plc's Patent* [1987] RPC 251.

[74] *Australian Mining & Smelting Europe Ltd v EC Commission* Case 155/79 [1982] ECR 1575; [1982] 2 CMLR 264.

Chapter 8

Patents Act 1992: Voluntary and Compulsory Licences

LICENCES AS OF RIGHT

[8.01] The proprietor of a patent may, under the Patents Act 1992 (PA 1992), at any time after the grant of the patent, apply to the Controller to indicate that licences as of right are available in respect of the patent.[1] This is a voluntary action by the proprietor. The advantages in taking this course of action are not just that it may attract potential licensees by virtue of publication of the licence as of right but also renewal fees are only one half of those normally payable.[2] On an application for a licence as of right, patentees must satisfy the Controller that they are not precluded by contract from granting licences under the patent.[3] Although it is stated that this must be verified by evidence,[4] there is no indication as to the form of the evidence required in this regard. In practice a simple statement by patentees that they are not so precluded will suffice. The Controller must direct the applicant to serve a copy of the application on any person entered on the Register as having an interest in the patent.[5] This would clearly include another licensee or a mortgagee.

[8.02] The effect of a licence of right entry is that any person may obtain a licence on terms to be agreed between the parties, or in default of agreement, on terms to be settled by the Controller.[6] An application in this regard cannot be made until the licence of right is entered on the Register. A licence granted by the Controller takes effect from the date on which terms are settled by the Controller.[7] Terms are settled when the Controller gives his final decision. The applicant can accept those terms and operate the licence without prejudice to any appeal. If an appeal by the applicant seeking more favourable terms succeeds, the effect is that the terms previously settled are varied in the applicant's favour.[8] If the royalty is increased on appeal, it will be backdated to the date of the original grant by the Controller by requiring a further royalty payment in respect of the increase.[9]

---

1. PA 1992, s 68(1).
2. PA 1992, s 68(2)(d).
3. PA 1992, s 68(4).
4. Patents Rules 1992 (SI 179/1992), r 46.
5. PA 1992, s 73(2).
6. PA 1992, s 68(2)(a).
7. *Allen & Hanburys Ltd v Generics (UK) Ltd* [1986] RPC 203.
8. *Allen & Hanburys (Salbutamol) Patent* [1987] RPC 327.
9. *Smith Kline & French (Cimetidine) Patents* [1990] RPC 203.

[8.03] An applicant may apply for a licence of right and still attack the validity of the patent in a defence to infringement proceedings. This does not constitute an admission of liability.[10] An infringer of a licence of right patent may undertake to accept a licence to be settled by the Controller. If this is done, no injunction will be granted and damages will be limited to double what the royalties would have been if the licence had been granted before the earliest infringement.[11]

[8.04] The procedure for application to the Controller for settlement of the terms of a licence of right is governed by r 47 of the Patents Rules 1992 and application may be made by the patentee, an existing licensee or a person requiring a licence. The application should be accompanied by a statement setting out the terms of the licence that the applicant is prepared to accept or grant, as the case may be.

[8.05] As stated by Lord Diplock in *Allen & Hanburys Ltd v Generics (UK) Ltd*:[12]

(a)   the Controller's 'discretion to impose limitations and conditions upon what the licence of right authorises the licensee to do is a wide one';

(b)   this discretion is not restricted to the amount of royalties and security for their payment. Terms that are settled by the Controller cannot, however, impose upon the licensee any positive obligation to do any of the acts so licensed, although such a positive obligation could be imposed by a contract relating to a licence of right granted by agreement between the patentee and licensee;

(c)   the Controller cannot settle terms to be incorporated in any one licence of right which would have the effect of debarring future applicants from applying for a similar licence.

These points have not been considered in Ireland, as an appropriate case has not yet come up for decision.

[8.06] In the UK, it was the practice, upon request, to include a prohibition on importation of the patented product, if the patentee itself manufactured that product within the UK.[13] However, the Court of Justice of the European Union (ECJ) has ruled that it is contrary to arts 34 and 36[14] of the Treaty on the Functioning of the European Union (the Treaty)[15] to discriminate between manufacturers in the UK and others in the EU. After this, terms were varied so as to limit import prohibitions only from outside the EU. In the UK, there has been an amendment to the provision corresponding to s 68(2)(c) of the PA 1992 that specifically states that if an infringer undertakes to take a licence on settled terms, an injunction can now only be granted in respect of importation 'otherwise than from another Member State of the EEC'. This amendment did not appear in the PA 1992 but an equivalent

---

[10] *EI Du Pont De Nemours & Co (Blades) Patent* [1988] RPC 479.

[11] PA 1992, s 68(2)(c) as amended by the Patents (Amendment) Act 2006.

[12] *Allen & Hanburys Ltd v Generics (UK) Ltd* [1986] RPC 203.

[13] *Ciba-Geigy's (FMC's Application)* [1986] RPC 403.

[14] Formerly EC Treaty, arts 28 and 30.

[15] [2010] OJ C83 of 30 March 2010.

amendment has now been included in this provision by the Patents (Amendment) Act 2006, which is in fact broader, as it limits the operation of that section to imports which are not from a country which is member of the World Trade Organisation (WTO).

[8.07] The ECJ has also held that it is contrary to EU law to prohibit a licensee from importing the patented product from a non-EU country where the patentee manufactures the product in the Member State concerned and to allow a licensee to import the patented product where the patentee works the patent by importing the product from another Member State.[16] This is because this would operate as an incentive for patentees to manufacture the product in the Member State concerned rather than in other Member States.

[8.08] In the UK, the Comptroller has refused certain contractual provisions in settling the terms of licences. These include a restriction preventing 'passing off'[17] and a requirement that the licensee should not indicate that the product has been licensed or approved by the patentee.[18] Provisions against assignment, sub-licensing or for termination in the event of a take-over of the licensee have been allowed in the UK.[19]

[8.09] There is no guidance in the PA 1992 as to how the Controller is to settle the financial terms of any licence, unlike in the UK where it is stated 'that the inventor or any other person beneficially entitled to a patent shall receive reasonable remuneration having regard to the nature of the invention'. Presumably, a similar general principle would be adopted by the Controller and the Irish courts. However, in this regard, s 42(2) of the Patents Act 1964 (PA 1964) relating to compulsory licences for food and medicines stated the need for patentees to derive a reasonable advantage from their patent right. The question is essentially a consideration of what a willing licensor and a willing licensee would have agreed upon as a reasonable royalty to be paid for the rights granted under the licence as of right.[20]

[8.10] In *JR Geigy's Patent*,[21] which was a compulsory licence case, it was held that the royalty fee payable should take into account three factors, namely: (1) recovery for research and development costs; (2) recoupment of promotional costs; and (3) an appropriate reward element. A further approach in calculating an appropriate royalty and one which is finding more favour is what is termed the 'comparables' approach. This involves simply looking at comparable licences where they exist on the basis that 'there is no better guide to what a willing licensor and a willing licensee would agree than what other licensors and licensees have in fact agreed in comparable cases'.[22] Less used is a 'profits available' approach. This asks the question

---

16 *Generics (UK) Ltd v Smith Kline & French Laboratories* [1993] FSR 592.
17 *Syntex Corpn's Patent* [1986] RPC 585.
18 *Hilti AG's Patent* [1988] RPC 51.
19 *Allen & Hanburys (Salbutamol) Patent* [1987] RPC 327.
20 *Allen & Hanburys (Salbutamol) Patent* [1987] RPC 327.
21 *JR Geigy's Patent* [1964] RPC 391.
22 *Smith Kline & French Laboratories (Cimetidine) Patents* [1990] RPC 203.

as to the likely profits to be earned by the licensee and then seeks to agree a division between the licensor and licensee, which is, of course, problematic in itself. The different approaches can lead to quite a divergence in the royalty rates.[23] It is, however, accepted that there are 'going rates' in specific industries.[24]

[8.11] An existing licensee under a patent may, subsequent to an entry of a licence of right, apply to the Controller to exchange the licence for a licence of right upon the settled terms.[25]

[8.12] A licensee under a licence of right, unless an agreed express contractual provision provides otherwise, may issue proceedings for infringement.[26] However, the licensee must first request the patentee to take the proceedings and the patentee must fail to do so within two months of the request. The patentee must be made a defendant but is not liable for costs unless he enters an appearance and takes part in the proceedings.[27]

[8.13] It is possible to cancel a licence of right entry.[28] The patentee must pay the balance of all renewal fees which would otherwise have been payable and the Controller must be satisfied that there are no existing licences or if there are, then there must be a consent to cancellation from the licensees.[29] Also, an interested party may seek cancellation of the licence of right on the grounds that the patentee was precluded by contract from granting licences under the patent.[30] In this regard, there is a time period of three months from the making of the relevant entry to apply for cancellation.[31] Any person may also oppose cancellation within three months from advertisement of the cancellation in the Official Journal.[32]

COMPULSORY LICENCES

[8.14] Unlike s 39(1) of the PA 1964, the PA 1992 does not use the words 'abuse of monopoly rights' in referring to the grounds under which a person may compel the granting of a licence. However, apart from the special provisions relating to foods and medicines in s 42 of the PA 1964,[33] there has been substantial re-enactment of the compulsory licence provisions.[34]

---

[23] *American Cyanamid Co's (Fenbufen) Patent* [1990] RPC 309.
[24] *Shiley Inc's Patent* [1988] RPC 97.
[25] PA 1992, s 68(2)(b).
[26] PA 1992, s 68(3).
[27] PA 1992, s 68(3).
[28] PA 1992, s 69.
[29] PA 1992, s 69(1).
[30] PA 1992, s 69(2).
[31] Patents Rules 1992, r 48(2).
[32] Patents Rules 1992, r 49(1).
[33] See *McDermott Laboratories Ltd v The Controller of Patents, Designs and Trade Marks* [1998] 2 EPC 276 for a discussion on when such an application can be filed.
[34] PA 1992, s 70(1) as amended by the Patents (Amendment) Act 2006.

[8.15] These provisions have been extensively amended by the Patents (Amendment) Act 2006. The main changes are as follows. Previously, a compulsory licence was available on the grounds that the demand for the invention was being met primarily through importation. Now, as long as the patentee is meeting demand for the invention either by manufacture in Ireland or by importation from a WTO country, no compulsory licence can be granted. Previously, compulsory licences could be sought on the grounds that an export market was not being satisfied by the patentee. As a result of TRIPS, such licences can no longer be granted, since compulsory licences are only available in any WTO country to satisfy a demand in that country itself. Previously, special public interest considerations had to be taken into account in setting a royalty rate where a compulsory licence was granted for a food or medicine. Because of the TRIPS requirement of equal treatment for all fields of technology, that provision no longer applies. Before applying for a compulsory licence, the patentee must now be approached seeking a licence on reasonable terms. Compulsory licences can now be assigned along with the goodwill of the business to which the licence relates.

[8.16] There is no positive requirement on a patentee to work the patent and indeed, he may not be able to do so through lack of resources or for some other reason. However, the compulsory licence provisions are an attempt to ensure that there should be the fullest practical use of the patented invention and that patent rights should be exercised without prejudice to the development of industry. Examples of prejudice often quoted but rarely substantiated are situations in which a party would either secure a patent or acquire a patent with a view to hindering a new product and thus maintaining the market for an existing conventional product. However, the compulsory licence provisions also apply in other situations such as where demand for a product is not being met on reasonable terms. Article 31 of TRIPS allows States to provide for use of the subject matter of a patent without the authorisation of the right holder but under certain conditions and with certain safeguards which include that 'such use may only be permitted if, prior to such use, the proposed user has made efforts to obtain authorisation from the right holder on reasonable commercial terms and conditions and that such efforts have not been successful within a reasonable period of time'. There is an exception in the case of a national emergency, other circumstances of extreme urgency or in cases of public non-commercial use.[35]

GROUNDS FOR A COMPULSORY LICENCE

[8.17] A compulsory licence cannot be applied for until after three years from the date of publication of grant of the patent, after which any person may apply for a licence under the patent and/or for an entry to be made on the Register to the effect that licences are available as of right. The grounds on which an application can be made are identified in s 70(2)[36] of the PA 1992 and the procedure is set out in rr 50–52 of the Patents Rules 1992. The grounds are as follows:

---

[35] PA 1992, s 73(1A) as inserted by the Patents (Amendment) Act 2006.
[36] As amended by the Patents (Amendment) Act 2006.

INSUFFICIENT DOMESTIC WORKING

[8.18] This requires that the patented invention, although being capable of being commercially worked in Ireland, is not being so worked or worked to the fullest extent that is reasonably practicable.[37] There is a definition of 'commercially worked' as the manufacture of the product or the carrying on of the process in or by means of a definite and substantial establishment or organisation, and on a scale which is adequate and reasonable in all the circumstances.[38] In *Hunter v Fox*,[39] Kenny J found, under the provisions of the Industrial and Commercial Property (Protection) Act 1927, that although the invention was not being worked on a commercial scale, a satisfactory reason for this had been given, namely that the manufacture of the patented sealing head in this country would have been grossly uneconomic. However, the PA 1992 does not provide for a defence by way of a satisfactory reason for non-working.

[8.19] In *Kamborian's Patent*,[40] consideration was given to what is meant by the expression 'fullest extent that is reasonably practicable' and it was considered to be the highest rate of production which is practicable and necessary substantially to meet the demand. The onus falls upon an applicant and it is therefore necessary to bring evidence to show what the demand for the invention might reasonably be expected to be and how far short production under the patent fails, as far as is practicable, to supply the demand.

[8.20] The working required is in relation to 'the subject of the patent'. If, for example, the patent claims a new improvement in a well-known machine, the patentee must manufacture the improvement and not necessarily the whole machine. However, if the patent claims the improvement in combination with a machine consisting of well-known parts, it may be that the patentee must, besides manufacturing the improvement, put together the whole machine in Ireland, or at any rate the combination claimed.[41] In *Smith Kline & French Laboratoires Ltd (Cimetidine) Patents*,[42] there was importation from Ireland into the UK of raw cimetidine, an important and highly successful drug used in the treatment of duodenal and gastric ulcers. The drug was then formulated in the UK. It was held that since the patent contained both product and process claims, commercial working was not met by the manufacture of the basic ingredient in a foreign country. However, it has now been made clear by the ECJ that it is contrary to art 34[43] of the Treaty to provide for the grant of a compulsory licence where the product is imported from an EU country rather than being manufactured domestically.[44]

---

[37] PA 1992, s 70(2)(a) as amended by the Patents (Amendment) Act 2006.

[38] PA 1992, s 2.

[39] *Hunter v Fox* [1965] RPC 416.

[40] *Kamborian's Patent* [1961] RPC 403.

[41] *Lake's Patent* (1909) 26 RPC 443.

[42] *Smith Kline & French Laboratoires Ltd (Cimetidine) Patents* [1990] RPC 203.

[43] Formerly EC Treaty, art 28.

[44] *EC Commission v United Kingdom* [1993] FSR 1. See also PA 1992, s 75(3).

Essentially, this means that references in s 70[45] of the PA 1992 to 'the State' should be deemed to be a reference to a Member State of the EU.

[8.21] The consideration of the adequacy of manufacture in Ireland does, no doubt, depend to some extent upon the local demand existing for the article. However, it does not follow that if there is no demand existing, there is a defence to an application for a compulsory licence.[46] Also the fact that there has at some stage been commercial working is not a defence, if this has ceased.[47]

Failure to meet demand or on reasonable terms or doing so by importation other than from a member of the WTO[48]

[8.22] Demand means public demand and not that of an individual person or company.[49] It must also be an actual demand and not merely one which the applicant for a licence hopes and expects to create if and when the licence is obtained.[50] Demand on reasonable terms is that which exists under the prevailing conditions, so that it is irrelevant that price cutting by a licensee might increase the existing demand. As stated by Hoffmann J in *Research Corpn's (Carboplatin) Patent*,[51] when considering corresponding UK provisions:

> demand not being met on reasonable terms, recognises that demand, unless wholly inelastic, must mean demand at a given price. If the price being charged by the patentee or the licensee is reasonable and the demand at that price is being fully met, it seems to me irrelevant to say (as one almost invariably could) that the demand would be greater at a lower price. The question is whether in all the circumstances the patentee is charging a reasonable price.

The circumstances would include the right to recoup research costs, fund further research in the public interest and make a profit from their monopoly.

[8.23] The original provisions of the PA 1992 also included a ground of 'refusal to grant a licence on reasonable terms'.[52] The Patents (Amendment) Act 2006 removed this as a separate ground, although the case law relating to this former ground may still be relevant where there is a failure to meet the demand on reasonable terms.

[8.24] The Supreme Court in *Hunter v Fox*[53] held that there was no abuse under the corresponding provision of the Industrial and Commercial Property (Protection) Act 1927 and that even though there was a void restrictive clause in an agreement, it did not

---

[45] As amended by the Patents (Amendment) Act 2006.
[46] *Boult's Patent* (1909) 26 RPC 383.
[47] *Gebhardt's Patent* [1992] RPC 1.
[48] PA 1992, s 70(1)(b) as amended by the Patents (Amendment) Act 2006.
[49] *Robin Electric Lamp Co Ltd* (1915) 32 RPC 202.
[50] *Cathro's Application* (1934) 51 RPC 75 and 475.
[51] *Research Corpn's (Carboplatin) Patent* [1990] RPC 663 at 695–696.
[52] PA 1992, s 70(2)(d) (now repealed).
[53] *Hunter v Fox* [1965] RPC 416.

result in demand not being met on reasonable terms. Such a restrictive clause would now fall foul of s 83 of the PA 1992.

By analogy with the 'refusal to grant licence on reasonable terms' cases, this failure must result in:

(a) an export market not being supplied;

(b) the working of another substantial invention being prevented or hindered; or

(c) the establishment of commercial or industrial activities in Ireland being unfairly prejudiced.

Similar provisions were also found in s 39(2)(d) of the PA 1964 and, therefore, older cases decided under the corresponding section of the UK Patents Act 1949 are still pertinent. A consideration of what is meant by reasonable terms involves a review 'of all the surrounding circumstances including the nature of the invention, the terms of existing licences, if any, the expenditure and liabilities of the patentee in respect of the patent, the requirements of the purchasing public and so on'.[54] Insistence that a licensee take out a licence in respect of a group of patents rather than just the particular patent might be reasonable in a given set of circumstances.

[8.25] Again, the effect of EU law is that importation from a Member State of the EU should be regarded as equivalent to manufacture in Ireland.[55] National law that equates a case where a demand for a patented product is satisfied on the domestic market by imports from other Member States (rather than by domestic production) to insufficient exploitation of the patent justifying imposition of a compulsory licence infringes art 34[56] of the Treaty. Similarly, TRIPS imposes similar obligations as regards member states of the WTO, which include all EU Member States. Thus, the scope of this section was broadened by the Patents (Amendment) Act 2006 to importation other than from other WTO countries.

Unfair prejudice to the establishment or development of commercial or industrial activities in the State[57]

[8.26] The PA 1992 originally included a similar ground, namely that commercial working in Ireland of the invention that is the subject of the patent is being prevented or hindered by the importation of a product that is protected by the patent. This differed from the corresponding UK section, which also includes importation of the product of a process protected under the patent. This provision was likely to have been regarded as contrary to EU law as it could operate as a measure equivalent to a quantitative restriction on imports from other EU Member States under art 34 of the Treaty.[58] Rather than widening this to allow imports from other EU Member States or WTO Member

---

[54] *Brownie Wireless Co Ltd's Application* (1929) 46 RPC 457.

[55] *EC Commission v United Kingdom* [1993] FSR 1. See also PA 1992, s 75(3) as amended by the Patents (Amendment) Act 2006.

[56] Formerly EC Treaty, art 28.

[57] PA 1992, s 70(1)(b).

[58] Formerly EC Treaty, art 28.

States in compliance with TRIPS, the Patents (Amendment) Act 2006 amended the wording to remove references to importation but retained the substance of the protection for Irish businesses. It must be assumed that this would be interpreted in accordance with the Treaty so as not to create a distinction between national manufacture and imports from other EU Member States.

[8.27] This provision is similar to part of the original s 70(2)(d) of the PA 1992 (refusal to grant licence on reasonable grounds). Therefore, some guidance may be found in the old case law on the point. In the UK case of *Penn Engineering and Manufacturing Corpn's Patent,*[59] Graham J allowed export of the patented article by the licensee under the terms of a compulsory licence. In this case, there had been no manufacture in the UK and accordingly, in the further absence of patents in export countries where there was likely to be a market, there was no justification to restrict export since that would prevent working to the fullest extent that was reasonably practicable. It was considered to be incumbent upon the patentee to ask for and justify an export restriction if he wished it to be inserted in a compulsory licence. The Controller, in a decision on 3 July 1995,[60] did not order the inclusion of provisions in a compulsory licence that would allow for export, but this was conceded without argument by the applicant for the licence.

[8.28] The phrase 'development of commercial or industrial activities' in s 70(2)(d)(iii) of the PA 1992 (now repealed) includes an increase in the size of a business.[61] In *Monsanto's CCP Patent,*[62] it was held that the onus was on an applicant for a compulsory licence to show that the licence offered by the patentee was not on reasonable terms. The mere allegation of advantages in a patent was not in itself conclusive evidence that commercial or industrial activity was being unfairly prejudiced.

Provisions removed by the Patents (Amendment) Act 2006

Unfairly prejudiced due to unreasonable conditions

[8.29] The PA 1992 also included a separate ground (now repealed) of unfair prejudice due to unreasonable conditions, where, as a result of conditions imposed by the proprietor on the grant of licences under the patent, or upon the purchase, hire or use of the product or process that is the subject of the patent, the manufacture, use or sale of materials not protected by the patent or the establishment or development of commercial or industrial activities in Ireland is unfairly prejudiced.[63] In *Monsanto's CCP Patent,*[64] the applicant for a compulsory licence wished to use a solvent. Although this was held to be a material not covered by the patent, it was proposed to import the solvent from France and it was accordingly held that the manufacture of the

---

[59] *Penn Engineering and Manufacturing Corpn's Patent* [1973] RPC 233.
[60] *Clonmel Healthcare Ltd* (3 July 1995, unreported).
[61] *Kamborian's Patent* [1961] RPC 403.
[62] *Monsanto's CCP Patent* [1990] FSR 93.
[63] PA 1992, s 70(2)(e).
[64] *Monsanto's CPP Patent* [1990] FSR 93.

solvent in the UK was not prejudiced unfairly or otherwise. The applicant had also failed to discharge the onus in the pleadings, which asserted that the royalty offered was unreasonable.

Null and void contractual provision[65]

[8.30] Under s 83 of the PA 1992, certain contractual provisions were unlawful and could be declared null and void. If such a provision related to the sale or lease of, or licence to use or work, any patented product or process, then it was grounds for a compulsory licence. This has not been retained after the amendments of the Patents (Amendment) Act 2006. It may be the case that the provisions read together would make it superfluous.

[8.31] Provisions corresponding to s 83 were considered in *Hunter v Fox*,[66] where the Supreme Court held that a consequence of finding such an unlawful clause resulted in the restriction being null and void *ab initio* and consequently should be treated as ineffective and indeed non-existent, which means that there could not be an abuse of monopoly rights. This, therefore, begs the question of whether or not this particular ground could ever be successfully argued.

Contribution to the art

[8.32] Under s 70(2)(d)(ii) of the PA 1992 (now repealed), where a patented invention making a substantial contribution to the art could not itself be exploited, the Controller would call for the applicant seeking a compulsory licence to cross-licence his own patent on reasonable terms.[67]

Specific provisions for food and medicine

[8.33] Section 70(3)(f) of the PA 1992 (now repealed) was a special provision dealing with patents relating to food or medicine. Under s 42 of the PA 1964, a patent in respect of a substance capable of being used as a food or medicine or in the production of food or medicine was vulnerable to a compulsory licence being granted. Somewhat surprisingly, this provision was not exploited until it was due to be repealed by the PA 1992. Under the transitional provisions of the PA 1992,[68] an application commenced under s 42 was dealt with under the PA 1964. The Controller, in *Clonmel Healthcare Ltd*,[69] did not find s 42 of the PA 1964 to be incompatible with Ireland's obligations under EU law and declined to refer the matter to the ECJ for a preliminary ruling under art 177 of TRIPS. Although a patent relating to food or medicine is no longer *per se* subject to a compulsory licence, it is a factor in determining the terms of a licence. The statutory obligation of the Controller in this regard is to endeavour to secure that food and medicine are available to the public at the lowest prices consistent with the proprietor of a patent deriving reasonable remuneration having regard to the nature of

---

65 PA 1992, s 70(2)(f) (now repealed).
66 *Hunter v Fox* [1965] RPC 416.
67 PA 1992, s 70(3)(c).
68 PA 1992, Sch 1, para 13.
69 *Clonmel Healthcare Ltd* (3 July 1995, unreported).

the invention. In the *Clonmel Healthcare* decision, the Controller accepted the principles laid down in *JR Geigy SA's Patent*,[70] which set out the following elements which the royalty should contain:

(a)   an element to take account of the patentee's expenditure on basic research and development;

(b)   an element to take account of the benefit which the licensee will derive from the promotion of the pharmaceutical product by the patentee; and

(c)   an element of profit to provide the patentee with an appropriate return on capital investment involved in basic research and development and in promotion.

Plant Varieties

[8.34] Directive 98/44/EC on the legal protection of biotechnological inventions[71] provides for compulsory licences and cross-licences between the proprietor of a patent and the holder of a plant variety right where one cannot be exploited without infringement of the other. In accordance with art 31(1) of TRIPS, art 12.3 of the Directive requires the applicant for the licence to show that he has applied unsuccessfully to the holder of the patent for a contractual licence and that the plant variety right constitutes a significant technical progress of considerable economic interest compared with the invention claimed in the patent.

TERMS OF A COMPULSORY LICENCE OR LICENCE AS OF RIGHT

[8.35] In making a determination on the terms of a licence, the Controller and ultimately the courts are given some guidelines by way of factors which should be taken into account.[72] There are also certain terms which may or must be included in the licence, dependant on the grounds for the compulsory licence.

[8.36] If the application for a licence is based on inadequate or non-commercial working in the State, the Controller may in fact adjourn the application if the time period to enable working has been insufficient.[73] In *Fette's Patent*,[74] there was a time period of six and a half years during which demand was met by importation. It was only when the application for a licence had begun that the patentee decided to commence local manufacture. It was held that the time period was a substantial proportion of the total life of the patent and that there was no defence to the licence application.

[8.37] The original s 70(3)(c) of the PA 1992[75] dealt with an application where a licence is required to permit the exploitation of a patent (the second patent) which

---

70   *JR Geigy SA's Patent* [1964] RPC 391.
71   [1998] OJ L213/13; SI 247/2000.
72   PA 1992, s 70(4) as amended by the Patents (Amendment) Act 2006.
73   PA 1992, s 70(3)(a).
74   *Fette's Patent* [1961] RPC 396.
75   Now repealed by the Patents (Amendment) Act 2006.

cannot be exploited without infringing another patent.[76] This was in conflict with art 31(L) of TRIPS whereby:

(i) the invention claimed in the second patent shall involve an important technical advance of considerable economic importance in relation to the invention claimed in the first patent;

(ii) the owner of the first patent shall be entitled to a cross-licence on reasonable terms to use the invention claimed in the second patent; and

(iii) the use authorised in respect of the first patent shall be non-assignable except with the assignment of the second patent.

The Patents (Amendment) Act 2006 introduced a new s 70(2) of the PA 1992 which mirrors these terms of TRIPS. It remains to be seen how these principles will be interpreted,

[8.38] Any licence granted under the compulsory licence provisions must be non-exclusive and may only be assigned with the prior authorisation of the Controller and with that part of the enterprise or goodwill which uses the patented invention.[77] Since a compulsory licence is predominantly granted to cater for the domestic market,[78] the Controller can, in the terms of a licence, preclude importation[79] but must, of course, take cognisance of EU law,[80] which would not allow a restriction on imports from another EU Member State, and TRIPS, which would impose the same obligation regarding Member States of the WTO.

[8.39] Reasonable remuneration was, in the view of the Controller, to be determined independently of what the licensee offers or could afford. It was an objective criterion. After hearing expert evidence on the issue, the Controller decided that a 40 per cent royalty figure was appropriate. He then went on to determine the basis of calculation of this figure. The applicant in *Clonmel Healthcare Ltd*[81] had proposed that the royalty be a percentage of the patentee's (Glaxo) selling price to wholesalers in Ireland. Glaxo sought a royalty of a fixed, inflation-adjusted sum *per* unit sold or supplied by Clonmel, calculated as a percentage of the Glaxo price to wholesalers at the date of the licence, but thereafter being independent of variations in Glaxo's price. The Controller accepted Glaxo's approach as having the merit of avoiding any possible disputes, at a later stage, between the parties as to net wholesale prices.[82]

[8.40] Glaxo had also argued that a licence, if granted, should prevent Clonmel from referring to the patentees, the patents or the licence, in their promotional activities. In response, it was stated:

---

[76] PA 1992, s 70(2)(d)(ii) (now repealed).

[77] PA 1992, s 70(3).

[78] TRIPS, art 31(8).

[79] PA 1992, s 70(3)(e).

[80] PA 1992, s 75(3).

[81] *Clonmel Healthcare Ltd* (3 July 1995, unreported).

[82] See also *Allen & Hanburys (Salbutamol) Patent* [1987] RPC 327.

It seems to me that in the course of trade, Clonmel may need to indicate how they are in a position to market a product which is protected by a patent without infringing the patent. For this purpose, it seems to me inevitable that reference must be made to the licence which results from these proceedings and thus to the patents in question. Clonmel may not, of course, market their product in any way which would cause it to be confused with a product of Glaxo and their product will have to carry their own logo; and I have decided to order the insertion of provisions to this effect in the licence. [83]

The Controller held against the inclusion of a most favoured licensee clause (which would prevent the patentee granting licences to others on more favourable terms) considering such to be more appropriate in the case of a voluntary licence.

[8.41] The Controller is required by statute to take into account certain matters when making a decision on the granting and terms of a compulsory licence. These are stated in s 70(4)[84] of the PA 1992, namely:

(a) the nature of the invention, how long the patent has been granted, and the measures taken by the patentee or any licensee to make full use of the invention;

(b) the ability of the proposed licensee to exploit the patent to the public advantage;[85] and

(c) the risks to be taken by the proposed licensee in providing capital and exploiting the patent.

[8.42] The Controller is not required to take into account matters subsequent to the application for a compulsory licence. This is not a mandatory requirement on the Controller but it is unlikely that the Controller would accept post-application efforts by the patentee in an attempt to remedy its position. In *Halcon's Patents*,[86] there was a refusal to order discovery of a licence agreement offered subsequent to the filing of an application.

[8.43] As to the obligation of an applicant to show its capacity to work the invention, in *Enviro-Spray Systems Inc's Patent*,[87] it was stated that:

It would clearly be unreasonable, before the grant of a licence, to require any applicant to show contracts or firm agreements with anyone for either finance or for the other forms of assistance which would be required to operate a licence. On the other hand, I have to be able to form some estimate of the ability of the applicants to work the inventions, at least to the extent of satisfying myself that the applicants are likely to have available to them the various resources, including technical expertise and know-how, which would be necessary to put the inventions into practice in a way which would benefit the public. It is in turn the responsibility of the applicants to explain as far as is reasonable what they expect to do, and also to put me in a position in which I can form some estimate of their likelihood of achieving it.

---

[83] *Clonmel Healthcare Ltd* (3 July 1995, unreported).

[84] As amended by the Patents (Amendment) Act 2006.

[85] *Monsanto's CCP Patent* [1990] FSR 93.

[86] *Halcon's Patents* [1989] RPC 1.

[87] *Enviro-Spray Systems Inc's Patent* [1986] RPC 147.

[8.44] Under the original terms of the PA 1992, an applicant for a compulsory licence was not prejudiced or estopped by virtue of the fact that it may already be a licensee.[88] This was not retained in the extensive amendments made by the Patents (Amendment) Act 2006. A licensee under a compulsory licence has the same power to sue for infringement as a licensee under a licence of right.[89] Under the original provisions of the PA 1992, if the Controller was satisfied that conditions imposed by the patentee on the grant of licences, or on the disposal or use of the patented product or process, unfairly prejudiced the manufacture, use or disposal of materials not protected by the patent, he could also order the grant of licences to customers of the applicant.[90] This was also not retained in the extensive amendments made by the Patents (Amendment) Act 2006. If the applicant is already a licensee, the Controller may amend the existing licence or order it to be cancelled and grant a new licence.[91] An application may also be made by any Minister of the government for an entry on the Register that a licence as of right is available.[92]

PROCEDURE ON APPLICATIONS FOR A COMPULSORY LICENCE OR BY A MINISTER FOR ENTRY OF A LICENCE AS OF RIGHT[93]

[8.45] The applicant must present a *prima facie* case to the Controller. If this is done, the application papers are then served on the patentee and any other interested party entered on the Register. The application is also advertised in the Official Journal. Within three months from advertisement, the application may be opposed by either the patentee or any other person.[94] The parties can agree to the appointment of an arbitrator[95] or the Controller may insist on such if the proceedings require a prolonged examination of documents or any scientific or local investigation which cannot conveniently be carried out by the Controller. If the whole proceedings have been referred to an arbitrator, unless otherwise agreed between the parties, an appeal lies from the arbitrator's award to the High Court. However, if the arbitrator is only to rule on a question or issue of fact, the arbitrator reports the finding to the Controller.[96] Before ruling, the Controller is obliged to give the parties an opportunity to be heard.[97] An appeal from the Controller's decision lies to the High Court.[98]

---

[88] PA 1992, s 70(5) (now replaced by the Patents (Amendment) Act 2006).
[89] PA 1992, s 70(5) as amended by the Patents (Amendment) Act 2006.
[90] PA 1992, s 71(1) (now replaced by the Patents (Amendment) Act 2006).
[91] PA 1992, s 71(2) as amended by the Patents (Amendment) Act 2006.
[92] PA 1992, s 72.
[93] PA 1992, s 73 as amended by the Patents (Amendment) Act 2006; Patents Rules 1992, rr 50–52.
[94] Patents Rules 1992, r 52.
[95] PA 1992, s 74(2).
[96] PA 1992, s 74(4).
[97] Patents Rules 1992, r 67; PA 1992, s 90.
[98] PA 1992, s 96(1).

USE OF INVENTIONS FOR THE SERVICE OF THE STATE

[8.46] A Minister of the government may acquire rights to a patented invention or to a patent application and can exploit such rights, including by granting a licence(s) and forming or promoting an incorporated company to develop, perfect or commercially work the invention.[99]

[8.47] It is permissible for a Minister of the government, his officers, servants, agents or persons authorised in writing, to use patented inventions for the service of the State without the consent of the patentee.[100] Certain acts which would otherwise amount to an infringement are not to be considered as such.[101] Service of the State is broadly defined to mean a service financed out of moneys charged on or advanced out of the central fund or moneys provided by the Oireachtas or by a local authority for the purposes of the Local Government Act 1941.[102]

[8.48] TRIPS recognises that a State may, in certain circumstances, use a patented invention without the authority of the right holder and on terms which include the right to be paid adequate remuneration taking into account the economic value of the authorisation. The terms governing State use are agreed between the parties or, failing which, the matter is referred to the High Court, which in turn can refer the whole matter or any question or issue of fact to an arbitrator.[103]

[8.49] Under s 77(4) of the PA 1992, if the invention prior to the filing or priority date has been recorded in a document by, or been tried by or on behalf of, a Minister, then the State may use such invention royalty free or without any other payment. Evidence of such documentary recordal or the trial may be given to counsel representing the patent applicant/proprietor, or to any agreed independent expert where the Minister determines that such disclosure would be detrimental to the public interest.

[8.50] Information as to the extent of State use should be provided by the Minister to the patent applicant or proprietor unless such would be contrary to the public interest.[104]

[8.51] If there are proceedings between the Minister and the proprietor of a patent under the provisions governing State use, then the patent can be challenged by the Minister.[105]

[8.52] The rights to State use under s 77 of the PA 1992 includes a power to dispose of, or sell, or offer to dispose of or sell, any products made in pursuance of such a right,

---

99 PA 1992, s 76(1).
100 PA 1992, s 77(1).
101 PA 1992, s 77(2).
102 PA 1992, s 77(10).
103 PA 1992, s 77(6).
104 PA 1992, s 77(5).
105 PA 1992, s 77(7).

which are no longer required for the service of the State.[106] Also covered are persons acquiring such products.[107]

[8.53] There are extended provisions for State use during a period where exceptional circumstances are in existence and it is desirable to do so in the interests of the community. In such circumstances, the government may by order empower the State to use the invention for any purpose which appears to be necessary or expedient for one or more stated reasons which are set out in s 78(1) of the PA 1992. These reasons include ensuring public safety and the preservation of the State, the maintenance and sufficiency of supplies and services essential to the life or well-being of the community and for assisting in the relief of suffering in any country outside the State that is in grave distress. This would presumably include instances such as a famine. However, included in the reasons are broadly stated objectives such as for promoting the productivity of commerce and industry including agriculture.

VOID CONDITIONS IN CONTRACTS

[8.54] Section 83 of the PA 1992 renders null and void certain restrictive conditions in contracts relating to the sale or lease of, or licence to use or work, a patent. This arises firstly where there is a prohibition or limitation of the use of a product supplied by, or of a patented process owned by, anyone other than the supplier or licensor or his nominee. Secondly, where there is a requirement to purchase from the patentee (or his nominee) a product not protected by the patent.

[8.55] However, such conditions can validly be included if the purchaser, lessee or licensee has the option of accepting the contract on reasonable terms without such restrictive conditions and relieve himself of his liability to comply with such conditions on giving the other party three months' notice in writing and on payment of compensation or royalty.[108] Section 83(4) makes the inclusion of a condition which is null and void a defence to infringement proceedings while the contract is in force. In *Hunter v Fox*,[109] the Supreme Court held that a scheme of licensing was contrary to the corresponding provision in the Industrial and Commercial Property (Protection) Act 1927. The facts of this case were that Hunter manufactured lids for jam jars and sealing heads for fixing the lids to the jars. They held a patent for the sealing heads but not in respect of the lids. The sealing heads were leased to Irish jam manufacturers subject to a covenant that the heads remain the property of the patentee and the hirer had no licence to use the sealing heads. However, supplies of lids contained a label licence to use the sealing heads. It was held that the effect of the agreement was to force the hirer of the sealing heads to purchase the lids from Hunter. Accordingly, the agreement between Hunter and the jam manufacturers was illegal and the relevant clause of the agreement was null and void *ab initio*, which meant that the jam

---

[106] PA 1992, s 77(8).
[107] PA 1992, s 77(9).
[108] PA 1992, s 83(1).
[109] *Hunter v Fox* [1965] RPC 416.

manufacturers were free to use lids from any source. There is no corresponding provision in the European Patent Convention (EPC) but licence agreements with such a restrictive condition would offend against art 101 of the Treaty[110] if they affect trade between Member States. In *Windsurfing International Inc v EC Commission*,[111] the ECJ considered clauses in a patent licence agreement and found objectionable, amongst others, a clause limiting a licence to manufacture to a country where a patent existed with the effect that royalties were to be paid even on products sold in parts of the EU where no patent existed.

[8.56] On the basis of art 101[112] of the Treaty, the European Commission has issued certain Regulations exempting certain licensing agreements from the application of art 101, most recently the Vertical Restraints block exemption, which can apply to patent licences and the Technology Transfer Block Exemption Regulation.[113] The block exemption applies to patent and/or know-how licences between two parties that contain one or more obligations that although generally restrictive of competition have positive attributes which fall within art 101. Included in the Regulation are obligations declared to be outside art 101. These are known as the black list, which are obligations in licence agreements that are definitely not exempted from art 101. The previous Technology Transfer Block Exemption Regulation[114] had a separate list of obligations which were regarded as generally not restrictive of competition, referred to as the white list, but this was not retained when the new Regulation replaced the old.

[8.57] It is also provided in s 83(3) of the PA 1992 that a licence agreement or lease allowing use on working of a patented product or process may be terminated by three months' notice in writing in the event that the relevant patent ceases to have effect. This is irrespective of any contractual agreement to the contrary. Section 83(5), which provides that certain conditions by way of exception are not void, may still fall foul of art 101 of the Treaty and the Competition Acts 2002 and 2006. These include an agreement containing a clause that prohibits a person from selling goods other than those of a particular person and a contract for hire or use of a patented product that reserves the right to supply new parts or repair. In *Fichera v Flogates Ltd*,[115] the provision of the UK Patents Act 1977 corresponding to s 83(5)(d) of the PA 1992 was held to be wide enough to provide an exception for a clause requiring the replacement of worn as well as damaged parts. A worn part needing to be replaced was considered a part required to keep the patented article in repair.

---

[110] Formerly EC Treaty, art 81.
[111] *Windsurfing International Inc v EC Commission* [1988] FSR 139.
[112] Formerly EC Treaty, art 81.
[113] Commission Regulation 772/2004/EC ([2004] OJ L123/15). See paras **[6.40]** and **[6.42]**.
[114] Commission Regulation 240/96/EC ([1996] OJ L31/2).
[115] *Fichera v Flogates Ltd* [1984] RPC 257.

Chapter 9

Introduction to Copyright

COPYRIGHT IN EARLY IRISH LAW

[9.01] The creation of any tangible object can be seen as an expression of skill, effort or individuality which raises in turn issues about ownership of that work, the freedom of others to imitate or utilise the work, or the right of the original creators of the work to control such imitations or uses. While these matters are now regulated by statute, early Irish manuscripts provide a well-known illustration[1] of this kind of conflict. Saint Columcille is recorded as having illicitly copied a gospel manuscript which belonged to Saint Fintan. When Saint Fintan discovered this unauthorised act of reproduction he claimed, before Dairmait, the King of Ireland, ownership of the copy. Dairmait, arguing by analogy, held 'for every cow its calf': thus 'to every book its copy'. Scholars dispute the true outcome of this copyright litigation; under some traditions it is said to have led to the battle of Cúil Dremne. One scholar at least is of the view that the entire 'decision' is probably fictitious[2] and Phillips is unable to identify any convincing proof that the trial of Columcille was actually about unauthorised copying.

HISTORICAL INTRODUCTION TO STATUTORY COPYRIGHT LAW

[9.02] The development of the modern law of copyright, addressing as it does an entire range of works and products, held in a diverse range of material (and sometimes intangible) formats, is the result of a number of economic, political and cultural factors. It would be a mistake to see copyright simply in terms of parliamentary recognition of an author's right to assert a 'property' in the work in question. Indeed, a brief survey of the development of statutory copyright,[3] particularly in relation to the book trade, reveals a somewhat convoluted political struggle between the Crown and Crown agents, on the one hand, and publishing entrepreneurs, on the other; a struggle within which the author or creator of a work had, at times, only an incidental role.

[9.03] The right to print not only Crown promulgations like statutes and royal proclamations but also common law books became seen as a part of the Royal Prerogative by the beginning of the sixteenth century, by which time it had devolved to

---

[1]   See Phillips, 'St Columba the Copyright Infringer' [1985] EIPR 350.
[2]   Kelly, A Guide to Early Irish Law (Dublin Institute for Advanced Studies, 1988), 239–240.
[3]   Patterson, Copyright in Historical Perspective (Vanderbilt University Press, 1968); Kaplan, An Unhurried View of Copyright (Columbia, 1967) 2–7; Feather [1988] EIPR 377; Saunders [1993] EIPR 452; Feather, Publishing, Piracy and Politics (Mansell, 1994).

the King's printer. Mary I provided that in relation to all existing and future common law books, the right to publish them would be a matter of a separate royal grant, and in 1556, Mary I, by Royal Charter ceded these rights to the Worshipful Company of Stationers of London, a body incorporated in that year. The Stationers Company, as an arm of the State, took over functions that had previously been the province of other institutions, in particular the Privy Council, which had been engaged in suppressing 'heretical' works imported into the Realm from Northern Europe. Through the Stationers Company, it was possible to regulate the publishing trade, in particular the right to establish presses and publish books and other works. Such a centralised supervisory system was therefore an important mechanism in controlling religious and political dissent.

[9.04] The Stationers Company,[4] the members being stationers or printers, established the practice of allowing its members to register the fact that a certain member had possession of the manuscript of a book and that such a manuscript had been read by the censor. This register of lawfully printed books soon evolved into a form of declaration of right, namely, that once the stationer had his name entered onto the register that stationer had the sole right to print copies of that book, infringement of such a right being a matter to be controlled by way of a fine imposed by the company. The basic equation established by the licensing system, namely, that registration equalled the sole right to make copies, was to survive both the attacks upon the Crown Prerogative and Cromwell's Protectorate. Upon the restoration of the Stuart dynasty the system was reaffirmed in the seventeenth century when the Licensing Act 1662 vested censorship functions and pre-publication clearance of manuscripts into the hands of the Secretary of State. However, this legislation, which reaffirmed the power of the copy holders to exclusive rights of publication of works, was not renewed by Parliament when it lapsed in 1695,[5] thereby removing the statutory rights of these early publishers to counteract piracy in printed books and pamphlets. While it appears that publishers were still able to utilise registration procedures and seek some remedy in damages against post-1694 pirates, the effective reliefs of search, seizure and injunction were no longer available in Chancery, although publishers were able to use the rules of the Stationers Company to base a claim of copyright infringement in the 1709 case of *Stationers Co v Partridge*.[6]

[9.05] At this stage it should be noted that the right to make, or authorise the manufacture of, copies in books was vested in the stationer, or publisher, such a right being proved, or established, via registration. The raw material for publication, the manuscript, was acquired by the stationer normally under a contract, and the idea that the author held or acquired any rights under the instruments which effected the Royal Prerogative, the procedures that had evolved in the Stationers Company, or under the

---

4 Blagden, The Stationers Company – A History (1960). The earliest preserved contract was lodged on 20 August 1667 by printer Samuel Simmons in respect of Milton's Paradise Lost. Milton was paid £5 at signing and another £5 for each 1,500 copies sold on a first edition print run of 4,500 copies.

5 Macaulay, in History of England, Vol 3 (Heron, 1967) 171–175 wrote entertainingly on the effects on the press and publishing trades of the consequences of non-renewal.

6 *Stationers Co v Partridge* (1709) 4 Burr 2329, 2381, 2402.

Licensing Act 1662, would be far from the mark. Agitation for recognition by Parliament of 'literary property' rights was successful and the Statute of Anne 1709,[7] gave the owner of a book the legal right to make copies. Both the notion of an owner – the author and his assigns – and the scope of the right, 'the sole right and liberty of printing books', were somewhat imprecise, and while the protection ran for 14 years from first publication, renewable if the owner was still alive at the end of this period for a further 14 years, the registration system and the operation of the anti-piracy provisions by the Stationers Company point to the statutory copyright as being a publishing right. This point is reinforced somewhat by the protection afforded to pre-published works; upon the passage of the Statute of Anne such works were protected for 21 years and in practice these rights were held by persons other than the author or the author's descendants.

[9.06] With the expiry of the statutory copyrights, particularly in relation to established and profitable literary and learned writers, the publishers attempted to persuade the courts that, apart from statutory copyright, the owners of 'literary property' could utilise common law rights of property not only to protect works from unauthorised publication but also to protect 'property' once the statutory copyrights ended. The Court of Chancery remedy of an injunction was available to publishers who objected to pirated versions of works that no longer enjoyed statutory copyright, although cases of this kind did not address directly the issue of whether a common law copyright, perpetual in nature, revived upon expiry of the statutory copyright. The common law cases that addressed this point accepted that the practice in equity was to grant injunctive relief on the basis of a perpetual copyright[8] and in *Millar v Taylor*[9] a majority of the Court of King's Bench, led by Lord Mansfield, accepted the concept of a perpetual property right which could be used against pirates. However, in *Donaldson v Beckett*[10] it was held[11] that for a published work copyright was a statutory right that did not survive expiry of a statutory right.

[9.07] Apart from copyright in books, there was agitation from other creative forces in society for protection of works against unauthorised reproduction. In 1734,[12] Hogarth was successful in obtaining a copyright for engravings that had previously been protected only through a subscription system which was ineffective once authorised copies had been put upon the market. Designs of fabric patterns also secured a limited statutory protection for some two months in 1787 and, a year later, protection for

---

[7] Ransom, The First Copyright Statute (University of Texas Press, 1956). Passed in 1709 but effective from 10 April 1710.

[8] *Eyre v Walker* (1735); *Molte v Falkner* (1735); *Walthoe v Walker* (1736) 1 Black W 332–1, cited in Saunders [1993] EIPR 452.

[9] *Millar v Taylor* (1769) 4 Burr 2303; see the earlier case of *Tonson v Collins* (1762) 1 Black W 332.

[10] *Donaldson v Beckett* (1774) 2 Bro Parl Cas 129. For a recent reappraisal see Deazley (2003) 62 Cam LJ 106.

[11] See, however, *Rooney v Kelly* (1861) 14 Ir CL Rep 138, which stresses that common law remedies survived the Statute of Anne.

[12] Hyatt-Mayor, Prints and People (Metropolitan Museum of Art, 1971) 550–555.

sculptures depicting the human figure were available. The Engraving Copyright Act 1734 (Hogarth's Act) and Sculpture Copyright Act 1798 provided protection for 28 years and two periods of 14 years respectively, thus providing a parallel with the copyright afforded to books under the Statute of Anne, this implicitly emphasising that in all three cases it was the work created by the author, the artist/engraver and the sculptor respectively that was worthy of protection. *Millar v Taylor*[13] focused on the issue of perpetual common law protection and, while ultimately the issue of perpetual protection was lost, the debate therein also highlighted copyright as being an author's right rather than an entrepreneur's right.

THE NINETEENTH CENTURY

[9.08] The nineteenth century also further enhanced this identification of copyright as an author's right when the Copyright Act 1814 extended the statutory copyright in published books to one period of 28 years or the author's life, whichever was the longer. As we shall see, the debate about the most suitable period of copyright protection is a contentious one, particularly at the present time, but, in the first half of the nineteenth century, parliament continued with an either/or approach by extending the copyright term in 1842[14] to the author's life and seven years, or 42 years post-publication, whichever was the longer. While the author's right conferred by statute could of course be effectively negated by way of a contractual assignment to a publisher there was no doubt that copyright was, in essence, a statutory right vis-à-vis a published work, and that when the statutory period expired, the work fell into the public domain and was thus freely exploitable by anyone, even if the author's dependants had not reaped an adequate return seven years after the author had passed on. Arguments for a longer period were in part based upon the public interest for under the either/or approach, authors were tempted to withhold works for posthumous publication in order to attract the fixed period tariff, thus depriving the public of certain literary works for some time.

[9.09] With the passage of the Copyright Act 1911, the UK was able to participate fully in the Berne Union, having not only embraced the principle of national treatment but also ending both the registration system and extending the period of protection to the Berne minimum of 50 years following the end of the year of death of the author.[15]

COPYRIGHT IN IRELAND

[9.10] Pollard, in her seminal work *Ireland's Trade in Books*, has provided a full account of both the structural and regulatory context within which Irish publishing developed up until the nineteenth century. The first Irish book was printed in 1551 and in practice the government recognised two printers during the sixteenth century, the position being

---

[13] *Millar v Taylor* (1769) 4 Burr 2303.

[14] Literary Copyright Act 1842.

[15] Under the Convention for the Protection of Literary and Artistic Works (the Berne Convention) (Berne, 9 September 1886).

regularised through the grant of letters patent to John Franckton in the 1604-1609 period. Franckton's monopoly over 'official publications, grammars, almanacs, the Bible' and 'all other books whatsoever' petered out in the early eighteenth century, and while later Irish publishers were given letters patent, a number of independent printers emerged. Seditious libel rather than a licensing system was used by government to secure censorship of publications – Pollard states that until the passing of the Stamp Act 1774 'the Irish press was unrestricted by statute law'[16] and increases in stamp duties on newspapers and the Press Act 1784 were unsuccessful measures aimed at stifling the unrest and dissention that ultimately led to the 1798 rising and the repression that followed hard upon it. The Act of Union of 1800 was followed by legislation in 1801 which extended the Westminster copyright legislation into Ireland and, in Pollard's words, 'removed the last remnants of the [Irish] book trade's autonomy'.[17] The Copyright Act 1801 integrated Irish book publishing into the structures that had been laid down by the Statute of Anne; copyright consisting of two renewable periods of 14 years, a system that operated until the Copyright Act 1814 brought in copyright for the life of the author or 28 years.

[9.11] In historical terms, Ireland and Scotland were seen as havens of book piracy. Efforts to counteract the piracy of well-known titles centred on both the courts[18] and the Irish Parliament,[19] and gradually the Westminster Parliament extended the structure of English copyright protection statutes to cover Ireland. With the foundation of the State, however, many of the cultural and economic patterns that had built up over the previous century continued to operate: academic and literary figures still tended to look to UK academic presses and commercial publishers to put their works before the world;[20] the Performing Rights Society, established in 1914, still functioned from London for the benefit of Irish composers and music publishers;[21] and even attempts to stimulate the publication of scholarship in the Irish language and early Irish history, for example, were frustrated by the size of the market, publishers' indifference and lack of technical resources.[22] With the establishment of the Irish Free State on 6 December 1921, Ireland lost all of the administrative structures and bodies that had caused the commercial and industrial property sectors of the economy to function – there was no Patent Office for example, and registration of a design copyright did not take place because there was no administrative body to accept applications for registration. Although the right to assert a copyright was afforded to an author as a common law right, it was only on the passing of the Industrial and Commercial Property (Protection) Act 1927[23] that design registration

---

[16] Pollard, *Ireland's Trade in Books* (Oxford, 1989) (hereafter Pollard).

[17] Pollard, p 31.

[18] *Pope v Curl* (1741) 2 Atk 342; see however *Fisher v Folds* (1838) 1 Jones 12.

[19] Print protection arrived via the Prints Copyright Act 1836 as extended in 1852 by the International Copyright Act 1852.

[20] See Senator WB Yeats in 8 Seanad Debates, Cols 599–610.

[21] This remained so until 1988 when the Irish Music Rights Organisation (IMRO) was established; total separation occurred in 1995.

[22] 8 Seanad Debates, Cols 599–610.

[23] An earlier Bill had been introduced in 1925 but was withdrawn to allow for revisions, which appeared in the 1926 Bill.

could take place so as to provide the author with a right to commence an action for breach of artistic design copyright.[24] The most significant feature of the 1927 legislation, Pt VI of which reproduced in substantive terms the Copyright Act 1911 which itself was repealed,[25] related to a discussion about the basis upon which copyright should be available to a citizen of Saorstát Éireann. Senator Dowdall sought to introduce an amendment that would have required Ireland to introduce a manufacturing clause similar to that found in the US and Canada that would have made the printing of a work (but not necessarily publication) a *sine qua non* for copyright protection. This amendment was defeated, not simply because of difficulties in relation to the Berne Convention, but because the amendment was castigated by WB Yeats in the Seanad as being tantamount to a vote for piracy[26] and likely to lead to the ruination of publishers and the death of academic scholarship in the country. In 1927, legislation was thus able to reconcile substantive law and administrative effectiveness[27] until it was replaced by the Copyright Act 1963, which in turn has been superseded by the Copyright and Related Rights Act 2000.

ECONOMIC AND CULTURAL IMPLICATIONS OF COPYRIGHT

[9.12] While the copyright system does not exactly parallel the patent system by giving the first into the field a statutory monopoly in every case – coincidental or simultaneous creation of two works creates two copyright works with no liability for either author once copying has been disproved[28] –a copyright does give the author, or right holder, quite substantial and enduring exclusive rights of exploitation. In justifying the scope and duration of statutory copyright, it is customary to defend the monopoly as being dependant upon the need to provide a satisfactory environment for investment and innovation. If works of authorship or derivative works, for example, are not protected then the creative and entrepreneurial sectors of society will have no incentive, or reward, for innovation or cultural or artistic progress. This argument is a powerful one,[29] particularly in the new digital environment where original works such as sound recordings, films and computer programs cost significant amounts to produce but can be reproduced with no discernible loss of quality, at a fraction of the original cost, by a counterfeiter. Certainly, at the level of international trade relations, the need to proscribe an economic and legal climate in which certain rogue states tolerated, or even tacitly supported, the counterfeiting of high volume and high value copyright works, was a

---

[24] The provision was retrospective.

[25] See paras **[21.01]–[21.02]** for an account of the relationship between the Copyright Act 1911 and the post-Treaty period.

[26] 8 Seanad Debates, Cols 599–610, 1107–1121.

[27] Eg see the background to effective enforcement of performance rights sketched in *PRS v Bray UDC* [1930] IR 509.

[28] Landes and Posner (1989) 18 JLS 325, at 344–347.

[29] The vibrancy of the Irish music industry and its potential for job creation make calls for improved copyright laws somewhat non-controversial (see, for example, 148 *Seanad Debates*, Col 1747 at 1813), at least until the issue of enforcement of performance rights comes to the fore.

central motivating factor for the position taken by the developed industrial economies in the Uruguay Round of the GATT.[30] Increased attention to strengthening criminal sanctions and civil remedies is a feature of the recently negotiated Anti-Counterfeiting Treaty Agreement (October 2010). The fact that few commentators would countenance a complete departure from a copyright regime does not mean, however, that there is some Panglossian consensus in favour of the broad levels of protection that generally operate within the Berne Convention tradition. Economic analysis of digital goods and services tends to suggest, for example, that data on the extent to which copyright compliance costs may actually frustrate innovation is incomplete.[31]

[9.13] Any monopoly, whether statutory or *de facto*, has distasteful implications; but the defenders of copyright in the traditional, paper-based literary fields argue that without an extensive period of copyright protection, and a power to obtain the assignment of copyright from an author to a publisher, it is not possible for the publishing industry adequately to exploit a published book due to the uncertainties of public taste, the ebb and flow of literary fashion, as well as the vagaries of a market in which rival works may appear to compete with, or even supplant, a work.[32] This approach, supported by the publishers of new works, justifies copyright protection for extensive periods of protection on the ground, *inter alia*, that production of unprofitable titles is subsidised by revenue obtained from more successful works and that such a subsidy must endure for a long rather than a short period of time. This argument is often regarded with some scepticism, for it tends to treat publishing as an altruistic rather than a commercial activity, and some commentators point to the evidence from countries which have traditionally extended short, but renewable, periods of protection. A leading US study, for instance, indicated that around 15 per cent of authors thought it worth while considering renewal following expiry of the 28-year copyright period.[33] Nevertheless, there are, from time to time, commentators who seriously argue that in order to protect the continual reinvestment needed to 'freshen' a work, copyright could become a perpetual right in certain instances.[34]

[9.14] While there will always be some works which will be modern classics and which will sell for whatever period of protection is decided upon, the reality for most works is that their commercial value is exhausted within a few years of initial publication, particularly in relation to academic, technical or scientific works, or new types of work such as computer programs where marketing or related factors such as advances in hardware make the work obsolete.[35] Indeed, Ricketson concludes that:

---

30 General Agreement on Tariffs and Trade (Marrekesh, 15 April 1994; Cm 3282), Annex 1A (Uruguay Round Agreements).
31 See Handke, *The Economics of Copyright* (May 2010) available at www.sabip.org.uk.
32 Ricketson (1992) 23 IIC 753 at 758–760.
33 Ringer (1963) 1 Studies in Copyright 583.
34 Landes and Posner, 'Indefinitely Renewable Copyright' (2003) 70 U Chicago LR 471.
35 Some games do enjoy a revival, eg the early Donkey Kong games in the 1970s were revived in the 1990s, albeit in more sophisticated form.

longer terms of protection probably do not play any part in the investment decisions of copyright investors such as publishers and the like although there is a need to investigate the effect that the prospect of future exploitation plays in their decisions.[36]

[9.15] It may of course be asked, if copyright protection for most works is a legal reality but an economic pipedream, why does this matter? The answer is of course that the onus lies upon those who assert the need for a copyright to justify that right, for the core of the copyright debate is one of public policy and the public interest. Macauley's observation[37] that 'monopoly is an evil that must not last a day longer than is necessary and that copyright, being a (necessary) tax on readers for the purpose of giving a bounty to writers', requires society to be vigilant in testing the monopoly which is thus obtained at a substantial social cost.

[9.16] Some commentators point to the fact that copyright keeps up the price of books by granting exclusive rights to one publisher, a matter which is compounded by resale price maintenance under the now mortally wounded Net Book Agreement.[38] Suggestions for the compulsory licensing of copyright works following upon first publication find support from the compulsory licensing provisions of the Berne Convention in relation to sound reproductions of musical works, the powers to republish works within developing countries, not to mention the broader public policy issues that the *Magill*[39] litigation seems to presage, but the retention of copyright as an exclusive right remains an article of faith to the copyright community:

> Copyright is a form of intellectual property. It is a species of property which is protected and recognised under the EC Treaty. The essential characteristic of intellectual property is that it gives to the owner a complete or partial monopoly over a creation of the human mind. In the case of copyright artistic works, it is the right to prevent others from copying that artistic work. The essence of intellectual property rights is the right to exclude and that means of course in relation to the subject matter of the intellectual property right the owner has, within the limits of the intellectual property right, a power to be the only trader. That is inherent in intellectual property rights and is sometimes referred to as the 'specific subject matter' of the right. This means that the owner of intellectual property rights can normally prevent a third party using his rights without permission. This means not just that the intellectual property owner can impose unfair terms on a potential infringer, it can refuse to offer any terms at all to the infringer and it can exclude the infringer from the market. To that extent he has a dominant position which he can use to suppress or eliminate competition.[40]

[9.17] Apart from the purely financial aspects that the monopoly produces, there are important cultural questions that remain at large when copyright is in issue. Parrinder[41] and others make the point that when a classic text remains in copyright publishers have

---

[36] (1992) 23 IIC 753 at 766.

[37] T Macauley, Speeches on Copyright 25.

[38] The British Publishers Association withdrew on 30 September 1995. *In Re Net Book Agreement 1957* [1997] EMLR 657.

[39] *Magill* [1995] FSR 530, Vinje [1995] EIPR 297.

[40] Laddie J in *HMSO v AA Ltd* [2001] ECC 272 at 278.

[41] Parrinder [1993] EIPR 391.

no incentive to produce newer, cheaper texts[42] but when such a work falls out of copyright, the public can often expect a range of newer, cheaper printings of the work (as occurred in relation to Joyce's works in the early 1990s). This has significant cost and quality advantages to students, libraries and others. One may also make the point that such public domain texts must also be worth reproducing or the publisher would steer clear of the text at all costs! The significant educational benefits of such printings is not the only cultural benefit from truncated or strictly controlled copyright protection. The estate or literary executor of a deceased author may have a separate agenda. There may be a dislike of either the form or the contents of a particular work, whether it be Richardson's famous nephew[43] or a relative concerned to safeguard the reputation or privacy of a third party, and in such a case the public may be deprived of a work on grounds which may have differing degrees of validity. Sometimes a refusal to grant permission to reproduce a work may not appear to be based on particularly strong ground, as occurred recently when permission to perform an extract from *Finnegans Wake* in a London musical recital was withheld by the Joyce Estate (the work having come back into copyright under the Term Directive[44]) on the ground that the permission request inserted an apostrophe between the 'n' and the 's' in 'Finnegans'.[45] This connection between the power that copyright cedes to the heirs of an author and the broader public interest in permitting access to a nation's literary heritage was eloquently put by Senator Norris in the Seanad debates accompanying the Copyright and Related Rights Bill 1999:

> What have the descendants of writers done to deserve to participate uniquely and dictatorially in the estate of a writer for 70 years after the writer's death? How far can this be stretched? Should I say I want to get something from every production of Dracula because Bram Stoker was my grandmother's cousin? It is absolute nonsense. I never met the man and have very little knowledge about him. Yet, I presume that genetically I could construct a claim. Why should a grandson, who until recently had never read a word written by his grandfather, suddenly have the right to dictate to everybody, to refuse permission to reprint or extract huge sums of money from anybody who dares to do so? …
> I am puzzled as to what right of inheritance in works of the imagination descendants can have. They can have it in terms of physical property, houses, stocks, shares and money, but a work of the imagination is different. It is the property of all people because it illumines all people. We must be careful in extending the right of proprietorship over this material if we are not to diminish ourselves as a cultural entity.[46]

[9.18] A related concept is the balance to be struck between copyright and freedom of expression, but, it is submitted, in the statutory framework that makes up copyright law, the fair dealing defences present a mechanism for resolving this question in most instances.[47]

---

42 Save when the work is serialised for television when a newer, more expensive printing of the text often results.

43 See Macauley's example in the House of Commons, cited by Ricketson (1992) 23 IIC 753, 769.

44 Council Directive 93/98/EEC ([1993] OJ L290/9).

45 'Dead Loss' (1995) Times, 21 September.

46 159 *Seanad Debates*, Col 454.

47 For the acquis communataire on this see recital (3) of the Information Society Directive: Council Directive 2001/29/EC ([2001] OJ L167/10).

HUMAN MOTIVATION AND THE DISTRIBUTION OF KNOWLEDGE

[9.19] It is often pointed out that authorship, which should be encouraged and promoted within society, is not always subject to the same motivating factors.[48] While the desire to see one's writings in print is a natural human ambition, the deeper reasons for this desire may differ. It may be simply a desire for financial reward, and Dr Johnson remarked that this is the only valid reason – 'no man but a blockhead ever wrote, except for money'.[49] There are of course areas of book and journal production where the author has no realistic expectation of financial reward; indeed some scientific publishers and journals require a financial contribution, often from the author, before a work can be printed, such is the limited market for even the most erudite work. Here the motivation is scholarship, the search for truth, or the advancement of reputation and career. In such a context, Breyer[50] asserts copyright is not a significant element and he argues for the more effective distribution of such works via grants or State subvention, a powerful argument given that most scientific research is publicly funded in any event. In Ireland, the tax exemption[51] given to the income on royalties is intended to provide a stimulus to cultural creation but the Revenue Commissioners have traditionally resisted extending this exemption to school or university texts (as distinct from novels) so this form of non-copyright stimulus does not always operate coherently in such a context. Although the copyright system has its critics, particularly amongst economic rights theorists who argue that copyright can be contrary to the public interest by keeping the cost of published works artificially high,[52] a survey by Landes and Posner[53] (in which the authors specifically examined the extent to which copyright law can be explained as a means for promoting efficient allocation of resources) can be said to be broadly supportive of the copyright system. Landes and Posner argued that the rights of an owner to prevent others from copying a work represent a trade off between the cost of limiting access to a work against the benefits of providing incentives towards the creation of a work in the first place. In such a context, positive doctrinal elements such as non-protection of ideas *per se*, fair use, and even the length of the protection, are seen as intuitively efficient in economic terms. It may be that Landes and Posner overstate their thesis and underestimate the strength of opposition towards an over-ready assimilation

---

[48] Plant (1934) Economica 167; Senator WB Yeats had this to say about the motivation of Irish scholars researching and writing in the fields of Old and Middle Irish: 'those books pay the author practically nothing at all. The learned man is satisfied merely that his scholarship should be given to the world' 8 *Seanad Debates*, Col 600 (11 March 1927).

[49] Boswell's Life of Johnson 5 April 1776.

[50] (1970) 84 Harv LR 281; contrast Tyerman (1971) 18 UCLA L Rev 1188, and Breyer's riposte at (1972) 20 UCLA Rev 75. See also Gordon (1989) 41 Stan LR 1343.

[51] Taxes Consolidation Act 1997, s 195. See *Revenue Comrs v Loinsigh* (21 December 1994, unreported), HC.

[52] Eg Plant (1934) Economica 167; Plant The New Commerce in Ideas and Intellectual Property (1953). Van den Berg [1998] IPQ 17 reviews much of the literature.

[53] (1989) 18 JLS 325.

of new economic and technological interests into copyright[54] but an economic defence of authors' rights is particularly opportune at this time.

COPYRIGHT WORKS AND THE RIGHTS OF THEIR CREATOR

[9.20] We have seen that, in historical terms, copyright evolved somewhat uneasily, from an entrepreneurial right into an author's right that can and often is abridged or transferred by way of contractual licence or contractual assignment. It is nevertheless argued that a copyright is necessary because it provides the author, or creator, of a work with statutory recognition of rights that are inherently based upon the causal link between the author and the work. The difficulty with supporting such a theory is that market forces and society generally do not reward or recognise the effort, imagination or skill that each author brings to bear on a work in any rational way. The author of a successful three-minute popular song, which was perhaps composed in under an hour, is likely to net considerably more in terms of fame and income than the author of a scholarly tome that represents a lifetime of endeavour and investigation. This point is side-stepped by those who assert the existence of copyright as an author's right by arguing that the true link is not between the author and the market as an economic relationship but between the author and the work as an expression of human personality. Such a perspective has found expression in the European Court of Justice (ECJ), which has forged together[55] the common law tradition of copyright as an exploitative economic right with the civilian idea that rights in an original work are authors' rights – the *droit d'auteur* – for the Court has said on several occasions, within the context of (old) art 36 of the EEC Treaty, that the essential function of copyright is to protect the moral rights in the work and ensure a reward for the creative effort in producing a work.

[9.21] While copyrights are in essence economic rights, both the common law origins of protection for unpublished works, and the statutory protections available in the form of moral rights, aim to safeguard the reputation of the author. Many creators see their work as being an essential part of their very being and use the more conventional legal mechanisms of contract and passing off to guard against damage that may have both financial and psychological implications. But constitutional law is also potentially applicable. The rights of a creator to maintain rights over a work are sometimes described as inherent rights in property but, as we have already seen, the publication of works brings such works into the realm of statutory rights only, according to English judicial decisions, and many economic commentators point to the differences between indeterminate and perpetual rights in real property and some tangibles, on the one hand, and the less compelling arguments vis-à-vis works of authorship on the other. Nevertheless, one Irish judge has stressed that the Irish Constitution does recognise intellectual property as property to be protected under the Constitution, thus opening up some prospect of control for a creator over a work, notwithstanding the non-application

---

[54] Breyer (1970) 84 Harv LR 281; Karnell (1995) 26 IIC 193. See also MacQueen (1994) 45 NILQ 30 for a specific discussion on software protection.

[55] In the most recent instance, *Magill* [1995] FSR 530.

or exhaustion of a statutory copyright. In *PPI v Cody and Princes Investments Ltd*,[56] Keane J considered a defence that recorded music that had been publicly performed in the defendant's premises had not been proved to be copyright material:

> Section 60(4) of the Act of 1963 provides that no right in the nature of copyright 'shall subsist otherwise than by virtue of this Act or of some other enactment in that behalf'. The right of the creator of a literary, dramatic, musical or artistic work not to have his or her creation stolen or plagiarised is a right of private property within the meaning of Articles 40.3.2 and 43.1 of the Constitution, as is the similar right of a person who has employed his or her technical skills and/or capital in the sound recording of a musical work. As such, they can hardly be abolished in their entirety, although it was doubtless within the competence of the Oireachtas to regulate their exercise in the interests of the common good. In addition, and even in the absence of any statutory machinery, it is the duty of the organs of the State, including the courts, to ensure, as best they may, that these rights are protected from unjust attack and, in the case of injustice done, vindicated. The statements in some English authorities that copyright other than by statutory provision ceased to exist with the abolition of common law copyright are not necessarily applicable in Ireland.[57]

COPYRIGHT AND THE COLLECTIVE ENFORCEMENT OF RIGHTS

[9.22] While copyright is clearly an individual right given to a human person in order to encourage and recognise the economic and cultural benefits of creating new works, the nature of copyright is in fact a collection of separate rights, the most important being rights to authorise or control physical reproduction of the work and public performance of the work. The first right is clearly important in relation to printed works and works of fine art, for example, while the performance right is critical for the authors of musical and dramatic works; but there are significant areas of cultural endeavour where both reproduction and performance rights will be of concern to the author. However, the individual nature of the right should not deflect attention from the reality behind the rights – they are extremely difficult to enforce on an individual basis. Even in cases where the author assigns copyright to an entity that possesses greater economic clout or expertise – a composer or songwriter assigning copyright to a music publisher for example – problems about detecting levels of use or reproduction make it worth while for right holders to consider collective action to bring about effective enforcement of these rights.

[9.23] In the area of publishing, Irish publishers have established a licensing body, the Irish Copyright Licensing Agency (ICLA). The agency administers the reproduction right for books and periodicals, giving individuals and institutions such as universities and schools the necessary permissions for photocopying and other reproduction activities, the revenue income being distributed to members of CLÉ, the Irish Publishers Association. The ICLA has been successful in obtaining a statutory licensing scheme

---

[56] *PPI v Cody and Princes Investments Ltd* [1994] 2 ILRM 241.
[57] *PPI v Cody and Princes Investments Ltd* [1994] 2 ILRM 241 at 247, reversed on another point at [1998] 4 IR 504.

under the Copyright and Related Rights Act 2000 (CRRA 2000)[58] in respect of the reprographic copying of literary works by educational establishments and the scheme also operates in respect of the digital scanning of works within the ICLA repetoire. In the area of musical copyrights, the Irish Music Rights Organisation (IMRO) and Phonographic Performance Ireland (PPI) enforce performance rights in musical works on behalf of composers and music publishers, and recording companies respectively. Recognition of the necessity and effectiveness of collective enforcement of rights is a matter of broad international and national agreement. Both the Berne Convention and GATT recognise these institutions, while the European Union (EU), in the Rental and Lending Directive,[59] expressly authorises collecting societies to administer rental and lending rights on behalf of authors. In a domestic context the role of the music collecting societies in the Irish economy has become a matter of controversy. However, the Competition Authority, while it has ruled that certain aspects of the initial IMRO standard assignment agreement are anti-competitive in nature, has upheld the general effect of compulsory licensing in the context of Irish society as being positive in nature:

> The notifying parties advanced a number of arguments in support of their claim that the arrangements notified met the above condition [ie, are not anti-competitive and contrary to the public interest]. These arguments may be summarised as follows. Effective protection of performing right [sic] is extremely labour intensive involving considerable expenditure on administrative and monitoring procedures. In view of the practical difficulties and expense involved, it is only through collective action that creators may ensure effective protection of their performing right. In the absence of the present arrangements, it would be impossible for creators to obtain a just reward for the performance of their works and, in that event, the incentive to produce musical works would be very significantly reduced, or licences to perform music might not so readily be made available, and these would be to the detriment of licensed users and of the general public, as ultimate consumers.

> The Authority accepts this reasoning. There are considerable practical difficulties involved in the administration and enforcement of performing rights, particularly in relation to the multiplicity of smaller users, and these difficulties do point to the need for a central collective licensing/enforcement system on behalf of creators and publishers many of whom are based outside the State. Substantial additional transaction costs would clearly be involved in any multiplicity of systems of administration of performing right based on licensing by individual creators. Compliant users would require a large number of licences while the cost of pursuit for non-compliance by individual creators/ publishers would make this activity totally uneconomic except in the case of major users or events. The pursuit of breaches of copyright by smaller users would become totally uneconomic.

> The Authority therefore accepts that a collective system of performing right administration involves efficiencies and these would be significant in the generality of cases. Assignment of the performing right to PRS is accepted as improving the provision of services.

> **Allowing consumers a fair share of the resulting benefit**

> Users benefit from the improved provision of services. Licensees (ie the users, such as radio and television broadcasters, discos, public houses etc) benefit from access to the

---

[58] CRRA 2000, s 173; SI 514/2002. See www.icla.ie.
[59] Council Directive 92/100/EEC (OJ L346/61).

PRS repertoire and from the avoidance of additional transaction costs which would be involved if they had to deal with a multiplicity of licensers. The ultimate consumers, the listening public, also share in this benefit as consumers of the various services, of which music forms part, provided by the intermediary undertakings. Consumers also benefit to the extent that a collective copyright arrangement has resulted in a greater supply and variety of musical works being available than would otherwise be the case. The Authority therefore considers that the collective copyright arrangements allow consumers a fair share of the benefit.[60]

[9.24] However, in many important sectors of the Irish business community, a substantial level of hostility to the music collecting societies can be identified.[61] While disgruntled users of copyright music do not publicly go so far as to call for the abolition of the music copyright system *per se*, the volume of dissatisfaction caused the Minister of State at the Department of Enterprise and Employment to review certain aspects of copyright law. Critics of the collecting societies describe their activities as resembling 'almost a legalised Mafia operation'[62] and 'parasitic',[63] and while one cannot accept such hyperbole, there is no doubt that the collecting societies have at times been forced onto the defensive[64] because the public perception often tends towards the view that the societies are multinational bodies that exercise monopoly powers. While this is somewhat unrealistic because the societies are made up of individuals who, by and large, do not have any substantial economic or contractual leverage, the societies will have to continue to react to comments that charges are arbitrary and unrealistically high, that the system of collection and distribution of income lacks transparency, particularly in relation to administrative costs, and that collection and enforcement mechanisms are intimidatory or based on using draconian legal measures such as the interlocutory injunction.

ANTI-COMPETITIVE PRACTICES AND COMMUNITY LAW

[9.25] The fact that authors' societies within the EU are organised territorially on the basis of individual Member States, and that there is in general one society for each Member State has long been a cause for concern within the EU. Cases that establish that collecting societies may be able to engage in anti-competitive practices and abuse a monopoly position have led both the European Commission and the European Parliament [65] to consider how best to counteract some activities that may benefit collecting societies at the cost of harming consumers and the competitiveness of European media interests and authors. The 1995 Green Paper,[66] which tentatively

---

[60] Competition Authority, Decision No 326, 18 May 1994.

[61] See *PPI v Controller* [1995] 2 ILRM 1 (SC); *Carrickdale Hotel Ltd v Controller* [2004] 2 ILRM 401.

[62] 136 *Seanad Debates*, Col 1098 (Senator Maloney).

[63] 136 *Seanad Debates*, Col 1100 (Senator Kiely).

[64] See the school concert debate in 464 *Dáil Debates*, Col 806.

[65] See, in particular, the Echerer Report, *Community Framework for Collecting Societies for Author's Rights* (Final 150478/2003).

[66] *Copyright and Related Rights in the Information Society*, COM (1995) 0382.

suggested that collecting societies operated in a less than transparent manner, was followed by a Commission communication on the management of copyright and related rights in the internal market[67] and a recommendation on the collective cross-border management of copyright and related rights for legitimate online music services.[68] These instruments and others reflect a reluctance on the part of the European Commission to legislate 'solutions' to these difficult questions. Indeed, the European Parliament has on several occasions adopted resolutions favouring the adoption of a Directive to liberalise the online sales of music market.[69] Some efforts to facilitate greater cross-border licensing have taken place, particular Commission Decisions under the Merger Regulation[70] whereby undertakings that seek to engage in practices that would concentrate market power in unacceptable ways may enter into a commission clearance mechanism to remove those competitive concerns. Perhaps the best known of these agreements is the *Universal/BMG Music Publishing Decision*.[71]

[9.26] A more controversial dispute between the European Commission and European music collecting societies remains in train as a result of the Commission Decision of 16 July 2008 relating to a proceeding under Article 81 of the EC Treaty and Article 53 of the EEA Agreement.[72] The European music collecting societies are members of CISAC, the International Association of Collecting Societies of Authors and Composers, and, as such, these collecting societies have engaged in contractual agreements using the CISAC model contract to conclude reciprocal representation agreements. The European Commission has objected to clauses that prevent composers from being eligible for multiple membership and which prevent collecting societies from dividing up its repertoire via sub-licensing mechanisms, as well as territorial delineation of each domestic market. These decisions have been challenged in a number of cases brought by the collecting societies (including IMRO) before the ECJ.[73] Even the European Parliament has complained about the European Commission's approach on the basis that the 16 July 2008 Decision:

> will be to preclude all attempts by the parties concerned to act together in order to find appropriate solutions – such as, for instance, a system for the clearing of rights at the European level – and to leave the way open to an oligopoly of a number of large collecting societies linked by exclusive agreements to publishers belonging to the worldwide repertoire; believes that the result will be a restriction of choice and the extinction of small collecting societies to the detriment of minority cultures.[74]

---

67 16 April 2004: COM (2004) 0261.

68 2005/737/EC ([2005] OJ L276/54) of 18 October 2005.

69 Parliament Resolution of 13 March 2007; Parliament Resolution of 25 September 2008.

70 Regulation (EC) No 139/2004 ([2004] OJ L24/1).

71 *Universal/BMG Music Publishing Decision* Decision of 22 May 2007 (Case Comp/M.4404).

72 *Commission Decision of 16 July 2008 relating to a proceeding under Article 81 of the EC Treaty and Article 53 of the EEA Agreement* Case COMP/C-2/38.698.

73 Eg. *Sacem v Commission* Case T-422/08 (30 September 2008).

74 Parliament Resolution of 25 September 2008.

DIGITISATION AND COPYRIGHT

[9.27] The digitisation of works and data has also had a significant impact on the reshaping of copyright law. When it became possible to convert words, images, sounds and data generally from an analogue form into digital representations – from atoms into bytes[75] – science had created a shock to the legal and cultural *status quo*, in every way as difficult to legislate for as the invention of the printing press some six centuries previously. Works can now be replicated inexpensively with no diminution in quality; when compression technologies and telecommunications networks facilitated the transfer of this kind of material at a distance and on-demand, the markets for such content defied national boundaries and the old rules on jurisdiction; contractual distribution models proved inappropriate and open to challenge under competition law and consumer protection law.

The creation of the World Wide Web and more recently m-commerce has facilitated a level of information access and transfer that was simply unimaginable less than 20 years ago. All of these factors provide a challenge to rights owners and vested interests, who are often accused of seeking to hang on to outmoded marketing patterns and business models, or at the very least, are believed to have been too slow to spot and react to technological change and shifts in consumer demand. In Ch 21 we provide a chronological survey of most of the important legislative initiatives, particularly in the area of international regulation and treaty law. At this juncture our intention is to take the reader into the relationship between the CRRA 2000 and digitisation, particularly in relation to content storage, and online distribution via the internet, by way of an introductory statement below.

[9.28] Copyright law has been amended to reflect the fact that digitisation does not, for example, present sounds as they were recorded, for a digital copy embodies a representation of sounds.[76] The law has also been adjusted to reflect the fact that works such as computer programs may be placed onto a physical support such as a disk, but the work itself is intangible.[77] New methods of commercialisation of a work have also led the law to embrace distribution patterns such as the public and private lending[78] of digital works (eg Video/DVD rental), as well as direct downloading of works.[79] Rights holders can therefore obtain remuneration and licence others to use or acquire copies of a work, something the older 1963 legislation could not have envisaged.

Digitisation, however, presents a lot of challenges that the legal system has not adequately addressed. The ability of users to make private copies for personal use is not covered by defences such as fair dealing; the copying is unlawful, but being able to

---

[75] Negroponte, *Being Digital* (1995); Negroponte is an enthusiast; contrast Rimner in *Digital Copyright and the Consumer Revolution: Hands off my iPod* (2007).

[76] CRRA 2000, s 2(1) definition of sound recording.

[77] CRRA 2000, s 2(1) definition of writing, and s 29(1) definition of copying.

[78] CRRA 2000 s 42 and 42A; however, Irish law does not include digital works in the public lending right – see www.plr.ie.

[79] CRRA 2000, ss 39 and 40.

prohibit such activity is quite another matter. The digital distribution of works through networks and via immaterial technologies such as satellite broadcasting directly challenges the competency of the courts to hear litigation and resolve issues in an effective way.[80] International consensus is difficult to create because the old certainties and accommodations are compromised by digitisation.

---

[80] See, however, Charleton J's forthright views on jurisdiction in *EMI and others v Eircom Ltd* [2010] IEHC 108.

Chapter 10

The Copyright Term

HISTORICAL INTRODUCTION

[10.01] The period of copyright protection under statute has fluctuated over the centuries but the trend has largely been an expansive one. The Statute of Anne 1709 initially provided for the protection of published books for 14 years, renewable for a further period of protection. The Copyright Act 1814 provided for a 28-year period or the life of the author, whichever was longer. The revision contained in the Literary Copyright Act 1842 extended the period of protection to the life of the author plus seven years, or 42 years, whichever was the longer. The Copyright Act 1911, intended as a measure which allowed the UK to implement the Berne Convention,[1] required a minimum of 50 years following the death of the author, a period of protection adhered to by the Irish State until 1995. Apart from literary copyright under the statute, the common law has provided substantial protection for unpublished works by fusing together notions of ownership of property and the law of confidence.[2] Injunctive relief has long been available in such cases.[3]

THE COPYRIGHT TERM UNDER THE COPYRIGHT ACT 1963[4]

[10.02] In accordance with the Berne Convention, the period of protection for protected works observed the minimum of 50 years *post mortem auctoris* (pma). However, this

---

[1]   Convention for the Protection of Literary and Artistic Works (Berne, 9 September 1886) (the Berne Convention).

[2]   *Perceval v Phipps* (1813) 2 Ves & B 19; *Jeffreys v Boosey* (1854) 4 HL Cas 815; *Prince Albert v Strange* (1849) 1 Mac & G 25; *Turner v Robinson* (1860) 10 Ir Ch R 510; *Caird v Sime* (1887) 12 App Cas 326; *Exchange Telegraph Co v Central News* [1897] 2 Ch 48; *Exchange Telegraph Co v Howard* (1906) 22 TLR 375.

[3]   *Granard v Durkin* (1809) 1 Ball & B 207. The fact that copyright protection may be more readily lost under Directives 93/98/EEC, as supplanted by 2006/116/EC, and the Copyright and Related Rights Act 2000 (CRRA 2000) is unlikely to change existing practices whereby the law of confidence (eg *Douglas v Hello! Ltd* [2003] 3 All ER 996), passing off (*Irvine v Talksport Ltd* [2003] 2 All ER 881) or inducement of breach of contract (*Arsenal Football Club plc v Elite Sports Distribution Ltd* [2002] All ER (D) 131 (Dec)), to name just three possible causes of action, may be used to secure compensation or an injunction against wrongful publication. Indeed, these reliefs may be available even when no copyright work has been infringed (eg *Creation Records v News Group Newspapers* [1997] EMLR 444).

[4]   For copyright protection for works that pre-exist the Copyright Act 1963 (CA 1963) see CA 1963, Schedules, and the CRRA 2000, Sch 1, for transitional provisions.

general principle cannot be relied upon as a universal rule because Irish law could produce significant variations on this theme, depending on the nature of the work and the kind of exploitative act that would trigger the running of the copyright term.

[10.03] A distinction was drawn depending upon whether the work was protected under the Berne Convention as an original work in Pt II of the Copyright Act 1963 (CA 1963), or was protected as a related or neighbouring right under Pt III of the Act.

Part II works

[10.04] In the case of an unpublished but original literary, dramatic or musical work, protection became available once the work was either made, or substantially made. Copyright protection could, theoretically, be perpetual, the period of 50 years pma only beginning to run once the work, or an adaptation of the work, was published, performed in public, records of the work were offered for sale to the public, or broadcast, these terms being defined in ss 2 and 3 of CA 1963.[5] The author had to be a qualified person (defined below at para **[10.05]**).

[10.05] In the case of a published original literary, dramatic or musical work, the protection became immediately available upon publication, even if the work was incomplete or part of a larger work such as an episode in a serialised work or a single volume of a series of encyclopaedia. Conditions of entitlement, however, were that the work was first published within the State or that the author was an Irish citizen, or Irish domiciled or resident at the date of publication. However, for works published before 1 October 1964, CA 1963 specifically provides that Irish copyright protection required first publication within the State, the qualified person provisions being excluded reflecting the Industrial and Commercial Property (Protection) Act 1927, s 171.[6]

[10.06] By analogy with unpublished literary, dramatic and musical works, an unpublished original artistic work was protected once the work had been made or substantially made, as long as the author of the work was a qualified person. Copyright protection would be lost once the artistic work was published unless the publication met the conditions set out in CA 1963, namely, that the first publication took place in the State, or the author was a qualified person at the time of publication or, if the author had died prior to publication, the author was a qualified person immediately before the author's death.[7]

[10.07] In the case of most published artistic works, the protection was available as from publication, even if the work was incomplete, as long as the first publication took place within the State or if the author was a qualified person as defined in CA 1963.[8]

---

[5] CA 1963, s 8(1) and (5).

[6] CA 1963, s 8(2). Other persons were protected under CA 1963, Pt VI and s 9(3).

[7] CA 1963, s 9(2) and (4). Publication, as defined in CA 1963, s 3, did not include exhibiting the artistic work.

[8] CA 1963, s 9(3) and (5).

[10.08] However, although an engraving (or etching) is a work of an artistic nature, a specific rule was laid down for such works, which were unpublished at the date of the death of the author. The period of protection for 50 years pma began to run as from the end of the year in which it was first published, thereby giving engravings a greater degree of protection than other posthumously published artistic works if, for example, the author of the engraving was not a qualified person.[9]

[10.09] In the case of photographs, art 7(4) of the Berne Convention permits countries of the Union to make specific provision for photographs, a desire being evinced to encourage the prompt exploitation of news photographs. Under CA 1963 the period of protection is 50 years following from the end of the year in which the photograph is first published.[10]

[10.10] In the case of works published anonymously or pseudonymously, the Berne Convention makes specific provision in art 7 for a modification of the above rules. Statutory protection for all CA 1963, Pt II works is to run for 50 years after the end of the year of first publication. This abridgement of the 50-year pma rule is not effective in cases where a person could, by reasonable enquiry, ascertain the identity of the author of the work.[11]

[10.11] In the case of CA 1963, Pt II works of joint authorship, that is, works of genuine collaboration by two or more authors, the period of protection is to run from the death of the last surviving author.[12] Where one or more of the joint authors of a work of joint authorship, which was published under two or more names, is, or becomes, identifiable by reasonable enquiry, then the period of protection is to be 50 years after the death of the disclosed or identifiable author, or the death of the last surviving disclosed or identifiable author.[13]

[10.12] It is therefore evident that under these rules, some works could enjoy perpetual copyright. Other works could enjoy a copyright, the duration of which would be triggered by either the death of an author, or by first publication. Protection would depend upon the status of the author as a qualified person or upon the place of first publication. While on this latter point the Berne principles of national treatment, as implemented by Pt VI of CA 1963 and the Copyright (Foreign Countries) Order 1978 and Copyright (Foreign Countries) (No 2) Order 1978,[14] were less important in practice, these rules could operate arbitrarily, particularly where the work was an artistic work that existed in several derivative forms, eg protection for photographs or engravings of a painting or sculpture all made by the one artist would enjoy different periods of

---

[9]   CA 1963, s 9(6). Compare CA 1963, s 9(4) on this point.

[10] CA 1963, s 9(7). However, in the case of pre-1 October 1964 photographs, the copyright period is 50 years from the end of the year in which it was taken: CA 1963, Sch 1, para 3.

[11] CA 1963, s 15.

[12] CA 1963, s 16(3).

[13] CA 1963, s 16(4).

[14] Copyright (Foreign Countries) Order 1978 (SI 132/1978); Copyright (Foreign Countries) (No 2) Order 1978 (SI 133/1978).

protection, depending upon the fact of publication, or not, and the medium in which the work was fixed.

Part III works

[10.13] The historical, theoretical and practical aspects of Part III rights are considered elsewhere in this book. For the purposes of the present chapter, it is sufficient to note that Irish law provided a somewhat extensive kind of protection in respect of most Part III rights.

(1)   In the case of sound recordings, CA 1963 provided a period of 50 years from the end of the year of first publication. Thus, an unpublished sound recording had perpetual copyright protection.[15]

(2)   In the case of cinematographic films, CA 1963 provided a period of 50 years from the end of the year of first publication, thus, an unpublished film had perpetual copyright protection.[16]

(3)   Where a television broadcast or a sound broadcast was made by Radio Éireann, copyright subsists in that broadcast for a period of 50 years from the end of the year in which the broadcast is first made.[17]

(4)   In the case of the publication of editions of one or more literary, dramatic or musical works the publisher's copyright in the typographical arrangement of such a work subsists for 25 years from the end of the year in which the edition is first published.[18]

THE COPYRIGHT TERM AFTER 1 JULY 1995

[10.14] The Term Directive of 29 October 1993[19] was transposed into Irish law through the European Communities (Term of Protection of Copyright) Regulations 1995.[20] While these Regulations were signed by the Minister on 23 June 1995, they came into operation as from 1 July 1995, the deadline set by the Directive itself. The decision to implement the Directive by way of statutory order, rather than via primary legislation, was a pragmatic one. The fact that these measures directly affect individual property rights made it necessary to ensure that the legislative changes necessary were in place by 1 July 1995, there being a fear that the State could well have been exposed to liability under *Francovich*[21] if the State had been tardy in respect of the deadline.

---

[15]   CA 1963, s 17(2). See CA 1963, Sch 1, paras 10 and 11 for transitional provisions for pre-1 October 1964 sound recordings which were mechanical musical instruments.

[16]   CA 1963, s 18(2). Pre-1 October 1964 films were not protected as films under CA 1963, s 18 but were protected as dramatic works. See CA 1963, Sch 1, paras 11 and 12 and CRRA 2000, Sch 1, paras 5 and 6.

[17]   CA 1963, s 19(2). See also SI 101/1991.

[18]   CA 1963, s 20(4).

[19]   Council Directive 93/98/EEC ([1993] OJ L290/9).

[20]   SI 158/1995. Von Lewinski (1992) 23 IIC 785; Dworkin [1993] EIPR 151.

[21]   *Francovich and Boniface v Italy* Cases C-6, 9/90 [1992] IRLR 84; Syszszczak (1992) 55 MLR 690.

[10.15] It is essential to note that there are no transitional measures in place under the European Communities (Term of Protection of Copyright) Regulations 1995 or CRRA 2000. The effect of the Regulations is to extend, renew, or abridge certain copyrights as a measure of harmonisation which is thought necessary if the EU objective of creating a single market is to be achieved. The Regulations also change in several respects the triggering events which mark the commencement of protection, and they also alter the identity of those persons whose lives measure the onset of the post mortem period for exploitation of several works. The Regulations also make provision for the resolution of difficulties that arise due to the exploitation of works that come back into copyright as the result of these provisions.

[10.16] Article 3 of the European Communities (Term of Protection of Copyright) Regulations 1995[22] override ss 8(4) and (5), 9(5), (6) and (7), and 51(3) and (4) by providing that the copyright term for literary, dramatic, musical or artistic works shall be the lifetime of the author of the work and 70 years pma, irrespective of the date when the work is published or otherwise lawfully made available to the public. This effects a considerable change for it is no longer directly relevant to the issue of protection whether or not a work was published. Therefore, the deliberate withholding of works for posthumous publication, or the discovery of a new unpublished work, cannot, as such, facilitate the descendants of the author in exploiting such a work if the author died more than 70 years previously. In this respect the Regulations can be said to abridge the old statutory copyrights in unpublished works, a situation that is not totally remedied by art 8 of the Regulations. This result, the loss of protection for unpublished works, is further underlined in art 5 of the Regulations. Article 4(1) of the 1995 Regulations extends the protection available in respect of anonymous or pseudonymous literary, dramatic, musical or artistic works, by extending the protection to 70 years following the first publication of the work or the work being lawfully made available to the public. Article 4(2) also deals with instances where the pseudonym adopted leaves no doubt as to the author's identity, or the author discloses his or her identity during the 70-year period: in such cases the 70-year period pma provided in art 4 is intended to act as updating s 15 of CA 1963. It is interesting to note that the Regulations, in art 4(2) depart significantly from the language of s 15(2)(b), thereby ensuring that the Regulations are in conformity with art 7(3) of the 1971 Paris Revision of the Berne Convention.

[10.17] In regard to related rights under Pt III of CA 1963, s 18 of CA 1963 is significantly broadened for CA 1963 gave a 50-year copyright in a cinematograph film to the maker of that film. The Term Directive,[23] which selected a 70-year period, is most effective in certain other EU States where the protection was for a lesser period (eg Spain). However, there are other significant features to reg 6 of the European Communities (Term of Protection of Copyright) Regulations 1995, which radically redefines the measuring standard vis-à-vis cinematographic works. Under the old law the older 50-year period was set off by first publication. Article 6 states that the copyright will subsist for 70 years after the death of the last of four categories of person

---

[22] SI 158/1995.
[23] Council Directive 93/98/EEC.

to survive, namely, the principal director, the author of the screenplay, the author of the dialogue and the composer of music specifically created for use in the film. This measure does not directly influence the issue of in whom copyright reposes, for the maker of a film is generally the producer of the film rather than one or more of the artistic talents behind the cinematographic work. This switch in emphasis can be seen as recognition that films represent a significant cultural as well as economic activity and that the artistically creative forces behind a film should be recognised as such. More pragmatically, once first publication was regarded as an unsuitable triggering event, some measuring lives had to be identified, for in practice the maker of a film may in many instances be a body corporate and therefore incapable of being a measuring life.

The copyright afforded to the producer of a sound recording under CA 1963, s 17 is not expanded by reg 7 of the European Communities (Term of Protection of Copyright) Regulations 1995 – a 50-year period in each case – but the triggering event is changed. The CA 1963 provided that first publication was to trigger the protection; under reg 7 it is to commence when the recording is made. However, if during this period the recording is published or communicated to the public, then a 50-year period of protection is to run from the date when the first of those two events occurs. Such an extension could prove a useful means of exploiting the forgotten or less meritorious recordings of artists by record companies. In relation to broadcasts and the copyright given to Radio Éireann by s 19 of CA 1963, it is not possible to interpret reg 7(3) as providing certain broadcasting organisations – local radio stations for example – with a copyright in their broadcasts. The statutory copyright in a broadcast is currently confined to radio and television broadcasts made by Radio Éireann, as defined in the Broadcasting Authority Act 1960, and local television and radio programmes made by bodies recognised[24] under the Radio and Television Act 1988. Article 7(3) of the 1995 Regulations, by providing that 'the term of protection as respects the rights of a broadcasting organisation' shall expire 50 years after first transmission, does not extend the scope of copyright to all broadcasting organisations, a generic concept that goes further than Radio Éireann, a specific entity, for the Term Directive was not intended to give new rights to unrecognised broadcasting organisations.[25]

[10.18] Regulation 8 of the European Communities (Term of Protection of Copyright) Regulations 1995[26] provides a *sui generis* exploitation right in respect of previously unpublished works, recordings, broadcasts or films. In cases where such protected works are within the public domain (eg an unpublished sound recording is not lawfully communicated to the public within 50 years of its making) any subsequent lawful publication or lawful communication to the public is to give that person rights which are to be equivalent to the (expired) economic rights of the author, maker or broadcasting organisation (as the case may be) for 25 years from the date of first publication or communication to the public. This new neighbouring right was proposed at a late stage in the legislative process in order to encourage the publication of previously unpublished

---

[24] SI 101/1991.

[25] The compelling argument against this is that the Term Directive, Council Directive 93/98/EEC, was not intended to create new rights *per se*.

[26] SI 158/1995.

works when copyright protection has expired. Presumably the exploitation of such works as between the right holder and any successors in title will become a matter of contractual negotiation in some instances, thus indirectly strengthening the bargaining position of the author vis-à-vis future exploitation of a work.

[10.19] Regulation 12 of the European Communities (Term of Protection of Copyright) Regulations 1995 addresses the vexed question of revival of rights. Because two EU Member States provided more extensive periods of protection than the Berne 50-year pma minimum (Spain provided 60-year pma protection while Germany provided for a 70-year period) the Term Directive[27] had to address the case of works within copyright in some Member States while being in the public domain elsewhere. Article 6 of the original proposal for a directive opted for a territorial or jurisdiction-specific approach that generally would have precluded a community-wide revival of copyright, that is, works that have fallen into the public domain would not become protected again, thereby envisaging that, for example, a work would be protected in Spain while being in the public domain elsewhere in the EU. The European Parliament proposed a different approach under which any work protected in at least one Member State on 1 July 1995 would be protected throughout the EU by way of a revival of rights. Cohen Jehorem has described the net effect thus, basing the argument on a combination of the Directive and the *Phil Collins*[28] decision:

> One small concrete example may be useful here. The famous Dutch painter Piet Mondriaan died on 1 February 1944. The copyrights in his paintings are still very lucrative because of all sorts of merchandising activities. His highly abstract expressions are still widely used as patterns for designs of fashionable rugs, textiles, place-mats etc: a regular Mondriaan industry. Now the copyrights in these works will lapse in the Netherlands, and in nearly all countries of the world, 50 years pma, ie on 1 January 1995. Since the Phil Collins decision it is clear, however, that the successors in title of Piet Mondriaan will enjoy another 20 years of copyright protection in Germany, with its term of 70 years pma. This means that on 1 July 1995, half a year after the rights have lapsed in the rest of the world, they still subsist in one Member State of the Community. Now through Article 10(2) [of Council Directive 93/98/EEC] this German copyright protection will trigger a revival of Mondriaan's rights in the rest of the Community, as of 1 July 1995, for another 19 the works will be in the public domain in the Netherlands and nearly everywhere in the Community. In that half year they can be freely exploited, as Article 10(3) provides, in order to protect acquired rights of third parties. The beauties of the EC directives are boundless.[29]

[10.20] However, the revival rule, favoured by the European Parliament, is balanced by a requirement that accrued rights, and lawful acts of exploitation, should be legally protected by Member States when these rights and acts conflict with the interests of the original, 'born again' copyright holder. In this regard, reg 14(1)(a) of the European Communities (Term of Protection of Copyright) Regulations 1995 provides that a person

---

[27] Council Directive 93/98/EEC.

[28] *Collins v Imtrat Handelsgesellschaft mbH* Cases C-92/92, 326/92 [1994] FSR 166. See Antill and Coles [1996] EIPR 379.

[29] (1994) 25 IIC 821, at 835–836.

who undertook the exploitation of a work before 29 October 1993 (the date of the adoption of the Draft Directive by the Council), that work then being in the public domain but copyright being subsequently revived by the Regulations, may avoid liability for copyright infringement and continue to exploit the work, notwithstanding the revival of copyright. Another situation covered by the Regulations is less clear for it deals with accrued rights in the period between adoption of the Term Directive[30] and its transposition. First, if exploitation, or preparations of a substantial nature in regard to exploitation, have occurred between 29 October 1993 and 1 July 1995, those acts of reliance may be legally significant. However, these factors are ambiguous: are all acts, or preparatory acts, sufficient or must substantial expenditure or work be involved? Is it necessary for legally significant actions to occur, eg the purchase of related rights necessary to effect the exploitation? These qualitative issues can only be tested via litigation. The second requirement set under reg 14(1)(b) is also problematic: the exploiter must prove that he or she was not aware, or had no reasonable grounds for suspecting, that copyright would be revived by the Regulations or any other enactment. The exploiter will presumably discharge this onus of proof on a negative basis, eg no legal advice was sought on copyright matters during the period in question, or a belief that the original proposal which was not intended of effect on EU revival of rights, remained the legal position. In fact, a newspaper report contemporary with the 1993 to 1995 exploitation period indicated that the Kenneth Grahame book, *The Wind in the Willows*, was currently being adapted for a new cartoon film and that two other television productions of the work were at an advanced stage of production, the belief being that these acts of exploitation would be protected by the then forthcoming UK transposition provisions,[31] which would have the effect of bringing the book back into copyright because Kenneth Grahame died 63 years ago. It is likely that similar acts of exploitation in Ireland, in relation to the works of James Joyce, for example, have taken place. Again, the effect of discharging the onus is to allow the exploiter to avoid liability to the copyright holder and allow exploitation to continue for the duration of the period of revival. It is by no means clear why the exploiter should have the right to continue to exploit the work for the entire period of the extension, and a fairer solution may well have been to permit exploitation only after a fair and reasonable payment has been arranged with the holder of the revived copyright.[32]

THE 50-YEAR BERNE MINIMUM

[10.21] The period of protection set by the Berne Convention as a minimum requirement is the lifetime of the author and 50 years after the author's death. The special rules that Berne recognises for certain other works generally result in the abridgement of this period of protection, but the 50-year pma general term is capable of being extended by

---

[30] Council Directive 93/98/EEC.

[31] (1995) Observer, 20 August.

[32] This approach has been adopted elsewhere, eg the UK and Germany. See, 'Hardy Pensioner waits far from movie crowd' (1996) The Times, 28 May, for an account of the windfall for certain Thomas Hardy heirs.

countries of the Berne Union. Within the context of the EU, however, Germany provides for a 70-year period of protection. Spain, since 1987, has made provision for a 60-year period, while France provides a 70-year period of protection in regard to musical compositions with or without words. Some countries, namely Belgium, Italy and France, have provided periodic extensions of the copyright term in respect of works that had not been adequately exploited due to the substantial disruption effected by the 1914–18 and 1939–45 Wars.

[10.22] The selection of a 50-year minimum period of protection represents a balancing process between, on the one hand, civilian legal traditions and certain sectoral interests (eg publishers) who perhaps favour unlimited or extensive periods of protection and, on the other hand, more pragmatic schools of thought who espouse the notion that the economic or cultural monopoly that flows from copyright should only operate where some compelling public interest can be justified by the putative right holder. The 50-year pma period is historically justified by claiming that the overriding concern that justifies such a period of protection is the safeguarding of the economic rights of the author and two generations of dependants that follow the author. The assumption is that the author's dependants must be protected for this later period although, as Ricketson has pointed out, the underlying assumption has never been challenged, save when there is agitation for an extension of copyright.[33] Ricketson concludes that the evidence in favour of selecting or continuing with a standard of protection that goes beyond even one generation of dependants is far from clear,[34] particularly when there is such a lack of clarity on whether we should be measuring the life of a dependant as being notional (eg up to 60–70 years) or simply a period of dependency (eg birth to adulthood or 20–25 years). Rather, Ricketson and others tend to favour the view that the selection of a standard pma protection may not be justifiable economically or culturally. The only significant comment made in Ireland on this point occurred during the Committee Stage of the Bill that became the Industrial and Commercial Property (Protection) Act 1927. A proposal to amend the 50-year pma period was made on the grounds that fixing a 30-year period instead would be 'the time which would allow children of the author to come to manhood' and that 'the monopoly rights of the writer ought to tend downwards rather than lengthen'.[35] The proposal was lost on the basis that the Berne Convention should prevail. Nevertheless, the trend towards expansion of the Berne minimum period of protection has accelerated in international copyright law. Further, the international community has tended to bring new objects of protection into the traditional copyright structure, the most striking example being the European Communities' decision to afford computer programs protection as a literary work (rather than *sui generis* protection) for 50 years pma and then 70 years pma.

---

[33] Ricketson, 'The Berne Convention for the Protection of Literary and Artistic Works 1886–1986' (1987) (CCLS) para 7.5.

[34] (1992) 23 IIC 751 at 762.

[35] *Per* Deputy Johnson, 17 *Dáil Debates*, Col 593.

THE TERM DIRECTIVE – WHY 70 YEARS PMA?

[10.23] The most important point to note about the Term Directive[36] is that it is a measure intended to effect the overriding commercial goal of bringing about a European single market in goods and services. Information products such as video cassettes are clearly within the first category, while a film retransmission organisation is clearly a service provider. However, in each of these cases, the rights of an importer to bring a product into a Member State,[37] or to retransmit in one Member State a signal lawfully transmitted in another Member State,[38] could be truncated by national copyright laws. The power of community law to compel some kind of harmonisation of Community copyright laws was finally shown to have no real muscle in *Patricia*:[39]

> ... that in the present state of Community law, which is characterised by a lack of harmonisation or approximation of legislation governing the protection of literary and artistic property, it is for the national legislatures to determine the conditions and detailed rules for such protection. Insofar as the disparity between national laws may give rise to restrictions on intra-community trade in sound recordings, such restrictions are justified under Article 36 of the [EEC] Treaty if they are the result of differences between the rules governing the period of protection and this is inseparably linked to the very existence of the exclusive rights.[40]

[10.24] In the light of *Patricia*[41] and the 1988 Copyright Green Paper[42] (which had alluded to the duration problem but had not emphasised this as a key topic for harmonisation) the 1991 Commission Action Plan[43] was able to compel a majority of Member States to agree to increase the standard copyright term by 20 years in those jurisdictions, even though there had been no significant debate on these issues in any Member State. The reasons advanced for this remarkable situation are set out in the explanatory memorandum accompanying the Directive and the recitals to the Term Directive.[44]

[10.25] First, *Patricia*[45] indicates that harmonisation of terms of copyright protection must occur, both in relation to the uniform periods of protection and standardisation of the events that trigger the protection, whether the events be the creation of the work, first publication, or the death of the author, as the case may be. The price to be paid for not harmonising these matters would be fragmented national markets and distortions and barriers to competition and free markets. A second justification for harmonisation was stated to be some desire on the part of 'interested circles' for greater uniformity and

---

[36] Council Directive 93/98/EEC, as supplanted by Directive 2006/116/EEC.
[37] *Warner Bros v Christiensen* Case 158/86 [1988] ECR 2605.
[38] *Coditel* Case 62/79 [1980] ECR 881.
[39] *EMI Electrola GmbH v Patricia* Case 341/87 [1989] ECR 79.
[40] *EMI Electrola GmbH v Patricia* Case 341/87 [1989] ECR 79 at 96.
[41] *EMI Electrola GmbH v Patricia* Case 341/87 [1989] ECR 79.
[42] Green Paper on Copyright and the Challenge of Technology (88) 172 Final.
[43] COM (90) 584 Final.
[44] Council Directive 93/98/EEC, replaced by Directive 2006/116/EC ([2006] OJ L372/12).
[45] *EMI Electrola GmbH v Patricia* Case 341/87 [1989] ECR 79.

certainty, thus easing collective management of rights and in particular aiding Community action against third-party piracy. Greater solidarity within the Community, so the argument ran, would heighten confidence within the European business community in relation to 'future investment in the sector of (sic) creativity in the Community'.[46]

[10.26] Non-discrimination on the basis of nationality case law has also strengthened the case for harmonisation. The interpretation placed upon national legislation in the area of copyright and neighbouring rights when national legislation uses nationality as the basis for prescribing entitlements to protection has tended to favour the grant of increased periods of protection. This is illustrated by the judgment of the European Court of Justice (ECJ) in *Land Hessen v G Ricordi & Co Bühnen und Musikverlag GmbH*.[47] German law (UrhG) provided that works produced by German nationals were entitled to copyright protection for 70 years pma whereas works of foreign authors that had not been published first in Germany were entitled to protection under foreign treaty law. The work in question here was Puccini's *La Bohéme*, unauthorised performances of which had taken place in Wiesbaden in the 1993–1994 and 1994–1995 seasons. As Puccini died in 1924 the 70 year German copyright expired at the end of December 1994. However, it was contended by Land Hessen that under the relevant treaty provision – art 7(8) of the Berne Convention, the comparison of terms provision – the duration of protection is determined by reference to the protection provided by the country of origin unless the law of the country in which protection has been sought provides to the contrary. As German law did not so provide another rule, the relevant law was Italian law which afforded a 56 year period of protection pma, that is, copyright expired in 1980 and the permission of Ricordi to mount the Wiesbaden performances was not necessary. After pointing to the *Phil Collins*[48] decision and the non-discrimination principle, the ECJ refused to be deflected by an argument that as Puccini's death occurred before the Community Treaty came into force on 1 January 1958, the non-discrimination principle in art 6 of that Treaty had no force. The ECJ, in particular, was critical of the failure of the German State to avail of the full scope of art 7(8) of the Berne Convention:

> since Article 7(8) of the Berne Convention permits the Federal Republic of Germany to extend to the rights of a foreign author the 70-year term of protection prescribed by German law, the mechanism of comparison of the terms of protection provided for in that provision cannot justify the difference of treatment as regards the term of protection, which is established by the abovementioned provisions of the UrhG between the rights of a German author and those of an author who is a national of another Member State.

[10.27] However, the real issue facing the Community was not whether to harmonise but, rather, how to harmonise. Should the term selected be in line with the term found in the majority of Member States, or some other term? Citing Community jurisprudence on accrued rights[49] and stressing that harmonisation downwards – to 50 years pma – was

---

46   Explanatory Memorandum accompanying Council Directive 93/98/EEC, art 29.
47   Case C–36/100; *Tod's SpA v Heyrand SA* Case C-28/04.
48   *Collins (Phil) v Instrat Handelsgesellschaft GmbH* Cases C-92/92, 326/92 [1994] FSR 166.
49   *Verli-Wallace v Commission* Case 159/82 [1983] ECR 2711; Case 159/82 *Simmenthal v Commission* Case 159/82 [1979] ECR 777.

only superficially attractive because the observance of accrued rights would mean extraordinary transitional measures for Spanish and German right holders, the result of which would be transitional periods that would 'necessarily be long and would lead to a corresponding delay in the actual creation of the internal market'.[50] In such a context, the only realistic option was clearly to harmonise up to the highest standard set by German law.

[10.28] However, the Commission advanced a number of ancillary points to justify this recommendation intellectually, although most commentators view these grounds as being spurious in the extreme. The first point is based upon the greater longevity of persons alive in the late twentieth century. If persons, including dependants, are living longer, then the period of protection should be extended. Critics of this argument point to the fact that automatic extension may not benefit the descendants of the author because rights may have been assigned previously, eg to a publisher, record company or film producer. Some limited support for this argument is to be found in the Irish implementing regulations, the European Communities (Term of Protection of Copyright) Regulations 1995,[51] which give the benefit of any revival or extension to the author or the author's personal representatives unless there has been an express reference in any assignment to renewal or extension of copyrights. However, the Commission failed to meet Ricketson's arguments[52] that there is little evidence to support two later generations. Many commentators feel that the length of a copyright term is not likely to effect either the substantive bargaining position of an author vis-à-vis a publisher and other entrepreneurs, or the decision of such persons when a work is about to be exploited.[53] Short-to-medium-term exploitation and income returns are the basis of investment decisions, rather than some hardly quantifiable estimate about the public's appetite for a work some 30, 50 or 70 years after its creator has passed on.

[10.29] The logic of the non-discrimination principle means that The Term Directive has been invoked even by 'creators' who are not traditionally identified with copyright. This is particularly so in relation to performers: recent ECJ case law allows non-EU nationals to invoke extended protection. In *Sony Music Entertainment (Germany) GmBH v Falcon Neue Medien Vertrieb GmbH*[54] the provisions of art 10(2) of Directive 2006/116/EC were held to allow protection to be claimed in respect of neighbouring rights, specifically the sound recording right, as long as the work in question was protected in at least one Member State on 1 July 1995. Protection was claimed by Sony over sound recording rights in several early Bob Dylan recordings. Despite the fact that the recordings had never been protected at any time in Germany, the jurisdiction in which

---

50 Explanatory Memorandum accompanying Council Directive 93/98/EEC, art 33.
51 SI 158/1995.
52 (1992) 23 IIC 753 at 761.
53 Cornish [1993] 52 CLJ at 51; Landes and Posner (1989) 18 JLS 325; MacQueen (1994) 45 NILQ 30 at 43; Dawson (1994) 45 NILQ 193. See also the Preface to Laddie, Prescott and Vitoria, *The Modern Law of Copyright and Designs, Vol 2* (2000).
54 *Sony Music Entertainment (Germany) GmBH v Falcon Nene Medien Vertrieb GmbH* Case C-240/07. See Owers [2009] JIPLP 321.

protection was claimed, the fact that the sound recordings were protected at the relevant date in the UK ('at least one Member State') was dispositive. Secondly, art 10(2) required the German courts to look at the national law in question: the fact that the beneficiary was, under that national law, entitled to protection, even if a national of a non-Member State, at that date could not be affected by the art 7(2) provisions, and the fact that the national legislation of the Member State in which protection was sought did not prevent the rights owner from benefiting from an art 10(2) revival of copyrights and related rights

[10.30] The decision to harmonise up, rather than down, while apparently justifiable in the view of EU Member States, has not, however, escaped criticism. One commentator has argued that the practice within the book trade has been to provide the public with new, cheaper editions of classical works only when copyright has expired and that the revesting of copyright in authors such as Yeats, Joyce, Hardy and DH Lawrence is unjustifiable and not in the public interest.[55] Other academic commentators have argued for a return to first principles, favouring the view that copyright terms should be shorter and selectively conferred, but these arguments seem destined to fall on deaf ears.[56] We shall leave the last word on this question to Laddie:

> The question to be asked is: what justification is there for a period of monopoly of such proportions? It surely cannot be based on the principle of encouraging artistic creativity by increasing the size of the carrot. No one is going to be more inclined to write computer programs or speeches, compose music or design buildings because 50, 60 and 70 years after his death a distant relative whom he has never met might still be getting royalties. It is noticeable that this expansion of term is not something which has only occurred in the last decade. On the contrary, it has been a trend which has been in evidence for the whole of this century. Before the 1911 Act [the Copyright Act 1911], the term of copyright in artistic works extended to seven years after the author's death. In 1911 this was extended to 50 years after death. The growth of term is in fact greater than these figures suggest. Life expectancy in 1910 was far shorter than it is now. The result is that a monopoly which was expected to last about four decades in 1910 should be expected to last on average more than three times as long.[57]

THE COPYRIGHT TERM UNDER CRRA 2000

[10.31] The European Communities (Term of Protection of Copyright) Regulations 1995[58] served their purpose in staving off non-implementation proceedings in respect of Council Directive 93/98/EEC. When the CRRA 2000 was initially presented to the Oireachtas the 1995 Regulations were replaced by what are now ss 24–36 of CRRA 2000. This means that in measuring the copyright term, commencement of protection for works created in recent years may be regulated by either CA 1963, the 1995 Regulations

---

55 Parrinder [1993] EIPR 391.
56 See the compelling arguments put by a group of learned US academic lawyers in Karjala [1994] EIPR 531.
57 Laddie 'Copyright: Over-Strength, Over-Regulated, Over-Rated?' [1996] EIPR 253, at 256.
58 SI 158/1995.

or CRRA 2000, and issues of authorship and ownership are generally resolved by reference to the law in force when the work was made. In fact, the transition from the 1995 Regulations to CRRA 2000 was made rather seamlessly. Schedule 1, para 9 to CRRA 2000 has two important provisions:

> Nothing in the [CCRA 2000] shall affect the duration of copyright in works in which copyright subsists on or before [1 January 2001]... And the duration of copyright in those works shall be determined, where applicable [by the European Communities (Term of Protection of Copyright) Regulations 1995];

> [CCRA 2000] shall apply to computer programs whether created before or after [1 January 1993].

[10.32] While CRRA 2000 repeals the European Communities (Term of Protection of Copyright) Regulations 1995[59] and ss 24–36 of CRRA 2000 make specific provision in respect of the duration of copyright, the CRRA 2000 does not simply constitute a re-enactment of the 1995 Regulations in the form of primary legislation. First of all, the 1995 Regulations dealt with the old CA 1963 forms of protected work, namely literary, dramatic, musical or artistic works (Part II works) as well as Part III works in the form of sound recordings, films, broadcasts and typographical arrangements of published editions. Because the scope of the notion of a protected work has expanded considerably, the duration provisions in CRRA 2000 have additional areas of application. In the area of literary works, for example, a work fixed on magnetic tape will be a literary work[60] while under the old law it was not.[61] The definition of an artistic work has been expanded to be an 'includes' definition and the new legislation includes collages and typefaces as artistic works. In this context the definition of a photograph is broadened to cover digital images. A film is similarly broadly defined.[62] The 1995 Regulations also pre-dated the Database Directive of 1996[63] and while some original databases were previously protected as literary works, the concept of an original database is much broader than under CA 1963.[64] Recognition by the Irish legislative draftsmen that copyright protection should be extended to cover cable programme services,[65] a concept taken from the UK Radio and Television Act 1988 which, while based on the diffusion service in CA 1963, also recognises the desirability of protecting the investment necessary in computer generated works.[66]

[10.33] Section 24(1) of CRRA 2000 provides that copyright in a literary, dramatic, musical or artistic work, or an original database, expires 70 years after the death of the author, irrespective of the date on which the work is first lawfully made available to the public.[67] This section re-enacts, with the reference to an original database, reg 3 of the

---

[59] SI 158/1995. See Council Directive 93/98/EEC, Sch 2, Pt II and Sch 1, Pt I, art 9(1).
[60] CRRA 2000, s 2 (definition of literary work).
[61] *Gormley v EMI Records (Ireland) Ltd* [1999] 1 ILRM 178.
[62] Even if it is not the same as in Council Directive 92/100/EEC ([1992] OJ L346/61), art 2.1.
[63] Council Directive 96/9/EC ([1996] OJ L77/20).
[64] For transitional provisions see CA 1963, Sch 1, Pt IV.
[65] CRRA 2000, s 28.
[66] CRRA 2000, s 30.

European Communities (Term of Protection of Copyright) Regulations 1995.[68] Section 24(2) and (3) of CRRA 2000 re-enacts the provisions of reg 4 in relation to anonymous or pseudonymous works,[69] but s 32(1) (rather otiosely) provides that if the author's identity becomes known or disclosed after the s 24(2) period of 70 years after the work has been made public, the s 24(1) 70 years pma is not to be triggered. Section 32(4) of CRRA 2000 defines the death of the author for the purposes of works of joint authorship.[70]

[10.34] In relation to the former CA 1963, Pt III rights, the provisions in the European Communities (Term of Protection of Copyright) Regulations 1995[71] relating to films remain in the same form, namely 70 years after the death of the last of the four measuring lives. However, this provision in CRRA 2000, s 25(1) is followed by a provision dealing with films that were not lawfully made available to the public until the running of that 70-year period. If the film is made available to the public during the 70-year period in question, then copyright will expire 70 years after the date of that 'making available' event.[72] This provision is modelled on the sound recording provision in the 1995 Regulations. That regulation[73] is re-enacted in the form of s 26 of CRRA 2000 and the broadcast provision in reg 7(3) is re-enacted in s 27(1). However, s 27(2) makes it clear that copyright in a repeat broadcast expires at the same time as the original broadcast. The duration of protection for the typographical arrangement of a published edition[74] was not addressed by the 1995 Regulations because this was not covered in the Term Directive.[75] Section 29 of CRRA 2000 extends the period of protection from 25 years to 50 years from the date the edition was first made available to the public.

[10.35] Of the newly protected copyright works, specifically the cable programme and the computer-generated work, different periods of protection are set. Cable programmes are in copyright for 50 years after the cable programme was first lawfully included in a cable programme service[76] with copyright in a repeat cable programme expiring at the same time.[77] This reflects the 'broadcast' rather than internet genesis of the concept. In relation to computer-generated works, where the right holder is likely to be an entrepreneur rather than a creative person or team of such persons,[78] copyright expires 70 years after the work is first lawfully made available to the public.[79]

---

[67] See CRRA 2000, s 40.

[68] SI 158/1995.

[69] SI 158/1995. See para **[10.16]** above.

[70] The issue of joint authorship of musical compositions is included in the Proposal to revise Directive 2006/116/EC as an effort to provide community-wide uniformity.

[71] SI 158/1995.

[72] CRRA 2000, s 25(2).

[73] SI 158/1995, reg 7.

[74] CA 1963, s 20(4).

[75] Council Directive 93/98/EEC.

[76] CRRA 2000, s 28(1).

[77] CRRA 2000, s 28(2).

[78] CRRA 2000, s 21(f).

[79] CRRA 2000, s 30.

[10.36] Two provisions that are intended to be of assistance to users of copyright works when the work is anonymous or pseudonymous are also included in CRRA 2000. If it is reasonable to presume that the author of a literary, dramatic, musical or artistic work, or an original database (or the last of the four measuring lives in relation to a film) has been dead for 70 years or more, copyright is not to subsist.[80] There is no clue as to how reasonableness is to be established – actuarial tables, or last reported whereabouts and health records of the author in question, for instance – but these provisions were added to the Bill to assist users faced with the difficult task of tracking down unknown individuals/authors.

[10.37] CRRA 2000 also contains a provision relating to unpublished works that was not found in the European Communities (Term of Protection of Copyright) Regulations 1995. It will be recalled that under CA 1963, copyright did not start to run until a work was published. The Directive intended to extinguish such rights and the wording of reg 3 of the 1995 Regulations[81] purported to do this. That Regulation, however, did not expressly extinguish copyright in an unpublished work.[82] Section 35 of CRRA 2000 does clearly extinguish copyright in a work if a work is not lawfully made available to the public within 70 years of its creation, if the work is a work that obtains copyright protection other than via the measurement of the life of an author (eg an anonymous literary work), the 25-year quasi-copyright provisions being exercisable by the person who lawfully makes the work available to the public after copyright has expired.[83]

[10.38] The provisions in CRRA 2000, ss 24 to 35 do not apply to government or Oireachtas copyright or the copyright of prescribed international organisations.[84]

CASE LAW ON THE DIRECTIVE DIRECTLY RELEVANT TO IRISH LAW

[10.39] As has been mentioned above, the European Communities (Term of Protection of Copyright) Regulations 1995[85] sought to balance the rights of persons who had begun to exploit public domain works, or who had begun to prepare for the work in question coming into the public domain.[86] Article 10.3 of Council Directive 93/98/EEC provided that:

> This Directive shall be without prejudice to any acts of exploitation performed before [1 July 1995]. Member States shall adopt the necessary provisions to protect in particular acquired rights of third parties.[87]

---

[80] CRRA 2000, s 32(2).
[81] SI 158/1995.
[82] Eg European Communities (Term of Protection of Copyright) Regulations 1995, reg 3 should have contained a phrase like 'regardless of whether the work is ever published' before 'irrespective'.
[83] CRRA 2000, s 34. See the presumption added by way of a new s 34A: SI 360/2006, reg 6.
[84] CRRA 2000, s 36.
[85] SI 158/1995.
[86] SI 158/1995, reg 14.
[87] Council Directive 93/98/EEC, recital 27.

Because Community law recognises acquired rights and the principle of legitimate expectation, the fact that Member States are afforded a considerable degree of freedom of movement in respect of transitional provisions does not mean that any such provisions in national law will pass muster. This is clear from the decision of the ECJ in *Butterfly Music Srl v Carosello Edizioni Musicale & Discographiche Srl*.[88] The relevant Italian transitional provisions provided that in respect of the exploitation of literary works being subsequently revived, such exploitation could continue for the remainder of the revived period of copyright. However, in the case of sound recordings, the period during which sound recordings could be distributed after revival of copyright was limited to three months. Butterfly continued to distribute recordings after expiry of the three-month period and pointed to the disparity of approach adopted by the Italian legislator in an attempt to have the three-month provision declared invalid. Both Advocate-General Cosmas and the Court were of the view that the amount of notice afforded by the Directive – from 29 October 1993 to 1 July 1995 (allied to the fact that the post-1 July 1995 period was 11 months due to an eight-month delay in transposition) was not inadequate or restrictive. The fact that literary works were treated in a different way was no basis for undermining the sound recording provision because Member States were free to treat different rights in different ways. However, Advocate General Cosmas warned that transitional provisions of this kind could be unlawful, for such provisions:

> by their nature, must be as narrow as possible, since they are equivalent to exceptions inserted into a general system for the protection of related rights which is created by the rules of the Directive.[89]

[10.40] Both the Advocate General and the ECJ hinted that while the sound recording provisions were acceptable and proportionate, the literary work provisions (which were not directly at issue) could well have difficulty in meeting the needs of Council Directive 93/98/EEC. The ECJ warned that the details of the transitional measures are:

> left to the discretion of the Member States, provided however, that they do not have the overall effect of preventing the application of the new term of protection on the date laid down by the Directive.[90]

[10.41] In *Sweeney v MacMillan Publishers Ltd*[91] the importance of this approach was graphically illustrated in the judgment of Lloyd J in the Chancery Division of the English High Court. The UK's transposition regulations were under scrutiny here in the context of a dispute over the exploitation of original manuscripts (still in copyright) and the published 1922 edition of James Joyce's *Ulysses*. The net point here was whether research work undertaken by the author, and a preparatory manuscript, along with unconcluded negotiations with publishers, could come within the term 'arrangements

---

[88] *Butterfly Music Srl v Carosello Edizioni Musicale & Discographiche Srl* Case C-60/98 [1999] ECR I-3939, [2000] 1 CMLR 587.

[89] *Butterfly Music Srl v Carosello Edizioni Musicale & Discographiche Srl* Case C-60/98 [1999] ECR I-3939, [2000] 1 CMLR 587 at 603.

[90] *Butterfly Music Srl v Carosello Edizioni Musicale & Discographiche Srl* Case C-60/98 [1999] ECR I-3939, [2000] 1 CMLR 587 at 609.

[91] *Sweeney v MacMillan Publishers Ltd* [2002] RPC 651.

for the exploitation of the work in question', the relevant UK 'accrued rights and legitimate expectation' test.[92] Lloyd J held that these acts could not themselves come within that phrase:

> Such an interpretation of the regulation would, in my judgment, be far too wide, even in its own terms, and the more so with the guidance of the European Court of Justice [in *Butterfly Music Srl v Carosello Edizioni Musicale & Discographiche Srl*[93]].[94]

[10.42] These two cases have, it is submitted, some significance for the Irish European Communities (Term of Protection of Copyright) Regulations 1995.[95] It will be recalled that reg 14(b) permits the full exploitation of the revived work, for the entirety of the revived period of copyright, without compensation to the right holder if, between 29 October 1993 and 1 July 1995:

(a) exploitation of the work had been undertaken or preparations of a substantial kind for such exploitation can be demonstrated;

(b) the work and surrounding materials was not copyright protected;

(c) that person can prove he was not aware, and had no reasonable grounds for knowing, that copyright would revive.

Regulation 14, it is submitted, would be extremely vulnerable save for the third point. It will be difficult to make out lack of knowledge, but, given the confusion that surrounded Council Directive 93/98/EEC on revival, there is some prospect of a user of a work being able to make out all three factors. But can the regulation survive after the analysis put forward in *Butterfly Music Srl v Carosello Edizioni Musicale & Discographiche Srl*,[96] as illustrated in *Sweeney v Macmillan Publishers Ltd*?[97]

[10.43] Regulation 14 of the European Communities (Term of Protection of Copyright) Regulations 1995[98] was not carried over into CRRA 2000. This is surprising, given the length of time for which the revival of copyright lasts under the 1995 Regulations. It may be that the drafters of the new statute felt that the transitional provision was 'spent', but such a view seems misplaced. Although the validity of SI 158/1995 was not directly put in issue in the Irish High Court case of *Sweeney v Cork University Press*,[99] because the High Court felt that the matters of interpretation raised by reg 14 were inappropriate to an application for interlocutory relief, Smith J listed four unresolved questions on the meaning of reg 14.[100] This air of uncertainty is exacerbated by Pt I of Sch 1 to CRRA 2000, which provides that the 1995 Regulations, notwithstanding their repeal, shall

---

[92] SI 1995/3295, reg 23(5).

[93] *Butterfly Music Srl v Carosello Edizioni Musicale & Discographiche Srl* Case C-60/98 [1999] ECR I-3939, [2000] 1 CMLR 587.

[94] *Sweeney v MacMillan Publishers Ltd* [2002] RPC 651 at 675–676.

[95] SI 158/1995.

[96] *Butterfly Music Srl v Carosello Edizioni Musicale & Discographiche Srl* Case C-60/98 [1999] ECR I-3939, [2000] 1 CMLR 587.

[97] *Sweeney v Macmillan Publishers Ltd* [2002] RPC 651.

[98] SI 158/1995.

[99] *Sweeney v Cork University Press* [2001] 1 ILRM 310.

[100] *Sweeney v Cork University Press* [2001] 1 ILRM 310 at 318.

determine the duration of copyright.[101] Regulation 14 does not determine duration but, rather, issues of infringement so our legislation is not entirely silent on issues of transition and the 1993 Term Directive.[102]

THE 2006 CONSOLIDATION DIRECTIVE

[10.44] Subsequent legislative developments in relation to the EU copyright *acquis* had a significant impact upon aspects of the Information Society Directive. Directive 93/98/EC,[103] art 11.2 made a technical amendment to art 3.2 in respect of revival of rights in respect of sound recordings, and with the passing of time some of the provisions such as those relating to commencement lacked clarity. For this reason the decision was taken to repeal Directive 93/98/EC in 'the interests of clarity and rationality,[104] and the term provisions have been consolidated and restated in Directive 2006/116/EC.[105] Changes to the text of the Directive also take account of the Database Directive (96/9/EC) and broader post-1993 developments, such as TRIPS's protection for collections (recital 13) and the WIPO Performances and Phonograms Treaty (PPT) (recital 9). This latter point has been used by the European Commission as leverage in its efforts to increase the period of protection available to some performers and phonogram producers. Recital 9 of Directive 2006/116/EC notes that the WIPO PPT 'took the form of a substantial update of the international protection of human rights' and the initiative to amend or broaden Directive 2006/116/EC is in part rooted in a desire to cut down perceived anomalies that exist in relation to the more limited period of protection that performers and phonograph producers enjoy vis-à-vis author's copyright. The 2006 Consolidation has been followed by European Commission efforts to extend protection for performers and phonogram producers from 50 to 70 years.

In an Irish context the Proposal for a European Parliament and Council Directive amending Directive 2006/116/EC[106] is conceptually puzzling because Irish law treats the right holders of sound recording copyright as authors, while all performers are regarded as having related rights. The Proposal follows the broader international treaty law practice as regarding sound recording producers and performers as having related rights.

[10.45] We will consider what the Proposal sets out in relation to performers in Ch 20. In the case of sound recordings, the producers of sound recordings appear to have persuaded the European Commission that falling revenues and reduced levels of investment in nurturing new talent, due to piracy and the shift to music downloading, had something to do with the limited period of (copyright) protection for sound recordings. The European Commission proposed that the term of protection should be extended from 50 years to 95 years and that a number of ancillary measures should be included, such as a 'use it or lose it' provision to incentivise the exploitation of a 'back

---

101 CRRA 2000, Sch 1, para 9(1).
102 Council Directive 93/98/EEC.
103 Council Directive 2001/29/EC ([2001] OJ L167/10).
104 Council Directive 2006/116/EC, recital 9.
105 OJ L. Coming into force on 15 January 2007.
106 COM/2008/0464 final (16 July 2008).

catalogue' of sound recordings. In truth, the motivation behind this proposal is a desire to align EU protection for sound recordings with those that prevail in the US, and the incentivisation argument that is often put forward in support of this proposal has not received widespread support from academic commentators.

US DEVELOPMENTS

[10.46] The duration of copyright protection in the US is resolved by the constitutional provision that mandates Congress to create protection 'for limited times'.[107] The first federal statute, based on the Statute of Anne 1709, provided for a 14-year term, renewable after 14 years. Extension of the fixed period to 28 years in 1831 led to later extensions of the renewal period to 28 years in 1909, 47 years in 1962, and 67 years in 1998. However, in 1976, Congress moved towards a Berne minimum provision of life of the author and 50 years pma. In 1998 the Copyright Term Extension Act[108] extended the pma period to 70 years for works in copyright in 1998 passed in order to ensure that copyright in Mickey Mouse did not lapse in 2002. The legislation was promoted because the US is a net exporter of copyright materials and because the extension served to promote reinvestment in existing works. Arguments about extending copyright because people are getting older has been described as making little sense unless we are concerned about the longevity of the author's heirs.[109]

[10.47] In *Eldred v Ashcroft*[110] the US Supreme Court by a 7:2 majority, held that the Copyright Term Extension Act 1998 (Sonny Bono Act) did not exceed Congress's power under the Constitution, nor was it a violation of the First Amendment. The majority pointed to the EU Council Directive 93/98/EEC and the need to match the Directive if US right holders were to receive equivalent protection in Europe, pointing as well to US commentators who supported the measure as a means of encouraging right holders to invest in the restoration and public distribution of their works.[111] In the light of these factors the extension was held to be a rational enactment that would not be second guessed by the majority of the Court. The fact that the US Supreme Court has upheld, by a majority, the Sonny Bono Act suggests that future efforts to challenge copyright extensions as being socially undesirable, economically inefficient and out of kilter with the avowed goal of allowing copyright in order to encourage creation may not be very successful. In fact Landes and Posner, in a recent article[112] published without the benefit of the Supreme Court Sonny Bono decision,[113] challenge the view that economic

---

[107] US Constitution, art I, s 8, cl 8.

[108] Copyright Extension Act 1998 (17 USC), ss 302–304 (the Sonny Bono Act).

[109] Landes and Posner (2003) 70 U Chicago LR 471, 492 at n 41. For other criticisms of the Copyright Extension Act 1998 see generally (2000) 18 Cardozo Arts & Ent LJ 651.

[110] *Eldred v Ashcroft* (2002) 56 IPR 608.

[111] Perlmutter (2002) 36 Loyola (LA) L Rev 3223.

[112] Landes and Posner, 'Indefinitely Renewable Copyright' (2003) 70 U Chicago LR 471. In submissions to Congress, interest groups such as the Songwriters Guild pressed for perpetual copyright rather than the proposed 20-year extension.

[113] *Eldred v Ashcroft* (2002) 56 IPR 608.

transaction costs and production incentive goals require copyright periods to be limited. The authors argue that many copyright works require re-investment and continuous remarketing – citing in particular the Disney phenomenon – and argue that because other intellectual property rights such as trademarks and publicity rights are potentially unlimited, copyright could be unlimited also. The authors suggest a system of renewable copyright (possible for US works via a registration system but impermissible under the Berne Convention) arguing that because most registrations would not be renewed this would actually encourage the creation of a larger public domain and facilitate the use of works (by permitting a system of exploitation of 'found' works). Such proposals would, however, facilitate the strengthening of monopoly, would shift the focus of copyright away from creation to investment and would require the international copyright system to be shifted to a registration system by the back door.

Chapter 11

Protected Works – Literary and Artistic Works

INTRODUCTION

[11.01] The protection afforded to an original work through the law of copyright is entirely dependant upon the statutory provisions of the Copyright Acts, for common law copyright protection has been held to have been swept away by copyright legislation.[1] Copyright protection for an original literary work, for example, will only be available if the subject matter in question is capable of satisfying the cumulative notion of an original literary work. The Copyright Act 1963 (CA 1963), however, did not provide any guidance on either the notion of originality or what may be considered to be a work. Section 2 of CA 1963 provided that the phrase 'literary work' included any written table or compilation. It is therefore necessary to scrutinise the cases in order to determine what the judges have considered to be an original literary work. Many of the older cases, however, must be viewed with some degree of caution because the earlier, pre-1911 legislative measures, did not, for example, in express terms require a literary work to be original; this requirement was implicit in the older case law. When the Copyright and Related Rights Act 2000 (CRRA 2000) came into operation on 1 January 2001, a number of significant changes to copyright law were made. In relation to literary works, for example, a compilation no longer falls within the definition of a literary work and such collections must now come within the definition of an original database or fall to be protected under the database right. Works in the form of words that are spoken are now clearly protected by the new definition of literary work. Some adjustments to the definitions of the constituent elements in an artistic work are also made by CRRA 2000 and the entire definition of an artistic work is more broadly based. CRRA 2000 also helpfully puts some of the restrictions upon eligibility for protection onto a statutory footing, in s 17. However, the key concept of an original work is otherwise not affected and it is to this definition that we shall now turn.

ORIGINAL

[11.02] Section 17(2)(a) of CRRA 2000 declares that copyright subsists in accordance with the Act in 'original, literary, dramatic, musical or artistic works'. The requirement that the work be original is intended to connect the work in question with the person responsible for its creation and its physical existence. In the leading case on originality, *University of London Press Ltd v University Tutorial Press Ltd*, Peterson J observed:[2]

---

[1] *Donaldson v Beckett* (1774) 4 Burr 2408; *Rooney v Kelly* (1861) 14 Ir CL Rep 158.
[2] *University of London Press Ltd v University Tutorial Press Ltd* [1916] 2 Ch 601 at 608–609.

The word 'original' does not in this connection mean that the work must be the expression of original or inventive thought. Copyright Acts are not concerned with the originality of ideas, but with the expression of thought, and, in the case of 'literary work' with the expression of thought in print or writing. The originality which is required relates to the expression of the thought. But the Act does not require that the expression must be in an original or novel form but that the work must not be copied from another work – that it should originate from the author.

[11.03] Later case law has described this as the 'not copied/originating from the putative author test'. Where the question of originality is put in issue, a number of factors may be involved. The work may be so commonplace that no spark of originality may be found therein. There may be evidence of a common origin for both the works in question to the extent that both are seen as derivative and lacking in any innovative quality such as may allow the court to condone those elements in the work that may have been directly copied. In general terms, the courts will look to the work as a whole and consider whether the work, as a whole, is original. An author may have taken inspiration for a work from a range of earlier works. While it may be possible to break up that work into its constituent parts and identify a relationship with earlier works or individual features, this will not be conclusive on the question of originality[3]. A court may also deny that a work is original for copyright purposes on the basis that the work subsists at a level of generality – an idea or principle – or to the extent that the work is a copy from a work that has previously been made available to the public: CRRA 2000, s 17(3) and 17(6). In particular, the originality test has been held not to require that there be a novelty in terms of idea or concept.[4] To quote from the judgment in one Australian case which discussed the issue of copyright residing in a standard form of contract, protection will be available for works, 'if they supply intelligible information and if mental effort and industry are required for their preparation'.[5] No less an authority than Sir Owen Dixon declared in *Victoria Park Racing and Recreation Grounds Co Ltd v Taylor* that a 'work need show no literary or other skill or judgment'; but it must originate with the author and be more than a copy of other material.[6] English cases express the same test.[7] The limited scope of the concept of an original work can be illustrated by comparing the position of a person who creates a poem with that of a literary editor who compiles an anthology of poems written and already published. In the former case copyright will be afforded to the poem if it has not been copied, or substantially copied, from the work of another person and it, as a piece of poetry, is original. However, in the latter case the anthology is derivative but may nevertheless be original, as an anthology, providing that such a compilation is not based upon some pre-existing work of compilation; some

---

3   *Ladbrooke (Football) Ltd v William Hill (Football) Ltd* [1964] 1 All ER 465 *per* Lord Reid at p 279; *Henkel KgaA v Holdfast* [2006] NZSC 102; *Electroquip Ltd v Craigco Ltd* [2008] NZHC 1371.

4   Eg *Walter v Lane* [1900] AC 539; *Sands and McDougall Pty Ltd v Robinson* (1917) 23 CLR 49.

5   *Reid Estate Institute of NSW v Wood* (1923) 23 SR(NSW) 439 at 352 *per* Street CJ.

6   *Victoria Park Racing and Recreation Grounds Co Ltd v Taylor* (1937) 58 CLR 479 at 51.

7   Eg *Bookmakers Afternoon Greyhound Services Ltd v Wilf Gilbert (Staffordshire) Ltd* [1994] FSR 723; *British Northrop Ltd v Texteam Blackburn* [1974] RPC 57.

degree of skill, discretion or choice must have been exercised in selecting the items to be included in the anthology.

The issue of originality, specifically whether there has been an exercise of labour, judgment or skill in the production of a work, arises most often in relation to compilations. In the leading case of *MacMillan & Co Ltd v K&J Cooper*,[8] the Privy Council observed that issues of this kind cannot be defined in precise terms and that the outcome in each case will depend largely on the facts of the case. However, the Privy Council there held that when the defendants edited or abridged the plaintiff's copyright work, North's translation of Plutarch's *Life of Alexander*, by leaving out the unimportant bits and deleting those parts of the work that were seen as verbiage, this was not of itself an act of creation. An original work, to exist, should demonstrate the exercise of skill or judgment; it should be an act of individuality. Even where a work is based upon a pre-existing literary work, the skill exercised in re-drafting, re-phrasing or reformatting the existing work may nevertheless involve sufficient skill or judgment so as to make the resulting work original.[9] The presentation of commonplace or prosaic kinds of factual material is sometimes denied copyright protection on the grounds of lack of originality, although these situations may just as conveniently be attributed to the non-literary quality of the work under review. The essential issue is whether the person who claims copyright has independently created the literary work or merely copied the efforts of others. A calligrapher who produces an ornamental piece of poetry by reference to a typed manuscript produced by a poet does not create an original literary work;[10] the only literary work in such a context remains the typed manuscript produced by the poet.

[11.04] The originality standard for a music work appears easy to satisfy. The eight bar organ introduction to 'A Whiter Shade of Pale', repeated twice with a slight variation on the second occasion, was added to the original song by the organist during rehearsals and was a part of the recording that was released with worldwide success[11]. The Court of Appeal held that the trial judge was correct to see the contribution as both original and worthy of giving the organist ownership of 40 per cent of the copyright, notwithstanding the fact that 'the melody would even strike a chord with an unworldly judge in its echoes of JS Bach, *Wachet Auf* and the second movement of his Keyboard Concerto No 5 in F Minor.'[12]

Originality in respect of a musical work may often focus on what is described as a 'hook', ie. 'that portion of the song that tends to stick in a listener's mind or memory; it can be a part of the music, a portion of the lyrics or both'.[13] Such a 'hook', even if

---

[8] *MacMillan & Co Ltd v K&J Cooper* (1923) 93 LJPC 113. See *Moffatt & Page Ltd v Gill & Sons Ltd* (1902) 18 TLR 547.

[9] *Express Newspapers plc v News (UK) Ltd* [1990] 3 All ER 376. This case also demonstrated that there may still be an infringement of copyright in the original.

[10] Is it a work of artistic craftsmanship?

[11] *Brooker v Fisher* [2008] EWCA Civ 287 (this point not appealed to the House of Lords).

[12] Per Mummery LJ in *Brooker v Fisher* [2008] EWCA Civ 287 at para 1. Originality and ownership were not at issue in the appeal to the House of Lords.

[13] *Larrikin Music Publishing Property Ltd v EMI Songs Australia Pty Ltd* (2010) 83 IPR 582, *per* Jackson J, citing *Drynan v Rostad* (1994) 59 CPR (3d) 8 at 18 and *Grignon v Roussel* (1991) 38 CPR (3d) 4 at 16.

limited to four bars, may constitute a substantial part of the work even if it does not necessarily constitute a substantial part of any infringing work. The test is an aural one, not a written one, for infringement purposes[14]

[11.05] The limited nature of the originality standard is in part due to the tendency of common law systems to provide copyright protection for creations which cannot be described as intellectually or culturally meritorious. The investment made in terms of time and effort is seen as worthy of protection because of the fact that the appropriation of another person's work cannot be satisfactorily addressed through traditional routes such as the criminal law[15] or tort – Irish law does not recognise a tort of unfair competition,[16] for example. The minimalist nature of the originality test, however, does contrast with that standard found in civilian jurisdictions and it may be that, in the context of purely factual works, the originality standard in US law, for example, is more demanding; but even in the English courts, the judges have stressed that it is not enough to confer the quality of originality on a work to show that labour and skill was expended in the process of copying or embellishing some pre-existing work.[17] Some independent product must be evident, even if the source of the independent product is identifiable.[18] In relation to translations, the question of originality is clearly measured by qualitative factors. The fact that a work has already been translated from one language to another will not mean that a subsequent translator's work will necessarily be characterised as a copy, even if the most recent translator consults earlier translations. A revision of vocabulary, for example, may make the translation 'flow' more easily than earlier translations, thereby demonstrating sufficient skill and judgment to confer the quality of originality. In *Drolet v Stiftung Gralsbotschaft*[19] the translation of one text from German into French was characterised as not simply being a copy of an earlier translation: the translator's work was said to have gone further than making cosmetic changes, altering the style of earlier translations to make it more literary and less literal, undoubtedly a sign of creativity.[20]

---

[14] *Austin v Columbia Gramaphone Co* [1923] Mac CC 398; *CBS Records v Gross* (1989) 15 IPR 385.

[15] Intangibles at common law cannot be stolen: see Clark, 'Computer Crime in Ireland' (1994) 2 Eur J Crime Cr L Cr J 252, at 257. See, now, the Criminal Justice (Theft and Fraud Offences) Act 2001.

[16] But see the Competition Acts 1991 to 2002: also *Samuelson v Producers Distributing Co* [1932] 1 Ch 201.

[17] *Per* Lord Oliver in *Interlego AG v Tyco Industries* [1988] 3 All ER 949 at 971.

[18] *Ladbroke (Football) Ltd v William Hill (Football) Ltd* [1964] 1 WLR 273; *Fortuity Property Ltd v Barcza* (1996) 36 IPR 529. For a spirited defence of originality in copyright, see Lea [1996] Ent LR 21.

[19] *Drolet v Stiftung Gralsbotschaft* [2009] FC 17.

[20] *Drolet v Stiftung Gralsbotschaft* [2009] FC 17, *per* de Montigny J at para 229.

ORIGINALITY – THE *INFOPAQ* DECISION

[11.06] Three Directives, the Computer Programs Directive,[21] the Database Directive[22] and the Term Consolidation Directive,[23] provide that, in respect of software, databases and certain photographs, the standard of protection is that of the work being the author's own intellectual creation. As the Community legislator had not sought to harmonise the originality standard for literary, dramatic or music works generally, the general belief was that the lower common law standard of originality could be retained and applied in the UK and Ireland. Some doubts have arisen on this point following the European Court of Justice (ECJ) decision in *Infopaq International A/S v Danske Dagblades Forening*.[24]

Infopaq provided an electronic information service by scanning newspaper articles without the permission of right holders, creating access to content in the form of strings of 11-word extracts to users. Within the context of art 2(a) of the Information Society Directive,[25] the issue was whether this activity was the reproduction of a substantial part of a work. After pointing out that the Information Society Directive did not define 'reproduction' or reproduction in part, the ECJ said that these concepts had to be interpreted in the context of both the Directive and international law. The use of the word 'work' in the Directive was held to indicate an intention to require the author's exclusive rights in respect of his or her 'works' to presuppose that the works are intellectual creations under the Berne Convention, art 2(5) and (8), a conclusion supported by the three Directives vis-à-vis software databases and certain photographs. The ECJ went on to hold that:

> in establishing a harmonised legal framework for copyright, Directive 2001/29 is based upon the same principle ... Copyright within the meaning of Article 2(a) of Directive 2001/29 is liable to apply only in relation to a subject matter what is original in the sense that it is its author's own intellectual creation.[26]

Read literally, the ECJ judgment can be said to have decided that in respect of works covered by the reproduction right in art 2(a), all such works must meet an intellectual creation test for eligibility for protection. It may be argued that the authors of art 2(a) had no such objective and there is nothing to suggest any intent on the part of the Community legislator to undertake a harmonisation exercise on any aspect of originality in Directive 2001/29/EC. Nevertheless, support for the harmonising effect of the Information Society Directive can be gleaned from *SAS Institute Inc v World Programming Ltd*.[27] In this complex case one issue that arose for consideration was whether the Community had in fact legislated in respect of the protection of ordinary literary works. Counsel for SAS contended that the Community had not legislated for

---

[21]   Directive 91/250/EEC ([1991] OJ L122/42), art 1(3).

[22]   Directive 96/9/EC ([1996] OJ L77/20), art 3(1).

[23]   Directive 2006/116/EC ([2006] OJ L 372/12), art 6.

[24]   *Infopaq International A/S v Danske Dagblades Forening* Case C-5/08 (16 July 2009).

[25]   Directive 2001/29/EC ([2001] OJ L 167/10).

[26]   *Infopaq International A/S v Danske Dagblades Forening* Case C-5/08, paras 36 and 37.

[27]   *SAS Institute Inc v World Programming Ltd* [2010] EWHC 1829 (Ch), (23 July 2010).

ordinary literary works so Community law was not relevant in determining how national courts were to interpret domestic legislation. Arnold J said:

> I do not accept this. The EU has legislated in relation to ordinary literary works, notably in the Information Society Directive. Whilst that is a measure of harmonisation and approximation of only some aspects of national copyright law as it affects literary works, it plainly brings ordinary literary works within the scope of the *acquis communitaire*. The ramifications of this can be seen from the ECJ's decision in *Infopaq*.

> It is now clear from *Infopaq* that there will only be reproduction of a substantial part of a literary work, including a compilation, where what has been reproduced represents the expression of the intellectual creation of the author of that literary work.[28]

Ironically, if the law of unintended consequences means that Directive 2001/29/EC has raised the originality threshold, the actual reasoning in *Infopaq* improves the prospect of copyright protection being extended into titles or headings that were previously regarded as not being copyright works. In *Infopaq* the ECJ considered that parts of a work, providing that the words in question 'contain elements that are the expression of the intellectual creation of the author of the work' may be eligible for protection. While words as such are ineligible,

> the possibility may not be ruled out that certain isolated sentences, or even certain parts of sentences in the text in question, may be suitable for conveying to the reader the originality of a publication such as a newspaper article, by communicating to that reader an element which is, in itself, the expression of the intellectual creation of the author of that article. Such sentences or parts of sentences are, therefore, liable to come within the scope of the protection provided for in Article 2(a) of that directive.

In the light of those considerations, the reproduction of an extract off a protected work which, like those at issue in the main proceedings, comprises 11 consecutive words thereof, is such as to constitute reproduction in a part within the meaning of art 2 of Directive 2001/29, if that extract contains an element of the work which, as such, expresses the author's own intellectual creation; it is for the national court to make this determination.[29]

LITERARY WORK

[11.07] Again, the leading case is *University of London Press Ltd v University Tutorial Press Ltd* where Peterson J said:[30]

---

[28] *SAS Institute Inc v World Programming Ltd* [2010] EWHC 1829 (Ch), paras 201 and 244.

[29] *Infopaq International A/S v Danske Dagblades Forening* Case-5/08, paras 47 and 48. See also *Fairfax Media Publications Pty Ltd v Reed International Books Australia Pty Ltd* [2010] FCA 984.

[30] *University of London Press Ltd v University Tutorial Press Ltd* [1916] 2 Ch 601 at 608. In one recent decision from the Australian courts copyright in a university medical school admissions test was established, even though half of the questions and answers had been sourced from existing materials. It is the selection and arrangement of materials rather than creation of individual questions that is the relevant aspect of originality in this context: *Boyapati v Rockefeller* (2008) 77 IPR 251.

In my view, the words 'literary work' cover work which is expressed in print or writing, irrespective of the question whether the quality or style is high. The word 'literary' seems to be used in a sense somewhat similar to the use of the word 'literature' in political or electioneering literature and refers to written or printed matter.

This view of the meaning of 'literary' was gathered from the long line of cases under the Literary Copyright Act 1842. In Irish law the decision of Peterson J, while far from being binding upon Irish judges either before or after the foundation of the State, has been cited with approval in the few cases in which the interpretation of the phrase 'literary work' has arisen. In developing the concept of literary as distinct from non-literary works, the English judgments have stressed that a literary work should convey, in the words of the Court of Appeal in the *Exxon* case,[31] 'information, instruction or pleasure'.

[11.08] The broad view taken of the concept of a literary work is no doubt explained by the concern of the judiciary to protect the effort and investment made by the putative copyright holder when others seek to take a free ride on the back of those efforts or investment. However is it not essential to show that the literary work has commercial value. In a recent Canadian, case the author of a learned treatise on the Old West successfully claimed for copyright infringement when parts of the thesis were used by the writer of a popular book on Canadian farming history. The fact that the thesis itself was not commercially exploitable did not preclude the plaintiff from asserting copyright in his work. It the work was created with no intent that it would ever be 'commercialised' this will not prevent a court from awarding significant levels of damages if the work should be appropriated by being used, for example, for a sensationalist publication in a newspaper[32] although injunctive relief is the normal remedy if publication has not taken place.[33] Other works that one would readily recognise as being literary efforts include the novels of Laurie Lee and the plays of Shaw, the letters of Swift and Pope, translated and annotated works of Plutarch, a John Osborne film script, and a learned scholar's annotation of an ancient Sanskrit text or the dead sea scrolls.[34] However, in the *University of London Press* case,[35] Peterson J emphasised that the word 'literary' was not to be interpreted 'in the sense in which that phrase is applied, for instance, to Meredith's novels and the writings of Robert Louis Stevenson', and for this reason the efforts of newspaper reporters who file copy for an evening newspaper on the mundane proceedings of Dublin's criminal courts,[36] the life of sporting celebrities,[37] or the British Royal family,[38] are considered to be literary works.

---

[31] *Exxon Corpn v Exxon Insurance Consultants International Ltd* [1981] 3 All ER 241; In Canada see *British Columbia v Mihaljevic* (1991) 36 CPR (3d) 445 and *Shewan v Canada (AG)* (1999) 87 CPR (3d) 475.

[32] *Nottinghamshire Healthcare v News Group Newspapers* [2002] RPC 962.

[33] *Breen v Hancock House Publishers Ltd* (1985) 6 CPR (3d) 433.

[34] *Kimron v Herschel Shanks* [1993] EIPR D-151.

[35] *University of London Press Ltd v University Tutorial Press Ltd* [1916] 2 Ch 601.

[36] *Hall v Crosbie* (1931) 66 ICTR 22.

[37] *Donoghue v Allied Newspapers* [1938] Ch 106.

[38] *Express Newspapers v News UK* [1990] 3 All ER 376.

The early Irish case of *Hodges v Walsh*[39] holds that law digests and reports are copyright protected[40] as literary works and a lawyer's precedents are also literary works.[41] Letters are literary works, regardless of the identity of the writer, and persons who write down a public speech or address, whether in long hand or shorthand, acquire a copyright in the document thus created, whether the speech is delivered in a perfect or garbled fashion, or the person taking down the speech demonstrates an ability to turn a halting or disjointed address into fluid prose or converts a flowing and coherent verbal presentation into a poorly constructed written format.[42]

[11.09] Judicial decisions have protected commercial documents that cannot be said to have any literary quality, in the popular sense of that phrase. Descriptive advertisements,[43] trade circulars and handbills,[44] consignment notes[45] and booksellers' and pharmacists' catalogues,[46] have all been held to be literary works. Maps and charts,[47] telegraphic codes devised to assist in transmitting telegraph messages,[48] railway guides and road guides,[49] football coupons,[50] lists of football fixtures and racing cards,[51] as well as radio and television listings,[52] are works which warrant copyright protection as long as an adequate level of skill or effort can be said to have gone into the production of that product.

[11.10] If there is insufficient skill or effort then the work will not be held to be literary. The unintelligible scribblings executed by a man whilst in a state of intoxication are not literary works, presumably because there was no information, entertainment or enjoyment conveyed by such a 'message'.[53] In the early case of *Bailey v Taylor*[54]

---

39   *Hodges v Walsh* (1840) 2 IR Eq R 266.
40   *Sweet v Benning* (1855) 16 CB 459; *Butterworth v Robinson* (1801) 5 Ves 709; *Saunders v Smith* (1838) 3 My & Cr 711.
41   *Co-operative Union Ltd v Kilmore Dairy Society Ltd* (1912) 47 ILTR 7.
42   *Walter v Lane* [1900] AC 539.
43   *Maple v Junior Army and Navy Stores* (1882) 21 Ch D 369; *Slumber Magic Co v Sleep King Bed Co* (1984) 3 CPR (3d) 81; *Ryan v Lum* (1989) 14 IPR 513 (packaging).
44   *Native Guano Co Ltd v Sewage Manure Co* (1889) 8 RPC 125; *Lamb v Evans* [1893] 1 Ch 218; *Comyns v Hyde* (1895) 72 LT 250.
45   *Van Oppen & Co Ltd v Van Oppen* (1903) 20 RPC 617.
46   *Collis v Cater* (1898) 78 LT 613; *Andrew Cash & Co v Porter* (1996) 36 IPR 309 (pawnbroker's ticket).
47   *Stannard v Lee* (1870) 6 Ch App 346; *Carey v Fadin* (1799) 6 Ves 24.
48   *Ager v Peninsula & Oriental Steam Navigation Co* (1884) 26 Ch D 637; *Anderson & Co v Lieber Code Co* (1917) 33 TLR 420.
49   *Kelly v Byles* (1879) 13 Ch D 682; *Leslie v Young* [1894] AC 335.
50   *Ladbroke (Football) Ltd v William Hill (Football) Ltd* [1964] 1 WLR 273.
51   *Canterbury Park Race Course Co v Hopkins* (1932) 49 NSWWN 27. Selections or forecasts are not copyright protected: *Chilton v Progress Printing* (1894) 71 LT 664; *Bookmakers Afternoon Greyhound Services Ltd v Wilf Gilbert (Staffordshire) Ltd* [1994] FSR 723.
52   *RTE v Magill TV Guide* [1990] ILRM 534.
53   *Fournet v Pearson Ltd* (1897) 14 TLR 82.
54   *Bailey v Taylor* (1824) 3 LJOS 66. This seems to be wrongly decided; see *Stevenson v Crook* [1938] Ex CR 299.

copyright protection for annuity tables was denied on the ground that these tables could have been calculated by a competent person in a matter of hours. Similarly, in *Page v Wisden*[55] a scoring sheet drawn up to record the scores in cricket matches was denied copyright protection because the format employed was commonplace and merely mathematical in nature. These two decisions do not sit easily with some more recent cases[56] in which the author has been held to be entitled to copyright protection in respect of mathematical formulae developed in order to allow gaming machines that operate via computer programmes to function satisfactorily, the author/programmer demonstrating a considerable level of skill and judgment. These remain cases where the court may conclude that the contribution lacks the requisite degree of expenditure of skill or judgment in relation to the fixation of the work itself. Colour coding of a grid template used by a bookmaker in presenting information lacks either literary or artistic content for copyright purposes: *Status Card Australia Pty Ltd v Rotondo*.[57]

[11.11] Even when the work is of its nature derivative, there can be copyright protection for such compilations. Most maps, anthologies, annotations, abridgements, translations and written transcriptions of a verbal address are nevertheless the subject of copyright protection in appropriate instances.[58] In this area of copyright protection for derivative works, the issue of copyright and editorially created texts such as the headnotes that accompany court judgments has proved extremely controversial. In the US the trend is to see such works as lacking the necessary spark of originality so as to constitute a literary work.[59] However, most common law jurisdictions that adopt the not copied, originating from the putative author test have rejected this standard. Most recently, the Canadian Federal Court of Appeal in *CCH Canadian Ltd v Law Society of Upper Canada*,[60] overruling a decision of the Ontario High Court, held that the reported decisions of a legal publisher, involving not just the judgment but editorial input, house style, the use of catchlines to highlight points and summary materials, were original works. Further, headnotes were not just summaries of reasons but original works in their own right. This view has been upheld by the Supreme Court of Canada on appeal.[61]

[11.12] The necessary skill, labour and judgment will include not only the skill, labour and judgment necessary to create the literary document but also efforts made to create a document that has commercial value or integrity. In *RTE v Magill TV Guide*[62] Lardner J said:

---

55   *Page v Wisden* (1869) 20 LT 435; *Kalamazoo (Aust) Ltd v Compact Business Systems Ltd* (1985) 5 IPR 213 suggests the test is one based upon whether the work is 'substantial'.

56   *Milwell Pty Ltd v Olympic Amusements Pty* (1999) 43 IPR 32.

57   *Status Card Australia Pty Ltd v Rotondo* [2008] QSC 181; Chesterman J in *Status Card* doubted whether *Kalamazoo* was correctly decided.

58   *Desktop Marketing Systems Pty Ltd v Telstra Corpn* (2002) 55 IPR 1.

59   *Feist Publications Inc v Rural Telephone Service* (1991) 20 IPR 129; *Bender v West* 158 F 3d 674 (1998 2nd Cir CA).

60   *CCH Canadian Ltd v Law Society of Upper Canada* (2002) 18 CPR (4th) 161.

61   *CCH Canadian Ltd v Law Society of Upper Canada* (2004) 30 CPR (4th) 1.

62   *RTE v Magill TV Guide* [1990] ILRM 534; contrast *Victoria Park Racing & Recreation Grounds Co v Taylor* (1937) 58 CLR 479.

I am satisfied that each weekly schedule is the result of a great deal of preliminary consideration and work and of the exercise of skill and judgment. It is the creation of RTE … the pattern and order in which the various programmes in each week are to be broadcast is determined by RTE – a determination which I am satisfied involves the exercise of skill and judgment.

It is arguable that on this point Lardner J's judgment may be open to attack. Some cases make the point that the skill and judgment that comes within the protectable sphere of copyright is the skill and judgment needed to create the literary work, not the investment that went into creating the underlying product. For example, the investment of time and effort put into creating a valuable design product is to be distinguished from the time and effort taken in putting the design onto paper.[63] However, the cases tend to err on the side of generosity whenever this argument surfaces, and originality is normally upheld.[64]

[11.13] In *Football League Ltd v Littlewoods Pools Ltd*,[65] Upjohn J considered that the considerable skill and judgment applied in ensuring that matches did not clash with local holidays, with other sporting events, and in meeting the wishes of each football league club, whenever possible, meant that such skill and judgment, when coupled with the lesser task of transcribing the decision on when each match was to take place, was such as to satisfy the 'literary work' concept. More recently, the complex task of calculating betting odds, as part of a pools or computerised gaming activity,[66] has been held to satisfy the 'skill, labour and judgment' requirement. Many of the cases in which the element of 'skill, labour and judgment' has been missing involve the compilation of works from pre-existing sources, the works in question possessing a factual element. In *Leslie v Young*,[67] the House of Lords held that the publication of railway timetables by the respondent, the timetables in question having been previously published by the appellant, was not an infringement of the appellant's copyright in these tables because the common source of each table was the railway company timetable – no independent work of significance had been done by either party. However, when the appellants had further processed information about railway journeys so as to compile a separate list of tours, this useful abridgement of information could be regarded as an independent literary work. The compilation of existing facts into a systematic course of instruction, for example, by adopting some kind of question and answer format, was held to be copyright protected, although the format was not the subject of a copyright in itself.[68] In the Canadian case of *Horn Abbot Ltd v WB Coulter Sales Ltd*,[69] the plaintiffs sought to protect their board game, 'Trivial Pursuit' from being substantially reproduced. The

---

63 *Elanco Products Ltd v Mandops* [1979] FSR 46.

64 *Autospin (Oil Seals) Ltd v Beehive Spinning (a firm)* [1995] RPC 683; *Football Dataco Ltd v Britten's Pools Ltd* [2010] EWHC 841 (Ch).

65 *Football League Ltd v Littlewoods Pools Ltd* [1959] Ch 637; *A-One Accessories Imports Pty v Off-Road Imports Pty* (1996) 36 IPR 306.

66 *BC Jockey Club v Standen* (1985) 8 CPR (3d) 283.

67 *Leslie v Young* [1894] AC 335.

68 *Jarrold v Houlston* (1857) 3 K&J 708.

69 *Horn Abbot Ltd v WB Coulter Sales Ltd* (1984) 77 CPR (2d) 145. Constrast *Wall v Horn Abbot Ltd* (2007) 256 NSR (2d) 34 (inital idea not copyright protected).

court was at pains to point out that a question and answer board game could not be protected as such, but because the defendants had produced their own product in a short period of time and because there was a substantial similarity in relation to the nearly 5,000 questions and answers, an inference of copying could certainly be drawn.

[11.14] Sometimes copyright protection is denied on the ground that the plaintiff is seeking to protect information obtainable from common sources, the form in which the information is held by the plaintiff being of secondary importance. In *Odham's Press Ltd v London and Provincial Sporting News Agency (1929) Ltd*[70] the plaintiffs employed at race meetings two persons to transmit by telephone to the plaintiffs the starting prices of the three placed horses. Information was obtained from bookmakers, from 'tic tac' men and other trade sources. However, the only written account of this exercise was a notebook that was clearly not a detailed or systematic record of the research undertaken for the plaintiffs; Eve J clearly viewed the entry as a random jotting in the nature of an *aide-mémoire*. In *GA Cramp & Sons Ltd v Frank Smythson Ltd*[71] the plaintiffs claimed that when the defendants reproduced in their 1942 diary some seven tables of factual material taken from the plaintiffs' 1933 diary, there was an infringement of the plaintiffs' copyright. The House of Lords, overruling a majority judgment of the Court of Appeal, held that there was no copyright owned by the plaintiffs in these seven tables as a compilation. There was no proof that each table had been compiled by the plaintiffs – indeed the tables were commonplace factual tables produced by organisations like the Post Office and the Automobile Association – and their Lordships found that tables of this kind were commonplace in diaries of this kind. The selection of these seven timetables was said by Lord MacMillan to be a collection 'of an obvious and commonplace character and I fail to detect any meritorious distinctness in it'.

TITLES, SLOGANS AND WORDS AS LITERARY WORKS

[11.15] It is difficult to obtain copyright protection for the title of a book, a song, an advertising slogan or word. In certain instances, a word or phrase may be a registered trade mark and in such a case the use of the word or phrase may give rise to a remedy for the proprietor of the mark.[72] Similarly, the law of passing off may give protection when the name or phrase is used in connection with goods or services in a misleading manner.[73] In principle, however, a short poem or a part of a larger work, such as the title

---

[70] *Odham's Press Ltd v London and Provincial Sporting News Agency* (1929) Ltd [1935] 1 Ch 672. See also *Victoria Park Racing & Recreation Grounds Co v Taylor* (1937) 58 CLR 479.

[71] *GA Cramp & Sons Ltd v Frank Smythson Ltd* [1944] AC 329; contrast *Artifakts Design Group v Rigg Ltd* [1993] 1 NZLR 196.

[72] *'High Life', Miller Brewing Co v Controller* [1988] ILRM 259. *'Bubble Up', Seven Up Co v Bubble Up Co* [1990] ILRM 204.

[73] *Valentine v Valentine* (1892) 31 LR Ir 488. The use of a title and other colourable imitations of another's work are protected under *Mack v Petter* (1872) LR 14 Eq 431; *Kelly v Byles* (1879) 13 Ch D 682, distinguishing *Metzler v Wood* (1878) 8 Ch D 606 and *Croft v Day* (1843) 7 Beav 84. Stone [1996] 7 Ent LR 178, 263, in two interesting articles considers both the copyright and passing off reliefs available for titles, character, names and catchphrases.

or chorus line of a song, can be copyright protected as an original literary work if the work is original and has sufficient definition to be regarded as a work. In *Francis & Day and Hunter Ltd v Twentieth Century Fox Corpn Ltd*[74] the Privy Council held that the use of the phrase, 'The man who broke the Bank at Monte Carlo' as the title of a feature film did not infringe the plaintiff's copyright in a song which bore that phrase as its title. The words of the song title were 'too insubstantial' to attract copyright, qua title. In the later case of *Canadian Olympic Association v Konica Canada Ltd*[75] the Canadian Federal Court of Appeal held that the phrase 'Guinness Book of Olympic Records' was also not copyright protected and that the infringement point was *a fortiori* within the *Man who broke the Bank at Monte Carlo* case.

[11.16] The balance of recent judicial authority in England favours the view that the selection of a title for a book from common phrases, or everyday words, cannot be regarded as exercising sufficient skill and judgment to warrant being held to be literary. In *Dicks v Yates*[76] the plaintiffs were assignees of copyright in a novel entitled 'Splendid Misery', which the plaintiff serialised in a weekly periodical. The defendant also published a serial entitled 'Splendid Misery'. Jessel MR held that these words are common English words and their combination was hackneyed, given that an earlier writer had used just this phrase in 1801 for the title of a novel. To similar effect is the recent Canadian decision in *Tomas v Boaden Catering Ltd*.[77] The defendants replicated 50 per cent of the plaintiff's two-page children's menu and were held to have infringed vis-à-vis the literary content of the menu, but the plaintiffs could not assert copyright over short phrases and titles that were 'generic' in nature. Nevertheless, should a combination of words be devised which is neither commonplace nor hackneyed, it is in law still possible to argue that copyright in that title may subsist. A central issue is the skill and judgment exercised in selecting the title in question rather than the time, skill or judgment exercised in reducing it into written form, which will be minimal. *McIndoo v Musson Book Co*,[78] a decision of the Ontario Court of Appeal, leaves this point open, for while the court held that copyright cannot subsist for a book title *simpliciter*, it may be that if the author can demonstrate that the title amounts to a literary, scientific or artistic composition, protection will be available. It is conceivable, therefore, that if the author demonstrates originality, or skill, or effort, copyright protection may be available to a title but the facts will have to be exceptional. In a recent New Zealand case, the slogan, 'Field Friendly – the best choice was field work', developed as a 'snappy memorable

---

[74] *Francis & Day and Hunter Ltd v Twentieth Century Fox Corpn Ltd* [1940] AC 112. In *Gormley v EMI Records Ireland Ltd* [1999] 1 IRLM 178, the phrase 'dirty auld squealer' was not copyright protected.

[75] *Canadian Olympic Association v Konica Canada Ltd* (1991) 24 IPR (3d) 216.

[76] *Dicks v Yates* (1881) 18 Ch D 76. See also *Licensed Victuallers Newspaper Co v Bingham* (1888) 38 Ch D 139. The earlier case of *Weldon v Dicks* (1878) 10 Ch D 247 seems incompatible with these decisions.

[77] *Tomas v Boaden Catering Ltd* (1995) 68 CPR (3d) 275.

[78] *McIndoo v Musson Book Co* (1916) 26 DLR 550. The point was also left open in *Shetland Times v Jonathan Wills* [1997] FSR 604; *Ward* [1997] CLSR 123. See now *Fairfax Media Publications Pty Ltd v Reed International Books Australia Pty Ltd* [2010] FCA 984.

phrase' to describe a system of marking electrical wires on site, was held to have been the result of independent skill, labour and judgment, the product itself having been redesigned to render it more user friendly 'in the field'.[79] The court placed much emphasis upon the slogan not being hackneyed and viewed it as conveying information associated with the product. It may be that the reasoning of the ECJ in *Infopaq International A/S v Danske Dagblades Forening*[80] also marks a more liberalising trend.

[11.17] Where the claim is brought in respect of a short phrase, whether it be to convey information[81] or advertise some product,[82] copyright protection is generally denied. In *Sinanide v La Maison Kosmeo*[83] the plaintiff, a beauty therapist, claimed copyright in a phrase, namely, that beauty was 'a social necessity, not a luxury'. The defendant later advertised his own beauty treatments with advertisements proclaiming that 'a youthful appearance is a social necessity'. While the case can be regarded as turning upon evidence that prior to the plaintiff's use of his phrase, a similar phrase had been constructed by yet another beautician (thus bringing the plaintiff's phrase within the notion of a commonplace or hackneyed expression and *Dicks v Yates*),[84] Scrutton LJ went further and observed that in the absence of a passing off or trade mark action, the quotation of a bit of a sentence is too small a matter to afford a ground for a copyright infringement action; in other words, the basis of this part of the judgment is that quotation of a tiny portion of a literary work – here, the advertisement as a whole – is not substantial reproduction. The case is suspect, not least because Scrutton LJ regarded both the professional involved and the dispute as unmeritorious,[85] but because all the Court of Appeal decided was that this phrase was not original nor had sufficient of the phrase been reproduced so as to constitute substantial reproduction of it; it clearly cannot be relied upon in an age when millions are apparently spent devising advertising slogans and phrases which cannot be considered to be hackneyed or commonplace, and which clearly serve to identify the advertiser's product or service. However, there are a number of cases in which the capture of the titles for newspaper articles by internet search engines, those titles being reproduced on a defendant's website, that site then

---

[79] *Sunlec International Pty Ltd v Electropar Ltd* (2008) 79 IPR 411; Sumpter [2009] EIPR 887.

[80] *Infopaq International A/S v Danske Dagblades Forening* Case C-5/08 (String of 11 words extracted from newspaper articles might be protected if words represent author's own intellectual creation).

[81] *Page v Wisden* (1869) 20 LT 435. The words 'Help-Help Driver in Danger-Call-Police-Ph.000', devised by the plaintiffs for a taxi driver duress situation, were held not to be copyright. Emmet J did not doubt that in some cases a title may be so extensive and of such significant character as to attract copyright protection. In this case, however, the words did no more than state an idea that a taxi driver was in peril. This was a case where the idea and the expressions merged and the words were thus not protected: *Victoria v Pacific Technologies (Australia) Pty* (2009) 81 IPR 524.

[82] On what product is being advertised see *Canadian Olympic Association v Konica Canadian Inc* (1991) 24 IPR 216.

[83] *Sinanide v La Maison Kosmeo* (1928) 44 TLR 574; *Rose v Information Services* [1987] FSR 254.

[84] *Dicks v Yates* (1881) 18 Ch D 76.

[85] See the opening passage of the Lord Justice's judgment at (1928) 44 TLR 574, 575.

permitting deep linking to the plaintiff's own site, has raised the issue of copyright infringement. If the act of infringement is reproduction of the headline of the defendant as distinct from infringement by way of caching or deep-linking or authorising infringement, then it is difficult to see how the reproduction of the title to the plaintiff's article *per se* can be an infringement unless the title is a literary work.[86] This subject may be in need of review should sentences or phrases found in newspaper headlines be capable of being protected even if protection here rests on a finding of systematic extraction of insubstantial parts of a work that may not of itself be within copyright.[87]

[11.18] Where the issue descends into the area of single words, whether they be ordinary words in English or some other language, or invented words, the balance of decided case law is against the word being copyright protected. In the *Wombles*[88] and *Kojak*[89] litigation the issue was regarded as being whether a proprietary right could exist in a word, whether actual or invented, and in both instances the same judge answered the question in the negative. While it is understandable that the courts should be wary about extending property rights over parts of the language, this does not appear to be at all powerful when the word is invented, and has been the subject of skill, judgment, investment or expertise in devising or selecting the word in circumstances where it can be concluded that an original literary work has been devised. Nevertheless, in *Exxon Corpn v Exxon Insurance Consultants International Ltd*[90] the Court of Appeal regarded the word 'Exxon' as incapable of being itself an original literary work for, as an invented word, it by itself, divorced from the context of a supply of goods or services, did not convey information, instruction or pleasure.[91] While Stephenson LJ was not prepared to rule that an invented word could never of itself be an original literary work, Oliver LJ and Sir David Cairns expressed no opinion on this question. Elsewhere, the view in Canada seems to be that the words 'Expo' and 'Expo 86' whether they be regarded as a single word, a name or a title of an event, are not copyright protected.[92] Cullabine, in his review of South African law, noted that the scant case law in that jurisdiction meant the point was still open.[93]

[11.19] The only recent sign that an invented word may be able to obtain copyright protection comes as an *obiter dictum* in the *Ninja Turtles* case[94] where Browne-

---

[86] *Shetland Times v Wills* (1996) 37 IPR 71. On the other hand, the Australian case of *Fairfax Media Publications Pty Ltd v Reed International Books Australia Pty Ltd* [2010] FCA 984 holds there is no per se exclusion but evidence of originality and authorship of headlines will be problematical. The *Infopaq* decision of the ECJ (Case C-5/08) certainly opens up the prospect of even minimal strings of words being regarded as 'works'.

[87] *Native Guano Co Ltd v Sewage Manure Co* (1889) 8 RPC 125.

[88] *Wombles Ltd v Wombles Skips Ltd* [1975] FSR 488.

[89] *Taverner Rutledge Ltd v Trexapalm Ltd* [1975] FSR 479.

[90] *Exxon Corpn v Exxon Insurance Consultants International Ltd* [1981] 3 All ER 241.

[91] Following Davey LJ in *Hollinrake v Truswell* [1894] 3 Ch 420 at 428; see Stephenson LJ at 248b, Oliver LJ at 249e.

[92] *British Columbia v Mihaljevic et al* (1991) 36 CPR (3d) 445.

[93] Cullabine [1992] 6 EIPR 205 at 210.

[94] *Mirage Studios v Counter Feat Clothing* [1991] FSR 145.

Wilkinson VC expressed the view that he saw no reason why such a word could not, in appropriate circumstances, be regarded as an original literary work. An Irish court has yet to address the point and the decision in *Reed v O'Meara*[95] which gave the plaintiffs a right to exclusivity in the use of the title 'The Grocer' would probably be regarded as a passing off rather than a purely copyright decision. The disgruntled novelist who finds that another writer has purloined a title must utilise passing off or rely instead on the substantive law of copyright infringement where the lifting of a plot or scenario constitutes copyright infringement in the work,[96] even if a different title is used. The use of a title to advertise a novel or play that does not bear any relationship with an earlier work – only the title, not the plot is copied – appears not to give the author of the first title any obvious remedy in copyright. If the word or phrase, however, appears in a distinctive form then protection of the stylised format may be available via artistic copyright.[97]

WHAT IS NOT AN ORIGINAL LITERARY WORK

[11.20] In the *Exxon* case[98] the Court of Appeal re-emphasised the notion that an original literary work must be able to convey information, instruction or pleasure. To this must be added the refinement that under CA 1963, for the work to be literary, it must be contained in print or writing.[99] The phrase must be regarded as essentially composite in nature[100] but there are elements of the phrase that can be divided up. Section 17 of CRRA 2000, however, contains a number of propositions that reflect a body of case law that denies copyright protection in certain instances. Section 17 states that copyright is not to extend to the ideas and principles that underlie any element in a work, nor to procedures, methods of operation or mathematical concepts.[101] Nor does copyright subsist in a work that infringes, or to the extent that it infringes, another work.[102] Nor does copyright subsist in a work to the extent that the work is a copy of a work that has been previously made available to the public.[103]

[11.21] Works which exist at a level of generality that permits a court to hold that it subsists at the level of an idea or a principle, include the 'commonplace' use of an archway in architectural drawings.[104] A chemical formula used to create a dye was also

---

[95] *Reed v O'Meara* (1888) 21 LR (Ir) 216; *Chappell v Sheard* (1855) 2 K&J 117.

[96] *Correlli v Gray* (1913) 30 TLR 116; *Zeccola v Universal City Studios* (1982) 46 ALR 189.

[97] *Paramount Pictures Corpn v Howley* (1991) 39 CPR (3d) 419.

[98] *Exxon Corpn v Exxon Insurance Consultants International Ltd* [1981] 3 All ER 241 at 248 and 249. *Kalamazoo (Aust) Ltd v Compact Business Systems Ltd* (1985) 5 IPR 213.

[99] *University of London Press Ltd v University Tutorial Press* [1916] 2 Ch 601 at 608, *per* Peterson J.

[100] *Exxon Corpn v Exxon Insurance Consultants International Ltd* [1981] 3 All ER 241, *per* Oliver LJ.

[101] CRRA 2000, s 17(3).

[102] CRRA 2000, s 17(5).

[103] CRRA 2000, s 17(6).

[104] *Jones v Tower Hamlets* [2001] RPC 407.

held to be an idea that could not attract copyright *per se*: *Tri Tex v Ghaly*.[105] There are also a number of cases that illustrate what is meant by a procedure or a method of operation. For instance, in *Boosey v Whight*,[106] perforated sheets to be used in mechanical pianolas were regarded as part of a mechanical contrivance for producing musical notes and as such were neither musical nor literary works, a decision that led to changes in copyright law via the UK Copyright Act 1911.

[11.22] In *Hollinrake v Truswell*,[107] copyright protection as a literary work was denied to a cardboard arm to be used as an aid to dressmaking. In *Libraco (Ltd) v Shaw Walker (Ltd)*[108] a system of colour coding a card index system was denied literary copyright on the ground that the cards merely gathered information under rubrics such as name and address. Copyright in a system of teaching by the use of sets of coloured rods was denied in the Canadian case of *Cuisenaire v South West Imports Ltd*,[109] a distinction being drawn between an explanatory book which could be copyright and the means of implementation, which was, in essence, an idea. Shadow cards or silhouettes were denied literary copyright on the basis that such a card was merely 'a child's toy',[110] while a Christmas card could be copyright protected via literary copyright in respect of the verse or sentiment therein.[111] The fact that a document contains or conveys information, instruction or pleasure does not guarantee the document the status of an original literary work if the document conveys such information or instruction in the only form in which that idea is capable of expression.[112] Mathematical formulae are also *per se* excluded from protection, but mathematical questions that form a part of a mathematics examination paper,[113] that are used in order to create a computer program or which are used in calculating a gaming machine's patterns of distribution will be copyright protected in an indirect sense.[114]

COMPILATIONS

[11.23] There is a significant difference between treatment of works of compilation under CA 1963 and the treatment of collections under CRRA 2000. Original compilations of works are to be treated as literary works under CA 1963, while collections of works, data and other materials that are original are denied protection as

---

[105] *Tri Tex v Ghaly* (1999) 1 CPR (4th) 160, following *Moreau v St Vincent* [1950] Ex CR198.
[106] *Boosey v Whight* [1900] 1 Ch 122.
[107] *Hollinrake v Truswell* [1894] 3 Ch 420; *Davis v Comitti* (1885) 52 LT 539.
[108] *Libraco (Ltd) v Shaw Walker (Ltd)* (1913) 30 TLR 22.
[109] *Cuisenaire v South West Imports Ltd* [1969] SCR 208; contrast *Church v Linton* (1894) 25 OR 131.
[110] *Cable v Marks* (1882) 47 LT 432.
[111] *Hildesheimer & Faulkner v Dunn & Co* (1891) 64 LT 452.
[112] *Kenrick v Lawrence* (1890) 25 QBD 99.
[113] *University of London Press Ltd v University Tutorial Press Ltd* [1916] 2 Ch 601.
[114] *Milwell Pty Ltd v Olympic Amusement Pty Ltd* (1999) 43 IPR 32; *Boyapati v Rockefeller* (2008) 77 IPR 251.

literary works but are to be treated as original databases under CRRA 2000. This treatment is due to the 1996 Database Directive[115] but, save for the scope of the definitions of 'database' and 'original database' (specifically 'original'), it is arguable that, under Irish law, this recent bifurcation is unlikely to bring about any radical differences because unauthorised use of the contents of a collection was regarded as an infringement of copyright in any respect. But, because of the possibility that CA 1963 will remain relevant for many years, it is necessary to provide readers with an analysis of rights in relation to compilations. Let us first of all deal with issues of definition.

[11.24] The otherwise unhelpful definition of literary work in s 2 of CA 1963 declares that the concept 'includes any ... compilation'. The section therefore makes it clear that existing forms of literary work, when in printed or written form, may be selected or arranged in such a way as to obtain a separate copyright for the compiler or arranger if sufficient skill or judgment can be shown to exist in relation to the selection or presentation of the compilation. This is difficult to establish in relation to factual material such as tables of tides or postal charges[116] or railway timetables[117] gleaned from one central source, which must be correct if they are to be of any value. The selection of factual information such as a person's name and address for inclusion in telephone, trade, professional or street directories has long been protected by the English courts, partly because these older cases tended to overlook the originality requirement which was an implicit requirement in the early statutory regimes. In contrast, however, the US Supreme Court[118] has ruled that purely factual data compiled by a telephone company about its subscribers and arranged in alphabetical form lacked the modicum of originality necessary to satisfy the US originality element. While the Supreme Court indicated that most compilations would easily pass such a test, there is some support for the view that the English courts may have to re-assess these directory decisions if, like the Australian courts, the view emerges that skill and judgment, rather than the expenditure of money and effort is to be the standard for copyright protection, particularly in a contemporary context where much of the labour and donkey work in producing factual or data rich compilations can be done by way of information technology.

[11.25] There is, of course, a requirement that any compilation of facts should pass an originality test because the idea/expression dichotomy would be nonsensical if one fact is not copyrightable but a grouping of 60 facts could be copyrightable. Predictable compilations, to be anticipated in the context in which the compilation is put, lack such originality[119] and the copyright protection for white pages and yellow pages telephone

---

[115] Council Directive 96/9/EC.

[116] *Cramp (GA) & Sons v Frank Smythson Ltd* [1944] AC 329.

[117] *Leslie v Young* [1894] AC 335.

[118] *Feist Publications Inc v Rural Telephone Service* (1991) 20 IPR 129. See note by Ginsberg (1992) 92 Col LR 338. *Feist* has also been followed in Canada. This is fully discussed at para **[14.03]**.

[119] *Cramp (GA) & Sons v Frank Smythson Ltd* [1944] AC 329.

directories has been removed by judicial decision.[120] Canadian case law[121] reaffirms that the originality standard can include industrious collection and that the basic test does not require creativity or originality of ideas. This is clearly put by Whitford J in *Gleeson v Denne Ltd*,[122] an artistic copyright case. After citing *Cramp (GA) & Sons v Frank Smythson Ltd*, Whitford J observed:[123]

> It has long been held in the field of literary copyright that, in order to secure protection, it is not necessary that there be any literary merit as such at all. If you work hard enough, walking down the streets, taking down the names of people who live at houses and make a street directory as a result of that labour, this has been held to be an exercise sufficient to justify you in making a claim to copyright in the work you ultimately produce.

[11.26] Where the material selected or arranged is not overtly factual[124] then there will be greater room for the exercise of skill, judgment, taste or some subjective (and thus individualistic) criteria – eg the compiler's 50 favourite poems on the theme of love or beauty. So a compilation of tables of football matches, grouped in such a way as to allow punters to place bets on the outcome of matches, was held to be an original work of compilation because the skill, judgment and labour exercised in selecting the bets could not be separated from the, admittedly less meritorious, effort expended in putting this onto paper.[125]

[11.27] A similar procedure is found in relation to television programme listings. The argument that a television company that compiles a list of programmes to be shown cannot acquire a copyright in information or a mere listing has been met by the argument that the skill and effort spent in devising a suitable schedule of programmes cannot be separated from the expression of that process of selection.[126] However, the compiler must, of course, obtain any copyright clearance necessary if the compiler is not also to be an infringer. An anthology of Elizabethan love poems will be a good deal easier to produce than a compilation of similar twentieth century poems, for obvious reasons.

[11.28] The fact that the English and Irish standard for originality is so low reflects the concern of the courts to prevent parasitic trading, which these jurisdictions find difficult to counteract for neither unfair competition nor passing off provide relief in such a

---

[120] *Telstra Corporation Ltd v Phone Directories Company Pty Ltd* [2010] FCA 44.

[121] Despite a flirtation with *Feist Publications Inc v Rural Telephone Service* (1991) 20 IPR 129 in both *Edutile Inc v APA* (2000) 6 CPR (4th) 211 and *Tele-Direct (Publications) Inc v American Business Information Inc* (1998) 154 DLR (4th) 328, the Federal Court of Appeal in *CCH Canadian Ltd v Law Society for Upper Canada* (2002) 18 CPR (4th) 161 has returned to the orthodoxy and the Supreme Court of Canada, on appeal, has also declined to follow *Feist*, (2004) 30 CPR (4th) 1.

[122] *Gleeson v Denne Ltd* [1975] RPC 471.

[123] *Gleeson v Denne Ltd* [1975] RPC 471 at 483.

[124] Eg *Slumber Magic Co v Sleep King Bed* (1984) 3 CPR (3d) 81.

[125] *Ladbroke (Football) v William Hill (Football)* [1964] 1 All ER 465.

[126] *Independent Television Publications v Time Out* [1984] FSR 64. Contrast *IceTV Pty Ltd v Nine Network Australia Pty Ltd* [2009] HCA 14.

context. The European Court of First Instance in *Magill*[127] clearly indicated that television listings were inappropriate matters for copyright protection by indirectly criticising the Irish originality standard, and it is noteworthy that the Database Directive[128] selects a higher originality standard than that posited in Irish copyright law.

LECTURES AND PUBLIC SPEECHES

[11.29] The distinction between the rights of a lecturer or speaker to control the right to publish or disseminate in literary form the contents of the lecture or speech, and the rights of others to record the lecture or speech is set out by Lord Halsbury in *Walter v Lane*.[129] The Lord Chancellor stressed the importance of maintaining the distinction:[130]

> ... between two very different things; one, the proprietary right of every man in his own literary composition; and the other the copyright, that is to say, the exclusive privilege of making copies created by the Statute.

[11.30] The proprietary right to control the public dissemination of one's own literary composition is generally controlled by common law principles.[131] The university professor who provides unpublished lectures to students gives the student the right to take notes of the lecture for study purposes, but in the absence of any implied contract, the student does not acquire a right to publish the lecture, whether the publication be a record of the lecture taken verbatim in perfect shorthand[132] or in garbled form.[133] In this context the right of the lecturer or speaker to exercise this proprietary right does not appear to depend on whether the lecture is delivered from notes or memory or extemporaneously.[134] However, when a lecture or speech is delivered, any person who records the speech, regardless of the question of the accuracy of the record, acquires copyright in that report, so that if there should be a number of persons who take down an account of a speech in written form (eg journalists at a press conference) the journalist and not the speaker is the author of the written account even if it be a word for word transcription of the words spoken.[135] The skill, labour and expense incurred in transcribing the speech of another is sufficient to provide the writer with copyright in this work.[136] *Walter v Lane* was decided before UK copyright law contained an originality requirement and some doubt has been cast on the decision in *Walter v Lane* when the reporter transcribes an oral statement without embellishment or reorganisation

---

[127] *RTE v EC Commission* [1991] 4 CMLR 586.
[128] Council Directive 96/9/EC.
[129] *Walter v Lane* [1900] AC 539.
[130] *Walter v Lane* [1900] AC 539 at 547.
[131] *Abernethy v Hutchinson* (1825) 1 H & Tw 28.
[132] *Nicols v Pitman* (1884) 26 Ch D 374.
[133] *Caird v Sime* (1887) 12 App Cas 326.
[134] *Caird v Sime* (1887) 12 App Cas 326; *Gould Estate v Stoddart Publishing* (1998) 80 CPR (3d) 161.
[135] *Walter v Lane* [1900] AC 539, subject to an employment relationship transferring ownership as in *Laidlaw v Lear* (1898) 30 OR 26.
[136] *Walter v Lane* [1900] AC 539 at 552, *per* Lord Davey.

of the speech;[137] there is also some doubt about whether the decision in *Walter v Lane* would extend to a case where the speaker had written out the speech prior to its delivery and the speech was delivered from the written text or from memory.[138] This question was recently considered by the Supreme Court in *Gormley v EMI Records Ireland Ltd*.[139] Here, the plaintiff, as a schoolchild, was asked to recount in her own words some Bible stories that her school teacher had recently related to the schoolchildren, these responses being tape recorded by the teacher. The teacher sold on the recordings to the defendant who used them to produce a successful commercial product. Did the plaintiff hold any copyright in her spoken word? The Supreme Court held that there were two obstacles to such a claim. Firstly, for the work to subsist as a literary work it had to subsist in the form of writing[140] or some other material form.[141] The Supreme Court reasoned that the necessary writing or material form had to be capable of being understood and a magnetic trace or a tape did not satisfy this test. Secondly, the child had not produced a literary work. She had merely recited a story she had been told albeit in her own words. Some of the key elements in her 'original' retelling – her Dublin accent, and phrases such as that 'dirty auld squealer' for Judas Iscariot for example, were not copyright works. The Supreme Court inclined towards the view that any literary creation that existed resided in the teacher's inspirational version of the Bible stories that had so magically captured the attention of the schoolchildren.

[11.31] Where, however, a person is engaged to produce a written account of spoken words (eg an audio typist or stenographer) the copyright is held by the speaker, the person transcribing this oral statement being regarded as an amanuensis.[142]

[11.32] After the decision in *Gormley v EMI Records Ireland Ltd*,[143] the publication of the Copyright and Related Rights Bill 1999 afforded the Oireachtas with the opportunity to re-examine the issue of whether copyright in spoken words could reside with the speaker. The solution adopted clarifies the law only in part. The definition of 'literary work' in s 22(1) of CRRA 2000 'means a work … which is written, spoken or sung'. This makes it clear that speech can be a literary work but it does not follow, it is submitted, that all speech is a literary work. The controlling issue is whether a work is in place. There is no useful insight in the Act into what a work is, but *Gormley* itself makes it clear that work can exist outside of any form; indeed, CRRA 2000 recognises this by stating that copyright in a work is not to subsist until it is recorded in writing or otherwise by or with the consent of the author.[144] It appears to follow, then, that conversational speech, extempore remarks, and so on, are not likely[145] to be works, but a

---

137 *Robertson v Lewis* [1976] RPC 169.
138 *Robertson v Lewis* [1976] RPC 169.
139 *Gormley v EMI Records Ireland Ltd* [1999] 1 ILRM 178.
140 CA 1963, s 2(1).
141 CA 1963, s 3(4).
142 *Cummins v Bond* [1927] 1 Ch 167; *Laidlaw v Lear* (1898) 30 OR 26.
143 *Gormley v EMI Records Ireland Ltd* [1999] 1 ILRM 178.
144 CRRA 2000, s 18(1).
145 *Falwell v Penthouse International* 218 US PQ 975 (1981); *Gould Estate v Stoddart Publishing* (1998) 80 CPR (3d) 161.

speech, lecture or announcement, for example, that has been deliberated upon (whether or not in 'bullet point' or on the 'back of an envelope' basis) may be a work, because of the intellectual effort expended in considering and creating the work in question. This is hardly a very clear or satisfactory situation. Nor is it entirely appropriate for protection to turn on whether the work has been recorded with the authority or consent of the speaker. If politician A covertly records politician B's wonderful oration and then memorises it and uses it in an 'off the cuff' address, it is difficult to see why politician B should be denied a remedy. In any event, it should be noted that s 89 of CRRA 2000 permits others to make notes or record words that have been spoken for the purpose of reporting current events or broadcasting or including the notes or recording in a broadcast or cable programme service without infringing any copyright in the spoken words.

FORMATS

[11.33] The possibility that copyright may be used to protect ideas or the outlines that go into producing a literary or dramatic work – the formula or format for a show or entertainment – was addressed in *Green v Broadcasting Corpn of New Zealand*.[146] The broadcaster, Hughie Green, sued the defendants who replicated the Opportunity Knocks talent show. Evidence before the New Zealand courts and the Privy Council established that, while a skeletal 'script' existed in the shape of the title, catchphrases and set methods of evaluating the performers, this structure for presenting a series of ever changing performance could be described as either a literary or a dramatic work. This, however, is a matter of degree, for once an idea finds a sufficient level of expression, the copying of that expression will infringe copyright; but the degree of character development in a script is vital and if the program, or character, lacks distinctiveness,[147] as in *Preston v 20th Century Fox Canada Ltd*,[148] the claim will fail. Some show formats such as the radio programme Desert Island Discs clearly have sufficient originality and precision of form to merit copyright protection, and show formats are franchised out, a practice which reflects the existence of rights in the devisor.[149]

---

[146] *Green v Broadcasting Corpn of New Zealand* [1989] 2 All ER 1056.

[147] *Hutton v CBC* (1992) 120 AR 291 (generic rock show; no copying); *Wilson v Broadcasting Corpn of New Zealand* [1990] 2 NZLR 565 illustrates that each case turns on its own facts.

[148] *Preston v 20th Century Fox Canada Ltd* (1990) 33 CPR (3d) 242. In general terms there will be a difficulty in establishing that the ideas and structure that go into a reality television programme, absent proof of copying and objective similarity as between the rival programmes, are protectable, particularly because the individuals are (presumably) not working to a script: *Nine Films Television Property v Ninox Television Ltd* (2005) 67 IPR46. Litigation over *X Factor/Big Brother* formats have not produced decisions granting protection in common law jurisdictions. Even if a work were protected, infringement might be difficult to make out: see *Knight v Beyond Properties Pty Ltd* (2007) 71 IPR 466.

[149] See generally Moran and Malbon, *Understanding the Global TV Format* (Intellect Books, 2006).

DRAMATIC WORKS

[11.34] Again, CA 1963 was somewhat unhelpful in terms of defining copyright works: s 2 provided that the phrase copyright works, 'includes a choreographic work or entertainment in dumb show if reduced to writing in the form in which the work or entertainment is to be presented'; film scripts and film scenarios are likewise included. Again, protection is based upon reducing the work into a protectable form; the introduction to a pantomime, which was the only written part of the drama, was protected as a dramatic work.[150] The question of distinguishing a dramatic work from a literary or musical work has arisen from time to time and the weight of precedent suggests that the presentation of a work with dramatic scenery or dramatic effect is an essential element: *Fuller v Blackpool Winter Gardens*.[151] More recently Lord Bridge in *Green v Broadcasting Corpn of New Zealand*[152] distinguished the literary nature of a script from its existence as a dramatic work. So the dramatic work must be capable of performance in the sense that elements such as music, movement, scenery, lighting and declaration may coalesce; of these elements movement seems to be the crucial element. So Beckett's *Waiting for Godot* is certainly a dramatic work while *Not I* may not be.[153] Although the definition of 'dramatic work' in CRRA 2000 is along similar lines to that found in CA 1963, referring specifically to choreography and mime, the common feature in both definitions is the fact that it is of an 'includes' nature.

Recent case law indicates that right holders are prepared to push at the boundaries of protection wherever possible.[154] Two obvious instances are in relation to sporting events and organised 'spectaculars'. Does the element of planning or organisation bring the event within the concept of choreography? In *Australian Olympic Committee Inc v Big Fights Inc*[155] Lindgren J held that the expression 'dramatic work' indicated that the work must be staged, contrived or directed. In this regard, the filming of track and field events at the 1956 Melbourne Olympics could not be held to be a dramatic work, notwithstanding the fact that films were protected prior to the creation of a specific film copyright, because in order to attract protection the film must attach to a work (eg a scripted event). The Canadian decision in *FWS Joint Sports Claimants v Copyright Board*[156] holds that despite the highly organised nature of the game and the intense coaching that goes on before and during the event, a sufficient degree of spontaneity remains in a Canadian football game and it cannot be a dramatic work. On the other

---

[150] *Lee v Simpson* (1847) 3 CB 871.

[151] *Fuller v Blackpool Winter Gardens* [1895] 2 QB 429; contrast *Russell v Smith* (1848) 12 QB 217.

[152] *Green v Broadcasting Corpn of New Zealand* [1989] 2 All ER 1056 at 1059.

[153] *The Complete Dramatic Works* (Faber and Faber, 1986). There is some debate about whether Brian Friel's work, *Molly Sweeney* is a dramatic work at all (three characters on stools speaking with little or no movement). But see *Kantel v Grant* [1933] Ex CR 84 (radio play).

[154] *Pastor v Chen* (2002) 19 CPR (4th) 206 (salsa dance steps held to be original dramatic works).

[155] *Australian Olympic Committee Inc v Big Fights Inc* (1999) 46 IPR 53.

[156] *FWS Joint Sports Claimants v Copyright Board* (1991) 22 IPR 429. US law is different but Nimmer, for example, doubts the correctness: see David Nimmer, *Nimmer on Copyright* (Matthew Bender, 1989), 209 [F].

hand, some spectacular sporting events, in the form of the opening ceremony of the Olympic Games, would appear to be dramatic works. However, the action should involve human movement rather than something like a firework display.[157]

[11.35] Problems of definition as distinct from the issue of authorship tend not to occupy the attention of the courts. The theatre owner or impresario who suggests a theme or plot to an author is not likely to be held to be an author or co-author of a dramatic work, for the basic test is whether there is some pre-conceived plan to create joint work from separate contributions, a 'joint labouring under a common design'.[158] The provision of some lines or scrutiny of the text written by an author following upon suggestions made will not suffice. It is essential that there be a substantial contribution to forming the written dialogue qua author, rather than qua muse,[159] critic[160] or editor.[161] Nor will the making of alterations to a settled text make the person making the alterations a joint author.[162]

MUSICAL WORKS

[11.36] The CA 1963 did not define a musical work; CRRA 2000 defines a musical work as 'a work consisting of music, but does not include any words or action intended to be sung, spoken or performed with the music'.[163] Words are protected via literary copyright while the action or gestures which are to accompany the music are protected as dramatic works. Protection of musical works against reproduction under the Statute of Anne was established in 1777,[164] and works that consisted of music and lyrics written by two distinct persons involved two separate copyrights. The addition of lyrics to an old, public domain tune or air may create a copyright in the air and accompaniment.[165] The addition of new elements may create a copyright in the product[166] but it is necessary to note that many 'arrangement' or 'adaptation' copyrights claimed may lack the necessary originality element to sustain a copyright. In *Hyperion Records Ltd v Sawkins*[167] a musicologist with unique knowledge of the composer Lalande (1657 to 1726) corrected and effectively reconstructed the (often lost) manuscripts in such a way as to make these works playable by a modern orchestra. This work was held not to be merely editorial work. The Court of Appeal rejected the view that new music only existed if new 'notes'

---

[157] *Nine Network Australia Pty v ABC* (1999) 48 IPR 333.
[158] Keating J in *Levy v Rutley* (1871) LR 6 CP 523; *Tate v Fulbrook* [1908] 1 KB 821; *Tate v Thomas* [1921] 1 Ch 503.
[159] *Shepherd v Conquest* (1856) 17 CB 427.
[160] *Wiseman v George Weidenfield & Nicholson Ltd* [1985] FSR 525.
[161] *Ashmore v Douglas-Home* [1987] FSR 553.
[162] *Shelley v Ross* (1871) LR 6 CP 53.
[163] CRRA 2000, s 2(1).
[164] *Bach v Longman* (1777) 2 Cowp 623. A performing right was added in the Literary Copyright Act 1842.
[165] *Leader v Purday* (1849) 7 CB 4; *Lover v Davidson* (1856) 1 CBNS 182.
[166] *Wood v Boosey* (1868) LR 3 QB 223; *CBS Records v Gross* (1989) 15 IPR 385.
[167] *Hyperion Records Ltd v Sawking* [2005] 3 All ER 636.

were written, saying it would be wrong in principle to single out the notes and ignore other contributions such as performing indications, tempo and performance practice indicators created by a person's effort, skill and time.[168] Openly derivative works may nevertheless be original.[169] The unauthorised use of an existing musical work will constitute an infringement of the original.[170] In practice, digital sampling of existing works will be a copyright infringement as long as there is a sufficient amount of the original work used to amount to a substantial taking.[171] Short snatches of a tune or a musical jingle are capable of being copyright protected.[172]

ARTISTIC WORKS

[11.37] Protection for artistic works under s 9(2) of CA 1963 is available only if it is an original artistic work; this means that the work must have been independently created and not copied from some pre-existing work.[173] The level of skill or artistry needed to execute the work is not uniformly drawn in the Act. Protection is available if the work falls into one of three categories, as long as it possesses a physical form. In *Creation Records Ltd v Newsgroup Newspapers*[174] the arrangement of objects and members of the group 'Oasis', made to produce an album cover, was denied the status of an artistic physical work, the English High Court drawing a distinction between the physical thing photographed and the photograph of that physical subject itself.

[11.38] In order to obtain protection under CRRA 2000, however, a much more fluid situation may be exploited by the putative rights owner. While s 9 of CA 1963 had a 'closed' list of works that the rights owner had to satisfy, s 2(1) of CRRA 2000 states that an artistic work 'includes a work of any of the following descriptions, irrespective of their artistic quality'. Both CA 1963 and CRRA 2000 use much the same conceptual language and the only kind of work that is recognised expressly in CRRA 2000 that was not included in CA 1963 is a work of collage.[175] The works included in the illustrative list include the following.

Photographs

[11.39] CRRA 2000 provides a definition that is very broad in so far as a photograph is 'a recording of light, or any other radiation or any medium on which an image is

---

[168] *Hyperion Records Ltd v Sawking* [2005] 3 All ER 636 *per* Mummery LJ at para 56. See generally Pila (2008) 71 MLR 535.

[169] *Brooker v Fisher* [2008] EWCA Civ 287, (4 April 2008).

[170] *ZYX Music v King* [1995] 3 All ER 1; *CBS Records v Gross* (1989) 15 IPR 385.

[171] *Redwood Music v Chappell* [1982] RPC 109.

[172] *Lawson v Dundas* (1985) Times, 13 June.

[173] Lord Oliver in *Interlego v Tyco Industries* [1988] 3 All ER 949 at 976. Merely mechanical efforts at creating an artistic work may not suffice: see *Reject Shop plc v Robert Manners* [1995] FSR 870; *Alwest Neon Signs v 464460 Alberta* (1994) 58 CPR (3d) 176.

[174] *Creation Records Ltd v News Group Newspapers* [1997] EMLR 444.

[175] See *Creation Records Ltd v News Group Newspapers* [1997] EMLR 444.

produced, or from which an image may by any means be produced and which is not part of a film'.[176] On the vexed question of originality the artistic quality reference does not take us very far, but after *Antiquesportfolio.com*,[177] the law changes significantly in one way: it appears that, apart from cases of slavish copying, or instances where the work originates with someone other than the putative author (eg the work is itself a photocopy of another's work), virtually any photograph will meet the required standard for protection. Indeed, cases also suggest that even where a photograph is the result of an exercise intended to recreate another scene, the resulting photograph may still require research, expertise and skill so as to negate a finding of slavish copying.[178]

Paintings

[11.40] A painting is not defined in either CA 1963 or CRRA 2000. Multi-media works involving a combination of paint, crayon, etc, will no doubt be protected. In *Merchandising Corpn of America v Harpbond*[179] it was, however, held that three stripes of face paint across both cheeks of a pop artist did not convert the singer's face into a painting. Whether this is due to the temporary nature of the work or because the concept of body art was foreign to the judge in question cannot be gleaned from the law report.[180]

Drawings

[11.41] No matter how commonplace the drawing,[181] it will be copyright protected as long as the necessary element of originality (not copied/originating with the putative author) is satisfied.[182]

Diagrams

[11.42] This is not defined but will include illustrative materials in a text[183] as well as technical diagrams.[184]

Maps

[11.43] Protection for maps dates back to 1790. The necessary element of originality can be made out by use of common sources and reliance upon conventional practice will not

---

[176] CRRA 2000, s 21(1).

[177] *Antiquesportfolio.com plc v Rodney Fitch & C Ltd* [2001] FSR 345.

[178] *Grosso v Seligman* [1911–16] MCC 219; *Ateliers Tango Argentin v Festival D'Espagne et d'Amerique* (1997) 84 CPR (3d) 56.

[179] *Merchandising Corpn of America v Harpbond* [1983] FSR 32, distinguished in *Australian Chinese Newspapers Pty Ltd v MCP* (2003) 58 IPR 1.

[180] On infringement, see *Hanfstaengl v Empire Palace* [1894] 2 Ch 1.

[181] *Green v Independent Newspapers and Freeman's Journal* [1899] 1 IR 386; *Miller & Lang Ltd v Polak* [1908] 1 Ch 433.

[182] *Interlego AG v Tyco Industries* [1988] 3 All ER 949.

[183] *Fasold v Roberts* (1997) 38 IPR 34.

[184] *British Leyland Motor Corpn v Armstrong Patents* [1986] AC 577.

deny the map the necessary originality.[185] Because of the breadth of one cartographer's latitude to use the conventional language of the skill, it is common for cartographers to provide proof of copying by building into a map errors that can provide direct evidence of copying as distinct from common or conventional sources.[186]

Charts

[11.44] Maritime charts have been protected for centuries but protection has often been given qua literary work.

Plans

[11.45] Architects' plans can be protected as such, whether they be of a building[187] or the floor layout of a house or building[188] or a shopfront.[189] Engineering plans are also artistic works.[190]

Engravings

[11.46] Copyright has been protected since Hogarth's Act of 1734.[191] Traditional engravings onto copper or steel sheets[192] were obviously the intended object of protection but the cases go much further.[193]

Etchings

[11.47] This presumably means exterior etched decoration on a surface as well as in a colloquial sense of print or other work (eg a brass rubbing).[194]

Lithographs

[11.48] This is a reproduction via paper receiving an image carved onto a stone surface.

---

[185] *Faden v Stockdale* (1797) 2 Bro CC 80n; *Sands and McDougall Pty Ltd v Robinson* (1917) 23 CLR 49; *Controller of HM Stationary Office v Green AMPS Ltd* [2008] EWCA Civ 588.

[186] *Geographia v Penguin Books* [1985] FSR 208.

[187] *Re Hansley* (1987) 10 IPR 367; *Ferntree Homes Pty v Bohan* (2002) 54 IPR 267.

[188] *Lend Lease Homes Pty v Warrigal Homes Pty* [1970] 3 NSWLR 265; *Eagle Homes Pty v Austec Homes Pty* (1999) 43 IPR 1; *Burke v Earlsfort Centre* (24 February 1981, unreported), HC.

[189] *Chabot v Davies* [1936] 3 All ER 221.

[190] *Netupsky v Dominion Bridge* (1972) 24 DLR (3d) 484.

[191] Copyright Act 1734.

[192] *Blackwell v Harper* (1740) 2 Atk 93, A screen print used on t-shirts is not an engraving: *Gabrin v Universal Music Operations Ltd* [2004] ECDR 18.

[193] *Wham-O-Manufacturing Co v Lincoln Industries Ltd* [1984] 1 NZLR 641; *Lilypak v Poly Containers* (1986) 8 IPR 363.

[194] Probably not protected as a 'slavish copy' of another work.

Woodcuts

[11.49] A master is carved from wood and the flat surface bearing the image is inked and then transferred to pages.[195]

Prints or similar works

[11.50] This seems to cover a variety of formats including prints created by photolithography.[196]

Collages

[11.51] Recent English case law suggests that some element of fixation rather than the random arrangement of objects is required.[197]

Sculptures (including any cast or model used therefor)

[11.52] This will include mass produced items such as plastic coins, frisbees or models produced from a cast or die, that cast or die being an engraving.[198] However, the English Courts have recently cast doubt on whether decisions such as those above are reliable.

In *LucasFilm Ltd v Ainsworth*[199] a strong Court of Appeal was concerned with the question whether the moulds created by a skilled craftsman, and the plastic body armour and helmets subsequently mass produced by injecting plastic in the moulds, for use in *Star Wars IV – A New Hope*, could be sculptures for the purposes of copyright protection. The Court of Appeal indicated that, for copyright purposes, a sculpture is a three dimensional work created by an artist's hand, being not merely utilitarian. The Court of Appeal said that a court should note the distinction in the use of the word 'sculpture', being descriptive of both the object created and the process by which the object is created; the analysis in this context should focus on the first aspect. The Court of Appeal distinguished this situation from instances where skills were deployed to create toys with artistic and aesthetic appeal.[200] The *Star Wars* figures, on the other hand were regarded as being functional reproductions of functional works created essentially as stage props. While the Court of Appeal conceded that some artistic works could still have functional characteristics – stage sets for films and ballets, and statues of saints created for the purpose of veneration in a church were two examples given – those borderline cases were not allowed to detract from the Court of Appeal's benchmark that a sculpture, like a painting (however good or bad it may be) connotes the work of the

---

[195] *Smith v New Publishing Co* (1897) 41 Sol Jo 367.

[196] *Theberge v Galerie d'Art du Petit Champlain* (2002) 210 DLR (4th) 385.

[197] *Creation Records v News Group Newspapers* [1997] EMLR 444.

[198] *Martin v Polyplas Manufacturers Ltd* [1969] 1 NZLR 1046; *Breville Europe v Thorn EMI Domestic* [1995] FSR 77.

[199] *LucasFilm Ltd v Ainsworth* [2010] EMLR 12.

[200] Lead models of real soldiers 'found by the judge to be artistic reproductions of the mounted yeoman they depicted': *Britain v Hanks* (1902) 86 LT 765.

artist's hand and a visual purpose on the part of the person creating that work.[201] The Court of Appeal indicated that some element of functionality did not disqualify the object from sculpture status[202] but rejected a long line of cases in which functional objects created with no artistic purpose being evident could be sculptures for copyright purposes.[203] The Court of Appeal enclosed a multi-factor test, devised by Mann J, to be used as guidelines in resolving what is, and what is not, a sculpture for copyright purposes.[204]

[11.53] The fact that the level of artistic skill is not significant is illustrated from the old Irish case of *Green v Independent Newspapers and Freeman's Journal*.[205] In that case an artist named Bownass produced a 'commonplace' drawing of Santa Claus on a poster which was reproduced without permission in an advertisement. Walker LJ[206] said that Bownass's drawing, reproduced in an evening newspaper without consent, must be given the same treatment 'as if the original drawing was by Millais and its copying by an engraving in the Art Journal'.

[11.54] However, there must be an act of independent creation, and the reproduction of an existing work will not suffice[207] to create an independent work, unless the transposition of the work into another form constitutes independent skill and judgment.[208] So my hastily taken wedding snaps are to be viewed as copyright protected, no matter how much red eye there is, and an unauthorised reproduction will be an infringement of my copyright.[209]

WORKS OF ARCHITECTURE BEING EITHER BUILDINGS OR MODELS FOR BUILDINGS

[11.55] The use of the word 'building' in CRRA 2000, defined as including 'any structure',[210] leaves open the question of how far the scope of protection can extend, particularly when there are no design drawings in existence. It has been held that a tennis court can be a building[211] as indeed can be a fibre glass swimming pool.[212] The

---

[201] *LucasFilm Ltd v Ainsworth* [2010] EMLR 12, para 70.

[202] Eg glass and wire 'critters' of a decorative nature that were also candleholders: *Wildash v Klein* (2004) 61 IPR 324.

[203] Eg *Lincoln Industries Ltd v Wham O Manufacturing* [1984] NZLR 641 (frisbee moulds); *Breville Europe v Thorn* EMI [1995] FSR 77 (heating panels in sandwich toasters).

[204] *LucasFilm Ltd v Ainsworth* [2008] EWHC 1878 (ch) at para 118.

[205] *Green v Independent Newspapers and Freeman's Journal* [1899] 1 IR 386.

[206] *Green v Independent Newspapers and Freeman's Journal* [1899] 1 IR 386 at 396.

[207] *Anvil Jewellery Ltd v Riva Ridge Holdings Ltd* [1987] 1 NZLR 35; *Krisarts v Briarfine* [1977] FSR 557.

[208] *Martin v Polyplas Manufacturers Ltd* [1969] NZLR 1046.

[209] See *Bauman v Fussell* (1953) [1978] RPC 485; *Warne v Genex Corpn Pty Ltd* (1996) 35 IPR 284; Lupton [1988] EIPR 257.

[210] CRRA 2000, s 2(1).

[211] *Half Court Tennis Pty Ltd v Seymour* (1980) 53 FLR 240.

[212] *Darwin Fibreglass Pty v Kruhse Enterprises Pty* (1998) 41 IPR 649.

unauthorised construction of a facsimile of a building which is of recent construction or the use of a design model to produce a building will infringe copyright in the original building or model for as long as the building or model is within copyright. While many cases involve copying from plans, taking the main features of a building that is itself innovative in design terms may infringe copyright as long as there is a 'substantial taking' of the original building.[213] In this context the moot issue will sometimes be who is the copyright holder – it may not be the owner of the building because the commissioned work exception in s 10(3) of CA 1963 (now repealed) does not cover architectural works – and it can transpire that substantial taking of design features in order to enhance an extension or addition to the original building may infringe the architect's copyright.[214]

WORKS OF ARTISTIC CRAFTSMANSHIP NOT WITHIN THE PRECEDING FORMS OF ARTISTIC WORK

[11.56] This distinct category of copyright law developed out of the protection afforded to fine arts works, which are protected under traditional statutory rules originating from 1790 onwards. Protection followed when the Art and Crafts movement in the nineteenth century made it clear that items that have decorative practical or aesthetic qualities, produced by artists and craftsmen, were worthy of protection from unauthorised imitation. However, a definition of artistic craftsmanship is absent from CRRA 2000 and in this context the courts have been engaged in addressing a number of complex issues. Firstly, who is to determine whether an object is a work of artistic craftsmanship? One Canadian judge has spoken for the judiciary generally when he observed that:[215]

> Artistic values cannot be weighted, for no universally acceptable unit or artistic weight has ever been agreed upon, nor have any so called artistic laws retained their sanctity for a protracted period of time. I think it unlikely that any legislature would be so addle-pated as to appoint the judiciary to decide whether Frank Lloyd Wright, Palladio, Pheidias, Corbusier or the plaintiff had produced buildings of artistic character or design in the sense that they are artistically good or artistically bad.

[11.57] Nevertheless, it will be for the court to decide what credibility or weight is to be given to expert testimony, public reaction to the work, as well as the intention and skill of the artist in creating the work. In *George Hensher Ltd v Restawhile Ltd*[216] the House of Lords indicated that the court is not to hold the plaintiff's claim to protection to be bad if a predominantly utilitarian reason is shown to explain the appeal of the item – the fusion of aesthetic beauty or 'delight'[217] in an item with its functionality is the very basis of the concept of artistic craftsmanship. Lord Simon in *Restawhile* considered that the protection of copyright should be established by reference to the craftsman's artistic skill

---

213 Eg *Beazley Homes Ltd v Arrowsmith* [1978] 1 NZLR 394; *LED Builders Ltd v Eagle Homes Pty* (1996) 35 IPR 215.

214 *Meikle v Maufe* [1941] 3 All ER 144.

215 Stewart J in *Hay and Hay Construction Ltd v Sloan* (1957) 27 CPR 132.

216 *George Hensher Ltd v Restawhile Ltd* [1974] 2 All ER 420.

217 See *Hay and Hay Construction Ltd v Sloan* (1957) 27 CPR 132 at 136.

and evidence of his intention; was it the craftsman's view that he was creating a work of art? While Lord Simon was later followed on this point in *Merlet v Mothercare*[218] by Walton J, one other member of the House of Lords in *Restawhile* emphasised that if public opinion viewed the work as pleasing in its appearance then artistic craftsmanship can be made out.[219] This resort to popular opinion 'by a show of hands or a card vote'[220] is not, it is submitted, very satisfactory and it is submitted that the 'vocational' test is a better one, even if it results in the works of Koons being afforded the same status as a Fabergé egg. Stewart J in *Hay Construction Ltd v Sloan* gave the following illustration:

> to interpret the Act properly, the tribunal should not attempt to exercise a personal aesthetic judgment but to consider the intent of the creator and its result. Suppose a man were to build himself a pig-pen garnished with fretted gingerbread and with four lovely turrets, yet firm and commodious. Let it stand in its multicoloured horror a mid-Victorian blot upon the landscape. Let us assume that no contemporary could accept this edifice as anything but an architectural excrescence of the most loathsome kind, yet to its creator it would well be a thing of beauty and to its inhabitants a porcine paradise. An attempt has been made to produce *venustas* and some originality displayed. This, in my view, is sufficient to render such building the subject matter of copyright.[221]

[11.58] *Burge v Swarbrick*[222] raised the question of whether a design model for a yacht could be a work of artistic craftsmanship. The High Court of Australia revisited *Restawhile*, favouring the analysis of Lord Simon on the inferences to be drawn when the craftsman operates within functional constraints. In such cases, where the design brief is dictated by technical or functional matters, there will be less scope for the manifestation of artistic expression. Clearly the yacht designer was an extremely skilled practitioner in the area of naval architecture, an engineering discipline, but the High Court of Australia indicated that there was little evidence of the designer being concerned with aesthetic matters; on the contrary, promotional literature for the finished product spoke to the performance of the vessel, not matters of visual or aesthetic appeal. A similar line of reasoning is evident in the decision of Mann J in *LucasFilm Ltd v Ainsworth*.[223] The moulds created in order to produced 'Stormtrooper' body armour and aviator helmets in the first *Star Wars* movie, and the armour and helmets themselves, were not works of artistic craftsmanship. Because the intention was not to appeal to the aesthetic but give a particular impression in a film (often by using fairly shoddy materials) the objects fell outside the test.

[11.59] The imprecision of the artistic craftsmanship notion makes it difficult to predict how an item will be judged; handprinted wallpapers, jewellery,[224] stained glass windows

---

[218] *Merlet v Mothercare* [1986] RPC 115.

[219] Lord Reid in *George Hensher Ltd v Restawhile Ltd* [1974] 2 All ER 420 at 424.

[220] *George Hensher Ltd v Restawhile Ltd* [1974] 2 All ER 420 at 435, *per* Lord Simon.

[221] *Hay and Hay Construction Ltd v* Sloan (1957) 27 CPR 132 at 137.

[222] *Burge v Swarbrick* (2007) 72 IPR 235.

[223] *LucasFilm Ltd v Ainsworth* [2008] EWHC 1878 (Ch); the Court of Appeal [2010] EMLR 12 was not called upon to consider this question.

[224] *Blayney v Clogau St Davids Gold Mines Ltd* [2003] FSR 361.

will have little difficulty but items of clothing or furniture will be marginal.[225] The *Restawhile* case[226] makes it very clear that functional items may attract registered design and artistic copyright, but when an item is mass produced or machine produced, there will be some difficulty in making out an artistic copyright claim, especially if the item is functional. While Chanel designed and produced dresses and Clarice Cliff tableware are, in their finished form, potential works of artistic craftsmanship, most means of production involve automation in terms of production of the work; but this should not invalidate an artistic craftsmanship copyright claim.

[11.60] This leads on to another point. If an item is produced via collaboration between two or more persons (eg a dress designer may produce the design but the finished product will only result from the work if skilled cutters and tailors are involved), can the designer still claim artistic copyright? Despite the decision in *Burke and Margot Burke Ltd v Spicers Dress Designs*,[227] most of the more recent authorities answer this in the affirmative if the designer is the employer of these persons[228] and the item so produced is original. In *Sheldon v Metrokane*[229] Conti J endorsed more recent Antipodean authorities holding that a work of artistic craftsmanship may be created by two or more persons operating at different times with different skills.

---

[225] *Bonz Group v Cooke* [1994] 3 NZLR 216; *Coogi (Aust) Pty Ltd v Hysport International Pty* (1997) 41 IPR 593; *Guild v Eskandar Ltd* [2001] FSR 645.

[226] *George Hensher Ltd v Restawhile Ltd* [1974] 2 All ER 420.

[227] *Burke and Margot Burke Ltd v Spicers Dress Designs* [1936] Ch 400, doubted in *Cuisenaire v Reed* [1963] VR 719.

[228] *Spyrou v Radley Gowns* [1975] FSR 455; *J Bernstein Ltd v Sidney Murray Ltd* [1981] RPC 303; *Merlet v Mothercare* [1986] RPC 115; *Thornton Hall Manufacturing v Shanton Apparel Ltd* [1989] 1 NZLR 239.

[229] *Sheldon v Metrokane* (2004) IPR 1, applying the New Zealand case of *BonzGroup v Cooke* [1994] 3 NZLR 216 and *Coogi Aust Pty Ltd v Hysport International Pty* (1997) 41 IPR 593.

Chapter 12

Protected Works – Non-Berne Works

THEORETICAL DISTINCTIONS

[12.01] The Berne Convention for the Protection of Literary and Artistic Works (Berne Convention) provides protection for authors' rights vis-à-vis works of authorship. It follows that certain kinds of exploitation or endeavour may not be works, even though they may be acts of exploitation or endeavour that are closely related to literary or artistic creation. Such rights are often described as neighbouring rights or entrepreneurial rights. Both expressions are informative. Neighbouring rights arise out of acts adjacent to the underlying copyright – filming a screenplay for example. Entrepreneurial rights often vest in an entity that has exploited or commercialised a work – for instance, a broadcaster transmitting a live reading by a famous poet. Prior to the Copyright Act 1963 (CA 1963), protection for neighbouring rights was largely absent. But CA 1963 introduced a distinction between 'classical' Berne Convention copyrights in Pt II of the Act and afforded a number of copyrights to works, in the form of Pt III copyrights. The Copyright and Related Rights Act 2000 (CRRA 2000) has swept away the distinction between Pt II and Pt III protection, and Pt II of the 2000 legislation recognises a number of works that constitute for the owner exclusive rights (save for sound recordings, which are the subject of licences of right under s 38 of the Act). This means that CRRA 2000 reserves the epithet of 'related rights' to the various performers' rights and the database right. We will now look at these works, turning first to the works that were, broadly speaking, protected by both CA 1963 and CRRA 2000.

SOUND RECORDINGS

[12.02] Sound recordings were protected under the Copyright Act 1911 and the Industrial and Commercial Property (Protection) Act 1927 (ICPPA 1927) by providing a copyright in mechanical contrivances that held a sound recording.[1] Under CA 1963 a sound recording was defined as being the aggregate in sounds embodied in, and capable of being reproduced in, a record.[2] As such, the recording need not be a recording of a work. A sound recording of birdsong, for instance, is copyright protected. Under CRRA 2000 the definition of a sound recoding has been expanded to cover not just the fixation of sounds but also the representation of sounds,[3] thus making it clear that digital sound

---

[1]   ICPPA 1927, s 169.

[2]   CA 1963, s 17. See generally Boytha (1993) 24 IIC 295. On the nature of this right, see *PPI v Somers* [1993] 1 IR 202.

[3]   CRRA 2000, s 2(1): see *Polygram Records v Raben Footwear Pty* (1996) 35 IPR 426.

recordings are within the definition. The definition changed significantly in respect of the soundtrack of a film. Soundtracks were not deemed sound recordings under CA 1963 and this provision has not been re-enacted in the CRRA 2000 legislation. Indeed, it is now provided that in respect of film soundtracks which were in copyright before 1 January 2001, the soundtrack, for the purposes of the new copyright provisions, is to be regarded as a sound recording;[4] copyright in the sound recording to last as long as the copyright in the film.[5] Copyright vests in the author and first owner of copyright in the film.[6] The owner of copyright in a sound recording is the producer of the sound recording,[7] subject to the old commissioned works provision in s 17(3) of CA 1963.[8] Infringement of a sound recording takes place by copying the work, but 'soundalike' recordings do not infringe.[9] Making the sound recording available to the public may involve acts of primary and secondary infringement, but s 38 limits the right to a remuneration right in performances in public contexts. Making an adaptation of the sound recording (eg sampling the sound recording) may involve infringements of both the sound recording right and underlying copyrights, as well as moral rights.[10] Copyright in a sound recording, under the new copyright provisions, begins to run from the making of the sound recording for 50 years, with an additional 50-year period of protection from the date of the sound recording being made available to the public within that 50-year period.[11]

FILMS

[12.03] Prior to CA 1963, copyright protection for films could be available if the film came within the definition of a dramatic work.[12] This depended upon the existence of scripted or choreographed performances so it was held that copyright protection for newsreels capturing the track events at the 1956 Melbourne Olympics was not available.[13] Similar reasoning applied to a film work created by cutting techniques rather than by the cinematographic capture of a real-time performance.[14] So, while it is correct to say that a true film copyright does not subsist prior to 1 October 1964 films,[15] original dramatic work copyright may subsist. Further, CRRA 2000 provides that the new copyright provisions apply in relation to photographs forming part of a film before 1 October 1964 as they apply to photographs not forming part of a film. The changes

---

4   CRRA 2000, Sch 1, Pt I, para 6(1).
5   CRRA 2000, Sch 1, Pt I, para 6(2).
6   CRRA 2000, Sch 1, Pt I, para 6(3).
7   CA 1963, s 17(10); CRRA 2000, s 21(a).
8   CRRA 2000, Sch 1, Pt I, para 8(2).
9   *CBS v Telmak* (1989) 9 IPR 440.
10 *Confetti Records v Warner Music Ltd* [2003] ECDR 336.
11 See CRRA 2000, s 26.
12 *DPP v Irwin* (25 October 1984, unreported), HC.
13 *Big Fights Inc v Australian Olympic Committee* (1999) 46 IPR 53.
14 *Norowzian v Arks Ltd (No 2)* [2000] FSR 363.
15 The date of commencement of CA 1963.

effected by CRRA 2000 in relation to film sound tracks should be noted. As is the case with sound recordings, the definition of 'film' has been broadened to include digital fixations. Indeed, in *Universal City Studios Inc v Mulligan*,[16] Laffoy J held that a video cassette could be within the old definition of 'cinematographic film'. Several cases have tested the question whether the screen displays and images produced by computer technology can be protected as films. While one Hong Kong case[17] and at least one Australian case[18] have answered this question in the affirmative, it is likely that these decisions do not represent the correct view, given the interactive nature of most screen displays.[19] Issues of ownership are generally resolved by reference to the law at the time the film was made. Under CA 1963 the author was the producer of the film while under CRRA 2000 the author is defined as including the producer and principal director.[20] Duration of copyright under CA 1963 was limited to a 50-year period while under CRRA 2000 a complex system of measuring lives and renewal upon making available operates.[21] Infringement of copyright may take place under CRRA 2000 via acts of primary and secondary infringement[22] and most acts of infringement will relate to the distribution of illegal video cassettes and DVDs.

BROADCASTS

[12.04] Under CA 1963, as first promulgated, the State monopoly held by Radio Éireann (as it then was) was recognised by copyright vesting in that body in respect of transmissions of radio and television signals from within the State.[23] Under the Radio and Television Act 1988, independent statutory broadcasters acquired copyright in their broadcasts.[24] No copyright exists, however, in respect of broadcasts made prior to 1 October 1964.[25] The definition of 'broadcast' under both pieces of legislation was broad, covering satellite and terrestrial broadcasting specifically, although CRRA 2000 requires direct public reception by wireless means, and the definition in s 2 (s 10 of CRRA 2000) specifically excludes multipoint microwave distribution systems. The reception and immediate retransmission of a broadcast will attract a separate broadcast copyright. Copyright vests in either the broadcaster or, in the case of immediate reception/ retransmission, the person who makes the retransmission;[26] and specific provision is made in respect of joint authorship[27] of a broadcast. Copyright expires in a broadcast

---

[16] *City Studios Inc v Mulligan* [1999] 3 IR 381.
[17] *Nintendo v Golden China* (1993) 28 IPR 313.
[18] *Sega Enterprises v Galaxy Electronics* (1996) 35 IPR 1.
[19] Contrast *Sony Computer Entertainment v Stevens* [2002] FCA 906.
[20] CRRA 2000, s 21(b), thus leaving open other claimants (eg cinematographers).
[21] CRRA 2000, s 25.
[22] CRRA 2000, ss 37 and 45–48; *Paramount Pictures v Cablelink* [1991] 1 IR 521.
[23] CA 1963, s 19(1) and (3).
[24] See SI 101/1991.
[25] CA 1963, Sch 1, Pt II, para 14.
[26] CRRA 2000, s 21(c). On digital terrestrial retransmission see the Broadcasting Act 2009, s 183.

made after 1 January 2001, 50 years after the broadcast is first lawfully transmitted and copyright in a repeat broadcast expires at the same time as copyright in the first lawful transmission expires.[28] It should be noted that the broadcast copyright relates to the signal *per se*.[29] Many broadcasts are broadcasts of scripted or literary material, and many of the programmes broadcast are themselves films or sound recordings which may indeed attract greater rights than the broadcast copyright which is, in practice, most valuable for 'live' transmissions of news stories or sporting events. Infringement of copyright may occur in respect of the copyright of a broadcast, the making available to the public of a broadcast and adapting a broadcast, as well as the secondary infringement provisions in ss 45 to 48 of CRRA 2000 (subject to defences such as time-shifting in s 101 of the Act). There are, however, a number of specific provisions in respect of the use of broadcasts and material to be included in a broadcast and these exceptions include time-shifting defences. However, the unauthorised interference with encrypted broadcast signals may be actionable by the broadcaster and others (CRRA 2000, s 372) as part of EU-wide measures to counteract 'signal piracy'.[30]

[12.05] 'Signal piracy', as a rhetorical device for characterising unauthorised access to broadcasts and signal content in a broadcast, may be counteracted by users who invoke other considerations such as consumer rights, freedom of expression and competition law. In an extremely significant reference to the European Court of Justice (ECJ), the English High Court, in *Football Association Premier League Ltd v QC Leisure*,[31] was asked to consider whether the defendants, who had supplied decoder boxes and decoder cards, intended by distributors for the Greek market, to UK customers in breach of licensing conditions, enabling purchasers to unscramble the Sky encrypted broadcast signal (and thus allow access to Premier League soccer matches), were in breach of national copyright laws. Particular attention[32] was paid to the Conditional Access Directive, Directive 98/84/EC, transposed into Irish law by CRRA 2000, s 372. Infringement by copying and communicating the works to the public, as well as authorising infringement were alleged. The defendants argued that the Conditional

---

[27] CRRA 2000, s 22(3).

[28] CRRA 2000, s 27; under CA 1963 the duration was for the same 50-year period.

[29] On the history of broadcast copyright, see *TCN Channel Nine v Network 10* (2004) 218 CLR 273. In that case the High Court of Australia rejected an argument that broadcast copyright could attach to each image included in a broadcast, distinguishing copyright or the absence of any copyright in material included in the broadcast from copyright in the broadcast itself. It was said that the policy behind broadcast copyright was to 'protect the cost to, and the skill of, broadcasters in producing or transmitting their programmes, in addition to what copyrights may have subsisted in underlying works used in those programmes' (para 29), judgment of McHugh ACJ, Gummow and Hayne JJ.

[30] CRRA 2000, ss 99–105.

[31] *Football Association Premier League Ltd v QC Leisure* [2008] EWHC 1411 (Ch); see also the summary judgment decision at [2008] EWHC 42 (Ch).

[32] Other Directives that were pleaded were the TV Without Frontiers Directive (as amended), Directive 89/552/EEC ([1989] OJ L298/23); the Cable and Satellite Directive, Directive 93/83/EC ([1993] OJ L248/15); and the Information Society Directive, Directive 2001/29/EC ([2001] OJ L 167/10).

Access Directive was only intended to apply to pirate decoder cards and that a number of EU general defences could be invoked on their behalf, in particular TFEU, arts 34–36, 56 and 101.[33] Kitchin J made an art 234 reference, noting the tension between Community policy in trying to create a common European audiovisual area and the principles of an internal market without frontiers, and the partition of markets by right holders 'to extract what they perceive to be the fair remuneration to which they are entitled'.[34] The outcome of this case should have significant consequences for European broadcasters and others.

CABLE PROGRAMME SERVICES

[12.06] Cable programme services are new to the Irish copyright landscape. While CA 1963 recognised that inclusion of a work in a diffusion service could be an infringing act, no separate copyright appears to have attached for the benefit of the service provider. Following upon the UK reforms of 1988, the Irish legislator adopted the UK provisions on cable programme services. In essence, a cable programme service involves services, including MMDS transmissions that transmit images, sounds and data through a telecommunications system, on demand for general public consumption. Unlike broadcasts, a material support, in the form of cable distribution, is likely to be the most common form of transfer of such images, sounds or data, but this will not necessarily be the case. Webcasting is likely to be within such a distribution technology but mobile communications delivery technology is making CRRA 2000 appear out of date even at this early stage.[35] Returning to the definition of 'cable programme service', certain uses of a telecommunications system are excluded, such as interactive systems in which receivers of the service transmit data in return, 'closed' internal telecommunications systems, such as company intranets, private security or CCTV systems, single occupation transmission of material in a building (non residential/professional) or cable programme and broadcasters using such technology for internal purposes.[36] The rules on authorship and infringement in respect of cable programme services mirror those applicable in respect of broadcasts.[37]

TYPOGRAPHICAL ARRANGEMENTS OF PUBLISHED EDITIONS

[12.07] Section 20 of CA 1963 introduced a copyright so as to provide a publisher with copyright protection in respect of the skill and effort that could be involved in the typographical layout of a book or other publication. Once the publication was made

---

[33] The defendants relied in particular on *Musik-Vertrieb Membran GmbH v GEMA* [1981] 2 CMLR 44, seeking to distinguish *Coditel I* [1980] ECR 81 on which the plaintiffs relied.

[34] *Football Association Premier League Ltd v QC Leisure* [2008] EWHC 1411 (Ch) at para 385.

[35] However in two recent cases, inclusion of material (literary content and sound recordings) was held to constitute including it in a cable programme: *Shetland Times v Wills* (1996) 37 IPR 71 and *Sony Music Entertainment (UK) Ltd v easyInternetcafe Ltd* [2003] IP & T 1059.

[36] CRRA 2000, s 21(1).

[37] CRRA 2000, ss 21(d), 28, 37–38, 45–48 and 99–105.

available to the public, protection against exact copying by photo-lithographic or similar means of copying the edition was available to the publisher for 25 years from the end of the year in which the literary, dramatic or musical work was first published. This typographical arrangement copyright[38] is not part of the EU *acquis* but the right was re-examined and expanded upon in CRRA 2000.

[12.08] Section 17(2)(c) of CA 1963 re-enacts the typographic arrangement copyright and the right is extended to facsimile reproduction of databases. In the definition of a published edition in s 2(1) of CRRA 2000 the duration of protection is extended to a period of 50 years after the date on which the published edition was first lawfully made available to the public.[39] Some of the 'fair dealing' and other defences are available under CRRA 2000 but the scope of the right has been considerably diminished by the decision of the House of Lords in *Newspaper Licensing Agency Ltd v Marks and Spencer plc*.[40] In this case their Lordships held that individual newspaper articles were not published editions and that for an infringement to be made out, a substantial amount of the newspaper had to be photocopied.

GOVERNMENT AND OIREACHTAS COPYRIGHTS

[12.09] Section 51 of CA 1963 gave to the government certain statutory rights in relation to literary, dramatic, musical or artistic works, sound recordings or cinematographic films that have been made by or under the control of the government or a Minister of State. The section provided that if no copyright otherwise would exist then a copyright shall exist, and in any case the government shall be entitled to the copyright in the work.[41] Chapter 19 of CRRA 2000 has built upon the concept of government copyright quite extensively and the Act distinguishes two kinds of copyright, government copyright and Oireachtas copyright. In relation to government copyright, a work created by an officer or employee of the government or of the State, in the course of his or her duties qualifies for copyright protection and the government is the first owner thereof.[42] Copyright expires 50 years from the end of the calendar year in which the work was made. The second copyright created by Ch 19 is Oireachtas copyright. Section 192(1) of CRRA 2000 provides that the copyright in any Bill or enactment vests in the Oireachtas, this copyright subsisting for the same 50-year period.[43] Works made by or under the direction or the control of either House also vests in the relevant House, with joint ownership provisions being in place in respect of works made for both Houses.[44] Again, a 50-year period of protection is available upon the making of the

---

[38] Not to be confused with the copyright protection afforded by CRRA 2000, ss 84 and 85 for typeface and the separate design right in the Industrial Designs Act 2001, s 2(1) (definition of product).

[39] CRRA 2000, s 29.

[40] *Newspaper Licensing Agency Ltd v Marks and Spencer plc* [2001] 3 All ER 977.

[41] CA 1963, s 51(1).

[42] CRRA 2000, s 191(2).

[43] CRRA 2000, s 192(2).

[44] CRRA 2000, s 193.

work. Where a work may be entitled to both forms of protection, Oireachtas copyright eliminates entitlement to government copyright.[45] Permissions to copy or make available works governed by Oireachtas copyright, upon conditions,[46] are under the control of the Ceann Comhairle and Cathaoirleach or their authorised officers[47] and any such conditions must be laid before each House as soon as may be after they have been imposed.[48] The commercial value of these copyrights must not be underestimated. For example, the maps, databases and other output of Ordnance Survey Ireland is protected by Oireachtas copyright[49] and a considerable amount of investment has gone into protecting these rights.[50]

PRESCRIBED INTERNATIONAL ORGANISATIONS

[12.10] Copyright in publications produced on behalf of the United Nations and the Organisation of American States, and other organisations prescribed by order were protected by Irish copyright law under s 44 of CA 1963. This system has been re-enacted, in modified form, in s 196 of CRRA 2000 but, to date, no orders prescribing the organisations in question have been made.

FOLKLORE

[12.11] Section 197 of CRRA 2000 provides a copyright in respect of 'anonymous works' as defined in s 2(1) but the note in the margin to s 197 more helpfully refers to folklore. By definition, works of cultural and traditional significance cannot be identified with an author. Where this is possible a copyright may well subsist via the adaptation of a public domain work. The s 197 right is afforded in respect of anonymous works that have a connection with a foreign country, territory or state. Enforcement within Ireland of the copyright in anonymous works may be ceded to designated bodies from outside the State and these may be recognised by the Minister. No orders have been made under s 197.

---

[45] CRRA 2000, s 191(7).
[46] CRRA 2000, s 194(1).
[47] CRRA 2000, s 194(2).
[48] CRRA 2000, s 194(3).
[49] Ordnance Survey Ireland Act 2001, s 4.
[50] See www.ordnancesurvey.ie.

Chapter 13

The Protection of Computer Programs as Copyright Works

INTRODUCTION

[13.01] In this chapter the primary focus will be on the extent to which Irish copyright law affords protection to computer programs; but the technology does not permit the analysis to end there. The boundaries between the protection of computer programs, works in electronic form, original databases and electronic protection measures used to restrict the ability of users (lawful and unlawful) to reproduce or gain access to works are not easy to draw. Many of theses issues are treated separately herein but the authors nevertheless consider it important to draw together the legislative framework in respect of copyright and electronic works, or works that are either in, or protected by, some electronic format.

PRE-2000 LEGISLATIVE PROTECTION

[13.02] Computer programs have been the subject of express legal protection as a result of the transposition of the Computer Programs Directive into Irish law by way of statutory instrument.[1] Protection was afforded to computer programs created before 1 January 1993, but the scope of this provision in the statutory instrument was and remains uncertain. This raises the potential of the Copyright Act 1963 (CA 1963) to afford protection to a computer program. Under the terms of Pt II of CA 1963, a copyright work could be protected as a literary work, a dramatic work, or an artistic work. The most obvious possibility in such a context was that the concept of an original literary work would be applicable to software. CA 1963 did not provide an extensive definition of literary work as s 2 stated that the definition includes a written table or compilation. In the High Court decision in *RTE v Magill TV Guide*[2] on the availability of interlocutory relief, Lardner J affirmed the traditional view that a literary work must be 'a printed or written work', thus echoing the leading English decision on this particular point.[3] This requirement will of course be difficult to comply with when the program exists in a form which does not communicate with human beings via print or writing but

---

[1] Council Directive 91/250/EEC ([1991] OJ L122/42). The 1991 Directive was codified and replaced by Council Directive 2009/24/EC OJL 111/16. Throughout this chapter reference is made to the original 1991 text.
[2] *RTE v Magill TV Guide* [1990] ILRM 534.
[3] *University of London Press Ltd v University of Tutorial Press Ltd* [1916] 2 Ch 601 at 608–609.

rather provides instructions to a machine – typically when the program exists in machine code and is provided to the consumer in that 'perfected', ready to use form.

[13.03] This central issue, can existing copyright regimes protect computer programs in the many forms in which such programs exist, has been a controversial one. Certain academic commentators have taken the view that the concept of a literary work can accommodate all computer programs[4] although many others take the view that this approach is too simplistic, for when a program exists in object code it cannot be said to be literary in any real sense[5] and, if anything, the program comes closer to a work that more properly answers the description of an audio-visual work or an industrial design. The Whitford Committee in 1977[6] examined this issue and reached a similarly ambivalent conclusion on the state of legal protection, noting that English law probably protected a programmer's original written work from direct copying but that, in the absence of case law, other possible abuses by unauthorised copying were only capable of redress via licensing conditions and the law of confidence – remedies that could not affect an innocent use of an unauthorised copy.[7] At the level of international treaties, both the Berne Convention for the Protection of Literary and Artistic Works (Berne Convention) and the Universal Copyright Convention of 1952 failed to address the question of protecting computer programs. Cornish argued that the central issue surrounding the implied protection afforded to computer programs turns on the scope of the Paris Act version of art 9(1) of the Berne Convention, the reproduction right,[8] but he noted that even if all unauthorised uses infringe the reproduction right this will not be of much use to the right holder if the program, in the relevant form, is not literary. However, the climate of opinion has been significantly changed by the Trade-Related Aspects of Intellectual Property Rights Agreement (TRIPS), art 10(1) of which obliges States which are party to the agreement to protect computer programs in both source code and object code as literary works under the Berne Convention. This has led World Intellectual Property Organisation (WIPO) experts looking at the possible protocol to the Berne Convention to reach 'practically unanimous agreement that computer programs, and in both source and object codes, were protected by copyright, and further, that the obligation to protect such programs at the same level as literary works could be deduced from the present text of the Berne Convention'.[9]

---

4   Eg Kindermann [1981] EIPR 6; Keplinger [1985] Copyright 119; for an analysis of case law see Drier (1989) 20 IIC 803.

5   Vaver (1986) 17 IIC 557; Cornish [1990] EIPR 131; Soltysinski (1990) 21 IIC 1.

6   Cmnd 6732.

7   Cmnd 6732, paras 479–482.

8   Cornish, 'Computer Program Copyright and the Berne Convention' in Lehmann and Tapper, *A Handbook of European Software Law* (Clarendon, 1995); Cornish [1990] EIPR 131. It should be noted that with effect from 2 December 2004 Ireland has lodged documents of accession to the Paris Act (1971) of the Berne Convention.

9   WIPO, Committee of Experts on a Possible Protocol to the Berne Convention, Fourth Session, Memorandum para 8. Nevertheless, the Protocol or First Treaty agreed in Geneva in December 1996 provides that computer programs in whatever form are literary works.

[13.04] Leaving the issue of interpretation of the Paris Act of the Berne Convention to one side, the debate in the national courts has tended to be somewhat inconclusive when the judges have been presented with national legislation that fails to declare expressly that computer programs are either literary works or are to be regarded as if they were literary works. Indeed, the pattern of judicial decisions in common law jurisdictions has tended to come out against an inclusive view of the protectability of computer programs when the judges have attempted to apply the words of the legislation to the technology before them.

Source code[10]

[13.05] This raises the question whether preparatory printed or written material is capable of being protected as an original literary work. Where a program is in written format in the sense that the operations the computer is required to perform is written in ordinary language, that language being accompanied by labels, mathematical symbols and/or flow-charts, it is clear that such high level language, preparatory material will be copyright protected. Such preparatory material is literary in the sense that it communicates information or instruction from one person in a way that another person can make sense of it. In the Australian case of *Computer Edge Property Ltd v Apple Computer Inc*[11] it was not contested, and indeed it was largely assumed, that such preparatory written material is capable of attracting copyright, as long as it is an original literary work.

[13.06] Whether the written statements are used to develop a source code, or whether the creation of a source code is the first step taken to develop a program, leads us on to the question as to whether source code is copyright protected. In *Computer Edge Property Ltd v Apple Computer Inc* the defendants contended that a source code written in an assembly code could not itself be capable of copyright protection. All members of the High Court of Australia rejected this submission. Citing the test of Davey LJ in *Hollinrake v Truswell*,[12] that is, a 'literary work is intended to afford either information and instruction, or pleasure, in the form of literary enjoyment', Gibbs CJ indicated that the test was satisfied on the facts of *Computer Edge*: the source code 'affords instruction to the operator keying in the machine that will convert the source code to object code'.[13] Opinion in other jurisdictions supports the view that source code can be the subject of copyright protection. In *Apple Computer Inc v Mackintosh Computers Ltd*[14] the alleged

---

[10] See the author's report in Jongen and Meijboom (eds) *Copyright Software Protection in the EC* (Kluwer, 1994).

[11] *Computer Edge Property Ltd v Apple Computer Inc* (1986) 60 ALJR 313.

[12] *Hollinrake v Truswell* (1894) 3 Ch 420 at 428.

[13] *Computer Edge Property Ltd v Apple Computer Inc* (1986) 60 ALJR 313 at 315; Mason and Wilson JJ in a joint judgment agreed, (1986) 60 ALJR 313 at 320; see also Brennan J at 324. Deane J at 329 did not find it necessary to decide this point.

[14] *Apple Computer Inc v Mackintosh Computers Ltd* (1987) 44 DLR (4th) 74, reasoning of both courts below affirmed by the Supreme Court of Canada at (1990) 71 DLR (4th) 95 in a short judgment.

infringers conceded before the Federal Court of Appeal that original computer programs written in assembly language were literary works within the meaning of the Federal Copyright Law.[15] Similarly, the English judiciary addressed this question during proceedings in which an interlocutory injunction was sought and the issue of whether copyright could subsist in a source code was held to be established, at least provisionally.[16] The most emphatic statement on which to base an assertion that source code is copyright protected appears in the New Zealand case of *IBM v Computer Imports Ltd*[17] where Smellie J concluded that whether source code is written down as a list of instructions, or keyed directly onto a computer and displayed onto a screen, it is an original literary work:[18]

> Source programs are the product of substantial originality and skill, they are expressed in writing, they are intended to convey and do convey information to human beings and they are expressed in a comprehensible form.

Object code

[13.07] When the source code is converted into machine-readable language, that is, the form in which the code is converted in order to make the computer read the source code, this has the effect of making the computer program, in this form, a program that is not in print or writing. The computer program, when it exists in object code or machine code, does not subsist in a form of notation. When the Irish CA 1963 stated that the definition of 'writing' includes any form of notation, it is clear that the statutory definition is not exhaustive, but, it is submitted, it is essential that the work should exist in some tangible or perceptible form at least. There is a significant distinction to be drawn between works consisting of electrical impulses that exist independently from the binary or hexadecimal notation that represents the impulses, and works where the static circuitry contains the program in a ROM chip. The first way in which protection may be sought is to argue that copyright may subsist in a series of impulses or in chip circuitry, as literary works. This first argument was decisively rejected in *Computer Edge Property Ltd v Apple Computer Inc*[19] by way of unanimous decision on this point. Gibbs CJ, in the leading judgment, rejected the view that a literary work itself need not be expressed in writing. Pointing out that a literary work is protected from the time it is reduced into writing or some other material form, the Chief Justice stated:[20]

> It seems to me a complete distortion of meaning to describe electrical impulses in a silicone chip, which cannot be perceived by the senses and are intended to convey any

---

[15] See judgment of Mahoney J (1987) 44 DLR (4th) 74 at 78.
[16] Goulding J in *Sega Enterprises v Richards* [1983] FSR 73. In *Thrustcode Ltd v WW Computing Ltd* [1983] FSR 502 a motion seeking an interlocutory injunction was heard on the assumption that copyright in a program could subsist; the only copyright material before the court was source code, [1983] FSR 502 at 506.
[17] *IBM v Computer Imports Ltd* [1989] 2 NZLR 395.
[18] *IBM v Computer Imports Ltd* [1989] 2 NZLR 395 at 409.
[19] *Computer Edge Property Ltd v Apple Computer Inc* (1986) 60 ALJR 313.
[20] *Computer Edge Property Ltd v Apple Computer Inc* (1986) 60 ALJR 313 at 316.

message to a human being and which do not represent words, letters, figures, or symbols as a literary work; still less can a pattern of circuits be so described.

[13.08] This approach was supported by Smellie J in *IBM v Computer Imports Ltd*.[21] In the Canadian case of *Apple Computer Inc v Mackintosh Computers Ltd*,[22] it was contended that the circuitry of a ROM chip could be a literary work but, as Gibbs CJ points out in the above extract from his judgment in the *Computer Edge* case,[23] information held in electronic circuitry is *a fortiori* not covered by copyright. It is a 'form' which does not contain a 'work'. A further argument that may be advanced in order to obtain protection is based upon the argument that if copyright protection is afforded to source code, then the object code version of the source code – assuming the program has not been written directly into a machine-readable format – represents an infringing use of the original and is thus a restricted act. The relevant restricted acts in s 8(6) of CA 1963 were as follows:

(a)   reproducing the work in any material form;

(b)   performing the work in public;

(c)   making any adaptation of the work. It appears from the decision of the Supreme Court in *Gormley v EMI Records (Ireland) Ltd*[24] denying copyright protection to speech recorded on magnetic tape that a similar conclusion would be reached by an Irish court if called upon to apply the 1963 legislation to object code.

It is of course necessary to point out that CRRA 2000 now includes object code as a literary work, a position that Irish law has taken under Directive 91/250/EC.

Reproduction under the Copyright Act 1963

[13.09] Proponents of the view that the words 'any material form' are to be given an extended definition use this argument to make the further point that if the infringing work is a reproduction of a literary work, then as long as it subsists in 'any material form', it does not matter that the reproduction itself is not a literary work. This argument was rejected in *Computer Edge Property Ltd v Apple Computer Inc* by Gibbs CJ, Deane and Brennan JJ on the ground that there was no similarity between the copyright work, the source program, and the alleged reproduction, the ROMs and EPROM. These judges also resisted the argument that copyright could subsist in the collocation of ideas represented in the written original, which was reproduced in ROMs/EPROM. In Brennan J's view:

> there is no resemblance between the Wombat ROMs and EPROM and the written compilations of the source programs. It is immaterial that the former were divided from the latter when there is no resemblance between them, for both resemblance and derivation are essential to reproduction.

21   *IBM v Computer Imports Ltd* [1989] 2 NZLR 395.
22   *Apple Computer Inc v Mackintosh Computers Ltd* (1987) 44 DLR (4th) 74.
23   *Computer Edge Property Ltd v Apple Computer Inc* (1986) 60 ALJR 313.
24   *Gormley v EMI Records (Ireland) Ltd* [1999] 1 ILRM 178.

Carrying out instructions in order to produce something in another material form is not a reproduction.[25]

[13.10] However, in the Canadian Federal Court of Appeal, a different approach was taken on the question of reproduction. The Federal Court of Appeal asked itself whether the chips, and in particular the programs, as embodied in ROM chips, were reproductions in material form of the source code. Mahoney, Hugesson and MacGuigan JJ took the robust view not only that reproduction in any material form meant that the reproduction did not have to be humanly readable (ie itself a literary work) but also implicitly rejected the view that reproduction involves similarity and a causal link. The Federal Court of Appeal failed to address the question of whether references to reproduction in any material form also distinguish between literary and 'dramatic or musical works' on the ground that dramatic or musical works are protected even if a written form is not needed, unlike literary works: see *Computer Edge Property Ltd v Apple Computer Inc*.[26]

Both the Canadian Federal Court of Appeal and Smellie J, in the New Zealand case of *IBM v Computer Imports Ltd*,[27] explained that the substantial objective similarity criteria, relied upon by the majority in the High Court of Australia, was purely evidentiary; once it could be established that there existed a causal link between an original literary work and an alleged unauthorised reproduction – eg running an object code through a dissembler program to produce source code, or by obtaining a print out, etc – then the comparison necessary in order to establish infringement by reproduction can be made. The *Computer Edge* decision has been departed from by the High Court of Australia in *Autodesk Inc v Dyason*,[28] the High Court holding that for an infringement of a computer program to be made out, it is not necessary that the derivative reproduction be itself a computer program.

Public performance

[13.11] In the Canadian case of *Apple Computer Inc v Mackintosh Computers Ltd*[29] the trial judge, Reed J, observed that she thought there was merit in the argument that the chips into which object code had been incorporated was a contrivance whereby the source code could be, as a work, 'delivered' to others, an infringement under the Canadian Copyright Act 1970, s 3(1)(d). This argument was doubted by Hugessen J in the Federal Court of Appeal on the ground that delivery was used in the legislation in the sense of communication by audible means. It is possible to advance the argument that the public display of a program which is embodied in object code, by way of display or delivery, may, in appropriate factual circumstances, be an infringement. The High Court of Australia, in *Data Access Corpn v Powerflex Services Pty Ltd*,[30] has reconsidered the

---

[25] *Computer Edge Property Ltd v Apple Computer Inc* (1986) 60 ALJR 313.

[26] *Computer Edge Property Ltd v Apple Computer Inc* (1986) 60 ALJR 313.

[27] *IBM v Computer Imports Ltd* [1989] 2 NZLR 395.

[28] *Autodesk Inc v Dyason* (1992) 173 CLR 330.

[29] *Apple Computer Inc v Mackintosh Computers Ltd* (1987) 44 DLR (4th) 74.

[30] *Data Access Corpn v Powerflex Services Pty Ltd* (1999) 45 IPR 353.

Court's earlier view on the definition of a substantial part of a computer program, but the reproduction point method in the context of *Computer Edge*[31] was not under discussion in the *Data Access* case. The argument here in favour of protection is to the effect that the public display of source code, by visual presentation, through object code produced by another person who copies the source code, may be a performance in public.[32] The issue is whether the act of visual presentation is proximate enough to the copyright work. We will return to this point below.

Adapting the work

[13.12] The possibility that copyright in source code may be infringed indirectly by reproducing in the form of object code, has been canvassed on the basis that any object code representation of the source code as a derivative of that source code may be an adaptation of the work. The definition of an adaptation in CA 1963, s 8(7) included 'a translation of the work'.

[13.13] This argument has been exhaustively reviewed in Australian, Canadian and New Zealand case law. The weight of judicial opinion is against the argument being successful. In the Australian case of *Computer Edge Property Ltd v Apple Computer Inc*,[33] the High Court of Australia, by a majority of 3:2, held that an object program, if derived from a source program, is not a translation of the source program. The word 'translation' was given the meaning 'the expression or rendering of something in another medium or form'. Gibbs CJ held that the definition required that the translated work must refer to the portrayal, utterance, representation, reproduction or depiction of the thing in a different form. The source code was a set of instructions effectuated by the electrical impulses in object code which causes a computer to function. Brennan J agreed in the sense that, while he held it was arguable that object code was a translation of source code, the argument failed because the adaptation itself had to be a work. A set of electrical impulses could not be a work. Deane J agreed that electrical impulses could not be held to be a translation or adaptation of a written source code.

[13.14] In the Canadian Federal Court of Appeal's decision in *Apple Computer Inc v Mackintosh Computers Ltd*[34] the Court emphatically rejected the argument, agreeing with Reed J at first instance that the conversion of source code into object code does not result in the creation of a new literary work, while disagreeing with Reed J's conclusion that such a conversion is a translation. Reed J advanced the analogy that a written message, when converted into Morse code by a telegraph operator, is a translation of the written message. The Federal Court of Appeal concluded, however, that such a process is not one of translation but is reproduction of the written message in a material form, namely, the dots and dashes that make up Morse code. A decision that goes the other

---

31 *Computer Edge Property Ltd v Apple Computer Inc* (1986) 60 ALJR 313.
32 See, by analogy, *Bookmakers Afternoon Greyhound Services Ltd v Wilf Gilbert (Staffordshire) Ltd* [1994] FSR 723.
33 *Computer Edge Property Ltd v Apple Computer Inc* (1986) 60 ALJR 313.
34 *Apple Computer Inc v Mackintosh Computers Ltd* (1987) 44 DLR (4th) 74.

way is that of Smellie J in the New Zealand case of *IBM v Computer Imports Ltd*,[35] but it is submitted that the reasoning advanced by the judge is at odds with the Australian and Canadian appellate decisions and, further, is based upon principles of statutory interpretation that depend heavily on New Zealand statute law.

[13.15] It should be noted in passing that UK case law has acknowledged that the conversion of a computer program from one language or code into another language or code is to be treated as an adaptation[36] but this conclusion is reached as the result of the direct effect of the 1985 and 1988 legislation.[37] It is also hardly surprising to note that computer program protection in those common law jurisdictions that addressed the issue via the courts has been introduced by specific statutory amendment to 'traditional' copyright legislative models. This forces us to conclude that prior to the transposition of the Directive, Irish copyright law probably afforded copyright protection to source code, but other forms in which a program was expressed were, in all probability, unprotected under CA 1963.

Transposition of the computer programs Directive into Irish law

Introduction

[13.16] Council Directive 91/250/EEC on the Legal Protection of Computer Programs was transposed into Irish law by the European Communities (Legal Protection of Computer Programs) Regulations 1993 (in this chapter the Computer Programs Regulations 1993)[38] made on the basis of the European Communities Act 1972. The validity or interpretation of these Regulations has not been tested by litigation although the Regulations were directly referred to in *News Datacom Ltd v Lyons*.[39] The statutory instrument was signed by the Minister for Enterprise and Employment on 2 February 1993, thus missing the implementation deadline. However, the Regulations were expressed to be retrospective and were to come into operation on 31 December 1992, although the implementation was not to result in the making or declaring of any acts to be unlawful if the act in question was lawful at the date of its commission. This provision against retrospective legislation and prejudice to accrued rights is a Constitutional imperative in both national and European Community law.

Literary works

[13.17] Although the entire scheme behind Council Directive 91/250/EEC is based upon the view that copyright protection, rather than any form of *sui generis* right or even an industrial design protection, is the preferred option because of the prospect of greater

---

[35] *IBM v Computer Imports Ltd* [1989] 2 NZLR 395.

[36] *John Richardson Computers Ltd v Flanders* [1993] FSR 497.

[37] Copyright (Computer Software) Amendment Act 1985, s 1(2); Copyright, Designs and Patents Act 1988, s 21(4). On the UK position see Bainbridge (1991) 54 MLR 643; (1993) 56 MLR 591; Chalton [1993] EIPR 138.

[38] SI 26/1993: see Jongen and Meijboom (eds), *Copyright Software Protection in the EC* (Kluwer, 1994); Tapper and Lehman, *A Handbook of European Software Law* (Clarendon, 1995).

[39] *News Datacom Ltd v Lyons* [1994] 1 ILRM 450; see [1995] EIPR D-70 (Hann).

international acceptance, the Irish mode of implementation is half-hearted on this central issue. The key regulation provided that for a computer program the Copyright Acts of 1963–87 'shall apply ... as if it were a literary work'.[40] For example, CA 1963, s 12 set out a number of 'fair dealing' provisions that, arguably, authorise certain acts that would otherwise be copyright infringements (or restricted acts under CA 1963, s 8(6)). The 'fair dealing' defences can be seen as covering much of the same territory as arts 5 and 6 of Directive 91/250/EEC, those articles being incorporated into Irish law by the Computer Programs Regulations 1993.[41] Thus, in a copyright infringement action involving computer software, the defendant could invoke both s 12 of CA 1963 and the customised defences found in the Computer Programs Regulations 1993 which are based on Directive 91/250/EEC, arts 5 and 6. Similarly, the restricted acts set out in s 8(6) of CA 1963 may be seen as similar in nature to the exclusive rights given to a right holder under art 4 of Directive 91/250/EEC but the regulations were clearly much broader in scope and the restricted acts closely tailored to the needs of the industry. It is doubtful, for example, whether the CA 1963 made the 'loading, displaying, running, transmission or storage' of a literary work a restricted act while the Computer Programs Regulations 1993 clearly gave the right holder authorisation rights to such acts in certain instances. However, the Computer Programs Regulations 1993 did not attempt to enhance the range of remedies available to a right holder, at least in procedural terms. The right holder who reasonably anticipated or feared that software has been unlawfully copied or pirated must have sought to rely on *Anton Piller* relief or on the search and seizure remedy given under s 27 of CA 1963, as amended by s 2 of the Copyright (Amendment) Act 1987. Indeed, it is understood that in *News Datacom Ltd v Lyons*[42] such reliefs were made available to the right holder prior to the hearing of the application for interlocutory relief.

Originality

[13.18] The standard set by both Council Directive 91/250/EEC and the Computer Programs Regulations 1993 are that the work must be the author's own intellectual creation. The regulations do not go further by insisting that 'no other criteria shall be applied to determine [the program's] eligibility for protection'.[43] While the view in the UK appears to be that the test simply reflects the lower common law threshold of originality,[44] the reference to 'intellectual effort' rather than 'original effort' *per se* can arguably posit an intermediate standard that is above the Irish and UK standard but considerably lower than the originality test applied in other EU States. This argument seems to have been overtaken by the decision of the ECJ in *Infopaq International A/S v Danske Dogblades Forening*,[45] the implications of which are uncertain. Nevertheless, some claims to copyright in software fail because the courts regard individual files as not being a 'substantial part' of a computer program. Also, it may be that the plaintiff

---

[40] SI 26/1993, reg 3.

[41] SI 26/1993, reg 6.

[42] *News Datacom Ltd v Lyons* [1994] 1 ILRM 450.

[43] Council Directive 91/250/EEC, art 2.1.

[44] Eg Tapper in *A Handbook of European Software Law*, p 6 of the UK Report.

[45] *Infopaq International A/S v Danske Dagblades Forening* Case C-5/08 (16 July 2009).

cannot make out any claim to authorship as downloading pre-existing source code suggests that the plaintiff's claim to authorship may be negated via 'common origin' arguments and s 17(5) of CRRA 2000. See, in particular, *Dais Studio Pty v Bullet Creative Pty*.[46]

Authorship

[13.19] On the question of who may be an author, Council Directive 91/250/EEC follows the civilian tradition in insisting that authors are human persons; the Directive provides that natural persons or groups of natural persons are authors unless a national law allows for designation of a legal person in such cases – which Irish law does not, in a direct sense. The central point here is that works created by computer programs – and programs can and do create other programs – cannot under the Directive benefit from the 'deemed authorship' provisions, such as are contained in the UK Copyright, Designs and Patents Act 1988. The existence of statutory rules on ownership still require a court to determine whether ownership extends into not just specific outputs from a contract but also the underlying and often pre-existing libraries of code. This was recently explored in the New Zealand case of *Pacific Software Technology Ltd v Perry Group Ltd*.[47] The New Zealand Court of Appeal, applying different statutory rules, held that a commissioner was entitled to copyright in source code, but that ownership did not extend into library code used by the programmer in producing source code. A non-revocable licence to use library code was nevertheless to be implied.

In general, however, the fact that a programmer has been engaged to write source code in order to enhance an existing program will not of itself give the commissioner a right to copyright in the source code, especially when there is an interoperability purpose behind the commission and other statutory means of gaining access are available: *Centrestage Management Pty Ltd v Riedle*.[48] The courts will regard the commissioner as having a right to use the program by way of a licence, but such licences are likely to be personal to the commissioner,[49] who may be obliged under the contract to pay a royalty[50] to the author of the program. Breach of the licence or any undertaking in relation to ownership or use of the program will be actionable in contract.[51] Most of the above cases involve bespoke or commissioned software. In the case of mass market software, the purchaser or licensee will be regarded as obtaining a licence to decompile the program under the Directive. In *SAS Institute Inc v World Programming Ltd*,[52] Arnold J said that where the licence is based on the Directive, art 5(3) should be a positive defence in an infringement action. This view is *obiter* as the matter has been referred to the ECJ.

---

[46] *Dais Studio Pty v Bullet Creative Pty* (2007) 74 IPR 512.

[47] *Pacific Software Technology Ltd v Perry Group Ltd* (2003) 57 IPR 145.

[48] *Centrestage Management Pty Ltd v Riedle* [2008] FCA 938; on joint ownership see *Fylde Microsystems Ltd v Key Radio Systems* (1998) 39 IPR 481.

[49] *Clearsprings Management Ltd v Businesslinx* [2006] FSR 3.

[50] *Wrenn Landamore* [2007] EWHC 1833 (Pat).

[51] *Cantor Gaming v Gameaccount Global* [2007] EWHC 1911 (Ch); *Visusoft Ltd v Harris* [2009] IEHC 543.

[52] *SAS Institute Inc v World Programming Ltd* [2010] EWHC 1829 (Ch).

Copyright in a computer program created by an employee

[13.20] An employer acquires copyright in computer programs created by an employee during the course of the employee's duties, subject to contrary provision by way of contract.[53] Even if the creator of the program is an independent contractor, recent case law suggests that the courts will readily infer an equitable trust that will give the employer, not the independent contractor, equitable title to the program created under contract.[54]

[13.21] In the specific context of computer programs, the Australian decision in *Intelmail Explorenet Pty Ltd v Vardanian (No 2)*[55] provides a very useful analysis of the process whereby the author of a work may find that ownership may be divested from the author by way of implied contract or equitable considerations. Vardanian was employed by Intelmail between the period 1987 to 1996 in order to write source code for software that Intelmail used in its automated mailing business, Intelmail supplying equipment and software to its customers. In 1996 and again in 1999 Vardanian renegotiated his relationship with Intelmail through his own company, agreeing to write enhancements and to supply the enhanced source code to Intelmail. After 2003, the relationship between the parties deteriorated and the issue of ownership of the post-1999 software enhancements arose for consideration. The parties were effectively silent on all issues of ownership and the Court had to imply a number of terms into the 1996 and 1999 agreements. Because of the statutory rules on ownership, which provide that an independent contractor, as distinct from an employee, enjoys legal ownership of a work, the court concluded that, as a matter of imputed intention, Intelmail would retain equitable ownership of the post-1996 and 1999 enhancements, notwithstanding that legal ownership was vested in Vardanian's company. However, Intelmail was entitled to call upon Vardanian's company to transfer equitable ownership as well as deliver up the source code that Vardanian had retained, in order to give effect to that imputed intention and perfect Intelmail's title to the software as a whole. It should be noted that one of the most critical points that triggers such an imputation is the level of consideration that is charged for the development work undertaken by the programmer. In *Vardanian's* case very significant fees were charged on the basis of the ability of the commissioner to pay. Where flat fees or a time and materials calculation is used, the law is reluctant to infer any transfer of rights, or indeed, that any licence arrangement is intended. In the case of source code written by a person who owes a fiduciary duty to a company, equitable ownership will be vested in the company: *Vitof Ltd Altoft.*[56]

[13.22] Of course, once works are created, ownership of those works can be held or transferred in the usual ways such as by way of an assignment under s 47 of CA 1963, as replaced by CRRA 2000, s 120. Rights owners may licence the use of computer programs and this possibility has produced a significant body of case law on the

---

[53] See CA 1963, s 10(3). See SI 26/1993, reg 4, however.

[54] *John Richardson Computers Ltd v Flanders* [1993] FSR 497.

[55] *Intelmail Explorenet Pty Ltd v Vardanian (No 2)* (2009) FCA 1018; see also *Ultraframe UK Ltd v GJ Fielding* [2004] RPC 439.

[56] *Vitof Ltd Altoft* [2006] EWHC 1678 (Ch).

question of whether such arrangements may result in the transfer of ownership via implied contract terms. In general, such arguments invoke a 'necessity' test and the decisions do not find for any such implied term.[57] The scope of any software licence is a matter of interpretation. A bare licence may be revocable at will,[58] some licences may be non-exclusive and personal to the licensee, while compelling circumstances and a writing requirement will have to be satisfied under s 122 of CRRA 2000 if a court is to be persuaded that a licence is exclusive and/or transferable to a sub-licensee.[59]

Infringement and defences

[13.23] We have already seen that under CA 1963, s 8(6), several of the acts of reproduction and use of a computer program would infringe copyright, as long as the program in question was a protected work under s 8 (ie a literary, dramatic or musical work). In order to address certain doubts about whether all prejudicial acts of exploitation would be caught by copyright law, Council Directive 91/250/EEC provided an extensive definition of the acts that the right holder is entitled to do, or authorise others to do; reg 5 of the Computer Programs Regulations 1993 thus provided word-for-word transposition of art 4 of the Directive. A less than faithful transposition of art 5 of the Directive was made. Under the Directive a distinction is drawn between acts of reproduction that constitute acts of loading and running necessary for lawful use by a lawful acquirer, and acts of error correction: these acts cannot be displaced by contract, for recital 17 in the Directive expressly so provides. However, while arts 5.1 and 9.1 generally provide that lawful acquirers do not need authorisation to do those things listed in art 4(a) and (b), specific contractual provisions may otherwise so direct. The implementing provision in reg 6 of the 1993 Regulations does not take account of the ambiguity in recital 17 and art 5.1 of the Directive although Ireland is not alone in this.[60] This is in contrast to the right to make a back-up copy and the right to run a program so as to observe, study or test a program, which cannot be excluded.[61]

Decompilation

[13.24] The decompilation provisions of Council Directive 91/250/EEC were transposed almost word for word by the Computer Programs Regulations 1993.[62] It is worth noting that the fair dealing defences were still available to these acts of creation (as well as the

---

57 *Ray v Classic FM* [1998] FSR 622; *Wrenn v Landamore* [2007] EWHC 1833 (Pat); *Meridian International Services Ltd v Richardson* [2008] EWCA Civ 609; *Centrestage Management Property v Riedle* [2008] FCA 938.

58 *Trumpet Software Property v Oz Mail Pty Ltd* (1996) 34 IPR 481.

59 *Wrenn v Landamore* [2007] EWHC 1833 (Pat); *SGI Games Ltd v Argonaught Games plc* [2006] Info TLR 175.

60 See Meijboom, in *Copyright Software Protection in the EC* (Kluwer, 1994), pp 12–13. Chalton [1993] EIPR 138 at 141.

61 Council Directive 91/250/EEC, art 9.1. On making back up copies of licensed software see *Racing and Wagering Western Australia v Software AG (Aust) Pty Ltd* (2008) 78 IPR 537. Note that the issue of contractual exclusion is one of the matters that Arnold J has referred to the ECJ in *SAS Institute Inc v World Programming Inc* [2010] EWHC 1829 (Ch).

62 Council Directive 91/250/EEC, art 6; SI 26/1993, reg 7.

observe, study and test rights expressly provided in reg 6.3). The UK Regulations, in contrast, exclude fair dealing defences in general copyright law from the UK measures implementing the Directive, despite the permissive nature of art 9.1 of the Directive itself.

Copyright protection under the 2000 legislation

[13.25] CRRA 2000 specifically repeals SI 26/1993[63] and provides that the Act is to apply to computer programs whether created before or after 1 January 1993.[64] It thus appears that even in respect of pre-1 January 2001 infringements[65] in regard to computer programs, the 2000 legislation applies. Section 2(1) provides that the definition of a literary work includes a computer program, further defined in the section as: 'a program which is original in that it is the author's own intellectual creation and includes any design materials used for the preparation of the program'.

[13.26] Most of the ownership issues raised under CRRA 2000 have been considered above, with the employee-created-works provisions in s 23 applying fully to computer programs. However, as many parts of a computer program are themselves computer-generated, computer-generated computer programs are owned by the persons responsible for making the arrangements necessary to generate the program: s 21(j).[66]

[13.27] Because of the integration of computer programs into the concept, and definition indeed, of a 'literary work'[67] the acts of infringement are:

(a) reproduction or copying the program, in the sense that a substantial part has been copied;

(b) making available to the public the computer program;

(c) adaptation of the computer program.[68]

Acts of reproduction include storing the program in any medium and transient and incidental copying vis-à-vis the program or any work[69] onto a server allowing internet downloading under both the internet provision in CRRA 2000[70] and the cable programme service provision.[71] Other commercial activities, such as renting copies of the computer program, will infringe.[72] The secondary infringement provisions in CRRA

---

63   CRRA 2000, Sch 2, Pt II.

64   CRRA 2000, Sch 1, Pt I, para 9(2).

65   The date of commencement of the CRRA 2000; SI 404/2000.

66   See CRRA 2000 s.2(1) for the definition of computer-generated work.

67   CRRA 2000, s 2(1).

68   CRRA 2000, s 37(1).

69   CRRA 2000, s 39(1)(a). It is dangerous to extrapolate case law from other jurisdictions where statutory definitions may differ: eg *Video Retailers Association Ltd v Warner Home Video* (2001) 53 IPR 242 (temporary RAM storage not a reproduction). Contrast *Gilham v R* [2009] EWCA Crim 2293.

70   CRRA 2000, s 40(1)(a).

71   CRRA 2000, s 40 (1)(d) as interpreted in *Sony Music Entertainment (UK) Ltd v easyInternetcafe Ltd* [2003] EWHC 62 (Ch).

72   CRRA 2000, s 40 (1)(j).

2000, ss 44 to 46 will also be very pertinent. File sharing activities and the distribution of computer programs may, for example, be non-commercial acts of distribution but it is possible to bring such activities both within secondary infringement provisions[73] and the authorising infringement concept in ss 37(1) and (2) of the Act.[74] It may be possible to view the 'authorising infringement' concept to be so wide as to cover acts of facilitation, such as providing information on the location of infringing works on the World Wide Web,[75] even if the infringing work is not available directly from that website. The right to control the adaptation of a computer program is given specific focus under s 43(2)(d), which states that a computer program includes a translation, arrangement or other alteration of the computer program in which it is converted into or out of a computer language or code or into a different computer language or code.

[13.28] Because of the availability of the defences to copyright infringement afforded to literary works, there are a significant number of situations in which an infringement claim will fail – eg fair dealing for research or private study, etc.[76] There are, however, specific defences in respect of computer programs that are attributable to Council Directive 91/250/EEC.[77] The first of these is the right of the lawful user to make a back-up copy where it is necessary for the lawful user to have such a copy for lawful use.[78] 'Lawful user' and 'lawful use' are defined in CRRA 2000, s 80(2) and those terms are of vital importance to s 82(1), a section that gives effect to the defence of permanent or temporary alteration of a computer program by a lawful user for the necessary and intended purpose of the program, including error correction. Section 82(2) gives effect to the right of the lawful user to observe, study or test the functioning of the program while operating the program in an authorised manner, when necessary to determine the underlying ideas and principles behind the program. It is submitted that contracting out of s 82 is not possible via licence agreements governed by Irish law notwithstanding the European Commission's views on the matter, as set out in both the Directive and the 2000 report on transposition of the Directive.[79]

---

[73] Eg CRRA 2000, s 45(d) (making available to the public to prejudice the rights of the copyright owner); s 46(2) (transmission in a network to facilitate copyright infringment).

[74] *Twentieth Century Fox Film Corporation v Newzbin* [2010] EWHC 608 (Ch); contrast *Roadshow Films Pty Ltd v iiNet Ltd (No 3)* [2010] FCA 24.

[75] *Grokster v MGM 545* US 913(2005) (a US vicarious liability case). See in Australia *Universal Music Australia Pty Ltd v Sharman Licence Holdings* (2005) 65 IPR 289 (authorising) and in England and Wales *Twentieth Century Fox Film Corporation v Newzbin* [2010] EWHC 608 (Ch) (authorising, procuring copyright infringement via a common design, communication of a work to the public). Liability will occur regardless of whether the user acquires the software directly or by downloading the software as a preliminary step to acquiring infringing copies of a work. The immunities afforded by s 40(3) and SI 68/2003 are considered elsewhere.

[76] See, however, CRRA 2000, s 50(5) in respect of the adaptation of a computer program: certain acts of adaptation are not within the research or private study fair dealing defence. See generally CRRA 2000, s 106.

[77] Council Directive 91/250/EEC, the Computer Programs Directive.

[78] CRRA 2000, s 80(1).

[79] COM(2000) 199 Final.

Section 81 of CRRA 2000 also sets out, mostly faithfully, the 'reverse engineering' right granted in order to compile an interoperable program; although the 'three step test' is omitted, much to the European Commission's dismay.[80] Acts of adaptation and copying may be available to a transferee of the program unless prohibited by express terms (eg in a licence agreement).[81] It should be noted that the English courts have denied the application of a repairer defence in relation to computer programs.[82] In *Microsoft Corporation v Commission of the European Communities*,[83] the Court of First Instance (CFI) considered the application of the interoperability provisions in Directive 91/250/EC and upheld the Commission's decision that refusal to provide protocols relating to Windows technology constituted an abuse of a dominant position under what is now TFEU, art 102. The CFI also upheld a complaint that 'bundling' the Windows PC operating system with Windows Media Player was similarly an abuse of a dominant position.[84]

[13.29] Directive 91/250/EEC[85] and CRRA 2000 cannot provide guidance on specific issues that arise in relation to the copyright protection of computer programs. Case law has developed a number of those points.

THE LIMITS OF THE COMPUTER PROGRAMS DIRECTIVE[86]

Proof of infringement

[13.30] In cases where the plaintiff alleges literal copying of a computer program, in the form of making another physical copy of the program by way of unauthorised reproduction of a tangible copy of that program, or through utilisation of knowledge or information previously acquired about the plaintiff's copyright work, the task facing the court will be to decide if copying has taken place. The fact that the defendant's program achieves the same results as the plaintiff's work, or that it supplants the plaintiff's product, does not signify copyright infringement, for first principles direct that the simultaneous or independent creation of works do not infringe any copyright. The issue of independent effort to create a derivative but superior competing product involves several complex legal and policy issues with which the courts in many countries are grappling. It is submitted that efforts towards the resolution of these difficulties have not been assisted by affording to computer programs the full blown status of literary copyright, and that the resolution of these difficulties may best be achieved by qualifying

---

80 COM(2000) 199 Final at 13.
81 CRRA 2000, s 86.
82 *Mars UK Ltd v Teknowledge Ltd* (1999) 46 IPR 248.
83 *Microsoft Corporation v Commission of the European Communities* Case T-201/04 [2007] 5 CMLR 829.
84 See Eagles & Longdin [2008] EIPR 205; Anderman [2008] EIPR 395; Dizon [2008] CTLR 213
85 Council Directive 91/250/EEC.
86 Council Directive 91/250/EEC.

the reproduction right afforded under the Berne Convention – something national laws may well do under art 9(2).[87]

[13.31] English case law has tended to focus attention on the objective similarities between the programs in question, and these decisions will clearly be influential in an Irish court.[88] However, the cases have not been free from difficulty and some decisions are clearly unreliable[89] as propositions of general principle. For example, it is clear that many computer programs are in fact made of a combination of existing code, routines and sub-routines. Despite doubts expressed in one English case,[90] the linking together of several distinct programs is clearly copyright protected as a compilation of works.[91] So, if copying is admitted but the issue before the court is whether the dependant has copied a work, an affirmative answer to this will normally be dispositive. It may be that the court may hold that the work was copyright and copying took place, but the defendant may avoid liability on the ground that no substantial copying took place. So in one case, *Data Access Corpn v Powerflex Services Pty Ltd*,[92] the reproduction of an error text program in the plaintiff's 'Data Flex' applications organisation program was not substantial infringement of the 'Data Flex' program because 'Data Flex' could function adequately without the error text program.

[13.32] Where such concessions are not made, the court will have to establish copying as a fact. The original work can be either reproduced substantially by the infringer, or rewritten into another programming language by the infringer, and in either case the infringement will be made out if the usual defence of independent creation does not prevail. In *Ibcos Computers Ltd v Barclays Mercantile Finance Ltd*,[93] the court concluded that there had been disk to disk copying by the defendant of the plaintiff's programs.[94] This made many of the learned judge's observations strictly *obiter*; in this area many doubts can only be resolved following clear decisions of the highest appellate tribunals. *Ibcos* complained that the defendant had copied their ADS accountancy work package. The defendant was responsible for developing ADS when engaged by *Ibcos*'s predecessor in title. On leaving that employment he developed a rival Unicorn package that competed with ADS. Jacob J rejected the blanket proposition that there could not be 'copyright in an idea', remarking that, if the 'idea' is applied to an 'original work', the

---

87 Cornish [1990] EIPR 129.
88 The only Irish decision to date is *News Datacom Ltd v Lyons* [1994] ILRM 450: Murray [1996] CLSR 157.
89 *Total Information Processing Systems Ltd v Daman Ltd* [1992] FSR 171.
90 *Total Information Processing Systems Ltd v Daman Ltd* [1992] FSR 171.
91 *Accounting Systems 2000 (Developments) Pty Ltd v CCH (Australia) Ltd* (1993) 27 IPR 133; *Ibcos Computers Ltd v Barclays Mercantile Highland Finance Ltd* [1994] FSR 275; *Trumpet Software Pty Ltd v Ozemail Pty Ltd* (1996) 34 IPR 481.
92 *Data Access Corpn v Powerflex Services Pty Ltd* (1999) 45 IPR 353. A careful study of *Ibcos Computers Ltd v Barclays Mercantile Highland Finance Ltd* [1994] FSR 275 also throws up instances of insubstantial copying.
93 *Ibcos Computers Ltd v Barclays Mercantile Highland Finance Ltd* [1994] FSR 275.
94 *Ibcos Computers Ltd v Barclays Mercantile Highland Finance Ltd* [1994] FSR 275 at 303.

enquiry goes beyond the general into the specific issue. He confined the utility of the proposition to certain situations:[95]

> For instance if all a defendant has done is to copy a general idea then it does not matter whether there is copyright in the plaintiff's work or whether the plaintiff owns that copyright.

[13.33] However, in *Ibcos*,[96] there was no mere taking of a general idea (ie compile an accounting package to be used in the financial workings of an agricultural dealership). Proof of copying by the defendant in creating Unicorn was established by pointing to the resemblance between the two programs in both essential and inessential matters. These similarities included common spelling mistakes, headings, the presence of otiose references to ADS programs in the Unicorn source code, use of ADS file records in Unicorn, as well as the presence of redundant or unexplained code in each program: from these factors the court deduced that acts of file to file, disk to disk copying had taken place. This comparative analysis was also utilised in *Prism Hospital Software Inc v Hospital Medical Records Institute*,[97] where a comparison of the original program, rewritten by the defendant in a more stable programming language than the original, was held to infringe as being both a reproduction and an adaptation of the original program. Unauthorised reproduction of a program by loading it onto a file transfer protocol site for downloading by others, or by distribution on diskette, either in original or adapted form, without consent, is a clear infringement.[98]

[13.34] The most comprehensive analysis of the infringement issue is the judgment of Pumfrey J in *Cantor Fitzgerald International v Tradition (UK) Ltd*.[99] While the defendant's employees were held to have infringed copyright by copying the plaintiff's bond-broking computer program when they left Cantor Fitzgerald to take up employment with the defendant, the entire program was later found to have been used by the defendant's employees to check the defendant's own program, which was independently written and was in the main a better and enhanced program.

Analysis of modules within the program identified at most some 3.3 per cent of suspect code. Pumfrey J explained that because the issue is whether the defendant has taken the plaintiff's skill and labour, it is too 'simplistic' to consider whether the system makes use of the copied code, or whether the system would work without the code.[100] In a case where the complaint relates to the taking of a specific part of a program, compiled from a specific set of inputs, and the complaint does not relate to the architecture of the program,[101] the substantiality of any copying must be viewed on the basis of the

---

[95] *bcos Computers Ltd v Barclays Mercantile Highland Finance Ltd* [1994] FSR 275 at 292.

[96] *Ibcos Computers Ltd v Barclays Mercantile Highland Finance Ltd* [1994] FSR 275.

[97] *Prism Hospital Software Inc v Hospital Medical Records Institute* (1994) 57 CPR (3d) 129: Honda (1995) 26 IIC 527.

[98] *Trumpet Software Pty Ltd v Ozemail Pty Ltd* (1996) 34 IPR 481; see Lambert (2000) EIPR 595.

[99] *Cantor Fitzgerald International v Tradition (UK) Ltd* [2000] RPC 95.

[100] *Cantor Fitzgerald International v Tradition (UK) Ltd* [2000] RPC 95 at 131, declining to follow *Autodesk Inc v Dyason* (1992) 173 CLR 330.

[101] See *Cantor Fitzgerald International v Tradition (UK) Ltd* [2000] RPC 95 at 134–135.

program, not its constituent parts. Again, like *Triolet*,[102] where the defendant was held not to have infringed copyright, notwithstanding the award of an interlocutory injunction against him, first impressions can be misleading.[103] Objective sequence similarities can be explained by looking at common sources (such as a manual)[104] or by reference to pre-existing code that the plaintiff cannot prove copyright in.[105] The fact that both programs may be written by the same person and therefore use similar names and techniques does not indicate copying.[106] It should be noted that the High Court of Australia, in *Data Access Corpn v Powerflex Services Pty*[107] has effectively overruled much of the reasoning in the two earlier *Autodesk* decisions.[108] The relevant test[109] for infringement of copyright in a computer program now resembles that established in English law.

Proof of infringement in interlocutory proceedings

[13.35] Within the context of a dispute involving computer software, the principles that govern the decision to grant relief by way of an interlocutory injunction have been stated somewhat controversially by Laddie J in *Series A Software v Clarke*.[110] In essence, Laddie J emphasised that *American Cyanamid*[111] principles are to be applied, but the learned judge made it clear that a court should have regard to the strength of each party's case while refraining from resolving difficult areas of fact or law. In this context, the strength of the case of each side will need to be resolutely set out in affidavit form and the court will have to assess the weight of such evidence in the usual way.[112] A failure to address specific allegations in the form of rebuttal statements in evidence will clearly be damaging. Affidavit evidence on similarity between the two programs can be provided by expert testimony that draws up conclusions reached as a result of the running of the two programs but such testimony will presumably be treated with caution if that expert has not had access to computer code, for example. Even where there is some evidence of

---

[102] *Carolian Systems International Inc v Triolet Systems Inc* (1989) 25 CPR (3d) 87.

[103] *Cantor Fitzgerald International v Tradition (UK) Ltd* [2000] RPC 95 at 196–197.

[104] *Cantor Fitzgerald International v Tradition (UK) Ltd* [2000] RPC 95 at 103.

[105] *Cantor Fitzgerald International v Tradition (UK) Ltd* [2000] RPC 95 at 105.

[106] *Cantor Fitzgerald International v Tradition (UK) Ltd* [2000] RPC 95 at 197.

[107] *Data Access Corpn v Powerflex Services Pty* (1999) 45 IPR 353.

[108] *Autodesk Inc v Dyason* (1992) 173 CLR 330; *Autodesk v Dyason (No 2)* (1993) 176 CLR 300. The second case was an application to vacate the earlier judgment. Mason CJ, dissenting, along with Deane J, would have allowed a rehearing on the issue of substantial taking. In *Data Access Corpn v Powerflex Services Pty* (1999) 45 IPR 353, Mason CJ's dissent was endorsed on the issue of substantiality.

[109] The earlier test being characterised as a 'but for' test: (1999) 45 IPR 353 at 373.

[110] *Series A Software v Clarke* [1996] 1 All ER 853. Irish Courts, however, have not favoured this approach: see *Symonds Cider and English Wine Co v Showerings (Ireland) Ltd* [1997] 1 ILRM 481 and *Miss World Ltd v Miss Ireland Beauty Pagent Ltd* [2004] IEHC 13. Contrast *Shelbourne Hotel Holdings Ltd v Torriam Hotel Operating Co Ltd* [2008] IEHC 376.

[111] *American Cyanamid v Ethicon Ltd* [1975] 1 All ER 504.

[112] Eg *Carolian Systems International Inc v Triolet Systems Inc* (1989) 25 CPR (3d) 87.

direct copying, the court will have to test whether the defendant has taken a substantial part.

In *Visusoft Ltd v Harris*,[113] an infringement case, there was no dispute about ownership of computer programs vesting in the plaintiff; the issues that arose were difficult questions of fact about when the defendant undertook independent work on developing a similar product and what his contractual status at that time was. Murphy J, after applying Jacob J's four-stage test in *Ibcos Computers Ltd v Barclay's Mercantile Highland France Ltd*,[114] was unable to find that the defendant had reproduced a substantial part of the plaintiff's program but held that the defendant was in breach of contract in not deleting parts of the program after leaving employment.

[13.36] If the program does not, objectively speaking, reveal any evidence of copying – and this can often only be achieved by submitting to the court evidence in the form of screen displays, print-outs, material that is the product of the program rather than the program itself – it may be very difficult to persuade a court that there is any evidence of copying. In the leading English case of *Thrustcode Ltd v WW Computing Ltd*,[115] Megarry V-C said:[116]

> In the normal case in which an infringement of literary copyright is alleged, it is possible to put side by side the written, typed or printed words in which the plaintiff claims copyright and the corresponding words which are said to infringe that copyright. The words can be seen and compared and discussed. In the case of computer programs, the software appears to consist of articles which by magnetic or electrical means will make the hardware do certain things, together with what is recorded on various tapes and discs. By means of this, the letters, signs and numbers of the program may be made to appear on a screen or on a print-out; and if this is done, then the familiar process of comparison is made possible. Yet where, as here, the claim is to copyright in the program itself, the results produced by operating the program must not be confused with the program in which copyright is claimed. If I may take an absurdly simple example, 2 and 2 make 4. But so does 2 times 2, or 6 minus 2, or 2 per cent of 200, or 6 squared divided by 9, or many other things. Many different processes may produce the same answer and yet remain different processes that have not been copied one from another. For computers, as for other things, what must be compared are the thing said to have been copied and the thing said to be an infringing copy. If these two things are invisible, then normally they must be reproduced in visible form, or in a form that in some way is perceptible, before it can be determined whether one infringes the other.
>
> In some cases, no doubt, it may be possible in some other way to demonstrate that one is a copy of the other, as where there is some evidence or some admission that when one computer was being programmed, someone was watching and was programming a rival

---

[113] *Visusoft Ltd v Harris* [2009] IEHC 543: Murphy J pointed to the common origin of computer code and the fact that code can be written by a computer as factors weakening the plaintiff's case. On computer-generated works see CRRA 2000, s 2(1). Murphy J seems to have regarded these factors as complicating proof of ownership.

[114] *Ibcos Computers Ltd v Barclays Mercantile Highland Finance Ltd* [1994] FSR 275.

[115] *Thrustcode Ltd v WW Computing Ltd* [1983] FSR 502, followed in *John Richardson Computers Ltd v Flanders* [1993] FSR 497.

[116] *John Richardson Computers Ltd v Flanders* [1993] FSR 497 at 505–506.

computer in the same or a similar way. Normally, however, what will be needed is a print-out or other documentary evidence of the program alleged to have been copied, and of the alleged infringing program, or sufficient parts of each. You must look at what the programs are, and not only at what they do or can do.

[13.37] In *News Datacom Ltd v Lyons*,[117] Flood J faced an even more difficult problem. The plaintiff produced a card that unscrambled an encrypted broadcast signal. The defendant produced a card that did the same thing but the defendant denied any copying of the plaintiff's program. All each card did was to cause the same screen display (ie Sky TV programmes) to appear. Asking whether there was a similarity in the screen display here was irrelevant, and in the absence of any procedure which would allow the court to appoint an expert to decompile each program for the purposes of independent analysis, the court was unable to grant the relief sought. After citing the *Thrustcode* case[118] Flood J examined the merits of the claim to injunction relief:[119]

> It is the plaintiffs' case that a card could be analysed by an electron microscope or similar device but no such examination has been carried out by the plaintiffs to thereby obtain a basis of comparison. Further the plaintiffs say in evidence that they changed the algorithm every few months to increase the security of their operation and in such an event according to the same affidavit the scrambling seeds will have been replaced by scrambling seeds based on a different algorithm and yet the plaintiffs admit that the defendants have produced within relatively short periods of time after such change a smart card which could operate to descramble the amended encrypted system. This to me seems to render even more unlikely – in fact highly improbable – the plaintiffs' only explanation for the functional similarity of the two cards namely, copying and to render highly probable the defendants' claim that they have in no way infringed or copied the plaintiffs' software.

> In my opinion the plaintiffs in the evidence tendered to the court at this stage have failed to show that they have sown the seed which could fructify at the hearing into a stateable case of infringement by copying of a copyright. At most they have merely shown the fruits of the software and not direct evidence of any similarities in the software itself or, if it had been more accurate to say so, they have simply shown the fruits of the respective algorithms used by the respective parties but have not shown direct evidence of any similarities between the algorithms.

NON-LITERAL INFRINGEMENT

[13.38] Where direct copying or direct adaptation of an original program has not been conceded, or shown to exist, the courts will have to consider whether non-literal copying of a program may be an infringement of copyright in some pre-existing work. Here it is not thought that the defendant has use of the source code in the original work but that the defendant has replicated either the structure of the program – sometimes expressed as being the structure, sequence and organisation of the program, or the user interface – the look and feel,[120] made up of the screen displays and menu hierarchy or menu sequence.

---

[117] *News Datacom Ltd v Lyons* [1994] 1 ILRM 450.

[118] *Thrustcode Ltd v WW Computing Ltd* [1983] FSR 502.

[119] *News Datacom Ltd v Lyons* [1994] 1 ILRM 450 at 456–457.

[120] Francis (1992) 18 MULR 584; Valasco (1994) 94 Col L Rev 242.

Structure of the program

[13.39] In the leading English structure and sequence case of *John Richardson Computers Ltd v Flanders*,[121] the defendant was an independent consultant who was engaged by the plaintiff to develop a program for the labelling of medicines that could run on a BBC computer (at the time a popular model) and be used by both Irish and UK pharmacists. The defendant ceased to work for the plaintiff and independently sought to produce a better program that would serve the Irish market and also function on IBM machines. These programs were written in different languages but when the plaintiff discovered that the defendant intended to distribute the new program in the UK, litigation ensued. After finding that the defendant's work was to be the property of the plaintiff via the law of trusts,[122] Ferris J outlined the nature of the plaintiff's complaint thus:

> What is said is that the defendants have taken the general scheme of the BBC program, including the detail of certain routines of an idiosyncratic nature. The case was likened by [counsel for the plaintiff] to one in which the plot of a book or other literary work has been taken.

[13.40] Apart from the cases cited[123] by counsel for the plaintiff, the case of *Correlli v Gray* is often referred to as being illustrative of the concept of non-literal copying of a work being held to be an infringement.[124] Miss Corelli wrote a novel called 'Temporal Power'. She claimed that the defendant's play or dramatic sketch, entitled 'The People's King' infringed copyright. The trial judge concentrated on six incidents in the play, which bore such a strong resemblance to the incidents in the plaintiff's work in terms of the identity or language of the work that he was unable to find any real prospect of coincidental creation. Although not one sentence in the plaintiff's novel had been reproduced by the defendant, both the trial judge and the Court of Appeal agreed that when the defendant wrote his work, the work of the plaintiff must have been present before him, either physically or in his memory.

[13.41] A more recent illustration of this can be found in the Australian case of *Peter v Coulter*.[125] The applicant wrote a novel, 'Monument of Stone'. He sought to establish a copyright infringement by the respondent when he wrote and produced a play 'Stretchmarks', citing some 25 instances of acts of reproduction of plot, character and events. The respondent sought to dismiss the applicant's statement of claim on the ground that it disclosed no cause of action. The motion to dismiss failed, Branson J

---

[121] *John Richardson Computers Ltd v Flanders* [1993] FSR 497. See also *Computer Aided Design v Bolwell* (23 August 1989, unreported), HC, *per* Hoffmann J; Sykes [1990] CLSR 30.

[122] Following *Massine v de Basil* (1938) Macg Cop Cas 223.

[123] *Rees v Melville* (1936) Macg Cop Cas 107; *Harman Pictures v Osborne* [1967] 1 WLR 723; *Nichols v Universal Pictures Corpn* 45 F 2d 119 (1930).

[124] *Correlli v Gray* (1913) 30 TLR 116.

[125] *Peter v Coulter* (1995) 33 IPR 450. See Jacobs [1994] EIPR 206.

agreeing with Jacob J in *Ibcos*[126] that in cases of this kind, '[i]n the end the matter must be left to the value judgment of the court'.[127]

[13.42] To return to the decision in *John Richardson Computers v Flanders*,[128] Ferris J, in examining this issue of non-literal copying of work, managed to combine the traditional English approach with the perspective given in several American cases where the judges sought to provide a means of drawing the line between non-copyright protected ideas and copyright protected expression. In essence, the issue is one of impression: at which stage do the plaintiff's efforts at fixing the idea into a work transform the idea into a stable and identifiable format that is original and distinctive enough to warrant protection via copyright? The approach favoured by Ferris J was that of the US Court of Appeals for the Second Circuit in *Computer Associates International Inc v Altai*.[129] In that case a programmer, previously employed by the plaintiff, wrote a rival program that not only produced the same kind of result, but also allegedly replicated the appearance to the user of the plaintiff's program. In that case the court developed an 'abstractions' test, which allowed it to side-step the defence argument that, because there was no evidence of direct copying, and because the defendants had written their program in a different language, there could be no copying in that instance. The court took the view that if non-literal copying could be established then a infringement would follow. This turned upon the abstractions test. The abstractions test, in essence, requires the court to engage in the following analysis. The extract reproduced below involves a discussion, by Ferris J, of the background to the decision of the Second Circuit Court of Appeals in *Altai*. After noting that the court in *Altai* had declined to follow *Whelan Associates Inc v Jaslow Dental Laboratory Inc*,[130] Ferris J continued:

> The Court of Appeals agreed with the District Judge's decision not to follow *Whelan*. It then became necessary for the Court of Appeals to formulate an alternative test. This it did by going back to what Judge Learned Hand had said in the *Nichols* case [*Nichols v Universal Pictures Corpn* 45 F 2d 119 (1930)]. It described this as the 'abstractions test'. In order to understand this label and the test itself it is necessary to read again part of the passage from *Nichols* which I have already read. As cited by the Court of Appeals in *Computer Associates* it is as follows:
>
> > 'Upon any work … a great number of patterns of increasing generality will fit equally well, as more and more of the incident is left out. The last may perhaps be no more than the most general statement of what the (work) is about, and at times might consist only of its title; but there is a point in this series of abstractions where they are no longer protected, since otherwise the (author) could prevent the use of his "ideas", to which, apart from their expression, his property never extended.'
>
> The Court of Appeals elaborated upon this process by saying that:
>
> > 'Initially, in a manner that resembles reverse engineering on a theoretical plane, a court should dissect the allegedly copied program's structure and isolate each level

---

[126] *Ibcos Computers Ltd v Barclays Mercantile Highland Finance Ltd* [1994] FSR 275; citing (1994) 24 IPR 25 at 49.

[127] *Peter v Coulter* (1995) 33 IPR 50 at 52.

[128] *John Richardson Computers v Flanders* [1993] FSR 497.

[129] *Computer Associates International Inc v Altai* (1992) 23 IPR 385.

[130] *Whelan Associates Inc v Jaslow Dental Laboratory Inc* [1987] FSR 1.

of abstraction contained within it. This process begins with the code and ends with an articulation of the program's ultimate function. Along the way, it is necessary essentially to retrace and map each of the designer's steps – in the opposite order to that in which they were taken during the program's creation.'

As an anatomical guide to this procedure, the following description is helpful:

'At the lowest level of abstraction, a computer program may be thought of in its entirety as a set of individual instructions organised into a hierarchy of modules. At a higher level of abstraction, the instructions in the lowest level modules may be replaced conceptually by the functions of those modules. At progressively higher levels of abstraction, the functions of the higher-level modules conceptually replaces the implementations of those modules until, finally, one is left with nothing but the ultimate function of the program ... A program has structure at every level of abstraction at which it is viewed. At low levels of abstraction, a program's structure may be quite complex; at the highest level it is trivial.'

That description is, I think, taken from a text book which had been cited to the Court of Appeals.[131]

In the test propounded in *Computer Associates* the discovery of a program's abstraction levels is the first step. The second step is to filter these abstractions in order to discover a 'core of protectable material'. In the process of filtration there are to be excluded from consideration (a) elements dictated by efficiency; (b) elements dictated by external factors and (c) elements taken from the public domain. Each of these categories is explained at some length. The essence of the 'elements dictated by efficiency' is that if there is only one way to express an idea the idea and its expression are inseparable and copyright does not prevent the copying of the expression. The exclusion of 'elements dictated by external factors' arises from the fact that if two persons set about the description of the same event there may be a number of particular facts which can only be described in a particular way. The Court of Appeals cited with evident approval the observation of Professor Nimmer (a well-known academic commentator on US copyright law) that:

'in many instances it is impossible to write a program to perform particular functions in a specific computing environment without employing standard techniques.'

As to 'elements in the public domain':

'plaintiffs may not claim copyright of an expression that is, if not standard, then commonplace in the computer software industry.'

The third step in the process suggested in the *Computer Associates* case is to compare what is left of the 'abstractions' made from the plaintiff's program after filtering out these elements with the program which is said to be an infringement of that program.[132]

[13.43] This ringing endorsement of the *Altai* decision[133] by Ferris J[134] has, of course, not been by any means representative of all reactions to the judgment, either by judges or

---

131 This is in fact David Nimmer, *Nimmer on Copyright* (Matthew Bender, 1989).

132 *John Richardson Computers v Flanders* [1993] FSR 497 at 525–526.

133 *Computer Associates International Inc v Altai* (1992) 23 IPR 385.

134 It has been pointed out that Ferris J concentrated more on the output of the program in order to test similarity and in this may have fallen into error: eg Grewal [1996] EIPR 454.

academic commentators. Some academics see the second stage to be too rigorous in so far as it can filter out too much[135] and, within the context of programs that are other compilations of existing code, this comment has much force. Other commentators generally support the *Altai* decision,[136] often with reservations.[137] Later US judicial decisions, however, have divided on the utility of the abstraction, filtration and comparison approach. Some courts have followed *Altai*[138] while in other cases that approach has not been followed. For example, in *Lotus Development Corpn v Borland International*[139] the Court of Appeal for the First Circuit observed that the *Altai* test has no real relevance to the basic issue of whether a work should be copyright protected at all.[140] While the *Altai* approach has been cited with approval in Canada,[141] the only support for this or any US tests in the English courts has come from Ferris J in *John Richardson Computers Ltd v Flanders*.[142] It must be noted, however, that while Ferris J supported *Altai* he did not really attempt to operate abstraction/filtration comparison himself, and as a general criticism of this entire US approach one must doubt whether tests that are so opaque that they cannot be operated by the judges are really worth persevering with at all. In any event, Jacob J in *Ibcos*[143] took the view that these US tests are unsuitable in an English context, basically because both the US copyright legislation and US judicial attitudes towards functional works and compilations have tended to differ from approaches and attitudes to such matters in English law. In this Jacob J is clearly correct. However, the filtration stage does at least allow the court to concentrate on aspects of the program that, seen individually, would not be seen as original works, thus facilitating clarification of the question of whether the programs, on the whole, are works and infringing works respectively.

It is submitted, therefore, that an Irish court should engage in the broad impressionistic approach canvassed by Jacob J but should still consider the relevance of looking at the program in a fragmented sense: how much code is conventional or standard 'boilerplate'?[144] Are symbols or words or 'macros' commonplace – '*scenes à faire*'.[145] Is

---

[135] Miller 106 Harv L Rev 977 (1992).

[136] Eg McCarthy (1993) 66 Temp L Rev 273.

[137] Eg Valasco (1994) 94 Col L Rev 242.

[138] Eg *Gates Rubber Co v Banab Chemical Industries* 9 F 3d 823 (1993); *Apple Computer Inc v Microsoft Corpn* 35 F 3d 1435 (1994).

[139] *Lotus Development Corpn v Borland International* (1995) 33 IPR 233.

[140] See also *General Universal Systems v Lee* 379 F. 3d 131 (2004) (5th Cir); *Dun & Bradstreet Software Services v Grace Consulting Inc* 307 F 3d 197 (2004) 3rd Cir). The decision of the Sixth Circuit in *Lexmark International v Static Control Components Inc* 387 F 3d 522 (2004) provides an interesting demonstration of the merger and *scènes a faire* doctrines within US law. See also *Hutchins v Zoll Medical Corporation* 430 F Supp 2d 24 (2007).

[141] *Carolian Systems Inc v Triolet Systems Inc* (1992) 47 CPR (3d) 1 and (2002) 17 CPR (4th) 289.

[142] *John Richardson Computers Ltd v Flanders* [1993] FSR 497.

[143] *Ibcos Computers Ltd v Barclays Mercantile Highland Finance Ltd* [1994] FSR 275.

[144] *Total Information Processing Systems Ltd v Daman Ltd* [1992] FSR 171. However, if the compilation of code is original, protection should be available, and on this point the *Daman* case has not been followed: see *Ibcos Computers Ltd v Barclays Mercantile Highland Finance Ltd* [1994] FSR 275 at 290.

[145] For original macros, see *Data Access Corpn v Powerflex Services Pty* (1999) 45 IPR 353.

there some common origin that does not involve an infringement of rights?[146] Is the expression of the idea only possible in one form, in which case the idea merges with the expression and no infringement can be established unless there is exact copying of the form in which that idea is expressed?[147] Merger is certainly an important part of the approach adopted by Ferris J in *John Richardson*[148] and it must be seen as a very relevant element in any 'filtering' process.

The question of whether similarities can be put down to individual skills or techniques rather than copying is the most significant feature of the filtering process, at least in regard to instances where the defendant has not been shown to have resorted to direct copying but rather is alleged to have reconstructed the look and feel of the sequence or structure of a program. The Canadian case of *Carolian Systems Inc v Triolet Systems Inc*[149] holds out some hope for a programmer who used individual skills, know-how and background knowledge on the features of the hardware, in order to create an independent but competing program. The English decisions, however, show that pleas of independent effort and skill by a defendant will be taken with some scepticism, and once sufficient evidence of objective similarity and opportunity are put before the court, the onus of proof will shift to the defendant.[150]

Programming languages and macros

[13.44] The High Court of Australia, in *Data Access Corpn v Powerflex Services Pty Ltd*[151] has held that where a programming language is compatible with the first language, there may not be a reproduction of a substantial part of the first language. In this case reserved words or commands in the first language, reproduced in the second, were not sets of instructions, nor could collections of such words be protected as compilations. In fact, several of the commands were English words so protection was further denied on the basis of lack of originality.

Copyright protection for screen displays

[13.45] In this context the most obvious scenario is as follows: the defendant takes the features of the plaintiff's work as set out in the screen display and reproduces these features so as to induce buyers and others to use the program. Ingenuity, investment and design skills go into creating a user interface and if competitors could replicate the

---

[146] Eg so-called 'Freeware': see *Trumpet Software Pty Ltd v Ozemail Pty* (1996) 34 IPR 481 at 485. See also Richardson [1996] EIPR 669.

[147] The merger doctrine, which in England was accepted in *Kenrick v Lawrence* (1890) 25 QBD 99, but explained with greater clarity by Jacob J in *Ibcos Computers Ltd v Barclays Mercantile Highland Finance Ltd* [1994] FSR 275 at 290–291.

[148] *John Richardson Computers Ltd v Flanders* [1993] FSR 497, especially in relation to the stock control features of each program at 555.

[149] *Carolian Systems Inc v Triolet Systems Inc* (1992) 47 CPR (3d) 1.

[150] *John Richardson Computers Ltd v Flanders* [1993] FSR 497 at 543; *Ibcos Computers Ltd v Barclays Mercantile Highland Finance Ltd* [1994] FSR 275 at 302–304.

[151] *Data Access Corpn v Powerflex Services Pty Ltd* (1999) 45 IPR 353; *Navitaire Inc v easyJet* [2004] EWHC 1725 (Ch).

screen display, which is an output from the program and not a program in itself, the plaintiff would face an element of unfair competition. For this reason copyright in the user interface is asserted but the display itself is not to be confused with the copyright in the underlying program; it may however provide proof of copying in the underlying code. In *John Richardson Computers Ltd v Flanders*, Ferris J put this issue very succinctly:[152]

> The two main ways, perhaps the only ways, in which a computer program can be made visible are by printing out the code on paper or by displaying on screen the prompts, entries, reports and other material which the program presents in visible form to the user. The latter is not, however, itself the program. It is a product of the program. The fact that two programs may produce a similar screen display may or may not be indicative of a similarity in the programs. The screen display is not itself the literary work which is entitled to copyright protection. A particular display may enjoy a separate copyright protection as an artistic work in the form of a photograph, or as a film, or as being a reproduction of an artistic work in the form of a drawing the copying of which will be, for copyright purposes the copying of the drawing. But no such copyright is relied on in this case. It appears to me, therefore that screen displays are only to be relied upon in this case to the extent that they demonstrate the contents of the underlying program in which the relevant copyright subsists.

[13.46] The question whether a screen display can be reproduced by a competitor without permission has raised directly the issue of whether a screen display is copyright protected as a literary work. In the US the decision in *Lotus Development Corpn v Borland International*[153] favours a negative answer to this question on the basis that a screen display, in the form of a menu hierarchy to guide the user through the software package, is a 'method of operation' that is not copyright protected under US law.[154] It is certainly possible now to regard *Borland* as highly relevant under the 2000 legislation. Section 17(3) of CRRA 2000 denies copyright protection to 'ideas and principles which underlie any element of a work, procedures, method *of operation* or mathematical concepts' (emphasis added).

[13.47] Where a screen display is reproduced (eg by running the program and causing moving images to be shown) an Australian case suggests that the person responsible for making the infringing program may be held to have infringed a separate copyright in a cinematographic film. In *Sega Enterprises Ltd v Galaxy Electronics Pty*,[155] the defendants were held to have infringed copyright in a cinematographic film when they reproduced two computer games by importing into Australia integrated circuits which 'housed' those games. The interactive nature of the video game was not an obstacle to giving the concept of a film a very broad meaning.[156] However, recent litigation has shifted away from this position. In both *Aristocrat Leisure Industries Pty Ltd v Pacific*

---

[152] *John Richardson Computers Ltd v Flanders* [1993] FSR 497 at 527.

[153] *Lotus Development Corpn v Borland International* (1995) 33 IPR 233: Schwarz [1995] EIPR 337.

[154] US Copyright Act 1976, s 102(b).

[155] *Sega Enterprises Ltd v Galaxy Electronics Pty* (1996) 35 IPR 161; *Avel Pty Ltd v Wells* (1992) 23 IPR 353.

Gaming Pty[157] and *Sony Computer Entertainment v Stevens*,[158] Australian courts have regarded it as inappropriate to view images generated by a computer as a film. However, there are cases concerning website displays and screen displays that have been held to merit protection by way of the underlying file and user interface.[159]

Non-textual copying – recent English cases

[13.48] 'Non-textual' copying of a computer program was at the heart of the action in *Navitaire Inc v easyJet Airline Co.*[160] Navitaire complained that when easyJet ceased to use its eRes booking software and commissioned another software house to write OpenRes, a program that replicated the look and feel of eRes and also involved identical commands and key strokes, as well as the screen output or reports, this constituted an infringement of copyright. Critically, it was accepted that the defendants had no access to Navitaire eRes source code. Pumfrey J rejected the argument that user command codes, commands themselves and user screen display layouts could be literary works in themselves. Individual command words and letters do not qualify[161] as literary works, and Pumfrey J departed from Jacob J's rejection of the idea/expression dichotomy in *Ibcos Computers* by observing that Directive 91/250/EC, in recitals 13–15, denied protection to underlying elements in computer programs and interfaces and characterised logic, algorithms and programming languages as non-protectable ideas and principles. In Irish law this reasoning is further supported by s 17(3), which provides a horizontal denial of copyright to 'the ideas and principles which underlie any element of a work, procedures, methods of operation or mathematical concepts'. While character based screen displays were regarded as not being protectable on the same basis as the other features of the user interface, the icons and logos displayed were held capable of protection by way of artistic copyright, and a limited infringement was made out. *Navitaire* also makes it clear that authorship may also be problematical when codes are keyed or 'authored' by persons unknown: this confirms existing case law.

A similar approach to the development of computer games was evident in *Nova Productions Ltd v Mazooma Games.*[162] Nova unsuccessfully argued that Mazooma had produced two computer games which copied Nova's game, all three games being based on pool. Again, there was no copying of source code and the infringement was alleged to have occurred because some features in Nova's game-pulsar bars – dotted lines to show shot direction, a rotating cue, shot values over the table pockets, etc – were a feature of

---

[156] The court cited para 93 of the Gregory Report: *Report of the Copyright Committee* (Cmnd 8662).

[157] *Aristocrat Leisure Industries Pty Ltd v Pacific Gaming Pty* (2000) 50 IPR 29.

[158] *Sony Computer Entertainment v Stevens* [2002] FCA 906.

[159] *Yapon AB v Joachin Akstron* [2002] ECDR 155 (Sweden); *Website Layout* [2003] ECDR 24 (Austria); *Navitaire Inc v easyJet* [2004] EWHC 1725 (Ch). In *Navitaire* Pumfrey J distinguished (non-protectable) text screen displays from icons and logos that could be protected via the artistic copyright underlying the icons and logos.

[160] *Navitaire Inc v Easyjet Airline Co* [2004] EWHC 1725 (Ch).

[161] Citing *Exxon Corp v Exxon Insurance Consultants International Ltd* [1981] 3 All ER 241.

[162] *Nova Productions Ltd v Mazooma Games* [2007] EWCA Civ 219.

the defendant's games. These features were held to be obvious, commonplace and a standard features in games of this kind. A strong Court of Appeal, in which the leading judgment was given by Lloyd LJ, followed and applied the reasoning in *Navitaire*, holding that even though Mazooma studied Nova's games, any copying was of ideas and principles and was insubstantial in scope.

Non-textual copying of software – ECJ ruling requested

[13.49] In a very important decision, handed down on 23 July 2010, Arnold J, in the English High Court has clarified several important points relating to the permissible use of existing computer programs by anyone seeking to produce a competing or 'drop in' program that replicates the functionality of the original program. The case, *SAS Institute Inc v World Programming Inc*,[163] concerned allegations of infringement when WPL produced a WPS program that could be used to support a number of the components that SAS supported via its SAS language. Both WPL and SAS language allowed users to undertake data manipulation, statistical analysis and graph plotting operations. What is important to note is that WPL at no time had access to SAS source code: this was an allegation that indirect copying of software had taken place and that this could infringe copyright. Arnold J referred a number of questions to the ECJ but gave his own views in a very forthright manner. In Arnold J's view, earlier cases like *Navitaire* and *Mazooma Games* have held that, in the absence of proof of direct copying of code, merely seeking to replicate the user's experience (in *Navitaire*, allowing a travel agent to book flights on easyJet by using commands/key strokes that were in the original program) will not infringe. In the world of gaming, the visual features of a game such as pool, or golf, are likely to be described as commonplace or generic, or (non-copyright protected) ideas and principles, rather than (copyright) expression. What makes SAS different is that WPL used SAS user manuals as well as its own research in creating WPS, and in creating WPL's own user manuals. As the SAS manuals are themselves literary works, did the use of these manuals infringe? The judge concluded that WPL's own manual writers did not copy directly from the SAS manuals, but, given identical functionality, WPL 'did not succeed in avoiding the use of very similar language'.

The judge said three issues arose:

1. The extent to which copyright protects ideas. UK law does not (unlike Irish law) specifically state that copyright does not extend to ideas, procedures, methods and mathematical expression. But the judge, using TRIPS, reached the same result, confirming that if the claim exists at a general level, it will be characterised as an idea, not protected expression.

2. Protection for programming languages, interfaces and functionality. In the judge's view neither the Software Directive[164] nor prior judicial decisions supported these claims to copyright. Without saying as much, the judge favoured the general policy of holding modules and strings of code, commands,

---

[163] *SAS Institute Inc v World Programming Inc* [2010] EWHC 1829 (Ch).
[164] Council Directive 91/250/EEC.

keystrokes, etc, as either being difficult to bring within the concept of authorship or notions of a 'literary work'.

3. When is there reproduction of a substantial part? Again, the judge took a pro user approach. Using the controversial ECJ *Infopaq* decision,[165] this will require the unauthorised use of the intellectual expression of the author. This will be hard to satisfy when the components of a program are fragmented, taken from common sources and anonymous.

The judge indicated that these principles applied to use of both the licensed software and the manuals. If using the software by running a program, for example, and copying outputs, the same reasoning will apply in relation to a manual. This is a very important perspective.

Copyright protection and computer-produced 'works'

[13.50] If something is produced by a natural force or by non-human intervention then that product cannot be a 'work', for a work requires the presence of an author. A work that is produced by a human being who produces that work by using a typewriter or work processor is clearly not deprived of protection because of the mechanical means used to fix the work, but problems arise in traditional copyright law where the work is created after a computer produces that work following upon a program being written and used in order to generate the work. In *Express Newspapers plc v Liverpool Daily Post and Echo*,[166] Whitford J regarded a group of numbers produced by way of a computer program to be a work, the computer as a machine being merely a tool by which the literary work could be produced via the operation of the computer program. However, where the work is produced by a machine – a satellite photograph or even some computer code generated by that machine with minimal human input – some difficulties will arise. A distinction between computer-aided (eg computer-aided designs) and computer-generated works is found in the literature and the distinction was approved in the South African case of *Payer Components South Africa Ltd v Bovic Gaskets*.[167] The importance of such a distinction is that works within the first category will be protected as original works while those in the second category will not. This issue is addressed in CRRA 2000, which specifically defines a computer-generated work as a work 'generated by computer in circumstances where the author of the work is not an individual'.[168] This means that a work can be computer-generated, but in all other respects the work must satisfy other criteria for eligibility. For example, certain kinds of work must satisfy the originality criteria – literary, dramatic, musical or artistic works must be original. In *Antiquesportfolio.com v Rodney Fitch & Co Ltd*,[169] Neuberger J discussed the originality standard in respect of a photograph of a static object. After holding the originality standard to be law, the judge left open the question of whether a

---

[165] *Infopaq International A/S v Danske Dagblades Forening* Case C-5/08 (16 July 2009).

[166] *Express Newspapers plc v Liverpool Daily Post and Echo* [1985] 1 WLR 1089.

[167] *Payer Components South Africa Ltd v Bovic Gaskets* (1995) 33 IPR 407.

[168] CRRA 2000, s 2(1).

[169] *Antiquesportfolio.com v Rodney Fitch & Co Ltd* [2001] ECDR 5.

copy created by a photocopier would be within copyright. It is submitted that even for a computer-generated artistic work the answer would have to be in the negative if the originality standard is to mean anything at all in this context. Ownership of the copyright in a computer-generated work, even a work that has to comply with an originality test, does not vest in the actual creator(s) of the work; under s 21(j) of CRRA 2000, the author is defined as the person by whom the arrangements necessary for the creation of the work are undertaken.[170]

Databases

[13.51] Works, data and other materials, collected and/or arranged in a systematic or methodical way, that are accessible electronically are protected by the concept of an original database (qua collection), and the unauthorised extraction and/or reutilisation of the contents of the database – even if insubstantial in scope in certain instances – will infringe the database right. The rights and obligations are examined in detail in the following chapter, but in the current context it should be noted that in respect of electronic original databases there is no fair dealing defence for persons who utilise the original database for research or private study.[171] However, it is conceivable that a defence of 'criticism or review' might be made out,[172] even in respect of the unauthorised use of electronic collections such as materials on a website, but the defence may not readily be inferred. In the 2001 case of *British Columbia Automobile Association v OPEIU Local 378*,[173] a trade union engaged in industrial action replicated the website established by the plaintiffs, infringing copyright in an artistic work. A fair dealing defence failed because 'the website contains no criticism of the BCAA website and it does not, as required by Statute, mention the source and author of the BCAA website'.[174] The reasoning of the Federal Court of Appeal may be vulnerable vis-à-vis the first reason: many cases establish that criticism of the philosophy or attitudes taken by the author are within the 'criticism or review' defence, just as much as criticism or review of the work.

Linking and copyright infringement

[13.52] It is certainly arguable that the creation of a link from one website to another, the link facilitating access to either the work of the right holder's copyright works or infringing content posted onto the web by a third party, could be an act of

---

[170] Protection expires 70 years after the work is first lawfully made available to the public (CRRA 2000, s 30).

[171] CRRA 2000, s 50(1).

[172] CRRA 2000, s 51(1) Defences are to be considered separately and may overlap: s 49.

[173] *British Columbia Automobile Association v OPEIU Local 378* (2001) 10 CPR (4th) 423.

[174] *British Columbia Automobile Association v OPEIU Local 378* (2001) 10 CPR (4th) 423 at 475, *per* Stone JA. There may be a defence of express or implied consent to copying. An employee who copies literary and artistic works from a computer onto a disk or USB key shortly after terminating a contract of employment, with the express purpose of observing express or implied terms to either delete or return materials that are copyright of the former employer, does not infringe the reproduction right: *Blackmagic Design v Overliese* (2010) 84 IPR 505.

infringement.[175] In *Roadshow Films Property Ltd v iiNet Ltd (No 3)*[176] the Federal Court of Australia indicated that liability via authorising infringement turns upon whether the defendant's site has the technical capacity to control links generated by others to its site when the defendant's site is serving as a portal onto other sites housing infringing material. This is fully considered in relation to filesharing below.

Technological protection measures

[13.53] Where works have been the subject of rights protection measures such as encryption of a work or an anti-copying technology, the copying, making available, or adaptation of the work, without the permission of the rights owner, may not necessarily constitute an infringement of copyright. For example, it may be that one of the fair dealing or other defences in the Act – recording a work for time-shifting purposes[177] is just such a situation – and the important point raised by anti-copying technologies and licensing terms that seek to deny users of a work to undertake acts that CRRA 2000 appears to leave open is of critical importance. Section 374 appears to authorise users to undertake acts of circumvention in order to undertake permitted acts in relation to copyright works, performances and databases, but in fact all s 374 does is to prevent ss 370 to 376 from impeding lawful acts by users. Section 374 does not as such authorise lawful acts of circumvention *per se*; s 374 is irrelevant in relation to the infringement defences. This subject, however, is addressed in the 2004 Regulations,[178] which give effect to the Information Society Directive,[179] where a provision of sweeping simplicity states by way of amendment to s 374, that:[180]

> [w]here the beneficiary is legally entitled to access the protected work or the subject matter concerned, the rightsholder shall make available to the beneficiary the means of benefiting from the permitted act, save where such work or other subject-matter has been made available to the public on agreed contractual terms in such a way that members of the public may access the work or other subject-matter from a place and at a time individually chosen by them.

Although one may feel that locating this provision in s 374 is not the best solution, the intent is clearly to give access in the broadest sense to works and protected material, even if in digital form, for all permitted purposes, unless the work is online or similarly available, and licensing conditions control access. In all other cases this provision, it is submitted, is intended to permit users the right to copy, adapt or gain access to a work, notwithstanding the existence of licensing conditions that purport to restrict such activities. However, it is likely that this provision will need to be tested in respect of the importation or manufacture of technologies that are capable of assisting in the manufacture of infringing copies as well as 'unlocking' protected works for otherwise legitimate uses.

---

[175] Via passing off or trade mark infringement as well as breach of copyright.

[176] *Roadshow Films Property Ltd v iiNet Ltd (No 3)* [2010] FCA 224.

[177] CRRA 2000, s 100.

[178] European Communities (Copyright and Related Rights) Regulations 2004 (SI 16/2004).

[179] Council Directive 2001/29/EC ([2001] OJ L 167/10).

[180] *Sony Computer Entertainment Inc v Owen* [2002] EMCR 742; *Kabushiki Kaisha Sony Computer Entertainment Inc v Ball* [2004] All ER (D) 334; *Gilham v R* [2009] EWCA Crim 229.

Chapter 14

Databases

INTRODUCTION

[14.01] The very term 'database' is somewhat ambiguous. Data, as a word, refers to the raw material that can be gathered or held by any person or organisation, regardless of its nature or content, and implicit in this term is the idea that some further refinement, processing or extraction will need to take place before information or knowledge can be obtained by a user. The database, in contrast, conjures up an image of a place, machine or material entity that holds or maintains data, whether it be a filing cabinet, a personal or mainframe computer, or a series of printed volumes, for example. In our information technology-driven world, a database most typically evokes the picture of a computerised information system, operated by way of a computer program, which can process, arrange or select words, sounds and images and project them onto a screen or print-out. Nevertheless, the older notion of a database still endures and newspapers, encyclopaedia and other journals are essentially databases in the sense that these information products have generally been created by a process of selecting existing works (whether copyright protected or not), by collecting facts and figures and commentary from other persons, and partly by independently commissioning contributions to the database. One need only think of a newspaper that serialises a politician's recently published memoirs, reprints a sonnet by Shakespeare, invites and publishes letters from readers to the editor, or carries cartoons by its resident cartoonist, for examples of these quite commonplace elements. It is the decision to select or not and the fact that these selected items are put before the public in such a format that makes the database a potential subject for copyright protection, regardless of the material form or support on which the database is held (paper/print or electronically). Protection for collections of works under the Copyright Act 1963 (CA 1963) was available as long as the database existed in some protectable form and the database met the originality test, protection being available via the concept of a literary work.

THE 1963 LEGISLATION

[14.02] It should be noted that copyright protection under CA 1963 was available for works that were secondary in the sense that the constituent parts of the works already existed, and s 2(1) provided a non-exhaustive definition of literary work as including 'any written table or compilation'. Thus, an anthology of poetry, or a selection of television programmes to be broadcast at a later date attracted literary copyright as long as the necessary element of skill or judgment was present in regard to the process of selection, arrangement, or both.[1] While the originality issue is addressed in Ch 11, it is sufficient for present purposes to note, firstly, that a compilation of factual material from some pre-existing source was less likely to attract copyright for the compilation. The aesthetic judgment or subjective elements in a process of selecting 50 love poems produces more latitude than the selection of tables setting out the movements of the tides: a table will be right or wrong and little or no skill or judgment arises in such a selection.[2] Secondly, a factual compilation (eg of names and addresses in a trade street directory), even if created by the person claiming copyright, may not have been copyright protected. There are no Irish cases on the point, but the balance of earlier[3] and more recent[4] English cases is to hold that if a body of factual material of this kind has been created by loading information into a compilation, the skill and effort involved will merit copyright protection. It has to be said that in both these later English cases, the analysis of each court was concerned not so much with the issue of originality but rather with issues of unfair utilisation by a trade competitor of the contents of a database. The leading modern US case of *Feist Publications Inc v Rural Telephone Service*[5] suggests that the American courts at least will not allow works that are compiled by reference to obvious criteria such as the alphabetical listing of surnames, without further refinement or selection criteria, from passing the selection and arrangement test necessary for purely factual compilations. While this approach has caused considerable alarm amongst many in the information industry, it must nevertheless be said that the *Feist* result has possibly been overstated, for O'Connor J remarked that even for factual databases, some limited modicum of selection, arrangement or classification would suffice to satisfy the originality requirement: mere alphabetical listing, which requires no skill or judgment but observance of an inflexible standard, will not be enough.[6]

[14.03] Recent case law suggests that the *Feist*[7] reasoning may be applicable outside the US, in other common law jurisdictions. In *Tele-Direct (Publications) v American Business Information*[8] the Federal Court of Canada denied copyright status to a yellow pages directory, which the defendants downloaded onto an electronic database and then used as the basis for their own, much enhanced database, which they marketed in parallel with the plaintiff's product. While McGillis J decided that there was no substantial infringement because the two works were not competing, or substantially similar, the basic reason why copyright protection was denied centred on the lack of

---

[1] *RTE v Magill TV Guide* [1990] ILRM 534.

[2] *Cramp (GA) & Sons v Frank Smythson Ltd* [1944] AC 329.

[3] *Morris v Wright* (1870) 5 Ch App 279, see also *Morris v Ashbee* (1868) LR 7 Eq 34 and *Lamb v Evans* [1893] 1 Ch 218.

[4] *Rose v Information Services* [1987] FSR 254; *Waterlow Directories Ltd v Reed Information Services Ltd* [1992] FSR 409.

[5] *Feist Publications Inc v Rural Telephone Service* (1991) 20 IPR 129; Geller (1991) 21 IIC 802; Schwarz [1991] EIPR 178.

[6] See *Bellsouth Advertising v Donnelley Information Publishing* 933 F 2d 952 (1991).

[7] *Feist Publications Inc v Rural Telephone Service* (1991) 20 IPR 129.

[8] *Tele-Direct (Publications) v American Business Information* (1996) 35 IPR 121, affirmed on appeal at (1997) 76 CPR (3d) 296.

originality of the plaintiff's directory: even the usual presumption of copyright protection was to no avail, the court choosing to follow the *Feist* reasoning, even in relation to a commercial yellow pages directory as distinct from a standard white pages directory. In *CCH Ltd v Law Society of Upper Canada*,[9] however, the Federal Court of Appeal has switched the analysis back to the traditional view of the originality standard and this approach, advocating a return to the 'not copied' standard, has been endorsed by the Supreme Court of Canada, who dismissed the publisher's appeal on this point.[10] In Australia in *Desktop Marketing Systems Pty Ltd v Telstra Corpn*,[11] an exhaustive review of the case law has led the Federal Court to conclude that both Australian and English law favours a lower standard than that set under the Database Directive.[12] However, *Desktop Marketing* is no longer regarded as good law in Australia following the decision of the High Court of Australia in *Ice TV Pty v Nine Network Pty Ltd*.[13] Ice TV created a subscription based online television schedule, beginning the work via independent efforts but ultimately checking the schedules against 'aggregator' listings released to aggregators by the television companies. Nine claimed that this constituted unauthorised copying of the weekly schedule (albeit via indirect copying) of a substantial part of the Nine weekly schedule. The High Court of Australia found that the claim to copyright turned upon Nine's skill and judgment in deciding on the content of its schedule as distinct from the skill and judgment exercised in putting the schedule into a protectable form. Ideas and information contained within the way in which the schedule had been described were not protectable. The High Court reasoned that the minimal skill and effort that went into creating the information about programme time and title did not attract copyright, so Ice TV did not infringe by copying those details. Clearly the High Court was concerned to free up the market for new innovative information products, and because the defendant had conceded that Nine weekly schedules were copyright protected, the High Court of Australia was not required to discuss the originality requirements to be met by Nine. A later case, however,[14] holds that white pages and yellow pages telephone directories do not enjoy copyright protection because of difficulties over proof of authorship of entries and insufficient intellectual effort. *Feist* was clearly influential in this context.

[14.04] The protection of compilations of works that of themselves are not literary was also not directly addressed by CA 1963. If the works are, or include, artistic works, for example, case law suggests that the compilation as a whole is to be regarded as literary[15] and it should be noted that the Berne Convention for the Protection of Literary and

---

9   *CCH Ltd v Law Society of Upper Canada* (2002) 18 CPR (4th) 161. See also a short report of British Telecom obtaining an injunction to prevent a German company from distributing a CD-ROM directory. 'BT Blocks Rivals Computer Phone List' (1996) The Times, 21 September.

10 (2004) 236 DLR (4th) 395.

11 *Desktop Marketing Systems Pty Ltd v Telstra Corpn* (2002) 55 IPR 1.

12 Council Directive 96/9/EC ([1996] OJ L77/20).

13 *Ice TV Pty v Nine Network Pty Ltd* [2009] HCA 14.

14 *Telstra Corp v Sensis Pty Ltd* [2010] FCA 44.

15 *Davis v Benjamin* [1906] 2 Ch 491; *Kalamazoo (Aust) Pty v Compact Business Systems* (1985) 5 IPR 213.

Artistic Works (Berne Convention), in art 2(5), sets out that 'collections of literary or artistic works such as encyclopaedias and anthologies which, by reason of the selection and arrangement of their contents, constitute intellectual creations shall be protected as such'. At the level of international treaty law, the protection available to database compilers has been broadened by the Agreement on Trade-Related Aspects of Intellectual Property Rights (TRIPS), the recent Geneva Protocol to the Berne Convention, the WIPO Copyright Treaty. These two provisions are set out towards the end of this chapter but they are seen as being of cardinal importance in protecting collections of works and/or data.

[14.05] The issue of creativity has proved to be a sensitive one in the UK. As the UK is the European industry leader, particularly in relation to online databases, the UK government has been extremely proactive in protecting electronic databases, the 1988 legislation being specifically drawn up so as to protect electronic databases as compilations,[16] and there is little doubt that the limited nature of the UK and Irish originality test, embracing as it does a 'sweat of the brow' element, gives copyright protection to data sets that represent a minimal amount of independent skill and labour. The European Commission's insistence upon retention[17] of an originality test that requires the database to 'constitute the author's own intellectual creation' pitches the originality standard above the UK/Irish threshold and somewhat below most European standards, representing a classical compromise but one that has been criticised nevertheless.[18] This situation in the UK has been complicated by the fact that a database is protected as a literary work and that literary copyright is available to 'a table or compilation other than a database'.[19] In *Football Dataco Ltd v Brittens Pools Ltd*,[20] the issue was whether the creation of fixtures lists for English League and Scottish League soccer matches could be protected by copyright. The High Court refused to ignore the preliminary work that the compilers of these lists put into the creation of the data, as distinct from the database, saying that such a selection or arrangement could be relevant for database copyright, as distinct from the *sui generis* right under the Directive. While an individual fixture[21] could not itself be a work, Floyd J regarded the exercise undertaken as being one in which a level of skill, effort and judgment could be exercised: the process was not purely deterministic and thus satisfied the author's own intellectual creation test. Floyd J specifically ruled that this was not a 'sweat of the brow' exercise. The judgment can be criticised as ignoring the need to isolate protection for facts and collections *per se* from copyright protection for expression, as well as drawing

---

[16] Copyright, Designs and Patents Act 1988, ss 1(1)(a), 3(1)(c) and 178: see Frome and Rowe [1990–91] CLSR 117.

[17] Article 3.1.

[18] Eg [1993] CLSR 4. For the pre-Directive view on German law, see Katzenberger (1990) 21 IIC 310.

[19] Copyright, Designs and Patents Act 1988, as amended.

[20] *Football Dataco Ltd v Brittens Pools Ltd* [2010] EWHC 841 (Ch) (trial of a preliminary issue on subsistence of copyright).

[21] 'Hull v Wigan at 7.45 pm on February 20': *Football Dataco Ltd v Brittens Pools Ltd* [2010] EWHC 841 (Ch) at para 69.

a curious distinction between selection and arrangement in relation to the database copyright and the *sui generis* right. The full implications of the decision that the fixture lists were protected by database copyright but not the *sui generis* right, or any other copyright, will only become clear in an infringement action.

CAN A DATABASE BE A WORK?

[14.06] Even if the originality standard can be overcome, the compiler of a database still faces other difficulties. If the material to be included within the compilation is copyright material, then reproduction without the consent of the author may be an infringement of copyright, certainly when the work is reproduced in a printed format. However, the situation is less certain if a database exists in an electronic form (eg online) and a user downloads the contents of the database onto another electronic format (eg the hard disk of a personal computer). It is by no means clear, under CA 1963, that the original database is itself copyright protected in that form because case law requires a literary work to exist 'in print or in writing'[22] and that it shall exist in a form that is perceptible to the human senses.[23] Further, an unauthorised act of downloading material into a digital format may not have been an act of reproduction under CA 1963, for, while the definition of 'reproduction' in s 2(1) is not exhaustive, the reference therein to 'records', which encapsulate sounds and 'cinematographic film', speaks to earlier technologies only.

[14.07] The uncertainty surrounding both the originality standard and the applicability of old concepts to these new methods of holding and distributing information were readily appreciated by the information industry. The UK legislated to bring electronic databases into copyright in 1988 and in the same year the European Commission Green Paper[24] canvassed European Community action in order to protect this significant, but underdeveloped, sector of European industry by creating a stable and secure legal environment for the information industry to develop within.[25]

COMMUNITY ACTION

[14.08] The 1988 Green Paper[26] was followed by a Commission hearing held in April 1990 in order to gather opinion on the need for harmonising legislation, and in the 1991 follow-up document,[27] Community legislation on databases was promised. Three major

---

[22] Peterson J in *University of London Press Ltd v University Tutorial Press* [1916] 2 Ch 601 at 609.

[23] *Computer Edge Property v Apple Computer Inc* [1986] FSR 537. Some support for the view that electronic databases were not literary works can be gleaned from *Gormley v EMI Records (Ireland) Ltd* [1999] 1 ILRM 178, denying literary copyright to speech recorded on 'a magnetic trace', *per* Barron J at 185.

[24] Com (88) 172 Final.

[25] See Huber [1993] CLSR 2.

[26] Com (88) 172 Final.

[27] Com (90) 584 Final.

versions of the proposed Directive appeared, namely the initial 13 May 1992[28] proposal,[29] the Amended Proposal of 4 October 1993,[30] and the Common Position adopted by the Council of Ministers on 10 July 1995. This illustrates that there have been significant shifts of perspective in the tortuous process of obtaining the agreement of Member States, and further adjustments by the Parliament have prolonged the process of getting agreement on this important document. The Directive on the Legal Protection of Databases was finally agreed, however, on 11 March 1996.[31]

[14.09] The motives behind the drafting of Directive 96/9/EC were clearly based upon internal market objectives and a desire to ensure that the European industry was not at a disadvantage vis-à-vis third countries such as the US and Japan. The Directive noted that the levels of protection were not clearly stated in all EU States at present and that such uncertainty could act as a brake upon the freedom to provide goods and services within the EU. Further, where protection existed, the protection took different forms (particularly in relation to the originality threshold) and for these reasons a harmonisation measure was seen as essential. The Directive also recognised the importance of providing a stable and uniform legal environment for the European information industry, acknowledging that levels of investment in the EU Member States were significantly lower than those in major competing States. The interests of both European industrial users of information products, and those seeking access to the Community's cultural heritage, necessitated legal measures to protect databases in the form of copyright protection and measures to counteract unfair competition. While there have been significant changes in the Directive during its path towards adoption, the main features are set out below.

SCOPE OF PROTECTION

[14.10] Article 1.2 of Directive 96/9/EC defines a database as 'a collection of independent works, data or other materials arranged in a systematic or methodical way and individually accessible by electronic or other means'. This broadening of the definition thus brings in raw data specifically – the original definition spoke only of 'materials' – and, significantly, brings in manually compiled databases, which are to be individually accessed by using the human eye and intellect. The materials must be a collection of works, data or other independent materials, so one act of downloading a film or scanning today's newspaper onto hard disk would not create a database.

However, the selection and arrangement of materials – print, sound, graphics – to create an electronic journal or newspaper, would be a collection of materials protected under Directive 96/9/EC as a compilation. The criteria of selection or arrangement may have the effect of excluding compilations that are created by reference to no real selection criteria, eg the mere downloading of printed matter perhaps to be selected and

---

[28] Common Position (EC) No 20/95.
[29] Com (92) 24 Final Syn 393.
[30] Com (93) 464 Final Syn 393.
[31] Council Directive 96/9/EC.

accessed by using software at a later date. In such a case the software may allow the database to meet the accessing criteria but the database itself will remain unstructured and possibly unprotected. Computer programs are not covered unless they are collections of independent materials, eg my 50 favourite Sega mega drive games.[32]

WHO IS PROTECTED?

[14.11] Directive 96/9/EC refers to the author of the database: the author in this context is the natural person or group of natural persons who create the database.[33] Thus, authorship can arise in a collective group, which of course was the position under s 16 of CA 1963. While the Directive allows Member States to nominate a legal person to be the right holder, this kind of provision does not appear in Irish legislation. The most significant omission on the issue of ownership is the failure of the Directive to deal with the ownership of computer-generated works, eg databases compiled by way of a computer program. While UK legislation currently provides that ownership vests in the person who makes the arrangements necessary to create the work, agreement could not be reached on this kind of problem in relation to the 1991 Computer Programs Directive,[34] so the issue was not pushed by the Commission.[35] Doubts exist about whether copyright provisions such as the aforementioned computer-generated work UK provision are permissible under the Directive,[36] the view being that such investment is protected under the *sui generis* right.

WHAT RIGHTS ARE GIVEN OR NOT GIVEN?

[14.12] The restricted acts in relation to Directive 96/9/EC are based upon traditional copyrights and employ also the broader rights found in the Software Directive.[37] Thus, temporary or permanent reproduction, in whole or in part, by any means, is a restricted act, as is the translation, adaptation, arrangement or other alteration of the database, public distribution (subject to a first sale of a tangible database within the Community exception), public communication, display or performance. These rights also apply in relation to translations and adaptations of the database.[38] These rights apply in relation to the database as a compilation of materials, so reproduction of the database, for example, infringes copyright in the compilation and not necessarily the individual works that form part of the database. Reproduction of individual works or data may constitute a breach of the *sui generis* right but not the copyright afforded to the author of the database under the Directive. As in the Software Directive, the expansion of the author's rights into acts

---

[32] CD compilations of musical performances are also not covered – Council Directive 96/9/EC, recital 19 – 'as a rule'.

[33] Council Directive 96/9/EC, art 4.

[34] Council Directive 91/250/EEC ([1991] OJ L122/42).

[35] Copyright, Designs and Patents Act 1988, s 9(3).

[36] See Kaye [1995] EIPR 583; Chalton [1995] CLSR 295.

[37] Council Directive 91/250/EEC; SI 26/1993.

[38] Council Directive 96/9/EC, art 5.

such as viewing a database or temporary reproduction may seem extreme[39] but it is necessary to protect the author's rights, and subject to qualification by the Directive in relation to lawful users of the database.

The lawful user's rights

[14.13] The provisions setting out the restricted acts would prevent any use at all if they were insisted upon, so there is an exception in the case of lawful users,[40] who are able to do all or any of the otherwise restricted acts that are necessary to access the contents of the database and that are a normal use of those contents. This right only applies to those parts of the database that are compatible with lawful use (ie parts publicly available or parts that the user has been permitted to use, by paying a subscription for example). Apart from this mandatory provision, Member States can go further by broadening the rights of individual users by taking advantage of certain permissive provisions in Council Directive 96/9/EC. Member States may extend existing natural laws on fair dealing[41] to the use of databases. Alternatively, there are tailor-made fair use provisions that an be utilised, which are instances of reproduction for private purposes of non-electronic databases, use for the sole purposes of teaching or scientific research[42] where such use is justifiable by non-commercial purposes,[43] or use for public security or the proper performance of administrative or judicial procedures.[44] These exceptions, however, are themselves conditioned by the overriding criteria that the use permitted by these provisions is not to allow a use that unreasonably prejudices the right holder's legitimate interests or conflicts with normal exploitation of the database[45] (eg leads to the parasitic and direct production of rival goods or services).

The *sui generis* right

[14.14] Council Directive 96/9/EC contains a further mechanism that permits the database creator to protect the contents of the database from being substantially used or reutilised by others. As long as the maker of the database can show that the creation of the database involved a substantial investment in terms of obtaining, verifying or presenting the contents of the database, any permanent or temporary extraction and/or reutilisation of the contents by making those contents available to the public will be held to constitute an infringement of the database creator's right.[46] This form of right to

---

[39] It is this issue that was to cause substantial problems at the 1996 Geneva Conference on the scope of the reproduction right, and exceptions thereto.

[40] Council Directive 96/9/EC, art 6.

[41] Ie CA 1963, ss 12 and 14.

[42] Defined so as to cover both natural and human sciences (Council Directive 96/9/EC, Recital 36).

[43] See, for example, *American Geophysical Union v Texaco* (1994) 29 IPR 381 and *Sweeney v Macmillan Publishers Ltd* [2002] RPC 651 at 660.

[44] Council Directive 96/9/EC, art 6(2)(c).

[45] Council Directive 96/9/EC, art 6(3).

[46] Council Directive 96/9/EC, art 7.

control copying or public distribution of contents is necessary because the raising of the originality threshold for some Member States, the fact that the copyrights afforded by the Directive apply to an author, and that those rights apply to the compilation qua compilation rather than elements within the database, made some kind of entrepreneurial right to protect investment in otherwise unprotected compilations a necessary corollary to copyright protection. This right provides an unfair competition right which is otherwise not available under Irish law and the measure is to be welcomed. The model for this provision comes from Scandinavian legislation that has apparently worked well; although not a substantial volume of case law has emerged from such provisions. The right is to operate for 15 years and an extension of the right can be obtained if the contents of the database are substantially changed during the period of protection. Again, in considering whether a substantial change has taken place that will justify a further 15-year extension, the core issue is whether there has been a substantial new investment. Thus, the relative shortness of the right is counterbalanced by the likelihood that changes to the contents and structure of a database are likely to satisfy the substantial change test and result in a further extension of rights.[47] While there are legitimate user exceptions[48] and fair dealing provisions[49] in the Directive, this twin-track approach represents an ingenious approach to reconciling users and producers as well as diverse legal traditions in the EU.[50]

THE WIPO TREATIES AND GATT/TRIPS

[14.15] At the level of international agreement, the climate is very much in favour of protecting compilations of works, or other material held electronically or in traditional formats, as being copyright protected as compilations. Article 10.2 of GATT/TRIPS[51] provides:

> Compilations of data or other material, whether in machine readable or other form, which by reason of the selection or arrangement of their contents constitute intellectual creations, shall be protected as such. Such protection which shall not extend to the data or material itself, shall be without prejudice to any copyright in the data or material itself.

[14.16] This approach to the compilation of both 'works' (whether in the public domain or copyright protected) and to non-copyrightable data (such as personal names, addresses and telephone numbers for example), has been further emphasised in work undertaken by the World Intellectual Property Organisation (WIPO) on the possible

---

[47] Council Directive 96/9/EC, art 10(3).

[48] Council Directive 96/9/EC, art 9.

[49] Council Directive 96/9/EC, art 9.

[50] See Huber [1993] CLSR 2. However, one commentator has doubted whether the Database Directive will alone provide the necessary protection available in relation to multimedia products: see Beutler [1996] Ent LR 317 for a critical look at Council Directive 96/9/EC in this context. For more praiseworthy comment see Thakur [2001] IPQ 100.

[51] Agreements on Trade-Related Aspects of Intellectual Property Rights including Trade in Counterfeit Goods.

Protocol to the Berne Convention. The Committee of Experts, by the end of 1994,[52] had concluded that compilations of works and data should be regarded as copyright protected as compilations when the necessary originality standard is satisfied, and that statements to this effect in the proposed Protocol should be regarded as declaratory in nature. The problem of protecting the database industry where the contents or criteria for selection fail to pass an originality test were also reviewed and the Committee considered the question whether such databases should be included in the provisions of the Protocol and what should be the nature and contents of those provisions. Those deliberations led to the evaluation of a database provision in the Protocol document, or First Treaty, which recognised that 'compilations of data or other material, in any form, which by reason of the selection and arrangement of their contents constitute intellectual creations are protected as such' (without prejudice to copyright protection of the contents, as such). No agreement was reached on a third treaty, put before the conference and modelled on the EU Directive, conferring *sui generis* rights, but efforts are in train at WIPO to agree such a treaty. However, the US is not keen on the database right, and the issue has been dropped by WIPO from its copyright agenda.

ORIGINAL DATABASES AND THE DATABASE RIGHT

Copyright in an original database and the Copyright and Related Rights Act 2000

[14.17] Copyright protection under CA 1963 for compilations as literary works is replaced in the Copyright and Related Rights Act 2000 (CRRA 2000) by copyright protection for original databases.[53] A database is a collection of independent works, data or other materials arranged in a systematic or methodical way which is individually accessible by any means.[54] While the definition seeks to draw a distinction between a database and computer programs that are used to make or operate the database, in practice such a distinction is difficult to draw and infringement actions may lead the plaintiff to allege the defendant has breached copyright in both a database and a computer program.[55] The database can be in any form and the means of access could be entirely physical (manual) or via an electronic search engine, for example. Infringement of copyright in a newspaper or a magazine will raise the issue of infringement of copyright in an original database. However, the critical point to note is that copyright in an original database relates to the 'selection or arrangement of the contents'.[56] In other words, it is the overall structure of the database that constitutes the work to be protected. For example, the person making a selection of 13 essays out of 127 essays written by Hazlitt will acquire copyright in the selection through the exercise of 'skill,

---

[52] WIPO, Fourth Session, 5–9 December 1994, BCP/CE/IV/2.
[53] CRRA 2000, s 17(2)(d).
[54] *Mars UK v Tecknowledge* [2000] ECDR 99.
[55] Definition of 'original database' in CRRA 2000, s 2(1).
[56] *Cambridge University Press v University Tutorial Press* (1928) 45 RPC 335.

discrimination, taste and judgment'.[57] The selection of pieces of classical music and production of a database in the form of 'play lists' will also be copyright protected as original databases because of the scholarly exercise of the skill and judgment of a compiler with an international reputation in the area.[58] However, the protection afforded by the original database copyright has rightly been described as 'thin' or 'quite scanty'[59] particularly in relation to informational works, but cases like *Cambridge University Press v University Tutorial Press*[60] reveal that for 'low authorship' works of selection it is difficult to make out a claim for infringement. Here, the defendant saved time by taking the plaintiff's selection of the most representational of Hazlitt's essays but avoided liability by adding another seven essays, rearranging the order of publication and supplementing the anthology with notes and commentary. Where the copyright is claimed because of arrangement of the materials then protection may be available for the headings[61] in a yellow pages directory or for a topical index to a series of law reports.[62] Fact-based works and raw information in the form of data must be capable of protection in the light of the definition of 'database' in CRRA 2000, even if the actual criteria used can be said to leave little or no room for the exercise of skill or judgment. However, there has to be a point at which there will not be copyright protection because s 2(1) requires the author to exercise some spark of creativity for the definition requires the database to constitute 'the original intellectual creation of the author'. It follows therefore that in respect of the kinds of factual directories that are universal in nature such as alphanumeric telephone directories,[63] trade directories of all members of a trade[64] or profession,[65] collections of railway timetables[66] and stud horses,[67] such databases are not entitled to protection as original databases unless there is some room for the exercise of skill or judgment[68] or some kind of 'value added' element in the work. The statutory definition, it is submitted, leaves no room for 'sweat of the brow' as the sole legitimate basis for protecting a database as an original database. Apart from the originality requirement, s 17(3) of CRRA 2000 makes it clear that copyright does not extend to the

---

57 *Cambridge University Press v University Tutorial Press* (1928) 45 RPC 335 at 340, *per* Maugham J.

58 *Ray v Classic FM* [1998] FSR 622.

59 Eg Ginsberg (1990) 90 Col LR 1865, at 1868; Ginsberg (1992) 92 Col LR 338.

60 *Cambridge University Press v University Tutorial Press* (1928) 45 RPC 335.

61 *Tele-Direct Publications Inc v American Business Information Inc* (1998) 154 DLR (4th). *Telstra Corp v Sensis Pty Ltd* [2010] FCA 44 has recently held no copyright protection is available in Australian law for headings in white and yellow pages telephone directories.

62 *CCH Canadian Ltd v Law Society of Upper Canada* (2002) 18 CPR (4th) 161, upheld on appeal to the SCC at (2004) 236 DLR (4th) 395.

63 *Feist Publications Inc v Rural Telephone Service* (1991) 111 SC 1282.

64 *Morris v Ashbee* (1868) LR 7 Eq 34.

65 *Waterlow Directories v Reed Information Services* [1992] FSR 409; *Waterlow Publishers v Rose* [1995] FSR 207.

66 *Blacklock v Arthur Pearson* [1915] 2 Ch 376.

67 *Weatherby v International Horse Agency and Exchange Ltd* [1910] 2 Ch 297.

68 Eg editorial work: *John Fairfax v Australian Consolidated Press* (1959) SR (NSW) 413. Judgment on 'ethnic' names: *Ital Press v Sicoli* (1999) 86 CPR (3d) 129.

contents of a database, as distinct from the selection or arrangement of that database. Many of the compilation copyright cases concern infringement by extracting content from a compilation rather than the reproduction of the parameters of the database and this point is central to understanding the database right. In fact even experienced judges may fall into error on this basic point. Witness the decision of Jacob J in *Mars UK v Tecknowledge*, the first decision in the UK on the database right.[69] A condition of protection is that the database must be recorded in writing or otherwise with the consent of the author.[70]

[14.18] Infringement of copyright in the original database is determined by the concepts of copying the work, making the work available to the public, and making an adaptation of the work, without the licence of the author of the original database.[71] Section 39 of CRRA 2000 sets out some provisions on the meaning of copying. For any database storing the work in any medium and transient or incidental copying in relation to some other use of the work are acts of copying unless the copier is a lawful user who can make out the defence of copying for the exercise of rights.[72] A similar lawful user defence exists for transient or incidental copying.[73]

[14.19] In relation to the making available right, the distribution of an original database in electronic form (eg by resale of the database when it is on some other platform to that on which the initial purchaser acquired it) may not infringe as long as the original purchased copy is no longer usable[74] and this provision extends on down the resale chain.[75] However, most licence agreements will prohibit resale transactions and in practice this provision will be difficult to rely on as a result. Where the infringement of copyright in the original database takes place by way of unauthorised adaptation of the original database – an adaptation being defined[76] as including 'a translation, arrangement or other alteration of the original database' – the use of search engines to extract headings or other structural features of the database (as distinct from content *per se*) may be viewed as both copying a substantial part of the original database and an adaptation of it.

[14.20] Apart from the ss 83 and 87 defences mentioned above, the full range of permitted acts, set out in Chapter 6 of Pt II of CRRA 2000, apply to original databases. It should be noted that an original electronic database obtains a considerable degree of additional protection because such a database does not come within the fair dealing for research or private study defence.[77] This is intended to prevent wholesale downloading

---

[69]   *Mars UK v Tecknowledge* [2000] ECDR 99.

[70]   CRRA 2000, s 18(1).

[71]   CRRA 2000, s 38.

[72]   CRRA 2000, s 83.

[73]   CRRA 2000, s 87(1). See also SI 16/2004.

[74]   CRRA 2000, s 86(2).

[75]   CRRA 2000, s 86(4).

[76]   CRRA 2000, s 43(2)(e).

[77]   CRRA 2000, s 50(1).

of electronic databases[78] but it can also be directed at any unauthorised use of the electronic database involving copying of the selection on arrangement of the original database.

Sui generis protection – the database right

[14.21] The 15-year *sui generis* right referred to in the Database Directive[79] is described as the 'database right' in CRRA 2000. While the Directive devotes only four articles to the *sui generis* right, coupled with six articles by way of common provisions, the Irish database right occupies 41 sections of CRRA 2000, most of those provisions being directed at licensing and registration by licensing bodies.[80]

[14.22] The right is described as a property right even though the basis of the database right is rooted in principles of unfair competition law.[81] Passing off, a tort, appears to be a more appropriate legal concept and the elevation of the database right to a full blown property right, with implications in Irish constitutional law, seems strange. The database right subsists where there has been a substantial investment in obtaining, verifying or presenting the contents of the database.[82] Investment exists whether it be of financial, human or technical resources,[83] so 'sweat of the brow' or 'industrious collection' of facts, by door-to-door enquiry, involving minimal outlay and no technical support will still attract protection. The investment must be substantial in terms of quantity or quality or a combination of both.[84] As Laddie J said in *British Horseracing Board v William Hill*[85] 'the investment must be substantial enough to justify protection'.[86] However, the judgments of the ECJ in both *William Hill* and the *Fixtures Marketing* decisions[87] have thrown the scope of the database right and the future of EU policy into confusion. While confirming that the database right is intended to protect investment, the ECJ drew a distinction between investment in creating the materials themselves and investment in presenting the data that results from the collection exercise; only the former is to be considered for the purposes of the database right. The ECJ indicated that the facts before

---

78 See Directive 96/9/EC, recitals 30 and 35 and art 6(2)(a). Directive 29/2001/EC (the Information Society Directive) ([2001] OJ L167/10) also distinguishes digital and analogue copying (recital 38); *Controller of HM Stationery Office v Green AMPS Ltd* [2008] EWCA Civ 588.

79 Council Directive 96/9/EC.

80 In fact only one organisation, the Irish Copyright Licensing Agency (ICLA), is currently registered.

81 See Directive 96/9/EC, recital 47 which states that the *sui generis* right is subject to Community and national competition rules.

82 CRRA 2000, s 321.

83 CRRA 2000, s 320(1).

84 CRRA 2000, s 320(1).

85 *British Horseracing Board v William Hill* [2001] RPC 612.

86 *British Horseracing Board v William Hill* [2001] RPC 612 at 625.

87 *British Horseracing Board v William Hill Organisation Ltd* C-203/02, [2005] RPC 13, *Fixtures Marketing Ltd v Oy Veikkaus Ab* C-46/02, *Fixtures Marketing Ltd v Svenska Spel AB* C-338/02, *Fixtures Marketing Ltd v OPAP* C-444/02, judgments delivered 9 November 2004.

it showed no protectable investment for database right purposes. The ECJ also suggested that while verification and the presentation of data will be qualifying investment, the test is qualitative and quantitative. It is again vital to stress that the database right exists even if all or any of the contents of the database are not protected works – personal data for example – or works that are in the public domain.[88] No copyrights exist as a result of the collection, verification or presentation of the contents of the database.[89]

[14.23] The database right exists in favour of the maker of the database, defined in CRRA 2000, s 322(1) as the person who takes the initiative in obtaining, verifying or presenting the contents of the database and assumes the risk of investing in the database. Section 322(5) makes joint ownership of the database possible. It is not clear whether investment in the cost of creation of the database, in the absence of some other elements of 'acting together', will allow the investor joint ownership of the database.

[14.24] Employees acting in the course of employment, subject to a contrary agreement, are not the makers of a database.[90] The employer is deemed the maker of the database and in relation to government or Oireachtas databases[91] ownership is claimed by the government or House or Houses of the Oireachtas and this is also the case in relation to prescribed international organisations.[92] The maker of the database, or, in cases of joint ownership, at least one of the makers, must be an EEA citizen, resident or domiciliary,[93] an EEA corporate body[94] with an EEA principal place of business or EEA registered office and operation, or have a genuine link with the Irish State.[95] Territories outside the EEA – accession or applicant countries affording comparable protection – may also be recognised by government order.[96] The time for testing the eligibility of the maker of the database is either the time of making the database (if it has not been lawfully made available to the public) or in cases of databases that have been made available to the public, the time of publication.[97]

[14.25] One of the most controversial aspects of the database right is its duration. CRRA 2000 follows Directive 96/9/EC by stipulating a period of 15 years from the end of the calendar year in which the database was completed.[98] Lawfully making the database available to the public within that 15-year period triggers another 15-year period of

---

[88] CRRA 2000, s 21(3).

[89] Directive 96/9/EC, recital 46 and art 8.4.

[90] CRRA 2000, s 322(2).

[91] CRRA 2000, s 322(3) officer or employee but not independent contractor.

[92] CRRA 2000, ss 322(6) and 196. See also CRRA 2000, s 326(2).

[93] CRRA 2000, s 326(1)(a).

[94] CRRA 2000, s 326(1)(b): partnerships and unincorporated associations are also capable of qualifying – CRRA 2000, s 326(1)(c).

[95] CRRA 2000, s 326(3).

[96] CRRA 2000, s 326(4).

[97] CRRA 2000, s 326(5).

[98] CRRA 2000, s 325(1); see Sch 1, Pt VI, which extends protection to databases completed on or after 1 January 1983.

protection from the end of the year of making the database available.[99] The prospect of a database being substantially changed, by additions, deletions or alterations, which lead to the conclusion that the changes represent a substantial new investment, means that the database that results from this substantial new investment is to qualify for its own term of protection.[100] The Act is silent on the question of whether investment to ensure that a database remains accurate but which does not result in a substantial change to the contents of the database will extend the period of protection, but recital 55 of the Directive appears to indicate that this was intended. This has been confirmed by the Advocate General but the ECJ declined to comment in the judgment in *William Hill*.

[14.26] Infringements[101] of the database right can take place in a number of ways. The exclusive rights given to the maker of the database are the rights to undertake or authorise others to undertake the extraction or reutilisation of a substantial part of the content of the database.[102] English case law holds that extraction means permanent or temporary transfer of the contents to another medium or form, while reutilisation means making the content available to the public.[103] Apart from infringement in respect of substantial parts of the database, repeated and systematic extraction or reutilisation of insubstantial parts of the database will also infringe if in conflict with the normal exploitation of the database or if such use is prejudicial to the interests of the database maker.

[14.27] Directive 96/9/EC gives lawful users the right to extract or reutilise insubstantial parts of the database for any purpose and invalidates contractual provisions to the contrary.[104] Such use must not infringe other copyrights and related rights, however.[105] The database right is more restrictive than the copyright provisions relating to original databases in so far as art 9 appears to mandate Member States to limit the range of exceptions to the *sui generis* right. For example, extraction for scientific research – defined in the Directive as applying to the natural and human sciences for non-commercial purposes – is consistent with fair dealing for research purposes, but CRRA 2000 goes further in identifying private study as another 'legitimising' purpose.[106] Other 'teaching' exceptions within art 9 of Directive 96/9/EC are also found in the Act[107] and CRRA 2000, ss 331 to 335 authorise the use of databases in ways that come within the public security or administrative or judicial procedure provisions of art 9(c) of Directive 96/9/EC.

---

99 CRRA 2000, s 325(2).

100 CRRA 2000, s 325(3).

101 CRRA 2000, s 324(2).

102 CRRA 2000, s 324(1).

103 See *British Horseracing Board v William Hill* [2001] RPC 612 at 663. Note the rejection of the argument that extraction must involve an act of removal or the taking away of the database.

104 CRRA 2000, s 327. This is not found in the articles in Directive 96/9/EC but see recital 49.

105 See Directive 96/9/EC, art 9(b) and recital 36.

106 CRRA 2000, s 329.

107 CRRA 2000, s 330. See also the pubic lending by educational establishments provisions in CRRA 2000, ss 58, 320(2) and (4) and the last sentence in Directive 96/9/EC, art 7.2.

[14.28] In relation to the remedies available for infringement of the database right, CRRA 2000, s 338 makes the provisions relating to damages and search and seizure in Ch 9 of Pt II applicable to the database right. As well as this, s 139 sets out a range of presumptions about subsistence of the right and ownership of databases. The provisions in the Act[108] relating to transfer of rights and licensing will be dealt with elsewhere in this book.

THE TRANSITIONAL PROVISIONS

[14.29] Because Directive 96/9/EC bifurcates copyright protection for a compilation into two new rights, copyright in the original database (the compilation right) and the *sui generis* right against unfair competition (extraction/reutilisation right), transitional provisions are in place in CRRA 2000.[109] These provisions have the effect of saving databases created on or before 27 March 1996 (the date of publication of the Directive in the Official Journal) as long as they were copyright works before the commencement of Pt V of CRRA 2000, that is, 1 January 2001.[110] This will require an examination of the relevant factors that determine entitlement to copyright protection under CA 1963 for compilations. Compilations that were copyright-protected retain copyright for the duration of the term, that is, the life of the author plus 70 years pma.[111] Such databases are not tested by reference to the new eligibility criteria set by CRRA 2000. However, there are going to be some databases that do not benefit from this saving provision. Databases created after 27 March 1996, and databases that consist of compilations of data, or sound recordings or film archives, for example – non-literary material – may arguably have to satisfy the eligibility criteria set out in CRRA 2000 even though 'the database' pre-dates the commencement of CRRA 2000 on 1 January 2001.[112]

ECJ CASE LAW ON THE DATABASE DIRECTIVE

[14.30] There have been a number of ECJ decisions in which national courts have sought to give guidance on what the expressions found in the Directive actually mean. In policy terms, the ECJ has given a narrow view of what 'substantial investment' means in relation to the *sui generis* right. As we shall see, a recent English case has not followed this approach on the separate question of what is relevant in relation to the necessary skill and labour in order to satisfy the author's own intellectual creation standard under art 2 of the Directive (ie for the compilation rights).

---

[108] CRRA 2000, ss 338, 340–361.
[109] CRRA 2000, Sch 1, Pt VI, para 45(1).
[110] CRRA 2000, Sch 1, Pt VI, para 45(2).
[111] Subject to a 'direct effect' argument.
[112] SI 404/2000.

'Substantial Investment' under art 7 of the Directive

[14.31] The *Fixtures Marketing* Cases[113] concerned the unauthorised use of football fixtures lists, produced by the English and Scottish Premier Leagues, by the defendants in their football pools wagering activities. The indirect replication of the fixtures lists could be considered to be infringing activities in relation to the *sui generis* right as long as the fixtures lists involved 'substantial investment' in the obtaining, verification or presentation of the contents of the database. In relation to 'obtaining', the ECJ ruled that a distinction had to be drawn between a substantial investment in acquiring content (eg buying in material or licensing use of material) as distinct from creating the content to be included in the database. In this latter case, such investment ('back' office costs and expenditure in producing the fixture list itself) was the wrong kind of investment. The plaintiffs also failed with their argument that changes to fixtures (eg television scheduling/bad weather cancellations) involved a 'substantial investment' in verifying or updating the fixtures; the ECJ held this to be too insubstantial to qualify the database for protection via the *sui generis* right. These cases must be read in the same context as the ECJ decision, handed down on the same day, in *British Horseracing Board v William Hill Organisation Ltd*.[114] This case also produced a restrictive interpretation on art 7. Here, a significant level of expenditure was undertaken by the British Horseracing Board as part of the process of creating and maintaining a database used by the UK horseracing industry and gambling entities such as William Hill. William Hill took daily 'feeds' of a small amount of the total information held without consent. On the question of 'substantial investment', the ECJ again indicated that expenditure and efforts made to obtain and collate reliable information was irrelevant to the art 7 issue, insofar as that investment was directed at creating data.

[14.32] The decisions in *Fixtures Marketing* and *William Hill*, particularly on the issue of 'substantial investment' caused significant levels of unease for database producers within the EU. The European Commission, in a 2005 Report on the impact of the Directive concluded that, while most of the received wisdom on the Directive after *William Hill* regarded that decision as having a negative impact vis-à-vis protecting the European database industry, there was no appetite for repealing the Directive and it remains in force.

[14.33] While *William Hill* and *Fixtures Marketing* provided a somewhat restricted perspective on what a database maker can bring in to establish whether there had been a substantial investment in the 'obtaining, verification or presentation of the contents' of the database, subsequent case law has shown that the ECJ has interpreted the rights of the database maker very broadly indeed. We examine this case law under four headings:

(a)   Extraction;
(b)   Article 7.5 – William Hill;
(c)   Substantial Part;
(d)   Substantial Investment for the Article 2 database right – an English view.

---

[113] *Fixtures Marketing Ltd v Oy Veikkaus Ab* Case C-46/02 (Greece); *Fixtures Marketing Ltd v Svenska Spel AB* Case C-338/02 (Sweden); *Fixtures Marketing Ltd v OPAP* Case C-444/02.
[114] *British Horseracing Board v William Hill Organisation Ltd* Case C-203/02, [2005] RPC 13.

Extraction

Extraction under Direct Media Publishing

[14.34] In *Direct Media Publishing GmbH v Albert Ludwigs Universität Freiberg*,[115] the ECJ gave a broad definition of the concept of extraction in art 7. In this case the defendant produced an anthology of poems that was in part the result of examining the plaintiff's earlier electronic database. Did 'extraction' include a visual analysis of the database and an individual assessment to transfer that data? The referring court sought assistance on whether extraction only concerned direct copying (eg cut and paste copying via an electronic database). The ECJ held that extraction had to be interpreted broadly. While a mere act of consultation is not an act of extraction, the ECJ reaffirmed that the maker of a database may restrict access to specific individuals or via payment mechanisms, and the ECJ also noted that competition law rules may also be relevant in cases where a rights owner sought to exclude access to information to the public. On the facts of this case, there was no question in relation to whether the extraction was of a substantial part as some 856 of the 1100 poems selected by the plaintiff found their way into the anthology of 1000 poems selected by the defendant.

Extraction under Apis-Hristovich

[14.35] In a reference from Bulgaria, *Apis-Hristovich Eood v Lakorda AD*,[116] Apis brought database right infringement proceedings against Lakorda, alleging that Lakorda had infringed certain modules of Apis's legal databases containing judgments, legislative texts and editorial materials relating to Bulgarian law. The Sofia City Court referred a number of questions relating to art 7 of Directive 96/9/EC to the ECJ. The ECJ grouped the questions under two headings, the first heading being regarded as relevant to determining the meaning of 'extraction' in the Directive, the second heading relating to the meaning of 'substantial part'.

The ECJ re-affirmed its position in *William Hill* and *Direct Media Publishing*, stating that 'extraction' had to be given a broad meaning: acts of temporary transfer from the original database are considered to be within the notion of extraction (eg temporary transfer to the operating memory of a computer) and the fact that a user modifies content taken from a protected database does not preclude a finding of extraction. The ECJ also observed that if a national court finds that the user of a protected database has transferred a substantial part of a database with a view to making modified content available to the public, this would constitute reutilisation, as well as extraction. Organisational similarities could also be investigated by a national court to consider whether there has been copying or not (ie use of prior sources by both parties). Although the ECJ decision was somewhat opaque on this point, it appears that only a short period of temporary extraction will be non-infringing and that while the motive of the user will be generally irrelevant on this question, motive may be pertinent in assessing the extent of the damage caused by that act to the maker of the database.

---

[115] *Direct Media Publishing GmbH v Albert Ludwigs Universität Freiberg* Case C-304/07, [2009] Bus LR 908; Christopher and Freeman [2009] EIPR 151.

[116] *Apis-Hristovich Eood v Lakorda AD* Case C – 545/07, [2009] 3 CMLR 3.

Article 7.5 – William Hill

[14.36] The repeated and systematic extraction/reutilisation of insubstantial parts provision in art 7.5 also received a narrow interpretation in *William Hill*.[117] The ECJ said that art 7.5 was aimed at preventing circumvention of the art 7.1 prohibition, but that for systematic extraction and reutilisation of an insubstantial part to infringe, this should result in the reconstruction of the database, or at the very least, reconstruction of a substantial part of it, without authorisation; because William Hill did not take a substantial part, their activities were non-infringing. This approach has created some discussion on whether taking very little, very often, comes within the prohibition when there is no attempt to reconstitute the database.

Substantial part

Apis-Hristovich on 'Substantial part'[118]

[14.37] On the meaning to be given to a 'substantial part' the ECJ noted that the question was asked within the context of a database that consisted of separate modules, constituting independent commercial products, within a body of materials. On the quantitative aspect of determining whether a 'substantial part' has been extracted or reutilised, the ECJ said that if a database actually constitutes a series of discrete databases or modules, each unauthorised act must be tested in relation to each discrete database. If this is not the case then the totality of the database and the proportion of the unauthorised use must be determined. On the qualitative test, the ECJ said that if part of a database has been obtained from sources not available to the public, then the resources deployed to obtain and make available those materials may affect the classification of those materials as a substantial part. Finally, the ECJ said that even if materials are contained in a public database, the national court must still inquire into whether there has been unauthorised use (judged on a quantitative or qualitative basis) of a substantial part of the protected database.

Substantial investment for the Article 2 right – an English view

[14.38] The English High Court, in *Football Dataco Ltd v Britten's Pools Ltd*,[119] has ruled that copyright protection for a database which created and contained English and Scottish Premier League fixture lists involved a sufficient exercise of skill and judgment on the part of the compilers to satisfy the author's own intellectual creation test. While Floyd J was careful to separate the preliminary work that went into creating the data from that which ultimately found expression in the completed database, the learned judge felt that such preliminary work was not irrelevant to an article 2 work. The selection or arrangement that went into producing these lists was not deterministic and there was sufficient room for individual choice to distinguish this as an act of authorship, as distinct from a 'sweat of the brow' exercise. No art 267 TFEU reference

---

[117] *British Horseracing Board v William Hill Organisation Ltd* C-203/02.
[118] *Apis-Hristovich Eood v Lakorda AD* Case C – 545/07.
[119] *Football Dataco Ltd v Britten's Pools Ltd* [2010] EWHC 841 (Ch).

was requested or made to the ECJ, but whether this position is compatible with the Directive is open to doubt.

INFRINGEMENT

[14.39] Infringement of the database right has been held to occur when a search engine is used to trawl the websites of newspapers, providing users with lists of newspaper headlines tailored to the search instructions and providing deep links into the newspaper sites, without the consent of the newspaper in question. Such competitive practices are clearly parasitical.[120] Similarly, a French court has held that the organisation of company press releases on a website, these being selectively downloaded and reutilised by a competing media and company information service, will infringe the database right on a qualitative, not quantitative basis: *SA PR Line v SA Communication and Sales*.[121] On the other hand, in *Noir D'Ivoire SPRL v Home Boutiques plc SPRL*[122] the replication of commonplace colours on a paint card used to assist buyers seeking to decorate their homes was held not to be an infringement at all because the defendant had not used all the colours selected by the plaintiff and had added other colours absent from the plaintiff's collection.

[14.40] The fear of some critics that the database right will preclude users of information from reutilising that information has not been borne out of subsequent national case law. In the Swedish case of *Fixtures Marketing Ltd v AB Svenska Spel*,[123] the plaintiff held the rights in respect of fixture lists for English and Scottish football matches. The defendant used the fixture lists in relation to these matches to create football pools games but at the trial of the action the defendant indicated that the source was teletext and/or a named publication. The trial court[124] found that while the skill and labour that went into devising the fixture lists merited copyright protection, the protection was 'thin' and only unauthorised copying or plagiarism could infringe. On appeal, the argument of the right holder was somewhat refined, the right holder invoking the database right, or catalogue/directory protection provision in Swedish law. In a short judgment the Appeal Court found that it had not been proved that the defendant had extracted the information from the plaintiff's database. In other words, once the information had been licensed to publishers and broadcasters, subsequent use of the information from that source, whilst indirectly reproducing the contents of the plaintiff's fixture lists was not an extraction or reutilisation of the plaintiff's database. However,

---

[120] *Danske Dagblades Forening v Newsbooster* [2003] ECDR 37 (Copenhagen City Court). In *Algemeen Dagblad BV v Eureka Internetdeinsten* [2002] ECDR 1, use of headlines was again held to be an unauthorised reproduction but in this case was justified under a 'press survey' defence.

[121] *SA PR Line v SA Communication and Sales* [2002] ECDR 10.

[122] *Noir D'Ivoire SPRL v Home Boutiques plc SPRL* [2003] ECDR 326 (Brussels CA).

[123] *Fixtures Marketing Ltd v AB Svenska Spel* [2002] ECDR 71.

[124] [2001] ECDR 406 (Grotland City Court).

Advocate General Stix-Hackl, in four opinions delivered on 8 June 2004,[125] has indicated that indirect copying (for example from other sources such as newspapers, magazines, teletext and the internet) will infringe the database right, a view endorsed by the ECJ in its judgment upholding the view that information *per se* cannot be protected, systematic and detailed copying of a database, even indirectly from other (licensed) sources, will infringe the database right. The ECJ in the *BHB* and *Fixtures Marketing* decisions[126] has also indicated that protection against indirect copying is available where the right can be invoked. On the other hand, the ECJ, in both *Direct Media Publishing* and *Apis-Hristovich*[127] has found that acts of consultation – merely reading the database – will not be infringing acts under the Directive.

---

[125] Joined Cases C-46, 203, 338, 444/02 *Fixtures Marketing Ltd v Oy Veikkaus Ab* (8 June 2004, unreported), Advocate General.
[126] Joined Cases C-46, 203, 338 and 444/02 (9 November 2004), ECJ.
[127] *Apis-Hristovich* [2009] CMLR 3.

Chapter 15

Ownership and Dealings in Copyright Works

INTRODUCTION

[15.01] The starting point in any examination of how a work may become the subject of subsequent transfers and dealings is of course the act of authorship, or making a correct attribution of authorship. The work must be literary, dramatic, musical or artistic, an original database, a sound recording, film, broadcast, or cable programme, or the typographical arrangement of a published edition if it is to be a work protected under the Copyright and Related Rights Act 2000 (CRRA 2000). These contemporary expressions have in most cases corresponding concepts in the Copyright Act 1963 (CA 1963). One major difference between CA 1963 and CRRA 2000 is that under CRRA 2000 protection is available for computer-generated works. This will mean that certain kinds of literary work and artistic work that are computer generated will be owned by 'authors' who are closer to the notion of a producer of a work than a traditional author: this will be particularly true of satellite photographs and computer programs, for example.[1] Both the 1963 and the 2000 legislation make provision for joint ownership of works and for the transfer of ownership under statutory rules on assignment, for example. CA 1963 also contained detailed provisions in relation to ownership of certain commissioned works but these have been removed from copyright law via CRRA 2000. Nevertheless, certain equitable concepts can be used to effect a transfer of ownership even after CRRA 2000.[2] Finally, contractual provisions may be used to alter or displace the effect of the statutory rules in many instances.

THE ORIGINAL VESTING OF COPYRIGHT

[15.02] We start from the proposition that ownership of copyright subsists in the author or co-author of a work.[3] Authorship was not generally defined in CA 1963 but this question has been teased out in many cases. In relation to musical works the composer of the piece, as a matter of statute, has copyright and the right is not lost by performance or use of that piece.[4] While the contribution of a lyricist in terms of a vocal contribution to

---

[1] See the distinction between computer-aided and computer-generated works in *Payen Components South Africa Ltd v Bovic Gaskets* (1995) 33 IPR 407 and *Voraarlberg Online* [2001] ECDR 417.

[2] *John Richardson Computers Ltd v Flanders* [1993] FSR 497; *Ultraframe UK Ltd v GJ Fielding* [2003] EWCA Civ 1805, [2004] RPC 479.

[3] CA 1963, ss 8(1) and 9(2).

[4] *Storace v Longman* (1788) 2 Camp 27n; *Chappell v Boosey* (1882) 21 Ch D 232.

347

the overall structure of a musical work may be compared to that of a musical instrument, one recent English case reaffirms the boundary between authorship of lyrics (a literary work) and authorship of a musical work.[5] Where, however, a piece has been produced as a result of interaction between an author, impresario and others, nice questions of judgment can arise. In *Tate v Thomas*,[6] Peterman suggested the title of a play to composers who he engaged to write music for the play. Peterman also engaged two others to write the libretto and during the writing of these pieces he suggested the names of the leading characters and some details of plot and incidental dialogue. On these facts, the court found that Peterman was not the author, or even a co-author of either element in the work. Persons who simply transpose speech into some other format, do not, unless there is sufficient skill or effort used to put the speech into a presentable form, thereby acquire a copyright in the work thus generated, nor does the *ex tempore* speaker acquire any rights.[7] If, however, a work exists which is then reworked or reformatted in such a way as to produce a derivative piece it may be possible to identify a separate copyright in the later piece[8] although any such piece may be itself an infringement of copyright in the original work.[9] In *Donoghue v Allied Newspapers Ltd*[10] a successful jockey was contracted to produce a number of newspaper articles about his 'racing secrets'. The defendant engaged a journalist to convert Mr Donoghue's racing anecdotes into literary form, often in the shape of conversations and dialogues. While the contract was silent on copyright, and it is clear that Donoghue supplied the content of each article, the journalist engaged by the newspaper gave the stories much of their shape and style. In this case the court held that Mr Donoghue was not the owner or even part-owner of the stories and could not therefore prevent the defendant from using the stories again.

[15.03] While there are situations where joint copyright may be held to exist,[11] the input of ghost-writers is normally addressed by contract. Where the work is subsequently altered by an editor or through editorial processes, express contractual provisions should be used to regulate both ownership and issues concerning editorial powers and subsequent utilisation.[12] Mere editorial input or critical advice in shaping the work will not allow that person to claim even a share in copyright.[13] However, in the case of artistic

---

5   *Peter Hayes v Phonogram Ltd* [2003] ECDR 11.
6   *Tate v Thomas* [1921] 1 Ch 503.
7   *Walter v Lane* [1900] AC 539; *Gould Estate v Stoddart Publishing* (1998) CPR (3d) 161 at 170.
8   *Springfield v Thame* (1903) 19 TLR 650.
9   *Ladbroke (Football) Ltd v William Hill (Football) Ltd* [1964] 1 All ER 465; *Express Newspapers plc v News UK Ltd* [1990] 3 All ER 376; *A-One Accessory Imports Pty Ltd v Off Road Imports Pty Ltd* (1996) 34 IPR 306.
10 *Donoghue v Allied Newspapers Ltd* [1937] 3 All ER 503; *Evans v Hutton (E) & Co* (1924) 131 LT 534; *Brumer Contractors v Mt Gambier Gorden Cemetery* (1999) 47 IPR 321.
11 *Heptulla v Orient Longman* [1989] FSR 598; *Beckingham v Hodgens* [2004] ECDR 46; *Neugebauer v Labieniec* [2009] FC 666.
12 *Samuelson v Producers Distributing* [1932] 1 Ch 201.
13 *Wiseman v Weidenfeld & Nicholson Ltd* [1985] FSR 525; *Ashmore v Douglas-Home* [1987] FSR 553; *Fairfax Media Publications Pty Ltd v Reed International Books Aust Pty* [2010] FCA 984.

works, the draftsman engaged to give artistic expression to the thoughts and ideas of a client may more readily be forced to yield any claim to sole copyright. In *Kendick v Lawrence*,[14] emphasis was placed on the need for the person giving instructions to the artist in some way to share in putting the work onto the paper: this seems to require an element of interaction and review of work in progress rather than physical execution of the drawing or artwork. In *Cala Homes (South) Ltd v Alfred McAlpine Homes East Ltd*,[15] the plaintiffs, who had engaged a firm of technical draughtsmen to assist in executing design drawings, were able to assert successfully that when the draughtsmen utilised those drawings to assist the defendant, they infringed copyright in the original drawings, which were acts of joint ownership. While the draughtsmen were solely involved in creating the drawings, the high degree of consultation and supervision undertaken by the plaintiffs, employee in the process of creating the drawings made the work a work of joint authorship.

[15.04] In relation to works of compilation[16] such as a newspaper or an encyclopaedia, persons who write the individual entries will generally be regarded as the author of the work, but the issue of ownership of copyright may be resolved by express terms or through an implied transfer of copyright due to the fact of commissioning and payment to the contributor.[17] Ownership of individual elements that form part of the collection should also be distinguished from the issue of ownership in the compilation. Even if the work of compilation consists of pre-existing material, the persons responsible for that work of compilation are the first owners of copyright.[18]

[15.05] The legislation contained, in CA 1963, a number of rules on ownership, specifically in relation to ownership of employee-authored works and commissioned works, as well as ownership of the entrepreneurial or Pt III copyright works. Ownership of a work, under the provisions of CRRA 2000 are, in general, to be determined by reference to the law applicable to the work at the time the work is made, as is the issue of authorship: CRRA 2000, Sch 1. These provisions will, therefore, remain important and for this reason the relevant provisions are dealt with later. However, CRRA 2000 sets out a number of specific provisions on authorship and first ownership of copyright.[19]

[15.06] An 'author' is defined[20] as the person who creates a work and the 'author' includes:

(a) the producer in the case of a sound recording;

(b) the producer and principal director in the case of a film;

---

14 *Kendick v Lawrence* (1890) 25 QBD 99.
15 *Cala Homes (South) Ltd v Alfred McAlpine Homes East Ltd* [1995] FSR 818; *Antill and Gourgey* [1996] EIPR 49; *Ray v Classic FM* [1998] FSR 622.
16 The definition of literary work 'includes' a compilation: CA 1963, s 2. CRRA 2000 alters this position.
17 *Lawrence & Bullen Ltd v Aflalo* [1904] AC 17.
18 *A-One Accessory Imports Pty Ltd v Off Road Imports Pty* (1996) 34 IPR 306.
19 CRRA 2000, ss 21–23.
20 CRRA 2000, s 21.

(c)   the broadcaster or relayer of that broadcast, in the case of a broadcast or broadcast relay by reception and immediate retransmission;

(d)   the cable programme service provider in the case of a cable programme;

(e)   the publisher in the case of the typographical arrangement of a published edition;

(f)   the person who makes the necessary arrangements to create the work if the work is computer-generated;

(g)   the individuals or group of individuals who made the database, in the case of an original database;

(h)   the photographer, in the case of a photograph.[21]

The CRRA 2000 also makes provision in respect of the joint ownership of works, including specific provisions for films and broadcasts and then goes on to provide rules on first ownership of copyright. Section 23 provides that the author shall be the first owner of the copyright unless the work is employee-created, in which case first ownership vests in the employer, subject to contrary agreement. First ownership is also denied to the author in cases of works that are subject to government or Oireachtas copyright or owned by a prescribed international organisation,[22] or a person or body by virtue of any statute.[23] First ownership of works created by journalists is also the subject of specific rules. The most important rule in practice relates to employee-created works under either CA 1963 or CRRA 2000.

Employees

[15.07] The relationship of employer and employee or master and servant gives rise to a number of common law duties and implied contractual rights, which in the field of intellectual property may be said to favour the employer. When an employee makes a discovery or creates something of value in the course of doing that which the employer has engaged him to do, the fruits of that employment will generally be the property of the employer and not the employee[24] save where it can be said that the discovery or product did not involve the use of the employer's time, information, trade secrets, or overlap with the contractual obligations or job description of the employed person.[25] In the area of copyright, s 10(4) of CA 1963 provided that where a work was made in the course of the author's employment by another person under a contract of service or apprenticeship, the employer was to be entitled to any copyright subsisting in that work.[26] It may be difficult at times to determine what kind of employment is involved

---

[21]   The old rule was that the author was the owner of the film: see *Gould Estate v Stoddart Publishing Co* (1998) 80 CPR (3d) 161 where the Canadian rule is the same.

[22]   CRRA 2000, s 23(1)(c).

[23]   Eg the National Standards Authority under the National Standards Authority of Ireland Act 1996, s 29.

[24]   *British Reinforced Concrete Co v Lind* (1917) 116 LT 243; *Sterling Engineering Co v Patchett* [1955] AC 534; *British Syphon Co v Homewood* [1956] 1 WLR 1190. See *Accountancy and Business College (Ireland) Ltd v Ahern & Plant* (1995) Irish Times, 4 February, HC.

[25]   *Re Selz Ltd* (1953) 71 RPC 158.

[26]   Subject to certain exceptions vis-à-vis journalistic employment and certain artistic works, mentioned below.

and the courts may have to distinguish between employee, independent contractor or even agent status in an extreme case.[27] The leading English case is *Stephenson Jordan and Harrison Ltd v MacDonald & Evans*.[28] In that case an accountant had written a number of public lectures and he had prepared the text of a study, while employed by the plaintiffs. The plaintiffs sought to prevent posthumous publication of these lectures, and the study, on the ground, *inter alia*, that copyright vested in the plaintiffs.

[15.08] In *Stephenson Jordan*[29] the Court of Appeal took the view that the accountant was not employed as a lecturer but, rather, was willing to give lectures outside the course of his employment to enhance his own position within the firm and provide positive publicity for the firm; the lectures and the text thereof were not caught by the statutory provision[30] although the separate item of text, compiled as a consequence of a specific task undertaken for the employer, was so caught. Indeed, even if a university teacher or professor is employed to give lectures, copyright in the text does not attach to the university that employs that person, according to *dicta* in *Stephenson Jordan*. The position of research students and teaching assistants is probably within these dicta also, unless the contract of employment specifically directs that the creation of literary texts is an element in the contractual duties of the employee. Some universities seek to claim ownership of research work via the regulations governing entry on a course of study, although it is submitted that these could be challenged via unconscionability concepts. In general, ownership of student works will vest with the student: *Boudreau v Lin*.[31] The course of employment exception applies also to many forms of artistic work and CA 1963, s 10(4) operated to transfer copyright to an employer in appropriate cases. In *Danowski v Henry Moore Foundation*,[32] the artist Henry Moore entered into a contractual arrangement with a limited company and registered charity to preserve his work. Sale and service agreements were struck under which Moore agreed not to carry on the business of sculptor for anyone other than the company, and further, vesting copyright in his works in the company. It was held that the company was entitled to ownership in all Moore's works, including a number of 'artist's copies', for these were made in the course of his employment. Most disputes in relation to the employment exception tend to centre on whether the person creating the work is an employee. These

---

[27] *Community for Creative Non-Violence v Reid* (1989) 17 IPR 367.

[28] *Stephenson Jordan and Harrison Ltd v MacDonald & Evans* [1952] 1 TLR 101; *Denny & Sons v Minister for Social Welfare* [1998] 1 IR 34.

[29] *Stephenson Jordan and Harrison Ltd v MacDonald & Evans* [1952] 1 TLR 101. Recent Canadian case law suggests that 'traditional' academics retain copyright, subject to the possibility of assignment in favour of the employer: *Dolmage v Erskine* (2003) 23 CPR (4th) 495, largely on the foot of custom and practice and academic freedom. Academics engaged specifically on research contracts are caught by the 'employee created works' provisions: *Hanis v Teevan* (1998) 162 DLR (4th) 414. See also the patents case of *University of Western Australia v Gray* (2008) 82 IPR 206.

[30] See also *Byrne v Statist Co* [1914] 1 KB 622.

[31] *Boudreau v Lin* (1997) 75 CPR (3d) 1.

[32] *Danowski v Henry Moore Foundation* [1996] EMLR 364; *Greenfield Products v Rover-Scott Bonnar* (1990) 17 IPR 417.

disputes involve a fastidious scrutiny of the contract and the incidental aspects of the relationship between the parties.[33]

[15.09] The fact that a person is an officer of a company will not prevent that person from also functioning as an employee.[34] Issues of this kind may be side-stepped by joining the author as a co-litigant.[35] In practice it is common for an employer, who somewhat belatedly realises that a diverse workforce – employees, independent contractors, volunteers, even – complicates ownership issues, to seek copyright releases and waivers.

Proof of title in respect of designs for large projects may be a difficult issue. The court may draw the conclusion that the plaintiff acquired copyright from employees and independent contractors through its general contractual practices, even if not all of the employees and contractors can be identified or shown to have been employees or to have expressly assigned copyright:

> one means of providing that a thing has been done is to show that there is a general practice that the thing be done…. It is not necessary to prove that the practice was invariable.[36]

Contributions to newspapers, magazines and similar periodicals

[15.10] Section 10(2) of CA 1963[37] provides for the sharing of a copyright when a literary, dramatic or artistic work is made in the course of employment and the author of that work is an employee or apprentice. The employer, as proprietor of a newspaper, magazine or similar periodical is to have copyright in that work, when made for those purposes, but the copyright so obtained is limited to republication in some other newspaper, magazine or similar periodical. Thus, the pirating of an article by some other proprietor will infringe the employer's copyright, and it is likely that if the employee or apprentice author sold that story for publication in another newspaper, magazine or similar periodical this would infringe the proprietor's copyright and possibly breach an implied term in the contract of employment or apprenticeship. However, the proprietor's copyright is limited, for the closing words of s 10(2) make it clear that, in all other respects, copyright is with the author. The requirement that the proprietor is entitled to assert copyright vis-à-vis a periodical is a limitation; the journalist may assert republication rights in an anthology, for example, but the notion of a periodical should

---

[33] *Beloff v Pressdram Ltd* [1973] 1 All ER 241. Many of these cases are tax and social welfare cases, eg *Graham v Minister for Industry and Commerce* [1933] IR 156; *Minister for Social Welfare v Griffiths* [1992] ILRM 667; *Denny & Sons v Minister for Social Welfare* [1998] 1 IR 34.

[34] *Re Beeton* [1913] 2 Ch 279; *Wilder Pump v Fusfield* (1985) 8 IPR 250.

[35] *University of London Press v University Tutorial Press* [1916] 2 Ch 601; *House of Spring Gardens v Point Blank Ltd* [1984] IR 611.

[36] Finkelstein J in *TS & B Retail v 3Fold Resources No 3* (2007) 72 IPR 492 at 515, citing *Connor v Blacktown District Hospital* [1971] 1 NSWLR 713; *Olga Investments Pty v Citipower* [1998] 3 VR 485.

[37] The predecessor of CA 1963, s 10(2) was considered in *Hall v Crosbie & Co* (1931) 66 ILTR 22.

also extend to publication in some form other than print medium. Although there is no case in point, the unauthorised use of copy by electronic republication on a bulletin board, for example, should infringe the publisher's copyright. The copyright is not shared if the journalist/contributor is a freelance or non-employed person and again the cases are of importance[38] in identifying employees and independent contractors. Section 10(2) does not apply to musical works here so the proprietor obtains copyright under the s 10(4) presumption. The effect of the s 10(4) provision is that where there is subsequent use of a newspaper article, by a clipping service, or in relation to photocopying of that work, the journalist owns the copyright. It is also arguable that in relation to other types of electronic reproduction, except in an electronic version of the newspaper in which the work appeared, which is published contemporaneously, it is the journalist not the proprietor who is the right holder.[39] We will return to this issue in a moment. Section 10(2) will clearly not apply if the photographer is a freelance photographer engaged by the newspaper, magazine or periodical.[40]

[15.11] Section 10(2) of CA 1963 can be displaced by contractual provisions to the contrary. In exceptional circumstances it may be that a court might consider that the level of payment and other surrounding circumstances transfer copyright to the employer under an implied contract or by way of an assignment in equity, but the facts would have to be very compelling in the light of s 10(2).

[15.12] Under CRRA 2000 the situation in respect of ownership of copyright has been changed very significantly. The shared copyright is abolished. Where the journalist or author is employed by the proprietor of a newspaper or periodical, as an employee, then any work created in the course of employment is treated in the same way as any other employee-created work. So where the work is created by a freelancer, or no employment relationship subsists at all (eg readers' letters to the editor) copyright remains with the author. Section 23(2) of CRRA 2000, however, provides where copyright vests in the propreitor/employer that the author has a right to use that work 'for any purpose' other than for the purpose of making the work available to other newspapers or periodicals without infringing the employer's copyright in the work. This is something of a compromise: what is intended by the evidence provided in Dáil debates concerning the subsection is a provision that would allow the author to use 'the story' in a broadcast or a book in the event that the proprietor did not publish the story or the author seeks a separate exploitation of his or her work (eg an anthology of pieces of journalism). In practice the subsection leaves open the question whether the use of the work by way of electronic publication is within the rights of the proprietor qua copyright owner or within the licence granted to the author by s 23(2).

Could the journalist author licence publication on a website, or in an electronic newspaper or journal without infringing the proprietor's copyright? There is no simple

---

[38] *Re Sunday Tribune* [1984] IR 505; *O'Riain v Independent Newspapers* UD 134/1978; *Kelly v Irish Press* (1986) 5 JISLL 170; *Allen v Toronto Star* (1995) 129 DLR (4th) 171.

[39] *De Garis v Neville Jeffress Pidler Pty* (1990) 18 IPR 292; *Nationwide News Pty v Copyright Agency* (1996) 34 IPR 53.

[40] *Allen v Toronto Star Newspapers Ltd* (1995) 63 CPR (3d) 517.

answer to this question. Firstly, if issues of authorship and first ownership of an existing work are resolved under CA 1963, works created before 1 January 2001 are to be exploitable under the shared copyright rule. It should therefore follow that any act of electronic publication of the work on an electronic site should be within the employer's share of the split copyright under CA 1963. If, however, the work is a pre-1 January 2001 work and the journalist has used 'the story' in creating a film or documentary, copyright here will clearly vest in the journalist. Difficult issues will arise, however. In the important recent French case of *Syndicat National des Journalistes v SA Plurimedia*,[41] France 3, a television station, entered into an agreement allowing Plurimedia, an internet service provider, the right to retransmit over the internet television programmes that had been scripted by journalists. The journalists had not given permission for this retransmission. Applying French law, of course, it was held that copyright had been infringed and that France 3 could not authorise the use of the work of the journalists in question. Under Irish law, if such facts were to appear before an Irish court, it is submitted that for pre-2001 existing works an Irish proprietor would not be able to authorise this kind of use (ie authorise a broadcaster to make a film, or authorise its distribution over the internet). However, in relation to post-1 January 2001 works, copyright vests in the proprietor, so a different conclusion is reached. However, the question whether a journalist could authorise the use of the work under s 23(2) would turn on whether inclusion of the film in an internet transmission is within the notion of a 'newspaper or periodical' (which it probably is not).

[15.13] In *Grisbrook v MGN*[42] the plaintiff, a freelance photographer, entered into a licensing agreement giving MGN a licence to use his photographs for MGN's purposes. The licence was breached in certain respects after the licensed images appeared in the original print version of the defendant's newspapers, but the defendant argued (in line with *Robertson v Thomson Corporation*)[43] that once a licence had been granted for print use, it was also valid and irrevocable for archiving and online distribution. The defendant also argued that the defendant's exploitation of its (original database/ compilation) copyrights trumped the plaintiff's own copyright in this photograph. Following *Ray v Classic FM*[44] the court held that the licence granted to the defendant covered archiving and the distribution of the plaintiff's images and that, accordingly, the electronic reproduction of these images for archiving purposes was not outside the scope of the licence, viewed in the context of newspaper industry custom and practice. However, exploitation by sale of images via back issue and merchandising websites was a new form of commercial exploitation that fell outside Lightman J's necessity test, ie it was an 'unexpected profitable opportunity not covered by the implied contract'. On *Robertson*, the court expressed the view that English law did not hold that a 'collective' copyright could 'trump' an author's right not to have his/her work included in a collection without consent.

---

[41] *Syndicat National des Journalistes v SA Plurimedia* [2002] ECDR 363; see also *SA Groupe Progress v SNDJ* [2001] ECC 62.
[42] *Grisbrook v MGN* [2009] EWHC 2520 (Ch).
[43] *Robertson v Thomson Corporation* [2006] SCC 43; D'Agostino [2007] EIPR 66.
[44] *Ray v Classic FM* [1998] FSR 622.

Commissioned photographs and certain other commissioned works

[15.14] Save in cases where the work was covered by CA 1963, s 10(2), the sharing of copyright provision as between an employed journalist and the proprietor, CA 1963 provided that where a person commissions the taking of a photograph,[45] a portrait[46] or the making of an engraving,[47] and the commissioner pays or agrees to pay for it in money or money's worth, the work so created is to be copyright of the commissioner. If a photographer invites persons to visit his studio in order to have portraits taken, a conclusion that the commissioner is bound to pay for the work done will lead to copyright being vested in the commissioner.[48] There are cases where the photographer has been successful even if the subject of the photograph obtains free copies of the work and later pays for copies of the work. In *Davis v Baird*[49] the plaintiff photographed a professional wrestler in his studio at a free sitting. Complimentary copies were given and the wrestler later ordered 50 copies of the portrait. In giving judgment for the plaintiff, Porter MR said that the circumstances surrounding the transaction pointed away from the portrait being the property of the subject. Should the contract stipulate that copyright is to vest in the author, notwithstanding the fact that it has been commissioned for money, CA 1963, s 10(3) could not prevent first copyright vesting in the photographer.[50]

Commissioned works generally

[15.15] The commissioned artistic works provision that has just been considered, is the exception that proves the rule; first ownership in a work that had been specifically ordered or commissioned, under CA 1963, vested in the author. There were, however, a number of situations where this conclusion was not to be reached. An entrepreneur who plants the seed of an idea does not *per se* acquire copyright[51] but it may be that where an entrepreneur commissions others to produce works, for a fee, and the circumstances do not point towards any attempt on the part of the authors to reserve copyright, then copyright as a matter of implied contract may subsist in the entrepreneur. The leading case is *Sweet v Benning*,[52] and, although the decision did not involve a dispute between an entrepreneur and a contributor but rather an entrepreneur and a pirate, it has passed into the literature as turning on drawing certain inferences of fact from the conduct of

---

45   *Gabrin v Universal Music Operations Ltd* [2004] ECDR 18.
46   *Leah v TwoWorlds Publishing* [1951] Ch 393.
47   *Con Planck Ltd v Kolynos* [1925] 2 KB 804; *Cape Allman v Farrow* (1984) 3 IPR 567.
48   *Boucas v Cooke* [1903] 2 KB 227; *Sasha v Stoenesco* (1929) 45 TLR 350. Consideration of some kind is essential; *Royal Doulton Tableware Ltd v Cassidy's Ltd* (1986) 1 CPR (3d) 214. A heart bypass operation will suffice; *Meskenas v ACP Publishing* [2006] FMCA 1136.
49   *Davis v Baird* (1903) 38 ILTR 23. Contrast *Desmaris v Edimay* (2003) 26 CPR (4th) 295.
50   CA 1963, s 10(5); *Christopher Bede Studios Ltd v United Portraits Ltd* [1958] NZLR 250.
51   *Tate v Thomas* [1921] 1 Ch 503.
52   *Sweet v Benning* (1855) 16 CB 459; *Lamb v Evans* [1893] 1 Ch 218. For musical works see *Wallerstein v Herbert* (1867) 16 LT 453.

the parties in each case. In *Lawrence & Bullen Ltd v Aflalo*,[53] the House of Lords affirmed that for copyright to vest in the commissioner, no written contract is needed and that express words are not needed to constitute such a bargain. The language of the House of Lords reflects a business efficacy, implied term, approach: the author must be taken to have intended to give copyright to the commissioner, as a reasonable person, for the author has been paid for creating the work on a bespoke basis,[54] and to allow the author to use the work again, to the prejudice of the commissioner's interests, would clearly not be reasonable. Advertisers[55] and certain clients of professional persons[56] have also benefited from this implied contract, particularly in relation to artistic copyright and design prototypes.[57]

[15.16] Apart from an implied contract argument, there are also equitable rules that may allow a person other than the author to claim that copyright in the work should be held, in equity, by the author, in trust for that other party who may be entitled to call for copyright to be assigned to them. The leading case is *Massine v de Basil*.[58] In that case a choreographer was engaged to produce ballets at Covent Garden and was held to be liable in equity to transfer any copyright to the director of the ballet. This equitable ownership has been held to apply to computer programmers engaged as independent contractors to work on specific projects,[59] to members of a partnership[60] and company officers in appropriate cases.[61] In *A-One Accessory Imports Pty Ltd v Off Road Imports Property Ltd*[62] two persons began work on a sales brochure intending to trade through the plaintiff company, which they were in the process of setting up. However, while this meant the plaintiff company was not first owner of copyright, the two founders of the plaintiff company had beneficial ownership of the works, which they held in trust for the plaintiff company. In appropriate circumstances equitable ownership by way of a constructive trust may be imposed upon the author. See *Bulan Bulan v R&T Textiles*

---

[53] *Lawrence & Bullen Ltd v Aflalo* [1904] AC 17. This is a very contentious issue for computer software; see, for example, *Wrenn v Landamore* [2007] EWHC 1833 (Pat); *Centrestage Management Pty Ltd v Riedle* [2008] FCA 938.

[54] On which see *PS Johnson v Bucko Enterprises* [1975] 1 NZLR 311 and *Pacific Software Technology Ltd v Perry Group* (2003) 57 IPR 145.

[55] *Harold Drabble Ltd v Hycolite Manufacturing Co* (1928) 44 TLR 264.

[56] *Chantrey, Chantrey & Co v Dey* (1912) 28 TLR 499. Contrast *Meikle v Maufe* [1941] 3 All ER 144.

[57] *PS Johnson v Bucko Enterprises* [1975] 1 NZLR 311; *Cope Allman v Farrow* (1984) 3 IPR 567; *Enzed Holdings v Wythnia Pty* (1984) 3 IPR 619; *Cselko Associates Inc v Zellers Inc* (1992) 44 CPR (3d) 56; *Griggs (R) Group v Evans* [2005] EWCA Civ 11; *Lucasfilm Ltd v Ainsworth* [2008] EWHC 1878 (Ch).

[58] *Massine v de Basil* [1936–45] Macg Cop Cas 223. A contract of service was held to exist in any event; see *Missing Link Software v Magee* [1989] FSR 361.

[59] *John Richardson Computers Ltd v Flanders* [1993] FSR 497; *Intelmail Explorenet Pty Ltd v Vardanian (No 2)* (2009) FCA 1018.

[60] *Roban Jig and Tool Co v Taylor* [1979] FSR 130; *Robert J Zupanovich Pty v B & N Beale Nominees Pty* (1995) 32 IPR 339.

[61] *Wilden Pump v Fusfield* (1985) 8 IPR 250.

[62] *A-One Accessory Imports Pty Ltd v Off Road Imports Pty Ltd* (1996) 34 IPR 306.

Pty,[63] and in certain instances the legal owner may be under fiduciary duties that contain his freedom in respect of use of the work.[64] It is likely that these general approaches to issues of ownership, via implied contract, equitable remedies and fiduciary duties will become increasingly important and that the authorship and ownership provisions in CRRA 2000 must be read subject to such propositions. Indeed, in *Griggs (R) Group Ltd v Evans*,[65] Deputy Judge Prescott has gone so far as to say that where a logo is designed for a client, the contract being silent on copyright ownership, it will be necessary to imply that copyright vests in the client so as to enable the client to defend the logo against improper use by others. A declaration of beneficial ownership was obtained by the applicants.

Beneficial ownership and wrongdoing

[15.17] English case law establishes that where a Crown servant owes a duty not to disclose information that is secret and confidential, and that duty is breached by publication in a literary work, equity may impose a duty upon that person to hold the fruits of the wrongdoing for the person to whom the duty was owed, namely the Crown.[66] The enforcement of statutory copyright ownership rights may be denied on public policy grounds if some wrongdoing such as an actionable conspiracy is disclosed in pleading infringement of copyright,[67] even where some superior private law right requires the subordination of copyright.[68] The Human Rights Act 1998 in the UK has had a significant impact upon copyright litigation, particularly upon issues such as the balance between property rights and freedom of expression; and these UK developments can be expected to impact upon Irish copyright litigation also. We will look at this subject generally in Ch 17.

ASSIGNMENT AND LICENSING

[15.18] It is important to distinguish between the concept of an assignment and a licence agreement. The assignment of rights will transfer ownership of rights and is itself further transferable, while a licence may be personal to the licensee and prevent the licensee from altering the work (eg editing parts of the work[69]). A transfer may be held to be in law an assignment of rights, although it is described as being a licence.[70] Requirements

---

63 *Bulan Bulan v R&T Textiles Pty* (1998) 41 IPR 513.
64 *Bulan Bulan v R&T Textiles Pty* (1998) 41 IPR 513.
65 *Griggs (R) Group Ltd v Evans* [2004] ECDR 165, affd [2005] EWCA Civ 11.
66 These observations are found by several judges in the *Spycatcher* litigation (*AG v Guardian Newspapers (No 2)* [1988] 3 All ER 545). More recent case law suggests an action for breach of contract may yield either 'disgorgement' damages or aggravated damages: *A-G v Blake (Jonathan Cape Ltd third party)* [2001] 1 AC 268; *Experience Hendrix LLC v PPX Enterprises Inc* [2003] 1 All ER (Comm) 635.
67 *Massie & Renwick Ltd v Underwriters Survey Bureau* [1940] 1 DLR 625.
68 *British Leyland v Armstrong Patents* [1986] AC 577.
69 *Frisby v BBC* [1967] Ch 932.
70 *Messager v BBC* [1929] AC 151.

of legal form attach to assignments, while licence agreements do not in themselves so require.[71] Because of the bewildering variety of rights that co-exist here, and the complexity of the law relating to express and implied licenses and assignments, the courts are reluctant to accede to expansive arguments in this area of law. The question of how to interpret an everyday business transaction arose in *Fisher v Brooker*,[72] the 'A Whiter Shade of Pale' case, which primarily concerned authorship but also raised issues of implied assignment. When the manager of the group, 'Procol Harem', assigned all recording rights in the work, did Fisher impliedly assign music copyright, gratuitously, without being expressly aware that such a transaction was taking place'? The House of Lords found in the negative, Fisher was one of five young men relying upon the record company[73]; any implied contract was unlikely to have been a gratuitous assignment if the touchstone was that of necessity/business efficacy. A limited licence for a reasonable payment would have been a more appropriate implied contract argument, their Lordships ruled.

Assignments – total and partial

[15.19] Section 47(2) of CA 1963 and CRRA 2000, s 120(2) both provide that an assignment may be limited by restricting the activity of the assignee to one or more, but not all, of the rights afforded by the Act to the assignor. The assignment may also limit the assignment geographically, restricting the right to one or more countries in relation to which the assignor has those rights and the assignment may be limited in terms of the duration of the assignment, giving the assignee rights in relation only to part of the period in which statutory copyright subsists.

[15.20] In the area of musical copyright, for example, the performing rights in Ireland are normally assigned by Performing Right Society (PRS) members to the Irish Music Rights Organisation (IMRO), while certain reproduction rights may be assigned by the same right holder to the Mechanical Copyright Protection Society. In one recent Canadian case it has been held that a composer who assigns performance and broadcasting rights to a company does not thereby assign reproduction rights.[74] In *Jonathan Cape Ltd v Consolidated Press Ltd*,[75] the plaintiff obtained an assignment of volume publication rights to cover a number of countries, including Australia, and was able to bring infringement proceedings against the defendant who reproduced the story without the plaintiff's permission.

[15.21] The question whether an assignment has been granted depends on the intention of the parties gathered from the words used. In *EW Savory Ltd v World of Golf*,[76] a

---

[71] Agreements not to be performed within one year under the Statute of Frauds 1695 could be a barrier in certain instances.

[72] *Fisher v Brooker* [2009] UKHL 41.

[73] Note also Baroness Hale's interesting discussion on the service contract and infancy issues.

[74] *Tele Metropole v Bishop* (1990) 20 IPR 318.

[75] *Jonathan Cape Ltd v Consolidated Press Ltd* [1954] 3 All ER 253; *Jung v Suh* (1991) 37 CPR (3d) 384.

[76] *EW Savory Ltd v World of Golf* [1914] 2 Ch 566; *Gabrin v Universal Music Operations Ltd* [2004] ECDR 18.

document referred to the sale of 'five original card designs inclusive of copyrights' and went on to state the subject of the cards. Proof by parole identifying the cards was possible. It was held that there was an assignment. Similarly, in *London Printing and Publishing Alliance Ltd v Cox*,[77] sale of a picture for a stated price which, 'includes sole and entire copyright nett' was held to assign total copyright to the buyer. In *Andritz Sprout Bauer Australia Pty v Rowland Engineering Sales Pty*,[78] a contract formed by way of an exchange of letters, which transferred business assets, was held, by implication, to transfer copyright in drawings to the purchaser of those assets. In contrast, the sale of electro blocks to a buyer who used them to print advertising posters was not an assignment but a mere personal licence to that buyer, who could not validly allow others to reproduce posters from those blocks.[79] In *JHP Ltd v BBC Worldwide Ltd*,[80] Norris J stressed that each case must be seen in context and warned against extrapolating from certain clauses (eg rights to 'revert' in certain instances) a generalised conclusion that an assignment was intended. Thus, a publishing agreement expressed as a 'grant' was not an assignment of copyright but an exclusive licence to publish a book.

[15.22] In the context of publishing agreements the separation of rights can be quite bewildering; in relation to reproduction alone, the right holder may carve up foreign language rights, serialisation rights, electronic publishing rights, talking book rights, film or adaptation rights, etc. Sometimes the act of reproduction may require a publisher and others to undertake certain specific tasks in relation to that work and in such a context a claim of joint ownership may emerge. An agreement as between an author and a publisher to publish a work on a profit-sharing basis does not assign copyright[81] unless the terms are clear, even if the word assignment is not used.[82] If, however, a work is published on terms whereby copyright is vested in two parties there can be certain difficulties. With one exception,[83] which relates to co-authors, the weight of opinion favours the view that co-ownership involves a joint tenancy in the copyright and that where a right is so shared the consent of each holder of a right must be obtained before any dealing in the work is lawful.[84] So, in *Cescinsky v Routledge & Sons*,[85] the plaintiff

---

77   *London Printing and Publishing Alliance Ltd v Cox* [1891] 3 Ch 291; *Lacy v Toole* (1867) 15 LT 512.

78   *Andritz Sprout Bauer Australia Pty v Rowland Engineering Sales Pty* (1993) 28 IPR 29. Contrast *Motel 6 Inc v No 6 Motel Ltd* (1981) 127 DLR (3d) 267.

79   *Cooper v Stephens* [1895] 1 Ch 567; *Tuck v Canton* (1882) 51 LJQB 363; *Marshall v Bull* (1901) 85 LT 77; *Hutchison Personal Communications Ltd v Hook Advertising Ltd* [1996] FSR 549.

80   *JHP Ltd v BBC Worldwide Ltd* [2008] EWHC 75 (Ch) (note also the licence by estoppel point).

81   *Stevens v Benning* (1855) 6 De GM & G 223; *Lucas v Moncrieff* (1905) 21 TLR 683; *Re Jude's Musical Compositions* [1906] 2 Ch 595.

82   *Ward Lock & Co v Long* (1906) 22 TLR 798; *Coleridge-Taylor v Novello & Co* [1938] Ch 608.

83   Said to be tenants in common in *Acorn Computers v MLS Microcomputer Systems* (1984) 57 ALR 389; *Dixon Projects Pty Ltd v Masterton Homes* (1996) 36 IPR 136.

84   *Powell v Head* (1879) 12 Ch D 686; *Lauri v Renad* [1892] 3 Ch 402.

85   *Cescinsky v Routledge & Sons* [1916] 2 KB 325; *Spiroflex Industries v Progressive Sealing* (1986) 34 DLR (4th) 201.

had published literary works on antique furniture with the defendant on the basis of equal copyright in the work by both parties. It was held that reproduction of part of that work by the defendant in another book, without the permission of the plaintiff, infringed the reproduction right of the plaintiff. No implied licence is possible in such a case. While these cases indicate that one co-owner cannot create a licence or assignment without the consent of the other co-owner, the cases hold that one co-owner can bring an infringement action without joining the other co-owner.[86] It is possible that an owner or a co-owner may lose rights to object to another's title through estoppel, as in the old Irish case of *Re Curry*.[87] Here a publisher's assertion of copyright on the title covers was not objected to by an author. Of course, these problems will not arise if the work is in reality a bundle of separate copyrights and these rights are identifiably the works of separate authors[88] (eg a film with dialogue, music, screenplay, etc). However, proof of separate creation should be put before the court and if it is not then the total output of the authors may be held to be works of joint authorship.[89]

Formal requirements for an assignment

[15.23] Section 47(3) of CA 1963 and s 120(3) of CRRA 2000 both provide that an assignment of copyright, whether in whole or in part, shall not be effective unless it is in writing, signed by or on behalf of the assignor. An assignment may be held to exist even if the issue of copyright does not appear to have arisen in the negotiations or in the instrument which sets out the transfer, as in a declaration that the parties intend to transfer 'all the right, title and interest', plus the goodwill of a publishing business,[90] but a mere sale of business equipment – moulds and master patterns for use in jewellery manufacturing – will not create an exclusive licence, much less a copyright assignment, without more.[91]

[15.24] If there is no written instrument of assignment the assignor will have to seek to enforce the assignment through a more circuitous route. In *Springsteen v Masquerade Music Ltd*,[92] assignments made in documentary form many years before had been lost. The plaintiff successfully adduced secondary evidence in the form of statements from his lawyer that the original documents had been lost. After making reasonable efforts to locate the originals the Court of Appeal upheld the decision of the court of first instance to consider this secondary evidence, remarking that the best evidence rule was to be consigned to legal history.

---

[86] *Mail Newspapers plc v Express Newspapers plc* [1987] FSR 90.

[87] *Re Curry* (1848) 12 Ir Eq R 382; contrast *Beckingham v Hodgens* [2004] ECDR 46.

[88] *Thibault v Turcot* (1926) 34 RNLS 415.

[89] *ATV Music Publishing of Canada v Rogers Radio Broadcasting Ltd* (1982) 134 DLR (3rd) 487.

[90] *Murray v King* (1984) 3 IPR 525. Contrast *Greenfield Products v Rover-Scott Bonnar* (1990) 17 IPR 417.

[91] *Anvil Jewellery Ltd v Riva Ridge Holdings Ltd* [1987] 1 NZLR 35. In *Larrikin Music Publishing Pty Ltd v EMI Songs Australia Pty* [2009] FCA 799 the rules of a song competition transferring 'property' in all entries to the organiser was consistent with property in the manuscript, not an assignment of copyright.

[92] *Springsteen v Masquerade Music Ltd* [2001] EMLR 654.

The assignment of future copyright[93]

[15.25] Both s 49 of CA 1963 and s 121 of CRRA 2000 make it possible for a person, who is the prospective owner of a copyright work in the sense that the work has yet to be created, to vest copyright in that putative work in another person.[94] Section 49(1) provides that where a contract to this effect is signed by or on behalf of the prospective owner and the agreement purports to assign copyright (wholly or partially in another) then on the coming into existence of copyright that copyright will vest in the assignee or his successor in title without further assurance.

[15.26] The key element in this subsection is that the vesting will only take place if the assignee would, without this subsection, be entitled to call for specific performance of the agreement. The assignee should be entitled to specific performance and thus an agreement made gratuitously (ie without consideration) or with an infant, or in restraint of trade (all circumstances where specific performance will be denied) will not satisfy CA 1963, s 49(1) or CRRA 2000, s 121(1).

Equitable assignments

[15.27] The writing requirements set out in relation to assignments of existing or future copyrights in CA 1963, ss 47 and 49 and CRRA 2000, ss 120 and 121 would appear to suggest that where these statutory provisions are not complied with there can be no other effective transfer of title, but there is judicial support for the view that equity will allow transactions of substance to be effective even if writing requirements in a statute are not satisfied.[95] Equitable assignments may be created when, for example, an independent contractor is engaged to create design drawings, verbally agreeing that copyright in those works will, upon their creation, be vested in the commissioner. If such an agreement can be made out then the artist will hold legal title for the assignee, who will have beneficial ownership, and the beneficial owner may call upon the legal owner to execute a written assignment to perfect legal and equitable title. In practice, there should be a written assignment in favour of the beneficial owner at some stage if the beneficial owner is to be able to not only seek interim relief[96] but also get final judgment against an infringer. While one English case suggests that the assignment of the legal title should take place prior to the issuing of a writ,[97] *Wah Sang Industrial Co v Takmay Industrial Co*,[98] a Hong Kong case, decided that if the assignment takes place after the writ has been issued, the assignee should either join the legal owners or commence a new action. Notwithstanding *Wah Sang Industrial Co v Takmay Industrial Co*, an equitable owner at the time of issue of the writ has been held to be capable of obtaining final judgment if

---

[93] For definitions see CA 1963, s 49(4) and CRRA 2000, s 121(4) respectively.

[94] The section is intended to remove the effect of *Performing Right Society Ltd v London Theatre of Varieties* [1924] AC 1.

[95] *Brooker v John Frend Ltd* [1936] NZLR 743.

[96] *Performing Right Society Ltd v London Theatre of Varieties* [1924] AC 1; *Merchant Adventurers v Grew* [1972] Ch 242.

[97] *Roban Jig & Tool Co v Taylor* [1979] FSR 130, applying *Creed v Creed* [1913] 1 IR 48.

[98] *Wah Sang Industrial Co v Takmay Industrial Co* [1980] FSR 303.

before judgment in the action he becomes the legal owner, by assignment, of that copyright.[99]

[15.28] If the work is in existence and this is not a future work, but the author agrees to assign copyright in the future, then *a fortiori* there will be an equitable assignment[100] and confirmation in the form of an assignment instrument may be expected.[101] But, if no such instrument is ever created, will the assignment be invalid? It appears that Irish law does not have a provision that corresponds with s 53(1)(c) of the English Law of Property Act 1925, which requires a disposition of an equitable interest or trust to be in writing signed by the person disposing of this interest, a provision that had been held to make verbal agreements to transfer equitable ownership ineffective.[102] However, *Wah Sang Industrial Co v Takmay Industrial Co*[103] makes it clear that an equitable interest of this kind can subsist without an instrument in writing being required and that as long as the equitable owner's title is perfected in accordance with statutory requirements relating to proof of legal title an equitable assignment for value will be recognised in law. *Batjak Production Inc v Simitar Entertainment (UK)* suggests that title can be perfected at any time up to final judgment.[104]

Licences

[15.29] In general, a licence to use or reproduce a copyright work can be created by way of express or implied contract. It may be, however, that the licence is granted gratuitously. In *Trumpet Software Property Ltd v Ozemail Pty Ltd*,[105] the plaintiff company produced an internet navigation software package, which it agreed to allow the defendant to distribute with its magazine as shareware to allow consumers to consider taking the program. The defendant modified the program and distributed it in that form. It was held that, as the permission to distribute was given without consideration moving from the defendant, the licence was bare and revocable at will. Even if the licence had not been revoked, distribution in a modified form constituted breach of the licence agreement.

[15.30] If the licence is contractual, the contract itself will determine its incidents, supplemented by any implied terms the court regards as being necessary to give the agreement business efficacy.[106] If the licence is express then it may not be revocable unless revocation is expressly or impliedly afforded to the licensor,[107] and it is difficult to

---

[99] *Batjak Production Inc v Simitar Entertainment (UK)* [1996] FSR 139.

[100] *Western Front Ltd v Vestron* [1987] FSR 66.

[101] *Kambrook Distributing Pty v Delaney* (1984) 4 IPR 79.

[102] *Roban Jig &Tool Co v Taylor* [1979] FSR 130.

[103] *Wah Sang Industrial Co v Takmay Industrial Co* [1980] FSR 303.

[104] *Batjak Production Inc v Simitar Entertainment (UK)* [1996] FSR 139.

[105] *Trumpet Software Property Ltd v Ozemail Pty Ltd* (1996) 34 IPR 481; Lambert [2000] EIPR 595; *McGill v S* [1979] IR 283. Reasonable notice, however, must be given to the bare licensee: *Beckingham v Hodgens* [2004] ECDR 46.

[106] *Ray v Classic FM* [1998] FSR 622; *Griggs (R) Group Ltd v Evans* [2004] ECDR 165.

[107] *Winter Garden Theatre (London) Ltd v Millennium Productions Ltd* [1948] AC 173; *Whipp v Mackey* [1927] IR 372.

persuade a court that a contractual licence can be impliedly revoked when the agreement is an exclusive licence.[108]

[15.31] An implied licence may be inferred from either the dealings that have taken place as between the parties or through some trade custom that operates within a particular industry. For example, is there a custom in the newspaper industry that allows one newspaper to reproduce, in substance, copy lifted from another publication?[109] It has certainly been held that submitting an article to the editor of a periodical with a view to its being adopted and paid for by the editor may give the editor an implied right to publish that piece without the need to revert to the author for any express permission.[110]

[15.32] It may be possible to infer a licence in cases where the right holder and the putative licensee have previously contracted to allow the licensee or his predecessors in title to use that work.[111] In one case,[112] the plaintiff produced artwork for a motel proprietor who had developed a distinctive sign to advertise the motel. The plaintiff registered copyright (probably unlawfully for the plaintiff was an employee) in the design. It was held that the dealings between the parties gave the motel proprietor, and the sign manufacturer engaged by the proprietor, irrevocable licences to use and reproduce the design. Third parties, however, may not acquire such rights as readily as persons who have commissioned or purchased that licence, thus leading to the conclusion that most licences are personal and non-transferable.[113]

[15.33] The implied licence argument has surfaced in several cases where architects have been engaged to prepare plans to be used in order to secure planning permission. In the event that these plans are completed and paid for, is there an implied licence that the person who ordered and paid for these plans can use them for any purpose they wish, including the construction of a building without necessarily engaging the architect to complete the work? Despite the breadth of the judgment in *Blair v Osborne and Tompkins*,[114] the Court of Appeal in *Stovin-Bradford v Volpoint Properties*[115] suggests that this licence will not be implied if the fee paid to the architect is not a full scale fee and, even if it is, such an implication will only be made if it is fair to both parties.[116] The

---

108 *Crown Industrial Products Co v IDI Electric (Can) Ltd* (1971) 2 CPR (2d) 1; *Pacific Software Technology Ltd v Perry Group Ltd* (2003) 57 IPR 145.

109 *Walter v Steinkopff* [1892] 3 Ch 489; *Express Newspapers v News (UK) Ltd* [1990] 3 All ER 376.

110 *Hall Brown v Illife & Sons* (1929) Macg Cop Cas 88. Copyright, of course, remains in the author: *Knaplock v Curl* (1722) 4 Vin Abr 278 pl 3.

111 Use is not unlimited: *Roberts v Candiware Ltd* [1980] FSR 352.

112 *Silverson v Neon Products Ltd* [1978] 6 WWR 512. See also *Pacific Software Technology Ltd v Perry Group Ltd* (2003) 57 IPR 145.

113 *Mateffy Perl Nagy Pty Ltd v Devefi Pty* (1992) 23 IPR 505.

114 *Blair v Osborne and Tompkins* [1971] 1 All ER 468.

115 *Stovin-Bradford v Volpoint Properties* [1971] 3 All ER 570.

116 *Stovin-Bradford v Volpoint Properties* [1971] 3 All ER 570 at 578, *per* Salmon LJ; *Dorans v Shard Partnership* [2003] Scots CS 313.

same approach is sometimes adopted in relation to designs and plans completed by structural engineers.[117]

[15.34] A licence may be created by way of laches or acquiescence. Certain acts of infringement may occur and if the right holder does not act promptly to obtain relief, the right holder may be denied protection because of the plaintiff's delay in seeking equitable relief. It may be that the plaintiff's failure to pursue the infringer is due to market circumstances – the *de facto* licensee may be acting in a way which is to the advantage of the right holder.[118] Conversely, the delay may be due to the absence of any real choice. In *Fisher v Brooker*[119] the House of Lords considered that while the plaintiff's delay of 38 years in claiming an entitlement to joint authorship in the work was extraordinary, neither the plaintiff's silence, nor his involvement in a transaction when withdrawing from the band, could ground an estoppel. The plaintiff's silence was due to a fear that had he raised issues of ownership at the time the sound recording was about to be released, he would have been expelled from the band and another version of the work released. The fact that Fisher had received no royalties since 1967 made it unconscionable to deprive him of his future copyright earnings. Declaratory orders requiring ownership to be noted by copyright collecting societies for the purpose of the distribution of future royalties were reinstated by the House of Lords.[120] In the context of copyright infringement, one English case provides a very broad basis upon which an apparent infringer may avoid liability. In *Film Investors Overseas Services SA v HomeVideo Channel Ltd*,[121] the licensee infringed the scope of a licence by showing films on a satellite channel over areas that the licence did not cover. The defendant sold decoders in areas outside the licence area, in breach of an implied term in the licence agreement. Nevertheless, Carnwath J held that the plaintiff could not complain because it suited the plaintiff to ensure that his films received broader distribution and exposure and that his delay in seeking relief was an acquiescence on the principle that 'it would be unconscionable for a party to be permitted to deny that which, knowingly or unknowingly, he has allowed or encouraged another to assume to his detriment'.[122] Similarly, if a licensor has committed a breach of warranty in using another's work in

---

[117] *Netupsky v Dominion Bridge Co* (1971) 24 DLR (3d) 484.

[118] *Dominion Rent a Car Ltd v Budget Rent a Car Systems (1970) Ltd* [1987] 2 NZLR 395.

[119] *Fisher v Brooker* [2009] UKHL 41.The Court of Appeal, at [2008] EWCA Civ 287, were held to have interfered with Fisher's property rights by holding it unconscionable that he should not be able to revoke his implied licence. Their Lordships thought this issue should be addressed in possible future litigation in the event that differences should cause Fisher to seek an injunction.

[120] *Fisher v Brooker* [2009] UKHL 41.

[121] *Film Investors Overseas Services SA v HomeVideo Channel Ltd* [1997] EMLR 347; *Masterton Homes Pty v LED Builders Pty* (1996) 33 IPR 417.

[122] Oliver J in *Taylor Fashions Ltd v Liverpool Victoria Friendly Society* [1982] 1 QB 133 at 151; *Gabrin v Universal Music Operations Ltd* [2004] ECDR 18.

creating the subject matter of the licence, equitable considerations may preclude an action for breach of warranty by the licensee.[123]

[15.35] There are some formal requirements in relation to licences that are granted where CRRA 2000 is the governing statute but these relate to the effectiveness of the licence vis-à-vis third parties rather than the validity of the licence itself. An exclusive licence,[124] that is, a licence that authorises the licensee, to the exclusion of all others, including the grantor of the licence, to exercise a right otherwise reserved for the rights owner, can have much the same effect as an assignment. If the exclusive licence is in writing signed by or on behalf of the owner or prospective owner of the copyright it will be binding on successors in title.[125] A verbal exclusive licence, on the other hand, like all other licences, is not binding on successors in title who are purchasers in good faith for valuable consideration without notice (actual or constructive) of the licence.[126]

[15.36] Where the author is entitled to receive equitable remuneration in respect of the rental right (part of the rights afforded to an author by s 42) and that right arises in relation to a film production, s 124 effects a statutory presumption of the rental right to the producer of the film, subject to any agreement to the contrary. The failure of the author to sign the agreement does not affect the validity of this assignment[127] and the agreement will be valid whether effected directly between themselves or through intermediaries such as managers or agents.[128] The transfer of the right does not affect the right to equitable remuneration, which is itself not assignable although it may devolve by testamentary disposition or by operation of law, in which case the right becomes assignable by the holder of the right.

[15.37] Licences granted by the owner of copyright are binding on every successor in title except a purchaser in good faith for valuable consideration and without notice, actual or constructive.[129] This provision also extends to licences of future copyrights.[130]

The licensing of use in copyright works

[15.38] Authorising persons to use a copyright work is of substantial benefit to the right holder and different methods of granting licences exist. At one extreme stands the practice of employing individuals to maximise the income that a work may generate. For example, the author of a literary work may engage a literary agent to negotiate the sale of publication rights with a publisher even before the work has been created, and even persons of limited literary expertise – celebrities, politicians, etc – engage in the business of touting memoirs and the like via an agent. The sale of future works to a

---

[123] *Walmsley v Acid Jazz Records* [2001] ECDR 29.
[124] See *Nomad Films International Pty v Export Development Grants' Board* (1986) 6 IPR 321.
[125] CRRA 2000, s 122.
[126] CRRA 2000, s 120(4).
[127] CRRA 2000, s 124(2).
[128] CRRA 2000, s 124(3).
[129] CA 1963, s 47(4); *Griggs (R) Group Ltd v Evans* [2004] ECDR 165.
[130] CA 1963, s 49(3).

publisher via a literary agent, even in the case of celebrated and talented authors, and the level of advance obtained, is viewed with great interest.[131] Sale and distribution practices in the fine arts field also can involve an artist agreeing to distribute works either via a dealer or some foundation, for a variety of motives. In some instances the right holder may engage an agent to control certain rights while employing others to deal with other rights. For example, in the area of dramatic works, the major British publishers such as Samuel French Ltd and Warner Chapell Ltd have distributed play texts and performance licences to Irish drama societies through agents in Ireland.[132] These arrangements, which involve close personal contact between the right holder's agent and the user, often represent the only practical means of ensuring that certain acts of exploitation by users lead to an income for the right holder but it must be pointed out that the market is somewhat haphazard and levels of income and efficiency in collection of revenues differ markedly from sector to sector.

Collective licensing

[15.39] The Register of Copyright Licensing Bodies[133] maintained under s 175 of CRRA 2000,[134] currently records the following bodies as being registered for licensing purpose:

- Newspaper Licensing Agency;
- Irish Visual Artists Rights Organisation;
- Association for the International Collective Management of Audiovisual Works;
- Phonographic Performance (Ireland) Ltd;
- The Authors' Licensing and Collecting Society Ltd;
- The Irish Copyright Licensing Agency;
- Irish Music Rights Organisation;
- Mechanical Copyright Protection Society (Ireland) Ltd;
- Newspaper Licensing Ireland Ltd;
- Ingenta UK Ltd;[135]
- The Screen Directors Collecting Society of Ireland;
- Motion Picture Licensing Company International.

The Register of Licensing Bodies for Performers' Property Rights, maintained under s 280 of CRRA 2000[136] currently has one registered body, Recorded Artists and Performers Ltd.

---

[131] Note the controversy surrounding Martin Amis and his £500,000 1996 two-book deal with Harper Collins, topped by a £1m four-book deal with Random House; (1996) Times, 17 December. *Proactive Sports Management Ltd v Rooney* [2010] EWHC 1807 (Ch) provides insights into image rights management practices.

[132] See 'Mister Copyright' (1994) Irish Times, 7 September.

[133] See www.patentsoffice.ie/copyright-bodies.

[134] See also SI 463/2002.

[135] Certificate of Registration expired on 31 August 2005.

[136] See also SI 306/2008.

Apart from bodies that are registered under the CRRA, it is understood that some bodies located in other jurisdictions do have collecting functions in relation to use of materials in Ireland.[137]

IMRO

[15.40] The most high profile area of third-party licensing is in the music sector. The right to authorise the public performance of a musical work – the performing rights – have traditionally been administered collectively, on behalf of composers and music publishers, by the Performing Right Society (PRS), a body established in 1914[138] to administer performing rights on behalf of the PRS membership. In 1988 PRS established the Irish Music Rights Organisation (IMRO) to act as the collecting body for the Republic of Ireland. The link between PRS and IMRO was broken in 1995 when the IMRO membership balloted to become independent of PRS, a move further enhanced by the resignation of PRS members from the board of IMRO during 1995. In essence, IMRO has the legally buttressed right to collect on behalf of its members as the result of an assignment of the performing rights by members to IMRO. The most recent financial statement in relation to IMRO appears in the 2008 Annual Report. Total revenue grew by 6.2 per cent to €40.1 million, with net distributable revenue of €34.4 million. Of this total revenue, some 92 per cent arose in Ireland. The breakdown of how the Irish-generated revenue was sourced by IMRO through its licensing agreements, set out in Table 2, is of interest.

Broadcast (excluding cable and satellite)	=	€9.0 million
Cable and satellite	=	€12.5 million
Public performance	=	€14.1 million
Online licensing (ringtones, etc)	=	€0.4 million[a]

a. Operated with MCPS: growth from a small base in 2007 stood at a 41 per cent growth rate.

Table 2: IMRO breakdown of Irish-generated revenue sourced through licensing agreements (Annual Report, 2008)

Some of the other collecting societies are less than forthcoming about the amount of money collected as part of licensing activities, often for sound commercial reasons, but this is one of the factors that leads many critics to question how transparent copyright collecting societies are.

[15.41] IMRO, as a company limited by guarantee, does not make a profit and it is committed to distributing all income to its members and to overseas affiliated bodies, after making deductions for administration costs. Distributions are periodic although concert promotion income is now distributed one month after the concert has been held. IMRO is currently engaged in developing a more aggressive approach to the relatively low level of membership income from certain other jurisdictions, particularly the US. IMRO, acting with the European Commission, obtained a WTO Panel decision holding that the business exemption found in s 110(5) of the US Copyright Act 1976, as

---

[137] Eg the UK Deign Artists Copyright Society – see www.dacs.co.uk.

[138] By several composers including Sir Edward Elgar.

amended, was inconsistent with the TRIPS Agreement, and a compensation award for European right holders has followed upon this decision. IMRO has also been a very vocal organisation in emphasising the importance of a stable and contemporary legal environment, especially in copyright matters, if the economic and employment potential of the Irish music industry is to be realised.[139]

MCPS

[15.42] The fact that IMRO regulates performing rights only on behalf of composers and publishers raises the issue of who regulates the right to reproduce the work, particularly the right to make recordings of a work. It should be recalled that under s 13 of CA 1963, the right to make a recording of a published musical work was given to anyone who was prepared to pay equitable remuneration to the right holder.[140] The rights to reproduce either the musical work itself on a record, or reproduce the author's copyright in a sound recording, are known as mechanical rights and these are administered in Ireland by the Mechanical Copyright Protection Society (MCPS). In essence, the members of MCPS are music publishers and composers and MCPS operates the mechanical right under contract, not assignment; these members deal with major commercial interests who seek to make recordings of copyright works. MCPS therefore deals with record companies, broadcasting organisations, video companies, film and advertising companies and agencies, record importers, indeed any person or body that wishes to reproduce a copyright musical work; even the reproduction of a musical work through door bell chimes or in a child's toy involve mechanical copyright. MCPS also has a substantial role to play in relation to mechanical reproduction abroad, and arrangements with affiliated societies in other countries are in place to allow collection and distribution to Irish members through mechanical reproduction that takes place abroad. Although MCPS, as a body, does not feature as a significant player vis-à-vis the Irish consumer, it is likely that, because digital distribution of works may give Irish consumers the chance to make digital copies of works (eg downloading onto a personal computer), MCPS may actually have a larger role to play in the years ahead. MCPS has taken a significant role in encouraging domestic law reform to counteract piracy.[141]

PPI

[15.43] The third significant collecting society is Phonographic Performance Ireland, or PPI. This company was established in 1968 by the leading UK and Irish recording companies and in effect represents all the leading multinational labels. This society administers the sound recording public performance copyright vis-à-vis all kinds of format – disk, tape, CD – in relation to public performance and broadcasting rights only; the reproduction rights are administered by the right holder directly via licensing agreements that allow the sound recording to be used in advertisements, etc. These public performance and broadcasting rights are quite distinct from the activities of

---

[139] See *A Strategic Vision for the Irish Music Industry* (Simpson Xavier Horwath Consulting); *Striking the Right Note* (Irish Business and Employers Confederation).

[140] This right was revoked in the CRRA 2000 but, in practice, continues to be administered by MCPS on a licensing basis.

[141] *Striking the Right Note* (Irish Business and Employers Confederation) Chs 3 and 4.

IMRO and this fact can be a source of confusion to the users of recorded music. The fact that two kinds of licence are needed if a hotelier or publican is to play recorded music on premises, allied to the traditionally higher tariff rate charged by PPI, makes collective licensing of music one of the most controversial aspects of copyright law in Ireland today. In the PPI case, however, the distribution of revenue amongst the companies that make up the PPI membership represents the scope of the right, for equitable remuneration is all the right holder may insist upon;copyright legislation[142] does not permit the right holder to refuse permission for public performance of a sound recording.

RAAP

[15.44] Prior to the 2000 legislation, in which performers are afforded neighbouring rights in respect of the fixation and use of performances, remuneration was provided to performers in respect of musical performances captured on a sound recording by agreements and ex gratia distributions by PPI and the Musicians' Union. A more formal system of collective licensing was made possible by CRRA 2000 and a collecting society, Recorded Artists and Performers Ltd (RAAP) has been established to administer the income right that arises when a performance captured on a sound recording is used in a public performance or broadcast. CRRA 2000 provides that PPI is required to function on behalf of both record producers and performers and distribute remuneration on behalf of these right holders. RAAP is responsible for negotiating the levels of remuneration to be paid to performers and ensuring that as wide a distribution of income as is possible can be made. RAAP also has an international role to play in ensuring the distribution of income to non-Irish performers for performances broadcast or publicly performed in Ireland, and vice versa.[143]

Miscellaneous

[15.45] In the area of film rights, which are normally held by film corporations, the statutory copyrights, at least in relation to reproduction and adaptation, are administered by the right holder directly. Public performance in the form of film distribution is also administered by the film company while private rental in the form of video is administered by specialist branches of these corporate bodies. In Ireland, many of these rights are protected in the form of an industry organisation, INFACT (Irish National Federation Against Copyright Theft), which is active in the area of counteracting video piracy in the form of importation and distribution of pirated copies, as well as domestic pirating of video products. INFACT also operates against those in the rental sector who distribute illegal products to the public. This policing role, carried out with the assistance of the gardaí and the Revenue Commissioners by using a number of legislative supports,[144] is generally regarded as being an area where new legislative measures are urgently required in order to strengthen the effectiveness of the law in relation to piracy.

---

[142] CA 1963, s 17; CRRA 2000, s 38.
[143] See www.raap.ie.
[144] Eg Video Recordings Act 1989 as well as the Copyright Acts and the Customs Acts.

[15.46] In contrast to the music industry, the traditional print media has not until recently been at the forefront of collective licensing in Ireland. Permission to reproduce substantial extracts from books, journals and other literature (when not within the fair dealing defence or one of the educational use exceptions) had to be obtained from the publisher, who often charged a tariff and imposed limiting conditions in relation to use. However, levels of compliance with copyright law in this sector have not been high and the use of photocopiers to reproduce both literary copyright works as well as the published edition typography copyright[145] has heightened concern about the extent to which these practices may prejudice right holders. The industry, through the Irish Book Publishers Association,[146] has established a licensing body that licences the use of portions of a copyright work on terms. That body, the Irish Copyright Licensing Agency (ICLA) has standard tariffs and standard licensing conditions that are to be observed. The Agency has been very successful in generating and distributing income that previously did not enure either to publisher or author, although as a body that operates on the cusp of fair dealing, exclusive rights, and educational or public interest use of copyright works, its opposition to unauthorised photocopying and scanning of books is voiciferous. CRRA 2000 has made it clear that most instances of photocopying will infringe copyright, and the ICLA has been recognised as a statutory body and has been charged with the task of administering a licensing scheme in respect of photocopying works by educational establishments.[147] The newspaper industry has also realised that the unregulated use of newspaper copy, through clippings services and others, as well as digital reproduction and electronic distribution, represents a substantial loss of revenue and, more broadly, a threat to its vital interests. The Irish national newspaper industry has established a licensing body to licence reproduction by the photocopying of newspaper materials.[148]

[15.47] The realisation that many right holders have not been able to obtain a full economic return for their copyright works, and the possibility that new forms of reproduction and distribution will create new markets for works, allied to the considerable benefits and economies that collective management of rights can produce, means that collective licensing of works will become more and not less important in the future. Further, the broadening of categories of right holders, particularly performers and film directors, will increase the prospect of concerted action by new right holders and this will no doubt lead to new forms of collective agreement or industry-wide negotiating practices, which will probably spawn renewed interest in collective management of rights. However, conflicts will also come into play and new mechanisms and compromises will have to be produced, if past experiences are anything to go by.

---

[145] CRRA 2000, s 17(1)(c).

[146] CLÉ Teoranta, trading as Publishing Ireland; www.publishingireland.com.

[147] SI 514/2002.

[148] In the UK, this is done by the Newspaper Licensing Agency which charges colleges, schools, press offices and businesses for the right to reproduce press clippings.

DISPUTE RESOLUTION

[15.48] The fact that most dealings in copyright works are the creature of contract law means that dispute resolution is often centred on the traditional court structure and that attempts to resile from agreements have relied on contract or contract-related doctrines. There have been a number of highly publicised cases in England where songwriters and composers of popular music have successfully challenged the effectiveness of certain management contracts, a prominent feature of which has often been the assignment of copyright in compositions to either a music publisher, a manager or management company, or a recording company. The legal basis for disturbing these contracts has differed somewhat, spanning the recognised concepts of restraint of trade, undue influence, as well as less firmly rooted notions such as inequality of bargaining power.[149]

[15.49] In some of these cases the plaintiff has sought to be relieved from the consequences of entering into one-sided publishing or recording contracts, in the form of a declaration that the contract is unenforceable[150] but it is likely that where such a declaration has been obtained, any copyright already transferred will not revest in the original author unless specific relief is sought along those lines. Even if copyright is revested in the composer, the court may, as part of its equitable jurisdiction in relation to restitution, allow the defendant some reasonable remuneration for work undertaken during the currency of the agreement.[151] It should be noted that while such agreements have been held to be in restraint of trade in appropriate cases,[152] one older Irish case holds the restraint of trade to be inapplicable to authors' contractual assignments, but this case is clearly too wide.[153] Other traditional concepts that have been successfully invoked have included undue influence[154] and breach of fiduciary duty.[155] Assignments made by persons labouring under the disability of infancy (in Ireland under 18 years of age) do not suffer the same degree of vulnerability[156] but the post-*Schroeder v Macaulay*[157] developments make this case, without more, somewhat unreliable.

---

[149] Eg *Zang Tumb Tuum Records Ltd v Johnson* [1993] EMLR 61 (Holly Johnson); *Silvertone Records Ltd v Mountfield* [1993] EMLR 152 (Stone Roses). See also the management contract decision in *Nicholl v Ryder* [2000] EMLR 632.

[150] *Zang Tumb Tuum Records Ltd v Johnson* [1993] EMLR 61 (Holly Johnson); *Silvertone Records Ltd v Mountfield* [1993] EMLR 152 (Stone Roses).

[151] *O'Sullivan v Management Agency & Music* [1985] 3 All ER 351.

[152] Eg *Schroeder v Macaulay* [1974] 3 All ER 616 (songwriter Tony Macaulay); *Clifford Davis v WEA Records* [1975] 1 All ER 237 (Fleetwood Mac). Contrast *Panayiotou v Sony* [1994] EMLR 229 (George Michael). Extended to sports stars and image rights managment contracts in *Proactive Sports Management Ltd v Rooney* [2010] EWHC 1807 (Ch).

[153] *Educational Co of Ireland v Fallon Bros* [1919] 1 IR 62.

[154] *Elton John v James* [1991] FSR 397.

[155] *O'Sullivan v Management Agency & Music* [1985] 3 All ER 351.

[156] *Chaplin v Leslie Frewin Publishers (Ltd)* [1966] Ch 71; *Stansfield v Sorereign Music Ltd* [1994] EMLR 224.

[157] *Schroeder v Macaulay* [1974] 3 All ER 616.

Performing rights and dispute resolution

[15.50] However, these cases and their complexity, as well as the expense involved in mounting litigation of this kind, help in some ways to point out the need for special methods of resolving disputes between right holders and others who deal in, or use, copyright materials. In the UK the Copyright Act 1956 set in train a tribunal system, the Performing Rights Tribunal, authorised to investigate complaints into the music industry and possible abuse of the power of collecting societies to seek payments in return for performing rights. CA 1963 adopted this initiative and, in introducing the Copyright Bill 1962 to the Seanad, the Minister for Industry and Commerce, Mr Lynch, had this to say of the need to provide control over copyright in musical works:[158]

> It is well known that the performing right in musical works is exercised by composers by means of an organisation set up for that purpose. This was probably inevitable, as it would be extremely difficult for an individual composer to keep track of all the various public performances that might be given of a work which he had published, and of which a copy could be bought in a shop. But the fact that the great bulk of what may be called popular music is within the control of one organisation, and that this music must be used by classes of persons such as cinema proprietors, dance promoters and entertainment organisers of various descriptions, has given rise to suggestions that there should be some means by which disputes between such an organisation of copyright owners and users of copyright works could be resolved. I may say that the use of gramophone records for playing in public is a similar case.

> The Bill, therefore, in Part V, proposes to set up an appeal body, consisting of the Controller of Industrial and Commercial Property, before whom cases of dispute may be brought. Royalties charged by an individual author for the use of his works will not be a matter that could be brought before the Controller but licensing schemes operated by an organisation of copyright owners can be reviewed at the instance of an organisation of persons requiring such licences.

[15.51] This appointment of the Controller, however, was not universally welcomed and Declan Costello TD (later to become the President of the High Court) was of the view that a tribunal of three persons would have been a better dispute resolution entity to determine these important issues of property rights.[159]

[15.52] Part V of CA 1963 proved to be extremely ineffective as a dispute resolution mechanism. In fact, the only utilised elements of Pt V were in relation to the public performance of musical works,[160] the mechanical right in relation to musical works,[161] Radio Telefís Éireann (RTE) use of music in a film[162] as well as equitable remuneration for the public performance of a musical work.[163] Use of Pt V was limited because of lack of clarity about the scope of several of the Controller's powers[164] under the legislation.

---

[158] 56 *Seanad Debates*, Cols 389–390.

[159] 200 *Dáil Debates*, Col 424, rejected because of the expense; Col 1460.

[160] CA 1963, ss 31(2) and 32.

[161] CA 1963, s 31(1).

[162] CA 1963, ss 31(4) and 48(2).

[163] CA 1963, s 31(3).

[164] See *PPI Ltd v Controller* [1996] 1 ILRM 1.

Even in instances where a reference to the Controller was validly made, the Controller had the power to refer the dispute to arbitration.[165] In fact, one substantial arbitration procedure between PPI and commercial users of recorded music in pubs and discotheques resulted in a decision on levels of equitable remuneration[166] but litigation in the High Court has followed upon this arbitration,[167] so even where the procedure has run its course the dispute may simmer on.

Dispute resolution and CRRA 2000

[15.53] CRRA 2000 introduces significant changes to the dispute resolution provisions found in CA 1963. For example, separate parts of the Act regulate the collective licensing of copyright works (ss 149 to 167), performer's rights (ss 266 to 279) and database rights (ss 340 to 354). In relation to copyright works, specific licensing provisions are in place in relation to licenses of right for sound recordings,[168] for reprographic copying[169] and cable retransmissions of works.[170] Individualised licensing of works is not within the statutory schemes because the Berne Convention for the Protection of Literary and Artistic Works (Berne Convention) prohibits the appropriation or regulation by the State of individual copyrights as being inconsistent with the relevant exclusive rights under Berne. However, the Controller of Patents, Designs and Trade Marks has significant powers to review proposed licensing schemes as well as schemes that are in place and may, by order, confirm or vary the scheme by reference to what the Controller determines to be reasonable in all the circumstances[171] and for such period as the Controller may determine.[172] The legislation determines what licensing bodies, representative organisations of users and aggrieved persons may seek to refer the dispute to the Controller. The power of the Controller to refer any reference so made to an arbitrator is retained in s 367 of CRRA 2000.

[15.54] While CRRA 2000, Pt VI sets out the jurisdiction of the Controller and in fact obliges the Controller to determine such disputes or references that are properly referred to the Controller within a reasonable period of time,[173] in practice these provisions are not working transparently at the present time. Several references and applications have been made under both CA 1963 and CRRA 2000. These relate to s 38(4) (licenses of right for sound recordings) and s 152 (licensing schemes). In the Annual Report for 2009,[174] the Controller only had one reference outstanding, having decided six cases in 2009, seven having been settled between the parties and two others being deemed

---

[165] CA 1963, s 31.
[166] *PPI v Discotheque Owners* (2004) unreported.
[167] *Carrickdale Hotel Ltd v Controller* [2004] 2 ILRM 401.
[168] CRRA 2000, s 38.
[169] CRRA 2000, s 163.
[170] CRRA 2000, ss 166 and 174.
[171] CRRA 2000, s 151(4).
[172] CRRA 2000, s 151(5).
[173] CRRA 2000, s 362.
[174] www.patentsoffice.ie/annual_reports (p 32).

withdrawn or invalid or closed. After a considerable period of delay, the Copyright and Related Rights (Proceedings before the Controller) Rules 2009[175] were made on 28 January 2009. The power of the Controller to refer, on a reference, to arbitration under s 367 was subject to a requirement that a decision be made within three months: s 367(2). This however, turned out to be unworkable so s 367(2) was repealed by s 48 of the Patents (Amendment) Act 2006.

[15.55] It is submitted that the current situation is entirely unsatisfactory and raises grave doubts about whether Irish law meets the requirements of art 49 of TRIPS and the need for administrative procedures to meet certain standards in respect of the costs of and speediness of remedies.

COMPETITION LAW

[15.56] Part of the controversy over music collecting societies is fuelled by allegations that these societies have monopoly powers that are being abused. Indeed, a suggested pro-competition law amendment to s 32(5) of CA 1963 was unsuccessful. It sought to give the Controller power to have regard to whether monopoly powers existed that were being abused; the amendment was lost even though the Minister of the day was clearly sympathetic to the amendment.[176] More recently, however, the Competition Acts have transformed the legal climate significantly.

[15.57] Section 4(1) of the Competition Act 2002, this Act having replaced the Competition Acts 1991 to 1996, prohibits and declares to be void all agreements between undertakings, decisions by associations of undertakings and concerned practices which have as their object or effect the prevention, restriction or distortion of competition in trade in any goods or services in the Irish State or in any part of the Irish State.

[15.58] Section 4(2) of the Competition Act 1991 provided that a licence could be granted by the Competition Authority where the Authority considered that an agreement contributed to the production of goods or provision of services, or the promotion of technical or economic progress, while allowing consumers a fair share of the resulting benefit, as long as the agreement did not impose on the undertakings concerned terms which were not indispensable to the attainment of those objectives, and did not afford to the undertaking the possibility of eliminating competition in respect of a substantial part of the products or services in question.

[15.59] Section 4(4) of the Competition Act 1991 empowered the Authority to declare that a notified agreement does not offend s 4(4) at all.

[15.60] The Competition Act 1991 and its 2002 successor have been modelled on European Community law, particularly (old) arts 85 and 86 of the EEC Treaty, now arts 101 and 102 of TFEU. The impact that Community law has had on the interpretation of

---

[175] SI 20/2009. On the issue of costs in relation to proceedings in which the Controller is involved, see CRRA 2000, s 364, and the Patents (Amendment) Act 2006, s 47.

[176] *Per* Declan Costello TD at 199 *Dáil Debates*, Col 1463.

the Competition Acts should not be underestimated. The Authority has given definitive rulings on a number of agreements notified to the Authority by PRS and IMRO. PRS/ IMRO sought to challenge the jurisdiction of the Authority in a number of ways. Firstly, agreements between PRS members and PRS were claimed not to be agreements between undertakings.[177] This has been roundly rejected on the basis that individual composers, lyricists and publishers (whether corporate or non-corporate) operate for gain and, as such, are undertakings and that resultant agreements on collective licensing represent agreements between undertakings. The Authority has also rejected the view that because Pt V of CA 1963 sets out a mechanism for resolving disputes, the Competition Authority has no jurisdiction. Notwithstanding these preliminary points, the Competition Authority ultimately resolved the substantive notification issues in favour of IMRO. In relation to the PRS standard assignment of copyright between individual creators and publishers, under which PRS members assigned performing rights and film synchronisation rights, the Competition Authority, in Decision No 326,[178] found against PRS on the ground that Competition Act 1991, s 4(1) was infringed. The market for musical works and the performing right therein was being restricted, distorted or inhibited by terms in the assignment, and related PRS rules and practices, particularly rules that prevented members from administering all or part of these rights themselves. Furthermore, the Authority impugned rules that prevented members from allowing organisations other than PRS to administer these rights, as well as deprecating the fact that standard licensing tariffs eliminated price competition for consumers. The fact that members could only be terminated at three-yearly intervals was also contrary to s 4(1). The Authority, while holding that collective licensing of copyright works has substantial benefits for both to the right holder and the public at large, could not bring these agreements into the licensing provisions in s 4(2). On this first point the Authority addressed the issue of whether collective licensing was the only way in which creators could ensure effective protection for their works, and while the Authority held that collective licensing was both efficient and beneficial to consumers, particularly smaller users who are thus able to avoid the substantial costs that would arise in negotiating separate licences, these assignments and related rules did not satisfy s 4(2). In particular, it could not be shown that the exclusivity provisions were indispensable to the effectiveness of PRS, the Authority noting that within the US, for example, licences could be obtained by members to administer part of their performing rights, on their own behalf, vis-à-vis individual users.[179] The Authority also ruled that the three-year membership tie was also not indispensable to the securing of the advantages offered by collective licensing.

Following on Decision No 326, a number of structural and organisational changes took place as between PRS and IMRO. In December 1994, IMRO separated from PRS

---

[177] As then defined the Competition Act 1991, s 3(1); see Decision No 5 of 30 June 1992 – PRS/ IMRO Transfer of Function Agreement. See now the Competition Act 2002, s 3(1).

[178] 18 May 1994.

[179] Eg concert promoters in relation to live performances by performer/composers of their own works.

and began to function independently as from January 1995.[180] In the wake of the decision to refuse to licence the PRS assignments, IMRO notified three assignments of copyright standard agreements in January 1995 between IMRO and writers, non-corporate publishers, and corporate publishers, respectively. These notified agreements, as well as the IMRO memorandum of association, articles of association and rules, were substantially different to those before the Authority in Decision No 326 and significant amendments were made to these documents even after they had been lodged in January 1995. The Authority noted a number of significant differences between these documents and the earlier PRS documents. Under the rules, the member could apply to obtain a non-exclusive licence allowing that member to administer all or any of the member's performing rights. The member could also resign membership after one year rather than at three-year intervals and, finally, the elimination of PRS nominees from the board of IMRO was held to bring these provisions into the 'indispensable' criteria set by s 4(2) of the Act. The licence thus granted[181] to run from 31 October 1995 for a period of 15 years, was to set clear the path for a number of separate but related agreements. Proceedings in the High Court to challenge these decisions were started[182] but later settled.

[15.61] While the PRS decision and the later IMRO assignment notifications reflect a tension between IMRO and some of the pop supergroups who pressed for the right to administer their own performing rights in relation to live concerts, the most political conflict in this area is between the collecting societies and commercial users of recorded music. This conflict formed the backdrop against which the IMRO standard public performance licence was tested by the Competition Authority. The IMRO public performance licence was attacked by bodies such as the Vintners Federation of Ireland through a representative body called IMUC.[183] IMUC and others alleged that a monopoly existed on the part of IMRO, that no effective appeal or review mechanism existed, that IMRO refused to negotiate individual agreements with most users and that charges were levied and raised unilaterally at excessive levels that did not take account of the user's ability to pay such charges. In the light of the changes made to IMRO's rules,[184] the fact that the user could play non-copyright music, the possibility of a non-Irish society granting a licence to a user, as well as the possibility that a competing society to IMRO could theoretically emerge, the Competition Authority granted a licence to IMRO in respect of its public performance licence.[185] One very significant feature of the decision, however, was the position taken by the Competition Authority on the main substantive objection to the licence provisions used by IMRO, namely, that

---

[180] Two PRS representatives sat on the IMRO board but this situation was changed on 31 October 1995 when PRS nominees were removed from the IMRO board.

[181] Decision No 445 of 15 December 1995.

[182] By members of the Vintners Federation of Ireland. See 'Publicans in Dispute over Music Rights' (1997) Irish Times, 25 February.

[183] Irish Music Users Council.

[184] Eg the possibility of individual right holders granting licences under the rules discussed in Decision No 445.

[185] Decision No 417 of 21 December 1995.

licence charges were excessive, unreasonable and placed a large financial burden on the business community. The Competition Authority, in effect, took the view that it did not have a broad consumer protection role to play:[186]

> the Authority's functions under s 4of the Competition Act are confined to considering whether or not an agreement 'prevents, restricts or distorts competition'. By and large, therefore, it is not the function of the Authority to adjudicate on the fairness of the terms of an agreement as between the parties, and, in particular, to arbitrate on matters such as prices. IMUC in its submissions also alleged abuses by IMRO of its dominant position. Such behaviour is prohibited under s 5 of the Competition Act. It is not the function of the Authority to take a view on any s 5 issues that might arise out of the notified arrangements.

[15.62] While not all the IMRO notified agreements were dependant upon the success of the notification of the standard assignment agreements,[187] Decision 445 cleared the way for the Authority to grant licences under s 4(2) of the Competition Act 1991 for the IMRO broadcast music licence with independent radio stations[188] and with RTE.[189]

[15.63] The activities of the MCPS, which acts in Ireland through its branch office of the Mechanical Copyright Protection Society Ireland (MCPSI), have also been the subject of a number of notifications. MCPS acts as a collection agency for its composer and publisher members and does not take an assignment of rights. However, in relation to a number of agreements between MCPS and its own members, MCPS and record producers, and MCPSI and music production companies for the schedule of fees relating to music production catalogues, for example,[190] a s 4(2) licence was granted on 8 October 1999 and the licence was declared to be in force for 15 years. Notifications in respect of MCPSI synchronisation and radio station licences have been held not to infringe s 4(1) of the Competition Act 1991[191] and in relation to MCPSI and a music production library side agreement a s 4(2) licence was granted for 15 years with effect from 7 October 1999.[192]

[15.64] Phonographic Performance Ireland (PPI) obtained a decision in respect of four notified agreements relating to the assignment by PPI members to PPI: in respect of performing rights; the PPI dubbing mandate; the licence terms made available by PPI to independent radio stations; and the PPI music video mandate. In each case a licence

---

[186] Decision No 451, para 28.

[187] Decision No 383 – IMRO and UK television companies and other copyright holders and Cable Relay and MMDS operators; Decision No 384 – IMRO and UK television companies/copyright holders.

[188] Decision No 449 of 18 December 1995.

[189] Decision No 456 of 21 December 1995. (The Competition Act 2002 abolishes the prior clearance mechanism but provides defences based upon criteria based upon principles enshrined in the legislation.)

[190] Decision No 569. Other users regulated by the decision include video producers, in-flight entertainment by air carriers, educational institutions, music production facility houses and companies.

[191] Decision No 570 of 8 October 1999.

[192] Decision No 573 of 15 November 1999.

under s 4(2) of the Competition Act 1991 was granted for a 10-year period commencing on 28 January 2000.[193]

[15.65] More generally, licensing agreements in respect of franchising operations have been made the subject of a category certificate/licence in respect of agreements between suppliers and resellers whereby one party grants to another the right to exploit a package of intellectual property rights, which can include copyrights.[194]

[15.66] The legal effects of these individual licenses under s 4(2) of the Competition Act 1991 are now somewhat uncertain. When the Competition Act 2002 replaced the 1991 legislation, provision was made for the saving of categories of agreements, decisions or concerted practices such as Decision No 528. Individual licenses, however, stood revoked on 1 July 2002. Nonetheless, it is submitted that the terms of these now legally ineffectual licences will have considerable value to a copyright owner who faces a challenge to the validity of licensing agreements, decisions and concerted practices under s 4 of the 2002 legislation. Given that the Competition Authority has tested such agreements, decisions and concerted practices by reference to the statutory criteria now found in s 4(5) of CRRA 2000, it is difficult to envisage viable challenges to collective licensing practices mounted by the musical copyright societies under Irish Competition law.

COMMUNITY LAW AND NATIONAL COPYRIGHT LEGISLATION

[15.67] The provisions of Community law apply to all intellectual property laws and although it is widely accepted that national laws granting and regulating intellectual property remain valid and dispositive in most areas, the growing incidence of Community sponsored legislation across the entire field of intellectual property, in the form of Council Regulations and Council Directives, hold out the prospect of a greater degree of legislative harmonisation than would have appeared possible 20 years ago. The application of TFEU to the exercise of national copyright is best understood within the broad context of Community law and industrial and commercial property rights – typically, patent, trade mark and industrial design law. The most obvious treaty provisions that could operate against national legislation conferring intellectual property rights are (old) arts 85 and 86 of the EEC Treaty, currently TFEU, arts 101 and 102 respectively. TFEU, art 101 invalidates agreements, decisions and concerted practices that distort or restrict competition within the Community; art 102 operates against rules and practices that allow an undertaking to abuse a dominant position.[195] Early decisions in the area of patent law[196] indicated that the mere exercise of statutory patent rights, in the absence of any evidence of an agreement or concerned practice ((old) art 85) or an

---

[193] Decision No 580 of 28 January 2000.
[194] Decision No 528 of 4 December 1998.
[195] In national law the Competition Act 2002, ss 4 and 5 are counterparts to TEU, arts 81(1) and 82(1).
[196] Eg *Parke, Davis v Centrafarm* [1968] ECR 55.

abuse of a dominant position ((old) art 86) could not result in conflict with either of those provisions.

Exhaustion of rights

[15.68] However, in drawing the distinction between the existence of an intellectual property right and the exercise of that right, the European Court of Justice (ECJ) indicated that it would be vigilant to ensure that rights were not abused by their exercise, but the current arts 81(1) and 82(1) of the TEU themselves provide only a limited power to control the fragmentation of markets, through the combined operation of national laws and contractual practices aimed at dividing up markets.

[15.69] In relation to the free movement of goods, however, art 30 of the EEC Treaty provided a much more interesting opportunity to counteract restrictions on the free flow of goods throughout the Community. Any quantitative restrictions on the importation of goods, and any measures having equivalent effect, are prohibited, and it is clear that national laws come within the art 30 prohibition. (Old) art 36, which provides an exception in the case of restrictions based on industrial and commercial property rights (*inter alia*) is a derogation principle that is strictly policed through the application of a proportionality test,[197] which allows a relaxation of the free movement of goods principle only in so far as it is justified for the purpose of safeguarding rights constituting the specific subject matter of that property.

The case that establishes the relevance of this approach in the area of copyright is *Deutsche Grammophon Gessellschaft GmbH v Metro*[198] (hereafter *Deutsche Grammophon*). In that case the plaintiff manufacturer of gramophone records in Germany sold copies of them to a French subsidiary company, who then passed them on to the defendant who proposed to sell them in Germany. German law gave the plaintiff a neighbouring right, which the plaintiff sought to exercise by obtaining an injunction restraining the resale in, or reimportation into, Germany, but the action failed on the ground that such a right could not be used to prevent the marketing, in a Member State, of products distributed by the right holder or under the consent of the right holder in another Member State, on the sole ground that the distribution did not take place on the national territory. A contrary conclusion would have defeated a central object of the Treaty, that is, the unification of national markets into a single market.

[15.70] This principle, therefore, will focus attention on the exercise of a right against the lawful marketing of goods within the Community rather than on the presence of restrictive contractual practices. First marketing of goods by the right holder, the right holder's agent or licensee, will exhaust, within the Community, any industrial property rights vested in the right holder.

---

[197] *Simminthal SpA v Italian Minister for Finance* [1976] ECR 1871; *Bristol-Myers Squibb v Paranova CH and Boehringer Sohn v Paranova* Joined Cases C-427/93, C-429/93 and C-436/93 [1996] ECR I-3457; *Merk & Co v Primecrown Ltd and Beecham Group plc v Europharm of Worthing Ltd* Case C-267/95 [1996] ECR-I 6285.

[198] *Deutsche Grammophon Gessellschaft GmbH v Metro* [1971] ECR 487.

[15.71] *Deutsche Grammophon* was applied directly to copyright in *Musik Vertrieb Membran v GEMA*.[199] Here an attempt by the German collecting society, GEMA, to levy a charge of 8 per cent in the form of a mechanical right royalty on recordings made under a voluntary licence in the UK, where a lower royalty charge of 6¼ per cent was imposed, was held to be unlawful. GEMA could not collect the difference between these two rates; when the right holder authorised the UK manufacturer in return for the lower rate of royalty, the right holder there and then consented to the Community wide distribution of that product on those terms. The notion of consent can become complicated where substantive rights differ from Member State to Member State. In *Warner Bros v Christiansen*,[200] Danish law gave the author or producer of a cinematographic work the right to regulate the commercial hiring out of that work. Christiansen purchased in London video-cassette copies of the film *Never Say Never Again* and imported them into Denmark. The Danish right holder sought to restrain the commercial hiring out of the film in that video-cassette format. The Danish High Court asked whether what are now arts 34 and 35 of TFEU applied vis-à-vis Danish national legislation, which gave the right holder the right to prevent hiring out of the works when they have been put onto the market in another Member State through first sale. The ECJ held that commercial rental was a significant commercial activity and that national laws regulating rental were not quantitative restrictions but measures having equivalent effect under art 34 of TFEU. However, the measure was justified under what is now art 36 of TFEU on the basis that if there was no method of regulating commercial rental, there was no certainty that authors and investors in films would secure an adequate return for work and investment. National laws which give collecting societies rights to collect supplementary reproduction fees, even if similar fees are not available under the law of the Member State where the work was first marketed, are also within the EEC Treaty.[201]

[15.72] The exhaustion principle does not apply to copies of works that are placed upon the market of a Member State because copyright has expired; in such a case the placement is clearly not consented to by the right holder, so, where goods were marketed in Denmark, copyright having expired, the importation into Germany of those works, copyright continuing to subsist there, could be prevented by the German right holder.[202] Cases of this kind served to persuade Member States to harmonise the duration of copyright but such problems will not automatically disappear[203] unless some other provision, such as the prohibition of discrimination on grounds of nationality, operate.

[15.73] In cases where the copyright is in the nature of a performing right the exhaustion rule does not apply. In *Coditel v Ciné Vog*,[204] Ciné Vog had a seven-year exclusive

---

[199] *Musik Vertrieb Membran v GEMA* [1981] ECR 147; *Merck v Stephar* [1981] ECR 2063; *Merk & Co v Primecrown Ltd* Case C-267/95 [1996] ECR I-6285.

[200] *Warner Bros v Christiansen* [1988] ECR 2605.

[201] *Basset v SACEM* [1987] ECR 1747.

[202] *EMI Electrola GmbH v Patricia* [1989] ECR 79.

[203] *Phil Collins v IMTRAT* [1993] ECR I-5415; Dworkin and Sterling [1994] EIPR 187; *Land Hessen v G Ricordi & Co Buhnen – und Musikverlag GmbH* [2002] ECR I-5089.

[204] *Coditel v Ciné Vog* [1980] ECR 881 (*Coditel I*).

licence to show the film *Le Boucher* in Belgium. The licence agreement also covered television transmission rights. The copyright holder granted the German television company, ARD, television performance rights in Germany. Coditel picked up the German signal and transmitted it via cable to its subscribers in Belgium. Ciné Vog sued Coditel *for* damages. Coditel pleaded that liability would conflict with what is now art 56 of TFEU guaranteeing free movement of services. The ECJ drew a distinction between the placing of copies of literary and artistic works onto a market and making a cinematographic film available to the public in the form of 'performances which may be infinitely repeated'. The Court reasoned that part of the essential function of copyright in a cinematographic work is to provide an income in the form of fees for the public performance of that work and art 59 did not therefore prevent the assignee from relying on copyright to regulate exhibition of that film. A similar position applies to the public performance of sound recordings.[205]

[15.74] While *Coditel I* and *Christiansen* lead to narrow distinctions in the form of different definitions of the specific subject matter of a film being exploited by performance (as opposed to commercial hiring of tangible copies) the exhaustion principle is very much confined to first sale of goods. In the follow up[206] to the Green Paper of July 1995[207] the European Commission had this to say about future legislative plans vis-à-vis distribution rights:

> The distribution right for authors should be harmonised with respect to *all* categories of works. Such harmonisation should provide that only the first sale in the Community by or with the consent of the right holder exhausts the distribution right.

> Furthermore, harmonised legislation should affirm that the principle of exhaustion applies to the distribution of goods only and not to the right applicable to the provision of services, notably not of on-line services. Such a measure, which would reflect the existing case law of the Court of Justice on the non-applicability of exhaustion to the provision of service, would enhance legal certainty across Member States.

[15.75] The geographical scope of the exhaustion principle is also important to note. Parallel imports[208] from non-EU countries are still capable of being excluded according to a significant line of recent case law.[209] The rules on national or international exhaustion of rights differ within the various Community Member States, and this issue, while not dealt with in GATT/TRIPS, is still a controversial one which surfaced in the December 1996 diplomatic conference on certain copyright and neighbouring rights questions, in the form of draft Article 8, which set out options for both national and international exhaustion rules. No agreement was reached on this matter. Irish law

---

[205] *Ministère Public v Tournier* [1989] ECR 2521.
[206] Com (96) 568 Final (November 1996) at 19. See art 4 of the Information Society Directive (Directive 2001/29/EC).
[207] Com (95) 382 Final (July 1995).
[208] Oliver, *Free Movement of Goods in the EEC* (3rd edn, Sweet & Maxwell, 1995); Rothnie, *Parallel Imports* (Sweet & Maxwell, 2003). Hays, *Parallel Importation under European Union Law* (Thomson Sweet and Maxwell, 2004).
[209] *KK Sony Computer Entertainment v Pacific Game Technology* [2006] EWHC 2509; *CD Wow* [2007] EWHC 533 (Ch).

certainly applies a national exhaustion principle in cases where the goods are not first marketed within either the Community or the European Economic Area.[210] This is illustrated by case law in 1992 when a Dublin bookseller imported from the US hardback copies of novels by best-selling authors, which had been published and sold in the US at heavily discounted rates, and were thus much cheaper than copies produced by the UK and Irish right holder. Injunctive relief was given against importation and sale.[211]

Exercising rights contrary to competition law

[15.76] Article 85 of the (old) EEC Treaty (art 101 of TFEU) provided a mechanism whereby a person affected by agreements and concerted practices that restrict competition in internal community trade may seek to have such agreements or practices invalidated. The ECJ, building on the distinction between the existence of a right and the exercise of that right, observed in *Coditel II*[212] that while a contract giving one party an exclusive right to exhibit a film may not itself infringe art 85, the exercise of that right may, in the context of the accompanying economic and legal circumstances, result in the restriction of competition. In consequence national courts must police licence agreements of this kind to prevent the creation of:

> barriers which are artificial and unjustifiable in terms of the needs of the cinematographic industry, or the possibility of charging fees which exceed a fair return on investment, or an exclusivity the duration of which is disproportionate to those requirements, and whether or not, from a general point of view, such exercise within a given geographic area is such as to prevent, restrict or distort competition within the common market.

[15.77] It should be noted that national courts in the UK and Ireland have been somewhat reluctant to find a breach of (old) EEC Treaty, art 85 although the point has been pleaded in a number of cases involving exclusivity agreements in the copyright field.[213] The European Commission, via its powers under (old) art 85 in the form of a licensing authority, has endorsed the view that certain types of provision such as no challenge clauses, non-competition clauses, royalty charges on products not protected by copyright, and certain kinds of title transfer clauses, may infringe (old) art 85.[214]

[15.78] The application of (old) art 86 of the EEC Treaty, on the other hand, has been extremely effective in judicial proceedings before the ECJ. The activities of collecting societies have been carefully scrutinised by the ECJ on a number of occasions in order to test whether the societies abuse any dominant position they may occupy by reason of any *de facto* monopoly they may enjoy in a given Member State. Membership rules and

---

[210] Apart from the 27 Member States of the Union, the Area includes Iceland, Liechtenstein and Norway. Switzerland has a separate arrangement.

[211] *Publishers Association v Gallagher* (1992) Irish Times, 25 and 29 September.

[212] *Coditel v Ciné-Vog Films* [1982] ECR 3381.

[213] *British Leyland v Armstrong Patents* [1986] AC 577; *Panayiotou v Sony Music* [1994] EMLR 229.

[214] See generally Korah, *Competition Law of the European* Community (2nd edn, LNUK, 2003); Keeling, *Intellectual Property Rights in EU Law*, Vol 1 (Oxford University Press, 2003).

distribution rules that may be arbitrary or oppressive may be open to challenge,[215] as may assignment provisions or provisions which restrict a member's right to choose another collecting society to represent that member outside the Community. Broader issues have also arisen in relation to third-party complaints that a collecting society has abused its dominant position by virtue of the levels of fee charged by it within a Member State. In the leading case of *Ministère Public v Tournier*,[216] the court held that a national collecting society which stood in a dominant position would be in breach of (old) art 86 when it imposed public performance tariffs on discotheques in one Member State which were significantly higher than those that would be charged by a similar collecting society in another Member State. Such differences could be justified if it could be shown that the society in question could point to objective qualitative differences in the level of service it provided to its members, as against the comparator societies in other Member States.

[15.79] The role of collecting societies[217] in the area of copyright is likely to expand and increase in the years ahead; it is a mistake to characterise these societies as anachronistic for new kinds of right and right holder – performers' rights, rental rights for performers and directors of cinematographic films, for example, will require collective licensing or exercise of these rights. Mechanical reproduction of musical works has survived the abolition of non-voluntary licences under s 13 of CA 1963. However, collecting societies will continue to be scrutinised by European Community institutions. In the most recent statements of European Commission policy on collecting societies,[218] the Commission has stressed the need to re-assess the management of copyrights in the light of digitisation and multimedia markets. Indeed, the Commission predicts that individual management of rights will become even less practicable in the future and that new central management or collective management structures may need to evolve. The fact that similar rights in Member States may be administered in different ways – some rights may be administered collectively in certain States but individually in others – will require the Commission to consider whether these differences create barriers to trade, which would impede the effective exploitation of rights across Member States. While the Commission has decided that the evolution of licensing schemes should be left for the market to develop, rather than insist on a legislative movement towards compulsory licensing or one-stop shop solutions, the Commission does not rule out Commission moves on regulating societies in Europe:[219]

---

[215] The Leading Commission Investigation in GEMA [1971] CMLR D35.

[216] *Ministère Public v Tournier* [1989] ECR 2521. See also *Lucazeau v SACEM* [1989] ECR 2811.

[217] See generally, Cohen Jehoram and others, *Collective Administration of Copyrights in Europe* (Kluwer, 1995); Hays, *Parallel Importation under European Union Law* (Thomson Sweet and Maxwell, 2004), ch 6 contains a useful summary of collecting society issues in EU law; Bellis, 'Collecting Societies and EEC Law' in Peeperhorn and C Van Riji, *Collecting Societies in the Music Business*.

[218] 'Copyright and Related Rights in the Information Society' COM (95) 382 Final: Follow-Up to the Green Paper on Copyright and Related Rights in the Information Society, COM (96) 568 Final.

[219] COM (96) 568 Final, pp 26 and 27.

As far as collective management is concerned, there are already indications for the need to define, both under the Single Market and the Competition Rules of the EC Treaty, at community level the rights and obligations of collecting societies, in particular, with respect to the methods of collection, to the calculation for tariffs, to the supervision mechanisms and to the application of the rules on competition to collecting societies and collective management.

However, the European Commission's decision of 16 July 2008 on anti-competitive clauses and practices (discussed in para **9.26** above) has injected a confrontational tone into this long-running debate in Europe.

(Old) Article 86 and licensing obligations

[15.80] It is established that (old) art 86 to the EEC Treaty (art 102 of TFEU) can operate so as to render the acquisition of an exclusive licence an abuse of an already dominant position.[220] In the area of registered designs the court has ruled that a refusal[221] to grant a licence to manufacture goods in accordance with a registered design is not *per se* an abuse of dominant position. The basic principles that operate in this area were stated in *Volvo v Veng*[222] to be that a motor vehicle manufacturer who refuses to licence others to manufacture spare parts does not as such abuse his dominant position, and that a manufacturer may assert a right to prevent third parties from creating products that incorporate the design without consent, which constitutes the very subject matter of his exclusive right. If that manufacturer was obliged to grant licences even for a reasonable royalty, this would deprive the manufacturer of his exclusive right. The court went on to state, however, that:

> the exercise of an exclusive right by the proprietor of a registered design in respect of car body panels may be prohibited by Article 86 if it involves, on the part of an undertaking holding a dominant position, certain abusive conduct such as the arbitrary refusal to supply spare parts to independent repairers, the fixing of prices for spare parts for a particular model even though many cars of that model are still in circulation, provided that such conduct is liable to affect trade between Member States.

Despite this balanced approach to the issue of art 86 and the emphasis placed by the court on the need to establish abusive or arbitrary conduct, the decision of the Commission and both European Courts in the *Magill TV Guide* litigation[223] has resulted in uncertainty about the scope of art 86 and the possibility that copyright holders may be prevented from exercising traditional copyrights such as the reproduction right, even where abusive conduct, within *Volvo v Veng*, does not appear to be present.

---

[220] *Europemballage Corpn & Continental Can Co v Commission* [1973] ECR 215; *Tetra Pak* ([1988] OJ L272/2).

[221] *Volvo v Veng* [1988] ECR 6211; *Maxicar v Renault* [1988] ECR 6039; Korah [1988] EIPR 381.

[222] *Volvo v Veng* [1988] ECR 6211.

[223] *RTE and ITP v EC Commission* [1995] FSR 530. See Walker [1996] IJEL 173.

[15.81] The decision in *Magill*[224] on old art 86 of the EEC Treaty has not been expanded in subsequent European case law. In *Tierce Ladbroke SA v Commission*[225] the Court of First Instance (CFI) upheld the decision of the European Commission in respect of the refusal of right holders to license the broadcasting of racing films for use in the applicants' betting shops. The CFI noted that, unlike *Magill*, the applicants were actually prominent in the applicable market (off-course betting shops) and, further, there was no real evidence that the right holders were actually in a dominant position in the market. However, the most serious application of *Magill* has occurred in the decision of the ECJ in *IMS Health GmbH v NDC Health GmbH*.[226] In this case a refusal to license the use of a copyright data management structure was the subject of an art 86 reference. The ECJ ruled that such a refusal may be an abuse of a dominant position if a refusal eliminates competition in a secondary market and the complainant can show that the intended use would have been to produce goods or services of a different nature from those offered by the right holders. In some ways this is a more sweeping decision than that of the ECJ in *Microsoft Corporation v Commission of the European Communities*,[227] discussed above in para **[13.28]**.

---

[224] *RTE and ITP v EC Commission* [1995] FSR 530.

[225] *Tierce Ladbroke SA v Commission* [1995] ECR II-2537. See also the essential facilities case of *Oscar Bronner GmbH v Mediaprint Zeitung* Case C-7/97, [1998] ECR I-7791.

[226] *IMS Health GmbH v NDC Health GmbH* Case C-418/01, [2004] 4 CMLR 28.

[227] *Microsoft Corporation v Commission of the European Communities* Case T-201/04 [2007] 5 CMLR 829.

Chapter 16

Infringement of Copyright and Related Rights

INTRODUCTION

[16.01] As a creature of statute, copyright infringement occurs whenever a person does something in relation to a copyright work that the Copyright and Related Rights Act 2000 (CRRA 2000) forbids. Right holders may seek to use some related cause of action, such as the law of contract, passing off, or a trademark infringement, and a successful plaintiff may be able to establish liability under a number of different heads.[1] However, in this chapter we are only concerned with infringement of copyright and performer's rights: separate attention is paid to those other issues in other parts of this book.

INFRINGEMENT UNDER CA 1963

[16.02] While the 1963 legislation has been repealed by CRRA 2000, the concept of infringement has not been altered significantly. Under both regimes the infringer uses the copyright work without the consent of the owner of the copyright, but the use in question must be proscribed by the statute. For example, reading a printed book will never infringe copyright, but photocopying the book may well be an infringing act. Where the work is an existing work, that is, the work was in existence on 1 January 2001, CRRA 2000 provides that the new copyright provisions apply in the same way that they apply in relation to works which come into existence after that date.[2] The most important exception to this relates to civil or criminal proceedings that have been initiated under the Copyright Act 1963 (CA 1963).[3] CA 1963 continues to govern those proceedings, so for such proceedings an understanding of the 1963 legislation is essential and is briefly set out here. Under CA 1963 copyright works were divided into Part II works and Part III works. This division reflects the boundary between 'true' copyrights, in which an author creates a work, as distinct from entrepreneurial copyrights where a producer or investor (often a corporation) may be the holder of such a copyright.

Infringement of CA 1963, Part II works

[16.03] Copyright infringement occurred in relation to literary, dramatic or musical works if a person did any of the following things without the consent of the right holder:

---

[1]   Eg *House of Spring Gardens Ltd v Point Blank Ltd* [1984] IR 611.
[2]   CRRA 2000, Sch 1, para 2.
[3]   CRRA 2000, Sch 1, para 3(6). For works covered by agreements, see para 3(7).

(a) reproducing the work in any material form;

(b) publishing the work;

(c) performing the work in public;

(d) broadcasting the work;

(e) transmitting the work via a diffusion service;

(f) making any adaptation of the work;

(g) doing anything listed in (a) to (e) to an adaptation of the work.[4]

[16.04] CA 1963 described these rights negatively as restricted acts. It should be noted that certain types of commercial activity were not regulated under the 1963 Irish copyright law (eg the rental or lending of a copyright work) and attempts were made by right holders to regulate these dealings by way of contractual provisions, with limited success.

[16.05] In relation to artistic works[5] the restricted acts in the 1963 regime comprised:

(a) reproducing the work in any material form;

(b) publishing the work;

(c) including the work in a television broadcast;

(d) including the work in a programme transmitted by a diffusion service. Many of these concepts were in part defined in CA 1963 but they can still cause substantial difficulties in their interpretation.

Reproducing ... in any material form

[16.06] In relation to literary, dramatic or musical works, s 2(1) of CA 1963 defined reproduction as including making a record or cinematographic film. It is generally agreed that the reproduction should produce something which can be discerned by the human senses, so prior to the implementation of the Software Directive,[6] it is likely that computer programs intelligible only to a machine were outside the concept of a reproduction. Reproduction, or copying, extends to expression of the work in other forms such as turning a novel into a ballet,[7] putting printed pages onto a word processor or computer,[8] using a photographic portrait in a newspaper,[9] or reworking newspaper articles into magazine articles.[10] The same is true of artistic works. So, using one artist's paintings in order to induce another artist to paint similar street scenes is, arguably, reproduction of the original work,[11] if the objective is to take the feeling and artistic character of the original. Infringement by copying of an artistic work, however, is much broader because the Act specifically provides that the two-dimensional reproduction of an artistic work which exists in three dimensions (eg drawing a sculpture) and vice

---

4 CA 1963, s 8(6).

5 CA 1963, s 9(8).

6 Council Directive 91/250/EEC ([1991] OJ L122/42).

7 *Holland v Van Damm* (1936) Macg Cop Cas 69.

8 *Waterlow Directories Ltd v Reed Information Services Ltd* [1992] FSR 409.

9 *Davis v Baird* (1903) 38 ILTR 23.

10 *Donoghue v Allied Newspapers Ltd* [1937] 3 All ER 503.

11 *Krisants v Briarfine* [1977] FSR 577. See also *Bauman v Fussell* [1978] RPC 485.

versa, are acts of reproduction. So, taking an artistic drawing such as a cartoon character and using the drawing to manufacture dolls and brooches of the character is an act of reproduction.[12] Furthermore, the taking of a three-dimensional object and the reproduction of that object (eg taking a sailing dinghy and copying its features) represents an indirect infringement of the original design drawings and is a reproduction[13] within the Act, even if the original drawings have not been used or seen by the copyist. In *Bookmaker's Afternoon Greyhound Services Ltd v Wilf Gilbert (Staffordshire) Ltd*[14] it was held that the display of a literary work, a greyhound race card, on a television monitor constituted a reproduction under the UK Copyright Act 1956, there being no need for the concept of material form to be given a restricted meaning. However, it is by no means clear that a digital representation of a work is necessarily within the definition of 'reproduction' and 'record' and although one Australian case decided that a CD is a record,[15] the court did not address the technological issues involved.[16] The *Gormley* decision[17] points away from digital works being within CA 1963.

Publishing the work

[16.07] This act of distribution, which in CRRA 2000 is perhaps more vividly described as issuing copies to the public, must be carefully regulated by the right holder, for once a copy of the work has been lawfully published, the right holder may find that the power to regulate further acts of distribution will be prejudiced[18] (eg in relation to musical works under CA 1963, s 13 and through the exhaustion of rights doctrine in EU law). CA 1963 directed that for the purpose of determining whether a work was published, no account was to be taken of any unauthorised act or unauthorised publication. The Act stated that the copyright owner's conduct or licence was to be the sole reference whereby publication was to be tested.[19] The place of publication was to be regarded as the place where the publisher invited the public to seek to acquire copies rather than the place where copies were received, otherwise there would be a multiplicity of places of publication[20] or the courts would have to ascertain where the first copy was received. A clandestine distribution to political sympathisers or friends is not intended to satisfy 'the public' and is thus not a publication,[21] even if the author's wishes are met by this kind of distribution.

---

[12] *King Features Syndicate Inc v Kleeman* [1941] AC 417.

[13] *Dorling v Honnor Marine* [1964] 1 All ER 241; *Allibert SA v O'Connor* [1981] FSR 613; *Plix Products v Frank M Winstone* [1986] FSR 63.

[14] *Bookmakers Afternoon Greyhound Services Ltd v Wilf Gilbert (Staffordshire) Ltd* [1994] FSR 723.

[15] *Polygram Records Inc v Raben Footwear Pty Ltd* (1996) 35 IPR 426.

[16] Works are 'represented' digitally: Negroponte *Being Digital* (Coronet, 1995) 14–17.

[17] *Gormley v EMI Records (Ireland) Ltd* [1999] I ILRM 178.

[18] *Turner v Robinson* (1860) 10 IR Ch R 510.

[19] CA 1963, s 3(3).

[20] *Francis Day v Feldman* [1914] 2 Ch 728; *British Northrop v Texteam Blackburn* [1974] RPC 57.

[21] *Bodley Head v Flegon* [1972] 1 WLR 680.

Performing the work in public

[16.08] This has been one of the most frequently litigated points of copyright law. Performing rights societies throughout the world seek to collect royalties in relation to the public performance of musical and dramatic works,[22] in particular, because the performance of a literary work (eg reading parts of a novel to an audience) is a restricted act.[23] In determining whether infringement has occurred, the courts stress that the vital distinction is between performances to a domestic or quasi-domestic audience, which do not infringe, as distinct from other kinds of performance, which do generally infringe. The basic issue is whether the audience come together as a result of some domestic or quasi-domestic tie. Even if this is so, as in *Duck v Bates*,[24] a case in which a play performed by amateurs to an audience of doctors, nurses, students and patients was held not to be in a place of public entertainment, the courts view the notion of a common tie as being somewhat restrictive. Membership of a club or institute and closed meetings of societies do not suffice[25] to make use of the work lawful. So musical performances by a band to members of a club[26] or to patrons of a hotel[27] are infringements and it does not make any difference whether a fee is paid for admission or not.

[16.09] The performance of recorded music to a captive audience of factory workers, even those engaged in vital assembly work in time of war, will still constitute an infringement of copyright, the courts emphasising that while the audience was gathered together for purposes other than entertainment this fact could not bring these performances into the domestic sphere.[28] Similarly, in *APRA v Commonwealth Bank*[29] the Federal Court of Australia held that the performance of recorded music on a training video, shown to a group of 11 employees outside of banking hours, was an infringing act. Gummow J held that the fact that the performance occurred as an adjunct to a commercial activity made such a performance likely to be regarded as a public performance.

[16.10] The courts here often emphasise that they are concerned to protect the statutory monopoly given to the right holder because of the diluting effect such performances have on other acts of distribution, particularly sales. It is no argument for the infringer to

---

22. See, for example, *SGAE v Ciudad de Vigo SL* [2001] ECDR 426 (Spain: televisions in hotel bedrooms); *Teosto v A taxi driver* [2004] ECDR 13 (Finland: music played in a taxi for customers).
23. But see CA 1963, s 12(4).
24. *Duck v Bates* (1884) 13 QBD 843.
25. *Jennings v Stephens* [1936] Ch 469.
26. *Harms (Incorporated) Ltd v Martans Club Ltd* [1927] 1 Ch 526.
27. *Performing Right Society Ltd v Hawthorns Hotel* [1933] Ch 855.
28. *Turner v Performing Right Society* [1943] Ch 167; *Performing Right Society v Rangers* [1975] RPC 626.
29. *APRA v Commonwealth Bank* (1992) 25 IPR 157. For performance in public of a literary work by display see *Bookmakers Afternoon Greyhound Services Ltd v Wilf Gilbert (Staffordshire) Ltd* [1994] FSR 723. The Premier League also charges bookmakers for using fixture lists for fixed odds betting – *Football Dataco Ltd v Brittens Pools Ltd* [2010] EWHC 841 (Ch).

say that performance in public may boost sales by increasing exposure of the work to the buying public.[30] Limited statutory exceptions were found in relation to the sound recording copyright.[31]

Broadcasting the work

[16.11] The broadcast must have been an RTE broadcast or a broadcast authorised under the Radio and Television Act 1988[32] if it was to be a protected broadcast under CA 1963. The notion of a broadcast, of sound or television, was based upon the Wireless Telegraphy Acts 1926 to 1988.[33] Broadcasting of a work was deemed not to be a performance of that work, nor an act of causing visual images or sounds to be seen or heard.[34]

Transmitting the work via a diffusion service

[16.12] The distributing of broadcasts via a cable service in the form of cable subscription services required the operator to obtain licences when copyright works were incorporated into broadcasts. CA 1963 specifically required the use of 'material substances' – copper wire or optical fibre, for example – and for the works to be comprised in the form of broadcast programmes or other programmes.

Acts of adaptation

[16.13] Acts of adaptation[35] – turning an artistic work into a literary work, or a musical work into a dramatic work, for example – overlap substantially with the concept of reproduction in any material form. Section 8(7) of CA 1963 defined an adaptation:

    (a)   in relation to a literary or dramatic work, means any of the following:

        (i)   in the case of a non-dramatic work, a version of the work, whether in its original language or a different language, in which it is converted into a dramatic work;

        (ii)   in the case of a dramatic work, a version of the work, whether in its original language or a different language, in which it is converted into a non-dramatic work;

        (iii)   a translation of the work;

        (iv)   a version of the work in which the story or action is conveyed wholly or mainly by means of pictures in a form suitable for reproduction in a book or in a newspaper, magazine or similar periodical; and

    (b)   in relation to a musical work, means of an arrangement or transcription of the work.

---

30 *Performing Right Society v Harlequin Record Shops* [1979] FSR 233.

31 CA 1963, s 17(8): *Phonographic Performance v Pontins Ltd* [1967] 3 All ER 736.

32 SI 101/1991.

33 See generally, Hall, *The Electronic Age: Telecommunications in Ireland* (Oak Tree Press, 1993).

34 CA 1963, s 2(2) and (5).

35 *Warne v Seebohm* (1888) 39 Ch D 73; *Holland v Van Damm* (1936) Macg Cop Cas 69.

[16.14] The notion of a translation did not extend to conversion of a printed work into an electronic format.[36] However, despite the early Irish case of *Turner v Robinson*,[37] the performance or reproduction of an artistic work by way of a *tableau vivant* was not an infringement under CA 1963. Following literary instructions in order to construct an item is not reproduction or adaptation.[38]

Infringement of Part III works under CA 1963

[16.15] The CA 1963, s 17 sound recording copyright, s 18 cinematographic film copyright, s 19 broadcast copyright and the typographical copyright in published editions of works provided by s 20, were the Part III works in question. As such, many of the concepts found in relation to Pt II infringements were applicable to Pt III infringements. However, it should be noted that restricted acts in relation to sound recordings included making a record embodying the sound recording, not to be confused with the author's mechanical right in s 13. The public performance infringement in relation to published sound recordings in CA 1963, s 17(4)(b) is only committed where the s 17 right holder refuses to pay, or undertake to pay, equitable remuneration.[39] There is no Irish decision on the question of whether a digital recording or remastering constituted a sound recording under CA 1963. It should also be noted that the infringement by copying of a broadcast includes a private copying exception[40] and that the public performance infringement provision requires the infringer to charge for admission.[41]

Secondary infringement

[16.16] The expression 'secondary infringement' was used to describe situations where the infringer handled infringing copies by way of importation, sale or letting, or by way of trade offered, exposed for sale, or exhibited, infringing copies.[42] Infringement covered not only copies that were counterfeit but copies that were legitimate but in the hands of the infringer in breach of the rights of the plaintiff. It thus applies to parallel imports that do not benefit from EU exhaustion rules, such as US published books imported into Ireland without the permission of the Irish right holder.[43] The secondary infringer must have, on an objective basis, known that the articles were infringing copies[44] and in practice problems of proof were side-stepped by putting the person trading in the goods on notice that the goods or packaging infringed copyright.[45] Secondary infringement also

---

[36] *Computer Edge Property Ltd v Apple Computer* (1986) 161 CLR 171.

[37] *Turner v Robinson* (1860) 10 IR Ch R 510.

[38] *Lambretta Clothing Co v Teddy Smith (UK)* [2003] FSR 728.

[39] *Phonographic Performance (Ireland) v Controller* [1996] 1 ILRM 1.

[40] CA 1963, s 19(5)(a) and (b).

[41] 'Broadcast ... by a paying audience': see s 19(5)(c) and (q).

[42] CA 1963, s 11.

[43] See 'Man Agrees not to sell US books' (1992) Irish Times, 29 February.

[44] *Infabrics v Jaytex* [1978] FSR 451.

[45] *Frank & Hirsch Pty v A Roopanand Bros* (1994) 29 IPR 465.

occurred in permitting a place of public entertainment to be used to mount a performance in public of a Part II work, subject to certain exceptions found in s 11(4) and (5) of CA 1963. Several of the provisions in s 54 of CA 1963 had direct relevance to secondary infringers all well as persons responsible for making the alterations in question.

INFRINGEMENT UNDER CRRA 2000

[16.17] In addressing issues of copyright infringement, the drafters of CRRA 2000 had to respond to legal, technological and commercial developments that were not anticipated in 1963 when the earlier legislation was passed. These legal considerations included the need to give effect to the Paris Act of the Berne Convention for the Protection of Literary and Artistic Works,[46] the TRIPS Agreement as well as a number of European Council Directives.[47] Because the texts involved required the State to extend protection in the form of identifying new kinds of work or enhancement of remedies, the infringement provisions had to be revised. Case law had also shown that certain dealings with works could not be regarded as acts of infringement.[48] Technological developments included the advent of satellite broadcasting and the digitisation of works, with Irish case law in certain instances demonstrating that infringement may not have been easy to make out under CA 1963.[49] New forms of commercialisation of works also proved to be a significant impetus for the review of copyright infringement. The electronic distribution of texts and images, not obviously covered by concepts such as 'broadcasting', or 'publication', was perhaps the clearest example, but ECJ case law also highlighted the fact that the commercial rental of works was a significant economic activity in the late twentieth century.[50]

[16.18] CRRA 2000 sweeps away the distinction between 'traditional' Berne Convention copyrights and the 'entrepreneurial' copyrights (or neighbouring rights) encapsulated in the Part II and Part III schema found in CA 1963. While most acts of infringement under the 1963 legislation will also be caught by the 2000 legislation, efforts to ensure that the legislation protects new forms of works and addresses acts of utilisation that were outside the 1963 legislation have been made by the Oireachtas. Many of those initiatives are based upon the EU Copyright Directives and the two 1996 Geneva treaties.

---

[46] On Ireland's failure to ratify this Convention before 1 January 1995 see *Commission v Ireland* [2002] ECDR 320.

[47] See the Long Title to CRRA 2000 for citations. Proceedings for non-transposition of those Directives have taken place: eg *Commission v Ireland* [2001] ECDR 174 (Database Directive).

[48] *News Datacom Ltd v Lyons* [1994] 1 ICRM 450. See now CRRA 2000, ss 371 and 372 and *Sony Computer Entertainment v Owen* [2002] ECDR 27.

[49] *News Datcom v Lyons* [1994] 1 ILRM 450; *Gormley v EMI Records (Ireland) Ltd* [1999] 1 ILRM 178; but contrast *Universal City Studios v Mulligan* [1998] 1 ILRM 438.

[50] *Warner Bros Inc v Christiansen* Case 158/86 [1988] ECR 2605.

Primary infringement

[16.19] Section 37(1) of CRRA 2000 provides that copyright in general is an exclusive right to undertake or authorise others to undertake all or any of the acts restricted by copyright[51] and CRRA 2000 stipulates that copyright is infringed[52] by any person who undertakes or authorises another to undertake a restricted act without the licence[53] of the right owner. The restricted acts are:

(a)   to copy the work;

(b)   to make the work available to the public;

(c)   to make an adaptation of the work or to undertake either of the above (a) and (b) actions in relation to an adaptation of the work.[54]

Copying the work

[16.20] This is known as the reproduction right. In general, the case law that has been decided under earlier legislation on the phrase 'reproduction in any material form' is relevant here[55] but CRRA 2000 goes further. Section 39(1)(a) provides that copying includes references to storing the work in any medium. So, electronic capture and/or storage of a work, without the permission of the right owner, will infringe.[56] Section 39(1)(b) also defines the scanning or caching of works (eg scanning onto the memory of a photocopier to generate paper copies or network transmission, or storage onto a personal computer) as acts of copying for the making of a copy that 'is transient or incidental to some other use of the work' will be an act of copying. Section 87 of the Act, however, provides a defence in certain instances, but the breadth of the reproduction right on this point is noteworthy. In relation to artistic works, three-dimensional reproduction of a work existing in two dimensions, and vice versa, are acts of reproduction.[57] In the recent case of *Theberge v Galerie d'Art du Petit Champlain*[58] the Supreme Court of Canada, by a 4:3 majority, decided that where an artistic work on a paper surface was lifted from that surface and placed onto a canvas surface no act of reproduction had taken place because this process did not lead to the multiplication of copies of the work. The dissenting justices argued strongly that if one work is 'rematerialised' this is an act of reproduction and the dissenting opinion on this point is

---

[51]   CRRA 2000, s 37(2).

[52]   CRRA 2000, s 37(3).

[53]   Licence is used in the sense of 'permission' rather than a formal licence.

[54]   CRRA 2000, s 37(1).

[55]   Eg *Reade v Conquest* (1862) 11 CBNS 479; *Ladbroke (Football) Ltd v William Hill (Football) Ltd* [1964] 1 All ER 465; *House of Spring Gardens Ltd v Point Blank Ltd* [1984] IR 611. Soundalike recordings do not infringe the copyright in a sound recording: *CBS Australia v Telmak* (1987) 9 IPR 440. On reshooting a photograph see *Ateliers Tango Argentin Inc v Festival d'Espagne* (1997) 84 CPR (3d) 56.

[56]   However, for electronic storage of a work of speech CRRA 2000 requires recording with the consent of the author before the work is in protected form: see CRRA 2000, s 18(1). This is very odd and could work an injustice in the case of covert recording of a work.

[57]   CRRA 2000, s 39(1)(b).

[58]   *Theberge v Galerie d'Art du Petit Champlain* (2002) 210 DLR (4th) 385.

to be preferred. Where the work is a film broadcast or cable programme, making a photograph of any part of an image will be an act of reproduction and the typographical arrangement copyright is infringed by reproduction in the form of photocopying. However, the decision of the House of Lords in *Newspaper Licensing Agency v Marks and Spencer plc*[59] establishes that 'the work' is the entire work, in this case a newspaper, and that selective reproduction of articles may not be substantial reproduction of the edition for the purpose of the typographical arrangement copyright.

[16.21] There is no doubt that when copyright material is transmitted via the internet, the person who copies the material by printing out an image, or by 'burning' a copyright sound recording, will infringe copyright in the image or sound recording, for example. This has been recently held by Peter Smith J in *Sony Music (Entertainment) (UK)Ltd v Easyinternetcafe Ltd*.[60] In this case it was held that this will be so even if the contents of the file, or the copyright status of the work, is unknown or unappreciated (eg because the person doing the copying is illiterate and cannot read the language in which the (literary) work is expressed). Whether internet service providers are also liable during the process of communication of the image over the network is governed by statutory instrument.[61] The liability of a person placing infringing material onto a server seems well established, although issues of liability of such a person in an Irish court if the server is located outside Ireland is less clear. *SOCAN v Canadian Association of Internet Providers*[62] appears to provide authority against liability being imposed here. But, in general, CRRA 2000, s 39(1), which defines an act of reproduction as covering storage of a work in any medium, and the making of even transient or incidental copies of a work, leaves no room for doubt on the issue of definition. Although the decision of Smith J in the *Easyinternetcafe* case was decided at a preliminary stage, the underlying issue is very important. The case also stresses that a purely innocent reproduction will be an infringing act. The most important 'defence' available in such a context is to be found in the European Communities (Copyright and Related Rights) Regulations 2004,[63] which amend s 87 of CRRA 2000 by substitution, by providing that temporary acts of reproduction which are transient or incidental and which are an integral and essential part of a technological process solely to transmit a work in a network between third parties by a telecommunications intermediary, or for lawful use, will not infringe the reproduction right. While the first part of this provision is only likely to be relevant to network operators, the second may be directly relevant to end users. The controlling part of this provision, however, is that the act of reproduction must have no independent economic significance, a factor that involves an analysis of both the impact on the right holder and the use intended by the user.

---

[59] *Newspaper Licensing Agency v Marks and Spencer plc* [2001] 3 All ER 977.

[60] *Sony Music (Entertainment) (UK)Ltd v Easyinternetcafe Ltd* [2003] EWHC 62 (Ch), [2003] IP & T 1059.

[61] SI 68/2003. Contrast the common carrier reasoning in the Canadian case of *SOCAN v Canadian Association of Internet Providers* (2002) 19 CPR (4th) 289; appeal allowed in part at (2004) SCC 45 by the Supreme Court of Canada.

[62] *SOCAN v Canadian Association of Internet Providers* (2002) 19 CPR (4th) 289.

[63] SI 16/2004.

[16.22] The reproduction right is also, in practice, extremely important in relation to photographic reprography of a work, particularly the photocopying of literary or artistic works. Again, CRRA 2000, s 39(1) specifically identifies reprographic copying as constituting an infringement of the typographical arrangement of a published edition:[64] *a fortiori* this will infringe any underlying literary or artistic copyright unless the photocopying is *de minimis* or within one of the statutory defences. Section 39 also re-enacts the idea that copyright in a two-dimensional artistic work is infringed by a three-dimensional reproduction, and vice versa. However, there are a number of important qualifications to this proposition. Where an artistic work consists of a building, a sculpture, a model for a building or a work of artistic craftsmanship on public display, it is not an infringement of copyright to, *inter alia*, print, draw, photograph or broadcast an image of that work.[65] Reproduction for the purposes of selling the artistic work is also permitted under s 94(1). However, recent case law suggests that the reproduction right is only infringed when more copies of a work result from the unauthorised utilisation of the work. So the lifting of an image from one physical support (paper) onto another (canvas) did not infringe the reproduction right.[66] Nor is the right infringed when copies of a work are incorporated into another work (eg mounting the plaintiff's advertising leaflet onto a competing leaflet).[67] A drawing created to show the location of stalls and utilities at a street market was held to have been an artistic work, the copyright being infringed when the drawing was downloaded and used by a trader in submitting an application to operate a similar business under a prospective lease of the same site: *Target Event Production Ltd v Cheung*.[68] Infringement of copyright in digital maps has been litigated in a number of jurisdictions in recent years with deliberate errors to detect infringement being very important[69] evidentiary factors.

[16.23] In respect of broadcasts and cable programme services,[70] the broadcaster and service provider continue to enjoy an ephemeral reproduction right, although the period in question is three months rather than six months as under CA 1963. Regulators are also able to copy broadcasts and cable programmes for their regulatory purposes although the precise identity of such a body is imprecise. While the Commission for Communications Regulation (ComReg) will be within this provision, what of non-statutory bodies such as

---

[64] CRRA 2000, s 17(1)(c). The issue of substantial reproduction, however, will often be moot: *Newspaper Licensing Agency v Marks and Spencer plc* [2001] 3 All ER 977.

[65] CRRA 2000, s 93.

[66] *Theberge v Galerie d'Art Petit Champlain* (2002) 210 DLR (4th) 385.

[67] *Benchmark Building Supplies Ltd v Mitre 10 (NZ)* (2004) 58 IPR 407.

[68] *Target Event Production Ltd v Cheung* (2009) 80 CPR (4th) 413. Warehouse plans which result in a building similar to dozens of others may still attract copyright: *Brookes v Ralph* (2009) 84 IPR 363 at 392.

[69] *Weetman (Beta Digital Mapping) v Baldwin* [2001] BCPC 0292 (British Columbia); *Virtual Map (Singapore) Pty v Singapore Land Authority* [2008] SGHC 42 (Singapore); Ong [2009] EIPR 17.

[70] CRRA 2000, ss 99 and 100(1).

the Internet Advisory Board or Office for Internet Safety? Archival copying is also specifically regulated under the CRRA 2000.[71]

[16.24] For users of broadcasts and cable programmes, a specific time-shifting provision is included in CRRA 2000. There is also a regulation in respect of time-shifting by establishments.[72] However, this provision has its limits because CRRA 2000 also provides that the copyright in a film, television broadcast or cable programme may be infringed by making a photograph of the whole or a substantial part of any image forming a part of the protected work.[73]

Making available to the public a work

[16.25] Under CA 1963 a number of public performance rights were ceded to a right holder. These have been updated in s 40 of CRRA 2000, that section providing that the making available to the public of a work includes all or any of the following specified acts. As an 'includes' definition, it is possible that other 'making available' actions without the permission of the right holder may infringe the making available right:

(a) making available to the public copies of a work, by wire or wireless means in such a way that members of the public may access the work from a place and at a time chosen by them (including via the internet). This provision specifies that placing works onto a server – acts of uploading – will be infringing acts;[74]

(b) performing,[75] showing or playing a copy of the work in public;

(c) broadcasting[76] a copy of the work;

(d) including a copy of the work in a cable programme service;[77]

(e) issuing copies of the work to the public;[78]

(f) renting copies of the work;[79]

---

[71] CRRA 2000, s 101(1).

[72] CRRA 2000, s 101(2), (3) and SI 407/2000.

[73] CRRA 2000, s 39(1)(d). But see the defence in CRRA 2000, s 102.

[74] On uploading, see *Universal Music Australia Pty Ltd v Cooper* [2005] FCA 972; *SGAE v Rafael Hotels* [2007] ECDR2; *Twentieth Century Fox Film Corporation v Newzbin Ltd* [2010] EWHC 608 (Ch); *Brown v McCasso Music Production* [2006] EMLR 26; *Disney Enterprises v Click Enterprises* (2006) 49 CPR (4th) 87. Uploading works onto a website generally involves infringement of both the reproduction right and the communication to the public right: *Universal Music Australia Pty Ltd v Cooper* [2005] FCA 972. This finding is the basis of Charleton J's judgment in *EMI Records v Eircom Ltd* [2010] IEHC 108. Contrast *Woolworths v Olson* (2004) 61 IPR 258.

[75] CRRA 2000, s 40(6); eg *APRA v Jain* (1990) 18 IPR 663.

[76] CRRA 2000, s 2(1); eg *Telstra v APRA* (1997) 37 IPR 294.

[77] CRRA 2000, s 2(1); *Shetland Times v Wills* (1996) 37 IPR 71.

[78] Known as the 'distribution right' under CRRA 2000, s 41(4); eg *Irvine v Rivero* (1992) 23 IPR 215. This right is important in relation to parallel importing of goods from outside the EEA: see *Euromarket Designs Inc v Peters and Clarke and Barrel Ltd* [2001] FSR 20; *KK Sony Entertainment v Pacific Game Technology* [2006] EWHC 2509 (Pat); *Independiente v CD Wow* [2007] EWHC 533 (Ch).

[79] Known as the rental right under CRRA 2000, s 42(6)(a).

(g)   lending copies of the work[80] without the payment of remuneration to the owner of copyright in the work.[81]

[16.26] The Copyright and Related Rights (Amendment) Act 2004[82] is a declaratory statute that provides that copyright is not infringed by the placing on display of a literary or artistic work, or a copy thereof, in a place to which the public has access. This amendment Act was thought necessary so as to make it clear that the use of the word 'showing' in s 40(1)(b) of CRRA 2000 was confined to audio-visual works and that the Oireachtas had not intended to introduce an exhibition right in s 40(1)(b).

[16.27] The right of the owner of copyright to regulate these actions is known as the 'making available right'.[83] Certain kinds of 'making available' are the subject of specific provisions. For example, the sound recording copyright is the subject of a licence of right under s 38 and the hotel bedroom exception in s 97 (which does *not* provide a defence vis-à-vis the underlying copyrights) is widely misunderstood. It should be noted also that the exception in respect of playing of sound recordings by clubs and societies for private purposes is not currently in force.[84] There are also exceptions in respect of the inclusion of a broadcast in a cable transmission service.[85] *Phonographic Performance (Ireland) Ltd v Ireland and the Attorney General*[86] concerned an application to have s 97(1) of CRRA tested before the ECJ for compatibility with the Rental and Lending Right Directive, art 8(2) and 10. Article 8(2), in particular, requires Member States to provide phonogram producers with a right to payment of 'a single equitable remuneration' when a commercially published sound recording is used in a broadcast, or for any communication to the public, the remuneration to be shared between the phonogram for private use and licenses of right (where compatible with the Rome Convention) insofar as the exceptions comply with the three-step test. Section 97(1) provides that it is not an infringement of copyright to cause a sound recording, broadcast or cable program to be heard or viewed:

(a)   in part of a premises where sleeping accommodation is provided for residents or inmates and

(b)   as part of the amenities provided exclusively or mainly for residents or inmates.

Section 246 of CRRA 2000 provides a similar exemption vis-à-vis performer's rights. The applicants isolated their complaint from instances where sound recordings were

---

[80] Known as the lending right under CRRA 2000, s 42(6)(b). For authors and performers, this is now covered by way of a public lending right via a new s 42A, inserted by the Copyright and Related Rights (Amendment) Act 2007 in respect of authors.

[81] The public lending right is administered by the Library Council and payments are made from monies voted by the Oireachtas: see www.plr.ie and SI 597/2008.

[82] Effective retrospectively unless proceedings were commenced before 26 May 2004: Copyright and Related Rights (Amendment) Act 2004, s 2.

[83] CRRA 2000, s 40(8).

[84] CRRA 2000, s 98. See SI 404/2000 and *South Tyneside Metropolitan Borough Council v PPL* (2000) 50 IPR 664.

[85] CRRA 2000, s 103.

[86] *Phonographic Performance (Ireland) Ltd v Ireland and the Attorney General* [2010] IEHC 79.

heard in parts of a hotel or guesthouse other than the bedroom and situations where the sound recording was available on demand or interactively. The complaint related to cases where television sets or radios receive a signal centrally, which is then relayed to guest bedrooms. As a matter of law, prior to the preliminary ruling, Finlay Geoghegan J found that Irish law exempted phonograms incorporated into a broadcast signal and piped into a bedroom from the equitable remuneration payment, observing that the exemption also applied to transmissions to hospitals, nursing homes, residential care facilities, prisons and other institutions.

[16.28] The applicants relied upon *SGAE v Rafael Hoteles SA*.[87] That case concerned hotel bedrooms also; but the legislative provision found in Spanish law was tested by reference to art 3(1) of the Information Society Directive rather than art 8(2) of the Rental and Lending Right Directive. The ECJ ruled that distribution of a signal to hotel guests via a television set located in guest bedrooms, by whatever means, is a 'communication to the public'. Further, the private nature of the hotel bedroom did not preclude art 3(1) from operation in such a context, the individuals using the room in sequence being 'the public'. The applicants sought to have the meaning given to a 'communication to the public' in *Rafael Hoteles* applied in a horizontal manner to the art 8(2) equitable remuneration right. Finlay Geoghegan J accepted submissions from the defendants that the court had to take into account 'the context of the provision and the purpose of the legislation in question'.[88] The defendants submitted that art 3(1) of the Information Society Directive concerned an author's right that originated in art 11*bis* (1) of the Berne Convention, and art 8 of the WIPO Copyright Treaty. In contrast, art 8(2) furthermore did not include a right to equitable remuneration on the 'making available to the public of a phonogram'. Finlay Geoghegan J concluded that it was necessary to make a request to the ECJ for a preliminary ruling so as to ensure that an autonomous and uniform meaning could be given to art 8(2) throughout the EU, remarking that the defendants had also submitted that art 8(2) should not be interpreted so as to allow a right holder to obtain single equitable remuneration from hotel operators in addition to the broadcaster (a 'double dipping' situation), particularly when the hotel operator remains liable when televisions are used in other areas of the hotel.

[16.29] Finlay Geoghegan J set forth five questions for the ECJ; it should be noted that the last two questions relate to physical or digital formats which can be played or heard via apparatus other than a television or radio (eg CD or DVD or digital streaming). These questions are:

(1) Is a hotel operator, which provides in guest bedrooms televisions and/or radios to which it distributes a broadcast signal, a 'user' making a 'communication to the public' of a phonogram which may be played in a broadcast for the purposes of art 8(2) of Codified Directive 2006/115/EC of the European Parliament and the Council of 12 December 2006?

(2) If the answer to paragraph (1) is the affirmative, does art 8(2) of Directive 2006/115/EC oblige Member States to provide a right to payment of equitable

---

[87] *SGAE v Rafael Hoteles SA* Case C-306/05 [2007] ECDR 2; Bateman [2007] EIPR 22.
[88] Following *SENA v Nederlandse Omroep Stiching* [2003] ECDR 125 at para 23.

remuneration from the hotel operator in addition to equitable remuneration from the broadcaster for the playing of the phonogram?

(3) If the answer to paragraph (2) is in the affirmative, does art 10 of Directive 2006/115/EC permit Member States to exempt hotel operators from the obligation to pay 'a single equitable remuneration' on the grounds of 'private use' within the meaning of Article 10(1)(a)?

(4) Is a hotel operator, which provides in a guest bedroom apparatus (other than a television or radio) and phonograms in physical or digital form which may be played on or heard from such apparatus, a 'user' making a 'communication to the public' of the phonograms within the meaning of art 8(2) of Directive 2006/115/EC?

(5) If the answer to paragraph (4) is in the affirmative, does art 10 of Directive 2006/115/EC permit Member States to exempt hotel operators from the obligation to pay 'a single equitable remuneration' on the grounds of 'private use' within the meaning of art 10(1)(a) of Directive 2006/115/EC?

Adapting a work

[16.30] CRRA 2000 provides that the unauthorised adaptation of a work constitutes an infringement of copyright. Case law determines that an adaptation consists of turning a novel into a play, or vice versa[89] or converting a work from one language into another.[90] More specifically, s 43(2) provides that the word 'adaptation', in relation to a literary or dramatic work, a film or sound recording, a broadcast or cable programme or typographical arrangement of a published edition includes: (i) a translation, arrangement or other alteration of the work; (ii) a dramatic work converted into a non-dramatic work, and vice versa; and (iii) picture reproduction of a work suitable for reproduction in that form. The section also provides that an adaptation of a musical work includes a translation, arrangement or other alteration of the work. An artistic work is also 'adapted' by including the work in a collage along with other works or by arrangement and other alteration of the work. An adaptation of an original database is defined so as to include a translation, arrangement or other alteration of the original database. An adaptation of a computer program is also defined so as to include a translation, arrangement or other alteration of the program, including conversion into different languages or computer codes[91] such as conversion from source code into object code.[92]

Secondary infringement

[16.31] CRRA 2000 draws a clear distinction between acts of primary infringement and those of secondary infringement. In essence, CRRA 2000 seeks to impose liability on persons who are engaged in the distribution of infringing copies of works by various

---

[89] Some acts of direct infringement may also look like acts of adaptation, eg *Anne of Green Gables Licensing Authority Inc v Avonlea Traditions Inc* (2000) 4 CPR (4th) 289.

[90] *Murray v Bogue* (1852) 1 Drew 353.

[91] CRRA 2000, s 43(3); *Microsoft v Business Post Pty* (2000) 49 IPR 573.

[92] Thus avoiding the impact of decisions such as *Computer Edge Pty Ltd v Apple Computer* (1986) 161 CLR 39. See, however, CRRA 2000, ss 80–82 and 106.

means. An infringing copy is defined as a copy, the making of which in the State constitutes an infringement of copyright, or importation of a work, the manufacture of which within the State would have infringed copyright.[93] This second situation is clarified by the Community exhaustion principle.[94] Section 45 of CRRA 2000 provides that copyright is infringed in a work where, without the licence of the copyright owner, a person does any of the following vis-à-vis a copy of a work which he or she knows or has reason to believe is an infringing copy:

(a)   sale, rental, loan, offering or exposing for sale rental or loan;

(b)   importation into the State otherwise than for his/her private and domestic use;

(c)   possession, custody or control, or making available to the public in the course of a business, trade or profession;

(d)   making available to the public (other than in the course of a business) to such an extent as to prejudice the interests of the owner of the copyright.

[16.32] Section 46 of CRRA 2000 also prescribed acts relating to the means whereby infringing copies may be made. Under earlier copyright legislation the possession of master copies ('plates' in the old terminology) could constitute infringing acts,[95] but these provisions go further in several respects. Possession of an 'article' could well include possession of a computer program that by-passes protection mechanisms as long as the putative infringer has the requisite degree of knowledge and that article in question has been specifically designed or adapted for making copies.[96] A 'stolen' computer program, for example, would come without this provision. Section 46(2) also addresses an electronic transfer of a work in the telecommunications system (eg file transfer within the State) to facilitate the making of infringing copies by others.

[16.33] Other acts of secondary infringement relate to the public lending of works, whether in places of public entertainment or not. Liability may be established against the person who permitted that place to be so used, subject to a knowledge requirement.[97] Liability may also be made out in respect of the supplier of any apparatus,[98] the owner or occupier of the premises who permitted the apparatus to be brought onto the premises,[99] as well as the supplier of a sound recording or file used in the infringement.[100]

[16.34] It should be noted that these secondary infringement provisions overlap significantly with other provisions in CRRA 2000 that relate to the technological

---

[93] CRRA 2000, s 44 (2)(a).

[94] CRRA 2000, s 44(3) eg *Deutsche Grammophon GmbH v Metro-SB-Grossmärkte GmbH & Co KG* Case 76/70 [1971] ECR 487; see generally Tritton, *Intellectual Property in Europe* (2007) ch 7.

[95] CA 1963, s 24(1) and (4).

[96] CRRA 2000, s 46(1).

[97] CRRA 2000, s 47.

[98] CRRA 2000, s 48(i).

[99] CRRA 2000, s 48(ii).

[100] CRRA 2000, s 48(iii).

protection of works and databases in Pt VII of the Act, as well as to criminal liability under ss 140, 371 and 376.

Authorising infringement

[16.35] The concept of infringement of copyright by authorising infringement by other persons was present in the UK Copyright Act 1911 but it sits somewhere in between the primary and secondary infringement notions. Under CRRA 2000 the infringement occurs when a person, without the consent of the right holder, can be said to authorise others to undertake a restricted act.[101] 'Authorise' has been judicially determined to occur when one person can be said to 'sanction, approve or countenance' infringement by another. While CRRA 2000 indicates[102] that the mere provision of facilities vis-à-vis the making available right is not itself an act of making available (eg server facilities), cases involving making available photocopying facilities from Australia suggest that the authorising infringement concept is quite broad.[103] Where, however, the defendant cannot control the infringement process (eg home copying of works) it may be more difficult to establish liability.[104] However, peer to peer copying of music by way of file swapping in which some intermediary role can be attached to a defendant, as in *Napster* situations, are likely to be actionable via the 'authorising infringement' concept. Most instances of liability involve situations where an employer or senior company official turns a blind eye to infringements by subordinates and can thus involve the inter-relationship with broader tortfeasor liability questions.[105]

Authorising infringement – The Filesharing Cases

[16.36] Where an internet service is a facilitator of copyright infringement, there is a possibility that some form of liability may be imposed upon that facilitator.[106] For example, providing a 'kiosk' service allowing access to internet files and 'burning' a CD for a user on a 'don't ask/don't tell' basis has been held to attract liability,[107] although the correctness of this decision in part has been challenged.[108] The most interesting line of case law has been provided by the Australian courts in relation to 'authorising infringement' on peer to peer networks. The first of these cases is *Universal Music Australia Pty v Cooper.*[109] Cooper provided internet users with a website that provided

---

[101] CRRA 2000, s 37(1).

[102] CRRA 2000, s 40(3); see, however, CRRA 2000, s 40(4).

[103] *Moorehouse v University of New South Wales* [1976] RPC 151; contrast *CCH Canadian v Law Society of Upper Canada* (2004) 236 DLR (4th) 395.

[104] Eg *CBS Inc v Ames Records and Tapes* [1981] RPC 407; *CBS Songs v Amstrad Consumer Electronics* [1988] AC 1013.

[105] *APRA Ltd v Jain* (1990) 18 IPR 663; *Foxtel Management Pty Ltd v The Mod Shop Pty Ltd* [2007] FCA 463; *Deckers Outdoor Corporation Inc v Farley (No 5)* [2009] FCA 1298.

[106] See generally Strowel, *Peer-to-Peer Filesharing and Secondary Liability in Copyright* (2009)

[107] *Sony Music Entertainment (UK) Ltd v Easy Internetcafe Ltd* [2003] IP and T 1059.

[108] Garnett [2003] EIPR 426

[109] *Universal Music Australia Pty v Cooper* (2005) 65 IPR 409; decision of Tamerlin J affirmed (2006) 71 IPR 1.

hyperlinks to other websites on which infringing music files were held. The website also provided information on music and lists of recordings, plus search engine facilities that allowed users to locate infringing files and download those files, as well as a facility allowing users to send hyperlinks to Cooper's website. Cooper made money from this operation by hosting advertising rather than charging access fees. While Cooper was held not to be liable for communicating the infringing files to the public – this was an unlawful activity that the remote websites were engaged in – he was held to be liable for authorising infringement in the sense that he had permitted others to gain access to infringing files. The notion of authorisation was held to have a mental element – knowledge or a reason to believe that infringement would take place – as well as a requirement that the defendant be able to control access. Cooper was held to have the requisite degree of knowledge as well as control, particularly in relation to hyperlinking. Third parties could have been denied access or required to link only to non-infringing files.

[16.37] The *Cooper* decision was followed by the landmark ruling of the Federal Court in *Universal Music Australia Pty Ltd v Sharman Licence Holdings Ltd*.[110] In this case the defendants provided Kazaa software to internet users who could use the program in order to access music files via remote access to those files held in the 'My Shared Folder' function on individual computers. The defendants knew that most files that Kazaa allowed access to were infringing but as their business model was based on advertising and maximising access to their website, the defendants had no incentive for filtering or disabling access. Indeed, their promotional material encouraged access and downloading. Wilcox J held that the necessary level of knowledge and control existed and ordered Sharman to adopt technical measures to block or disable access. In the event, Sharman closed down the infringing facility. It is important to note that in these cases the Australian courts required the defendants to do more than simply facilitate access by others. The defendants knew that their facilities (website, hyperlink function, software) would be used for predominantly infringing purposes. A direct commercial benefit to the defendants, in each case advertising fees, flowed from the facilitation, and positive exhortations to use the facility were made to users. While the infringing files were located elsewhere in cyberspace, a level of control over users was possible and a failure to exercise such control was at the core of liability as an 'authoriser'.

[16.38] The limits of infringement by authorisation have been set by Cowdroy J in *Roadshow Films Pty Ltd v iiNet Ltd (No 3)*.[111] The defendant was a large internet service provider (third biggest in Australia) that was alleged to have authorised its subscribers and other internet users to infringe copyright in audio visual works, principally films, via connectivity to the internet. There was no doubt that iiNet subscribers were downloading films without the permission of rights owners, but what was at issue was iiNet's liability, as an authoriser. The critical difference between the defendants in the *Kazaa* litigation and iiNet was that iiNet did not provide the means of copying to its subscribers; nor was there any element of exhortation or encouragement to infringe.

---

[110] *Universal Music Australia Pty Ltd v Sharman Licence Holdings Ltd* (2005) 65 IPR 289.
[111] *Roadshow Films Pty Ltd v iiNet Ltd (No 3)* [2010] FCA 24.

The technology employed by iiNet users was the Bit Torrent system, or Bit Torrent protocol, which consisted of software that would engage with torrent files identifying the film or music files being requested by the user, the .torrent file in turn locating and tracking the work requested by the user. Cowdroy J indicated that iiNet could not be said to have provided the means of infringement because Bit Torrent was the means whereby iiNet users infringed copyright. iiNet had no control of any kind over Bit Torrent and were not 'sanctioning, approving or countenancing copyright infringement'. After commenting that all iiNet did was to provide an internet service to its users, Cowdroy J said this stood in contrast to *Cooper* and *Kazaa*, where the respondents intended copyright infringements to occur, in circumstances where the website and software respectively were deliberately structured to achieve this result.

Cowdroy J cautioned against holding internet service providers liable for authorising infringement by others 'merely because it is felt that '"something must be done" to stop the infringements'. Cowdroy J went on to stress that liability for authorising infringement is 'based upon a fundamental assumption that the alleged authoriser is the one who provides the true "means" of infringement'[112]

The Irish Pirate Bay decision

[16.39] When the Swedish Courts convicted four defendants who operated Pirate Bay of the offence of assisting in making copyright content available to others (17 April 2009) the decision had important consequences in Ireland.

[16.40] Charleton J's decision in the *Pirate Bay* application is controversial. CRRA 2000, s 40(3) provides that it is not an infringement of copyright merely to provide the means whereby another person might infringe copyright. Section 40(4) however qualifies this immunity somewhat. The service provider will be held to be liable in the same way as the infringer if the right holder of the work concerned notifies the service provider that the services are being so used and the service provider fails to remove this infringing material 'as soon as practicable'.

In 2008, s 40(4) was used by EMI in an action against Eircom, the action being settled in January 2009. As a result of the settlement, Eircom agreed to implement what became known as a 'graduated response', or 'three strikes' mechanism which involved a process of notifying Eircom subscribers that illegal filesharing was suspected, the subscriber being given opportunities to investigate and terminate any illegal activity, the ultimate sanction being access rights being withdrawn. Following upon the publicity surrounding the Swedish *Pirate Bay* prosecutions and convictions late in 2009, EMI responded by seeking orders requiring Eircom to terminate Eircom subscriber access to Pirate Bay.[113] In these circumstances, with Eircom not contesting the EMI application, Charleton J granted the order sought. Whether s 40(4) is an appropriate basis for this kind of remedy remains an open question. Certainly, the legislative history of s 40(4) suggests it was a 'notice and take down' procedure applying to identifiable works. In a subsequent case in

---

[112] *Roadshow Films Pty Ltd v iiNet Ltd (No 3)* [2010] FCA 24 at para 381.
[113] *EMI Records and Others v Eircom Ltd* [2010] IEHC 108.

which Charleton J received the benefit of a more comprehensive debate between counsel, *EMI Records Ireland Ltd and Others v UPC Communications (Ireland) Ltd*[114] the learned judge has ruled that s 40(4) cannot be used other than in a notice and take down context and the earlier *Pirate Bay* ruling was said to have been incorrectly made. Charleton J reached the conclusion that Irish law does not currently allow a court to injunct ISPs caught up in p2p filesharing and that the 'mere conduit' defence is available to ISPs under art 14 of Directive 2000/31/EC. Charleton J was critical of UPC insofar as it was viewed as profiting from illegal acts by others. In contrast, Cowdroy J in *iiNet* refused to infer that .torrent files predominantly carried copyright materials that infringed copyright (the Bit Torrent protocol carries large volumes of authorised material), nor did the *iiNet* Court assume that *Pirate Bay* carried a majority of files that related to the plaintiff's films. Nor was there any direct commercial advantage to iiNet in having its bandwidth used to transfer infringing material, a key issue in *Kazaa* and *Cooper*.

[16.41] English decisions on the legal consequences of electronic file transfers have been generally confined to criminal prosecutions. The judgement of Kitchin J in *Twentieth Century Fox Film Corporation v Newzbin Ltd*,[115] however, has explored a number of ways in which civil liability may be established. This case involved the use of Usenet, a bulletin board messaging technology that allows persons to exchange text and binary content by posting these materials for open access. While Usenet has been supplanted by the web for most purposes, it remains popular with newsgroups. File transfer via Usenet newsgroups can be somewhat difficult, but Newzbin developed very sophisticated indexing and support services for Newzbin subscribers, allowing subscribers to create safe and reliable files containing infringing copies of films, software, ebooks, video games, etc. The plaintiffs brought proceedings which the defendants resisted, arguing that most of the Newzbin content was textual, not binary content, and that Newzbin was simply providing an indexing system for its Usenet subscribers. Kitchen J characterised these defences as misleading factually and found that Newzbin personnel were providing functionality to 'crack' Blu Ray formats, thus being actively aware of user infringements of copyright. Both the indexing facility and the file transfer mechanism were provided to Newzbin subscribers with knowledge that 'a very large proportion of the movies category is commercial and so very likely to be protected by copyright'. Newzbin could have fitted filtering software, but, as in *Cooper* and *Sharman*, Newzbin's commercial interests were advanced by ignoring copyright issues. Approving *Cooper* and *iiNet*, Kitchin J found that Newzbin was authorising infringement in the narrower sense of purporting to grant its subscribers a right to copy any film in its movies 'portofolio'.

In addition, Kitchin J held that Newzbin had participated with its subscribers in a common design to infringe copyright, rendering it liable jointly and severally with the

---

[114] *EMI Records Ireland Ltd and Others v UPC Communications (Ireland) Ltd* (11 October 2000, unreported) HC.

[115] *Twentieth Century Fox Film Corporation v Newzbin Ltd* [2010] EWHC 608 (Ch).

actual primary infringer.[116] Kitchen J also held that, following *Rafael Hoteles*,[117] the defendant had actively provided facilities to subscribers in the 'full knowledge' that its subscribers would infringe copyright. Newzbin had thus effected an unauthorised communication to the public contrary to art 3(1) of the Information Society Directive.[118]

THE BOUNDARIES OF INFRINGEMENT

[16.42] If a competitor does not copy from the work of a rival no copyright infringement occurs. Problems, however, arise when a right holder asserts that there has been a substantial taking, a claim denied by the defendant who must attribute any objective similarity between the works to coincidence. A defence of coincidental creation is effective where it can be made out, but it can be difficult to sustain. Witness the action in the courts of the US[119] where George Harrison was held to have infringed copyright when his song, 'My Sweet Lord' involved a substantial taking from The Chiffons's earlier hit, 'He's So Fine'. More recently, controversies broke out[120] over the Irish 1995 Eurovision entry 'Dreamin', when substantial similarities were detected with the Julie Felix seventies hit, 'Moonlighting'. The same scenario reappeared in 1996 with allegations that the British Eurovision song had plagiarised an earlier work[121] and the Irish 2003 Eurovision entry was again at the centre of plagiarism allegations.[122] Such allegations can be dangerous, however, leading to countersuits.[123] Literary figures such as the Duchess of York and Ian McEwan have also produced works that have been thought to bear similarities with earlier works in relation to plot structure, but plot structure in a literary work is eminently open to coincidental creation. Of course there may be an entirely simple explanation for the similarity of the works in question: one party may be hoping to free-ride on the popularity of another work such as the 'Harry Potter' phenomenon.[124]

In the *Da Vinci Code* case,[125] the question was whether Dan Brown had taken substantial parts from a book, described as 'a work of historical conjecture' by its authors, when writing his 'thriller', *The Da Vinci Code*. The claim was related to

---

[116] Applying, *inter alia*, *CBS Songs Ltd v Amstrad Consumer Electronics plc* [1988] AC 1013; *Unilever plc v Gillette (UK) Ltd* [1989] RPC 583; *Sabaf SpA v MFI Furniture Centres Ltd* [2003] RPC 264.

[117] *SGAE v Rafael Hoteles SA* Case C-306/5 [2006] ECR I-11519 [2007] ECDR 2; Bateman [2007] EIPR 22.

[118] Directive 2001/29/EC ([2001] OJ L167/10).

[119] *ABKCO Music Inc v Harrisongs Music* 722 F 2d 988 (1983).

[120] See (1995) Irish Times, 6 May.

[121] 'Dispute over British Eurovision Song' (1996) Irish Times, 8 March.

[122] The EBU, however, ruled the entry original for competition purposes (2003) Irish Times, 21 March.

[123] See 'Lloyd-Webber Sues Songwriter for $78' (1996) The Times, 5 June.

[124] *Rowling v Uitgeverij Byblos BV* [2003] ECDR 23, affirmed at [2004] ECDR 61. Not all cases, however, involve parasitic practices; an author may also use copyright to maintain control over a work when the defendant has in turn sought to create new content: see Sanders [2009] EIPR 45 (*RDR Brooks* Case).

[125] *Baigent v Random House Group Ltd* [2007] EWCA Civ 247.

allegations of copying the central theme in the plaintiffs' work, and based on some similarities in language in certain places of the two texts. The claim failed because the plaintiffs were unable to identify what the central theme in their book was, and the case established that the rights owner must be able to identify what the claim to copyright consists of, and how it has been infringed.[126] Any central theme that existed in the plaintiffs' work in this case existed at the level of ideas, abstraction, or (non-protectable) fact. While Dan Brown had clearly taken themes from the plaintiffs' book, as well as other sources there was no substantial taking.

[16.43] The leading English case dealing with this issue is the Court of Appeal decision in *Francis Day & Hunter Ltd v Bron*.[127] The plaintiff alleged infringement of a musical copyright by the defendant who wrote another song which, the defendant conceded, had similarities with the plaintiff's song. In considering whether infringement has occurred in a literary, dramatic or musical work the Court of Appeal held that two elements must be present: sufficient objective similarity between the copyright work and the later 'infringing' work or a substantial portion thereof, and evidence that the copyright work is the source from which the infringing work is derived – a causal link. Intention, or knowledge, is not relevant to the issue of infringement although these factors may be considered later in relation to the award of damages. The Court of Appeal endorsed Wilberforce J's assessment of the three principal conclusions a court may reach in an infringement action, namely, conscious copying, unconscious copying, and coincidence. The first two conclusions represent infringement while the third does not. After eliminating conscious copying in the case at bar, the Court of Appeal endorsed Wilberforce J's assessment of the factors that are relevant to the enquiry into unconscious copying: these are the degree of familiarity with the plaintiff's work, the character of the work and its qualities in impressing on the mind of the listener, objective similarity, the inherent probability of coincidence, ie the influence of other factors on the mind of the defendant, and the defendant's evidence on influences upon the defendant's work.[128] Without any evidence of the defendant having had access to the plaintiff's work,[129] it will be difficult for a court to avoid the conclusion that two people each had the same general idea as the starting point for developing a copyright work: *Obisanya v Ellis*.[130]

[16.44] Many of the factors are also relevant to an enquiry into the likelihood that the defendant consciously copied the plaintiff's work. However, unless there has been a substantial taking from the original work, no infringement can be made out. If the element of the work taken is commonplace or itself derivative then infringement will not

---

[126] See also *Henkel KgaA v Holdfast* [2006] NZSC 102; *Electroquip Ltd v Craigco Ltd* [2008] NZHC 1371.

[127] *Francis Day & Hunter Ltd v Bron* [1963] Ch 587. Contrast *Malmstedt v EMI Records Ltd* [2004] ECDR 162.

[128] *Per* Willmer LJ in *Bron* [1963] Ch 587 at 614.

[129] See McKillop, *The Spinster and the Prophet* (2002), discussing the HG Wells plagiarism case of *Deeks v Wells* [1931] 4 DLR 533 (PC appeal dismissed).

[130] *Obisanya v Ellis* [2008] EWHC 884 (Ch) (similarities in the title of a work not proof of infringement).

occur, while if the plaintiff's work is original, a small percentage of the total work will be a substantial taking, particularly if memorable or distinctive.[131]

COPYRIGHT INFRINGEMENT – THE NATURE OF THE RESTRICTED ACT

[16.45] For an infringement to be made out by a right holder, it will be necessary to establish that the infringer has committed the infringing act – it is not enough to show that the defendant has acted in a way that strikes at the economic integrity of the right holder's investment. In *News Datacom Ltd v Lyons*,[132] the defendant manufactured computer smart cards that decoded the plaintiff's encoded broadcast signal of SKY television subscription channels. In an infringement action seeking interlocutory relief, the plaintiff asserted that in order to achieve this result the defendant must have reproduced the algorithm, in whole or in part, that was contained in the smart card. Flood J, however, was faced with evidence only that the defendant's card could achieve the same result as the plaintiff's and, on this basis, functional similarity was not enough to establish the probable 'fact' of copying. Copyright law is not intended to deter competition but, rather, it is intended to prevent others from taking a competitive advantage from the efforts and talents of others by copying the tangible products of original skill, talent or innovation. If parasitic copying were facilitated the law would be tolerating anti-competitive practices. The defendant, in *News Datacom*, may not have copied the algorithm but he certainly embarked upon a trading practice that was regarded by the plaintiff as unfair competition, which is not an independently actionable common law tort in Ireland.

[16.46] Volume is not a determining factor: small snatches of a song or novel – even one line from a poem may be protectable, while titles, no matter how distinctive, are not protected.[133]

[16.47] The case of *Ravenscroft v Herbert*[134] has proved influential in filtering some of the factors necessary to examine substantial infringement. Whitford J approved counsel, Mr Laddie's, observations on the principal factors which are relevant:[135]

> First the volume of the material taken, bearing in mind that quality is more important than quantity; secondly, how much of such material is the subject matter of copyright and how much is not; thirdly, whether there has been an animus furandi on the part of the defendant; this was treated by Page Wood VC in *Jarrold v Houlston* (1857) 3 K&J 708 as equivalent to an intention on the part of the defendant to take for the purpose of saving

---

[131] *Hawkes & Sons v Paramount Film Service* [1934] Ch 593. In *Campbell v Acuff-Rose Music Inc* 510 US 569 (1994) (Pretty Woman) only the title and opening bass riff were taken but this was clearly a substantial taking. Other examples come to mind. The opening chords of Eric Clapton's 'Layla' are really the only memorable part of the composition. Contrast *Malmstedt v EMI Records Ltd* [2004] ECDR 162.

[132] *News Datacom Ltd v Lyons* [1994] 1 ILRM 450; see *British Sky Broadcasting Group Ltd v Lyons* [1995] FSR 357 for a follow-up case in the UK.

[133] *Francis Day & Hunter Ltd v Twentieth Century Fox* [1939] 4 All ER 192.

[134] *Ravenscroft v Herbert* [1980] RPC 193.

[135] *Ravenscroft v Herbert* [1980] RPC 193 at 201.

himself labour; fourthly, the extent to which the plaintiff's and the defendant's book are competing works.

Volume of work taken

[16.48] This is always a question of fact and although both quality and quantity are relevant, the quality of the taking seems more important. In *CCH Canadian Ltd v Law Society of Upper Canada*,[136] the Canadian Federal Court of Appeal provided valuable guidelines on the qualitative and quantitative aspects of delimiting substantial taking from insubstantial taking.[137] Photocopying an entire work is a substantial taking; photocopying the index of a volume is a substantial taking of the volume because it is an integral part of the work. Photocopying a lot of unimportant pages in a volume may not infringe while copying a few important pages will infringe.[138] A headnote to a reported court decision will, qualitatively, be a substantial part of the reported decision. However, if the work is a newspaper and the copyright that is being allegedly breached is the copyright in the typographical arrangement of the edition, mere reproduction of an entire article or a number of articles may not infringe the copyright in the edition – this appears to be a predominantly quantitative issue.[139] In the case of literary works, in particular, it is often possible for the parties to rely on expert testimony from academic[140] or publishing[141] specialists. Expert testimony will be particularly important in infringement actions involving computer programs but the cases tend to reveal that there is ample room for fundamental disagreement between expert testimony on this point in particular.[142] However, the most significant problem in this field is raised by one of definition. Copyright protects the creator of forms of expression or articulation. Copyright does not protect ideas *per se*, such as ideas that have not been expressed in a protectable form previously, or ideas that by their nature are limited to one form of articulation. The judges, however, echo academic commentators by saying that while this is a truism, the boundary between protectable expression and a non-protectable idea depends on what is meant by an idea. The level of abstraction at which the idea is pitched is of particular significance here. If an idea is capable only of one form of expression then actual copying of that form of expression will need to be shown.[143] The leading case on this point involved an artistic copyright infringement whereby a hand

---

[136] *CCH Canadian Ltd v Law Society of Upper Canada* (2002) 18 CPR (4th) 161. On appeal, the Supreme Court of Canada did not have to consider these points: 236 DLR (4th) 396.

[137] See also *Silletoe v McGrath Hill Book Co* [1983] FSR 545.

[138] *Neale v Harmer* (1897) 13 TLR 209 (use of three architectural drawings from 200 held to infringe).

[139] *Newspaper Licensing Agency Ltd v Marks and Spencer plc* [2002] RPC 225.

[140] *International Writing Institute v Rimila Property Ltd* (1993) 27 IPR 546; *House of Spring Gardens Ltd v Point Blank Ltd* [1984] IR 611.

[141] *Silletoe v McGraw Hill Book Co* [1983] FSR 545.

[142] See *John Richardson Computers Ltd v Flanders* [1993] FSR 497 and *Ibcos Computers Ltd v Barclays Finance Ltd* [1994] FSR 275.

[143] *Kenrick v Lawrence* (1890) 25 QBD 99, criticised in *Ibcos Computers Ltd v Barclays Finance Ltd* [1994] FSR 275.

pointed to a square on an electoral ballot paper indicating how to cast a vote. Wills J said that such an idea is the common property of the world:[144]

> the mere choice of subject can rarely, if ever, confer upon the author of the drawing an exclusive right to represent the subject ... something special in the way of artistic treatment even of this simple operation, if it existed, might be the subject of copyright but nothing of the kind has been suggested.

[16.49] In the field of artistic copyright the essence of such a work is said to be that which is 'visually significant'.[145] It should be noted that the idea/expression dichotomy may also be relevant here: the plaintiff who puts forward a drawing as the basis of an infringement action may fail if the court thinks the drawing fails clearly to identify distinguishing features other than commonplace ones: *Gleeson and Gleeson Shirt Co Ltd v HR Denne Ltd*.[146] The leading case on infringement of artistic copyright is now *Designers Guild Ltd v Russell Williams (Textiles) Ltd*.[147] In this case, which involved the copying of a textile design, the House of Lords indicated that where it is found that the defendant has copied the plaintiff's design, in most cases this will also dispose of the issue of whether the defendant has taken a substantial part. It should also be noted that in artistic copyright cases the infringement test is broad. Copying may take place via the three-dimensional reproduction of a two-dimensional work (eg the defendant manufacturing goods that objectively correspond with the plaintiff's design drawings) even if there is no evidence that the defendant had access to those drawings as distinct from the plaintiff's finished products manufactured to the drawings.[148] But a redesign exercise may nevertheless still create a new work even when the defendant concedes on intention to rely on an earlier drawing: *Jules Rimet Cup Ltd v Football Association Ltd*,[149] a case in which a redesign exercise of the *World Cup Willie* character did not infringe. If the court characterises the references in the later work as being non-copyrightable artistic techniques, a degree of similarity as between the works may not be enough to constitute copying.[150] In *Ateliers Tango Argentin Inc v Festival d'Espagne et d'Amerique Latin Inc*[151] it was held that the use of a publicity photograph to reset or recreate an image, similar to the original, in the same location and using similar subject

---

[144] *Kenrick v Lawrence* (1890) 25 QBD 99 at 102.

[145] *Rose Plastics GmbH v William Beckett & Co* [1989] FSR 113 cited with approval in *Interlego AG v Tyco Industries* [1988] 3 All ER 949.

[146] *Gleeson and Gleeson Shirt Co Ltd v HR Denne Ltd* [1975] RPC 471.

[147] *Designers Guild Ltd v Russell Williams (Textiles) Ltd* [2001] 1 All ER 700; *Nouveau Fabrics Ltd v Voyage Decoration Ltd* [2004] EWHC 895 (Ch).

[148] *LB (Plastics) Ltd v Swish Products Ltd* [1979] RPC 551; *Frank M Winstone (Merchants) Ltd v Plix Products Ltd* [1985] 1 NZLR 376; *British Leyland Motor Corpn v Armstrong's Patents* [1986] 1 All ER 850.

[149] *Jules Rimet Cup Ltd v Football Association Ltd* [2007] EWHC 2376 (Ch), applying *Designers Guild*. For views on the necessary vagueness of *Designers Guild* see *Spence and Endicott* (2005) 121 LQR 657.

[150] *Cummins v Vella* [2002] FCAFC 218.

[151] *Ateliers Tango Argentin Inc v Festival d'Espagne et d'Amerique Latin Inc* (1997) 84 CPR (3rd) 56.

matter was a colourable imitation of the original and thus an infringing act. Where the work is literary, the quality of the work may be thematic, and several older cases make it clear that taking the plot of a story so as to serve as the outline of a play or film could be a substantial taking, even though there is no copying or reproduction of the original script, or even if shifts in time, place or theme occur. These cases will, of course, need to address the issue of coincidental creation[152] but they suggest that the idea/expression dichotomy can be difficult to draw in the context of dramatic works at least. Protection tends to be extensive when a court opts to protect an investment from unfair copying, as distinct from looking to the level of reproduction by the infringer, and, despite *dicta* to the contrary, there are a number of cases that allow the protection of literary works because of the level of investment made in creating a work even if this results in protection of information *per se*.[153]

How much is copyright protected?

[16.50] Apart from the idea/expression dichotomy, considered above, the courts must distinguish between the defendant's use of non-copyright information and the defendant's reliance upon the plaintiff's work, which is not always the same thing. While an edited or annotated edition of a literary work that itself is copyright protected will create a copyright in that edited or annotated edition, the use of parts of the 'public domain' element of the work will not infringe copyright in the edition. In *Warwick Film v Eisinger*[154] the plaintiff's copyright in an edited version of the trial of Oscar Wilde was not infringed when the defendant was shown to have used the trial transcript as distinct from the plaintiff's edited work.

[16.51] There may be some reliance by a defendant on the plaintiff's work without a copyright infringement being shown. If the plaintiff's work is factual then a plaintiff may not complain if the defendant uses the historical facts to assist in creating an independent work of fiction – knowledge is meant to be built upon – but the plaintiff can complain if the structure of such a work, and theories and speculations of the author are lifted by a novelist.[155] Use by the defendant of a common source is not an infringement.[156] In the case of factual works like maps or television listings, the external similarities will be excused upon proof of independent work or common sources.[157]

---

152 *Robl v Palace Theatre Ltd* (1911) 28 TLR 69; *Corelli v Gray* (1913) 30 TLR 116; *Vane v Famous Players* (1928) Macg Cop Cas 6.

153 Eg are these ideas hackneyed, scenes à faire, etc? *Elanco v Mandops* [1979] FSR 46. See also the TV listings cases such as *RTE v Magill TV Guide* [1990] ILRM 534. Contrast the Dutch case of *De Telegraaf v NOS* [2002] ECDR 97.

154 *Warwick Film v Eisinger* [1969] 1 Ch 508.

155 *Ravenscroft v Herbert* [1980] RPC 193; *Harman Pictures NV v Osborne* [1967] 1 WLR 723.

156 *Geographia Ltd v Penguin Books Ltd* [1985] FSR 208.

157 *TV Guide Inc v Publications La Semaine Inc* (1984) 9 CPR (3d) 368; *Spiers v Brown* (1858) 6 WR 352.

The intention to take the plaintiff's work

[16.52] Once it has been shown by the plaintiff that the defendant intended to use the plaintiff's work it may be difficult for the defendant to argue that the use was not an infringement, certainly in cases where the use is not transformative in nature. If little or nothing remains of the original then the defendant may be held to have created a separate and independent work that not only attracts a separate copyright but also is a new work that does not infringe earlier works, even if the earlier work was inspirational.[158] Where the defendant has merely taken the plaintiff's work without alteration in order to save time and effort, this will not free the defendant from liability, even if the information set out in the plaintiff's work, eg a trade directory[159] or advertising material,[160] refers to individuals who have in some way consented to personal details of this kind being reproduced. Substantial problems may arise where the defendant is actually the person who created or contributed towards the plaintiff's copyright work (eg an employee or assignor), who subsequently uses his expertise or skill to create a similar work. In the software engineering industry or in technical areas such as cartography, liability has been negative when the similarities have been ascribed to the personal qualities or conventions found in the relevant sector.[161] Wholesale reliance on other works, however, will not be excused.[162] An author, even one who has assigned copyright, is free to create an independent work but it is common for many contracts to provide anti-competition clauses, which prevent an author from creating a competing work. These clauses are seen to be of doubtful constitutional validity and arguably are not likely to be enforceable under domestic competition law, so the earlier Irish case of *Educational Co of Ireland v Fallon*,[163] in which a restraint clause of this kind was upheld, may no longer be reliable.

[16.53] The courts will be hostile to attempts to use the plaintiff's work while modifying its literal features by colourable alterations.[164] The leading case in Ireland is *House of Spring Gardens Ltd v Point Blank Ltd*.[165] In that case, the defendants sought to avoid liability for copyright infringement by re-designing a bullet-proof vest that the plaintiffs had sold to the Libyan government, the re-designing exercise being undertaken following settlement of earlier litigation. The re-design exercise took place in consultation with lawyers and accountants acting for the defendants but the product that

---

[158] *Williamson Music v Pearson* [1987] FSR 97.

[159] *Morris v Ashbee* (1868) LR 7 Eq 34.

[160] *Allied Discount Card v Bord Failte* [1990] ILRM 534. In relation to the published edition copyright issues of intention raise different concerns: see *Nationwide News Pty Ltd v Copyright Agency* (1996) 34 IPR 53.

[161] *Delrina Corpn v Triolet Systems* (1993) 47 CPR (3d) 1; *Geographia Ltd v Penguin Books Ltd* [1985] FSR 208.

[162] *Sands & McDougall v Robinson* (1917) 23 CLR 49.

[163] *Educational Co of Ireland v Fallon* [1919] 1 IR 62.

[164] *Elanco v Mandops* [1979] FSR 46.

[165] *House of Spring Gardens Ltd v Point Blank Ltd* [1984] IR 611.

emerged was held to have been a substantial reproduction of the original work. McCarthy J in the Supreme Court viewed the re-design exercise with:[166]

> dismay that solicitors and counsel should consider it proper to be so personally involved with such a matter. I assume that neither the Law Society of England nor the Inns of Court in London provide tuition or require any aptitude in tailoring or cognate disciplines.

Competition between two works

[16.54] This factor remains significant, particularly in the areas of professional or trade directories,[167] television listings cases,[168] the computer programs sector[169] and the newspaper industry, where case law[170] suggests that the plaintiffs have sought to enforce copyright in order to protect market position or repulse 'literary larceny'.[171] The decision of the ECJ in *Magill*,[172] however, suggests that this desire to avoid 'undesirable' monopolies may take on a rather more active role where copyright is used to protect the right holder's market position, at a cost to the consumer in terms of quality of product. In an instructive Canadian case,[173] the defendant was held to have infringed the plaintiff's copyright in his doctoral thesis on the history of the Canadian West when parts were used by the defendant in a book on ranching; the non-commercial nature of the thesis was a factor in the court's decision not to award damages. But, in general, the possibility that an anti-competitive use of copyright may be countered by invoking competition law will generally revolve around the use of *Magill*.

[16.55] The effect of *Magill*[174] has been explored by Laddie J in *HMSO v Automobile Association Ltd*.[175] The Crown claimed copyright in Ordnance Survey road maps,[176] maps which included Crown copyright material in relation to road building. The defendants sought to use this material in their other roadmaps but would not agree to the royalty payments sought by HMSO, the relevant licensing agency for the Crown. The defendants sought to amend their defence to an action for infringement by arguing an

---

[166] *House of Spring Gardens Ltd v Point Blank Ltd* [1984] IR 611 at 708.

[167] *Kelly v Morris* (1866) LR 1 Eq 697; *Morris v Ashbee* (1868) LR 7 Eq 34; *Rose v Information Services* [1987] FSR 254; *Waterlow Directories v Reed* [1992] FSR 409; *Waterlow v Rose* [1995] FSR 207; *Tele-Direct (Publications) Inc v American Business Information* (1996) 35 IPR 121.

[168] *BBC v Wireless League* [1926] Ch 433; *Independent Television v Time Out Ltd* [1984] FSR 64; *RTE v Magill TV Guide* [1990] ILRM 534.

[169] See generally **Ch 13**.

[170] *Express Newspapers v News (UK)* [1990] 3 All ER 376.

[171] *Per* North J in *Walter v Steinkopff* [1892] 3 Ch 489 at 496.

[172] *Radio Telefís Éireann v European Commission (Intellectual Property Owners Inc, intervening)* Joined Cases C-241/91P and C-242/91P [1995] ECR I-743, [1995] FSR 530.

[173] *Breen v Hancock House Publishers Ltd* (1985) 6 CPR (3d) 433.

[174] *Radio Telefís Éireann v European Commission (Intellectual Property Owners Inc, intervening)* Joined Cases C-241/91P and C-242/91P [1995] ECR I-743, [1995] FSR 530.

[175] *HMSO v Automobile Association Ltd* [2001] ECC 272.

[176] In Ireland, Ordnance Survey Ireland maps are covered by government copyright: see CRRA 2000, s 191 and Ordnance Survey Ireland Act 2001, s 4(2)(i).

abuse of a dominant position under new art 102 of TFEU[177] and that other users, specifically Ordnance Survey, did not have to pay to use the copyright material in producing Ordnance Survey maps. In declining to permit the amendment of the defence so as to raise the art 82 defence, Laddie J found most of the abuse arguments to lack any merit. In particular, the learned judge indicated that the Crown was to be treated as one entity and the fact that one part of the same entity permitted 'free use while charging competitors for the material did not amount to discrimination as between the entity and third parties'. Laddie J said that the 'hub' of the complaint was that the defendants sought a royalty agreement with a zero rate of royalty, using *Magill* as the authority for such an anti-competitive practice argument. Laddie J wrote of *Magill*:[178]

> It has always been regarded as an exceptional case, but what the European Court of Justice said was that in the very peculiar facts of that case, where copyright was being used to bolster this dominant position in relation to the co-operation and information needed by the third party, the provisions of article 82 come into play and in particular it would not be open to the proprietor of the intellectual property rights, in that case, copyright to prevent the third party putting its television guide on the market. In effect it said that the television companies had to submit to a compulsory licence. It is interesting to note that even in that case, which, as I said, is treated as being quite exceptional, the European Court of Justice did not abolish by the backdoor the intellectual property right. What it did was say that the intellectual property right had to be licensed on reasonable terms to the infringer.

[16.56] In *HMSO v Automobile Association Ltd*,[179] after commenting on the factual differences between *Magill*[180] and the case at bar, specifically the lack of factual material supporting discriminatory treatment and the willingness of HMSO to licence use of the copyright material, Laddie J returned to *Magill*. After commenting on the willingness of the defendants to take a licence:[181]

> as long as the rate is zero. The royalty rate of zero means effectively that the intellectual property right might just as well not exist. There is no authority that I know that would suggest that even in the most favourable climate *Magill* could be stretched to any such length. It would amount to Article 82 [of the EC Treaty] being used to destroy intellectual property rights.

[16.57] One of the more recent ECJ decisions also contains compelling insights on *Magill*.[182] In *Oscar Bronner v Mediaprint*,[183] Advocate General Jacobs argued that in *Magill* the decision to require the television companies to grant licences was based on

---

[177] Formerly EC Treaty, art 86.

[178] *HMSO v Automobile Association Ltd* [2001] ECC 272 at 278–279. But see *Intel Corpn v Via Technologies* [2003] ECC 93 and *IMS Health GmbH v NDC Health GmbH* Case C-418/01 [2004] ECDR 123 (Advocate General's opinion).

[179] *HMSO v Automobile Association Ltd* [2001] ECC 272.

[180] *Radio Telefis Éireann v European Commission (Intellectual Property Owners Inc, intervening)* Joined Cases C-241/91P and C-242/91P [1995] ECR I-743, [1995] FSR 530.

[181] *HMSO v Automobile Association Ltd* [2001] ECC 272 at 284.

[182] *Radio Telefis Éireann v European Commission (Intellectual Property Owners Inc, intervening)* Joined Cases C-241/91P and C-242/91P [1995] ECR I-743, [1995] FSR 530.

[183] *Oscar Bronner v Mediaprint* Case C-7/97 [1998] ECR I-7791.

exceptional circumstances. Firstly, the individual guides produced by the television companies were inadequate, especially when compared to the guides available in other countries. Secondly, copyright protection for television listings was a disproportionate right seen in the light of the need to provide an incentive for creative effort. Thirdly, because listings had a short life span, the copyright was a permanent barrier to market entry.[184] The view that a refusal to license use of a copyright is of itself not an abuse of a dominant position has been reaffirmed in *IMS Health Inc v Commission*.[185] Here a German company developed a database and information management system, declining to licence a competitor to use the database and management system, a German court having held the database and system were copyright. The Court of First Instance was of the view that the decision of the European Commission, namely that the refusal to licence was likely to eliminate competition and was therefore within *Magill*, ignored significant factual differences between the two situations. The Advocate General has, however, opened up a more radical approach, which the ECJ has broadly endorsed.[186]

[16.58] Post-*Magill* debate has tended to focus on the extent to which circumstances external to the exercise of an exclusive right can constitute a basis for interfering with the intellectual property right. Situations in which the intellectual property constitutes an industry standard – protected by a patent, copyright or design right – trigger an analysis of the 'essential facilities' doctrine. The refusal to license may become an abuse if, for example, the applicant is seeking to produce something for which there is no actual or proximate substitute, especially where the rights owner does not satisfy a demand for that product. Apart from circumstances of market failure, the rights owner may be required to explain or justify the refusal to grant or licence.[187] Should the refusal be seen as an interference with an adjacent or secondary market – in *Magill*[188] the primary RTE market was television programmes and on-screen advertising, not magazines – and the effect is to preclude market entry, then an abuse may be made out.

OTHER ASPECTS OF INFRINGEMENTS – TECHNICAL PROTECTION

[16.59] Section 370 is the central provision in CRRA 2000 relating to the protection of copyright works by way of rights protection measures. The section is drawn from s 296 of the Copyright, Designs and Patents Act 1988 (UK), art 11 of the World Intellectual Property Organisation Copyright Treaty (WCT) and art 18 of the World Intellectual Property Organisation's Phonograms and Performances Treaty (WPPT). Minor adjustments in the definitions have been made to reflect the language of the Information

---

[184] *Oscar Bronner v Mediaprint* Case C-7/97 [1998] ECR I-7791 at 7812–7813.

[185] *IMS Health Inc v Commission* [2001] ECR II-3193.

[186] Advocate General Tizzano: *IMS Health GmbH v NDC Health GmbH* Case C-418/01 [2004] ECDR 123.

[187] *Sea Containers/Stena Sealink* Commission Decision 94/19/EC ([1994) OJ L15/8). Contrast *Tierce Ladbroke v Commission* [1997] ECR II-923.

[188] *Radio Telefís Éireann v European Commission (Intellectual Property Owners Inc, intervening)* Joined Cases C-241/91P and C-242/91P [1995] ECR I-743, [1995] FSR 530.

Society Directive.[189] In essence, where a work, recording of a performance, or a database has been subject to rights protection measures and then made available to the public so as to prevent acts of infringement by a secondary infringer, both the rights owner and any person issuing those works, recordings of performers and databases may proceed against the secondary infringer if he/she is engaged in distribution of a protection defeating device. Because secondary infringement normally relates to the infringing copies or infringing performances, CRRA 2000, s 370 goes further in addressing technical means of 'locking' a work, a recording of a performance or a database. The impact of s 370 is illustrated by *Sony Computer Entertainment v Owen*.[190] The plaintiffs had produced Playstation 2 consoles but had 'regionalised' them so as to produce one format for Japan, one for North America and one for (effectively) the rest of the world. Each CD-ROM issued by Sony had a code that was read by the console and if the appropriate regional code was not on the disc, or if the disc was unauthorised (produced via a CD burner) the game would not play on the console. The defendant imported 'Messiah' chips, which when fitted to the console would bypass the coding reader in the console and the game would run. Sony argued that the code attached to each of their regionally issued CD-ROMs was a copy protection device and that the Messiah chip was a protection defeating device. Given the breadth of these definitions in UK[191] and Irish[192] law there was no doubt that these points were not really in dispute, but what Jacob J had to decide was whether the fact that there could be 'legitimate' uses for the Messiah chip altered the situation. Jacob J held that the fact that the Messiah chip could interact with works other than Sony products was irrelevant. More importantly, Jacob J held that most users would be utilising the chip to read pirated CDs, the very thing that the Sony codes were intended to prevent – the making and distribution of pirated Playstation 2 games.[193] The fact that there may be a right to import works for private and domestic use (eg buy Sony games in the US and Japan) did not mean that any importer could also play the game on a UK issue console. Such a restriction was far-reaching but on a contractual level it existed in the light of the restrictive licensing conditions attached to Sony games sold in the US and Japan. Even if some lawful uses of 'Messiah' products could be identified, the fact that there were such uses would not take the chip outside the definition of a protection defeating device.[194]

---

[189] Council Directive 29/2001/EC.

[190] *Sony Computer Entertainment v Owen* [2002] ECDR 742.

[191] 'Copy protection' includes 'any device or means': Copyright Designs and Patents Act 1988, s 296(4).

[192] Rights protection measure means 'any process, treatment, mechanism or system': CRRA 2000, s 2(1).

[193] But in Australia the definitions of 'technological protection measure' and 'circumvention device' are narrower, referring to devices, products and components – physical things by implication. See *Kabushiki Kaisha Sony Computer Entertainment v Stevens* (2002) 55 IPR 497, reversed at (2004) 57 IPR 161.

[194] *Kabushiki Kaisha Sony Computer Entertainment v Stevens* (2002) 55 IPR 497, reversed at (2004) 57 IPR 161; in *Nintendo Co Ltd v Lik Sang International Ltd* (2003) 58 IPR 187 the Hong Kong High Court answered such an argument with a 'substantial purpose' test. For an illustration of the need to keep this legislation under review see *Kabushiki Kaisha Sony Computer Entertainment Inc v Ball* [2004] All ER (D) 334.

[16.60] Some guidance may be expected from the ECJ on how these measures on technological protection attaching to underlying works are to be interpreted. In *Football Association Premier League Ltd v QC Leisure*[195] and *UEFA v Euroview Sport Ltd*[196] the plaintiffs were the organising body behind the English Premier League and the UEFA Champions League/Europa League respectively. Their complaint related to the use of decoder cards, lawfully put on the market in Greece and Germany, with permission for use in those countries only. When these cards were purchased and used in the UK, in breach of the licence, could rights owners utilise community law such as the Conditional Access Directive, Directive 98/84/EC, to counteract such activities? In the *QC Leisure* Case some 10 questions were referred, including issues relating to whether these decoder cards, lawful in their country of origin, were 'illicit devices' under Directive 98/84/EC. In the *Euroview Sport* case novel issues under Directive 2001/29/EC were referred to the ECJ on whether encryption *per se* is a 'technological measure' for the purposes of protection; the ECJ has also been asked to consider whether use of a decoder card that has been lawfully issued in a Member State amounts to 'circumvention' when use takes place in another Member State.

CRIMINAL LAW

Criminal law protection for copyright works

[16.61] Right holders have been very active in pressing governments to provide additional enforcement mechanisms in the guise of the criminal law. Even in civil proceedings judges can use the language of 'copyright theft'; see for example Charleton J in *EMI Records (Ireland) Ltd v Eircom Ltd*.[197] Infringement of copyright may at one time have appeared to be an inappropriate subject for the criminal law, but in recent years organised crime has turned to the business of piracy and counterfeiting as very lucrative and relatively low risk commercial activities. On the international stage the criminal law has been touted as the most cost-effective method of grappling with CD and video piracy, brand counterfeiting and image right infringement, activities that often involve copyright issues. Note that the presumptions on copyright and ownership under CRRA 2000 apply in relation to criminal copyright infringement proceedings.[198] The most important provision in CRRA 2000 is s 140 which sets out four offences.

[16.62] The first offence is committed by a person who, without the consent of the copyright owner:

    (a)   makes for sale, rental or loan;

    (b)   sells, rents, lends or offers or exposes for sale, rental or loan;

---

[195] *Football Association Premier League Ltd v QC Leisure* [2008] EWHC 1411 (Ch) of 11 July 2008, now Joined Cases C-403/08 and C-429/08.

[196] *UEFA v Euroview Sport Ltd* [2010] EWHC 1066 (Ch).

[197] *EMI Records (Ireland) Ltd v Eircom Ltd* [2010] IEHC 108; Loughlan [2007] EIPR 401. See generally Tapper, 'Criminality and Copyright' in *Intellectual Property in the New Millennium* (eds Vaver and Bentley (CUP)).

[198] CRRA 2000, s 139.

(c)   imports into the State, otherwise than for his or her private and domestic use;

(d)   in the course of a business, trade or profession, has in his or her possession custody or control, or makes available to the public; or

(e)   otherwise than in the course of a business, trade or profession, makes available to the public to such an extent as to prejudice the interests of the owner of the copyright

a copy of a work which is, and which he or she knows or has reason to believe[199] is, an infringing copy of the work,[200] shall be guilty of an offence.[201]

[16.63] This offence is committed in relation to the manufacture or distribution of infringing copies: if no infringing copy exists then no offence can be made out. So a copy created within CRRA 2000, s 50 – a copy of a work created for research, for example – will not involve infringement, and because of the definition of 'loan' in CRRA 2000, s 140(2) a subsequent transfer to another person may also avoid criminal liability (eg a loan to a friend).

[16.64] The second offence is the related offence that arises from infringement of the making available right.[202] Here, copyright is infringed by:

(a)   the public performance of a literary, dramatic or musical work,

(b)   the playing or showing in public of a sound recording, artistic work, original database or film, or

(c)   broadcasting a work or including a work in a cable programme service

and the person who caused the work to be so infringed is guilty of an offence if he or she knew or had reason to believe an infringement would occur.[203] Again, this offence may only be made out if an infringement is established; if, for example, the performance of a musical work occurs within the limits of the school concert defence,[204] no offence is committed.

[16.65] Section 140(6) of CRRA 2000 at first sight merely reinforces this by providing that both of these offences are incapable of being committed by undertaking an act that may take place without infringing copyright in the work.

[16.66] The third offence found in CRRA 2000, s 140 relates to manufacture, sale or rental or loan,[205] importation into the State or possession of a protection defeating device,[206] knowing or having reason to believe that it has been or is to be used to

---

[199] *LA Gear Inc v Hi Tech Sports plc* [1992] FSR 121; *Husqvarna Forest & Garden Ltd v Bridon NZ Ltd* (1997) 38 IPR 513; *Vermaat Powell v Boncrest (No 2)* [2002] FSR 331.

[200] CRRA 2000, s 44.

[201] CRRA 2000, s 140(1). See *Gilham* [2009] EWCA 229.

[202] CRRA 2000, s 40.

[203] CRRA 2000, s 140(5).

[204] CRRA 2000, s 55(1).

[205] CRRA 2000, s 140(4).

[206] *Husqvarna Forest & Garden Ltd v Bridon NZ Ltd* (1997) 38 IPR 513.

circumvent rights protection measures. This offence is likely to be used in respect of devices or computer programs that bypass anti-copying or access-limiting technologies such as the Messiah Chip[207] or the De CSS program.[208] But the scope of the offence is uncertain. In some respects it is very broad. For example, importation for private and domestic use[209] is not a defence under this subsection. But what if the user is seeking to deploy the device in order to use the protected work for a permitted purpose, eg record an otherwise unrecordable cable programme to watch at a later time under s 101 of CRRA 2000? The fact that the s 140(6) defence is not available here suggests there is no defence, but it is arguable that because the definition of 'rights protection measure' refers to the exercise of rights given to the right holder by the Act, the absence of the s 140(6) defence may not be dispositive. It has also been held by the English courts that in relation to a trade mark prosecution, a conviction cannot be obtained in respect of an action that does not constitute a trade mark infringement.[210]

The fourth offence relates to the manufacture, sale, rental or loan, importation or possession of an article specifically designed or adapted for making infringing copies.[211] The problem of determining whether an article has been 'specifically designed' has been addressed robustly by the courts. The fact that an article might be capable of allowing access to a protected work as distinct from facilitating copying is unlikely to prevail if the predominant purpose behind the article is unauthorised copying.[212] In *R v Gilham*[213] the English Court of Appeal side-stepped arguments about the loading of insubstantial parts of a game onto the RAM games console on the basis that images presented to the player were themselves artistic works that had been pirated.

[16.67] Persons convicted of offences under CRRA 2000, s 140 face, on summary conviction, fines of up to €1,900 for each copy or offence, as the case may be, or imprisonment for up to 12 months, or both, and upon indictment a fine of up to €125,000 or a term of imprisonment of up to five years, or both.[214]

[16.68] There are two further offences in the CRRA 2000 that are related to s 140. Section 140(4)(b) for example, would enable a conviction to be secured against a service provider who assisted a person to receive an encrypted broadcast by either providing information or rendering a service. Section 371 creates an offence of unlawful reception of a rights protected broadcast or cable programme (eg a webcast with access code

---

[207] *Sony Computer Entertainment Inc v Owen* [2002] EMLR 742.

[208] *Public Prosecutor v Johansen* [2003] ECDR 309.

[209] *Helliwell v Piggot-Sims* [1980] FSR 582; *Irvine v Rivero* (1992) 23 IPR 215.

[210] *R v Johnstone* [2003] ETMR 1. See also CRRA 2000, s 374, as amended by SI 16/2004.

[211] CRRA 2000, s 140(3).

[212] *Sony Computer Entertainment v Owen* [2002] ECDR 742; *Kabushiki Kaisha Sony Computer Entertainment v Stevens* (2003) 57 IPR 161.

[213] *R v Gilham* [2009] EWCA Crim 2293.

[214] CRRA 2000, s 140(7) and (8).

protection). The offence is committed by the person receiving the broadcast or cable programme.[215]

[16.69] Section 376 of CRRA 2000 creates offences relating to the removal or alteration of rights management information on works, recordings of performances or databases and their subsequent distribution in changed form. Offences are to be proceeded with summarily or on indictment.[216]

Miscellaneous offences

[16.70] It is an offence for a person to claim to enjoy a copyright for financial gain when he or she knows or has reason to believe that the claim is false. Proceedings are on indictment.[217] A similar provision exists in relation to performances[218] but not in relation to the database right. The CRRA 2000 also makes provision for criminal liability for collecting societies that are not registered when so required by the Act.[219] Offences may be committed by bodies corporate[220] and members of a partnership.[221]

[16.71] The process of gathering evidence so as to disturb the distribution of infringing items and enhance the right holder's prospects of bringing about a conviction is assisted by s 143 of CRRA 2000. This enables an application to be made to the District Court to obtain a warrant authorising the gardaí to enter any premises or place where an offence is believed, on reasonable grounds, to have been committed, or is about to be committed, and gather evidence. Search and seizure of infringing works, copy manufacturing articles and protection defeating devices is authorised and delivery up to the District Court of these items is required. In *DPP v McGoldrick*[222] the Court of Criminal Appeal stressed that the requirements of Article 40.5 of the Constitution require the legal conditions set by CRRA 2000 to be 'strictly met'. Errors on a printed form accompanying the search warrant, and on the warrant itself, as well as textual ambiguities, meant that the warrant was invalid. Offences of obstruction or refusal to provide information are also prescribed.[223] Similar seizure and delivery up powers exist in relation to persons, upon conviction, arrest and charge, who are in possession of infringing items.[224] There is a six-year limitation period in respect of these

---

[215] A response to *News Datacom v Lyons* [1994] ILRM 450; on summary conviction, maximum penalty is €1,900 per infringing item.

[216] CRRA 2000, s 376(2).

[217] CRRA 2000, s 141.

[218] CRRA 2000, s 259.

[219] CRRA 2000, ss 181, 286 and 361.

[220] CRRA 2000, s 12.

[221] CRRA 2000, s 13.

[222] *DPP v McGoldrick* [2005] IECCA 8. For new District Court forms see the District Court (Intellectual Property) Rules 2010 (SI 421/2010).

[223] CRRA 2000, s 143(3). For performances see CRRA 2000, s 261(3).

[224] CRRA 2000, s 142. For performances see CRRA 2000, s 263.

proceedings.[225] The ultimate fate of infringing items, that is, infringing copies, copy manufacturing articles and protection defeating devices, may be decided by an application to the appropriate court by a right owner who may seek to have the goods forfeited to the copyright owner or destroyed or otherwise dealt with as the court may direct.[226] The court may make such an order as is appropriate and it is not unknown, in the case of clothing or footwear, for the court to order that infringing articles be donated to an Irish or overseas charity.

---

[225] CRRA 2000, s 144(3) and (4). For performances see CRRA 2000, s 263.
[226] Often after the offending logos and trade marks have been removed or obscured.

Chapter 17

Defences to Copyright Infringement

INTRODUCTION

[17.01] Irish copyright legislation provides a range of circumstances and situations in which certain dealings in, or use made of, a copyright work will not be actionable by the right holder. Many of these provisions are based upon the traditions that can be traced back to the Berne Convention 1886 which attempts to strike a balance between the interests of right holders and users, particularly when the use is for certain special circumstances defined by national law that does not unreasonably prejudice the right holder,[1] or where use is in the public interest or has an educational purpose.[2] However, the introduction of new technology, particularly the photocopier and the digitisation of information, which allow for perfect copies to be taken from all kinds of works, require a re-assessment of international and national law provisions on these various 'fair use' type of defences. As we have seen in **Ch 16**, there has been a very significant expansion of the criminal law in relation to the protection of works, a development that reflects the ease with which electronic products such as DVD films and recorded music may be pirated, with significant economic losses resulting to right holders. The development of technical protection technologies and electronic rights management systems have the potential for disturbing these traditional checks and balances and recent Irish legislation has addressed these complex issues in an extremely robust manner.

EXPRESS OR IMPLIED AUTHORISATION BY THE RIGHT HOLDER

[17.02] Because copyright normally consists of an exclusive right to do, or authorise others to do, certain things in relation to a work,[3] it follows that where the right holder has authorised such user there can be no infringement. The onus of showing that permission or consent has been given rests on the person alleging the agreement.[4] An Australian case in which an alleged oral licence was pleaded by way of defence, held that the court should enquire about whether consent was given rather than embark upon

---

[1] Berne Convention for the Protection of Literary and Artistic Works (Paris Act), art 9. Ireland ratified the Paris Act on 2 December 2004.

[2] Berne Convention (Paris Act), arts 10 and 10bis.

[3] CA 1963, ss 7(1) and 11(2); CRRA 2000, s 37(1).

[4] *Blair v Osborne and Tompkins* [1971] 1 All ER 468; *Computermate Products v Ozi-Soft Property* (1988) 12 IPR 487; *Pacific Software Technology Ltd v Perry Group Ltd* (2003) 57 IPR 145.

a contractual analysis of the case.[5] It is perfectly possible for a court to hold that the right holder has been granted an implied licence to use the work, particularly if the right holder has been commissioned to create architectural drawings[6] or a database;[7] the commissioner may not hold copyright but will have an implied licence to use the work in question. The scope of the licence may be personal or even limited in space or time.[8] In *Richie v Sawmill Creek Golf and Country Club*[9] a golf club member transferred an album of photographs to the defendant organisation for use in publicity purposes. Differences arose between them and the plaintiff alleged that certain uses were infringements of copyright. It was held that the transfer of the album was an irrevocable licence from which the plaintiff could not resile.[10] Although there is no clear case law on the point it is arguable that if a right holder puts copyright works onto a server without attaching technical protection measures or restricting certain kinds of use, it would be possible to infer general consent by the right holder to acts of downloading that do not constitute or facilitate competing commercial use.[11]

FAIR DEALING

[17.03] This is the broadest exception to the right holder's exclusive rights in literary, dramatic or musical works. The user must bring the use, or intended use, within one of the excepted activities, and the court must determine whether on the facts the use was a fair dealing. If, for example, the fair dealing is for the purpose of research or private study or criticism or review then no infringement takes place.

Research or private study[12]

[17.04] The making of one copy of a copyright work for research or private study, a broadly educational use, has been upheld as a fair dealing, but the statutory defence is narrowly construed. The making of several copies for distribution within a school or business is not within this defence and it has been held in a recent New Zealand case that the defence cannot be made out where a master copy is made available to allow students to photocopy that item themselves.[13] The Copyright and Related Rights Act 2000 (CRRA 2000) envisages that where copying is undertaken on behalf of the researcher or student, then the copiers may 'adopt' the purposes of the researcher or student. In *CCH*

---

[5] *Clune v Collins, Argus & Robertson Publishers Property Ltd* (1992) 25 IPR 246.
[6] *Blair v Tomkins and Osborne* [1971] 1 All ER 468; *Tucker v Bentley* (1996) 36 IPR 243.
[7] *Ray v Classic FM* [1998] FSR 622; *Cyprotex Discovery Ltd v University of Sheffield* (2003) 89 Con LR 109.
[8] *Strahan v Graham* (1868) 17 LT 457; *Ray v Classic FM* [1998] FSR 622.
[9] *Richie v Sawmill Creek Golf and Country Club* (2003) 27 CPR (4th) 220; *Pacific Software Technology Ltd v Perry Group Ltd* (2003) 57 IPR 145.
[10] Some licences may be revoked: *Bowden Bros v Amalgamated Pictorials* [1911] 1 Ch 386.
[11] On which see *Shetland Times v Wills* (1996) 37 IPR 71; *Sony Music Entertainment (UK) Ltd v Easyinternetcafe* [2003] IP & T 1059.
[12] CA 1963, s 12(1)(a).
[13] *Copyright Licensing Ltd v University of Auckland* [2002] 3 NZLR 76.

Canadian Ltd v Law Society of Upper Canada[14] the defendant, upon request, faxed an individual copy of various legal materials to practitioners to assist them in research and thus advising clients. The Ontario Court of Appeal indicated that on these facts the defence was not *per se* unavailable and the Supreme Court of Canada has gone further in holding the defence is made out, but this is a controversial view to take.[15] The term 'research' was unqualified and so research for commercial purposes by the lawyer was nevertheless research. Private study, however, cannot be made out if the results of the study are generally made available to others.[16] Under CRRA 2000, there are specific rules applicable to librarians and archivists, considered below, but if the copier is not the researcher, a librarian or an archivist (eg a fellow student or friend), any copying for research or private study purposes will not be fair if the copyist knows, or has reason to believe, that his or her conduct will result in that material being substantially available to more than one person at approximately the same time and for the same purpose (eg the copy will be shared). While individual research for commercial purposes may still be a legitimate and fair dealing, the making available of multiple copies to a number of researchers will not be a fair dealing.[17] The provision of extracts from news broadcasts by a commercial news monitoring entity to commercial customers who in turn use the material for their own commercial purposes is also not within the defence, for here there is a simple appropriation of another's work for a commercial profit.[18] Similarly, the substantial taking of extracts from novels or plays for incorporation in 'cramming' guides sold to students cannot be within the defence for these activities clearly prejudice the legitimate interests of the right holder – the use diminishes the market for the original.[19] The photocopying of sheet music for research or private study purposes is, however, not permitted.[20]

[17.05] One significant factor that will be of great practical importance for this defence is the availability of contractual licences from publishers; since 1992 the Irish Copyright Licensing Agency has sought to regulate unauthorised reproduction of printed materials on behalf of Irish publishers. While the Agency has been anxious to deal with mass photocopying by schools, universities and other institutions, it is certainly arguable that individual users may find that the availability of permission upon payment of a fee may well make unauthorised private copying of printed material something other than a fair dealing.[21] There are other specific educational copying defences considered below.

---

[14] *CCH Canadian Ltd v Law Society of Upper Canada* (2002) 18 CPR (4th) 161.

[15] *CCH Canadian Ltd v Law Society of Upper Canada* (2004) 236 DLR (4th) 395.

[16] Eg *Hager v ECW Press* (1998) 85 CPR (3d) 289. This is a very sweeping statement and cannot be taken literally.

[17] *American Geophysical Union v Texaco* (1994) 29 IPR 381; *Fairfax Media Publications Pty Ltd v Reed International Books Aust Pty Ltd* [2010] FCA 984 (transformative use upheld).

[18] *TVNZ v Newsmonitor* (1993) 27 IPR 441; *Basic Books Inc v Kinko's Graphics* (1991) 23 IPR 565.

[19] *Sillitoe v McGraw Hill Book Co* [1983] FSR 545.

[20] European Communities (Copyright and Related Rights) Regulations 2004 (SI 16/2004).

[21] See *American Geophysical Union v Texaco* (1994) 29 IPR 381 where the licensing terms were described as fair, hence a refusal to comply with them made unauthorised copying unlawful.

Criticism or review

[17.06] Under the Copyright Act 1963 (CA 1963), the use of substantial extracts from a literary, dramatic or musical work for the purpose of criticism or review of the work is permitted.[22] The 'criticism or review' defence is to be interpreted broadly. Use in relation to another work may include use to illustrate a review of criticism (eg of cheque-book journalism) without being confined to a specific criticism or review of an identifiable edition: criticism of a genre which is made up of 'works' appears to be within the defences.[23] CRRA 2000 covers all works. One early case indicated that where a work is unpublished, that is, the author has not put the work before the public, the defence should not be available[24] but this view has not prevailed in recent cases,[25] which hold that the publication status of the original work is only a factor in the fair dealing issue. The English Court of Appeal has ruled recently, that a 'criticism or review' defence will not be made out if the publication that takes place is a newspaper making use of a private diary that has only been circulated to a small group of friends: *Associated Newspapers Ltd v HRH Prince of Wales*.[26] In the same case the English Court of Appeal resisted an argument that if a newspaper published a work within the reporting of current events defence, it could then also invoke a criticism or review defence for a subsequent republication. Lord Phillips of Worth Maltravers said that such a defence was not possible if only one publication was created with no subsequent review or critique being made. However, under CRRA 2000, s 50(4), which provides a definition of fair dealing, it is specifically stated that the making use of the work must relate to a work 'which has already been lawfully made available to the public' so the use of unpublished letters or photographs, for example, will not be available if the CRRA 2000 is the governing legislation.

[17.07] If the 'critical' work makes use of the original text so as to compete with the original work this will prevent the defence from being available[27] but reproduction of an entire work may still be within the defence.[28] It is clear that the concept of 'criticism or review' is not to be confined to criticism or review of the work as a work; in *Hubbard v Vosper*[29] the defence was available to a critic of the Church of Scientology who used the works of the founder of the Church to criticise the ideas and philosophy behind the Church. Similarly, in *Time Warner v Channel 4 Television Corpn*[30] a television documentary that was in part critical of the sociological thesis behind Kubrick's *Clockwork Orange* was held to be within this defence, even if the critique ran the risk of

---

[22] CA 1963, s 12(1)(b). *Wigginton v Brisbane TV* (1992) 25 IPR 58.
[23] *Pro Sieben Media AG v Carlton UK Television Ltd* [1999] 1 WLR 605; *Fraser – Woodward Ltd v BBC* [2005] EWHC 472 (Ch).
[24] *British Oxygen Co Ltd v Liquid Air Ltd* [1925] Ch 383.
[25] *Beloff v Pressdram Ltd* [1973] 1 All ER 241; *Ashdown v Telegraph Group* [2001] 4 All ER 666.
[26] *Associated Newspapers Ltd v HRH Prince of Wales* [2006] EWCA Civ 1776.
[27] *Silletoe v McGraw-Hill Book Co (UK) Ltd* [1983] FSR 545.
[28] Per Megaw LJ in *Hubbard v Vosper* [1972] 1 All ER 1023.
[29] *Hubbard v Vosper* [1972] 1 All ER 1023.
[30] *Time Warner v Channel 4 Television Corpn* (1993) 28 IPR 454.

misrepresenting or possibly giving a distorted view of the original film. Personal criticism of the Prime Minister, as distinct from any speech he or she may have delivered is not within a criticism or review defence.[31] The test of fairness in this specific context is a combination of objective and subjective elements, requiring the court to take a balanced view of the likely impact the use of the plaintiff's work will have on the target audience or market, as well as the motives of the user.[32] Some activities will be difficult to bring within the criticism or review context, such as photocopying materials for students[33] which have not been requested by the students or compiling factual materials.[34] The recent Australian decision in *TCN Channel Nine Pty Ltd v Network Ten Pty Ltd*[35] concerned the rebroadcasting by the defendants of extracts from some of the plaintiff's broadcasts, and a very strong Federal Court divided on the applicability of the 'criticism or review' defence. It appears that both the English and the Australian courts are of the view that a trial judge's findings on these matters will only be disturbed if 'clearly unsustainable'[36] on the basis that 'fair dealing involve questions of degree and impressions on which different minds can reasonably come to different conclusions'.[37] While this may well be an appropriate position to take, it should nevertheless be remembered that the purpose of the 'criticism or review defence' is, in the words of Lightman J, 'to protect a critic or reviewer who may bona fide wish to use the copyright material to illustrate his review or criticism'.[38]

[17.08] There must be a sufficient acknowledgment of not only the source of the work but the author of the work.[39]

For the purpose of reporting current events[40]

[17.09] The public is entitled to be informed about matters of controversy or contemporaneous events such as political stories, celebrity lifestyles or sporting or cultural features, and the use of literary, dramatic or musical works that have appeared in a newspaper or similar periodical, with sufficient acknowledgments, or in a broadcast or film, is not an infringement if the use is within the fair dealing context. However, if there is no real contemporaneous event, such as the death of a celebrated actor or the opening of a new play, the section may not be satisfied. So in *Associated Newspapers Group plc*

---

31   *Ashdown v Telegraph Group Ltd* [2001] 4 All ER 666.
32   *Pro Sieben AG v Carlton Television Ltd* [1999] 1 WLR 605.
33   *Copyright Licensing Ltd v University of Auckland* [2002] 3 NZLR 76 at 83, *per* Salmon J.
34   *De Garis v Neville Jeffress Pidler Pty* (1990) 18 IPR 292.
35   *TCN Channel Nine Pty Ltd v Network Ten Pty Ltd* (2002) 55 IPR 112.
36   *Pro Sieben Media AG v Carlton UK Television Ltd* [1999] 1 WLR 605; *Aldi Stores Partnership v Frito-Lay Trading Co* (2001) 54 IPR 344; *TCN Channel Nine Pty Ltd v Network Ten Pty Ltd* (2002) 55 IPR 112.
37   *Per* Sundberg J in *TCN Channel Nine Pty Ltd v Network Ten Pty Ltd* (2002) 55 IPR 112 at 113.
38   *Banier v News Group Newspapers Ltd* [1997] FSR 812 at 815.
39   *Express Newspapers plc v News (UK) Ltd* [1990] 3 All ER 376; *Pro Sieben Media AG v Carlton Television Ltd* [1999] 1 WLR 605. In Ireland, see interlocutory proceedings arising from the Bishop Casey controversy: (1993) Irish Times, 20 and 23 March.
40   CA 1963, s 12(12); CRRA 2000, s 51(2).

v News Group Newspapers,[41] the death of the Duchess of Windsor was not an event which justified the unauthorised publication of correspondence written many years before between herself and her husband. The courts are suspicious of this defence, on the ground that sensational stories puffed up by way of copyright material used without permission to sell newspapers is unmeritorious. However, in relation to injunction proceedings arising out of the unauthorised use of extracts from Annie Murphy's book on her relationship with the former Bishop of Galway, Dr Casey, a fair dealing defence under s 12 was used, with some success.[42] In *Hyde Park Residence Ltd v Yelland*[43] the English Court of Appeal held that publication in September 1998 of stills taken from a security film on the afternoon prior to the death of Princess Diana in August 1997 could be regarded as a publication for reporting current events because the investigation into the death of the Princess was continuing and had an element of currency. Further, the September 1998 publication was within the current events formula because it was relevant to allegations of wrongdoing by Mohamed Al Fayed, which were clearly contemporaneous with the September 1998 publication.[44] It should also be noted that under s 89 of CRRA 2000, there is an absolute defence to the recording, by notes or otherwise, of spoken words for the purpose of reporting current events or broadcasting or including the recording in a cable programme service unless the speaker has prohibited the recording in question.

Fair dealing

[17.10] In *TVNZ v Newsmonitor*,[45] Blanchard J commented that fair dealing is simply reasonable use. Echoing the words of Denning MR in *Hubbard v Vosper*,[46] Blanchard J indicated that the important issues are an examination of the nature of the work, the purpose for which the defendant has used them, the quantity of the material taken, and the effect that the defendant's activity has on the plaintiff's work; in particular does the defendant's use have a depreciating effect? A substantial use of some 10 per cent of the original may be upheld as in the *Clockwork Orange* case,[47] and the use of the most important elements (such as film of the goals in a soccer match) may be within the defence.[48] It will be extremely difficult to make out the defence in cases where the

---

[41] *Associated Newspapers Group plc v News Group Newspapers* [1986] RPC 515.

[42] (1993) Irish Times, 20 and 23 March.

[43] *Hyde Park Residence Ltd v Yelland* [2001] Ch 143.

[44] The Court of Appeal, however, found against the defendant on the fair dealing issue, not the purpose issue. It should be noted that photographs are not amenable to the current events defence (CRRA 2000, s 51(2)).

[45] *TVNZ v Newsmonitor* (1993) 27 IPR 441.

[46] *Hubbard v Vosper* [1972] 1 All ER 1023.

[47] *Time Warner v Channel 4 Television Corpn* (1993) 28 IPR 454.

[48] Even if the user has an arguable case in respect of criticism or review, or the reporting of current events the fairness of the fair dealing element will be difficult to make out where the plaintiff has spent much literary or artistic endeavour in making out a specific identity for a product, only to find it appropriated by a competitor for competing commercial purposes: *IPC Media v News Group Newspapers* [2005] EMLR 23; *Media Works NZ Ltd v Sky Television Network* (2007) 74 IPR 205, distinguishing *BBC v British Satellite Broadcasting* [1991] 3 All ER 833.

defendant intends some 'parasitic'[49] or competing user with the plaintiff. These observations are reinforced by s 51(4) of CRRA 2000 which states that, under CRRA 2000, fair dealing can only be available where the work has already been lawfully made available to the public and the purpose behind the use by the defendant is a 'purpose and to an extent which will not unreasonably prejudice the interests of the owner of the copyright'. Downloading an entire set of Ordnance Survey maps, the user taking the attitude that we will 'get the data and argue about the terms of the licence afterwards' clearly did not impress the English Court of Appeal as consistent with a fair dealing for the purpose of research: the Court of Appeal indicated that a fair minded and honest person would not have dealt with the work in the way this defendant did.[50]

SCOPE OF THE FAIR DEALING PROVISIONS

[17.11] When the governing legislation is CA 1963, it should be noted that the fair dealing defence is applicable to the use of literary, dramatic and musical works[51] and to artistic works[52] as defined in CA 1963. CRRA 2000 is much broader,[53] applying as it does also to films, sound recordings, broadcasts, cable programmes, non-electronic original databases and the typographical arrangements of published editions.[54]

INCIDENTAL INCLUSION

[17.12] A specific defence of incidental inclusion is available under CRRA 2000, s 52(1); incidental inclusion of one work in another work (eg a film camera capturing the page of a text or the exterior of a new sculpture) will not infringe, nor will the issue of copies of that later work to the public.[55] The test is one of unreasonable prejudice to the right holder.[56] Parasitic use is clearly not going to come within the defence[57] and although this is not *per se* a fair dealing defence, it can be expected to be used in conjunction with these defences. The 'incidental inclusion' defence involves an examination on whether the inclusion is incidental to some other purpose in the ordinary sense of the word. A direct link to a commercial purpose may not satisfy this requirement[58] whereas inclusion to illustrate a link with some other defence or legitimising factor may satisfy this test.[59] It should be noted that the Irish defence is

---

[49] *TVNZ v Newsmonitor* (1993) 27 IPR 441.
[50] *Controller HM Stationery Office v Green AMPS Ltd* [2008] EWCA Civ 588.
[51] CA 1963, s 12.
[52] CA 1963, s 14.
[53] CRRA 2000, s 50(4).
[54] See also CRRA 2000, s 50(2).
[55] CRRA 2000, s 52(2).
[56] CRRA 2000, s 52(3).
[57] *Football Association Premier League Ltd v Panini UK Ltd* [2003] 4 All ER 1290.
[58] *Football Assocation Premier League Ltd v Panini UK Ltd* [2003] 4 All ER 1290.
[59] *Fraser-Woodward Ltd v BBC* [2005] EWHC 472 (Ch) (note Mann J's different treatment of the Beckham photographs in paras 79-87 of the judgment).

broader than the UK defence insofar as specific selection does not preclude the defence in Irish law.

REPRODUCTION FOR THE PURPOSE OF PUBLIC ADMINISTRATION

[17.13] Under CA 1963, in the case of literary, dramatic and musical works, the reproduction of such works for the purpose of judicial proceedings[60] is not an infringement. This exception also applies to artistic works,[61] cinematographic films[62] and sound and television broadcasts.[63] A judicial proceeding is defined in CRRA 2000, s 2(1) as a proceeding before any court, tribunal or person having by law power to hear, receive and examine evidence on oath. CRRA 2000 re-enacts those provisions, extending the immunity in respect of all works, as defined in the Act.[64]

There is one recent English decision[65] which holds that the use of material for planning purposes is not within the public administration defence in relation to use for judicial proceedings. Given the definition of 'judicial proceedings' in s 2(1), substantially the same as in English law, the user must show that the material was used to decide on any matter affecting the legal rights or liabilities of a person. While such proceedings might determine whether the applicant has a right to undertake a particular development, the English High Court held that this is 'not a question of deciding any matter affecting a person's legal rights or liabilities. It is a question of dealing with additional facilities or entitlements … whether they should be granted a right to undertake a particular activity'. However, the 2000 legislation extends the immunity to acts done for the purpose of parliamentary proceedings or the reporting of those proceedings.[66] A specific provision has been inserted to provide for proceedings in, and reporting of, statutory enquiries.[67]

[17.14] Material in public records,[68] or material open to public inspection or on a statutory register[69] may also be copied and actions authorised under statutory authority (eg the photocopying of documents by law enforcement bodies) will be immune from liability for breach of copyright,[70] subject to any defences available under any other enactment.[71]

---

[60] CA 1963, s 12(3); this also applies to reports of such proceedings.

[61] CA 1963, s 14(6).

[62] CA 1963, s 18(5).

[63] CA 1963, s 19(11).

[64] CRRA 2000, ss 2(1) and 71(1) and (2): see *A v B* [2000] EMLR 1007.

[65] *Controller of HM Stationery Office v Green AMPS Ltd* [2008] EWCA Civ 588.

[66] Note that European Parliament proceedings are also covered: CRRA 2000, s 2(1). See also CRRA 2000, s 75.

[67] CRRA 2000, s 72.

[68] CRRA 2000, s 73.

[69] CRRA 2000, s 74.

[70] CRRA 2000, s 76(1).

[71] CRRA 2000, s 76 (1) and (2).

EDUCATIONAL USAGE

[17.15] The fair dealing exceptions in ss 12 and 14 of CA 1963 addressed the issue of individual fair dealings in works. There were other provisions that can broadly be described as educational use exceptions. The use of short passages from a copyright Part II work was permitted if the passages were included in a compilation intended for use in schools under stringent conditions laid down in the Act.[72] This exception was available to publishers of school texts. The Act also allowed for reproduction of Part II works by teachers or pupils in the course of instruction as long as the reproduction did not take place by a duplicating process – a photocopier, for example. Reproduction for examination purposes was also permitted.[73] Reproduction exceptions in CRRA 2000 are limited. In relation to literary, dramatic, musical or artistic works, or the typographical arrangement of published editions, copying in the course of instruction,[74] or preparation for instruction, does not infringe copyright as long as the copying is done by or on behalf of the instructor or student, and the copy is accompanied by a sufficient acknowledgment.[75] Copying via reprography such as photocopying, faxing, scanning and then email or internet transmission is not permitted however. A similar provision exists in relation to sound recordings, films, broadcasts, cable programmes and original databases[76] but in such instances the copying must result in only a single copy being made.[77] More latitude is given to usage of a work for setting, communicating and answering examination questions[78] but reproducing a copy of a musical work by reprography is not permitted for examination purposes.[79] The use of short passages from literary, dramatic or musical works, and original databases by a publisher for inclusion in a published collection for use in educational establishments is also permitted on rather stringent conditions.[80] It may be that any publisher considering such a venture might also seek to rely on the more 'open' provisions in s 52(4) of CRRA 2000. Section 56(1) of CRRA 2000 authorises educational establishments to make a copy of a broadcast or a cable programme for the educational purposes of the establishment without infringing copyright. It is arguable that an internet communication is within the definition of a cable programme – two courts have arguably so found (*obiter*) in the United Kingdom[81] but, it is submitted, such an interpretation could open up the possibility of abuse by

---

72 CA 1963, s 12(5).

73 CA 1963, s 53.

74 CRRA 2000, s 53(1) and (2).

75 On which see CRRA 2000, s 51(3).

76 CRRA 2000, s 53(3).

77 CRRA 2000, s 53(4)(b).

78 CRRA 2000, s 53(5).

79 CRRA 2000, s 53(6).

80 CRRA 2000, s 54 (most of the work must not be in copyright and no more than two pieces from one author over five years).

81 *Shetland Times v Wills* (1996) 37 IPR 79 (Scotland); *Sony Music Entertainment (UK) Ltd v Easyinternetcafe Ltd* [2003] FSR 882.

educational establishments and it might be prudent to hold that this exception applies to simultaneous broadcasts and webcasts rather than all internet-based communications. The issue of photocopying by educational establishments, save where the copying is done by the student under the research or private study fair dealing exception, is regulated by way of a statutory licensing scheme that took effect from January 2003.[82] Under this scheme educational establishments pay a fixed annual fee, *per* student, and in return for this fee permission is given to photocopy materials covered by the conditions set by the licensing agency; the Irish Copyright Licensing Agency, a collecting society established by CLÉ (the Irish Book Publishers Association). Apart from this licensing scheme, reprographic copying by librarians or archivists on behalf of either the library community or library users, is regulated by ss 59–70 of CRRA 2000. In brief, copying for replacement purposes, preparing catalogues and the like are possible under strict conditions. Coping by librarians or archivists for users of the library is also possible, but a system of statutory declarations and restrictions on the number of copies that can be supplied are in place.[83] It is understood that these rules are under review.

PUBLIC PERFORMANCE EXCEPTIONS

[17.16] A number of somewhat diverse infringement exceptions and defences were found in CA 1963. For the sake of ease of analysis, these are being grouped together. The reading or recitation of reasonable extracts from a published literary or dramatic work, when sufficiently acknowledged, was not an infringement.[84] In the case of sound recordings, persons who caused the recording to be heard in public, broadcast, or communicated on a diffusion service did not infringe copyright if that person undertook to refer the dispute about payment of equitable remuneration to the Controller under s 31 of the Act.[85] A person who caused a sound recording to be heard in public by hotel guests, and the like, or in clubs or associations that were charitable in nature[86] likewise did not infringe copyright if strict conditions were met.[87] In the cases of films that are newsreels, infringement did not occur if the newsreel was seen or heard in public, or broadcast after the end of 50 years in which the events depicted occurred.[88] Where a sound or television broadcast was heard in public, the person so causing the broadcast to

---

[82] Copyright and Related Rights (Certification of Licensing Scheme for Reprographic Copying by Educational Establishments) (The Irish Copyright Licensing Agency Limited) Order 2002 (SI 514/2002).

[83] CRRA 2000, ss 61–63 and the Copyright And Related Rights (Recording for Purposes of Time-Shifting) Order 2000 (SI 407/2000). On the history of the library exemptions see Sherman and Wiseman (2010) 73 MLR 240.

[84] CA 1963, s 12(4) and (12). See 199 *Dáil Debates*, Cols 1420–1422.

[85] CA 1963, s 17(5).

[86] CA 1963, s 17(8); see *Phonographic Performance Ltd v Pontins Ltd* [1968] Ch 290.

[87] CA 1963, s 17(9).

[88] CA 1963, s 18(7). Where a film incorporates CA 1963, Part II material but copyright in the film expires, public performance of the film does not infringe the underlying copyrights: CA 1963, s 18(6).

be heard in public did not infringe copyright in the sound recording[89] and a similar exception was provided for persons who, by receiving a broadcast, cause a film to be seen or heard in public.[90] An even broader exception, covering CA 1963, Pt II copyrights, as well as a cinematographic film copyright, operated vis-à-vis authorised broadcasts distributed by way of a diffusion service.[91]

CRRA 2000 retains many of these provisions. For example, s 55(1) makes provision for the possibility that a literary, dramatic or musical work would be performed before an audience limited to persons directly connected with the educational establishment – students, teachers and other staff[92] – either in the case of instruction or possibly in fundraising activities. CA 1963 also had such a provision[93] but during the course of the debates on what is now CRRA 2000, s 55(1), the Irish Music Rights Organisation (IMRO) gave an undertaking[94] that it would not seek to licence school concerts by using s 55(1) save in cases where its interests would be prejudiced. In the light of this undertaking, enforcement of s 55(1) by IMRO will be problematical. Audiences of students and staff are not part of 'the public' for the purposes of infringement by playing or showing a work in public.[95] Section 90(1) of CRRA 2000 permits the reading or recitation of any reasonable extract from a literary or dramatic work carefully made available to the public, as did s 12(3) of CA 1963, but CRRA 2000, s 90(2) goes further in providing that any fixation or broadcasting of the performance or recitation will not infringe copyright. Section 97 of CRRA 2000 re-enacts the exemption in respect of causing a sound recording broadcast or cable programme in a place where residents or inmates sleep, but this widely misunderstood exemption does not authorise 'public performances' of musical works, films or dramatic works in the form of television set use in hotel bedrooms.[96] Interestingly, the new form of the exemption in respect of playing sound recordings by clubs and societies has not yet come into force.[97]

REPRODUCTION EXCEPTIONS

[17.17] Exceptions to an author's right to authorise reproduction of CA 1963, Part II works were again somewhat diverse. In the case of publicly available manuscripts unpublished but made 100 years previously, the author having died 50 years previously,

---

[89] CA 1963, s 52(1); the author's copyright as distinct from the phonogram producer's copyright is, however, so infringed; *Performing Right Society v Rosses Point Hotel Co High Court* (20 February 1967, unreported).

[90] CA 1963, s 52(2).

[91] CA 1963, s 52(3). See *Performing Right Society v Marlin Communal Aerials* [1982] ILRM 269.

[92] Parents are not 'directly connected' with the activities of the educational establishment.

[93] CA 1963, s 53(3)–(5).

[94] The 'Gaffney' letter given by IMRO Chief Executive Adrian Gaffney.

[95] CRRA 2000, ss 40(1)(b) and 55(2); Copyright and Related Rights (Amendment) Act 2004.

[96] See para **[16.27]** above.

[97] CA 1963, s 17(8)(b); CRRA 2000, s 98. See *Phonographic Performance Ltd v South Tyneside Metropolitan Borough Council* [2001] RPC 594 (sound recordings at aerobics classes not covered by exemption).

copyright was not infringed by publishing the work in accordance with directions made by the Minister.[98] The reproduction of a literary, dramatic or musical work, which RTE has been authorised to broadcast by way of an ephemeral recording, made entirely for broadcast purposes, did not infringe copyright if RTE complied with the requirements of the Act.[99] A similar exemption operated in relation to the sound recording copyright.[100] The most significant reproduction right exception in relation to sound and television broadcasts was the right of persons to make a recording for private purposes, whether this be by way of a film[101] or a television broadcast (eg a video recording) or a sound recording[102] of a sound broadcast (eg cassette taping of a radio broadcast). Again, this does not authorise an infringement of any Part II rights held by others (eg the composer of music used in the broadcast) or infringement of the s 17 sound recording copyright. Finally, in relation to the s 20 copyright in the typographical arrangement of a published edition, reproduction in the form of a photographic reproduction (photocopy) did not infringe that copyright if undertaken for private research or study purposes.[103]

[17.18] CRRA 2000 has not re-enacted the Ministerial power to regulate the publishing of previously unpublished manuscripts. Broadcast organisations and cable programme service providers are permitted to use their own facilities to make copies of a work when licensed by the right holder to use the work, but these records must now be deleted after three months rather than six months as before.[104] There is a specific provision giving authorised broadcasters and cable programme service providers the right to maintain supervision and control over programme[105] and regulators such as ComReg have similar powers.[106] In relation to the home taping of broadcasts and cable programmes solely for private and domestic use, s 101(1) specifically authorises 'time-shifting' by individuals, and s 101(2) makes similar provision in respect of establishments, defined in the legislation as multiple occupancy residence units housing students, patients, etc.[107] Making a photograph for private and domestic use of any image contained in a broadcast, cable programme or film will not infringe copyright in the broadcast or cable programme, or film contained therein.[108]

[17.19] Immediate reception and retransmission of a broadcast from within the State via a cable programme service does not infringe copyright in the broadcast if done under statutory authority and the broadcast is intended for reception in the same area, not being

---

[98] CA 1963, s 12(6); see SI 158/1995, which is subject to CA 1963, s 12(6); for national archives see National Archives Act 1986, s 17.

[99] CA 1963, s 12(7) and (8).

[100] CA 1963, s 17(11) and (12).

[101] CA 1963, s 19(5)(a).

[102] CA 1963, s 19(5)(b).

[103] CA 1963, s 20(6).

[104] CRRA 2000, s 99(1).

[105] CRRA 2000, s 99(2).

[106] CRRA 2000, s 100(1).

[107] CRRA 2000, s 100(2); SI 407/2000.

[108] CRRA 2000, s 102.

a satellite or encrypted transmission.[109] 'Not for profit' organisations that modify works to meet special needs are also given statutory protection from liability but these provisions[110] have not been followed by a s 104 designated bodies Order.

[17.20] In relation to the ephemeral recording exceptions given to RTE in relation to the authorised use of literary, dramatic and musical works in CA 1963, s 12, and the similar exception in relation to RTE's use of sound recordings in s 17, the obligation to destroy such recordings within six months did not apply if the recording was stored as being one of exceptional documentary character. This has been replaced by s 105 of CRRA 2000, which permits a designated body to make fixations of broadcasts or cable programmes of a designated class without infringing any copyrights relating thereto. CRRA 2000 has entirely new provisions authorising designated bodies to made fixations of performances of anonymous works of folklore as long as no other copyrights are infringed and the performer does not prohibit the fixation,[111] the fixation being maintained in an archive. Certain provisions relating to copying by archives relate to preserving or replacing works in the permanent collection of the archive.[112]

ARTISTIC WORKS

[17.21] A specific exception to the reproduction right was also expressly provided for where a sculpture or a work of artistic craftsmanship is permanently situated in a public place or public venue; the work might be photographed, painted, drawn, or an engraving of it might be made. Such a work might also be included in a broadcast or a film. The same freedoms existed for architectural works. Publication of the result was also not an infringement of copyright.[113]

[17.22] A broader exception, applicable to all artistic works included in a film or television broadcast existed where inclusion is for background purposes or is incidental to the main purposes behind the film.[114] An artist who used a drawing or a model, for example, in creating a work, who later uses the same drawing or model to create a subsequent work does not infringe copyright in the first work unless the subsequent work repeats or imitates the main design in the earlier work.[115] In relation to architectural works, reconstruction of a building in accordance with the original or with drawings of the original building does not infringe copyright.[116] The ephemeral reproduction right given to RTE was applicable to artistic works, as was the archival exception for works, having exceptional documentary character. CRRA 2000 also makes provision in respect of the reproduction of buildings, sculpture and works of artistic craftsmanship[117] and the

---

[109] CRRA 2000, s 103.
[110] CRRA 2000, s 104.
[111] CRRA 2000, s 92; see SI 407/2000.
[112] Eg CRRA 2000, s 65.
[113] CA 1963, s 14(3) and (5).
[114] CA 1963, s 14(4).
[115] CA 1963, s 14(8).
[116] CA 1963, s 14(9) and (10).
[117] CRRA 2000, s 93.

broader incidental inclusion defence in s 52 applies to all works, including artistic works. The fair dealing defence for the purpose of reporting current events does not apply to photographs.[118] The provision in CA 1963 on the use of drawings or models in order to create another work is not repeated,[119] probably because of the demise of the commissioned work provision, but s 95 provides that where the author is not the copyright owner (eg an employee created work or copyright has been assigned) it is not an infringement to copy the work as long as the main design is not repeated or imitated.[120] The reconstruction of buildings provision is re-enacted in CRRA 2000, s 96. There is a new provision in relation to the copying of an artistic work for the purpose of copying it and releasing copies of the work, for the purpose of advertising the sale of the work.[121]

NON-VOLUNTARY LICENCES FOR RECORDINGS OF MUSICAL WORKS

[17.23] A very substantial exception to a composer's right to authorise the reproduction of a musical work was found in s 13 of CA 1963. Under this section any person may manufacture a record of a musical work, or an adaptation of that work in the State as long as that musical work has previously been made or imported into the State for retail sale by the right holder or with the right holder's licence. This exception was developed in order to allow the public to gain access to recordings of musical works while providing the composer and publisher with a right to equitable remuneration. There were a number of procedural requirements laid down in the Act – notice must be given to the right holder prior to manufacture and the manufacturer must intend to work for retail sale – and an agreed royalty (normally around six per cent of the ordinary retail selling price of the record) should be paid to the right holder. The right to manufacture reproductions of a musical work is generally known as the mechanical right and the licensing of this right was and is exercised by the Mechanical Copyright Protection Society (MCPS) on behalf of right holders. The Act contained a dispute resolution procedure[122] and envisaged that where copyright in the musical work and any literary work (ie the lyrics of a recorded song) were held by different persons, apportionment of the royalty paid by the manufacturer should be agreed as between these right holders.[123] A manufacturer does not infringe copyright in either the musical work or any literary copyright if the manufacturer complies with CA 1963, s 13. The s 13 provisions, as compulsory licenses, have appeared increasingly anachronistic and CRRA 2000 did not re-enact them. However, transitional measures were in place where notice was served under CA 1963, s 13. In such cases a one-year period, commencing on 1 January 2001 enabled the person serving the notice to manufacture records to the limit set in the notice as intended to be sold.

---

[118] CRRA 2000, s 51(2).

[119] CA 1963, s 14(4).

[120] CRRA 2000, s 95.

[121] CRRA 2000, s 94; CA 1963, ss 14(11)–(14).

[122] CA 1963, s 13(2). For legislative history, see 199 *Dáil Debates*, Cols 1425–1429.

[123] CA 1963, s 13(5).

[17.24] The Information Society Directive[124] necessitated two important changes to the 2000 legislation.[125] The first is really one of form. Sections 87 and 244 of CRRA 2000 are amended so as to bring the language of the exception into line with the Directive. Electronically cached copies of a work, or 'saved' copies of a work in electronic form may be reproduced in a network transmission by an internet service provider without infringing copyright as long as certain requirements are met. The second exception effects an amendment to s 374 requiring use of technological protection devices to comply with fair dealing and other defences unless the protection device is attached to online works and the terms restricting access have been the subject of contractual provisions.

PUBLIC POLICY

[17.25] Although copyright is an exclusively statutory regime, there are a number of situations in which a right holder may find that the courts are not prepared to uphold a copyright when this would conflict with some compelling or competing policy objective.[126] Firstly, the courts have declined to allow right holders to proceed against infringers in equity when the work in question, which has undoubtedly been pirated, is itself regarded as obscene, or a work calculated to injure the public.[127] Even at common law, a scandalous work which had been pirated by another could be outside the protection of the courts[128] and in the leading modern English case of *Glyn v Weston*[129] the novel *Three Weeks* by Elinor Glyn, which had been denounced as encouraging free love and adultery, in cases where the marriage tie had merely been made irksome, was not protected from an act of infringement by the defendant. More recently, however, the American courts have departed from this kind of position, describing these defences as the vestiges of a bygone era.[130] In the Canadian case of *Aldrich v One Stop Video*[131] the view was expressed that only in clear cases should a court opt to use this residual jurisdiction to protect the social or economic well-being of the public, observing that the Berne Convention does not support content-based denials of copyright in works. The court indicated that unlawful distribution of a work rather than obscenity should be the central issue when a court declines to allow copyright to be enforced against an infringer by refusing to award damages to the right holder. The use of the 'clean hands' doctrine to deny an injunction to restrain unauthorised distribution of the work by a pirate may, in

---

[124] Council Directive 2001/29/EC ([2001] OJ L167/10).

[125] SI 16/2004.

[126] For an unsuccessful Irish attempt see *Hodges & Smith v Welsh* (1840) 2 IR Eq R 266.

[127] *Southey v Sherwood* (1817) 2 Mer 435; *Lord Byron v Dugdale* (1823) 1 LJOS Ch 239; *Baschet v London Illustrated* [1900] 1 Ch 73.

[128] *Stockdale v Onwhyn* (1826) 5 B & C 173.

[129] *Glyn v Weston* [1916] 1 Ch 261; See Phillips (1977) 6 Anglo Am L Rev 138.

[130] *Mitchell Bros Film Group v Cinema Adult Theatre* 604 F 2d 852 (1979). In *Venus Adult Shops v Fraserside Holdings Ltd* (2006) 70 IPR 517 it was held that there was no basis for denying protection because of content; availablity of discretionary remedies may be influenced by content however.

[131] *Aldrich v One Stop Video* (1987) 39 DLR (3d) 362.

any event, be a somewhat short-sighted response; the infringer or pirate can continue to distribute the work to a wider audience with relative impunity!

[17.26] Public policy also intervenes when a right holder seeks to use the monopoly powers given by the Copyright Acts to protect its own market interests while at the same time harming the community as a whole. For this reason the House of Lords in *British Leyland v Armstrong Patents*[132] prevented British Leyland from enforcing artistic copyright in parts used in constructing motor vehicles, on the ground that the sale of vehicles by British Leyland ceded to a purchaser the inherent right to have the vehicle maintained and repaired in the most economical way possible, even if the purchaser and subsequent owners resorted to persons such as the defendant who have manufactured identical replacement parts that competed with the plaintiff's own spare parts. The House of Lords noted that while it was novel to apply the principle that a grantor should not derogate from his grant so as to preclude the enforcement of a statutory right to which the grantor was *prima facie* entitled, the principle could apply to this novel set of circumstances. The Hong Kong Court of Appeal, in *Green Cartridge Co (Hong Kong) Ltd v Canon*,[133] applied the repairer principle to a case where the plaintiffs sought to prevent the defendants from reverse engineering the replaceable toner cartridges provided by the plaintiffs in their printers and photocopiers in order for the defendants to produce a cheaper rival product. Because the owner of a computer printer is entitled to repair that printer, the majority of the court reasoned that this gave a right to repair the printer in the most convenient manner, which in this case involved the right to select a replacement cartridge.

[17.27] However, on appeal to the Privy Council the decision of the Hong Kong Court of Appeal was revised[134] because the *British Leyland defence*[135] was a limited one that should not be extended to consumable items that the market anticipated would have a short life before being replaced. In *Mars UK Ltd v Teknowledge Ltd*,[136] Jacob J indicated that in respect of infringement actions in which breach of national law transposing the computer programs and database directives was alleged, it was inappropriate for the court to construct a repairer defence when both the European and national legislators had declined to include such provisions into the relevant legislation. Nevertheless, signs of a 'repairer' defence can be detected in a recent majority decision of the Supreme Court of Canada where four of the judges held that the owner of an artistic work did not infringe copyright by transferring the image from a paper backing onto a canvas backing.[137] The only Irish case in which this species of defence has been explored is the Supreme Court decision in *Re Hunter's Patent*.[138]

---

[132] *British Leyland v Armstrong Patents* [1986] FSR 221. For copyright misuse defences in the US see *Hanna* (1994) 46 Stanford LR 401. So far these defences have not prevailed in UK computer cases; *Ibcos Computers Ltd v Barclays Finance Ltd* [1994] FSR 275.

[133] *Green Cartridge Co (Hong Kong) Ltd v Canon* (1996) 34 IPR 614.

[134] *Green Cartridge Co (Hong Kong) Ltd v Canon* [1997] AC 728.

[135] *British Leyland v Armstrong Patents* [1986] FSR 221.

[136] *Mars UK Ltd v Teknowledge Ltd* (1999) 46 IPR 248.

[137] *Theberge v Galerie d'Art du Petit Champlain Inc* (2002) 210 DLR (4th) 385.

[138] *Re Hunter's Patent* [1965] RPC 416.

[17.28] The Electronic Commerce Directive (Directive 31/2000/EC), as transposed by SI 68/2003, affords an intermediary service provider – basically an internet service provider – with some defences and immunities. These are applicable in a copyright context although most cases are decided in the context of defamation actions.[139] The most important defences relate to an internet service provider being a 'mere conduit'[140] and requiring an internet service provider to act expeditiously when aware, or made aware, of infringing material.[141] In *EMI Records Ireland Ltd and Others v UPC Communications Ireland Ltd*[142] s 40(4) was said not to legitimise stopping material in transit via a network, as distinct from removing access to material at a specific location over which the ISP has access. Charleton J was critical of the rather limited language used in relation to s 40(4). Contrasting this with the permissive provisions found in the Electronic Commerce Directive, recital 47, and art 8(3) of the Information Society Directive, Charleton J was respectful of the fact that the European legislature, had provided a considerable degree of latitude for national legislators and was unable to construe Community law in such a was as to afford a remedial power to disable access to a third party. Charleton J drew attention to Directive 2009/140/EC, to be transposed before 26 May 2011, which will require ComReg to address issues of this kind. Charleton J himself suggested a District Court access termination procedure could serve a useful purpose.

PARODY

[17.29] The fact that an existing work has been used to create a separate work which is intended to parody that work is regarded in the US as within the 'fair use' doctrine.[143] English case law does not recognise parody as a legitimate defence[144] but approaches the issue by considering whether the use of the original work is such as to create a new, separate work, little or nothing of the original remaining. This seems to ignore the fact that a parody can only be effective if the parody mirrors the original. This factor, and the moral rights implications of treating the original work to derogatory treatment, will have to be considered in future cases. The Irish legislator was afforded the opportunity to introduce a parody defence when transposing the Information Society Directive[145] but declined to do so. It might be possible for the parody to come within one of the 'fair dealing' defences or the incidental inclusion defence, of course, but a specific parody

---

[139] *Bunt v Tilley* [2006] EWHC 407 (Ch); *Mulvaney v Betfair* [2009] IEHC 133.

[140] SI 68/2003, reg 16.

[141] SI 68/2003, reg 18; *Mulvaney v Betfair* [2009] IEHC 133.

[142] *EMI Records Ireland Ltd and Others v UPC Communications Ireland Ltd* [2010] IEHC 000 (11 October 2010).

[143] *Acuff Rose Music v Campbell* (1994) 114 SC 1164; *Depel* [1994] EIPR 358.

[144] *Joy Music Ltd v Sunday Pictorial* [1960] 1 All ER 703; *Williamson Music v Pearson* [1987] FSR 97.

[145] Council Directive 2001/29/EC, art 5.3(k). This defence rarely succeeds: *Productions Avanti Cine Video Inc v Favreau* (1999) 1 CPR (4th) 129; *BC1 Automobile Association v PEIU Local 378* (2001) 10 CPR (4th) 423; *Canwest Mediaworks Publications Inc v Horizon Publications* [2008] BCSC 1609.

defence would have been an appropriate means of giving statutory effect to freedom of expression. Most instances where parody has been pleaded involve a commercial appropriation and in such situations the defence is difficult to make out in the face of considerable financial gain to the defendant.

[17.30] In *Rowling v Uitgeverij Byblos BV*[146] preliminary injunctive relief was given against a Dutch translation of a Russian book, titled in English *Tanya Grotter and the Magic Double Bass*. The author and publisher of *Harry Potter and the Philosopher's Stone* pointed to significant plot similarities and the Amsterdam District Court, after finding that infringement of copyright via the making of an unauthorised adaptation of the Harry Potter book could be made out, rejected the defence of parody because humour was not adequately evoked by the defendant's work and thus there was no new and original work.

A PUBLIC INTEREST DEFENCE IN IRISH LAW?

[17.31] Notwithstanding the decision of the majority of the Court of Appeal in *Yelland*[147] in which it was observed that there was no room in UK copyright law for a public interest defence when the defendant reproduced a substantial part of the plaintiff's work, a different Court of Appeal has held that in exceptional circumstances such a defence may be available.[148] Freedom of expression and the public interest may well require such a defence to be made out, but the Court of Appeal indicated that precise categorisation of the circumstances in which the defence would be available would not be attempted. However, in most cases the application of the standard fair dealing defences would provide the necessary means of judging whether publication of another's work would be permitted. The Court of Appeal emphasised that this common law defence, whereby the enforcement of copyright would be declined on the grounds of the public interest, is specifically mandated by s 171(3) of the Copyright, Designs and Patents Act 1988. It is submitted that even though CRRA 2000, like its predecessor, did not contain such a provision, an Irish court would be likely in exceptional cases to follow the English position as mapped out in *Ashdown v Telegraph Group Ltd*.[149] A public interest defence in actions for breach of confidence has been expressly approved by the Supreme Court in *National Irish Bank Ltd v RTE*.[150] On the other hand, there is something to be said for removing the element of subjectivity from copyright law by a court declining to proscribe a work on the basis of offensiveness or indecency.

[17.32] In *Venus Adult Shops Pty Ltd v Fraserside Holdings Ltd*,[151] an infringement action where the defendants infringed copyright in pornographic films, the Federal

---

[146] *Rowling v Uitgeverij Byblos BV* [2003] ECDR 245, affd [2004] ECDR 61.

[147] *Hyde Park Residence Ltd v Yelland* [2000] RPC 604.

[148] *Ashdown v Telegraph Group Ltd* [2002] RPC 235.

[149] *Ashdown v Telegraph Group Ltd* [2002] RPC 235.

[150] *National Irish Bank Ltd v RTE* [1998] 2 IR 465. See Fenwick and Phillipson (2004) 55 NILQ 118.

[151] *Venus Adult Shops Pty Ltd v Fraserside Holdings Ltd* (2006) 70 IPR 517. *Sims* [2008] EIPR 189.

Court of Australia affirmed that in Australia there is no statutory basis for holding that copyright does not subsist because the content of the work offends against community values or standards. The content of the work may inform a court's discretion to award certain remedies. Where the claim is for conversion damages, the fact that the goods in question cannot lawfully be sold will be relevant but the onus rests upon the defendant to show the absence of a lawful market.

RELATED ARGUMENTS

[17.33] While not defences, *per se*, copyright legislation provides a potential infringer with other mechanisms and arguments whereby liability may be avoided.

[17.34] It may be possible to challenge the subsistence of copyright by arguing that the use of the plaintiff's work extends only to ideas and principles underlying the work; that the use extends to procedures, methods of operation and mathematical concepts only,[152] (non-protected content, in other words). The defendant may also argue that the plaintiff's action is based upon the work of another author[153] and that protection should not be available to the extent that this is an infringing use.

[17.35] Where the work has been published anonymously or pseudonymously, CRRA 2000, s 32(2) provides that, in respect of such literary, dramatic, musical or artistic works or an original database, copyright is not to subsist where it is reasonable to presume that the author has been dead for 70 years or more and that a similar rule applies to films.[154]

[17.36] English case law demonstrates that, on occasion, efforts are made to persuade the courts to carve out new defences based on EU law.[155] For example, the Reuse of Public Sector Information Regulations[156] set out mechanisms and procedures whereby a public body may be required to allow others to make use of materials generated by that public body. The Regulations do not give the user a defence to copyright infringement.[157]

---

[152] CRRA 2000, s 17(3).

[153] CRRA 2000, s 17(5) and (6): *A-One Accessory Imports Pty v Off Road Imports Pty* (1993) 34 IPR 306 332.

[154] CRRA 2000, s 32(3).

[155] Eg *Mars UK v Teknowledge* [2000] FSR 138 (an unsuccessful effort to create a software repairer defence); *Controller of HM Stationery Office v Green AMPS Ltd* [2008] EWCA Civ 588 (downloading maps for re-use of public sector materials)

[156] SI 279/2005, transposing Directive 2003/98/EC.

[157] *Controller of HM Stationery Office v Green AMPS Ltd* [2008] EWCA Civ 588.

Chapter 18

Remedies for Copyright Infringement

INTRODUCTION

[18.01] In general terms, the Copyright Acts provide the right holder with a number of specific remedies, while emphasising that the primary reliefs are the same as those available to a person who issues proceedings in respect of an infringement of other proprietary rights – breach of confidence, passing-off, and trade mark infringement, for example; this is hardly surprising given the overlap between copyright and these related causes of action. The range of remedies and the methods of enforcing these remedies can be somewhat complex, representing as they do a curious amalgam of self-help remedies, civil enforcement procedures and reliefs, and criminal and customs law. In recent years the emphasis upon effective remedies, a process commenced in the 1988 European Commission Green Paper[1] and the Trade-Related Aspects of Intellectual Property Rights (GATT), in the form of the provisions of Part II of the TRIPS Agreement[2] has forced the Oireachtas to overhaul the legislative framework in respect of the range of remedies available to a right owner following upon a copyright infringement. The unsatisfactory state of Irish copyright law was the basis of a complaint, under the TRIPS Agreement to the World Trade Organisation (WTO), by the US and although the proceedings were discontinued the WTO reference forced the Irish government to act very promptly in passing the Intellectual Property (Miscellaneous Provisions) Act 1998. This Act was something of a transitional measure in the sense that the Act strengthened the presumptions applicable in respect of works and ownership of works, thus bypassing the Supreme Court decision in *Phonographic Performance (Ireland) Ltd v Cody*[3] as well as stiffening up the criminal penalties that may be imposed upon persons convicted of criminal offences in respect of copyright works. The Intellectual Property (Miscellaneous Provisions) Act 1998 has been replaced by the Copyright and Related Rights Act 2000 (CRRA 2000). The European Commission has revisited the issue of remedies in the form of the Enforcement Directive.[4]

---

[1] 'Copyright and the Challenge of Technology' (1988) COM(88) 172 final.
[2] Agreement on Trade-Related Aspects of Intellectual Property Rights.
[3] *Phonographic Performance (Ireland) Ltd v Cody* [1994] 2 ILRM 241, [1998] 4 IR 504.
[4] Council Directive 2004/48/EC ([2004] OJ L195/16); see SI 360/2006. The Directive adds little new or more effective to Irish law; see *Duhan v Radius Television Production* [2007] IEHC 292.

COMMENCEMENT OF PROCEEDINGS

[18.02] The Copyright Act 1963 (CA 1963) specifically stated[5] that infringements of copyright are to be actionable at the suit of the owner of the copyright, a provision re-enacted by s 127(1) of CRRA 2000. Transfer of ownership from the original creator should take place on the foot of a written assignment and where the assignment is a partial assignment of rights, eg by a composer of the performing rights in a musical work to the Irish Music Rights Organisation (IMRO), then only the owner, in this case, IMRO, may sue and obtain the full reliefs. In cases where the owner has granted an exclusive licence which is currently in force the exclusive licensee can enforce the same rights of action as the owner (save against the owner) and these rights in respect of most reliefs[6] are concurrent with those of the owner. Except where the court directs otherwise, the owner or exclusive licensee who issues proceedings cannot proceed with the action unless the other party is joined as a plaintiff in the action or added as a defendant.[7] If, however, the relief sought is an interlocutory injunction then either the owner or the exclusive licensee may proceed with such an action.[8] Should the action be proceeded with by one party only, then damages are to be assessed by reference to liabilities that the plaintiff (if the exclusive licensee) may be subject to (in the form of royalties or otherwise) or any other pecuniary remedy already awarded or any remedy that the other party may have against the defendant.[9] Where the relief sought is an account of profits then such apportionment as between owner and exclusive licensee as the court thinks just may be ordered (subject to any arrangement made by those parties of which the court is aware).[10] Where an owner or exclusive licensee has already obtained judgment under the legislation in respect of the same infringement, no subsequent order in favour of the other party may be made where the orders sought or already obtained relate to damages or an account of profits.[11] These provisions are clearly intended to prevent the defendant from being exposed to double jeopardy and to encourage all the parties to be before the courts and thus shorten litigation. For example, the defendant is to have as against the exclusive licensee any defence that could be validly asserted against the owner (such as consent).[12] Where the owner or exclusive licensee is not joined as a plaintiff but is added as a defendant that joined defendant is not to be liable for any costs

---

[5] CA 1963, s 22(1).

[6] CA 1963, s 25(2); CRRA 2000, s 135(2).

[7] CA 1963, s 25(3); CRRA 2000, s 136(1). For a compelling illustration, see *Dixon Projects Pty v Masterton Homes Pty* (1996) 36 IPR 136. The question whether proceedings for infringement of copyright may proceed against an infringer brought by an exclusive licensee without joining the exclusive licensor was fully considered in *Flashback Holdings Pty v Showtime DVD Holdings Pty* (2008) 79 IPR 2007.

[8] CA 1963, s 25(4); CRRA 2000, s 136(3).

[9] CA 1963, s 25(6); CRRA 2000, s 136(3).

[10] CA 1963, s 25(7); CRRA 2000, s 136(4).

[11] CA 1963, s 25(8); CRRA 2000, s 136(4).

[12] CA 1963, s 25(5); CRRA 2000, s 135(3).

in the action unless he enters an appearance and takes part in the action.[13] Save in these cases of exclusive licensing, the Act does not prevent a work that is jointly owned by two or more persons from being protected by way of legal action by one of them acting without the other owner or owners.[14] In cases of equitable interests or equitable titles, proceedings may be commenced by such a person in order to obtain an interlocutory injunction[15] but that final relief will not be made until the equitable title has been perfected or the legal owner joined as co-plaintiff (or possibly co-defendant). [16]

Identifying the correct defendant

[18.03] Persons who, without the consent of the owner, do or authorise others to do restricted acts, are the correct defendants.[17] In cases of primary infringement it is possible for a number of joint tortfeasors to be sued and rendered liable under the Civil Liability Act 1961.[18] The leading English case is *CBS Songs Ltd v Amstrad Consumer Electronics plc*,[19] favouring a test of two or more persons acting in concert pursuant to a common design. It may be that a company officer such as an executive director is personally liable for instructing or requiring other company personnel to infringe copyright,[20] thus making the company and that director each separately liable. However, the precise test in establishing liability remains uncertain for recent lines of authority in both Canada and Australia tend to favour a test which is higher than that set in the traditional English cases; a test which requires the court to decide not simply whether the director has committed or directed the tort so deliberately or recklessly that he has made the tort his own. The leading English case in recent years is *MCA Records Ltd v Charly Records Ltd*,[21] applied in *Tommy Hilfiger Europe v McGarry*.[22]

---

13 CA 1963, s 25(9); CRRA 2000, s 136(2).
14 *Lauri v Renad* [1892] 3 Ch 402; *Dixon Projects Pty v Masterton Homes Pty* (1996) 36 IPR 136.
15 *Merchant Adventurers Ltd v Grew* [1972] 1 Ch 242; *John Richardson Computers Ltd v Flanders* [1993] FSR 497.
16 *Performing Right Society v London Theatre of Varieties* [1924] AC 1; *Batjak Productions Inc v Simitar Entertainment (UK)* [1996] FSR 139.
17 For music performance problems see *Phonographic Performance NZ v Lion Breweries* [1980] FSR 1; *Warne v Genex Corpn* (1996) 35 IPR 284 illustrates that a wrong choice can be made.
18 *Ravenscroft v Herbert* [1980] RPC 193; *House of Spring Gardens Ltd v Point Blank Ltd* [1984] IR 611.
19 *CBS Songs Ltd v Amstrad Consumer Electronics plc* [1988] 2 All ER 484.
20 *C Evans v Spritebrand* [1985] 1 WLR 317; *APRA v Valamo Property Ltd* (1990) 18 IPR 216.
21 *MCA Records Ltd v Charly Records Ltd* [2002] FSR 401. *Mentmore Manufacturing Co v National Merchandising Manufacturing Co* (1978) 89 DLR (3d) 195; *Apple Computer Inc v Mackintosh Computer Inc* (1986) 8 CIPR 153; *King v Milpurrurru* (1996) 34 IPR 11; *Mentmore* was cited by Costello J with approval in *House of Spring Gardens.*
22 *Tommy Hilfiger Europe v McGarry* [2005] IEHC 66.

Presumptions of title

[18.04] The right holder obtained the benefit of a number of presumptions under s 26 of CA 1963. Copyright was presumed to exist in a work and it is to be vested in the plaintiff if the defendant does not put these matters in issue.[23]

[18.05] The presumptions contained in the CA 1963 were, in practice, of limited use to the plaintiff. The presumptions were effective in relation to the subsistence of copyright and the plaintiff's ownership of copyright only if the defendant did not put these matters in issue. All the defendant had to do was contest either or both of these points and the presumption in question was negated. In *Phonographic Performance (Ireland) Ltd v Cody*,[24] Keane J held that the plaintiff could prove issues of title upon affidavit rather than by direct evidence and witnesses. This decision was reversed by the Supreme Court,[25] holding that where a defendant *bona fide* sought the attendance of witnesses for cross-examination, the trial judge had no discretion under the Rules of Superior Courts 1986[26] to allow these facts to be proved by affidavit. The Intellectual Property (Miscellaneous Provisions) Act 1998 replaced the 'put in issue' criteria with a range of presumptions that are now set out in CRRA 2000 and they apply to any proceedings, whether civil or criminal, for infringement of copyright.[27] Copyright is presumed to subsist in a work until the contrary is proved.[28] In general, where copyright in a work is proved, admitted or presumed under the Act, the plaintiff is presumed to be the owner or exclusive licensee of the copyright until the contrary is proved.[29] The presumptions mentioned previously in respect of works under CA 1963 in relation to the making of certain works have been upgraded and are applicable to all works where the work bears a name purporting to be that of the author[30] or the person who first lawfully made the work available to the public.[31] Presumptions of ownership for joint authors and deceased or unknown authors[32] are also found in CRRA 2000.[33]

Authorising infringement

[18.06] In the leading case[34] the concept of authorising an infringement has been summarised as granting or purporting to grant, expressly or by implication, the act of

---

[23] CA 1963, s 26(1)(a) and (b).

[24] *Phonographic Performance (Ireland) Ltd v Cody* [1994] 2 ILRM 241, [1998] IR 504.

[25] *Phonographic Performance (Ireland) Ltd v Cody* [1998] 4 IR 504 at 518.

[26] Specifically O 39, r 1.

[27] CRRA 2000, s 139(1).

[28] CRRA 2000, s 139(2).

[29] CRRA 2000, s 139(3).

[30] CRRA 2000, s 139(4). See also s 139(5) for certain consequential presumptions.

[31] CRRA 2000, s 139(6); CA 1963, s 26(3).

[32] CRRA 2000, s 139(8); CA 1963, s 26(6).

[33] For presumptions relating to performers' rights and the database right see CRRA 2000, ss 211 and 339.

[34] Atkin LJ in *Falcon v Famous Players Film Co* [1926] 2 KB 474 at 499, approved in *CBS Songs v Amstrad* [1988] 2 All ER 484.

infringement which is complained of. An implied grant will occur when the defendant cedes to the user the apparent right to do the thing complained of when that usage is the only real use contemplated, eg renting a film to a cinema owner who shows it to the public.[35] Some element of active participation or failure to control the boundary between lawful and unlawful use of the work should be shown, such as indifference to controlling photocopying machines[36] where these are within the power of the defendant. Hiring out records or machines while being indifferent as to whether someone else infringes, is not to authorise, for the hirer cannot exercise control over the record or machine.[37] Cynical advertising of the infringement potential of a machine in order to encourage sales will not 'authorise' infringement.[38]

SEARCH AND SEIZURE REMEDIES

[18.07] There are a number of procedures which can be used to limit or control the distribution of infringing copies of copyright material, and although these powers mostly have a statutory basis, the provisions of the Irish Constitution require that these powers be exercised in accordance with constitutionally mandated norms and values.

[18.08] Section 27(1) of CA 1963 sets out a number of specific offences, which relate to the manufacture, sale, exhibition or importation of infringing copies of a work. Section 27(2) sets out offences in relation to the distribution of infringing copies while s 27(3) makes possession of a plate an offence. In such a context CA 1963, as amended in 1987, sets out a procedure whereby the owner of a work may apply to the District Court for an order authorising a member of the Garda Siochána to seize copies without warrant and bring these copies before the court. This power to authorise without warrant was exercised where there was a reasonable ground for believing that infringing copies were being hawked, carried about, sold or offered or exposed for sale, let for hire or offered or exposed for hire, and following upon the delivery up to the court of any infringing copies seized, the District Justice could either order the destruction of these infringing copies or otherwise deal with them as the court saw fit.[39] These provisions really dealt with retail, sale or distribution on the street and are to be so construed. Subsection (5), however, went further by allowing the District Court, in cases where there was a reasonable ground for believing that offences under s 27(1), (2), (3) or (8) had been committed on premises, to authorise a search warrant to a named garda to enter those premises, seize infringing copies and deliver them up to be dealt with by the

---

35 *Falcon v Famous Players Film Co* [1926] 2 KB 474.

36 Contrast *CCH Canadian Ltd v Law Society of Upper Canada* (2004) 236 DLR (4th) 395 with *Moorehouse v University of NSW* [1976] RPC 151; *APRA Ltd v Jain* (1990) 18 IPR 663.

37 *CBS Inc v Ames Records and Tapes* [1981] 2 All ER 812; *Vigneux v Canadian Performing Right Society* [1945] AC 108.

38 *A & M Records v Audio Magnetics* [1979] FSR 1; *CBS Songs v Amstrad* [1988] 2 All ER 484; *Performing Right Society v Bray UDC* [1930] IR 509. No mental element is needed in authorising infringement: *King v Milpurrurru* (1996) 34 IPR 11 but later filesharing cases do suggest this is a factor.

39 CA 1963, s 27(4) as amended by Copyright (Amendment) Act 1987, s 2.

District Justice in the manner already outlined[40] under sub-s (4). These powers were not to be exercised against persons or vehicles.[41] In relation to copyright in films where video piracy is involved, the copyright holder is likely to be represented by the Irish National Federation Against Copyright Theft (INFACT) and the courts have accepted proofs of ownership and capacity to act on the part of right holders.[42]

[18.09] These search and seizure provisions have been replaced in CRRA 2000 by much more far-reaching search and seizure powers. In relation to the possession, custody or control of infringing copies of works,[43] or articles specifically designed or adapted to make infringing copies, or protection defeating devices, s 131 of CRRA 2000 sets out a procedure whereby the copyright owner may seek from the appropriate court[44] an order that the infringing article be delivered up to that person or whoever the court may direct. Section 132 re-enacts the District Court's power to order the seizure of infringing copies that are being hawked, carried about and mandated.[45] However, s 132 relates to articles specifically designed or adapted to making infringing copies and protection defeating devices as well as infringing copies. The exercise of this order is to be carried out by a member of the Garda Síochána not the right holder and the infringing item must be brought before the District Court for such disposal as the court sees fit.[46] The application under s 132 may be grounded on hearsay evidence from a witness or deponent,[47] who is not obliged to indicate the source of his or her information.[48] These quite sweeping provisions, however, have to a limited extent been balanced by a statutory right to obtain damages, if, following upon the execution of a District Court order, the appropriate court is satisfied that no infringement of copyright took place and the information given to the copyright owner was given maliciously,[49] for example, by a disgruntled former employee of the person against whom the order was obtained.

[18.10] CRRA 2000 also contains a self-help remedy for a copyright owner in cases where it would be impracticable to seek a s 131 order in respect of infringing copies, articles or devices. Where these are being hawked, carried about or marketed – on street corners or at car boot sales, for example – the copyright owner or trade representative can seize and detain the items in question[50] but is obliged to apply to the District Court

---

[40] CA 1963, s 25(5) and (6).

[41] *Roche v District Justice Martin and the DPP* [1993] ILRM 651.

[42] *Roche v District Justice Martin and the DPP* [1993] ILRM 651.

[43] An exception for a copy held for private and domestic use is implicit.

[44] CRRA 2000, s 2(1) (determined by the financial limits of the jurisdiction of the court).

[45] CA 1963, s 27(4) was the original provision – the language of the section vis-à-vis the activity in question has been altered.

[46] This could involve handing over to a charity: see 'Charities to get bogus clothing' (2002) Irish Times, 22 May.

[47] CRRA 2000, s 132(3).

[48] CRRA 2000, s 132(4).

[49] CRRA 2000, s 132(5).

[50] CRRA 2000, s 133(1). The form of notice to be used at the time of seizure of infringing materials and copy protection defeating devices under CRRA 2000, ss 13 and 257 is set out in SI 440/2009. See also SI 421/2010 for other District Court forms.

for disposal by the court within 30 days of seizure. Notice of the impending seizure must be given to the gardaí within that locality. While exercise of this power may permit that person to enter public places, seizure cannot take place at any person's regular or permanent place of business, trade or profession, nor may any force be used in the seizure. CRRA 2000 also sets out provisions whereby a contested seizure may be resolved by way of application to the District Court.[51] A remedy in damages may be available following upon a seizure where the appropriate court is satisfied that no infringement of copyright had been made out and the person seizing the items had no reasonable grounds for seizing the items in question.[52] These provisions relate to interim right holder reliefs. Final disposal of items seized under ss 131 and 132 is made by the appropriate court under s 145 of CRRA 2000.

[18.11] Apart from these specific search and seizure provisions the right owner may also seek to exercise injunctive relief or some other form of civil remedy such as the collection of documentary or other evidence of infringement of copyright. For example, the possibility that an infringer might seek to destroy evidence of infringement led the English courts to evolve a specific procedure, the *Anton Piller* order[53] which allows right owners and their representatives to enter and search premises and seize any evidence of infringement. The Irish courts have given *Anton Piller* orders on several occasions[54] and in the most recent reported case of *Microsoft Corpn v Brightpoint Ireland Ltd*,[55] Smyth J gave valuable guidance on the appropriate steps to be taken in relation to the obtaining and execution of an *Anton Piller* order.

[18.12] Another valuable form of relief is an order requiring disclosure of information, eg on the source of supply of infringing items, even where it is clear that the person in question was blameless and unaware that an infringement of copyright has taken place. These orders are known as *Norwich Pharmacal*[56] orders and their ever expanding application is a matter of considerable controversy. However, these orders have been given by Irish courts on occasion[57] as part of the process of discovery. The first *Eircom* decision[58] involved an application for a *Norwich Pharmacal* order, which Kelly J granted on 8 July 2005, and a number of related applications were made some days later. In granting *Norwich Pharmacal* relief, Kelly J indicated that, in his view, intellectual property rights must hold sway over privacy rights where infringement threatens to erode intellectual property rights. During 2008, Eircom found that the recording industry had changed tack by using s 40(4) of CRRA 2000 in order to obtain injunctive relief to require filtering software to be fitted to the Eircom network and/or disable access to

---

51 CRRA 2000, s 133(7)–(11).
52 CRRA 2000, s 133(2).
53 *Anton Piller KG v Manufacturing Processes Ltd* [1976] Ch 55.
54 Eg *House of Spring Gardens Ltd v Point Blank Ltd* [1984] IR 611 and *News Datacom Ltd v Lyons* [1994] 1 ILRM 450.
55 *Microsoft Corpn v Brightpoint Ireland Ltd* [2001] 1 ILRM 540; *Sky Channel Pty v Yahmoc Pty* (2003) 58 IPR 63.
56 *Norwich Pharmacal Co v Customs and Excise Comrs* [1974] AC 133; *Ashworth Hospital Authority v MGN Ltd* [2002] 1 WLR 2033.
57 *Megaleasing UK Ltd v Barrett* [1993] ILRM 497; *IO'T v B* [1998] 2 IR 321.
58 *EMI Records (Ireland) Ltd v Eircom* [2005] 4 IR 148.

suspect websites and also to disconnect Eircom subscribers. This litigation was settled, by agreement reached between the parties, in January 2009. Details of the protocol put together after the settlement can be found in Charleton J's judgment in *EMI Records (Ireland) Ltd v Eircom Ltd,*[59] and it is against the background of this settlement that Charleton J gave an *ex tempore* judgment in an application brought by EMI to require Eircom to disable subscriber access to *Pirate Bay.*[60]

[18.13] Where disclosure is sought in the context of discovery proceedings against an alleged infringer, the court may be required to balance the plaintiff's rights to test whether proprietary rights have been infringed with the defendant's interests in protecting any intellectual property that the defendant has independently created. This is a sensitive issue when the plaintiff and the defendant are competitors. Most cases will allow disclosure in a conditional form with the court requiring the plaintiff to restrict access to those persons who can provide assistance on the issue of infringement in exceptional situations: see the order of Kelly J in *Koger Inc and Koger (Dublin) Ltd v O'Donnell and Others.*[61]

[18.14] It should be noted that the power of the court to grant an *ex parte* application or interlocutory application, which will result in the entry and search of premises, such as an *Anton Piller* order, may be grounded on hearsay evidence.[62]

[18.15] The importation of infringing copies of published literary, dramatic or musical works, or sound recordings, may be controlled by a right holder by giving notice to the Revenue Commissioners requesting them to treat copies of the work as prohibited goods.[63] The notice is to be in prescribed form[64] and should not last for more than five years or the length of the period of copyright. The prohibition does not apply to copies imported by a person for private or domestic use. Such importation, however, does not create a criminal offence, nor is the importer liable to any penalty under the Customs Consolidation Acts other than secondary seizure. However, acts of importation, sale or exhibition may be secondary infringements and thus lead to liability thereunder.[65]

DAMAGES

[18.16] The principles which underlie the award of damages following a copyright infringement are based upon the principle of compensation, although there are other possibilities, as we shall see. While CA 1963 afforded little or no guidance to a court on

---

[59] *EMI Records (Ireland) Ltd v Eircom Ltd* [2009] IEHC 411.

[60] *Pirate Bay* [2010] IEHC 108.

[61] *Koger Inc and Koger (Dublin) Ltd v O'Donnell and Others* [2009] IEHC 385, applying, *inter alia, Warner Lamber Co v Glaxo Laboratories Ltd* [1975] RPC 354; contrast *Sport Universal v ProZone Holdings Ltd* [2003] EWHC 204 (Ch).

[62] CRRA 2000, s 132(3); SI 421/2010.

[63] CRRA 2000, s 147, replacing CA 1963, s 28.

[64] SI 231/1964. This is the form used under CRRA 2000.

[65] See the importation of brochures point in *House of Spring Gardens Ltd v Point Blank Ltd* [1984] IR 611.

the appropriate measure of damages, the CRRA 2000 legislation has been deliberately left open-ended, with the judge having a number of pecuniary reliefs available for use, including aggravated and punitive damages, the judge simply being directed to 'award such damages as, having regard to all the circumstances of the case, it considers just'.[66] At a later stage in this work we will consider the extent to which copyright damages and an award for breach of confidence may overlap.[67] It sometimes occurs that the issue of damages is not central to the litigation – the establishment of infringement of a right may be more important to a plaintiff and some judges may simply award a figure without any enquiry into loss.[68]

Measure of loss

[18.17] The measure of damages following on from an infringement of copyright is sometimes said to be a matter which is left 'at large' – that the award is a matter for the court's judgment and discretion.[69] However, it is accepted that the plaintiff will normally seek to obtain the amount by which the value of the copyright of the plaintiff has been diminished as a chose in action; this is often calculated by looking at the volume of sales made by the defendant of the pirated work and deducting the cost of production from the income made by the defendant by way of the unauthorised reproduction and sale.[70] This approach, however, does not always provide adequate compensation to the plaintiff, even if it has the merit of being simple and compatible with the principles of unjust enrichment. The plaintiff may be able to show that his product was more expensive and had a higher profit margin that the pirated work, so merely giving the plaintiff the defendant's profit may not compensate the plaintiff for lost volume of sales. This is particularly important and some cases hold that where the defendant's product undercuts the plaintiff's product, this should be reflected in the compensation award.[71]

[18.18] The leading case dealing with the evidentiary problems that confront a plaintiff who is seeking damage for lost volume sales is *Columbia Pictures v Robinson*.[72] The plaintiffs sought to obtain damages based upon the lost profits which they claimed was the result of the defendant's release onto the market of cheaper, inferior versions of their video cassette product. Disputed figures on how the film cassette would have sold but for the pirated version led Scott J to direct that the normal measure of damages would be pitched between the minimum number of pirated copies sold and a maximum of the

---

66 CRRA 2000, s 128(1).
67 See Ch 24.
68 *H Blacklock & Co v Pearson* [1915] 2 Ch 376.
69 Particularly where estimates are approximate: *Schindler Lifts v Milan Debalak* (1989) 15 IPR 129.
70 As in *Allied Discount Card Ltd v Bord Failte* [1990] ILRM 811; *Star Micronics Property Ltd v Five Star Computers Property* (1991) 22 IPR 473.
71 *Birn Bros Ltd v Keen & Co Ltd* [1918] 2 Ch 281; *International Writing Institute Inc v Rimila Pty* (1994) 30 IPR 250 at 254; *Polygram Records Inc v Raben Footwear Pty* (1996) 35 IPR 426 at 444; *Retail Systems Technology v McGuire* [2007] IEHC 13.
72 *Columbia Pictures v Robinson* [1988] FSR 531. For performer's rights and sound recording copyright see *Experience Hendrix LLC v Times Newspapers* [2010] EWHC 1986 (Ch).

number of legitimate copies that could have been anticipated to have been sold in order to meet the commercial expectations of the film. Further, the pirate cannot expect to put the plaintiff to precise proof of normal or reasonable commercial expectations, and upon proof of the existence of pirated copies, and in the absence of another explanation for the diminished success of the film, the right holder is entitled to attribute the shortfall in sales to the activity of the pirate.

Aggravated, exemplary or punitive damages

[18.19] Apart from the normal compensatory principle based upon lost volume of sales, general principles of compensation permit a court to take cognisance of any aggravated damage that the plaintiff has suffered, such as loss of reputation,[73] mental stress or emotional injury that the defendant's conduct has produced.[74] The important Australian decision in *Milpurrurru v Indofern Pty*[75] holds that ordinary damages awards under the Australian equivalent provision to CA 1963, s 22 make it possible to compensate the plaintiff for suffering and humiliation experienced within a particular artistic community, on basic compensatory principles.

[18.20] Apart from aggravated damages which are broadly compensatory anyway, there is also some scope for the award of exemplary or punitive damages where the plaintiff's award will provide compensation but still leave the defendant with a sizeable profit.[76] Under Irish law a similar rule has been used in defamation cases[77] and a general principle, intended to prevent unjust enrichment, has been canvassed.[78] CA 1963, in s 22(4) included a provision, taken from the UK Copyright Act 1956, which gave the High Court the power to award 'additional' damages. Fortunately s 128(3) of CRRA 2000 has replaced CA 1963, s 22(4) with a clearer provision permitting the award of aggravated damages or punitive damages, or both. However, for existing claims brought under the 1963 legislation the meaning of s 22(4) may still be important to glean. While the Gregory Committee regarded the provision as a form of exemplary damages, *Beloff v Pressdram*,[79] *obiter*, stated that this provision constituted a basis for aggravated damages rather than exemplary damages, but the terminology is unhelpful. Note that the section uses the word 'additional' rather than 'aggravated' or 'punitive' or some other descriptive term. The leading Irish case on this provision is *Folens v O'Dubhghaill*,[80] where the defendant infringed the plaintiff's copyright in textbooks for use in schools by

---

[73] *Star Micronics Property Ltd v Five Star Computers Property* (1991) 22 IPR 473.

[74] See *Flamingo Park Property Ltd v Dolly Dolly Creations* (1986) 6 IPR 431; *Amalgamated Mining Services v Warman Int* (1992) 24 IPR 461.

[75] *Milpurrurru v Indofern Pty* (1994) 30 IPR 209.

[76] *Cassell v Broome* [1972] AC 1027; *Ravenscroft v Herbert* [1980] RPC 193. See generally O'Dell [1993] DULJ 27.

[77] *Cassell v Broome* [1972] AC 1027 was followed in *Garvey v Ireland* [1981] IR 75 which was not a defamation case, but a wrongful dismissal case.

[78] *Hickey v Roches Stores* (14 July 1976, unreported), HC.

[79] *Beloff v Pressdram* [1973] 1 All ER 241.

[80] *Folens v O'Dubhghaill* [1973] IR 255.

using part of the text to produce another book when the school course syllabus changed. The High Court awarded £1 in damages, saying that the change in syllabus had made the breach a technical one but awarded £250 in punitive damages under s 22(4). The Supreme Court rejected this approach on the grounds that the High Court was erroneous in not deciding whether an injunction could have been an adequate remedy. The basic fact is that s 22(4) of CA 1963 was badly drafted, limiting the court's power to award punitive damages, a point made in Dáil Éireann by Deputy Costello, later a President of the High Court. Deputy Costello remarked that in his experience Irish courts were slow to give exemplary damages and that the use of words like 'flagrancy' in the section did not improve matters.[81] Despite the *Folens* case, however, Laffoy J, in *Universal City Studios Inc v Mulligan (No 3)*[82] awarded punitive damages of £50,000 against a defendant who had been engaged in a series of counterfeiting activities, this sum outweighing the compensatory measure of £25,000 awarded at the same time. The Australian courts have consistently used their provision, s 115(4) of the Copyright Act 1968, to award punitive damages.[83] The fact that the English equivalent of s 22(4) of the Irish Act was so curiously worded inhibited judicial behaviour in England and it is no surprise to discover that when the UK Copyright Act 1956 was revised, a new statutory power to give additional damages 'as the justice of the case may require' was included in s 97(2) of the Copyright, Designs and Patents Act 1988. In *Cala Homes (No 2)*[84] this statutory provision was likened to a power to give exemplary damages. Indeed, this broad provision is one of the basic reasons why the UK Parliament did not renew the conversion damages provisions in 1988.

The licensing measure

[18.21] An alternative measure of compensation that is sometimes used is the licensing measure. Under this approach the court considers what figure would have been an appropriate amount had the reproduction taken place on foot of a licensing agreement between the parties. This measure of compensation is frequently used where copyright in

[81]   200 *Dáil Debates*, Cols 421–427.

[82]   *Universal City Studios Inc v Mulligan (No 3)* [1999] 3 IR 407.

[83]   *Concrete Systems Pty v Devon Symonds Holdings* (1978) 20 ALR 677; *Autodesk Australia Pty v Cheung* (1990) 17 IPR 69; *Bailey v Namol Pty* (1994) 30 IPR 147; *Milpurrurru v Indofern Pty Ltd* (1994) 30 IPR 209; *Columbia Pictures v Luckins* (1996) 34 IPR 504; *Polygram Records Inc v Raben Footwear* (1996) 35 IPR 426. A cynical and flagrant exploitation of a competitor's copyright by defendants acting in concert under a tacit agreement led to damages of A$450,000 being awarded, these being damages that were additional to compensatory damages of A$44,800: *Aristrocrat Technologies Australia Pty v Global Gaming Supplies* (2009) 84 IPR 222.

[84]   *Cala Homes (South) Ltd v Alfred McAlpine Homes East Ltd (No 2)* [1996] FSR 36: suggests that punitive damages under the Copyright, Designs and Patents Act 1988, s 97 may be added to an account of profits but this decision has been disapproved by the House of Lords in *Redrow Homes v Bett Bros* [1999] 1 AC 197. See also, on punitive damages in England, *Nottingham Healthcare NHS Trust v News Group Newspapers Ltd* [2002] RPC 962.

architectural drawings is infringed. The measure is not the profit the plaintiff would have made on the commission but the reasonable fee the right holder could have charged if he had licensed the architect to do the work using the right holder's design.[85] Where the work has been licensed to others then the fee thus charged is normally the measure against an infringer[86] although in cases where the infringement is heavy handed the court's discretion can come into play. In *Hay and Hay Construction v Sloan*,[87] reproduction of design drawings was expressly forbidden by the plaintiff although isolated permissions to reproduce at a small fee of £60 were allowed. Damages were assessed at £650 in excess of the fee permitted, because of the surrounding circumstances, particularly the flagrant disregard of the plaintiff's wishes and profits made by the defendants and additional damages because of the flagrant nature of the infringement. This approach has been endorsed in *Columbia Pictures Industries v Luckins*,[88] a secondary infringement by importation case, where the Federal Court of Australia held the licensing measure to be inappropriate where it was clear that a licence would never be granted and where the infringer acted in direct competition with the plaintiff. In actual copyright licensing cases, where a rights holder finds that the licensee has breached the terms of the licence, damages will reflect the arrangement that the parties would have made in terms of a reasonable commercial bargain. In *Rutter v Brookland Valley Estate*[89] the licensee continued to use copyright material in marketing wine produced on his estate after the licence had expired and for a range of products not envisaged by the licence itself. Damages could include a figure to reflect the success of the campaign, due in part to use of the plaintiff's work. Additional damages to reflect the flagrant breach of rights were also awarded.

[18.22] The English case of *Blayney v Clogau St David's Gold Mine Ltd*[90] adds a further dimension to the licensing measure of compensation. Even if the plaintiff cannot show that a normal rate of profit was anticipated from the business, nor that a licensing practice was attached to the business, the plaintiff will still be entitled to a notional royalty by virtue of the defendant's invasion of the plaintiff's right of property; see, in particular, s 17(1) of CRRA 2000, which specifically describes copyright as a property right. In *Retail Systems Technology v McGuire*[91] Kelly J followed the *Blayney* decision, holding that where lost sales could be shown, the measure of damages was the profit on those sales lost by the plaintiff where no lost sales could be directly traced back to the infringement. Kelly J said that damages to reflect the infringement of the plaintiff's copyright were to be awarded, based upon a national licence. Kelly J also endorsed the

---

[85] *Stovin-Bradford v Volpoint* [1971] Ch 1007, applying *Chabot v Davies* (1936) 53 TLR 61; *Dixon Investments Property Ltd v Hall* (1990) 18 IPR 490.

[86] *Performing Right Society v Bradford Corpn* (1921) Macg Cop Cas 309.

[87] *Hay and Hay Construction v Sloan* (1957) 27 CPR 132.

[88] *Columbia Pictures Industries v Luckins* (1996) 34 IPR 504.

[89] *Rutter v Brookland Valley Estate* (2009) 81 IPR 549.

[90] *Blayney v Clogau St David's Gold Mine Ltd* [2003] FSR 361.

[91] *Retail Systems Technology v McGuire* [2008] 1 IR 541.

convoyed goods principle[92] whereby lost sales of non-infringing products (eg hardware), which were bundled with the infringing works (eg software), could be the subject of a damages award.

[18.23] Apart from the general provisions in respect of compensatory damages, s 24(1) of CA 1963 and s 134(1) of CRRA 2000 give a court the power to award damages in conversion. This attaches under CRRA 2000 to infringing copies of the work, articles used to make infringing copies, and protection defeating devices. The court is required to award conversion damages after taking account of all the circumstances of the case and is to award such a sum as the court considers just.[93]

Conversion damages

[18.24] Some judges have drawn a distinction between cumulative and overlapping awards,[94] which is an important reference point in this process. According to the English leading cases,[95] the deemed ownership of the original pattern or model (the plate) and the copies thus manufactured, will provide the right holder with damages based upon the value of the infringing copies thus sold and not merely the profit margin recovered by the pirate after allowing for production costs. The fact that the infringement does not cause market confusion – the infringing product and copy do not compete with or diminish the reputation of the plaintiff – cannot influence such an award and the court will resist a plea for it to impose the reasonable licensing measure as an alternative,[96] because the general damages provision is subordinate to the conversion measure, although the standard of proof needed to establish conversion damages is higher[97] and, where damages overlap, the conversion damages should be reduced.[98] Conversion damages have been abolished in the UK following adverse comments by both Whitford and senior judicial figures, but an Irish plaintiff may, under both the 1963 and 2000 Acts, select the conversion measure along with 'ordinary' damages, leaving it to the court to limit the award to avoid overcompensation. Australian courts have shown a reluctance to permit conversion damages in cases where the effect would be ludicrous or disproportionate, arguing that for conversion damages to apply, the plaintiff must establish a realistic value for the converted goods, which will probably be the price for which the goods have been sold.[99] At times, conversion damages and punitive damages

---

[92] Following *Gerber Garment Technology Inc v Lectra Systems Ltd* [1997] RPC 443 (a patent case). The Enforcement Directive (2006/48/EC), art 13 also allows a degree of choice to plaintiff or the court: see Blackburne J's judgment in *Experience Hendrix LLC v Times Newspapers* [2010] EWHC 1986 (Ch).

[93] CRRA 2000, s 134(5).

[94] *Graves v Pocket Publications Ltd* (1938) 54 TLR 952.

[95] *Caxton Publishing Co v Sutherland Publishing Co* [1939] AC 178; *Infabrics v Jaytex* [1982] AC 1.

[96] *Lewis Trusts v Bamber Stores* [1983] FSR 453. See, however, *Alwinco Products Ltd v Crystal Glass Industries* [1985] 1 NZLR 716.

[97] *Columbia Pictures v Robinson* [1988] FSR 531.

[98] *Lewis Trusts v Bamber Stores* [1983] FSR 453.

[99] *WH Brine Co v Whitton* (1981) 37 ALR 190; *Autodesk Inc v Yee* (1996) 35 IPR 415.

may overlap. *Sony Entertainment (Australia) Ltd v Smith*[100] illustrates how conversion damages may be used in order to mark the court's disapproval of the conduct of the defendants. In this case the defendants released copies of sound recordings on a CD, persisting in selling the recordings even after they were told that some of the tracks were unauthorised and threatening record company executives with serious physical harm. Because the court had no basis for awarding compensatory damages, Australian statute law affords a discretion to overcome the risk that conversion damages may operated harshly where the object released contains infringing and non-infringing material, for in such cases, the court may be required to hold that the value of the entire object must be awarded.[101] Irish law does not overtly contain provisions allowing apportionment, but, it is submitted, the general discretion contained in s 128(3) is equally applicable to conversion damages under s134 of CRRA. *Sony Entertainment (Australia Ltd) v Smith* is also of interest because the court awarded additional damages for the threats made, and absence of contrition shown, by the defendants.[102]

THE INNOCENT INFRINGER DEFENCE

[18.25] The legislation provides that where it is proved or admitted that the defendant infringer, at the time of the infringement, was not aware and had no reasonable grounds for suspecting that copyright existed in the work, then damages shall not be awarded. The plaintiff is, however, to be entitled to an account of profits, notwithstanding the success of the innocent infringer defence.[103]

[18.26] The defence does not apply where the defendant mistakenly believes that copyright is held by X who has apparently consented to the defendant's use of the work. In *Performing Right Society v Bray UDC*[104] the honest belief that a band had been given permission to perform works to the Bray public from PRS was not within the similar defence set by the Copyright Act 1911.

[18.27] Similarly, in *Byrne v Statist Co*[105] the defendants reproduced verbatim the text of an advertisement, which the plaintiff had independently translated for reproduction in a newspaper. The original advertisement had appeared in a Brazilian newspaper and it had been translated by Byrne for publication in the *Financial Times* with a translation by-line of F Byrne. The defendants who 'lifted' the *Financial Times* advertisement pleaded the

---

[100] *Sony Entertainment (Australia) Ltd v Smith* (2005) 64 IPR 18; *Boyapati v Rockefeller (No 2)* (2008) 78 IPR 600.

[101] *Infabrics Ltd v Jaytex Shirt Co Ltd* [1982] AC 1; *WH Brine v Whitton* [1981] 37 ALR 190.

[102] See also *Aristocrat Technologies Australia Pty Ltd v Global Gaming Supplies* (2009) 84 IPR 222.

[103] CRRA 2000, s 128(2) replacing CA 1963, s 22(3).

[104] *Performing Right Society v Bray* UDC [1930] IR 509.

[105] *Byrne v Statist Co* [1914] 1 KB 622: *John Lane, Bodley Head Ltd v Associated Newspapers* [1936] 1 All ER 379. Contrast the broader Australian defence, discussed in *Golden Editions Pty v Polygram* (1996) 334 IPR 84. It is not possible to view an anonymously published work as a work to which no copyright attaches: *Imperial Parking Ltd v Barrington* (1995) 66 CPR (3d) 269; *Retail Systems Technology v McGuire* [2007] IEHC 13.

defence, based upon an alleged lack of copyright in an advertisement and the fact that the Brazilian authorities who placed the Portuguese original had apparently consented. Bailhache J said the section:

> ... is no protection to a person who, knowing or suspecting that copyright exists, makes a mistake as to the owner of copyright and under that mistake obtains authority to publish from a person who is not in fact the owner.

[18.28] The defence has been made out successfully where a right owner could be said to have intimated by way of a licensing tariff that consent had been given.[106] It is sometimes possible for the defendant to consider that the length of time a work has been published and the fact that it may be of foreign origin or difficult to trace the right holder, if any, may be factors that could assist in establishing the defence. There are also more complete defences available under s 31 of CRRA 2000, specifically the defence in sub-s (2), which denies the subsistence of copyright in a work where it is reasonable to presume that the author has been dead for 70 years or more.

[18.29] The innocent infringer defence is also available in relation to conversion damages under CA 1963, s 24. So, in *Allibert SA v O'Connor*[107] an innocent importer of items that infringed artistic copyright was held to be able to shelter behind s 24(3)(a) but the supplier from abroad was not.

ACCOUNT OF PROFITS

[18.30] CA 1963 acknowledges that where an infringement of copyright has occurred, the right holder has a right to seek an account of profits on the same basis as any infringement of other rights.[108] Further, where an innocent infringer defence has been made out the only realistic financial remedy may be an account of profits.[109] As an equitable remedy, however, there is no *per se* entitlement to an account of profits and it is within the discretion of the court to order the account or decline to do so. An account is ordered on the basis that the infringer's misuse of copyright material renders the infringer liable to disgorge the profits made. The leading Irish case is *House of Spring Gardens Ltd v Point Blank Ltd*.[110] In that case Griffin J in the Supreme Court observed that the basic principle upon which an account should be ordered is the prevention of unjust enrichment, affirming the prevailing English view that:[111]

> the object of ordering an account ... is to deprive the defendants of the profits which they have improperly made by wrongful acts committed in breach of the plaintiff's rights and to transfer such profits to the plaintiffs.

---

[106] *Spelling Goldberg Productions v BPC Publishing* [1981] RPC 283.

[107] *Allibert SA v O'Connor* [1982] ILRM 40.

[108] CA 1963, s 22(2).

[109] CA 1963, s 22(3).

[110] *House of Spring Gardens Ltd v Point Blank Ltd* [1984] IR 611.

[111] Slade J in *My Kinda Town Ltd v Soll* [1983] RPC 15 at 49.

[18.31] The order made should enable the court to compel the surrender of profits made in breach of the plaintiff's rights, and in *My Kinda Town Ltd v Soll*, Slade J, *obiter*, indicated that where part of the profit is unlawfully made, a proportion thereof can be transferred to the right holder. Normally, the process of ordering an enquiry into profits is a complex and expensive one. However, in exceptional circumstances the court, where accounts are already in evidence before the court, may order the payment over of the difference between the price of the infringing goods sold, minus manufacturing and transportation costs.[112] Some allowances for the benefits, talents and skills of the infringer in providing services may be permitted.[113] An account may be declined in the event of delay, because of the trivial nature of the breach of right, or condonation of the infringement.[114]

[18.32] The decision whether to seek to obtain an account or damages is a somewhat difficult one, for in the leading case of *Caxton Publishing v Sutherland Publishing*,[115] Lord Porter indicated that once the election is made and ordered the plaintiff loses any right to seek damages, whether general damages or conversion damages. In the English case of *Island Records v Tring International plc*,[116] Lightman J had to consider the general question of when a plaintiff had to elect as between these remedies. The plaintiff was seeking summary judgment under O 14 of the Rules of the Supreme Court[117] in respect of the defendant's uncontested infringement in sound recordings. Lightman J, starting from the position that the plaintiff could not obtain damages for infringement and an account for profits, and that the plaintiff should not be required to exercise the election until he was in a position to make an informed choice, was of the view that the judiciary should develop flexible procedures to facilitate the reconciliation of these two principles. In rejecting the defendant's view that the election should take place at the hearing of the motion for summary judgment, Lightman J ordered the defendant to provide an audited schedule of sums received and sales figures within two months. Such a procedure should greatly enhance the use of the election procedure in cases of large-volume piracy infringements.[118]

---

[112] *House of Spring Gardens Ltd v Point Blank Ltd* [1984] IR 611; *Zupanovich Pty Ltd v B & N Beale Nominees Pty* (1995) 32 IPR 339 contains a very scholarly analysis of the remedy by Carr J in the Federal Court of Australia in which he stresses the restitutionary and equitable characteristics of the remedy, citing extensively from Bently [1991] EIPR 5. See also *Apand Pty Ltd v Kettle Chip Co* (1999) 43 IPR 225.

[113] *Redwood Music v Chappell & Co* [1982] RPC 109; *O'Sullivan v Management Agency & Music Ltd* [1985] 3 All ER 351.

[114] *Van Camp Chocolates v Aulsebrooks Ltd* [1984] 1 NZLR 354. An account of profits is unlikely to be granted in a breach of contract action: *Experience Hendrix LLC v PPX Enterprises Inc* [2003] 1 All ER (Comm) 830, a breach of licence case.

[115] *Caxton Publishing v Sutherland Publishing* [1939] AC 178.

[116] *Island Records v Tring International plc* [1995] 3 All ER 444.

[117] SI 1965/1776.

[118] Lightman J relied heavily on *Minnesota Mining and Manufacturing Co v C Jeffries Property Ltd* [1993] FSR 189.

INJUNCTIVE RELIEF

[18.33] An extensive review of the principles governing the granting of injunctive relief is inappropriate to a work of this kind but the main features of the exercise of the equitable discretion to award an injunction can be briefly described at this point. There are several different kinds of injunction.

Perpetual injunction

[18.34] A perpetual injunction is considered at the close of the actual hearing of the merits of the dispute between the parties. The injunction is given to finally resolve the issues before the court and it may be awarded even if there is little or no prospect that infringement will occur again. All that is needed is a judicial apprehension that the defendant has infringed the plaintiff's rights previously; what is at issue is the resolution of the dispute on a permanent basis, so an injunction may be appropriate because the final resolution of the conflict makes this a prudent if somewhat empty relief. The relief will be given if the injury is continuous and recurring and damages will not be an adequate remedy.[119] Delay does not generally preclude the award of a perpetual injunction.

Interlocutory injunction

[18.35] This kind of injunction is, in practice, the most important relief for not only are the parties free to treat the injunction application at interlocutory stage to be the hearing of the action, but also the successful award of an injunction may, in practice, resolve the matter because the defendant's commercial activities will be stopped or abridged by the grant of the injunction. The injunction is sought by an applicant who asserts that irreparable damage to the applicant before the trial of the action will result from the activities of another and that surrounding circumstances make the award of an injunction necessary to preserve the *status quo* until the hearing of the action. Normally, service of the proceedings will be necessary four days before the hearing of the application, although in extreme cases where damage is immediate an *ex parte* application can be made and an interim injunction can be given until the hearing of the application for interlocutory relief or some other date or event. The application will be made on affidavit and the court will have to decide whether facts disclosed in the affidavit indicate to the court that there is a serious issue to be tried;[120] the claim must not be frivolous or vexatious and unless the material before the court discloses that at the hearing of the action the plaintiff has no real prospect of obtaining a perpetual injunction the court will, after concluding that damages will not be an adequate remedy for either party, go on to consider the issue of where the balance of convenience lies.

[18.36] The governing principle here is whether the plaintiff, in succeeding in establishing an infringement in the main action, is capable of being adequately

---

[119] *Evans Marshall & Co v Bertolla* [1973] 1 All ER 992.

[120] *American Cyanamid v Ethicon* [1975] AC 396; *News Datacom Ltd v Lyons* [1994] 1 ILRM 450; *Series A Software Ltd v Clarke* [1996] 1 All ER 853; *Smithkline Beecham plc v Genthan BV* (28 February 2003, unreported), HC.

compensated in damages. The applicant must give an undertaking that it will compensate the defendant should the defendant succeed, while the defendant may of course assert either that the plaintiff will not be able to compensate the defendant adequately or that the defendant's loss will be irreparable, which is much the same kind of issue. In *PPI Ltd v Chariot Inns Ltd*,[121] interlocutory relief was awarded in the form of an order closing down a discotheque for non-payment of licensing fees because at the hearing of the action the various discotheque proprietors involved in the representative action may have transferred ownership to other entities to avoid making the payment. Damages may be an inadequate remedy for either party, in which case an injunction will issue.[122] Sometimes the parties may avoid the grant of an injunction pending trial by giving an undertaking not to use the infringing materials but this may not be successful if the undertaking offered is not acceptable.[123] Apart from factors such as delay, which may lead the court to decline to exercise its discretion,[124] the courts do consider factors such as a citizen's freedom to communicate information and other constitutionally mandated factors within this balancing process.[125] The English courts have similarly prevented gagging a defendant through the award of an interlocutory injunction when the public interest so requires.[126] Where the plaintiff is a large industrial entity with the largest market share there may be a trend towards allowing competitors to enter the market by refusing to grant interlocutory relief although the adequacy of the defendant's ability to meet a claim in damages if unsuccessful will of course be crucial here.[127] Threatened or apprehended infringements of rights are remediable via an interim or interlocutory injunction or a *quia timet* (because he fears) basis. This relief may be very important in counteracting unspecified or prospective infringements particularly if the work in question does not yet exist. The courts in Ireland have been active in protecting the future repertoires of collecting societies when broadcasters may appear to intend broadcasting works to the public in the short to medium term – an important factor in the ephemeral world of popular music. Damage will be inferred where a breach of right is reasonably apprehended.[128]

[18.37] The power of a court to award injunctive relief against unknown persons, who will infringe contractual rights or commit torts such as passing off, has been a feature of the common law in several situations. Most of these cases are merchandising cases that do not necessarily involve copyright infringement. However, the power of a court

---

[121] *PPI Ltd v Chariot Inns Ltd* (8 October 1992, unreported), HC. The fact that the defendant is not a mark was important in *Mirage Studios v Counter Feat Ltd* [1991] FSR 145.

[122] *Elanco v Mandops* [1979] FSR 46; *Waterlow Directories Ltd v Reed Information Services Ltd* [1992] FSR 409.

[123] *Elanco v Mandops* [1979] FSR 46; *Waterlow Directories Ltd v Reed Information Services Ltd* [1992] FSR 409.

[124] *Lennon v Ganley* [1981] ILRM 84.

[125] *A-G for England and Wales v Brandon Brooks* [1987] ILRM 135.

[126] *Fraser v Evans* [1969] 1 QB 349; *Woodward v Hutchins* [1977] 2 All ER 751; *Lion Laboratories v Evans* [1984] 2 All ER 417.

[127] *Kelloggs Ltd v Dunnes Stores* (1995) Irish Times, 12 April.

[128] *C & A Modes and C & A (Ireland) v C & A (Waterford) Ltd* [1976] IR 198.

exercising its inherent jurisdiction to fashion equitable relief against unknown persons who are infringing copyrights, or who in the future will undoubtedly do so, in this case cable operators who will rebroadcast without authorisation, has been recently reaffirmed in the Indian case of *TEJ Television Ltd v Rajan Manda*[129] granting 'John Doe' orders. Orders of this kind should be seen as part of the broader inherent jurisdiction of the High Court and they are clearly to be regarded as linked to *Norwich Pharmacal* orders discussed below.

DENIAL OF INTERNET ACCESS – THE GRADUATED RESPONSE AGREEMENT (2009)

[18.38] In *EMI Records (Ireland) Ltd v Eircom*,[130] Kelly J granted a *Norwich Pharmacal* order to the plaintiffs, requiring Eircom, Ireland's largest internet service provider, to reveal to the plaintiffs the name and addresses of Eircom subscribers whose IP address was suspected of being used to infringe sound recording copyrights. In the light of the fact that the Enforcement Directive (Directive 2004/48/EC) contains provisions requiring persons to disclose information concerning infringement of intellectual property rights, this overlapping provision[131] means that there are Community law aspects to this kind of mechanism.

[18.39] In *Productores de Musica de Espana v Telefonica de Espana (Promusicae)*[132] the ECJ stressed that Member States were not required by the laws on data protection to legislate for the disclosure of traffic data in civil proceedings, but that any legislation should reflect the principle of proportionality: the means used to counteract the infringement of intellectual property rights must not be excessive or disproportionate. The courts should strive to balance these conflicting rights and not give primacy to one of them.

[18.40] Even though the ECJ judgment in *Promusicae* was not cited in his judgment, Charleton J, in *EMI Records and Others v Eircom*[133] has ruled that the graduated response agreement, or the 'three strikes' settlement between Eircom and the Irish recorded music industry, does not infringe data protection legislation. The viability of the Graduated Response Agreement must be in doubt following upon Charleton J's decision in *EMI Records and Others v UPC*.[134] As Charleton J has ruled that the Irish High Court has no jurisdiction to injunct an ISP in respect of peer to peer filesharing by its subscribers, the legal basis for the Graduated Response Agreement appears very uncertain. Indeed, in *EMI Records (Ireland) Ltd and Others v UPC Communications*

---

129 *TEJ Television Ltd v Rajan Manda* [2003] FSR 407.

130 *EMI Records (Ireland) Ltd v Eircom* [2005] 4 IR 148.

131 See SI 360/2006, reg 3.

132 *Productores de Musica de Espana v Telefonica de Espana (Promusicae)* Case C-275/06: See Kuner [2008] EIPR 199; Davies & Helman [2008] EIPR 307.

133 *EMI Records and Others v Eircom* [2010] IEHC 108.

134 Decision handed down on 11 October 2010. See para **[17.28]** above.

(Ireland) Ltd.[135] Charleton J has expressed the view that his earlier judgment in *EMI Records (Ireland) Ltd v Eircom Ltd,*[136] the data protection judgment is not affected by his decision[137] in relation to the application to have Eircom discontinue subscriber access to Pirate Bay. Charleton J, in the *UPC Case*[138] has held that the earlier Eircom Pirate Bay order was incorrectly made on the basis of an incorrect interpretation of s 40(4) of the 2000 Act.

---

[135] *EMI Records (Ireland) Ltd and Others v UPC Communications (Ireland) Ltd* (11 October 2010, unreported) HC.

[136] [2010] IEHC 108.

[137] [2009] IEHC 411.

[138] (11 October 2010, unreported) HC.

Chapter 19

Moral Rights and the *Droit de Suite*

MORAL RIGHTS

Introduction to moral rights

[19.01] The historical development of copyright within the book publishing industry in England during the eighteenth century[1] saw the notion of copyright as a publishing right that was vested initially in the author under the Statute of Anne. Dealings in copyright works, particularly as between the author and the publisher, both then and now, frequently involve the transfer or assignment of many, if not all, of the author's statutory rights. If copyrights are seen as being personal property which can be totally transferred to others, then it follows that upon the total assignment of copyright the author/transferor cannot enjoy any remaining copyrights: the transferee holds any or all such rights and is free to deal in the work in any way the transferee sees fit within the English common law tradition. Certainly after the Statute of Anne, copyrights are seen as exclusively statutory when the work in question is a published work: the common law gives no additional rights and it is the role of the courts to provide remedies where statutory rights are infringed. Thus, copyrights are economic rights that are, in general, freely transmissible. It is nevertheless interesting to note that Canada, the first copyright country to introduce moral rights legislation in 1931, had previously provided protection via the criminal law[2] in respect of the correct attribution and integrity of dramatic works and that a very interesting internal debate on moral rights had preceded the 1931 Canadian legislation. In contrast, however, the civilian tradition, particularly in French legal theory, copyright, or the *droit d'auteur*, is seen as an author's right, based upon an act of creation by the author or artist. The work thus produced is seen as a part of the identity, personality or integrity of the author or artist and, as such, subject to economic *and* moral laws.[3] Thus, the civilian tradition recognises a *droit moral*. Article 6*bis* of the Berne Convention for the Protection of Literary and Artistic Works (Berne Convention) makes due provision for the balancing of economic rights by reference to certain essential interests of the author of the literary or artistic work in question:

---

[1] Feather [1988] EIPR 377.

[2] The Criminal Code 1915, s 508B amendment. See generally Adeney (2001) 15 IPJ 205.

[3] Roeder (1940) 53 Harv L Rev 554; Dworkin (1981) 14 IIC 476; Chang [1995] CLP 243; Dietz (1994) 25 IIC 177; Deitz (1995) 19 Colum VLA JL & Arts 199 and Dworkin (1995) 19 Colum VLA JL & Arts 229 provide contrasting looks at civil law and common law systems. For moral rights in cyberspace see Pessach (2003) 34 IIC 250.

Article 6*bis*

(1) Independently of the author's economic rights, and even after the transfer of the said rights, the author shall have the right to claim authorship of the work and to object to any distortion, mutilation or other modification of, or other derogatory action in relation to, the said work, which would be prejudicial to his honour or reputation.

(2) The rights granted to the author in accordance with the preceding paragraph shall, after his death, be maintained, at least until the expiry of the economic rights, and shall be exercisable by the persons or institutions authorised by the legislation of the country where protection is claimed. However, those countries whose legislation, at the moment of their ratification of or accession to this Act, does not provide for the protection after the death of the author of all the rights set out in the preceding paragraph may provide that some of these rights may, after his death, cease to be maintained.

(3) The means of redress for safeguarding the rights granted by this Article shall be governed by the legislation of the country where protection is claimed.[4]

Moral rights for authors and artists

[19.02] It must be said at the outset that the existence of moral rights within certain legal traditions are hotly debated subjects of controversy, which cause opponents of these rights to argue that the mere existence of residual moral rights, which are essentially uncertain and subjective in nature, represent a substantial barrier to the 'sensible' exploitation of a work, which is not in the interest of right holders or authors. However, it is certainly impossible to point to any substantial body of case law that supports such a view: French case law, for example, is not voluminous and one recent French decision indicates that moral rights are far from absolute and must, in certain instances, be subject to a judicial balancing exercise in which the broadest public interest may be a dispositive factor.[5]

[19.03] The debate on moral rights in some countries that share the traditional English approach to such rights, namely Canada[6] and Australia,[7] has led parliament in those countries towards adoption of *droit moral*, based in the main on an appreciation that authors and creators do need some additional measures of protection: the position taken by the UK Gregory Committee in 1952[8] is no longer shared in those countries and even

---

[4] See Ricketson, *The Berne Convention for the Protection of Literary and Artistic Works 1886–1986* (Centre for Commercial Law Studies QMC, London, 1987).

[5] *Foujita v Sarl Art Conception Realisation ACR* [1988] FSR 523. See generally Sarraute (1986) Am JCP 465 and Walravens (2004) 197 Revue Internationale du Droit d'Auteur 3.

[6] Canada introduced moral rights in 1931 and began a revision exercise in the 1970s. See Keyes and Brunst: *Copyright in Canada: Proposals for a Revision of the Law* (1977). Vaver (1983) 14 IIC 329 reviews the law of moral rights for authors in Canada.

[7] Ricketson [1990] 17 MULR 463; Strauss (1995) 4 AJCL 506. The Pearce Committee made recommendations for the adoption of moral rights in Australia and the Copyright Amendment (Moral Rights) Act 2000, amending the Copyright Act 1968, introduces very detailed moral rights provisions, with general effect from 21 December 2000.

[8] Report of the Copyright Committee (Cmnd 8662), paras 219–226.

in the UK the 1977 Whitford Report[9] came out in favour of legislation to implement the Berne minima.[10] New Zealand legislated a moral rights regime in the Copyright Act 1994; see *Benchmark Building Supplies Ltd v Mitre 10 (NZ) Ltd.*[11]

[19.04] There is a significant body of case law that supports the general thrust of the Gregory Committee's conclusion that existing protections are significant. However, the scope of these rights is either uncertain or limited in nature.

Constitutional protection

[19.05] It is quite difficult to identify those aspects of Irish constitutional law that may be pertinent to this enquiry. However, a few may be advanced as relevant.

The right to privacy

[19.06] It is sometimes speculated that the right to paternity implicitly raises the issue of a right to anonymity or a right to disclaim authorship.[12] Irish case law has recognised that the Irish Constitution contains an implicit right of privacy, and it may be suggested that this right could be utilised by an author in appropriate circumstances. However, the case law that exists and explores this right to privacy does so in the context of communications between citizens (*Kennedy and Arnold v Ireland and AG*),[13] in matters of sexual freedom (*McGee v AG, Norris v AG*),[14] and in relation to abortion services (*A-G v X*),[15] where a State law, a State agency or a Minister of Government purports to impinge upon the affairs of citizens.[16] Nevertheless, it is possible to foresee situations where an author's privacy interest could be infringed by publication or treatment of works that could perhaps prove to be an embarrassment to the author.[17]

Good name and property rights of a citizen

[19.07] Article 40.3.2° of the Irish Constitution provides that 'the State shall, in particular, by its laws protect ... and vindicate the ... good name and property rights of the citizen'. This article, and Article 43, controls the extent to which personal rights to property can be affected by legislation. Property will clearly include intellectual

---

9 Copyright and Designs Law 1977 (Cmnd 6732), paras 51–57.

10 See generally Dworkin (1981) 4 IIC 476, at 490–492.

11 *Benchmark Building Supplies Ltd v Mitre 10 (NZ) Ltd* (2004) 58 IPR 407.

12 For privacy in making broadcasts see Broadcasting Authority Act 1960, s 19 and the Radio and Television Act 1988, s 9; Broadcasting Act 2001, Pt III. For telecommunications privacy see the Communications Regulation Act 2002, s 12; see the interesting Greek case of *Konbareli v Volatos* [2003] ECDR 197.

13 *Kennedy and Arnold v Ireland and AG* [1987] IR 587.

14 *McGee v AG* [1974] IR 284, *Norris v AG* [1984] IR 36.

15 *AG v X* [1992] ILRM 401.

16 See *O'Reilly v Ryanair* [2003] 1 ILRM 14.

17 See now *Peck v United Kingdom* [2003] EMLR 15, a case in which broadcasting of film capturing images of the plaintiff were held to be embarrassing and an infringment of ECHR, art 8.

property rights. In *PPI v Cody and Princes Investments Ltd*[18] Keane J characterised the rights of an author not to have a work stolen or plagiarised as being rights which could be protected under the Constitution, independent of any statutory right. While this is an *obiter* statement, it presents a tantalising scenario within the context of future constitutional litigation: does the notion of plagiarism extend to unfair appropriation, eg by parody? Moral rights provisions could conceivably lead to circumstances in which a right holder, eg a publisher who has obtained copyright, could challenge an exercise of a moral right by an author on the ground that the legislation inhibits the exercise of property rights and as such moral rights represent an unjust attack on the property rights of the copyright holder.

[19.08] In relation to an artistic work that has been altered since the author parted with possession of the work, s 54(4) of the Copyright Act 1963 (CA 1963) made it a contravention of the Act to publish, sell, let for hire, or, in the course of trade, to offer or expose for sale or hire of the work, as altered, as being the unaltered work of another, or do any of these acts in relation to a reproduction, when it is known by that person not to be so unaltered. Section 54(6) created a similar contravention in relation to artistic works that were published, sold, let for hire, trade offer or trade exhibit as being reproductions made by the author when the reproductions were not reproductions of the author.[19] When the Gregory Committee reviewed[20] the area of moral rights in 1952 the specific protection afforded to artistic works was cited with approval but it was not built upon by the UK Parliament in the 1956 Act. Instead, the UK Parliament passed a rather curious provision which makes it actionable for a person to do any of the following things to a literary, dramatic, musical or artistic work:

(a)   fixing the name of that person to the work in a way which implies that that person, not the author, is the author of that work;

(b)   publication, sale, letting for hire, the making of trade offers, exposure for sale or hire, or trade exhibit, of a work on which another person's name appears if to the knowledge of the offender that other person is not the author of the work;

(c)   doing any of the above in relation to a reproduction of the work;

(d)   public performance or broadcasting of a work when aware that the work as represented is the work of another author.

[19.09] The Irish draftsman lifted this provision from the UK Copyright Act 1956 (CA 1956)[21] and imported it into CA 1963.[22] The precise effect of this provision was not readily understood as the following parliamentary exchange indicates:

Mr Cosgrave: There is another matter referred to in the Minister's speech in relation to s 53 of the Bill. He says the Bill provides that offences under the section will be

---

[18]   *PPI v Cody and Princes Investments Ltd* [1994] 2 ILRM 241, later overruled but on another point.

[19]   These provisions in fact go back to the Fine Arts Copyright Act 1862; see *Carlton Illustrators v Coleman* [1911] 1 KB 771.

[20]   Report of the Copyright Committee (Cmnd 8662).

[21]   CA 1956, s 43.

[22]   CA 1963, s 54(2).

prosecuted, not by the Minister as at present but by the person to whom the work has been falsely attributed or, if he is dead, by his personal representative. Take a person who has a large number of literary or artistic productions to his credit, say a well-known author like the late Bernard Shaw, who wrote over a long period and who has now been dead for some years. Is it his personal representative who has the right to take action? Is there any reason why under this proposed Act the change is being made under which this right is vested in the person or his personal representative rather than in the Minister?

Mr A Barry: I am not clear about the third point Deputy Cosgrave raised. Why should a person to whom work has been falsely attributed initiate a prosecution? Surely it would be the person who wrote the work. I am not clear why the Minister should use those words.

Mr J Lynch: If Deputy Barry were a composer of note, composing works of high musical content and somebody composed what might be called a Tin Pan Alley ditty and put Deputy Barry's name under it, Deputy Barry in those circumstances would be an aggrieved party and would have the right to prosecute the person who composed this Tin Pan Alley ditty.

Mr A Barry: It does not relate to the pirating of my works?

Mr J Lynch: No, on the contrary.

Mr A Barry: I thought it was protection against the pirating of works.

Mr J Lynch: No, it is false attribution, that is, having the work falsely attributed to somebody other than the real author.[23]

[19.10] It is important to note that CA 1963, s 54 was actionable as a breach of statutory duty at the suit of the person named or, if deceased, his or her personal representatives. In this latter situation damages recoverable devolved as part of the estate: s 54(8) and (9). This section proved to be a most useful support to the common law actions for breach of contract and misrepresentation but they are very limited. Neither the section nor those common law causes of action correspond to a right of paternity: these remedies simply provide that another person cannot seek to affix that person's name to the copyright work of another in circumstances where third parties would believe that other person to be the author – a kind of passing off in reverse.[24]

Statutory protection for works outside the field of copyright

[19.11] Consumer protection legislation affords indirect protection for works if, for example, the work is incorrectly described, marked or labelled. The Consumer Information Act 1978 creates several criminal offences relating to false or misleading descriptions so it is possible to invoke the criminal law if works are misdescribed: indeed conspiracy charges may be possible in cases of serious racketeering in pirated goods.

---

[23] 198 *Dáil Debates*, Cols 246–247. For a case which is clearly wrongly decided see *Adams v Quasar Management Services Pty* (2002) 56 IPR 385.

[24] See *Moore v News of the World* [1972] 1 QB 441; *Clark v Associated Newspapers* [1998] RPC 261.

Statutory protection in CA 1963

[19.12] Section 54 of CA 1963 made provision for protecting artistic works from being falsely described as being the work of a particular person. Section 54 was based upon the protection found in the Fine Arts Copyright Act 1862[25] and was the only provision in the Copyright Acts that allowed the artist to proceed against another person who misdescribes an artistic work as being unaltered. This provision was therefore a hybrid right between a right of integrity and a right of paternity.

Miscellaneous causes of action

[19.13] Opponents of moral rights legislation point to the availability of other causes of action which go some way towards achieving the primary object of *droit moral* – the preservation of the reputation and honour of the creator of a work. While these causes of action do not answer every situation, the common law system does provide various means of redress to an author who finds that the activities of others threaten to diminish the author's standing or reputation within the community:

(a) *Defamation*: The wrongful publication of a false statement about a person, which tends to lower that person in the eyes of right thinking members of society, or causes that person to be held up to ridicule or contempt, or causes that person to be shunned and avoided by right thinking members of society, is actionable through the tort of defamation.[26] In some cases the publication of works protected by copyright may take place in circumstances where publication is defamatory. To wrongfully attribute authorship to a person when the work in question is a scandalous or obscene publication, for example, may be defamatory.[27] Similarly, to publish a work written by an author in a format which does not advance the reputation of the author but rather threatens to injure the reputation of the author is actionable.[28]

(b) *Passing off*: To pass off a book as being the work of another, a celebrated author, for example, is clearly a misrepresentation which can be actionable by the person misrepresented as the author.[29]

(c) *Injurious falsehood*: It may be an injurious falsehood to claim that a particular work is the work of another person.[30]

---

[25] Finally repealed by the Industrial and Commercial Property (Protection) Act 1927: see, however, Industrial and Commercial Property (Protection) Act 1927, s 186.

[26] See generally, McMahon and Binchy, *Irish Law of Torts* (3rd edn, Butterworths, 2000).

[27] *Ridge v English Illustrated Magazine* (1913) Macg Cop Cas 91.

[28] *Archbold v Sweet* (1832) 1 Mood & R 162; *Lee v Gibbings* (1892) 67 LT 263.

[29] *Wood v Butterworth* (1901) Macg Cop Cas 16; *Samuelson v Producers Distributing* [1932] 1 Ch 201. See also *Sweeney v Macmillan Publishers* [2002] RPC 651.

[30] Per *Archbold v Sweet* (1832) 1 Mood & R 162. See generally *Meridian Communications Ltd v Eircell Ltd* [2002] IR 17.

The law of contract

[19.14] If we start from the position that copyright vests in the author of a work following upon the creation of that work, it is arguable that the author should be able to protect that work by using the methodology of contractual protection against prejudicial treatment of that work by a publisher, broadcaster, or other persons. While in theory this may be so, there are practical reasons why the law of contract may not be operative. Firstly, an assignment may have already taken place of the copyright even in a future work. Secondly, some editorial work may be an implicit right for a publisher to assert in relation to a manuscript and, finally, to claim that authors and artists are financially or legally able to address problems of great technical complexity is disingenuous.[31] While the courts[32] have recently overturned a number of copyright assignments and contractual arrangements by using concepts such as breach of fiduciary duty, undue influence and restraint of trade, the balance of power and expertise will still tend to rest upon the entrepreneur rather than the creator of a work. There are some examples of contractual arrangements being struck, which enable the author to protect the integrity of a work against unauthorised structural alterations of a text, but such clauses must be specifically included in a contract.[33] There is little or no room for implied terms in such a context.[34]

[19.15] CRRA 2000 re-enacts the provisions in CA 1963 in relation to false attribution of authorship and also sets out a paternity right, an integrity right and a statutory right to privacy in relation to photographs and films. While this last right owes much to a virtually identical provision in the UK Copyright, Designs and Patents Act 1988,[35] and drafting of the paternity and integrity rights were clearly influenced by that legislation, it would be a mistake to see the Irish provisions as reflecting the UK model. In several aspects the Irish provisions are markedly different. The Irish paternity right,[36] unlike the UK right,[37] does not have to be asserted by the author; in Ireland the right arises automatically. Unlike the UK legislation the integrity right may be invoked in Ireland against a translation of a work that the original author considers to be derogatory action. These are just two examples of how far the Irish legislation reaches beyond the UK model.[38]

---

[31] Exceptionally, some writers are fastidious and learned on copyright matters, eg Anthony Trollope, J P Donleavy.

[32] *Schroeder v Macauley* [1974] 3 All ER 616; *O'Sullivan v Management Agency Ltd* [1985] QB 428; *John v James* [1991] FSR 397. Contrast *Panayiotou v Sony Music Entertainment (UK) Ltd* [1994] EMLR 229.

[33] *Joseph v National Magazine* [1959] Ch 14; *Frisby v BBC* [1967] Ch 932.

[34] See the controversy on the publication of the book, *Cré na Cille* in an edition of which the author's surviving relatives did not approve: (1996) Irish Times, 19 September.

[35] Copyright, Designs and Patents Act 1988, s 85.

[36] CRRA 2000, s 107.

[37] Copyright, Designs and Patents Act 1988, s 78.

[38] Indeed, the Copyright and Related Rights Bill 1999, on introduction, extended moral rights so as to include sound recordings, films and broadcasts. This was probably a drafting error and the right is now confined – see below and CRRA 2000, s 2(1) in the definition of 'work'.

[19.16] Section 107(1) of CRRA 2000 states:

> the author of a work shall have the right to be identified as the author and the right shall apply in relation to an adaptation of the work.

Unfortunately, there is no guidance in CRRA 2000 about how this right is to be vindicated other than a provision in s 107(2, which relates to instances where the author uses a pseudonym, initials or other form of identification. Must the right apply at first point of sale or distribution? Must the work be marked? If the work is being performed must each performance be the subject of an identification process? It is likely that the right is directed at copying and forms of distribution of the work as a product, rather than a performance, but the Act is not clear on the limits of the right. Because of the highly political nature of moral rights, one can be excused for thinking the lack of precision is intentional. CRRA 2000 contains a number of exceptions. The right does not apply in relation to works where copyright vests in the employer under s 23.[39] Nor does the right apply to a work made for the purpose of reporting current events.[40] A work made for a newspaper, a periodical, an encyclopaedia, a dictionary, a yearbook or other collective work of reference, or a work appearing in such a publication and intended to be made available to the public, with the licence of the author, is also denied any paternity right.[41] Nor does the paternity right arise in relation to works in which government or Oireachtas copyright subsists or where copyright is vested in a prescribed international organisation unless previous copies have identified the author.[42]

[19.17] Infringement of the paternity right (as distinct from situations in which the right simply does not arise) are also the subject of some special exceptions.[43] A defence of incidental inclusion is available and in relation to the use of a work for examination purposes a paternity right is not capable of being infringed, other than photocopying a musical work for use by an examination candidate. The right is also not infringed by use in parliamentary or judicial proceedings or in the reporting thereof. Statutory enquiries and those reporting those enquiries are simply free to use works without infringement of the paternity right. Hardly surprisingly, where a work is anonymous or pseudonymous, or it is reasonable to assume copyright has expired, use of that work will not infringe the paternity right if the author is not identified.[44] The paternity right, as it stands in CRRA 2000, is a right to be acknowledged as the author of the work. The statute, like the common law, does not confer rights of anonymity or the right to 'repent' of an earlier work, or stop distribution of that work to the public.[45] The case law suggests that the contribution of the author should be acknowledged by naming the author – a reference to

---

[39] CRRA 2000, s 108(2). The reference should be to CRRA 2000, s 23(1)(a) only.

[40] CRRA 2000, s 108(3).

[41] CRRA 2000, s 108(4).

[42] CRRA 2000, s 108(5).

[43] CRRA 2000, s 108(1).

[44] The right subsists for as long as the copyright in the work: CRRA 2000, s 115.

[45] *Harris v Warren and Phillip* [1918] WN 173; *Chaplin v Leslie Frewin* [1966] Ch 71; *Harrison and Starkey v Polydor* [1977] FSR 1.

'a colleague' is not enough[46] – and the modification of a work so as to leave out the signature of the artist, for example, will infringe.[47] One recent Canadian case indicates that whether attribution is required may turn on the individual facts of the case at bar. In *Ritchie v Sawmill Creek Golf and Country Club*,[48] the defendants were held not to have been required to attribute authorship to the plaintiff when loading photographs onto their website, the defendants having been accused of theft of the photographs, presumably on the basis that any attribution could have been prejudicial to the defendant's prospects of avoiding a conviction. There is little guidance on the level of damages that should be awarded for breach of moral rights. In *Meskenas v ACP Publishing Ltd*,[49] a non-attribution case where the author's complaints were treated dismissively, the judge indicated that damages would not be broken down into separate heads, awarding $1,100 for breach of copyright/moral rights and $8,000 in aggravated damages arising out of post breach events. The court regarded it as unlikely that there was a loss of reputation to the plaintiff, a distinguished portrait painter.

[19.18] The integrity right[50] affords the author of a work:

> the right to object to any distortion, mutilation or other modification of or other derogatory acting in relation to the work which would prejudice his or her reputation and that right shall also apply in relation to an adaptation of the work.[51]

The right to object applies also to treatment of parts of a work that have already been stripped away from the author's original work if that additional treatment to the part is attributed to, or likely to be regarded as the work of, the author.[52] Like the paternity right, there are exceptions. The integrity right does not arise in relation to treatment for the purpose of reporting current events[53] or works made or made available under licence of the author, for newspapers, periodicals, encyclopaedia, dictionaries, year books, or other collective works of reference.[54] Nor does subsequent use of such a work, without alteration, result in breach of the integrity right.[55] For example, if author X finds words of her poem have been adapted in a newspaper article published by Z and that article is then loaded onto a website by A, without alteration, X has no integrity rights in respect of Z or A and their respective use of the work. Infringement of the integrity right does not arise in relation to the use of a work if the use in question comes within any s 51 fair dealing defence vis-à-vis an action for infringement of copyright. So, regardless of

---

46   *Eisenman v Qimron* [2001] ECDR 73 (Israel).

47   *Theberge v Galerie d'Art Petit Champlain* (2002) 210 DLR (4th) 385; *Faranda v Italian Post Office* [2001] ECDR 177; *Maria Isabel PR v Viproga SA* [2003] ECDR 331.

48   *Ritchie v Sawmill Creek Golf and Country Club* (2003) 27 CPR (4th) 220.

49   *Meskenas v ACP Publishing Ltd* [2006] FMCA 1136.

50   CRRA 2000, s 109(1).

51   CRRA 2000, s 109(3). Note that the right is defined to address reputation only: the reference to 'honour or reputation' in the Berne Convention, art 6*bis* is obviously wider.

52   CRRA 2000, s 109(2).

53   CRRA 2000, s 110(1)(a).

54   CRRA 2000, s 110(1)(b).

55   CRRA 2000, s 110(1)(c). See more broadly *Benchmark Building Supplies Ltd v Mitre 10 (NZ) Ltd* (2004) 58 IPR 407.

whether the underlying copyright is with the original author or someone else – a publisher by way of assignment, for example – fair dealing for the purposes of criticism or review or for the purposes of reporting current events[56] with a sufficient acknowledgment[57] cannot infringe the integrity right. Nor will use of an anonymous or pseudonymous work, or use of a work where it is reasonable to assume that copyright has expired, infringe the integrity right.[58] More controversially, defences of legal necessity were added to the original draft legislation. Apart from providing a defence in respect of treatment for the purpose of avoiding any contravention of the civil or criminal law (eg to avoid defamation or incitement to racial hatred)[59] or for compliance with a statutory duty,[60] authorised broadcasters or authorised cable programme service providers may do anything with the work if the inclusion would be likely to offend public morality or be likely to encourage or initiate crime or lead to pubic disorder. This 'editorial' or 'censoring' provision can only be used if the author is identified at the time of the action, or has previously been identified, and the author has disclaimed the action taken by the broadcaster or service provider in question.[61]

[19.19] Where the copyright in the work vests in the author's employer under CRRA 2000, s 23, or the work is copyright of the government, the Oireachtas or a prescribed international organisation,[62] the integrity right will not apply to anything done with the work, with the licence of the copyright owner,[63] unless prior to the act in question the author has previously been identified in or on copies lawfully made available to the public, or the author is identified at the time of the act concerned.[64] If the right applies, the right is not infringed if there is a sufficient disclaimer.[65]

[19.20] Because the test in CRRA 2000 is one of injury to reputation, the basis of the moral right is much diminished. It will be necessary for the author to establish, first of all, that there has been some distortion, mutilation or other modification of, or derogatory action to, the work. 'Distortion' would occur through the casting of actors for a play that is at odds with the author's specific instructions[66] or the addition of music to a performance.[67] Some actions may be both a 'distortion' and a 'mutilation' of the work, as in the case of *Snow v Eaton Centre Ltd*,[68] where ribbons tied to a sculpture were held

---

[56] Other than use of photograph – CRRA 2000, s 51(2).

[57] CRRA 2000, s 51(3).

[58] CRRA 2000, s 88.

[59] CRRA 2000, s 110(2)(b)(i).

[60] CRRA 2000, s 110(2)(b)(ii).

[61] CRRA 2000, s 110 (3), (4).

[62] No organisations have yet been prescribed.

[63] Ie the employer, government, Oireachtas or prescribed international organisation.

[64] CRRA 2000, s 111.

[65] CRRA 2000, s 110(4).

[66] CRRA 2000, s 109(1).

[67] *SA Argos Films v Ivens* [1992] FSR 547.

[68] *Snow v Eaton Centre Ltd* (1982) 70 CPR (2d) 105. See also *Smt Mann Bhandoari v Kala Vikas Pictures* [1987] 3 All India Reps 13 and *Pollock v CFCN Productions Ltd* (1983) 73 CPR (3d) 204.

to infringe the integrity right. Cases involving the 'sampling' of musical works and the possibility that these activities will infringe have also been explored, somewhat inconclusively.[69] English case law has been very 'generous' in respect of the use of artistic works for advertising purposes[70] and European case law is, hardly surprisingly perhaps, more pro-author.[71] Nevertheless, public interest considerations are also important here because large construction projects such as the Athens Olympic Games should not be sacrificed for the sake of protecting the reputation of the architect unless compelling grounds can be set forth.[72] Whether the treatment will be prejudicial to the reputation of the author is a difficult question. English case law suggests that a purely subjective approach is not to be supported and the views of the author of the impact of use of the work must be reasonably held – *per* Rattee J in the *Bill Tidy* case,[73] suggesting a predominantly objective test. Some case law in other jurisdictions draws a distinction between the sensibilities of the author and the views of the author's heirs on suitability of treatment meted out to the work in question.[74] It is also evident from some English case law that the author must have a reputation in the first place. In *Confetti Records v Warner Music UK Ltd*[75] the plaintiffs complained that when the defendant added a 'rap' line to a piece of music that he had sampled from the plaintiffs under licence, there had been a mutilation or distortion of the work. Lewison J held that mutilation or distortion *per se* did not ground an action – such mutilation or distortion had to be prejudicial to the author's honour or reputation. On whether this had been made out Lewison J said:

> The nub of the original complaint ... is that the words of the rap (or at least that part contributed by Elephant Man) contained references to violence and drugs. This led to the faintly surreal experience of gentlemen in horsehair wigs examining the meaning of such phrases as 'mish mish man' and 'shizzle (or sizzle) my nizzle'.

Lewison J dismissed that claim for lack of evidence on what the lyrics were, or meant, and the lack or evidence of prejudice to the author's reputation and indeed whether the author had any reputation at all. In *Ritchie v Sawmill Creek Golf and Country Club*[76] the enlargement of photographs by the defendant was also held not to be prejudicial to the plaintiff's honour and reputation given that there had been no appropriate diminution in the quality of the defendant's print.

[19.21] Apart from infringement of the integrity right by distortion, mutilation or other modification of, or other derogatory action prejudicial to, the reputation of the author,[77] as discussed above, s 112 of CRRA 2000 sets out a number of acts of secondary

---

69 *Holst v RCA* (1977) Times, 18 May; *Schott Music International GmbH v Colossal Records* (1996) 36 IPR 267; *Confetti Records v Warner Music* [2003] ECDR 336.

70 *Tidy v Trustees of the Natural History Museum* (1995) 39 IPR 501; *Pasterfield v Denham* [1999] FSR 168.

71 Eg *Faranda v Italian Post Office* [2001] EDCR 177.

72 *Architecture Studio v OEK* [2002] ECDR 385; *Le Regie Nationale des Usines Renault v Dubuffet* [1982] ECC 7.

73 *Tidy v Trustees of the Natural History Museum* (1995) 39 IPR 501.

74 *Fuensanta v Antra 3TV* [2001] ECDR 317.

75 *Confetti Records v Warner Music UK Ltd* [2003] ECDR 336.

76 *Ritchie v Sawmill Creek Golf and Country Club* [2003] 27 CPR (4th) 220.

77 CRRA 2000, s 109.

infringement. These involve sale or other distribution of the works,[78] importation other than for private and domestic use,[79] the possession in the course of a business, trade or profession,[80] and making available to the public[81] such a work or a copy of such a work.[82]

[19.22] The false attribution right enacted in s 54 of CA 1963 is broadly speaking re-enacted in s 113 of CRRA 2000. The section in question applies to all works.[83] According to s 115(2), the right subsists for 20 years after the death of the person who enjoys this right.

[19.23] The new privacy right in relation to photographs and films applies to commissioned works when the commission takes place for private and domestic purpose, and the resulting photograph or film is within copyright.[84] Even though the copyright may vest in the photographer[85] (unless of course some kind of case for equitable ownership can be made out) the person who commissioned the photograph or film has the right not to have the work or copies of it made available to the public.[86] Infringement takes place by issuing copies and by authorising others to issue copies.[87] Defences available are incidental inclusion, issuing copies for parliamentary and judicial proceedings, use by statutory enquiries, actions undertaken under statutory authority and issuing anonymous or pseudonymously created photographs or films.[88] It may be that, while s 114 is narrowly drawn, the release of photographs to the public may be actionable by the subject as a breach of confidence even where there is no copyright dispute or act of commissioning involved.[89] The Canadian courts have gone further by suggesting that infringement of privacy or personality rights may follow from the unauthorised use of a person's image[90] in the form of a photograph on a commercial product, and passing off[91] may also be made out.[92]

[19.24] The most controversial aspect of the new moral rights provisions has proved to be the extent to which these rights are inalienable. In France the transfer of rights of this kind by contract is prohibited.[93] Pressure from the holders of the entrepreneurial

---

78 CRRA 2000, s 112(a).
79 CRRA 2000, s 112(b).
80 CRRA 2000, s 112(c).
81 CRRA 2000, s 112(d).
82 CRRA 2000, s 113(2) sets out infringements that are secondary infringements but there is no marginal note to this effect. *Quaere*: does CRRA 2000, s 113(2) set out the only liability?
83 The right lasts for as long as copyright in the work: CRRA 2000, s 115(1).
84 See *Antiquesportfolio v Rodney Fitch* [2001] FSR 345.
85 CRRA 2000, s 21(h). On joint commissioned works see CRRA 2000, s 117(4).
86 CRRA 2000, s 114(1).
87 CRRA 2000, s 114(2).
88 CRRA 2000, s 114(3).
89 *Warne v Genex Corpn* (1966) 35 IPR 284; *Creation Records v Mirror Group Newspapers* (1997) 39 IPR 1; *Campbell v MGN* [2004] 2 All ER 995.
90 *Bogazewicz v Sony of Canada Ltd* (1995) 128 DLR (4th) 530.
91 *Henderson v Radio Corpn* [1969] RPC 218; *Irvine v Talksport* [2003] 2 All ER 881.
92 The right lasts for as long as the copyright: CRRA 2000, s 115(1).

copyrights, in particular broadcasters and film producers, forced the legislation to shift towards an 'opt out' philosophy. CRRA 2000 envisages that a waiver of rights may be effective, preferably in writing,[94] signed by the right holder. Even a failure to execute such a formal waiver will not preclude an informal waiver via contract[95] or the law of estoppel,[96] and consent to the use of the work by the right owner is also a defence.[97] The only sense in which moral rights are inalienable is that the rights are personal rights incapable of assignment or alienation, by sale, for example,[98] although they do become transmissible on the death of the right owner.[99]

[19.25] There are specific provisions in CRRA 2000 regarding moral rights which relate to works of joint authorship.[100]

[19.26] The new rights under CRRA 2000, ss 107–109 do not apply to a literary, dramatic, musical or artistic work where the author died before 1 January 2001, or to a film, broadcast or typographical arrangement made before that date. Similar immunities are provided in respect of pre-existing assigned or employer-owned works in CRRA 2000, Sch 1.[101]

DROIT DE SUITE

[19.27] The Berne Convention, specifically art 14*bis* in the 1948 Brussels Revision, permits members of the Berne Union to enact legislation that allows artists to share in the profits made upon subsequent sales of artistic works; artistic works are generally unique – many are not reproduced or capable of mass reproduction so that when the work is sold on it may normally be expected to increase in value. In such circumstances, if the artist has originally sold the work to a dealer who then profits from the fame or investment potential of an artistic work, it is thought only right that a percentage of the resale profits should enure to the benefit of the artist or the artist's estate. While the identity and traditions of the first jurisdictions to enact the resale right, France and Belgium,[102] tend to suggest that the right is historically civilian in tone, recent developments in the EU and the US suggest that while only a minority of Berne Union states have enacted resale rights, there is the prospect of renewed interest in the *droit de suite* on the international front. There are isolated instances of the *droit de suite* taking

---

93 See the Cour de Cassation decisions of 10 July 2002 (Jean Ferrat) (2002) 195 Revue Internationale du Droit D'Auteur 338.

94 CRRA 2000, s 116(2). On waiver and joint authors see CRRA 2000, s 117(2).

95 Eg the Greek case of *Architecture Studio v OEK* [2002] ECDR 385.

96 CRRA 2000, s 116(4).

97 CRRA 2000, s 116(5).

98 CRRA 2000, s 118.

99 CRRA 2000, s 119. The false attribution right, however, does not devolve but is actionable by the personal representatives of the deceased right owner: CRRA 2000, s 119(5).

100 CRRA 2000, s 117.

101 CRRA 2000, Sch 1, Pt 1, para 12.

102 In 1920 and 1921 respectively.

root in common law jurisdictions, the most noteworthy being California. In California the right, introduced in 1976 and later amended in 1982, provides that a five per cent tariff of the consideration is to be payable to the artist or the artist's agent when a work of fine art has been sold. The sale may take place at auction by a dealer, broker, museum or gallery but does not apply to purely private transactions; there are a number of quite substantial exemptions such as first sale by the artist and where the resale results in a loss for the dealer. The right applies to sales that take place in California and can be claimed by US citizens or persons resident in California for a minimum of two years.

[19.28] The optional nature of the right in the Berne Convention and the lack of precision on the scope of the resale right assist in throwing up significant differences in national laws on how the right is to function. Some jurisdictions restrict the right to artists and blood dependants[103] while most other jurisdictions make the right freely transmissible under national inheritance legislation. The question of duration has also caused significant differences of approach. Because some countries regard the right as a matter of copyright, it enures for the duration of the artist's other economic rights, namely life and 70 years pma.[104] In California, the right lasts for the author's life and 20 years pma. Further points of departure involve the definition of original works, for there is no agreed definition, and where the work is not unique – an engraving, print or lithograph for example – the basis of protection is uncertain. Even unique items, such as an author's original literary manuscript, are normally excluded even though such items do enjoy a vibrant resale market. The economic implications of the right for fine arts businesses, as well as national interests, in supporting a vibrant national and international market for fine arts are highlighted by an examination of the kinds of transaction that are either caught or exempted from the *droit de suite*.

Should all public auction sales and dealer/broker sales be caught? A small number of countries even include private sales, for example Brazil, although aspirational and unworkable provisions of this kind are thought to have contributed towards making the *droit de suite* completely ineffective in such jurisdictions. The picture is further complicated by exempting the first sale and certain fairly immediate resales by a dealer from the right (for example in California). International debate on the essential nature of the right is also inconclusive, for while most regard the right as an author's right it is often characterised by opponents as a tax, a perception that is often sharpened by the State's intervention in some collection mechanisms and by the flat nature of the levy.

[19.29] However, the most trenchant criticisms of the *droit de suite* tend to concentrate on the unrealistic and inefficient nature of the right. While accepting that measures that sponsor and encourage a realistic return to the artist are of themselves 'a good thing',

---

[103] France: see the *Utrillo* decision discussed in Pierredon Fawcett, *Droit de Suite* (Centre for Law and the Arts, Columbia University School of Law (1991)).

[104] The period provided in the Term Directive (Council Directive 93/98/EEC ([1993] OJ L290/9)): see **Ch 10**.

several critics have observed that the economic and cultural climate has moved on since the nineteenth century. As Price observed in 1968:[105]

> The *droit de suite* springs from a nostalgic recollection of the late nineteenth century. It is a case, not unusual, of legislation passed or posed to correct a situation that no longer exists with the intensity that provoked reform.

> The *droit de suite* evolved from a particular conception of art, the artist and the way art is sold. At its core is a vision of the starving artist, with his genius unappreciated, using his last pennies to purchase canvas and pigments which he turns into a misunderstood masterpiece. The painting is sold for a pittance, probably to buy medicine for a tubercular wife. The purchaser is a canny investor who travels about artists' hovels trying to pick up bargains which he will later turn into large amounts of cash. Thirty years later the artist is still without funds and his children are in rags. Meanwhile his paintings, now the subject of a Museum of Modern Art retrospective and a Harry Abrams parlour-table book, fetch small fortunes at Park-Bernet and Christie's. The rhetoric of the *droit de suite* is built on this peculiar understanding of the artist and the art market. It is the product of a lovely wistfulness for the nineteenth century with the poor artist starving in his garret, unappreciated by a philistine audience and doomed to poverty because of the stupidity of the world at large. The *droit de suite* is *La Boheme* and *Lust for Life* reduced to statutory form. It is an expression of the belief that (1) the sale of the artist's work at anything like its 'true' value only comes late in his life or after his death; (2) the postponement in value is attributable to the lag in popular understanding and appreciation; (3) therefore the artist is subsidising the public's education with his poverty; (4) this is an unfair state of affairs; (5) the artist should profit when he is finally discovered by the new sophisticated market.

[19.30] It is sometimes pointed out that sponsorship of the artistic community by levying taxes on resale is inefficient because of the probability that many sales will be undetected, will take place in order to take advantage of exemptions and will fail to provide any income at all to the heirs of the artist because the dictates of fashion may simply make most artists unsaleable at certain stages, particularly when the market is subject to cyclical economic patterns. Far better to provide subsidies, bursaries and grants during the artist's creative life, so the argument runs. However, the debate on the *droit de suite* in Europe has taken on a different aspect in recent years because the European Commission has investigated this topic with a view to considering whether the presence of a *droit de suite* in some Member States[106] constitutes a distortion of competition in so far as the art market in non-*droit de suite* jurisdictions operates at a competitive advantage due to the absence of the *droit de suite* 'levy' on sales in those countries. While the Commission has not been specific in its assertion that economic data exists to verify this position, the Commission probably has in mind the analogous situation of differential VAT or sale tax rates and how such imbalance can lead to market

---

[105] (1968) 77 Yale LJ 1333 at 1335: see generally Ulmer (1975) 6 IIC 12; for California see Neumann (1992) 23 IIC 45: Kretsinger [1993] Hastings Comm & Ent LJ 967; Merryman [1997] IPQ 16.

[106] France, Belgium, Italy, Germany, Portugal, Luxembourg, Spain, Denmark, Finland, Sweden and Greece. However, the *droit de suite* has not been implemented in Austria, the Netherlands, Ireland and the UK.

displacement.[107] In the *Joseph Beuys* case[108] decided in Germany by the Dusseldorf Court of Appeals in 1992, a decision to sell paintings by that artist in London rather than Germany was made by a collector on the basis of absence of *droit de suite* in the UK. The heirs of Joseph Beuys unsuccessfully claimed on the *droit de suite* because the sale was held to have been in London and thus the right could not be asserted in such circumstances. This displacement argument has been highlighted by the *Phil Collins* case,[109] which allows EU nationals to claim *droit de suite* in *droit de suite* states but does not allow *droit de suite* nationals to claim in respect of sales taking place in non-*droit de suite* Member States. Traditional UK opposition to legislation is in part due to the hostility of the Whitford Committee[110] to the introduction of a *droit de suite*, a feeling that measures of this kind may actually harm the position of young, unknown artists but, most important of all, a fear that the fine arts market may be displaced to Switzerland and the main US centres where *droit de suite* does not exist.

[19.31] In Australia, the issue of introduction of a *droit de suite* was considered in 1989 by the Australian Copyright Council.[111] This empirical study of art resale in Australia reached the conclusion that creative endeavour would be encouraged via a mechanism of this kind, which would give visual artists a share in the accumulating value of their original creative work. However, the practical constraints behind this right were not ignored by the Copyright Council and the royalty rate was to be set at a level which did not discourage sales of fine art or encourage avoidance via placing these sales on overseas markets. However, there are no real signs of legislative action in Australia at the present time; but the cautionary note set in the 1989 Report finds a significant echo in the work of the European Commission in its 13 March 1996 document on the Resale Right.[112]

The Directive

[19.32] The debate within Europe on the need for a measure to approximate laws on resale rights started in earnest following a European Parliament Resolution of 13 May 1974 calling upon the European Commission to propose measures to harmonise laws on the protection of cultural heritage. The European Commission responded in 1975 with a plan for priority action which included approximation of national laws on copyright and neighbouring rights, particularly the resale right. The 1976 Working Document, 'Community Action in the Cultural Section' placed the *droit de suite* within the classification of neighbouring rights. That report asserted that *droit de suite* had the

---

[107] In Ireland, for example, differential VAT rates on bloodstock sales as between the UK and Ireland have led to reports about higher sales volumes in Ireland because VAT in 1994 and 1995 was much lower on such sales.

[108] *Joseph Beuys Works* (1993) 24 IIC 139.

[109] *Collins (Phil) v Imtrat Handelsgesellschaft mbH* Joined Cases C-92/92 and 326/92 [1993] ECR I-5145.

[110] Cmnd 6732, Ch 17.

[111] '*Droit de Suite*: the Art Resale Royalty and its Implications for Australia' (1989).

[112] Proposal for a European Parliament and Council Directive on the Resale Right for the Benefit of the Author of an Original Work of Art (Com) 96 97 Final.

effect of transferring sales to Member States where no resale right existed and legislative action was commenced in the form of a public announcement in late 1977, the European Commission calling a hearing of interested parties to discuss the possible contents of a Council Directive. This meeting, held on 20 June 1980, revealed significant opposition from sections of the art market and opposition from the UK. The proposal was mothballed until 1991 when the *droit de suite* re-emerged in the follow up to the 1988 Copyright Green Paper. Following upon a series of legal and economic studies and a process of consultation, a proposed Council Directive was presented by the Commission on 13 March 1996.[113] The basis of the Community Action was said by the Directive to be distortion of competition and unequal treatment of artists within the (old) art 100A of the EC Treaty, thus facilitating a decision by the Council on the basis of a qualified majority. Given the strength of opposition to the Proposed Directive from the UK, aided and abetted by Ireland and the Netherlands, this is an important point. Throughout the legislative process, the text underwent significant alternations and revisions.[114]

[19.33] Directive 2001/84/EC[115] consists of mandatory and optional provisions. In this paragraph we will set out the mandatory provisions. Article 1.1 defines the right as an inalienable and unwaivable right which attaches to the author of an original work of art. Article 2 harmonises the definition of works of art to which the Directive applies. Article 3 requires Member States to set a threshold minimum sale price before the resale right will apply – this is not to be above €3,000. The royalty is fixed by reference to five bands. For that portion of the price up to €50,000, 4% is payable. A 3% royalty is payable for that portion of the price from €50,000 to €200,000. The third band of 1% attaches to the portion of the sale price from €200,000 to €350,000. The royalty for the portion of the price that falls within €350,000 to €500,000 is 0.5%, with the sale price in excess of that sum attracting a royalty of 0.25%. However, no royalty can ever exceed a 'cap' of €12,500. This means that sales in excess of €2m will exhaust the royalty right. Third-country nationals are to enjoy the right on a reciprocity basis by reference to a Commission list system – art 7. The resale right lasts for the duration of the artist's economic rights and art 9 gives to artists rights of information on resales made by art market professionals.

[19.34] The optional provisions have attracted considerable attention. It is giving nothing away to say that the position of the UK and Ireland has been lukewarm on the Directive. A considerable degree of 'watering down' has occurred, not just on the modest nature of the royalty rate but also on several of the optional provisions. For example, an exception in respect of guaranteed sales made by the artist to a gallery was introduced in art 1.3. This has the effect of eliminating the right if resold within three years for less than €10,000. The minimum price threshold of €3,000 can be reduced.[116] The Directive also allows Member States to increase the bottom band of four per cent (ie

---

[113] Proposal for a European Parliament and Council Directive on the Resale Right for the Benefit of the Author of an Original Work of Art (Com) 96 97 Final.

[114] For an excellent analysis see Duchemin (2001) 191 Revue Internationale de Droit d'Auteur 3.

[115] Council Directive 2001/84/EC ([2001] OJ L272/32).

[116] Council Directive 2001/84/EC, art.3.2. In the UK the threshold was reduced to €1,000

the first €50,000) to five per cent.[117] A further 'optional' provision in the Directive, of a rather different kind, relates to the issue of eligibility. Ireland and three other Member States that did not operate a resale right system were permitted to apply the scheme to living artists, adjudged on the date of adoption of the Directive. ie 13 October 2001. In the period between 1 January 2006 and 1 January 2010 the resale right was not to be available to beneficiaries of a deceased artist; a further two year maximum derogation was provided for, if the 'economic operators' were able to make out an argument that the extension of the resale right in respect of deceased artists would prejudice their economic viability.[118]

[19.35] When the date for transposition arrived, no legislative text had been presented to the Oireachtas. In response to this apparent inactivity, the leading Irish artist Robert Ballagh brought an action against the State, arguing that non-transposition had led to income losses on the sale of his works at auction in the first six months of 2006. Damages of €5,000 were awarded.[119] In response to the *Ballagh* action the government pushed through a statutory instrument[120] that gave effect to the mandatory provisions in the Directive. Optional provisions were not exercised in this piece of secondary legislation because of Constitutional difficulties that secondary legislation presents when policy choices are implemented in that manner.[121] While the government promised that a fuller consideration of policy matters would be undertaken and that primary legislation would follow, there are no signs of a Bill being presented to the Oireachtas in the near future (August, 2010). Thus, the sales threshold remains set at the high level of €3,000 and the bottom band is set at four per cent rather than the optimal rate of five per cent.

[19.36] The 2006 Regulations provide that the author of an original work of art is to have a resale right: a royalty on any sale of a work that is subsequent to the original sale or disposition by the artist. This right is inalienable and not assignable. Any charge on a resale right is void as is any waiver or agreement to share or repay the royalty. A resale may be in existence even if there is no consideration, in money or otherwise. An art market professional must be involved in the sale and the UK experience is that eBay sales are regarded as qualifying sales.[122] The Regulations place the obligation on the seller to pay the royalty even though the Directive, and custom and practice, seem to place this onus on the art market professional and seller as being jointly and severally liable.[123] The Regulations also provide for information on sales to be made available to artists by art market professionals. The Regulations, like the Directive, envisage collective management of the right by artists, but the Regulations do not identify any collecting body, something that can cause delays in making payment as the seller can

---

[117] Council Directive 2001/84/EC, art 4.2
[118] Council Directive 2001/84/EC, art 8.2 and 8.3
[119] 'Ballagh gets €5,000 damages for loyalties lost' (2006) The Irish Times, 1 July.
[120] SI 312/2006.
[121] Eg *Maher v Minister for Agriculture* [2001] 2 IR 139.
[122] See www.dacs.org.
[123] *Ibid* for UK practice.

withhold the payment until entitlement is established. The Irish Visual Artists Organisation (IVARO) was created by Visual Artists Ireland as a collecting society. IVARO has entered a number of reciprocal agreements so as to facilitate collection of the resale right royalty from other collecting societies in respect of the use of the works of Irish artists outside Ireland. While Irish auctioneers are broadly compliant with the law, IVARO still faces some hostility from gallery owners for a number of reasons.[124] Perhaps one of the most commonly heard complaints is that the resale right tends to be paid to already highly successful artists, and a newspaper article indicates that 10 artists receive two thirds of the monies collected.[125] Gibbons[126] has questioned whether the resale right is an efficient method of supporting artistic creation, but at a time when government support in the form of bursaries and grants is in decline, the resale right does represent some, albeit clumsy, mechanism for supporting artists.

[19.37] The possibility of Ireland obtaining a derogation of a further two years, as provided for under art 8.3 of the Directive, became a reality when Ireland followed the UK in seeking to argue that the art market faced significant problems in 2009. The European Commission agreed to these requests for an extension of the rules restricting payments to living artists only until 1 January 2012. Some of the *droit de suite* jurisdictions are now complaining that the UK and Ireland now actually have a competitive advantage in the fine arts market and some EU Member States are believed to be pressing for some adjustments to be made to national resale rights regimes (eg making the payment available only to living artists). Ironically, France is believed to have its rules under review.

---

[124] See 'Artists to sue gallery owners over royalties' (2010) Sunday Times, 4 July.

[125] 'Rich get richer in new arts bonanza' (2007) Sunday Times, 25 November. See Kawashima [2006] IPQ 225.

[126] Gibbons [2007] EIPR 163.

Chapter 20

Rights in Performances

INTRODUCTION

[20.01] International intellectual property law has been slow to recognise the contribution that performers, as interpreters of protected copyright works, may bring to bear in respect of the aesthetic, cultural or commercial value of intellectual property. There are a number of reasons for this. One reason is the evanescent nature of a performance. In contrasting author's rights with the rights of performers Lord Denning MR wrote:[1]

> No matter how brilliant the performance, which no one else could rival, nevertheless it is so intangible, so fleeting, so ethereal that it is not protected by the law of copyright. The actual musical work which they play or sing may itself be the subject of copyright, but the performers have no right in that musical work itself. It may be out of copyright. It may be the work of an old composer who died long ago. Or it may be the copyright of a modern composer or owner who has already been paid his due. The important thing to notice is that the performers themselves have no copyright.

[20.02] Strictly speaking, the 2000 legislation, which affords considerable rights to performers in respect of performances does not alter Lord Denning's view of the law vis-à-vis copyright. Performer's rights are the central concern of that part of the Copyright and Related Rights Act 2000 (CRRA 2000) devoted to related rights (often described also as neighbouring rights) as distinct from copyright, and rights in performances are treated separately in Pt III of CRRA 2000. The distinction between authorship and interpretation of a work of authorship is difficult to draw. It is common for the contributor to press the boundaries in the hope that the court may view a contribution as one of joint authorship, but the courts must insist that the contribution of a composer to a copyright work of authorship is to be distinguished from that of a performer. In *Barrett v Universal-Island Records Ltd*,[2] Aston Barrett, one of the members of 'The Wailers' claimed co-authorship of two of Bob Marley recordings based on a 'musical bridge' authored during a performance. Lewison J held that the contribution was both insubstantial and in conformity with the remainder of the composition. In contrast, in *Bamgboye v Reed*,[3] contributions to the definition of the baseline were held to assist in contributing to the melody and the additional performance contributions by way of drum

---

[1] *Ex p Island Records* [1978] 3 All ER 824 at 827.
[2] *Barrett v Universal-Island Records Ltd* [2006] EWHC 1009 (Ch).
[3] *Bamgboye v Reed* [2002] EWHC 2922.

patterns were classified as co-authorship elements entitling Bamgboye to one third of the copyright, applying the tests found in *Hadley v Kemp*.[4]

INTERNATIONAL LAW CONTEXT AND THE 1968 LEGISLATION

[20.03] Ireland has ratified the primary international treaty protecting performers, the Rome Convention for the Protection of Performers, Producers of Phonograms and Broadcasting Organisations of 1961 (Rome Convention), but while the two latter entities described in the title in this Convention were afforded copyrights under Part III of the Copyright Act 1963 (CA 1963), performers were treated differently by giving them rights affording them the possibility of preventing unauthorised fixation and broadcasting of a performance rather than exclusive rights to authorise and permit such actions by others. The Performers' Protection Act 1968 (PPA 1968) allowed persons engaged in performance – defined as 'a performance of any actors, singers, musicians, dancers or other persons who act, sing, deliver, declaim, play in or otherwise perform literary, dramatic musical or artistic works' – some form of right other than a copyright. PPA 1968 provided that the gardaí could proceed against persons who made, dealt in or used unauthorised recordings of performances[5] or films[6] or who broadcast a performance without the consent of the performer,[7] who were deemed guilty of a criminal offence.[8] The penalties for infringement were modest and there were a substantial range of defences such as private use in the case of unauthorised recordings. The reasons for this limited protection were in part due to the often unorganised nature of performers and their limited bargaining power in crafts or professions where supply often exceeds demand, a reluctance by right holders to benefit performers because of the supposed complexity that could result if performers obtained exclusive rights that could impede exploitation of copyright works, and the view that efficient protection and recognition can best be afforded by way of contractual arrangements for remuneration between broadcasters and actor and musician unions. The fact that US law affords performers few rights is often cited as a reason for continuing with this approach and US opposition to the broadening of performers' rights has long been an impediment to a broader international instrument than the Rome Convention. However, it should be noted that US domestic law, via a law of publicity, does provide some measure of protection for celebrity performers who, for example, have their performances recorded.[9]

---

4   *Hadley v Kemp* [1999] EMLR 589 (QB). The fact that a contribution has been made to the version of a work that has already been recorded will not prevent the contribution from being one of authorship vis-à-vis a second version of the work/new sound recording: *Fisher v Brooker* [2009] UKHL 41.

5   PPA 1968, s 2.

6   PPA 1968, s 3.

7   PPA 1968, s 5.

8   See Cohen Jehoram (1990) 15 Colum VLA JL & Arts 75 for a discussion of the performer as a special case.

9   *Zacchini v Scripps Howard Broadcasting* 433 US 562 (1976) (unauthorised filming of human cannonball): see generally, Gordon (1960) 55 NUL Rev 553; Frazer [1983] EIPR 139 and (1983) 99 LQR 281 and Klink [2003] IPQ 363.

[20.04] Even within the confines of PPA 1968 it was possible for a performer to seek to use the civil courts to prevent the unauthorised recording of a performance (bootlegging) and, more realistically, the distribution of copies of the recording. The precise judicial basis of this right has been explored in a series of English cases. The net result of these cases[10] indicates that the right is available to the performer and that the recording company has no *locus standi* to seek to enforce the performer's right, which exists by virtue of performers' protection legislation and is thus personal to the performer. In the leading case of *Rickless v United Artists*[11] the estate of Peter Sellers obtained relief in the civil courts against the use of out-takes from the 'Pink Panther' series in order to produce a new film, action which Peter Sellers actually opposed during his lifetime. The Court of Appeal followed the earlier cases and found that because the intention behind the UK legislation was to give effect to the Rome Convention, the legislation had to be viewed as granting civil relief to the performer. While the Court of Appeal conceded that the result was somewhat anomalous – it was not clear when the performer or the performer's estate would lose such rights to object because the right is not defined in such terms in the legislation – this strengthening of the performer's rights is certainly sympathetic with the wider objectives of the Rome Convention.

[20.05] It remains to be seen just how an Irish court would respond to a similar action brought by or on behalf of a performer. Mannion has argued[12] that, while the legislative history of PPA 1968 indicates that there was no government intention to give performers a property right enforceable in the civil courts, the Rome Convention and the constitutional rights of a citizen to earn a livelihood in the face of illegal conduct together would compel a court to follow *Rickless* in some shape or form.

[20.06] A second, but more indirect, route for the performer would be to utilise some other cause of action, such as wrongful intervention in business relations. A copyright holder[13] or even a collecting society acting on behalf of a copyright owner[14] could proceed against pirates and bootleggers. In some cases unauthorised use of the performer's image (eg on labelling) might ground a passing-off action at least where the use of the image misrepresents the possibility of product endorsement by the performer.[15] Privacy law has also been brought into play in such circumstances by the Canadian courts[16] although no Irish decision in this area exists.

---

[10] *Island Records v Corkindale* [1978] FSR 505; *Lonrho v Shell* [1982] AC 173; *RCA v Pollard* [1983] Ch 135.

[11] *Rickless v United Artists* [1987] FSR 362.

[12] Mannion (1992) 10 ILT (ns) 276.

[13] Despite *Lonrho v Shell* [1982] AC 173 the performer will presumably often perform the works of an author or composer, unauthorised recording of which will breach copyrights.

[14] *Carlin v Collins* [1979] FSR 548.

[15] Eg *Irvine v Talksport* [2003] 2 All ER 881.

[16] *Bogajewicz v Sony of Canada* (1995) 128 DLR (4th) 530.

THE RENTAL AND LENDING RIGHTS DIRECTIVE

[20.07] The rather uneven pattern of protection afforded to European Community performers – Member States had interpreted and transposed the provision of the Rome Convention unevenly and in some instances not at all – made the issue of performers' rights a matter for the Community legislator. In the Rental and Lending Rights Directive, Directive 92/100/EC, a number of significant provisions were included so as to create a single market form of protection for performers as therein defined.[17] Performers were afforded exclusive rights to authorise the fixation of their performances and the exclusive right to authorise the issuing of copies of these fixations to the public. An exclusive right in respect of the broadcasting of a performance is also afforded to performers in respect of their performances. The CRRA 2000 legislation reflects the scope of these provisions but the Directive is not the sole reference point. It should also be noted that the international community has gone some way towards providing performers with substantial rights in the form of provisions set out in the Geneva Treaty on Performers' Rights and Phonogram Producers (1996)[18] by granting exclusive rights to authorise the fixation, reproduction, distribution and communication to the public of aural performances – thus giving musical performers rights analogous to copyright. This Treaty broadens the concept of performer, so as to include performers of folklore, for example,[19] and the Treaty also clearly covers digital fixations of performances.

[20.08] This last part is extremely important because the post-1992 explosion of performance distribution via the internet made the provisions of the 1992 Directive appear to be silent on the issue. The drafters of the 2000 legislation took the Geneva WPPT into account when drafting CRRA 2000, particularly in relation to Article 10 of the Treaty, giving performers an exclusive right of authorising the making available to the public of performances fixed on phonograms and made available via 'on demand' services such as the internet.

THE CRRA 2000 AND 'PERFORMANCE' DEFINED

[20.09] A performance is defined as a

> performance of any actors, singers, musicians, dancers or other persons who act, sing, deliver, declaim, play in, interpret or otherwise perform literary, dramatic, musical or artistic works or expressions of works of folklore, which is a live performance given by one or more individuals, and shall include a performance of a variety act or any similar presentation.[20]

---

[17] Council Directive 92/100/EC ([1992] OJ L346/61).

[18] The World Intellectual Property Organisation's Phonograms and Performances Treaty (WPPT), agreed at a World Intellectual Property Organisation (WIPO) Diplomatic Conference held in Geneva, 2–20 December 1996.

[19] WPPT, art 2.

[20] CRRA 2000, s 202(1).

[20.10] While this is a broad definition of performance there are still criteria to be met. For example, the performance should be of a work or a variety act. It appears that *ex tempore* or ad lib performances may not be protected unless the performer can show some underlying work was involved. Cases involving speech *per se* allow a distinction between unprotected speech and protected speech in the form of lectures and sermons, for example.[21] Performances by sportsmen and sportswomen are unscripted[22] and even highly choreographed sports in which particular moves are 'coached' will not bring the players into the category of a performer.[23] Choreographed works and works of mime are included in the definition of dramatic works, so dancers and mime artists are clearly included.[24] It is also suggested that because of the broad, 'includes' nature of the definition of artistic work, a performance artist engaged in the recreation of a performance could invoke protection against, for example, the unauthorised filming of the performance under both copyright law and the performers' protection provisions in CRRA 2000. For performances to be protected, the performance must be a qualifying performance, that is, a performance given by an Irish, EEA or WTO citizen, resident or domiciliary, or be a performance given in one of those countries.[25] Irish law is unclear on the question whether a 'qualifying country' can include a country that, at the time the performance was given, was not, for example a member of the EU at the time the performance was given.[26] English case law suggests not only that the relevant legislation has retrospective effect, but also that the legislation will be effective even if the performer was deceased at the time the qualifying performance legislation replaced performers' protection legislation.[27]

SCOPE OF PERFORMERS' RIGHTS

[20.11] Performers are given exclusive rights in respect of the making of a recording of the whole or a substantial part of a qualifying performance directly from the live performance,[28] the live broadcasting/cable programme inclusion of the whole or a substantial part of a qualifying performance,[29] or the making of a recording from a live broadcast/cable programme transmitting the performance, live or otherwise.[30] Infringement occurs by doing, or the authorising of others to undertake, these actions

---

[21] Eg *Gould Estate v Stoddard Publishing Co* (1998) 80 CPR (3d) 161; *Gormley v EMI Records (Ireland) Ltd* [1998] 1 ILRM 126 and [1999] 1 ILRM 178.

[22] *Australian Olympic Committee Inc v Big Fights Inc* (1999) 46 IPR 53.

[23] Eg Canadian Football players have been held not to be engaged in participating in a dramatic work.

[24] See also CRRA 2000, s 202(3).

[25] CRRA 2000, ss 287–290.

[26] See *Experience Hendrix LLC v Purple Haze Records* [2005].

[27] *Experience Hendrix LLC v Purple Haze Records Ltd, Miller and Hillman* [2007] EWCA Civ 501.

[28] CRRA 2000, s 203(1)(a).

[29] CRRA 2000, s 203(1)(b).

[30] CRRA 2000, s 203(1)(c).

without the consent of the performer.[31] Performers also enjoy the right to authorise reproduction of recordings from an original recording – the reproduction right – whether the reproduction takes place directly or indirectly[32] and temporary or permanent copying or storage come within the scope of the right.[33] The making available to the public of copies of a recording is also an exclusive right under CRRA 2000, s 205, but in respect of recordings of performances that are played in public or included in a broadcast or cable programme service, the exclusive right is deemed to be satisfied by the payment of equitable remuneration.[34] This 'making available right' also extends to internet access to a recording in which a qualifying performance is fixed and sub-s (5) sets out the scope of the making available right, giving seven examples of what the right consists of.[35] Infringement of the s 203 right is addressed by s 209 which makes it an infringement to show or play in public the qualifying performance or broadcast, or include the performance in a cable programme service by way of a recording which that person knows or has reason to believe is a recording made without the consent of the performer. The making available right under s 205 is infringed by any person who without the consent of the performer undertakes or authorises another person to undertake any of the restricted acts coming within s 205.[36] The s 206 distribution right, which is, strictly speaking, part of the making available right, is infringed by the issuing of copies of a recording of whole or a substantial part of a recording of a qualifying performance.[37] However, s 226 exempted public lending establishments in respect of this aspect of the distribution right. Section 226 has been limited to educational establishments by the Copyright and Related Rights (Amendment) Act 2007. As the PLR Scheme[38] does not apply to works other than books, enforcement of this right is not possible in any realistic way.

Secondary infringement

[20.12] The CRRA 2000 makes it possible for persons who are facilitating infringement to be primarily liable,[39] but there are also significant secondary infringement provisions in relation to the importation, possession and distribution of illicit recordings,[40] providing the means of making illicit recordings,[41] and permitting or facilitating the public performance of infringing performances.[42]

---

[31] CRRA 2000, s 203(1), (2).

[32] CRRA 2000, s 204; see *Bassey v Icon Entertainments* [1995] EMLR 596.

[33] CRRA 2000, s 204(6).

[34] CRRA 2000, ss 205(2) and 208.

[35] On demand access, showing or playing the recording in public, broadcasting, cable programme service inclusion, issuing copies to the public, rental and lending of copies.

[36] CRRA 2000, s 205(6).

[37] CRRA 2000, s 206(4) and (6).

[38] See www.plr.ie

[39] CRRA 2000, s 205(8) (providing facilities for making available infringing copies, etc).

[40] CRRA 2000, s 212.

[41] CRRA 2000, s 213.

[42] CRRA 2000, s 214. On damages see *Experience Hendrix LLC v Times Newspapers* [2010] EWHC 1986 (Ch).

RECORDING RIGHTS

[20.13] As we have seen, the old provisions in relation to performers' protection did not give the maker of a sound recording the right to obtain an injunction to prevent the unauthorised fixation of a performance; 'bootleg' performances could be the subject of a sizeable industry amongst fans of performers like the Grateful Dead or Pearl Jam, bands who did not object to 'bootleg' recordings. The UK legislation in 1988, the Copyright, Designs and Patents Act 1988, addressed this situation by affording recording rights to record companies and CRRA 2000 has adopted a similar approach. In short, if a performer signs an 'exclusive recording contract' giving the record company the right to make recordings of one or more of the performer's performances, with a view to commercial exploitation, the fixation of a performance or the issue of copies of that recording will infringe the recording right. If the fixation or use is to be lawful, the consent of either the performer or the right holder is necessary,[43] and the usual primary and secondary infringement provisions apply in relation to recording rights.

PERMITTED ACTS

[20.14] CRRA 2000 re-enacts many of the defences available in respect of the reproduction or use of copyright works so as to make these defences available in respect of the use of a performance or a recording. Fair dealing for the purposes of criticism or review or for the purpose of reporting current events is permitted[44] as is an incidental inclusion defence.[45] The copying of a recording for instruction or examination performances is also permitted[46] as is the playing or showing of a sound recording, film, broadcast or cable programme service in which a performance is fixed for instruction or school purposes,[47] and the exemption extends also into the fixation of a broadcast or cable programme containing a performance.[48] Provisions regulating copying by librarians and archivists are also found in CRRA 2000[49] and in the regulations governing educational establishments and librarians and archivists.[50] The public administration exceptions are applicable to performances and recordings of performances.[51] Recordings that exist in electronic form and that enable the purchaser to make further copies may be similarly reproduced by a transferee.[52] The use of recordings of the spoken word is also regulated[53] and technical reproduction of a performance or recording may also be

---

[43] CRRA 2000, ss 215–219. On transmission and duration, see ss 301 and 308.
[44] CRRA 2000, s 221; note that there is no sufficient acknowledgment requirement.
[45] CRRA 2000, s 222.
[46] CRRA 2000, s 223.
[47] CRRA 2000, s 224.
[48] CRRA 2000, s 225.
[49] CRRA 2000, ss 227–336; see s 45 and folklore archives.
[50] SI 409/2000 and SI 427/2000.
[51] See CRRA 2000, ss 237–241 and SI 411/2000 in respect of international organisations.
[52] CRRA 2000, s 242.
[53] CRRA 2000, s 243.

permitted on the basis of necessity for caching purposes.[54] An exemption is also provided in respect of the use of a sound recording, broadcast or cable programme containing a performance in residential or inmate premises[55] but the controversial provision in respect of the playing of sound recordings for the private activities of a club is not yet in force.[56] A range of broadcast exemptions are found in ss 248 to 253 covering activities such as supervision of broadcasts, cable retransmission, time-shifting, meeting the needs of disabled persons and designated archives.[57]

REMEDIES

[20.15] CRRA 2000 contains search and seizure reliefs both in civil[58] and in criminal[59] proceedings with the usual provision in relation to final disposal of the seized articles.[60] Apart from the infringement of performers' rights provisions mentioned earlier, the legislation makes several of these acts of primary and secondary infringement criminal offences where the individual knows or has reason to believe that the article in question is either an illicit recording,[61] an article specifically designed or adapted to make illicit recordings,[62] or is a protection defeating device to be used in circumvention of rights protection measures.[63] Entitlement to damages for breach of most of these rights is available via s 304 and these damages may include aggravated or exemplary damages as well as damages for financial loss.[64] The rights afforded in respect of the fixation of a performance, the broadcasting of a performance, and the making of a recording or cable programme from such a performance,[65] as well as the s 208 equitable remuneration right and the recording right are actionable as breach of statutory duty[66] and an application for damages may be made in such a context.[67] Restrictions on the availability of certain reliefs such as injunctive relief are set out in the legislation.[68]

---

[54] CRRA 2000, s 244, as amended by SI 16/2004.

[55] CRRA 2000, s 245; on time-shifting see s 250 and SI 407/2000.

[56] CRRA 2000, s 247 and SI 404/2000.

[57] See SI 405/2000.

[58] CRRA 2000, ss 255–257.

[59] CRRA 2000, ss 260, 261.

[60] CRRA 2000, s 264.

[61] CRRA 2000, s 258(1).

[62] CRRA 2000, s 258(2).

[63] CRRA 2000, s 258(3). Information provided or services rendered to the same end are also within the offence.

[64] CRRA 2000, s 304(3). An innocent infringer defence is also available: s 304(2).

[65] CRRA 2000, s 203.

[66] CRRA 2000, s 308(1).

[67] CRRA 2000, s 308(2).

[68] Eg CRRA 2000, s 305 (licences of right).

TRANSMISSION OF RIGHTS

[20.16] The rights can be the subject of licence agreements. However, the transmission of these rights via an assignment depends on whether the rights are property or non-property rights. The reproduction right, the making available right, the distribution right and rental and lending rights are property rights and are freely transmissible and assignable whereas the fixation rights in CRRA 2000, ss 203, 209 and 212 are non-property rights and are personal to the performer but capable of testamentary and non-testamentary disposition.[69]

DEALINGS WITH PERFORMERS' RIGHTS

[20.17] It should be remembered that performers' rights break down into two kinds of right; rights that are property rights and rights that are non-property rights. The property rights[70] are the performers' reproduction right,[71] the making available right,[72] the distribution right[73] and the rental and lending right.[74] In contrast, the performers' non-property rights are the fixation of a live performance, on the making of a recording of the said broadcast/cable programme.[75] Also, CRRA 2000 identifies the public performance or use in a broadcast or cable programme service of a s 203 illicit recording of a live performance as an infringement[76] as are the acts of secondary infringement in the form of importation, possessing or dealing in s 203 illicit recordings.[77] This dichotomy is not exhaustive of performers' rights, however, and there are some rights that are not classed as performers' property and non-property rights such as the s 208 right to equitable remuneration for the exploitation of a sound recording that contains a qualifying performance.

[20.18] In terms of the ability of a performer to transfer the property rights afforded under CRRA 2000, these rights are treated in the same way as true copyrights. The rights are transmissible by assignment, by testamentary disposition, or by operation of law, as personal or moveable property.[78] The rights are divisible by way of partial transmission, that is, some performances but not all may be the subject of a transfer and the transfer could be for a limited period of the performer's economic rights.[79] Any assignment is ineffective unless in writing, signed by or on behalf of the assignor,[80] defective transfers

---

69   CRRA 2000, s 300.
70   CRRA 2000, s 203.
71   CRRA 2000, s 204.
72   CRRA 2000, s 205.
73   CRRA 2000, s 206.
74   CRRA 2000, s 207.
75   CRRA 2000, s 300.
76   CRRA 2000, s 209.
77   CRRA 2000, s 212.
78   CRRA 2000, s 293(1).
79   CRRA 2000, s 292(2).
80   CRRA 2000, ss 292, 293.

or verbal transfers having the effect of an equitable assignment in the usual way. Assignment of future performance rights is also possible.[81] Licences of performers' property rights are also governed by the same approach as those adopted by the legislature in relation to copyright licences, with exclusive licenses that are in writing and signed by or on behalf of the performer being binding on the performer's successors in title.[82] A statutory presumption of transfer of the performer's rental right (part of the s 207 property right) in the case of film production performances, with extremely 'liberal' provisions in relation to defective execution of any film production agreement[83] and third-party representation of the performer are found in ss 297 and 298 of CRRA 2000. The right to equitable remuneration subsequent to a transfer of the rental right cannot be assigned other than a collecting society for administrative purposes, but when the right is transferred by testamentary disposition or by operation of law, the holder can assign the right to equitable remuneration.[84]

[20.19] The performer's right to equitable remuneration in respect of the exploration of a sound recording, provided to performers under CRRA 2000, s 208 is similarly not assignable other than to a collecting society for administrative purposes.[85] When the right devolves by testamentary disposition or by operation of law the holder may assign the right to equitable remuneration.[86]

THE COLLECTIVE ADMINISTRATION OF PERFORMERS' RIGHTS

[20.20] The exercise of the right to equitable remuneration[87] for the purpose of the rights of performers in respect of the use of sound recordings which are played in public or used in a broadcast or cable programme is in practice assigned to a collecting society. The society that exists for this purpose is the Recorded Artists and Performers Organisation (RAAP) and RAAP negotiates with PPI in relation to the division of fees as between record producers and recording artists.

MORAL RIGHTS

[20.21] The European Commission has not entered into the subject of moral rights in respect of either copyright or performers, and obviously the provisions of the Berne Convention for the Protection of Literary and Artistic Works (Berne Convention), Article 6*bis* are inapplicable to performers. However WPPT, art 5 provides:

> (1) Independently of a performer's economic rights, and even after the transfer of those rights, the performer shall, as regards his live aural performances or performances fixed in

---

[81]   CRRA 2000, s 294.
[82]   CRRA 2000, s 295; contrast s 293(4) and (5) for non-exclusive licenses.
[83]   CRRA 2000, s 297(2).
[84]   CRRA 2000, s 298.
[85]   CRRA 2000, s 208(2).
[86]   CRRA 2000, s 209(3).
[87]   See WPPT 1996, art 15.

phonograms, have the right to claim to be identified as the performer of his performances, and to object to any distortion, mutilation or other modification of his performances that would be prejudicial to his reputation.

(2) The rights granted to a performer in accordance with paragraph (1) shall, after his death, be maintained, at least until the expiry of the economic rights, and shall be exercisable by the persons or institutions authorised by the Contracting Party where protection is claimed. However, those Contracting Parties whose legislation, at the moment of their ratification of or accession to this Treaty, does not provide for the protection after the death of the performer of all the rights set out in the preceding paragraph may provide that some of these rights may, after his death, cease to be maintained.

(3) The means of redress for safeguarding the rights granted by this Article shall be governed by the legislation of the Contracting Party where protection is claimed.

[20.22] While art 5 of the WPPT only required Ireland to apply moral rights to sound recording performances, CRRA 2000 went further than the WPPT required by allowing moral rights to be available to all performers within the ambit of CRRA 2000. The rights in question are the paternity right,[88] the integrity right,[89] and a right not to have a performance falsely attributed to him or her as a performer.[90] These rights are the subject of significant limitations and in particular may be the subject of written waiver,[91] contractual limitation or estoppel.[92]

SUBSISTENCE OF PERFORMERS' RIGHTS

[20.23] Performers' rights subsist for 50 years from the end of the calendar year in which the performance takes place, or where a recording of the performance is made available to the public within that period, 50 years after that date.[93] This is the same position in respect of performers' moral rights.[94] In order to protect the income of featured performers and session musicians who were professionally active between 1957 and 1967 (those performers being adversely affected by the fact that the sound recordings onto which performances were fixed are about to enter the public domain) the European Commission proposed[95] to extend the term of protection for performers and phonogram producers from 50 years to 95 years. Session musicians, it is proposed, are to receive income from a fund to be established by the European Commission and financed from royalties from phonogram producers. The proposal also contains a 'use it or lose it' clause whereby rights in a sound recording may transfer to a performer in the

---

88 CRRA 2000, s 309.
89 CRRA 2000, s 311.
90 CRRA 2000, s 314.
91 CRRA 2000, s 316(1).
92 CRRA 2000, s 316(4).
93 CRRA 2000, s 291; on rental and lending rights see CRRA 2000, Sch 1, Pt V.
94 CRRA 2000, s 315.
95 Proposal for a European Parliament and Council Directive amending Directive 2006/116/EC Com/2008/464 Final –COD 2008/0157.

extension period. There are objections to the extension of protection. The Gowers Report[96] in the UK examined this question but found no link between extension of protection and incentivising artists and composers and the proposal has been likened to a social security measure rather than copyright and related rights legislation.[97]

---

[96] Gowers, *Review of Intellectual Property* (December 2006): Groves 2007 Enter 150; Rahmatan [2007] EIPR 353; Miller [2007] EIPR 244.

[97] See generally Helberger [2008] EIPR 174; Opinion [2008] EIPR 341; Hilty [2009] EIPR 59.

Chapter 21

Copyright – Past, Present and Future Legislative Developments

IRISH LAW AND THE FOUNDATION OF THE STATE

[21.01] With the establishment of Saorstát Éireann as a result of the Anglo-Irish Treaty of 6 December 1921, and the resulting legislation,[1] the issue of the status of the Copyright Act 1911 (CA 1911) arose for debate in Saorstát Éireann. Legislation to consolidate and amend existing legislation in the intellectual property field was initiated in the form of an Industrial and Commercial Property (Protection) Bill, which was introduced in 1925, but this legislation was withdrawn and re-introduced the following year by another omnibus measure which became the Industrial and Commercial Property (Protection) Act 1927 (ICPPA 1927). The provisions of Part VI on copyright broadly reflected the provisions set out in the 1911 legislation. Thus, copyright in published works was given, if the work was first published in the State, and in the case of an unpublished work, copyright subsisted if at the time of making the work the author was a citizen of, or resident in the State.[2] Save in cases where international conventions provided to the contrary, a power was given to extend copyright to foreign citizens through the Governor General by order made on the advice of the Executive Council.[3] Through this mechanism, copyright protection for works published other than within the British Dominions[4] or in the Berne Union would be given as long as there was reciprocity of treatment. At this time the US was regarded as the most significant jurisdiction outside either the British Copyright Union or the Berne Convention for the Protection of Literary and Artistic Works ('Berne Convention'). The provisions in ICPPA 1927 on the nature of copyright, the kinds of infringement and duration of copyright, including the compulsory licensing exceptions[5] were also based on CA 1911. Issues that had to be dealt with even included the granting of a State copyright[6] and the lodging of new books with certain copyright libraries within the State and in Britain.[7] Apart from attempts by some well-meaning parliamentarians who sought to introduce a manufacturing clause in relation to the printing of books, debates on ICPPA 1927 were

---

[1]   Eg Irish Free State (Agreement) Act 1922.
[2]   ICPPA 1927, s 154.
[3]   This procedure was amended by the Industrial and Commercial Property (Protection) (Amendment) Act 1929.
[4]   On which, see ICPPA 1927, s 175.
[5]   ICPPA 1927, ss 156 and 157.
[6]   ICPPA 1927, s 168.
[7]   ICPPA 1927, s 178.

relatively unexceptional and it was certainly the view that this Act repealed and replaced CA 1911 within the State. However, in a remarkable piece of litigation, the status of CA 1911 was called into question by the Supreme Court although this decision was in turn overruled by the Judicial Committee of the Privy Council in *Performing Rights Society v Bray UDC.*[8] In that case, the defendant permitted a band to perform two musical works in the course of a number of summer concerts in 1926. Despite assurances to the contrary given to the defendant by the band, the band did not have a performing rights licence from the plaintiff. The works had been written before 6 December 1921 but assignments took place after that date in favour of PRS. The issue before the Irish courts was whether CA 1911 was in force after the foundation of the State for, if it was not, no infringement could have taken place in the summer of 1926. The Supreme Court[9] held that the Irish Free State, as a self-governing dominion, had not declared CA 1911 to be in force[10] and thus CA 1911 was not carried over into Irish law. The Judicial Committee of the Privy Council held that the phrase, 'self-governing dominion', within CA 1911, had a specific meaning and that the Irish Free State could not come within it. Their Lordships also noted that a schedule to ICPPA 1927 certainly repealed CA 1911, an unnecessary measure if the Supreme Court's reasoning was correct. No remedy other than costs was available to the PRS, however, because in the period between ICPPA 1927 and the Supreme Court's decision[11] the Oireachtas had passed amending legislation which had revested copyright as from 5 December 1921, but that legislation had also declared that no remedies were to be available prior to implementation of this amending statute.[12]

[21.02] The ICPPA 1927 continued to be the primary copyright law until replaced by the Copyright Act 1963 (CA 1963). After the *Bray UDC* litigation,[13] pressure for amending legislation seems to have been virtually non-existent. The Industrial and Commercial Property (Protection) (Amendment) Act 1929 made significant amendments to the foreign national procedure and introduced licensing provisions in respect of translations of works into Irish in an attempt to stimulate interest in the Irish language, and those provisions were also the primary copyright matters contained in the Industrial and Commercial Property (Protection) (Amendment) Acts of 1957 and 1958.

[21.03] The Copyright Bill 1962 was introduced into Dáil Éireann on 28 November 1962 for a number of reasons. First, ICPPA 1927, itself based on CA 1911, clearly had outlived its usefulness and the Minister for Industry and Commerce, Mr Jack Lynch, indicated that the UK Copyright Act 1956 took account of modern developments whereby ideas can be conveyed by radio, television, films and recordings as well as the print media; this 1956 legislation had proved a model for other countries and 'it is the

---

[8]   *Performing Rights Society v Bray UDC* [1930] IR 509.
[9]   *Performing Rights Society v Bray UDC* [1928] IR 506.
[10] CA 1911, s 25(1).
[11] Handed down on 7 July 1928.
[12] Copyright (Preservation) Act 1929 (24 July 1929).
[13] *Performing Rights Society v Bray UDC* [1928] IR 506, [1930] IR 509; see discussion in para **21.02**.

basis upon which much of the present Bill has been prepared'. The second factor mentioned by Mr Lynch was the influence of international conventions and international agreements. While Ireland was party to both the Berne Convention and the Geneva Convention,[14] legislation to give greater protection to broadcasts was of particular importance in such a context. The Minister also indicated that the Rome Convention on International Protection of Performers, Producers of Phonograms and Broadcast Organisations of October 1961 (Rome Convention) required legislative changes to be made. Part III of CA 1963 gave films and recordings specific copyrights, qua films and recordings and not entitlement as a kind of dramatic or musical work. The Minister noted that such a move was not only internationally mandated but a matter of good sense because 'there is frequently no personal author in the sense in which the word is used in relation to dramatic or musical works'.[15] Although CA 1963, by recognising broadcast copyright, made a significant advance, CA 1963 defined broadcast organisations so as to include the national broadcasting agency, Radio Telefís Éireann (RTE), and in fact it was only in 1991 that independent broadcasting services established under the Radio and Television Act 1988 were given a copyright in respect of broadcasts.[16]

[21.04] Even though ICPPA 1927 had been used to extend protection to foreign nationals, eg the Copyright (Foreign Countries) Order 1959,[17] the technological and economic importance of copyright was pointed to by the Supreme Court in *PRS v Marlin Communal Aerials Ltd*.[18] In that case, PRS claimed infringement of copyright by a licensed wireless retransmission company that, in diffusing the boosted signal of UK television companies, was causing the PRS repertoire to be heard contrary to s 8(6)(e) of CA 1963. However, the authors of these works, not being qualified persons, had to rely on international rights available under the Berne Convention but no order had been made under s 43 of CA 1963 at this time. The relevant order[19] under ICPPA 1927 did not make cable diffusion of works a restricted act. The Supreme Court declined to interpret the transitional provisions in CA 1963 as having the effect of supplanting a s 43 order. The legally correct, but embarrassing, situation for the Irish State was ultimately resolved by a number of statutory orders made one year later.[20] A number of separate orders were made to deal with copyright for countries not covered by the Berne Convention or international organisations within s 44 of CA 1963.[21] However, the Copyright (Foreign Countries) Order 1996[22] provides copyright protection in respect of the authors of literary, dramatic, musical or artistic works and the makers of films as long as the author

---

[14] Ie the Universal Copyright Convention (Paris, 1974). The earlier Universal Copyright Convention (Geneva 1952) is binding on Ireland.

[15] 198 *Dáil Debates*, Col 242.

[16] SI 101/1991 as from 23 April 1991.

[17] SI 50/1959.

[18] *PRS v Marlin Communal Aerials Ltd* [1977] FSR 51.

[19] SI 50/1959 as amended by CA 1963, Sch 1, para 35.

[20] SI 132/1978; SI 133/1978 and SI 134/1978, effective as from 9 May 1978.

[21] Eg Copyright (Republic of Indonesia) Order 1988 (SI 155/1988).

[22] SI 36/1996.

or maker, as the case may be, are citizens of countries of the Berne Union, UCC States, or members of the World Trade Organisation on or after 30 January 1996.

SUBSTANTIVE LAW REFORM AND UK INFLUENCES

[21.05] Since ICPPA 1927 was passed, the main features of Irish copyright law, in terms of substantive law, remained largely unaltered until 2000. Even the introduction of the CA 1963 Part III copyrights did not mark any significant departure from the primary features of the UK CA 1911, and the history of legislative debate on both ICPPA 1927 and CA 1963 point to the fact that the principles which shaped Irish law were largely externally determined. Efforts to introduce manufacturing clauses into what became ICPPA 1927 were resisted because of the Berne Convention and some otherwise very sensible efforts to abridge the duration of copyright itself similarly foundered during those debates.[23] Since CA 1963 was passed, the first piece of primary legislation on copyright to go through the Oireachtas[24] was the Copyright (Amendment) Act 1987, a short two-section Act that improved powers of search and seizure of counterfeit goods and amended the law on artistic copyright to take functional designs out of copyright. On this second point, the solution adopted follows the UK approach, but it was not accompanied by the introduction of an unregistered design right along the lines of the UK unregistered design right. The 1987 amendment to artistic copyright has been further refined by the Copyright and Related Rights Act 2000 (CRRA 2000) and the Industrial Designs Act 2001 (IDA 2001); again, some features of these reforms can be said to have been shaped by UK legislation. However, the protection of unregistered designs is now (after March 2003) governed by the Community unregistered design right considered in further detail below. Nevertheless, the structure, if not always the content, of CRRA 2000 reflects UK legislation, partly because of the strength of historical and conceptual links between the two copyright regimes and also because of strong commercial relations in place in key media and other industrial sectors.

[21.06] The changes recently made to the UK copyright law could be expected to have some impact upon the 2000 Irish legislation for a number of reasons. The Copyright, Designs and Patents Act 1988 (UK) (CDPA 1988) was the result of a prolonged process of review and debate in the UK, most significantly through the Whitford Report,[25] the Green Paper,[26] and the White Paper 'Intellectual Property and Innovation'[27] of 1986. The 1988 legislation, therefore, can be said to represent a relatively up-to-date benchmark and its merits, in terms of substantive law reform, are many. For example, the expansion of literary copyright to cover speech,[28] the expansion of rights to cover issuing copies of

---

[23] 17 *Dáil Debates*, Cols 544 and 591.

[24] A Copyright (Amendment) Bill 1984 was introduced by the government but this modest Bill, to enhance CA 1963, s 27 infringement penalties, grew by one further section to become the Copyright (Amendment) Act 1987.

[25] Copyright – Copyright and Design Law (Cmnd 6732, 1977).

[26] Reform of the Law Relating to Copyright, Designs and Performers Protection (Cmnd 8302, 1981).

[27] Cmnd 9712.

[28] CDPA 1988, s 3(1).

works to the public[29] as distinct from publication *simpliciter*, the clarification of primary and secondary infringement concepts and the strengthening of civil and criminal laws aimed at counteracting piracy, such as providing protection against unauthorised broadcast reception,[30] were only a few of the measures that were useful to adapt to Irish conditions. However, the CDPA 1988 has many critics because of the length and complexity of the Act and the drafting style adopted. Laddie, Prescott and Vitoria[31] observed that, while the CDPA 1988 does not confine itself simply to copyright matters:

> diversity of subject matter does not account for all of its greatly increased length. Consider, for example, Chapter III of Part I of the 1988 Act. Here one may find no less than 49 sections setting forth in (too great) detail what are the exceptions to copyright protection. Some of these regulations will soon be out of date, and an embarrassment. Others can only have been invented by persons who did not think out properly what they were supposed to be achieving. How much better the Americans do it with their simple, flexible 'fair use' exception! (A concept which originated on these shores by the way).[32]

In the first edition of this work, written at a time when the Copyright and Related Rights Bill 1999 had not been published, the authors expressed the hope that criticisms of this kind would be taken to heart by the drafters of the forthcoming Irish legislation.[33] Alas, this was not to be. The 1999 Bill, an introduction to the Oireachtas, totalled some 355 clauses: the final product is 376 clauses long and has three schedules. While some verbosity is to be expected because of the complexity and technical nature of the subject matter, other parts of the legislation are unnecessarily wordy and entire chapters (eg on licensing and collecting societies/dispute resolution) are repetitive, recalling Shaw's observation that he did not have time to write a short letter so he had to apologise for writing a long one. Nevertheless, CRRA 2000 houses most of Irish substantive copyright law under one roof with only a minimum amount of secondary legislation in place. Indeed, the European Communities (Copyright and Related Rights) Regulations 2004[34] that gave effect to some of the outstanding issues of definition created by the Information Society Directive of 2001[35] contain a mere three regulations of a substantive nature. This contrasts with the UK Copyright and Related Rights Regulations 2003[36] that contain 40 regulations. It is now widely accepted that the UK copyright law is now hopelessly unmanageable and structurally unintelligible and in urgent need of consolidation.

[21.07] Nevertheless, at least the UK engages in a process of review and adjustment of its copyright legislation as the 2006 Gowers Review and the Digital Economy Act 2010

---

[29] CDPA 1988, s 16.

[30] CDPA 1988, ss 297–299: contrast *News Datacom v Lyons* [1994] 1 ILRM 545.

[31] Laddie, Prescott and Vitoria, *The Modern Law of Copyright and Designs* (2nd edn, Butterworths, 1995). This work is now in a third edition.

[32] Laddie, Prescott and Vitoria, *The Modern Law of Copyright and Designs* (2nd edn), Preface.

[33] Clark and Smyth, *Intellectual Property Law in Ireland* (1997), para 20.06.

[34] SI 16/2004.

[35] Council Directive 2001/29/EC ([2001] OJ L167/10).

[36] SI 2498/2003.

attest. Although the 2000 legislation is far from perfect there is no national debate on copyright law revision/reform.

Irish government policy, in the form of 'smart economy' initiatives, however, does not appear to identify copyright law reform as part of an action area for boosting the Irish knowledge economy.[37] While this is in part due to the primary role that the EU has taken on via the development of copyright law, there are some areas of copyright law that are not clear or immune from scrutiny – ownership of research outputs, educational use and orphan works, to give just three examples. Current policy on stimulating the knowledge economy via legislation appears to be driven by adjustments to taxation[38] which, while welcome, do not address some underlying failures in copyright legislation. An inquiry into the role of intellectual property legislation as a boost to the smart economy is urgently needed.[39]

EU LEGISLATION

[21.08] In a legal context, the impact of EU law in the field of intellectual property law tends to focus upon the importance of competition rules and related concepts such as exhaustion of rights.[40] The general principles of EU law and how they affect intellectual property rights (which, in this field, are largely national in operation) are not allowed to hamper Community trade, wherever possible. However, given the fact that, despite the Berne and Rome Conventions, Member States do operate under quite diverse laws of copyright, it is inevitable that the ECJ should take the view that national restrictions on free movement of goods and, perhaps, services are permitted in certain instances. In such a context, the focus, in recent years, has switched dramatically to the possibility of approximation, and even harmonisation, of national laws on copyright and neighbouring rights. In terms of legislative competence, the engine behind these initiatives must be the need to complete the internal market and in the area of intellectual property legislation generally, Directorate General III (DG III), later reorganised and merged with DG XV, took on the task of producing draft legislation in accordance with a set of priorities identified in 1988 by the Commission in the document 'Green Paper on Copyright and the Challenge of Technology – Copyright Issues Requiring Immediate Action'.[41] While the Green Paper rightly disclaimed any pretensions toward comprehensiveness in relation to copyright issues requiring immediate attention, it has, despite protestations to the contrary, proved to be a blueprint for Community action between 1988 and 1992.

---

[37] See eg 'Summary of Progress and Future Priorities' (March 2010); 'Building Ireland's Smart Economy – Progress Report' (March 2010); see www.taoiseach.ie. Similar criticisms are applicable to 'The National Development Plan 2007-2013, Transforming Ireland – A Better Quality of Life for All'.

[38] Eg Finance Act 2009, ss 13 and 25; on intellectual property generally see www.revenue.ie.

[39] The Intellectual Property Unit in the Department of Enterprise, Trade and Innovation is currently engaged in a particular law review (July 2010)

[40] See Tritton, *Intellectual Property in Europe* (2nd edn, Sweet & Maxwell, 2002); Oliver, *Free Movement of Goods in the European Community* (4th edn, Thomson Sweet & Maxwell, 2003).

[41] Com (88) 172 Final.

The issues identified and addressed in the 1988 Green Paper were seen as priorities for immediate action although several of the problem areas such as legislation to improve anti-piracy laws within Member States were outside the legislative competence of the European Community.

[21.09] The Commission published a follow-up to the Green Paper in January 1991[42] and in this document the Commission set out a number of proposed actions. In terms of specific legislation, legislation harmonising copyright in such areas as software protection, database protection, duration of copyright, the harmonisation of neighbouring rights, legislation on commercial rental of works, and legislation on the co-ordination of copyright and neighbouring rights applicable to satellite and cable broadcasting. The follow-up document also recommended that the Council should make a decision requiring all Member States to accede to the 1971 Paris Act of the Berne Convention and the 1961 Rome Convention by the end of 1992.

[21.10] Although the legislative timetable in the follow-up document suggested that such legislative action would be taken before 31 December 1991, this timetable proved to be somewhat over-ambitious[43] in terms of the substantive topics to be covered and the time needed to process draft legislation through the Co-operation procedure.[44] Nevertheless, the success rate achieved by the Commission looks extremely impressive and Community legislation in certain key areas of harmonisation of copyright have proved extremely influential. This, of course, is to state the obvious. The need to transpose the Directives is an obligation under Community law and the substantive terms of the Directives of necessity were reflected in CRRA 2000. However, the size and complexity of the task of reform meant that, apart form the Software Directive[45] and the Term Directive,[46] Ireland fail to meet the transposition deadline for the other Directives, thus triggering proceedings and judgments against Ireland for breach of the EC Treaty.[47]

[21.11] For the sake of completeness, the measures adapted in the form of Directives via CRRA 2000 are as follows:

The Software Directive

[21.12] This Directive, agreed on 15 May 1991,[48] gave protection to computer programs as literary works in whatever form the program existed. Thus, object code became protected as a literary work. This Directive has been transposed into Irish law[49] and is discussed elsewhere in this book.[50]

---

[42] Com (90) 584 Final.
[43] Action on home copying of works, for example, never got off the ground but this is addressed in Council Directive 2001/29/EC.
[44] See EEC Treaty, art 100A.
[45] Council Directive 91/250/EEC ([1991] OJ L122/42).
[46] Council Directive 93/98/EEC ([1993] OJ L290/9).
[47] Eg [2002] ECDR 320, proceedings in respect of non-ratification of the Paris Act of the Berne Convention.
[48] Council Directive 91/250/EEC.

The Directive on Rental, Lending and Neighbouring Rights

[21.13] The Directive on Rental, Lending and Neighbouring Rights,[51] agreed on 19 November 1992, gives the authors of works exclusive rights to authorise rental and lending of those works, as defined in the Directive. Rental is defined as 'making available for use, for a limited period of time and for direct and indirect economic or commercial advantage' but it is not intended that this covers the distribution of films for public performance or broadcasting.[52] The distribution of physical copies is involved here and the Directive is not intended to cover the distribution of online information or other forms of electronic rental such as video-on-demand services. Lending of works is also covered and this is defined as making available for use, for a limited period of time and not for direct or indirect economic advantage, when it is made through establishments which are accessible to the public, but this does not cover inter-establishment lending (eg strict inter-library loans).[53]

[21.14] The public lending provisions were included to ensure that commercial rental was not endangered by unfair competition from publicly funded institutions. The Directive on Rental, Lending and Neighbouring Rights does not apply to the rental or lending of buildings and works of applied art, that is, industrial designs. Works protected in a Member State on 1 July 1994 qualify for these rental and lending rights.[54] However, the provisions that give effect to the rental right for copyright owners and performers, Part V of Sch 1 to CRRA 2000, required notice of an intention of exercise of those rights to be given before various dates. Needless to say, the post hoc nature of these provisions has largely subverted the ability of stakeholders of works affected by the rental right to assert and control these rights.

[21.15] Another new area that Directive 92/100/EEC addresses is the possible introduction of a public lending right. Irish law does not give the authors of books (much less all literary works, musical works, dramatic works, artistic works, sound recordings or films) any remuneration from the lending to the public of these works. Article 5 of Directive 92/100/EEC opens the door to this possibility for it provides that States may derogate from the lending right – that is, not implement this right as exclusively an authors' right – but the State must give remuneration to the authors of works made available via lending. In giving effect to the Directive, however, the government effectively denied authors any remuneration right.[55] Whether this is a faithful transposition of Directive 92/100/EEC is in doubt.

---

49 SI 26/1993. See now CRRA 2000, ss 2, 80–82 and 87.
50 See Ch 13.
51 Council Directive 92/100/EEC ([1992] OJ L346/61). See generally Reinbothe and Von Lewinski, *The EC Directive on Rental and Lending Rights and Piracy* (Sweet & Maxwell, 1993).
52 Directive 92/100/EEC, art 1.2 and recital 13; CRRA 2000, s 42(3).
53 Directive 92/100/EEC, art 1.3; CRRA 2000, s 42(4).
54 Directive 92/100/EEC, art 4.4.
55 CRRA 2000, s 58.

PUBLIC LENDING RIGHT

[21.16] In the last edition of this book the authors opined that the legality of the decision to exempt public lending establishments is in doubt.[56]

The decision to exempt educational establishments and public libraries from the obligation to pay remuneration in respect of public lending in CRRA 2000[57] was held by the ECJ to be an incorrect interpretation and transposition of the cultural purposes exemption in Directive 92/100/EC[58].

The government moved to adjust the law by deleting the exemptions in respect of authors and performers when books are the subject of lending by public establishments. The exclusive right to authorise lending, however, is replaced by a remuneration right that is based upon figures compiled about borrowings from public libraries.[59] The scheme is administered by a public lending unit in the Library Council.[60] Authors need to register in order to receive an income from the public lending right and the scheme has been criticised as providing no right to remuneration in respect of authors who had predeceased the commencement of the scheme in Spring 2009.[61] The scheme is funded entirely from the Exchequer and first distribution of payments. Payments for Irish authors in respect of both the UK and the Dutch public lending schemes are made by the Irish Copyright Licensing Agency.[62]

[21.17] One of the most controversial aspects of Directive 92/100/EEC is the broad definition of author – it includes film directors vis-à-vis cinematographic films.[63] Performers also acquire rights but the Directive contains presumptions and methods whereby these rights will, or may, under national legislation, be assigned to film producers, publishers, record companies and the like. These presumptions reflect the comparative weakness of authors and performers vis-à-vis other industry sectors, and ss 124–126 of CRRA 2000 effect a transfer of rental rights for authors while ss 297 and 298 address performers' rights in relation to film production agreements. However, the assignment or transfer cannot displace the author's right to equitable remuneration[64] and such rights will ultimately be administered for performers and authors by collecting societies: see CRRA 2000, ss 125(2) and 298(2) for authors and performers respectively. This right, however, was not introduced until 1 July 1997. Authors who had concluded contracts to exploit their works after the date of adoption of the Directive but before the implementation deadline (ie between 19 November 1992 and before 1 July 1994) must

---

56 Second edition, para 21.14.
57 CRRA 2000, ss 58 and 226.
58 *Commission v Ireland* Case C- 175/05 [2007] ECRI-3.
59 Copyright and Related Rights (Amendment) Act 2007 (SI 597/2008).
60 www.plr.ie. Cheques began to issue in December 2009
61 Clark [2009] JIPLP 833.
62 www.icla.ie.
63 CRRA 2000, s 21(6). See generally, Kamina, *Film Copyright in the European Union* (Cambridge, 2002).
64 Directive 92/100/EEC, art 4; CRRA 2000, s 125.

have asserted their rental right before 1 January 1997 or the right could not be available.[65]

[21.18] Chapter II of Directive 92/100/EEC, which is a harmonisation measure that aims to create equivalent rights in respect of performers, sound recordings, films and broadcasts, has less of an impact on Irish law because CA 1963 broadly implemented the provisions of the 1961 Rome Convention. However, the granting of neighbouring rights to performers is extremely significant.[66] In fact CRRA 2000 goes further in some respects such as through the introduction of moral rights to performers.

The Directive on Satellite Broadcasting and Cable Retransmission

[21.19] The Directive on Satellite Broadcasting and Cable Retransmission,[67] agreed on 27 September 1993, addresses several of the copyright issues that the earlier Television without Frontiers Directive[68] failed to resolve. Although a primary objective of that Directive was the distribution and promotion of European television programmes, Directive 89/552/EEC did not address differences in national copyright laws, nor did it address the question of which law or laws governed issues of copyright clearance. The 1993 Satellite and Cable Directive regulates the communication to the public by satellite broadcasts and it makes it clear that the broadcasting right conferred under Directive 92/100/EEC, considered above, is to be within the concept of a broadcast, whether the satellite broadcast is a direct broadcast satellite (DBS) or point-to-point satellite communication.[69] Directive 93/83/EEC provides a choice of origin rule whereby the law of the country where the broadcaster introduces the programme carrying signals intended for reception by the public in an uninterrupted chain is to apply vis-à-vis the clearance of authors' rights that are exploited in the broadcast.

[21.20] Chapter II of Directive 93/83/EEC gives the author the exclusive right to authorise communication to the public by satellite of copyright works and because art 2 requires all Member States to give authors such a broadcasting right, if the act of communication occurs in a Member State, copyrights and copyright clearances will be uniform.[70] However, if the act of communication to the public takes place in a third country that does not give these Chapter II rights, evasion is avoided by rules which direct that either the Community State where the uplink station is located or, failing that, the Member State where the broadcasting organisation has its principal establishment, should be deemed to be the place where communication to the public occurs. Article 4 of Directive 93/83/EEC gives the right of communication to the public by satellite to performers, phonogram producers and broadcast organisations.

---

65 Directive 92/100/EEC, art 13; CRRA 2000, Sch 1, Pt V.
66 CRRA 2000, ss 309–319.
67 Council Directive 93/83/EEC ([1993] OJ L248/15).
68 Council Directive 89/552/EEC ([1989] OJ L298/23).
69 See Dietz (1989) 20 IIC 135; Kern [1993] EIPR 276.
70 Compulsory licensing is not possible and Directive 93/83/EEC, art 3 envisages collective licensing of rights under contract.

[21.21] Ireland failed, along with a number of other Member States, to meet the transposition deadline.[71] The broadcast provisions in Directive 93/83/EEC have been implemented in CRRA 2000, specifically in ss 2, 6, 17 and 203, but there are a number of specific broadcast provisions that the Directive does not mandate, such as the fair dealing and other defences found in respect of authors and performers.

[21.22] The other major area of concern relates to cable retransmission by cable operators of television and radio broadcasts originally from another Member State. In cases of simultaneous retransmission of that signal, Directive 93/83/EEC applies but if there is any retransmission delay, or the cable operator produces independently a cable service of programmes, the Directive does not apply. Directive 93/83/EEC requires that authors, performers, phonogram producers and film producers should have their copyrights respected but these rights are to be exercised through collecting societies who may act even on behalf of right holders who refuse to transfer such rights to a collecting society.[72] Broadcast organisations, however, are free to refuse to allow their broadcast signal to be retransmitted.[73]

[21.23] This area of cable retransmission or inclusion of a work in a cable service[74] is a controversial one in Ireland and it is clear that belated implementation of Directive 93/83/EEC had serious economic consequences for right holders for many cable operators in the south and south west did not comply with licensing schemes then in operation in Ireland.[75]

The Directive on Copyright Duration

[21.24] The Directive on Copyright Duration,[76] agreed on 27 October 1993 and now replaced by Directive 2006/116/EC,[77] broadly extends the duration of copyright for Part II[78] works to 70 years pma and confirms the duration of Part III[79] works to 50 years while it changes certain of the 'triggering' conditions. It was transposed into Irish law by SI 158/1995,[80] with effect from 1 July 1995, the due date for transposition, thus ensuring that Ireland was not the subject of default procedures brought by the European

---

[71] It should have been implemented before 1 January 1995. Article 169 letters have been sent to defaulting States – see OJ L 303/34. See *Commission v Ireland* Case C-212/98 [1999] ECR I-8571.

[72] Directive 93/83/EEC, art 9: CRRA 2000, s 174.

[73] Directive 93/83/EEC, art 10. But see CRRA 2000, s 103.

[74] CRRA 2000, s 2(1) (cable programme service).

[75] See the discussion in the IMRO/Cable Broadcast Decision No 384 by the Competition Authority.

[76] Council Directive 93/98/EEC.

[77] See Ch 10.

[78] CA 1963, Pt II.

[79] CA 1963, Pt III.

[80] See Ch 10.

Commission. SI 158/1995 was replaced by primary legislation contained in Pt II, Ch 3 of CRRA 2000.

The Database Directive

[21.25] The Database Directive,[81] eventually agreed on 11 March 1996, provides significant additional protection for compilations of works through copyright and a separate right to prevent extraction and/or reutilisation of the contents of a database.[82] CRRA 2000 removes the protection of compilations from the 'literary work' concept and places protection within the framework of the original database.[83] The *sui generis* protection provisions, defined as the database right, are found in CRRA 2000 and it is classified as a neighbouring or related right.[84]

Other European Commission initiatives and CRRA 2000

[21.26] As we shall see, there are two more recent Directives that await transposition into Irish law while a third Directive, which has been largely anticipated by CRRA 2000, has been the subject of secondary legislation in 2004. The long title to CRRA 2000 acknowledges that the primary purpose of CRRA 2000 is to give (belated) effect to the EU Directives, and to give effect to related matters. However, while the formal legislative programme of the European Commission has been largely achieved, other proposals or initiatives flagged in the January 1991 follow-up document[85] did not proceed into legislative form, whether draft or otherwise. Studies that were to prepare the ground for an evaluation of the need for further reforms addressed the areas of moral rights, reprography[86] the resale right (or *droit de suite*) and collective management of rights. In relation to those studies, the Commission held a number of follow-up public hearings, the most important of which, on moral rights, concluded that there was no consensus in Europe for further action. The resale right debate has also raged across the Community, with the UK and Ireland being resistant to the introduction of such a right but a proposed Directive emerged in 1996.[87] This proposed Directive was the subject of considerable debate and in somewhat diluted form the Directive was adopted in 2001.[88]

---

[81] Council Directive 96/9/EC ([1996] OJ L77/20). Late transposition was the subject of action and an adverse ECJ ruling: see *Commission v Ireland* [2001] ECDR 119.
[82] See Ch 14.
[83] CRRA 2000, ss 2(1) and 17(2)(d).
[84] CRRA 2000, Pt V.
[85] Com (90) 584 Final.
[86] Ie photocopying.
[87] Com (96) Final.
[88] Council Directive 2001/84/EC ([2001] OJ L272/32).

INTERNATIONAL STIMULI FOR CHANGES IN IRISH LAW AND CRRA 2000

[21.27] Apart from EU initiatives towards harmonisation of copyright there are a number of international treaties that provide the Irish legislature with additional reasons for making significant changes in copyright law. While Ireland is a member of the Berne Union, Irish law did not give effect to the most recent version of the Berne Convention, that is, the Paris Act 1971. EEA Treaty obligations required ratification of the Paris Act before 1 January 1994. In January 2000 the European Commission brought proceedings[89] against Ireland under art 226 of the EEC Treaty for failure to adhere to the Paris Act, as required by the EEA Agreement[90] and art 228(7) of the EEC Treaty.[91] The ECJ, rejecting an argument that there was no jurisdiction to rule on non-implementation of the Berne Convention because this was an international text as distinct from a Community harmonisation text, declared that Ireland was in breach of the EEA Agreement. In the face of a threat of daily fines, Ireland lodged ratification documents with WIPO on 2 December 2004, four days before fines were to be imposed. The entire climate for international treaty revisions and developments has been transformed by the adherence of the US, China and many of the former Eastern Block States to the Berne Union – the US joined in 1989 – and the successful conclusion of the GATT/TRIPS Agreement[92] has added a further element of broad agreement on the shape of copyright within the international community of States. While the copyright provisions of the GATT/TRIPS Agreement do not require any legislative changes for Ireland[93] (the obligation to ratify the Paris Act[94] excludes the moral rights provisions in art 6*bis* of the Berne Convention), the expansion of neighbouring rights for broadcasting organisations, performers and phonogram producers hold out the prospect for greater concerted action against copyright pirates. The GATT/TRIPS Agreement is being used by the US, along with threats of ending most favoured treatment, against States which are perceived to condone wholesale piracy, the most visible instances being the dispute between the US and China in relation to pirated software and sound recordings. The EU has also used the threat of trade sanctions to force Thailand to address what the EU see as Thai indifference to wholesale piracy of sound recordings, and proceedings before the WTO under Part V of TRIPS have been commenced by the EU in relation to Japanese reluctance to meet obligations in relation to sound recordings for EU citizens.[95]

---

89 *Commission v Ireland* Case C-13/00 [2002] ECDR 320.

90 EEA Agreement, Protocol 28, art 5.

91 Now art 218 of TFEU.

92 Agreement of Trade-Related Aspects of Intellectual Property Rights Including Trade in Counterfeit Goods (15 December 1993).

93 Ireland ratified the WTO Agreement, including TRIPS on 15 November 1994; *Allen & Hanburys Ltd v Controller* [1997] 1 ILRM 416.

94 Berne Convention, arts 1–21 and the Appendix – see the GATT/TRIPS Agreement, art 9. On the TRIPS generally, see Worthy [1994] EIPR 195.

95 See 'EC wants Japan to pay for Old Hits' (1996) The Times, 24 February.

However, the most significant international events took place at a diplomatic conference in Geneva in December 1996.

The Berne Convention and the 1996 Geneva Treaties

[21.28] Work commenced in 1989 on preparing a Protocol to the Berne Convention in order to clarify existing international copyright norms, as found in the Paris Act 1971, and also to consider whether new international norms were needed. WIPO had then proposed establishing a Committee of Experts to examine the issue of revision but by 1992 it had been resolved[96] to establish two such Committees, one being charged[97] with examining the possible Protocol to the Berne Convention (hereafter 'the Protocol') and the second Committee addressing[98] the provisions of a possible New Instrument, or separate treaty (hereafter 'the New Instrument') on the protection of the rights of performers and the producers of phonograms. The work of these Committees was based upon preparatory documents provided by the International Bureau of WIPO. Acting upon a recommendation made to the Committees of Experts, a diplomatic conference was convened, in Geneva, between 2 December 1996 and 20 December 1996. Work on the texts of the Conference was entrusted to the chairman of the Committee of Experts and those texts were circulated to the States involved in the proposed conference by the WIPO International Bureau, who then in turn produced the draft final clauses of the treaty or treaties. In fact, three treaties were before the December 1996 conference: the two documents mentioned above, ie the Protocol[99] and the New Instrument[100] were joined by a draft treaty on databases.[101] When the conference closed and the smoke cleared, two treaties had been agreed in the form of the Protocol and the New Instrument. However, agreement could not be reached on the third treaty nor on the central issue posed in the New Instrument, namely, whether the performers' rights provisions should extend beyond performances in relation to sound recordings and embrace audio-visual performances also.

[21.29] Despite the fact that the issues of broadening performers' rights and the expansion of database protection have been under active consideration in WIPO, no formal instruments have been adopted by WIPO Member States. Other initiatives and issues, post the two adopted Geneva treaties, have in fact taken on a significant profile, the most important of which is the issue of the protection of broadcasts, an extremely important subject in the light of convergence of delivery technologies. WIPO has been examining this matter since 1998 with a view to providing protection for broadcast signals. This involves a delicate balancing exercise with the majority of proposals seeking to afford exclusive rights to broadcasters as long as these rights do not prejudice competing interests such as the rights of content providers and performers, for example.

---

96 By the Assembly and the Conference of Representatives of the Berne Union.
97 Seven sessions were held between 1991 and May 1996.
98 Six sessions were held between 1993 and May 1996.
99 WIPO document CRNR/DC/4 (30 August 1996).
100 WIPO document CRNR/DC/5 (30 August 1996).
101 WIPO document CRNR/DC/6 (30 August 1996).

A consolidated text has been prepared by WIPO, with a view to the adoption of a proposed Treaty[102] but this subject has been stalled at WIPO for several years – see www.wipo.org for developments.

[21.30] To return to the 1996 Treaties, the first Treaty or Protocol to the Berne Convention (the WIPO Copyright Treaty 1996)[103] is a special agreement within art 20 of Berne Convention and it is to have no connection with any Convention[104] other than the Berne Convention, and is not to derogate from any of the provisions of Berne itself.[105]

[21.31] Some of the provisions of the Copyright Treaty repeat provisions found in the TRIPS Agreement:[106] for example, the provisions declaring that copyright protection extends to expressions and not ideas, procedures, methods of operation or mathematical concepts as such.[107] The WIPO Copyright Treaty 1996, art 4 makes provision for the protection of computer programs as literary works, as defined in art 2 of the Berne Convention 'whatever may be the mode or form of expression' and art 5 of the WIPO Copyright Treaty 1996 provides protection to compilations of data or other material in any form if their selection and form constitutes intellectual creations. This software and database protection mirrors art 10 of TRIPS but the Protocol provisions are wider in certain respects.[108]

[21.32] Article 6(1) of the WIPO Copyright Treaty 1996 provides that authors shall enjoy an exclusive right of authorising the making available of the original and copies of their works through sale or other transfer of ownership. This provision thus adds a distribution right to authors, the international treaties previously not recognising this right. The controversial issue of exhaustion of rights is addressed in art 6(2), which retains the existing position whereby this is a matter of national competence. The proposed options in the preliminary draft treaty, in art 8 of the draft, have been dropped, as has the reference to an importation right in one of the proposed drafts.

[21.33] Article 7 of the WIPO Copyright Treaty 1996, addresses the question of rental rights and this issue, while often regarded as an aspect of distribution rights in some countries, is dealt with along the lines set out in art 11 of TRIPS; the Berne Convention does not address the issue at all. The authors of computer programs, cinematographic works and works embodied in phonograms are to enjoy an exclusive right of authorising commercial rental to the public of the originals or copies of their works.[109] Efforts to broaden the rental right to cover all works (with some opt-out provisions) foundered due

---

102 Consolidated Text for a Treaty on the Protection of Broadcasting Organisations SC RR/11/3.

103 WIPO document CRNR/DC/89 (20 December 1996).

104 WIPO Copyright Treaty 1996, art 1(1).

105 WIPO Copyright Treaty 1996, art 1(2), ie the Paris Act, art 1(3). See, however WIPO Copyright Treaty 1996, art 10.

106 Eg WIPO Copyright Treaty 1996, art 10 on limitations and exceptions mirrors TRIPS, art 13.

107 WIPO Copyright Treaty 1996, art 2; CRRA 2000, s 17(3).

108 TRIPS mentions programs in source or object code only: see, however, the Draft Agreed Statement Convening Treaty No 1.

109 The Rental and Lending Directive, 92/100/EEC, goes much further of course; CRRA 2000, s 40.

to strong resistance from the US and some other States. The inclusion of phonograms is, however, a positive move but national competence is reserved for determining what works are to come within this category. The exclusive right is not to apply where the computer program is not the essential object of the rental (eg hardware is rented also) and the right in relation to films is limited by the so-called impairment test found in the TRIPS Agreement.[110] Opt-out provisions[111] for countries that had and continue to have equitable remuneration for authors of phonograms that have been rented out may continue to operate under this system.[112]

[21.34] Article 8 of the WIPO Copyright Treaty 1996, is an important provision for authors in so far as the authors of works may find that works may be communicated to the public by wire or wireless means. The distribution of works in electronic form such as the digital diffusion of a work – digital distribution of musical works by cable or to a personal computer via telecommunications link or by satellite, online distribution of literary works, video on demand, to name just three examples – do not, arguably, come within existing reproduction or broadcasting rights. Article 8, therefore, in giving the author an exclusive right of this kind gives to authors protection against many kinds of commercial exploitation of a work, particularly on-demand distribution systems in which a tangible copy of the work is not transferred. This right does not prejudice provisions in the Berne Convention that also deal with 'communication to the public'.[113] However, failure to agree at the conference on a definition of the reproduction right so as to cover digital works is regrettable; although the conference apparently had no difficulty with regarding a digital representation of a work as being a reproduction, agreement could not be reached on temporary or ephemeral reproductions and exceptions to the reproduction right, so the article[114] was not carried over into the WIPO Copyright Treaty 1996, but art 10 of the Treaty allows Member States to address issues of this kind, consistent with the Berne Convention itself.[115] CRRA 2000 does so in the making-available right in s 40.

[21.35] Articles 11 and 12 of the WIPO Copyright Treaty 1996 address two important matters, namely, the issues of technological methods of exercising the author's exclusive right and technological methods of rights management. States are obliged to provide adequate and effective legal remedies against persons who attempt to render such initiatives ineffective or less effective (eg remove electronic 'tags' from a work). Part VII of CRRA 2000, as amended by the European Communities (Copyright and Related Rights) Regulations 2004 (SI 16/2004), gives effect to these provisions as well as the requirements of the Information Society Directive.[116]

---

[110] The right only applies if 'such commercial rental had led to widespread copying of such works materially impairing the exclusive rights of reproduction'. This does not feature in CRRA 2000.

[111] WIPO Copyright Treaty 1996, art 7(3).

[112] Crucial date is 15 April 1994, the date the GATT/TRIPS Agreement came into force.

[113] Berne Convention, arts 11(1)(ii), 11*bis* (1)(i) and (ii), 11*ter* (1)(ii), 14(1)(ii) and 14*bis* (1).

[114] Article 7 of the draft in document CRNR/DC/4.

[115] See the Draft Agreed Statements Conveying Treaty No 1 on Article 10 and the Resolution on the Reproduction Right.

[116] Council Directive 2001/29/EC.

[21.36] The second treaty, the WIPO Performances and Phonograms Treaty 1996,[117] provides the international community with an opportunity to expand the rights of performers and record companies in accordance with both the Rome Convention[118] and GATT/TRIPS. The second treaty is not to allow contracting parties to the Rome Convention to derogate from any of the obligations set out in that Convention.[119] The definitions found in art 2 are extremely significant. The definition of a performer goes further than that found in the Rome Convention by including performers of expressions of folklore, and the definition of phonogram makes it clear that digital representations of a work are to be included in the term 'phonogram': doubts had been expressed about whether traditional definitions of a 'record' were broad enough to deal with digital technology.[120] The definition of 'fixation' also covers digital representations of sound and the definition of 'broadcasting' similarly is recast to cover the broadcasting of digital works. Satellite transmissions are also included in the definition of broadcast, as are encrypted signals where the public have been given the means of decrypting the signal by the broadcasting organisation, or with its consent.[121] The definition of 'communication to the public' is also of crucial importance for it makes it clear that cable transmissions, which are outside the notion of a broadcast (eg works made available via the internet), are also to be regulated under this Treaty. In relation to the beneficiaries of the Treaty, the Rome Convention is used whereby coverage to nationals of other contracting parties is to be available to performers and phonogram producers on the basis of a national treatment rule,[122] although reservations are possible in relation to the art 15 right[123] to equitable remuneration for use made in connection with broadcasts or communication to the public.

[21.37] Article 5 of the WIPO Performances and Phonograms Treaty 1996 makes provision for moral rights in relation to performers in respect of live aural performances, by which is meant performers who speak or sing a work or expression of folklore. Audio-visual performers are not covered by this provision, which is modelled on Berne Convention, art 6*bis*. Therefore, performers are to enjoy rights of paternity and integrity in accordance with the legislation of the contracting party where the protection is claimed.[124]

---

[117] WIPO Document CRNR/DC/90 (20 December 1996) (hereafter the WIPO Performances and Phonograms Treaty 1996).

[118] International Convention for the Protection of Performers, Producers of Phonograms and Broadcasting Organisation (Rome, 26 October 1961) (Rome Convention).

[119] WIPO Performances and Phonograms Treaty 1996, art 1(1).

[120] See our outdated definition in CA 1963, s 2(1), replaced in CRRA 2000 by 'fixation'.

[121] WIPO Performances and Phonograms Treaty 1996, art 2; CRRA 2000, s 205(2).

[122] WIPO Performances and Phonograms Treaty 1996, arts 3 and 4.

[123] WIPO Performances and Phonograms Treaty 1996, art 15.

[124] WIPO Performances and Phonograms Treaty 1996, art 5. Article 22(2) permits States to limit the moral rights provision to performances that occurred after entry into force of the Treaty. Performers' moral rights in CRRA 2000 are not limited to aural performers and these rights apply to 'new' performances (ie after 1 January 2001): CRRA 2000, Pt IV.

[21.38] Articles 6, 7 and 8 of the WIPO Performances and Phonograms Treaty 1996 give performers exclusive economic rights in relation to authorising the broadcasting, communication to the public and fixation of their unfixed performances,[125] the authorisation of reproductions of performances fixed in phonograms[126] and authorisations of distributions of an original or copies of fixed performances on phonogram through sale to the public or other transfer of ownership.[127] These performers' exclusive rights go much further than either the Rome Convention or the TRIPS provision, which only gave performers 'the possibility of preventing' such acts when they were undertaken without the authorisation of the performer. Article 9 also gives performers an exclusive right to authorise commercial rental to the public of performances fixed in phonograms, subject to national law of contracting parties and the possibility of displacement by prior[128] national regimes giving equitable remuneration.

[21.39] Article 10 of the WIPO Performances and Phonograms Treaty 1996 addresses the issue of distribution of fixed performances by way of satellite or digital diffusion to members of the public who may access these performances from a time or place individually chosen by them. Digital diffusion services of this kind are now subject to the performer's exclusive right to authorise the making available of such works, and the right thus given by art 10 of this Treaty mirrors art 8 of the World Intellectual Property Organisation Copyright Treaty (WCT), which was given to the authors of works made available by way of 'on demand' services of this kind.

[21.40] These provisions on performers' rights are far-reaching but it is significant that the definition of performer and phonogram were drawn up so as to exclude performances by way of audio-visual fixations, largely because of opposition by the film industry based in certain countries. Phonogram producers, on the other hand, found that exclusive rights to authorise reproduction of a recording 'in any manner or form',[129] rights of authorisation of sales of the original or copies of a recording,[130] commercial rental[131] and authorising wire or wireless accessing by the public of recordings, including on demand services,[132] were obtained during the conference with only a few amendments being made to these provisions, which are much more extensive than either the Rome or TRIPS provisions in relation to sound recording rights. Article 15 of the WIPO Performances and Phonograms Treaty 1996 in essence repeats[133] the performers and phonogram producers' right to single equitable remuneration if a phonogram which has been published commercially is broadcast or communicated to the public. This is

---

[125] WIPO Performances and Phonograms Treaty 1996, art 6; CRRA 2000, s 203(1).

[126] WIPO Performances and Phonograms Treaty 1996, art 7. The right covers direct or indirect reproduction, thus covering reproduction by a person who uses a telecommunications network. CRRA 2000, s 204(1).

[127] WIPO Performances and Phonograms Treaty 1996, art 8; CRRA 2000, s 205(1).

[128] Prior to 15 April 1994: see WIPO Performances and Phonograms Treaty 1996, art 9(2).

[129] WIPO Performances and Phonograms Treaty 1996, art 11.

[130] WIPO Copyright Treaty, art 12.

[131] WIPO Copyright Treaty, art 13.

[132] WIPO Copyright Treaty, art 14.

[133] See Rome Convention, art 12.

payable by the person who makes direct or indirect use of the phonogram. Performers' protection is to run for 50 years following the end of the year in which the performance was fixed in the phonogram[134] while the phonogram producers' right runs for 50 years following on the year of publication, absent which, 50 years from the end of the year in which fixation was made.[135] Articles 18 and 19 set out the same technological protection of rights measures and rights management information provisions as are found in the WIPO Copyright Treaty 1996 vis-à-vis authors' rights.

[21.41] Both Treaties[136] require an Assembly to be created. States are to appoint one delegate each and the Assembly is to deal with matters concerning the maintenance and development of the Treaties. Each Treaty is open for signature by any WIPO Member State and the EU until 31 December 1997 and will enter into force three months after 30 instruments of ratification or accession have been deposited with the Director General of WIPO. The Copyright Treaty entered into force on 6 March 2002, following upon the accession of Gabon to the Treaty. The Phonograms and Performances Treaty entered into force on 20 May 2002 with the accession of Honduras.

[21.42] The EU ratified the Treaties on 14 December 2009 and the Treaties became operative (ie as a contracting party) within the EU on 24 March 2010. Ireland ratified and became a contracting party on those same dates. On 10 August 2010, there were 88 contracting parties to the Copyright Treaty and 86 contracting parties to the Performers and Phonograms Treaty.[137]

[21.43] Work at producing a broadcast treaty at WIPO,[138] to update and modernise existing treaty law in the form of the Rome Convention of 1961, has been in progress since 1998 but as only a minority of WIPO Member States are signatories of the Rome Convention itself, so-called 'rights based' legislation is by no means an obvious solution to problems of 'signal theft', the unauthorised decryption of broadcasts and post fixation or downstream reutilisation of content rights being vested in the broadcast organisation. Even though the webcasting question was stripped away from the proposed treaty in 2006, significant differences remain and a diplomatic conference to agree a new treaty is some way off.[139]

Opposition to providing a new right in respect of broadcasts that would give broadcast organisations the power to proceed against the use of content after the fixation of a signal, as distinct from straightforward piracy of the signal itself, is deep rooted. Stronger broadcast copyright, particularly the extension of such a copyright in respect of webcasts over the internet is opposed by civil liberties groups, educationalists and researchers, podcasters and bloggers who argue that existing treaty provisions are

---

134 WIPO Performances and Phonograms Treaty 1996, art 17(1).

135 WIPO Performances and Phonograms Treaty 1996, art 17(2).

136 WIPO Copyright Treaty 1996; WIPO Performances and Phonograms Treaty 1996.

137 See www.wipo.org.

138 See www.wipo.org.

139 See the Informal Paper prepared by the Chairman of the SCCR on the WIPO Treaty on the Protection of Broadcasting Organisations (17th Session) SCCR/17/INF/1.

adequate. A rights-based treaty provision is also seen as anti-consumer, particularly in the context of time-shifting and private copying rights under national laws.[140]

[21.44] Other work that is currently being undertaken within WIPO includes support for a proposal for a treaty relating to exceptions and limitations for 'print-disabled' persons; the text was prepared by the World Blind Union. Further consideration is being given to making further progress on concluding a new instrument giving better protection to performers in respect of audiovisual performances. While the 1996 Performers and Phonograms Treaty only dealt with aural performers, a 2000 diplomatic conference reached agreement on all matters save for the critical issue of transfer of rights from the performer to the producer and, 14 years later, this matter remains to be resolved.

THE TRIPS REFERENCE

[21.45] Perhaps one further measure, albeit coercive, needs to be mentioned in order to understand the origins of CRRA 2000. Concern in certain industrial sectors (particularly the software industry) about the rather toothless nature of CA 1963 was expressed to the government of the US. The enforcement provisions in the TRIPS Agreement were clearly not being complied with by Ireland at this time, and the US administration made two complaints in 1997[141] and 1998 to the WTO dispute dettlement body. The US, in particular, indicated displeasure with the criminal and civil reliefs available to the right holder and the evidentiary difficulties that a right holder had to overcome in the Irish courts. Negotiations between the US, Ireland, and the European Communities led to a settlement of these disputes, the US being satisfied with the passing of two Acts, the Intellectual Property (Miscellaneous Provisions) Act 1998, and CRRA 2000. The parties reached agreement on 6 November 2000 and the two complaints were withdrawn.

[21.46] The Intellectual Property (Miscellaneous Provisions) Act 1998 was an interim measure that directly addressed the most pressing enforcement issues. The first of these matters was the effectiveness of presumptions concerning the subsistence of copyright and the ownership of copyright. Section 26 of CA 1963 gave the putative right holder the benefit of presumptions unless the defendant put these matters 'in issue', at which stage the presumptions lost any real value. This weakness was exacerbated, from the perspective of right holders, by the decision of the Supreme Court in *Phonographic Performance (Ireland) Ltd v Cody*.[142] The Supreme Court held that evidence of title could not be made out solely on the basis of affidavits sworn by right holders. The approach adopted to these two points by the drafters of the 1998 legislation was to make the relevant presumptions effective 'unless the contrary is proved'. These presumptions were to be operative in civil cases only, although it should be noted that these presumptions, which have been re-enacted in CRRA 2000,[143] are applicable in both civil

---

[140] See SCCR 19th Session Report (20 April, 2010).
[141] WT/DS82/ 1, 14 May 1997.
[142] *Phonographic Performance (Ireland) Ltd v Cody* [1998] 4 IR 504, [1998] 2 ILRM 21.
[143] CRRA 2000, ss 139 (copyright), 211 (performers), 339 (database right).

and criminal proceedings for infringement of copyright.[144] The 1998 Act also amended s 27 of CA 1963, thereby making it possible for proceedings to be brought on indictment as well as by way of summary prosecution. Penalties were also significantly enhanced by the 1998 legislation. Again, CRRA 2000 has supplanted these provisions.

THE POST-2000 DIRECTIVES

[21.47] Three Directives have been agreed since the 2000 copyright legislation, CRRA 2000, was passed by the Oireachtas. One of these, the Resale Right Directive of 2001,[145] is examined separately in Ch 19 of this book. We will briefly address the state of play in respect of the other two Directives.

[21.48] The Information Society Directive of 22 May 2001[146] represents a significant advance in the European Commission's harmonisation agenda. While in some respects the Directive represents an updating of the Community *acquis* in the light of the 1996 Geneva Treaties,[147] the Directive goes much further in effecting a harmonisation of the reproduction right, the communication to the public right, and the distribution right. These provisions in the Directive are addressed by ss 37–42 of CRRA 2000. Article 5 of Directive 2001/29/EC, however, sets out a 'closed' list of exceptions and limitations to these rights with, in many cases, the right holder having rights to fair compensation upon the exercise of these rights. The Directive was transposed into Irish law, on a horizontal and literal basis, by SI 360/2006. With the exception of the provision on publicising judicial decisions finding that an infringement has taken place – see reg 5 – little is achieved by the Directive.

In *Duhan v Radius Television Production Ltd*,[148] Herbert J indicated that the court would continue to use the provisions of the Rules of the Superior Courts in relation to discovery when it appeared that SI 360/2006 was possibly late and defectively transposed on the basis that 'the discovery procedure provided by the terms of Ord 31, r 12 of the Rules of the Superior Courts is manifestly more favourable to right holders as more extensive in the scope of its application'. This 'closed' list of exceptions means that Member States were required to delete exceptions and limitations that fell outside the list. Articles 6 and 7 of Directive 2001/29/EC also required Member States to provide for the protection of technological measures and rights management information, affording to the right holder the possibility that technology could be used to 'lock-out' certain uses of a work, even by lawful acquirers or users of the work.

[21.49] Transposition of Directive 2001/29/EC took place mostly by way of CRRA 2000, notwithstanding the fact that the Directive was only finally agreed many months after the passing of CRRA 2000. The drafters of CRRA 2000 were of the view that all that was required, post Information Society Directive, was a minor change to certain

---

[144] CRRA 2000, s 139(1).
[145] Council Directive 2001/84/EC.
[146] Council Directive 2001/29/EC.
[147] WIPO Copyright Treaty 1996; WIPO Performances and Phonograms Treaty 1996.
[148] *Duhan v Radius Television Production Ltd* [2007] IEHC 292.

technical definitions found in CRRA 2000[149] and this was achieved by way of SI 16/ 2004. Perhaps the most significant provision in the statutory instrument is the view of the drafters that art 6.4 of Directive 2001/29/EC required Member States to strengthen national laws to prevent technological measures to override permitted acts, the person benefiting from the exception being able to apply to the High Court to require compliance. While this provision is limited – it does not apply to online access on contractual terms that effect a lock-out – it remains to be seen whether this view of the Directive will prevail in the light of Commission scrutiny under Directive 2001/29/EC, art 12.

[21.50] The other Directive, adopted by the Council of Ministers in 2004, is the Enforcement of Intellectual Property Rights Directive.[150] Consideration of this text is outside the scope of a chapter directed at copyright developments because the Directive addresses the entire field of intellectual property rights, but it had proved controversial, not least because general respect commentators have argued that the case has not been made out for civil law remedial measures to be devoted to intellectual property rights, as well as conflict with the principle of subsidiarity.[151] The Enforcement Directive was transposed by SI 360/2006. However, in the copyright arena many of the provisions in the Directive are already a feature of CRRA 2000 – indeed Irish law goes much further in several respects – and even controversial provisions such as the art 9 right to information provision represent a 'statutory' articulation of *Norwich Pharmacal* type reliefs,[152] already available under Irish civil procedure.[153]

[21.51] On 7 October 2010, the secret negotiations on the Anti Counterfeiting Treaty Agreement concluded. The text reflects USA domestic law and a desire to adopt criminal reliefs and statutory damages. While the Treaty provisions have been diluted somewhat, it is a text that appears to reflect the policital fate of the Obama Administration rather than a balanced world view on copyright law.

---

[149] Changes to CRRA 2000, ss 2(1), 50, 87, 244 and 374.

[150] Directive 2004/48/EC ([2004] OJ L195/16).

[151] See Cornish et al [2003] EIPR 447.

[152] *Norwich Pharmacal Co v Customs and Excise Comrs* [1974] AC 133.

[153] Eg *Re MK, SK and WK* [1999] 2 ILRM 321; *Lough Neagh Exploration Ltd v Morrice* [1999] 4 IR 515.

Chapter 22

Semiconductor Chip Protection

INTRODUCTION

[22.01] Semiconductor chips are products that perform electronic or related functions. Semiconductors are elements or compounds that in part allow (or prevent) electricity being conducted and they stand between conductors (eg metals) and insulators (eg rubber). Common semiconductors include silicon and gallium arsenide. Those products are made by a photographic process that builds a pattern of circuits upon layers or wafers of semiconducting material. This process allows the design or mask work – normally a glass disc with the circuit pattern engaged upon it – to be produced as a composite product. More recent technology dispenses with the use of physical masks and relies upon an etching process whereby light or laser technology can etch a mask onto each layer of the chip. It is the physical mask and the information that goes into creating the circuit by means of digital plots that represent the intellectual property which is the subject matter of protection.[1] The technology allows the development of integrated circuits that can perform a number of logical or analogue functions, which increase the processing power of computers, reduce production costs and save both space and energy. Apart from obvious applications in the computer games industry, many semiconductors are now embedded into a number of consumer goods, from fuel efficiency elements in motor vehicles to microwave ovens and personal computers. Chips are valuable in themselves, as can be seen from the growth of computer chip thefts from offices and other commercial premises, and worthy of protection. The investment needed to produce semiconductor products is substantial, but reverse engineering techniques allow a pirate to replicate a legitimate product at a fraction of the cost of developing that product. Notwithstanding this, protection for semiconductor chips is rarely relied upon or enforced.[2]

[22.02] In describing the problems of providing protection, Hart drew a parallel between this technology and the earlier problem of protecting the layout of a printed circuit board.[3] Design protection by means of the law of copyright could be available under artistic copyright, but Hart drew attention[4] to the danger that a three-

---

[1] Hart [1985] EIPR 258; Hart (1986) 2 YLCT 93; Laddie, Prescott and Vitoria, *The Modern Law of Copyright and Designs* (3rd edn, 2000), ch 58.

[2] For an analysis of the possible reasons, see Karnell, 'Protection of layout designs (topographies) of integrated circuits: RIP?' (2001) IIC 32(6), 648–658.

[3] Hart [1985] EIPR 258 at 260.

[4] This was prescient: see the reasoning of the majority of the High Court of Australia in *Computer Edge Pty v Apple Computer* (1986) 60 ALJR 313.

dimensional replication of the two-dimensional design may fail to pass the non-expert test[5] whereby a non-expert would be able to see a link between works – the masks or digital plots – and the infringing chip. So, even if artistic copyright could be available under Berne Convention principles,[6] there were problems of proof that were not easily overcome. In any event, this was a theoretical problem, as no Irish cases arose on the point, and it disappeared altogether when s 2 of the Copyright (Amendment) Act 1987 removed artistic copyright from purely functional designs that had been used to manufacture more than 50 copies of the product. Given that the protection available for registered design protection under the Industrial and Commercial Property (Protection) Act 1927 required the design to satisfy an eye appeal test, purely functional or hidden design features of the kind that the semiconductor mask work epitomises were unlikely to be protected via either copyright or design law. The repeal of the Copyright (Amendment) Act 1987 by the Copyright and Related Rights Act 2000 (CRRA 2000) did not affect this position because s 79(2) of CRRA 2000 re-enacted the non-expert test. However, it should be noted that the Industrial Designs Act 2001 (IDA 2001) repealed s 79(2) of CRRA 2000, leaving it possible, under s 78A of CRRA 2000, for the design drawing or prototype to be protected via artistic copyright as a design document or model. It is unlikely that most semiconductor chips would be patentable, as they are usually modifications of the prior art, and thus it can be difficult to show an inventive step. In addition, the length of time required for patent searches and prior art comparisons usually negates the benefit of seeking patent protection for semiconductor chips, which have a very short lifespan and quickly become obsolete.[7] Whether the design itself will be protected under design law is uncertain because certain requirements of IDA 2001 will be difficult to satisfy, eg the requirement that a part of a complex product should be visible in use under s 14 of IDA 2001. A further possibility is that protection under the Community unregistered design right may be available because, while it was initially intended to exclude chip protection, the final legislative instruments on Community design law appear permissive on this question.

INTERNATIONAL DEVELOPMENTS

[22.03] In the international arena the World Intellectual Property Organisation (WIPO) produced a treaty on integrated circuits and layout designs, the Treaty on Intellectual Property in respect of Integrated Circuits (the IPIC Treaty or Washington Treaty)[8] in

---

5   In Ireland, see the Copyright Act 1963 (CA 1963), s 14(7).

6   Berne Convention for the Protection of Literary and Artistic Works, art 2(1) – 'illustrations, maps, plans, sketches and three dimensional works relative to geography, topography, architecture or science'.

7   See Irish H-Yu Chiu and Will W Shen, 'A sui generis intellectual property right for layout designs on printed circuit boards? An analysis of current intellectual property laws and proposal for reform', (2006) EIPR 28(1), 38–50.

8   Washington, 26 May 1989.

1989 but no EU Member States have to date signed this Treaty and the two major semiconductor producing States outside the EU actually opposed the adoption of the Washington Treaty, so the prospects of this Treaty obtaining international acceptance are slender indeed.[9] The reasons for this can be gleaned from the fact that some national legislation and Directive 87/54/EEC on the legal protection of topographies of semiconductor products[10] had already introduced *sui generis* measures of protection that differed quite radically from the Washington Treaty. The Washington Treaty departed significantly from pre-existing national legislation in relation to definitions of protected works, the period of protection, the nature of the infringing acts and the possibility of compulsory non-exclusive licences. As of 1 July 2010, the Washington Treaty has not yet entered into force.

The US Semiconductor Chip Protection Act 1984

[22.04] Rather than wait for developments at the level of an international treaty in the form of a WIPO Treaty or via the Berne Convention, the US created an entirely new international context by passing legislation which protected 'mask works', namely 'images ... having or representing the pre-determined three-dimensional pattern of metallic, insulating or semiconductor material ... of a semiconductor chip product'.[11] If the work is original, first exploited in the US, or elsewhere by a US national or domiciled person, that person acquires an exclusive right to reproduce, import or distribute the mask work or products containing the work. The right lasts for 10 years from the registration of the work or its first commercial exploitation, whichever is the earlier. In the light of US anti-trust and fair use laws, the US Semiconductor Chip Protection Act 1984 has generous reverse engineering provisions which all competitors may use to produce compatible (and thus competing) products or improved products. Substantial investment and originality must be shown if the competitor is to justify the use of the pre-existing mask work design for independent creation not mere plagiarism, which is the reasoning behind the legitimisation of reverse engineering in this context.

[22.05] The real significance of the US legislation is found in the area of geographical scope. Because semiconductor products were not within the Berne system and because international industrial design law was still in its infancy, no problem of national treatment arose for non-US citizens or non-US domiciles. Thus, foreign (eg EU) rights holders could not come within US protection rules in this most vital of markets, unless their countries had entered into treaty agreements with the US government under which those countries granted US citizens with equivalent protection in national law on the basis of reciprocity. By setting this agenda, the US hoped to be able quickly to force the pace in creating a new world regime on

---

9   Many of these Treaty provisions, not least the provisions in IPIC Treaty, art 2–7 (excluding art 6(3), the compulsory licensing provision) are acceptable, for TRIPS, arts 35–38 obliges the World Trade Organisation (WTO) States to implement some of the IPIC Treaty provisions.

10   Council Directive 87/54/EEC ([1987] OJ L24/36).

11   US Semiconductor Chip Protection Act 1984, Title 17, ch 9, p 901.

a bilateral treaty basis.[12] This objective has broadly been realised, as the result of the reluctance of the EU[13] to allow a trade war or protectionism to disfigure international trade in computer chip and chip enhanced products.

Council Directive 87/54/EEC

[22.06] Council Directive 87/54/EEC of 16 December 1986 on the Legal Protection of Topographies of Semiconductor Products[14] was processed very quickly by the EU institutions as a matter of urgency.[15] This Directive required all Member States to adopt legislative provisions conferring exclusive rights in respect of semiconductor product topographies. Ireland adopted legislation enacting this in the form of the European Communities (Protection of Topographies of Semiconductor Products) Regulations 1988,[16] Regulations which came into effect on 13 May 1988[17] in Ireland. These Regulations[18] provide an exclusive right, called a topography right, in favour of the creator of a topography of a semiconductor product.[19] The Regulations do not define a semiconductor product but art 1 of the Directive defines a semiconductor product thus:

    (a)   a 'semiconductor product' shall mean the final or an intermediate form of any product:

        (i)   consisting of a body of material which includes a layer of semiconducting material; and

        (ii)   having one or more other layers composed of conducting, insulating or semiconducting material, the layers being arranged in accordance with a predetermined three-dimensional pattern; and

        (iii)   intended to perform, exclusively or together with other functions, an electronic function.

The same article goes on to define a topography as:

    a series of related images, however fixed or encoded;

    (i)   representing the three-dimensional pattern of the layers of which a semiconductor product is composed; and

    (ii)   in which series, each image has the pattern or part of the pattern of a surface of the semiconductor product at any stage of its manufacture.

---

[12] Stern (1986) 17 IIC 486; Dreier (1988) 19 IIC 427.

[13] Cohen Jehoram [1987] EIPR 35.

[14] Council Directive 87/54/EEC.

[15] The proposal was published in December 1985: [1985] OJ C360/14.

[16] SI 101/1988.

[17] The deadline set for implementation under the Directive was 7 November 1987. Only France, Germany and the Netherlands met the deadline.

[18] SI 101/1988.

[19] SI 101/1988, regs 2(1) and 3(1).

[22.07] Regulation 3 of the European Communities (Protection of Topographies of Semiconductor Products) Regulations 1988[20] defines the conditions for entitlement as depending upon the typography being able to satisfy an originality test which has since become part of the *acquis communitaire,*[21] namely that the topography must be 'the result of the creator's own intellectual effort'.[22] The Regulations reinforce this by requiring that the topography not be 'commonplace within the industry'. The term 'commonplace' implies some objective assessment and has been held in the UK to include any design that was trite, trivial, common-or-garden, hackneyed or of the type which would excite no peculiar attention in those skilled in the relevant art.[23] The Regulations go on to provide that where the topography consists of elements that are commonplace, protection under the Regulations exists 'only to extent that the combination of such elements, taken as a whole, fulfils' the non-commonplace standard. The requirement that the topography must be viewed as a whole is important, for many topographies will consist of standard cell or pre-existing configurations, and by analogy with compilations of pre-existing works in areas like compilations and computer programs produced from standard code, it is the totality of the work that may produce protection.[24] Whether computer-generated works may satisfy the originality standard is open to debate, and the answer may turn on the distinction between computer-aided and computer-generated works, which are matters of fact.[25]

[22.08] For the creator[26] of the topography who overcomes such problems, protection under the European Communities (Protection of Topographies of Semiconductor Products) Regulations 1988 will turn on whether a nationality test set by the Regulations can be satisfied. The individual creators must be, according to reg 3(3):

(a) natural persons who are nationals of a Member State or who habitually reside in the territory of a Member State, or

(b) persons having a real and effective industrial or commercial establishment in the territory of a Member State.

[22.09] Regulation 3(3)(b) of the European Communities (Protection of Topographies of Semiconductor Products) Regulations 1988 is obviously intended to confer rights

---

[20] SI 101/1988.
[21] The cumulative total body of EU law.
[22] This originality standard resurfaced later in both the Computer Program Directive (Council Directive 91/250/EEC ([1991] OJ L122/42)) and the Database Directive (Council Directive 96/9/EC ([1996] OJ L77/20)).
[23] *Ocular Sciences Ltd. & Anr. v Aspect Vision Care Ltd & Ors* [1997] RPC 289; see also *Farmers Build Ltd (In Liquidation) v Carier Bulk Materials Handling Ltd* [1999] RPC 461.
[24] Eg *A-One Accessory Imports Pty v Off-Road Imports Pty* (1996) 34 IPR 306; *Ibcos Computers v Barclays Mercantile Highland* [1994] FSR 275.
[25] Eg. see the South African case of *Payen Components South Africa Ltd v Bovic Gaskets* (1995) 33 IPR 407.
[26] The right is assignable, eg to a company, and where the creator is an employee, or it has been commissioned, the employer or commissioner owns the right.

on a person or company who takes the exclusive right by virtue of an assignment from an employee or through commissioning that topography, where the person(s) creating the topography are not EU nationals or habitually resident in the EU. Further, even if these tests of nationality or residence are not satisfied, reg 3(5) provides protection if the rights holder markets the topography via an EU national or person resident in the EU, the topography is first exploited commercially[27] in a Member State and that agent is exclusively authorised to exploit the topography throughout the EU. However, Directive 87/54/EEC makes it clear that protection is available to the persons who are within reg 3(3) of the European Communities (Protection of Topographies of Semiconductor Products) Regulations, as distinct from the EU rights holder who has authorised the EU national who is exclusively authorised to exploit commercially the work within the EU.[28] As soon as the topography is a protected work within these provisions, the protection is available to any successor in title, regardless of nationality or habitual residence.[29]

[22.10] The exclusive rights given by the European Communities (Protection of Topographies of Semiconductor Products) Regulations 1988 relate to reproduction and commercial exploitation in Ireland or importation for the purpose of commercial exploitation.[30] The same regulation sets out an exception to the reproduction right in respect of non-commercial reproductions and reproduction for analysis or evaluation or teaching purposes. A further exception is given in relation to reproduction which results in the evaluation of another topography which in turn is the intellectual creation of the person who is responsible for that resulting topography. The doctrine of exhaustion under EU law applies to such rights.[31]

[22.11] The commencement and duration of these rights are also fixed by the European Communities (Protection of Topographies of Semiconductor Products) Regulations 1988. Regulation 5 provides:

> (1) A right to protection in a topography shall commence:
>
> (a)   when the topography is first fixed or encoded, provided, however, these Regulations shall not apply to any topography created before the coming into operation of these Regulations, or
>
> (b)   in a case falling within Regulation 3(5) of these Regulations, from the date of first commercial exploitation anywhere in the world.
>
> (2) The rights subsisting in a topography by virtue of these Regulations shall come to an end 10 years from the end of the calendar year in which the topography is first commercially exploited anywhere in the world, or, where it has not been commercially

---

27   See Council Directive 87/54/EEC, art 1(c).

28   Council Directive 87/54/EEC, art 3(4).

29   Council Directive 87/54/EEC, art 3(5); European Communities (Protection of Topographies of Semiconductor Products) Regulations 1988, reg 3(6).

30   European Communities (Protection of Topographies of Semiconductor Products) Regulations 1988, reg 4.

31   European Communities (Protection of Topographies of Semiconductor Products) Regulations 1988, reg 4(4).

exploited anywhere in the world, within a period of 15 years from its first fixation or encoding.

[22.12] Infringement of rights is actionable by of the owner of the topography right but there is an innocent infringer defence,[32] which limits the innocent infringer to being liable in damages only. Further, damages are to be measured by reference to a licensing measure, namely a reasonable royalty payment.[33]

[22.13] While Directive 87/54/EEC provided that Member States could impose registration of rights and deposit of materials procedures as a precondition to protection,[34] the Irish Regulations do not make provision for this, apart from reg 7 of the European Communities (Protection of Topographies of Semiconductor Products) Regulations 1988, which provides that a semiconductor product manufactured using a protected topography may be marked with the letter T*. The topography right does not exist in relation to topographies created prior to 13 May 1988, but topographies created after that date acquire protection under the regulation from the time of fixation or encoding, or in the case of topographies that acquire protection under reg 3(5), from the date of first commercial exploitation. Protection lasts for 15 years from the date of fixation or encoding if there is no subsequent commercial exploitation of the topography anywhere in the world, but if the work is so commercially exploited, protection ends 10 years after first commercial exploitation.[35] The limited originality test in the 1988 Regulations makes any enhanced product likely to attract new and distinct rights in any event, as these rules seem quite adequate for exploitative purposes.

Reciprocity and international requisition of rights

[22.14] The US position under the Semiconductor Chip Protection Act 1984 permitted protection to non-US nationals or domiciles if, by means of Presidential proclamation, the President of the US is satisfied that the foreign State in question affords protection to US owners of mask works. This reciprocity requirement is moderated by provisions that give the US Secretary of Commerce the power to issue interim orders giving protection to countries which are, *inter alia*, making progress toward enacting legislation that would trigger the issuing of a Presidential proclamation. The EU Member States and others have benefited from this interim order procedure while the US has also been the subject of a number of interim measures in the form of Council Decisions.[36] The President, with effect from 1 July 1995, issued the necessary

---

[32] See CA 1963, s 24(3).

[33] European Communities (Protection of Topographies of Semiconductor Products) Regulations 1988, reg 6: *Stovin-Bradford v Volpoint* [1971] 3 All ER 570.

[34] Council Directive 87/54/EEC, art 4(1).

[35] European Communities (Protection of Topographies of Semiconductor Products) Regulations 1988, reg 5(2). The European Communities (Protection of Topographies of Semiconductor Products) Regulations 1988 put the expiry events the other way around, as does Council Directive 87/54/EEC.

[36] 87/532/EEC; 90/511/EEC; 93/16/EEC; 94/4/EC; 94/373/EC; 95/237/EC.

proclamation[37] of protection to EU Member States and that proclamation extended protection to all WTO Members with effect from 1 January 1996. A Council Decision of 22 December 1994 extended topography protection in EU Member States to all members of WTO with effect from 1 January 1996,[38] so the Irish permanent and temporary protection orders[39] have effectively been superseded by EU legislation.

---

[37] Proclamation 6780 to Implement Certain Provisions of Trade Agreements Resulting from the Uruguay Round of Multilateral Trade Negotiations.
[38] 94/824/EC ([1994] OJ L349/201).
[39] SI 208/1988; SI 318/1991; SI 310/1993.

Chapter 23

Industrial Designs

INTRODUCTION AND FORMER DESIGN LAW

[23.01] Most countries have a system of registration whereby it is possible to protect a new design applied to a product but the dilemma is how to pitch such protection between that afforded by a patent and copyright in an artistic work. With the increasing liberalisation of trade mark laws, it is also now possible to register certain shapes of goods or their packaging, which before would have been the sole prerogative of design law. It is possibly the overlap with other forms of intellectual property and uncertainty as to the boundaries of design law that have led to the low profile and under-utilisation of the system of design registration.[1] Design law is based on a recognition that, similar to the position with inventions, there are many instances where much time, energy and effort is injected into the design of a product, which, once disclosed, can be copied at minimal cost.

[23.02] Prior to the Industrial Designs Act 2001 (IDA 2001), the principal legislation dealing with registered industrial designs was to be found in Pt IV of the Industrial and Commercial Property (Protection) Act 1927 (ICPPA 1927). ICPPA 1927 dealt with patents, copyright, trade marks and designs but, prior to 1 July 2002, only remained in force in so far as it related to designs and a provision dealing with the overlap with copyright law.[2] It was this overlap in s 172 of the ICPPA 1927 that was fundamental in the consideration of industrial design law. Section 9 of the Copyright Act 1963 (CA 1963) provided for protection in respect of artistic works and this includes protection against reproduction by turning a two-dimensional work into a three-dimensional form and vice versa, subject to the lay recognition test. This lay recognition test was contained in s 14(7) of CA 1963 and stated that the making of any object of any description which is in three-dimensional form, shall not be taken to constitute an infringement of the copyright in an artistic work in two dimensions if the object would not appear to persons who are not experts in relation to objects of that description to be a reproduction of the artistic work. In practice, it was difficult for a defendant to raise this defence.[3] In *King Features Syndicate Inc v OM Kleeman*,[4] the House of Lords, in dealing with corresponding provisions of the UK law, held that the production of 'Popeye The Sailor

---

1   There were 414 applications filed in 2001. In 2009 the number of national applications was only 44, due in the main to the popularity of the Community-registered design right.
2   ICPPA 1927, s 172.
3   *Dorling v Honnor Marine Ltd* [1964] RPC 160; *Allibert SA v O'Connor* [1981] FSR 613.
4   *King Features Syndicate Inc v OM Kleeman* [1941] AC 417.

Man' dolls amounted to copyright infringement because, without consent, there had been reproduction of the drawings in a material form albeit in a different dimension. The making of an article depicted in a drawing infringed the copyright under the concept of what has become known as indirect copying.

[23.03] An author/artist had to consider very closely whether or not their artistic work was capable of being registered as a design because there could not be duality of protection. Under s 172 of ICPPA 1927, copyright protection was denied in respect of designs that were capable of being registered under the 1927 Act, and which were used or intended to be used as models or patterns to be multiplied by an industrial process. An illustration of how this worked in practice can be seen in *Pytram Ltd v Models (Leicester) Ltd*,[5] which considered the design of a wolf cub's head used on totem poles. Under the then equivalent provisions of UK law, Clawson J held that there was neither copyright nor design protection. Copyright did subsist but protection was denied because the work was capable of being registered as a design. A design only returned to the category of works protected by copyright if it was one that was not used or intended to be used as a model or pattern to be multiplied by any industrial process. This was not the case in respect of the newly designed totem poles and, since design registration had not been sought, the plaintiff was stripped of all forms of protection.

[23.04] It was the artist's intention when the original drawings were created that determined whether or not it was the intention that such be used as a model or pattern to be applied by an industrial process. If a work enjoyed copyright protection under CA 1963, it did not then lose such protection simply because it was subsequently used as a model for mass production.[6]

[23.05] ICPPA 1927 protected the appearance of a specific article to which the design had been applied in respect of which it had been registered. The definition of design was stated in s 3 of the 1927 Act as:

> ... only the features of shape, configuration, pattern, or ornament applied to any article by any industrial process or means, whether manual, mechanical, or chemical, separate or combined, which in the finished article appeal to and are judged solely by the eye, but does not include any mode or principle of construction, or anything which is in substance a mere mechanical device.

The word 'article' was defined in s 3 as 'any article of manufacture and any substance, artificial or natural or partly artificial and partly natural'. This was very broad and applied to a wide range of articles such as, for example, containers, furniture, lamp shades, vehicles, chocolates and cutlery. A design registration was not restricted to three-dimensional articles and could, for example, be surface decoration applied to clothing or wallpaper. The definition of a design was considered by Costello J in *Allibert SA v O'Connor*.[7] Costello J broke down the definition into two parts, the first providing that a 'design' means, *inter alia*, those features of the shape and configuration of the

5   *Pytram Ltd v Models (Leicester) Ltd* [1930] 1 Ch 639.
6   *King Features Syndicate Inc v OM Kleeman* [1941] AC 417.
7   *Allibert SA v O'Connor* [1981] FSR 613.

finished article that appeal to and are judged solely by the eye. The second part excluded from the definition anything that is in substance a mere mechanical device. At issue in the *Allibert* case was the plaintiff's claim to ownership of copyright in drawings relating to fish boxes. The plaintiff also owned registered designs in relation to such but introduced evidence to show, *inter alia*, that the novelty in the shape of the boxes was dictated by its function of improved nesting and stacking. Costello J applied the statement of Luxmore J in *Kestos Ltd v Kempat Ltd*[8] that a mere mechanical device is a shape in which all the features are dictated solely by the function or functions that the article has to perform. If the shape does not possess some features beyond those necessary to enable the article to fulfil the particular purpose, then the drawing cannot be regarded as a design within s 3 of ICPPA 1927.[9] Costello J went on to hold that the designs of the plastic fish boxes should not have been registered under the 1927 Act because all of the features were dictated by their function. As a consequence, copyright subsisted under s 9 of CA 1963.

[23.06] The definition of a design was amended in England by s 1(3) of the Registered Designs Act 1949 and in *AMP Inc v Utilux Proprietary Ltd*,[10] the House of Lords considered the definition, which included reference to visual appeal. It was held that an electric terminal for a washing machine was not registrable. The terminal was located inside the machine and was not visible except to someone servicing the machine. Lord Porter stated:

> no doubt another shape of fuse and another type of machine could be invented to perform the same task. However, that may be, the only object of using the registered shape now under discussion is to perform the functional purpose of making the machine work.

THE COPYRIGHT (AMENDMENT) ACT 1987

[23.07] The effect of the judicial interpretation of the statutory provision[11] that denied registered design protection to functional designs meant that the owners of such could rely on copyright in the original drawings and enjoy protection under CA 1963. Therefore, functional designs enjoyed protection for the life of the author plus 50 years, far exceeding that of either registered designs or patents. This created a number of problems, particularly for manufacturers of spare parts and components. Also, because copyright under CA 1963 is an unregistered right, it is often very difficult to determine ownership. The UK courts had to grapple with the difficult problem of spare parts in *British Leyland Motor Corpn v Armstrong Patents Co*[12] on the issue of copyright protection in original drawings of vehicle exhaust pipes. The court of first instance and the Court of Appeal adopted the traditional copyright line that by copying a British

---

8   *Kestos Ltd v Kempat Ltd* (1935) 53 RPC 139 at 151.
9   *Stenor Ltd v Whitesides (Clitheroe) Ltd* (1948) 65 RPC 1.
10 *AMP Inc v Utilux Proprietary Ltd* [1972] RPC 103 at 114.
11 Definition of design: ICPPA 1927, s 3.
12 *British Leyland Motor Corpn v Armstrong Patents Co* [1986] FSR 221, [1986] 2 WLR 400.

Leyland exhaust pipe in order to supply the market with competing spares, the defendant infringed copyright in the original drawings. The House of Lords, by a majority, accepted that copyright did exist in original drawings of functional designs such as a car exhaust pipe but nevertheless felt that this was so anti-competitive that copyright could not be allowed to interfere with the rights of car owners to repair their vehicles. Lord Templeman likened allowing motor manufacturers to monopolise the spare parts market to the consequence that car owners then 'sell their souls to the company store' because a manufacturer could charge what it wished and the car owner would have no alternative but to buy from this source.

[23.08] The Irish courts were not called upon to address this problem and did not have to do so by virtue of s 1 of the Copyright (Amendment) Act 1987. Under the 1987 Act, protection was denied under CA 1963 to artistic works reproduced in three dimensions where the shape, configuration and pattern that appeared in the work and were applied to the object, were wholly or substantially functional. A second requirement was that the object must be one of a number, in excess of 50, of identical objects, which had been manufactured and made commercially available by the owner of the copyright or by a person authorised by him in that behalf. This effectively meant that mass-produced functional designs were no longer protected under copyright law. They also could not be protected by way of a registered design or under trade mark law.[13] In some instances, patent protection could be sought and it is conceivable that a case of passing off might be made in an exceptional set of circumstances.

NEW DESIGN LAW

[23.09] The new design law is contained in the Industrial Designs Act 2001 and its Regulations.[14] The Act came into force on 1 July 2002 and, apart from modernising the former design law dating back to 1927, it gave effect to the EU Directive on the Legal Protection of Designs.[15] The Act also gives effect to the Geneva Act of the Hague Agreement concerning the International Registration of Industrial Designs, adopted at Geneva on 2 July 1999. It is also necessary to read the Act in conjunction with the EU Regulation on Community Designs,[16] which was adopted on 12 December 2001 and came into force on 6 March 2002. The Regulation introduces for the first time Community-wide design protection by way of both an unregistered and registered Community design.

---

[13] Trade Marks Act 1996, s 8(2)(b).
[14] SI 280/2002; SI 275/2002.
[15] Council Directive 98/71/EC ([1998] OJ L289/28).
[16] Council Regulation 6/2002/EC ([2002] OJ L179/31).

WHAT IS REGISTRABLE AS A DESIGN?

[23.10] A design is defined in s 2 of IDA 2001 as:

> the appearance of the whole or a part of a product resulting from the features of, in particular, the lines, contours, colour, shape, texture or materials of the product itself or its ornamentation.

The word 'product' is also defined in s 2 as 'any industrial or handicraft item, including parts intended to be assembled into a complex product, packaging, get-up, graphic symbols and typographical typefaces, but not including computer programs'. A complex product is itself defined as a product that is composed of multiple components, which can be replaced, permitting disassembly and reassembly of the product. The component part is protected only if it remains visible during normal use of the component.[17] The definition of a product is extremely broad and can be applied to a wide range of products such containers, furniture, vehicles, chocolates, phones and cutlery. A design registration is not restricted to three-dimensional products and can, for example, be surface decoration applied to clothing or wallpaper or more modern design features, such as screen displays or key pads on computer equipment or mobile devices. Under ICPPA 1927, registration could be obtained for designs applied to particular articles by means of an industrial process and which had some aesthetic eye appeal. Under IDA 2001, protection is conferred upon the design itself rather than a particular article. There is no longer any reference to any industrial process and no eye appeal requirement.[18] The new legislation embraces non-physical products such as get-up and graphic symbols thus increasing the overlap with trade mark law. Because the design need no longer be applied to an article, many designs are being registered in respect of digital products, screen displays for mobile technology and computers. The Explanatory Memorandum to the Directive and Regulation stressed that features such as weight, flexibility and tactilicity may be protected.

Novelty and individual character

[23.11] In order to be registrable, a design must be new and have an individual character.[19] Novelty is defined differently from that which prevails under patent law but does introduce into Irish design laws the concept of universal novelty. Novelty requires that the design must not be identical to a design that is made available to the public prior to the application or any priority claim.[20] English and Australian case law[21] tends to favour the view that a statement of novelty creates 'what amounts to an estoppel against the proprietor', or, at least, will make it difficult for the proprietor, in an attempt to expand the scope of a registration, to deny that certain features are novel when

---

[17] IDA 2001, s 14.

[18] See *Allibert SA v O'Connor* [1981] FSR 613.

[19] IDA 2001, s 11(1).

[20] IDA 2001, s 12(1).

[21] *Sommer Allibert (UK) Ltd v Flair Plastics Ltd* [1987] RPC 599; *Chiropedic Bedding Pty Ltd v Radburg Pty* (2009) 83 IPR 275.

previously asserted in the statement of novelty.[22] However, the registration procedure itself does not require the applicant to provide a statement of novelty or individual character; a deliberate adjustment to the law so as to allow greater flexibility.[23]

[23.12] Designs shall be deemed to be identical if their features differ only in immaterial details.[24] What is considered as 'made available to the public' is determined by reference to the definition of such in IDA 2001, s 2(1) and its exceptions in s 2(7). Novelty in patent law is also determined by reference to what has already been made available to the public, defining such to be the state of the art. In a similar vein, novelty under design law is broadly defined, and is determined by reference to any prior disclosure including disclosure by way of publication, exhibition or use in trade. However, a disclosure falls outside the definition where it could not reasonably have become known in the normal course of business to the circles specialised in the sector concerned, operating within a Member State of the EEA. Apart from this exception, the main feature which differentiates the concept of novelty from that under patent law is the grace period of one year during which the designer can make the design available by way of, for example, test marketing and without prejudice to subsequent registration. A design is also deemed not to have been made available to the public where it has been disclosed in confidence[25] or made available without authorisation of the author.[26] Those exceptions to the definition of being 'made available to the public' underline the dangers in exhibiting models and prototypes at trade fairs in major markets like the US and Germany, for example: *Central Vista (M) SDN BHD v Pemi Trade sro*.[27] Provision for certification purposes to a government department will not trigger the 12-month novelty grace period: *World of Technologies (Aust) Pty v Temp (Aust) Pty Ltd*.[28]

[23.13] The second criterion for registrability is that the design must also have individual character. This is a concept new to Irish intellectual property law. Individual character in a design arises if the overall impression it produces on informed users differs from the overall impression produced on such a user by an earlier design.[29] An assessment of individual character involves a consideration of the degree of freedom enjoyed by the author in the development of the design.[30] In *Wuxi Kipor Power Co v Honda Giken Kogyo Kabushiki*[31] the product, inverter generators for use in mobile homes, caravans, etc, was said to give a lot of room to the designer; protection was denied on the basis that all the designer did here was to take the prior product and

---

[22] *Russell-Clarke & Howe on Industrial Designs* (7th edn, 2005) para 3-284

[23] See SI 574/2004, amending SI 280/2002.

[24] IDA 2001, s 12(2), eg the capacity of a container, scale adjustments to models: *Central Vista (M) SDN BHD v Pemi Trade sro* [2009] ECDR 21.

[25] IDA 2001, s 2(7)(a).

[26] IDA 2001, s 2(7)(c).

[27] *Central Vista (M) SDN BHD v Pemi Trade sro* [2009] ECDR 21.

[28] *World of Technologies (Aust) Pty v Temp (Aust) Pty Ltd* (2007) 71 IPR 307.

[29] IDA 2001, s 13(1).

[30] IDA 2001, s 13(2).

[31] *Wuxi Kipor Power Co v Honda Giken Kogyo Kabushiki* [2009] ECDR 4.

incorporate differences – called colourable imitations under the 1927 legislation. Older case law suggests that where there is little design freedom, minor adjustments to the prior art will be more likely to trigger design protection.[32]

[23.14] The informed user, as the new benchmark for assessing whether a design has individual character, has produced a significant body of case law. The cases suggest that design circumstances will change the focus on the individual 'informed user'. In *Woodhouse UK plc v Architectural Lighting Systems*[33] Deputy Judge Fysh said that the informed user in relation to street lighting would, firstly, be a person to whom the design is directed – not a manufacturer or 'the man in the street'. Secondly, the user must be informed – be familiar with 'what's about in the market' and have an awareness of product trend and basic technical considerations. Judge Fysh cautioned against applying patent standards or what he described as 'nerd-like' personal knowledge. In *Karen Millen Ltd v Dunnes Stores*[34] the informed user, in respect of three designs for fashion shirts and tops, was said to be a notional person, was the end user for the purposes of wearing the items in question, was aware of similar designs, that is, be a woman with a keen sense of fashion for these kinds of items and their design, and be alert to design issues and better informed than the average consumer in design law. The informed user should also have a basic appreciation of the functional aspects of limitations upon design freedom. In this context Finlay Geoghegan J followed *Proctor & Gamble Co v Reckitt Benkiser UK Ltd.*[35] The case concerned design features for an air freshener product and the Court of Appeal indicated that in such a context the informed user will have a more extensive knowledge than an average consumer in possession of average information, awareness and understanding, in particular the informed user will be open to design issues and fairly familiar with them.

Bailey v Haynes,[36] a case involving fishing bait equipment, suggests that for everyday small value purchases the informed user – in that case an enthusiastic angler – will not be too far away from a notional consumer. In *Wuxi Kipoor Power Co v Honda Giken Kogya Kabushiki*,[37] inverter generators for use in caravans and the like were described as technical equipment, the informed user being a person who habitually purchases such an item and puts it to its intended use. The user will have become informed on the subject of inverter generators through browsing through catalogues, visiting relevant stores and downloading information from the internet. The visual comparison that such an informed user would carry out on technical equipment will focus on the attractiveness and practicability of the device.

---

[32] *Albion Hat and Cap Co Pty Ltd* (1989) 21 IPR 558; *Re Apple Computer* (2007) 74 IPR 164.

[33] *Woodhouse UK plc v Architectural Lighting Systems* [2006] RPC 1.

[34] *Karen Millen Ltd v Dunnes Stores* [2008] 2 ILRM 368.

[35] *Proctor & Gamble Co v Reckitt Benkiser UK Ltd* [2008] FSR 8.

[36] *Bailey v Haynes* [2006] EWPPC 5.

[37] *Wuxi Kipoor Power Co v Honda Giken Kogya Kabushiki* [2009] ECDR 4. The 'informed user' test has been imported into Australian law. For USB connectors on 'keys' the informed user is an ordinary computer user, not a person with particular knowledge about how computer peripherals are to be set out (eg set up a LAN connection: *Re Apple Computer* (2007) 74 IPR 164).

[23.15] A design in respect of a component part of a complex product can only fulfil the criteria of novelty and individual character if it remains visible during normal use of the complex product.[38] Normal use is defined to mean use by the end user excluding maintenance, servicing or repair work.[39]

[23.16] A scenario may arise whereby a design, although the subject of a prior design right, has not yet been published and would not therefore constitute part of the prior art destroying novelty in the subsequent design. However, in such a scenario, the earlier design is deemed to be a conflicting design and makes the later design unregistrable.[40]

DESIGNS DICTATED BY THEIR TECHNICAL FUNCTION AND DESIGNS OF INTERCONNECTIONS

[23.17] Section 16 of IDA 2001 implements art 7 of the Designs Directive[41] and excludes a design right from subsisting in features of a design that are wholly functional[42] or constitute a must-fit.

[23.18] Recital 14 of the Designs Directive[43] states the rationale behind excluding protection in respect of features of a product that are solely dictated by the technical function as being to prevent the hampering of technological innovation. However, it is not a requirement that a design must have an aesthetic quality. There is also no exclusion simply because the design, which performs a new function, is also the subject of a patent. The exclusion allows competition by copying of a design feature that is technically essential. The term 'dictated' means that a design is not excluded provided it can be made in some other shape to fulfil the same function.[44] The leading case is *Landor and Hawa International Ltd v Azure Design Ltd*.[45] Features that were incorporated into the design of suitcases that had an expandable section were held to be protectable on the basis that for a design feature to be disqualified from protection it must be solely dictated by technical function. Many design features may be capable of being replicated in other ways and some design features with a technical function may also be characterised as decorative.

[23.19] The must-fit provisions contained in s 16(2) of IDA 2001 limit protection for spare parts in cases of mechanical interconnection. The impetus for this exclusion lies primarily in the automobile industry and caters for a scenario such as that which arose in *British Leyland v Armstrong*.[46] The defendant manufactured replacement exhaust pipes for British Leyland motor vehicles, which replicated certain design features in order to

---

[38] IDA 2001, s 14(1).

[39] IDA 2001, s 14(2).

[40] IDA 2001, s 15.

[41] Council Directive 98/71/EC.

[42] IDA 2001, s 16(1).

[43] Council Directive 98/71/EC.

[44] *Philips Electronics NV v Remington Consumer Products* [2001] RPC 745, at paras 31–38.

[45] *Landor and Hawa International Ltd v Azure Design Ltd* [2007] FSR 9.

[46] *British Leyland v Armstrong* [1986] FSR 221.

fit the underside of the vehicle. It is only the interconnecting features themselves and not the whole part that is excluded from protection. A special case arises for the mechanical fittings of modular products, and under s 16(3) they escape the exclusion. The most obvious is a building block toy.[47] The Oireachtas also expressed its intention to facilitate the development of an Irish 'spare parts' manufacturing base for motor vehicles by providing in s 42(5) that the design right shall not apply to the use of a component part of a complex product for the purpose of repair of that product so as to restore its original appearance: this is known as the 'must match' exemption.[48]

OWNERSHIP

[23.20] The author of a design is treated as the first proprietor.[49] An exception arises in the case of a design created by an employee in the course of employment. In this case, the employer is considered as the first proprietor unless there is an agreement to the contrary. The author is the person who creates the design.[50] Where a design is computer generated, the author is the person who arranged for the computer generation.[51] Joint authorship arises in circumstances where a design is produced by two or more authors in which the contribution of each author is not distinct from that of the other author(s).[52] One of the consequences of joint ownership is that a licence must have the consent of all owners.[53] There is no automatic vesting of a design right in favour of a party who commissions the design and, consequently, it is important that any commissioned work is accompanied by a contract that expressly assigns the rights in any design if, as is usual, this would have been the intention of the parties if it had been addressed. This proposition has been confirmed by the ECJ. In *Fundacion Espanola para la Innovacion de la Artesania* Case C- 32/08,[54] the question of ownership of an unregistered design right when the design was created on the basis of a commission contract was held not to be governed by the employee created work rule in art 14(3) of Regulation 6/2002/EC, and, unless national law applies the employee created works rule to commissioned works the right to the Community design vests in the designer unless it has been assigned by the designer to his successor in title. A design right is a property right[55] and an application for registration is also treated as such[56] and may be assigned by the first proprietor[57] and then subsequently assigned. However, in circumstances where the

---

[47] LEGO; DUPLO.

[48] For a discussion on this see 542 *Dáil Debates*, Col 241.

[49] IDA 2001, s 19.

[50] IDA 2001, s 17(1).

[51] IDA 2001, s 17(2) and (3).

[52] IDA 2001, s 18(1).

[53] IDA 2001, s 18(3).

[54] *Fundacion Espanola para la Innovacion de la Artesania (FEIA) v Cul de Sac Espacio Creativo SL and Acierta Product & Position SA* Case C-32/08 [2009] ECR I-05611.

[55] IDA 2001, s 42.

[56] IDA 2001, s 22(1).

[57] IDA 2001, s 19(2).

author is not the first proprietor, such as in the case of an employee, the author does have the right to be cited as the author in any application for registration.[58] Unlike the position under the Community Designs Regulation,[59] there is no provision to substitute the names of individuals with a team name in circumstances of joint authorship. An assignment should be recorded on the Register, otherwise the instrument of transfer may not be admitted by a court[60] and thus title may be denied. It is important to ensure that the registration is obtained by the person entitled to register the design. A recent English case holds that if a commissioner incorrectly obtains registration, the registration may be cancelled: *Woodhouse UK plc v Architectural Lighting Systems*.[61]

IRISH DESIGN REGISTRATION PROCEDURE

[23.21] Registration of a design effective in Ireland can be either through the Community Designs Regulation 6/2002/EC of 12 December 2001 resulting in a European Community-wide registration or, alternatively, a national right obtained under the provisions of IDA 2001 and administered by the Irish Patents Office based in Kilkenny. There are minimal formalities in the registration of a design before the Irish Patents Office.

[23.22] The application must be made by the proprietor[62] and, in order to achieve a filing date, apart from full particulars of the applicant, the request for application must be accompanied by the prescribed fee and a representation of the design in a form suitable for reproduction.[63] The Industrial Designs Regulations 2002[64] schedule the prescribed form of application. When registering a design, it is necessary to identify the product or products against which the design is used and to classify such product(s) according to the Locarno Classification, the system of design identification and registration maintained by WIPO since 1968. Classification is to be treated as an administrative exercise important for issues such as searching. Unlike under the former Act, ICPPA 1927, the rights granted by a design registration are not limited to the product against which the design is registered. There is no longer any requirement for a statement of novelty.[65]

[23.23] In addition to the mandatory requirements, in order to achieve a filing date, there are certain additional elements which may also arise in an application. It is possible to request a deferment of publication for up to 30 months[66] and to claim priority from a foreign design application under the Paris Convention for the Protection of Industrial

---

58 IDA 2001, s 19(3).
59 Council Regulation 6/2002/EC.
60 IDA 2001, s 41(4).
61 *Woodhouse UK plc v Architectural Lighting Systems* [2006] RPC 1.
62 IDA 2001, s 20(1).
63 IDA 2001, s 25.
64 SI 280/2002.
65 SI 574/2004.
66 IDA 2001, s 32; Industrial Designs Regulations 2002 (SI 280/2002), reg 25.

Property (Paris Convention).[67] The priority period is six months from the date of first application and its effect is that the priority date is to be considered as the filing date for the purposes of determination of grounds such as novelty, individual character, disclosure and prior use.[68] However, any priority claim does not affect the effective date of registration, which is the filing date.[69]

[23.24] It is possible to register a number of designs under one application[70] subject to a maximum of 100 designs and payment of additional fees. This is termed a multiple application. It is a requirement that the products all fall into the same class of the Locarno Classification although such a condition is not imposed in respect of an ornament and design. There is no requirement that the designs be similar or applied to products which are used together. Multiple applications can be a considerable cost saving for an applicant and there is no requirement for multiple designs to share a common priority date.

[23.25] Unlike the trade mark system, there is no opposition procedure and a party wishing to challenge a design, for example one based on lack of novelty or individual character, must do so by way of invalidity proceedings.[71] The grounds upon which the Controller may refuse an application are stated in IDA 2001, s 21. These grounds include a design that is contrary to public policy or to accepted principles of morality. It can be expected that such will only rarely arise[72] such as, for example, on the grounds of offence to religious beliefs. Works protected by copyright constitute a basis for refusal of a design as do designs which consist of or include protected national or international symbols which would fall for refusal under ss 9, 62 or 63 of the Trade Marks Act 1996.

Register of designs

[23.26] During the application stages it is not normally possible to obtain information pertaining to the design. An exception arises by virtue of IDA 2001, s 39(4), which allows a third party who has been threatened with infringement upon registration to obtain particulars of the design even in circumstances where the applicant has requested deferment of publication. In cases where an application has been refused or abandoned, particulars pertaining to that application are not published or available for public inspection.[73] It is possible to make an application before the Controller to record a registrable transaction[74] on foot of a design application[75] but recordal will not be entered on the Register until registration.[76]

---

67 IDA 2001, s 26.
68 IDA 2001, s 28.
69 IDA 2001, s 29.
70 SI 280/2002, reg 19.
71 IDA 2001, s 47.
72 *Masterman's Application* [1991] RPC 89.
73 IDA 2001, s 39(5).
74 IDA 2001, s 41.
75 IDA 2001, s 22(2) and (3).
76 SI 280/2002, reg 13(3).

[23.27] There is no prescribed time period within which details of a design are open for public inspection by way of publication. Publication occurs in the Patents Office Journal and upon registration,[77] unless an applicant has requested a deferment of publication,[78] for up to 30 months from the date of filing or the priority date. The information that the Controller must provide by way of publication is stated in reg 24 of the Industrial Designs Regulations 2002[79] and includes the reproduction of a representation of the design and a statement of the product or products to or in which the design is to be applied or incorporated.

[23.28] The Register of Designs includes information such as full particulars of the proprietor and registrable transactions, which are specifically stated in IDA 2001, s 30(2) and further information, which is prescribed under SI 280/2002, reg 22. No notice of any trust may be entered on the Register.[80] There is a right of public inspection of the Register.[81] It is also possible to request the Controller to carry out a search to establish the existence of a registered design on the Register.[82] Regulation 31 does impose certain limitations on the right to obtain information. This includes information that the Controller considers should be treated as confidential or any documentation that may prejudice a person's reputation.

[23.29] An aggrieved person may apply either to the Controller or to the High Court[83] for rectification of the Register. Such a rectification can include the substitution on the Register of the true owner of a design. Any new entry on the Register as a result of rectification has effect from the date on which it should have been made[84] and an entry deleted is deemed never to have had effect.[85] The Controller also has power to correct errors on the Register including at the behest of an interested party, who must provide a statement of the reasons why correction has been sought.[86]

[23.30] A person who acquires proprietary rights or an interest in a design right or a share of the design right is required to record such on the Designs Register.[87] An interest includes as a mortgagee or licensee. Particulars of the instrument by which a person acquired their rights are entered on the Register. Failure to record a title or interest means that the document purporting to show the title or interest will not be admitted in court unless the court otherwise directs. An exception to inadmissibility arises in cases of an application to rectify the Register.[88] Until application to record an entitlement is

---

[77]   IDA 2001, s 32(1).
[78]   IDA 2001, s 32(2).
[79]   SI 280/2002.
[80]   IDA 2001, s 30(4).
[81]   IDA 2001, ss 38 and 39; SI 280/2002, reg 30(1).
[82]   IDA 2001, s 40; SI 280/2002, reg 30(2).
[83]   IDA 2001, s 33.
[84]   IDA 2001, s 35(a).
[85]   IDA 2001, s 35(c).
[86]   SI 280/2002, reg 29(d).
[87]   IDA 2001, s 41(1).
[88]   IDA 2001, s 41(4).

made to the Irish Patents Office it is ineffective as against a person acquiring a conflicting interest.[89]

Effect of registration

[23.31] A design right subsisting in a registered design is a property right[90] the ownership of which resides in the registered proprietor.[91] The scope of protection extends to designs that do not produce on the informed user a different overall impression from the registered design, taking into consideration the degree of freedom the author had in developing the design.[92]

[23.32] A registered design grants a monopoly right to prevent any unauthorised person from making, offering, supplying, importing, exporting or using any product incorporating or applying the design.[93] There is no requirement that the unauthorised party should have copied from the proprietor or had any knowledge of the design.

[23.33] A thin line is sometimes drawn between the unauthorised act of manufacture and the act of repair. In the patent case of *Solar Thomson Engineering Co v Barton*[94] the Court of Appeal held that there was an implied licence to repair. However, the House of Lords in *United Wire Ltd v Screen Repair Services*[95] held the concept of an implied licence distracted attention from the real question of distinguishing between the mutually exclusive concepts of manufacture and repair. Lord Hoffmann stating:

> As a matter of ordinary language, the notions of making and repair may well overlap but for the purposes of the Statute, they are mutually exclusive. The owner's right to repair is not an independent right conferred upon him by licence, express or implied.

Although registration of designs in respect of spare parts is permitted and there is no implied licence to repair, s 42(5) of IDA 2001 precludes the assertion of a design right in cases of use of a component part to effect repairs to restore the original appearance of a complex product.

[23.34] The maximum duration of a registered design is 25 years, renewable at five-year intervals.[96] There is provision for a six-month grace period within which to pay an overdue renewal fee and if renewal is paid during this grace period, the design right is deemed never to have expired. However, a court may refuse to award damages or an account of profits for infringement between the normal renewal date and the late renewal. It is also possible for a design right to be restored within 12 months from the date on which the design right expires provided the proprietor can illustrate to the

---

[89] IDA 2001, ss 76(4) and 78(1).

[90] IDA 2001, s 42(1).

[91] IDA 2001, s 42(2).

[92] IDA 2001, s 42(3).

[93] IDA 2001, s 42(4).

[94] *Solar Thomson Engineering Co v Barton* [1977] RPC 537.

[95] *United Wire Ltd v Screen Repair Services* [2001] RPC 439.

[96] IDA 2001, s 43.

satisfaction of the Controller that they had taken all reasonable care to ensure renewal.[97] Consequently, the failure to renew must be inadvertent. The Controller may impose conditions on restoration. Section 45 provides certain safeguards to third parties who, prior to publication of the notice of restoration, acted in good faith believing the design right to have expired. A design right can be surrendered[98] by the proprietor, who must certify that they are not contractually precluded from such surrender.[99] Persons entered on the Register as having an interest must be given three months' notice of the intention to surrender and not have raised any objection.

[23.35] Although there is no opposition procedure, once a design has been registered, an interested party may apply to the Controller for invalidation. The grounds are stated in s 47 of IDA 2001 and include a wrongly made claim to proprietorship, lack of novelty or individual character and features of appearance of a product that are solely dictated by the technical function. Also included amongst the grounds is any design contrary to public policy or morality. An invalidity action based on a design in conflict with a prior design can be pursued on the initiative of the Controller. Invalidity may arise by virtue of the inclusion in the design of a distinctive sign registered as a trade mark but the Controller does have power to amend the design by exclusion of the sign[100] or entry of a partial disclaimer.[101]

INFRINGEMENT

[23.36] A registered design confers exclusivity in favour of the registered proprietor.[102] Article 12 of the Harmonisation Directive[103] expands on what is meant by use to embrace, in particular, the making, offering, putting on the market, importing, exporting or using of a product in which the design is incorporated or to which it is applied or stocking such a product for those purposes. Secondary infringement can occur in circumstances of certain specifically stated unauthorised acts relating to a product, which is known to be or there is reason to believe is an infringing product. Section 52 of IDA 2001 states the unauthorised acts, and s 53 further makes it possible to take action against a person who facilitates infringement by providing the means to others to make infringing products. What is meant by an infringing product is itself defined in s 54.

[23.37] The design right is not infringed by reproduction of a feature of the design which is not taken into account in determining whether the design is registrable.[104] Thus, the scope of protection afforded to a design right only extends to those aspects of the design as registered that are novel and have individual character. Importation of what would

---

[97] IDA 2001, s 44; SI 280/2002, reg 35.
[98] SI 280/2002, reg 36.
[99] SI 280/2002, reg 36.
[100] IDA 2001, s 47(11).
[101] IDA 2001, s 47(12).
[102] IDA 2001, s 51(1); IDA 2001, s 42(4).
[103] Council Directive 98/71/EC.
[104] IDA 2001, s 51(2).

otherwise be considered as an infringing product is permitted in circumstances where the proprietor's first marketing has amounted to an exhaustion of rights.[105]

[23.38] An infringement action is not possible until issuance of the certificate of registration granting the design. In proceedings a party who is neither resident nor carrying on business in the State may be called upon to give security for costs.[106]

[23.39] Section 48 of IDA 2001 implements art 13 of the Designs Harmonisation Directive[107] and lists certain acts that are stated as not amounting to an infringement, namely:

1.   acts done privately and for non-commercial purposes;
2.   acts done for experimental purposes;
3.   acts of reproduction for the purposes of making citations or of teaching.

In relation to the latter exclusion, it is further stated that the act must be compatible with fair trade practice and must not unduly prejudice the normal exploitation of the design.[108] The exclusion does not provide the teaching profession generally with a defence to a claim of infringement but only in instances where the teaching pertains to the subject matter of the design itself. Further exclusions relate to the temporary visit to the State of ships and aircraft, of vehicles and are designed to ensure, in accordance with art 5*ter* of the Paris Convention, that intellectual property is not a barrier to freedom of movement.

[23.40] There is a right of continuous use, which subsists in favour of a third party who can establish that before the filing date of the design or any priority claim, they had commenced use within the State or had made serious preparations to that end.[109] Unlike art 22 of the Designs Regulation,[110] there is no requirement that the user has acted in good faith although it is necessary that the prior user is in respect of a design that has not been copied from the registered design. It is likely that the provision will be interpreted in such a way that the continued activity must amount to substantially the same as the prior user both technically and commercially.[111] A possible occurrence of this provision would arise if a third party independently reproduces the design during the grace period of a design that is subsequently registered. The right of continued user is a personal right that cannot be transmitted.

[23.41] Once a design has been registered, it is possible for any person to apply to the Controller for a compulsory licence[112] on the ground that a demand in the State for a product incorporating the design is not being met or is not being met on reasonable terms. The demand can be met by importation provided it is from a member country of

---

[105] IDA 2001, s 54(2).
[106] IDA 2001, s 81(2).
[107] Council Directive 98/71/EC.
[108] See TRIPS, art 26(2).
[109] IDA 2001, s 41(1).
[110] IDA 2001, s 41(4).
[111] IDA 2001, ss 76(4) and 78(1).
[112] IDA 2001, s 49.

the World Trade Organisation (WTO). It is possible for the terms of the licence to be varied or for the licence to be cancelled if the circumstances which led to the granting of the licence in the first instance have changed.

REMEDIES

[23.42] An infringement on foot of a design right itself is actionable by the registered proprietor of the design,[113] an exclusive licensee[114] or a licensee generally where the registered proprietor refuses to take action.[115] The general remedies by way of injunction, damages or account of profits are available.[116] In cases where a defendant can show innocent infringement, no award of damages or account of profits will be made.[117] Innocent infringement is not a defence to an infringement suit.[118] A court may award aggravated damages and/or exemplary damages.[119]

[23.43] In any infringement proceedings, it would be common for a plaintiff to encounter a counterclaim seeking invalidity of the registered design. In such circumstances, if a court finds the design to be validly registered then it may grant a certificate of validity. The effect of such a certificate is that in subsequent proceedings, the party relying on validity would normally be granted solicitor-and-client costs.[120]

[23.44] Similar to the position in both patent and trade mark legislation, a complainant should be aware that an infringement claim could result in an aggrieved party seeking their own relief by way of action for groundless threats.[121] The aggrieved person would normally be the person against whom the threat to take proceedings is directed but the statutory provision is not so limiting. The threatened party becomes the plaintiff to proceedings and can obtain remedies such as an injunction against continuance of threats and damages. The onus falls on the plaintiff to show the design is invalid. It is possible to put a third party on simple notice of the registered design without offending the groundless threats provision and the provision does not extend to a person making or importing any object.

[23.45] An order for delivery-up of infringing products or articles can be sought provided manufacture of the offending products or articles is not over six years old.[122] This six-year period is extendible in circumstances where the proprietor is under a disability or has been prevented by fraud or concealment from discovering facts, which

---

[113] IDA 2001, s 57(1).
[114] IDA 2001, s 63(1).
[115] IDA 2001, s 65(1).
[116] IDA 2001, s 57(3).
[117] IDA 2001, s 58(1).
[118] IDA 2001, s 58(3).
[119] IDA 2001, s 59.
[120] IDA 2001, s 55.
[121] IDA 2001, s 56.
[122] IDA 2001, ss 61(1), (2) and 71(1).

would have entitled the proprietor to an order for delivery.[123] The onus to prove that the infringing product or article is over six years old resides with the defendant.[124] It is also possible for the registered proprietor to make an application to the District Court for seizure without warrant of products or articles that the proprietor has reasonable grounds to believe to be an infringement. The District Court is permitted to receive hearsay evidence and without any obligation on a witness to reveal the source of information upon which that witness formed the belief that material could be found in a particular location.[125] Following a court order for delivery-up or seizure, a court may make a further order of forfeiture, destruction or even release of the infringing product or article to a third party.[126]

[23.46] A registered proprietor may notify the Revenue Commissioners as to the existence of their registered design, and hence infringing products or articles are to be treated as prohibited goods and importation other than for private or domestic use is to be prohibited.[127] The effect is that the goods are to be treated as counterfeit and such goods can be forfeited.[128]

LICENCES AND ASSIGNMENT

[23.47] A distinction is drawn between an exclusive and non-exclusive licence. An exclusive licensee is essentially put in the same position as the registered owner and enjoys the same rights and remedies once application to record the licence has been made.[129] Indeed, in some in instances, damages may be higher in favour of a licensee because of the royalties that they are paying to a design owner.[130] The rights of an exclusive licensee are concurrent with those of the registered proprietor.[131] An exclusive licence is defined in s 77 of IDA 2001 and means 'a licence authorising the licensee, to the exclusion of all other persons including the person granting the licence'. In the case of a non-exclusive licensee, there is an entitlement to invite the registered owner to take infringement proceedings and if there is a refusal or if within two months no action is taken by the registered owner, then the licensee may take proceedings in his or her own name.[132] It is a condition that application for recordal of the licence has been made to the Irish Patents Office.[133]

---

123 IDA 2001, s 71(2).
124 IDA 2001, s 71(4).
125 IDA 2001, s 62.
126 IDA 2001, s 72(1).
127 IDA 2001, s 73.
128 European Communities (Counterfeit and Pirated Goods) Regulations 1996 (SI 48/1996); see new Regulation SI 1383/2003, para [32.64].
129 IDA 2001, s 63(1).
130 IDA 2001, ss 63(4) and 64(4).
131 IDA 2001, s 63(2).
132 IDA 2001, s 65(2).
133 IDA 2001, s 76(4)(b).

[23.48] A design right is transmissible by assignment, testamentary disposition or operation of law, as personal or movable property.[134] Where there is more than one registered proprietor of a design, it is necessary for all proprietors to consent to any licence, assignment or mortgage.[135] An assignment can be partial as to rights and duration.[136]

CRIMINAL OFFENCES

Fraudulent use of a registered design

[23.49] Under s 66 of IDA 2001 it is an offence to carry out certain specified acts when there is no authorisation by way of licence from the registered proprietor. The specified acts are use or importation other than for private or domestic use, manufacture for sale or rental, selling, hiring, export or possession and custody or control during the course of business. In all cases, it is a requirement that the offending party knows or has serious reason to believe that the product is an infringement. An offence can only occur in respect of an action that constitutes an infringement.[137] Certain specified acts relating to articles specifically designed or adapted for use in the manufacture of infringing products are also protected.

[23.50] On summary conviction, the liability is to a term of imprisonment not exceeding 12 months and/or a fine not exceeding €1,905 in respect of each infringing product or article. On conviction on indictment liability is to a term of imprisonment not exceeding five years and/or a fine not exceeding €127,000.

Falsification of the register

[23.51] Under s 67 of IDA 2001, it is an offence to make a false entry in the Register knowing or having reason to believe the entry to be false. It is also an offence to produce a document which falsely purports to be an entry on the Register.

False representation

[23.52] Under IDA 2001, s 68, it is an offence to represent falsely a design applied to a product as being registered when for valuable consideration disposing of the product within the State. The false claim includes the application to the product of the word 'Registered', by stamping, engraving, impression or otherwise, unless it can be shown that the design is registered in another jurisdiction. False representation extends to a registered design that has expired.[138]

---

[134] IDA 2001, s 76(1).
[135] IDA 2001, s 76(5).
[136] IDA 2001, s 76(6).
[137] IDA 2001, s 66(3).
[138] IDA 2001, s 66(4).

REMEDIES IN CRIMINAL PROCEEDINGS

[23.53] A court can order delivery-up of a product or article being an infringement of a registered design. This can arise either upon conviction or on the court being satisfied that there is a *prima facie* case to answer.[139] A court cannot make the order if six years have expired from the initiation of the proceedings[140] or where it appears to a court that an order for disposal will be made.[141]

[23.54] A district court may authorise the Garda Síochána by warrant to search premises, and powers including the seizure of products or articles suspected of being an infringement. A warrant may also authorise the owner of the registered design or their representative to accompany and assist the Garda Síochána in executing the warrant or in collating any inventory or other evidence.[142]

THE COMMUNITY DESIGN

[23.55] Under Council Regulation 6/2002/EC, similar to the position in relation to trade marks, it is now possible to register a design before the Office for Harmonisation in the Internal Market (OHIM)[143] thus providing a system for centralised registration covering all countries of the EU. Registrations are published in the Community Designs Bulletin which is only in electronic format and is accessible via the internet.[144] The system allows for multiple applications, ie one filing that includes several designs. No upper limit exists for the number of designs included in a multiple application. Applicants have to indicate at least one product to which the design is applied. In relation to a multiple application, all products indicated for all designs in the application have to fall into the same main class of the Locarno Classification except where the designs concern ornamentation.

[23.56] Under the community design, examination is restricted to formalities. There is no substantive examination and no opposition procedure. After registration, a third party may seek invalidity based on grounds that include lack of novelty or individual character.

[23.57] It is possible for community design to be filed either directly before OHIM or through the Irish Patents Office on payment of an additional fee.[145] The Irish High Court has been designated as a Community Design court of first instance in accordance with art 80(1) of the Designs Regulation[146] and the Supreme Court as a Community Design

---

139 IDA 2001, s 69.
140 IDA 2001, ss 69(2)(a) and 71(3).
141 IDA 2001, s 69(2)(b).
142 IDA 2001, s 70. See SI 421/2010.
143 12 December 2001; (2001) OJ L3/1.
144 http://oami.europa.eu/bulletin/rcd/rcd_bulletin_en.htm.
145 European Communities (Community Designs) Regulations 2003 (SI 27/2003), art 3.
146 Council Regulation 6/2002/EC.

court of second instance.[147] The Controller has been designated as the national authority for the purpose of art 71 of the Designs Regulation, which deals with the enforcement of decisions of OHIM affixing the amount of costs.[148]

UNREGISTERED DESIGN RIGHT

[23.58] The Community Designs Regulation[149] entered into force on 6 March 2002 and from that date introduced for the first time into Irish law the concept of an unregistered design right. The unregistered design right enables the right holder to prevent third parties from using the same or similar design. It attaches a presumption of validity to designs first made available to the public after 6 March 2002. Protection is valid for three years from the date on which the design was first made available to the public. There is a requirement of novelty, but infringement can only occur by copying. An unregistered design right cannot be asserted against an independently created design.

[23.59] In *Karen Millen*[150] Finlay Geoghegan J held that for the purpose of establishing individual character, the court must look to individual designs that have been made available to the public prior to the launch of the plaintiff's product. The only evidential burdens on the design owner are that the design was made available to the public within three years (UCD) and the submission of indicia of the elements constituting individual character. The Federal Court of Australia has also followed the decision of Finlay Geoghegan J, in *Karen Millen*, on the relevant test for distinctiveness. The court is not to compare the design in question to the prior art base as a whole but individually to each relevant piece of prior art.[151]

---

[147] European Communities (Community Designs) Regulations 2003 (SI 27/2003), art 4.

[148] European Communities (Community Designs) Regulations 2003 (SI 27/2003), art 5.

[149] Council Regulation 6/2002/EC.

[150] *Karen Millen Ltd v Dunnes Stores* [2008] 2 ILRM 368.

[151] *LED Technologies Pty Ltd v Elecspess Pty Ltd* (2008) 80 IPR 85.

Chapter 24

The Duty of Confidence

INTRODUCTION

[24.01] The duty to observe a confidence is an important element in the overall legal structure that recognises and protects intellectual property rights. Where such a duty exists it can overlap with certain copyright, patent and contractual remedies available to a right holder, but in certain circumstances the law relating to confidence can take on a life of its own. For example, duties to observe express or implied terms in a contract or licence cannot bind third parties who are strangers to the contract unless some agency, fiduciary or trust relationship can be located. Further, because the law of copyright protects against unauthorised dealings in works that exist in a certain form, copyright cannot protect against the unauthorised use of information or an idea that exists in an unprotectable format (ie it has not been written down or drawn).[1] In these and other situations, the courts have developed the notion that a duty of confidence may exist although, as we shall see, this area of judge-made law is not without its uncertainties and contradictions, so much so that the English Law Commission, for example, has called for legislation to put the duty of confidence onto a statutory footing.[2] Academic commentators have also argued that some legislative measures would be useful in clarifying this somewhat arcane but policy-fraught area of intellectual property law.

[24.02] The modern law of confidence has evolved from a number of different sources, although it is generally recognised that the basic rationale behind both the cause of action and the available remedies is equitable in nature.

[24.03] It is the decision of the Lord Chancellor, Lord Cottenham, in *Prince Albert v Strange*[3] that represents the clearest early case in which the duty is recognised. Prince Albert and Queen Victoria arranged to have certain etched plates that they had created

---

[1] *Fraser v Thames Television* [1983] 2 All ER 101. Note however that the inherent vagueness of the underlying idea may be held fatal to a confidence action: *De Maudsley v Palumbo* [1996] FSR 447; Phillips [1997] IPQ 135. Note the Irish courts' refusal to rule that a patent application may waive a copyright claim: *House of Spring Gardens v Point Blank Ltd* [1984] IR 611.

[2] Law Com No 110 Breach of Confidence (1981). See generally, Gurry, *Breach of Confidence* (Oxford University Press, 1984); Lavery, *Commercial Secrets* (Round Hall Sweet & Maxwell, 1996); Lang [2002] CTLR 193.

[3] (1849) 1 Mac & G 25. For a contemporary repetition of not dissimilar facts arising out of the printing of a 'Harry Potter' book see *Bloomsbury Publishing Group Ltd v News Group Newspapers* [2003] FSR 812.

sent to Brown, a printer in Windsor, so as to allow etchings to be made therefrom, the etchings to be kept for their own private amusement. Middleton, an employee of Brown, wrongfully kept copies for his own purposes and these copies came into the possession of Strange who arranged a catalogue intending to exhibit these works to allow the public to 'admire … the eminent artistic talent of both' – a likely story! While these facts would clearly be seen today as involving a primary infringement of copyright in an unpublished work by Middleton, and an act of secondary infringement by Strange in so far as the unauthorised impressions made by Middleton, and the catalogue describing them, would be reproductions in a material form or adaptations of the plaintiff's works, Lord Cottenham granted injunctions restraining the circulation of the catalogues and the holding of the exhibition, because the defendants had dealt in the works in 'breach of trust, confidence or contract'. It is the notion that equitable remedies can be used to enjoin a threatened breach of contract that marks this decision as an important one, although the fact that the Lord Chancellor identified the basis of the duty as resting upon a property right in the etching plates can be seen as a limiting circumstance. In the Irish case of *Turner v Robinson*,[4] the defendant paid sixpence in order to view the painting, 'the Death of Chatterton' by Wallis, exhibited by the plaintiff in order to raise demand for copies in the form of engravings. The defendant thereafter arranged a group of persons so as to reproduce the scene in the picture in order to photograph it, thereby undercutting any market for the engraving. An action to restrain the defendant from selling photographs or slides was taken in the Irish Courts of Chancery because statute law relating to copyright at that time did not protect paintings. The action was described by Brady LC as resting upon the author's rights of ownership in personal property and he described the decision in *Prince Albert v Strange* as proceeding upon the principle that there is:

> peculiar property in such works of art as drawing and etchings remained in the authors, so long as they kept them for their own private use, or allowed them to be copied under any restrictions.[5]

[24.04] In fact the plaintiff in *Turner v Robinson*[6] had warned that attempts at reproduction by others would be met by legal proceedings, thus making it clear that the owner's right of property would be insisted upon. The Court of Appeal in Chancery thus affirmed the decision of the Master of the Rolls to grant an injunction restraining further publication.

[24.05] While the actual decision in *Turner v Robinson*[7] is narrower in scope than *Prince Albert v Strange*[8] in so far as principles of common law, copyright and even implied contract are discernible, these two decisions demonstrate great judicial willingness to fill in gaps when other statutory reliefs are of perhaps doubtful utility.

---

4   *Turner v Robinson* (1860) 10 Ir Ch R 121, 510. The painting is now in the Tate Gallery.
5   (1860) 10 Ir Ch R 121, 510, at 514.
6   *Turner v Robinson* (1860) 10 Ir Ch R 121, 510.
7   *Turner v Robinson* (1860) 10 Ir Ch R 121, 510.
8   *Prince Albert v Strange* (1849) 1 Mac & G 25.

[24.06] Some of the earlier cases that had been relied upon in *Prince Albert v Strange*,[9] however, do not seem to rest on either implied contract or property rights, perhaps the most graphic being Lord Eldon's *dicta* that if one of George III's physicians had kept a diary of what he heard and saw, the Courts of Chancery would not have permitted publication during the King's lifetime.[10] Such conduct would clearly be professionally unethical, possibly even if publication took place after the Monarch's death, but this example serves to point up the privacy or confidentiality based aspects of the jurisdiction, based on notions of duty or trust. In *Morison v Moat*,[11] the plaintiff's partner communicated verbally the details of a secret recipe for an unpatented medicine to the defendant in breach of a contractual duty of confidentiality. It was observed that the communication here took place in breach of faith and could thus be the subject of an injunction restraining use of this secret recipe. It is clear, however, that the property theory and the implied contract theory cannot adequately explain the diverse range of circumstances in which the equitable jurisdiction operates, and it is accepted that it is the judgment that the defendant stood in a confidential relationship with the plaintiffs, or one of them, that is the basis of the equitable duty of confidence.[12] As we shall see, the modern cases throw up a diverse range of relationships and circumstances within which the equitable duty will arise.

CONTEMPORARY JUDICIAL VIEWS ON THE DUTY OF CONFIDENCE

[24.07] In *A-G v Guardian Newspapers Ltd (No 2)*[13] Lord Griffiths had this to say about the law of confidence:

> It is judge-made law and reflects the willingness of the judges to give a remedy to protect people from being taken advantage of by those they have trusted with confidential information.[14]

[24.08] Lord Goff of Chieveley, without purporting to provide an exhaustive study of the subject, stated the following broad principle:

> a duty of confidence arises when confidential information comes to the knowledge of a person (the confidant) in circumstances where he has notice, or is held to have agreed, that the information is confidential, with the effect that it would be just in all the circumstances that he should be precluded from disclosing the information to others. I have used the word 'notice' advisedly, in order to avoid the (here unnecessary) question of the extent to which actual knowledge is necessary, though I of course understand knowledge to include circumstances where the confidant has deliberately closed his eyes to the obvious. The existence of this broad general principle reflects the fact that there is such a public interest in the maintenance of confidences, that the law will provide remedies for their protection.

---

9 *Prince Albert v Strange* (1849) 1 Mac & G 25.
10 In *Wyatt v Wilson* (1820), cited in *Prince Albert v Strange* (1849) 1 Mac & G 25, 46.
11 *Morison v Moat* (1851) 9 Hare 241.
12 See *El du Pont de Nemours Powder Co v Masland* 244 US 100 at 102 (1917) *per* Holmes J.
13 *A-G v Guardian Newspapers Ltd (No 2)* [1988] 3 All ER 545.
14 *A-G v Guardian Newspapers Ltd (No 2)* [1988] 3 All ER 545 at 648.

I realise that, in the vast majority of cases, in particular those concerned with trade secrets, the duty of confidence will arise from a transaction or relationship between the parties, often a contract, in which event the duty may arise by reason of either an express or an implied term of that contract. It is in such cases as these that the expressions 'confider' and 'confidant' are perhaps most aptly employed. But it is well-settled that a duty of confidence may arise in equity independently of such cases; and I have expressed the circumstances in which the duty arises in broad terms, not merely to embrace those cases where a third party receives information from a person who is under a duty of confidence in respect of it, knowing that it has been disclosed by that person to him in breach of his duty of confidence, but also to include certain situations, beloved of law teachers, where an obviously confidential document is wafted by an electric fan out of a window into a crowded street, or when an obviously confidential document, such as a private diary, is dropped in a public place, and is then picked up by a passer-by. I also have in mind the situations where secrets of importance to national security come into the possession of members of the public, a point to which I shall refer in a moment.[15]

[24.09] To be sure, this decision of the House of Lords raised specific problems on the scope of the law of confidence that involve significant issues of constitutional law and public policy that have not yet been broadly addressed in Ireland. The basis of the duty of confidence has, however, been considered by the High Court and the Supreme Court in *House of Spring Gardens Ltd v Point Blank Ltd*.[16] In that case the plaintiffs sought damages for breach of contract, infringement of copyright and breach of confidence by the defendants who had variously used confidential information acquired during the process of developing a bullet-proof vest as part of a venture involving the plaintiffs, who held various rights, including copyrights in drawings as artistic works, in the products in question. In his examination of the claim relating to the misuse of confidential information, Costello J, in the High Court, examined the leading English cases and summarised the law as resting upon a moral obligation.[17] While the Supreme Court endorsed Costello J's assessment of the law relating to misuse of confidential information, McCarthy J, in his judgment, observed, somewhat elliptically, that 'the obligation of secrecy, whilst enforced by equitable principles, depends more upon commercial necessity than moral duty'.

[24.10] The significance of this observation will become evident when we come to consider the 'springboard' doctrine below.

THE LAW OF CONFIDENCE AND BROAD DUTIES OF SECRECY

[24.11] While the duty of confidence was a stable and recognised equitable principle by the end of the last century,[18] most explanations for the concept at this time adopt an implied contract theory even though other judges present breach of trust or breach of the

---

[15] *A-G v Guardian Newspapers Ltd (No 2)* [1988] 3 All ER 545 at 658–659.

[16] *House of Spring Gardens Ltd v Point Blank Ltd* [1984] IR 611.

[17] *House of Spring Gardens Ltd v Point Blank Ltd* [1984] IR 611 at 663–664.

[18] *Tipping v Clark* (1843) 2 Hare 383; *Merryweather v Moore* [1892] 2 Ch 518; *Robb v Green* [1895] 2 QB 315.

general duty as either an alternative or the true judicial basis[19] for relief in equity. Once we disentangle contract, copyright and other related legal concepts such as non-derogation of grant[20] from the range of possible explanations for judicial activism, we can see that the moral, commercial, and public and private interest considerations that shape this cause of action are indeed complex.

[24.12] In *A-G v Guardian Newspapers Ltd (No 2)*,[21] the House of Lords indicated that while in most instances the plaintiff obtains relief because breach of the duty will result in financial detriment to the confider, there are instances where the duty will arise in cases where the right to personal privacy will be of legitimate concern for the courts. Indeed, Lord Keith indicated that 'the right to personal privacy is clearly one which the law should in this field seek to protect'.[22] The signs are that this area of equitable duty is being used in the English courts, and to a lesser extent in Ireland, to make up for the absence of overt constitutional or statutory means of guarding the privacy of individuals. In these instances the individual can invoke equitable relief not because the statement or information is untrue and harmful (as in defamation) but because the information is probably true and harmful and is to be disclosed against the wishes of the person who confided it to others. Even after the passing into law of the UK Human Rights Act 1998 (HRA 1998), UK case law recognises the fact that a right to privacy does not exist in UK law.[23] English judges have been willing to press the law of confidence into service[24] rather than develop an entirely new common law cause of action.

[24.13] In the context of communications between a husband and wife it has been held that the law of confidence may prevent one of the partners from disclosing these communications as part of the relationship of trust that exists as between them, even if the proposed disclosure is to take place within the context of an acrimonious divorce case.[25] This principle was reshaped and extended further in *Stevens v Avery*[26] where Browne-Wilkinson VC refused to strike out an action in which the plaintiff invoked the law of confidence against a close friend who had passed on to a Sunday tabloid newspaper confidential information concerning the plaintiff's lesbian relationship with the victim of an unlawful killing, which resulted in a much publicised trial in which the victim's husband was convicted of manslaughter. Browne-Wilkinson VC rejected a submission that the law of confidence would not protect information about sexual proclivities, save where married partners are involved, and the learned judge observed

---

[19] Eg *Tuck & Sons v Priester* (1887) 19 QBD 629; *Pollard v Photographic Co* (1880) 40 Ch D 345; *Exchange Telegraph Co v Gregory* [1896] 1 QB 147; *Exchange Telegraph Co v Central News Ltd* [1897] 2 Ch 48.

[20] *Trego v Hunt* [1896] AC 7; *Gargan v Ruttle* [1931] IR 152.

[21] *A-G v Guardian Newspapers Ltd (No 2)* [1988] 3 All ER 545.

[22] *A-G v Guardian Newspapers Ltd (No 2)* [1988] 3 All ER 545 at 639.

[23] *Wainwright v Home Office* [2003] UKHL 53, [2003] 4 All ER 969; see *Hosking v Runting* [2004] NZCA 34. This decision has been criticised for the uncertainty the tort so created engenders: *Rogers v TVNZ Ltd* [2007] NZSC 91.

[24] Eg *Douglas v Hello! Ltd (No 3)* [2003] 3 All ER 996.

[25] *Duchess of Argyll v Duke of Argyll* [1967] Ch 302; *D v L* [2004] EMLR 1.

[26] *Stevens v Avery* [1988] 2 All ER 477.

that information about a person's sex life is 'high on their list of those matters which they regard as confidential'.[27] However, the absence of any general right of privacy in English law has led some courts to deny a plaintiff any remedy on the ground that a duty of confidence cannot arise as between a person seeking to make a private communication, on the one hand, and the communications organisation or individuals generally, on the other hand.[28] In a number of important decisions the English courts, in particular, have broadened the equitable duty of confidence to apply to disclosure situations where sensitive personal information falls into the hands of an individual or organisation and the person in question advances a privacy argument to restrain the use or disclosure of that information. The decision of the Court of Appeal in *Kaye v Robertson*[29] in 1991 indicated that while neither privacy nor confidentiality *per se* could fashion an injunction for the applicant, the tort of malicious falsehood could be called into play. But the fact that such an artificial argument was allowed to prevail constituted judicial acknowledgment that English law was clearly deficient in respect of affording general statutory or tortious protection for individual privacy.

[24.14] Isolated instances of privacy protection can, however, be identified. In wardship proceedings, injunctive relief may be given to preserve the anonymity of a child who is thus afforded a degree of protection from intrusive media activities arising out of criminal acts perpetrated by a parent.[30] 'Supergrasses' who are afforded new identities may also be entitled to protective injunctions.[31]

[24.15] However, decisions such as *Kaye v Robertson*[32] and *Malone v Metropolitan Police Comr*[33] represent the low water mark in the debate in English law over the protection of privacy. It is certainly evident from the view taken by the Court of Appeal in the proceedings brought to obtain interlocutory relief in *Douglas v Hello!*[34] that some members of the Court of Appeal were prepared to look at the privacy issue afresh. However, while English law still does not provide a tort of invasion of privacy, a number of legislative reliefs have transformed the landscape in UK law. HRA 1998, acting in concert with the European Convention on Human Rights (ECHR) and the recognition of freedom of expression as an important common law principle, requires a balance to be drawn between privacy rights (ECHR, art 8) and freedom of expression (art 10). Section 12 of HRA 1998 addresses the application of injunctive or other reliefs that affect

---

[27] *Stevens v Avery* [1988] 2 All ER 477 at 481.

[28] *Malone v Metropolitan Police Comr* [1979] 2 All ER 620. In *Malone v United Kingdom* (1984) 7 EHRR 14, the European Court of Human Rights found the UK to be in breach of the European Convention on Human Rights (ECHR), art 8. This led to the passing of the UK Interception of Communications Act 1985. In Ireland, see the Interception of Postal Packets and Telecommunications Messages (Regulation) Act 1993.

[29] *Kaye v Robertson* [1991] FSR 62. For a review of privacy rights in the common law see Moreham (2005) 121 LQR 628.

[30] *Re X (a minor)* [1984] I WLR 1422.

[31] *Nicholls v BBC* [1999] EMLR 791.

[32] *Kaye v Robertson* [1991] FSR 62.

[33] *Malone v Metropolitan Police Comr* [1979] 2 All ER 620.

[34] *Douglas v Hello!* [2001] FSR 732 (interlocutory proceedings).

freedom of expression and requires the court to consider a number of factors such as the likelihood that at the trial of the action the applicant will establish that publication should not be allowed.[35] In addition, of particular regard is the extent to which journalistic, literary or artistic material has or is about to become available to the public, whether it is in the public interest for the material to be published, and the terms of any privacy code.[36] It is of interest to note that in the cases that have followed on from HRA 1998, the English courts have tended to retain the view that the privacy interest is still to be subsumed within the law of confidence. Lord Phillips MR, however, in *Campbell v MGN Ltd*,[37] mapped out a new approach when he observed that the:

> development of the law of confidentiality since HRA 1998 came into force has seen inspiration described as 'confidential' not where it has been confined by one person to another, but where it relates to an aspect of the individual's private life which he does not choose to make public. We consider that the unjustifiable publication of such information would be better described as breach of privacy rather than breach of confidence.[38]

[24.16] The cases in which freedom of expression has been abridged by reference to the law of confidence/privacy are compelling ones. In *Venables v News Group Newspapers Ltd*,[39] Butler-Sloss P held that the High Court had jurisdiction to restrain publication about the personal circumstances of Venables and Thompson, the persons convicted of the murder of Jamie Bulger. Disclosure of details about the whereabouts of the applicants would result, in particular, in the risk of serious harm or death to the applicants, thus raising not just privacy considerations under art 8 of ECHR but also art 2, the right to life. In the later case of *X (A woman formerly known as Mary Bell) and Y v O'Brien*,[40] lifetime injunctions to restrain publication of information concerning X, a person convicted of two still notorious child murders and Y, her daughter, were obtained on the basis of the risk of apprehended harm to X, her physical and mental state. Award of the injunction to protect Y was merited on the basis that her situation was to all practical effects indistinguishable from that of her mother. In contrast, freedom of expression has taken precedence over privacy concerns in relation to allegations of sexual misconduct by a then married soccer player, Gary Flitcroft,[41] and by the television presenter, Jamie Theakston.[42] There are cases in which the privacy interest has been

---

35 HRA 1998, s 12(3); a negative answer precludes the grant of relief on whether the claimant is 'likely' to establish at trial that publication should not be allowed: see *Cream Holdings Ltd v Banerjee* [2003] Ch 650. See Irvine J in *Murray v Newsgroup Newspapers Ltd* [2010] IEHC 248 on the relevance of *Cream Holdings* in Ireland.

36 HRA 1998, s 12(4).

37 *Campbell v MGN Ltd* [2003] 2 WLR 80.

38 *Campbell v MGN Ltd* [2003] 2 WLR 80 at 90.

39 *Venables v News Group Newspapers Ltd* [2001] Fam 430; contrast *WB v H Bauer Publishing Ltd* [2002] EMLR 145.

40 *X (A woman formerly known as Mary Bell) and Y v O'Brien* [2003] EWHC 1101 (QB), [2003] EMLR 850.

41 *A v B plc* [2003] QB 195; *Terry v Persons Unknown* [2010] EWHC 119 (QB).

42 *Theakston v MGN Ltd* [2002] EWHC 137; see, however, *Barrymore v News Group Newspapers* [1997] FSR 600. (contd.../)

legitimately invoked by a celebrity but the freedom of the press has been upheld. In *Mills v News Group Newspapers Ltd*,[43] Heather Mills was unsuccessful in seeking an injunction to restrain *The Sun* from publishing details of her address, citing fears for her safety in the light of her relationship with Sir Paul McCartney and the attacks on two other members of the Beatles. More controversially still, the Court of Appeal denied damages to Naomi Campbell[44] in respect of the use of information about involvement in a drug rehabilitation program but the House of Lords,[45] by a majority of three to two, has reinstated the finding of the High Court that the use of photographic images of the plaintiff leaving a drug treatment centre infringed her right of privacy, and publication in this case could not be justified in the public interest. The limited decisions to date suggest that the English courts will incline towards upholding freedom of expression save in respect of instances of a real and appreciable risk of physical or mental harm or where the media intend to use information that is clearly in breach of a relevant code of practice. It should also be recalled that the use of confidentiality clauses, either in a formal contract document of the kind that is to be expected by a celebrity or a public figure[46] or in respect of certain kinds of employment,[47] may still be of great utility in inhibiting the use of unauthorised photographs or other confidential information. The leading case is *Douglas v Hello! Ltd*[48] in which Lindsay J took the view that the plaintiffs' celebrity wedding, by invitation only, was a private event. When photographs were covertly taken, in breach of the wishes of the plaintiffs, this constituted a trespass by defendants who were aware that their conduct was unconscionable. In such circumstances Lindsay J felt that the freedom of expression of the defendants was overborne by the plaintiffs' right to maintain confidence in information relating to their wedding. The *Douglas* case clearly finds that privacy can be supported via a cause of action for breach of confidence although the trial judge was anxious to stress that he was

---

42. (\...contd) Mr Theakston's transgressions were really 'public space' events. In contrast, a reasonable expectation of privacy in respect of private sexual conduct, especially when there is some covert recording of the details of this activity will not be trumped by freedom of expression unless a public interest test can be satisfied and the publication is proportionate: *Mosley v News Group Newspapers Ltd* [2008] EWHC 1777. Difficulties about a person's marriage will be privacy protected: *X and Y v Persons Unknown* [2006] EWHC 2783 (QB); *McKennitt v Ash* [2007] 3 WLR 194.

43. *Mills v News Group Newspapers Ltd* [2001] EWHC 412 (Ch), [2001] EMLR 957.

44. *Campbell v MGN Ltd* [2003] 2 WLR 80. The plaintiff pleaded breach of ECHR rights and liability under the UK Data Protection Act 1998; see in Ireland the Data Protection (Amendment) Act 2003, s 21 and the ECJ decision *Criminal Proceedings Against Lindqvist* Case C-101/01 [2004] 1 WLR 1385.

45. *Campbell v MGN Ltd* [2004] 2 All ER 995.

46. See 'Lady Archer wins gag order on Surgery' (2002) The Times, 16 March in which information about cosmetic surgery received by Lady Archer was the subject of injunctive relief and reported at [2003] EMLR 869. See also 'Jagger seeks Satisfaction in Court' (2002) Daily Telegraph, 13 June in which Mick Jagger sought to restrain a book of memoirs written by his former chauffeur.

47. *Douglas v Hello! Ltd (No 3)* [2003] 3 All ER 996.

48. *Donnelly v Amalgamated Television Services Pty* (1998) 45 NSWLR 570.

not making any findings in relation to a law of privacy. The sense of humiliation that follows on from intrusive photography has also been held to be a relevant consideration, but not illegal means *per se*.[49]

[24.17] Information obtained by law enforcement agencies may also be the subject of duties of confidence. In *DPP (Commonwealth) v Kane*[50] advices from the DPP were inadvertently sent to counsel for the defendant. The duty of confidence was imposed on defence counsel who were required to deliver up the documents in question. In *Hellewell v Chief Constable of Derbyshire*,[51] the duty of confidence was held to apply to the police who fingerprinted and photographed the plaintiff in connection with theft offences for which he was later convicted. The police later released the photographs to traders who were concerned to identify persons who may have been involved in a spate of shoplifting and harassment of shopkeepers in the Nottingham area. Laws J held that a duty of confidence could exist, after the *Spycatcher* litigation,[52] simply out of a relationship between the parties without a need for express notice. The police were thus under a duty, which in this instance required them to make reasonable use of such information as they possessed. Laws J concluded, however, that there were sufficient surrounding circumstances to justify the limited disclosure that had taken place.

[24.18] It is also evident that the police owe a duty to provide informants with protection against the public disclosure of information provided in confidence.[53] This may arise out of the duty of confidence itself or may be enforceable via an action in negligence, as in *Swinney* where there was a relationship between the police and the informant that gave rise to a duty of care. Prior to the judicial development of a right to privacy, Irish judges had resorted to developing a duty of care in negligence when members of An Garda Siochána carried out their duties in a way that could cause distress and embarrassment, specifically leaking information to the media.[54] In *Gray v Minister for Justice*,[55] the wrongful disclosure of confidential and sensitive information about a convicted sex offender residing in the home of the plaintiffs was held to be a violation of their constitutional right to privacy, following *Kennedy and Arnold v Ireland*.[56] The situation was held not to be one in which a careful and deliberate decision was made in order to protect others[57] but, rather, the gardaí confirmed the details of the information when asked to do so by a news reporter.[58] Once the right to privacy is engaged in these circumstances, the balancing exercise will require the court to consider the risks posed

---

49 *ABC Ltd v Lenah Game Meats Pty* (2001) 54 IPR 161.
50 *DPP (Commonwealth) v Kane* [1997] 140 FLR 468.
51 *Hellewell v Chief Constable of Derbyshire* [1995] 4 All ER 473. See Fenwick and Phillipson (1996) 55 CLJ 447; Wee Loon [1996] EIPR 307.
52 *A-G v Guardian Newspapers Ltd (No 2)* [1988] 3 All ER 545.
53 *Swinney v Chief Constable of Northumbria (No 2)* (1999) Times, 25 May.
54 *Hanahoe v Hussey* [1998] 3 IR 69.
55 *Gray v Minister for Justice* [2007] 2 IR 654.
56 *Kennedy and Arnold v Ireland* [1987] IR 587
57 *R v Chief Constable of North Wales Police* [1999] 1 QB 396; *R (Ellis) v Chief Constable of Essex Police* [2003] EWHC 1321.
58 Contrast *Murray v Newsgroup Newspapers Ltd* [2010] IEHC 248.

by the criminal and potential harm that the criminal may experience should information be put into the public domain. The issue generally involves a proportionality exercise to be undertaken on a case-by-case basis,[59] although some statutory provisions have recently been added by s 62 of the Garda Síochána Act 2005.

[24.19] The most highly publicised recent advance in relation to the duty of confidence has occurred in England and in other common law jurisdictions, including Ireland, when the State, in the form of state security agencies, has tried to restrain former operatives from profiting from memoirs that may compromise the interests of national security. In *A-G v Guardian Newspapers Ltd (No 2)*,[60] the House of Lords indicated that a member of MI5, Peter Wright, owed a life-long, world-wide duty of confidence to the Crown, which he had breached by publishing his book *Spycatcher*, initially in the US, an act which Lord Jauncey described as one that 'reeked of turpitude'. Their Lordships had to consider the extent to which newspapers that had either reported or reviewed the book, or overseas proceedings intended to restrain overseas publication, or serialised the work, could be restrained by injunction in the English courts. In affirming the decision of the Court of Appeal, their Lordships endorsed a number of earlier cases in which civil servants[61] and Cabinet Ministers,[62] who sought to put confidential information into the public domain by publication with a third party, were caught by the equitable duty but that publication could be permitted unless the State can show that publication would be harmful to the public interest. It may be that a privacy interest and another legitimate interest, such as the desire to ensure the efficient and dignified administration of justice, may combine to counterbalance the broader public interest in freedom of the press.[63] It is certainly arguable that most public documents should be published and the Australian courts have inclined towards drawing a distinction between government documents and commercial documents: *Minister for Mineral Resources v Newcastle Newspapers Pty.*[64] On the other hand, the Freedom of Information Acts 1997–2003 could be said to mark the boundaries of the public interest on this matter and how an Irish court will address this policy factor remains to be seen.

[24.20] One of the significant features of the *Spycatcher* litigation[65] concerned the extent to which one State would uphold a duty of confidence owed not to its own State but to those of a friendly democratic State.[66] In Australia, the High Court held that an Australian court should decline to accept jurisdiction to enforce a duty of confidence owed to a foreign government. The New Zealand decision in *A-G v Wellington Newspapers Ltd*[67] suggested that jurisdiction would be taken but no real public interest

---

59 *Callaghan v Independent News & Media Ltd* [2009] NIQB 1.
60 *A-G v Guardian Newspapers Ltd (No 2)* [1988] 3 All ER 545; *R v Shayler* [2002] UKHL 11, [2003] 1 AC 247, [2002] 2 WLR 754.
61 *Commonwealth of Australia v John Fairfax & Sons Ltd* (1980) 32 ALR 485.
62 *A-G v Jonathan Cape Ltd* [1975] 3 All ER 484.
63 *Wiggington v Brisbane TV Ltd* (1992) 25 IPR 58.
64 *Minister for Mineral Resources v Newcastle Newspapers Pty* (1997) 40 IPR 403.
65 *A-G v Guardian Newspapers Ltd (No 2)* [1988] 3 All ER 545.
66 *A-G (UK) v Heinemann Publishers Australia Property* (1988) 78 ALR 449.
67 *A-G v Wellington Newspapers Ltd* (28 April 1988, unreported), HC.

to justify the award of an injunction was evident. In Ireland the approach taken by Carroll J in *A-G for England and Wales v Brandon Books*[68] is broadly in sympathy with the view that Irish constitutional requirements outweigh the secrecy interests of foreign powers, for here the High Court refused to grant an injunction to restrain the defendant from publishing *One Woman's War*, the memoirs of a British security operative during the 1939–45 War. Carroll J observed of the duty of secrecy visited on Crown employees in the context of Irish law:

> The publication which is sought to be prevented here is not a private confidence or trade information but information shared between a government and a private individual. It seems to me that a distinction can and should be drawn between a government and a private person. This was considered in the Australian case *Commonwealth of Australia v John Fairfax & Sons Ltd*.[69] Mason J says as follows:
>
> > 'The equitable principle has been fashioned to protect the personal, private and proprietary rights of the citizen, not to protect the very different interests of the executive government. It acts, or is supposed to act, not according to standards of private interest, but in the public interest. This is not to say that equity will not protect information in the hands of the government, but it is to say that when equity protects government information it will look at the matter through different spectacles.
> >
> > It may be a sufficient detriment to the citizen that disclosure of information relating to his affairs will expose his actions to public discussion and criticism. But it can scarcely be a relevant detriment to the government that publication of material concerning its actions will merely expose it to public discussion and criticism. It is unacceptable in our democratic society that there should be a restraint on the publication of information relating to government when the only vice of that information is that it enables the public to discuss, review and criticise government action.
> >
> > Accordingly, the Court will determine the government's claim to confidentiality by reference to the public interest. Unless disclosure is likely to injure the public interest, it will not be protected.' (at p 51)
>
> I consider that correctly states the law. Mason J was talking there in the context of the Government of Australia asking the courts of Australia to restrain publication where the question of public interest did arise and which would arise here if the Government of Ireland were the plaintiff. But here the plaintiff is the representative of a foreign government. There is no question of the public interest of this State being affected. The considerations which would move the courts in the United Kingdom in this matter are different to the considerations here.'[70]

[24.21] Two recent cases underline the importance of being able to utilise a breach of contract action rather than the law of confidence. Private law transactions between secret service operatives on the one hand and the government on the other are freely enforceable and may lead to the award of restitutionary or 'disgorgement' damages.[71] In

---

[68] *A-G for England and Wales v Brandon Books* [1987] ILRM 135.
[69] *Commonwealth of Australia v John Fairfax & Sons Ltd* (1980) 147 CLR 39.
[70] *A-G for England and Wales v Brandon Books* [1987] ILRM 135 at 136–137.
[71] *A-G v Blake* [2001] 1 AC 268.

contrast to the *Brandon Books* case,[72] the Attorney-General for England and Wales has been successful in using basic contract law to enforce an agreement in the New Zealand courts, which was entered into by a serving officer in the SAS and the Crown.[73] *Brandon Books* seems to reflect the correct approach in Ireland, however, freedom of the press 'the right to say things which "right thinking people" regard as dangerous or irresponsible ... is subject only to clearly defined exceptions laid down by common law or statute'[74]. Where the right to communicate information, as distinct from opinions, is concerned, the weight of opinion appears to favour the view that Article 40.6.1° of the Constitution protects dissemination of information as well as the expression of convictions and opinions. In *Mahon v Post Publications*,[75] a majority of the Supreme Court declined to award injunctive relief in respect of information provided to the Mahon Tribunal on the basis of an understanding that it would be kept confidential. Information was being leaked to the press but the Supreme Court held that assurances made to disclosees on confidentiality could not of themselves make out the necessary 'clearly defined exception' to freedom of expression. After providing a cogent analysis of the law of confidence the Supreme Court, agreeing with Kelly J at first instance,[76] held that much of the material did not have the necessary quality of confidence and that the relief sought was not proportionate.

[24.22] Whether Irish law will develop along the same lines as the more recent English decisions vis-à-vis the privacy interest is perhaps in doubt. Irish constitutional law recognises a number of personal rights such as the right of a citizen to a good name[77] and the right to a livelihood[78] as well as the right to protect property.[79] In an important contractual action, *O'Keeffe v Ryanair Ltd*,[80] Kelly J in the High Court upheld the validity of a contract between an airline and a customer in which the consideration that moved from the customer was the forbearance to exercise rights of privacy and anonymity and a willingness to be involved in a publicity campaign with the airline. These rights must be balanced and are not such as to require the State to provide absolute guarantees to citizens, so many of the factors that are relevant in a confidence action are broadly relevant to judicial activism under these constitutional parameters. While case law on Articles 40.3.2° and 43 of the Constitution of Ireland are somewhat inconclusive on many points of detail concerning these express constitutional rights, the courts have identified an unenumerated personal right to privacy in Article 40.3. While

---

72 *A-G for England and Wales v Brandon Books* [1987] ILRM 135.
73 *A-G for England and Wales v R* [2002] 2 NZLR 91, affirmed by the Privy Council at [2003] UKPC 22.
74 Hoffmann L.J. in *R v Central Independent Television plc* [1994] 3 WLR 20, followed by Fennelly J in *Mahon v Post Publications* [2007] 3 IR 338.
75 *Irish Times v Ireland* [1998] 1 IR 349; *Murphy v IRTC* [1999] 1 IR 12.
76 *Mahon v Post Publications* [2005] IEHC 307 (4 October 2005); see also *Cogley v RTE* [2005] IEHC 180.
77 Constitution of Ireland, art 40.3.2°: eg *Re Haughey* [1972] IR 217.
78 Constitution of Ireland, art 40.3.2°: eg *Lovett Transport v Gogan* [1995] 2 ILRM 12.
79 Constitution of Ireland, arts 40.3.2° and 43.
80 *O'Keeffe v Ryanair Ltd* [2003] 1 ILRM 14.

the decisions on this initially addressed privacy within the context of marital and sexual privacy,[81] the decision in *Kennedy and Arnold v Ireland*[82] involved a case where Ministerial authorisation of wiretapping which failed to meet a number of internal administrative guidelines was conceded to be unlawful by the State. However, Hamilton P went further in finding the State had infringed the citizens' right to privacy and damages were awarded to the plaintiffs. Hamilton P indicated that the right is not absolute and is subject to the requirements of public order and morality. On the facts of this case there was no real attempt to argue that the State security interest would take priority over the citizens' privacy right. *Kennedy and Arnold*, however, highlights a different solution to the privacy plea that was so unsuccessful in the High Court in England in *Malone v Metropolitan Police Comr*,[83] at least on the issue of the possibility of a plea of invasion of privacy as a specific cause of action.[84]

[24.23] In *X v Drury*,[85] interlocutory injunctions were sought by a young woman who had been the complainant in a sexual abuse case. She had given interviews to members of the press, including the defendant and sought to prevent publication on the grounds, *inter alia*, that the journalists had not respected her constitutional right to privacy. Costello J expressly distinguished the older English case law on privacy, pointing out that constitutionally protected rights to privacy were at issue in the instant proceedings. While referring to the contrasting interests of freedom of the press and the right of journalists to communicate and carry out their professional duties, the balance of convenience lay in protecting the privacy rights of the plaintiff vis-à-vis her family life. It should be noted that this case goes further than *Stevens v Avery*[86] in so far as the decision of Browne-Wilkinson VC was simply that the confider's action to protect her confidence was not to be struck out. In *X v Drury* the court was more proactive in granting a broad measure of interlocutory relief. However, *X v Drury* is not the last word on this point for in *MM v Drury*[87] O'Hanlon J limited the concept of marital privacy by holding that such rights could not prevent an estranged husband from giving to the press details about his wife's sexual affair with a Roman Catholic priest: here the balancing process was held to favour the freedom of the press and the approach of O'Hanlon J in *MM v Drury* appears to be in sharp contrast to the English decision of *Duchess of Argyll v Duke of Argyll*.[88]

[24.24] In *Herrity v Independent Newspapers Ltd*[89] the defendants, with the assistance of the plaintiff's estranged husband, published newspaper articles and photographs

---

[81] *McGee v A-G* [1974] IR 284; *Norris v A-G* [1984] IR 36.

[82] *Kennedy and Arnold v Ireland* [1987] IR 587.

[83] *Malone v Metropolitan Police Comr* [1979] 2 All ER 620.

[84] The decision in *Malone v United Kingdom* (1984) 7 EHRR 14, however, made it necessary for Irish administrative practices on telephone tapping to be put on a statutory footing through the Interception of Postal Packets and Telecommunications Messages (Regulation) Act 1993.

[85] *X v Drury* (19 May 1994, unreported), HC.

[86] *Stevens v Avery* [1988] 2 All ER 477.

[87] *MM v Drury* [1994] 2 IR 8.

[88] *Duchess of Argyll v Duke of Argyll* [1967] Ch 302.

[89] *Herrity v Independent Newspapers Ltd* [2008] IEHC 249.

detailing the plaintiff's romantic involvement with a Roman Catholic priest. Information was gathered from telephone conversations recorded by Mr Herrity without the plaintiff's permission and contrary to s 98 of the Postal and Telecommunications Services Act 1983, as amended. While Dunne J was prepared to acknowledge that the defendants had a right to freedom of expression and that in some circumstances the public interest might be served by outlining the failings of a person such as a priest who enjoys a position of public trust, the purpose behind these publications was to make use of materials obtained from Mr Herrity to violate the plaintiff's privacy rather than inform the public that the priest was having an affair. Because the Oireachtas had provided legislative protection against private telephone conversations being recorded without consent, the right to privacy should prevail over any freedom of expression interest claimed by either the defendants or Mr Herrity, even in circumstances where the information is accurately reported. Dunne J dealt with the public interest argument by referring back to s 98 of the 1983 Act: 'I can see no basis for saying that the public interest arising on the facts of this case could be such as to set at naught the restriction on the disclosure of telecommunications messages prohibited by s 98'.[90] The learned judge also placed some emphasis on the weight of the publications being directed at the plaintiff's post-marital behaviour rather than any clerical misconduct. This balancing exercise is also evident in *Oblique Financial Services v Promise Production Co*,[91] where the publishers and editor of *Phoenix* magazine were the subject of interlocutory proceedings brought to prevent the firm publishing confidential information that was the subject of an express contractual provision between the plaintiffs and the defendants' sources. Keane J held that the constitutional rights of citizens to convey information arose under Article 40.3.1° and that this right could be subject to other rights and duties, particularly the right to confidentiality. The injunction was granted. This balancing exercise will not always come out in favour of a confidentiality clause being upheld because countervailing constitutional principles, to say nothing of the restraint of trade doctrine, may be invoked to tilt the balance the other way. The fact that the contract contains covenants against misuse of confidential information does not weaken any clause preventing a former employee from taking up employment with a competitor. Difficulties in determining what is confidential and whether a breach has occurred makes the non-compete clause enforceable if it satisfies the restraint of trade doctrine.[92]

THE DUTY OF CONFIDENCE IN A COMMERCIAL CONTEXT

[24.25] While the discussion in the preceding paragraphs suggests an enhanced role for the law of confidence, it should be noted that most of the modern cases have addressed the duty within the context of commercially valuable information, a context that does

---

[90] *Herrity v Independent Newspapers Ltd* [2008] IEHC 249, distinguishing *A v B plc* [2003] QB 195.

[91] *Oblique Financial Services v Promise Production Co* [1994] ILRM 74. See also *A-G (Australia) v Burton* (2003) 58 IPR 268.

[92] *Littlewoods Organisaton v Harris* [1977] 1 WLR 1472; *Turner v Commonwealth v British Minerals Ltd* [2000] IRLR 114; *Dyson Techonology v Strutt* [2005] EWHC 2814 (Ch).

not readily raise privacy or other human rights issues. The decision of the Court of Appeal in *Saltman Engineering Ltd v Campbell Engineering Co Ltd*,[93] decided in 1948, represents the most significant reformation of the equitable duty, for later cases, particularly in the extremely active period between 1963 and 1969, defer to this case as the most influential summary of the law in such a context. The plaintiffs provided the defendants with access to design drawings needed by the defendants in furtherance of a contract whereby the defendants would manufacture machine tools on behalf of the plaintiffs. The defendants used the drawings for their own purposes and were the subject of proceedings for breach of contract and breach of confidence. Lord Greene MR characterised the rights of action as existing without the necessity of there being a contractual relationship and he approved, as the basic principle, that where:

> a defendant is proved to have used confidential information, directly or indirectly obtained from a plaintiff, without the consent, express or implied, of the plaintiff, he will be guilty of an infringement of the plaintiff's rights.[94]

Lord Greene's reference to 'express consent' requires a short consideration of how non-disclosure agreement may abridge the scope of the equitable duty. There is Canadian authority suggesting that where a non-disclosure agreement sets a non-disclosure threshold that is higher than that set by principles of confidentiality, the contract will modify both the relationship and the extent of the confidentiality obligation[95] in the sense that the low threshold for equitable protection may be irrelevant when a non-disclosure agreement indicates that disclosure use of low level information is permissible.

[24.26] In contrast, publication is not likely to be inhibited unless a clearly defined exception in law or an overriding public interest will be made out[96] In contrast to the successful plaintiff in *Gray v Minister for Justice*,[97] the plaintiff in *Murray v Newsgroup Newspapers Ltd*[98] was unsuccessful in obtaining sweeping injunctive reliefs to prevent newspapers from publishing photographs and information upon the plaintiff's whereabouts; the plaintiff had a history of committing serious sexual offences in the UK and within the State, and a number of newspapers were featuring information about the plaintiff. While pleading a constitutional right to privacy as well as some incitement and harassment offences, the plaintiff also invoked ECHR jurisprudence, arguing, in particular, that the restrictions in art 10.2 should be applied. Irvine J. distinguished this case from *Venables v News Group Newspapers*[99] and *Callaghan v Independent News and*

---

93 *Saltman Engineering Ltd v Campbell Engineering Co Ltd* (1948) 65 RPC 203. The case was decided in 1948 but more widely reported at [1963] 3 All ER 413.

94 *Saltman Engineering Ltd v Campbell Engineering Co Ltd* (1948) 65 RPC 203 at 211, cited with approval by O'Higgins CJ in *House of Spring Gardens v Point Blank Ltd* [1984] IR 611.

95 *Cadbury Schweppes Inc v FBI Foods Ltd* [1999] SCC 142; *Aram Systems Ltd v NovAtel Inc* (2008) 76 CPR (4th) 175, leave to appeal to SCC has been refused.

96 *Mahon v Post Publications* [2007] 3 IR 338.

97 *Gray v Minister for Justice* [2007] 2 IR 654; *Callaghan v Independent News and Media Ltd* [2009] NIQB 1.

98 *Murray v Newsgroup Newspapers Ltd* [2010] IEHC 248.

99 *Venables v News Group Newspapers* [2001] Fam 430.

Media on the basis that no exhortation to do violence to the plaintiff had been set out and that the plaintiff, unlike *Callaghan*, had provided little in the form of cogent evidence that he was unlikely to offend again. Prior restraint orders of the kind he sought necessitated the plaintiff showing that there was a real threat to his life or that he was likely to succeed at the trial of the action. Irvine J. also put the public interest in knowing the whereabouts of the applicant into the scales on the side of allowing freedom of expression. It is necessary however to clearly distinguish the various applicants. In the light of recent developments, O'Hanlon J's judgment in *MM v Drury*[100] may be said to have undervalued the privacy interests of the children of the marriage: see in particular *Murray v Big Pictures (UK) Ltd*[101] on balancing family members' interests.

[24.27] Lord Denning MR in *Seager v Copydex Ltd*[102] followed the judgment of Lord Greene MR in *Saltman Engineering*[103] and observed that:

> The law on this subject does not depend on any implied contract. It depends on the broad principle of equity that he who has received information in confidence shall not take unfair advantage of it. He must not make use of it to the prejudice of him who gave it without obtaining his consent.[104]

[24.28] However, in an Irish context, the decision of Megarry J in *Coco v AN Clark (Engineers) Ltd*[105] and the decision of the same judge in *Thomas Marshall (Exports) Ltd v Guinle*[106] provide the basis for formulating the leading judicial statement on what must be provided to sustain a breach of confidence action.

[24.29] In *House of Spring Gardens v Point Blank Ltd*,[107] Costello J said:

> The court, it should be borne in mind, is being asked to enforce what is essentially a moral obligation. It must firstly decide whether there exists from the relationship between the parties an obligation of confidence regarding the information which has been imparted and it must then decide whether the information which was communicated can properly be regarded as confidential information. In considering both (i) the relationship and (ii) the nature of the information, it is relevant to take into account the degree of skill, time and labour involved in compiling the information. As to (i), if the informant himself has expended skill, time and labour on compiling the information, then he can reasonably regard it as of value and he can reasonably consider that he is conferring on its recipient a benefit. If this benefit is conferred for a specific purpose then an obligation may be imposed to use it for that purpose and for no other purpose. As to (ii), if the information has been compiled by the expenditure of skill, time and labour by the informant then, although he has obtained it from sources which are public, (in the sense that any member of the public with the same skills could obtain it had he acted like the compiler of the

---

[100] *MM v Drury* [1994] 2 IR 8.

[101] *Murray v Big Pictures (UK) Ltd* [2008] WLR 1360; *Hosking v Runting* [2004] NZCA 34.

[102] *Seager v Copydex Ltd* [1967] 1 WLR 923.

[103] *Saltman Engineering Ltd v Campbell Engineering Co Ltd* (1948) 65 RPC 203.

[104] *Seager v Copydex Ltd* [1967] 1 WLR 923 at 931, cited with approval by Griffin J in *House of Spring Gardens v Point Blank Ltd* [1984] IR 611.

[105] *Coco v AN Clark (Engineers) Ltd* [1968] FSR 415.

[106] *Thomas Marshall (Exports) Ltd v Guinle* [1978] 3 All ER 193.

[107] *House of Spring Gardens v Point Blank Ltd* [1984] IR 611.

information) the information may still, because of its value, be regarded as 'confidential' information and subject to an obligation of confidence. Furthermore, the court will readily decide that the informant correctly regarded the information he was imparting as confidential information if, although based on material which is accessible to the public, it is of a unique nature which has resulted from the skill and labour of the informant. Once it is established that an obligation in confidence exists and that the information is confidential, then the person to whom it is given has a duty to act in good faith, and this means that he must use the information for the purpose for which it has been imparted, and he cannot use it to the detriment of the informant.[108]

[24.30] This approach must be regarded as the definitive Irish statement on the general judicial approach to breach of confidence actions for in the Supreme Court O'Higgins CJ specifically endorsed this part of Costello J's judgment[109] while Griffin J concurred with the Chief Justice on the basic approach to be adopted, confining himself to issues of assessment and quantum. It is to the specific issues that Costello J's judgment addresses that we must now turn.

The relationship between the parties – does it create an obligation of confidence vis-à-vis the information imparted?

The contract

[24.31] The most obvious relationship in which the duty may arise is a contractual relationship. Clearly, if the parties have a contractual relationship which raises a number of positive obligations, breach of those obligations, express or implied, will be actionable contractually and under the duty of confidence. Thus, giving design drawings,[110] preparatory material like moulds,[111] plates,[112] lists of clients and customers,[113] trade samples and specimen products,[114] levels of commission or profit margins,[115] a recipe for a clam and tomato soup,[116] or instruction on how to teach innovative dance steps[117] for the use of others, imports express/implied duties of confidence. Specific contractual relationships, however, create a range of circumstances in which there may or may not be commensurate duties of confidence. In the arena of employment contracts, for example, an employee owes a duty of fidelity to the employer and while the major features of this duty depend upon the existence of the contractual relationship, there are certain duties that survive the termination of the employment relationship and it is also possible, of course, for the scope of these duties to be

---

108 *House of Spring Gardens v Point Blank Ltd* [1984] IR 611 at 663.
109 In *House of Spring Gardens v Point Blank Ltd* [1984] IR 611.
110 Eg *Tuck & Sons v Priester* (1887) 19 QBD 629.
111 *Ackroyds (London) Ltd v Islington Plastics Ltd* [1962] RPC 97.
112 *Prince Albert v Strange* (1849) 1 Mac & G 25; *Banco de Portugal v Waterlow* (1933) 47 TLR 214.
113 *Forkserve Property Ltd v Fenely* (2001) 52 IPR 563.
114 *X Ltd v Nowacki* [2003] EWHC 1928 (Ch).
115 *Indata Equipment Supplies Ltd v ACL Ltd* [1998] FSR 248.
116 *Cadbury Schweppes Inc v FBI Foods Ltd* [2000] FSR 491.
117 *Pastor v Chen* (2002) 19 CPR (4th) 206.

broadened, both in scope and duration, by express agreement. Thus the employee, during the currency of the contract, is not to use his master's time and facilities to further his own interests by making use of information[118] soliciting customers of the master,[119] even if the employee intends to do business with those persons after the termination of the contract. Nor is the employee to compete with the master during the currency of the employment contract or aid a competitor by 'moonlighting' outside of contracted hours.[120] The duty is based upon the relationship of trust and confidence that is a consequence of the contract. However, the ability of the employer to rely upon this implied duty to protect information from post-termination use by an employee is now circumscribed by the decision of the Court of Appeal in *Faccenda Chicken Ltd v Fowler*,[121] a case which tilts the balance in favour of allowing information, which is not seen as a trade secret but rather part of the general mode of doing business, to be used by competitors when an employment contract is at an end.

[24.32] The Court of Appeal, in *Faccenda Chicken*, limited the scope of the implied contractual term against disclosure of commercially valuable information to two instances:[122]

[i] While the employee remains in the employment of the employer the obligations are included in the implied term which imposes a duty of good faith or fidelity on the employee. For the purpose of the present appeal it is not necessary to consider the precise limits of this implied term, but it may be noted: (a) that the extent of the duty of good faith will vary according to the nature of the contract (see *Vokes Ltd v Heather* [[1997] FSR 34]); (b) that the duty of good faith will be broken if an employee makes or copies a list of the customers of the employer for use after his employment ends or deliberately memorises such a list, even though, except in special circumstances, there is no general restriction on an ex-employee canvassing or doing business with customers of his former employer (see *Robb v Green* [1895] 2 QB 315; [1895–99] All ER Rep 1053 and *Wessex Diaries Ltd v Smith* [1935] All ER Rep 75).

[ii] The implied term which imposes an obligation on the employee as to his conduct after the determination of employment is more restricted in its scope than that which imposes a general duty of good faith. It is clear that the obligation not to use or disclose information may cover secret processes of manufacture such as chemical formulae (see *Amber Size and Chemical Co Ltd v Menzel* [1913] 2 Ch 239), or designs or special methods of construction (see *Reid Sigrist Ltd v Moss Mechanism Ltd* (1932) 49 RPC 461), and other information which is of a sufficiently high degree of confidentiality as to amount to a trade secret. The obligation does not extend, however, to cover all information which is given to or acquired by the employee while in his employment, and in particular may not cover information which is only 'confidential' in the sense that an unauthorised disclosure

---

[118] *Robb v Green* [1895] 2 QB 1; *AF Associates v Ralston [1973] NI 229; Universal Thermosensors Ltd v Hibben* [1992] FSR 361; *X Ltd v Nowacki* [2003] EWHC 1928 (Ch).

[119] *Robb v Green* [1895] 2 QB 1; *Wessex Dairies v Smith* [1935] 2 KB 80; *Libra Rollaroy Pty Ltd v Angeli* (1997) 39 IPR 549.

[120] *Hivac Ltd v Park Royal Scientific Instruments* [1946] Ch 169.

[121] *Faccenda Chicken Ltd v Fowler* [1986] 1 All ER 617. *Purvis and Turner* [1988] EIPR 3; Hull [1989] EIPR 319; Stewart [1989] EIPR 88 cites *Faccenda* and its use in other jurisdictions.

[122] *Faccenda Chicken Ltd v Fowler* [1986] 1 All ER 617 at 625, *per* O'Neill LJ.

of such information to a third party which the employment subsisted would be a clear breach of the duty of good faith.

[24.33] This decision is a controversial one, and it has not been followed by later judges in all respects.[123] However, the implied term, as a judicially constructed device, does possess the merits of flexibility and responsiveness. The nature of the term, the duration of the term, and the boundary between compliance and breach, can be set on a case by case basis.[124] The most important instances of unauthorised appropriation of information in the context of breaches of implied terms have involved the unauthorised dissemination of information by subscribers to an information service. Third-party disclosure that prejudiced the interests of the service provider was held to constitute a flagrant breach of an implied contract. These decisions,[125] while over a century old, will prove very pertinent in the age of electronic database subscription services. The absence of a contract may be a significant obstacle; however, the important English decision in *PCR Ltd v Dow Jones Telerate Ltd*[126] suggests that the fact that information is provided to subscribers only will neither raise an implied term, nor will it of itself communicate to third parties actual or even constructive knowledge that the information itself is confidential. Similarly, in *Mars UK v Teknowledge Ltd*[127] the fact that information itself was encrypted did not *per se* communicate to users the message that this information was confidential. If the information is not commercially sensitive or there are no real efforts taken to safeguard the database or confine access to senior personnel then confidentiality will be difficult to establish.[128]

[24.34] Whether the scope of the duty will be universal in the sense that all employees will be caught by it to the same degree is unlikely. Clearly an employee who comes into contact with trade secrets, confidential information and the like will be caught by the duty, but where the employee is menial,[129] as distinct from being a director or managing director,[130] there may be no obvious commercial interest worthy of protection. Later cases suggest *Faccenda*[131] cannot be taken too far. In *Wallace Bogan & Co v Cove*[132] the appellants left the employment of the respondent firm of solicitors and established a new practice. The appellants wrote to clients of the respondent firm to inform these clients about this fact and the areas of specialisation. The respondent objected to these acts of solicitation and obtained an interlocutory injunction. The Court of Appeal discharged

---

[123] *Systems Reliability Holdings plc v Smith* [1990] IRLR 377.

[124] *Liverpool City Council v Irwin* [1977] AC 239.

[125] Eg *Exchange Telegraph v Gregory* [1896] 1 QB 147; *Exchange Telegraph v Central News* [1897] 2 Ch 48.

[126] *PCR Ltd v Dow Jones Telerate Ltd* [1998] EMLR 407.

[127] *Mars UK v Teknowledge Ltd* (1999) 46 IPR 248.

[128] *IF Asia Pacific Pty v Galbally* (2003) 59 IPR 43.

[129] *Nova Plastics v Froggatt* [1982] IRLR 146.

[130] *Roger Bullivant Ltd v Ellis* [1987] FSR 172. *Balston Ltd v Headline Filters Ltd* [1990] FSR 385; *Marshall v Industrial Systems and Control Ltd* [1992] IRLR 294.

[131] *Faccenda Chicken Ltd v Fowler* [1986] 1 All ER 617.

[132] *Wallace Bogan & Co v Cove* [1997] IRLR 453. See also *Co-ordinated Industries Pty v Elliot* (1998) 43 NSWLR 283.

the injunction because, in the absence of an express contractual term restraining a former employee from competing with the former employer, the only circumstance in which *Faccenda* would warrant preventing a former employee from using confidential information is where the information amounts to a trade secret. Even if the information in question has this character it may be that an injunction will not be available if the employee's claim is overstated or the trade secret, or its equivalent, cannot be readily distinguished from other information that the employee is free to use.[133] Certain employees are not to be the subject of intimidatory injunctive proceedings where they simply propose to compete, even if some preparatory acts take place during the currency of the employment contract.[134] Although some cases seem to be unduly favourable to employers, in so far as injunctions have been awarded when little or no legitimate interest was disclosed in the proceedings,[135] the courts are generally vigilant to permit former employees to compete whenever possible, *pace Faccenda*, even if the employee has expressly agreed not to compete after leaving employment. The general view is that the employer may, by express contract, obtain additional protection from misuse of information by a former employee and attention has been drawn to the fact that *Faccenda* was based upon the implied duty of confidentiality only. But even relatively unskilled employees who deliberately compile lists of the customers of the employer, the customer connection being the core of the business in question, will be prevented from doing so on the basis that equity will not countenance such deliberate breaches of duty.[136] Express restraints, which specifically seek either to prevent former employees from using both trade secrets and know-how, or which attempt to prevent former employees from using that information or skill by way of blanket non-competition clauses are subject to the restraint of trade doctrine but they remain valid[137] and, indeed, are encouraged by the judges because clauses of this kind are subject to the reasonableness tests within the restraint of trade doctrine.[138] However, the success of such clauses requires precise and very skilful drafting if they are either to broaden the implied duty or survive the restraint of trade clause. In both *Ixora Trading Inc v Jones*[139] and *Triangle Corpn v Carnsew*[140] the express clauses forbidding disclosure were held not to add to the *Faccenda* duty. *Ixora* goes further by showing that, save in trade secrets or soliciting cases or cases where the non-competition clause can be justified in context, express clauses are not likely to be very effective,[141] thus making the implied duty of great importance.[142]

---

[133] *AT Poeton (Gloucester Plating) Ltd v Horton* [2001] FSR 169.

[134] *Ixora Trading Inc v Jones* [1990] FSR 251.

[135] Compare *Hivac Ltd v Park Royal Scientific Instruments Ltd* [1946] Ch 169 with *Laughton v Bapp Industrial Supplies Ltd* [1986] ICR 634.

[136] *Forkserve Property Ltd v Fenely* (2001) 52 IPR 563, applying *Forkserve Pty Ltd v Pacchiarotta* (2000) 50 IPR 74.

[137] See *Printers and Finishers Ltd v Holloway* [1964] 3 All ER 731 at 736.

[138] *Balston Ltd v Headline Filters Ltd* [1987] FSR 330 at 351–352; *Pastor v Chen* (2002) 19 CPR (4th) 206; *IF Asia Pacific Pty v Galbally* (2003) 59 IPR 43.

[139] *Ixora Trading Inc v Jones* [1990] FSR 251.

[140] *Triangle Corpn v Carnsew* (1994) 29 IPR 69.

[141] Eg *John Orr Ltd and Vescom BV v John Orr* [1987] ILRM 702.

[142] See Stewart [1989] EIPR 88.

[24.35] Bona fide disputes concerning the ownership of information are not altogether uncommon. The issue of ownership of business contacts arose in *Pennwell Publishing (UK) Ltd v Ornstien*.[143] Where a journalist was employed as a publisher and conference chairman for a leading international business to business media information company, the status of his business contact address book became an issue upon his departure from that employment. The address book was maintained upon his employer's Outlook system and contained a diverse amount of information, some of which related to pre-employment journalistic contacts as well as individuals with whom the journalist had interacted in his role as a Pennwell employee. Applying both the general law and database legislation,[144] the English High Court held the address book was the property of Pennwell as it was maintained on Pennwell equipment and created in the course of employment. The court distinguished this situation from one in which a sales employee sought to hive off an employer's business contacts, which would clearly be unlawful. The employee, as a journalist, would have been entitled to compile a record of both his pre-employment journalistic contacts and key contacts built up during employment as well as other personal sources; the journalist, however, could not claim exclusivity for the list insofar as it contained his employer's business contacts and related information. The High Court, in a helpful judgment, stressed how prudent it is for an employer to establish clear rules and practices in this kind of situation, particularly via computer and internet use policies.

[24.36] Other contractual relationships that have produced duties of confidence involve agents and sub-contractors,[145] and banker–customer.[146] The law relating to fiduciaries is also invoked although the recent expansion of confidence makes this less necessary.[147] Even though the categories of relationship in which a fiduciary duty may be held to arise are not closed,[148] arm's length relationships such as a finance broker to a finance house are unlikely to create a fiduciary relationship.[149] If the essence of the complaint is misuse of confidential information, breach of confidence will be the appropriate cause of action.[150] Fiduciary duties are extremely useful to an employer in thwarting an employee's preparatory acts of direct competition. In *Crowson Fabrics v Rider*[151] the defendants were senior employees who during the service of their notice period copied commercial documents and made approaches to the claimant's customers advising that the defendants would be starting a new business in competition with the claimants. Their defence was that use of the claimant's resources to create lists of possible customers saved a few hours in getting names and addresses from competitor websites. Activities

---

[143] *Pennwell Publishing (UK) Ltd v Ornstien* [2007] IRLR 700.
[144] SI 1997/3032 (UK).
[145] Eg *Fortuity Property Ltd v Barcza* (1995) 32 IPR 517.
[146] *Tournier v National Provincial and Union Bank of England* [1924] 1 KB 461.
[147] For a case involving sales agents and the interaction of these various heads of action, see *Ecrosteel Pty Ltd v Perfor Printing Pty* (1996) 37 IPR 22.
[148] *Lac Minerals Ltd v International Corona Resources Ltd* [1990] FSR 441 at 483, *per* Sopinka J.
[149] *Indata Equipment Supplies Ltd v ACL Ltd* [1998] FSR 248.
[150] *Lac Minerals Ltd v International Corona Resources Ltd* [1990] FSR 441 at 486, *per* Sopinka J.
[151] *Crowson Fabrics v Rider* [2007] EWHC 2492 (Ch).

undertaken during the notice period were only preparatory to post-termination trading. After finding that these individuals were under a fiduciary duty, as distinct from being only bound by a duty of employee fidelity, the court went on to apply a recent line of cases[152] that distinguishes the duty of fidelity from that relating to breach of a fiduciary duty, observing that in the case of a fiduciary the employer will find it easier to establish that activities in preparation for competition will themselves breach the fiduciary obligation. On the facts the defendants had been actively canvassing for business and diverting opportunities during the notice period and were in fact in breach of both duties. A substantial body of Australian case law also serves to incentivise an employer, who finds that either confidential information has been misused[153] or that an employee failed to disclose to the employer a useful idea or application during employment, to go down the fiduciary duty route[154], but where the information becomes assimilated with that of the employee's own knowledge or skill, liability will be difficult to make out qua fiduciary.[155]

Proposed joint ventures

[24.37] The fact that information has been disclosed as part of a negotiating process that does not result in the formation of a contract between the parties is not an impediment to the application of the duty of confidentiality.[156] In *Coco v AN Clark*,[157] the plaintiff designed a moped engine, disclosing details of its operation to the defendants, including a prototype of the engine. No agreement was reached about development of the engine and the defendants proposed to make their own moped engine to a different design. The plaintiff complained that the defendant was using confidential information for the defendants' own purpose without the consent of the plaintiff. Megarry J imported the duty of confidence as an equitable obligation because in his view the 'circumstances of the disclosure in this case seem to me to be redolent of trust and confidence'.[158] The strength of the duty here is that the confider is able to utilise the duty even if the information disclosed does not exist in some other protectable form. In *Fraser v Thames Television Ltd*,[159] the plaintiffs provided a script writer and television company with the idea for a television comedy drama series upon condition that the plaintiffs had the right to appear in and contribute music towards the programme. The defendants ultimately used the ideas to create a successful television series but did not use the plaintiffs, arguing that the mere idea was not copyrightable and could not be the subject of a duty of confidence because of its tentative character. The defendants were nevertheless held

---

[152] Employees are not normally fiduciaries: *Hanco ATM systems Ltd v Cashbox* [2007] EWHC 1599 (Ch); *University of Nottingham v Fishel* [2000] IRLR 618; *Helmut Integrated Systems Ltd v Tunnard* [2007] IRLR 126; Hull [2009] EIPR 623.

[153] Eg *Breen v Williams* (1996) 186 CLR 71; *P & V Industries Pty Ltd v Porto* (2006) 14 VR 1; *Levy v Bablis* [2007] NSWSC 565.

[154] *Blackmagic Design Pty Ltd v Overliese* (2010) 84 IPR 505.

[155] *Futuretronics.com.au Pty v Graphix Labels Pty Ltd* [2009] FCAFA 40.

[156] *Saltman Engineering Ltd v Campbell Engineering Co Ltd* (1948) 65 RPC 203.

[157] *Coco v AN Clark* [1968] FSR 415; Lavery [1998] EIPR 93.

[158] *Coco v AN Clark* [1968] FSR 415 at 424.

[159] *Fraser v Thames Television Ltd* [1983] 2 All ER 101; *Gupta v Dasgupta* [2003] FSR 337.

liable for the idea was sufficiently developed and original even though it was not copyright protected.

[24.38] Confidential information that is co-owned and is to be used to raise capital, for example, can create difficulties if one of the co-owners seeks to use the information unilaterally. The recent decision in *Murray v Yorkshire Fund Managers*[160] indicates that use of information without the consent of all the owners will breach the confidentiality obligation. The question whether a co-owner could disclose confidential information to competitors was extensively considered in the Supreme Count of Victoria in *Centaur Mining and Exploration Ltd v Anaconda Nickel Ltd.*[161] Centaur and Anaconda had created valuable scientific data as part of a joint venture proposal that was never finalised. Centaur went into receivership and the receivers sought to disclose this data, on the foot of confidentiality agreements, to competitors of Anaconda. Warren J upheld the confidentiality agreement and declined to permit the release of this data on the basis that even selective release would destroy the confidential nature of the data and do significant harm to Anaconda.[162] This is an important decision on an extremely common commercial situation and the solution reflects the primacy of contract law solutions when these can be put in place.

Involuntary relationships

[24.39] Special considerations arise where the relationship exists by force of circumstance, as in cases where information is obtained on the foot of a court order, eg discovery,[163] or under the exercise of police search powers[164] or powers of arrest and enquiry.[165] In *Hellewell*,[166] Laws J observed that the police, when photographing suspects during investigations into criminality, were not free to do whatever they thought proper with that photograph:

> The circumstances in which the photograph is taken when the suspect has no choice save to insist that physical force be not used upon him, impose obligations on the police, breach of which may sound in an action at private law ... they [the police] may make reasonable use of it for the purpose of the prevention and detection of crime, the investigation of alleged offences and the apprehension of suspects or persons unlawfully at large ... they must have these and only these purposes in mind and must, as I have said, make no more than reasonable use of the picture in seeking to accomplish them.[167]

---

160 *Murray v Yorkshire Fund Managers* [1998] 2 All ER 1015; *Oblique Financial Services Ltd v Promise Production Co* [1994] ILRM 74.

161 *Centaur Mining and Exploration Ltd v Anaconda Nickel Ltd* 29 June 2001 (5767 of 2001).

162 Applying, *inter alia*, *Saltman Engineering Co Ltd v Campbell* (1948) 65 RPC 203; *Delta Nominees Pty Ltd v Viscount Plastics Products Pty* [1979] VR 167 and *Mobil Oil Australian Ltd v Guina Development Pty Ltd* [1996] 2 VR 34 (a discovery case).

163 *Distillers Co (Biochemicals) Ltd v Times Newspapers Ltd* [1975] QB 613; *Riddick v Thames Board Mills Ltd* [1977] QB 881.

164 *Marcel v Metropolitan Police Comr* [1992] 1 All ER 72.

165 *Wiggington v Brisbane TV Ltd* (1992) 25 IPR 58; *Hellewell v Chief Constable of Derbyshire* [1995] 4 All ER 473.

166 *Hellewell v Chief Constable of Derbyshire* [1995] 4 All ER 473.

167 *Hellewell v Chief Constable of Derbyshire* [1995] 4 All ER 473 at 478–479.

Bona fide third-party defendants

[24.40] Can a defendant avoid the application of the duty of confidence on the ground that the defendant unwittingly came into possession of confidential material, having paid full value for this information? In *Stevenson Jordan & Harrison Ltd v MacDonald and Evans*,[168] the trial judge declined to accept the validity of such a plea. It is arguable that where a defendant does not actually know of the breach of confidence by another, or is in breach of duty negligently, without owing a contractual duty to the confider, there are few grounds upon which to visit a duty of conscience upon that defendant.[169] Lord Denning MR in *Fraser v Evans*[170] indicated that the duty can attach to the innocent recipient of information once that person gets to know that the information was originally given in confidence. We will return to the issue of the 'innocent infringement' in the next chapter.

The requirement that the information must be secret – not in the public domain

[24.41] In *A-G v Guardian Newspapers (No 2)*[171] Lord Goff observed:

> once information has entered what is usually called the public domain (which means no more than that the information in question is so generally accessible that, in all the circumstances, it cannot be regarded as confidential) then, as a general rule, the principle of confidentiality can have no application to it.[172]

Lord Goff considered this to be a limiting principle or a defence, but it is perhaps more proper to regard this as a necessary proof for the successful maintenance of a breach of confidence action.[173] Where the plaintiff is seeking to restrain a defendant from breaching the duty of disclosure, the action of the plaintiff may prejudice any such claim. The leading case is *O Mustad & Son v Dosen*.[174] In that case the plaintiff sought to prevent a manufacturing process from being disclosed by a former employee. However, the plaintiff had successfully filed a patent in relation to this process and was thus held not to be entitled to an injunction, for once the secret has been confided by the confider to the world 'the secret, as a secret, has ceased to exist'.[175] However, Lord Buckmaster indicated that if the plaintiff can show that the disclosee had obtained knowledge of ancillary secrets not disclosed in the patent invention but which would be of service in exploiting the information publicly available, then the duty of confidence will remain in place.

---

[168] *Stevenson Jordan & Harrison Ltd v MacDonald and Evans* (1951) 68 RPC 190. This defence was not at issue; *Stevens v Avery* [1988] 2 All ER 477.

[169] *Weld-Blundell v Stephens* [1920] AC 956; see Law Commission no 110 at paras 3.8 and 4.14.

[170] *Fraser v Evans* [1969] 1 QB 349 at 361.

[171] *A-G v Guardian Newspapers (No 2)* [1988] 3 All ER 545.

[172] *A-G v Guardian Newspapers (No 2)* [1988] 3 All ER 545 at 659.

[173] See Law Commission Report no 110 at para 4.15.

[174] *O Mustad & Son v Dosen*, decided in 1928 but reported in [1963] 3 All ER 416.

[175] *O Mustad & Son v Dosen* [1963] 3 All ER 416 at 418, *per* Lord Buckmaster; *Franchi v Franchi* [1967] RPC 149.

[24.42] In *House of Spring Gardens Ltd v Point Blank Ltd*,[176] Costello J applied the *dicta* by holding that despite the fact that two patents had been applied for in which much of the confidential information held by the disclosees was thus in the public domain, other valuable secrets not included in the patent specifications remained in the possession of the defendants who had misused it. The natural reluctance of the courts to allow one person to trade on the back of another explains the somewhat limited view of 'the public domain' in this particular context. Even if the information is a trade secret that could not be patentable because it would be obvious, once disclosed, this fact is no bar to the continued application of the duty.[177] Nor does the fact that information is a known element in the state of the art, for an expert, prevent that information from being caught by the duty vis-à-vis a lay or non-specialist confidant.[178] The courts may hold that even though information could be compiled from other sources or created by using research skills and data analysis, this will not prevent the duty from being applicable once it appears that the confidant eschewed the opportunity to obtain or create the information in this way. In *Under-Water Welders and Repairers Ltd v Street*[179] a simple cleaning technique for cleaning ships could be protected even though others had the means and opportunity to use their brains so as to produce the same result through honest endeavour. The basic issue is whether the secret is known to the trade or particular to the confider.[180] In contrast, commercially valuable materials such as computer source code may not attract a duty of confidentiality if left in a location where the material could be accessed by employees or members of the public without breaching the law, and no other serious steps to protect the material were undertaken. If some of the materials had a dubious entitlement to copyright and the materials could be readily obtained or recreated then no quantity of confidence may exist: *Dais Studio Pty Ltd v Ballet Creative Pty*.[181] Conversely,

> In determining whether the information in question has the necessary quality of confidentiality, the fact that the information is jealously guarded by the claimant, that it is not readily made available to employees and that it could not, without considerable effort and risk, be acquired by others, is a relevant consideration. The fact that considerable skill and effort was actually expended to acquire the information is also a relevant consideration: *Wright v Gasweld Pty Ltd* (1991) 22 NSWLR 317.[182]

[24.43] Perhaps the most controversial element in the law of confidence centres around the problem of unauthorised disclosure of confidential information by someone other than the confider. If information is put into the public domain by the confidant, or a third

---

[176] *House of Spring Gardens Ltd v Point Blank Ltd* [1984] IR 611.
[177] *House of Spring Gardens Ltd v Point Blank Ltd* [1984] IR 611 at 664.
[178] *House of Spring Gardens Ltd v Point Blank Ltd* [1984] IR 611 at 664.
[179] *Under-Water Welders and Repairers Ltd v Street* [1968] RPC 498.
[180] *Triplex Safety Glass Co v Scorah* (1938) 55 RPC 21; on the protection of the mundane via the springboard doctrine see Lavery [1998] EIPR 93. On television formats see *Gupta v Dasgupta* [2003] FSR 337.
[181] *Dais Studio Pty Ltd v Ballet Creative Pty* (2007) 74 IPR 512.
[182] Emmett J in *Bluescope Steel Ltd v Kelly* (2007) 72 IPR 289 at 309, citing *Wright v Gasweld Pty Ltd* (1991) 22 NSWLR 317 at 334; 20 IPR 481 at 498.

party, can the duty survive? The narrow approach to this issue depends upon judicial willingness to characterise the defendant as someone who is likely to profit unscrupulously from the privileged position they were previously in, rather than being a mere member of the public who is free to compete with others. The moral nature of the law of confidence is highlighted by several judicial statements that deny to the confidant the right to use 'public domain' information to steal a march on competitors, a view often described as the 'springboard' doctrine.

[24.44] In *Terrapin Ltd v Builders Supply Co (Hayes) Ltd*,[183] the plaintiff designed portable buildings, which were obviously open to use and inspection by others. The defendant manufactured these buildings on the plaintiff's behalf but then began to manufacture similar and competing products. Roxburgh J held for the plaintiff:

> a person who has obtained information in confidence is not allowed to use it as a springboard for activities detrimental to the person who made the confidential communication, and springboard it remains even when all the features have been published or can be ascertained by actual inspection by any member of the public ... the possessor of the confidential information still has a long start over any member of the public.[184]

[24.45] It should be noted that in this case there had not been a complete and full disclosure to the public, for the central plank in the defence was that the disclosure by the plaintiff of brochures describing the buildings was tantamount to publication of plans, specifications and other know-how. Roxburgh J rejected this, noting also that, while a skilled carpenter could dismantle these buildings and thus see how they were built, this possibility was not a publication that would discharge the confidential obligation. The defendant's 'head start' thus justified the 'special disability' they were under as against a trade competitor who could possibly imitate the plaintiff's product.[185] In later cases the *Terrapin* decision[186] was expressly followed on this notion of a limited concept of public domain information. In *Cranleigh Precision Engineering Ltd v Bryant*[187] the defendant, having acquired information about a Swiss patent application during his employment with the plaintiff company, suppressed this information from the plaintiff, with the intention of using the confidential information and the patent information for his own purposes. In awarding relief to the plaintiff, Roskill J characterised the release of information as being a third-party release that was not caught by the decision in *O Mustad & Son v Dosen*,[188] even though it was of course open to him to argue that it was the advantage gleaned from his position of trust and confidence that allowed Bryant to profit from information about the Swiss patent he would otherwise not have come across. While *Cranleigh* has been criticised because of

---

[183] *Terrapin Ltd v Builders Supply Co (Hayes) Ltd* [1960] RPC 128 at 130.

[184] *Terrapin Ltd v Builders Supply Co (Hayes) Ltd* [1967] RPC 375.

[185] Of course artistic copyright may counteract even this possibility. For an interesting decision which pushes out the boundaries on both fronts, see *Creation Records Ltd v News Group Newspapers* [1997] EMLR 444.

[186] *Terrapin Ltd v Builders Supply Co (Hayes) Ltd* [1960] RPC 128.

[187] *Cranleigh Precision Engineering Ltd v Bryant* [1964] 3 All ER 289.

[188] *O Mustad & Son v Dosen* [1963] 3 All ER 416.

Roskill J's willingness to take an easy, but intellectually unsatisfying, way out through distinguishing the *Mustad* decision, the *Cranleigh* decision is supportable if only because the evidence revealed a breach of trust and confidence in using secret and commercially useful information that this defendant, firstly, could not show had been acquired legitimately and, secondly, the breach of trust clearly gave a commercial advantage over others. On this basis Lord Goff of Chieveley in the *Spycatcher* case[189] approved of Roskill J's judgment as representing nothing more than an extension of the springboard doctrine.

[24.46] The balance between preventing the free use of publicly available information and unfair use of information is at times a delicate one. In *Seager v Copydex Ltd*[190] Denning MR, who gave the leading judgment for the Court of Appeal, considered the scope of these principles where the information is mixed in the sense that some is publicly available (ie patented) while the remainder was disclosed confidentially (ie for purposes of joint development negotiations). Denning MR said:

> when the information is mixed, being partly public and partly private, then the recipient must take special care to use only the material in the public domain. He should go to the public source and get it or, at any rate, not be in a better position than if he had gone to the public source. He should not get a start over others by using the information which he received in confidence. At any rate, he should not get a start without paying for it.[191]

[24.47] At this juncture the approach of the courts comes closer to the approach to an infringement of copyright claim as distinct from one of patent infringement, and proof of misuse is unlikely to be excused by a claim that the material was publicly available. In *Roger Bullivant Ltd v Ellis*[192] the defendant took a card index containing his employer's customers' names and addresses intending to use them for his own purposes. The Court of Appeal held that even accepting that some of these names and addresses could have been recalled or found in other public sources, the 'ready and finite'[193] list of potential customers was still a valuable short cut for the defendant in his canvassing activities; Nourse LJ made short shrift of the public domain defence:

> having made deliberate and unlawful use of the plaintiff's property he cannot complain if he finds that the eye of the law is unable to distinguish between those whom he could, had he chose, have contacted lawfully and those whom he could not.[194]

[24.48] The springboard doctrine, properly understood, turns upon a finding that the defendant has not used the publicly available source and this fact, combined with the use of information collected from another confidential source, makes it improper to allow the defendant to steal a march on others. It is a limited qualification of the *Mustad* decision[195] but after the *Spycatcher* litigation,[196] in which the House of Lords accepted

---

189 *A-G v Guardian Newspapers Ltd (No 2)* [1988] 3 All ER 545.
190 *Seager v Copydex Ltd* [1967] 1 WLR 923.
191 *Seager v Copydex Ltd* [1967] 1 WLR 923 at 933.
192 *Roger Bullivant Ltd v Ellis* [1987] FSR 172.
193 *Roger Bullivant Ltd v Ellis* [1987] FSR 172 at 181 following *Robb v Green* [1895] 2 QB 315.
194 *Roger Bullivant Ltd v Ellis* [1987] FSR 172 at 181.
195 *O Mustad & Son v Dosen* [1963] 3 All ER 416; Lavery [1998] EIPR 93.
196 *A-G v Guardian Newspapers Ltd (No 2)* [1988] 3 All ER 545.

both *Mustad* and post-*Terrapin*[197] developments, there can be no real doubt about the usefulness of 'springboard' as being an essentially moral imperative, as well as a notion that ensures economic probity in terms of countering unfair competition while avoiding any taint of punishing a defendant. The primary relief of an injunction is to last only for so long as the advantage may reasonably be expected to continue – to cancel the headstart the defendant would otherwise get. This is a matter of fact tested by reference to any express terms, implied terms and the like in each individual case.[198] However, the approach of Lord Goff of Chieveley in the *Spycatcher* case tends to eliminate from the springboard doctrine two somewhat irrational features of it. Lord Goff doubted[199] whether the obligation of confidence could survive if a third party put the confidential information, *in toto*, into the public domain. In so doing, Lord Goff was clearly not able to support the decision in *Cranleigh Precision Engineering*,[200] in so far as it rests upon the distinguishing of the *Mustad* case. Lord Goff also indicated that the duty of confidence will not survive an act of publication by the confidant (ie Peter Wright and his publishers in overseas locations), the learned judge indicating that *Speed Seal Products Ltd v Paddington*[201] could not be supported. Lord Goff was the only member of the House of Lords in *Spycatcher* to address these features of the springboard doctrine and he was prepared to canvass the possibility that while the information so disclosed may lose its confidential nature, some kind of springboard doctrine could be used to prevent the confidant from benefiting from his own iniquity. The problem for the UK government in this case was the unsatisfactory nature of the pecuniary and other remedies because Wright and his overseas publishers were outside the jurisdiction of the 'English courts'.[202]

The public interest

[24.49] The equitable principle operates because of the circumstances in which information was provided by the confider and not because the information was 'owned' by the confider; ownership in information is not possible under the Larceny Act 1916, although some limited movement in this direction is in evidence in the Oireachtas[203] and in the recent deliberations of the Law Reform Commission.[204] However, in this area of judge-made law, the courts have traditionally balanced the interests of persons from being taken advantage of by those to whom they have entrusted confidential information with the broader public interest in counteracting serious misconduct and maintaining the integrity of the State. In *Spycatcher* Lord Goff of Chieveley compared existing English

---

[197] *Terrapin Ltd v Builders Supply Co (Hayes) Ltd* [1960] RPC 128.

[198] *Potters Ballotini Ltd v Weston-Baker* [1977] RPC 202; *Harrison v Project & Design Co (Redcar) Ltd* [1978] FSR 81; *Fisher-Karpark Industries Ltd v Nichols* [1982] FSR 351.

[199] *A-G v Guardian Newspapers Ltd (No 2)* [1988] 3 All ER 545 at 661–662.

[200] *Cranleigh Precision Engineering Ltd v Bryant* [1964] 3 All ER 289.

[201] *Speed Seal Products Ltd v Paddington* [1986] 1 All ER 91.

[202] See Lord Goff in *A-G v Guardian Newspapers Ltd (No 2)* [1988] 3 All ER 545 at 664.

[203] Criminal Damage Act 1991. See now the Criminal Justice (Theft and Fraud Offences) Act 2001, s 2(1) (definition of 'property').

[204] *Report on Dishonesty* LRC 43 (1992); *Report on Aggravated, Exemplary and Restitutionary Damages* LRC 60 (2000), especially Ch 14.

law or freedom of expression and the duty of confidence (as contrasting English law principles), with art 10 of the ECHR, remarking that in the jurisprudence of the European Court of Human Rights the right to freedom of expression is qualified by restrictions based on pressing social need and noting also that the English courts qualify the duty of confidence by reference to similar considerations. However, recent case law indicates that different approaches are to operate depending on whether the information is concerned with private law secrets or government secrets; in the first case the onus will lie in favour of upholding confidence while in the second, the case for secrecy will have to be made out.

[24.50] The basis of the public interest exception is normally attributed to the words of Wood VC in *Gartside v Outram*:[205]

> there is no confidence as to the disclosures of iniquity. You cannot make me the confidant of a crime or a fraud and be entitled to close up my lips upon any secret which you have the audacity to disclose to me relating to any fraudulent intention on your part; such a confidence cannot exist.[206]

[24.51] While cases in the early parts of this century have doubted the existence, not to say the scope, of such a principle[207] when the confidant sought to invoke it to excuse the publication of libellous material or information that would disclose the basis of some other kind of private civil cause of action, there is no doubt that a wider duty owed to the State or to other citizens could, in a proper case, outweigh the contractual or equitable basis of the duty of confidence. The trick has always been where to draw the line in this area, as well as in analogous fields such as denying a plaintiff a successful cause of action for breach of contract because of some common law defence such as illegality or restraint of trade. In *Initial Services Ltd v Putterill*,[208] the plaintiffs sought to strike out a defence to their action for breach of contract, brought against a former employee who had taken away with him, when he left employment, documents which tended to show involvement in a price-fixing cartel which was a restrictive practice. The defendant passed these documents on to the second defendant, a national newspaper. Counsel for the plaintiffs relied heavily on *Weld-Blundell v Stephens*[209] arguing that, even if proved, their conduct was neither a crime nor a fraud. Lord Denning MR's view, although he may have misunderstood[210] the plaintiffs' argument, was:

> The exception should extend to crimes, frauds and misdeeds, both those actually committed as well as to those in contemplation, provided always, and this is essential, that the disclosure is justified in the public interest.[211]

---

[205] *Gartside v Outram* (1856) 26 LJ Ch 113.

[206] *Gartside v Outram* (1856) 26 LJ Ch 113 at 114.

[207] Eg Warrington LJ in *Weld-Blundell v Stephens* [1919] 1 KB 520 at 535.

[208] *Initial Services Ltd v Putterill* [1968] 1 QB 396.

[209] *Weld-Blundell v Stephens* [1919] 1 KB 520.

[210] See *Initial Services Ltd v Putterill* [1968] 1 QB 396 at 400D and Salmon LJ at 409A; contrast Denning MR at 405E.

[211] *Initial Services Ltd v Putterill* [1968] 1 QB 396 at 405.

[24.52] Counsel's reliance on earlier cases was also directed at the identity of the person who is informed, in breach of confidence; was a national newspaper a proper person to be informed of the 'iniquity'? While the Court of Appeal accepted this proposition they were ultimately unprepared to strike out the defence for neither facet of it was such as to be unarguable. Later cases indicate that this public interest exception does not extend towards revelations that a particularly obnoxious military government elsewhere in Europe has engaged a firm of public relations consultants to improve its public image in other parts of Europe, even if the regime itself has a poor human rights record.[212] On the other hand, the disclosure of details about courses devised by the head of a religious organisation who was prepared to countenance powerful coercive methods to maintain the integrity of the church was certainly a powerful enough interest to deny interlocutory relief to the head of that church in confidence/copyright proceedings.[213]

[24.53] The case that establishes the public interest defence in English law, with greater clarity and precision than any other case, is *Lion Laboratories Ltd v Evans*,[214] a decision of the Court of Appeal that fully examined both the nature of the iniquity and the factors relevant to the balancing process.

[24.54] The Home Office had approved an intoximeter produced by Lion Laboratories for use by the police in detecting drunk drivers. The defendants, who were technicians employed by Lion Laboratories, leaked information, which revealed that these devices were not completely reliable and this information appeared in the national press. Leonard J gave an interlocutory injunction restraining disclosure or use of confidential information but, following use of this information by the press, an application to have the injunction discharged was sought in the Court of Appeal. In the light of the much fuller argument in the Court of Appeal, that court stated that the relevant principles necessitated the discharge of the injunction. While the Court of Appeal agreed with Leonard J that there were two primary interests to be balanced, namely, the protection of confidential documents and the freedom of the press to investigate matters of public concern, there were other relevant factors to be brought into play. Firstly, the Court of Appeal pointed out that there is a wide difference between what is interesting to the public and what is in the public interest vis-à-vis open disclosure of facts; private matters may interest the public but be matters of no real public concern. Secondly, newspapers have a separate interest – boosting readership and circulation – which is not to be used to confuse the public interest issue. Thirdly, the public interest may often best be served by discretion in the sense that details should be given to the police or other bodies charged with investigative powers. Fourthly, the basic rule against a confidence being maintained in an iniquity was of importance. Using these supplementary rules, the Court of Appeal held that the balancing exercise should work in favour of disclosure. While the plaintiff company was not itself the author of an iniquity – it merely manufactured the device and unlike the Home Office did not specifically control its use – the failure to meet a manufacturing standard would raise the possibility of wrongful convictions and loss of

---

[212] *Fraser v Evans* [1969] 1 All ER 8.

[213] *Hubbard v Vosper* [1972] 1 All ER 1023.

[214] *Lion Laboratories Ltd v Evans* [1985] QB 526.

liberty for citizens. On the issue of the appropriateness of resorting to the media, the Court of Appeal allowed a degree of latitude. Stephenson LJ went so far as to say that in a case of this kind the media may be under a duty to publish, even if information has been obtained in flagrant breach of confidence and even if some other motive (such as vengeance) could be shown to exist on the part of the informer. However, press freedom cannot be pushed too far; a countervailing interest that is similarly powerful is the public interest in facilitating the proper administration of justice through a leakproof system of discovery, for example.[215] The removal of the duty of confidence from a defendant using the iniquity exception will only be tolerated if the removal of the duty presents the only realistic way in which 'the press' can put this information, on a matter of public interest, before the public.[216] While an exegesis of the law relating to press freedom would be out of place at this juncture it should be recalled that third-party disclosees who happen to be journalists cannot invoke any special privilege against disclosure of sources.[217]

[24.55] Nevertheless, a public interest defence is available to the Irish media. In *National Irish Bank Ltd v RTE*[218] the plaintiffs sought to prevent RTE from broadcasting confidential information about investment accounts operated by the plaintiffs, which tended to show wrongdoing in the form of banking activities that facilitated widespread tax evasion. While the Supreme Court indicated that a duty of confidentiality existed as between banker and customer which could extend to third parties such as RTE in this case, on the basis that: 'there is a public interest in the maintenance of such confidentiality for the benefit of society at large',[219] the Supreme Court, endorsing the public interest defence cases such as *Lion Laboratories*,[220] also observed that:

> There is also a public interest in defending wrongdoing and where the publication of confidential information may be of assistance in defending wrongdoing then the public interest in such publication may outweigh the public interest in the maintenance of confidentiality.[221]

However, the breadth of the disclosure that is sought is an extremely relevant factor. It may be that a distinction is to be drawn in respect of limited disclosure and worldwide publication such as loading confidential documents onto a website. In *Imutran Ltd v Uncaged Campaigns Ltd*,[222] the plaintiffs complained about the defendants' acts of uploading copyright and/or confidential documents onto a website. These documents

---

[215] *Distillers Co v Times Newspapers Ltd* [1975] QB 613.

[216] See, in particular, Templeman LJ in *Schering Chemicals Ltd v Falkman Ltd* [1981] 2 All ER 321 at 347 where he noted both the financial motive of the journalist and the 'public domain' nature of much of the information.

[217] Carolan and O'Neill, *Media Law in Ireland* (Bloomsbury, 2010).

[218] *National Irish Bank Ltd v RTE* [1998] 2 IR 465; see Fenwick and Phillipson (2004) 55 NILQ 118.

[219] *Per* Lynch J, giving the judgment of the majority of the Supreme Court: *National Irish Bank Ltd v RTE* [1998] 2 IR 465 at 494.

[220] *Lion Laboratories Ltd v Evans* [1985] QB 526.

[221] *National Irish Bank Ltd v RTE* [1998] 2 IR 465 at 494.

[222] *Imutran Ltd v Uncaged Campaigns Ltd* [2002] FSR 26; *Jockey Club v Buffham* [2003] EMLR 111.

raised serious issues about animal research and the supervision of such research by the Home Office. Morritt VC held that there were a sufficient number of agencies and bodies seised with the responsibility of investigating these areas of concern; the fact that the documents were often highly technical and scientific, and thus broadly unintelligible to the general public also militated against the breadth of publication sought by the defendants. Interlocutory relief was obtained and contained in favour of the plaintiffs.

[24.56] One case of some controversy arose out of the pre-publication release of the *Thatcher Memoirs* by the *Daily Mirror* newspaper prior to the Conservative Party conference in 1993. Forbes J ruled that the *Sunday Times* and Harper Collins, who owned the serialisation and publication rights respectively, could not obtain an injunction against Mirror Newspapers because it was in the public interest that the public be aware of tensions within the government party at a time when that party was attempting a show of unity which the memoirs tended to give the lie to. Forbes J followed *Lion Laboratories*.[223] While the Master of the Rolls dismissed this appeal on different grounds, the decision was a cause of great surprise to many, especially the *Sunday Times*.[224] The fact that the confidant himself intends to make the information known at some time in the near future may undermine the confider's efforts to obtain an injunction, for as part of the balancing process a public interest argument may thus outweigh what is in essence an effort to protect the commercial value of the information rather than its secrecy.[225] The balance will go the other way if a legitimate privacy interest is at stake[226] although in some cases publication will be allowed if the confider cannot show that the confidant was really the recipient of 'exclusive' information and the information related to a person in the public eye who has acted improperly in a public place.[227] If there is any real risk of the public being physically harmed as a result of upholding the confidence then a public interest defence may prevail for it will be evident in some cases that the real interests of the public and the parties to the information may coincide.[228] After the implementation of HRA 1998 the public interest defence has been to a certain extent overshadowed by the s 12 issue, which has no real counterpart in Irish law. Nevertheless, the trend towards permitting publication of information, save where a compelling privacy interest, or a direct contractual relationship, can be brought into play by the confider, suggests that Irish law and other common law jurisdictions will produce broadly similar jurisprudence notwithstanding points of difference by way of statute law.

---

[223] *Lion Laboratories Ltd v Evans* [1985] QB 526; *London Regional Transport v Mayor of London* [2003] EMLR 88; *Jockey Club v Buffham* [2003] EMLR 111.

[224] See 'For Authors Back to the Law of the Jungle' (1993) Sunday Times, 10 October.

[225] This was the basis of Bingham MR's decision in the *Thatcher Memoirs* appeal: *Times Newspapers v MGN Ltd* [1993] EMLR 443, CA; 'For Authors Back to the Law of the Jungle' (1993) Sunday Times, 10 October.

[226] *Francome v Mirror Group Newspapers Ltd* [1984] 2 All ER 408.

[227] Contrast *Woodward v Hutchins* [1977] 2 All ER 751 with *Stevens v Avery* [1988] 2 All ER 477 and *X v Y* [1988] 2 All ER 648.

[228] *W v Edgell* [1989] 1 All ER 1089.

[24.57] Where the information in question is held by the government, as distinct from being 'private' information, a rather different emphasis has been placed on the availability of relief via the law of confidence. In *A-G v Jonathan Cape Ltd*,[229] the Attorney-General sought an injunction to restrain the publication of the *Crossman Diaries* on the ground that certain Cabinet discussions were relayed therein, in breach of confidence. However, it was for the Attorney-General to show not only that publication would breach confidence but also that the public interest required that publication be restrained and that other facets of the public interest were not present that contradicted or were more compelling than the public interest requiring secrecy. This approach has been endorsed both in the High Court of Australia[230] and by various members of the House of Lords in *Spycatcher*.[231] In *Spycatcher*, however, the public interest in maintaining the integrity of the secret service was held clearly to outweigh any countervailing public interest in investigating wrongdoing (although it should be recalled that neither Wright nor his publishers were before the English courts to argue this point). Had the issue been whether an injunction should be given to restrain first publication in the UK there is no doubt that the Attorney-General would have prevailed but in *Spycatcher* the issue was whether publication should be restrained when the work was widely available due to overseas publication and widespread importation into the UK. In the view of the House of Lords, broad injunctive relief would not be appropriate, for no confidence remained due to Wright's breach of duty and its worldwide dissemination. If, however, there is no allegation that the information provided to the Crown servant was secret or confidential, the decision of Scott VC in *A-G v Blake*[232] indicates that the Crown interest in maintaining an air of secrecy around the security services will not of itself be sufficient to warrant an injunction: the countervailing public interest in freedom of speech and a person's right to earn a living will be predominant unless contractual duties arise.

[24.58] This issue has arisen in recent times as a result of publication of the memoirs of former SAS members, the most important instance being Chris Ryan's *The One that Got Away*, televised in February 1996 and based on Chris McNab's *Bravo Two Zero*. The lack of activity in the form of attempts to injunct publication presumably indicates that this kind of publication is thought by the Attorney-General to fall on the other side of the *Spycatcher*[233] line, even though some danger to serving members is apprehended in certain circles.[234] Despite the force of the earlier cases in which the onus was placed on

---

[229] *A-G v Jonathan Cape Ltd* [1976] QB 752.
[230] *A-G v Blake* [1996] 3 All ER 903. See in particular Mason J in *Commonwealth of Australia v John Fairfax and Sons Ltd* (1980) 32 ALR 485 at 492–493.
[231] *A-G v Guardian Newspapers Ltd (No 2)* [1988] 3 All ER 545: see Lord Keith at 642; Lord Griffiths at 650–651; Lord Goff at 660.
[232] *A-G v Blake* [1996] 3 All ER 903.
[233] *A-G v Guardian Newspapers Ltd (No 2)* [1988] 3 All ER 545.
[234] See 'He who dares faces a law suit' (1996) Observer, 25 February. The article indicates that confidentiality agreements with members are actively being considered to provide a firmer legal basis for enforcing confidentiality. *A-G for England and Wales v R* [2003] UKPC 22, a Privy Council decision affirms the effectiveness of a contractual solution.

the State, Australian case law,[235] has tended to emphasise that even if a public interest defence in exposing criminality is invoked against an agency of the Federal government, the defendant will have to go some way towards substantiating this claim if he is to be relieved of the contractual duty to keep confidence as a government employee.

Skill, time and labour in compiling the information

[24.59] In *House of Spring Gardens Ltd v Point Blank Ltd*,[236] Costello J indicated that in determining the nature of the relationship and the information, the expenditure of skill, time and labour in compiling the information is relevant in determining whether the duty of confidence arises. Costello J was, of course, considering these factors in the context of industrial trade secrets, some of which were already in the public domain and these remarks are therefore to be seen in context. In general terms, however, if the information is seen as being management data rather than a trade secret the action will fail.[237] If the information is seen as being an essential part of the personal skill and know-how of the confidant[238] the duty will not arise thus making express clauses against competition necessary.[239] Although the memory test is not a part of English law,[240] evidence that a confidant has taken or copied documents will tend towards a conclusion that the confidant knew that the information had been given within a relationship of confidence and subject to a duty to use it only for certain purposes or not at all,[241] unless that information is characterised as little more than gossip or tittle-tattle.[242] If the information is vaguely expressed or little more than an idea this may point away from there being anything confidential at all, as in the case of an idea for a nightclub theme.[243]

REMEDIES IN RELATION TO BREACH OF CONFIDENCE

[24.60] The remedies available in relation to a threatened or actual breach of confidence, a broadly equitable doctrine, are closely linked to the traditional range of equitable remedies such as declaratory orders, injunctions and account of profits. While the basic principles that operate in relation to these remedies vis-à-vis other intellectual property rights are generally applicable, there are specific problems in key area, which make it

---

[235] *DCT v Rettke* (1995) 31 IPR 457.

[236] *House of Spring Gardens Ltd v Point Blank Ltd* [1984] IR 611.

[237] *Herbert Morris Ltd v Saxelby* [1916] 1 AC 688; *Ixora Trading Corpn v Jones* [1990] FSR 251.

[238] *Printers and Finishers Ltd v Holloway* [1965] 1 WLR 1; *AT Poeton (Gloucester Plating) Ltd v Horton* [2001] FSR 169.

[239] Eg *Triangle Corpn v Carnsew* (1994) 29 IPR 69.

[240] See Heydon, *The Restraint of Trade Doctrine* (1971) 91–92. *Crowson Fabrics v Rider* [2004] EWHC 2942 (Ch) has reaffirmed the distinction between information obtained and 'kept in the head' of an employee and documentary information as a basic rule of thumb on what is proprietary information and what is not.

[241] *AF Associates v Ralston* [1973] NI 229; *Roger Bullivant Ltd v Ellis* [1987] FSR 172.

[242] *Beloff v Pressdram Ltd* [1973] 1 All ER 241.

[243] *De Maudsley v Palumbo* [1996] FSR 447.

desirable for the law to be put on a statutory footing, particularly in relation to the remedy of damages.

Injunctions

[24.61] The principles expounded in *American Cyanamid Co v Ethicon Ltd*[244] have been accepted as governing this area of law although certain of the leading cases pre-date the decision of the House of Lords on this point.[245] It is by no means clear whether a defendant who is intent on pleading that disclosure was made in the public interest can be the subject of an interlocutory injunction. In *Hubbard v Vosper*[246] the Master of the Rolls, Lord Denning, said:

> We never restrain a defendant in a libel action who says he is going to justify. So, in a copyright action, we ought not to restrain a defendant who has a reasonable defence of fair dealing. Nor in an action for breach of confidence if, the defendant has a reasonable defence of public interest. The reason is because the defendant, if he is right, is entitled to publish it; and the law will not intervene to suppress freedom of speech except where it is abused.[247]

[24.62] It has to be said that Lord Denning was the most enthusiastic exponent of this view and other judges have tended to decide not to award injunctions on the balance of convenience issue[248] rather than by reference to this rule, and there must be significant doubt about the existence of any such rule in the light of subsequent decisions in which interlocutory relief was given.[249] Factors that affect the balance of convenience in favour of upholding the confidence via an interlocutory injunction include whether publication would result in a breach of the criminal law[250] and whether damages would not be an adequate remedy for the plaintiff.[251] Injunctions are less likely where the defendant is innocent and has changed his position irrevocably[252] but *bona fide* purchasers are not immune from injunctions.[253] As long as the *American Cyanamid*[254] test is applied, the fact that the defendant is likely to be driven out of business as a result of upholding the confidence via an interlocutory injunction is not a barrier to the relief.[255] Nor is an injunction to be denied simply because the loss to the defendant is hard or impossible to

---

[244] *American Cyanamid Co v Ethicon Ltd* [1975] AC 396.

[245] Eg *Amber Size and Chemical Co v Menzel* [1913] 2 Ch 239; *Coco v AN Clark Ltd* [1968] FSR 415.

[246] *Hubbard v Vosper* [1972] 2 QB 84.

[247] *Hubbard v Vosper* [1972] 2 QB 84 at 96–97.

[248] *Woodward v Hutchins* [1977] 1 WLR 760.

[249] *Schering Chemicals Ltd v Falkman Ltd* [1982] QB 1.

[250] *Francome v Mirror Group Newspapers* [1984] 2 All ER 408.

[251] *ECI European Chemical Industries Ltd v Bell* [1981] ILRM 345.

[252] *Seager v Copydex Ltd* [1967] 2 All ER 415.

[253] *Stevenson, Jordan and Harrison Ltd v MacDonald and Evans* (1952) 69 RPC 10.

[254] *American Cyanamid Co v Ethicon Ltd* [1975] AC 396.

[255] *Roger Bullivant Ltd v Ellis* [1987] FSR 172.

quantify for, as Keane J said in *Oblique Financial Services Ltd v Promise Production Co:*[256]

> If that proposition were correct, then it would follow that in cases where breach of confidentiality arises it would, in effect, be impossible for the courts to grant interlocutory relief, however unjust the consequences, if the respondents were, as in the present case, publishers in magazines or periodicals of a large volume of information and comment other than the impugned material.[257]

Other equitable relief may be sought in the form of an order, given by the court within the context of equitable principles, whereby the name of the person responsible for breaching the confidence may be disclosed to the applicant by the third-party defendant. Again, knowledge, actual or constructive, of the breach of confidence appears to be a precondition to relief.[258] *Anton Piller* orders are available in respect of breach of confidence actions[259] as are *Norwich Pharmacal* orders,[260] including 'John Doe' orders.[261]

[24.63] For breach of equitable duties the permanent injunction is a primary remedy that will only be refused in exceptional circumstances or where the information has entered the public domain.[262] Although the trend in all common law jurisdictions favours the award of damages for breach of the equitable duty of confidence, many claimants may seek to obtain injunctive relief; this remedy may afford the plaintiff a measure of protection against competition although there is an increasing awareness that this is not a desirable situation for the courts to promote. In *Certicom Corp v Research in Motion Ltd*,[263] the Ontario High Court issued in injunction preventing the defendant from using confidential information it had obtained improperly in order to launch a hostile takeover. The court stressed that damages would not be an adequate remedy and that the public interest in ensuring confidentiality and standstill agreements would be advanced by injunctive relief in this case. Courts continue to award injunctive relief in conjunction with delivery up remedies, on the chance that a defendant might remember parts of the information.[264] Even though information taken in hard copy or digital form may not be obviously confidential, the courts will still require a defendant to deliver it up, generally regarding an argument that the information has no or limited value with suspicion: 'It is an unattractive plea. If it was of such little use I cannot understand why it was taken or retained'.[265] Even where trade secrets have been misappropriated, the courts are increasingly reluctant to infer that the misappropriation must necessarily involve the

---

[256] *Oblique Financial Services Ltd v Promise Production Co* [1994] ILRM 74.
[257] *Oblique Financial Services Ltd v Promise Production Co* [1994] ILRM 74 at 80.
[258] *NEAP Pty v Ashton* (1995) 33 IPR 281.
[259] *Elvee Ltd v Taylor* [2002] FSR 738.
[260] *Norwich Pharmacal Co v Customs and Excise Comrs* [1974] AC 133.
[261] *Carlton Film Distributors Ltd v VCI plc* [2003] FSR 876.
[262] *Vestergaard Frandsen A/S v Bestnet Europe Ltd* [2010] FSR 2.
[263] *Certicom Corp v Research in Motion Ltd* (2009) 71 CPR (4th) 278.
[264] *Blackmagic Design Pty Ltd v Overliese* (2010) 84 IPR 505.
[265] *Per* Peter Smith J in *Crowson Fabrics Ltd v Rider* [2007] EWHC 2942 (Ch), applying *Robb v Green* [1895] 2 QB 315 and *Bullivant (Roger) Ltd v Ellis* [1987] FSR 172.

award of an injunction to prevent the distribution of the defendant's products that allegedly incorporate the trade secret in question. Efforts to limit the springboard doctrine to cases where there has been either a threatened disclosure or use, or continued use of material in manufacturing a product, are based upon the view that a defendant should not be regarded as a wrongdoer when there is no longer any use or the information has passed into the public domain. Denial of an injunction will be an exceptional step[266] for a court to take but even if the injunction is issued it will be narrowly tailored in the current judicial climate.[267] A strong trend towards awarding damages for breach of an equitable duty of confidence is evident in England.[268]

Damages

[24.64] While damages are awarded in cases of breach of confidence, the position of a plaintiff seeking damages who has no contractual link with the defendant is somewhat perilous as the authorities now stand. The issue of the measure of damages is somewhat more satisfactorily settled. The award of damages for breach of a Constitutional right to privacy are capable of being assessed by reference to three headings, namely, ordinary compensatory damages, aggravated damages and punitive damages[269]. In *Herrity v Independent Newspapers Ltd,*[270] Dunne J awarded €60,000 under the compensatory and aggravated damages heads, with an additional €30,000 being awarded as punitive damages to mark the blatant use of unlawfully obtained transcripts of telephone conversations.

Quantum of damages

[24.65] The case that is most frequently cited on the issue of quantum is the Court of Appeal's decision in *Seager v Copydex (No 2).*[271] In this case the defendants were approached by an inventor who wanted the defendants to licence others to use a carpet grip that he had devised; the defendants used information thus received to make their own product which competed with a carpet grip that the plaintiff himself sold, although the two products were different in design. The plaintiff sought compensation for the loss to his business that he suffered as a result of giving the defendants information which they had exploited, albeit innocently, to the detriment of the plaintiff's business. Denning MR said that the approach to be taken was to be based on the analogy provided by damages for conversion or trover. Once damages are paid, the property becomes that of the defendant, a satisfied judgment having the effect of transferring property to the defendant; the problem was one of valuing the 'property':

---

[266] *Occular Sciencess Ltd v Aspect Vision Care Ltd* [1997] RPC 289.

[267] *Vestergaard Frandsen A/S v Bestnet Europe Ltd* [2010] FSR 2; *Penwell Publishing (UK) Ltd v Ornstien* [2007] IRLR 70.

[268] *Douglas v Hello! Ltd (No 3)* [2008] 1 AC 1.

[269] See Finlay CJ in *Conway v INTO* [1991] 2 IR 305 at 317; Murray C J in *Shortt v Commissioner of An Garda Síochána* [2007] IESC 9.

[270] *Herrity v Independent Newspapers Ltd* [2008] IEHC 249.

[271] *Seager v Copydex (No 2)* [1969] 2 All ER 718.

If there was nothing very special about it, that is, if it involved no particular inventive step but was the sort of information which could be obtained by employing any competent consultant, then the value of it was the fee which a consultant would charge for it; because in that case the defendant company, by taking the information, would only have saved themselves the time and trouble of employing a consultant. But, on the other hand, if the information was something special, as for instance if it involved an inventive step or something so unusual that it could not be obtained by just going to a consultant, then the value of it is much higher.[272]

[24.66] In this judgment Lord Denning MR considered that the approach to take is to look to an appropriate figure; thus on the lower end of the scale, ie where the information is 'not special' the consultant fee basis would be the quantum, while at the other end of the scale Lord Denning MR had in mind the possibility of looking to the royalty that confidential information could have attracted and then capitalising the value of that royalty, presumably over the commercial life of that information, that is, the lead-in time before competitors could enter the market and use this information for themselves.

[24.67] However, Lord Denning MR's speech in *Copydex (No 2)*[273] has not fared well and it has been held in subsequent cases[274] not to lay down any rule which qualifies the broad compensatory principle by which damages are calculated. In *Dowson and Mason Ltd v Potter*,[275] the Court of Appeal considered *Copydex (No 2)* in the context of an action where the first defendant gave to his new employer, the second defendant, information concerning technical equipment which he acquired while in the plaintiffs' employment. In finding a breach of confidence the defendants were ordered to compensate the plaintiffs for their loss of profits resulting from the wrongful disclosure. The defendants appealed, characterising the information disclosed as being within the first category stated by Lord Denning MR, ie information available elsewhere, as distinct from information within the exclusive control of the plaintiff. In such a case, the defendants argued, the damages should be the value of the article (the information) as between a willing buyer and a willing seller. The Court of Appeal, relying upon the decision of the House of Lords in *General Tire and Rubber Co v Firestone Tyre and Rubber Co*[276] restated the basic principle that in economic torts the purpose of an award of damages would be to put the plaintiff in the position he would have been in if the plaintiff had not sustained the wrong. The Court of Appeal added to the *Copydex (No 2)* test a requirement to look to the particular position of the plaintiff. If, as in *Copydex (No 2)*, the plaintiff is prepared to allow others to use information for a fee, on a non-exclusive basis, then that fee should be the quantum. If, however, the information is not to be licensed, even if others could ultimately discover and use the information from other sources, the non-exclusive nature of that information, or relatively prosaic nature

---

[272] *Seager v Copydex (No 2)* [1969] 2 All ER 718 at 719–720.

[273] *Seager v Copydex (No 2)* [1969] 2 All ER 718.

[274] Eg *Talbot v General Television* [1981] RPC 1.

[275] *Dowson and Mason Ltd v Potter* [1986] 2 All ER 418.

[276] *Tire and Rubber Co v Firestone Tyre and Rubber Co* [1975] 2 All ER 173, especially Lord Wilberforce at 177.

of the information, is not to deprive the plaintiff of the profit he would have obtained as a result of being ahead of the competition via the exclusivity of the information, judged at the time of the wrong done to him. Slade LJ, in particular, drew a contrast between the relevant quantum where the plaintiff did not intend to manufacture the finished products; the relevant measure here should be a licensing measure. In contrast, where the plaintiff did manufacture that item, the licensing measure would be inappropriate, for it is manufacturing profits that the plaintiff has lost. A similar attempt to restrict damages, in *House of Spring Gardens Ltd v Point Blank Ltd*,[277] was unsuccessful, for the plaintiffs, in opting for an account of profits, which were multi-million pound figures, were able to side-step the defendants' assertion that as between a willing seller and buyer the information would be worth around £630,000 under a royalty agreement.

[24.68] The nature of the information, however, may be important in the final analysis of just how much of the defendant's business can be attributed to the nature of the defendant's misuse of information. Certainly, where the information consists of customer names and addresses, the plaintiff is often given the benefit of the doubt, but if in the assessment of damages it is found that the defendant used little or no confidential information and that the defendant's success is down to other factors then nominal damages and a successful counterclaim may result.[278] If the breach of confidence leads to the loss of a business opportunity then damages for that lost opportunity will be awarded. This amount will generally be much lower than any estimate as to lost profits.[279]

[24.69] Where the plaintiff's claim is based on a contractual relationship with the defendant, the award of damages may be possible because of that contractual link. However, where the plaintiff is bringing an action against someone with whom there is no such link (eg a third-party disclosee) then the issue arises whether damages are possible. Certainly, in cases of a threatened breach of confidence, where the plaintiff seeks interlocutory relief, the court has a discretion to award damages 'in lieu of or in addition to an injunction' under the Chancery Amendment Act 1858 (Lord Cairns' Act), a reforming piece of legislation intended to rationalise litigation by allowing a common law remedy to be available in a court of equity in circumstances where an injunction would be within the jurisdiction of the court, but an inappropriate or inadequate relief in the case at bar. Several of the leading cases are to be regarded as cases where the court awarded damages in lieu of an injunction,[280] the damages being awarded to cover loss occasioned by previous and possible future breaches of confidence. It is, however, necessary for the non-contractual claimant to seek to prove that the claimant had some claim to an injunction for if there is no real prospect of an injunction being awarded, as where the breach of duty has already occurred and an injunction is not necessary to deter

---

[277] *House of Spring Gardens Ltd v Point Blank Ltd* [1984] IR 611, especially the judgment of Griffin J on this point.

[278] *Universal Thermosensors Ltd v Hibben* [1992] FSR 361.

[279] *Indata Equipment Supplies Ltd v ACL Ltd* [1998] FSR 248.

[280] See Slade J's view of *Seager v Copydex* ([1969] 2 All ER 718) in *English v Dedham Vale Properties Ltd* [1978] 1 WLR 93 at 111.

future breaches of duty, then, in the absence of some other cause of action for damages, there seems no prospect of Lord Cairns' Act being applicable.[281] This issue was considered extensively in the Northern Ireland case of *O'Neill v DHSS*.[282] In that case the plaintiff made an application to her local DHSS office for maternity benefit. She was unmarried at the time and, apart from the father of the child and her doctor, no other person was aware of the pregnancy. Shortly after this application was made, the plaintiff miscarried. A neighbour later indicated that he knew that she was pregnant indicating that the source of this information was his sister who had dealt with the plaintiff's initial maternity benefit claim. This caused the plaintiff to be upset and she told the salient facts to her mother as a result of this distress, although she initially wanted to withhold her condition from her mother. While the DHSS accepted that information of this kind was given in confidence and while Carswell J held that the facts came within the *Coco v AN Clark*[283] threefold test, Carswell J indicated that there is no common law tort of breach of confidence and because there was no prospect of the plaintiff getting an injunction in the case before him, damages in lieu of an injunction were not possible. Carswell J also observed that if the disclosure made by the DHSS clerk was made negligently then there may have been a further obstacle to awarding damages for in his view any such tort should be limited to deliberate disclosures. Carswell J also took the view that while the DHSS clerk may well have been within a *Hedley Byrne*[284] special relationship, or also in the position of a fiduciary, liability under such headings for true statements would cause difficulties for the plaintiff. Carswell J also opined that mere nervous shock, aside from some other sustainable claim to protect other interests, is not recoverable *per se*. The plaintiff was also not able to fix the State with liability since the wrong done was outside the concept of vicarious liability and protected by Crown immunity.

[24.70] While Capper[285] has made valiant efforts to suggest that a more pro-plaintiff spin can be put on both the facts and the law, *O'Neill v DHSS*[286] represents an almost unimpeachable argument for statutory modification of the remedial aspects of the equitable duty of confidence.

[24.71] The decision in the *O'Neill* case[287] also raises the issue of non-pecuniary loss. Had the plaintiff made out a cause of action, could there be an award of damages for distress, vexation, injured feelings and annoyance caused by the breach of duty? In cases where the information is commercial in nature, transferred within a context of this kind, general principles may dictate that financial distress rather than injury to feelings is the foreseeable kind of loss, and the Irish courts on both sides of the border have taken the

---

[281] *Proctor v Bayley* (1889) 42 Ch D 390; *Malone v Metropolitan Police Comr* [1979] 2 All ER 620; contrast Harman J in *Nichrotherm Electrical Co v Percy* [1957] RPC 207.

[282] *O'Neill v DHSS* [1986] 5 NI 290.

[283] *Coco v AN Clark* [1968] FSR 415 at 420–421.

[284] *Hedley Byrne v Heller* [1964] AC 465.

[285] Capper (1986) 37 NILQ 273; (1994) 14 Legal Studies 313.

[286] *O'Neill v DHSS* [1986] 5 NI 290.

[287] *O'Neill v DHSS* [1986] 5 NI 290.

view that injury to feelings and mental stress is not generally recoverable.[288] If, however, the nature of the confidence is such that no pecuniary or financial interest can be shown to have been prejudiced, then damages, if available at all, should be assessed so as to compensate the plaintiff for injury to reputation, anxiety, loss of self-esteem and general distress caused by the breach of duty, certainly in cases of deliberate disclosure even if the facts disclosed are true. The appropriate analogy here is with holiday cases[289] and the many decisions involving 'the wedding reception from hell'.[290] Recent case law suggests that damages for injury to feelings are recoverable, regardless of whether the cause of action is breach of an implied contractual duty or the equitable duty of confidence.[291] Similar uncertainties surround the availability of punitive damages (save in cases of State misuse of confidential information) or damages intended to prevent unjust enrichment of a plaintiff under the *Hickey v Roches Stores dictum*[292] that damages for breach of contract or some other wrong can be assessed to deprive a '*mala fide*' defendant of the fruits of his wrongdoing.

[24.72] There are of course several cases in which the plaintiff is able to make out a number of different causes of action, breach of confidence being only one of them. It is clear that the plaintiff cannot obtain damages under each cause of action, for damages are cumulative. The plaintiff has some opportunity to nominate both the cause of action and the relevant measure, but the courts may determine that the appropriate measure of damages in breach of confidence is the actual value of the information rather than profits earned by the defendant. In *Interfirm Comparison v Law Society of NSW*,[293] the plaintiff was able to support actions for breach of confidence and infringement of copyright. The plaintiff was held entitled to one lot of damages to cover two breaches of obligation, and it was held that the normal copyright measure, that is, the depreciation caused by the infringement to the chose in action – the copyright work – is not a universal measure. In that case the court compared the work, as an unpublished work, to an unauthorised disclosure in breach of confidence, and said that the relevant measure is the value of the information disclosed in breach of duty. In *Fortuity Property Ltd v Barcza*[294] this approach was taken even further for here the court held that either measure was impossible to calculate so a reasonable sum by way of damages was ordered as compensation for the defendants' breaches of duty. Where breach of the fiduciary duty

---

[288] *Kelly v Crowley* (5 March 1985, unreported), HC. However, Keane J in the later case of *Lennon v Talbot Ireland* (20 December 1985, unreported), HC awarded modest damages for 'general anxiety and inconvenience' caused by premature termination of a motor dealership. In Northern Ireland see *Smith v Huey* [1993] 8 NIJB 49.

[289] *Jarvis v SwansTours* [1973] QB 233.

[290] Eg *Hotson v Payn* [1988] CLY 409.

[291] *Cornelius v De Taranto* [2002] EMLR 112; Stewart [2001] EIPR 302; *Giller v Procopets* (2008) 79 IPR 485.

[292] *Hickey v Roches Stores* (14 July 1976, unreported), HC; (1978) 26 NILQ 128.

[293] *Interfirm Comparison v Law Society of NSW* (1975) 6 ALR 445.

[294] *Fortuity Property Ltd v Barcza* (1995) 32 IPR 517; appeal against liability dismissed at (1996) 36 IPR 529.

is made out, recent case law suggests that damages may be awarded via equitable compensation on a rather more expansive basis that contract damages.[295]

An account of profits

[24.73] This is an equitable remedy that the plaintiff may elect to choose, in contrast to the remedy of damages. The election is to take place at a time prior to the conclusion of the litigation although English case law has indicated that the plaintiff is entitled to make an informed choice, which will necessitate the defendant providing details of accounts prior to the election.[296] Most judicial opinion is of the view that an account of profits is a messy and unsatisfactory business.[297] In more recent times, however, the English and the Irish courts have extolled the virtue of an account of profits in cases where the courts have already obtained access to the accounts of the defendant, and the ordering of an account will have the additional advantage of deterring wrongdoers who are thus denied any incentive to breach the confidence and hope that damages will not disgorge from the defendant all his ill-gotten gains.[298] Furthermore, because the plaintiff need only elect after adequate information has been provided by the infringer, new lines of authority suggest the courts may order a form of discovery, or require affidavits from responsible persons, which will serve to inform the plaintiff of the likely outcome of the account.[299] However, practical difficulties may arise in sorting out the profits made legitimately from those made as a result of the breach of confidence, and in such cases the court's discretion may lead to the award of damages.[300]

[24.74] In *A-G v Blake*[301] a majority of the House of Lords held that an account of profits could, in the exceptional circumstances before their Lordships' House be awarded so as to deny a contract breaker the profits he would otherwise make from his breach of contract. Blake was a member of the British Security forces who signed in 1944 a non-disclosure agreement which was lifelong. He was convicted of spying for the USSR, escaped from prison and in 1989 wrote a memoir. The Attorney-General sought to prevent Blake from receiving advances from the publisher. Because the information used in 1989 was no longer confidential the Attorney-General pursued an argument based on breach of contract, the difficulty being that the Crown was not seeking compensation but the amount Blake sought to gain from his breach of contract. Lord Nicholls, giving judgment for the majority of the Law Lords, held that there were

---

[295] *Vawdrey Australia Pty Ltd v Kruger Transport Co* (2008) 79 IPR 81, *RBC Dominion Securities Ltd v Merrill Lynch Canada* (2008) 68 CPR (4th) 401; *Deeson v Cox* (2009) 82 IPR 521.

[296] *Island Records Ltd v Tring International plc* [1995] 3 All ER 444; *Tang Man Sit v Capacious Investments Ltd* [1996] 1 All ER 193.

[297] Eg *Siddell v Vickers* (1892) 9 RPC 152; *Wedderburn v Wedderburn* (1838) 4 My & Cr 41.

[298] *Peter Pan Manufacturing Corpn v Corsets Silhouette Ltd* [1964] 1 WLR 96; *House of Spring Gardens Ltd v Point Blank Ltd* [1984] IR 611.

[299] *Island Records v Tring* [1995] 3 All ER 444; *LED Builders Pty v Eagles Homes Pty (No 2)* (1996) 36 IPR 293. *Stenner v Scotia McLeod* (2007) 62 IPR 1; *Tenderwatch Pty Ltd v Reed Business Information* (2008) 78 IPR 329.

[300] *Fortuity Property Ltd v Barcza* (1995) 32 IPR 517, appeal dismissed (1996) 36 IPR 529.

[301] *A-G v Blake* [2001] 1 AC 268.

exceptional instances where equity would grant an account of profits and that this could be extended into claims arising from a breach of contract, *pace Wrotham Park Estate Co v Parkside Homes Ltd,*[302] a decision rooted in Lord Cairns' Act. In a vigorous dissent Lord Hobhouse objected that this was an unsound departure from the compensatory principle and he predicted that if the principle of awarding non-compensatory damages were to extend into commercial law the consequences would be 'far reaching and disruptive'. The decision in *Blake* has attracted a significant volume of comment, much of it adverse (for a variety of reasons). The New Zealand Court of Appeal in *A-G for England and Wales v R* has, *obiter*, indicated that in the case of a solider who gives a contractual commitment not to publish his account of the Bravo Two Zero in the first Gulf war, such a commitment is contractually binding and that any publication is in breach of contract or in an account of profits and damages.[303] Whether a contract will be able to procure for the plaintiff both damages and an account of profits is just one of the many points of uncertainty that will be tested in this post *Blake* environment.

[24.75] It has been suggested that where confidential information has been used to create a trading or business opportunity it may be possible to argue that either the profits or the business itself may be held on a constructive trust for the beneficial ownership of the confider.[304] For this possibility to arise the House of Lords has held that trust property or traceable proceeds of trust property must exist.[305] In *Satnam Investments Ltd v Dunlop Heywood & Co*[306] the Court of Appeal held that the fact that a third party comes into possession of confidential information by way of a fiduciary does not of itself create liability of that third party vis-à-vis the proprietor.

SUBSEQUENT DEVELOPMENTS IN IRELAND

[24.76] There have been a number of recent legislative and other initiatives that provide ancillary means of protecting confidential information. The possibility that information may be stolen and the criminal law brought into play is strengthened by the Criminal Justice (Theft and Fraud Offences) Act 2001.[307] In relation to the issue of using personal data, particularly by the media, specific reliefs are afforded to data subjects by the Data Protection (Amendment) Act 2003 and the Data Protection Commissioner has ruled in favour of celebrities and family members being entitled to privacy even in public places. However, the increased emphasis upon human rights, particularly rights of privacy under

---

302 *Wrotham Park Estate Co v Parkside Homes Ltd* [1974] 2 All ER 321.

303 *A-G for England and Wales v R* [2002] 2 NZLR 91 at paras 112–113, *per* Keith J, citing the provisions in the agreement signed by the respondent. Appeal to the Privy Council was dismissed [2003] UKPC 22; see O'Sullivan (2003) 62 Cam LJ 554.

304 *LAC Minerals Ltd v International Corona Resources Ltd* (1989) 6 DLR (4th) 14; *Fortuity Property Co v Barcza* (1995) 32 IPR 517.

305 *Royal Brunei Airlines Sdn Bnd v Tan* [1995] 2 AC 378.

306 *Satnam Investments Ltd v Dunlop Heywood & Co* [1999] 3 ALL ER 652.

307 Property is defined so as to include things in action and other intangible property (Criminal Justice (Theft and Fraud Offences) Act 2001, s 2(10)). See the s 4 theft offences and Criminal Justice (Theft and Fraud Offences) Act 2001, s 9 (dishonest use of computers).

art 8 of ECHR, will no doubt stimulate increased litigation in Ireland *pace* the UK HRA 1998 and the UK cases[308] in which infringement of the data protection principles have proved to be ancillary causes of action. The incorporation of art 8 of ECHR into Irish domestic law will also trigger increased interest in the jurisprudence of the European Court of Human Rights in arts 8 and 10, in particular. Apart from the fact that Irish Constitutional law has recognised an unenumerated right to privacy, which can be used against the State and the media, as well as providing consideration in a private law bargain, the Law Reform Commission Report *Privacy, Surveillance and the Interception of Communications*[309] has pressed for further statutory innovation. The Law Reform Commission recommended the enactment of a new tort of Privacy – Intrusive Surveillance. The Commission was at pains to stress that it was not recommending the creation of a general privacy tort protecting informational privacy *per se* but was seeking to 'enhance the protection provided by the privacy shield against intrusion'.[310] The tort would provide a 'reasonable expectation' of privacy and would require a balancing exercise to be carried out by the courts. The report set out a list of indicative factors on a non-exhaustive basis. These factors are generally recognisable to anyone familiar with general privacy legislation and case law from other jurisdictions. They are:

(a)   the place of surveillance, public or private;
(b)   the object or occasion of surveillance;
(c)   the purpose of collection, including publication;
(d)   the means employed (eg covert devices or long-lens cameras);
(e)   the status or function of the person being monitored;
(f)   the conduct of the person prior to surveillance;
(g)   the overall context.[311]

Surveillance is broadly defined so as to cover all acts of aural or visual surveillance including acts of interpretation and participant/third-party monitoring, as defined in the report; the casual overhearing of a conversation on a bus was also considered to be within the recommended new tort so, despite the restriction to 'surveillance', the tort is very close to providing an informational privacy tort. Although a more far reaching Privacy Bill was published in 2006,[312] with a view to providing a tort of violation, no progress has been made towards this.

---

[308] *Campbell v MGN Ltd* [2004] 2 All ER 995; *Ewing v Times Newspapers* [2010] NIQB 7.
[309] LRC 57 (1998).
[310] LRC 57 (1998), para 7.06.
[311] LRC 57 (1998), ch 2.
[312] [Seanad] Bill No 44/2006.

Chapter 25

Remedies in Tort

PASSING OFF

The relationship with trade mark law

[25.01] The common law tort of passing off is regarded as an independent cause of action that is in no way subordinate to the statutory regime in relation to trade marks. The history of passing off demonstrates that the common law cause of action is much more flexible and can be operated by the courts so as to produce quite different results. Ní Shuilleabháin[1] draws attention to the impact that the law of passing off has even within modern trade mark regimes.

[25.02] In *Inter Lotto (UK) Ltd v Camelot Group plc*[2] the claimants had used the name 'Hot Pick' in connection with lotteries it ran on behalf of charities. The UK National Lottery started to use 'Hot Picks' and obtained a trade mark registration. The claimants argued that the registration was in conflict with their earlier use and that they could maintain an action for passing off. The defendants argued that the claimants could not utilise post-registration trading activities in establishing goodwill because in the face of registration this trading was unlawful, the common law rights of the claimant being subordinate to and inferior to a trade mark registration. Both these points were rejected, the Court of Appeal reaffirming that in order to sustain an action in passing off, the claimant must establish goodwill at the time at which the acts of the defendant, which the claimant complains of, have commenced. The claimant may establish goodwill even by pointing to trading activities that postdate a rival's application to register a trade mark.

Historical origins[3]

[25.03] While the basic features of the cause of action for passing off have been clearly identified in modern jurisprudence as resting upon the law relating to misrepresentation, this rationalisation has not always been agreed upon. In historical terms, the approach of equity and the common law courts did not coalesce until the end of the nineteenth century, and the early cases demonstrate a variety of possible motives for judicial intervention when goods or services were offered or supplied by a defendant in controversial circumstances. There are also examples of cases in which the courts

---

[1]   Ní Shuilleabháin (2003) 34 IIC 722.
[2]   *Inter Lotto (UK) Ltd v Camelot Group plc* [2004] RPC 186; see the Trade Marks Act 1996, s 7(2); Jolly [2004] Ent LR 25.
[3]   See Wadlow, *Passing Off* (3rd edn, Sweet and Maxwell, 2002), ch 1.

pressed into service a number of related concepts and causes of action such as injurious falsehood or defamation so as to afford a plaintiff relief from damage to trade or reputation: see, for example, *Seeley v Fisher.*[4]

[25.04] In two early seventeenth century cases,[5] Dodderidge J gave as an early instance of the vitality of the common law in this field an earlier Tudor case in which a Gloucester clothier's mark of reputation was fixed upon cloth inferior to that of the Gloucester clothier by the defendant. Dodderidge J observed that an action could lie upon the wrong of the defendant although it is by no means clear that the action was available to the user of the mark or a purchaser of the inferior cloth who relied upon the mark.[6] However, the nineteenth century cases that followed made it clear that the action at law was available to the trader whose mark had been used by the defendant and that the basis of the right to common law damages[7] is deceit on the part of the defendant. In equity, however, the availability of injunctive relief proceeded on somewhat different grounds. Early cases like *Blanchard v Hill*[8] indicated that one trader could not injunct another trader from using the plaintiff's mark, although Lord Hardwicke LC observed *obiter* that, while use of the mark *per se* could not ground relief, doing so with fraudulent intent to either sell bad goods or draw away customers from the plaintiff could merit relief. By the beginning of the nineteenth century, however, equity had awarded injunctive relief to protect authors from having inferior works sold under the author's name[9] and to prevent traders from occupying premises previously used by the plaintiff and imitating their nature and mode of business.[10] The decision in *Millington v Fox,*[11] however, suggested that equity was not simply following the law in regarding intention to deceive as an essential proof, for in this case an injunction was given to restrain the defendant from using the plaintiff's mark even though the original use was innocent, in so far as the defendant did not know it was the plaintiff's mark but rather, a technical or descriptive mark. So, while innocent original use was not a defence in equity, the approach at common law was fully considered in *Perry v Truefitt.*[12]

[25.05] In *Perry v Truefitt*, the plaintiff successfully manufactured and sold a hair product under the name 'Perry's Medicated Mexican Balm' for several years. The defendant produced a rival product which he described as 'Medicated Mexican Balm'. The plaintiff complained that in the mind of the public the phrase 'Medicated Mexican Balm' was connected with Perry. Lord Langdale declined to give an injunction saying, however:

---

4   *Seeley v Fisher* (1841) 11 Sim 581.
5   *Southern v How* (1618) Cro Jac 468; *Dean v Steel* (1626) Lat 188 reported in law French.
6   See Wadlow, *Passing Off* (3rd edn, Sweet and Maxwell, 2002).
7   *Sykes v Sykes* (1824) 3 B & C 541; *Crawshay v Thompson* (1842) 4 Man & G 357.
8   *Blanchard v Hill* (1742) 2 Atk 484.
9   *Byron v Johnston* (1816) 2 Mer 297.
10 *Crutwell v Lye* (1810) 17 Ves 335.
11 *Millington v Fox* (1838) 3 My & Cr 338.
12 *Perry v Truefitt* (1842) 6 Beav 66 at 418.

A man is not to sell his own goods under the pretence that they are the goods of another man; he cannot be permitted to practice a deception, nor to use the means which contribute to that end. He cannot, therefore, be allowed to use names, marks, letters or other indicia, by which he may induce purchasers to believe that the goods which he is selling are the manufacture of another person.[13]

[25.06] The observation of Lord Langdale MR about the basis of the action being a desire to counteract deception is heightened by his doubts about the possibility of there being any property right in a name or a mark, and his Lordship also observed that the principle is the basis of both common law and equitable reliefs. In Ireland, *Perry v Truefitt*[14] was followed in *Foot v Lea*[15] some eight years later. The well known Dublin firm of *Lundy Foot & Co*[16] sought an injunction to prevent a former employee from selling 'A Lea Dublin Snuff', the defendant advertising the fact that he was a former employee of the plaintiff who manufactured 'Lundy Foot & Co Irish Snuff'. The labels used by the defendant were said by the court to have been made so as to intentionally mislead the public, but on these facts an injunction would not be issued. The jurisdictions at law and in equity were said to be one and the same, *pace Perry v Truefitt*, and the liability of the defendant was left to be tested in a trial of the action. Shortly after *Foot v Lea* an Irish court held that an agreement to allow persons to trade in products that deceive the public would be unenforceable as a fraud on the public.[17]

[25.07] The emphasis on misrepresentation or deception was not the only rationalisation, however. In a number of cases, Lord Westbury gave the view that the basis of the plaintiff's cause of action in relation to trade marks was a right of property[18] and this view was espoused by an Irish judge in *Wheeler v Johnson*.[19] In that case the plaintiffs had bottled water using an ancient well in Belfast under the name Cromac Springs, a geographical appellation. The defendants began to sell water using the name Cromac Springs pointing to the number of wells and springs in that area. Chatterton VC had no doubt that a geographical name of this kind could become a trade mark, observing that rights to marks acquired by usage and reputation are in the nature of property rights and he granted an injunction restraining the defendants from using the phrase Cromac Springs in such a way as to indicate a connection with the plaintiffs' business.

[25.08] However, the property right rationalisation did not take root and after *Singer Manufacturing Co v Loog*[20] little is heard of the Westbury view. By the end of the nineteenth century the Irish courts had given a considered view of the basis of the cause

---

13 *Perry v Truefitt* (1842) 6 Beav 66 at 73.
14 *Perry v Truefitt* (1842) 6 Beav 66.
15 *Foot v Lea* (1850) 13 IR Eq R 484.
16 Mentioned by James Joyce in *Ulysses*.
17 *Oldham v James* (1863) 14 IR Ch R 81.
18 Eg *Hall v Barrows* (1863) 4 De GJ & Sm 150; *Leather Cloth Co v American Leather Cloth Co* (1865) 11 HL Cas 523.
19 *Wheeler v Johnson* (1879) 3 LR Ir 284.
20 *Singer Manufacturing Co v Loog* (1882) 8 App Cas 15.

of action in two cases. In *Bodega Co v Owens*,[21] Chatterton VC adopted the view of James LJ in *Levy v Walker*[22] that a person:

> has a right to say, you must not use a name, whether fictitious or real, you must not use a description, whether true or not, which is intended to represent, or calculated to represent to the world that your business is my business, and so, by a fraudulent misstatement deprive me of the profits of the business that would otherwise come to me. That is the principle and the sole principle on which this court interferes.

[25.09] Chatterton VC extended this *dictum* by allowing the plaintiff to succeed even without any proof of fraud, holding that both the fact of registration and the undoubted reputation of the plaintiffs gave them rights to their trade name independent of any statute. The Vice Chancellor held that:

> On the evidence now before me, to the use of the word [Bodega] as a trade name in connection with his trade and business: this, however, does not give him an exclusive right to it, but only the right to restrain any other person from using it in such a way as to represent that the business carried on by that person is his business.[23]

The modern basis for passing off

[25.10] In *Jameson v Dublin Distillers Co*,[24] the plaintiff carried on the business of whiskey distilling under the name of John Jameson & Son Ltd. There was another distillery which distilled and sold whiskey under the name of William Jameson and Co. Both companies had been founded in the eighteenth century. However, after the defendant company acquired William Jameson and Co it began to trade under the style of Jameson's Whiskey, dropping the prefix of William from the product label. The plaintiff asserted that the William Jameson product was inferior and cheaper in price and that 'Jameson's Whiskey' in the public mind was associated with it. Chatterton VC gave an injunction to prevent the defendant trading in the product without prefacing the phrase 'Jameson's Whiskey' with the name of William. In treating this case as turning solely on the misuse of a name, Chatterton VC indicated that a court of equity would protect a person whose name has been used in trade or manufacture from use by others if such use leads others to think that the trade of the person using the name is that of the plaintiff and that for such relief to be obtained it is enough to show that the conduct complained of will tend to mislead ordinary persons. While Chatterton VC throughout this judgment refers to fraud, parallel developments in England suggest that some English judges were also persuaded that deceit remained at the heart of a passing-off action.[25] However, in *AG Spalding v AW Gamage Ltd*[26] the true basis of a passing-off action was enunciated by Lord Parker. In that case the learned Lord of Appeal observed

---

21 *Bodega Co v Owens* (1888) 23 LR Ir 371.
22 *Levy v Walker* (1879) 10 Ch D 436 at 448.
23 *Bodega Co v Owens* (1888) 23 LR Ir 371 at 389–390.
24 *Jameson v Dublin Distillers Co* [1900] 1 IR 43, 73, 466.
25 Eg Lord Davey in *Edge & Sons v Gallon & Son* (1900) 17 RPC 557 at 566.
26 *AG Spalding v AW Gamage Ltd* (1915) 32 RPC 273.

that the basis of the relief is a false representation by the defendant and he reformulated the basis of the cause of action thus:

> A cannot, without infringing the rights of B, represent goods which are not B's goods or B's goods of a particular class or quality to be B's goods or B's goods of that particular class or quality.

[25.11] While rejecting the notion of deceit and noting that reliefs could be obtained even against innocent defendants, Lord Parker observed that the right that the plaintiff may invoke is a right of property. The right is not a right of property in the name, mark or other indicia but, rather, a right of property in the business or goodwill that the plaintiff has created.[27] Lord Parker thus provided not only a more satisfying rationale for passing off as a strict liability economic tort, he also provided a more flexible basis for relief when the misrepresentation is not linked to names, marks, etc, but to non-trade mark material such as a shape[28] or an advertising campaign.[29] The *Spalding* decision[30] is seen as the basis of the most influential of all recent appellate utterances on liability for passing off, for the formula devised by Lord Parker in *Spalding* came into its own in a series of cases in which marks *per se* were not used by the defendants but the defendants were seen to be appropriating the reputation and integrity of the plaintiff's goods by misdescribing their own products. Judges distinguish what they describe as the 'classic' form of passing off, in which the plaintiff seeks to show that the plaintiff has built up the goodwill personally by dint of commercial activity or that goodwill has been around from a predecessor. In the 'extended' form of the tort, on the other hand, it is the legitimate entry into a trade by an individual (often an association member using a geographical or entirely descriptive term in connection with goods or services) that provides the basis of the action. The first case in this sequence, *Bollinger v Costa Brava Wine Co*[31] involved an action brought by producers of champagne from the Champagne district of France, who produced this wine from particular grapes by a particular method of production, who sought to prevent the defendants from using the phrase 'Spanish Champagne' to describe their own beverage. In that case Danckwerts J held that the misdescription would enable each and every shipper of sparkling wine from the Champagne region, whose wines met the requirements of the appellation, to protect the goodwill built up in England from damage caused by the defendants' misrepresentation to, and deception of, the public. This approach was extended in later cases to the producers of sherry from Jerez[32] and Scotch whisky.[33] The leading case that upholds the integrity of these decisions, which afford to producers collective and individual rights to protect the integrity of a descriptive term that is used to market goods so as to exploit the public's esteem for those goods, is the *Advocaat* case.[34] In that case, the manufacturers of

---

[27] Following on this point Lord Herschell in *Reddaway v Banham* [1896] AC 199 at 209.

[28] *Reckitt and Colman Products v Borden* [1990] 1 All ER 873.

[29] *Cadbury Schweppes v Pub Squash* [1981] 1 All ER 213.

[30] *AG Spalding v AW Gamage Ltd* (1915) 32 RPC 273.

[31] *Bollinger v Costa Brava Wine Co* [1960] Ch 262.

[32] *Vine Products Ltd v MacKenzie* [1968] FSR 625.

[33] *Walker (John) and Sons v Henry Ost & Co* [1970] 2 All ER 106.

[34] *Warnink v Townsend & Sons (Hull)* [1979] AC 731.

an egg and gin drink, made to Dutch governmental standards, sought to prevent the defendants who were marketing a cheaper product made up from a mixture of eggs and wine, from selling this as 'Old English Advocaat'. The plaintiffs, who were the market leader for the Dutch Advocaat were able to show that the name Advocaat had a significance and a reputation in England and that the defendants' product, being wine-based rather than spirit-based, did not meet consumer expectations and that, accordingly, the public would be deceived, to the detriment of the plaintiffs.

[25.12] *Taittinger v Allbev Ltd*[35] emphasises the 'inferior' nature of the defendant's product. But this will not be a requirement of succeeding in an extended passing-off action. In *Chocosuisse Union des Fabricants Suisses v Cadbury Ltd*[36] the defendants marketed a chocolate bar under the name 'Swiss Chalet'. It was established that the public associated the words 'Swiss chocolate' with a distinct and superior product, and, on the evidence, a significant portion of the public believed that the words 'Swiss Chalet' indicated not just a descriptive phrase but 'chocolate made in Switzerland' about which individual manufacturers could not complain. Laddie J at first instance rejected evidence that there was no discernible difference between the taste of the competing products as irrelevant; the Court of Appeal agreed that the issue was whether Swiss chocolate had established a distinct reputation as chocolate made in Switzerland to a Swiss recipe.[37] In the extended form of the tort the English courts have accepted that this approach affords to the proprietor(s) of the right a property right that represents a powerful marketing or branding tool once the otherwise descriptive generic or geographical appellation has been used by someone not recognised as entitled to use the appellation. As the most recent example of this form of extended passing-off protection illustrates,[38] the brand leader in relation to Vodka can maintain an action against a misleading name, here VODKAT, when the name, marketing and get up of a different product has the actual effect of misleading the public. No obvious geographical link need be shown, nor is it necessary to demonstrate that the class of goods seeking to be protected has a 'cachet' denoting superior quality.

[25.13] In his speech in the *Advocaat* case, Lord Diplock, with whom the other Law Lords concurred,[39] identified five elements in the tort of passing off:

(1) a misrepresentation;

(2) made by a trader in the course of trade;

(3) to prospective customers of his or ultimate customers or ultimate consumers of goods or services supplied by him;

(4) which is calculated to injure the business or goodwill of another trader (in the sense that this is a reasonably foreseeable consequence); and

---

[35] *Taittinger v Allbev Ltd* [1993] FSR 641.

[36] *Chocosuisse Union des Fabricants Suisses v Cadbury Ltd* [1998] RPC 117.

[37] *Chocosuisse Union des Fabricants Suisses v Cadbury Ltd* [1999] RPC 826.

[38] *Diageo North America Inc v Intercontinental Brands ICB Ltd* [2010] EWHC 17 (Ch).

[39] Lords Dilhorne, Salmon and Scarman concurred with both Lord Diplock and Lord Fraser's speeches but Lord Fraser's speech is more narrowly focused and has not proved influential.

(5)   which causes actual damage to a business or goodwill of the trader by whom the action is brought or (in a *quia timet* action) will probably do so.[40]

[25.14] In *Reckitt and Colman Products Ltd v Borden*,[41] Lord Oliver addressed the issue of the essential elements in passing off:

> [The plaintiff] must establish a goodwill or reputation attached to the goods or services which he supplies in the mind of the purchasing public by association with the identifying get-up (whether that consists simply of a brand name or trade description or the individual features of labelling or packaging) under which his particular goods or services are offered to the public, such that the get-up is recognised by the public as distinctive, specifically as the plaintiff's goods or services. Second, he must demonstrate a misrepresentation by the defendant to the public (whether or not intentional) leading or likely to lead the public to believe the goods or services offered by him are the goods or services of the plaintiff ... Third, he must demonstrate that he suffers or in a *quia timet* action that he is likely to suffer damage by reason of the erroneous belief engendered by the defendant's misrepresentation that the sources of the defendant's goods or services is the same as the sources of those offered by the plaintiff.[42]

[25.15] Lord Jauncey, in a concurring judgment, gave his view of the proofs needed to succeed in the tort of passing off:

> In a case such as the present, where what is in issue is whether the goods of A are likely to be passed off as those of B, a plaintiff, to succeed, must establish
>
> (1)   that his goods have acquired a particular reputation among the public,
>
> (2)   that persons wishing to buy his goods are likely to be misled into buying the goods of the defendant and
>
> (3)   that he is likely to suffer damage thereby.[43]

[25.16] Lord Oliver's formulation in *Reckitt and Colman*[44] has the merit of being more elaborately structured and it has been endorsed in recent English litigation as a valuable restatement of the Diplock approach. In *Consorzio del Prosciutto di Parma v Marks & Spencer plc*,[45] Nourse LJ regarded the approach of both Lord Oliver and Lord Jauncey in *Reckitt and Colman* as signalling a welcome return to the classical approach to the elements of a passing-off action, an observation endorsed by Harman J in the *Fortnum & Mason* case[46] when he observed that the judgments of Lords Oliver and Jauncey are to the same effect 'save that the Scotsman compresses it more than the Englishman'.

---

[40]   *Warnink v Townsend & Sons (Hull)* [1979] AC 731 at 742.

[41]   *Reckitt and Colman Products Ltd v Borden* [1990] 1 All ER 873; *Neutrogena Corpn v Golden Ltd* (1995) 34 IPR 406.

[42]   *Bodega Co v Owens* [1990] 1 All ER 873 at 880.

[43]   *Reckitt and Colman Products Ltd v Borden* [1990] 1 All ER 873 at 880.

[44]   *Reckitt and Colman Products Ltd v Borden* [1990] 1 All ER 873.

[45]   *Consorzio del Prosciutto di Parma v Marks & Spencer plc* [1991] RPC 351.

[46]   *Fortnum & Mason plc v Fortnum Ltd* [1994] FSR 438.

[25.17] Modern Irish pronouncements on passing off have tended to follow the classical English approaches in cases such as *Reddaway v Banham*,[47] *Spalding*[48] and the *Advocaat*[49] case.[50] The most expansive statement on passing off is in the judgment of Budd J in *Polycell Products Ltd v O'Carroll*:[51]

> To establish merchandise in such a manner as to mislead the public into believing that it is the merchandise or product of another is actionable. It injures the complaining party's right of property in his business and injures the goodwill in his business. A person who passes off the goods of another acquires, to some extent, the benefit of the business reputation of the rival trader and gets the advantage of his advertising.[52]

As we shall see this observation must be noted in its context of being a case involving get-up rather than use of names or marks. More recently, Laffoy J, in *DSG Retail Ltd v PC World Ltd*[53] has favoured Lord Oliver's three essential elements test. However, Laddie J, in *Chocosuisse Union des Fabricants Suisses v Cadbury Ltd*[54] appears to have favoured the Diplock test over the more simplified versions, at least in cases where the tort complained of is the 'extended' form of the tort, in which the complainant is seeking to protect goodwill established by collective development of 'a brand' or a range of products.

Goodwill

[25.18] In the *Polycell* case,[55] Budd J emphasised that the vital interest that is being protected is a property right in the business or trade carried on by the plaintiff. It must therefore be established by the plaintiff that goodwill exists, defined in the leading English tax case of *IRC v Muller & Co's Margarine Ltd*[56] as:

> the benefit and advantage of the good name, reputation, and connection of a business. It is the attractive force which brings in custom. It is the one thing which distinguishes an old established business from a new business at its first start'.[57]

It must also be established that the plaintiff is responsible for developing any reputation and goodwill, and passing off will fail if it is shown that the words that provoke the

---

47 *Reddaway v Banham* [1896] AC 199.

48 *AG Spalding v AW Gamage Ltd* (1915) 32 RPC 273.

49 *Warnink v Townsend & Sons (Hull)* [1979] AC 731.

50 Eg Murphy J in *Falcon Travel Ltd v Owners Abroad Group plc* [1991] 1 IR 175; Kinlen J in *An Post v Irish Permanent* [1995] 1 ILRM 336.

51 *Polycell Products Ltd v O'Carroll* [1959] Ir Jur Rep 34.

52 *Polycell Products Ltd v O'Carroll* [1959] Ir Jur Rep 34 at 36.

53 *DSG Retail Ltd v PC World Ltd* (13 January 1998, unreported), HC.

54 *Chocosuisse Union des Fabricants Suisses v Cadbury Ltd* [1998] RPC 117, affirmed by the Court of Appeal at [1999] RPC 826.

55 *Polycell Products Ltd v O'Carroll* [1959] Ir Jur Rep 34.

56 *IRC v Muller & Co's Margarine Ltd* [1901] AC 217, followed in *Independent Newspapers Ltd v Irish Press Ltd* [1932] IR 615.

57 *IRC v Muller & Co's Margarine Ltd* [1901] AC 217 at 213. For a recent case where an attempt to argue that goodwill was concurrent failed, see *Hotel Ciprani and Others v Ciprani (Grosvenor Street) Ltd* [2010] EWCA Civ 110.

litigation are slang or colloquial terms, in common usage, that the plaintiff could not have contributed towards the language, as in 'the box' to describe television-related products and services: *Box Television Ltd v Box Magazines Ltd*.[58] This case turns upon the fact that the phrase in question does not have a secondary meaning arising out of the activities of the plaintiff. If, however, the court finds the words are not entirely descriptive, interlocutory relief at least will be available. So, in *DSG Retail v PC World*,[59] Laffoy J held that while 'PC' might be descriptive of personal computers, the phrase 'PC World' was not entirely so and relief was afforded to the plaintiff in passing off. In *Diageo North America Inc v Intercontinental Brands ICB Ltd*,[60] the defendant sought to defend its use of the word VODKAT in relation to its mixed vodka and neutral fermented alcohol drink of 22% ABV on the bases that vodka itself was not a clearly defined class of goods and that 'vodka' did not have a reputation giving rise to goodwill amongst a significant section of the public. Arnold J. referred to Community legislation referring to alcoholic strength (37% to 37.5% ABV) and evidence from experts and the trade that vodka is perceived to be 'a clear, tasteless, distilled, high strength spirit ... that can alcoholically enhance any chosen mixture without detracting from the taste of the mixer'. Lack of consumer knowledge on contents of manufacture or geographical origin were not important and reputation and consequent goodwill were easily made out.

[25.19] While goodwill and a business activity are generally present when the plaintiff is successful, there are instances where goodwill can subsist even if the plaintiff does not have a business, eg trading has recently ceased. In order to establish the element of goodwill, the plaintiff must demonstrate a trading presence within a locality or with the public. In *Stannard v Reay*,[61] the plaintiff traded as a mobile fish and chip shop in holiday resorts on the Isle of Wight for several weeks before the defendant started his own enterprise using the same business name. Even though the business itself was peripatetic and the composition of the customer body, many of them being holidaymakers or trippers, hardly constant, an interlocutory injunction was given because trade in this seasonal kind of business had built up very quickly. Goodwill will be easier to establish, even if trading has not been carried out for a long period of time, if the business is distinctive in terms of its trading sphere or business image.[62] There are

---

[58] *Box Television Ltd v Box Magazines Ltd* (1997) Times, 1 March. The Canadian cases of importance include *Ciba Geigy Canada Ltd v Apotex Inc* (1992) 44 CPR (3d) 289 in which Lord Oliver's test was favoured by Gonthier J at 297 in the Supreme Court of Canada.

[59] *Retail v PC World* (13 January 1998, unreported), HC; see also *Mecklermedia v DC Congress* [1997] FSR 627.

[60] *Diageo North America Inc v Intercontinental Brands ICB Ltd* [2010] EWHC 17 (Ch).

[61] *Stannard v Reay* [1967] RPC 589. In *Bignell v Just Employment Law Ltd* [2007] EWHC 2203 (Ch) 'Just Employment' as a trade name for an employment lawyer in Surrey built up local goodwill; not infringed by same trade name for similar operation in Glasgow. It may be that neither party can establish goodwill; *Nationwide Building Society v Nationwide Estate Agents* (1987) 8 IPR 609. A trade promotion board does not trade; *An Bord Tráchtála v Waterford Foods* [1994] FSR 316.

[62] *Compatibility Research Ltd v Computer Psyche Co* [1967] RPC 201; contrast *BBC v Talbot Motor Co* [1981] FSR 228.

cases where a defendant has sought to avoid liability by arguing that the plaintiff, as a professional person[63] or non-profit-making entity, has no goodwill because customers rely on that person's professional and personal skills rather than any trading reputation. In the case of charities, churches, clubs and associations[64] and the like, the absence of any direct market or business motivation has been invoked by defendants. In both instances these defences have been ineffective for professional persons, no more than the charity, church or club, may find their reputation and professional standing tarnished if others may appropriate their name. In *Arabian Muslim Association v Canadian Islamic Centre*,[65] the Alberta Court of Appeal emphasised that the plaintiffs had provided not just a mosque but a school and recreational facilities for over 40 years. The possibility that members of an association or the association itself may be subject to some later legal liability has also been used to justify the grant of interlocutory relief in *BMA v Marsh*.[66] The basis upon which an unincorporated association may bring an action in passing off was explored by Lawrence Collins QC in *Artistic Upholstery Ltd v Art Forma (Furniture) Ltd*.[67] A guild of furniture manufacturers had mounted a series of successful trade exhibitions over many years. Differences arising between members of the association, the defendants obtained trade marks in respect of a phrase connected to the exhibition and the association expelled the defendants and sought an injunction to restrain the defendants from using the phrase in connection with exhibition services. Lawrence Collins QC, sitting as a Deputy Judge of the English High Court, indicated that associations held property on the basis of express and implied contracts, revolving around the rules of the association. The property that such associations were entitled to protect could include the ability to raise revenue by way of subscriptions, in the case of charitable associations,[68] the possibility that actual or prospective members may leave or refrain from joining the association[69] or the protection of a profit made from the activities of the association, as in the *Artistic Upholstery* case itself, where the exhibitions returned levels of profit to the association. In these cases the association does not bring proceedings; these are brought by individual members in a representative capacity.

[25.20] The traditional view in respect of political parties has been that they do not trade and cannot thus maintain passing-off actions. However, in *Burge v Haycock*,[70] the Court

---

[63] *Burchell v Wilde* [1900] 1 Ch 551.

[64] *British Diabetic Association v Diabetic Society Ltd* [1995] 4 All ER 812; *AG (Elisha) v Holy Apostolic and Catholic Church of the East (Assyrian) NSW* (1989) 16 IPR 619; *British Legion v British Legion Club (Street) Ltd* (1931) 48 RPC 555; BMA v Marsh (1931) 48 RPC 565.

[65] *Arabian Muslim Association v Canadian Islamic Centre* (2004) 36 CPR (4th) 6.

[66] *BMA v Marsh* (1931) 48 RPC 565; Inglis and Stevens [1996] EIPR 166.

[67] [1999] 4 All ER 277.

[68] *British Diabetic Association v Diabetic Society Ltd* [1995] 4 All ER 812, applying *British Legion v British Legion Club (Street) Ltd* (1931) 48 RPC 555.

[69] A point clearly made by Warrington J in *Society of Accountants and Auditors v Goodway* [1907] 1 Ch 489 at 502 (an incorporated body case); *BMA v Marsh* (1931) 48 RPC 565.

[70] *Burge v Haycock* [2002] RPC 553. On political parties running a bogus candidate, see *Devinder Shory Campaign v Richard* (2008) 71 CPR (4th).

of Appeal has taken the previous decisions, relating to fund-raising charities, churches and voluntary bodies that are intended to be of benefit to humanity, such as Dr Barnardos and veterans' associations, a step further. Here, the Countryside Alliance, an apolitical association intended to provide a lobby for rural preservation and development, was able to prevent a former British National Party activist from standing in elections as a Countryside Alliance candidate because of the damage that would occur to the goodwill that had been built up through the work of the Alliance. No trading activity needed to be made out.

[25.21] It is also difficult for an author to make out a passing-off action in respect of the unauthorised use of a manuscript because the courts are reluctant to extend the 'class of product' approach to an individual 'producer' in the form of one author.[71] Passing off in the form of imitation of the 'get-up' of a series of books or articles may, however, be more likely to be successful.[72] Even so, the essentials of the action will have to be satisfied. The author of children's books produced in the early 1990's under the name 'Mythbusters' had subsequently been unsuccessful in persuading television companies to convert the books into a television series. A television series under the title 'Mythbusters' that went to air in September 2004 was held not to be an actionable passing off. Any reputation the author had in 2004 was with television executives, not the consumer. Given that the products were so different there was no misrepresentation.[73] However, recent developments in relation to passing off in the form of 'false endorsement' actions may bring about some changes to the law in relation to celebrity authors.[74]

[25.22] The plaintiff may establish the existence of a substantial reputation and an established goodwill via trading activities over a relatively short period of time. In *Guinness Ireland Group v Kilkenny Brewing Co Ltd*,[75] the defendant incorporated a company using the name 'Kilkenny' in connection with beer. The plaintiff's objection was based upon prior use of the name in selling ale in Europe from 1987 and in the UK from 1994, with the product being launched in Ireland in July 1995. Sales in Ireland reached £1.8m between July and December 1995. In the light of the reputation obtained from both direct advertising in Ireland and the availability of the plaintiff's product in Europe and the UK, Laffoy J held that even before launch onto the Irish market 'the product was known to consumers in Irish public houses'. Where the plaintiff has ceased to trade or has perhaps abandoned the use of some trading indicia, then the plaintiff may find it difficult to establish any goodwill or reputation sufficient to sustain a passing-off

---

[71] *Sweeney v Macmillan Publishers Ltd* [2002] RPC 651.

[72] *Biddulph v De Vries* (1998) 43 IPR 144; *Clark v Associated Newspapers* [1998] 1 All ER 959.

[73] *Knight v Beyond Properties Pty Ltd* (2007) 71 IPR 466.

[74] In *Independent Newspapers Ltd v Irish Press Ltd* [1932] IR 615, Meredith J observed that 'Mr [WB] Yeats could not transfer the goodwill of his business as a poet'. See, however, the copyright case of *Anne of Green Gables Licensing Authority Inc v Avonlea Traditions Inc* (1999) 4 CPR (4th) 289 and *Jane Austen Trade Mark* [2000] RPC 879.

[75] *Guinness Ireland Group v Kilkenny Brewing Co Ltd* [1999] 1 ILRM 531; see also *Electro Cad Australia Pty v Mejati* [1998] FSR 291.

action. In *Independent Newspapers Ltd v Irish Press Ltd*,[76] the plaintiffs had acquired the title in the *Evening Telegraph* newspaper in 1925 but until the date of the application for a quia timet injunction, the plaintiffs had not since 1925 published a newspaper under that name; they, however, reserved the right to use the title at some time in the future. The defendants announced their intention to retitle their evening newspaper, the *Evening Press*, as the *Evening Telegraph*. Meredith J declined to grant the injunction sought, pointing out that, particularly in quia timet cases, the onus of showing an appropriation of goodwill and damage was a heavy one for a plaintiff. Meredith J saw a distinction between a trader using premises vacated by a plaintiff for similar trading purposes and using an abandoned business name; in the latter case a business name has a peculiar function – to designate and identify. While there could not be a proprietary right in a name *simpliciter*, the seven-year interval in trading and the remote possibility that purchasers who had recently returned to Ireland, following a long absence abroad, might be misled into thinking the new evening paper was the plaintiff's product made the injunction inappropriate given the improbability of damage.[77] While some vague intention to continue or return to trade is not sufficient, evidence that the plaintiff is active in trying to return to a trading situation will be influential,[78] but at issue is whether the business actually has any goodwill left. A temporary interruption in trading while relocating to other premises[79] or due to planning or other difficulties will not eliminate goodwill. So, in *Ad-Lib Club v Granville*[80] an injunction was issued to restrain the defendant from opening a club under the name Ad-Lib Club, even though the plaintiff had spent five years unsuccessfully trying to find premises in which he could resume to trade as a place of entertainment under the same name. The selection of the name by the defendant was held to indicate that some reputation must have survived the (temporary) closure of the plaintiff's club and because the name had no geographical or activity-based point of reference, the plaintiff was entitled to exploit this residual goodwill.[81] An attack upon the reasoning behind the *Ad Lib Club* decision was unsuccessfully mounted in a recent case in which two bands contested a passing-off claim in respect of the name 'Liberty'.[82] The plaintiffs were members of a band called 'Liberty', which had been formed in the late 1980s and had been at its peak between 1993 and 1996. It had only released three records and had not been commercially successful. In contrast, a 'manufactured' pop group, also called 'Liberty' had been created out of the 'Pop Stars' television contest of 2000 and this group had been successful in getting a six-record recording contract, releasing two hit singles in 2001. The issue was whether the earlier 'Liberty' had any residual goodwill to protect in Spring 2001, when the new 'Liberty'

---

[76] *Independent Newspapers Ltd v Irish Press Ltd* [1932] IR 615.

[77] Leave to re-enter the application if proof of damages could be shown was reserved.

[78] *Star Industrial v Yap* [1976] FSR 256.

[79] *Berkeley Hotel v Berkeley International* [1971] FSR 300.

[80] *Ad-Lib Club v Granville* [1971] 2 All ER 300.

[81] See also *Elders IXL Ltd v Australian Estates Pty* (1987) 10 IPR 575.

[82] *Sutherland v V2 Music Ltd* [2002] EMLR 28; Dennis [2002] EIPR 331. Contrast *Norman Kark Publications Ltd v Odhams Press Ltd* [1962] 1 All ER 636 which seems wrongly decided after *Ad-Lib*.

began to 'trade' on the Liberty name. The defendants argued that *Ad Lib* was wrongly decided because the requirement that the misrepresentation should cause damage could not be satisfied in the *Liberty* case[83] and that *Ad Lib* ignored this point; 'old' Liberty had effectively disbanded so no damage could be inflicted by the defendants' use of the name Liberty. Laddie J rejected this view. Goodwill, where it exists, may be based upon past trading activities, but it also has a prospective nature. Future business opportunities could well arise and such goodwill as 'old' Liberty could muster in the view of the public and the music industry could be protected five years after the band had ceased to perform as a band. At some stage, however, goodwill will cease because the business will cease to be distinctive.[84]

Goodwill and reputation contrasted

[25.23] A number of leading English and Australian cases draw a distinction between goodwill and reputation. Where the plaintiff is able to establish that his product has a reputation or cache in the minds of the public, then the orthodox view is that this alone will not justify intervention by the courts, for a reputation may exist in isolation from any business activity, but goodwill, the appropriate basis for protection, can only arise and subsist through trading activities.[85] It must be doubted whether this distinction is a hard and fast one, for many judges use the word reputation to describe the plaintiff's obligation to show distinctiveness as well as the likelihood that the public is likely to be misled. Indeed in *Muckross Park Hotel Ltd v Randles*,[86] Barron J observed that:

> 'Goodwill' is a term used in some of the reported cases. However, it seems to me that 'reputation' is a more correct word in the context of passing off. 'Goodwill' is essentially a balance sheet term. It is an intangible asset. It is in my view, inter alia, the additional sum which would be paid for premises to carry on a particular business there which has either now or in the past been carried on and which will accordingly have a fund of customers already in existence. The value in the name is in the same position. Its importance lies in the number of people who know it and what it stands for.[87]

[25.24] Barron J, in preferring 'reputation' is not alone for even in *Jif Lemon*,[88] Lords Jauncey and Oliver talked about 'reputation' and 'goodwill and reputation' respectively but the Law Lords were probably using the word 'reputation' in the context of distinctiveness. It is, however, likely that Barron J's preference will attract judicial support in Ireland and elsewhere because the courts in most common law jurisdictions are increasingly prepared to protect traders and corporations with international or regional trading reputations from parasitic or imitative trading, even though the plaintiff

---

83 *Sutherland v V2 Music Ltd* [2002] EWHC 14 (Ch); *McPhail and Doyle v Bourne and Sargeant* [2008] EWHC 1235 (CH) (The Busted Case).

84 On the converse issue of whether liability can be avoided if the defendant pleads no intention to trade, see the discussion by Karet [1996] EIPR 47 and cases cited therein.

85 *Anheuser-Busch Inc v Budejovicky Budvar NP* [1984] FSR 413 (the *Budweiser* case); *Athlete's Foot Marketing Associates Inc v Cobra Sports Ltd* [1980] RPC 343.

86 *Muckross Park Hotel Ltd v Randles* (10 November 1992, unreported), HC.

87 *Muckross Park Hotel Ltd v Randles* (10 November 1992, unreported), HC at p 12 of transcript.

88 *Reckitt and Colman Products v Borden Inc* [1990] 1 All ER 873.

may only be able to demonstrate a reputation within that jurisdiction. A typical case is point is the decision of the Federal Court of Australia in *Al Hyat Publishing Co v Sokarno*[89] where efforts to launch a newspaper with the *Al Hyat* title in Australia were the subject of successful interlocutory relief proceedings by the UK parent company that published this title internationally, even though the plaintiffs could only show reputation, and not the fact of trading, in Australia. In the context of global markets, international advertising and brand and consumer awareness, the English view, as espoused in *Budweiser*,[90] looks increasingly archaic. This will be considered below. Future goodwill (in the sense that the plaintiff seeks to show that its reputation must be viewed in the light of plans to expand in the future) is regarded with suspicion where the evidence indicates insufficient current trading activities to establish goodwill and the plaintiff is inviting the court to speculate on what its reputation and goodwill may be in the future. However, an expanding business is entitled to seek protection against threats to its goodwill even in fields where it may not intend to expand at the time of the complaint.[91]

[25.25] The basic principle upon which the courts operate is that the plaintiff must establish goodwill within the jurisdiction in which relief is sought. A person cannot complain about customers being deceived if he has no customers[92] or no reputation with the public[93] who do business with the plaintiff. Whether goodwill exists on the part of the manufacturer, importer, distributor, retailer or some other person responsible for putting the goods or services before the public, is a question of fact. Some of the early cases indicate that the plaintiff should have some kind of trading presence within the jurisdiction but this is not the current state of the law. In *Grant v Levitt*,[94] the defendant proposed to trade in Dublin under the style of Globe Furnishing Company. The plaintiffs traded in Liverpool under that name, a significant element in their business being mail order customers in Ireland who were targeted through advertising in Ireland. To similar effect is *C&A Modes Ltd v C&A (Waterford) Ltd*[95] when the plaintiff company, who traded in Northern Ireland, but had no retail business within the Republic, obtained an injunction to force the defendant to discontinue trading under the 'C&A' style of the plaintiff. The plaintiff's advertising within the UK reached into the homes of residents of the Irish Republic and shopping expeditions to the plaintiff's Belfast store were extremely popular until 1969 and, although business had declined from the Republic, the Supreme Court accepted that the plaintiff enjoyed a significant goodwill in their C&A symbol in the Irish Republic. In *Guinness Ireland Group v Kilkenny Brewing Co Ltd*,[96]

---

[89] *Al Hyat Publishing Co v Sokarno* (1996) 34 IPR 214; *Con Agra Inc v McCain Foods (Aust) Pty* (1992) 23 IPR 193.

[90] *Anheuser-Busch Inc v Budejovicky Budvar NP* [1984] FSR 413.

[91] *Lego Systems A/S v Lego M Lemelstrich Ltd* [1983] FSR 155; *Teleworks Ltd v Telework Group plc* [2002] RPC 535.

[92] See Oliver LJ in the *Budweiser* case: *Anheuser-Busch Inc v Budejovicky Budvar NP* [1984] FSR 413.

[93] *Petals v Winners Apparel* (1999) 2 CPR (4th) 92 (cheap discount store: no reputation).

[94] *Grant v Levitt* (1901) 18 RPC 361.

[95] *C&A Modes Ltd v C&A (Waterford) Ltd* [1976] IR 198.

[96] *Guinness Ireland Group v Kilkenny Brewing Co Ltd* [1999] 1 ILRM 531.

Laffoy J was presented with evidence of a relatively brief trading pattern in Ireland, made up of both advertising and sales over a period of less than one year but it is clear that considerable weight was afforded to earlier trading patterns in mainland Europe and the UK. The learned judge found that even before the product was launched in Ireland patrons in licensed establishments in Ireland asked for 'Kilkenny' or 'a pint of Kilkenny'. Whether the plaintiffs would have obtained an injunction, even absent the launch of the product in Ireland, cannot of course be determined, but, it is submitted, Laffoy J clearly inclined towards this possibility. This particular point was pleaded in *DSG Retail Ltd v PC World Ltd*[97] where the plaintiffs argued that the scope of their advertising and the reputation established in Ireland, which had attracted a substantial number of Irish customers to their UK computer superstores, entitled them to an injunction, regardless of the existence of their first store in Blanchardstown. Applying the *C&A* case, Laffoy J found that there was a serious issue to be tried on the passing-off argument. Irish law therefore readily identifies 'foreign' goodwill (in the sense that an Irish court will allow a non-Irish trading activity to protect its goodwill amongst Irish consumers) as a legitimate aspect of passing off. This stands in stark contrast to English law which has recently been characterised as discriminatory under EU law[98] even though it is arguable that the *Athlete's Foot*[99] decision marks a more liberal position[100] than that sketched in *Bernadin v Pavilion Properties* (the *Crazy Horse* case).[101] In this case it was held that the plaintiffs, proprietors of the famous Crazy Horse Saloon in Paris, could not obtain an injunction to prevent the defendant from using that name in England. The distribution of promotional literature in England to create or enhance a reputation in the hope that English visitors to Paris would patronise the plaintiffs' establishment was insufficient to establish a customer base in England. However, this decision was not followed in *Maxim's v Dye*,[102] where Graham J permitted the proprietors of Maxim's in Paris to prevent the defendant from trading in Norwich under that name. The judge was unable to distinguish the *Crazy Horse* case but nevertheless took the view that on the facts a sufficient reputation and goodwill could be established in England by the plaintiff. Further, a decision denying relief simply because the plaintiff did not trade in England would be contrary to art 59 (old) of the EEC Treaty by inhibiting the plaintiff from setting up any future business in England. In the *C&A* case, the Supreme Court disapproved of the distinction between trading within a State and advertising within a State and declined to follow the reasoning in the *Crazy Horse* case. The *Crazy Horse* case, however, has not been disapproved in England, at least within the context of cases without a European Community context. In *Athlete's Foot Marketing Associates v Cobra Sports Ltd*,[103] Walton J declined to give an injunction to an American company who

---

[97] *DSG Retail Ltd v PC World Ltd* (13 January 1998, unreported), HC.

[98] Cohen and Schmit [1999] EIPR 88. See *HG Investment Managers Ltd v HIG European Capital Partners LLP* [2009] FSR 26.

[99] *Athlete's Foot Marketing Associates v Cobra* [1980] RPC 343.

[100] See Ní Shuilleabháin (2003) 34 IIC 722 at 745–746.

[101] *Bernadin v Pavilion Properties* [1967] RPC 581; *Enterprise Car and Truck Rentals v Enterprise Rent a Car Co* (1998) 79 CPR (3d) 45.

[102] *Maxim's v Dye* [1978] 2 All ER 55.

[103] *Athlete's Foot Marketing Associates v Cobra Sports Ltd* [1980] RPC 343.

found that the name for their chain of sports footwear shops was being used by the defendant for a shop in London. While Walton J disapproved of the Irish Supreme Court's rejection of the *Crazy Horse Saloon* distinction, the actual decision in *Athlete's Foot* is supportable. While some English customers may have patronised the plaintiff's stores in the US, there was no evidence of any efforts to advertise or franchise the plaintiff's name in England, much less create a reputation or goodwill in relation to its retailing activities. Some preliminary advertising, expenditure or preparatory work, which indicates the possibility of goodwill being created via consumer expectations, may, however, be enough to persuade a court that there is a serious issue to be tried.[104]

[25.26] Attention should be drawn to the fact that the debate on whether customers within one country can be identified is a somewhat sterile approach. In essence, we should be considering the likelihood that customers who know of the plaintiff are going to be deceived by a defendant when the customer seeks out the kind of product that the plaintiff offers because the customer believes, wrongly, that it is the plaintiff who is offering that product. For high value, branded products where quality is important, the *Crazy Horse* decision[105] seems inappropriate[106] because it damages the marketability of the plaintiff's name in potential future markets. Where a mark has an international reputation however, protection will be available even if there is no targeted advertising. It will be enough if nationals use the services/goods whilst abroad. In *Hotel Cipriani Srl and Others v Cipriani (Grosvenor Street) Ltd and Others*,[107] the English Court of Appeal has addressed this point in relation to services, holding that a significant percentage of the rooms occupied in the Hotel Cipriani in Venice (some 30 per cent) in the 2000–2007 period were by British guests. The Court referred to the traditional significance of the direct bookings test but stated that as websites now allow for different methods of reserving services and facilities it will be necessary to reconsider this test at some future date.[108] A Hong Kong court in *Tan Ichi Co v Jancar Ltd*[109] has gone even further in preventing a Hong Kong restaurant from using the name and trading style of an up-market chain of Japanese tempura restaurants on the ground that a considerable volume of Japanese tourists may easily visit Hong Kong and that such persons may believe they were trading with the plaintiff. Here the case goes much further than the *C&A* case because there was no evidence that the plaintiff company advertised or sought to cultivate any market for its services in Hong Kong nor was there any evidence of an intention to trade in Hong Kong in the immediate future, much less expenditure to create goodwill in this regard. If the plaintiff trades within a number of cities or a region within

---

[104] *My Kinda Bones Ltd v Dr Pepper's Store Co* [1981] FSR 228.

[105] *Bernadin v Pavilion Properties* [1967] RPC 581.

[106] See *Apple Computer Inc v Apple Leasing Industries Ltd* (1991) 22 IPR 257; *Calvin Klein Inc v International Apparel Syndicate* [1995] FSR 515.

[107] *Hotel Cipriani Srl and Others v Cipriani (Grosvenor Street) Ltd and Others* [2010] EWCA Civ 110.

[108] For direct bookings see *Wadlow*.

[109] *Tan Ichi Co v Jancar Ltd* [1990] FSR 151; in Canada see the decision in *Enterprise Car and Truck Rentals v Enterprise Rent a Car Co* (1998) 79 CPR (3d) 45.

a particular jurisdiction, the defendant will be unlikely to persuade a court not to grant relief because the defendant intends only to trade in another city or region where the plaintiff is not active, for markets and customers are flexible and modern advertising and communications make the likelihood of reputations spreading beyond a trading sphere to be somewhat inevitable[110] unless the business only has a localised appeal[111] or lacks distinctiveness.

[25.27] The Trade Marks Act 1996 alters this position significantly in order to protect well-known marks[112] that are the property, not simply of EU nationals (the *Maxim* case)[113] but of persons who are nationals of Paris Convention States when those marks are well-known. Section 2 of the GATT/TRIPS Agreement is also relevant here.

Who owns the goodwill?

[25.28] It may also be of the utmost importance to establish who enjoys the goodwill in question. Where goods are manufactured to the order of a seller, the goodwill vests in the seller rather than the manufacturer, unless the manufacturer alone is held out as the sole trader involved or the defendant falsely asserts authorised distributor status.[114] Where a foreign manufacturer appoints a local distributor then the foreign manufacturer, if identified, will generally possess the goodwill[115] unless the local distributor or representative is identified as the source of the goods, the foreign manufacturer being undisclosed to purchasers.[116] Where a licensee obtains rights of manufacture under a licensing agreement then the licensor obtains goodwill vis-à-vis third parties.[117] The case of *Colgate Palmolive Ltd v Markwell Finance Ltd*[118] points out the importance of joining all parties as co-plaintiff since the late joinder of a parent company had a deleterious effect on the award of costs to the successful plaintiff in the action.

---

[110] *Chelsea Man Menswear Ltd v Chelsea Girl Ltd* [1987] RPC 189; *The Last Aussie Fish Caf Pty Ltd v Almove Pty Ltd* (1989) 16 IPR 376.

[111] *Clock Ltd v Clock House Hotel Ltd* (1936) 53 RPC 269; *A Levey v Henderson-Kenton (Holdings) Ltd* [1974] RPC 617.

[112] So-called Marque Notoire – TMA 1996, s 61.

[113] *Maxim's v Dye* [1978] 2 All ER 55.

[114] *Hirsch v Jonas* (1876) 3 Ch D 584; *Nishika Corpn v Goodchild* [1990] FSR 371.

[115] *Manus (A/B) v RJ Fulwood & Bland Ltd* (1949) 66 RPC 71; *Gromax Plasticulture v Don and Law Nonwovens* [1999] RPC 367. In the recent Irish 'Miss World' case interlocutory relief was given to the franchisor of 'Miss Ireland' against a franchisee who continued to use 'Miss Ireland' in describing a beauty contest after the franchise had ended: *Miss World Ltd v Miss Ireland Beauty Pageant Ltd* (2004) Irish Times Law Reports, 10 May.

[116] *Sturtevant Engineering Ltd v Sturtevant Mill Co* [1936] 3 All ER 137; *Grange Marketing Ltd v M & Q Plastic Products Ltd* (17 June 1976, unreported), HC distinguishing *Dental Manufacturing Co v de Trey & Co* [1912] 3 KB 76.

[117] *Alfred Dunhill Ltd v Sunoptic* [1979] FSR 337.

[118] *Colgate Palmolive Ltd v Markwell Finance Ltd* [1990] RPC 197.

MISREPRESENTATION

[25.29] The basis of passing off is a false representation by the defendant that goods or services offered by him are the goods of another person. Once, however, the 'get-up' begins to target prominent graphic or name factors that associate the defendant's product with the plaintiff product – as in the use of a puffin bird graphic and the name puffin in a deliberate parody of the penguin brand for chocolate sandwich bars – the public may well infer either a common manufacture of each bar or some other association.[119] In contrast, in *Specsavers International Healthcare Ltd v Asda Stores Ltd*,[120] Mann J held that the use of Specsavers 'lookalike' marks and variations on Specsavers slogans (eg 'You should have gone to Asda') by the defendants in their larger Asda Stores did not constitute a passing off. While the defendants acknowledged that they were 'living dangerously' in mounting an advertising campaign that so closely resembled the trading practices of Specsavers, they were held not to have crossed over the line into having made an actionable misrepresentation. The judgment contains some interesting observations on how a design exercise may allow non-infringing use of a competitor's marks. It is generally true to say that express misrepresentations are not the most frequent instances of passing off, but examples exist where the defendant supplies customers with the goods of a third party when the customer requested the plaintiff's goods by name and has not consented to third-party goods as a substitution.[121] In most cases, however, the misrepresentation takes place because marks, names, get-up or the image or marketing techniques used by the defendant are likely to cause confusion in the mind of customers about the source of the product, or, in the case of merchandise licensing, about whether the plaintiff has licensed or authorised the defendant to produce the goods in question. The misrepresentation must take place in a context whereby the statements are calculated, ie likely to deceive. The plaintiff cannot assert an infringement by passing off simply because the defendant uses a mark, name or other indicia that is identified as the 'property' of the plaintiff if no misrepresentation takes place.[122] The issue of whether a misrepresentation has been made is a question of fact on which an appellate court may be entitled to express a view only. So in *Premier Luggage and Bags Ltd v Premier Co (UK) Ltd*,[123] the Court of Appeal overruled the trial judge on the issue of misrepresentation because the tags attached to the defendant's products suggested it was the branded product of the defendant company and in the absence of any evidence of actual deception, no misrepresentation was made on tags attached to the goods that the plaintiff could complain of.

[25.30] It may be that the defendant is doing nothing more than using, trading or advertising materials that are common or universal within a trade or profession as in the

---

[119] *United Biscuits (UK) Ltd v Asda Stores Ltd* [1997] RPC 513.

[120] *Specsavers International Healthcare Ltd v Asda Stores Ltd* [2010] EWHC 2035(Ch).

[121] *British Leather Cloth Manufacturing v Dickens & Cooper Ltd* (1914) 31 RPC 337; *Procea Products Ltd v Evans & Sons* (1951) 68 RPC 210.

[122] *Singer Manufacturing Co v Loog* (1882) 8 App Cas 15.

[123] *Premier Luggage and Bags Ltd v Premier Co (UK) Ltd* [2003] FSR 69.

case of *Hennessy & Co v Keating*,[124] where the use by the defendant of brandy labels, which featured a grape and leaf motif but did not incorporate any of the Hennessy marks, was held not to constitute a passing off. In contrast, in the recent VODKAT case, the English High Court was clearly influenced by both the use of the name and misleading get up to find that the marketing of VODKAT was calculated to deceive a substantial number of members of the public that they were purchasing vodka, the court also taking into account similar conduct in relation to brandy, gin, rum and scotch 'soundalike' products.[125] The defendant, for example, is entitled to truthfully describe his present or former link with the plaintiff company[126] but to describe the defendant company incorrectly as agent of or the successor to the plaintiff company when there is no link and the plaintiff company is still in existence, is a passing off.[127] It is also a misrepresentation to represent goods that have been withdrawn from sale by the manufacturer as sub-standard, as being the latest version of that product.[128] Filling branded product containers with inferior versions of that product is also clearly a misrepresentation.[129] The range of, and possibilities for, potential misrepresentation cannot be catalogued; suffice it to say that if the statement is false and likely to deceive the public and damage the plaintiff, then it is in all probability actionable. So, in *Allergan Inc v Ocean Healthcare Ltd*,[130] the defendants used the name BOTINA in connection with a cosmetic product that was applied as a cream to the skin of the user, promising wrinkle reduction. The plaintiffs were the rights owners in respect of Botox. The packaging of BOTINA replicated a hyperdemic syringe on the side of the pack, the packaging looking more like a clinical medication than a cosmetic product. McGovern J saw the defendants' product as piggy-backing on Botox and granted interlocutory relief.

[25.31] While it is not necessary to show an intention to defraud in order to establish passing off because there is no mental element involved in the cause of action, the plaintiff may find it useful to establish dishonest intent by a defendant, for the courts will readily infer from intent that the defendant has achieved its objective of deceiving members of the public by way of the misrepresentation.[131] In *Guinness Ireland Group v Kilkenny Brewing Co Ltd*, Laffoy J said:

> I am satisfied that the name Kilkenny Brewing Company Ltd was chosen innocently and without any consciousness of the possibility of confusion being created in consumers minds of a connection between the defendant and the plaintiffs. Moreover, on the evidence I am satisfied that the plaintiffs' efforts to procure that the defendant's name be changed

---

[124] *Hennessy & Co v Keating* [1908] 1 IR 43 at 73 affirmed by the House of Lords, [1908] 1 IR 466.

[125] *Diageo North America Inc v Intercontinental Brands ICB Ltd* [2010] EWHC 17 (Ch) see judgment, para 228.

[126] *Pompadour Laboratories v Frazer* [1966] RPC 7.

[127] *Kent Adhesive Products Co v Ryan* (5 November 1993, unreported), HC.

[128] *Spalding v Gamage* (1915) 32 RPC 117; contrast *Revlon Inc v Cripps & Lee* [1980] FSR 85.

[129] *Jameson (John) & Sons Ltd v Clarke* (1902) 19 RPC 255.

[130] *Allergan Inc v Ocean Healthcare Ltd* [2008] IEHC 189.

[131] *Parker-Knoll Ltd v Knoll International* [1962] RPC 265; *Telmac Teleproducts Aust Pty Ltd v Coles Myer Ltd* (1989) 12 IPR 297; *Con Agra v McCain Foods* (1992) 23 IPR 193.

prior to and in these proceedings have been resisted in the bona fide belief that the plaintiffs are not entitled to require the defendant to change its name. The defendant's state of mind is wholly irrelevant to the existence of the cause of action of passing off.[132]

This statement, however, is not entirely accurate. Proof that the defendant intended to appropriate the plaintiff's reputation is clearly of probative value. Evidence of subjective intent may also be relevant. A redesign exercise intended to parody the get-up of another product in order to create a 'brand beater' can be dangerous. Robert Walker J, in such a case, said the defendants were 'aiming to avoid what the law would characterise as deception, they were taking a conscious decision to live dangerously. That is not in my judgment something that the court is bound to disregard'.[133] If the defendant is an innocent infringer, this may operate so as to lead the court not to infer the likelihood of deception or damage[134] and an innocent infringer will be inhibited from trading by way of an injunction, but there may be some effect on the right to damages or an account of profits. The innocent infringer, once put on notice, will be liable to compensate the plaintiff for post-notice damages but older cases indicate that because fraud was a proof in common law passing-off cases, only nominal damages are available against the innocent infringer.[135] The basic standard by which the misrepresentation is to be tested is whether the misrepresentation is likely, on an objective basis, to deceive a 'careless and casual person'.[136] However, the nature of the goods and services may be relevant. Consumers are often 'brand-conscious'[137] and liable to exercise greater care over expensive items than casual purchases.[138] The defendant may seek to justify its conduct by stressing that the public, as an educated body of persons, would inspect and compare the goods and not be deceived, but the courts will, however, consider whether a substantial body of persons would nevertheless be likely to be deceived. In *Taittinger v Allbev Ltd*[139] the effect of this test was graphically illustrated. The defendant manufactured a non-alcoholic drink called Elderflower Champagne which he sold at £2.45 *per* bottle. The drink was sold in the thick heavy bottles associated with champagne and foil caps and mushroom shaped corks were also incorporated. The plaintiff, a champagne house, brought a representative action alleging, *inter alia*, a passing off. At first instance, Mervyn Davies J found a misrepresentation but held that there was no likelihood of damage. Before the Court of Appeal, the defendant cross-

---

[132] *Guinness Ireland Group v Kilkenny Brewing Co Ltd* [1999] 1 ILRM 531. See also *Smithkline Beecham plc v Antigen Pharmaceuticals Ltd* (25 March 1999, unreported), HC.

[133] *United Biscuits UK Ltd v Asda Stores Ltd* [1997] RPC 513 at 531.

[134] *Grange Marketing Ltd v M & Q Plastic Products Ltd* (17 June 1976, unreported), HC; *Petersville Sleigh Ltd v Sugarman* (1987) 10 IPR 501.

[135] *Crawshay v Thompson* (1842) 4 Man & G 357; *Draper v Trist* [1939] 3 All ER 513.

[136] *Per* Holmes LJ in *Hennessy v Keating* [1908] 1 IR 43 at 101; applying *Singer Manufacturing Co v Loog* (1882) 8 App Cas 15 at 18 *per* Lord Selborne ('ignorant and unwary').

[137] *Dr Martens Australia Pty v Figgins* (1999) 44 IPR 281.

[138] *Teleworks v Telework Group* [2002] RPC 535; *British Sky Broadcasting Group plc v Sky Home Services* [2007] FSR 14. The juxtaposition of the defendant's trade name in directories will constitute a misrepresentation when causing confusion, even though otherwise the plaintiff's own trading style may be descriptive or generic : *Evans v Graham* (2009) 84 IPR 127.

[139] *Taittinger v Allbev Ltd* [1994] 4 All ER 75.

appealed that the judge had been incorrect in holding a material misrepresentation, arguing that members of the public, seeing a bottle of this kind at £2.45 would inspect the product and conclude that it was not champagne or linked with champagne. Peter Gibson LJ agreed with Mervyn Davies J who had observed that a simple unworldly person may know nothing of Elderflower Champagne as an old cottage drink and may know nothing of champagne prices. Such persons are not a majority of the public or even a substantial sector of the public, but there must be many persons who would think that Elderflower is champagne. The other members of the Court of Appeal indicated that the real danger is that persons could believe this beverage was in some way associated with French champagne and thus 'dilute' the goodwill in champagne.[140]

[25.32] The need for the defendant to make a representation to customers or potential customers of the plaintiff has been a significant factor in limiting the scope of a successful passing-off action. In the absence of any registered trade mark or copyright or design right protection, the courts permit imitative or even derivative trading if the plaintiff's own badges of trade are not distinctive, are generic, or attributable to a fashion that the plaintiff cannot identify as being of his making. In *Adidas Sports Schuhfabriken Adi Dassler KA v Charles O'Neill & Co*,[141] O'Higgins CJ said of the plaintiff's right to prevent the defendant from using a three-stripe design on its own sportswear when that design was, on the evidence, not associated in the public mind with Adidas products and no other trader:

> In this case, if the complaint had been that the name 'Adidas' or a name similar thereto or an imitation thereof had been used in association with O'Neill's goods, although no Adidas products were on sale in this country, I have no doubt that a goodwill and a potential in relation to customers would have been established and protection given. We are dealing, however, not with a well known name but with a particular design and its exclusive association with the goods of Adidas in Ireland must be established if the claim made is to succeed. One other matter should be mentioned. The fact is that Adidas have, over the years, projected their products with the three-stripe design in every advertising medium available. This fact, however, does not give title to Adidas to complain if a trader, attracted by the design or susceptible to the fashion which its prominence creates, decides to copy or imitate. The mere copying of a design or the anticipation of a fashion or the taking advantage of a market or demand created by another's advertising is not of itself sufficient to support an action for passing off if the trader against whom the complaint is made has sufficiently distinguished his goods so that confusion is not created.[142]

[25.33] In contrasting the use of a name as distinct from a design, O'Higgins CJ is emphasising that certain badges of trade are more effective than others in allowing the plaintiff to establish that its products and services are distinctive of the plaintiff's trade. The use of the plaintiff's trade marks or logo (or deceptively similar marks), names, descriptive terms or geographical statements of origin are the most frequent sources of the misrepresentation but impersonation of goods by adopting the style or get-up of the plaintiff's goods without using the plaintiff's marks or in conjunction with distinguishing terms or names identifiable with the defendant, may suffice to ground

---

[140] Carty (1996) 112 LQR 632.

[141] *Adidas Sports Schuhfabriken Adi Dassler KA v Charles O'Neill & Co* [1983] ILRM 112.

[142] *Adidas Sports Schuhfabriken Adi Dassler KA v Charles O'Neill & Co* [1983] ILRM 112 at 116–117.

liability, as in *Gabicci plc v Dunnes Stores*[143] where sweaters produced by the defendant were made up in the same factory as the plaintiff's branded goods, sold at half the price under the defendant's St Bernard label. Carroll J held an injunction should be granted for at point of sale the public could not distinguish these garments, thinking that the defendant must have got the plaintiff's goods under an arrangement at a special price. Similarly in *R Griggs Group v Dunnes Stores*,[144] the actual get-up of a Doc Martens shoe was replicated by the defendant's product, but for the sake of injunction proceedings, the misrepresentation relied upon was a verbal description given by the defendant's employees of the disputed product being 'Docs'. The misrepresentation may be made out, notwithstanding the presence of indicators that could negative the misrepresentation. The use of 'Swiss Chalet' in connection with chocolate could induce a significant proportion of the public to believe the chocolate bar is made in Switzerland, notwithstanding the presence of 'Cadbury' branding which would induce an association with Bourneville in England, the Cadbury centre of operations.[145]

Names

[25.34] Authors' names will become part of the stock in trade of the author[146] and it makes no difference if the name was devised by the defendant if it has become identified with the plaintiff author or performer; goodwill will be with the plaintiff[147] as long as the plaintiff can demonstrate the existence of protectable goodwill.[148] While the plaintiff cannot assert a proprietary right in his personal name he is entitled to trade in his own name even if the use of that name is likely to result in some confusion.[149] This right is limited to cases where the person uses his name as a style of trading and it is a very limited concession for it is generally agreed that the defence is available to natural persons who do nothing further, which could cause confusion and who act honestly.[150]

---

[143] *Gabicci plc v Dunnes Stores* (31 July 1991, unreported), HC.

[144] *R Griggs Group v Dunnes Stores* (4 October 1996, unreported), HC; *Primark Ltd v Lollypop Ltd* [2001] FSR 638.

[145] *Chocosuisse Union des Fabricants Suisses de Chocolat v Cadbury Ltd* [1999] RPC 826.

[146] *Landa v Greenberg* (1908) 24 TLR 441.

[147] *Hines v Winnick* [1947] 2 All ER 517. Because most disposals of a business will involve the transfer of the goodwill in the business, such a transaction will preclude the vendor from resuming to trade in the old name, even upon expiry of a non-competition clause: *Newman (IN) Ltd v Adlem* [2006] FSR 16.

[148] *Serville v Constance* [1954] 1 All ER 662.

[149] Older cases assert this right but more modern decisions suggest otherwise, *Taylor Bros Ltd v Taylors Group Ltd* (1990) 14 IPR 353; *Guccio Gucci SPA v Paolo Gucci* [1991] FSR 89; for older cases that suggest the right subsists see, in particular, *Rodgers v Rodgers* (1924) 41 RPC 277; *Marengo v Daily Sketch* (1948) 65 RPC 242.

[150] *Parker-Knoll Ltd v Parker Knoll International Ltd* [1962] RPC 265; *Boswell-Wilkie Circus Pty v Brian Boswell Circus Property Ltd* [1985] FSR 434, affirmed at [1986] FSR 479; *Noel Leeming Television Ltd v Noel's Appliance Centre Ltd* (1985) 5 IPR 249. This issue resurfaced in England when the Forte hotel and restaurant chain discontinued proceedings against a Winchester tea-room proprietor who traded in his own name of 'The Forte Tea-rooms' (1996) Times, 8 August. Wadlow doubts the existence of any such exception to this confusion principle (Wadlow, *Passing Off* (3rd edn, Sweet and Maxwell, 2002).

This requirement of acting honestly and *bona fide* is an important one and there are several Irish cases in which the defendant has been prevented from trading in its own name because of the context within which the name has been used. Indeed, in *Reed Executive plc v Reed Business Information Ltd*[151] an own name defence was denied to the defendant once it was acknowledged that the defendant knew of a risk of deception in fact. After citing Romer J in *Rodgers v Rodgers*[152] and Lord Greene in *Marengo v Daily Sketch*,[153] Pumfrey J said that Lord Greene was simply restating Romer J's test in other words:

> if there is passing off then that is enough. In other words, the only defence is 'no passing off', because there is no deception leading to damage to the relevant goodwill.[154]

While the Court of Appeal[155] has overturned Pumfrey J on another ground, there is no reason to doubt the correctness of his judgment on this point.

[25.35] In *Valentine v Valentine*,[156] the plaintiffs had previously traded as Valentine & Co, tea merchants at 23 Corn Market, Belfast. When their lease expired the defendants obtained a lease of those premises and traded as J Valentine & Co, also as tea merchants. It was held that such conduct was calculated to deceive the public. In *Glenny v Smith*,[157] the defendant used his own name to describe his business but added that he was 'FromT&G' his former employer. The use of the former employer was held to have been misleading and upon proof of persons being misled, the use of the phrase was restrained by injunction and the view that persons should not describe goods sold by way of a surname that may mislead has been endorsed in Irish case law,[158] although, even if the defendant is held to be liable for passing off, injunctive relief will be limited to discontinuing the misleading usage: the defendant may still be able to use his own name[159] but the adoption of a surname that has no link with any of the defendants will be regarded as an attempt to appropriate the name of a reputable trader[160] unless businesses are dissimilar and the company name is explained away.[161]

[25.36] The 'own name' defence to a passing off action was most recently considered by the English Court of Appeal in *Hotel Cipriani Srl and Others v Cipriani (Grosvenor Street) Ltd and Others*.[162] The various plaintiffs traded in respect of hotels and

---

[151] *Reed Executive plc v Reed Business Information Ltd* [2003] RPC 207.

[152] *Rodgers v Rodgers* (1924) 41 RPC 277.

[153] *Marengo v Daily Sketch* [1992] FSR 1.

[154] *Reed Executive plc v Reed Business Information Ltd* [2003] RPC 207 at 251.

[155] *Marengo v Daily Sketch* (2004) 148 Sol Jo 298.

[156] *Valentine v Valentine* (1892) 31 LR Ir 488. Contrast *Burgess v Burgess* (1853) 3 De GM & G 896 and *Turton v Turton* (1889) 42 Ch D 128.

[157] *Glenny v Smith* (1862) 2 Drew & Sm 476.

[158] *Jameson v Dublin Distillers Co* [1900] 1 IR 43.

[159] *Dickson v Dickson* [1909] 1 IR 204.

[160] *Lloyds & Dawson Bros v Lloyds, Southampton Ltd* (1912) 29 RPC 433; *Dockrell v Dockrell* (1941) 75 ILTR 226.

[161] *Fortnum & Mason plc v Fortnam Ltd* [1994] FSR 438.

[162] *Hotel Cipriani Srl and Others v Cipriani (Grosvenor Street) Ltd and Others* [2010] EWCA Civ 110. See also *Stenner v Scotia McLeod* (2007) 62 IPR 1.

restaurants, and related establishments, in various parts of the world. The Hotel Cipriani in Venice, and Harry's Bar, also in Venice, were the only establishments that were held to have any reputation in England at the time when the defendants opened a restaurant in London, in 2004 under the name, Cipriani London. Harry's Bar, whilst enjoying a reputation in England, did not have a sufficient connection with Cipriani to establish goodwill in England, so, for the purpose of a passing off action, the relevant goodwill related to Cipriani, a trading name that was protected by domestic and community trade marks. One of the defendants who had set up Cipriani London had the surname Cipriani. Could any of the defendants use an own name defence? The Court of Appeal revisited two earlier decisions,[163] in which the Court of Appeal were said to have decided that for a corporate defendant the only own name defence available relates to the precise corporate name and not any abbreviated or trading name. The Court of Appeal, however, said that these cases did not go that far. Clearly, where a corporate entity is established with a trade name that closely resembles that of an established entity, any newly adopted trade name will be available only insofar as that trade name is its correct corporate name. However, if a company has used a trade name in business for a considerable period of time the defence might be available; the corporate name only rule was said by Lord Justice Lloyd, giving judgment for a unanimous Court of Appeal to be 'not absolute':

> By comparison, in principle an individual ought to be able to use the defence in relation to an adopted name by which he or she is known for business purposes or generally, for example an actor's stage name or a writer's nom de plume. That being so, I find it difficult to see why a corporate entity should not be able to do so, if it can show that it sues a distinct name for trading purposes. To take one example, a company, even a newly formed company, might acquire an existing business carried on under a trade name and wish to carry it on under the same name. I do not see why it should not do so.[164]

However, as the first defendant's employees described the business as 'Cipriani's' on its own, with no efforts being made to stop or clarify this usage, the own name defence was not made out. The other defendants, including the second defendant, did not trade so they were not entitled to the defence (relevant to a trade mark infringement issue).

[25.37] Even if the trader uses its own name in a *bona fide* manner, and there are few cases that actually establish this as a positive finding of fact, the plaintiff can still succeed if the defendant has marked or marketed goods or services by reference to a mark that is distinctive of the plaintiff's goods or services. In *Baume & Co v Moore (AH) Ltd*,[165] the marketing of watches, which were factually correctly identified by a mark that was similar to the plaintiff's mark, was the subject of an injunction even though the defendant was held to have acted honestly. His failure to attempt to distinguish, or

---

[163] *Asprey and Garrard Ltd v WRA (Guns) Ltd* [2001] EWCA Civ 1499; *Premier Luggage and Bags Ltd v Premier Co (UK) Ltd* [2002] EWCA Civ 387. In this later case the defence failed in respect of employees who identified the defendants as 'Premier', 'Premier Luggage' or 'Premier Luggage Company'.

[164] *Hotel Cipriani Srl and Others v Cipriani (Grosvenor Street) Ltd and Others* [2010] EWCA Civ 110 at para 66.

[165] *Baume & Co v Moore (AH) Ltd* [1958] Ch 907. See 'Restraining Orders Put on Firm Marketing Footwear Dryer', (1997) Irish Times, 1 May.

disclaim, his goods from those of the plaintiff was a significant element here. Initials may also be distinctive and protected via injunction[166] when these have become distinctive.

Descriptive words

[25.38] Where the defendant has used a word or phrase to describe or identify its goods or services, the plaintiff may complain that the use of that descriptive phrase may confuse customers into believing that the goods or services are connected with the plaintiff's business. The plaintiff is required to establish that the phrase has acquired a secondary meaning. The leading case is *Reddaway v Banham*.[167] Here, the plaintiff manufactured a product called 'camel hair belting' and was in fact the market leader. A former employee set up his own business manufacturing camel hair belting made up from camel hair. The House of Lords held that it had been established that in the minds of purchasers this product was identified as the product of Reddaway for here the phrase went beyond being merely descriptive in so far as it was connected with the business of the plaintiff. Some phrases, however, will be so common that they will not be capable of producing a secondary meaning. In *Office Cleaning Services Ltd v Westminster Office Cleaning Association*,[168] the House of Lords held that the only possible mark was the activity of cleaning offices; that as a mark this was a non-starter because it was simply a description of what each party did. The plaintiff should be able to point to a name, which identifies what the goods or services provided actually are, and at the same time point to a descriptive phrase or brand that is distinctive of the plaintiff's trading activities. Each case turns on its own facts. If the evidence indicates that a phrase has been identified in the minds of the public with the source of origin of goods or services, the phrase will be neither descriptive nor generic. In *Associated Newspapers Ltd v Express Newspapers*,[169] the plaintiff was the proprietor of the *Daily Mail* and *Mail on Sunday*, holding trade marks which included 'The Mail'. The defendant proposed to launch an evening newspaper in the London region under the name of either the 'Evening Mail' or the 'London Evening Mail'. Laddie J held that colloquial use of the phrase, 'The Mail' by the plaintiff's customers and indeed the defendant's employees in describing the relevant publications provided evidence of confusion, on the one hand, and a misrepresentation

---

[166] *Kinahan v Bolton* (1863) 15 IR Ch R 75; *C&A Modes Ltd v C&A (Waterford) Ltd* [1976] IR 198.

[167] *Reddaway v Banham* [1896] AC 199. See 'Golden Pages gets injunction against publisher' (1996) Irish Times, 11 July when injunctions against the use of the words 'Golden' and 'Yellow' pages were given against an internet-based advertiser. The Supreme Court later discharged these injunctions.

[168] *Office Cleaning Services Ltd v Westminster Office Cleaning Association* [1946] 1 All ER 320n; *County Sound v Ocean Sound* [1991] FSR 367.

[169] *Associated Newspapers Ltd v Express Newspapers* [2003] FSR 909. Use of a similar magazine title *per se* may not be a passing off, but use of content that had previously appeared in the plaintiff's publication without distinguishing the publications may merit injunctive relief: *Pacific Publications Pty v IPC Media Pty* (2003) 57 IPR 28. See (2004) Irish Times, March 3 for a case in which *Buy and Sell* magazine restrained publication of *Mayo Buy and Sell*.

on the other. The phrase, 'The Mail', was not descriptive because newspapers were not described as 'mails'. The strong likelihood that the public and advertisers would connect the defendant's proposed publication with the plaintiff's titles, to the detriment of the plaintiff's business, warranted interlocutory relief, *quia timet*. In the absence of such proofs the plaintiff may find that the defendant can use descriptive phrases such as 'oven chips'[170]'vacuum cleaner',[171] 'linoleum',[172] for here the phrase will be held to be descriptive or generic in nature and thus not distinctive. A striking example of a successful argument for a secondary meaning can be found in *Kettle Chip Co Pty Ltd v Apand Pty Ltd*.[173] The plaintiffs, in 1989, manufactured potato chips by reference to a particular method of cooking by hand in batch cookers and sold those chips under the name of Kettle Chips. The defendants later made chips of a similar texture using different methods of cooking but described the product as Kettle style chips. Holding that the word 'Kettle' does not naturally describe a potato chip the court held that the word had acquired the status of a brand. Even if the word was descriptive, in so far as it referred to the method of cooking, it had also acquired a secondary meaning with the Australian public in so far as it was linked to the plaintiff's potato chip products.

[25.39] Descriptive words such as 'Solartint' for sunglasses[174] are inherently descriptive. Some descriptive words have been categorised as being distinctive rather than descriptive, such as Fantasyland for an amusement park.[175] Foreign words may be held to be descriptive as in the case of 'Chi Yip' which means 'acquire property', thus a descriptive phrase in the area of real estate companies in Hong Kong.[176] It is not necessary to establish that the public exclusively associates the name in dispute with the plaintiff before an injunction or other relief will be obtained. In *DSG Retail Ltd v PC World Ltd*,[177] Laffoy J indicated that the fact that other entities have traded under the PC World name raised a serious issue to be tried but could not of itself negate the plaintiff's argument that the name 'PC World' was exclusively distinctive of the plaintiff's business in Ireland.

Geographical names

[25.40] Place names, whether local, national or international, are clearly capable of distinguishing or identifying the plaintiff's goods or services. In *Montgomery v Thompson*,[178] the town of Stone was the place of the plaintiff's brewery and his beers

---

[170] *McCain International v Country Fair Foods Ltd* [1981] RPC 69.

[171] *British Vacuum Cleaner Co v New Vacuum Cleaner Co* [1907] 2 Ch 312.

[172] *Linoleum Manufacturing Co v Nairn* (1878) 7 Ch D 834.

[173] *Kettle Chip Co Pty Ltd v Apand Pty Ltd* (1993) 27 IPR 321.

[174] *Dodds Family Investments v Lane Industries* (1993) 26 IPR 261.

[175] *Walt Disney Productions v Fantasyland Hotel Inc* (1994) 31 IPR 233.

[176] *Land Power International Holdings Ltd v Inter-Land Properties Ltd* (1995) 31 IPR 163; See also *Bodega Co v Owens* (1888) 23 LR Ir 371.

[177] *DSG Retail Ltd v PC World Ltd* (13 January 1998, unreported), HC. See also *Roadside Garages (Cotex) Ltd v Roadside Motors (Coleraine) Ltd* [1999] NI 195.

[178] *Montgomery v Thompson* [1891] AC 217.

were sold as Stone Ales. The defendant was prevented from building his own brewery and selling his ales under the name of Stone Ales. In the case of *Muckross Park Hotel Ltd v Randles*,[179] the plaintiffs were able to show that the reputation of their long established hotel in Muckross, Co Kerry was such that 'the Muckross' was known nationally and internationally as connoting the Muckross Park, so that when the defendants changed the name of their hotel from the Dromhall Hotel, following refurbishment and an extension of the premises, to the 'Muckross Court Hotel' the geographical fact that their premises were in the district of Muckross and situated on the Muckross Road could not provide a justification for this user for a secondary meaning had been established. It will not, however, always be possible to establish a secondary meaning for products as in *My Kinda Town v Soll*,[180] where the phrase 'Chicago Pizza' was held not to be such as to conjure up a secondary meaning.

Get-up

[25.41] The whole visible external appearance of the goods, as they are presented to the public prior to purchase, is capable of being misrepresented. Where the external appearance of the goods is in essence due to the shape, colour, size and composition of the container, the leading English decision, the *Jif Lemon* case[181] illustrates that once a distinctive reputation is established as a matter of fact, then the defendant may be prohibited from trading in goods that are packaged in an imitative way, even if the defendant does not use the plaintiff's trade mark and some efforts have been made to distinguish the defendant's goods by way of its own mark or distinctive labelling. The external appearance of goods and the similarity between them does not, in itself, provide the plaintiff with an open and shut case of passing off, for the courts tend towards the view that buyers are likely to purchase by reference to brands and brand names rather than a possibly generic appearance. In Ireland, the cases involving misdescription by way of packaging have tended to go in favour of the plaintiff. In *Grange Marketing Ltd v M&Q Plastic Products Ltd*,[182] the products in question were exercise machines, which were being sold by the defendants in boxes that were the same size and shape as that of the plaintiffs, with point of sale material copied from the plaintiffs' own material and using the plaintiffs' box design and advertising slogan. In *Polycell Products Ltd v O'Carroll*,[183] the defendants sold wallpaper paste in packages similar to those used by the plaintiff and while the brand names were quite dissimilar, the danger of confusion was such as to merit interlocutory relief. Injunctions have also been obtained to prevent the sale of non-dairy spreads from being sold in containers under a get-up that closely resembles another product already in the market but in these cases the defendant's brand

---

179 *Muckross Park Hotel Ltd v Randles* (10 November 1992, unreported), HC.
180 *My Kinda Town v Soll* [1983] RPC 407.
181 *Reckitt and Colman Products v Borden Inc* [1990] 1 All ER 873; *Dalgety Spillers Foods Ltd v Food Brokers Ltd* [1994] FSR 504; Mills [1994] EIPR 307.
182 *Grange Marketing Ltd v M&Q Plastic Products Ltd* (17 June 1976, unreported), HC.
183 *Polycell Products Ltd v O'Carroll* [1959] IR Jur Rep 38.

name itself has tended to be very close to the plaintiff's name.[184] In some cases the court is able to find parasitic copying of the packaging and get-up as a deliberate act by the defendant and where this occurs relief can be expected.[185] Where, however, the shape or style of the goods themselves is at issue, there are few cases in which the plaintiff has succeeded when the extent of the copying relates to functional items as distinct from decoration.[186] Even where decoration is involved, the decision in the *Adidas* case[187] suggests that distinctiveness may not be easy to establish. In the case of pharmaceutical products, the size, shape and colour of the product itself is the only real method of distinguishing, for the medicines themselves may be much the same as between brands.[188] Generally, mixtures of colours will be held to be much more distinctive than single colours unless the colour of the item or get-up has significance for the customer (eg the market is an illiterate one that buys in ignorance of brands or in reliance on colour or get-up alone).[189] Reproduction of the visual features of a website via the use of identical colours, layout and site structure to that developed by the plaintiff has been held to be passing off in *British Columbia Automobile Association v OPEIU, Local 378*.[190] However, the Court of Appeal, in *Reed Executive plc v Reed Business Information*,[191] has rejected the view that the use of metatags could constitute a passing off; a similar conclusion was reached in *British Columbia Automobile Association*. The view that the comparison between the products in 'get-up' passing off is essentially based on first impression was reaffirmed by Clarke J in *Jacob Fruitfield Food Group Ltd v United Biscuits (UK) Ltd*.[192] The way in which goods will be presented for sale and the likelihood that the average consumer will seek out a brand, or not, will also be relevant.

Inverse passing off

[25.42] If the misrepresentation made by the defendant is to the effect that the goods or services the defendant is providing are the defendant's when in fact they are those of another, recent case law indicates that such cases of 'inverse passing off' may be

---

[184] *Mitchelstown Co-operative Agricultural Society Ltd v Goldenvale* (12 December 1985, unreported), HC; *R & C Products v Sterling Winthrop* (1993) 27 IPR 223.

[185] *Cantrell & Cochrane Ltd v Savage Smith & Co* (16 October 1975, unreported), HC.

[186] *Edge (William) & Sons Ltd v William Niccolls & Sons* [1911] AC 693; *Tot Toys v Mitchell* (1992) 25 IPR 337.

[187] *Adidas Sports Schuhfabriken Adi Dassler KA v Charles O'Neill & Co* [1983] ILRM 112; see Phillips (1983) 5 DULJ (ns) 105. Lack of distinctiveness may arise because artwork on a product may be common within the genre: *GM Radio Holdings Ltd v Tokyo Project Ltd* [2006] FSR 15.

[188] *Hoffman La Roche v DDSA Pharmaceuticals* [1972] RPC 1; *Beecham Group v Eiraj Pharmaceuticals Ltd* (1985) Irish Times, 28 March; *Ciba-Geigy Canada Ltd v Apotex Inc* (1992) 24 IPR 652.

[189] On colour in connection with petroleum sales see *John Kelly Ltd v Amoco* [2002] FSR 87.

[190] *British Columbia Automobile Association v OPEIU, Local 378* (2001) 10 CPR (4th) 423.

[191] *Reed Executive plc v Reed Business Information* (2004) 148 Sol Jo LB 298.

[192] *Jacob Fruitfield Food Group Ltd v United Biscuits (UK) Ltd* [2007] IEHC 368.

relieved against, as where the defendant's advertising material claimed that ornamental conservatories produced by the plaintiff were in fact produced by the defendant.[193]

The likelihood of deception and damage

[25.43] The likelihood of confusion is not enough; absent a misrepresentation the leading modern case is *HFC Bank plc v Midland Bank plc*.[194] HFC was in the personal lending sector, not retail banking. It had a low level of brand recognition amongst the UK public. When Midland Bank, a part of the Hong Kong and Shanghai Banking Corporation, started to rebrand itself as HSBC from late 1998, HFC sought an injunction alleging passing off. The action failed for the simple reason that HFC could not establish brand recognition and thus goodwill and because Midland Bank had in its advertising sought to demarcate its operations from HFC; non-actionable confusion as distinct from actionable misrepresentation was the most that the plaintiff could establish before the English High Court. Similarly in *Teleworks Ltd v Telework Group plc*[195] the generic nature of 'telework', descriptive of electronics-based commercial activities, was a source of confusion but only in relation to entities that did not know either party. In this case the complainant was a very sector specific company operating at a much lower billing or price level to the defendant company, and while both companies were in the same broad sector, any apparent confusion based upon name would have been dispelled by the time the customers of each company reached the position of being ready to do business with the respective company. The plaintiff will have to prove, in a number of different ways, that its reputation is such that the defendant's trading activity is likely to cause the public to believe that the defendant is providing goods or services that are linked with those provided by the plaintiff, thus causing substantial damage to the plaintiff's property in the goodwill of his business. In *Stringfellow v McCain Foods*,[196] the plaintiff was the proprietor of a night club in London, which was at that time successful and popular with the affluent and glamorous sector of London society. The defendant used the name Stringfellow to launch an oven chip product that was long and thin in shape. The advertising campaign for the product involved scenes from a discotheque and in the view of the Court of Appeal involved an element of misrepresentation. However, there was no proof of damage; the word Stringfellow could have a reference to the 'stringy' nature of the chip. In *Newsweek Inc v BBC*,[197] the title 'Newsweek' was adopted by the BBC for its current affairs programme. The proprietors of *Newsweek* magazine sought to prevent this usage claiming it would deceive the public into thinking that the publication was in some way involved. However, it was held that the BBC would distinguish the broadcast by way of distinctive titles, credits and BBC logos, thus avoiding any deception. If the defendant seeks to trade in competition with a brand leader by putting

---

[193] *Bristol Conservatories v Conservatories Custom Built Ltd* [1989] RPC 455; Carty [1993] EIPR 370. See also *John Robert Powers School Inc v Tessensohn* [1995] FSR 947 (a Singapore case).

[194] *HFC Bank plc v Midland Bank plc* [2000] FSR 176; see also *Marcus Publishing plc v Hutton-Wild Communications plc* [1990] RPC 576.

[195] *Teleworks Ltd v Telework Group plc* [2002] RPC 535.

[196] *Stringfellow v McCain Foods* [1984] RPC 501.

[197] *Newsweek Inc v BBC* [1979] RPC 441.

onto the market goods that are produced in a similar get-up, the likelihood of confusion may, in most cases, be avoided by emphasising different brand names[198] or by selling the goods in different markets.[199] Where evidence of this kind is before the court, passing off will not be established for it is likely that 'only a moron in a hurry' would be deceived.[200] The strength of the plaintiff's own brand has been held to negative misrepresentation. Where Mars asserted that a rival manufacturer of malt balls confectionary, sold in a similar packaging to 'maltesers' but under the brand 'Delfi', amounted to misrepresentation, the Court opined that the plaintiffs' famous brand 'maltesers' served to distinguish each product – the trial judge held that the plaintiffs were 'the victims of their own success'. The Full Federal Court of Australia has affirmed that in get-up cases it is permissible to refer to the strength of the plaintiff's own mark: *Mars Australia Pty Ltd v Sweet Rewards Pty Ltd*.[201] Get-up that is common in the trade will not attract liability for the user. First use will not confer a monopoly so long as any subsequent use by another trader will not be likely to deceive the reasonable consumer. In some markets, where the consumer may be expected to purchase cheaper consumer products that will promote a healthy lifestyle, for example, it may be that the purchaser will look quickly for a brand and not be misled by get-up alone.[202] The plaintiff will have to establish confusion, even overcoming the hurdle of showing reputation established via get-up as distinct from a name or logo, for example.[203]

[25.44] The courts will tend to infer damage in cases where fraudulent trading is established or where the plaintiff can show a falling volume of sales. Damage is normally made up from a reduction in the volume of sales,[204] injurious association with the defendant because the defendant's goods are inferior or because the plaintiff may become embroiled in disputes with others or suffer loss of goodwill. An illustration of this occurred in *Associated Newspapers plc v Insert Media Ltd*.[205] The proprietors of two national newspapers objected to the practice of inserting advertising leaflets into their daily newspapers. After finding that there was an element of misrepresentation – that the

---

[198] *Rizla Ltd v Bryant & May Ltd* [1986] RPC 389.

[199] *Financial Times v Evening Standard* [1991] FSR 7; *Borthwick v Evening Post* (1888) 37 Ch D 449.

[200] *Morning Star Co-operative Society Ltd v Express Newspapers* (1978) 1A IPR 661. For confusion due to illiteracy or inability to read English, the goods being placed on a foreign market, see *White Haden & Co Ltd v Asian Organisation Ltd* [1965] 1 All ER 1040 and *Lee Kar Choo v Lee Lian Choon* [1966] 3 All ER 1000. Where a product is intended for a foreign market (eg Irish Whiskey for sale in Russia) evidence of the likelihood of confusion in that marketplace may be dispositive: *Irish Distillers Ltd v Cooley Distillery plc* [2008] IEHC 236.

[201] *Mars Australia Pty Ltd v Sweet Rewards Pty Ltd* (2009) 84 IPR 12.

[202] *Natural Waters of Viti Ltd v Artesian Waters Ltd* (2007) 7 IPR 571; *Nutrient Water Pty Ltd v Baco Pty Ltd* (2010) 84 IPR 452.

[203] *Ricegrowers Ltd v Real Foods Pty Ltd* (2008) 77 IPR 32.

[204] *Singer v Loog* (1888) 8 App Cas 15. Damages may be awarded in respect of lost sales and also in respect of the effects the misrepresentation may have had in terms of the loss of distinctiveness: *Diageo North America Inc v Inercontinental Brands (ICB) Ltd* [2010] EWHC 17(Ch).

[205] *Associated Newspapers plc v Insert Media Ltd* [1991] 3 All ER 535.

leaflets formed a part of the newspaper – Browne-Wilkinson VC went on to consider whether there was any evidence of substantial damage[206] occurring if this practice were permitted:

> The evidence disclosed that, on occasion, readers who had responded to advertisements in the plaintiff's newspapers and had been less than satisfied with the results had complained to the publishers, who had taken steps, usually effectively, to right wrongs which the readers suffered. It is true that such letters of complaint cannot be tied in with any one reader ceasing to take the plaintiff's newspapers though, as the judge held, that is not decisive. If the third defendant can procure newsagents to make inserts without the knowledge and approval of the plaintiffs, there must be a real risk that the Daily Mail will be thought by the readers to be responsible for the accuracy and honesty of those advertisements. The publishers will have no control over the nature of the advertisements, or their honesty or their quantity. There is therefore an obvious, appreciable, risk of loss of goodwill and reputation by the publishers.[207]

Despite *Taittinger v Albev*, a majority of the Court of Appeal has reiterated the view that if the public is not likely to be confused by the use of a name, but such use has the danger of harming the plaintiff's reputation but not the plaintiff's goodwill, this is not sufficient to sustain a passing off action: *Harrods v Harrodian School*.[208]

The Budweiser litigation

[25.45] The international trade mark and passing-off litigation between Anheuser-Busch and the Budejovicky Budvar organisation, a contest between a US corporation and a Czech company in respect of the use of the name, 'Budweiser', has, at the last count, led to proceedings being brought in 40 countries, as well as in the Benelux, since 1966.[209] Such claims generally revolve around allegations of trade mark infringement and passing off although in one early English case the action failed on the basis that in the early 1970s Budweiser was not a product that enjoyed any reputation or goodwill in England, a position that has dramatically changed in recent years, so much so that the US 'Budweiser' mark is regarded as a well-known mark within international treaty law.[210] However, in the two most recent instances of litigation in the common law world, different conclusions were reached on the passing off issue. In the Australian case, Allsop J found that the labels and get-up of the Czech product created and reinforced a product distinct from that of the US applicant, but that the use of the word 'Budweiser' on the front label (notwithstanding use of the words 'Budejovicky Budvar' on the same labelling) constituted a passing off.[211] In contrast, the New Zealand Court of Appeal held

---

[206] See Peter Gibson LJ in *Taittinger v Allbev* [1994] 4 All ER 75 at 83.

[207] *Associated Newspapers plc v Insert Media Ltd* [1991] 3 All ER 535 at 542.

[208] *Harrods v Harrodian School* (1996) 35 IPR 355.

[209] See Allsop J in the Australian case of *Anheuser Busch Inc v Budejovicky Budvar* (2002) 56 IPR 182 at 203.

[210] Paris Convention for the Protection of Industrial Property 1893, art 6*bis*; see [2003] 1 NZLR 472 at 502. The early English case is *Anheuser Busch v Budejovicky Budvar* [1984] FSR 413.

[211] *Anheuser Busch Inc v Budejovicky Budvar* (2002) 56 IPR 182.

that on examination of the Czech product as a whole, the get-up of that product did not increase the likelihood of deception beyond that inherent in the use of the trade marks.[212]

[25.46] The requirement that there be substantial damage may help to explain the decision in the Irish case of *B & S v Irish Auto Trader*.[213] There the plaintiffs sought an injunction to prevent the defendants from launching an Irish edition of their magazine *Auto Trader*. The plaintiffs had produced a magazine, which had used the word 'Autotrader' as a heading for their used car section. An injunction was refused because McCracken J held that it was unlikely that car dealers would be deceived but that if members of the public examined the defendants' magazine thinking it was the plaintiffs', they would quickly realise that this was not the case.

[25.47] The most interesting Irish decision on damage is the decision of Murphy J in *Falcon Travel Ltd v Owners Abroad Group*.[214] The plaintiff, a small retail travel agency, had traded under the name Falcon Travel since 1970. In 1988 the defendants started to sell package holidays, as tour operators, on the Irish market using the name Falcon. This caused market confusion in so far as the plaintiff complained that 'I am afraid that everybody thinks I am the defendants'. Was confusion enough or did the plaintiff have to show a real tangible risk of damage resulting from the confusion? While damage is normally an essential proof,[215] Murphy J held that in cases where the plaintiff can show that the defendant has appropriated the plaintiff's reputation, submerging that reputation into that of the defendant, the tort is completed, whether or not any other damage has been shown to follow from 'that invasion of the right of property'. The reasoning in this decision must be regarded as incorrect, for damage to goodwill is the basis of liability rather than appropriation of any supposed property right. Rather than awarding nominal damages, Murphy J awarded damages as a rough estimate of loss intended to allow the plaintiff to advertise and re-establish its identity with the public and the trade.

Proof of damage

[25.48] If damage is not inferred, and several Irish cases indicate that this may well occur when improper use is proved,[216] the plaintiff will have to establish the likelihood of deception and damage.[217] If the action is *quia timet* then proof may be impossible to obtain. While some cases involve the testimony of traders, wholesalers and the like, this

---

[212] *Anheuser Busch Inc v Budejovicky Budvar NC* [2001] 3 NZLR 666.

[213] *B & S v Irish Auto Trader* [1995] 2 ILRM 252; see also *Private Research Ltd v Brosnan* [1995] 1 IR 534.

[214] *Falcon Travel Ltd v Owners Abroad Group* [1991] 1 IR 175; Carty [1996] EIPR 487.

[215] Citing *Unitex Ltd v Union Texturing Co* [1973] RPC 119.

[216] *C & A Modes v C & A (Waterford) Ltd* [1976] IR 198 and *Falcon Travel Ltd v Owners Abroad Group* [1991] 1 IR 175. This is also the Canadian view: see *British Columbia Automobile Association v OPEIU Local 378* (2001) 10 CPR (4th) 423.

[217] See in particular *Harrods v Harrodian School* (1996) 35 IPR 355 at 369–370 *per* Millett LJ; Lai (1996) 146 NLJ 874. Several cases hold that where there is no likelihood of confusion then there will also be no likelihood of damage, eg *Baywatch Production Co v Home Video Channel* [1997] FSR 877; *Harding v Smilecare* [2002] FSR 589. Even if confusion is established there may be no proof of damage: *Irvine v Talksport Ltd* [2003] 2 All ER 881.

evidence may not always be admissible, for the basic issue will be whether, at the point of sale, a customer is likely to be deceived and the judges have tended to say that the hypothetical customer is a more suitable point of reference for this test than someone actively involved in business; although actual evidence of deception is helpful, the independent judgment of the court should always be exercised.[218]

Codes of practice

[25.49] There are codes of practice that can be called into play to challenge the accuracy or propriety of certain product advertisements. The Advertising Standards Authority for Ireland (ASAI Codes) has governed print and broadcast advertising and a contrary ruling by the Authority may attract significant levels of adverse publicity.[219] The Broadcasting Act 2001 has created a new body, the Broadcasting Commission of Ireland (BCI) and it has recently produced a code of practice directed, in particular, at regulating broadcast advertisements towards children.[220] One recent example of the 'knock on' effect that ASAI complaints may have occurred when Hunky Dorys crisps were found to have committed a 'grave breach' of the code when using scantily clad female rugby players to advertise their products. The advertisements were regarded as demeaning to women – because of the strap lines mostly – and they were withdrawn. The Irish Rugby Football Union, it is understood, hinted at legal action because of a perception that the advertisements implied that the company was a significant sponsor of Irish rugby.[221]

Character merchandising

[25.50] One important area of commercial activity relates to the practice of character merchandising and the possibility that the defendant may appropriate the persona or image of a real or invented character for his or her own ends. In this context, the act of appropriation, with consent, does not lead the courts to impute damage to the plaintiff's goodwill. The plaintiff will generally have to prove that members of the public would believe the plaintiff had licensed the use of the image or character in circumstances where damage to the goodwill in the business would be prejudiced. The licensing of an image or an invented character is as much a commercial enterprise as the actual sale of goods or services. At first, English courts struggled with recognition of this problem. Radio personalities and actors who found that their reputation or name had been appropriated to promote a product with which they had no conceivable point of contact could not point to any cause of action because their goodwill was based upon their 'business' as entertainers – there was no common field of activity, for example, in relation to the plaintiff's professional persona and the defendant's marketing of a

---

[218] *Payton & Co v Snelling Lampard & Co* [1901] AC 308; *Symonds Cider & English Wine Co v Schwepps (Ireland)* (10 January 1997, unreported), HC.

[219] Eg 'Guinness goodness' ad rejected: (2002) Irish Times, 24 April.

[220] 'New Code will restrict adverts aimed at children' (2004) Irish Times, 20 April. The code is effective from 1 January 2005.

[221] See 'Complaints against crisps ads upheld over 'grave beach'" (2010) Irish Times, 7 July.

breakfast cereal.[222] Similarly, the impersonation of a distinguished actor's voice in order to promote products by way of radio advertisements was held not to be actionable despite evidence that listeners thought that the voice was that of the plaintiff.[223] English courts adhered to this approach in cases involving the pop group ABBA,[224] the fictional detective Kojak[225] and the Wombles.[226] These cases suggested that the creators of an image or a character could not control unauthorised use of that image unless some artistic copyright, design right or trade mark had been used in replicating the character and that mere use of a name could not be actionable, without more.

[25.51] For protection to be available in respect of the misuse of an invented character under the traditional approach, it will be necessary to put forward some underlying intellectual property right. Passing off requires the plaintiff to establish goodwill or reputation; a misrepresentation and resulting damage to other intellectual property rights will also suffice. In cases of copyright, for example, it will often be a drawing that the defendant replicates. In *Cie Générale des Etablissements Michelin – Michelin & Cie v CAW Canada*,[227] the defendant trade union, during an industrial dispute, reproduced the Michelin man figure, Bibendum, in anti-employer leaflets and was held to have infringed copyright, a defence of parody being rejected. In these cases the court will be required to consider basic copyright issues. It may be, for example, that a defence of coincidental creation may be established, as in *United Artists v Clarke*,[228] where United Artists were unsuccessful in preventing a motor vehicle retailer from using a cat-like figure dressed in a jacket and bow tie in promotional literature. The fact that there was a strong resemblance to the plaintiff's 'Pink Panther' character was not of itself evidence of infringement of artistic copyright: contrast *NBA v Gaunt*.[229] Images may also be held to be generic or generally descriptive of an animal species rather than a specific character.[230] Infringement may also occur if, for example, a literary character is fully described by the author and a three-dimensional replication of the character is successful in capturing the essence of that character, according to the Canadian case of *Anne of Green Gables Licensing Authority Inc v Avonlea Traditions Inc*.[231] However, where the underlying work comes within the definition of a design document there may be the possibility of a defence prevailing in certain circumstances.[232]

---

[222] *McCulloch v May* [1947] 2 All ER 845; doubted in *Harrods Ltd v Harrodian School* (1996) 35 IPR 355.

[223] *Sim v HJ Heinz* [1959] 1 All ER 547.

[224] *Lyngstad v Anabas Products Ltd* [1977] FSR 62.

[225] *Tavener Rutledge v Trexapalm* [1977] RPC 275.

[226] *Wombles Ltd v Wombles Skips Ltd* [1975] FSR 488.

[227] *Cie Générale des Etablissements Michelin - Michelin & Cie v CAW Canada* (1996) 71 CPR (3d) 348.

[228] *United Artists v Clarke* (1998) 41 IPR 425.

[229] *NBA v Gaunt* (1998) 44 IPR 225.

[230] *Universal City Studios Inc v M & R Hamersfield Pty Ltd* (1997) 40 IPR 196.

[231] *Anne of Green Gables Licensing Authority Inc v Avonlea Traditions Inc* (1999) 4 CPR (4th) 289.

[232] Copyright and Related Rights Act 2000, s 78A, inserted by the Industrial Designs Act 2001, s 89; *BBC Worldwide Ltd v Pally Screen Printing Ltd* [1998] FSR 665.

[25.52] In cases of trade mark registrations, the use of images such as the 'Thomas the Tank Engine' characters as part of the trading image of a children's toy store has been injuncted at the behest of the owners of the rights in 'Thomas'.[233] Similarly, a wrestler who donned the garb of 'Super Mario' was prevented from infringing the Nintendo trade mark via interlocutory proceedings.[234] It is possible, however, that the validity of the trade mark may itself be challenged, *inter alia*, on the ground that the mark refers directly to the subject matter of the goods or services.[235]

[25.53] Even the law of confidence could be brought into operation to prevent the defendant from appropriating characters sketched out in the form of a pilot for a television series or film, for example .[236]

[25.54] But in the absence of an underlying intellectual right, it is difficult to obtain protection for the use of a name, image or personality trait *per se*.

[25.55] In the *ABBA* case,[237] the group had begun to fix the group's name and image to a limited range of products but unfortunately for them they had not diversified into clothing, T shirts or bedlinen, and thus could not show any likelihood of confusion. In the case of the *'Kojakpop'* lollipop,[238] the defendant was in fact claiming to be an authorised licensee of the right holder in the Kojak character but this did not prevent Walton J from granting an injunction in favour of the plaintiff, who had no such authority and happened to be the first to exploit the Kojak name. Walton J was clearly sceptical of both the scope and public benefit of the practice of character licensing, observing that the person in the street would not conclude from the mere use of an invented character's name that the defendant had been given a licence to use that name and that the use of the name carried a guarantee of quality in the product.[239] This attitude has survived in the English courts until recent times. The Spice Girls were unable to obtain an injunction to stop the unauthorised distribution of stickers bearing their image on the ground that the Spice Girls were not 'traders'.[240]

[25.56] However, a line of Australian cases has in effect subverted the earlier English approach. The first in this sequence, *Henderson v Radio Corpn*,[241] involved an application for an injunction restraining the defendant from releasing an album of dance music under a cover which reproduced a photograph of the plaintiffs, professional ballroom dancers. No copyright infringement in the photograph occurred but the defendant, in using the photograph, was held to indicate 'sponsorship'[242] of the

---

[233] *Britt v Miller* (2000) 49 IPR 7.

[234] *Nintendo Co Ltd v Care* (2000) 52 IPR 34.

[235] *Tarzan Trade Mark* [1970] RPC 450.

[236] Eg *Fraser v Thames Television Ltd* [1983] 2 All ER 101; *Gupta v Dasgupta* [2003] FSR 337.

[237] *Lyngstad v Anabas Products Ltd* [1977] FSR 62.

[238] *Tavener Rutledge v Trexapalm* [1977] RPC 275.

[239] The *Judge Dredd* case is an honourable exception to the English line of authority; see *IPC Magazines v Black & White Music Corpn* [1983] FSR 348.

[240] *Halliwell v Panini SpA* (6 June 1997, unreported); see Jones [1999] E IPR 28, at 30.

[241] *Henderson v Radio Corpn* [1969] RPC 218.

[242] *Henderson v Radio Corpn* [1969] RPC 218, *per* Manning J.

defendant's products. More significantly, while there was a common field of activity as between the parties, in so far as the album would be used in dance and dance tuition, activities in which both parties had a commercial interest, the Supreme Court of New South Wales distanced itself from both the common field of activity test and the result in *McCulloch v May*,[243] and the court argued for a return to basic principle, namely:

> once it is proved that A is falsely representing his goods as the goods of B or his business to be the same as or connected with the business of B, the wrong of passing off has been established and B is entitled to relief.[244]

[25.57] The crucial factor here is whether there is some commercial connection between the plaintiff and the defendant by way of the use by the defendant of the image or indicia. In *Hogan v Pacific Dunlop*,[245] the defendants sold leather shoes by utilising the knife scene in the film *Crocodile Dundee* although the actor playing the role of Mick Dundee in the advertisement could not be confused with the plaintiff, Paul Hogan. The Federal Court of Australia found a misrepresentation, for the public would be deceived into thinking that the shoes had some authorised link with *Crocodile Dundee*, perceived to be a persona of the plaintiff by the Australian public, in Burchett J's view. The Australian courts have also granted injunctions to restrain the unauthorised marking of T shirts with the 7 Up Fido-Dido character, a decision that is important because it was followed by Browne-Wilkinson VC in *Mirage Studios v Counter-Feat Clothing Co*.[246] In that case, the plaintiff obtained an injunction to prevent the defendant from trading in sportswear that depicted humanoid turtles engaged in sporting rather than martial arts activities, but the evidence indicated a similarity with the plaintiff's Ninja Turtles characters and the fact that the defendant's artwork was derived from that of the plaintiff via a redesign exercise. While the actual decision is a somewhat narrow one, in so far as the plaintiff could point to artistic copyright infringement, the Vice Chancellor indicated that the evidence was that the public was now much more sophisticated in relation to character merchandising than previously:[247]

> The critical evidence in this case is that a substantial number of the buying public now expect and know that where a famous cartoon or television character is reproduced on goods, that reproduction is the result of a licence granted by the owner of the copyright or owner of other rights in that character. Mr Smith, the defendant, accepted that evidence subject to this; he said that was only true where the reproduced matter was an exact reproduction of the character in the cartoon or television show, whereas in his case the defendants' turtles were different. I cannot accept that. If, as the evidence here shows, the public mistake the defendants' turtles for those which might be called genuine plaintiffs'

---

[243] *McCulloch v May* [1947] 2 All ER 845.

[244] *McCulloch v May* [1947] 2 All ER 845, *per* Evatt CJ and Myers J. The full Court of the High Court of Australia has approved *Henderson* in *Campomar Sociedad, Limitada v Nike International Ltd* (2000) 46 IPR 481 at 511.

[245] *Hogan v Pacific Dunlop* (1989) 12 IPR 225, 14 IPR 398; *Hogan v Koala Dundee Pty Ltd* (1988) 12 IPR 508.

[246] *Mirage Studios v Counter-Feat Clothing Co* [1991] FSR 145.

[247] Or possibly that Walton J in the *Kojak* case (*Tavener Rutledge v Trexapalm* [1977] RPC 275) took an unrealistic view of the character merchandising phenomenon, even in 1977.

Turtles, once they have made that mistake they will assume that the product in question has been licensed to use the Turtles on it. That is to say, they will connect what they mistakenly think to be the plaintiffs' Turtles with the plaintiffs. To put on the market goods which the public mistake for the genuine article necessarily involves a misrepresentation to the public that they are genuine. On the evidence in this case, the belief that the goods are genuine involves a further misrepresentation, namely that they are licensed.[248]

[25.58] On the other important point of proof of damage, Browne-Wilkinson VC said that where the plaintiff can show that a part of its business profile involves the licensing of others to use the character, then the plaintiff will establish depreciation in the value of the image and thus damage to the licensing right. In following the trend set out in Australian case law,[249] the Vice Chancellor indicated that while both the *ABBA* case[250] and the *Wombles* case[251] were probably still good law in so far as there was no use made of copyright material, the decision in *Kojak*,[252] based on the evidence of consumer awareness before the Vice Chancellor, was simply not reliable and could only be defended on the ground that there could be no copyright in a name. However, the *Ninja Turtles* case[253] does not suggest that the proprietor of rights in a character or image will always succeed in a passing-off action when the defendant has used that character to produce a rival, for the requirement of misrepresentation may operate as an obstacle. In *Tot Toys Ltd v Mitchell*,[254] the plaintiff was the proprietor of a 'Buzzy Bee' toy, which the defendant used to produce a rival product which he marketed as 'Kiwi Bee'. Significantly, design right protection for the 'Buzzy Bee' had expired and no copyright protection could be claimed. The plaintiff was thus forced to argue that there was a deception which injured, *inter alia*, the plaintiff's character merchandising rights. Fisher J, however, refused to follow the Australian decisions for two reasons: firstly, it could not be shown in all character merchandising cases that a deception had been practised and, secondly, the argument that the defendant is damaging the plaintiff's merchandising rights assumes that a right always exists – a circular argument. Fisher J observed that the Australian courts were guilty of turning passing off into a cause of action based more on a property right than deception, and he approved of certain academic comments, which described the Australian cases as being based in unfair competition or appropriation of personality rather than misrepresentation.[255] One English commentator also sees the Australian cases as jettisoning goodwill and protecting the plaintiff because of loss of future merchandising opportunities.[256] In any event, Fisher J, in *Tot Toys*, held that the plaintiff's claim did not succeed because the defendant had taken adequate steps to distinguish its product from the 'Buzzy Bee'. Notwithstanding this cautionary New

---

[248] *Mirage Studios v Counter-Feat Clothing Co* [1991] FSR 145 at 155.
[249] *Children's Television Workshop Inc v Woolworths (NSW) Ltd* [1981] RPC 187 and *Fido-Dido Inc v Venture Stores Retailers* (1988) 16 IPR 365.
[250] *Lyngstad v Anabas Products Ltd* [1977] FSR 62.
[251] *Wombles Ltd v Wombles Skips Ltd* [1975] FSR 488.
[252] *Tavener Rutledge v Trexapalm* [1977] RPC 275.
[253] *Mirage Studios v Counter-Feat Clothing Co* [1991] FSR 145.
[254] *Tot Toys Ltd v Mitchell* (1992) 25 IPR 337.
[255] Terry (1991) 65 ALJ 587; Howell (1991) 6 IPJ 197.
[256] Carty (1993) 13 LS 289. Note, however, that in the *Ninja Turtles* case, Browne-Wilkinson VC seems to have regarded market entry as a *sine qua non*.

Zealand decision, English courts are making significant strides in favour of broad brand or name protection since the repudiation of the common field of activity element in the tort.[257] The character merchandising protection available in respect of imaginary persons may also extend to character goods, ie goods that are not traded in but which are associated with a character. In *Twentieth Century Fox v South Australian Brewing*,[258] Homer Simpson's favourite tipple, Duff Beer, was poached by the defendants without the consent of The Simpsons' right holder. Applying *Hogan v Pacific Dunlop*,[259] the Federal Court of Australia found both a misrepresentation in the form of conjuring an association between the product and the plaintiffs and damage in the form of lost licensing opportunities.

Appropriation of personality

[25.59] Until comparatively recently, where the defendant has misappropriated the image of real personalities for product endorsement, the plaintiff has generally been unsuccessful,[260] save in the *Crocodile Dundee* case[261] where the Hogan/Dundee persona have tended to be regarded as the same. In one Australian case, the artist Michael Jackson sought to prevent the unauthorised release of recordings on the ground that this would infringe Jackson's right to publicity, but the application failed because Australian law does not recognise any such right.[262] Lockhart J in the Federal Court of Appeal resisted the temptation to enquire into whether cases such as *Henderson v Radio Corpn* could be the basis of such a right in Australian law. In essence, the evolution of a cause of action for misappropriation of personality resides in the tort of passing off with the need for a misrepresentation being the central requirement. Other English cases, however, suggest that nascent privacy rights will afford room for further remedies in appropriate cases. Beverly-Smith is also of the view that a degree of hybridisation will mark future English law development.[263]

[25.60] In Ireland, the constitutional protections in relation to property and a good name would arguably assist any Irish litigant whose name has been used prejudicially in obtaining vindication in the courts, but there is no judicial recognition of any tortious right to personality in Irish case law.

[25.61] That the active participation of an individual in the marketing of goods and services is itself a tradable commodity was recognised by Kelly J in *O'Keeffe v Ryanair Ltd*.[264] The plaintiff was approached as she checked in for a flight with Ryanair and was

---

[257] Eg *Lego System v Lego M Lemelstritch Ltd* [1983] FSR 155.

[258] *Twentieth Century Fox v South Australian Brewing* (1996) 34 IPR 225.

[259] *Hogan v Pacific Dunlop* (1989) 12 IPR 225, 14 IPR 398.

[260] *10th Cantanac Pty v Shoshana Pty* (1987) 10 IPR 289; *Wickham v Associated Pool Builders Property* (1986) 7 IPR 392; *Honey v Australian Airlines* (1990) 18 IPR 185.

[261] *Hogan v Pacific Dunlop* (1989) 12 IPR 225, 14 IPR 398; *Hogan v Koala Dundee Pty Ltd* (1988) 12 IPR 508.

[262] *Sony Music Australia Ltd and Michael Jackson v Tansing* (1993) 27 IPR 649. See also *Gould Estate v Stoddart Publishing* (1996) 30 OR (3d) 520.

[263] Beverly-Smith, *Commercial Appropriation of Personality* (2002) 322–329.

[264] *O'Keeffe v Ryanair Ltd* [2003] 1 ILRM 14.

offered the opportunity to gain free flights for life if she agreed to participate in a 'millionth passenger' promotion She accepted the offer and engaged in photographic and television promotions for Ryanair. Kelly J held that she provided consideration in the form of participation and giving up rights of privacy; if an unknown member of the public could surrender such rights, *a fortiori* product endorsement by a celebrity is clearly more valuable. In one Irish High Court case the athlete Mary Peters sued Ark Life for use of her image in promoting pension products, the case settling for a reported five-figure payment.[265] Similarly, the unauthorised use of Bono's image in a Smurfit annual report (this being controversial because of allegations about environmental damage and human rights abuses by the Smurfit Group) was the subject of a strong complaint. Even though the photograph in question had itself been lawfully acquired, Bono/U2 complained that use of the photograph could be interpreted as a false endorsement of the Smurfit Group.[266]

[25.62] In some jurisdictions the appropriation of aspects of a human personality, whether it be image, voice name or other indicia of identity, may be actionable if that person's identity is filched by others for commercial objectives.

[25.63] This route to protection is problematical, and the most reliable means of obtaining protection is by way of a trade mark registration.[267] The uncertainty surrounding the availability of relief is based on identifying the cause of action itself. Canadian case law, in particular, has established that a well-known sports celebrity has 'a proprietary right in the exclusive marketing for gain of his personality, image and name',[268] this decision being important because the court rejected any passing-off claim.[269] The application of the tort of appropriation of personality has been considered in relation to the use of a musician's image and in such cases the action failed because of the grant of a licence[270] or because the use was directed at explaining the personality of the musician rather than product endorsement.[271] At least the Canadian case sees the unauthorised use of a musician's image as involving the infringement of rights of privacy.[272] The Jamaican decision in *Robert Marley Foundation v Dino Michelle Ltd*[273] is to the same effect.

---

[265] See 'Action by athlete against Ark Life settled' (2001) Irish Times, 3 March.

[266] See 'U2 dissociates itself from use of Bono's image in Smurfit report' (2001) Irish Times, 12 May.

[267] Eg registration of a trade mark such as THORPEDO for swimwear by Ian Thorpe: [2003] FCA 901; see [2004] Ent LR 59 on the downside of sports personality endorsements.

[268] *Athens v Canadian Adventure Camps Ltd* (1977) 80 DLR (3d) 583, following *Krouse v Chrysler Canada* (1973) 40 DLR (3d) 15 (a case where privacy rights were identified).

[269] See Beverley-Smith, *Commercial Appropriation of Personality* (2002) 115–122.

[270] *Shaw v Berman* (1997) 72 CPR (3d) 9; appeal dismissed at 167 DLR (4th) 576.

[271] *Gould Estate v Stoddard Publishing* (1996) 30 OR (3d) 520, appeal dismissed at (1998) 80 CPR (3d) 161.

[272] *Bogajewicz v Sony of Canada Ltd* (1995) 63 CPR (3d) 458; *Debrulle v Dubrulle French Culinary School Ltd* (2000) 8 CPR (4th) 180.

[273] *Robert Marley Foundation v Dino Michelle Ltd* (12 May 1994, unreported), HC; see Hytton and Goldson (1996) 55 CLJ 56.

[25.64] In England, the decision of Laddie J in *Irvine v Talksport Ltd*[274] has suggested that it is through the law of passing off that the misappropriation of personality will be examined. In this case Eddie Irvine, at that time a very successful Ferrari F1 driver, was used in sales promotional material for a radio station, without his permission. An action in passing off was successful, Laddie J preferring to follow the Australian *Henderson*[275] line of authority. The Court of Appeal endorsed Laddie J's analysis of substantive law, but both decisions leave open considerable scope for debate and future development. In *Irvine* there was a discussion in both courts about the existence of a misrepresentation where recipients of the communication would perhaps conclude that the 'doctoring' of a photograph was so obvious that no misrepresentation would be inferred; room for a parody defence may also be possible. Further, *Irvine* appears limited to cases of false endorsement of a product rather than appropriation of an image *per se*. Whether the passing-off action can be maintained by the estate of a deceased person must be open to doubt; Laddie J in *Irvine* gave an example of posthumous use of a celebrity's image on products[276] opining that no misrepresentation would be made out in such a case. This is in contrast to the Canadian and Jamaican view, where personality rights survive the death of the celebrity. *Irvine*, like similar Australian passing-off actions,[277] holds that damages are to be measured by reference to what has been lost, which is a reasonable endorsement fee, although, as the Court of Appeal in *Irvine* demonstrated, this can differ depending on the image rights being marketed by the celebrity. It is also possible to make the case for damages being capable of compensating the celebrity for being associated with unsavoury products or products that the celebrity clearly disapproves of, such association either causing injury to reputation, feelings, or causing distress – aggravated damages, in other words.

[25.65] New Zealand case law is sparse but 'counterfeit' products can be seized under an order not unlike a *Norwich Pharmacal*[278] order.[279]

PRIVACY LAW

[25.66] The development of a right to privacy, actionable by the individual whose name, likeness or personal life is laid open to others without permission is clearly relevant to this question of the appropriation of personality. The decision of the majority of the House of Lords, in *Campbell v MGN Ltd*,[280] suggests that, via the extended action for breach of confidence, a balancing exercise should be carried out in order to determine whether the competing interests of free speech and privacy can be reconciled and, if not, which holds primacy in the case at bar.[281] *Campbell* distinguishes public interest

---

[274] *Irvine v Talksport Ltd* [2002] 2 All ER 414.

[275] *Henderson v Radio Corpn* [1969] RPC 218.

[276] *Mirage Studios v Counter-Feat Clothing Co* [2002] 2 All ER 414 at 427 (Elvis Presley).

[277] *Henderson v Radio Corpn* [1969] RPC 218; *Talmax Pty Ltd v Telstra Corpn* (1996) ATPR 41–484.

[278] *Norwich Pharmacal Co v Customs and Excise Comrs* [1974] AC 133.

[279] *Tony Blain Property v Splain* [1993] 3 NZLR 185.

[280] *Campbell v MGN Ltd* [2004] UKHL 22, [2004] 2 All ER 995.

[281] Eg *Hosking v Runting* [2003] 3 NZLR 385.

information from the private or mundane, as well as surveillance[282] from the recording of everyday streetscapes.[283]

INJURIOUS OR MALICIOUS FALSEHOOD

[25.67] Some practices in trade that harm the plaintiff may not be protected via passing off and, in the absence of broader laws on unfair competition, the plaintiff may have to resort to one of the lesser torts to vindicate his business reputation. Trade libels, whereby the defendant deliberately disparaged the goods or business of the plaintiff, were possible[284] but the decision of the House of Lords in *White v Mellin*[285] indicated that statements which simply praise the defendant's goods as superior to the plaintiff's brand are not actionable as an injurious falsehood and that the general elements of the tort are narrow in order to minimise the scope of liability in the cut and thrust of business practices. The classic statement on liability is that the plaintiff must prove three elements:

(1)　that the statements complained of were untrue: in terms of actionability, Walton J, in *De Beers Abrasive Products Ltd v International General Electric Co of New York*[286] set out two polar positions: first, where the trader is merely 'puffing' his or her own goods, as distinct from, second, the case of obvious denigration – 'my goods are better than X's, because X's are absolute rubbish'. Walton J went on to state:

> Between these two kinds of statements there is obviously still an extremely wide field; and it appears to me that, in order to draw the line, one must apply this test, namely, whether a reasonable man would take the claim being made as being a serious claim or not. A possible alternative test is to ask whether the defendant has pointed to a specific allegation of some defect or demerit in the plaintiff's goods. This is, I think, the test favoured by the learned editors of the last few editions of *Salmond on Torts* ... I think that as the law now stands, the cases are probably fully consistent with the adoption of either test.[287]

(2)　that they were made maliciously – ie without just cause or excuse: the issue of malice is generally regarded as requiring an analysis of the mental element in the tort. At one extreme stand cases where the law is equated to an action in deceit, where the standard is knowledge of falsity, or recklessness.[288] The Court

---

[282] *Aubrey v Editions Vice-Versa* (1998) 78 CPR (3d) 289; *Peck v United Kingdom* (2003) 36 EHRR 719.

[283] *Hosking v Runting* [2004] 2 LRC 65. See dataprivacy.ie for Case Study 6 of 2006.

[284] Eg *Herman Loog v Bean* (1884) 26 Ch D 306.

[285] *White v Mellin* [1895] AC 154. See *Cooke v McGuigan* (1926) 61 ILTR 45 and more recently *British Airways plc v Ryanair* [2001] FSR 541; *Meridian Communications Ltd v Eircell Ltd* [2001] IEHC 195.

[286] *De Beers Abrasive Products Ltd v International General Electric Co of New York* [1975] FSR 323.

[287] *De Beers Abrasive Products Ltd v International General Electric Co of New York* [1975] FSR 323 at 329.

[288] Eg *Shapiro v La Morta* (1923) 40 TLR 201; *De Beers Abrasive Products Ltd v International General Electric Co of New York* [1975] FSR 323; *Schindler Lifts Australia Pty Ltd v Milan Debelak* (1989) 15 IPR 129; *Palmer Bruyn and Parker Pty Ltd v Parsons* (2001) 208 CLR 388.

of Appeal in England has recently affirmed the view that before pleadings for either fraud or malicious falsehood are drafted there must be both clear instructions and reasonably credible admissible evidence of fraud.[289] On the other hand, there are wider statements of liability, which indicate that even a *bona fide* belief of the truth of a statement will not provide a defence if the statement be false and made with the intention to harm the plaintiff.[290] In *British Airways plc v Ryanair*,[291] Jacob J took a robust view of a Ryanair comparative advertising campaign holding that advertisements were either 'vulgar abuse' or not false, the learned judge indicating that a reasonable person, in such a context, would know that price comparisons, in particular, would involve the selection of prices that broadly would favour the advertiser. The importance of industry codes and industry practices is an important element in this judgment.

In a recent Irish High Court case involving Louis Le Brocquy, reproduction on the walls of a restaurant of some of Mr Le Brocquy's works was conceded to be an infringement of copyright. Interestingly, a claim for slander was added to the claim because the defendants publicised the action to stir up interest in the restaurant, thus 'disparaging and denigrating [the plaintiff's] claims'. The case was settled in favour of the plaintiff.[292]

(3) that the plaintiffs have suffered special damage thereby:[293] this requirement is very liberally interpreted from the viewpoint of the plaintiff.

[25.68] If the statement is false it matters not that the plaintiff is not likely to suffer any loss of reputation or public esteem as long as his business contacts or customer base is likely to be dissuaded from contracting with him, eg by falsely asserting that the plaintiff intends to cease trading either generally or specifically.[294] However, *Allason v Campbell*[295] held that special damage need not be specifically pleaded under the Defamation Act 1961, s 20(1). Damages for malicious falsehood are capable of including damages on an aggravated loss basis after the decision of the Court of Appeal in *Khodaparast v Shad*.[296]

[25.69] There is some limited support for the view that where the defendant intends to plead justification then an injunction will not issue[297] although injunctive relief is relatively easy to obtain if the defendant acts outrageously to damage the reputation of the plaintiff.[298]

---

[289] *Cornwall Gardens Pte Ltd v RO Gerrard & Co* (2001) Times, 19 June.

[290] *Wilts United Dairies Ltd v Thomas Robinson & Sons Ltd* [1957] RPC 220.

[291] *British Airways plc v Ryanair* [2001] FSR 541.

[292] See 'Restaurant apologises to artist for copyright breach' (2001) Irish Times, 2 August.

[293] Lord Davey in *Royal Baking Powder Co v Wright, Crossley & Co* (1900) 18 RPC 95 at 99.

[294] *Radcliffe v Evans* [1892] QB 524; *Gregory v Portsmouth City Council* [2000] 1 AC 419.

[295] *Allason v Campbell* (1996) Times, 8 May.

[296] *Khodaparast v Shad* [2000] 1 All ER 545; *Sallows v Griffiths* [2001] FSR 88.

[297] *Alan H Reid Engineering v Ramset Fasteners* (1990) 20 IPR 15.

[298] *Kaye v Robertson* [1991] FSR 62.

UNLAWFUL INTERFERENCE WITH ECONOMIC RELATIONS

[25.70] It is beyond the scope of this book[299] to explore the history of this particular tort although the Irish courts have had occasion to consider whether it exists at all from a somewhat early date. In *Higgins v O'Donnell*[300] it was held that the obstruction of the plaintiff's customers by the defendant to the prejudice of the plaintiff's business was not actionable because no interference with a proprietary right or contract could be pointed to. Later Irish courts have tended to the view that this tort certainly exists within the sphere of employment contracts[301] and despite some judicial ambivalence on this point,[302] the Supreme Court has recently affirmed that this tort is part of Irish law. In *Charles O'Neill & Co v Adidas Sports Schuhfabriken*,[303] the plaintiffs complained that the defendants had provided sports shirts for a charity event but, finding that none of theirs were suitable, they used shirts manufactured by the plaintiffs and put Adidas symbols on the shirts in two places. Blayney J dismissed the plaintiffs' application for injunctive relief and damages for the tort of unlawful interference in the plaintiffs' business interest on the basis that there was no evidence that the defendants intended to harm the business of the plaintiffs. In the Supreme Court, Finlay CJ endorsed the analysis of the tort in *Clerk and Lindsell on Torts*[304] where three ingredients of the tort are set out, namely:

(1)　interference by unlawful means with a person's trade or activities of an economic or commercial nature;

(2)　with the intent to damage the plaintiff;

(3)　and which causes such damage.

In the view of the Supreme Court, the plaintiff had failed to make out either of factors (2) or (3) to the satisfaction of Blayney J at first instance, and the trial judge was therefore entitled to dismiss the action.

[25.71] At times this tort is described as being divisible into two separate causes of action,[305] unlawful interference with economic relations and unlawful interference with a contract. This second form of the tort was considered in *Premier League Ltd v Elite Sports plc*,[306] a case suggesting the tort may be useful in counteracting piracy on a commercial scale.

---

[299] See Carty (1988) 104 LQR 250.

[300] *Higgins v O'Donnell* (1869) Ir R 4 CL 91.

[301] *Cooper v Millea* [1938] IR 749.

[302] *Bula Ltd v Tara Mines (No 2)* [1987] IR 95; *Pine Valley Developments Ltd v Minister for the Environment* [1987] ILRM 747.

[303] *Charles O'Neill & Co v Adidas Sports Schuhfabriken* (25 March 1992, unreported), SC, *ex tempore* (1992) Irish Times Law Report, 17 August.

[304] *Clerk and Lindsell on Torts* (15th edn, 1982), 747.

[305] Eg *Lineal Group Ltd v Atlantis Canadian Distributors Inc* (1998) 42 OR (3d) 157 (Ont CA).

[306] *Premier League Ltd v Elite Sports plc* [2003] FSR 450.

Chapter 26

Introduction to Trade Mark Law

INTRODUCTION

[26.01] Under Irish law, rights in a trade mark are governed by the provisions of the Trade Marks Act 1996 (TMA 1996), [1] the Community Trade Mark Regulation[2] or by use of a mark leading to goodwill sufficient to sustain an action for passing off. The statutory protection does not affect the laws of passing off[3] and, indeed, until TMA 1996, passing off was the only legal remedy available to the owners of marks[4] used in respect of services. Registration under TMA 1996 and earlier trade mark legislation enables a trade mark proprietor to produce a certificate of registration showing that they are the *prima facie* owner of the mark and, subject to certain limitations, can claim exclusivity to that mark and sue for any infringement thereof. The existence of a trade mark register also assists parties in determining what rights, if any, exist in a particular mark and the scope of protection thereof.

COMPANY NAMES AND BUSINESS NAMES

[26.02] Rights in a trade mark do not exist by virtue of the incorporation of a company under a particular name[5] under the Companies Acts 1963–2009 or the existence of a business name registration under the Registration of Business Names Act 1963.[6] Under s 21 of the Companies Act 1963,[7] there is a provision whereby the Registrar of Companies may, within six months after incorporation, compel a company to change its corporate name if the name is too similar to that of a company which has already been incorporated. The Registrar of Companies adopts a liberal attitude towards the approval of company names and will generally approve any name unless it is identical, or extremely close, to that of a company name already on the Register. Unfortunately, there is no cross-searching between the Company Names Register and the Register of Trade Marks. The Registrar of Companies will approve a company name even though a third

---

[1] Which implements the Trade Mark Harmonisation Directive, Council Directive 2008/95/EC ([2008] OJ L 299/25), which repealed and replaced Directive 89/104/EEC ([1989] OJ L40/1).

[2] Council Regulation 207/2009/EC ([2009] OJ L78/1) which repealed and replaced Council Regulation 40/94/EC ([1994] OJ L11/1).

[3] TMA 1996, s 7(2).

[4] The words 'trade mark' and 'mark' can be used interchangeably.

[5] *Volkswagen Leasing GmbH* [2001] ETMR 101.

[6] See para [26.04].

[7] As amended by the Company Law Enforcement Act 2001, s 86.

party already holds a trade mark registration for such. The effect of this is that, even though a party may incorporate a company under a particular name, use of that name could constitute trade mark infringement[8] and/or passing off.[9] Indeed, the Irish courts have gone even further and have held that the mere incorporation of a company under a name can also amount to passing off. In the Supreme Court, in *C&A Modes v C&A (Waterford) Ltd,*[10] Kenny J stated:

> the legal wrong known as passing off includes the incorporation in the Republic of Ireland of a company with a name likely to give the impression to the public that it is a subsidiary or branch of or is associated or connected with another company which has an established goodwill, whether the latter company is incorporated in the Republic or outside it. The incorporation with the name selected may have been with the intention of creating that impression, *Lloyds and Dawson Bros v Lloyds (Southampton) Ltd* (1912) 29 RPC 433; *Harrods Ltd v R Harrod Ltd* (1923) 41 RPC 74 or innocently without knowing the existence of the well-known company, *Ewing v Buttercup Margarine Co Ltd* [1917] 2 Ch 1. In either event, the wrong of passing off may be restrained by the company with the established goodwill.

This *obiter dictum* was approved as 'a sound statement of the law' by Carroll J in the unreported case of *Rittal Werk Rudolph Loh GmbH v Rittal (Ireland) Ltd.*[11] In that case the defendant was ordered to change its corporate name even though it was not trading and had undertaken not to trade in the plaintiff's field of activity.

[26.03] In *Guinness Ireland Group v Kilkenny Brewing Co Ltd,*[12] Laffoy J accepted that the defendant acted in good faith when incorporating under the offending company name, but nevertheless granted the relief sought, approving the statement of Kenny J in *C&A Modes,* and held that neither intention nor a degree of knowing culpability is a necessary ingredient in the tort of passing off. Laffoy J also reinforced the earlier judicial precedent that the boundaries of the law of passing off extend to a cause of action against even the mere incorporation of an offending company name stating:

> I think it is somewhat disingenuous to argue that there is no likelihood of confusion or giving the wrong impression because the defendant will merely be a land holding company. Under section 114 of the Companies Act 1963, every company has certain statutory obligations in relation to the publication of its name – on the exterior of every premises in which it carries on business, on its letterheads, cheques, invoices etc. Moreover, the evidence is that the primary objects clause in the defendant's Memorandum of Association is deliberately broad in scope because of a realisation that the regulatory authorities might require it to be so, for instance, if the defendant was applying for a licence in the future. In my view it is unrealistic to assume that the name of the defendant can be immured from the public perception so as to avoid giving a wrongful impression of a connection with the plaintiffs' business.

---

[8]   *Celine SARL v Celine SA* [2007] ETMR 80; see also *PEBEX* [2004] ETMR 14.
[9]   *Hotel Cipriani Srl v Cipriani (Grosvenor Street) Ltd* [2010] EWCA Civ 110.
[10] *C&A Modes v C&A (Waterford) Ltd* [1976] IR 198.
[11] *Rittal Werk Rudolph Loh GmbH v Rittal (Ireland) Ltd* (11 July 1991, unreported), HC.
[12] *Guinness Ireland Group v Kilkenny Brewing Co Ltd* [1999] ETMR 807.

[26.04] Under the Registration of Business Names Act 1963, the registration of a business name is a legal requirement imposed upon a person who uses a name which is different from his own individual or corporate name or, in the case of a firm, the names of all partners.[13] The purpose of such a registration is that the public can carry out a search in the Register of Business Names and ascertain who is behind a particular business name at a particular address. The registration of a business name does not confer any proprietary rights in the name. Section 14(3) specifically states that the registration shall not be construed as authorising the use of that name if, apart from such registration, the use thereof could be prohibited. The Registrar of Business Names has no power to refuse a registration based on what is already on the Business Names Register, only on the basis that registration of the business name is undesirable in the opinion of the Minister for Enterprise, Trade and Innovation. A multiplicity of different and unconnected persons can, and often do, hold identical or confusingly similar business name registrations.

DOMAIN NAMES

[26.05] Similar to the position in relation to a company name, the mere existence of a domain name does not grant any proprietary rights and the ability to trade through a website utilising a particular domain name is subject to trade mark rights, which may be held by others through trade mark registration and/or use. However, the nature of a borderless internet and intellectual property rights hold considerable potential for conflict, particularly in a scenario where domain names are unique and generally allocated on a 'first-come, first-served' basis. This conflict led to the foundation in 1998 of the Internet Corporation for Assigned Names and Numbers (ICANN) and the introduction in 1999 of the Uniform Domain Name Dispute Resolution Policy (UDRP). ICANN is a non-profit-making body that manages the general top level domain names (gTLD) such as .com, .net, .org, .biz and .info. The UDRP allows an aggrieved trade mark owner to challenge a third party's registration of a domain name, which incorporates or is confusingly similar to its registered or unregistered trade mark, where the domain name registration was made in bad faith. The UDRP is very popular and is seen by trade mark owners as providing a fast and inexpensive system to address the issue of cybersquatting and certain other forms of domain name abuse. The UDRP only applies to generic top level domain names, unless a country which administers a country code top level domain name voluntarily adopts the UDRP (which Ireland has done with some small alterations). gTLD domain name registrants contractually submit to the UDRP when registering their domain name. However, the UDRP does not have any binding effect other than on the registrar of the domain name in dispute. Decisions under the UDRP do not prejudice subsequent court proceedings.

---

[13] Registration of Business Names Act 1963, s 3.

[26.06] Under the UDRP, a complainant must establish all of the following:

- the respondent's domain name is identical or confusingly similar to the complainant's trade mark;
- the respondent has no rights or legitimate interest in the domain name; and
- the respondent must have registered, and must be using, the domain name in bad faith.[14]

Proceedings under the UDRP are conducted by three ICANN-approved dispute resolution providers namely:

- WIPO (World Intellectual Property Organisation);
- NAF (National Arbitration Forum); and
- ADNDRC (Asian Domain Name Dispute Resolution Centre).

There is a fourth ICANN-approved dispute resolution provider that deals exclusively with .eu domain names, namely the Czech Arbitration Court Arbitration Center for Internet Disputes.

[26.07] A complainant initiates UDRP proceedings before any ICANN-approved provider and must designate whether they wish the dispute to be conducted before a three-member panel or by a single-member panel. The respondent has a right to elect a three-member panel where the complainant has elected a single-member panel. In such a scenario, the respondent must contribute towards the fees. The fees vary between the providers and are dependant on the number of panellists elected and the number of domain names in dispute. Remedies are limited to the cancellation or transfer of the respondent's domain name registration and there is no provision for fines or punitive damages. Generally, a respondent has 20 days before the commencement of proceedings within which to file a response and the panel issues its decision within 14 days of the appointment. The panel's decision is implemented by the ICANN-approved registrar with whom the respondent has registered their domain name.

[26.08] The requirement of a complainant to prove the existence of their own trade mark rights is generally accomplished by providing evidence of a trade mark registration, irrespective of the jurisdiction in which the trade mark is registered. However, a complainant may also rely on unregistered (common law) trade mark rights but the evidential burden in such cases is more difficult to satisfy.

[26.09] A lack of rights or legitimate interests in respect of a domain name is generally proven by a statement that a respondent does not have a trade mark right of their own and that the complainant's trade mark has a well-known reputation so that the respondent must have known of its existence. The respondent can establish rights or legitimate interests by proving any one of the following three circumstances:

---

[14] See 'WIPO Overview of WIPO Panel Views on Selected UDRP Questions', (http://www.wipo.int/amc/en/domains/search/overview/index.html) for a summary of the WIPO position on many contentious issues.

(a)   a *bona fide* use of the domain name;

(b)   a common use of the domain name in connection with the domain name holder;

(c)   a legitimate non-commercial or fair use of the domain name.

[26.10] The issues that cause the biggest problems for a complainant are the burden of proving registration of the domain name in bad faith[15] and use of the domain name in bad faith. Examples of registration in bad faith are offers to sell the domain name, a pattern of conduct blocking trade mark owners from using their marks in corresponding domain names, registration of the domain name primarily for the purpose of disrupting the business of a competitor, creating a likelihood of confusion or even attracting internet users to the website for commercial gain.[16]

[26.11] The registry for .ie internet domain names is called the IEDR[17] and has its origins in the computing and services department of University College Dublin. It is an independent not-for-profit organisation and manages the .ie country code top level domain name (ccTLD).[18] The IEDR is one of the few remaining ccTLD registries in Europe that requires a registrant to have a real and substantive connection with the country in question. The requirements to prove such a connection vary according to the category of registrant. A new .ie dispute resolution policy (ieDRP) was launched on 31 July 2003 and follows the UDRP model with some small alterations. Complaints are filed with and administered by the WIPO Arbitration and Mediation Center.[19] The ieDRP applies to all .ie domain names registered after 31 July 2003 and to the remaining .ie domain names upon their renewal. The basis for a complaint under the ieDRP is that:

- the .ie domain name is identical or misleadingly similar to a protected identifier in which the complainant has rights;
- the registrant has no rights in law or legitimate interests in the domain name;[20]
- the domain name has been registered or is being used in bad faith.[21]

THE FUNCTION OF A TRADE MARK

[26.12] The reason why persons seek to protect their trade mark(s) must be considered in the context of the functions that a trade mark performs. Perhaps the most immediate function that springs to mind is that the trade mark is an indication as to the origin of the goods or services and thus, for example, in the Trade Marks Act 1963 (TMA 1963), the statutory definition of a trade mark was:

---

15   *Meat and Livestock Commission v David Pearce* [2004] ETMR 26.

16   *PARMA HAM* [2004] ETMR 27.

17   The full name of the domain name registrar is IE Domain Registry Ltd.

18   See www.domainregistry.ie.

19   See arbiter.wipo.int/domains/cctld/ie/index.html.

20   *Tesco Stores Ltd v Elogicom Ltd* [2006] ETMR 91.

21   As opposed to bad faith use and registration under the UDRP.

a mark used or proposed to be used in relation to goods for the purpose of indicating, or so as to indicate, a connection in the course of trade between the goods and some person having the right either as proprietor or as registered user to use the mark, whether with or without any indication of the identity of that person.

[26.13] As a consequence of this definition, in many instances, the courts felt compelled to adopt a narrow interpretation of a trade mark and issues such as whether 'an inference of identity of origin would be drawn'[22] were raised in determining issues of similarity between marks. The English courts refused registration of a cartoon character 'Holly Hobbie'[23] by an applicant because the owner intended to grant licences in such a way that the mark was being dealt with primarily as a commodity in its own right and so there would be no real trade connection between the owner of the mark and the goods to which the mark was to be applied. Both the UK Trade Marks Act 1938 and the Irish TMA 1963 included a provision against facilitating trafficking in a trade mark.[24]

[26.14] In a group of cases involving parallel imports of re-packaged pharmaceuticals, the Court of Justice of the European Union (ECJ) reaffirmed that the essential function of a trade mark is to guarantee to the consumer or end user the identity of the trade marked product's origin by enabling them to distinguish it without any risk of confusion from products of different origin. That guarantee of origin means that the consumer or end user can be certain that a trade marked product offered to them has not been subject at a previous stage of marketing to interference by a third party, without the authorisation of the trade mark owner, in such a way as to affect the original condition of the product.[25] In the ECJ decision in *Arsenal Football Club v Matthew Reed*,[26] the importance of a trade mark as a guarantee of origin was so sacrosanct that infringement arose even in circumstances where the unauthorised use would be perceived as a badge of support for or loyalty or affiliation to the proprietor of the mark. It was not a requirement for infringement that the contested use be trade mark use in the sense that the use indicated the origin of the goods. It was sufficient that the contested use was likely to damage the property rights of the trade mark proprietor.[27]

[26.15] The ECJ has drawn attention to a further function of a trade mark which is to guarantee certain attributes of goods and/or services and thus ensure customer satisfaction. Recognition of this guarantee function can be seen in *SA CNL-Sucal N V v Hag AG:*[28]

trade marks reward the manufacturer who consistently produces high quality goods and they thus stimulate economic progress. Without trade mark protection, there would be

---

[22] *McDowell's Application* (1926) 43 RPC 313.

[23] *American Greetings Corpn's Application* [1984] RPC 329.

[24] TMA 1963, s 36(6).

[25] *Bristol-Myers Squibb v Paranova; Eurim-Pharm v Beiersdorf; MPA Pharma v Rhône-Poulenc* [1997] FSR 102.

[26] *Arsenal Football Club v Matthew Reed* [2003] RPC 144.

[27] See Court of Appeal in *Arsenal Football Club v Matthew Reed* [2003] RPC 696.

[28] *SA CNL-Sucal NV v Hag AG* [1990] 3 CMLR 571.

little incentive for manufacturers to develop new products or to maintain the quality of existing ones. Trade marks are able to achieve that effect because they act as a guarantee, to the consumer, that all goods bearing a particular mark have been produced by, or under the control of, the same manufacturer and are therefore likely to be of a similar quality.

[26.16] The recognition of the function of a trade mark as a commodity in its own right can now be seen in TMA 1996, which grants rights to prevent dilution by use of a third party even in respect of goods and/or services which are dissimilar to those in which the trade mark owner trades. However, this has only arisen in a limited number of instances and it is the product/service differentiation function of a trade mark which is now prevalent under TMA 1996, namely a trade mark should distinguish the goods or services of one undertaking from those of other undertakings.[29]

[26.17] Given these important functions of a trade mark and increased consumer awareness due to extensive advertising, there has been an increased awareness in the importance of trade marks which has resulted in attempts to value brands. In 2009, Interbrand valued the COCA-COLA brand at US$68.7 billion and the IBM brand at US$60.2 billion.

REGISTRATION

[26.18] Most countries, including Ireland, have taken steps to protect trade marks through a system of registration rather than relying solely on common law rights that may exist, and which have limitations such as the need to show damage or a likelihood of damage. The evolution of trade mark statute law up to 1927 was summarised by Johnston J in *Fry-Cadbury (Ireland) Ltd v Synott*.[30] The Industrial and Commercial Property (Protection) Act 1927 dealt with intellectual property matters generally and Pt IV of the Act dealt with trade marks. The first trade mark to be advertised in the Irish Patents Office Journal was DÉANTA IN ÉIRINN logo which was held by the Industrial Development Association. As far as trade marks were concerned, the 1927 Act was repealed by TMA 1963 which had a two-part Register, Part A and Part B, depending on whether or not a trade mark was adapted to distinguish or capable of distinguishing.

[26.19] One of the principal shortcomings of TMA 1963 was the failure to provide for the registration of marks in respect of services. Although this has been dealt with under TMA 1996, Ireland was in fact the last EU Member State to provide for such marks and the commencement date of the 1996 Act, 1 July 1996, was long after the implementation date set down by the Trade Mark Harmonisation Directive,[31] namely 31 December 1992.

---

[29] TMA 1996, s 6(1).

[30] *Fry-Cadbury (Ireland) Ltd v Lynnott* [1936] IR 700.

[31] Council Directive 2008/95/EC ([2008] OJ L 299/25), which repealed and replaced Directive 89/104/EEC ([1989] OJ L40/1); see Smyth, 'Service Mark Registrations in Ireland' [1994] 4 EIPR 167.

[26.20] In 1993, the Irish Patents Office started to accept receipt of service mark applications and indeed, prior to TMA 1996, it is estimated that approximately 7,000 such applications had been filed. These applications were all simply held in abeyance and although given a number, were not given an official filing date. The transitional provisions of TMA 1996[32] provided that all of these applications were to be given the same date, 1 July 1996, the commencement date of TMA 1996, and examined under that Act. The fact that those applications had the same date meant that none were earlier rights compared to the rest and so, could not form the basis of an opposition against another such mark.[33] This also means that for many service mark applications, there was a loss of rights from the filing date. The situation was further worsened by the State's failure to implement TMA 1996 prior to 1 April 1996, which was the effective date of the Community Trade Mark Regulation. This means that in many cases, owners of Community trade marks (CTMs) have service mark registrations that were effective in Ireland before it was possible to secure such registrations nationally. Also, if a CTM is abandoned, it can be converted into a national application in Ireland and retain the CTM date of application. It is regrettable that the State's failure to introduce the new trade mark law prior to the Directive's[34] implementation date and, worse still, the effective date of the CTM, left in its wake a legal quagmire. In fact, Michael McDowell, TD introduced a Private Member's Trade Marks Bill 1993[35] which would have implemented the provisions of the Directive in a timely fashion and introduced service marks. This Bill was withdrawn when the Irish Government produced its own Bill, the Trade Marks Bill 1995, which was enacted as TMA 1996.

---

[32] TMA 1996, Sch 3, para 15.

[33] The same applies to CTM applications which were given the same date on commencement, see for example OHIM Opposition Division Decision No. 398/1999 TOPMAN Device.

[34] Council Directive 89/104.

[35] No 12 of 1993.

Chapter 27

Irish Trade Mark Law and International Conventions

THE PARIS CONVENTION

[27.01] Under the Paris Convention for the Protection of Industrial Property 1883 (the Paris Convention),[1] 'trade marks, service marks, trade names, indications of source or appellations of origin, and the repression of unfair competition' are all specifically stated as being industrial property rights and for which the objective is to provide protection. Similar to the position in relation to other forms of industrial property, nationals of all Member States should enjoy the same rights as those which prevail in a particular State. No requirement as to domicile or establishment may be imposed.[2] Article 2 of the Agreement on Trade-Related Aspects of Intellectual Property Rights (TRIPS) requires Member States to comply with arts 1–12 and 19 of the Paris Convention.

[27.02] There are several references to the Paris Convention in the Trade Marks Act 1996 (TMA 1996) and it is specifically defined in s 60(1)(a). Reference is also made to a Convention country,[3] which simply means a State (other than Ireland) which is party to the Convention.

[27.03] The Paris Convention provides for 'priority' and this is set out in s 40(1) of TMA 1996. A claim to priority means that where any person who has filed a trade mark application in a Convention country, if they or their successor in title subsequently file in Ireland within six months of the first application, they can claim rights from the date of the first application. The Irish trade mark application must correspond to the first application in that the trade marks must be the same and the goods or services must fall within the specification of the first application. The Irish application is not dependant on the outcome of the application from which priority is claimed.[4] The purpose of priority is to enable trade mark owners to file just one trade mark application and preserve their position for at least six months knowing that they can, during this time, market products and services under a trade mark, carry out market research and undertake searches, etc, and yet avoid being pre-empted by filing in other States within the six-month period.

---

[1]   See Ch 2.
[2]   Paris Convention, art 2(2).
[3]   TMA 1996, s 2(1).
[4]   Paris Convention, art 4(3), TMA 1996, s 40(3).

Priority in relation to trade marks is not as important as in relation to patents because pre-application trade mark use does not invalidate any subsequent registration.

[27.04] Under the Trade Marks Act 1963 (TMA 1963),[5] the effect of claiming priority was that the date of registration was the same date as the date of the application from which priority was claimed. However, under s 40(2) of TMA 1996, the date of registration is the date of the actual Irish application but 'the relevant date for the purposes of establishing which rights take precedence, shall be the date of filing of the first Convention application'. This means that when carrying out trade mark searches and subsequently filing an application, one cannot provide any certainty for a period of six months that a third-party right may take precedence even with a subsequent Irish filing date. Strictly speaking, the Irish Patents Office, when examining an application, should refrain from carrying out searches against earlier rights for a period of six months from the date of filing, in order to be sure that all prior conflicting applications/ registrations are on record, but in practice this does not occur.

[27.05] In certain circumstances, a subsequent Convention application will be treated as the first Convention application where the previous application has been withdrawn, abandoned or refused without having been laid open to public inspection and without leaving any rights outstanding.[6] It must also not have served as a basis for claiming a right to priority.[7]

The applicant for the Irish application does not have to be the same as that for the Convention application, since under s 40(6) of TMA 1996, provision is made for an assignment or transmission of the application from which priority is claimed. It is also provided that the provision relating to priority also extends to a Community trade mark (CTM) application and could extend to non-Convention countries in certain instances. [8] It is possible to claim priority from a CTM application.

[27.06] The transitional provisions of TMA 1996 raise some interesting issues by virtue of their failure to address the position as regards a claim to priority from a trade mark that is dated prior to 1 July 1996, being the commencement date of TMA 1996. A person who was fortunate enough to file a Convention application after 1 January 1996 and claim priority will find that they have a priority date pre-dating the commencement date of TMA 1996 for a type of registration that did not exist under the old law and that could pre-empt applications that bear the commencement date of TMA 1996. If we take, for example, an application in respect of a trade mark for the shape of goods or their packaging which was unregisterable under TMA 1963, an application for a mark not claiming priority and filed prior to 1 July 1996 would have been refused registration and the only possibility would have been to convert the application so that it would have been examined under the new law. The effect of conversion was that the applicant lost the filing date, which was replaced by 1 July 1996, which is subsequent to the priority date

---

5   TMA 1963, s 70.
6   TMA 1996, s 40(4)(a).
7   TMA 1996, s 40(4)(b).
8   TMA 1996, s 41.

afforded to an applicant of a Convention application fortunate enough to have a priority claim dating from within the six months prior to 1 July 1996. The inequity of this is even stronger in relation to service marks where the Controller had accepted applications since 1993 but under para 15 of Sch 3 to TMA 1996, these were all given the date of 1 July 1996. However, it was possible to claim a priority date in a service mark pre-dating this date by virtue of a priority claim in respect of an application dated after 1 January 1996.

[27.07] The position as regards an applicant who claimed priority from an Irish service mark filed prior to 1 July 1996 is far from certain. Although the Controller allotted an application number, no date of application was afforded to such, and Sch 3, para 15 of TMA 1996 (the transitional provisions) states that the date of filing is to be the commencement date, ie 1 July 1996. However, it could be argued that under the Paris Convention, a national filing simply means 'any filing that is adequate to establish the date upon which the application was filed in the country concerned, whatever may be the subsequent date of the application'. In other words, it is the *filing* date that is important, not the *application* date afforded by a national Patents Office.

[27.08] There is no requirement for a home application or registration in order to prosecute and register a mark in other Convention countries.[9]

Well-known trade marks

[27.09] The term 'well-known trade marks' appears in art 6*bis* of the Paris Convention, and s 61 of TMA 1996 gives statutory effect to this provision, which allows the owner of a well-known trade mark, whether or not they carry on business or have any goodwill in the State, to obtain injunctive relief against the use of an identical or similar mark in relation to identical or similar goods or services where the use is likely to cause confusion. The trade mark must be well-known in the State. Section 11(1)(c) also includes such a mark as an earlier mark, which forms the basis for opposing or seeking invalidity of a conflicting mark. It could be argued that the rights granted to a well-known trade mark under statute in fact simply reflect the position at common law, as illustrated in the Supreme Court decision in the case of *C&A Modes v C&A (Waterford) Ltd*.[10] In that case the Supreme Court criticised the UK authorities and held that the plaintiff possessed a protectable reputation in the State, even though it did not trade in the State. The law of passing off is not dependant on use within the State and if we equate reputation with a mark being well-known as appears to have been done in the *C&A* case, then a legal remedy was available prior to TMA 1996. In the *C&A* case, Finlay J actually used the words 'well-known' when referring to the reputation through advertising circulating in the State and this was repeated by Kenny J in the Supreme Court. The decision would also suggest that the level of recognition required of a trade mark to make it well-known should not be equated with too high a level of notoriety. As stated by Henchy J:

---

9   Paris Convention, art 6(2).
10 *C&A Modes v C&A (Waterford) Ltd* [1978] FSR 126.

if there are in this State sufficient customers of a plaintiff's business to justify his claim to have a vested right to restrain and expand that custom, then there is ample authority in principle and in the decided cases for the conclusion that, no matter where the plaintiff's business is based, he is entitled to be protected against it being taken away or dissipated by someone whose deceptive conduct is calculated to create a confusion of identify in the minds of existing or potential customers.

An obvious way of trying to show how well a mark is known is by way of survey evidence,[11] but apart from being expensive, given the number of variables, surveys are not the result of exact science. For example, who is to be surveyed? Presumably, although not stated, the term 'well-known' is to be directed towards likely consumers and not necessarily to the population generally.

[27.10] The rights granted to a well-known trade mark under s 61 of TMA 1996 are limited to an injunction and, for example, do not include damages although damages can be included as part of a claim in respect of passing off. Section 61(3) differs from para 3(2) of the transitional provisions[12] and there appears to be an inconsistency because under the transitional provisions, it is not an infringement under TMA 1996 to continue to do an act which was not an infringement under TMA 1963. However, in relation to well-known trade marks, use before TMA 1996 came into effect must also be *bona fide*.

[27.11] Although a well-known trade mark under the Paris Convention is deemed to be an 'earlier trade mark' for opposition or invalidity purposes, a different phrase, 'earlier right', is used in s 15 of TMA 1996 to determine if there exists a defence to infringement proceedings. What is strange is that for a well-known trade mark to be embraced within the phrase 'earlier right', which one would expect, the whole of the State must be viewed as a 'locality' under s 15(3); a strange interpretation of this word.[13]

National and state emblems

[27.12] Article 6*ter* of the Paris Convention deals with national and international organisation emblems, including flags, and is dealt with in ss 62–64 of TMA 1996, complying with art 3(1)(h) and 3(2)(c) of the Harmonisation Directive.[14]

[27.13] Essentially, flags, armorial bearings, State emblems, official signs or hallmarks of Convention countries cannot be registered without authorisation from the appropriate authority. In relation to flags, the Controller can dispense with such authorisation 'if it appears to the Controller that use of the flag in the manner proposed is permitted without such authorisation'.[15] No such exception exists in relation to armorial bearings or State emblems which are notified in accordance with art 6*ter*.[16] Protection is afforded under

---

[11] See paras **[32.43]**–**[32.47]**.

[12] TMA 1996, Sch 3, para 3(2).

[13] *Nieto Nuno v Monlleo Franquet* [2008] ETMR 12.

[14] Council Directive 2008/95/EC ([2008] OJ L 299/25), which repealed and replaced Directive 89/104/EEC ([1989] OJ L40/1).

[15] TMA 1996, s 62(1); see para **[32.76]** regarding unauthorised use of State emblems.

[16] TMA 1996, s 62(2).

the Paris Convention to official signs or hallmarks adopted by a Convention country, which indicates control and warranty, although the restriction on registration applies only in relation to goods or services of the same or a similar kind to those in relation to which it indicates control or warranty.[17]

[27.14] The restrictions do not apply to applications made by a national of a country who is authorised to make use of a State emblem or official sign or hallmark of that country, notwithstanding that it is similar to that of another country.[18] Injunctive relief is available to restrain use of a mark that could not be registered without authority.[19]

In relation to national flags, State emblems, official signs or hallmarks, the protection also extends to imitations from an 'heraldic point of view'.[20] This alludes to the system of granting of coats of arms which has its roots in the Laws of Arms, an English law dating back hundreds of years. In Ireland, coats of arms are registered with the Chief Herald of Ireland, whose office falls under the National Library of Ireland by virtue of the National Cultural Institutions Act 1997.[21] The original purpose of this system was to enable different families to use a coat of arms on shields, etc, so that it was clear in battle or at a distance which soldiers were under the control of which family. This purpose gradually became less important and it became more a matter of tradition and honour, with coats of arms now used on stationery, cutlery, etc. A grant of a coat of arms is actually for the description of the design, rather than a particular representation of same. The National Cultural Institutions Act 1997 provides that the Chief Herald has copyright in any grants of arms and therefore, copyright would appear to be the basis of any protection of these grants in Ireland. There are no rules governing the relationship between coats of arms and third-party intellectual property rights. Disputes in England relating to granting of coats of arms or use thereof are under the jurisdiction of the Court of Chivalry. This is not part of the general court system and the Law of Arms is not a part of the common law. There is no equivalent forum for resolution of disputes in Ireland. This subject can be relevant to trade marks because the ground for refusal or invalidity based on whether a sign is an imitation from an heraldic point of view may technically require a consideration of the Law of Arms as it applies in the country concerned.[22]

[27.15] The position as regards armorial bearings, flags or other emblems and abbreviations or names of international inter-governmental organisations and any imitations of an emblem from an heraldic point of view is that a Member State is not compelled to prevent registration or use where such is probably 'not of such a nature as

---

[17] TMA 1996, s 62(3).

[18] TMA 1996, s 62(5).

[19] TMA 1996, s 62(6).

[20] TMA 1996, s 62(4).

[21] This part of the Act was only commenced in 2005 and there has been controversy as to whether the power of the Chief Herald to grant coats of arms survived the enactment of the Irish Constitution; see Cox, 'The Office of the Chief Herald of Ireland and Continuity of Legal Authority' (2007) 29 DULJ 84-110.

[22] See *Manchester Corporation v Manchester Palace of Varieties* [1955] All ER 387 for a discussion of the Law of Arms in a modern context.

to mislead the public as to the existence of a connection between the user and the organisation'.[23] The fact that a mark also contains a word element does not of itself preclude the application of art 6*ter* of the Paris Convention.[24] Again, these emblems must be protected under the Paris Convention, a pre-requisite of which is notification in accordance with art 6*ter*.[25] The Irish government has lodged particular shamrock and harp devices as protected State emblems under art 6*ter*. In *American Clothing Associates SA v OHIM*,[26] the ECJ considered refusal of a Community trade mark consisting of a maple leaf with the letters 'RW' below it. The ECJ did not accept any distinction between a trade mark for goods and service marks and held that art 6*ter* also applies to elements of marks that include or imitate State emblems.

Unauthorised applications

[27.16] Article 6*septies* of the Paris Convention is implemented by s 65 of TMA 1996 and deals with a situation where, without permission, a trade mark application is made by a person who is an agent or representative of the owner of the trade mark in another Convention country. In such a situation, the State is obliged to refuse registration upon opposition. Irish law also allows for a declaration of invalidity against such a registration[27] or for the proprietor to be substituted as the registered proprietor.[28]

[27.17] There is a defence by which the agent or representative can justify their actions. Article 6*septies* of the Paris Convention provides that 'domestic legislation may provide an equitable time limit within which the proprietor of a mark must exercise the rights provided'. In this regard, Irish law provides for a three-year time limit, which runs from knowledge of the registration.[29] The proprietor can also obtain an injunction to restrain use by the agent or representative.[30] It is likely that in a case of this type, there would also be a claim for breach of a contractual relationship between the parties.

Unfair competition

[27.18] Article 10*bis* of the Paris Convention is a provision that must be complied with under the TRIPS Agreement[31] and requires the State to provide effective protection against unfair competition, which is stated to be 'any act of competition contrary to honest practices in industrial or commercial matters'. Article 10*bis* goes on to give the following examples, namely:

---

23   Paris Convention, art 6ter(1)(c); TMA 1996, s 63.
24   *Concept v OHIM* [2004] ETMR 81.
25   TMA 1996, s 64.
26   *American Clothing Associates SA v OHIM* [2010] ETMR 3.
27   TMA 1996, s 65(3)(a).
28   TMA 1996, s 65(3)(b); see also *Zoppas Trade Mark* [1965] RPC 381.
29   TMA 1996, s 65(6).
30   TMA 1996, s 65(4).
31   See para **[27.20]**.

(1) all acts of such a nature as to create confusion by any means whatever with the establishment, the goods, or the industrial or commercial activities, of a competitor;

(2) false allegations in the course of trade of such a nature as to discredit the establishment, the goods, or the industrial or commercial activities, of a competitor;

(3) indications or allegations, the use of which in the course of trade is liable to mislead the public as to the nature, the manufacturing process, the characteristics, the suitability for their purpose, or the quantity, of the goods.

[27.19] It could be argued that the State has not fulfilled its obligation under TRIPS by failing to include provisions in TMA 1996 corresponding to art 10*bis*. However, the Irish courts have shown a willingness to expand the traditional horizons of the law of passing off to cover such scenarios. In *C&A Modes*,[32] Henchy J stated 'it is to prevent unfair competition of that kind that the action for passing off lies'. Essentially, in so far as the concept of unfair competition exists under Irish law, it does so in the form of passing off, defamation and injurious falsehood.

THE TRIPS AGREEMENT

[27.20] TRIPS is the Agreement on Trade-Related Aspects of Intellectual Property, including trade in counterfeit goods. TRIPS was opened for signature on 15 April 1994 and is the intellectual property portion of the Uruguay round of the World Trade Organisation's agreements, which amended the General Agreement on Tariffs and Trade (GATT). TRIPS resulted from the desire stated in the preamble:

> ... to reduce distortions and impediments to international trade, and taking into account the need to promote effective and adequate protection of intellectual property rights, and to ensure that measures and procedures to enforce intellectual property rights do not themselves become barriers to legitimate trade.

TRIPS sets forth minimum international standards concerning the availability, scope and use of trade-related intellectual property rights, including trade marks and geographical indications. Members must treat nationals of all Member States, including their own, equally with regard to intellectual property rights and must comply with arts 1–12 and 19 of the Paris Convention.

[27.21] Trade marks are dealt with in Pt II, s 2 of the TRIPS Agreement (arts 15–21). Article 15 is headed 'Protectable Subject Matter' and defines what may constitute a trade mark in terms that are already reflected in TMA 1996, namely signs capable of distinguishing the goods or services of one undertaking from those of other undertakings. Section 6(1) of TMA 1996, which requires that a sign be capable of being represented graphically, is an option allowed to Member States who may require that signs be visually perceptible. Where signs are not inherently capable of distinguishing the relevant goods or services, Member States may make registrability dependant on distinctiveness acquired through use. Actual use cannot be a condition for filing a trade

---

[32] *C&A Modes v C&A (Waterford) Ltd* [1978] FSR 126 at 139.

mark application but it can be a prerequisite to registration. However, an intent to use application must not be refused solely on the ground that the intended use has not taken place before the expiry of a period of three years from the date of the application. Under art 6*quinquies* of the Paris Convention, it is permissible to deny registration of marks that designate the kind, quality, intended purpose, value or place of origin of the goods or that are considered contrary to morality or public order. However, the nature of the goods or services to which the trade mark is to be applied cannot be a bar to registration. Trade marks must be published and a reasonable opportunity afforded to third parties to seek cancellation. Member States can also provide for opposition (as Irish law has done) but pre-registration opposition proceedings are not mandatory.

[27.22] Article 16 of TRIPS deals with the rights conferred by a trade mark registration and these are already reflected under Irish law. The owner has the exclusive right to prevent third parties from using identical or similar signs for goods or services that are identical or similar to those for which the trade mark is registered where such use would result in a likelihood of confusion.[33] If signs are identical, the likelihood of confusion is assumed.

[27.23] TRIPS applied art 6*bis* of the Paris Convention dealing with well-known trade marks and extends such protection to service marks. In addition, if a mark is well-known and its use by a third party indicates a connection with the trade mark owner, and the interests of the trade mark owner are likely to be damaged, then its use may be prohibited even if it is being used for dissimilar goods or services. Section 14(3) of TMA 1996, which also provides for infringement in respect of dissimilar goods/services, appears to be stricter in requiring proof that the use is detrimental to the distinctive character or the reputation of the trade mark. There is no definition of 'well-known' in the Paris Convention or TMA 1996 but there is a statement in art 16(2) of TRIPS that in determining whether a trade mark is well-known, account shall be taken of the relevant sector of the public's knowledge of the trade mark, including knowledge obtained as a result of the promotion of the trade mark.

[27.24] TRIPS allows Member States to make registered trade marks subject to any existing prior rights, which has been implemented by s 15 of TMA 1996. Rights may also exist on the basis of use, such as passing off under Irish law.

[27.25] Article 17 of TRIPS allows limited exceptions to the rights conferred by a trade mark, such as fair use of descriptive terms, provided that such exceptions take account of the legitimate interests of the owner of the trade mark and of third parties. This can be seen in s 15(2) of TMA 1996, which provides for certain exceptions to infringement provided that the 'use is in accordance with honest practices in industrial and commercial matters'.

[27.26] The minimum term of protection is dealt with in art 18 of TRIPS, which allows for renewal indefinitely. Initial registration and each renewal must be for not less than seven years.

---

[33] *Anheuser-Busch v Budejovicky Budvar* [2005] ETMR 27.

[27.27] Under art 19 of TRIPS, use may be required to maintain a registration and registrations may be cancelled for non-use, but only after a minimum of three years unless valid reasons based on the existence of obstacles to such use are shown by the trade mark owner. Circumstances arising independently of the will of the owner, such as government restrictions or other requirements, are recognised as valid reasons for non-use. This is the position under s 51(1)(b) of TMA 1996, as governmental restrictions would be considered proper reasons for non-use. The non-use period under Irish law is five years. When subject to the control of its owner, use of a trade mark by another person shall be recognised as use of the trade mark for the purpose of maintaining the registration.

[27.28] Article 20 of TRIPS provides that members cannot unjustifiably encumber the manner in which a trade mark is used. Examples given of such are requirements to use a trade mark in conjunction with another trade mark or in a special form. It is, however, possible to impose a requirement prescribing the use of the trade mark identifying the undertaking producing the goods or services along with, but without linking it to, the trade mark distinguishing the specific goods or services in question of that undertaking.

[27.29] Provisions dealing with the licensing and assignments of trade marks are contained in art 21 of TRIPS. The owner of a registered trade mark has a right to assign the trade mark with or without the transfer of the business to which the trade mark belongs. This differs from the Paris Convention, which required the transfer of the business or goodwill.

[27.30] TRIPS explicitly prohibits compulsory licensing of trade marks. Article 6 states that any provisions dealing with the issue of the exhaustion of intellectual property rights are outside the scope of the TRIPS Agreement.

[27.31] Part III of TRIPS contains enforcement provisions. Enforcement procedures must be fair and equitable and must not be unnecessarily complicated, costly or entail unreasonable time limits or unwarranted delays. The remedies must include injunctive relief and damages. In the case of wilful trade mark counterfeiting, criminal penalties must be provided for, including monetary fines and/or imprisonment as well as seizure, forfeiture and destruction of infringing goods.

THE TRADEMARK LAW TREATY

[27.32] The Trademark Law Treaty[34] (the TLT) came into effect on 1 August 1996. Although it started out with more ambitious aims, it is essentially an international treaty harmonising procedural aspects of the filing of trade mark applications and their maintenance. It is directed principally at countries where there are cumbersome and expensive procedural requirements. Thirty-six countries, not including Ireland, signed the draft treaty on 27 October 1994. By 27 October 1995, more than 50 countries had signed the Treaty including the Member States of the EU. The TLT became effective on 1 August 1996 being three months after deposit by seven States.[35]

---

[34] Concluded in Geneva on 27 October 1994.

[35] Moldova, Ukraine, Sri Lanka, Czech Republic, the UK, Monaco and Guinea.

[27.33] The TLT applies to marks, which are described as visual marks, and also to three-dimensional marks where a contracting State allows for registration of such. The TLT does not apply to holograms, sound, or to collective or certification marks.

[27.34] Article 3 of the TLT provides for certain maximum requirements in the filing of a trade mark application. In certain countries, it is necessary to furnish a certificate or an extract from a local chamber of commerce and, in other countries, evidence of a corresponding registration in other jurisdictions. These requirements are not permitted under the TLT.

[27.35] A contracting State must allow for the filing of a multi-class application covering both goods and/or services resulting in a single registration. Irish law already provides for such under TMA 1996. The CTM Regulation 207/2009/EC[36] also allows for multi-class applications and registrations. Under art 7, trade mark owners can divide applications in those cases where, for example, certain classes encounter opposition. The divided application maintains the filing date of the initial application and the benefit of priority, if any. The TMA 1996 already allows for such division.[37]

[27.36] Article 9 of the TLT outlaws the practice in some countries[38] of allowing registration in respect of a specification reading 'all goods/services in class ...'. It is necessary to identify the specific goods and/or services by name. The practice of the Controller under TMA 1963 was to allow a registration covering all goods in a given class but only in exceptional circumstances where an applicant was able to show trading or an intent to trade in an extremely broad range of goods in that class. Goods/services will not be considered under Irish law to be similar just because they have the same class number. Also goods/services will not be considered dissimilar just because they have different class numbers.

[27.37] Article 13 of the TLT deals with duration and renewal. The duration of the initial period of the registration and the duration of each renewal period must be 10 years. Trade mark offices cannot require proof of use at renewal or a re-examination of the mark as to its validity. Proof of use can, however, be required at times other than renewal and this is the position under current US law.

[27.38] The TLT regulations establish standard forms for applications, renewals, change of address, change of name or ownership and powers of attorney. These must be accepted by the national trade mark offices when presented in the manner prescribed by the TLT.

[27.39] The only substantive features of the TLT are that all contracting parties must comply with the provisions of the Paris Convention concerning marks and allow for the registration of marks in respect of services.

---

[36] Council Regulation 207/2009/EC ([2009] OJ L78/1), which repealed and replaced Council Regulation 40/94/EC.

[37] Trade Marks Rules 1996 (SI 199/1996), r 28.

[38] Particularly Scandinavian countries such as Denmark, Finland, Norway and Sweden.

THE SINGAPORE TREATY

[27.40] The Singapore Treaty on the Law of Trademarks came into force on 16 March 2009 following its ratification by 10 States. Ireland has not, at the time of writing,[39] ratified the Singapore Treaty, although it is under consideration. The Department of Enterprise, Trade and Innovation issued a consultation document in 2009 calling for comments on the advantages and/or disadvantages of ratification and the desirability of proceeding with ratification at this stage. The Singapore Treaty is intended to revise and update, but not replace, the TLT, to allow for streamlining and simplification of administrative procedures and for electronic filing and communication. Ireland already complies with most of the mandatory provisions of the Treaty and, therefore, ratification is likely to have little effect other than in the areas of licences[40] and time limits.[41]

[27.41] Article 17(1)(ii) provides that the information required for recordal of the licence can be a certified extract from the licence or an uncertified statement,[42] which is less onerous than r 45(1)[43] of the Trade Marks Rules 1996 under which a certified copy of the licence agreement is required. Article 17(4) specifically states that neither the licence contract nor an indication of the financial terms thereof can be required. Article 18 covers requests for amendment of a recordal of a licence, which are not covered by the Trade Marks Rules at present. Article 19(2) provides that recordal of a licence cannot be required as a condition for any right of the licensee to obtain damages in any infringement proceedings. This is in conflict with s 29(4) of TMA 1996, which provides that unless an application to record a licence is made within six months of the transaction (unless a court is satisfied that it was not practicable to apply during that period), the licensee will not be entitled to damages or an account of profits for any period before the application was filed.

[27.42] Article 14(2) of the Singapore Treaty requires that one or more of the specified relief measures must be provided. Ireland already permits one of these, namely extensions of time after a deadline has been missed by virtue of r 63(4) of the Trade Marks Rules 1996. However, such late extensions are at the Controller's discretion and the Controller must be satisfied with the explanation for the delay and that the extension would not disadvantage any other person or party. The Treaty provides in art 14(5) that no requirements other than a fee can be imposed to avail of this relief. Therefore, if the Treaty is to be ratified, the Trade Marks Rules would have to be changed to remove these additional requirements. Alternatively, one or both of the other relief measures, continued processing or reinstatement of rights, which are both available at CTM level, could be introduced.

---

[39] 1 July 2010.
[40] Articles 17, 18 & 19.
[41] Article 14(2).
[42] Rule 10(2) of the Regulations under the Treaty; consists of (1) a certified extract from the licence or (2) an uncertified statement of licence signed by the registered proprietor or applicant and the licensee.
[43] As amended by the Trade Marks (Amendment) Rules 2010 (SI 410/2010).

[27.43] The UK amended its similar legislation when it implemented the Singapore Treaty to provide that recordal of a licence would be required for a licensee to claim costs in an infringement action (s 25(4) of the Trade Marks Act 1994) and to allow for an extension after a deadline had been missed where the request was made within two months of the deadline, with no mention of discretion, explanations, justice or equity (r 77 of the Trade Marks Rules 2008). It remains to be seen whether the Irish government will decide to amend Irish law in a similar fashion to permit ratification, or maintain the *status quo*.

THE MADRID AGREEMENT

[27.44] The Madrid Agreement Concerning the International Registration of Marks of 14 April 1891 (the Madrid Agreement) entered into force on 13 July 1892 and a number of revisions have been made subsequently.[44] It would be fair to say that the title to the Agreement is somewhat a misnomer. The Agreement provides a centralised system for registering a trade mark in states that are party to the Agreement. It is not truly international and many countries, particularly in South America and Africa, are members of neither the Madrid Agreement nor Protocol. The US became a party to the Protocol on 2 November 2003. Both the Agreement and Protocol are closed systems, which means that the users of the systems must be citizens or legal entities from a Member State, which includes a company, regardless of its place of incorporation, that has a real and effective industrial and/or commercial establishment in a Member State.

[27.45] The purpose of the Madrid Agreement is to enable the owner of a national registration to obtain protection in other Member States by way of a single application.

Procedure

[27.46] The first requirement is the holding of a home national registration. Once this is acquired, then an application for an international registration can be filed with the national registry of the country of the applicant. The application is directed to the World Intellectual Property Organisation (WIPO) based in Geneva. The application seeks extension of the home registration to Member States, which the applicant designates. Once the national registry has examined the application as to formalities, it is then forwarded to WIPO. The goods and/or services must correspond with or be more limited than the home registration. WIPO will only make a formal examination, which is mainly restricted to checking on the specification of goods/services and classification. WIPO will allocate a number and publish the registration in the journal: *Les Marques Internationales*. WIPO also notifies the national registries of all countries designated by an applicant.

[27.47] Each national registry will then treat the national registration as if it was filed as a national application. This means, for example, that the German designation of the

---

44   Brussels, 14 December 1900; Washington, 2 June 1911; The Hague, 6 November 1925; London, 2 June 1934; Nice, 15 June 1957; Stockholm, 14 July 1967.

international registration can be refused by the German Patent Office or can be opposed by the owners of earlier conflicting marks on the National German Register. However, each national registry has only a period of 12 months within which to refuse registration. Such refusal can be provisional or final. In the absence of a notification of refusal within the 12 months, registration is deemed to have been accepted by that country.

[27.48] Although what results is a bundle of national registrations, renewals, changes of name, licences and assignments are all dealt with centrally through WIPO. An accepted international registration enjoys exactly the same protection as a national registration and the major advantage of the Madrid Agreement is a considerable cost saving from the alternative of filing individual national applications. This cost saving includes the possibility of filing multi-class applications, which is not possible when filing nationally in some Member States. It is also possible to extend protection to other countries at any time by way of the simple formality of a subsequent designation. The Agreement has proved a great success and is heavily utilised, particularly in Germany, Benelux, France, Switzerland, Italy, Spain and Portugal.

Dependency on national registration

[27.49] The international registration remains dependant on the basic home national registration for the first five years of its existence. If, during that five-year period, the national mark ceases to enjoy protection whether by voluntary withdrawal, non-renewal or cancellation, the international registration is no longer valid in those countries for which the mark has been accepted. After the five-year period has expired, the international registration becomes independent from the basic national registration. This provision is often referred to as the dependency clause or the central attack system.

PROTOCOL TO THE MADRID AGREEMENT[45]

[27.50] For many years, WIPO tried to attract a wider membership of the Madrid Agreement, especially important industrial countries that remained outside despite the advantages offered by the Agreement. The principal reasons for non-membership could not be addressed by amendment to the Agreement because such amendments would have suppressed some of the main advantages of the Madrid Agreement itself. Therefore, a separate Agreement was concluded and is termed the Protocol. Ireland became a member of the Protocol on 19 October 2001.[46] Where possible, the Protocol followed the terms of the Madrid Agreement itself; the following are the main differences.

Home application instead of home registration is sufficient

[27.51] This was perceived to be necessary because in countries where there was a more substantive examination, nationals would be disadvantaged by the consequential delays

---

[45] 28 June 1989.
[46] Trade Marks (Madrid Protocol) Regulations 2001 (SI 346/2001).

in obtaining the basis upon which to found a Madrid Agreement registration. The innovation of the Madrid Protocol is that while a home registration is still accepted as a basis for a Madrid Protocol application, it is not a requirement. A home application is sufficient although it must mature to registration.

Extended time limit for refusing registration

[27.52] Under the Madrid Protocol, notification of refusal of protection by the national registry where protection is sought can be extended to 18 months, and even later in the event of opposition. Ireland has exercised this option.[47] Again, like the Madrid Agreement, if there is no notification of refusal during the time period allowed, registration is deemed automatic.

Fees for extending protection to given country can be equal to national filing fees instead of flat fee *per* country

[27.53] National registries were concerned about the considerable loss of income incurred by joining the Madrid Agreement because the fees charged for a designation via Madrid were often much lower than the official fees charged for national applications. Indeed, this is one of the main advantages of the Madrid Agreement. Unfortunately, such an advantage had to be sacrificed so that national registries could maintain, at their option, the same charges irrespective of whether an application is under the Madrid Protocol or a national application. The UK, Sweden, Norway, Finland and Denmark have all struck individual designation fees, which are very close to the national filing fees. The individual designation fees for Ireland are 372 Swiss Francs for one class and 106 Swiss Francs for each additional class. This compares to national fees of €247 for one class and €70 for each additional class. These include both official application and final registration fees.

Conversion following central attack

[27.54] The Madrid Protocol retains the principle of central attack but in certain circumstances, a Protocol trade mark can be transformed into a national trade mark application and still retain the date of filing of the Protocol mark.[48] In this way, cancellation of a home national registration may not necessarily lead to a loss of rights in countries, although it will be necessary to file an application under each national system of interest.

Duration

[27.55] The duration of a Protocol mark is every 10 years as opposed to a 20-year renewal under the Madrid Agreement.

---

47   Trade Marks (Madrid Protocol) Regulation 2001 (SI 346/2001), r 9.
48   Madrid Protocol, Article 9*quinquies*.

Languages

[27.56] Under the Madrid Protocol, applications can be filed in French, English or Spanish and publications will occur in all three languages.

Link between Madrid Agreement and Protocol

[27.57] There is no relationship between countries who are only members of the Madrid Agreement and countries who are only members of the Madrid Protocol because, although having many common elements, they are to be viewed as separate and distinct conventions. However, in a situation where a country is a member of both conventions, it is the Madrid Agreement that prevails[49] and therefore, by way of example, the country where protection is sought must send its refusal notification within 12 months of the date of the international mark as provided in the Madrid Agreement as opposed to 18 months under the Protocol.

Link with CTM

[27.58] The Madrid Protocol provides for a link with the CTM system on the basis that the EU is an inter-governmental organisation. Since 1 October 2004 an applicant with an existing registration or application in a Protocol country may file a single application at WIPO in Geneva and designate the CTM system.

Infringement

[27.59] As an international or Madrid Protocol mark is essentially a bundle of national rights, enforcement of a right is dependant on the national laws of the country concerned in the same way as infringement of a national registration. Invalidity proceedings are dealt with in the same way but details of any invalidity, cancellation, etc, are recorded on the National Register. Use in each designated State is required to maintain validity.

[27.60] The Protocol came into force on 1 April 1996. Section 59 of TMA 1996 enabled the Minister to give effect to the provisions of the Madrid Protocol and, by virtue of the Trade Marks (Madrid Protocol) Regulation 2001,[50] Ireland became a party to the Protocol on 19 October 2001.

---

49 Madrid Protocol, Article 9*sexies*.
50 SI 346/2001.

Chapter 28

The Community Trade Mark

INTRODUCTION AND BRIEF HISTORY

[28.01] The objective of the Community trade mark (CTM) is to fulfil the recognised need for a system for trade marks whereby undertakings can obtain a single registration to which uniform protection is given, and which has effect throughout the entire area of the EU. It does not replace the national trade mark laws of the various EU countries but is a complimentary system for undertakings that require a more cost effective and streamlined system for protecting trade marks in a number of EU countries. Prior to the CTM, an Irish company wishing to register its trade mark throughout the EU had to file, prosecute and register through the national trade marks office of each country, the only exception being a single Benelux registration covering the Netherlands, Belgium and Luxembourg.

[28.02] The Regulation governing the CTM took a long time to be agreed. The major obstacles to adoption were political, namely the location of the Community Office and the selection of the official languages. On 29 October 1993, the EU Council of Ministers decided that the Community Trade Marks Office, or, to give it its correct but cumbersome name, The Office for Harmonisation in the Internal Market (OHIM) would be located in Spain and later the Spanish authorities decided on establishment in the city of Alicante in south-east Spain. The language problems were resolved on 7 December 1993.

[28.03] On 20 December 1993, the Council of the EU issued Regulation 40/94/EC.[1] The Regulation was published in the Patents Office Journal on 14 January 1994 and came into force on 15 March 1994. It was repealed and replaced in 2009 by Council Regulation 207/2009/EC[2] on the Community trade mark. Although OHIM accepted applications from January 1996, the effective date for all applications filed between January 1996 and the commencement of the Regulation was 1 April 1996.[3] However, similar to the transitional provisions in the Irish Trade Marks Act 1996 (TMA 1996), it was still possible to claim Paris Convention for the Protection of Industrial Property (the Paris Convention) priority of an earlier filed application and thus effectively secure a priority date earlier than 1 April 1996.

---

[1]   Council Regulation 40/94/EC ([1994] OJ L11/1).
[2]   Council Regulation 207/2009/EC ([2009] OJ L78/1).
[3]   The number of applications filed before OHIM during 1996 exceeded most expectations and was in excess of 40,000.

[28.04] The CTM has proved to be a very attractive cost-effective method of registering a trade mark throughout the EU. Between the years 1996–2009 the number of CTM applications amounted to 825,094. The biggest users of the system are from the US, amounting to approximately 20 per cent of all applications. Over 7,500 applications had originated from Ireland by the end of 2009.

PRINCIPAL FEATURES OF THE CTM

Unitary character

[28.05] Article 1(2) of Regulation 207/2009/EC provides:

> A Community trade mark shall have a unitary character. It shall have equal effect throughout the Community; it shall not be registered, transferred or surrendered or be the subject of a decision revoking the rights of the proprietor or declaring it invalid, nor shall its use be prohibited, save in respect of the whole Community.

It is thus not possible to hold a CTM registration excluding one or more EU countries. It is all or nothing. A single prior conflicting earlier trade mark, for example, on the national register in just one EU Member State can form the basis for opposition against the entire CTM application. If an opposition is successful, an applicant may convert the failed CTM application into national trade mark applications and enjoy the same date of filing and priority or seniority as the CTM application.

Who may apply

[28.06] Under art 5 of Regulation 207/2009/EC, both natural and legal persons can apply for and hence own a CTM registration. Legal persons are covered by a broad definition. Companies or firms and other legal entities shall be regarded as such if, under the terms of the law governing them, they have the capacity in their own name to have rights and obligations of all kinds, to make contracts or accomplish other legal acts and to sue and be sued.

Definition of a CTM

[28.07] Article 4 of Regulation 207/2009/EC provides as follows:

> A Community trade mark may consist of any signs capable of being represented graphically, particularly words, including personal names, designs, letters, numerals, the shape of goods or of their packaging, provided that such signs are capable of distinguishing the goods or services of one undertaking from those of other undertakings.

This broad definition corresponds to art 2 of the Harmonisation Directive[4] and s 6 of TMA 1996. The explanatory memorandum to the earlier Regulation 40/94/EC stated that 'no type of sign is automatically excluded from registration' and this would therefore include colours, sounds, smells, phrases, slogans, gestures, surnames, get-up

---

[4]   Council Directive 2008/95/EC ([2008] OJ L 299/25), which repealed and replaced Directive 89/104/EEC ([1989] OJ L40/1).

and trade dress. However, for registration purposes, all signs must be capable of distinguishing the goods or services of one undertaking from those of other undertakings. The explanatory memorandum to Regulation 207/2009/EC states that the purpose of these words is to focus attention on the question whether:

> ... the relevant sign is capable of performing the basic function of a trade mark. That function in economic and legal terms, is to indicate the origin of goods or services and to distinguish them from those of other undertakings.

Languages

[28.08] The provision as regards languages was a compromise position and is therefore quite intricate. Under art 119 of Regulation 207/2009/EC[5], the OHIM official languages are English, French, German, Spanish and Italian.[6] However, an application for a CTM may be filed in any one of the official EU languages including Irish but an applicant must always select a second language, which must be one of the five OHIM languages. If the applicant is the sole party to any proceedings, then the language of these proceedings is the language used for filing. If, however, the language used for filing is not one of the five official OHIM languages, then OHIM may choose the second language as the language for communication. All notices of oppositions and all applications for revocation or invalidity must be in one of the official OHIM languages and are determined by reference to the language(s) governing the trade mark registration.[7]

ABSOLUTE GROUNDS FOR REFUSAL

[28.09] Because a trade mark registration grants exclusivity of use, there is an examination as to whether or not the trade mark fulfils the requisite requirement of being distinctive and it must also be capable of distinguishing the goods or services of one undertaking from those of other undertakings, and that there is therefore no inconsistency with the rights being conferred. There is an exhaustive list of the absolute grounds for refusal[8] and these are as follows:

(A) Marks falling outside the definition of a sign in art 4.[9]

(B) Trade marks which are devoid of any distinctive character.

(C) Trade marks which consist exclusively of signs or indications:

– which may serve in trade, to designate the kind, quality, quantity, intended purpose, value, geographical origin or the time of production of the goods or of rendering of the services or other characteristics of the goods or services; and/or

---

5 Formerly Council Regulation 40/94/EC, art 115.
6 *Christina Kik v OHIM* [2004] ETMR 30.
7 *Chef Revival USA Inc v OHIM* [2004] ETMR 8.
8 Council Regulation 207/2009/EC, art 7.
9 Council Regulation 207/2009/EC: see para **[28.07]**.

- have become customary in the current language or in the *bona fide* and established practices of the trade. Thus, generic marks are excluded.

(D) Signs being exclusively shapes either resulting from the nature of the goods, necessary to obtain a technical result or give a substantial value to the goods.

(E) Trade marks contrary to public policy or morality.[10]

(F) Deceptive trade marks.

(G) Trade marks pursuant to art 6*ter* of the Paris Convention.

(H) Public interest badges, emblems or escutcheons.

(I) Trade marks for wines or spirits, which contain or consist of a geographical indication and where the wine or spirit does not have this origin.[11]

(J) Trade marks, which contain or consist of a designation of origin or a geographical indication registered in accordance with Council Regulation 510/2006/EC on the protection of geographical indications and designations of origin for agricultural products and foodstuffs.

These absolute grounds apply notwithstanding that the basis for non-registrability pertains only in part of the EU.[12] This could arise, for example, because of the meaning of the word in just one language.[13] In relation to (B) and (C) above, use can be taken into account and if the trade mark can be shown to be distinctive through use, then registration will be allowed. Because of the principle of the unitary character of the CTM, in order to be accepted for registration, a sign must possess a distinctive character throughout the Community.[14] Even considering the two native English-speaking countries, evidence of use in the UK will not be deemed to extend to cover the position in the Republic of Ireland on the basis of spill-over; this, despite evidence showing extensive use of a sign in the UK, where the population of approximately 60 million represents 93 per cent of the total number of native English-speakers in the EU.[15] Thus, in certain instances, the CTM is not an appropriate vehicle through which to seek registration, and where, in particular, the mark contains a word that may be descriptive in certain languages and not others.[16] Proving acquired distinctiveness through use must be done in all countries of the EU sharing the language.[17]

[28.10] It is not possible to file an opposition to a CTM application on any of the absolute grounds. However, it is possible to file observations following publication on absolute grounds. An application to register a trade mark, which is made in bad faith, is not contrary to public policy or to accepted principles of morality and thus an opposition cannot be filed against such an application under art 7.[18]

---

[10] See *Couture Tech Ltd's Application* [2010] ETMR 45.
[11] See *Abadia Retuerta SA v OHIM* [2010] ETMR 43.
[12] Council Regulation 207/2009/EC, art 7(2).
[13] *Patak (Spices) Ltd* [2007] ETMR 3.
[14] *Ford Motor Co v OHIM* [2000] ETMR 554 (OPTIONS).
[15] *Medline Industries Inc's Community trade mark Application* [2004] ETMR 97.
[16] *Matratzen Concord GmbH v OHIM* [2003] ETMR 31.
[17] *Bovemij Verzekeringen NV v Benelux-Merkenbureau* [2007] ETMR 29 (EUROPOLIS).
[18] *Durferrit v OHIM* [2004] ETMR 32.

SEARCHES

[28.11] OHIM does not cite prior conflicting marks on the CTM or any national register as a basis for refusing registration and this practice differs from the examination before certain national trade mark offices, including examination under TMA 1996. OHIM will conduct a search of prior CTMs. Given that there are no citations, there are a large number of oppositions and owners of marks have to be vigilant, and monitor applications that have been approved and published for opposition purposes. Many trade mark owners retain trade mark watch surveillance services for these purposes.

[28.12] A search system is in place since 10 March 2008 whereby OHIM conducts a mandatory search of CTMs under art 38(1),[19] reports to the applicant and notifies the proprietors and applicants of those rights that may be regarded as identical or similar to their own in relation to the goods and services covered by the application. National searches are optional[20] and are subject to a fee;[21] and a number of Member States have opted out of the search system with only 11 participating States remaining as of 1 July 2010. Many applicants decide against requesting national search reports from the Member States due to the lack of detailed information provided and the small number of Member States involved.

OPPOSITIONS AND RELATIVE GROUNDS FOR REFUSAL

[28.13] Within three months following publication, the proprietor or authorised licensee of an earlier trade mark and other specified persons can lodge an opposition to the CTM application.[22] An opposition may be brought on the basis of any or all of the relative grounds for refusal[23] in art 8 of Regulation 207/2009/EC. An 'earlier trade mark' is defined as:

- a CTM;
- a national trade mark in an EU Member State or the Benelux; and
- an international (Madrid Agreement or Madrid Protocol) trade mark effective in an EU Member State.

Article 8(2)(c) of Regulation 207/2009/EC also provides for opposition based on a trade mark which is well-known in an EU Member State under art 6*bis* of the Paris Convention. Under art 8(4), opposition is also possible by the proprietor of an unregistered trade mark used in the course of trade and of more than mere local significance. In *McCann Erickson Advertising Ltd's Application*,[24] it was held that use

---

[19] Formerly Council Regulation 40/94/EC, art 37(1).

[20] Council Regulation 207/2009/EC, art 38(2), formerly Council Regulation 40/94/EC, art 37(2).

[21] Currently €12 per Member State as of 1 July 2010.

[22] Council Regulation 207/2009/EC, art 41, formerly Council Regulation 40/94/EC, art 42.

[23] Council Regulation 207/2009/EC, art 8.

[24] *McCann Erickson Advertising Ltd's Application* [2001] ETMR 52.

of an unregistered trade mark in the UK was a use that was of more than mere local significance. The Opposition Division of OHIM stated:

> An individual assessment must be made on the particulars of each case and cannot be based on geographical criteria alone. An important element is the intensity of the marketing and the volume of sale made. The amount of population concerned is also a criterion to be taken into account.

The unregistered trade mark must have been acquired before the CTM application or its priority date. The law in a particular EU Member State must be such as to confer a right on the proprietor to prohibit the use of a subsequent trade mark.[25] In *Fianna Fáil Ltd's Trade Mark Application*,[26] Fianna Fáil failed in opposition because of a lack of evidence showing use in the course of trade. OHIM stated 'use of a sign as a trade mark implies use for the trading of specific goods and services'.

[28.14] Normally, opposition is based on a trade mark that is identical or similar and is protected for identical or similar goods/services to those of the opposed trade mark. However, art 8(5) of Regulation 207/2009/EC provides for opposition by the proprietor or licensee of an earlier trade mark registered for goods/services that are not similar to those of a CTM application where, in the case of an earlier CTM, the mark has a reputation in the EU and, in the case of an earlier national trade mark, the mark has a reputation in the State concerned. It is also necessary for the opponent to show that the use, without due cause, of the trade mark applied for would take unfair advantage of, or be detrimental to, the distinctive character or the repute of the earlier trade mark.

[28.15] The opponent can elect to conduct the opposition proceedings in either of the two official languages that were selected by the applicant and indicated in the advertisement appearing in the official bulletin. Regulation 207/2009/EC provides for a streamlined opposition procedure, including a time frame within which the parties may resolve the dispute. This is referred to as the 'cooling-off period'. If the application is withdrawn during the cooling-off period, there is no award of costs. Awards of costs by OHIM are, in any event, on a nominal scale.[27] Such awards of costs are enforceable by the High Court in Ireland pursuant to the European Communities (Enforcement of Community Judgments on Trade Marks and Designs) Regulations 2006.[28] The Regulation imposes an obligation on OHIM to ensure that 'Decisions of the Office shall state the reasons on which they are based'.[29]

[28.16] If an opponent bases its opposition on an earlier trade mark which is over five years old, the applicant can put the opponent on proof of use.[30] The evidence of proof of use must consist of indications concerning the place, time, extent and nature of use of the opposing trade mark for the goods and services in respect of which it is registered

---

25 *Gill v Frankie Goes to Hollywood* [2008] ETMR 4.

26 *Fianna Fáil Ltd's Trade Mark Application* [2008] ETMR 40; see also [2008] ETMR 41 and 42.

27 Commission Regulation 2868/95/EC, r 94.

28 SI 646/2006.

29 *Institut für Lernsysteme GmbH v OHIM* [2004] ETMR 17 (ELS).

30 Council Regulation 207/2009/EC, art 42(2), formerly Council Regulation 40/94/EC, art 43(2).

and on which the opposition is based.[31] If the opponent fails to provide the requisite evidence, the opposition will be rejected and many oppositions fail on this basis.[32] The rationale is to restrict the number of conflicts between two marks, in so far as there is no sound economic reason resulting from an actual function of the mark on the market.[33]

DURATION AND RENEWAL[34]

[28.17] A CTM registration has a registration period of 10 years from the date of filing of the application and may be renewed for further 10-year periods. No evidence of use is required for renewal. In *Rodd & Gunn Australia Ltd v OHIM*, a trade mark owner who missed the renewal deadline applied for *restitutio in integrum*. The General Court[35] upheld the decision of the Board of Appeal in rejecting the application and reiterated the two conditions for *restitutio in integrum*, first, that the party acted with all due care required by the circumstances and, second, that the non-observance of the time limit by that party had the direct consequence of causing the loss of any right or means of redress.[36]

AMENDMENT OF APPLICATION

[28.18] A CTM application can only be amended by correcting the name and address of the applicant, errors of wording or of copying, or obvious mistakes, provided such correction does not substantially change the trade mark or extend the list of goods or services.[37]

EXTENT OF PROTECTION CONFERRED BY CTM

[28.19] A CTM registration confers an exclusive right to prevent others from using, in the course of trade, an identical or confusingly similar sign on identical or similar goods/services anywhere in the EU.[38] Rights can also extend to prevent use in respect of dissimilar goods/services where the CTM has a reputation in the EU and where the unauthorised use, without due cause, takes unfair advantage of, or is detrimental to, the distinctive character or repute of the CTM. The rights conferred by a CTM can be

---

[31] Commission Regulation 2868/95/EC, r 22(3).

[32] *Chassot AG's Application (Opposition by Pfizer Inc)* [1999] ETMR 295; *Payless Car Rental System Inc's Trade Mark Application* [2000] ETMR 1136.

[33] *Goulbourn v OHIM* [2004] ETMR 16 (SILK COCOON).

[34] Council Regulation 207/2009/EC, arts 46 and 47.

[35] Formerly known as the Court of First Instance.

[36] *Rodd & Gunn Australia Ltd v OHIM* [2010] ETMR 39.

[37] Council Regulation 207/2009/EC, art 43 formerly Council Regulation 40/94/EC, art 44; *Blueco Ltd's Application* [1999] ETMR 394; *Packard Bell NEC Inc's Application* [1999] ETMR 570; *Signal Communications Ltd v OHIM* [2002] ETMR 38 (TELEYE).

[38] Council Regulation 2007/2009/EC, art 9.

enforced against third parties from the date of publication of registration of the CTM. However, damages can be claimed from the date of publication of the application.

[28.20] In relation to an infringement claim in respect of a non-identical trade mark and/or goods/services where no reputation of the earlier mark is invoked, it is necessary to prove that 'there exists a likelihood of confusion on the part of the public'. It is further stated that 'the likelihood of confusion includes the likelihood of association between the sign and the trade mark'. This corresponds to the provision in s 14(2) of TMA 1996. Likelihood of association is a concept which, in particular, has been developed by Benelux case law. Benelux law recognises that the function of a trade mark is not just as an indication of origin but also as a carrier of reputation and goodwill. The public may be in a position to distinguish the respective marks but may nevertheless associate the trade marks and attribute the goodwill to one and the same source and presume an economic or contractual link between the owners of the respective marks. In the early years of the CTM Regulation, a question arose as to whether likelihood of confusion is a separate criterion to be satisfied, or whether likelihood of association is sufficient. In the preamble to the earlier Regulation 40/94/EC, the following statement appears:

> Whereas an interpretation should be given of the concept of similarity in relation to the likelihood of confusion; whereas the likelihood of confusion, the appreciation of which depends on numerous elements and, in particular, on the recognition of the trade mark on the market, the association which can be made with the used or registered sign, the degree of similarity between the trade mark and the sign and between the goods or services identified, constitutes the specific condition for such protection.

[28.21] This, in very tortuous language, appeared to indicate that the likelihood of confusion forms the basis for protection and the likelihood of association was simply one of the determining factors. In the UK case of *Wagamama Ltd v City Centre Restaurants plc*,[39] Laddie J concluded that 'confusion' is meant to be confusion as to the source or origin of the goods. He did not accept a concept of likelihood of association that would mean that it would be trade mark infringement if, on seeing the alleged infringing sign, the registered trade mark would be called to mind even if there was no risk of confusion as to the origin of the goods.

[28.22] Given the divergence of interpretation, it did not take long for the ECJ to be asked to rule on the corresponding provision in art 4(1)(b) of the Trade Mark Harmonisation Directive.[40] In *Sabel BV v Puma AG*,[41] the ECJ held that 'the mere association which the public might make between two trade marks as a result of their analogous semantic content is not in itself a sufficient ground for concluding that there is a likelihood of confusion'.

---

[39] *Wagamama Ltd v City Centre Restaurants plc* [1995] FSR 713.
[40] Council Directive 2008/95/EC ([2008] OJ L 299/25), which repealed and replaced Directive 89/104/EEC ([1989] OJ L40/1).
[41] *Sabel BV v Puma AG* [1998] ETMR 1.

[28.23] Article 9(2) of Council Regulation 207/2009/EC contains a non-exhaustive list of acts that can be considered to be use of a trade mark in the course of trade. The following may constitute infringement:

- affixing a sign to the goods or to the packaging thereof;
- offering the goods, putting them on the market or stocking them for these purposes under that sign, or offering or supplying services thereunder;
- importing or exporting the goods under that sign; or
- using the sign on business papers and in advertising.

[28.24] The registration of a CTM does not entitle the proprietor to prohibit the use of that trade mark in relation to goods that have been put on the market in the EU under that trade mark by the proprietor or with his consent.[42] Parallel imports of products covered by the CTM registration from countries that are not members of the EU are not subject to this rule and this limitation, with the exception of those countries party to the agreement on the European Economic Area. This exhaustion principle does not apply where there exist legitimate reasons for the proprietor to oppose further commercialisation of the goods, especially where the condition of the goods is changed or impaired after they have been put on the market.

JURISDICTION

[28.25] Jurisdiction for proceedings relating to infringement and the validity of a CTM is governed by Regulation 207/2009/EC,[43] and also Council Regulation 44/2001/EC on jurisdiction and the recognition and enforcement of judgments in civil and commercial matters.[44] Jurisdiction for proceedings other than infringement and validity is governed solely by Regulation 44/2001/EC on the basis that the CTM is treated as if it were a national trade mark registration.[45]

[28.26] Regulation 207/2009/EC does not set up a special court to deal with CTM matters but rather each Member State is obliged to nominate a limited number of courts and tribunals in their own jurisdiction entitled to handle CTM cases.[46] These are referred to as 'Community trade mark Courts' and the courts so nominated by the Irish government are the High Court and the Supreme Court.[47] These courts have exclusive jurisdiction for proceedings relating to CTM infringement and validity actions, declarations of non-infringement (if allowed under national law) and counterclaims for revocation or for a declaration of invalidity.

---

[42] Council Regulation 207/2009/EC, art 13.

[43] Council Regulation 207/2009/EC, arts 95–98, formerly Council Regulation 40/94/EC, arts 91–94.

[44] Which superseded the Brussels Convention of 27 September 1968 on Jurisdiction and the Enforcement of Judgments in Civil and Commercial Matters (Brussels Convention).

[45] Council Regulation 207/2009/EC, art 106(1), formerly Council Regulation 40/94/EC, art 102(1).

[46] Council Regulation 207/2009/EC, art 95(1), formerly Council Regulation 40/94/EC, art 91(1).

[47] Trade Marks Act 1996 (Community Trade Mark) Regulation 2000 (SI 229/2000), r 7.

[28.27] Article 102(1)[48] of Council Regulation 207/2009/EC provides:

> Where a Community trade mark court finds that the defendant has infringed or threatened to infringe a Community trade mark, it shall, unless there are special reasons for not doing so, issue an order prohibiting the defendant from proceeding with the acts which infringed or would infringe the Community trade mark. It shall also take such measures in accordance with its national law as are aimed at ensuring that this prohibition is complied with.

In *Nokia Corp v Wardell*[49] the ECJ held that the 'special reasons' do not include the mere fact that the risk of further infringement or threatened infringement is not obvious or is otherwise merely limited.

[28.28] Essentially, the jurisdiction of a Community trade mark court is governed by either domicile or where the act of infringement is taking place. Firstly, in relation to jurisdiction based on domicile, the following rules apply:

(a) the proceedings must be brought in the CTM court of the Member State in which the defendant is domiciled or, if it is not domiciled in any Member State, in which it has an establishment, which means a real and effective industrial or commercial establishment;

(b) if the defendant is not domiciled and does not have an establishment in any Member State, the proceedings must be brought in the CTM court of the Member State in which the plaintiff is domiciled or, if the plaintiff is not domiciled in any Member State, in which the plaintiff has an establishment; and

(c) if neither the defendant nor the plaintiff is domiciled or has an establishment in any Member State, the proceedings shall be brought in the Spanish CTM courts since OHIM has its seat in Alicante, Spain.[50]

[28.29] The parties can agree that a different CTM court has jurisdiction and then art 23(1) of Regulation 44/2001/EC applies, namely:

> If the parties, one or more of whom is domiciled in a Member State, have agreed that a court or the courts of a Member State are to have jurisdiction to settle any disputes which have arisen or which may arise in connection with a particular legal relationship, that court or those courts shall have jurisdiction. Such jurisdiction shall be exclusive unless the parties have agreed otherwise. Such an agreement conferring jurisdiction shall be either:
>
> (a) in writing or evidenced in writing; or
>
> (b) in a form which accords with practices which the parties have established between themselves; or
>
> (c) in international trade or commerce, in a form which accords with a usage of which the parties are or ought to have been aware and which in such trade or commerce is widely known to, and regularly observed by, parties to contracts of the type involved in the particular trade or commerce concerned.

---

[48] Formerly Council Regulation 40/94/EC, art 98(1).

[49] *Nokia Corp v Wardell* [2007] ETMR 20.

[50] Council Regulation 207/2009/EC, art 97, formerly Council Regulation 40/94/EC, art 93.

[28.30] In addition, if a defendant enters an appearance before a CTM court that would not otherwise have jurisdiction, then art 24 of Regulation 44/2001/EC applies. This means that this CTM court has jurisdiction provided that the defendant has not entered an appearance solely to contest jurisdiction.

In all cases where jurisdiction is based on art 97(1) to (4), namely domicile/establishment, submission/agreement to a jurisdiction and entry of an appearance other than to contest jurisdiction, the CTM court decision has extra-territorial effect.[51]

[28.31] An infringement claim can always be brought in a CTM court in the EU Member State in which infringement is occurring or threatened. In such a case, the decision of the CTM court does not have extra-territorial effect. The remedies, such as injunctions, will only extend to acts in that EU Member State.

[28.32] Article 103[52] of Regulation 207/2009/EC provides for 'provisional relief'. An interim or interlocutory injunction may be sought in a CTM court or a national court in the same way as would be available if the proceedings were in respect of a national trade mark. If such an action is based on the rules of domicile, then extra-territorial provisional relief can be granted.

[28.33] Validity may only be put in issue in proceedings before a CTM court by way of a counterclaim or by way of defence. If a person wishes to challenge the validity of a CTM other than in infringement proceedings, then the action must be taken before OHIM for revocation or a declaration of invalidity.

[28.34] Article 100(7)[53] of Regulation 207/2009/EC provides that a CTM court hearing a counterclaim for revocation or declaration of invalidity may, on application, stay proceedings and require the defendant to submit the matter to OHIM for its decision on revocation or a declaration of invalidity. The CTM court may also make an order for provisional relief pending the outcome of the application to OHIM. Article 99[54] provides that in the case of a defence, a defendant may put validity in issue only to the extent that the plea relates to non-use of the CTM in issue or an earlier right of the defendant (and, for example, not on absolute grounds), otherwise the CTM court must treat the CTM as being valid. The validity of a CTM may not be put in issue in an action for a declaration of non-infringement.

[28.35] Article 109(2)[55] of Regulation 207/2009/EC states:

> The court hearing an action for infringement on the basis of a Community trade mark shall reject the action if a final judgment on its merits has been given on the same cause of action and between the same parties on the basis of an identical national trade mark valid for identical goods or services.

---

[51] Council Regulation 207/2009/EC, art 98, formerly Council Regulation 40/94/EC, art 94.
[52] Formerly Council Regulation 40/94/EC, art 99.
[53] Formerly Council Regulation 40/94/EC, art 96(7).
[54] Formerly Council Regulation 40/94/EC, art 95.
[55] Formerly Council Regulation 40/94/EC, art 105(2).

In *Prudential Assurance Co Ltd v Prudential Insurance Co of America*,[56] the Court of Appeal had to consider whether the English courts could hear an infringement action once the French Cour d'Appel had ruled in French opposition proceedings. They ruled that since the case before the Cour d'Appel related to a national trade mark, it differed from the CTMs at issue before the English courts and consequently the requirement of dual identity was not satisfied. However, the Court of Appeal did not make any determination on the issue of whether art 109(2) only applied where both the earlier proceedings and the sequential or successive proceedings were actions for infringement.

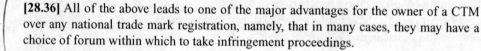

[28.36] All of the above leads to one of the major advantages for the owner of a CTM over any national trade mark registration, namely, that in many cases, they may have a choice of forum within which to take infringement proceedings.

ASSIGNMENT

[28.37] A CTM may be assigned in respect of some or all of the goods/services but only for the whole of the EU. A CTM cannot be assigned for individual Member States.[57] The assignment must be in writing and executed by both parties. Until recordal of the assignment is entered on the Register, rights cannot be invoked by the assignee and third parties without knowledge of the transfer will not be affected. Assignments need not include the goodwill but must not mislead the public.

LICENSING

[28.38] A CTM may be licensed for some or all the goods/services and for the whole or part of the EU.[58] A licence may be exclusive or non-exclusive. The holder of an exclusive licence may bring infringement proceedings if the proprietor, after formal notice, does not itself bring the proceedings.

REVOCATION AND INVALIDITY

[28.39] Both an application for revocation and for a declaration of invalidity can be made to OHIM or before a national CTM court by way of a counterclaim in infringement proceedings.[59] The grounds of revocation are as follows:

    (1)   A CTM registration will be revoked if there is non-use during a five-year period.[60] The trade mark must have been put to genuine use in the EU in connection with the goods or services for which it is registered and provided

---

[56] *Prudential Assurance Co Ltd v Prudential Insurance Co of America* [2003] ETMR 69.

[57] Council Regulation 207/2009/EC, art 17.

[58] Council Regulation 207/2009/EC, art 22.

[59] Council Regulation 207/2009/EC, arts 51–53, formerly Council Regulation 40/94/EC, arts 50–52.

[60] Council Regulation 207/2009/EC, art 15.

there are not proper reasons for non-use. The five-year period runs from the date of registration. A resumption of use can cure previous non-use but a three-month period before the revocation action or a counterclaim is filed is discounted. The genuine use must be in the EU and thus use in only a single EU Member State may suffice.[61] This is a significant advantage of the CTM system over both the national trade mark and international registration (Madrid) systems.

(2)   As a consequence of the inactivity of the proprietor, the trade mark has become the common name in the trade for a product or service for which it is registered, ie the mark has become generic.[62]

(3)   As a consequence of the use by the proprietor, or with its consent, the mark is liable to mislead the public.

[28.40] The absolute grounds for refusal[63] are a basis for invalidity but usage after registration may be taken into account in determining whether the trade mark has acquired a distinctive character. A CTM may be declared invalid where the applicant was acting in bad faith when he filed the application. In cancellation proceedings on absolute grounds, the Cancellation Division is reluctant to overrule a decision made by the Examination Division unless there has been a clear mistake.[64] No such reluctance arises in cancellation proceedings on relative grounds.[65] Under art 56(3)[66] of Council Regulation 207/2009/EC, an application for revocation or for a declaration of invalidity shall be inadmissible if an application relating to the same subject matter and cause of action, and involving the same parties, has been adjudicated on by a court in a Member State and has acquired the authority of a final decision.[67] In *Lancôme Parfums et Beauté & Cie SNC v OHIM*,[68] the ECJ upheld invalidity proceedings on absolute grounds that had been applied for by a law firm and also concluded that there was no need for a party to have an actual interest, economic or otherwise, in bringing such invalidity proceedings.

[28.41] The registration of a CTM may also be declared invalid because the mark conflicts with earlier rights of third parties. Article 53(2)[69] of Regulation 207/2009/EC sets out a non-exhaustive list of some earlier rights, which include right to a name,[70] a right of personal portrayal, a copyright and an industrial property right. Article 8(4) lays

---

61   But see the controversy raised by the Benelux and Hungarian courts in 2010 and the statement released by OHIM in response on 27 January 2010 (http://oami.europa.eu/ows/rw/news/item1273.en.do).

62   *Alcon v OHIM* [2004] ETMR 6.

63   Council Regulation 207/2009/EC, art 7.

64   *Cahill May Roberts* [2000] ETMR 794.

65   *Société France Cartes v Naipes Heraclio* [2002] ETMR 92.

66   Formerly Council Regulation 40/94/EC, art 55(3).

67   See para **[31.05]**.

68   *Lancôme Parfums et Beauté & Cie SNC v OHIM* [2010] ETMR 34.

69   Formerly Council Regulation 40/94/EC, art 52(2).

70   *USP Brands* [2008] ETMR 48.

down requirements which must be satisfied cumulatively to successfully claim invalidity based on unregistered trade mark rights:

  (i) the earlier right must be a non-registered trade mark or similar sign;
  (ii) the sign must be used in the course of trade;
  (iii) the use must be of more than mere local significance;
  (iv) the right must be acquired prior to the filing date of the contested mark;
  (v) the proprietor of the sign must have the right, under the terms of the national law governing this right, to prohibit the use of the contested mark.

In *Kehoe v Williams-Sonoma Inc*,[71] OHIM held that use in Maynooth and Mullingar was not more than mere local use.

ACQUIESCENCE

[28.42] If the proprietor of a CTM or national registration has acquiesced for five years in the use of a later CTM, the owner of that earlier CTM or national mark is barred from applying for a declaration that the later CTM is invalid and from opposing the use of the later CTM in respect of goods or services for which it is being used, unless the registration of the later CTM was applied for in bad faith.[72]

CONVERSION INTO NATIONAL APPLICATION

[28.43] A CTM application or registration may be converted into separate national applications and retain the CTM filing date, priority or seniority as appropriate.[73] Conversion cannot take place if there has been revocation on the grounds of non-use.

SENIORITY

[28.44] The owner of a CTM may claim the seniority of one or more national registrations in those EU countries where the trade mark is registered nationally.[74] A claim to seniority requires the applicant to be the actual proprietor of the national registration from which the seniority is claimed even if it was not the registered proprietor.[75] The trade marks should also correspond[76] and the goods/services of the national registration should be identical with or contained within the specification of the

---

71 *Kehoe v Williams-Sonoma Inc* [2005] ETMR 74.
72 Council Regulation 207/2009/EC, art 54, formerly Council Regulation 40/94/EC, art 53.
73 Council Regulation 207/2009/EC, art 112, formerly Council Regulation 40/94/EC, art 108; Trade Marks Act 1996 (Community Trade Mark) Regulation 2000, rr 8–11; *Cardiva SL v Cardima Inc* [2009] ETMR 1.
74 Council Regulation 207/2009/EC, art 34; Trade Marks Act 1996 (Community Trade Mark) Regulation 2000, rr 3, 4.
75 *Batmark Inc's Application* [1998] ETMR 448.
76 *Thinkpad* [1998] ETMR 642.

CTM. The claim to seniority may be made either at the time of the CTM application, within two months of the filing date or after registration. If seniority is claimed and the proprietor surrenders his national registration or allows it to lapse, he will continue to have the same rights as he would have had if his earlier national registration had been retained.

OVERVIEW

[28.45] A CTM registration arises through a single application and examination. Only one renewal is required and recordal of assignments, change of name, licences, etc, can all be done centrally before OHIM. It is also particularly advantageous to trade mark owners who are only using a mark in some but not all EU countries. Genuine use in one EU Member State may constitute use throughout the EU. Unlike the international registration (Madrid) systems, there is no requirement for a national registration or application. Opposition proceedings are through one forum, ie OHIM, and OHIM does not raise objections based on relative grounds. The decision of a single CTM court can have effect throughout the EU. Seniority will, in some cases, allow a trade mark owner to tidy up their portfolio and maintain just a single registration without loss of rights. With a CTM, a single certificate can be used for filing with customs authorities in order to activate customs' monitoring.[77]

[28.46] Because a single national conflicting prior right can form the basis of opposition, there is an opposition rate before OHIM of approximately 16 per cent of all applications. There is a two-month 'cooling off' period within which parties can reach settlement before entering the adversarial part of the proceedings, and a large number of oppositions are settled.

---

[77] Council Regulation 1383/2003/EC ([2003] OJ L196/7) concerning customs action against goods suspected of infringing certain intellectual property rights and the measures to be taken against goods found to have infringed such rights.

Chapter 29

Trade Marks Act 1996 – Registrability

INTRODUCTION

[29.01] The Trade Marks Act 1996 (TMA 1996) had a commencement date of 1 July 1996[1] and apart from generally modernising the statutory law as regards trade marks, it enabled the State to fulfil its obligations under EU law. The substantive provisions regarding the types of marks which are registrable, grounds upon which to oppose and seek invalidity, scope of protection, user requirements and the new concept of acquiescence are all requirements under the First Council Directive of 21 December 1988 to approximate the laws of the Member States relating to trade marks.[2] The TMA 1996 introduced registration in respect of marks used for services[3] and for collective marks. It also introduced a new concept into Irish law that the scope of protection granted by a registration extends beyond the exact goods/services and in some cases, to dissimilar goods/services. It provided for rights to a trade mark through registration effective in the State to be secured under the Community Trade Mark Regulation[4] and the Protocol Relating to the Madrid Agreement Concerning the International Registration of Marks 1989 (the Madrid Protocol).[5] Procedurally, it introduced the ability to file multi-class applications and simplified procedures relating to licensing and assignments. Renewals are now every 10 years. For trade mark applications after 1 July 1996, the distinction between Parts A and B of the Register no longer exists. Although the Trade Marks Act 1963 (TMA 1963) is repealed, the transitional provisions provide that it still applies to the validity of existing registrations and therefore the distinction between an old Part A and Part B registration may still be important. This is an example of a difference between the Irish TMA 1996 and its UK counterpart.[6] The rigid registered user requirements are gone and use with the consent of the proprietor can defeat revocation on the ground of non-use. Associations are no longer imposed and when agreed between parties (for example, by a letter of consent), the Controller has no discretion to refuse to allow identical or confusingly similar marks held by different

---

[1] SI 199/1996.
[2] Council Directive 2008/95/EC ([2008] OJ L 299/25), which repealed and replaced Directive 89/104/EEC ([1989] OJ L40/1).
[3] See paras **[26.19]** and **[26.20]**.
[4] Council Regulation 207/2009/EC ([2009] OJ L78/1), which repealed and replaced Council Regulation 40/94/EC of 20 December 1993 ([1994] OJ L11/1) on the Community trade mark.
[5] TMA 1996, s 58 and 59. See para **[27.50]**.
[6] The Trade Marks Act 1994, which came into effect in the UK on 31 October 1994.

proprietors to co-exist on the Register. The TMA 1996 also gives effect to certain provisions of the Paris Convention for the Protection of Industrial Property.[7]

DEFINITION OF A TRADE MARK

[29.02] Section 6(1) of TMA 1996 defines a trade mark as:

> Any sign capable of being represented graphically which is capable of distinguishing goods or services of one undertaking from those of other undertakings.

A non-exhaustive list of examples are given such as 'words (including personal names), designs, letters, numerals or the shape of goods or their packaging'. This definition and the non-exhaustive list of examples are taken from art 2 of the Trade Mark Harmonisation Directive.[8] The definition imposes three requirements for a trade mark to be registrable:

(a)   it must be a sign;

(b)   it must be capable of being represented graphically; and

(c)   it must be capable of distinguishing goods or services of one undertaking from those of other undertakings.

The word 'sign' is to be interpreted broadly. The UK White Paper[9] includes a quote from an explanatory memorandum issued by the European Commission in relation to the corresponding provision of the earlier CTM Regulation[10] (which was then in draft form) as follows:

> No type of sign is automatically excluded from registration as a Community trade mark. Article 3 lists the types of signs used most frequently by undertakings to identify their goods or services, but is not an exhaustive list. It is designed to simplify the adoption of administrative practices and court judgments to business requirements and to encourage undertakings to apply for Community trade marks.

> Depending on the circumstances, therefore, the Trade Marks Office, the National Courts, or in the last resort, the Court of Justice, will be responsible for determining whether, for example, solid colours or shades of colours, and signs denoting sound, smell or taste, may constitute Community trade marks.[11]

In *Dyson Ltd v Registrar of Trade Marks*,[12] the trade mark was described as 'a transparent bin or collection chamber forming part of the external surface of a vacuum cleaner as shown in the representation'. The ECJ ruled that this did not constitute a 'sign' under art 2 of the Directive. The rationale behind such a decision is that the holder

---

[7]   TMA 1996, ss 60–65.

[8]   Council Directive 2008/95/EC ([2008] OJ L 299/25), which repealed and replaced Directive 89/104/EEC ([1989] OJ L40/1).

[9]   Reform of Trade Marks Law (September 1990).

[10] Council Regulation 40/94/EC.

[11] Bulletin of the European Communities, Supplement 5/80.

[12] *Dyson Ltd v Registrar of Trade Marks* [2007] ETMR 34.

of a trade mark relating to a non-specific subject matter would obtain an unfair competitive advantage.

[29.03] The requirement that the sign must be capable of being represented graphically is logical in order that parties are aware of the scope of protection and, for example, by carrying out searches can ascertain rights which exist under trade marks either pending or registered. Also, trade marks are advertised for opposition purposes and the Patents Office Journal must be able to represent the trade mark exactly. This is a procedural requirement of registration and is confirmed by s 2(2) of TMA 1996, which states that:

> ... references in this Act to use (or any particular description of use) of a trade mark, or of a sign identical with, similar to, or likely to be mistaken for a trade mark, include use (or that description of use) otherwise than by means of a graphic representation

Examples of trade marks which are *prima facie* registrable but which may be difficult to represent graphically, are sound marks, smells and tastes. A mere description, not conveying the clear and precise appearance of the mark itself, cannot be considered to be a reproduction.[13] It is, however, not always necessary that the graphic representation be a visual representation depicting an image of the mark.[14]

Sounds

[29.04] In relation to sounds, the US practice has been simply to describe them as, for example, 'for the mark consisting of the sound of a creaking door' or 'the mark consists of the sound of clop, clop, clop, moo'. In some instances, the mark can be described by reference to the name of a well-known song or musical work such as, for example, Bach's *Air on the G String*, immediately recognisable from advertising campaigns for Hamlet cigars. The perceived problem with simply using musical notation is that part of the distinctiveness may lie in the emphasis given to a particular instrument and whether or not it is accompanied by vocals. In some cases, it will be necessary to accompany musical notation with a written description. In *Shield Mark BV v Kist*,[15] the ECJ ruled that the requirement of graphic representation is satisfied where the sign is represented by a musical stave divided into measures and showing, in particular, a clef, musical notes and rests whose form indicates the relative value and, where necessary, accidentals. A mere sequence of notes is not sufficient. Graphic representation was not considered satisfied by way of a description using only written language such as by means of a simple onomatopoeia without any addition, for example 'cock-a-doodle-doo'.

Smells/gustatory[16] signs

[29.05] During the passage of the UK Trade Marks Bill, which was enacted as the Trade Marks Act 1994, there was much discussion over whether or not a smell can be

---

13 *Antoni and Alison's Application* [1998] ETMR 460.
14 *Swizzels Matlow* [2000] ETMR 58.
15 *Shield Mark BV v Kist* [2004] ETMR 33; see also *Metro Goldwyn Mayer Lion Corp's Community trade mark Application 'Roar of a lion'* [2004] ETMR 34.
16 Meaning 'relating to taste'.

represented graphically in such a way that the scope of protection can be determined. There are various classification systems for odorants such as chromatography and methods of chemical analysis, which can be detailed. However, to a searcher, such an analysis is unlikely to assist in determining the nature of the smell without performing the chemical analysis itself. Therefore, it may well be decided that the graphic representation in itself does not adequately portray the sign. It can be argued that a smell can be graphically represented by a description, such as in the US case of a registration in respect of embroidery yarn for 'a high-impact, fresh floral fragrance reminiscent of plumeria blossoms'.[17] An application in respect of 'the smell of fresh cut grass' for tennis balls was approved by the Board of Appeal before the Office for Harmonisation in the Internal Market (OHIM)[18] but the 'smell, aroma or essence of cinnamon' in respect of furniture was rejected by the UK Intellectual Property Office.[19] The UK Intellectual Property Office distinguished the earlier OHIM decision by ruling that the description did not stand on its own but relied upon the reader's previous experience of the sign. In the ECJ decision of *Ralf Sieckmann v Deutsches Patent-und Markenamt*[20] it was held that in respect of an olfactory sign, the requirements of graphic representation are not satisfied by a chemical formula, by a description in written words, by the deposit of an odour sample or by a combination of those elements. Such a statement would suggest that there is no currently available means by which a smell or a gustatory sign[21] can be graphically represented, thus casting doubt over the decision by the OHIM Board of Appeal to allow registration in respect of a trade mark such as 'the smell of fresh cut grass'.[22]

Colours

[29.06] Even under TMA 1963, colour has been held to be a registrable trade mark. In *Parke Davis and Co's Application*,[23] Kenny J allowed registration in Part A of the Register of a coloured band around a capsule containing a pharmaceutical preparation. In almost all cases where colour is sought to be registered as a trade mark, it will be necessary to show acquired distinctiveness through use, which would include showing that there is no compelling need to use a particular colour and that the colour serves no utilitarian or functional purpose.[24] It is necessary to use an explicit and correct description of the colour claim and to furnish colour representations[25] preferably also utilising PANTONE reference numbers. It may be easier for a single colour to be

---

[17] US Registration No. 1,639,128, subsequently cancelled because of failure to file evidence of use.

[18] *Vennootschap Onder Firma* [1999] ETMR 429.

[19] *John Lewis of Hungerford* [2001] ETMR 36 and 104.

[20] *Ralf Sieckmann v Deutsches Patent-und Markenamt* [2003] ETMR 37.

[21] *Eli Lilly* [2004] ETMR 4.

[22] *Eden SARL v OHIM (Smell of ripe strawberries)* [2006] ETMR 14.

[23] *Parke Davis and Co's Application* [1976] FSR 195; see also *Smith Kline & French Laboratories Ltd v Sterling-Winthrop Group Ltd* [1976] RPC 511.

[24] *KWS Saat AG v OHIM* [2003] ETMR 23.

[25] *Orange Personal Communications' Application* [1998] ETMR 337.

distinctive in relation to services rather than goods.[26] The registrability of a single colour has been the subject of consideration by the ECJ in *Libertel Groep BV v Benelux-Merkenbureau*.[27] The ECJ confirmed that a colour *per se*, which is not spatially delimited, may in respect of certain goods and services have a distinctive character provided that it is:

> represented graphically in a way that is clear, precise, self-contained, equally accessible, intelligible, durable and objective. The latter condition cannot be satisfied merely by reproducing on paper the colour in question, but may be satisfied by designating that colour using an internationally recognised identification code. In assessing the potential distinctiveness of a colour as a trade mark, regard must be had to the general interest in not unduly restricting the availability of colours for the other traders who offer for sale goods or services of the same type as those in respect of which registration is sought.

Even in the case of a combination of colours, the applicant may not be able to show distinctiveness, particularly if such colours are commonly used in respect of the goods the subject of the application.[28]

Slogans

[29.07] The registrability of a slogan under TMA 1996 has been considered by Kelly J in *Masterfoods Ltd v Controller*.[29] One of the two slogans under consideration, 'TOP BREEDERS RECOMMEND IT', had earlier been the subject of a High Court decision under TMA 1963 and had been refused on the grounds that such words should be open for use by traders generally. Kelly J quoted extensively from the ECJ decision in the *BABY DRY* case[30] and concluded that it is only where the proposed trademark amounts to no more than the usual way of designating the relevant goods or their characteristics that it can be said to be devoid of distinctive character. He stated:

> In determining whether or not to refuse to register a trade mark worries or concerns about the impact on competitors do not appear to me to be appropriate matters for consideration having regard to the provisions of Section 15 of the 1996 Act, it now seems clear that rivals of the plaintiff cannot be prevented from using the words in suit for descriptive or informative purposes rather than as a means of brand identification.

The Controller's decision[31] had emphasised that the slogans always appeared in conjunction with a house mark PEDIGREE CHUM. However, Kelly J considered that this served to strengthen rather than weaken the case that the slogans were associated with the plaintiff's product and he found in favour of registrability both inherently and by virtue of use. In the English decision, *I CAN'T BELIEVE IT'S YOGHURT* Trade

---

[26] *KWS Saat AG v OHIM* [2003] ETMR 23.

[27] *Libertel Groep BV v Benelux-Merkenbureau* [2003] ETMR 63; see also *Heidelberger Bauchemie GmbH* [2004] ETMR 99.

[28] *VIKING-UMWELTTECHNIK GmbH v OHIM* [2003] ETMR 17.

[29] *Masterfoods Ltd v Controller* [2003] ETMR 84.

[30] *BABY DRY case* [2002] ETMR 3.

[31] *Master Foods Ltd's Application 'Top Breeders Recommend It'* [2001] ETMR 62.

Mark,[32] emphasis was placed on the fact that the slogan was used on its own without any other trade mark and 'as seen on a pot of yoghurt, the public will take the phrase to be a brand name'. In a second English decision, *HAVE A BREAK Trade Mark*,[33] the slogan was viewed as no more than an exhortation to buy, i.e., a phrase used purely in an advertising sense and not therefore in a trade mark sense at all. The issue of whether or not distinctiveness can be acquired as a consequence of use in conjunction with another mark was the subject of a referral to the ECJ.[34] The ECJ[35] concluded that the distinctive character of a mark may be acquired in consequence of the use of that mark as part of or in conjunction with a registered trade mark. There is a recognition that some slogans serve both functions but as stated in the *I CAN'T BELIEVE IT'S YOGHURT* decision, 'it may be necessary to show by evidence that there is a branding function in addition to there being an advertising slogan'. This distinction drawn by the English courts appears to be artificial given that a trade mark need not actually be applied to goods and that advertising is clearly trade mark use. The OHIM Board of Appeal approved the registration of the slogan BEAUTY ISN'T ABOUT LOOKING YOUNG BUT LOOKING GOOD[36] emphasising that a trade mark seen as a promotional text should be considered in a positive vein, as it serves not only to identify the origin of the goods or services to which it relates but also a marketing function in that it draws attention to them. However, in *Sykes Enterprises v OHIM*[37] the General Court rejected a slogan REAL PEOPLE, REAL SOLUTIONS because it contained nothing beyond its promotional meaning that would enable the public to memorise the slogan easily and instantly as a distinctive trade mark for the services designated. The OHIM Board of Appeal rejected an application in respect of the slogan THE WORLD'S BEST WAY TO PAY AND BE PAID, stating that the rhyme in the mark was obvious and banal and did not detract from the crude directness of the statement in the mark.[38] Descriptiveness must be assessed on the basis of all of the elements appearing in the slogan.[39] It may be important for an applicant to restrict the trade mark application to services alone should that application be rejected in respect of the goods.[40]

[29.08] The recent decision of the ECJ in relation to the mark VORSPRUNG DURCH TECHNIK[41] has been perceived as relaxing the strict approach to slogans taken by some previous decisions. The ECJ confirmed that a slogan cannot be required to display imaginativeness or conceptual tension, which would create surprise and make a striking

---

[32] *I CAN'T BELIEVE IT'S YOGHURT Trade Mark* [1992] RPC 533.

[33] *HAVE A BREAK Trade Mark* [1993] RPC 217.

[34] *Societe des Produits Nestle SA v Mars UK Ltd 'HAVE A BREAK'* [2003] ETMR 101, [2005] ETMR 96.

[35] *Societe des Produits Nestle SA v Mars UK Ltd 'HAVE A BREAK'* [2005] ETMR 96.

[36] *BEAUTY ISN'T ABOUT LOOKING YOUNG BUT LOOKING GOOD* [1999] ETMR 750; see also *WHERE SINGLES CLICK* [2007] ETMR 45.

[37] *Sykes Enterprises v OHIM* [2003] ETMR 57.

[38] *VISA International Service Association's Application* [2000] ETMR 263.

[39] *Erpo Mobelwerk GmbH* [2002] ETMR 39.

[40] *Fieldturf Inc. v OHIM* [2004] ETMR 86.

[41] *Audi AG v OHIM* [2010] ETMR 18.

impression. It also held that a slogan cannot be refused registration merely because it is perceived by the relevant public as a promotional formula and could, in principle, be used by other entities due to its laudatory nature. The particular mark at issue had a number of meanings, constituted a play on words and would be perceived as imaginative, surprising and unexpected and thus be easily remembered, which were further factors likely in this case to lead to a finding of distinctive character. The ECJ also made reference to marks that possess a certain originality or resonance, requiring little in the way of interpretation by the relevant public or setting off a cognitive process in the minds of that public as being likely to have capacity to be an indicator of origin. More controversially, the ECJ also held that the fact that the mark was a widely-known slogan, which has been used for many years, could mean that members of the public are accustomed to establishing the link between that slogan and the motor vehicles manufactured by the applicant, which the court believed could also make it easier for the public to identify the commercial origin of the goods or services covered by the application, even though many of those goods and services did not have any connection with motor vehicles.

The shape of goods or their packaging

[29.09] Given the specific inclusion of the shape of goods or their packaging in s 6(2) of TMA 1996, it is readily apparent that the House of Lords decision in *Coca-Cola*,[42] where the bottle shape was refused registration, would now be decided differently. There is no longer a requirement that a 'sign' must consist of something that is different from the goods themselves, as had been the practice of the Irish Patents Office. For example, the Coca-Cola bottle shape is in fact also used graphically on labelling and this would already have been registrable, even under TMA 1963. It has been stated by the OHIM Board of Appeal:[43]

> It is normal, indeed common place, to use not only a word mark but also a logo, a colour or scheme of colours, and a particular shape for the goods or their packaging, as a means of creating a distinctive visual image that will enable consumers to identify goods emanating from a particular commercial source. This point is certainly well understood by product imitators, as is demonstrated by the well-known practice of marketing 'look-alike' products. This practice is familiar to anyone who has visited a supermarket: alongside the leading brand sits a competing product which has the same shape and the same colour scheme but an entirely different word mark. Clearly the manufacturers of such 'look-alike' products do not assume that the average consumer focuses exclusively on word marks. On the contrary, they are well aware that many consumers identify products on the basis of their overall appearance, in particular their shape.

There is an obvious overlap between the provision that allows for registration in respect of the shape of goods[44] and registered design law, which also allows for registration of such designs under the Industrial Designs Act 2001. The additional requirement for

---

[42] *Coca-Cola* [1986] RPC 421.

[43] *Cabot Safety Intermediate Corp's Three Dimensional Trade Mark Application* [2001] ETMR 85; see also *Henkel v OHIM* [2005] ETMR 56.

[44] *Josef Rupp GmbH's Community trade mark* [2002] ETMR 35.

trade marks of capacity to distinguish may mean that at least in the initial years of a new shape, it may be necessary to rely on the protection afforded to a registered design unless the mark departs significantly from the customs of the sector,[45] particularly given the somewhat tortuous rationale in considering factors for registrability, such as the changing shape of the product when used.[46] The possibility that the average consumer might have become accustomed to recognising an applicant's product by reference to its shape alone[47] cannot render inapplicable the absolute ground for refusal based on the absence of distinctive character. This is only a factor taken into account when claiming acquired distinctiveness through use. A sign consisting of a combination of elements, each of which is devoid of any distinctive character, can be distinctive provided that concrete evidence, such as, for example, the way in which the various elements are combined, indicates that the sign is greater than the mere sum of its constituent parts.[48]

[29.10] A question that will arise is in relation to get-up or trade dress that is not packaging. Examples would be the decor of a restaurant or a petrol station forecourt.[49] Again, provided that the criterion as to capability of distinguishing is satisfied, there is no reason why such should not be registrable simply because it comprises a number of signs. It has certainly been the practice in the US to allow such registrations.[50]

Capable of distinguishing

[29.11] Graphical representation is only one requirement and it is still necessary to show a capability of distinguishing goods or services of one undertaking from those of other undertakings. The expression 'capable of distinguishing' is not new and, under TMA 1963, the Register was divided into two parts. Part A of the Register was for marks that were considered to be 'adapted to distinguish' whereas Part B was for marks 'capable of distinguishing'.[51] It could therefore be argued that the test under TMA 1996 should correspond to the criteria for Part B registration under TMA 1963, including the important factor that where a mark is shown to be distinctive in fact, it will be registrable. This was a concept with which the English courts struggled, but in the Irish Supreme Court decision in *WATERFORD Trade Mark*,[52] the English authorities were rejected and, despite its geographical signification, registration of WATERFORD was

---

[45] *Bang Olufsen A/S v OHIM* [2006] ETMR 46.

[46] *Procter & Gamble's Irish Trade Mark Application (Shaped Soap)* [2000] ETMR 703.

[47] *Mag Instrument Inc v OHIM* [2002] ETMR 61 and *Bang Olufsen A/S v OHIM* [2005] ETMR 46.

[48] *Nestle Waters France v OHIM* [2004] ETMR 41.

[49] For example, UK trade mark registration No 2256239, registered on the basis of acquired distinctiveness through use, which has the description 'The mark consists of the colours green and yellow (as shown in the representation) used together, the green predominating, applied to a visually substantial proportion of the exterior surface of structural elements of vehicle service stations'.

[50] See Hudis and Signore, 'Protection of industrial designs in the United States' (2005) EIPR 27(7), 256–264.

[51] TMA 1963, ss 17 and 18.

[52] *WATERFORD Trade Mark* [1984] FSR 390.

allowed in respect of cut crystal glassware. It was accepted that the mark had been used continuously since 1952 and that when used in relation to cut crystal glassware, had in fact achieved 100 per cent factual distinctiveness. O'Higgins CJ, in reviewing the English authorities, stated:

> Eighteen years later, however, in *Liverpool Electric Cable Co's Application* [1929] 46 RPC 99, the same Court, having accepted that factual distinctiveness had been established in relation to the words LIVERPOOL CABLES, held that the word being geographical in part, lacked capacity to be distinguished in law ... I feel that in relation to the Part B application the Court at the time had turned against geographical words and faced with the fact that no discretion to refuse was possible under the section once the factual distinctiveness was established, introduced a requirement of 'capacity in law' which was not within the words used in the section ... The *Liverpool* case and similar cases were followed in subsequent decisions and the line of authority which these represent, no doubt led to the recent House of Lords decision in *York TM*.[53] It involves interpreting section 10(2)(b) of the United Kingdom Trade Marks Act 1938 (which is identical in terms with section 18(2)(b) of the Trade Marks Act 1963) as if it only applied to words which could be regarded as 'capable in law' of distinguishing. It seems to me, as I have already indicated, that this is to ignore the plain words which are used or to seek to alter the meaning. I cannot accept such a view as being correct so far as this jurisprudence is concerned.

[29.12] The mark must be considered in the context of its meaning to the ordinary member of the Irish public likely to purchase such goods or services. In *Schweppes (Overseas) Ltd*,[54] Kenny J pointed out that 'the meaning must be determined by reference to ordinary speech and not by the views of lexicographers'. In *KIKU TM*,[55] the Irish Supreme Court had to determine whether a foreign (Japanese) dictionary word should be considered as having a direct reference to the goods under TMA 1963. O'Higgins CJ observed:

> The qualifying word 'direct' was first introduced in the Trade Marks Act 1905 because earlier decisions have tended to prevent the registration of words having a merely indirect reference to the character or quality of the goods. What is sought to be registered is 'KIKU' not 'CHRYSANTHEMUM'. KIKU either spoken or written denotes nothing. One has to be told that it is a word. Even as a word and accepted as such, it still denotes nothing to those unacquainted with the language from which it came. In order that its meaning can be conveyed, it has to be translated, which means that another word has to be used to convey the meaning. This seems to me to be the very antithesis of 'direct reference'. To my mind, to have such a reference, the word itself must refer and must carry the association to the person who hears it spoken or sees it written. If something additional or separate is to be done such as a translation, then the word itself does not directly refer.

The ECJ has ruled that the Trade Mark Harmonisation Directive does not preclude registration in a Member State, as a national mark, of a term borrowed from the language of another Member State in which it is devoid of distinctive character or

---

[53] *York TM* [1982] FSR 111.

[54] *Schweppes (Overseas) Ltd* [1970] IR 209.

[55] *KIKU TM* [1978] FSR 246; see also *Ajlan Bin* [2000] ETMR 710 and *SHISH* [2005] ETMR 19.

descriptive, unless the relevant parties in the Member State in which registration is sought are capable of identifying the meaning of the term.[56]

[29.13] The criteria in TMA 1996 differ from TMA 1963 in that there is no longer a requirement of a connection in the course of trade between the goods and a person entitled to use the mark, ie use as a means of denoting the source or origin of the goods[57] so that consumers recognise the goods bearing the mark as emanating from the same source.[58] The new criteria moves from treating a trade mark as an indicator of origin to a means of distinguishing, which somewhat ironically was the test used in the past when assessing whether or not a trade mark was adapted to distinguish and so worthy of Part A registration under TMA 1963. As stated by Kenny J in *Mothercare Ltd's Application:*[59]

> I think that this must mean that there is some feature of the word which makes it suitable to distinguish the goods of one trader from another.

[29.14] The tendency in considering this criterion may be to maintain the view of a trade mark as an indicator of origin/source and simply consider the function of distinguishing as a means of achieving this objective. The Trade Mark Harmonisation Directive,[60] after all, in its preamble, describes the function of a trade mark as being, in particular, an indication of origin. A mark which does no more than represent a characteristic of the goods does not fulfil the function. Thus for example, the name of a band may not be registrable in respect of goods such as posters because the name of the band appearing on the posters is the subject matter of the goods which itself is an essential characteristic of such goods.[61]

[29.15] Prior to TMA 1996, and principally because of the absence of service mark registrations, many trade mark owners sought to maintain a footing on the Register by registering what was essentially a service mark but in respect of goods. Thus banks, insurance and car hire companies used to register their trade marks in respect of printed publications (Class 16). The validity of a number of these registrations must be questionable given that such registrations still remain to be determined under TMA 1963,[62] and hence the trade mark proprietor needs to show a connection in the course of trade with the goods of registration. It is true that the Supreme Court, in *ITT World Directories Inc v Controller,*[63] did retreat from Kenny J's statement that 'the goods which are to bear the trade mark must be sold in the course of trade'[64] and did not require an actual sale but if, for example, the use on printed publications is simply a means

---

[56] *Matratzen Concord v Hukla* [2006] ETMR 48.

[57] *Bismag v Amblins (Chemists) Ltd* (1940) 57 RPC 209.

[58] *McDowell's Application* (1926) 43 RPC 313.

[59] *Mothercare Ltd's Application* [1968] IR 359; contrast with *American Home Products Corporation's Application 'FLU-SHIELD'* [2001] ETMR 51.

[60] Council Directive 2008/95/EC ([2008] OJ L 299/25), which repealed and replaced Directive 89/104/EEC ([1989] OJ L40/1).

[61] *LINKIN PARK* [2005] ETMR 17.

[62] TMA 1996, s 13, Sch 3.

[63] *ITT World Directories Inc v Controller* [1985] ILRM 30 (GOLDEN PAGES Trade Mark).

[64] *Bank of America National Trust & Savings Association's Trade Mark* [1977] FSR 7.

of advertising services on different goods, then the requisite connection in the course of trade does not exist.[65] This is also the position likely to be adopted under TMA 1996 and, to quote from the UK White Paper:

> The goods 'of' an undertaking can in this context only sensibly mean the goods which the undertaking makes or sells – in short, goods which it deals with in the course of trade – and not for example goods which it merely repairs or delivers. Likewise, the services 'of' an undertaking mean those services (banking, repairing, cleaning, etc) which the undertaking is in the business of providing.[66]

RETAIL SERVICES

[29.16] During the passage of the UK Trade Marks Bill, which was enacted as the Trade Marks Act 1994, attempts were made to include a specific provision allowing for the registration of marks in respect of retail services. Under the UK Trade Marks Act 1938, which corresponded to the Irish TMA 1963, registration in respect of retail services was refused but the decision was primarily based on the wording of the 1938 Act, as amended by the UK Trade Marks (Amendment) Act 1984, which required that the provision of a service had to be for money or money's worth; no longer a requirement under the UK Trade Marks Act 1994 or the Irish TMA 1996. This was not the only reason for refusal: the Court of Appeal in *DEE Corporation plc's Application*[67] also expressed the view that the specification 'retail services' was too indefinite and that the activities were merely ancillary to the business of trading in goods in the stores. In the initial years of TMA 1996, the Patents Office decided to refuse applications in respect of retail services, which is in keeping with the statements for entry in the minutes of the Council Meeting at which the earlier CTM Regulation[68] was adopted, and which states with regard to art 1(1):

> The Council and the European Commission consider that the activity of retail trading in goods is not as such a service for which a Community trade mark may be registered under this Regulation and retail services is also not a specific entry in the Nice Classification of goods or services.

[29.17] However, in the late 1990s, the Irish Patents Office began to find that their position on the refusal of retail service marks could no longer be reconciled with the needs of trade mark owners and the increasing number of other countries who allowed for such registration. In the *Golden Pages*[69] decision, the Irish Supreme Court had already determined registrability, not on the basis of what is actually sold but on the substance of the products provided to customers. There was no logical distinction between other services, such as restaurants and photocopying, where charges were made in respect of goods supplied on site.

---

65 See *KODAK Trade Mark* [1990] FSR 49.
66 Reform of Trade Marks Law (September 1990).
67 *DEE Corporation plc's Application* [1990] RPC 159.
68 Council Regulation 40/94/EC.
69 *Golden Pages* [1985] FSR 27.

[29.18] A considerable impetus for the Irish Patents Office to change its practise arose from the OHIM Board of Appeal decision in *GIACOMELLI SPORT*.[70] Prior to this decision, OHIM had also been refusing registration in respect of retail service marks. The Board of Appeal explained the basis for the need for this retail service mark protection in the statement:

> It is a matter of common experience that the consumer prefers the service provided by one particular shop over that of another. It may be the totality of the services offered which influences choice. There may be different factors which go to make up the retail services offered, for example, the range of goods provided; the way in which the goods are laid out; the location; the overall convenience it affords; the attitude and commitment of the staff; the attention given to customers; and so on. The extent or quality of the service, however, is not a matter to be taken into account in assessing an application. The fact that a retail store is, for example, 'self service', should not lessen the prospects of gaining trade mark registration as a retail service. By and large, the goodwill of a retail business is built on the service it provides.

The Board of Appeal did enter a proviso that it is necessary for an applicant to furnish a comprehensible description of the services, including a reference to the field in which the service is rendered, for example, 'retail services in the field of sports goods'. This is the current practice of the Irish Patents Office and registration of retail services is allowed in Class 35 of the International Classification, provided the nature of the retail service activities is also identified. The rationale for requiring such identification is the concern over the scope of protection which is to be afforded to a registration in respect of retail services. A scenario can arise where a trade mark can be held to be devoid of distinctiveness and exclusively descriptive for goods but not for retail-related services such as customer services for mail order sales.[71]

[29.19] For a while there was an inconsistent approach between the Irish Patents Office, who allowed registration of retail service marks with identification as to the nature of such activities and OHIM, which allowed for registration in respect of retail services *per se*. However, OHIM shares the same concern over the scope of protection and this is reflected in its President's communication:

> 'As regards conflicts between services and goods, OHIM takes the view that, while a similarity between goods sold at retail and retail services cannot be denied in the abstract, the risk of confusion is unlikely between retail services on the one hand and particular goods on the other except in very particular circumstances, such as when the respective trade marks are identical or almost so and well established in the market. Each case that arises will of course be dealt with on its merits.'[72]

---

[70] *GIACOMELLI SPORT* [2000] ETMR 277; see *Land Securities plc v Registrar of Trade Marks* [2008] ETMR 67.

[71] *Ellos AB v OHIM* [2004] ETMR 7.

[72] Communication No 3/01 of the President of OHIM of 12 March 2001, OJ OHIM 6/2001, p 1223, see also Communication No 7/05 of the President of OHIM of 31 October 2005, OJ OHIM 1/2006, p 15.

[29.20] In *PRAKTIKER,*[73] the ECJ concluded that it is necessary for a specification to provide details with regard to the goods or type of goods to which the retail services relate. Thus, it is now a requirement before both OHIM and the Irish Patents Office. The English High Court[74] has gone a step further and accepted that an application for the services of a shopping centre operator could be registrable, even though the activity of bringing together of a variety of retail outlets (rather than goods) was not strictly speaking within the wording of the PRAKTIKER decision. The Court considered that the guidance given in the PRAKTIKER decision was general enough to encompass these services.

USE OR INTENTION TO USE

[29.21] There is no requirement of actual usage to secure registration under Irish law. The TMA 1963 stated that the mark had to be 'used or proposed to be used in relation to the goods'.[75] Section 37(2) of TMA 1996 provides that an applicant must state that the trade mark is being used or that the applicant has a *bona fide* intention that it should be so used. This provision appears to have no teeth because it is not specifically identified as one of the absolute grounds for refusing registration. However, it must follow that an application to register without a *bona fide* intention to use is likely to be considered as an application made in bad faith.[76] The registration of a 'ghost mark' is not *bona fide* as evidenced in the case of *Imperial Group Ltd v Philip Morris & Co Ltd.*[77] In that case, the plaintiff wished to use the word MERIT in respect of cigarettes but understandably considered the word to be unregistrable as being laudatory. In order to gain a footing on the Register, they registered the word NERIT and also made token use with the objective that the registration would not be liable to cancellation on the ground of non-use. This failed and it was held that there was no *bona fide* use, the Court of Appeal equating the words '*bona fide*' with the need for use to be genuine use, ie use in the context of a course of trading embarked upon as an end in itself and not as embracing an activity which, although in the nature of trading, is in reality subordinate to a wholly independent objective.

[29.22] One major advantage of TMA 1996 for trade mark owners is that the applicant for registration no longer has to be the actual or intended user of the mark, or file a simultaneous registered user application. An applicant and subsequent registered proprietor can be a holding company. However, since invalidity of registrations dated prior to 1 July 1996 is determined under TMA 1963, this is still an important issue for Part B registrations.[78] An application invalidly filed under TMA 1963 because of failure to include the user by way of a simultaneously filed registered user application, cannot

---

[73] *Praktiker Bau- und Heimwerkermarkte AG v Deutsches Patent- und Markenamt* [2005] ETMR 88.

[74] *Land Securities Plc v Registrar of Trade Marks* [2008] ETMR 67.

[75] TMA 1963, s 1.

[76] TMA 1996, s 8(4)(b).

[77] *Imperial Group Ltd v Philip Morris & Co Ltd* [1982] FSR 72.

[78] TMA 1963, s 21.

be subsequently remedied by filing a registered user application, since the requirement under s 37(1)(b) of TMA 1963 was for the registered user application to accompany the trade mark application itself.[79] An application filed under TMA 1963 by a licensee or authorised user is open to refusal under s 25 of TMA 1963 as it was not filed by the proprietor.[80]

---

[79] See *Gillette Co's Application* ([1972] Supp OJ No 1160/9). This decision was affirmed on appeal by the High Court.

[80] *'MARIE CLAIRE'* Application No 157500, unreported decision of the Controller, February 2003.

Chapter 30

Trade Marks Act 1996: Absolute Grounds for Refusal of Registration

INTRODUCTION

[30.01] Because a trade mark registration grants the proprietor exclusivity, it is not unnatural that there are limitations on what is registrable. Grounds for refusal can be divided into *absolute* grounds and *relative* grounds. Absolute grounds for refusal mean grounds that are not dependant on earlier rights. Relative grounds are a basis for refusal because of earlier rights and not because of something inherently wrong with the trade mark itself.

[30.02] The absolute grounds for refusal are set out in s 8 of the Trade Marks Act 1996 (TMA 1996). Sections 62 and 63 of TMA 1996 deal with flags and emblems under art 6*ter* of the Paris Convention for the Protection of Industrial Property (Paris Convention). These provisions implement the compulsory grounds for refusal under art 3 of the Trade Mark Harmonisation Directive[1] and also most of the optional grounds. TMA 1996 did not include provisions to implement art 3(2)(b) of the Directive allowing refusal of a trade mark which 'covers a sign of high symbolic value, in particular, a religious symbol' and only included limited provisions to implement art 3(2)(c) allowing for refusal in respect of badges, emblems and escutcheons of public interest but outside art 6*ter* of the Paris Convention.[2]

[30.03] Similar to the position under the Trade Marks Act 1963 (TMA 1963), but in contrast to the position before the Office for Harmonisation in the Internal Market (OHIM), opposition proceedings in Ireland can be sustained on absolute grounds. Thus for example, in *Masterfoods v Nestlé Purina Petcare (UK) Ltd*[3] the Controller found in favour of the opponent who had opposed the registration of the device of a dog's head in respect of goods including pet food, finding that there was nothing about the image that displayed the type of individual character required to make it distinctive in the context of the relevant goods.

[30.04] The absolute grounds are mandatory, but in contrast to TMA 1963, TMA 1996 states the specific grounds for refusal rather than laying down positive requirements

---

[1] Council Directive 2008/95/EC ([2008] OJ L 299/25), which repealed and replaced Directive 89/104/EEC ([1989] OJ L40/1).

[2] See TMA 1996, s 9(2).

[3] *Masterfoods v Nestlé Purina Petcare (UK) Ltd* (2 September 2003, unreported).

necessary for registration. This would suggest that there is a presumption of registrability.

SIGNS WHICH ARE NOT TRADE MARKS

[30.05] Under s 8(1)(a) of TMA 1996, it is necessary that a sign falls within the definition of a trade mark contained in s 6(1)[4] and it must therefore be capable of being represented graphically and capable of distinguishing the goods or services of one undertaking from those of other undertakings. An aspect of this ground of refusal is that evidence of use even showing factual distinctiveness is not sufficient to overcome this particular objection. A broader view of what is capable of distinguishing must be taken than that which existed under TMA 1963. Geographical place names must generally be viewed as capable of distinguishing because they can acquire a distinctive character through usage as recognised in the proviso to s 8(1).[5] The Irish Supreme Court in the *WATERFORD trade mark*[6] decision had already allowed for the registration of a well-known place name upon evidence of factual distinctiveness through usage but the English courts proceeded differently.[7]

TRADE MARKS DEVOID OF DISTINCTIVE CHARACTER

[30.06] The ECJ has ruled that a mark that has distinctive character either by its nature or by its use must also have a capacity to distinguish.[8] A trade mark can be devoid of distinctive character at a particular moment in time but may earn distinctiveness through usage. A mark is devoid of distinctive character if it falls within any one or more of s 8(1)(b), (c) and (d) of TMA 1996. These absolute grounds are not to be applied cumulatively.[9] In assessing registrability, any acquired distinctiveness through usage must be shown to have arisen before the date of application.[10]

[30.07] The determination of whether a trade mark is distinctive is by reference to the goods/services for which registration is sought and not by guessing such goods/services or in the abstract,[11] so factors such as the price of the product concerned, which will not be an element of the registration, cannot be taken into account in evaluating distinctiveness.[12] In addition, it is important to avoid analysis of a mark by means of a separate analysis of each element, since what is important is the overall perception.[13]

---

[4]   See para **[29.02]**.
[5]   See also *WATERFORD Trade Mark* [1984] ILRM 565.
[6]   *WATERFORD Trade Mark* [1984] ILRM 565.
[7]   *YORK Trade Mark* [1982] FSR 111.
[8]   *Koninklijke Philips Electronics v Remington* [2002] ETMR 81.
[9]   *Harbinger Corporation v OHIM 'TRUSTEDLINK'* [2001] ETMR 2.
[10] *ECOPY Inc v OHIM* [2003] ETMR 99.
[11] *Chemfinder Cambridgesoft Corp's Community trade mark Application 'CHEMFINDER'* [2000] ETMR 250; *Inter-Ikea Systems v OHIM* [2009] ETMR 17.
[12] *AXION v OHIM* [2005] ETMR 72.
[13] *SAT.2* [2005] ETMR 20.

[30.08] Under TMA 1963, the Controller determined whether or not the ordinary signification of a word was that of a surname by consideration of the number of times the word appeared in both the Irish and a number of foreign telephone directories, a practice that the Irish courts considered could not be applied too rigidly.[14] This practice is no longer followed by the Controller but is even less likely to be an important consideration for the courts since the prohibition does not result from the fact of being a surname but from such being devoid of distinctive character.[15] OHIM does not raise objection to surnames unless it has a further meaning, which takes it into the realm of lacking distinctiveness, eg 'farmer' in respect of agricultural products, and the ECJ, in *NICHOLS*,[16] has ruled that even a well-known surname should not be treated any differently from the normal criteria in assessing distinctive character.

[30.09] Personal names are specifically stated in s 6(2) of TMA 1996 as being an example of a trade mark and under German law the registration of even well-known surnames is allowed, one of the arguments being that the very purpose of a surname is as a means of distinguishing between persons. It is true that surnames have a capacity to distinguish, eg FORD, COLMANS, MURPHYS, but should registration of a common name as a trade mark simply be granted on a first come, first served basis? In the *NICHOLS* case,[17] the ECJ ruled that the fact that a given name may be a common surname does not necessarily mean that the name is to be regarded as not having the requisite distinctiveness to function as a trade mark. It should be borne in mind that the registration of a surname cannot be asserted to stop a third party from using their own name provided that such use is honest.[18] It is not necessarily the position that a name that is unique to a particular person must by definition have distinctive character as a trade mark. Where a famous name is concerned, there is a possibility that the name will serve to signify not the trade source of the goods/services but merely the subject matter. Thus, the Court of Appeal in *ELVIS PRESLEY*[19] stated:

> In my judgment the Judge was right to conclude that the ELVIS mark has very little inherent distinctiveness ... members of the public purchase Elvis Presley merchandise not because it comes from a particular source, but because it carries the name or image of Elvis Presley.

This case has also been quoted as rejecting the proposition that there is a 'personality right' whereby a person can claim an exclusive and unqualified right to use their name for commercial purposes.[20]

[30.10] The word 'devoid' suggests that if the trade mark has a number of elements, then the existence of a single distinctive element in the composition should make the overall

---

[14] *Kreuzer* [1978] FSR 239.

[15] *MISTER LONG* [1999] ETMR 406.

[16] *NICHOLS* [2005] ETMR 21.

[17] *Nichols Plc's Trade Mark Application (No 2241892)* [2003] ETMR 15; see also *Thomson v Thomson Finance SA* [2007] ETMR 32.

[18] TMA 1996, s 15(2)(a).

[19] [1999] RPC 567.

[20] *DIANA, PRINCESS OF WALES Trade Mark* [2001] ETMR 25; see para **[29.13]**.

trade mark registrable. Thus, for example, although the word *COMPLETE*[21] was refused registration, it was because of the absence of any additional element that could be regarded as arbitrary, fanciful, imaginative or inventive. However, simplicity itself is not a ground for objection.[22] In *Daishowa Seiki Co Ltd's Application*,[23] the OHIM Board of Appeal allowed the registration of the words BIG PLUS, considering the application to be for two words presented in an analytical and elliptical manner giving no clear and unambiguous sense in relation to the specialist goods, ie metal machine tools. A compound mark consisting of, for example, a number of words, must be considered as a whole but this principle is not incompatible with an examination of each of the individual components in turn.[24]

[30.11] There is an increasing liberalisation as to trade marks which, although enjoying a low level of distinctiveness, pass the threshold of being trade marks that are not devoid of distinctive character.[25] OHIM allowed registration of the word 'PEERLESS' because of its derivation from the word 'PEER' suggested that the adjective was used in relation to persons and not things.[26] Another example of this can be seen in respect of two-letter trade marks. Such marks, in the absence of distinctiveness through use, were not registrable under TMA 1963 or initially before OHIM. Now two-letter trade marks are generally registrable,[27] unless they have some specific meaning, for example, XL representing the words extra large would be refused registration in respect of clothing. However, single digit trade marks are still generally regarded as unregistrable.[28]

[30.12] It is common for practitioners to argue against a non-distinctiveness objection by the use of precedent registrations[29] already achieved including those in other jurisdictions. However, these tend to be of little persuasive value unless it amounts to an identical situation receiving dissimilar treatment from which there is no objective justification.[30] The two trade marks must be so similar as to require identical treatment.

[30.13] A device mark may be suggestive and may actually depict the goods against which it is to be used but at the same time be distinctive because the same idea can be conveyed in numerous ways.[31]

[30.14] A colour *per se* is normally considered to be devoid of distinctive character. Consumers are not generally accustomed to making an assumption about the origin of goods based on their colour or the colour of their packaging in the absence of a graphic

---

[21]   *COMPLETE* [1999] ETMR 664.
[22]   *Tong Hwei Enterprise Co Ltd's Community Trade Mark Application* [2001] ETMR 86.
[23]   *Daishowa Seiki Co Ltd's Application* [2002] ETMR 36.
[24]   *Robert Bosch v OHIM [2003] ETMR 79; Best Buy Concepts v OHIM* [2004] ETMR 19.
[25]   *YES Trade Mark* [2000] ETMR 883.
[26]   *Peerless Systems Corp's Application* [2006] ETMR 28.
[27]   *FUJI PHOTO FILM CO LTD'S Trade Mark Application* [1998] ETMR 343.
[28]   *CATERHAM CAR SALES* [2000] ETMR 14.
[29]   *BURSTADVISOR* [2000] ETMR 89.
[30]   *XTRA Trade Mark* [1998] ETMR 562; *Streamserve Inc v OHIM* [2003] ETMR 59.
[31]   *FERTIN A/S's Application* [2000] ETMR 652.

or textual element.[32] A single colour is generally considered to belong in the public domain and forming part of the store of signs available to traders generally[33] but free availability is not a factor to be taken into account in assessing the distinctive character of a colour.[34]

[30.15] A trade mark may be devoid of distinctive character in relation to certain goods/services but pass the threshold of distinctiveness in relation to others.[35] A minimum degree of distinctive character is sufficient[36] and thus in *Daimler Chrysler's Application*[37] the General Court upheld the registrability of a figurative sign depicting a radiator grille in respect of vehicles as being capable of leaving an impression on the memory of the target public as an indication of commercial origin.

DESCRIPTIVE TRADE MARKS

[30.16] In s 8(1)(c) of TMA 1996, descriptive trade marks are defined as:

> Trade marks which consist exclusively of signs or indications which may serve, in trade, to designate the kind, quality, quantity, intended purpose, value, geographical origin, the time of production of goods or of rendering of services, or other characteristics of goods or services.

For a sign to fall within the scope of the prohibition, it must suggest a sufficiently direct and concrete link to the goods or services in question to enable the public concerned, immediately and without further thought, to perceive a description of the category of the goods and services in question or of one of their characteristics.[38]

[30.17] The rationale behind this provision is essentially that marks which should legitimately be open to use by traders in general cannot be registered.[39] However, there need not be a real, current and serious need for a sign to be available for use by others in order to be excluded from registration.[40] The question often asked is whether the registration of the trade mark would confer on the proprietor an unjustified monopoly over linguistic elements that belong to the public domain, thereby unfairly depriving other undertakings of the right to promote their goods and services by using ordinary

---

[32] *WM WRIGLEY'S Trade Mark Application* [1999] ETMR 214; *Sunrider Corporation v OHIM 'VITALITE'* [2001] ETMR 56.

[33] *TYNANT SPRING WATER* [1999] ETMR 974.

[34] *ZIELINSKY R785/2000–4* (28 August 2002); see para **[29.06]**.

[35] *SIECLE 21* [1999] ETMR 781; *PERFECT BROW* [2000] ETMR 174.

[36] *Eurocool Logistik GmbH v OHIM* [2003] ETMR 4.

[37] *Daimler Chrysler's Application* [2003] ETMR 87.

[38] *DKV v OHIM (EUROHEALTH)* [2001] ETMR 81.

[39] *THE PERFECTIONISTS Trade Mark* [1997] ETMR 505; *NEW ZEALAND LOTTERIES COMMISSION'S Application* [1998] ETMR 569; *PC CONNECTION* [2000] ETMR 362; *IDEAL* [2000] ETMR 382; *LITE* [2002] ETMR 91.

[40] *Audi AG v OHIM* [2004] ETMR 59.

descriptive terms that form part of the store of words available to traders in general.[41] Thus in *Sealed Air Corpn v Controller*,[42] Smyth J refused registration of the trade mark *BUBBLE WRAP*, being satisfied that it amounted to no more than the usual way of designating the relevant goods. The use of the word 'exclusively' indicates that use of a descriptive word in conjunction with other elements means that the overall mark would fall outside this prohibition.[43] This appears to be the position but the mark can still fall foul of s 8(1)(b) of TMA 1996 as being devoid of any distinctive character.[44] What is different from s 8(1)(b) is that a trade mark could be viewed as distinctive by consumers but may nevertheless be trade terminology and accordingly refused. Even operating under the former law, the trade mark *SUPERWOUND*[45] was refused registration in respect of guitar strings. The evidence showed that the word 'wound' was used by the trade and was therefore descriptive. In *Fry-Cadbury (Ireland) Ltd v Synott*,[46] an application was brought seeking cancellation of the trade mark *'CRUNCH'* in respect of confectionery. Both the High Court and Supreme Court agreed that the trade mark was essentially descriptive. Many of the Controller's decisions[47] on trade marks having a direct reference to the character or quality of the goods under TMA 1963 would still apply under TMA 1996. There is also no reason to believe that phonetic equivalents to descriptive words will not be caught under this provision.[48] The proviso to s 8(1) of TMA 1996 applies to s 8(1)(c) and therefore use showing a distinctive character will be sufficient to overcome an objection, eg BUDGET for care hire. It is only pre-application use which can be taken into account in determining the question of distinctiveness under the proviso.

[30.18] The fact that a trade mark is a created name that does not exist in a dictionary does not preclude the trade mark from being descriptive.[49] An examiner should have regard to the overall impression created by the mark as a whole, taking into account the nature of the goods or services, the level of awareness of the likely consumers[50] and any other relevant factors.[51] In principle, the splitting of a multiple word mark or a compound mark into its components is to be avoided when considering descriptiveness. In *Cuisine Express Fresh Foods Ltd v Cuisine de France Ltd*[52] the Controller, in rejecting an opposition on absolute grounds that the words CUISINE EXPRESS were non-distinctive, stated:

---

41 *ENVIRO-CHEM* [1999] ETMR CN845 (Monsanto Company's Application, OHIM Board of Appeal Case R87/1998-1).

42 *Sealed Air Corpn v Controller* (29 July 2003, unreported).

43 See *Deutsche Post Euro Express v OHIM (EUROPREMIUM)* [2006] ETMR 52.

44 See paras **[30.06]–[30.15]** above.

45 *SUPERWOUND* [1988] RPC 272.

46 *Fry-Cadbury (Ireland) Ltd v Synott* [1936] IR 700.

47 See Tierney, 'Irish Trade Marks Law and Practice' (Gill & Macmillan, 1987).

48 *Electrix Ltd's Application* [1959] RPC 283; *Siemens AG's Application* [1999] ETMR 146.

49 *Pilkington plc's Application* [2002] ETMR 17.

50 *Ford Motor Co* [2000] ETMR 679.

51 *Poly Pads Trade Mark Application* [1999] ETMR 234.

52 *Cuisine Express Fresh Foods Ltd v Cuisine de France Ltd* [2008] ETMR 35.

The market economy has developed to a point where the average consumer is exposed to the use of trade marks in almost every aspect of his daily life so that he has come to perceive and assimilate the overall impressions created by trade marks intuitively and subliminally. In trying to assess whether a given trade mark has the requisite distinctiveness to permit [its] registration, one must therefore attempt to gauge the likely 'gut reaction' of the consumer to it and to ask whether he is likely to perceive it as an indication of specific commercial origin or merely as a product describer.

It is not necessary that a word be wholly meaningless and a word can be suggestive or allusive without being denied registration under s 8(1)(c)[53] of TMA 1996. A trade mark may be distinctive if it merely hints at the character or quality of the goods providing it does not describe them.[54]

[30.19] It is very hard to reconcile the rationale between certain decisions and hence establish a consistent practice. In *BABY-DRY Trade Mark*,[55] registration in respect of diapers was approved by the ECJ overruling the General Court stating:

descriptiveness must be determined not only in relation to each word taken separately but also in relation to the whole which they form. Any perceptible difference between the combination of words submitted for registration and the terms used in the common parlance of the relevant class of consumers to designate the goods or services or their essential characteristics is apt to confer distinctive character on the word combination ... whilst each of the two words in the combination may form part of the expressions used in everyday speech to designate the function of nappies, their syntactically unusual juxtaposition is not a familiar expression in the English language, either for designating babies' nappies or for describing their essential characteristics.

In contrast, and even following the *BABY-DRY* decision, the Boards of Appeal before OHIM still have no problem in holding that in terms of distinctiveness, the whole of a trade mark is no greater than the sum of its parts.[56] The BABY-DRY decision is also in sharp contrast to the ECJ's own ruling in *DOUBLEMINT*[57] that descriptive signs may be freely used by all and cannot be reserved to one undertaking alone. For a descriptiveness objection to arise, it is not necessary that the sign is already in use by others or that it has a number of different possible meanings. As a general rule, a mere combination of elements, each of which is descriptive of the goods or services for which registration is sought, remains descriptive of those characteristics even if the combination creates a neologism. Just bringing descriptive elements together without any unusual variation, for example, as to syntax or meaning, does not prevent a sign from being descriptive.[58]

[30.20] In the absence of sufficient use, well-known geographical locations may still be refused registration. However, because the test is based on the legitimacy of the likely

---

[53] *OILGEAR* [1999] ETMR 291; *NETMEETING* [1999] ETMR 386; *SWIFTCALL* [2005] ETMR 83.

[54] *VISION DIRECT* [2000] ETMR 934.

[55] *BABY-DRY Trade Mark* [2002] ETMR 3; see also *Dart Industries Inc v OHIM 'ULTRAPLUS'* [2003] ETMR 32.

[56] *EUROFLEET* [2003] ETMR 80.

[57] *OHIM v WM Wrigley Jnr Co 'DOUBLEMINT'* [2004] RPC 327, [2004] ETMR 88.

[58] *Campina Melkunie BV v Benelux Merkenbureau (BIOMILD)* [2004] ETMR 58.

wish by traders to use the trade marks where there is no plausible connection between the goods and the geographical location, registration should be allowed.[59] The fact that a word is a geographical name does not automatically mean that it serves as an indication of geographical origin when used in trade.[60]

[30.21] A trade mark application for a protected designation of origin or geographical indication should also be refused registration under s 8(1)(c) of TMA 1996, at least in so far as the application relates to an agricultural product or foodstuff covered by Regulation 510/2006/EC.[61] Article 14 of Regulation 510/2006/EC specifically provides for refusal in relation to 'the same class of product' if the trade mark application is dated subsequent to the publication of approval of the protected designation or geographical indication.

CUSTOMARY LANGUAGE IN A TRADE

[30.22] Under s 8(1)(d) of TMA 1996, an absolute ground for refusal arises in respect of:

> Trade marks which consist exclusively of signs or indications which have become customary in the current language or in the *bona fide* and established practices of the trade.

In *Merz & Krell*,[62] the ECJ confirmed that for a trade mark to be barred from registration on the ground that it is part of the current language of the trade, it need not also be descriptive of those goods or services to which it is applied. Some commentators have equated this provision with a trade mark being generic but, unlike the revocation provision in s 51(1)(c) of TMA 1996, the words 'common name' are not used, which are also the words used in Council Regulation 510/2006/EC dealing with geographical indications or designations of origin. The word 'customary' suggests a somewhat lower standard than 'common' and certainly a lower standard than 'well-known' which were the words used in TMA 1963.[63] However, similarly to TMA 1963, the test under TMA 1996 is trade use, not use by the general public, which decides this issue.[64] Unlike s 8(1)(c) of TMA 1996, it is what traders are actually doing that is relevant as opposed to what they may be likely to wish to do at a future date. What is in current language should be by way of reference to modern dictionaries[65] or other reference materials. It is for the party alleging that a mark has become generic to bring substantive evidence to that

---

[59] *Windsurfing Chiemsee Products v Huber* [1999] ETMR 585; *Nordic Saunas Ltd's Trade Mark* [2002] ETMR 18; *PEEK & CLOPPENBERG* [2006] ETMR 33; *Nordmilch EG v OHIM* [2004] ETMR 70.

[60] *WIMBELDON* [2006] ETMR 36.

[61] Council Regulation 510/2006 of 20 March 2006 on the protection of geographical indications and designations of origin for agricultural products and foodstuffs ([2006] OJ L 93/12) which repealed and replaced Council Regulation 2081/92/EEC.

[62] *Merz & Krell* [2002] ETMR 21; see also *Alcon Inc v OHIM* [2005] ETMR 69.

[63] TMA 1963, s 23.

[64] *Daiquiri Rum* [1969] RPC 600; *Gramaphone Co's Application* [1910] 2 Ch 423.

[65] *MINI CLAW* [1999] ETMR 505.

effect.[66] It is not just words that might fall foul of this provision. In the *Cimetidine Trade Mark* case,[67] Smith Kline & French Laboratories Ltd sought to register the colour pale green as a trade mark for pharmaceutical preparations on varying shapes of tablets. Registration was denied, it being found to be common practice for pharmaceutical tablets to be supplied in a visible single colour, although not pale green. If this case had been decided under TMA 1996, it is unlikely that it would be held to fall foul of s 8(1)(d), given that it was not customary in the trade to use pale green. The fact that the trade mark owner has misused the trade mark by using it in a descriptive sense[68] may make it devoid of distinctive character but it is not customary trade usage and, although it may lead to cancellation at a future date, this is not a basis for refusal under s 8(1)(d). It is, however, a factor that is likely to be taken into account in determining whether or not an applicant can avail of the proviso to s 8(1) allowing use to show that a trade mark has in fact acquired a distinctive character.[69] If an applicant is using a word as a name of an article and not as a trade mark, then distinctiveness cannot be proven. Dependant on the type of industry, use by a small number of traders may be sufficient to uphold this ground of refusal.

[30.23] In *Gillette Co's Application*,[70] the OHIM Cancellation Division had to consider invalidity proceedings against a trade mark DLC being the standard abbreviation for 'diamond like carbon' in respect of goods including razors. It was argued that the term was only known to a limited number of technicians and scientists and consequently not the public generally. This argument was rejected on the basis that scientists must also be considered as part of the general public as they would also purchase and utilise the product.

ACQUIRED DISTINCTIVENESS THROUGH USAGE

[30.24] The absolute grounds for refusal under s 8(1)(b), (c) and (d) of TMA 1996 can be overcome in circumstances where, before the date of application, the trade mark had in fact acquired a distinctive character as a result of use. In assessing distinctive character the following factors should be taken into consideration:[71]

> the market share held by the mark; how intensive, geographically widespread and long standing use of the mark has been; the amount invested by the undertaking in promoting the mark; the proportion of the relevant class of persons who, because of the mark, identify goods as originating from a particular undertaking; and statements from chambers of commerce and industry or other trade and professional associations

---

[66] *Du Pont de Nemours (EI) and Company v AMA Antoon Michielsen Automobiles 'TEFLON'* [2001] ETMR 70.
[67] *Cimetidine Trade Mark case* [1991] RPC 17.
[68] *Shredded Wheat Co Ltd v Kelloggs* (1940) 57 RPC 137.
[69] *Portogram Radio Electrical Co's Application* (1952) 69 RPC 241.
[70] *Gillette Co's Application* [2002] ETMR 65.
[71] *Windsurfing Chiemsee Products v Huber* [1999] ETMR 585.

In *Interdigital Com Corporation's Application*,[72] the applicant argued that the relevant public would recognise the mark as distinctive of the applicant because it was the originator of the technology embodied in the product identified by the mark. This application was rejected because the evidence furnished did not support the claim and only showed that the applicant was an operator of the technology.

[30.25] In the English case of *1–800 Flowers Inc v Phonenames Ltd*,[73] reliance was placed on internet use. Jacob J was circumspect and questioned such use with an example:

> a fishmonger in Bootle who put his wares and prices on his own website, for instance for local delivery, can hardly be said to be trying to sell fish to the whole world or even the whole country … the mere fact that websites can be accessed anywhere in the world does not mean, for trade mark purposes, that the law should regard them as being used anywhere in the world. It all depends on the circumstances, particularly the intention of the website owner and what the reader will understand if he accesses the site.

Acquired distinctiveness through use must be evaluated in relation to the goods and from the perspective of an average consumer of those goods, who is reasonably well informed, reasonably observant and circumspect. In *Glavabel SA v OHIM*,[74] the General Court was critical of an attempt to shift the average consumer to professionals since the average consumer was still part of the target public in relation to patterned glass and glass sheets.

SHAPES

[30.26] The definition of a trade mark in s 6 of TMA 1996 includes the 'shape of goods or of their packaging'. When assessing the distinctiveness of a three-dimensional shape of goods the tests to be applied should be no stricter than with other types of trade marks.[75] There are, however, certain shapes that will be excluded from registration and these are set out in s 8(2), which states:

> A sign shall not be registered if it consists exclusively of—
>
> (a)   the shape which results from the nature of the goods themselves; or
>
> (b)   the shape of goods which is necessary to obtain a technical result; or
>
> (c)   the shape which gives substantial value to the goods.

[30.27] The rationale behind these provisions is a compromise. Firstly, there was a view that to allow the registration of the shape of goods or containers would lead to an unacceptable restriction on the choice of shapes available to traders, ie an attempt to expand the boundaries of intellectual property and to convert a protective law into a source of monopoly.[76] The law already provides for a monopoly right for a shape by way

---

[72]   *Interdigital Com Corporation's Application* [1999] ETMR 758.

[73]   *1–800 Flowers Inc v Phonenames Ltd* [2000] ETMR 369.

[74]   *Glavabel SA v OHIM* [2008] ETMR 37.

[75]   *Linde AG, Winward Industries Inc, Rado Uhren AG (joined applications)* [2003] ETMR 78.

[76]   *Coca-Cola* [1986] RPC 421; see also *Linde AG, Winward Industries Inc, Rado Uhren AG (joined applications)* [2003] ETMR 78.

of a registered design under the Industrial Designs Act 2001. However, the shape must be new and, upon expiry of the maximum 25-year duration, it enters the public domain. The concept of registered trade mark protection for a shape contrasts strongly with this, and therefore sits uncomfortably with registered design law, by not requiring any novelty and being indefinite in duration. A second and contrasting view is reflected in para 2.18 of the UK White Paper:[77]

> It is a fact of the market place, however, that some shapes are recognised by consumers as distinctive of the products of a particular trader. Allowing the registration of such shapes would therefore not be conferring a monopoly – it would merely recognise that a *de facto* monopoly already exists.

[30.28] In the *Jif Lemon* case,[78] the House of Lords held that the JIF lemon shape was protected under the law of passing off since all of the ingredients to sustain such an action were present, including get-up in terms of the shape, which was associated in the minds of substantial numbers of the purchasing public specifically and exclusively with the JIF lemon juice. The reluctance with which the House of Lords reached their decision can be seen in the following statement of Lord Bridge of Harwich:

> The result seems to be to give the respondents a *de facto* monopoly of the container as such which is just as effective as *de jure* monopoly. A trader selling plastic lemon juice would never be permitted to register a lemon as his trade mark, but the plaintiffs have achieved the result indirectly that a container designed to look like a real lemon is to be treated, *per se,* as distinctive of their goods. If I could find a way of avoiding this result, I would. But the trial judge's findings of fact, however surprising they may seem, are not open to challenge.

The ECJ in *Koninklijke Philips Electronics v Remington*[79] ruled that where a trader has been the only supplier of particular goods to the market, extensive use of a sign, which consists of the shape of those goods, may be sufficient to give the sign a distinctive character in circumstances where, as a result of that use, a substantial proportion of the relevant class of persons associates that shape with that trader and no other undertaking or believes that goods of that shape come from that trader. The English courts have taken a strict approach to such marks and in *Nestlé v Unilever*,[80] Jacob J suggests that evidence of 'trade mark significance' is required to register a shape mark and mere recognition of the shape is not enough. In relation to three-dimensional trade marks consisting of the packaging of goods, such as liquids, which are packaged in particular ways for reasons linked to the very nature of the product, the ECJ has ruled that the packaging must enable consumers to distinguish the product concerned from those of other undertakings without conducting an analytical or comparative examination and without paying particular attention.[81]

---

77 Reform of Trade Marks Law (September 1990).
78 *Reckitt & Colman Products Ltd v Borden Inc* [1990] RPC 341.
79 *Koninklijke Philips Electronics v Remington* [2002] ETMR 81.
80 *Nestlé v Unilever* [2003] ETMR 53.
81 *Deutsche Sisi-Werke v OHIM* [2006] ETMR 41.

[30.29] Section 8(2) of TMA 1996 relating to registrability of shapes is taken from art 3(1)(e) of the Trade Mark Harmonisation Directive,[82] which has its roots in the corresponding provisions of the Benelux Trade Marks Act.[83] The Benelux Court of Justice, in the case involving BURBERRY tartan patterns,[84] held that shapes only cover three-dimensional and not two-dimensional designs. In the minutes to the earlier Community Trade Mark Regulation,[85] it is also stated 'the Council and the European Commission consider that where goods are packaged, the expression "shape of the goods" includes the shape of the packaging'.

[30.30] When looking at the exceptions, it should be noted that these only arise if the trade mark consists exclusively of the shape. It is possible that the inclusion of further matter to the mark may still not be sufficient to avoid refusal under s 8(1)(b) of TMA 1996, ie due to lack of distinctive character.[86]

The shape which results from the nature of the goods themselves

[30.31] This involves consideration of both the shape and the goods and would cover, for example, the shape of a pineapple in respect of pineapples. A mark consisting of the shape of a pineapple for ice buckets would however be registrable. Because of the words 'which results from the nature of', it is broader than a mere representation of the product itself and may, for example, cover a caricature of a pineapple, again in respect of pineapples. A bottle shape would not generally come under this provision because its contents, being the goods, are not reflected in the shape itself. This is not always the case and one could, for example, have orange juice in a bottle resembling an orange. Some guidance on this issue can be taken from US law[87] but the issue of whether the exclusion is limited to naturally-occurring shapes rather than artificially-created shapes still remains undecided.[88] The rationale behind this exception is that one cannot impose on the industry or the trade, restrictions on the use of a shape which is indispensable to the manufacture or the distribution of the product.

The shape of goods which is necessary to obtain a technical result

[30.32] In *Koninklijke Philips Electronics v Remington*,[89] the ECJ had to consider a claim to invalidity in respect of the graphic representation of the shape and configuration of the head of a shaver comprising three circular heads with rotating

---

82 Council Directive 2008/95/EC ([2008] OJ L 299/25), which repealed and replaced Directive 89/104/EEC ([1989] OJ L40/1).
83 Benelux Trade Mark Law 1971, art 1(2).
84 *Burberrys v Bossi* [1992] NJ 596.
85 Council Regulation 40/94/EC which was repealed and replaced by Council Regulation 207/2009/EC ([2009] OJ L78/1).
86 *BP's Application OIL CONTAINER* [1999] ETMR 282.
87 *North American Philips Corpn* 217 USPQ 926 (1983) relating to the face plate of a three-headed electric razor.
88 *Nestlé v Unilever* [2003] ETMR 53.
89 *Koninklijke Philips Electronics v Remington* [2002] ETMR 81, [2006] ETMR 42.

blades in the shape of an equilateral triangle. The equivalent to s 8(2)(b) of TMA 1996 was interpreted to mean that the essential functional features of the shape must not be attributable only to the technical result. In addition, the fact that a product could possess a different functional shape while still performing the same technical result does not make that shape non-functional.[90] In *Mega Bloks Inc v Kirkbi A/S*,[91] OHIM Cancellation Division considered a LEGO brick and concluded that the term 'necessary' must be interpreted as meaning that the respective shape or element of the shape is necessary in the sense of a condition *sine qua non*[92] for achieving the result.

[30.33] In the Irish design case of *Allibert SA v O'Connor*,[93] Costello J considered the shape of a fish box and whether or not a valid registered design existed in that shape. The test used by Costello J was whether all the features were dictated by the function to be performed, which in this case was ease of stacking. In most cases it is unlikely that the whole shape will be unprotectable. The provision provides for an exception to registrability only to the extent that there is no freedom as regards arbitrary elements of design since almost all three-dimensional items will fulfil a certain technical function.

The shape which gives substantial value to the goods

[30.34] This provision is likely to be extremely difficult to interpret and certainly would seem to cover a large number of products, which are often bought for their aesthetic qualities such as jewellery, ornaments, china, bags and fashion items. If a person's reason for purchasing a product is its aesthetic qualities, then it appears to be caught by this provision. These very aesthetic qualities make it more likely to be a suitable candidate for a registered design. Although there is no prohibition on a shape being protected by both a registered design and a trade mark registration, a court may be persuaded by such registrations for the same design that it is the aesthetic quality in the shape that gives substantial value to the goods. However, a shape can serve as a trade mark and also be aesthetic. The question which might appropriately be asked is, which factor influenced the purchase? The answer may be a combination of factors. In the Dutch Supreme Court case of *Wokkels*,[94] it was held that the shape of a particular cracker did increase market share but the intrinsic value was in the actual taste, which was accordingly the determining factor. It would be strange if a manufacturer of a product with expensive packaging was to be penalised by being refused registration in respect of an attribute to the product which assists in its promotion but which, in most cases, must be secondary to the product itself. In a case involving the BURBERRY tartan pattern in the Benelux,[95] it was held that if the effect on the market value has its origin in the attractive power connected with the shape's reputation as a distinctive sign

---

[90] *Lego Juris v OHIM* [2009] ETMR 15; decision affirmed by the ECJ in *Lego Juris v OHIM* Case C-48/09 (14 September 2010, unreported).

[91] *Mega Bloks Inc v Kirkbi A/S* [2005] ETMR 87.

[92] Indispensable, literally 'without which there is nothing'.

[93] *Allibert SA v O'Connor* [1981] FSR 613.

[94] *Wokkels* [1985] BIE 23.

[95] *Burberrys v Bossi* [1992] NJ 596.

and not in the aesthetic attractiveness of the shape, the exception to registrability should not apply. Certainly, in the US, the aesthetic function is no longer viewed as the correct criterion for registrability of product shapes.[96] Some guidance can be obtained from the English decision in *Julius Samann Ltd v Tetrosyl Ltd*,[97] where Kitchen J stated:

> the mark may have a large goodwill associated with it derived from sales and advertising. This will no doubt have a substantial value. But it is not relevant. It is the shape itself which must add substantial value. Secondly, it is relevant to make a comparison with the shapes of equivalent articles. It is only if the shape in issue has a high value relative to such other shapes that it will be excluded from registration.

In *Benetton Group SAS v G-Star International BV*,[98] the ECJ ruled that a shape of a product cannot constitute a trade mark even where, prior to the application for registration, it acquired distinctiveness as a result of its recognition as a distinctive sign following advertising campaigns presenting the specific characteristics of the product in question.

[30.35] Section 8(2) of TMA 1996 does not have a proviso similar to s 8(1) and consequently an applicant cannot avoid refusal in respect of a shape by showing that the shape has, in fact, acquired a distinctive character through use.

TRADE MARKS CONTRARY TO PUBLIC POLICY OR ACCEPTED PRINCIPLES OF MORALITY

[30.36] This provision in s 8(3)(a) of TMA 1996 is unlikely to be interpreted very differently than that part of s 19 of TMA 1963 which provided for mandatory refusal of marks 'contrary to law or morality or any scandalous design'. Although public policy is specifically included, it was also the rationale behind the provision in TMA 1963 that it existed not merely for the benefit of traders but for the benefit of the public at large.[99] The section would also presumably prevent registration in respect of marks which would cause offence to a section of the public on matters such as race, sex, religious belief and even general matters of taste and decency. It is also likely to cover art 3(2)(b) of the Trade Mark Harmonisation Directive,[100] which was an optional provision relating to refusal on the grounds that 'the trade mark covers a high symbolic value, in particular, a religious symbol' but given that this is an additional ground, it must at least have been perceived that not all trade marks of 'high symbolic value' were also necessarily contrary to public policy. The *HALLELUJAH Trade Mark*[101] was refused registration in

---

[96]   *DC Comics Inc* 689 F 2d 1042 (1982).
[97]   *Julius Samann Ltd v Tetrosyl Ltd* [2006] ETMR 75.
[98]   *Benetton Group SAS v G-Star International BV* [2008] ETMR 5.
[99]   *Livron* (1937) 54 RPC 161.
[100] Council Directive 2008/95/EC ([2008] OJ L 299/25), which repealed and replaced Directive 89/104/EEC ([1989] OJ L40/1).
[101] *HALLELUJAH Trade Mark* [1976] RPC 605; see also *Basic Trade Mark SA's Application (trade mark JESUS)* [2006] ETMR 24.

respect of women's clothing, and the following observation was made by the UK Registrar:

> to be contrary to morality the use of a mark would, I think, have to offend the generally accepted mores of the time, while the adverse use of the Registrar's discretion would be warranted if registration would be reasonably likely to offend persons who might be in a minority in the Community, yet be substantial in number.

[30.37] In the English design case of *Masterman's Design*,[102] a design for a kilted doll with mimic male genitalia was allowed, it being considered that simply because a section of the public would find it distasteful was not a valid reason for refusal. However, in *Ghazilian's Application*,[103] registration of the trade mark TINY PENIS was refused, the offence residing in the fact that an accepted social and family value was likely to be significantly undermined. This social and family value was considered to be the belief that the correct anatomical term for parts of the genitalia should be reserved for serious use and should not be debased by use as a smutty trade mark for clothing. This is in contrast to the OHIM Board of Appeal Decision when considering the trade mark DICK & FANNY,[104] which held that the mark did raise a question of taste but not one of public policy or morality. The Enlarged Board of Appeal before OHIM applied, in consideration of a trade mark SCREW YOU,[105] the standards of a reasonable person with normal levels of sensitivity and tolerance. On this basis, registration was approved for some goods such as condoms but rejected for others. Public safety is a matter of public policy and therefore the question arises as to whether or not it is a ground for refusal to register where the trade mark is identical or confusingly similar to an existing trade mark, where co-existence may be of concern to public safety. An example of such is the case of trade marks for pharmaceutical purposes, but it could also arise in respect of dissimilar goods, where the Controller's searching would not raise the earlier mark as a citation. In *JARDEX Trade Mark*,[106] application for JARDEX in respect of disinfectants was refused upon opposition by the owners of the trade mark JARDOX in respect of extract of meat despite the possibility of a serious accident being remote and unlikely to occur without negligence on the part of one or more persons. The UK Assistant-Comptroller stated:

> I do think that I can take cognisance of the fact that negligence is a human failing from which few, if any, of us are entirely free, and the consequence of a mistake such as that just referred to, might be so disastrous, that it is obviously necessary for me to consider carefully whether, as a public official exercising a discretionary power, I ought to take any step that would encourage the placing upon the market of a food and a poisonous disinfectant sold under almost identical marks, knowing that the two articles may ultimately come to be used in proximity with each other.[107]

---

[102] *Masterman's Design* [1991] RPC 89.

[103] *Ghazilian's Application* [2002] ETMR 57.

[104] *Dick Lexic Ltd's Application* [2005] ETMR 99; see also *FCUK* [2007] ETMR 8.

[105] *Application of Kenneth (Trading as Screw You)* [2007] ETMR 7.

[106] *JARDEX Trade Mark* (1945) 63 RPC 19: see also *UNIVER Trade Mark* [1993] RPC 239.

[107] See also *Motorine* (1907) 24 RPC 585.

[30.38] The difference between TMA 1996 and TMA 1963 is that in TMA 1963, there was a definite dual obligation on the Controller, not just to protect the owners of earlier marks, but to avoid confusion amongst the public. This was evidenced by s 31 of TMA 1963 and the association requirement, whereby owners of identical or similar marks could only assign associated marks together, preventing them from being held by different owners. In TMA 1996, there is no association requirement and, indeed, the transitional provisions remove the requirement for existing registrations.[108] Section 10(6) is more salient in that consent by the owner of an earlier trade mark is sufficient to overcome any objection by the Controller on the relative grounds of refusal based on an earlier conflicting right. However, s 10(6) of TMA 1996 is limited to objections under s 10 itself and therefore appears to be overridden by public policy considerations including public safety objectives. Article 4(5) of the Trade Mark Harmonisation Directive[109] allows for consent as an optional provision but only in 'appropriate circumstances', and refusal based on public policy is mandatory under art 3(1)(f).

[30.39] The General Court has ruled that the fact that a party is prohibited from trading, for example, without a gambling licence, is of no consequence to an examination of the intrinsic qualities of the trade mark and therefore whether it is contrary to public policy or accepted principles of morality.[110]

DECEPTIVE TRADE MARKS

[30.40] Section 8(3)(b) of TMA 1996 provides for refusal if a trade mark 'is of such a nature as to deceive the public, for instance, as to the nature, quality or geographical origin of the goods or services'. Section 19 of TMA 1963 also provided for refusal in respect of trade marks 'likely to deceive or cause confusion'. It was common practice for the Controller to raise objection on this basis and applicants were often faced with the dilemma of a trade mark, which was either descriptive of the goods or, alternatively, was deceptive in that it described an attribute of a product which did not apply to the goods in question. The often quoted *UK ORLWOOLA Trade Mark*[111] is a good illustration of this point, Fletcher Moulton LJ finding that the trade mark ORLWOOLA for textile goods was utterly unfit for use as a trade mark as being directly descriptive for goods that were all wool and deceptive of goods that were not. The TMA 1996 puts applicants in the same position by virtue of a possible descriptiveness objection[112] and/or a deceptiveness objection.[113] However, no amount of use can overcome a deceptiveness objection under s 8(3)(b). The device of a crocodile was held by the High Court and affirmed by the Supreme Court as being deceptive of clothing and footwear not made from genuine

---

108 TMA 1996, Sch 3, para 2(3).

109 Council Directive 2008/95/EC ([2008] OJ L 299/25), which repealed and replaced Directive 89/104/EEC ([1989] OJ L40/1).

110 *Sportwetten GmbH Gera v OHIM* [2006] ETMR 15.

111 *UK ORLWOOLA Trade Mark* (1909) 26 RPC 681.

112 TMA 1996, s 8(1)(c).

113 TMA 1996, s 8(3)(b).

crocodile skin.[114] In the Irish case of American Cyanamid's application to register *STRESSTABS*,[115] it was held that the mark was likely to deceive or cause confusion if it was used on goods that were not in the form of tablets for the relief of physical stress. Examples of decisions relating to deceptiveness as to the nature of the goods are *CHINA-THERM*[116] for insulated cups and tumblers made of plastic, which misdescribed the character of the goods since people were likely to believe the goods were made of china; *CONSARC*[117] in respect of electrical welding apparatus and electric furnaces on the grounds that the mark suggested arc welding apparatus; *SOFLENS*[118] for contact lenses, which was held to be deceptive if used for hard contact lenses; and WINE OH! for water and non-alcoholic drinks.[119]

An example of deceptiveness as regards quality can be seen in *SAFEMIX*[120] in respect of thermostatically controlled valves for mixing hot and cold water. It was held that the use of the word 'SAFE' as part of the mark was deceptive and could be regarded as inducing purchasers to believe that goods bearing the mark were safe to use, whereas the goods were of a kind which could be possibly dangerous to a user.[121] The issue of deception is directed to 'the public' but it is likely that this will be interpreted as deceptive to the public who are likely to purchase the goods or avail of the services in question. Trade marks in respect of goods in a specialised market directed to persons engaged in a particular trade and not goods sold to the general public for consumption and domestic use should be considered accordingly.[122] However, the fact that the goods are not bought without due enquiry is not of itself sufficient to avoid an argument of deceptiveness. In the *BLACK MAGIC Trade Mark*,[123] Morton J stated 'the mark must be held to offend if it is likely to cause confusion or deception in the minds of persons to whom the mark is addressed, even if actual purchasers will not ultimately be deceived'.

[30.41] In relation to marks falsely suggesting a particular geographical origin, it is not the use of the place name itself which is objectionable. Whether the use of a place name is in fact deceptive will in part depend on the nature of the product and the likelihood of it being thought of as coming from the place suggested.[124] Other factors that have been considered relevant are that the mark is an invented term, which does not hold out any promise to the consumer that the products are expected to have specific characteristics, and that it is unlikely that the average consumer would be influenced in his purchasing

---

[114] *La Chemise Lacoste* (1974, unreported) No 38 Sp.

[115] *American Cyanamid's application to register STRESSTABS* ([1980] Supp OJ No 1367/11), decision affirmed on appeal to the High Court (unreported).

[116] *CHINA-THERM* [1980] FSR 21.

[117] *CONSARC* [1969] RPC 179.

[118] *SOFLENS* [1976] RPC 694.

[119] *WINE OH! LLC's Application* [2006] ETMR 95.

[120] *SAFEMIX* [1978] RPC 397.

[121] See also *VITASAFE* [1963] RPC 256.

[122] *GE Trade Mark* [1973] RPC 297.

[123] *BLACK MAGIC Trade Mark* (1940) 58 RPC 91.

[124] *MADGECOURT* [2000] ETMR 825.

decision by the use of the word alluding to a particular geographical origin.[125] The trade mark ROMAN HOLIDAY[126] was accepted for registration in respect of perfumes, on the basis that the fact that the mark would indicate a connection with the modern city of Rome to some persons did not mean that such persons would believe that the connection had anything to do with the origin of the goods. In the Australian case of *Re Bali Brassiere Co Inc's Application*,[127] Windeyer J commented as follows:

> There is no evidence that any one has thought that BALI BRAS are made in Bali. It seems to me most unlikely that members of the public who buy brassieres in Australia, would think so. Bali is not famed or known as a country where such goods are made. Balinese women are not notable for wearing brassieres.

[30.42] In a decision of the OHIM Board of Appeal, registration of a trade mark *DUQUE DE VILLENA* was refused registration in respect of wines because in Spain, *VILLENA* was a protected indication of origin, and the goods were not of such origin.[128]

[30.43] The *ADVOKAAT Trade Mark*[129] was refused registration in respect of an alcoholic beverage from Belgium because Advokaat of Dutch origin enjoyed such a reputation, and a substantial number of the purchasing public associated that alcoholic drink with Dutch origin. It was common practice under TMA 1963 to overcome a deceptiveness objection due to geographical origin by agreeing to a condition of registration that would read:

> It is a condition of registration that the mark shall be used only in relation to goods manufactured in …[130]

[30.44] Under the transitional provisions of TMA 1996,[131] these conditions ceased to have effect. Another way of overcoming a deceptiveness objection is to simply add a statement in the specification itself, ie '… all being goods of … origin' or '… all being goods emanating from …'.

An application should also be refused registration in respect of a protected designation of origin or geographical indication under Regulation 510/2006/EC governing agricultural products and foodstuffs.

[30.45] The list of possible deceptive characteristics contained in s 8(3)(b) of TMA 1996 is not exhaustive. It would presumably cover references in a trade mark to protection by way of other forms of intellectual property which cannot be justified, such as 'patent', 'copyright', 'design', etc. This was specifically provided for in r 12 of the Trade Marks Rules 1963.[132] Rule 15 of the Trade Marks Rules 1996[133] grants the Controller a

---

[125] *Lidl Stiftung & Co KG's Application* [2009] ETMR 2.
[126] *ROMAN HOLIDAY Trade Mark* [1964] RPC 129.
[127] *Re Bali Brassiere Co Inc's Application* (1968) 118 CLR 128.
[128] *DUQUE DE VILLENA Trade Mark*: R 1220/2000–2 (11 December 2002, unreported).
[129] *ADVOKAAT Trade Mark* [1978] RPC 252.
[130] See *TONINO* [1973] RPC 568.
[131] TMA 1996, Sch 3, para 2(4).
[132] SI 268/1963.
[133] SI 199/1996.

discretion to refuse to accept any application in which the word 'patent', 'patented', 'registered', 'copyright' or any other word or any symbol with a like signification appears. Marks may be refused registration that falsely suggest affiliation or sponsorship. An example of this can be seen in the Australian case of *Radio Corpn Pty Ltd v Disney*.[134] In this case, the name 'MICKEY MOUSE' was denied registration in respect of radio transceiving sets as it suggested in some way an association with Walt Disney. There may be an overlap with the provisions for refusal on absolute grounds and s 10 because a mark conflicting with an earlier right can deceive as to origin. Nonetheless, s 19 of TMA 1963 was often pleaded in opposition proceedings and this is also the position under s 8(3)(b) of TMA 1996. If it can be shown that the result of the use of the mark will be that a number of persons will be caused to wonder whether it might not be the case that the two products come from the same source, this is an example of deception.[135]

[30.46] The absence of the word 'likely' in s 8(3)(b) of TMA 1996, which appeared in s 19 of TMA 1963, might suggest that actual deception must be shown. This is unlikely to be interpreted in this way because a trade mark application can be based on intent to use and it is only when actual use commences that actual instances of deception will become apparent. Also, in many instances, an Examiner will not have any knowledge of whether or not there is actual usage.

[30.47] The Consumer Protection Act 2007 makes it an offence to engage in misleading or prohibited commercial practices. A wide range of conduct is included within the definition of a commercial practice, including courses of conduct or representations by a trader in relation to a promotion or supply of a product to a consumer. Any such conduct or representation can be made or engaged in before, during or after the transaction. Misleading practices include those likely to cause the average consumer to confuse a competitor's product with the trader's product or trade marks, where the practices are likely to lead to the consumer making a transactional decision which he or she would not otherwise make.[136] Such practices can be the subject of a court order prohibiting the practice, which can be sought by any person,[137] or an action for damages, including exemplary damages, by an aggrieved consumer.[138] The aggrieved consumer's action for damages is particularly far-reaching as it can be directed against any director, manager, secretary or other officer of the trader who authorised or consented to the practice. There is a presumption that directors and employees whose duties included making decisions that, to a significant extent, could have affected the management of the trader consented to the practice.[139] The Consumer Protection Act 2007 also includes many measures that do not deal directly with trade marks but which could have an effect on trade mark owners, such as a prohibition on misleading information, which includes information as

---

[134] *Radio Corpn Pty Ltd v Disney* (1937) 57 CLR 448.
[135] *JELLINEK'S Application* (1946) 63 RPC 59: see also *SMITH HAYDEN* (1946) 63 RPC 97.
[136] Consumer Protection Act 2007, s 44(1).
[137] Consumer Protection Act 2007, ss 67 and 71.
[138] Consumer Protection Act 2007, s 74(2).
[139] Consumer Protection Act 2007, s 71(5).

to the nature of the product or its geographical or commercial origin.[140] All provisions of the Consumer Protection Act 2007 came into effect on 1 May 2007. The old Merchandise Marks Acts and the Consumer Information Act 1978 were repealed. These provisions are in addition to labelling Directives which aim to prevent deception by purchasers as to the product characteristics.[141]

TRADE MARKS, THE USE OF WHICH IS PROHIBITED BY LAW

[30.48] Section 8(4)(a) of TMA 1996 provides that a trade mark shall not be registered if or to the extent that the use is prohibited in the State by any enactment or rule of law or by any provision of EU law. This is an optional provision contained in art 3(2)(a) of the Trade Mark Harmonisation Directive.[142] Examples of Irish legislation that prohibit use of certain trade marks are the Red Cross Act 1938, as amended by the Red Cross Act 1954, which disallows use of the heraldic emblem of the Red Cross on a white background formed by reversing the federal colours of Switzerland or the words 'Cross Dearg', 'Cross Na Geineibhe', 'Red Cross' or 'Geneva Cross'. In the National Lottery Act 1986, there is a prohibition on use in relation to a lottery game other than the National Lottery of the names 'Irish National Lottery' or 'National Lottery' or of their equivalents in the Irish language or names so closely resembling them 'as to be reasonably capable of leading to the belief that either of those names or either of those equivalents is being referred to'. Applications should only be refused under s 8(4)(a) on the basis of the mark viewed in isolation from earlier marks, ie whether the use of the mark is specifically prohibited by law rather than merely liable to be prevented, for example, by the law of passing off.[143]

[30.49] Under EU law, there are already a number of regulations governing what are considered to be protected names. The Community Trade Mark Regulation 207/2009/EC includes as an absolute ground for refusal:

> Trade marks for wines or for spirits which contain or consist of a geographical indication identifying wines or for spirits which contain or consist of a geographical indication identifying spirits with respect to such wines or spirits not having that origin.

[30.50] Both 'champagne'[144] and 'cognac' are protected names. The European Commission has also considered a large number of trade marks for which protection was

---

[140] Consumer Protection Act 2007, s 43.

[141] Council Directive 2000/13/EC ([2000] OJ L109/29); *YANNICK GEFFROY* [2001] ETMR 1: see also *Federation Nationale d'Agriculture Biologique des Regions de France (FNAB) v Council of the European Union* [2003] ETMR 100.

[142] Council Directive 2008/95/EC ([2008] OJ L 299/25), which repealed and replaced Directive 89/104/EEC ([1989] OJ L40/1).

[143] *Veolia Water Operations Ireland Ltd v Dublin City Council* [2007] ETMR 50.

[144] *Taittinger SA v Allbev Ltd* [1993] FSR 641.

sought in respect of geographical indications and designations of origin for agricultural products and foodstuffs.[145]

TRADE MARKS APPLIED FOR IN BAD FAITH

[30.51] Section 8(4)(b) of TMA 1996 contains a prohibition in respect of trade mark applications to the extent that they were applied for in bad faith. The words 'to the extent' suggest that the bad faith may only relate to a part of the application such as, for example, a specification which includes goods/services for which there is no *bona fide* intention to use the mark in accordance with s 37(2)[146] of TMA 1996. So-called 'ghost' marks,[147] registered simply to block a competitor or to secure a footing on the Register to protect an unregistrable mark, would be examples of trade marks applied for in bad faith. The rationale was stated by Smyth J in *Unilever plc v Controller*[148] as being 'if there is no real or genuine intention, there is the risk that the purposes of the Act could be defeated, as speculative applications could be made to block off the Register'. An honest but mistaken statement that the applicant intends to use the mark is not considered bad faith.[149]

[30.52] It is bad faith for an application to be made by an agent or representative of a trade mark proprietor.[150] This is also a basis for opposition under s 65 of TMA 1996, which may be more attractive for a proprietor, due to the fact that bad faith is an absolute ground to be taken into account by the Controller on examination. The question is how will the Controller be aware of any such agent/representative relationship without opposition? This can be done by way of observations to the Controller. A dilemma for the Controller is that he or she is obliged to refuse an application if he or she suspects that the application has been made in bad faith but, at the same time, must allow an applicant to present their own evidence in this regard. It is therefore unlikely that this particular aspect of bad faith will be raised at examination stage but will be left to opposition proceedings, except if the trade mark is also well-known under s 61 of TMA 1996.

[30.53] TMA 1963 required an applicant to make a claim as to proprietorship of the trade mark. In *Al Bassam Trade Mark*,[151] the Court of Appeal considered that all that was required at the time of application was that the claim was *bona fide*, ie an honest belief

---

145 Council Regulation 510/2006/EC ([2006] OJ L93/12), which repealed and replaced 2081/92/EEC.

146 Contrast with *OHIM – TRILLIUM* [2000] ETMR 1054; *Decon Laboratories v Fred Baker Scientific* [2001] ETMR 46; *POTTERY BARN* [2005] ETMR 74.

147 *Imperial Group Ltd v Philip Morris & Co Ltd* [1982] FSR 72.

148 *Unilever plc v Controller* [2006] IEHC 427.

149 *Application of Robert McBride Ltd* [2005] ETMR 85 applying the principle in *CHINAWHITE, Harrison v Teton Valley* [2004] 1 WLR 2577.

150 *R82 A/S v ATO Form GmbH* [2006] ETMR 81; see also *Shamrock Sea-Cal Ltd v Marigot* [2008] ETMR 25.

151 *Al Bassam Trade Mark* [1995] RPC 511.

that it had a good claim to be registered.[152] Whether or not there is a *bona fide* application is a question of whether the applicant was aware of proprietary rights of a third party. These rights could be other intellectual property rights such as copyright[153] or registered designs, a geographical indication[154] or an employer's rights against an application by an employee.[155]

[30.54] The mere fact that another party has a trade mark registration or has used their trade mark in other countries does not mean an application has been made in bad faith.[156] The proprietary right, if it exists from outside the State, must be as a consequence of a reputation which nevertheless exists within the State.[157] However, an earlier proprietary right through use is a separate ground of opposition. In *Gaines Animal Foods' Application,*[158] the use was not deemed to be sufficient to establish a reputation but, nevertheless, the conduct of the applicant in attempting to register a number of different marks used in the US illustrated bad faith. A further illustration is the *RAWHIDE Trade Mark*[159] where, again, reputation for the goods was not proven but bad faith arose because the applicant chose the trade mark in the hope of gaining some benefit from the publicity through television broadcasts of the opponent's film. Cross J drew the following distinction:

> It is one thing to say that a man who is using or proposes here and now to use a mark on his goods is entitled to be registered notwithstanding that his reason for choosing that mark is the hope of getting the benefit of publicity for which he has not paid, but it is quite another thing to say that a man can put himself in the position of reaping the advantage of any publicity which may subsequently attach to the name though he has no intention of making any substantial use of the mark unless and until it is clear that publicity will attach to it.

In *Pizza Caesar Ltd v Little Caesar Enterprises, Inc,*[160] the Controller determined that bad faith should not be regarded from a solely subjective aspect nor confined to an assessment of the motives of the applicant. Whether an applicant had acted in bad faith should not turn on the applicant's own perception of his actions and their likely consequences. However, generally, trade marks are registered on a territorial basis and that is why the only exception which exists is limited to well-known trade marks under art 6*bis* of the Paris Convention.[161] In *MONTEX*[162] O'Sullivan J accepted that the test of ownership in the mark under TMA 1963 is that the ownership vests in the party first

---

[152] *Senso Di Donna* [2001] ETMR 5.
[153] *Karo Step* [1977] RPC 255.
[154] *VELASCO BAQUEDANO* [2008] ETMR 21.
[155] *Casson's Trade Mark* (1910) 27 RPC 65.
[156] *Zockoll Group v Controller* [2007] ETMR 26.
[157] *C&A Modes* [1976] IR 198; however see *Chocoladefabriken Lindt v Franz Hauswirth GmbH* [2009] ETMR 56 at para **[30.55]**.
[158] *Gaines Animal Foods' Application* [1958] RPC 312.
[159] *RAWHIDE Trade Mark* [1962] RPC 133.
[160] *Pizza Caesar Ltd v Little Caesar Enterprises, Inc* [2004] ETMR 78.
[161] TMA 1996, s 61.
[162] *MONTEX* [2000] ETMR 658, [2002] ETMR 24.

using it in the jurisdiction. The applicant was the first user in the State and hence *prima facie* the owner. The issue of *bona fides* arose because the applicant had not explained the derivation of the trade mark. However, the decision can be criticised because even if the derivation had been with the knowledge of the opponent's mark, this arguably should not have amounted to bad faith in the absence of a relationship between the parties or a proprietary right in Ireland and held by the opponent. Thus in *Jaguar Cars Ltd v Controller*,[163] Clarke J held that, since the extent to which the JAGUAR trade mark was used in Ireland in relation to watches was limited, there were no proprietary rights in relation to such goods and there was no inappropriate behaviour by the applicant in seeking to register the JAGUAR trade mark in relation to such goods. In the *MONTEX* decision the issue of lack of *bona fides* was appealed to the Supreme Court but there was no consideration of the issue by the Supreme Court and the application was refused on the basis of s 19 of TMA 1963.

[30.55] In *Chocoladefabriken Lindt v Franz Hauswirth GmbH*,[164] the ECJ held that an applicant's intention at the relevant time is a subjective factor, which must be determined by reference to the objective circumstances of the particular case. Thus the intention to prevent a third party from marketing a product may be bad faith, particularly if it is apparent that the applicant applied without any intention to use.

If an opponent raises an issue that the applicant has applied to register the mark in bad faith, then the question arises as to the onus of proof. It appears that it may at least be incumbent on the applicant to explain the derivation of the trade mark in rebuttal of the bad faith claim.[165] In *Gromax Plasticulture v Dun & Low Nonwovens*, Lindsay J stated that the definition of bad faith:[166]

> includes dishonesty and, as I would hold, includes also some dealings which fall short of the standards of acceptable commercial behaviour observed by reasonable and experienced men in the particular area being examined.

It is not necessarily bad faith to adopt a trade mark that is similar to an earlier trade mark even with full knowledge of the earlier trade mark. This may be considered as no more than a normal and legitimate act of commercial competition provided there is no likelihood of confusion.[167] An applicant is not bound or constrained by the unfulfilled intentions of an opponent.[168]

INVALIDITY AND OPPOSITION ACTIONS ON ABSOLUTE GROUNDS

[30.56] Unlike the position under art 41 of the Community Trade Mark Regulation,[169] opposition to an Irish trade mark application can be based on the absolute grounds of

---

[163] *Jaguar Cars Ltd v Controller* [2006] ETMR 72.

[164] *Chocoladefabriken Lindt v Franz Hauswirth GmbH* [2009] ETMR 56.

[165] *KUNDRY SA's Application* [1998] ETMR 178.

[166] *Gromax Plasticulture v Dun & Low Nonwovens* [1999] RPC 367.

[167] *McDermott Laboratories Ltd* [2006] ETMR 17.

[168] *Veolia Water Operations Ireland Ltd v Dublin City Council* [2007] ETMR 50.

[169] Council Regulation 207/2009/EC, formerly Council Regulation 40/94/EC, art 42.

refusal in s 8 of TMA 1996. Also, when registered, an invalidity action is possible on absolute grounds.[170] There is also a recognition that a trade mark, which might have been invalid at the time of application, may have acquired distinctiveness post-registration. This implemented the optional provision in art 3(3) of the Harmonisation Directive[171] and allows post-registration use to be taken into account in relation to an invalidity action that claims lack of distinctiveness,[172] descriptiveness[173] or customary language in a trade mark.[174]

REGISTRATIONS PRIOR TO TMA 1996 (TRANSITIONAL PROVISIONS)

[30.57] Paragraph 13 of the transitional provisions in Sch 3 to TMA 1996 exercised the option available to States under art 3(4) of the Trade Mark Harmonisation Directive[175] and provides:

> The old law shall continue to apply as regards the validity of the registration of an existing registered mark; and no objection to the validity of such a registration may be taken on the grounds of failure to satisfy the requirements of this Act.

The reasoning for this provision, which differs from the position taken in the UK, was stated by the Minister in the Dáil Debates as simply being due to advice given by the Attorney-General concerning a possible constitutional challenge that the basis upon which personal property rights were being held was to be varied. This view was not shared by Deputy Michael McDowell who pointed out that:

> there is no constitutional law which states, when one has acquired a property right under the Trade Marks Act, that the right cannot be qualified, varied, reduced, affected or prejudiced if the State considers it has a good reason to do so. There is every good reason to introduce a single law of invalidity in respect of existing and future marks. They should all be decided by the same canons of validity.[176]

[30.58] The effect of the transitional provision is that the grounds for invalidity under TMA 1963 remain for trade marks registered under TMA 1963. This means that for pre-TMA 1996 registrations, the distinction between Part A and Part B of the Register is still important. Under s 21 of TMA 1963, registration of a trade mark in Part A of the Register is conclusive as to validity after the expiration of seven years from the date of registration unless the registration was obtained by fraud or offended against s 19 of TMA 1963. On the other hand, a Part B registration could always be declared invalid irrespective of the time it had been on the Register. Section 19 of TMA 1963 concerns

---

[170] TMA 1996, s 52(1).
[171] Council Directive 2008/95/EC ([2008] OJ L 299/25), which repealed and replaced Directive 89/104/EEC ([1989] OJ L40/1).
[172] TMA 1996, s 8(1)(b).
[173] TMA 1996, s 8(1)(c).
[174] TMA 1996, s 8(1)(d).
[175] Council Directive 2008/95/EC ([2008] OJ L 299/25), which repealed and replaced Directive 89/104/EEC ([1989] OJ L40/1).
[176] 462 Dáil Debates, Col 683.

marks that are likely to deceive or cause confusion[177] and such a mark, even on Part A of the Register, can be removed from the Register although it has been on it for over seven years. This arises even if the trade mark was validly registered but has subsequently become likely to deceive or cause confusion.[178]

[30.59] However, the further grounds of invalidity under TMA 1963 will remain indefinitely in the case of Part B registrations for pre-TMA 1996 registrations. This includes trade marks which, although invalidly registered at the time of application, have become distinctive through usage.[179] This contrasts with the proviso in s 52(1) of TMA 1996, which allows for acquired distinctiveness through use. Ironically, it was noticeable that in anticipation of TMA 1996, the Irish Patents Office had already relaxed examination criteria and many trade marks were approved in Part B of the Register even though, on a strict interpretation of TMA 1963, registration should have been refused. It was this very liberalisation of the registrability requirements under TMA 1996, which prompted the Irish Patents Office into a more pro-registration position but, as a consequence, the validity of a number of marks under the 1963 criteria would be questionable. This would include well-known surnames or geographical place names[180] allowed upon evidence of minimal use and also three-letter trade marks not forming a pronounceable word,[181] without sufficient evidence of distinctiveness through usage at the date of application. Three-letter trade marks forming a pronounceable word were allowed under TMA 1963.[182]

[30.60] A number of trade marks, which would be invalid under the 1963 requirements, are those which did not comply with the definition of a trade mark in s 2 of TMA 1963, namely:

> A mark used or proposed to be used in relation to goods for the purpose of indicating, or so as to indicate, a connection in the course of trade between the goods and some person having the right either as proprietor or as Registered User to use the mark, whether with or without any indication of the identity of that person ...

This definition, in conjunction with s 25 of TMA 1963, meant that the applicant for registration must be the actual or intended user of the mark or, at the time of application, there must have been in place a registered user identifying an actual or intended user. Without such a registered user, an application, for example by a holding company, would be invalid and could not be saved later by a subsequent user entry. Such a registration in Part B under TMA 1963 will continue to remain invalid. Even if there was a registered user entry, it does not necessarily save the position following the reasoning of the House of Lords in *Holly Hobbie*,[183] which refused registration on the grounds of trafficking in

---

[177] *MONTEX* [2000] ETMR 658.
[178] *Sterling Winthrop Group Ltd v Farbenfabriken Bayer AG* [1976] RPC 469.
[179] *TABASCO Trade Mark* [1998] ETMR 100.
[180] *DENT Trade Mark* [1979] FSR 205.
[181] *SFD Trade Mark* [1975] RPC 607.
[182] *SAF Trade Mark* [1982] ILRM 207; see also *ACEC Trade Mark* [1964] IR 20.
[183] *Holly Hobbie* [1984] FSR 199.

the trade mark.[184] This was a case of character merchandising where the owner intended to grant licences in such a way that the mark was being dealt with primarily as a commodity in its own right and there was no real trade connection between the owner of the mark and the goods to which the mark was to be applied.

SPECIALLY PROTECTED EMBLEMS

[30.61] In s 9 of TMA 1996, there is a prohibition on registration of a trade mark consisting of or containing any State emblem without consent from the Minister. The prohibition also extends to marks that are so nearly resembling an emblem, that they may be mistaken to be one. Various State emblems of Ireland have been notified under art 6*ter* of the Paris Convention, namely arms of Ireland, harp and shamrock symbols and escutcheons in various forms as used by the State.

[30.62] Article 7 of the Irish Constitution defines the Irish flag as the tricolour of green, white and orange. There is no general prohibition as to registration of trade marks consisting of or containing the Irish flag except to the extent that such is misleading or grossly offensive. To this extent, the protection afforded to the Irish flag is less than that given to the flags of other Paris Convention countries where registration is to be refused without authorisation from the authorities in that country 'unless it appears to the Controller that use of the flag in the manner proposed is permitted without such authorisation'.[185]

[30.63] The Controller also has a discretionary power to refuse to register a trade mark, which consists of or contains any badge, device or emblem of a public authority unless there is consent to such.[186] What is strange with s 9 of TMA 1996 is that it sits in isolation and, unlike the corresponding provision in the UK Act,[187] it is not listed as one of the absolute grounds of refusal and is not therefore a ground of invalidity under s 52.

---

[184] TMA 1963, s 36(6).
[185] TMA 1996, s 62(1).
[186] TMA 1996, s 9(3).
[187] Trade Marks Act 1994.

Chapter 31

Trade Marks Act 1996: Relative Grounds for Refusal of Registration

INTRODUCTION

[31.01] The relative grounds for refusal of registration of a trade mark are based on prior conflicting rights owned by proprietors of earlier trade marks or other earlier rights. The sections in the Trade Marks Act 1996 (TMA 1996) dealing with relative grounds for refusal are as follows:

> Section 10 – Statement of the basic prohibition.
> Section 11 – Definition of what is meant by an earlier trade mark.
> Section 12 – Exception to the prohibition based on honest concurrent use.
> Section 52(2) – Earlier trade mark or earlier right as a basis of invalidity of a registration.

Sections 10, 11 and 52(2) are based on art 4 of the Trade Mark Harmonisation Directive.[1] Section 12, dealing with honest concurrent use, is modelled on the corresponding provision in the Trade Marks Act 1963 (TMA 1963).[2] The relative grounds should be read in conjunction with s 61, which provides for prior rights based on trade marks which are well-known,[3] and s 65 where there is an agent/representative relationship with the trade mark proprietor.[4]

[31.02] There are numerous sources available to assist in the interpretation of the statutory provisions. In many cases, it is possible to look at decisions decided under TMA 1963 and its UK counterpart, the UK Trade Marks Act 1938, because prior trade marks, which formed a basis for opposition and invalidity under TMA 1963, included not just identical marks for identical goods but also identical or similar marks for similar goods. In addition, TMA 1996 includes prior rights, which can be raised even where there is dissimilarity of goods/services. Decisions of OHIM and the ECJ on the interpretation of the corresponding provision in art 8 of the Community Trade Mark Regulation[5] are important. Since the main thrust of the relative grounds are based on

---

[1] Council Directive 2008/95/EC ([2008] OJ L 299/25), which repealed and replaced Directive 89/104/EEC ([1989] OJ L40/1).
[2] TMA 1963, s 20(2).
[3] Paris Convention for the Protection of Industrial Property (1893) (Paris Convention), art 6bis.
[4] Paris Convention, art 6*septies*.
[5] Council Regulation 207/2009/EC ([2009] OJ L78/1), which repealed and replaced Council Regulation 40/94/EC ([1994] OJ L11/1).

mandatory provisions in the Trade Mark Harmonisation Directive,[6] decisions by courts in other EU countries are likely to be drawn upon, particularly in the Benelux upon whose law prior to the Directive certain of these provisions have been based. There will also need to be consistency in decisions based on the infringement provisions in s 14 of TMA 1996 because the scope of protection afforded by a registration corresponds with the relative grounds of refusal. This differs from TMA 1963 where the scope of protection afforded to a registration was limited to the exact goods of registration but refusal extended to a question of similarity of goods.

[31.03] Conflicts with earlier trade marks or rights can arise at three different stages in the life of a trade mark. Firstly, the Controller carries out a search upon examination of a trade mark application and can raise a conflicting mark as a basis for refusing registration. This *ex officio* search and citation procedure is not a mandatory requirement under EU law and many EU countries, including Germany, France, Benelux and Italy do not carry out such official action. Also, OHIM, under the Community Regulation, does not cite prior conflicting marks on either the Community trade mark (CTM) or national registers and leaves it to the owner of a prior trade mark to institute opposition proceedings.

[31.04] Secondly, an application for registration can be opposed on relative grounds following publication in the Patents Office Journal.[7] This opposition must be filed within three months of publication in the Patents Office Journal with no extension of time permissible.[8]

[31.05] Thirdly, even when registered, the relative grounds are a basis for securing cancellation or partial cancellation of a registration due to invalidity.[9] In *Special Effects Ltd v L'Oreal SA*,[10] the Court of Appeal held that unless there was an abuse of process, it is possible for a defendant to raise, in defence or counterclaim to a declaration of invalidity, matters which were raised in opposition proceedings and which were found against it.

The prior trade marks or rights that can form the basis for a refusal of an application or invalidity of a registration on relative grounds are as follows.

---

6   Council Directive 2008/95/EC ([2008] OJ L 299/25), which repealed and replaced Directive 89/104/EEC ([1989] OJ L40/1).

7   TMA 1996, s 43.

8   Trade Marks Rules 1996 (SI 199/1996), r 18(1); *NOLAN'S Application* [2000] ETMR 208; the three month period includes the date of publication, ie the opposition period expires the day before the three month anniversary of publication. Thus, an opposition filed on the three-month anniversary date is out of time.

9   TMA 1996, s 52(2).

10   *Special Effects Ltd v L'Oreal SA* [2007] ETMR 51.

EARLIER TRADE MARK

[31.06] An earlier trade mark can be a trade mark registered or pending[11] on the Irish Register, the CTM Register or the International Register. A trade mark on the International Register, by virtue of s 58 of TMA 1996, means a trade mark that has been registered with the International Bureau of the World Intellectual Property Organisation (WIPO) under the Protocol Relating to the Madrid Agreement Concerning the International Registration of Marks 1989 (Madrid Protocol), and protection for which has been extended to the State. Whether a trade mark is to be deemed earlier, is determined by the filing date or any priority date if claimed under the Paris Convention.[12]

[31.07] Also included in the list of earlier trade marks is a later filed CTM but with a valid seniority claim bearing an earlier date. Under arts 34 and 35 of the CTM Regulation,[13] the proprietor of an Irish registered trade mark who applies for and secures registration for an identical trade mark under Council Regulation 207/2009/EC may surrender or allow the Irish registration to lapse but retain seniority for such. This means that the trade mark proprietor is deemed to continue to have the same rights as if the earlier Irish registration had been maintained.[14]

[31.08] Under s 11(1)(c) of TMA 1996, reference to an earlier mark also includes a mark that is not registered but which at the priority date of the mark in question, was entitled to protection under the Paris Convention as a well-known trade mark.[15] A question that may arise is whether or not the Irish owner of an unregistered mark can rely on this provision because s 61 refers to the mark of a national of a 'Convention country' which, in s 60, excludes the State itself. Ironically, this means that an Irish trade mark may have to rely on s 10(4)(a) with the possible heavier evidential burden of having to show rights equivalent to sustain an action for passing off. The ECJ has ruled that the earlier trade mark must be well-known throughout the territory of the Member State of registration or in a substantial part of it.[16]

[31.09] It is still necessary to take into account earlier trade marks on the pertinent Register, which may have lapsed. This is because of s 11(3) of TMA 1996 and includes, as an earlier trade mark, a registration which has expired within the previous 12 months unless the Controller is satisfied that there was no *bona fide* use of the trade mark during the two years immediately preceding the expiry. This provision does not wholly reflect the optional provision in art 4(4)(f) of the Trade Mark Harmonisation Directive,[17] which

---

11 TMA 1996, s 11(2).
12 TMA 1996, s 40.
13 Council Regulation 207/2009/EC.
14 TMA 1996, s 11(1)(b).
15 TMA 1996, s 61.
16 *Nieto Nuno v Monlleo Franquet* [2008] ETMR 12.
17 Council Directive 2008/95/EC ([2008] OJ L 299/25), which repealed and replaced Directive 89/104/EEC ([1989] OJ L40/1).

limits the relevance of such a mark as an earlier right to a situation where the expiry was only because of non-renewal and can be avoided if 'the proprietor of the earlier trade mark gave his agreement for the registration of the later mark or did not use his trade mark'.

[31.10] If there is an earlier trade mark as defined, then the issue is one of comparison with the conflicting mark.

IDENTICAL MARKS FOR IDENTICAL GOODS OR SERVICES

[31.11] Whether or not two marks are identical is not as straightforward an issue as might be perceived. This is because a mark rarely appears in isolation. In *AAH Pharmaceuticals Ltd v Vantagemax*,[18] Pumfrey J considered the question of identity to be 'a question for the eye of the Judge' and in coming to a conclusion of identity, discounted use of descriptive words 'rewards' and 'points'. The ECJ in *LTJ Diffusion SA v Sadas Vertbaudet SA*[19] ruled that the concept of identity must be interpreted strictly and that the elements compared should be the same in all respects:

> There is therefore identity between the sign and the trade mark where the former reproduces without any modification or addition, all the elements constituting the latter. However, the perception of identity between the sign and the trade mark must be assessed globally with respect to an average consumer who is deemed to be reasonably well informed, reasonably observant and circumspect. The sign produces an overall impression on such a consumer. That consumer only rarely has the chance to make a direct comparison between signs and trade marks and must place his trust in the imperfect picture of them that he has kept in his mind. Moreover, his level of attention is likely to vary according to the category of goods or services in question (see, to that effect, case C-342/97 *Lloyd Schuhfabrik Meyer* [1999] ECR I-3819, paragraph 26). Since the perception of identity between the sign and the trade mark is not the result of a direct comparison of all the characteristics of the elements compared, insignificant differences between the sign and the trade mark may go unnoticed by an average consumer.

 It is the advantage of not having to show a likelihood of confusion, which is attractive to the owner of an earlier trade mark availing of this section.

SIMILAR OR IDENTICAL TRADE MARKS FOR SIMILAR OR IDENTICAL GOODS/SERVICES[20]

[31.12] Section 10(2) of TMA 1996 covers the following:

(a) where the respective marks are identical and the goods or services are similar;

(b) where the respective marks are similar and the goods or services are identical;

(c) where the respective marks are similar and the goods or services are similar.

---

18 *AAH Pharmaceuticals Ltd v Vantagemax* [2003] ETMR 18.
19 *LTJ Diffusion SA v Sadas Vertbaudet SA* [2003] ETMR 83.
20 See para **[32.30]** et seq.

In all cases, there is a requirement that there exists a likelihood of confusion, which includes the likelihood of association.

[31.13] It is the concept of similarity that is the key factor and in TMA 1996, as under TMA 1963, there is no legislative statement as to what is meant by this term. The wording is taken from art 4(2) of the Harmonisation Directive[21] and some guidance can be drawn from a recital in the Directive, which states that the likelihood of confusion depends on a number of elements and in particular:

  (a) the recognition of the trade mark on the market;

  (b) the association which can be made with the used or registered sign; and

  (c) the degree of similarity between the respective marks and the goods/services.

[31.14] Assistance can be drawn from decisions of the Irish and English courts in determining the issue under s 20 of TMA 1963 and its UK equivalent.[22] Section 20 prohibited registration of an identical trade mark or a mark so nearly resembling an existing trade mark as to be likely to deceive or cause confusion for the same goods or goods of the same description.[23]

In *Maynards Confectionery v Nestle*,[24] the Controller stated the test to be applied in the following manner:

> imagine a typical purchasing scenario involving the average person who already knows the product sold under the earlier trade mark and ask yourself whether it is likely that he will select and purchase a product bearing the mark put forward for registration in the mistaken belief that it is the product he knows by the earlier mark (direct confusion) or that it is related to that product (indirect confusion by association)

SIMILARITY OF THE RESPECTIVE MARKS

[31.15] The words 'nearly resembles' in TMA 1963 and 'similar' in TMA 1996 are not to be interpreted very differently. The Irish Supreme Court in *Coca-Cola v F Cade & Sons Ltd*[25] applied the tests expounded by Parker J in *PIANOTIST*[26] and stated:

> You must take the two words. You must judge of them, both by their look and by their sound. You must consider the goods to which they are to be applied. You must consider the nature and kind of customer who would be likely to buy the goods. In fact, you must consider all the surrounding circumstances; and you must further consider what is likely to happen if each of those trade marks is used in a normal way as a trade mark for the goods of the respective owners of the marks. If, considering all those circumstances, you come to the conclusion that there will be a confusion – that is to say, not necessarily that one man will be injured and the other will gain illicit benefit, but there will be a confusion in the

---

21 Council Directive 2008/95/EC ([2008] OJ L 299/25), which repealed and replaced Directive 89/104/EEC ([1989] OJ L40/1).

22 UK Trade Marks Act 1938, s 12(1).

23 *Seixo v Provezende* (1865) 1 Ch App 192.

24 *Maynards Confectionery v Nestle* [2007] ETMR 40.

25 *Coca-Cola v F Cade & Sons Ltd* [1957] IR 196.

26 *PIANOTIST* (1906) 23 RPC 774.

minds of the public which will lead to confusion in the goods – then you may refuse the registration, or rather you must refuse the registration in that case.

[31.16] The need to consider all the surrounding circumstances is repeated by the ECJ in *Sabel BV v Puma AG*[27] emphasising that the likelihood of confusion must be appreciated globally taking into account all factors relevant to the circumstances of the case. This global appreciation includes an assessment of the respective marks from a visual, aural and conceptual perspective bearing in mind their distinctive and dominant components. The ECJ went on to caution that average consumers normally perceive a mark as a whole and do not proceed to analyse the various details.

[31.17] In analysing the visual, aural or conceptual similarities between respective marks, it is important to bear in mind that such an analysis cannot be taken in isolation and without consideration of the interplay due to the identity or closeness of similarity between the respective goods/services. In *CANON v METRO-GOLDWYN-MAYER*[28] the ECJ emphasised this interdependence:

> A global assessment of the likelihood of confusion implies some interdependence between the relevant factors, and in particular a similarity between the trade marks and between the goods or services. Accordingly, a lesser degree of similarity between the goods or services may be offset by a greater degree of similarity between the marks, and vice versa.

CONCEPTUAL SIMILARITY

[31.18] It has been long established that the idea or image conveyed by the respective marks is a primary consideration. As stated in *Kerly's Law of Trade Marks,*[29] 'two marks, when placed side by side, may exhibit many and various differences, yet the main idea left on the mind by both may be the same'. In *Broadhead's Application,*[30] the trade mark ALKA-VESCENT was refused in the face of the trade mark ALKA-SELTZER given that the suffix VESCENT suggested effervescence and so conveyed the same underlying idea as the ALKA-SELTZER fizzy alkaline tablet. In *Harry Reynolds v Laffeaty's LD,*[31] the suffix MATIC was common but similarity was found to exist between the trade mark AQUAMATIC and WATERMATIC in respect of water pistols as both brought the same idea to mind.

In *MERRY MAYERS-HEAD Trade Mark Application*, the trade mark COMFORT AND JOY was considered to be more than a mere collocation of the two words COMFORT and JOY and sufficiently known as a phrase in its own right so as to be distinguishable from the word JOY.[32]

Trade marks can, however, be viewed as similar even if they convey two different meanings. In *Beecham Group Ltd v Goodalls of Ireland,*[33] Kenny J held that TANG was

---

[27] *Sabel BV v Puma AG* [1998] ETMR 1.
[28] *CANON v METRO-GOLDWYN-MAYER* [1999] ETMR 1.
[29] *Kerly's Law of Trade Marks* (14th edn, 2005), para 17-028.
[30] *Broadhead's Application* (1950) 67 RPC 209.
[31] *Harry Reynolds v Laffeaty's LD* [1958] RPC 387.
[32] *MERRY MAYERS-HEAD Trade Mark Application* [1997] ETMR 577.
[33] *Beecham Group Ltd v Goodalls of Ireland* (1977, unreported), HC.

likely to deceive or cause confusion with the trade mark TANGO, both being used in respect of non-alcoholic beverages. Even though marks are conceptually similar, the fact that they are neither visually nor phonetically similar may be sufficient to differentiate them.[34] Whether or not a conceptual similarity alone is unlikely to lead to confusion is largely dependent on whether the earlier mark has a particularly distinctive character, either *per se* or because of the reputation it enjoys with the public.[35] In *Loewe SA's Application*[36] the common feature was the single letter 'L', lacking distinctiveness *per se*, and therefore the visual and stylistic manner in which each sign was presented became more significant and, despite the common element, also conveyed a different conceptual impression. The ECJ has also held that:

> where the meaning of at least one of the two signs at issue is clear and specific so that it can be grasped immediately by the relevant public, the conceptual differences observed between those signs may counteract the visual and phonetic similarities between them.[37]

In *Cofresco Frischalteproduckte GmbH & Co KG v Controller*,[38] Finlay Geoghegan J placed significant emphasis on the conceptual dissimilarity between the word 'TOPPITS' and 'TUB-ITS' and was able to distinguish a decision in the Benelux on the basis of linguistic differences.

IMPROPER RECOLLECTION

[31.19] In *Sandow Ltd's Application*,[39] Sarjant J cautioned against over-reliance on a detailed examination of the respective trade marks side by side as follows:

> The question is not whether if a person is looking at two trade marks side by side there would be a possibility of confusion; the question is whether the person who sees the proposed trade mark in the absence of the other trade mark, and in view only of his general recollection of what the nature of the other trade mark was, would be liable to be deceived and to think that the trade mark before him is the same as the other, of which he has a general recollection.

[31.20] It is the first impression that is the important factor. The customers, whose imperfect recollection is to be considered, are persons of ordinary intelligence and memory who are not to be credited with any high perception or habitual caution but, on the other hand, stupidity or exceptional carelessness may be disregarded.[40]

[31.21] The average consumer normally perceives a mark as a whole and does not proceed to analyse its various details since he only rarely has the chance to make a direct

---

[34] *DINKOIDS* [1999] ETMR 882.

[35] *Sabel BV v Puma AG* [1998] ETMR 1.

[36] *Loewe SA's Application* [2000] ETMR 40.

[37] *Ruiz-Picasso v OHIM* [2006] ETMR 29 'PICARO/PICASSO', deriving the principle from *Phillips-Van Heusen Corp v OHIM* [2004] ETMR 60 'PASH/BASS' and subsequently endorsed in *Mülhens GmbH & Co KG v OHIM* [2006] ETMR 57 'ZIRH/SIR'.

[38] *Cofresco Frischalteproduckte GmbH & Co KG v Controller* [2007] ETMR 63.

[39] *Sandow Ltd's Application* (1914) 31 RPC 196.

[40] *Australian Woollen Mills v FS Walton* (1937) 58 CLR 641.

comparison between the different marks but must place his trust on the imperfect picture of them that he has kept in his mind.[41]

TRADE MARKS AS A WHOLE/COMMON ELEMENTS

[31.22] Regard should be had to the trade mark as a whole and the trade mark should not be divided into segments. In *Bailey's Application*,[42] Farwell J refused registration of ERECTIKO in the face of a prior mark ERECTOR, both for toys, and stated:

> I do not think it is right to take a part of the word and compare it with a part of the other word; one word must be considered as a whole and compared with the other word as a whole ... I think it is a dangerous method to adopt to divide the word up and seek to distinguish a portion of it from a portion of the other word.

In the case of a composite trade mark comprising both graphic and word elements, the word elements are normally, but cannot systematically be, regarded as dominant.[43]

[31.23] Where an element, which is common to marks under comparison, is descriptive or in common use,[44] generally or in the trade, its presence must to some extent be discounted in deciding on confusing similarity. It is common practice to carry out a trade investigation and a search of other marks on the Register[45] to determine the existing state of the Register concerning marks with the same common element. The Supreme Court found that the trade mark PHILCO[46] was not likely to deceive or cause confusion because of prior trade marks for the same description of goods consisting of the same prefix PHIL, and Kennedy CJ cautioned against the extent to which a registration of a mark with a common element can be used to prevent others from adopting marks also including such a common element.[47] Similarly, the Supreme Court found that the trade mark CADA COLA was not confusingly similar with COCA COLA, the common feature being the descriptive word COLA.[48]

[31.24] In *Crecon Spiel-und Hobbyartikel GmbH v Ohio Art Co*,[49] the OHIM Board of Appeal upheld confusing similarity between the trade marks BETTY and BETTY LA

---

[41] *Lloyd Schuhfabrik Meyer & Co v Klijsen Handel BV* [1999] ETMR 690.

[42] *Bailey's Application* (1935) 52 RPC 136.

[43] *L & D SA v OHIM* [2008] ETMR 62.

[44] *Real Media Inc's Application* [2002] ETMR 59.

[45] In the case of Ireland, the relevant registers are the Irish Patents Office Register and the OHIM Register.

[46] *Philadelphia Storage Battery Co v Philips* [1935] IR 575; see also *Mediline AG's Application* [1970] IR 169.

[47] See also *Madaus AG v OHIM* [2006] ETMR 76 'ECHINAID/ECHINACIN' and *CureVac GmbH v OHIM* [2010] ETMR 11 'RNAIFECT/RNACTIVE'.

[48] *Coca-Cola v F Cade & Sons Ltd* [1957] IR 196; see also *Coca-Cola Co (Canada) Ltd v Pepsi-Cola* (1942) 59 RPC 127.

[49] *Crecon Spiel-und Hobbyartikel GmbH v Ohio Art Co* Dec No 44/2002-1 (16 December 2002, unreported); see also *ODC Enterprises Ltd v Tommy Hilfiger* [2006] ETMR 78; see also *Harman International v OHIM* [2009] ETMR 38.

MALICE in respect of dolls, considering that the consumer will tend to remember the first or the most simple element in a trade mark composed of several words.

In *Medion AG v Thomson Multimedia*,[50] the ECJ ruled that a likelihood of confusion can arise in circumstances of adding a company name to a registered trade mark since such a registered trade mark still has an independent distinctive role in the combination.

Importance of First Syllable/Prefix

[31.25] In *London Lubricants*,[51] Sarjant LJ observed the tendency of persons using the English language to slur the termination of words, which had the inevitable effect that the beginning of words is accentuated in comparison. Consequently, the first syllable of a word is, as a general rule, the most important for the purpose of assessing similarity.[52] In *Unilever plc v Controller*,[53] Smyth J reiterated the importance of the first word or prefix as the predominant sound and the visual impact of a trade mark. However, if the latter part of a word is more unusual and distinctive, then emphasis is likely to be placed on that part.[54] The visual consideration of a monosyllabic trade mark may require that greater significance be attached to the first letter of the mark.[55]

Visual and aural comparison necessary

[31.26] The respective trade marks must be judged by both their look and sound.[56] Trade marks can be similar phonetically although visually very different. This is a recognition that in many cases, products are bought over the telephone.[57] It is possible that mere aural similarity may create a likelihood of confusion[58] but this must be treated with caution.[59] Conceptual differences counteract limited visual and aural similarity.[60] The use of a figurative element does not normally play a significant role in distinguishing respective trade marks since a consumer may often refer to a mark orally.[61] However, in certain sectors, such as clothing, customers may rely more on figurative elements[62] and there may be instances in which a figurative element may be considered dominant in

---

50   *Medion AG v Thomson Multimedia* [2006] ETMR 13.
51   *London Lubricants* (1925) 42 RPC 264.
52   *ISENBECK and BECK* [1999] ETMR 225; see also *Jose Alejandro SL v OHIM* [2004] ETMR 15 'BUD/BUDMEN' and *Allergan Inc v Ocean Healthcare Ltd* [2008] ETMR 72.
53   *Unilever plc v Controller* [2006] IEHC 427.
54   *Parker-Knoll Ltd v Knoll International* [1962] RPC 265.
55   *FIF Trade Mark* [1979] RPC 355; contrast with *Funk* [2000] ETMR 685.
56   *SODEXHO/SODECO* [1999] ETMR 402.
57   *Morcream Products Ltd v Heatherfresh (Foods) Ltd* [1972] RPC 799.
58   *Lloyd Schuhfabrik Meyer & Co v Klijsen Handel BV* [1999] ETMR 690.
59   *Muhlens v OHIM* [2006] ETMR 57.
60   *Philips Van Heusen Corpn v OHIM* Case T-292/01 [2004] ETMR 60; *BEAUTY SHOP Application* [1999] ETMR 20; *Muhlens GmbH v OHIM* [2004] ETMR 101.
61   *HUMIL SA's Application* [1999] ETMR 26; *Miles Handelsgesellschaft International* [2006] ETMR 5.
62   *MARC BROWN's Application* [2002] ETMR 60.

relation to written elements.[63] Conversely, figurative elements in a complex mark have been considered in the context of jeans labels to be decorative, non-dominant features, which allow the word elements to have dominance.[64] There is an argument that with modern shopping, where goods are for the most part picked up in circumstances where the marks will be clearly visible, the question of sound is perhaps becoming of diminishing importance.[65] There are also circumstances where, despite phonetic similarity, the trade marks will not be confused because of the nature of the goods. In *Lancer*,[66] it was held that there was no risk of confusion between LANCER and LANCIA for cars since a car is unlikely to be purchased over the telephone and the matter will usually be considered with some care, assisted by an abundance of literature. In *Oro-Produkte Marketing GmbH v Elida Lever Ireland Ltd*,[67] the Controller, in comparing the trade mark ORO (stylised) and OMO, concluded:

> the aural resemblance between the respective marks in this case is not such as to outweigh the clear visual differences between them. There is no general prohibition on the registration of marks that sound like other registered marks; it is only where the use or registration of such a similar sounding mark would be likely to lead to confusion in the minds of the relevant public that registration is prohibited.

It is important not to carry out a fragmented analysis, syllable by syllable. The comparison should be by pronunciation of the word as a whole[68] as well as having regard to the goods.[69]

[31.27] In *Pinewood Laboratories Ltd v Novartis*,[70] the Controller stressed the importance of avoiding a bias when assessing the similarity between invented words compared to the assessment of similarity between common words. However, the rationale used by the Controller in avoiding this bias can be questioned because if two words being compared have very different conceptual meanings, then this by itself can outweigh any visual similarity.

[31.28] Another factor to be considered is a comparison of the respective marks as they would be seen in actual usage when fairly and honestly used.[71] It is also possible for a word mark to be viewed as similar to a device mark. In *Dewhurst's Application*,[72] the words THE GOLDEN FAN BRAND were refused registration in the face of a prior mark of a fan which was coloured gold in usage.

---

63   *Shaker Di Laudato & C SA v OHIM* [2006] ETMR 51; see also *Koipe Corporacion v OHIM* [2008] ETMR 8.

64   *Claudia Oberhauser v OHIM* ('MISS FIFTIES') [2003] ETMR 58.

65   *Mars GB Ltd v Cadbury Ltd* [1987] RPC 387 at 395.

66   *Lancer* [1987] RPC 303; see also *Claude Ruiz-Picasso v OHIM* [2006] ETMR 29.

67   *Oro-Produkte Marketing GmbH v Elida Lever Ireland Ltd* (15 September 2003, unreported).

68   *MYSTERY DRINKS* [2004] ETMR 18.

69   *Arnotts plc (NEMANN v NEW MAN)* [2004] ETMR 45.

70   *Pinewood Laboratories Ltd v Novartis* [2010] ETMR 36.

71   *Lyle & Kinahan's Application* (1907) 24 RPC 37 and 249.

72   *Dewhurst's Application* [1896] 2 Ch 137; see also *Baldwin & Walker v Prescott* ([1941] Supp OJ No 384/76).

FAMILY OF MARKS DOCTRINE

[31.29] It is reasonably common for traders to adopt and register a series of trade marks with a common element such as, for example, the same prefix but a suffix which denotes a particular product in the range of products for which the prefix is the source indicator. In *SEMIGRES Trade Mark*,[73] the opponent had a number of SEM prefixed marks and it was accepted that evidence showed that SEM used as a prefix in relation to flooring tiles, indicated their products. In *FRIGIKING*,[74] Whitford J commented on the decision in *Ravenhead Brick v Ruabon Brick & Terra Cotta*:[75]

> It can, I think, be said upon the basis of the judgment in the *Ravenhead Brick* case that it is not necessary to success in an objection of this character that the objector should be able to establish the use of a series of marks if he has in fact used some mark which is highly distinctive or some mark which has some highly distinctive part, but only used one such mark, for, if somebody comes along and takes that highly distinctive mark and adds something to it or takes a highly distinctive mark or part of the mark and makes an addition or a substitution, then it may still be possible that people will be confused and will think that the new mark indicates the same source of origin – the same sort of connection – as the old mark indicated. This sort of approach does necessarily involve some enquiry as to the inherent distinctiveness of the part which is common to both marks under consideration.

The emphasis in these instances is the distinctiveness of the common element in its own right. In *FRIGIKING,* the earlier mark was THERMOKING and the basis of the complaint was the common element, being KING, which was held not to be highly distinctive, and hence, to succeed, the opponent would have had to show a reputation in a series of KING suffixed marks. However, in SEMIGRES, it was considered that the common element SEM was capable of standing on its own as a trade mark. In *TURBOGAZ*,[76] an application to register the mark in respect of blow torches was opposed by the proprietor of an earlier TURBOTORCH registration. It was claimed that since the applicant had a series of GAZ suffixed trade marks, it indicated the source of origin and was simply one more of a series of marks. It was held that since *GAZ* was the French for the word gas, it was not highly distinctive and did not sufficiently detract from the prefix TURBO so as to make the whole mark distinguishable from TURBOTORCH.

[31.30] There have been a number of cases in Australia where the courts have allowed an opponent to call on a combination of elements of different marks which they held. Opposition was upheld against FIBROBESTOS on the basis of trade marks FIBROLITE and DURBABESTOS.[77] In a similar manner, CAT-TRAX was refused on the basis of the opponent's use of CAT and TRAXCAVATOR.[78] The basis of these decisions is that a

---

[73] *SEMIGRES Trade Mark* [1979] RPC 330.

[74] *FRIGIKING* [1973] RPC 739.

[75] *Ravenhead Brick v Ruabon Brick & Terra Cotta* (1937) 54 RPC 341.

[76] *TURBOGAZ* [1978] RPC 206.

[77] *James Hardie & Co Ltd v Asbestos Products Ltd* (1937) 7 AOJP 767.

[78] *Freestone v Caterpillar Tractor* (1985) AIPC 90–237.

compound of earlier marks could 'bridge over' the distinction between the earlier marks themselves and create confusion. Stretching the principle even further is the UK case of *Taylor Drug Co Ltd's Application,*[79] where an application to register the word GERMOCEA was refused on the grounds of the existence of two registered marks GERMOLINE and HOMOCEA, held by different proprietors on the grounds that the new word bridged over the distinction between the two registered marks and might create confusion between the goods offered for sale under each of the marks. This has not yet been followed in Ireland.

[31.31] The Cancellation Division of OHIM, in *VEIGA'S Application,*[80] recognised the family of marks doctrine and defined it as:

> a plurality of marks having a common distinctive feature like a surname which makes the consumer public associate not only the individual marks, but the family 'surname' and so the whole family of marks with the trade mark owner.

It is incumbent upon the opponent to submit evidence of use or, even more importantly, of the relevant public's perception or recognition of the common element in its trade marks.[81] In *Il Ponte Finanziaria SpA v OHIM,*[82] the ECJ recognised the concept of a family of similar trade marks but only if actual use can be established of a significant number of marks being perceived by the average consumer as forming a series. In *Easybroker International Ltd v EasyGroup Intellectual Property Licensing Ltd,*[83] the UK Intellectual Property Office rejected an opposition based on a family of marks prefixed with the word 'EASY' holding that a company does not necessarily have universal claim on an element which is common to a number of trade marks that they hold. However, unlike reputation, the assessment of inherent distinctive character does not have to be proven as a matter of fact.[84]

SIMILARITY OF GOODS OR SERVICES

[31.32] The division of goods and services into different classes is primarily an administrative exercise. The fact that goods or services might fall into different classes does not of itself mean that they are dissimilar.[85] The word 'similar' used in the context of goods or services is something to which the Irish courts and the Patents Office have already become attuned by virtue of s 20(1) of TMA 1963, and the determination whether or not respective goods were 'of the same description'. The test followed by the

---

[79]   *Taylor Drug Co Ltd's Application* (1923) 40 RPC 193.

[80]   *VEIGA'S Application* [2000] ETMR 939.

[81]   *LIFESOURCE* [2001] ETMR 106.

[82]   *Il Ponte Finanziaria SpA v OHIM* [2008] ETMR 13.

[83]   *Easybroker International Ltd v EasyGroup Intellectual Property Licensing Ltd* (20 June 2003, unreported); see also *Innodis Plc's Application; Opposition of Financière Batteur Plc, Cour d'appel de Paris ALGO SLIM* [2004] ETMR 36 and Decision of the Controller of 12 July, 2007 concerning Application No. 226996 *EASYMOVES Device* (unreported).

[84]   *Societe Provencale d'Achat et de Gestion (SPAG) SA v OHIM* [2005] ETMR 116.

[85]   *Idom Consulting Ltd* [2006] ETMR 32; see also *El Corte Ingles SA v OHIM* [2007] ETMR 81.

Irish courts has been that propounded in *Jellinek's Application*,[86] namely a comparison of:

(a)   the nature and composition of the goods;

(b)   the respective uses of the articles; and

(c)   the trade channels through which the commodities are bought and sold respectively.

It is a question of fact in each case and it is not necessary for all three elements to be satisfied.

[31.33] The UK *Jellinek* decision was reached long before the introduction of service mark registration in the UK, but the UK Intellectual Property Office adopted the principles in respect of a comparison of services as follows:

(a)   the nature of the services;

(b)   the purpose of the services;

(c)   the users of the services; and

(d)   whether the two services could be provided in the course of normal business relations.

If any two or more of these were the same, then this was regarded as an indication that the services were of the same description.

The factors to be considered in assessing similarity of goods and services were held by the ECJ in *CANON v METRO-GOLDWYN-MAYER*[87] to include their nature, intended purpose[88] and method of use and whether they are in competition with each other or are complementary. Goods are complementary if one is indispensable or important for the use of the other so that consumers may think that the same undertaking is responsible for the production of both goods.[89] The words 'in particular' used in a specification are indicative of an example and not of a limitation.[90]

[31.34] These are only guidelines and there is no single conclusive test for deciding whether or not goods are similar. Ultimately, the matter is one of judgment and degree. This was the view expressed by Jacob J[91] in allowing registration for different fungicides, one for the pharmaceutical trade and the other for agricultural purposes. The nature of the goods was the same but the uses and trade channels were different. It is an open question whether or not this decision would be the same under the UK Trade Marks Act 1994 corresponding to the Irish TMA 1996. It could be argued that similarity should be a lesser test than a determination of whether or not goods are of the same description. Two products could be similar but the same description would not be

---

86   *Jellinek's Application* (1946) 63 RPC 59; see also *DAIQUIRI RUM* [1969] RPC 600.

87   *CANON v METRO-GOLDWYN-MAYER* [1999] ETMR 1.

88   Not 'end users', which was an incorrect translation in the original English text of the decision.

89   *Sergio Rossi v OHIM ('SISSI ROSSI')* Case T-169/03 [2005] ECR II-685.

90   *SCIL Proteins GmbH v OHIM* [2009] ETMR 30.

91   *INVICTA* [1992] RPC 541; see also *CASA GIRELLI SPA's Application* [2002] ETMR 66 in holding dissimilarity between coffee and alcoholic drinks.

applied to them.[92] The counter-argument is that it would be unreasonable to look at similarity in isolation. For example, certain instances of similarity such as colour, size, weight, etc, might all exist but are not determining factors and, in many cases, can be disregarded. Trade channels and actual usage can be particularly important. In *SEAHORSE Trade Mark*,[93] an application for the trade mark in respect of inboard marine engines exceeding 5,000 bhp was allowed despite the existence of an identical mark for outboard motors. The similarity that both goods powered vessels was outweighed by the sizes and prices of engines and the different vessels to which they would be applied, so that there was no real and tangible risk of confusion. In *Lidl Stiftung v Heinz Iberica SA*,[94] the OHIM Board of Appeal confirmed that the relevant consumer of pet food for trade mark purposes is the purchaser and not the animal. In *Lidl Stiftung & Co KG v OHIM*,[95] the General Court determined that an average consumer would pay particular attention in distinguishing between alcoholic and non-alcoholic drinks (even though they could be mixed) since some consumers cannot drink alcohol.

[31.35] The question of similarity of goods or services cannot be answered without reference to the mark in issue and any reputation that might exist. As stated by the ECJ in *Canon v Metro-Goldwyn-Mayer*:[96]

> a global assessment of the likelihood of confusion implies some interdependence between the relevant factors, and in particular a similarity between the trade marks and between these goods or services. Accordingly, a lesser degree of similarity between these goods or services may be offset by a greater degree of similarity between the marks, and vice versa.

It is also sufficient if any of the goods covered by the application are similar to any of the goods covered by the earlier mark. It does not matter if most of the goods covered by the application or the prior mark are not similar if there is a small residue that is similar.[97] In *Choay SA v Boehringer*,[98] the OHIM Board of Appeal refused to apply a stricter comparison in relation to pharmaceutical products on the basis that similarity would be offset by the intervention of qualified professionals, which would reduce the likelihood of mistakes. The degree of similarity between services provided by a retail trader and goods increases when it can be established that the retail services concern the same goods as the contested trade mark.[99]

 [31.36] Section 10(3)(b) requires a comparison of the goods or services of the later mark with those for which the earlier trade mark is 'protected' as opposed to the Directive's statement that the comparison is with the goods or services of the earlier mark as

---

[92] *Pedro Díaz, SA v OHIM* [2004] ETMR 42 ('*CASTILLO*').
[93] *SEAHORSE Trade Mark* [1980] FSR 250.
[94] *Lidl Stiftung v Heinz Iberica SA* [2003] ETMR 25.
[95] *Lidl Stiftung & Co KG v OHIM* [2005] ETMR 98.
[96] *Canon v Metro-Goldwyn-Mayer* [1999] ETMR 1; see also *Cobra Beer Ltd's Application* [2000] ETMR 638.
[97] *Bensyl* [1992] RPC 529.
[98] *Choay SA v Boehringer* [2001] ETMR 64; see also *Madaus OG v OHIM* [2006] ETMR 76.
[99] *Venticinique Ltd v Oakley Inc* [2005] ETMR 115.

'registered'. Protection extends beyond the exact goods or services of a registration where there exists a likelihood of confusion.[100] It could be argued that since 'protection' extends to similar goods or services, the comparison to establish if there is dissimilarity is to be made between the exact or similar goods or services of an earlier trade mark and the goods or services of the contested mark.

LIKELIHOOD OF CONFUSION

[31.37] In addition to the requisite similarity between the respective trade marks and the goods or services, it is also a requirement under s 10(2) of TMA 1996 that:

> there exists a likelihood of confusion on the part of the public, which includes the likelihood of association of the later mark with the earlier trade mark.

This provision is derived from art 4(1)(b) of the Harmonisation Directive[101] and modelled on art 13A of the Uniform Benelux Trade Mark Law of 1971. The test adopted by the Benelux Supreme Court in interpreting their law does not focus on the question of confusion but whether the public are likely to draw an association between the respective marks. ANTI-MONOPOLY was held likely to be associated with the trade mark MONOPOLY on board games. Even though there was no confusion as to the origin of the products, there was a calling to mind of the earlier case of *MONOPOLY Trade Mark*.[102] The decisive factor was not the use of the trade mark as an indicator of origin, but instead its function as a means of encapsulating goodwill. The Irish Supreme Court has already viewed likelihood of association as a ground for maintaining an action for passing off. In the *C&A Modes* case,[103] Kenny J stated:

> the legal wrong known as passing-off includes the incorporation in the Republic of Ireland of a company with a name likely to give the impression to the public that it is a subsidiary or branch of or is associated or connected with another company which has a substantial goodwill.

[31.38] The issue of association refers to the extent to which the public call to mind the earlier trade mark. In *HP Bulmer Ltd v J Bollinger SA*,[104] the UK Court of Appeal cautioned that not every type of connection will amount to passing off and quoted with approval Harman J in the *Treasure Cot*[105] case, that what was required was a connection in the mind of the public that the goods were 'something for which the plaintiffs were responsible'. However, the Irish High Court has approved Kenny J's statement in the *C&A* case[106] and compelled a company to change its corporate name even though it was

---

[100] TMA 1996, s 10(2).

[101] Council Directive 2008/95/EC ([2008] OJ L 299/25), which repealed and replaced Directive 89/104/EEC ([1989] OJ L40/1).

[102] *MONOPOLY Trade Mark,* Dutch Supreme Court [1978] BIE 39; see also *Union v Union Soleure* [1984] BIE 137 and *Always v Regina* [1993] IER 22.

[103] *C&A Modes v C &A (Waterford) Ltd* [1976] IR 198.

[104] *HP Bulmer Ltd v J Bollinger SA* [1978] RPC 79.

[105] *Treasure Cot* (1950) 67 RPC 89; see also *LEGO* [1983] FSR 155 and *GLENLIVET* [1993] RPC 461.

not trading.[107] The use of the term 'mere incorporation' by Kenny J would suggest that to succeed in a passing-off action, it is sufficient that an association can be drawn by the public even if that association does not result in an actual belief that an offending product originated from the same source as the owner of the reputation. As stated by Carroll J in the *RITTAL* case, approving of the statement made by Kenny J:[108]

> It is urged on behalf of the defendants that this should not be adopted as the law because it is *obiter dictum*. However, it seems to me whether it is obiter or not it is a sound statement of the law. The company was incorporated with the purpose of gaining an advantage from the use of the word RITTAL. It had to be in the context that it would give the impression that it was a subsidiary or branch or was associated or had a connection with the plaintiffs. The defendants have therefore committed the tort of passing off. While the plaintiffs have a proven reputation for excellence in a particular field both in this country and internationally in my opinion the company is not limited to trading only in that field. If it expands its business it is entitled to use its market name and the defendants are not entitled to appropriate the name for any purpose.

[31.39] In a similar vein, in the case of *Guinness Ireland Group v Kilkenny Brewing Co Ltd*[109] the defendant was ordered to change its company name. The defendant argued that it was to be a land holding company but Laffoy J nevertheless held that given company legislative compliance requirements, it was unrealistic to assume that the name of the defendant could be immured from the public perception so as to avoid giving a wrongful impression of a connection with the plaintiffs' business.

[31.40] The distinctive character of the earlier trade mark and, in particular, its reputation must be taken into account in any determination as to whether the similarity between the goods or services covered by the two trade marks is sufficient to give rise to a likelihood of confusion. Registration of a trade mark may be refused, despite a lesser degree of similarity between the goods or services covered, where the marks are very similar and the earlier mark, in particular its reputation, is highly distinctive.[110] Thus in *Pfizer v Eurofood Link*,[111] emphasis was placed on the interdependence of the similarity of the trade marks and the similarity of the goods or services. Given the reputation enjoyed by the trade mark VIAGRA in respect of a particular pharmaceutical, it could result in a likelihood of confusion with use of a trade mark VIAGRENE on a drink which was to be marketed as an aphrodisiac.

[31.41] The wording in s 10(2) of TMA 1996 is ambiguous because it is not clear whether the likelihood of association is an additional requirement to a likelihood of confusion or whether the likelihood of association is simply an example of an instance of

---

[106] *C&A Modes v C &A (Waterford) Ltd* [1976] IR 198.

[107] *Rittal Werk Rudolf LOH GmbH & Co KG v Rittal (Ireland) Ltd* (11 July 1991, unreported) HC, Carroll J; see para **[26.02]**.

[108] *Rittal Werk Rudolf LOH GmbH & Co KG v Rittal (Ireland) Ltd* (11 July 1991, unreported) HC, Carroll J.

[109] *Guinness Ireland Group v Kilkenny Brewing Co Ltd* [1999] ETMR 807; see para **[26.03]**.

[110] *CANON v METRO-GOLDWYN MAYER* [1999] ETMR 1.

[111] *Pfizer v Eurofood Link* [2000] ETMR 896.

the likelihood of confusion. The problem with the first interpretation is that it is hard to envisage a situation where there is a likelihood of confusion but not necessarily association. The second interpretation was preferred by Laddie J, in *Wagamama Ltd v City Centre Restaurants plc*,[112] who stated 'it is unconventional use of language to provide that the smaller (ie likelihood of confusion) includes the larger (ie likelihood of association)'. Significantly, Laddie J rejected any obligation to draw any inference from interpretation by the Benelux courts and stated:

> if the broader scope (ie likelihood of confusion) were to be adopted, the Directive and our Act would be creating a new type of monopoly not related to the proprietor's trade but in the trade mark itself. Such a monopoly would be likened to a quasi-copyright in the mark. However, unlike copyright, there would be no fixed duration for the right and it would be a true monopoly effective against copyist and non-copyist alike.

Laddie J went on further to state:

> if it had been the intention to make the Directive identical with Benelux law on this important issue, it could have said so. Indeed, in view of the fact that to have done so would have been significantly to expand trade mark rights and thereby significantly restrict the freedom of traders to compete. I would have expected any such expansion to have been stated in clear and unambiguous words so that traders throughout the European Union would be able to appreciate that their legislators had created a new broad monopoly … It follows that this Court cannot follow the route adopted by the Benelux on this issue … Nevertheless, the natural inclination to come to a conclusion which would further harmony on this issue is not so strong that I am prepared to agree that a new millstone round the neck of traders has been created when that is not my view.

[31.42] The broad interpretation already given to the law of passing off indicates that likelihood of association without likelihood of confusion is not as radical as might at first be perceived. However, the ECJ held in *Sabel BV v Puma AG*[113] that the concept of likelihood of association is not an alternative to the likelihood of confusion, but serves to define its scope. Thus, the mere association that the public might make between two trade marks as a result of their analogous semantic content is not in itself a sufficient ground for concluding that there is likelihood of confusion. A likelihood of confusion can, however, arise even if there is a public perception that the goods or services have different places of production. In *L'Oreal SA v Bellure NV*,[114] Lewison J used an analysis described as 'the three degrees'. The degree of similarity required is not the same in respect of each kind of infringement. In that decision, the English court derived from *Sabel v Puma* three kinds of possible links between the mark and sign:

(1) Where the public confused the sign and the mark in question (likelihood of direct confusion).

(2) Where the public makes a connection between the proprietors of the sign and those of the mark and confuses them (likelihood of indirect confusion or association).

---

[112] *Wagamama Ltd v City Centre Restaurants plc* [1995] FSR 713.
[113] *Sabel BV v Puma AG* [1998] ETMR 1.
[114] *L'Oreal SA v Bellure NV* [2007] ETMR 1.

(3)   Where the public considers the sign to be similar to the mark and there is a perception of the sign which calls to mind the memory of the mark, although the two are not confused (likelihood of association in the strict sense).

A link in either of the first two categories is necessary for infringement under s 14(2). The third category is sufficient for infringement under s 14(3).

The ECJ went on to emphasise that the more distinctive the earlier mark, the greater will be the likelihood of confusion.[115] Distinctive character in the earlier mark can exist either *per se*[116] or because of the reputation it enjoys with the public.

[31.43] In *British-American Tobacco Ltd's Application,*[117] it was considered that smokers are loyal customers to the brands they favour and that, consequently, there was a diminished likelihood of confusion. When goods are expensive, consumers contemplating purchase give greater consideration and this also reduces the likelihood of confusion.[118] In *Newmans Chocolates Ltd v Nestle*[119] the Controller held the average consumer to be a child of reading age in circumstances where the nature of the trade marks being compared (MILKBEARS v NESTLE MILKY BAR) and the goods made it clear to whom the goods were primarily directed. In *Zaklady v Leaf,*[120] the Controller held that confectionery and sweets were relatively low cost, impulse purchases and therefore the degree of attentiveness and consideration applied by the average consumer in the typical purchasing scenario must be assumed to be relatively low.

SIMILAR OR IDENTICAL TRADE MARKS FOR DISSIMILAR GOODS/SERVICES[121]

[31.44] Section 10(3) of TMA 1996 incorporates both a mandatory provision in art 4(3) and an optional provision in art 4(4)(a) of the Harmonisation Directive.[122] The mandatory provision required Member States to recognise that, in some instances, an earlier Community mark can be a basis for opposition or invalidity even if the later identical or similar contested mark is in respect of dissimilar goods or services. The optional provision allowed Member States to extend this principle to earlier national trade mark registrations. The requirement in s 10(3) is that if the earlier mark is a CTM, then there must be a reputation in a substantial part of the EU. In *PAGO International GmbH v Tirolmilch,*[123] the ECJ had to consider a Community trade mark registration in respect of the PAGO trade mark having a reputation in Austria and held that the territory of the single Member State in question, Austria, may be considered as a substantial part

---

[115] *Canon v Metro-Goldwyn Mayer* [1999] ETMR 1.

[116] *Belvedere's Application* [2007] ETMR 18.

[117] *British-American Tobacco Ltd's Application* [1999] ETMR 32.

[118] *GTR Group's Application* [1999] ETMR 164.

[119] *Newmans Chocolates Ltd v Nestle* [2006] ETMR 89.

[120] *Zaklady v Leaf* [2009] ETMR 31.

[121] See para **[32.36]** et seq.

[122] Council Directive 2008/95/EC ([2008] OJ L 299/25), which repealed and replaced Directive 89/104/EEC ([1989] OJ L40/1).

[123] *PAGO International GmbH v Tirolmilch* [2010] ETMR 5.

of the territory of the EU. If it is a national (Irish) registration, there must be a reputation in the State. The use of the later mark must also be without due cause and take unfair advantage of, or be detrimental to, the distinctive character or the repute of the earlier trade mark.

[31.45] There is a divergence from the Directive in that s 10(3)(a) comes into play in respect of an 'earlier trade mark' which, as defined in s 11, includes well-known trade marks under the Paris Convention. The Directive does not provide for this and therefore, the proprietor claiming an earlier trade mark by virtue of a well-known mark and who seeks to rely on s 10(3) may find a challenge that the statutory provision is in breach of EU law.

[31.46] Initially there was uncertainty as to whether or not s 10(3) of TMA 1996 requires the contested trade mark to cause a likelihood of confusion. Although no such criterion is identified in s 10(3), it had been considered an enigma that a likelihood of confusion is a requirement in the case of similar goods or services but not in respect of dissimilar goods or services.[124] This can be contrasted with the *obiter dicta* of the ECJ in *SABEL BV v PUMA AG*,[125] where the court stated that art 5(2) of the Harmonisation Directive:[126]

> permits the proprietor of a trade mark which has a reputation to prohibit the use without due cause of signs identical with or similar to his mark and does not require proof of likelihood of confusion, even where there is no similarity between the goods in question.

The ECJ in *Davidoff v Gofkid*[127] ruled that the provision in s 10(3), which provides a stronger form of protection for well-known registered trade marks, also applies in a scenario where goods/services are identical or similar and is not limited to dissimilar goods/services. However, a 'link' is required between the marks even though there is no confusion.

[31.47] In *Intel Corp Inc v CPM United Kingdom Ltd*,[128] the ECJ was cautious in not extending the boundaries and held that the establishment of a link did not automatically mean that use of the later mark takes unfair advantage of or is detrimental to the distinctive character or repute of the earlier mark, going on to state:

> proof that the use of the later mark is or would be detrimental to the distinctive character of the earlier mark requires evidence of a change in the economic behaviour of the average consumer of the goods or services for which the earlier mark was registered consequent on the use of the later mark, or a serious likelihood that such a change will occur in the future.

---

[124] *BASF plc v CEP (UK) plc* [1997] ETMR 51; *Baywatch Production Co Inc v Home Video Channel* [1997] FSR 22.

[125] *SABEL BV v PUMA AG* [1998] ETMR 1; see also *Pfizer v Eurofood Link* [2000] ETMR 896 and *Premier Brands UK Ltd v Typhoon Europe Ltd* [2000] ETMR 1071.

[126] Council Directive 2008/95/EC ([2008] OJ L 299/25), which repealed and replaced Directive 89/104/EEC ([1989] OJ L40/1).

[127] *Davidoff v Gofkid* [2003] ETMR 42; *Adidas v Fitnessworld* [2004] ETMR 10.

[128] *Intel Corp Inc v CPM United Kingdom Ltd* [2009] ETMR 13.

This can be contrasted with a decision of the General Court in *Mäurer + Wirtz v OHIM*,[129] which held that particularly in the case of a trade mark with exceptionally high reputation, detriment or unfair competition may be so obvious that an opponent does not need to put forward and prove any other fact to that end.

[31.48] Registration of the trade mark *VISA*[130] in respect of condoms was refused before the UK Intellectual Property Office on the basis of reputation of the opponent in relation to credit card services. It was considered that the daily use of the VISA trade mark in connection with many and varied consumer products would cause the public to wonder whether there is a connection in trade between the opponent's and dissimilar consumer goods under the same mark.[131]

[31.49] The requirement to show a reputation under the earlier trade mark will undoubtedly draw upon principles established under the law of passing off in determining whether or not there is the requisite reputation. In broad terms, as expressed by O'Higgins CJ in the Supreme Court decision in *Adidas v Charles O'Neill & Co Ltd*,[132] it arises where the trade mark 'is clearly associated in the public mind with its products, and with those of no other trader', and the degree to which the same or a similar mark has been used by third parties is important. At a practical level, the question of reputation is a matter of fact which takes into account the duration, extent and geographical area in which the trade mark is used together with the amount spent on advertising and channels of trade. Evidence of market share is a useful indicator of reputation but is not imperative.[133] In *Pinewood Laboratories Ltd v Glaxo Group Ltd*,[134] the Controller found that the opponent had a protectable goodwill sufficient to ground an opposition under s 10(4)(a) but that nevertheless the requisite reputation under s 10(3) was not proven. The ECJ in *Antartica SRL v OHIM*[135] found that the NASDAQ trade mark enjoyed a reputation amongst the public generally because of the interest of a large part of the general public in developments in the financial markets.

[31.50] In *Audio Medical Devices Ltd's Application*[136] the UK Intellectual Property Office held that the onus is on an opponent to show that use of the contested mark will take unfair advantage of and/or be detrimental to the opponent's earlier mark or its reputation. If he succeeds in doing so, the applicant must, in order to avoid the refusal of the application, show that they nevertheless have due cause to use the contested mark.

[31.51] The ECJ, in *General Motors v Yplon SA*,[137] held that an earlier mark enjoys sufficient reputation if it is known, by a significant part of the public concerned, by the

---

[129] *Mäurer + Wirtz v OHIM* [2010] ETMR 40.

[130] *VISA* [1999] ETMR 519. See also *Inlima SL's Application* [2000] ETMR 325.

[131] Contrast with *EVEREADY* [1999] ETMR 531.

[132] *Adidas v Charles O'Neill & Co Ltd* [1983] FSR 76 at 84.

[133] *Floris (J) Ltd v Istrad Ltd* [2005] ETMR 8.

[134] *Pinewood Laboratories Ltd v Glaxo Group Ltd* [2009] ETMR 44.

[135] *Antartica SRL v OHIM* [2009] ETMR 47.

[136] *Audio Medical Devices Ltd's Application* [1999] ETMR 1010; see also *Intel Corp v Sihra* [2004] ETMR 44.

[137] *General Motors v Yplon SA* [1999] ETMR 950.

products or services which it covers. It added that in examining whether the condition is fulfilled, all the relevant factors of the case must be considered and, in particular, the market share held by the trade mark, the intensity, geographical extent and duration of its use and the size of investment made by the undertaking in promoting it. In *Pebble Beach Co Ltd v Lombard Brands Ltd*[138] it was held that the reputation required was not amongst the public at large but the public interested in golf.

[31.52] Very similar evidential requirements were imposed under the Trade Marks Rules 1963[139] in order to show distinctiveness through usage, and it is this possible dilution to the distinctive character or reputation of the earlier mark that is the rationale behind this provision. In *Taittinger SA v Allbev Ltd,*[140] the plaintiffs were champagne producers who succeeded in preventing the use of the trade mark 'Elderflower Champagne' on a non-alcoholic soft drink on the basis of passing off. Bingham LJ in the Court of Appeal stated:

> a reference to champagne imports nuances of quality and celebration, a sense of something privileged and special. But this is the reputation which the champagne houses have built up over the years, and in which they have a property right. It is not in my view unfair to deny the defendants an opportunity to exploit, share or (in the vernacular), cash in on that reputation, which they have done nothing to establish. It would be very unfair to allow them to do so if the consequence was, as I am satisfied, it would be, to debase and cheapen that very reputation.

Even if reputation is proven, it is not an entitlement to blanket protection against use of a similar trade mark in relation to virtually any kind of product. Reputation is just one of several conditions to be proven.[141]

[31.53] In *Ferrero SpA v Kindercare*[142] the OHIM Board of Appeal described the scenario of unjust enrichment or unfair advantage as occurring when:

> a third party exploits the reputation of the earlier mark to the benefit of its own marketing efforts. In practice, the third party 'hooks on to' the renowned mark and uses it as a vehicle to incite consumers' interest in its own, albeit different, products. The advantage for the third party is a substantial saving on investment in promotion and publicity for its own mark, since it benefits from that which has made the earlier mark highly famous, and it is unfair because it is done in a parasitic way.

[31.54] The concept of detriment to the distinctive character equates with that of dilution under US law and from which guidance can be sought. Anti-dilution laws in the US are designed to prevent the gradual whittling away or the dispersion of the identity and hold upon the public mind. If we take the case of champagne, its use upon non-alcoholic beverages, then confectionery items and then restaurants, etc, would gradually erode and make the trade mark commonplace thus losing its identity. Detriment to the repute arises in the scenario of a possible damage to the positive attributes that may be enjoyed under

---

[138] *Pebble Beach Co Ltd v Lombard Brands Ltd* [2003] ETMR 21.
[139] SI 268/1963, r 20(2).
[140] *Taittinger SA v Allbev Ltd* [1993] FSR 641.
[141] *Ferrero OHG mbH v Beekenkamp* [2004] ETMR 20.
[142] *Ferrero SpA v Kindercare* [2005] ETMR 6.

a trade mark. This is recognised under Benelux law, and in *Claeryn v Klarein*,[143] the owner of CLAERYN Dutch gin was able to prevent the use of KLAREIN in respect of a household cleaning product.[144] In *Hollywood SAS v Souza Cruz SA*,[145] the OHIM Board of Appeal held that the earlier right registered in respect of chewing gum was seen as likely to be sullied or debased if the applicant was to use its trade mark in respect of tobacco. This was referred to as being dilution by tarnishment. The words 'without due cause' in s 10(3) of TMA 1996 would suggest that there are some instances where it is possible to take unfair advantage of an earlier mark. This is hard to imagine except where there has been consent from the owner of the earlier mark or there has been honest concurrent use under s 12. Taking 'unfair advantage' may include an act that is likely to prevent a product diversification. In *Lego System v Lego M Lemelstrich Ltd*,[146] it was described by Falconer J as follows:

> because of the reputation of LEGO (meaning the plaintiffs' toy construction products), there would be an opportunity for licensing or franchising the mark LEGO in other fields, that, because of the nature of the LEGO products, primarily plastic bricks, the plastic area would be a likely one to exploit and that garden implements would be an ideal market for franchising LEGO … Obviously, the possibility of licensing or franchising another trader to use LEGO in the gardening equipment area would be lost if the defendants are allowed to continue using LEGO in this country in relation to their products. The effect, therefore, of the defendants continuing to use LEGO in this country in relation to their products would be to destroy that part of the plaintiff's reputation in their mark LEGO and goodwill attached to it which extends to such goods.

The courts will have to determine in many cases whether or not loss of exclusivity to the proprietor of an earlier mark is the taking of an unfair advantage.

Detriment to the distinctive character arises where the earlier mark is no longer capable of arousing immediate association with the goods for which it is registered and used. Detriment to the repute is made out where the goods for which the contested mark is used appeal to the public's senses in such a way that the earlier mark's power of attraction is diminished.[147]

EARLIER RIGHTS/UNREGISTERED TRADE MARKS

[31.55] The right to oppose a trade mark application based on an unregistered mark existed under s 19 of TMA 1963, which provided that:

> it shall not be lawful to register as a trade mark or part of a trade mark any matter the use of which would, by reason of its being likely to deceive or cause confusion or otherwise, be disentitled to protection in a Court of Law or would be contrary to law or morality, or any scandalous design.

---

[143] *Claeryn v Klarein* (1976) 7 IIC 420.
[144] See also *Parfums Givenchy v Designer Alternative Labels* [1994] RPC 243.
[145] *Hollywood SAS v Souza Cruz SA* [2002] ETMR 64.
[146] *Lego System v Lego M Lemelstrich Ltd* [1983] FSR 155.
[147] *Spa Monopole v OHIM* [2005] ETMR 109.

Unlike s 10(4)(a) of TMA 1996, no reference to passing off was made. Indeed, under s 19 of TMA 1963, the evidential burden for an opponent to a trade mark registration was not as heavy as to sustain as an action for passing off. The Irish courts[148] have applied the statement of Evershed J in *Smith Hayden & Co Ltd's Application:*[149]

> having regard to the reputation acquired by the [earlier mark], is the Court satisfied that the mark applied for, if used in a normal and fair manner in connection with any goods covered by the registration proposed, will not be reasonably likely to cause deception and confusion amongst a substantial number of persons.

Unlike passing off, it was not necessary to prove a likelihood of damage caused by the deception. Indeed, in *BALI Trade Mark,*[150] Lord Upjohn went further and stated: 'I think the learned Judge was wrong to use the words 'reputation acquired by', it should have been 'the user of'. Lord Upjohn went on to say:

> it is not necessary ... to prove that there is an actual probability of deception leading to a passing off ... It is sufficient if the result of the registration of the mark will be that a number of persons will be caused to wonder whether it might not be the case that the two products came from the same source. It is enough if the ordinary person entertains a reasonable doubt, but the Court has to be satisfied not merely that there is a possibility of confusion; it must be satisfied that there is a real tangible danger of confusion if the mark which it is sought to register is put on the Register.[151]

[31.56] The difference between s 10(4)(a) of TMA 1996 and s 19 of TMA 1963, although both allow opposition based on unregistered rights, is nevertheless quite significant. In *Montex,*[152] the Irish High Court, and on appeal the Supreme Court, interpreted s 19 as not requiring any element of blameworthiness on the part of the applicant. At the time of application both parties had been using their trade mark for a number of years so confusion was seen as inevitable despite the fact that the applicant was the first user of the trade mark in the State and was consequently entitled *prima facie* to be registered as the owner. The requirement under s 10(4)(a) is that the owner of the claimed earlier right must be able to show that he would have a legal basis for prohibiting use of the later mark. The legal basis is described as 'by virtue of any rule of law (in particular, the law of passing off)'. Section 10(4)(a) requires the owner of the claimed earlier right to submit proofs in the same way as would be required to prove passing off, putting the later mark into the notional position as if it was being used. This is meant to reflect the optional provision in art 4(4)(b) of the Harmonisation Directive[153] but does not do so entirely. The Directive makes it clear that the basis of the claim to a non-registered trade mark must have been acquired prior to the date of application or priority date of the later mark. The Directive refers to 'rights to a non-registered trade

---

[148] *Zockoll Group Ltd (formerly Phonenames Ltd) v Controller of Patents, Designs and Trade Marks* [2007] ETMR 26.

[149] *Smith Hayden & Co Ltd's Application* [1946] 63 RPC 97 at 101.

[150] *BALI Trade Mark* [1969] RPC 472.

[151] See also *Pioneer Hi-Bred Corn Co v Hi-Line Chicks Pty Ltd* [1979] RPC 410.

[152] *Montex* [2000] ETMR 658.

[153] Council Directive 2008/95/EC ([2008] OJ L 299/25), which repealed and replaced Directive 89/104/EEC ([1989] OJ L40/1).

mark' which 'confers on its proprietor the right to prohibit the use of a subsequent trade mark'. This would include certain statutes that prevent certain names from being used such as, for example, under the Industrial Research and Standards Act 1961 and the National Lottery Act 1986.

[31.57] In *Last Minute Network v OHIM*,[154] the General Court highlighted the particular characteristics of a passing off action and stated:

> It is clear from the national case law that in an action for passing off the misleading nature of the representation of the defendant's goods and services must be assessed with regard to the claimant's customers and not to the abstract notion of the average consumer ... The property protected by an action for passing off is not property in a word or name, which third parties are restrained from using, but the very customer base which is undermined by the usage in question (Parker J. in *Burberrys v Cording* (1909) 26 RPC 693), since the reputation of a trade mark is the power of attraction which brings in custom and the criterion which distinguishes an established business from a new business (*IRC v Muller & Co's Margarine Ltd* [1901] AC 217).

OTHER INTELLECTUAL PROPERTY RIGHTS

[31.58] Section 10(4)(b) of TMA 1996 implements the optional provision in art 4(4)(c) of the Harmonisation Directive,[155] and prohibits registration if use could be prevented by virtue of an earlier right 'in particular, by virtue of the law of copyright, registered designs or any other law relating to a right to a name, a right of personal portrayal or an industrial property right'. Essentially, the owner of an earlier right has to show that he would have a legal basis for prohibiting use.[156] In the case of copyright, this would entail showing that he is a qualified person and the owner of an original work and that the contested mark amounts to a reproduction of a substantial part of the work. However, in exceptional circumstances the normal proof requirements may not be imposed, particularly when there is no denial by the applicant.[157] Under provisions corresponding to s 19 of TMA 1963, the English courts have allowed copyright in an artistic work as a basis for revocation of a registration of a device mark which was deemed 'contrary to law'.[158] A registered design arises by virtue of the Industrial Designs Act 2001 or Council Regulation 6/2002/EC on Community Designs, and provides protection by way of registration in respect of novel features of the product.[159] The shape of goods or their packaging may be registrable as trade marks[160] subject to certain limitations.[161] Even though a certain shape may not itself be registrable as a trade mark, for example, being

---

[154] *Last Minute Network v OHIM* [2010] ETMR 35.

[155] Council Directive 2008/95/EC ([2008] OJ L 299/25), which repealed and replaced Directive 89/104/EEC ([1989] OJ L40/1).

[156] *EINSTEIN* [2000] ETMR 952.

[157] *TEAM LOTUS VENTURES* [1999] ETMR 669.

[158] *KARO STEP* [1977] RPC 255; see also *OSCAR* [1979] RPC 173.

[159] See Ch 23.

[160] TMA 1996, s 6(2).

[161] TMA 1996, s 8.

'a shape which gives substantial value to the goods',[162] it may nevertheless be a registered design and form the basis for opposition or invalidity. Once the registered design right expires, so will the basis for opposition or invalidity. A Community design may be declared invalid if a registered trade mark is incorporated in that design.[163] The right to a name or the right of personal portrayal are matters that would generally fall under the law of passing off and so fall outside s 10(4)(b) and into s 10(4)(a), the effect of which is the same. Unauthorised character merchandising using a name can amount to passing off.[164] In *Hogan v Koala Dundee*[165] and *Hogan v Pacific Dunlop,*[166] the actor Paul Hogan obtained injunctions against a retail shop displaying pictures of a koala bear with a bush hat and a crocodile tooth necklace and a television advertisement for shoes, which parodied a scene from the *Crocodile Dundee* film. Rights to a name that would fall outside the field of passing-off would be rights of privacy and against defamation.[167]

[31.59] Section 10(6) of TMA 1996 provides that a consent from the proprietor of an earlier mark shall dispense with the prohibition based on any of the relative grounds for refusal. In practice, this means that there are a large amount of requests for consent to owners of earlier trade marks, which may have been cited by the Controller. If the cited mark is vulnerable to cancellation on the grounds of non-use, then a consent is likely to be forthcoming. In many cases, a consent is furnished in return for undertakings which may, for example, restrict the form of the trade mark to be used and the goods or services of use and registration. There is also no legal prohibition on the owner of an earlier trade mark from seeking a consideration in excess of their costs in return for furnishing a consent, and refusing to provide such if it is not forthcoming. Apart from the danger of a likelihood of confusion, before giving a consent, the proprietor of an earlier trade mark should bear in mind that under s 51(1)(d), it is possible for their own registration to be revoked on the grounds that the consent has resulted in use which is liable to mislead the public. A licence confers no proprietary rights on a licensee[168] and, therefore, no opposition or revocation action is possible by a licensee on relative grounds if the registered proprietor has given consent to such trade mark application/registration.

---

[162] TMA 1996, s 8(2)(c).

[163] *Compagne Gervais Danone SA v Piotrowski* [2007] ETMR 42.

[164] *Childrens' Television Workshop v Woolworths, Muppets Case* [1981] RPC 187.

[165] *Hogan v Koala Dundee* (1988) 12 IPR 508.

[166] *Hogan v Pacific Dunlop* (1989) 14 IPR 398.

[167] See Bolger, 'The Common Law and the Tort of Appropriation of Personality Parts I & II' (1999) 3 (1) IIPR 16 and Part II (1999) 3 (2) IIPR 2; Carty, 'Advertising, publicity rights and English law' (2004) IPQ 3, 209–258; and McLean and Mackey, 'Mosley v News Group Newspapers Ltd: how sadomasochism changed the face of privacy law: a consideration of the Max Mosley case and other recent developments in privacy law in England and Wales'(2010) EIPR 32(2), 77–89.

[168] *Northern & Shell plc v Conde Nast & National Magazine Distributors Ltd* [1995] RPC 117.

HONEST CONCURRENT USE

[31.60] The provisions dealing with honest concurrent use are contained in s 12 of TMA 1996. These were introduced during the passage of the Bill, where it was argued at committee stage for a provision corresponding to that previously contained in s 20(2) of TMA 1963. Essentially, honest concurrent use allows for an otherwise conflicting mark to be registered, and is designed to reflect on the Register the reality of the market place and a situation where the proprietor of an earlier mark is not prepared to furnish a consent. Section 12(3) of TMA 1996 expressly states that the criteria as to what constitutes honest concurrent use are to be determined in accordance with s 20(2) of TMA 1963 and, therefore, it is clear that appropriate case law under s 20(2) of TMA 1963 and the equivalent UK provision can have value as precedent.[169] The leading authority is the House of Lords decision in *Alexander Pirie & Sons Ltd*,[170] where Lord Tomlin identified the factors which may be taken into consideration. These are:

(a) the extent of use of the mark for which registration is sought. Extent would include duration of use, quantity and geographical spread within the State;
(b) the degree of confusion likely to arise;
(c) the honesty of the concurrent use;
(d) whether any instances of confusion have been proven; and
(e) the relative inconvenience if the mark was allowed registration.

[31.61] These are only guidelines and every case is decided on its own merits. In *PEDDIES Application*,[171] two-and-a-quarter years was sufficient and in *GRANADA Trade Mark*,[172] two years and 10 months was held to be a comparatively short period for the exercise of such a discretion but was nevertheless allowed. Because it is a discretionary provision, there is considerable reluctance to allow a trade mark under this honest concurrent use provision in a situation of what is termed triple identity, ie if the respective marks, goods/services and geographical areas of trade are all identical. In the case of triple identity, confusion is deemed to be inevitable.[173] However, even in cases of triple identity, discretion has still been exercised.[174] Honest concurrent use recognises and takes into account the fact that the relevant public can, by familiarity brought about by concurrent use, learn that two similar marks are in use.[175] In *BULER*,[176] the goods were in each case watches but the respective customers were different because of the considerable price divergence, and so the risk of confusion was slight. In that case, the applicant's trade was in fact larger than the opponent's trade, but this is not a requirement.[177]

---

[169] UK Trade Marks Act 1938, s 12(2).
[170] *Alexander Pirie & Sons Ltd* (1933) 50 RPC 147.
[171] *PEDDIES Application* (1944) 61 RPC 31.
[172] *GRANADA Trade Mark* [1979] RPC 303.
[173] *LION Brand* (1940) 57 RPC 248.
[174] *BUD* [1988] RPC 535.
[175] *L'AMY* [1983] RPC 137.
[176] *BULER* [1975] RPC 275.
[177] *BAINBRIDGE* (1940) 57 RPC 248.

[31.62] There are some factors that differentiate s 12 of TMA 1996 from s 20(2) of TMA 1963. Firstly, it is restricted to honest concurrent use alone and does not provide for 'other special circumstances' to be taken into account. Secondly, it may be more difficult to distinguish marks because, unlike TMA 1963, no limitations or conditions can be imposed, except a limitation by consent under s 17 of TMA 1996. In *Bass Ratcliffe & Gretton Ltd v Nicholson & Son Ltd,*[178] the fact that there was a limitation in the form of different containers differentiated the goods and was a determining factor, but this may no longer afford the degree of comfort that a court might require before exercising its discretion in favour of an honest concurrent user. Thirdly, it was not clear under TMA 1963 whether or not an honest concurrent user could apply where the earlier trade mark had been used but not registered. Section 12 makes it clear that both registered trade marks and unregistered earlier rights can be overcome by an honest concurrent user.

[31.63] To establish how the honest concurrent use provision will apply in practice, it is important to look at s 12(2) of TMA 1996, which indicates that if the Controller establishes honest concurrent use, he or she will allow the application to proceed to advertisement but an opponent with an earlier trade mark or right may still pursue opposition proceedings despite the existence of honest concurrent use. In *Henry J Archer & Sons Ltd v Diageo Brands BV*[179] the Controller held that upon opposition by the owner of the cited earlier trade mark, the acceptance of the trade mark application will be withdrawn. The procedure that follows is that the trade mark application reverts to the status of an application under objection in accordance with s 10 of TMA 1996.

[31.64] The EU Trade Mark Harmonisation Directive[180] does not provide for honest concurrent use and there is an argument that the inclusion of this is a breach of the State's obligations under EU law. Article 4 expressly states that a trade mark shall not be registered when it conflicts with an earlier trade mark or right as defined. The provision of consent is an option and exception provided in art 4(5) of the Directive but the addition of a further exception by way of honest concurrent use is not provided for. The owner of an earlier trade mark or right could challenge a decision to allow a registration based on honest concurrent use or seek invalidity of any such registration as being in breach of the Directive, although such an action could face difficulties in terms of the lack of horizontal direct effect of most Directive provisions. The other side of the argument is that honest concurrent use is simply being used as a criterion in determining the question of a likelihood of confusion under art 4(1)(b) or whether the later mark takes unfair advantage or is detrimental to the earlier mark under art 4(3).

---

[178] *Bass Ratcliffe & Gretton Ltd v Nicholson & Son Ltd* (1932) 49 RPC 88.

[179] *Henry J Archer & Sons Ltd v Diageo Brands BV* Decision of the Controller of 30 July 2007, unreported, regarding opposition to application No 224939.

[180] Council Directive 2008/95/EC ([2008] OJ L 299/25), which repealed and replaced Directive 89/104/EEC ([1989] OJ L40/1).

[31.65] The Harmonisation Directive[181] in fact uses the words 'a trade mark shall not be registered or if registered, shall be liable to be declared invalid' on the basis of an earlier conflicting trade mark or right. In most EU countries, the national trade marks offices do not cite earlier trade marks as a basis for refusal and it is up to the owners of an earlier trade mark to oppose or seek invalidity. The State can therefore argue that its decision not to cite an earlier trade mark because of honest concurrent use but to allow such to proceed to advertisement is not in breach of the Directive. There is, in fact, no statutory obligation on the Controller to carry out searches of prior trade marks either on the Irish or Community Registers but this is provided for in the Rules[182] and policy in this regard may vary.

[31.66] The Department of Enterprise, Trade and Innovation opened a consultation process in late 2009 on the issue of whether examination of trade mark applications on relative grounds should be maintained, and issued its conclusion in June 2010. The decision was made to retain the relative grounds examination. Responses to the consultation were largely in favour of retaining the *status quo* on the basis that it ensures, in so far as possible, that the Register is clean and free of potentially conflicting marks. It also provides a degree of certainty as to who has exclusive rights in a mark as against other prospective users and is more beneficial for proprietors who are not in a financial position to vigilantly police and enforce their trade mark rights. The Department was also of the view that Ireland is not out of step with Europe in having a relative grounds examination as 12 other EU Member States have a relative grounds examination, including major economies such as Sweden, Portugal, Poland and the Czech Republic. It was also a factor that the ownership of an Irish trade mark registration is a defence to a trade mark infringement action in Ireland so a relaxation of the examination requirements would make the defence more widely available and reduce the effectiveness of the trade mark infringement action. It was not considered that the existence of the relative grounds examination in Ireland is a major factor in encouraging companies to file Community trade marks instead. Those in favour of a change had argued that other national offices are moving away from relative grounds examination and that retaining the relative grounds examination might put Irish trade mark applicants at a disadvantage over applicants for Community or International marks; that there are many Community trade marks that cover Ireland but may never be used here or where the owners of those registrations have no real concern as regards Ireland, but which may prevent Irish applications becoming registered and that applicants who have an application refused on relative grounds can be successful in attaining a Community trade mark that becomes effective in Ireland anyway. These reasons were not considered sufficient to overcome the benefits of retaining the current system. The Department stated that the international community is still divided on this matter and that it will be monitoring developments and will keep the matter under review.

---

[181] Council Directive 2008/95/EC ([2008] OJ L 299/25), which repealed and replaced Directive 89/104/EEC ([1989] OJ L40/1).

[182] Trade Marks Rules 1996, r 16.

Chapter 32

Trade Marks Act 1996: Infringement and Remedies

INTRODUCTION

[32.01] A trade mark registration confers on the proprietor exclusive rights in the trade mark in the country in question[1] and there is no requirement to prove a reputation or to show actual or likely damage, which are constraints under the law of passing off. It could be argued that the wording in s 13(1) of the Trade Marks Act 1996 (TMA 1996) does not correctly transpose art 5(1) of the Trade Mark Harmonisation Directive[2] because art 5(1) appears to be broader in that the right to prevent unauthorised use is only part of the overall entitlement granted by virtue of a registration. Under s 13(1), the exclusive right is limited to prevention of unauthorised use of the trade mark. It is customary to focus on the exclusivity of use but a trade mark is a proprietary right and, as such, rights extend beyond mere usage and to, for example, other dealings such as assignments or security interests. In addition, the protection afforded under s 14 of TMA 1996 includes infringing acts which do not amount to trade mark usage.

[32.02] It is not possible to bring infringement proceedings prior to the date of publication of registration[3] but the effective date of registration is the application date[4] and therefore damages for infringement of an Irish trade mark registration can be claimed from this date.

[32.03] The proprietor of an Irish trade mark registration can only sue on foot of infringement within the State.[5] However, s 14(4)(c) of TMA 1996 contains a prohibition against infringing use by way of export under the offending trade mark. In *George Ballantine & Son Ltd v Ballantyne Stewart & Co Ltd,*[6] it was held that the likelihood of deception is to be considered as regards the public in the country where the article is to be sold. The Irish High Court in *Irish Distillers Ltd v Cooley Distillery plc*[7] also took into account evidence as to the likelihood of confusion in the Russian market on foot of a Community trade mark registration in relation to goods exported from Ireland. Section 61 deals specifically with the rights of the proprietor of a well-known trade mark, which

---

[1] TMA 1996, s 13(1); in the EU in the context of a Community trade mark.
[2] Council Directive 2008/95/EC ([2008] OJ L 299/25), which repealed and replaced Directive 89/104/EEC ([1989] OJ L40/1).
[3] TMA 1996, s 13(4)(a).
[4] TMA 1996, ss 13(3) and 45(3).
[5] TMA 1996, ss 13(1) and 101.
[6] *George Ballantine & Son Ltd v Ballantyne Stewart & Co Ltd* [1959] RPC 273.
[7] *Irish Distillers Ltd v Cooley Distillery plc* [2009] ETMR 8.

arise irrespective of registration.[8] Similarly, s 65 grants the proprietor a right of action against unauthorised acts of an agent or representative.[9]

INFRINGEMENT

[32.04] The Trade Marks Act 1963 (TMA 1963) limited the scope of protection by way of an infringement action to the goods embraced by the registration. Section 14 of TMA 1996, in implementing art 5 of the Trade Mark Harmonisation Directive,[10] increases the scope of such protection to unauthorised use of an identical or similar sign on goods or services similar to that of the registration and, in some instances, even to dissimilar goods or services.[11] To this extent, the grounds of infringement correspond to those for determining whether or not an earlier trade mark right exists under s 10 of TMA 1996. However, the infringement provisions in s 14 also require not just a comparison of the respective marks and the goods/services but also an examination of the nature of the allegedly infringing act and, despite the constraints of TMA 1963, the Irish courts were already moving in this direction. In *Gallaher (Dublin) Ltd v Health Education Bureau,*[12] Costello J found infringement by use on printed matter by virtue of a registration in respect of tobacco products. The defendant used the identical trade mark on an imitation cigarette packet containing printed matter used as an aid to stop smoking. This was held to be use in relation to cigarettes and thus an infringement.

[32.05] In *Levi Strauss & Co v Casucci SpA,*[13] the ECJ ruled that account must be taken of the perception of the public concerned at the time when the offending mark began to be used since:

> If the likelihood of confusion were assessed at a time after the sign in question began to be used, the user of that sign might take undue advantage of his own unlawful behaviour by alleging that the product had become less renowned, a matter for which he himself was responsible or to which he himself contributed.

[32.06] Under s 14 of TMA 1996, an infringing act requires use of a sign in the course of trade. An issue that will have to be determined by the Irish courts is whether or not s 14 embraces non-trade mark usage where such usage is not within the accepted limitations on effects of registered trade marks under s 15 of TMA 1996. Many cases under TMA 1963 and the corresponding provision in the UK Trade Marks Act 1938 were decided on this issue. In *Mars (GB) Ltd v Cadbury Ltd,*[14] the registered trade mark

---

8   Paris Convention for the Protection of Industrial Property (1883) (Paris Convention), art 6bis.
9   Paris Convention, art 6*septies*.
10   Council Directive 2008/95/EC ([2008] OJ L 299/25), which repealed and replaced Directive 89/104/EEC ([1989] OJ L40/1).
11   TMA 1996, s 14(3); *BASF plc v CEP (UK) plc* [1996] ETMR 51.
12   *Gallaher (Dublin) Ltd v Health Education Bureau* [1982] ILRM 240.
13   *Levi Strauss & Co v Casucci SpA* [2006] ETMR 71.
14   *Mars (GB) Ltd v Cadbury Ltd* [1987] RPC 387.

TREETS in respect of confectionery was deemed not to be infringed by the use of the words 'treat size' as these words were not used as a trade mark. In *Mothercare (UK) Ltd v Penguin Books Ltd*,[15] it was stated by Dillon LJ as follows:

> Indeed it stands to reason that a Trade Marks Act would only be concerned to restrict the use of a mark as a trade mark or in a trade mark sense, and should be construed accordingly. If descriptive words are legitimately registered in Part A of the Register, there is still no reason why other people should not be free to use the words in a descriptive sense, and not in only a trade mark sense.

[32.07] In *Unidoor Ltd v Marks & Spencer plc*,[16] the plaintiff held a Part B registration for COAST TO COAST in respect of articles of clothing. The defendants used COAST TO COAST as a slogan on their own T-shirts and it was held that this was not use in a manner that constituted trade mark usage.

[32.08] In *Trebor Bassett Ltd v Football Association*,[17] the plaintiff manufactured candy sticks the packaging of which included collectable insert cards. Some of these cards depicted soccer internationals in English team jerseys on which the Football Association logo appeared. The plaintiff was granted a declaration of non-infringement and Rattee J found that the logo was not being used as a 'sign' in respect of its cards.

[32.09] There are certainly arguments as to why these cases might still apply under the current law. The preamble to the Harmonisation Directive[18] states 'whereas the protection afforded by the registered trade mark, the function of which is in particular to guarantee the trade mark as an indication of origin'. The definition of a trade mark in s 6(1) of TMA 1996 reinforces this statement and s 13 refers to infringement as being in relation to use of that trade mark. In contrast, the definition of 'use' in s 2(2) distinguishes between a trade mark and a sign and envisages both by using the word 'or'. In the first decision in the English courts that addressed this issue, Jacob J in *British Sugar plc v James Robertson & Sons Ltd*[19] held that the section covers non-trade mark use and considered the important matter to be the language of the Directive, which has not been exactly transposed into either UK or Irish law. Jacob J did not view the language corresponding to s 13 as of assistance in interpreting s 14 being 'really no more than a chatty introduction to the details set out in s 14, itself adding no more than that the acts concerned must be done without consent'.

[32.10] Section 14(4) of TMA 1996 includes a non-exhaustive list of examples of what constitutes use of a sign, namely:

---

[15] *Mothercare (UK) Ltd v Penguin Books Ltd* [1988] RPC 113 at 118–119.
[16] *Unidoor Ltd v Marks & Spencer plc* [1988] RPC 275.
[17] *Trebor Bassett Ltd v Football Association* [1997] FSR 211.
[18] Council Directive 2008/95/EC ([2008] OJ L 299/25), which repealed and replaced Directive 89/104/EEC ([1989] OJ L40/1).
[19] *British Sugar plc v James Robertson & Sons Ltd* [1996] RPC 281.

(a) affixing it to goods or the packaging thereof;[20]
(b) offering or exposing goods for sale, putting them on the market or stocking them[21] for those purposes under the sign, or offering or supplying services under the sign;
(c) importing or exporting goods under the sign; or
(d) using the sign on business papers or in advertising.

Even under TMA 1963, the trade mark did not have to appear at the point of sale.[22] In *CHEETAH Trade Mark*,[23] it was held that use of a registered trade mark on invoices and delivery notes was just as much an infringement as stamping the mark on a container for the goods. Also, the use of a registered trade mark on an invoice, even if rendered long after sale and delivery, was still use in the course of trade. The infringing activities should take place within the State and the simple existence of advertising that may circulate in the State or use on the internet does not necessarily amount to infringement.[24] In relation to internet use, in the Scottish case of *Bonnier v Smith and Kestrel Trading Co*[25] Lord Drummond Young stated as follows:

> the person who sets up the website can be regarded as potentially committing a delict in any country where the website can be seen, in other words, in any country in the world. It does not follow that he actually commits a delict in every country of the world, however. It is obvious that the overwhelming majority of websites will be of no interest whatsoever in more than a single country or a small group of countries. In my opinion a website should not be regarded as having delictual consequences in any country where it is unlikely to be of any significant interest. That result can readily be achieved by a vigorous application of the maxim *de minimis no curat praetor*; if the impact of a website in a particular country is properly regarded as insignificant, no delict has been committed there.

In *Beaumatic International v Mitchell International Pharmaceuticals Ltd*,[26] the defendants were not liable in respect of a trade mark applied to packaging that was to be sent abroad to be used on goods. In *Montex Holdings Ltd v Diesel SpA*,[27] the ECJ ruled that goods in transit from Poland (not then in the EU) through Germany destined for Ireland where the DIESEL trade mark was not registered were not an infringement.

[32.11] The infringement provisions require use in the course of trade. 'Trade' is defined in s 2 of TMA 1996 to include any business or profession, and use includes otherwise than by means of a graphic representation.[28] Thus, oral use can amount to an infringement, which was not possible under TMA 1963, which required 'use of a printed or other visual representation of the mark'. However, use in the course of trade was a requirement under TMA 1963 and therefore recourse can be made to decisions under

---

[20] *Beautimatic v Mitchell International* [1999] ETMR 912.
[21] *Sony v Nuplayer* [2006] ETMR 46.
[22] *Esquire Electronics Ltd v Roopanand Bros* [1991] RPC 425.
[23] *CHEETAH Trade Mark* [1993] FSR 263.
[24] *Euromarket Designs Inc v Peters (Crate and Barrel)* [2000] ETMR 1025.
[25] *Bonnier v Smith and Kestrel Trading Co* [2002] ETMR 86.
[26] *Beaumatic International v Mitchell International Pharmaceuticals Ltd* [1999] ETMR 912.
[27] *Montex Holdings Ltd v Diesel SpA* [2007] ETMR 13.
[28] TMA 1996, s 2(1).

that Act. The High Court adopted a broad interpretation in *Gallaher (Dublin) Ltd v Health Education Bureau*[29] and conferred protection against any use that damaged the trade mark. This can be contrasted with the UK decision in *M Ravok (Weatherwear) Ltd v National Trade Press Ltd*[30] in which the defendant incorrectly attributed ownership of a trade mark in a directory. It was held that there was no infringement, since the defendant had not used the mark in the course of trade in the goods for which it was registered.

[32.12] Use of trade marks on the internet has been an area of significant contention. The issue of metatag use was considered by Jacob LJ in *Reed Executive plc v Reed Business Information Ltd*.[31] Leaving open the question of whether metatag use constituted use of a trade mark, Jacob LJ concluded that causing a site to appear in a search result, without more, does not suggest any connection with anyone else.

[32.13] The issue of sponsored search results on internet search engines has been particularly controversial. The legality of the practice of sale and purchase of sponsored search results was the subject of conflicting decisions at national level in the European courts and elsewhere (see for example the decisions in the UK regarding MR SPICY[32] and in France relating to Google).[33] In 2010, the ECJ ruled that Google's lucrative AdWords business does not breach trade mark law.[34] The case involved several parties, including Louis Vuitton, who objected to Google's sale of keywords of their major brand names to competitors or imitators, including in combination with terms such as 'imitation' or 'copy'. The ECJ held that Google was not infringing trade mark rights by selling these keywords because Google does not use the brand or trade mark in its own commercial communication. Instead, Google merely allows keyword purchasers to use the trade marks without Google using them itself. The decision also held that keyword purchasers are not infringing trade mark rights so long as the advertisements which appear in the sponsored links are not misleading, vague or difficult to understand in terms of the origin or source of the goods or services in question. The trade mark owners' claims that keywords harm their ability to advertise their brands were rejected on the basis that their websites would still appear at or near the top of the normal or 'natural' search results section. Therefore, the visibility of their brands is guaranteed.[35]

[32.14] This decision also dealt with Google's role as a service provider in storing and transmitting the content of the advertisements. If Google remains neutral in these

---

[29] *Gallaher (Dublin) Ltd v Health Education Bureau* [1982] ILRM 240.
[30] *M Ravok (Weatherwear) Ltd v National Trade Press Ltd* (1955) 72 RPC 110.
[31] *Reed Executive plc v Reed Business Information Ltd* [2004] ETMR 56.
[32] *Wilson v Yahoo! UK Ltd* [2008] ETMR 33.
[33] See Cornthwaite, 'To key or not to key? The judgment of the European Court of Justice in the Google France Adwords cases' (2010) EIPR 32(7), 352–359.
[34] *Google France v Louis Vuitton* [2010] ETMR 30.
[35] See *Portakabin Ltd and Portakabin BV v Primakabin BV* [2010] ETMR 52 regarding use of keywords by resellers of genuine second-hand goods and the use of misspellings and *BergSpechte Outdoor Reisen und Alpinschule Edi Koblmuller GmbH v Guni* [2010] ETMR 33 on the use of keywords either identical or similar to the trade mark by third party advertisers who do not have a connection to the goods of the trade mark.

activities, it has no knowledge or control of the content so it is not liable for it. However, Google could become liable if it takes an active role in those activities. In particular, the ECJ left it to the national courts to decide whether Google's activities in suggesting text for the advertisements meant that it took on an active role. This neutrality versus active role test is an attempt by the ECJ to strike a balance between service providers, their customers and trade mark owners. In the ECJ's keenness to balance those rights, it stretched the usual limits of interpretation of the law in creating this test from a statement of intent in the non-binding 'background' recitals of the E-Commerce Directive 2000/31/EC.[36]

[32.15] Section 14(5) of TMA 1996 provides for contributory infringement in circumstances where a person applies a registered trade mark to certain materials where that person knew or had reason to believe that such application was unauthorised. The words 'had reason to believe' were considered in the case of *LA Gear Inc v Hi-Tech Sports plc*[37] and were held to involve the concept of knowledge of facts from which a reasonable person would arrive at the relevant belief and that knowledge of facts from which a reasonable person might suspect the relevant conclusion was not enough. It was stated by Morritt J that 'the phrase does connote the allowance of a period of time to enable the reasonable man to evaluate those facts so as to convert the facts into a reasonable belief'.

Comparative advertising[38]

[32.16] There are different forms of comparative advertising and this is defined in Directive 2006/114/EC concerning misleading and comparative advertising[39] as 'any advertising which explicitly or by implication identifies a competitor or goods or services offered by a competitor'. In some instances, comparative advertising does not refer to a specific competitor and, for example, a slogan which states a courier service to be faster than the rest or a supermarket to be better value is a form of comparative advertising. There were differing views as to whether or not comparative advertising should be allowed and, for example, historically German law tended to be very restrictive in this regard. The matter was never tested in the Irish courts under TMA 1963 and, indeed, the earlier Council Directive 97/55/EC of 6 October 1997 amending Directive 84/450/EEC concerning misleading advertising so as to include comparative advertising was never implemented in Ireland as the view of the Irish government was that the pre-existing provisions of Irish law covered the same principles, which was arguably not the case. However, there is no reason to believe that the principles adopted by the English courts would not have been equally applicable in this jurisdiction. It is

---

[36] Directive 2000/31/EC ([2000] OJ L178/16).

[37] *LA Gear Inc v Hi-Tech Sports plc* [1992] FSR 121.

[38] See para **[33.15]**.

[39] Directive 2006/114/EC ([2006] OJ L 376/21), implemented in Ireland by the European Communities (Misleading and Comparative Marketing Communications) Regulations 2007 (SI 774/2007). In addition, a comparative advertisement could also contravene the provisions of the Consumer Protection Act 2007 on unfair or misleading commercial practices.

clear that comparative advertising is not just a question of trade mark law and, in cases of false or misleading statements, involves the issues of trade libel or injurious falsehood. In *Kaye v Robertson*,[40] Glidewell LJ stated the essential requirements in the tort of injurious or malicious falsehood, namely:

> that the defendant has published about the plaintiff words which are false, that they were published maliciously, and that special damage has followed as the direct and natural result of their publication ... Malice will be inferred if it be proved that the words were calculated to produce damage and that the defendant knew when he published the words that they were false or was reckless as to whether they were false or not.

[32.17] Comparative advertising can result in an action for passing off in circumstances where there is a misrepresentation whereby customers are deceived into believing that the defendant's product is that of the plaintiff. In *McDonald's Hamburgers Ltd v BurgerKing (UK) Ltd*,[41] the defendant advertised by way of a card with the words 'It's not just Big, Mac' beside a reference to their own hamburger called the 'WHOPPER'. Whitford J held that there was passing off, the words conveying the impression that the burger being advertised was an improved version of the BIG MAC or drew an association between the BIG MAC and the defendant. Whitford J came to the conclusion that a significant number of people reading the advertisement would find in it a misrepresentation as to the possible source or origin from which the BIG MAC could be obtained and stated 'advertisements are not to be read as if they were some testamentary provision in a will or a clause or in some agreement with every word being carefully considered and the words as a whole being compared'.

[32.18] In *Ciba-Geigy plc v Parke Davis & Co Ltd*,[42] the defendant only referred to the plaintiff's trade mark in an indirect manner while emphasising the equivalent quality but cheaper price for its own product. It was held that there was no actual misrepresentation because the advertisement made it clear that the product came from the defendant. Although the defendant used the device of an apple which was associated with the plaintiff, the advertisement did not result in confusion as to the source of the defendant's product. Aldous J quoted from the House of Lords decision in *Erven Warnick BV v J Townend & Sons (Hull) Ltd*[43] and the statement by Lord Diplock that:

> exaggerated claims by a trader about the quality of his wares that they are better than those of his rivals, even though he knows this to be untrue, have been permitted by the common law as venial puffing which give no cause of action to a competitor even though he can show that he has suffered actual damage to his business as a result.

The difficulty of showing passing off in the case of comparative advertising is that, in many cases, there is no question of customer confusion as to the origin of the product. This is particularly so in cases where the advertisement refers indirectly to the attributes of a rival product. Examples given by Aldous J in *the Ciba Geigy* case were 'A's flour is

---

[40] *Kaye v Robertson* [1991] FSR 62; see also *Compaq Computer Corpn v Del Computer Corpn Ltd* [1992] FSR 93.

[41] *McDonald's Hamburgers Ltd v BurgerKing (UK) Ltd* [1986] FSR 45.

[42] *Ciba-Geigy plc v Parke Davis & Co Ltd* [1994] FSR 8.

[43] *Erven Warnick BV v J Townend & Sons (Hull) Ltd* [1979] AC 731.

as good as B's' or 'A's flour can be substituted in all recipes for B's flour'. The position under the law of passing off was mirrored for registered trade marks prior to TMA 1963.[44] However, s 12(1)(b) of TMA 1963 extended protection to prevent use in advertising issued to the public in the course of trade. This was considered by the Court of Appeal under the corresponding provision in the UK Trade Marks Act 1938 in *Bismag Ltd v Amblins (Chemists) Ltd.*[45] It was held that although the section was obscure, it essentially prevented traders from using registered trade marks of others as a springboard to the promotion of their own products, even in cases where there was no confusion as to origin.[46] The only way around the provision for a person wishing to engage in comparative advertising was to avoid using a registered trade mark. In *Duracell International Ltd v Ever Ready Ltd,*[47] the defendant used the corporate name of its competitor and a black and white picture of a battery similar to the get-up of the plaintiff's goods, but in neither case infringed a registered trade mark. A possible defence under TMA 1963 available to a defendant engaged in comparative advertising was s 13(2) of TMA 1963, in circumstances where the trade mark was registered in Part B of the Register. This was a statutory defence to infringement proceedings where the defendant could show that, despite the use being made, it was not likely to deceive or cause confusion or indicate a connection in the course of trade with the proprietor.[48]

[32.19] The position now under s 14(6) of TMA 1996 is that it is permissible to engage in comparative advertising by use of another person's registered trade mark for the purpose of identifying the goods or services of the proprietor of the registered trade mark or their licensee.[49] However, such use must be in accordance with honest practices in industrial or commercial matters and should not without due cause take unfair advantage of, or be detrimental to, the distinctive character or reputation of the trade mark. In *Siemens AG v VIPA Gesellschaft,*[50] the ECJ ruled that use of a company's product code known in specialist circles did not take unfair advantage of the reputation of the distinguishing mark. Section 14(6), although mimicking the provisions in s 10(6) of the UK Trade Marks Act 1994, is not taken directly from any particular single provision of the Harmonisation Directive[51] but draws from both arts 5(5) and 6(1) of the Directive, the words '*bona fide* and established practices of the trade' also being used in the Paris Convention.

[32.20] Attempting to strike a balance between allowing comparative advertising in the interests of consumers but at the same time limiting the extent to which the products of a

---

44 See *Irving's Yeastvite Ltd v Horsenail* (1934) 51 RPC 110.

45 *Bismag Ltd v Amblins (Chemists) Ltd* (1940) 57 RPC 209.

46 *Chanel Ltd v Triton Packaging Ltd* [1993] RPC 32.

47 *Duracell International Ltd v Ever Ready Ltd* [1989] FSR 71.

48 *Montana Wines Ltd v Villa Maria Wines Ltd* [1985] FSR 400; see also *Pompadour Laboratories v Frazer* [1966] RPC 7.

49 *O2 Holdings Ltd v Hutchinson 3G UK Ltd* [2008] ETMR 53.

50 *Siemens AG v VIPA Gesellschaft* [2006] ETMR 47.

51 Council Directive 2008/95/EC ([2008] OJ L 299/25), which repealed and replaced Directive 89/104/EEC ([1989] OJ L40/1).

competitor, through its trade mark, can be denigrated means that the courts have a very difficult task in interpreting s 14(6)[52] of TMA 1996. The courts may look at practices in accordance with standards operated in different industries and where, for example in the car industry, it is more common to engage in comparative advertising than in, for example, the food industry. In *De Landtsheer Emmanuel SA v CIVC*,[53] the ECJ ruled that a comparison between goods with designation of origin status and goods without that status or a comparison between goods with different designations cannot be regarded as a homogenous comparison.

[32.21] It would be difficult for the courts to adopt varying standards depending on the product/service line. Such an approach would certainly make it very difficult for guidelines to be interpreted from judicial pronouncements. Some guidance can be found in Directive 2006/114/EC, which states that comparative advertising will be permitted provided that it objectively compares the features of the competing goods and services and that it:

(a) is not misleading;

(b) compares goods or services meeting the same needs or intended for the same purpose;

(c) objectively compares one or more material, relevant, verifiable and representative features of those goods and services, which may include price;

(d) does not discredit or denigrate the trade marks, trade names, other distinguishing marks, goods, services, activities or circumstances of a competitor;

(e) for products with designation of origin, relates in each case to products with the same designation;

(f) does not take unfair advantage of the reputation of a trade mark, trade name or other distinguishing marks of a competitor or of the designation of origin of competing products;

(g) does not present goods or services as imitations or replicas of goods or services bearing a protected trade mark or trade name;

(h) does not create confusion among traders, between the advertiser and a competitor or between the advertiser's trade marks, trade names, other distinguishing marks, goods or services and those of a competitor.[54]

Any comparison referring to a special offer must indicate in a clear and unequivocal way the date on which the offer ends. A price comparison does not entail the discrediting of a competitor nor does the reproduction of a competitor's logo.[55] In *Lidl Belgium GmbH v Etablissementen Franz Colruyt NV*,[56] the ECJ held that comparative advertising claiming that the advertiser's general price is lower where the comparison relates to a sample of products may be misleading for a number of reasons including if the advertisement does

---

[52] *British Airways plc v Ryanair Ltd* [2001] ETMR 24.

[53] *De Landtsheer Emmanuel SA v CIVC* [2007] ETMR 69.

[54] Council Directive 2006/114/EC, art 4.

[55] *Pippig Augenoptik v Hartlauer* [2004] ETMR 65.

[56] *Lidl Belgium GmbH v Etablissementen Franz Colruyt NV* [2007] ETMR 28.

not reveal that the comparison related only to such a sample and not to all the advertiser's products. In *L'Oreal v Bellure*,[57] the Court of Appeal was critical of aspects of the Comparative Advertising Directive but nevertheless, following guidance from the ECJ, felt bound to rule that even if a defendant was up-front and truthful, that their product amounted to an imitation or replica, they forfeited the right to rely on the Comparative Advertising Directive as a defence to an infringement claim.

[32.22] In *O2 Holdings v Hutchinson 3G UK Ltd*,[58] the ECJ ruled that even if the comparative advertisement does not satisfy all the conditions under which comparison is permitted, there is still a requirement in cases of similar marks or similar goods/services to prove a likelihood of confusion for infringement to occur.

[32.23] The word 'honest' would lean towards a subjective test but the courts in the UK have already been faced with the difficulty of such a test in interpreting the words '*bona fide*'. In *Provident Financial plc v Halifax Building Society*,[59] it was observed by Aldous J that:

> the test of *bona fide* use as enunciated by the Court of Appeal is subjective, namely whether the defendant honestly thought that no confusion would arise and had no intention of wrongfully diverting business to himself. I have always found it difficult to believe that this was the correct test, because the test tends to the result that the uninformed fool could have a defence ... whereas the properly informed reasonable man would not.

When the word 'honest' is read in conjunction with 'practices' as appearing in s 14(6) of TMA 1996, the courts are likely to adopt an objective as opposed to a subjective test by reference to the trade. In *Barclays Bank plc v RBS Advanta*,[60] Laddie J held that it was indeed an objective test, which depended on whether the use would be considered honest by members of a reasonable audience and possibly even in circumstances where the information upon which the comparison was made was ultimately found to be incorrect.[61] In *O2 Ltd v Hutchinson 3G UK Ltd*,[62] Pumfrey J cautioned against the need to perform a minute analysis of every aspect of a particular advertisement. It was more important to concentrate on the 'take home' message of the advertisement in question.

[32.24] It could be argued that comparative advertising is in fact covered by s 14(4)(d) of TMA 1996 (infringing use of a mark in advertising), but the minutes of the Council Meeting at which the earlier Community Trade Mark Regulation[63] was adopted specifically stated that the corresponding art 9(2)(d) 'does not cover the use of a Community trade mark in comparative advertising'. Section 14(6), in extracting the wording from art 5(5) of the Harmonisation Directive[64] and requiring without due cause an unfair advantage or an act detrimental to the distinctive character or reputation of the

---

57 *L'Oreal v Bellure* [2010] ETMR 47.
58 *O2 Holdings v Hutchinson 3G UK Ltd* [2008] ETMR 55.
59 *Provident Financial plc v Halifax Building Society* [1994] FSR 81.
60 *Barclays Bank plc v RBS Advanta* [1996] RPC 307.
61 *Cable & Wireless plc v BT* [1998] FSR 383.
62 *O2 Ltd v Hutchinson 3G UK Ltd* [2005] ETMR 61.
63 Council Regulation 40/94/EC ([1994] OJ L11/1).
64 Council Directive 2008/95/EC ([2008] OJ L 299/25), which repealed and replaced Directive 89/104/EEC ([1989] OJ L40/1).

registered trade marks, means that reference can be had to the interpretation of ss 14(3) and 10(3) of TMA 1996. The use of these words is strange in this context because it appears to suggest that it is only proprietors of well-established trade marks, by virtue of a reputation, who can prevent comparative advertising. A more logical explanation is that the legislative provision is designed to protect disparaging or negative advertising, which is likely to have a detrimental effect and which, by its very nature, detracts from the registered trade mark. It was stated by Laddie J in *Barclays Bank plc v RBS Advanta*[65] that:

> if the use without due cause takes unfair advantage of, or is detrimental to, the distinctive character or repute of the trade mark in most cases adds nothing of significance to the first part of the proviso. An advertisement which makes use of a registered mark in a way which is not honest will almost always take unfair advantage of it and vice versa. At the most these final words emphasise that the use of the mark must take advantage of it or be detrimental to it. In other words the use must either give some advantage to the defendant or inflict some harm on the character or repute of the registered mark which is above the level of *de minimis*.

In *Vodafone Group plc v Orange Personal Communications Services Ltd*[66] Jacob J applied the test in *Barclays Bank plc v RBS Advanta* and affirmed that the primary objective of s 14(6) of TMA 1996 is to facilitate comparative advertising, provided that it is honest. In the *Vodafone* case, the contested advertisement, which was directed to mobile phone users, stated 'On average, Orange users save £20 a month compared to Vodafone and Cellnet equivalent tariffs'. Vodafone sued both for malicious falsehood, and infringement and failed on both counts. In relation to the claim as to malicious falsehood it was held that as a notional jury, the judge had to decide upon a single natural and ordinary meaning of the words taking into account the fact that the public expect a certain amount of hyperbole in advertising. However, the more precise and specific the claim, the more likely it was that the public would take it seriously. Jacob J accepted that the most likely meaning was that asserted by Orange, ie, Orange users would save £20 a month compared to what they would be paying if they made the same use of their telephones but using the Vodafone network to make calls. That meaning was not false. If the slogan had been misleading then infringement would have occurred.

[32.25] Both art 6(1)(c) of the Trade Mark Directive[67] and the case law of the ECJ uphold the principle that use of another's trade mark may be lawful if it is necessary to inform the public of the nature of the products or intended purposes of the services offered.[68] The use of a third party's trade mark is necessary to indicate the intended purpose of a product if it constitutes the only means of providing consumers with complete information as to the possible uses of the product in question.[69]

---

[65] *Barclays Bank plc v RBS Advanta* [1996] RPC 307.
[66] *Vodafone Group plc v Orange Personal Communications Services Ltd* [1997] FSR 34.
[67] Council Directive 2008/95/EC ([2008] OJ L 299/25), which repealed and replaced Directive 89/104/EEC ([1989] OJ L40/1).
[68] *BMW v DEENIK* [1999] ETMR 339.
[69] *Gillette Co v LA-Laboratories Ltd OY* [2005] ETMR 67.

[32.26] Advertising standards are in the main ensured by means of self-regulation, the principal body being the Advertising Standards Authority for Ireland which administers the Code of Standards for Advertising, Promotional and Direct Marketing in Ireland. The advertising of certain subject matter is regulated directly by specific legislation, for example relating to tobacco[70] or alcohol[71] or distributed through broadcast media.[72]

[32.27] Under the European Communities (Misleading and Comparative Marketing Communications) Regulations 2007,[73] an individual can apply to the Circuit Court or High Court for an injunction to prevent a trader engaging in or continuing to engage in a misleading marketing communication or a prohibited comparative marketing communication. The onus is on the trader making a factual claim to prove on the balance of probabilities that it is true, if its veracity is challenged.

[32.28] The Consumer Protection Act 2007 makes it an offence to engage in misleading or prohibited commercial practices. Such practices can be the subject of a court order prohibiting the practice. An order can be sought by any person including but not limited to the National Consumer Agency[74] and an action for damages, including exemplary damages, can be sought by an aggrieved consumer. [75]

Infringement proceedings pursuant to s 14(1)

[32.29] Infringement under s 14(1) of TMA 1996 arises in circumstances where the respective marks are identical and the goods or services under the contested mark fall within the scope of the registered trade mark. In such a case, there is no requirement to show any likelihood of confusion. There is, for example, no defence available corresponding to that which existed for Part B registration under TMA 1963 where a defendant could show that its use is not likely to deceive or cause confusion or to be taken as indicating a connection in the course of trade. In *Arsenal Football Club plc v Matthew Reed*,[76] the ECJ ruled that infringement arises even in the context where the offending sign is perceived as a badge of support for or loyalty or affiliation to the trade mark proprietor. On the question of identity of goods/services, reference should be made to corresponding provisions in s 10(1) relating to the refusal on relative grounds.[77] In *British Sugar plc v James Robertson & Sons Ltd*,[78] Jacob J held that a spread was not a dessert sauce or a syrup and stated:

---

[70] The Public Health (Tobacco) Act 2002, the Public Health (Tobacco) (Amendment) Act 2004, the Tobacco Products (Control of Advertising, Sponsorship and Sales Promotion) Regulations 1991, as amended and EU legislation on the issue; see the Office for Tobacco Control website, www.otc.ie.

[71] Licensing Acts 1833 to 2008.

[72] Broadcasting Act 2009.

[73] SI 774/2007.

[74] Consumer Protection Act 2007, s 71.

[75] Consumer Protection Act 2007, s 74(2).

[76] *Arsenal Football Club plc v Matthew Reed* [2003] ETMR 19.

[77] See para **[31.11]**.

[78] *British Sugar plc v James Robertson & Sons Ltd* [1996] RPC 281.

when it comes to construing a word used in a trade mark specification, one is concerned with how the product is, as a practical matter, regarded for the purposes of trade. After all a trade mark specification is concerned with use in trade.

The ECJ in *LTJ Diffusion SA v Sadas Vertbaudet SA*[79] ruled:

> that a sign is identical with the trade mark where it reproduces, without any modification or addition, all the elements constituting the trade mark or where, viewed as a whole, it contains differences so insignificant that they may go unnoticed by an average consumer.

In *International Business Machines Corporation v Web-Sphere Ltd*,[80] the difference that arose was a hyphen and the question asked was whether the existence of the hyphen was so insignificant as to go unnoticed by the average consumer. The English High Court considered there to be identity.

Infringement proceedings pursuant to s 14(2)[81]

[32.30] Section 14(2) of TMA 1996 is divided into two parts, ie, an identical sign and similar goods or services in s 14(2)(a) and a similar sign for identical or similar goods or services in s 14(2)(b). Both are treated equally and in each case, there must exist a likelihood of confusion on the part of the public because of the identity or similarity. The provision in s 14(2) introduced a major change from TMA 1963 and, for the first time, extended infringement to goods or services not covered by the registration. The wording is taken from art 5(1)(b) of the Harmonisation Directive[82] and some guidance can be obtained from the preamble, which states that the likelihood of confusion:

> depends on numerous elements, and in particular, on the recognition of the trade mark on the market, of the association which can be made with the used or registered sign, of the degree of similarity between the trade mark and the sign and between the goods or services identified.

[32.31] The ECJ in *Sabel BV v Puma*[83] quoted from the preamble and went on to say that the likelihood of confusion must be appreciated globally, taking into account all factors relevant to the circumstances of the case:

> that global appreciation of the visual, aural and conceptual similarity of the marks in question must be based on the overall impression given by the mark, bearing in mind, in particular, their distinctive and dominant components ... the perception of the marks in the mind of the average consumer of the type of goods or services in question plays a decisive role in the global appreciation of the likelihood of confusion. The average consumer normally perceives a mark as a whole and does not proceed to analyse its various details.

The comparison is between the defendant's sign as used and the plaintiff's registered trade mark.[84] However, the plaintiff's use leading to a reputation increases distinctiveness and therefore the likelihood of confusion. The concept of 'likelihood of

---

[79] *LTJ Diffusion SA v Sadas Vertbaudet SA* [2003] ETMR 1005.

[80] *International Business Machines Corporation v Web-Sphere Ltd* [2004] ETMR 94.

[81] See para **[31.12]** et seq.

[82] Council Directive 2008/95/EC ([2008] OJ L 299/25), which repealed and replaced Directive 89/104/EEC ([1989] OJ L40/1).

[83] *Sabel BV v Puma* [1998] ETMR 1.

association' was developed by Benelux case law, a point made in the Council minutes at which the first Community Trade Mark Regulation[85] was adopted. In the Benelux case of *Union v Union Soleure*,[86] it was stated that:

> there is similarity between a trade mark and a sign when, taking into account the particular circumstances of the case, such as the distinctive power of the trade mark, the trade mark and the sign, each looked at as a whole and in relation to one another, demonstrate such auditive, visual or conceptual resemblance, that associations between sign and trade mark are evoked merely on the basis of this resemblance.

[32.32] Thus, calling to mind that an association is not to be equated with confusion as to origin, which is well illustrated with the case of *Monopoly v Anti-Monopoly*[87] where the Benelux court held that ANTI-MONOPOLY used on a game infringed the MONOPOLY trade mark even though, given the very different nature of the ANTI-MONOPOLY game, it was highly unlikely that the public would be confused into believing that the games came from the same source. The infringement lay in the association and not public confusion. The English courts showed their reluctance to follow this broad interpretation as 'creating a new type of monopoly not related to the proprietor's trade but in the trade mark itself',[88] and the ECJ has ruled that the mere association is not in itself a sufficient ground for concluding that there is a likelihood of confusion.[89]

[32.33] It is important to determine the distinctiveness of the claimed earlier mark because distinctiveness enhances the likelihood of confusion. In *Lloyd v Klijsen Handel*,[90] the ECJ ruled:

> In determining the distinctive character of a mark and, accordingly, in assessing whether it is highly distinctive, it is necessary to make a global assessment of the greater or lesser capacity of the mark to identify the goods or services for which it has been registered as coming from a particular undertaking, and thus to distinguish those goods or services from those of other undertakings. In making that assessment, account should be taken of all relevant factors and, in particular, of the inherent characteristics of the mark, including the fact that it does or does not contain an element descriptive of the goods or services for which it has been registered. It is not possible to state in general terms, for example, by referring to given percentages relating to the degree of recognition attained by the mark within the relevant sector of the public, when a mark has a strong distinctive character.

[32.34] On the question of similarity of goods/services, the courts have already had much experience through their interpretation of s 20 of TMA 1963, where they had to determine what was meant by goods of the same description. The English courts have

---

[84] *Portakabin Ltd v Powerblast Ltd* [1990] RPC 471; see also *Origins Natural Resources Inc v Origin Clothing Ltd* [1995] FSR 280.

[85] Council Regulation 40/94/EC.

[86] *Union v Union Soleure* [1984] BIE 137.

[87] *Monopoly v Anti-Monopoly* [1978] BIE 39.

[88] *Wagamama Ltd v City Centre Restaurants plc* [1995] FSR 713.

[89] *Sabel BV v Puma AG* [1998] ETMR 1; see also *Marca Mode CV v Adidas AG* [2000] ETMR 723.

[90] *Lloyd v Klijsen Handel* [1999] ETMR 690.

drawn on the older cases, and in *British Sugar plc v James Robertson & Sons Ltd,*[91] Jacob J used the following criteria:

(a)   the respective uses of the respective goods or services;

(b)   the respective users of the respective goods or services;

(c)   the physical nature of the goods or acts of service;

(d)   the respective trade channels through which the goods or services reach the market;

(e)   in the case of self-service consumer items, whether in practice they are found or likely to be found in supermarkets and, in particular, whether they are, or are likely to be, found on the same or different shelves; and

(f)   the extent to which the respective goods or services are competitive.

This enquiry may take into account how those in trade classify the goods, eg, whether market research companies, who act for industry, put the goods or services in the same or a different sector. These tests are very much a modern version of the old *JELLINEK*[92] criteria, namely the nature of the goods, their uses and the trade channels.

[32.35] There is a general tendency in considering the issue of likelihood of confusion to consider separately the similarity of the respective marks and then the goods/services and, therefore, to treat each component as a separate issue in its own right. The ECJ has warned against such an analytical approach:[93]

> A global assessment of the likelihood of confusion implies some interdependence between the relevant factors, and in particular, a similarity between the trade marks and between their goods or services. Accordingly, a lesser degree of similarity between these goods or services may be offset by a greater degree of similarity between the marks, and vice versa.

Having regard to the interdependence of the similarity of the trade marks and the similarity of the goods or services, there is no automatic bar to a finding of infringement under s 14(2) of TMA 1996 merely because the goods on which the defendant is using the mark are in some respects dissimilar to those for which the plaintiff's mark is registered.[94]

Infringement proceedings pursuant to s 14(3)[95]

[32.36] Section 14(3) of TMA 1996 implements the optional provision in art 5(2) of the Harmonisation Directive[96] and extends infringement to use of an identical or similar sign on dissimilar goods in circumstances where the registered trade mark has a reputation in the State and the use of the sign is without due cause and takes unfair advantage of, or is detrimental to, the distinctive character or the reputation of the registered trade mark.

---

[91]   *British Sugar plc v James Robertson & Sons Ltd* [1996] RPC 281.

[92]   *JELLINEK* (1946) 63 RPC 59. See also *DAIQUIRI RUM* [1969] RPC 600.

[93]   *Canon v Metro-Goldwyn Mayer* [1999] ETMR 1.

[94]   *Pfizer v Eurofood Link* [2000] ETMR 896.

[95]   See para **[31.44]** et seq.

[96]   Council Directive 2008/95/EC ([2008] OJ L 299/25), which repealed and replaced Directive 89/104/EEC ([1989] OJ L40/1).

The ECJ in *Davidoff v Gofkid*,[97] held that s 14(3) equally applies in respect of an identical or similar trade mark registered in respect of identical or similar goods/services. A trade mark with reputation enjoys protection against the use of identical or similar signs without requiring proof of any likelihood of confusion. Infringement arises where the degree of similarity is such that the relevant section of the public establishes a link between the mark and the sign, even though it does not confuse them. The owner of a trade mark enjoying a reputation cannot necessarily invoke s 14(3) to prevent the use of a sign that is viewed by the relevant public purely as a decoration.[98] Essentially, the provision is a recognition of possible dilution, which is a concept long recognised by the Benelux courts and certain US State laws and arises in instances of damage despite the absence of any confusion. There are a number of aspects pertaining to the concept of dilution and this includes a blurring of the distinctiveness of a mark towards non-distinctiveness. The Benelux courts have found dilution, for example, in relation to DUNHILL for glasses and MARLBORO for cosmetics. In *HP Bulmer Ltd v J Bollinger SA*,[99] Buckley LJ moved towards recognising dilution when he stated:

> the exclusivity of the association of the name, mark or get-up with A's business might, perhaps, be shown to be itself a valuable asset as a powerful means of bringing A's goods to the notice of the public, thus maintaining and promoting A's competitive position on the market.

[32.37] The more recognisable cases are where there is damage to the positive attributes that the mark conveys to the public. In the Benelux, the proprietor of a Dutch gin under the trade mark *CLAERYN* prevented the use of KLAREIN in respect of a liquid cleanser.[100] In the British case of *Taittinger SA v Allbev Ltd*,[101] the defendant sold as 'Elderflower Champagne', a non-alcoholic fruit drink in a bottle of a same shape, size and colour as champagne, with labels and wired corks similar to those used for champagne. The Court of Appeal upheld an injunction in favour of the champagne producers and the Master of the Rolls, Sir Thomas Bingham stated:

> The first plaintiffs' reputation and goodwill in the description Champagne derive not only from the quality of their wine and its glamorous associations, but also from the very singularity and exclusiveness of the description, the absence of qualifying epithets and imitative descriptions. Any product which is not Champagne but is allowed to describe itself as such must inevitably, in my view, erode the singularity and exclusiveness of the description Champagne and so cause the first plaintiffs damage of an insidious but serious kind.

[32.38] It was regarded as strange that the protection afforded under s 14(3) of TMA 1996 by use on dissimilar goods could be argued to be stronger than that under s 14(2) because there is no requirement to show any likelihood of confusion. Initially, this argument was rejected in *Baywatch Production Co Inc v Home Video Channel*.[102] Mr M

---

[97] *Davidoff v Gofkid* [2003] ETMR 42; see also *Adidas v Fitnessworld* [2004] ETMR 10.

[98] *Adidas v Fitnessworld* [2004] ETMR 10.

[99] *HP Bulmer Ltd v J Bollinger SA* [1978] RPC 79 at 94.

[100] *Claeryn v Klarein* (1976) 7 IIC 420.

[101] *Taittinger SA v Allbev Ltd* [1993] FSR 641.

[102] *Baywatch Production Co Inc v Home Video Channel* [1997] FSR 22; see *Davidoff v Gofkid* [2003] ETMR 42.

Crystal QC, sitting as a deputy judge of the Chancery Division, held that it would be illogical for the UK equivalent to s 14(3) to give a greater protection to non-similar goods or services by dispensing with the ingredient of a likelihood of confusion than the protection afforded to similar goods under s 14(2). The court reconciled this by deciding that the requirements under s 14(3) must include a likelihood of confusion on the part of the public. In *BASF plc v CEP (UK) plc*,[103] Knox J also held that confusion is an essential ingredient for infringement to occur under s 14(3).[104]

[32.39] However, the ECJ in *Sabel BV v Puma AG*,[105] by way of *obiter dicta*, did not consider proof of likelihood of confusion to be a requirement. In *BT plc v One in a Million Ltd*, Aldous LJ[106] also expressed the view that there was neither a requirement of the use to be trade mark use nor that it must be confusing use. The ECJ, in *Adidas v Fitnessworld*,[107] ruled that infringement under art 5(2) of Directive 89/104/EC (now replaced by Directive 2008/95/EC is not conditional on a finding of a likelihood of confusion. It is sufficient for the degree of similarity between the mark with a reputation and the sign to have the effect that the relevant section of the public establishes a link between the sign and the mark. In *L'Oreal SA v Bellure NV*,[108] the ECJ clarified the types of injury[109] against which art 5(2) of the Directive provided protection, namely:

- detriment to the distinctive character also referred to as 'dilution', 'whittling away' or 'blurring' caused when use of an identical or similar sign by a third party leads to dispersion of the identity and hold upon the public mind of the earlier mark;

- detriment to the repute also referred to as 'tarnishment' or 'degradation' caused when the third party goods may be perceived by the public in such a way that the trade mark's power of attraction is reduced;

- unfair advantage also referred to as 'parasitism' or 'free-riding' which relates not to the detriment caused to the mark but to the advantage taken by a third party amounting to an exploitation on the coat-tails of the mark with the reputation.

[32.40] In relation to the requirement to show a reputation, the Irish Supreme Court has already held, in *C&A Modes v C&A (Waterford) Ltd*,[110] that this can arise even though there is no actual use in the State. The factors taken into account by the courts in determining reputation are likely to be similar to those in a passing-off action and may include:

---

[103] *BASF plc v CEP (UK) plc* [1996] ETMR 51.
[104] For a contrasting view see Martino, Trade Mark Dilution (Clarendon Press, 1996).
[105] *Sabel BV v Puma AG* [1998] ETMR 1, para 20.
[106] *BT plc v One in a Million Ltd* [1999] ETMR 61 at 92; see also *Pfizer v Eurofood Link* [2000] ETMR 896 and *Premier Brands UK Ltd v Typhoon Europe Ltd* [2000] ETMR 1071.
[107] *Adidas v Fitnessworld* [2004] ETMR 10.
[108] *L'Oreal SA v Bellure NV* [2009] ETMR 55.
[109] Just one of the three types of injury is sufficient, see *Intel Corporation* [2009] ETMR 13.
[110] *C&A Modes v C&A (Waterford) Ltd* [1978] FSR 126.

(a)   the degree of inherent or acquired distinctiveness of the mark;

(b)   the duration and extent of use of the mark in connection with the goods or services;

(c)   the duration and extent of advertising and publicity of the mark;

(d)   the geographical extent of the trading area in which the mark is used;

(e)   the channels of trade for the goods or services within which the proprietor's mark is used;

(f)   the degree of recognition of the proprietor's mark in its and the defendant's trading areas and channels of trade;

(g)   the nature and extent of use of the same or any similar sign by third parties.

What is meant by use 'without due cause' will have to be determined by the courts but could presumably embrace claims such as prior rights, authorisation by the trade mark proprietor, necessity due to legal requirements or the trade mark proprietor's abuse of a dominant position.

[32.41] The ECJ considered the reputation required and how such reputation may be established in *General Motors Corpn v Yplon SA*.[111] A court must take into consideration the market share held by the trade mark, the intensity, geographical extent and duration of its use, and the size of the investment made by the undertaking in promoting it. The ECJ stated:

> The public amongst which the earlier trade mark must have acquired a reputation is that concerned by that trade mark, that is to say, depending on the product or service marketed, either the public at large or a more specialised public, for example traders in a specific sector.

The trade mark must be known by a significant part of the public to which it is directed.

[32.42] In *BT plc v One in a Million Ltd*, the Court of Appeal considered a claim of infringement under the UK equivalent of s 14(3) of TMA 1996 in the context of a number of internet domain name registrations incorporating the marks of certain well-known companies and concluded that such were registered to take unfair advantage of the distinctive character or reputation of the marks.[112]

Survey evidence

[32.43] Apart from the reliability of survey evidence, a question arises as to whether such is *prima facie* hearsay. A person answering a questionnaire is not on oath and unless called cannot be cross-examined. An unsworn questionnaire is not itself admissible, as illustrated in *LANCER Trade Mark*,[113] following the practice established in the *Glastonbury's* case,[114] where Lord Russell of Killowen stated:

> The applicants circularised ninety-one members of the public asking them to answer the following question: if you were offered in the ordinary way of trade slippers described as

---

[111] *General Motors Corpn v Yplon SA* [1999] ETMR 950.

[112] *BT plc v One in a Million Ltd* [1999] ETMR 61.

[113] *LANCER Trade Mark* [1987] RPC 303 at 319.

[114] *Bailey & Co Ltd v Clark, Son & Morland* (1938) 55 RPC 253.

Glastonbury Slippers what would the word Glastonbury mean to you? They received eighty three replies. To save expense they only filed affidavits by eleven of those who had replied; but in order to prove that the eleven were a proper and fair sample of the bulk, the remaining seventy-two replies were exhibited to an affidavit. This procedure was the subject of severe comment in the Court of Appeal. No doubt it was technically wrong; but the appellants not unnaturally shrank from the great expense of filing some seventy affidavits. It will be wiser perhaps in a similar case in the future to file an affidavit merely stating the number of the other answers which have been received, and that they are open to inspection by the other side's advisers. The Court will then be protected from the embarrassment of being in possession of documents which are in no sense evidence of the facts stated therein.

At face value there appears to be no better way of illustrating to a court the reputation enjoyed by a trade mark or the likelihood of confusion between respective marks than by producing survey evidence. However, the weight and reliance placed by the courts on such evidence, which is usually undertaken at great expense, is generally so minimal as to raise the question whether it is a futile exercise. In *Imperial Group plc v Philip Morris Ltd*,[115] Whitford J observed as follows:

> However satisfactory market research surveys may be in assisting commercial organisations as to how they can best conduct their business, they are by and large, as experience in other cases has indicated, an unsatisfactory way of trying to establish questions of fact which are likely to be matters of dispute.

The dilemma for litigants is that despite statements such as those by Whitford J, the courts often find such surveys helpful and of evidential value. In *Unilever plc's Trade Mark*[116] Falconer J criticised the absence of such evidence.

[32.44] In the New Zealand case of *Custom Glass Boats Ltd v Salthouse Bros Ltd*,[117] Mahon J concluded that survey evidence was admissible as being an exception to the strict hearsay rule and 'as proving an external fact, namely, that a designated opinion is held by the public or a class of public, which is not a matter of hearsay at all'.

[32.45] What is readily apparent is that it is the methodology behind any survey that is closely scrutinised and which is usually the crux of the issue as to the acceptability of survey evidence.[118] In *Imperial Group plc v Philip Morris Ltd*,[119] Whitford J set out the following criteria for surveys:

(1)   The interviewees must be selected to represent a relevant cross-section of the public.

(2)   The size of the sample must be statistically significant.

(3)   The survey must be conducted fairly.

(4)   All the surveys carried out must be disclosed, including the number carried out, how they were conducted, and the totality of persons involved.

---

[115] *Imperial Group plc v Philip Morris Ltd* [1984] RPC 293 at 302.

[116] *Unilever plc's Trade Mark* [1984] RPC 155 at 181.

[117] *Custom Glass Boats Ltd v Salthouse Bros Ltd* [1976] RPC 589.

[118] *Safeway Stores plc v Hachette Filipacchi Presse* [2000] ETMR 311.

[119] *Imperial Group plc v Philip Morris Ltd* [1984] RPC 293.

(5) The totality of the answers given (and the requisite details) must be made available to the opposite party before trial.

(6) The questions must not be leading nor should they lead the person answering into a field of speculation he would never have embarked upon had the question not been put. In *Scott Ltd v Nice-Pak Products Ltd*,[120] the interviewees were shown the defendant's product and asked questions about it. However, the product in question was not available in the UK. It was held that the entire premise upon which the questions were put was false.

(7) The exact answers and not some abbreviated form must be recorded.

(8) The instructions to the interviewers as to how to carry out the survey must be disclosed.

(9) Where the answers are coded for computer input, the coding instructions must be disclosed.

[32.46] It is important that the survey is not made under conditions remote from the conditions in which people are going to look at marks when they are in a shop. Thus in the *Laura Ashley* case,[121] Whitford J rejected evidence by way of the results of readings from a tachistoscope, which is an instrument used in perception studies. A tachistoscope comprises a viewing chamber and an eyepiece. Material is exposed on an illuminated screen by an operator. Over a period of time the image gradually becomes clearer and records are kept of the time period taken for recognition of the trade mark. Whitford J held that 'trademarks had to be considered in a business context and not in the context of laboratory experiments' and such was rejected as being a 'perfectly useless exercise'.[122] A typical way of conducting a survey in a real context is to approach purchasers having made a purchase or potential purchasers picking up and examining a product.[123] It is also important that a subject is given ample time to consider their response.[124] Where a device element appears in a trade mark the person surveyed should be shown the mark rather than be referred to such orally.[125]

[32.47] Survey evidence can be important for marginal cases. This is reflected in the statement of Jacob J in *Neutrogena Corpn v Golden United*:[126]

> Ultimately the question is one for the court, not for the witnesses. It follows that if the judge's own opinion is that the case is marginal, one where he cannot be sure whether there is a likelihood of sufficient deception, the case will fail in the absence of enough evidence of the likelihood of deception. But if that opinion of the judge is supplemented by such evidence then it will succeed. And even if one's own opinion is that deception is unlikely though possible, convincing evidence of deception will carry the day.[127]

---

[120] *Scott Ltd v Nice-Pak Products Ltd* [1989] FSR 100.

[121] *Laura Ashley Ltd v Colorol Ltd* [1987] RPC 1.

[122] See also *Saville Perfumery Ltd v June Perfect Ltd* (1941) 58 RPC 147.

[123] *Reckitt & Colman v Borden* [1987] FSR 505.

[124] *Unilever plc v Johnson Wax Ltd* [1989] FSR 145.

[125] *Neil King's Application* [2000] ETMR 22.

[126] *Neutrogena Corpn v Golden United* [1996] RPC 473 at 482.

[127] Cited with approval in *Neutrogena Corpn v Golden United* [1996] RPC 473 at 492.

Jacob J also stated the preference for evidence in chief by direct oral examination[128] and, indeed, the costs of survey evidence often make the oral evidence of a small number of witnesses a more attractive proposition for many litigants.[129]

Without prejudice correspondence

[32.48] The without prejudice rule is a rule governing the admissibility of evidence founded on the public policy of encouraging litigants to settle their differences rather than litigate them to a finish.[130] It is important that communications be specifically stated to be 'without prejudice' since a court will be reluctant to imply such to be the case.[131]

Expert witnesses

[32.49] It is possible to produce expert witness evidence on issues of which a judge may be unaware and which may impact on the likelihood of confusion, such as distinctiveness through use and special features of the market in which the trade mark is in use. However:

> It is not legitimate to call such witnesses merely in order to give their opinions whether the two signs are confusingly similar. They are experts in the market, not on confusing similarity.[132]

Transitional provisions (Third Schedule)

[32.50] The transitional provisions are contained in Sch 3 to TMA 1996. In relation to the rights conferred by a registration, as and from the date of commencement of TMA 1996,[133] the distinction between Part A and B of the Register is removed and, consequently, the Part B defence under TMA 1963 no longer applies, ie, it is not a defence for the defendant to show no likelihood of deception or confusion.[134] However, for use occurring prior to 1 July 1996, TMA 1963 applies in determining whether or not there is infringement.[135] It remains questionable if a Part B defence is available in such an instance because the use was still deemed an infringement and the Part B defence only provided for denial of injunctive or other relief and accordingly was not a defence to the infringement itself. For acts of infringement after 1 July 1996, it is necessary to determine if the plaintiff's mark is an 'existing registered mark' within Sch 3, para 1(1).

---

[128] See also *Wagamama Ltd v City Centre Restaurants plc* [1995] FSR 713.

[129] See also Smith and Wheeler, 'Trade marks: "pilot" customer surveys in trade mark cases are "experiments"' (2006) EIPR 28(7), n127; and Niedermann, 'Surveys as evidence in proceedings before OHIM' (2006) IIC 37(3), 260–276.

[130] *Rush & Tompkins Ltd v GLC* [1989] AC 1280 at 1299.

[131] *Prudential Assurance v Prudential Insurance* [2004] ETMR 29.

[132] *European Ltd v Economist Newspaper Ltd* [1998] ETMR 307; see also *O2 Ltd v Hutchinson 3G* [2006] ETMR 54.

[133] 1 July 1996.

[134] TMA 1963, s 13(2).

[135] TMA 1996, Sch 3, para 3(2).

This is defined as 'a trade mark or certification trade mark, within the meaning of the Act of 1963, registered under that Act, immediately before commencement'. Consequently, in most cases, it will be clear if the plaintiff's mark is an existing registered mark. The difficulty lies in cases where a trade mark application had been filed under TMA 1963 but had not proceeded to registration by 1 July 1996. Such a mark does not appear to be caught by the definition of an existing registered mark because it was not registered 'immediately before commencement'. Under Sch 3, para 1(2), it would be treated as pending by virtue of not having been finally determined. It is unfortunate that 'finally determined' is not defined but, presumably, it would at least mean the expiry of the opposition period following advertisement and no opposition having been encountered.

[32.51] As from 1 July 1996, the rights conferred on an existing registration are those under TMA 1996.[136] However, it is not an infringement of an existing registered mark to continue after 1 July 1996 any use that did not amount to an infringement under TMA 1963.[137] This provision also extends to a registered trade mark of which the distinctive elements are the same or substantially the same as those of an existing registered mark and which is registered for the same goods or services.[138] This is designed to protect a defendant against a plaintiff who applies to register the same mark and who, in the absence of this provision, could allege infringement of the second registration. The reference to 'services' is erroneous because it is not possible to have an existing registered mark in respect of services since such marks were not provided for under TMA 1963.

[32.52] A defendant claiming use prior to 1 July 1996, and thus a defence to infringement under TMA 1963, must show a use which has 'continued'. The words 'continuously used' appeared in s 15 of TMA 1963 and reference to court decisions interpreting those words could be made. Although there must be more than occasional use of the mark, it can still be somewhat intermittent.[139]

REMEDIES FOR INFRINGEMENT

[32.53] The TMA 1996 provides for both civil and criminal remedies for infringement of a trade mark.

Civil remedies

[32.54] An infringement is actionable by the trade mark proprietor.[140] It is also possible for an exclusive licensee to take an infringement action in specified circumstances.[141] Although rights extend from the date of filing, no infringement action is possible until

---

[136] TMA 1996, Sch 3, para 3(1).
[137] TMA 1996, Sch 3, para 3(3).
[138] TMA 1996, Sch 3, para 3(3)(b).
[139] *Smith Bartlett & Co Ltd v British Pure Oil, Grease & Carbide Co Ltd* (1933) 51 RPC 157.
[140] TMA 1996, s 18(1).
[141] TMA 1996, s 34.

the trade mark is registered.[142] Section 18(2) of TMA 1996 provides that damages, injunctions, accounts of profits and other reliefs are available as in the case of infringement of any other intellectual property right.

Damages

[32.55] An award of damages is essentially an attempt to put the proprietor into the same position as if the infringement had not occurred. The methodology used to calculate damages in other areas of intellectual property is often by reference to the notional reasonable licence. In other words, if the infringer was a licensee under an arm's length agreement, what royalty would have been expected? This is generally less suitable in cases of trade mark infringement where damages are more likely to be calculated based on lost sales to the proprietor, but it is unlikely that every infringing sale will be viewed as a loss to the plaintiff.[143] Innocence on the part of an infringer is no defence to a claim to damages.[144] Damages can also include an amount for corrective advertising being a sum representing the costs of publishing advertisements to counter the effect of infringement.[145] The European Communities (Enforcement of Intellectual Property Rights) Regulations 2006 [146] also provide for an order by way of appropriate measures at the defendant's expense for the dissemination and publication of a judgment that intellectual property rights have been infringed.

Account of profits

[32.56] This is an alternative remedy to damages and, being an equitable remedy, it is discretionary. It is essentially an accountancy exercise and deprives the defendant of profits made as a result of the infringing activity. When a plaintiff elects in favour of an account of profits, he will in the normal case get an account of what the defendant expended upon manufacturing the goods, the price received for their sale and obtain an order for the difference.[147]

Injunctions

[32.57] The normal criteria governing injunctive relief apply in relation to trade mark infringement. The Irish courts apply the decision of the Supreme Court in *Campus Oil Ltd v Minister for Energy (No 2)*[148] in determining whether or not to grant an interlocutory injunction. The test applied is, firstly, whether a *bona fide* question has been raised by the person seeking relief. Secondly, the court considers the balance of convenience, and thirdly, what irreparable damage would follow from any denial of the interlocutory injunction to the plaintiff. A decision on trade mark infringement and/or passing off at the interlocutory stage, although designed to preserve the *status quo* pending a full hearing, tends to finally determine the issue, particularly for a defendant

---

[142] TMA 1996, s 13(3) and (4).

[143] *Dormeuil Frères SA v Feraglow Ltd* [1990] RPC 449.

[144] *Gillette UK Ltd v Edenwest Ltd* [1994] RPC 279.

[145] *Spalding v Gamage* (1918) 35 RPC 101; *Roadrunner* [2000] ETMR 970.

[146] SI 360/2006.

[147] *House of Spring Gardens Ltd v Point Blank Ltd* [1983] FSR 489.

[148] *Campus Oil Ltd v Minister for Energy (No 2)* [1983] IR 88.

against whom an injunction has been granted. The reality of the market is that a defendant will usually relaunch a product under a different trade mark and is unlikely to pursue an action in respect of a trade mark that has now been superseded. The balance of convenience will usually favour the plaintiff unless there has been undue delay as it is impossible to calculate damages to the reputation of a plaintiff's trade mark by the existence of the defendant's product on the market since issues such as product quality come into focus as well as the obvious diminution of market share, which may not be recoverable. The balance of convenience will not favour a plaintiff where there has been co-existence between the respective trade marks over a reasonable period of time without any actual instances of confusion being brought to the court's attention.[149] The plaintiff who obtains an interlocutory injunction has to give a cross-undertaking as to damages to compensate the defendant for any damage caused by the injunction if it is lifted at a full hearing.

If interlocutory relief is denied, a court may nevertheless impose undertakings on a defendant such as, for example, informing customers that they have no connection with the plaintiff and to keep detailed records of all transactions certified by auditors.[150] The latter allows for ease of calculation of damages in the event that an injunction is granted at any full hearing. Other injunctive reliefs available are set out below.

Anton Piller Order

[32.58] An *Anton Piller* order[151] arises where there is a serious risk that a defendant will destroy documents or evidence upon notice of the proceedings. It is consequently *ex parte* and the jurisdiction of the court to make such an order is found under s 28 of the Judicature (Ireland) Act 1877. The order authorises entry and inspection and directs the defendant to give permission for this.

The need for an *Anton Piller* order is somewhat diminished by virtue of the European Communities (Enforcement of Intellectual Property Rights) Regulations 2006,[152] which provide for an order requiring an infringer to disclose certain stated information, including the name and address of the manufacturer or distributor of infringing goods.

Mareva injunction

[32.59] A *Mareva* injunction is a court order freezing the defendant's assets to ensure that they are not dissipated up to a certain value pending the trial of the action. Again, the basis for this injunction is to be found in s 28 of the Judicature (Ireland) Act 1877. It must be just and convenient, which means that the balance of convenience lies with the plaintiff.[153] The presence of money or assets within the State does not automatically confer a jurisdiction on the court to grant a *Mareva* injunction.[154]

---

[149] *Smith Kline Beecham v Antigen Pharmaceutical Ltd* [1999] ETMR 512.

[150] *DSG Retail Ltd v PC World Ltd* [1998] ETMR 321.

[151] *Anton Piller KG v Manufacturing Processes Ltd* [1976] Ch 55.

[152] SI 360/2006.

[153] *Harry Fleming v Ranks (Ireland) Ltd* [1983] ILRM 541.

[154] *Serge Caudron v Air Zaire* [1986] ILRM 10.

Quia Timet injunction

[32.60] This is an order preventing a defendant from carrying out a threatened act in violation of a plaintiff's right, even though such an act has not yet taken place. The proof required is 'a well founded apprehension of injury – proof of actual and real danger – a strong probability almost amounting to a moral certainty'.[155]

ORDERS

Erasure of offending sign

[32.61] This remedy is to be found in s 19 of TMA 1996 and only arises in cases where infringement has been found. As an alternative to delivery up, the High Court may instead order the offending sign to be removed from the infringing goods. If this is not reasonably practicable, then the High Court may order destruction. In the event of non-compliance or if the court believes non-compliance is likely, an order may direct delivery to an authorised person for compliance.

Order for delivery up of infringing goods, material or articles

[32.62] Sections 20, 22 and 23 of TMA 1996 should be read together. Section 20 enables the trade mark proprietor to obtain a court order[156] for delivery up of any infringing goods, material or articles. Subject to certain exceptions concerning the disability of the trade mark proprietor or fraud or concealment on the part of the infringer, an order cannot be made after the end of a period of six years from the date on which the trade mark was applied to the goods, their packaging or the material or, in the case of articles, the date on which they were made.[157] In interpreting similar delivery up provisions in the UK Copyright, Designs and Patents Act 1988, it was held in *Lagenes Ltd v It's At (UK) Ltd,*[158] that an order may be made against a person who has an infringing copy in his possession in the course of business regardless of the existence of any knowledge on the part of that person that the copy is an infringing copy. All that is required is that 'a person' has possession, custody or control in the course of business, and that person may not be the actual infringer. Thus, orders for delivery up could be made against persons engaged in storage or transportation. Section 20 does not limit the granting of an order to a situation in which infringement has been found to have occurred, unlike the position under s 19 dealing with erasure. No order will be made unless the court also makes, or it appears to the court that there are grounds for making, an order for destruction or forfeiture under s 23. If there has been an order for delivery up and no order for destruction or forfeiture, then the infringing goods, material or articles are retained by the person to whom there has been delivery up until a determination by the court.[159]

---

[155] *A-G v Rathmines Joint Hospital Board* [1940] 1 IR 161.
[156] Includes Circuit Court: TMA 1996, s 96.
[157] TMA 1996, s 22.
[158] *Lagenes Ltd v It's At (UK) Ltd* [1991] FSR 492.
[159] TMA 1996, s 20(3).

Order for disposal of infringing goods, material or articles

[32.63] Where an order for delivery up has been made under s 20 of TMA 1996, the High Court or the Circuit Court[160] may also order destruction or forfeiture.[161] In determining whether to grant such an order, the court will have regard to whether other remedies are available, which would be adequate to compensate and to protect the interests of the proprietor and any licensee[162] and, for example, a court may determine that damages are sufficient and order return of the goods, material or articles.[163] Section 23 sets out procedures whereby any person with an interest in the goods, material or articles must be notified and is entitled to appear in both proceedings for an order or an appeal against such an order.

Infringing goods, material or articles

[32.64] The provisions dealing with the various remedies refer to infringing goods, material or articles. These are defined individually in s 21 of TMA 1996.

Infringing goods

[32.65] This includes the goods themselves or their packaging, which bears a sign identical or similar to a registered trade mark. The application of the sign to the goods or their packaging must amount to an infringement. It is also provided that infringing goods include goods or their packaging, which have been or are proposed to be imported into the State in circumstances where application of the mark in the State would constitute infringement. This is subject to the doctrine of exhaustion under EU law.[164] In consideration of a similar provision under UK copyright law, it was held that the relevant person to be considered is the person making the goods abroad and notionally this was taken to have been done in the UK to determine if there is infringement.[165] Infringing goods also include a situation where a sign has otherwise been used in relation to the goods in such a way as to infringe the trade mark registration.

Infringing material

[32.66] This covers use on packaging, labelling, business paper and advertising material. Again, the material should bear a sign identical or similar to the registered trade mark in such a way as to infringe or it must be intended to be so used and such use would amount to an infringement.

Infringing articles

[32.67] This covers articles specifically designed or adapted for making copies of an identical or similar sign and would, for example, include printing plates, moulds,

---

160 TMA 1996, s 96.
161 TMA 1996, s 23(1).
162 TMA 1996, s 23(2).
163 TMA 1996, s 23(5).
164 See paras **[33.18]**–**[33.33]**.
165 *CBS United Kingdom v Charmdale Record Distributors* [1981] Ch 91.

photographic negatives, etc. These must be in the possession, custody or control of a person who knows or has reason to believe that they have been, or are to be, used to produce infringing goods or material. Once such a person is put on notice, then they have the requisite knowledge. In a scenario where a person who has control of the articles has the requisite knowledge but the person in possession does not, the articles are still deemed to be infringing articles.

Power of seizure and search

[32.68] Section 25 of TMA 1996[166] was introduced during the passage of the Trade Marks Bill through the Dáil and allows the District Court, by way of an order, to authorise a member of the Garda Síochána to seize infringing goods, material or articles without a warrant and by way of a warrant to enter premises. The goods, material or articles must then be brought before the Court, which can order delivery up, destruction or forfeiture or that the goods are to be dealt with in any other way the court thinks fit.

Order for disclosure of information and for recall, removal or destruction

[32.69] The European Communities (Enforcement of Intellectual Property Rights) Regulations 2006[167] provide for additional remedies not found in TMA 1996. These remedies include an order to disclose certain stated information on infringing activities, including information relating to the price paid for infringing goods. In addition, a court may order a defendant to recall infringing goods from channels of commerce.

Seizure by Customs Authorities

[32.70] Council Regulation 1383/2003/EC concerning customs action against goods suspected of infringing certain intellectual property rights and the measures to be taken against goods found to have infringed such rights[168] and its implementing Regulation, Regulation 1891/2004/EC,[169] have been implemented by the European Communities (Customs Action against Goods Suspected of Infringing Certain Intellectual Property Rights) Regulations 2005.[170] It is necessary to submit evidence of ownership of the requisite intellectual property, and notification is valid for a maximum of 12 months. The application can cover the EU or selected Member States. The application can be made by the right holder, authorised user or representative. The normal procedure is for

---

[166] Extends to CTM: see Trade Marks Act 1996 (Community Trade Mark) Regulation 2000 (SI 229/2000), r 6.

[167] SI 360/2006.

[168] Council Regulation 1383/2003/EC ([2003] OJ L196/7); also applies to international registrations, see *Zino Davidoff SA v Bundesfinanzdirektion* [2009] ETMR 57.

[169] Commission Regulation 1891/2004/EC ([2004] OJ L328/16) of 21 October 2004 laying down provisions for the implementation of Council Regulation 1383/2003/EC concerning customs action against goods suspected of infringing certain intellectual property rights and the measures to be taken against goods found to have infringed such rights.

[170] SI 344/2005; these replace the earlier Council Regulations 3295/94/EC and 1367/95/EC and the European Communities (Counterfeit and Pirated Goods) Regulations 1996 (SI 48/1996).

the Revenue Commissioners to supply a sample of goods taken from a consignment so that it can be confirmed that it is indeed an infringing product. It is necessary for an applicant to indemnify the Revenue Commissioners by way of security against all actions, proceedings, claims or demands consequent upon detention of the goods. Criminal sanctions are imposed against any person who makes a declaration for the release for free circulation, for export or for re-export in respect of goods found to be infringing goods. Article 11 of Council Regulation 1383/2003/EC provides for an optional simplified procedure under which rights holders can request destruction of the goods without initiating infringement proceedings, where the importer agrees or does not object to the destruction. Some Member States such as the UK, France and Germany have enacted legislation relating to this simplified procedure, but Ireland has not done so to date.[171] Member States are free to impose penalties such as fines on the parties responsible for the importation of the goods, even where the simplified procedure has been used.[172] In *Adidas AG's Reference*,[173] the ECJ held that a national law could not prohibit the disclosure of the identity of the counterfeiter to the trade mark owner. The Regulation also applies to goods in transit between two countries not belonging to the EU,[174] but in *Rioglass*,[175] the ECJ held that transit of lawfully manufactured goods from one Member State (Spain) through a further Member State (France) en route to a non-Member State was not an infringement and the detention by the French customs authority was not justified.

Criminal remedies

[32.71] Criminal remedies exist in respect of certain acts, identified in ss 92 to 94 and s 97 of TMA 1996, as follows.

Fraudulent use of a trade mark

[32.72] Under s 92 of TMA 1996, it is an offence to carry out specified acts when there is no entitlement to use the mark in relation to the goods in question or there is no authorisation by a person who is so entitled. The specified acts are the application, selling, hiring, offering, exposing for sale or hire or the distribution of goods bearing a registered trade mark or to materials used or intended to be used for labelling, packaging or advertising goods. Use of a slight variant of the registered trade mark will not be a defence because the provision also includes a mark so nearly resembling a registered trade mark. Also covered within the specified acts stated to constitute an offence is the

---

[171] As of 1 July 2010. For the UK procedures, see The Goods Infringing Intellectual Property Rights (Customs) (Amendment) (No 2) Regulations 2010 and the notes by Montagnon and Wilson in (2010) EIPR 32(7) n59–62. Generally, see Peets and Hanley, 'European Border Detention Orders' November, 2009, Trademark World #222.

[172] *Schenker SIA v Valsts Ienemumu Dienests* [2009] ETMR 35.

[173] *Adidas AG's Reference* [1999] ETMR 960.

[174] *Seiko KK v Bajrami Sinavere* [2000] ETMR 401; *Polo/Lauren v PT Duidua* [2000] ETMR 535.

[175] *Administration des Douanes et Droits Indirects v Rioglass SA* [2004] ETMR 38; see also *Montex Holdings Ltd v Diesel SpA* [2007] ETMR 13 and *Nokia Corp v Revenue & Customs Commissioners* [2009] ETMR 59.

use of material bearing the mark in the course of a business for labelling, packaging or advertising the goods. It is also an offence to possess, in the course of a business, goods or materials with a view to carrying out any of the offences or in order to assist a third party in doing so, knowing or having reason to believe that the third party has no entitlement to use the mark. There is no requirement that the goods upon which the offending mark is being used actually fall within the specification of a registered trade mark. However, it is a defence to show a belief on reasonable grounds that there was an entitlement to use the mark on the goods in question. Counterfeiters would be unlikely to be in a position to avail of this defence but if there was legal uncertainty on issues such as whether or not the contested mark was similar to the registered trade mark or the goods were identical or similar, then there is considerable scope for the defence to operate. An offence only arises if a person acts with a view to gain for himself or another, or with intent to cause a loss to another. Both inevitably arise in the case of counterfeit products. There is no specific provision for criminal liability in respect of unauthorised use of a mark in relation to services. Under s 13(4)(b) of TMA 1996, no offence arises in respect of acts carried out prior to publication of registration of the mark. On summary conviction, the liability is to a term of imprisonment not exceeding six months or a fine not exceeding €1,250,[176] or both. On conviction on indictment, the liability is to a term of imprisonment not exceeding five years or a fine not exceeding €125,000,[177] or both.

[32.73] In *R v Johnstone*,[178] the UK Court of Appeal (criminal division) held in consideration of the UK Trade Marks Act 1994 that unless there was also civil infringement, there could be no offence under the criminal provisions even though it was not possible to challenge validity in criminal proceedings. In the House of Lords[179] it was observed that the fact that a performer's name appeared on a compact disc did not necessarily equate to use as a badge of origin.

Falsification of the register

[32.74] Under s 93 of TMA 1996, it is an offence to make a false entry on the Register knowing or having reason to believe such to be false. It is also an offence to produce a document that falsely purports to be an entry in the Register.

Falsely representing a trade mark as being registered

[32.75] Under s 94 of TMA 1996, it is an offence to falsely represent a trade mark as being registered, knowing or having reason to believe that the representation is false. This includes use of the word 'registered' or any other word or device importing a reference to registration, express or implied. This would include an abbreviated term of the word registered such as 'regd' and also, presumably, the symbol ®, which is a recognised abbreviation for registered. The initials TM simply stand for trade mark. They do not imply registration and consequently, no offence arises in Ireland where TM

---

[176] Euro Changeover (Amounts) Act 2001.
[177] Euro Changeover (Amounts) Act 2001.
[178] *R v Johnstone* [2003] ETMR 1, [2003] FSR 748.
[179] *R v Johnstone* [2004] ETMR 2.

is used in conjunction with an unregistered trade mark. There is no offence if it can be shown that the reference is in fact to registration outside the State for the goods or services for which the trade mark is so registered.[180] In *Pall v Dalhausen*,[181] it was held that a provision in German unfair competition law, which prohibited the circulation of goods with the ® symbol where the mark was not registered, contravened art 36 of the Treaty on the Functioning of the European Union (the Treaty).[182] This defence in s 94(2) is not limited to instances where the trade mark is only registered in another EU Member State. In the English case of *Johnson v Puffer*,[183] an interlocutory injunction was denied in a passing-off action where the plaintiff falsely indicated its trade mark as being registered, but questions have been asked as to whether this is still good law and whether it would be likely to be followed at any full hearing of an action.[184] A person guilty of an offence under this section is liable on summary conviction to a fine not exceeding €1,250 and in the case of a continuing offence, to a further fine not exceeding €125 for every day during which the offence continues.[185]

Unauthorised use of State Emblems of Ireland

[32.76] Under art 6*ter* of the Paris Convention, the Irish government has registered both the harp and shamrock devices as being State emblems. These emblems or any future emblems that may be registered by the State cannot be used in connection with any business without the authority of the Minister.[186] The prohibition also extends to emblems so closely resembling the State emblems as to be calculated to deceive or to lead to the belief that there is authorisation. The Minister can seek an injunction against such use.[187] A defence to the prohibition arises if the user is the owner of a registered mark containing the emblem.[188] Indeed, there are a large number of trade mark registrations on the Irish Register containing the shamrock device. Under the Trade Marks Rules 1963,[189] the Controller had a discretion to refuse a mark in which the device of a shamrock or where the word 'shamrock' appeared in relation to goods other than goods expressly of Irish origin.[190] This meant that if the trade mark proprietor amended the specification to indicate Irish origin or made it a condition of registration that the goods were of Irish origin, the Controller allowed the application. Under TMA 1996, if the Minister refuses to give consent to an application containing a State emblem, then the trade mark application must be refused.[191] At least in relation to the device of a

---

[180] TMA 1996, s 94(2).

[181] *Pall Corpn v PJ Dalhausen & Co* [1990] ECR I-4827.

[182] Formerly art 30 of the Treaty Establishing the European Community (EC Treaty).

[183] *Johnson v Puffer* (1930) 47 RPC 95.

[184] Kerly's Law of Trade Marks (14th edn, 2005), para 20.056; *Jamieson v Jamieson* (1898) 15 RPC 169 at 191.

[185] TMA 1996, s 94(3).

[186] TMA 1996, s 97(1).

[187] TMA 1996, s 97(3).

[188] TMA 1996, s 97(4).

[189] SI 268/1963.

[190] SI 268/1963, r 12(1)(b).

[191] TMA 1996, s 9.

shamrock, this is really more an indication of Irish origin and provided that an applicant undertakes to use the trade mark on goods or services of Irish origin, there is no reason for the Minister to refuse to consent to registration and/or use of what is already a heavily utilised trade mark by many Irish entities.

[32.77] The Minister also has power to issue proceedings abroad against the use or registration of trade marks that are deceptive if not used in relation to Irish goods or services.[192] This is not limited to emblems registered under art 6*ter* of the Paris Convention. It would, for example, include the words 'Ireland' or 'Irish'.

Offences committed by partnerships and bodies corporate

[32.78] Proceedings in respect of any offence committed by a partnership under TMA 1996 must be brought against the partnership in the name of the firm and not in that of the partners.[193] Every partner is also subject to proceedings and will be punished if there has been an offence by the partnership unless they can prove that they were ignorant of the commission of the offence or attempted to prevent it.[194] In relation to a company, if the offence was committed with the consent, connivance of or is attributable to any neglect by a director, manager, secretary or similar officer, then that person is subject to the same set of proceedings and fines as against the company.[195] Because corporations can only act through natural persons, it is no defence for a corporation to prove that an employee who carried out the offending act was acting contrary to orders and had been properly trained, supervised and monitored.[196]

Groundless threats of infringement proceedings

[32.79] Section 24 of TMA 1996 makes provision for certain forms of relief in the event of groundless threats of infringement. Similar provisions exist under the Patents Act 1992 and formerly under the Patents Act 1964. Prior to TMA 1996, relief had to be sought through the laws of trade libel and it was necessary to show not just that the threat was calculated to injure the plaintiff's trade or to diminish the value of his goods but also that the party had acted in bad faith.[197] In *Bestobell Paints Ltd v Bigg*,[198] Oliver J stated that:

> no interlocutory injunction will be granted in defamation proceedings, where the defendant announces his intention of justifying, to restrain him from publishing the alleged defamatory statement until its truth or untruth has been determined at the trial, except in cases where the statement is obviously untruthful and libellous.

and extended this principle to trade libel.

An interlocutory injunction was granted to restrain threats of passing off in *Essex Electric (Pte) Ltd v IPC Computers (UK) Ltd*,[199] it being held that there is jurisdiction in

---

[192] TMA 1996, s 98.
[193] TMA 1996, s 95(1).
[194] TMA 1996, s 95(3).
[195] TMA 1996, s 95(4).
[196] *British Telecom v Nextcal* [2000] ETMR 943.
[197] *Coley v Hart* (1890) 7 RPC 101; *Speed Seal v Paddington* [1986] 1 All ER 91.
[198] *Bestobell Paints Ltd v Bigg* [1975] FSR 421 at 430.
[199] *Essex Electric (Pte) Ltd v IPC Computers (UK) Ltd* [1991] FSR 690.

a court to restrain, either completely or partially, the commencement of proceedings, which the court would regard as an abuse of its process and as a corollary, there must likewise be jurisdiction to restrain, in some instances, the making of threats to commence proceedings.[200] Also, the normal rules for granting an interlocutory injunction may apply if the plaintiff's case is based on a defendant's unlawful interference with the plaintiff's contractual relations with third parties.[201] The statutory provision appears to be primarily designed to protect against threats made to parties other than an alleged primary infringer. A typical example would be a manufacturer's customer who may be more inclined to switch suppliers rather than risk an infringement suit with the resultant loss of business. No right of action for groundless threats exists where the alleged infringement is said to arise out of:

(a)   the application of the mark to goods;[202]
(b)   the importation of goods to which the mark has been applied; or
(c)   the supply of services under this mark.[203]

The rules relating to 'without prejudice' correspondence may in some circumstances render the letter containing the threat inadmissible.[204] What remain are a number of instances where a trade mark owner or their legal representative must be extremely cautious in the issuance of a cease and desist letter threatening proceedings for trade mark infringement. These includes instances where the alleged infringer is affixing the mark to packaging and using the mark in advertising, and would cover wholesalers, retailers and distributors.

[32.80] The relief available to the aggrieved party are an injunction to stop the threats from continuing, a declaration that the threats are unjustified and damages sustained as a result of the threats. A defendant will usually plead justification and counterclaim for infringement. At an interlocutory stage, an injunction will be decided upon by virtue of the balance of convenience. In almost all cases, it will be readily apparent as to whether or not a person is an aggrieved party. It would obviously include the persons against whom the threat is made and manufacturers, suppliers or distributors of the pertinent goods. The relief is equally available to the owner of a CTM and an international mark entitled to protection in the State.[205] Particular care must be taken when drafting cease and desist letters based on such marks as the recipient may have a range of countries in which it can take a groundless threats action, being any country, which a reasonable recipient of the letter would consider to be a likely forum for an infringement action.[206]

---

[200] See also *Landi Den Hartog BV v Sea Bird (Clean Air Fuel Systems) Ltd* [1976] FSR 489.

[201] *Microdata Information Services Ltd v Rivendale Ltd* [1991] FSR 681.

[202] This differs from the wording of the equivalent UK provision, s 21(1)(a) of the Trade Marks Act 1994, which refers to application of the mark to goods or their packaging. It remains to be seen whether this will be regarded as a significant difference in practice.

[203] For example, this exception would not cover threats relating to offering services under a mark; see *Best Buy Co Inc and another v Worldwide Sales Corp España SL* [2010] EWHC 1666 (Ch).

[204] *Best Buy Co Inc and another v Worldwide Sales Corp España SL* [2010] EWHC 1666 (Ch).

[205] TMA 1996, ss 57(4), 59(3).

[206] *Best Buy Co Inc and another v Worldwide Sales Corp España SL* [2010] EWHC 1666 (Ch).

The onus is on a defendant to show that the threats were justified and that the contested acts constitute an infringement.[207] If the plaintiff can prove invalidity or revoke the registration in any relevant respect, then there is an entitlement to the relief.[208]

[32.81] A mere notification that a trade mark is registered or that an application for registration has been made, does not constitute a threat. Since the threat must be made against another, a general threat placed in an advertisement and not directed to a particular person is not actionable. A court will decide on what constitutes a threat through the eyes of a reasonable and normal recipient. Verbal statements can amount to threats.[209] It has not yet been decided under Irish law whether the professional advisor who issues the letter containing the threat may be liable aside from the client, although this tactic is often attempted (usually unsuccessfully) in the UK.[210] The fact that it is not explicit that infringement proceedings will be taken is not conclusive, because a threat can be veiled or implied just as much as it can be explicit. In *L'Oreal (UK) Ltd v Johnson & Johnson*,[211] a letter was found to be:

> the work of a master of Delphic utterances who uses all his skills to say everything and nothing to convey an enigmatic message which has the same effect on the recipient as a threat or adverse claim whilst disclaiming to be neither.

And who as a consequence:

> should not be surprised if the Court holds that it is at least arguable that there is a threat or adverse claim.

A communication may constitute a threat against a person other than the recipient.[212] What is strange is that apart from the law of trade libel and abuse of process, there is no prohibition on threats to take an action for passing off or criminal proceedings for counterfeiting. However, if a party threatens passing off and in the same communication notifies the recipient of the existence of trade mark registrations, this could be viewed as an implied threat of infringement proceedings and thus actionable.

[32.82] In *Symonds Cider & English Wine Co Ltd v Showerings (Ireland) Ltd*,[213] Laffoy J had cause to consider s 24 of TMA 1996, which was raised by way of a counterclaim in defence of proceedings seeking an interlocutory injunction, and commented:

> At the time the defendant initiated its application under Section 24 the jurisdiction conferred by Section 24 was spent. The jurisdiction conferred by Section 24 relates to threats of proceedings. When as happened here, a threat of proceedings burgeons into an action in this court against the party threatened, in my view, it is not open to the party against whom the action has been taken to retaliate by invoking Section 24. It is true that

---

[207] TMA 1996, s 24(3).

[208] TMA 1996, s 24(4).

[209] *Luna Advertising Co Ltd v Burnham & Co* (1928) 45 RPC 258.

[210] See Davies and Scourfield, 'Threats: Is the current regime still justified?' (2007) EIPR 29(7), 259–265; see also *Reckitt Benkiser UK Ltd v Home Pairfum Ltd, Hubert Willem Maat, Josephine Bernadette McCarthy* [2005] ETMR 94.

[211] *L'Oreal (UK) Ltd v Johnson & Johnson* [2000] ETMR 691.

[212] *Bowden Controls Ltd v Acco Cable Controls Ltd* [1990] RPC 427.

[213] *Symonds Cider & English Wine Co Ltd v Showerings (Ireland) Ltd* [1997] ETMR 238.

on this construction of Section 24 a party threatening proceedings may pre-empt an application under Section 24 by issuing a plenary summons. However, I believe this is what the legislature intended in enacting Section 24. Once a plenary summons is issued, the matter is within the seisin of this court and, if necessary, the party who was threatened can invoke the rules of procedure of this court to ensure that the issue between him and the party who issued the threat is dealt with.

[32.83] In *Trebor Bassett Ltd v Football Association*,[214] the plaintiff successfully brought an action for groundless threats and obtained a declaration of non-infringement. The defendant's cross-action for infringement was held to be an abuse of the process of the court and was struck out.

---

[214] *Trebor Bassett Ltd v Football Association* [1997] FSR 211.

Chapter 33

Trade Marks Act 1996: Limitations On Rights Conferred

USE OF A REGISTERED TRADE MARK

[33.01] The provisions of s 15(1) of the Trade Marks Act 1996 (TMA 1996) are similar to those of s 12(4) of the Trade Marks Act 1963 (TMA 1963) and provide a defence to an infringement action in circumstances where there is concurrent registration by the defendant and use of the mark on goods or services covered by the defendant's registration. This provision is subject to s 52(6) of TMA 1996 and where the defendant's mark is subsequently declared invalid, then, to the extent of the invalidity, the registration is deemed never to have been made. The section should be narrowly interpreted and is likely to require use by the defendant in the exact form in which its trade mark is registered. There is no equivalent to s 51(2), which allows for use in a form differing in elements which do not alter the distinctive character of the mark. For this reason, it is particularly important to register a mark in the exact form in which it is used. It will also be necessary for the defendant to use its registered trade mark in respect of the exact goods and/or services covered by the registration. Use outside the goods of registration will mean this defence is not available in respect of those particular goods and/or services. It should be noted that this particular defence is not provided for under the Trade Mark Harmonisation Directive[1] and, consequently, it could be argued that this is in breach of EU law. Indeed, it does not fit easily into the system under the Community Trade Mark Regulation[2] whereby there is no citation of a prior registered mark and it is left to the proprietor of an earlier registration to formally oppose following advertisement. This requires proprietors of registered marks to be vigilant, not just in the market place, but by closely observing the Irish register otherwise they may find that at least interlocutory relief will be denied and no remedy will be available until the conclusion of an invalidity action. However, in *Allergan Inc v Ocean Healthcare Ltd*,[3] the High Court has held that the s 15(1) defence was only in respect of an infringement action bought in respect of an Irish registered trade mark and not a Community trade mark. This statutory defence does not affect the position at common law and consequently a possible action for passing off.

---

[1] Council Directive 2008/95/EC ([2008] OJ L 299/25), which repealed and replaced Directive 89/104/EEC ([1989] OJ L40/1).

[2] Council Regulation 207/2009/EC ([2009] OJ L78/1), which repealed and replaced Council Regulation 40/94/EC ([1994] OJ L11/1).

[3] *Allergan Inc v Ocean Healthcare Ltd* [2008] ETMR 72.

[33.02] Section 15 of TMA 1996 should also be considered in conjunction with s 14(6), which allows the use of a registered trade mark in accordance with honest practices by any person for the purpose of identifying goods or services as those of the proprietor or a licensee. In *PAG Ltd v Hawke-Woods Ltd*,[4] Pumfrey J had to consider the defendants' use on reconditioned battery packs and casings and considered that this was in fact a new product and therefore they could not be considered as 'goods of the proprietor' as referred to in s 14(6).

DESCRIPTIVE USES

Use of one's own name and address

[33.03] Section 15(2)(a) of TMA 1996 provides that the use by a person of his own name or address shall not amount to an infringement of a registered trade mark. A similar provision existed under s 16 of TMA 1963, which required that such use be *bona fide*. A proviso to s 15(2) of TMA 1996 requires that the use be in accordance with honest practices in industrial and commercial matters, which is the wording used in art 6(1)(a) of the Trade Mark Harmonisation Directive,[5] except that the word 'or' is used as opposed to 'and'. However, this is unlikely to have any significance in practice. What will have to be determined by the courts is whether or not use by a company of its incorporated name amounts to a defence. It would still have to fulfil the criteria of being an honest practice and this is likely to exclude parties who had knowledge of the plaintiff's rights. There is a duty to act fairly in relation to the legitimate interests of the trade mark proprietor.[6] This is consistent with the law of passing off and whereby *bona fide* use of one's own name is not a defence if the name is used to describe or mark goods so as to represent that the goods are the goods of another.[7] The ECJ has considered the issue of what is in accordance with honest practices in *Celine SARL v Celine SA*,[8] and stated the following:

> in assessing whether the condition of honest practice is satisfied, account must be taken first of the extent to which the use of the third party's name is understood by the relevant public, or at least a significant section of that public, as indicating a link between the third party's goods or services and the trade mark proprietor or a person authorised to use the trade mark, and secondly of the extent to which the third party ought to have been aware of that. Another factor to be taken into account when making the assessment is whether the trade mark concerned enjoys a certain reputation in the Member State in which it is registered and its protection is sought, from which the third party might profit in marketing his goods or services.

---

4   *PAG Ltd v Hawke-Woods Ltd* [2002] ETMR 70.
5   Council Directive 2008/95/EC ([2008] OJ L 299/25), which repealed and replaced Directive 89/104/EEC ([1989] OJ L40/1).
6   *Celine SARL v Celine SA* [2007] ETMR 80; see also *Anheuser-Busch Inc v Budvar* [2005] ETMR 27.
7   *Rodgers v Rodgers* (1924) 41 RPC 277; *Asprey & Garrard Ltd v WRA (Guns) Ltd* [2002] ETMR 47.
8   *Celine SARL v Celine SA* [2007] ETMR 80.

In *Parker-Knoll Ltd v Knoll International Ltd,*[9] the defence was held to extend to the *bona fide* use by a company of its incorporated name with or without use of its corporate status, eg, 'Ltd'. This appears to remain the position despite the minutes of the Council Meeting at which the earlier Regulation 40/94/EC[10] was adopted, and which stated that the Council and the European Commission consider that the words 'his own name' apply only in respect of natural persons.[11] The defence is available even if there is some actual confusion with a registered trade mark. The amount of confusion which can be tolerated is a question of degree.[12]

Description of the goods or services

[33.04] Section 15(2)(b) of TMA 1996 provides as follows:

> (2) A registered trade mark shall not be infringed by ...
>
> (b)   the use of indications concerning the kind, quality, quantity, intended purpose, value, geographical origin, the time or production of goods or of rendering of the service or other characteristics of goods or services ...

Again, this is subject to the proviso that such use is in accordance with honest practices in industrial and commercial matters. The wording is taken from art 6(1)(b) of the Harmonisation Directive.[13] The difference between this provision and s 16(b) of TMA 1963 is that to avail of the defence under TMA 1963 it was necessary to show that the *bona fide* description was not likely to impart a reference as having the right to use the mark by virtue of being the registered proprietor or registered user. The type of question which will arise to be determined under s 15(2)(b) of TMA 1996 is the question of using a third party's trade mark to describe, for example, an ingredient in a product or that it is compatible with a particular product. In *Adam Opel AG v Autec AG,*[14] the ECJ had to consider a trade mark used on a scale model car identical to that used on that make of vehicle. The ECJ held that art 6(1)(b) did not apply even in circumstances where use of the trade mark was merely 'an element in the faithful reproduction of the original vehicles'. It is necessary to read s 15(2)(b) in conjunction with s 14(6), which generally allows use of a third party's trade mark for the purpose of identifying goods or services of the registered proprietor. Taking the example of identification of an ingredient in a finished product by reference to a registered trade mark, this would come under s 14(6). As for the finished product itself, the use is not use as a trade mark in relation to the

---

9   *Parker-Knoll Ltd v Knoll International Ltd* [1962] RPC 265; see also *Euromarket Designs Inc v Peters (Crate and Barrel)* [2000] ETMR 1025.
10   Repealed and replaced by Council Regulation 207/2009/EC.
11   Compare *Scandecor Development AB v Scandecor Marketing AB* [2001] ETMR 74 with *NAD Electronics Inc v NAD Computer Systems Ltd* [1997] FSR 380; see also *Premier Luggage and Bags v Premier Co (UK) Ltd* [2002] ETMR 69; *Anheuser-Busch Inc v Budvar* [2005] ETMR 27.
12   *Reed Executive plc v Reed Business Information Ltd* [2004] ETMR 56.
13   Council Directive 2008/95/EC ([2008] OJ L 299/25), which repealed and replaced Directive 89/104/EEC ([1989] OJ L40/1).
14   *Adam Opel AG v Autec AG* [2007] ETMR 33.

finished product but it is attributing a certain characteristic to the finished product and would consequently be a defence (or more properly, an exclusion from infringement) under s 15(2)(b). It may be advisable not to give undue prominence to the registered trade mark, otherwise it is arguable whether or not the use is honest. The courts will have to proceed with caution and it will be noted that unlike s 15(2)(c), which deals with use of a trade mark for accessories and spare parts, there is no statement in s 15(2)(b) that there can be use of a trade mark, but what is being allowed is use of an *indication*. The difference in wording between the two provisions in (b) and (c) suggests that (b) could be more limited on its scope of application, although this was not regarded by the ECJ as excluding use of a trade mark from the defence.[15] There will be instances in which what might normally have been considered an indication has, through usage, acquired a distinctiveness and become registrable as a trade mark. The courts may consider this as no longer an indication when used on products not genuinely having a characteristic due to the trade mark owners' own product/service even if it is, for example, a quality or quantity descriptor or describes the geographical origin of the goods/services. In *British Sugar plc v James Robertson & Sons Ltd,*[16] Jacob J considered the corresponding section under the UK Trade Marks Act 1994[17] and held that if a word was being used as a trade mark for the defendant's goods, then it would not be covered by the defence, even if outside the context of such use it was descriptive. Neuberger J reached a similar conclusion in *Beaumatic International v Mitchell International Pharmaceuticals Ltd,*[18] where it was held that if the trade mark is not descriptive, it would take an exceptional set of circumstances for this defence to be pleaded successfully. However, the ECJ did not consider that any different standard should apply if the geographical indication also operates as a trade mark.[19] Where, in interlocutory proceedings, a defendant raises a defence of honest use of a geographical indication, a plaintiff will have to show not only that the contested acts constitute an infringement but also that these same acts are not *prima facie* permissible under the terms of that defence.[20] In the ECJ decision of *Gerolsteiner Brunnen GmbH & Co v Putsch GmbH,*[21] the case at issue from a referral of the German Federal Supreme Court was whether or not a label KERRY SPRING, used as an indicator of origin, could be prohibited because of a danger of tonal confusion with a national German registration GERRI. The ECJ interpreted art 6(1)(b) of the Directive to mean that the holder of a trade mark registration can only prohibit the use of an indication of geographical origin if use does not correspond to honest practices in commerce or in trade matters.

---

[15] *Gerolsteiner Brunnen GmbH & Co v Putsch GmbH* [2004] ETMR 40.

[16] *British Sugar plc v James Robertson & Sons Ltd* [1996] RPC 281.

[17] UK Trade Marks Act 1994, s 11(2).

[18] *Beaumatic International v Mitchell International Pharmaceuticals Ltd* [1999] ETMR 912.

[19] *Gerolsteiner Brunnen GmbH & Co v Putsch GmbH* [2004] ETMR 40.

[20] *Allied Domecq Spirits v Murray McDavid* [1998] ETMR 61.

[21] *Gerolsteiner Brunnen GmbH & Co v Putsch GmbH* [2004] ETMR 40.

[33.05] In *Adidas AG v Marca Mode CV*,[22] the ECJ considered the question of whether the requirement of availability of a sign for use by other economic operators should be a factor and held that it

> cannot be one of those relevant factors. As is apparent from the wording of Art 5(1)(b) of the Directive and the case law cited, the answer to the question as to whether there is a likelihood of confusion must be based on the perception by the public of the goods covered by the mark of the proprietor on the one hand and the goods covered by the sign used by the third party on the other.

Use of a trade mark to indicate intended purpose: accessories and spare parts

[33.06] Section 15(2)(c) of TMA 1996 provides:

> (2) A registered trade mark shall not be infringed by …
>
> (c)   the use of the trade mark where it is necessary to indicate the intended purpose of a product or service, in particular, as accessories or spare parts: provided that such use is in accordance with honest practices in industrial and commercial matters.

This provision corresponds to art 6(1)(c) of the Harmonisation Directive.[23] A problem for a defendant in seeking to rely on this provision is the requirement that such use must be 'necessary'. The provision in s 12(3)(b) of TMA 1963 used the words 'reasonably necessary' and a court will have to determine if an absolute necessity is required under s 15(2)(c). In *Philips v Remington*,[24] Aldous J concluded:

> The purpose of this subsection is to allow such use as 'This film is suitable for a Kodak camera'. The purpose is not to allow use of valid trade marks … except where 'necessary' to indicate the purpose.

Even if this restrictive interpretation becomes generally adopted by the courts, it may not have too profound an impact because, in most instances, a defendant will be entitled to avail of the defence in s 15(2)(b) as an indication of the intended purpose.

[33.07] Because a trade mark registration grants exclusivity, the proprietor cannot rely on this right in circumstances where a third party, in the course of negotiations, reveals the origin of the goods that he has produced himself and uses the sign in question solely to denote the particular characteristics of the goods he is offering for sale so that there can be no question of the trade mark being perceived as a sign indicative of the undertaking of origin. In *Michael Holterhoff v Ulrich Friesleben*,[25] the ECJ considered the sale of precious stones in which the claimants' trade marks were indicative of the stones' style of cut. The court considered that the oral use of another's trade mark, in a

---

[22] *Adidas AG v Marca Mode CV* [2008] ETMR 44.

[23] Council Directive 2008/95/EC ([2008] OJ L 299/25), which repealed and replaced Directive 89/104/EEC ([1989] OJ L40/1).

[24] *Philips v Remington* [1999] ETMR 816.

[25] *Michael Holterhoff v Ulrich Friesleben* [2002] ETMR 79.

situation where it was clear the mark was not being used to suggest the origin of that person's goods, did not infringe the rights in it.

Repair and maintenance

[33.08] The proprietor of a trade mark registration cannot prohibit a third party from using the mark in order to inform the public that they carry on business in the repair and maintenance of goods put on the market by the proprietor. However, the mark must not be used in such a way as to suggest some connection with the trade mark owner's own distribution network.[26]

Honest practices in industrial and commercial matters[27]

[33.09] All of the defences in s 15(2) of TMA 1996 require that the defendant's use be in accordance with honest practices in industrial and commercial matters. These words were totally new to Irish trade mark law when TMA 1996 was enacted and there were no definitions as an aid to interpretation. The courts have to address this question not just under s 15(2) but also under s 14(6) which also uses the words 'honest practices'. In *Barclays Bank plc v RBS Advanta*,[28] Laddie J held that this test is objective and is determined by reference to members of a reasonable audience and that the court should not look to statutory or industry agreed codes of conduct to determine whether the advertisement is honest. Laddie J went on to hold that 'honesty has to be gauged against what is reasonably to be expected by the relevant public'. This interpretation seems to ignore the reference to industrial and commercial matters, which requires the courts to apply a subjective test by reference to trade practices. The reluctance to apply a subjective test leads to an anomaly, which was expressed by Aldous J in *Provident Financial plc v Halifax Building Society*,[29] namely, that it results in an uninformed fool having a defence whereas a properly informed reasonable person would not. However, the difference between TMA 1996 and the provision in s 16 of TMA 1963 is that the actions of the defendant must be compared against what would be considered honest practice in a particular trade. In most cases, what is dishonest applies right across industry generally and decisions under TMA 1963, where there was *male fides* or dishonesty, would still be useful precedent in relation to the application of s 15.[30] However, instances will arise where trade practices are such that the conduct of a defendant will not be viewed as dishonest and, for example, in the computer industry, it is the norm to prominently refer to another company's trade mark in the context of compatibility.

---

[26] *BMW v Deenik* [1999] ETMR 339; see also *Michael Holterhoff v Ulrich Friesleben* [2002] ETMR 7 and 79.

[27] See also para **[33.03]** and *Celine SARL v Celine SA* [2007] ETMR 80.

[28] *Barclays Bank plc v RBS Advanta* [1996] RPC 307.

[29] *Provident Financial plc v Halifax Building Society* [1994] FSR 81 at 93.

[30] *Teofani Co Ltd v Teofani* (1913) 30 RPC 446; *IZAL Trade Mark* (1935) 52 RPC 399.

Use of an earlier right

[33.10] Section 15 of TMA 1963 provided a defence to infringement in the case of continuous use by the defendant from a date prior to registration or use by the registered proprietor. A somewhat similar, but more limited, provision exists under s 15(3) of TMA 1996 which provides:

> A registered trade mark shall not be infringed by the use in the course of trade in a particular locality of an earlier right which applies only in that locality.

It is still a requirement that use by the defendant be continuous but it is limited to a particular locality, although it is still necessary for a defendant to show an earlier right by way of any rule of law and, in particular, the law of passing off, which would protect use in that particular locality.

[33.11] Section 15(3) of TMA 1996 implements art 6(2) of the Harmonisation Directive[31] but in doing so, does not follow the same exact wording. The Directive indicates that the earlier right is a defence to an infringement claim whereas s 15(3) states that use of the earlier mark does not actually amount to an infringement and thus no cause of action arises in the first place. Section 15(4) defines what is meant by an earlier right for the purposes of s 15(3). An earlier right under s 15(3) of TMA 1996 means an unregistered trade mark or other sign, which has been continuously used in relation to goods and services from a date prior to the use of the registered trade mark or its registration, whichever is the earlier.

[33.12] Article 6(2) of the Harmonisation Directive[32] states:

> The trade mark shall not entitle the proprietor to prohibit a third party from using, in the course of trade, an earlier right which only applies in a particular locality if that right is recognised by the laws of the Member State in question and within the limits of the territory in which it is recognised.

There is no definition in either the Directive or TMA 1996 as to what is meant by a locality and it remains to be decided if in fact it can embrace a whole country. It is notable that no similar provision exists under the CTM Regulation.[33] The concept of the CTM is alien to that of local trade marks and treats the whole of the EU as one territory. If a national registration was treated on the same footing, then the whole of Ireland would not be viewed as a locality. The rationale of the provision is to cater for the position where there are localised earlier rights and, to this limited extent, co-existence is tolerated. If the earlier rights extend to the whole State, then an action for invalidity is appropriate under s 52(2) of TMA 1996 or, alternatively, there may be a defence that a likelihood of confusion does not exist.

---

[31] Council Directive 2008/95/EC ([2008] OJ L 299/25), which repealed and replaced Directive 89/104/EEC ([1989] OJ L40/1).

[32] Council Directive 2008/95/EC ([2008] OJ L 299/25), which repealed and replaced Directive 89/104/EEC ([1989] OJ L40/1).

[33] Council Directive 207/2009/EC, which repealed and replaced Council Regulation 40/94/EC; see *Compass Publishing BV v Compass Logistics Ltd* [2004] RPC 41.

[33.13] What is meant by continuous use, in the context of s 15(4) of TMA 1996, in determining whether or not an earlier right exists, will have to be decided in conjunction with the requirement that the use is such that it would sustain an action for passing off. This would mean that use can be somewhat interrupted. There are many instances in which plaintiffs have succeeded in passing off actions where their businesses have been shut down for some time.[34] The courts are likely to look at any circumstances surrounding the interrupted use and whether this has affected the goodwill rather than simply taking a literal meaning of the word 'continuous'. Even the words 'continuously used' in s 15 did not carry this literal interpretation.[35] It is somewhat of an anomaly that the continuous use must be in relation to the goods or services of the registration and does not extend to similar goods or services that are now protected by way of registration under s 14(2). This is unlikely to have been the intention of the legislature because if there is an earlier right that meets the other criteria in s 15(4), then there is an even stronger case that it should be a defence against an action for infringement based on similar goods.

[33.14] Although s 15(3) of TMA 1996 requires continuous use prior to use or registration by the proprietor, it does not state that the goodwill must exist at that time. A scenario could exist whereby there was a small amount of continuous use prior to registration or use by the proprietor but the defendant's goodwill accrued through subsequent usage. Again, it is doubtful that this was the intention of the legislature but it arises from a failure to properly define an earlier right as necessitating that the requisite goodwill exists prior to the registrant's own rights, which appears to be the position under art 6(2) of the Harmonisation Directive.[36]

Use in order to identify proprietor's own goods or services

[33.15] Section 14(6) of TMA 1996 provides for a defence to infringement in circumstances where there is:

- use for the purposes of identifying the goods or services of the trade mark owner or licensee; and
- where such use without due cause, does not take unfair advantage of or is detrimental to, the distinctive character or reputation of the trade mark.

It is quite legitimate to use another person's trade mark to describe the compatibility or suitability of a particular product being, for example, a spare part or accessory. In the computer industry, it is common to identify software or hardware compatibility by reference to another company's trade mark. A common instance of use of another's mark is in comparative advertising.[37] This defence was successfully raised in the case of

---

[34] *Ad-Lib Club Ltd v Granville* [1972] RPC 673; *A Levey v Henderson-Kenton (Holdings) Ltd* [1974] RPC 617.

[35] *Smith, Bartlett & Co v British Pure Oil Grease and Carbide Co* (1933) 51 RPC 157 at 163.

[36] Council Directive 2008/95/EC ([2008] OJ L 299/25), which repealed and replaced Directive 89/104/EEC ([1989] OJ L40/1).

[37] See paras **[32.16]– [32.28]**.

Barclays Bank plc v RBS Advanta,[38] where, in considering the corresponding section in the UK Trade Marks Act 1994, the High Court held that the primary objective was to allow for comparative advertising. So long as the use of the competitor's mark is honest, there is nothing wrong with informing the public of the relative merits of competing goods or services and using registered trade marks to identify them. What qualifies as honest practices was held to be an objective test by reference to members of a reasonable audience. It was stated by Laddie J:

> The fact that the advertising pokes fun at the proprietor's goods or services and emphasises the benefits of the defendant's is a normal incidence of comparative advertising. Its aim will be to divert customers from the proprietor. No reasonable observer would expect one trader to point to all the advantages of its competitor's business and failure to do so does not *per se* take the advertising outside what reasonable people would regard as 'honest'. Thus mere trade puffery, even if uncomfortable to the registered proprietor, does not bring the advertising within the scope of trade mark infringement. Much advertising is recognised by the public as hyperbole. The Act does not impose on the courts an obligation to try to enforce, through the back door of trade mark legislation, a more puritanical standard. If, on the other hand, a reasonable reader is likely to say, on being given the full facts, that the advertisement is not honest, for example, because it is significantly misleading, then the protection from trade mark infringement is removed.

The nature of the goods or services may affect the reasonable perception of what advertising is honest. There is no requirement to identify the owner or licensee of the trade mark or that it is in fact a trade mark by, for example, use of the initials TM. Section 14(6) does not apply to a retailer of parallel imported goods.[39]

ACQUIESCENCE

[33.16] This is a totally new concept to Irish trade mark legislation and its introduction in s 53 of TMA 1996 is by way of implementation of art 9 of the Trade Mark Harmonisation Directive.[40] Under s 53, acquiescence arises where the proprietor of an earlier trade mark or right has acquiesced for a continuous period of five years in the use of a later registered trade mark in the State. It is required that the proprietor of the earlier trade mark or right was aware of such usage. The effect of acquiescence is that it is no longer possible to seek invalidity of the later registration or to oppose continued use for those goods or services in relation to which there has been acquiescence. It would not prevent an action against use on similar goods/services to those for which the acquiescence took place. Essentially, what takes place if s 53 is invoked is an enforced co-existence of trade marks, since even in the case of acquiescence, the proprietor of the later mark cannot invoke its mark against use of the earlier mark or exploitation of the earlier right. Each party must tolerate each other's usage. A claim of acquiescence will

---

[38] *Barclays Bank plc v RBS Advanta* [1996] RPC 307.

[39] *Levi Strauss v Tesco Stores* [2002] ETMR 95.

[40] Council Directive 2008/95/EC ([2008] OJ L 299/25), which repealed and replaced Directive 89/104/EEC ([1989] OJ L40/1).

not be upheld if it can be shown that the registration of the later trade mark was applied for in bad faith.

[33.17] Acquiescence is stated to deny the proprietor of the earlier trade mark or right the ability 'to oppose the use of the later trade mark'. This strange wording leaves open an argument that all that is denied is injunctive relief, and that damages or other remedies may still be available, which is a bizarre scenario with which the courts are unlikely to find favour. The acquiescence must be to the use of a registered mark. However, the knowledge required is in relation to *use* as opposed to *registration*. Thus, a situation could possibly exist where the owner of the earlier trade mark may know of the existence of a registration for over five years but will not have acquiesced where their knowledge of use of the later registered mark is less than five years. Although the courts are likely to adopt constructive notice as a criterion, it is reasonably common for many marks to be registered for some time before being used. Therefore, the mere fact of registration should not constitute constructive notice that the mark is in actual use. There is no statutory provision for acquiescence where the later trade mark is unregistered. Section 53 of TMA 1996 is limited to acquiescence in the use of the mark that is on the Register. The statutory effect of acquiescence does not extend to an action for passing off, although delay could result in equitable remedies being denied. Prior to s 53 the courts were reluctant to uphold a claim as to acquiescence[41] except as a factor in deciding on the balance of convenience when seeking interlocutory relief.

EXHAUSTION OF RIGHTS/PARALLEL IMPORTS

[33.18] This limitation on the right to enforce a trade mark is common to intellectual property law in general. The doctrine is specifically stated in s 16 of TMA 1996 and art 7 of the Trade Mark Harmonisation Directive.[42] A registered proprietor cannot pursue an infringement action if the goods are the proprietor's own goods, which have been put onto the market in the European Economic Area either by the proprietor or with its consent, for example, by a subsidiary or licensee. The doctrine is a reconciliation between the right to enforce an intellectual property right weighed against the objective of allowing the free movement of goods throughout the EU. Article 34 of the Treaty on the Functioning of the European Union (the Treaty)[43] provides that: 'Quantitative restrictions on imports and all measures having equivalent effect shall be prohibited between Member States'. Normally this means that goods lawfully put on sale in one EU Member State must be acceptable throughout the EU and national laws cannot prohibit free movement. Article 36 of the Treaty[44] provides for a derogation on several grounds, which include the protection of industrial and commercial property, ie, intellectual property, where this does not constitute a means of arbitrary discrimination or a

---

[41] *Electrolux Ltd v Electrix Ltd* (1954) 71 RPC 23; Daimler Chrysler AG v Javid Alavi [2001] ETMR 98.

[42] Council Directive 2008/95/EC ([2008] OJ L 299/25), which repealed and replaced Directive 89/104/EEC ([1989] OJ L40/1).

[43] Formerly EC Treaty, art 28.

[44] Formerly EC Treaty, art 30.

disguised restriction on trade between Member States. Thus, art 36 recognises that the owner of a national trade mark registration can rely on the protection afforded by that article to prevent the importation of goods under a trade mark which infringes that national registration even though the trade mark is legitimately used in other countries of the EU. However, if the goods are those of the proprietor or a licensee, then any attempt to prevent importation by the proprietor is, in effect, a disguised restriction on trade. What is permitted is control by the proprietor of the first marketing in the EEA.

[33.19] Initially, cases were decided under the anti-competition laws of the former EC Treaty. In *Grundig and Consten v Commission*,[45] an agreement was held by the ECJ to be a deliberate attempt to use trade marks to prevent price competition by way of parallel imports. The agreement was between the German manufacturer, Grundig, and its sole distributor in France, Consten. Under the agreement, the distributor was allowed to register in its own name, the trade mark GINT. Grundig not only applied its own GRUNDIG trade mark to products but also the trade mark GINT and thus the distributor claimed infringement when a parallel import occurred. The ECJ considered that the aim of the agreement was to isolate the French market for Grundig products and distort competition. The ECJ went on to draw a distinction between recognition of the existence or ownership of intellectual property rights and the exercise of such rights, which can be curtailed in certain circumstances such as anti-competitive agreements. The early cases saw a general hostility to trade marks as being exclusive rights, which are limited by national registrations, and in *Sirena Srl v Eda Srl*,[46] the ECJ stated:

> The exercise of a trade mark right is particularly apt to lead to a partitioning of markets, and thus to impair the free movement of goods between states which is essential to the common market. Moreover, a trade mark right is distinguishable in this context from other rights of industrial and commercial property in as much as the interests protected by the latter are usually more important, and merit a higher degree of protection, than the interests protected by an ordinary trade mark.

[33.20] The European Commission considered a complaint against Bayer for failure to meet all orders placed by Spanish and French wholesalers on the grounds that the UK subsidiary of Bayer was suffering a substantial loss of turnover due to parallel imports from both France and Spain. The European Commission found that there was the operation of an export ban through an agreement with its wholesalers contrary to art 101 of the Treaty,[47] which deals with anti-competitive agreements between undertakings. However, the ECJ concluded that the existence of an agreement contrary to art 101 cannot be based on what is only the expression of a unilateral policy on the part of one party, which that party can put into effect without the assistance of others.[48]

[33.21] Continuing with the principle of distinguishing between the existence and exercise of an intellectual property right, the ECJ considered subsequent cases under arts

---

[45] *Etablissements Consten SARL and Grundig-Verkaufs-GmbH v European Commission* [1966] ECR 299.

[46] *Sirena Srl v Eda Srl* [1971] ECR 69.

[47] Formerly EC Treaty, art 81.

[48] *Bundesverband v Bayer* [2004] ETMR 100.

28 to 30 of the EC Treaty (now arts 34 and 36 of the Treaty) and developed the doctrine of exhaustion. In *Deutsche Grammophon v Metro-SB*,[49] which was a copyright case, the ECJ held that a German record company could not rely on copyright to stop a supermarket from selling sound recordings bought from the record company's French distributor. The application of the doctrine of exhaustion to trade marks was illustrated in *Centrafarm BV v Winthrop BV*,[50] where the ECJ gave a definition as to what the court viewed as the specific subject matter of a trade mark:

> In relation to trade marks, the specific subject matter of the industrial property is the guarantee that the owner of the trade mark has the exclusive right to use that trade mark, for the purpose of putting products protected by the trade mark into circulation for the first time, and is therefore intended to protect him against competitors wishing to take advantage of the status and reputation of the trade mark by selling products illegally bearing that trade mark.

This narrow interpretation of the function of a trade mark led to a rigorous application of the doctrine of exhaustion in *Van Zuylen Frères v Hag Ag (Hag I)*,[51] which is a heavily criticised decision of the ECJ and its attempt to deal with what is termed 'trade marks of common origin'. Prior to the Second World War, a German company owned the HAG trade mark in Germany and a subsidiary of the German company held the registration in Belgium. After the Second World War, the rights in Belgium were sequestrated and assigned to Van Zuylen. The German company commenced selling goods under the trade mark in Belgium and it was claimed that this amounted to infringement. The ECJ held that because the registrations had a common origin, the German product was to be considered as a parallel import and did not constitute infringement. The ECJ viewed the basic function of a trade mark as being to guarantee to consumers that the product has the same origin. In *Terrapin v Terranova*,[52] the ECJ emphasised that national trade mark rights held by different undertakings could prevent importation, provided that there were no agreements restricting competition and no legal or economic ties between the undertakings, and their respective rights had arisen independently of one another. A national registration can even be used to stop importation under a non-distinctive trade mark, as illustrated in *Deutsche Renault AG v Audi AG*,[53] where the word QUATTRO meaning the number four in Italian was registered in Germany on evidence being provided of distinctiveness through usage.

[33.22] The ECJ has more recently recognised the importance of trade marks, not just to owners but to consumers, and has relaxed the boundaries of the doctrine of exhaustion by emphasising the need for full consent by the trade mark proprietor or its licensee to the first marketing. This was already recognised under patent law where a compulsory licence was not viewed as a consent.[54] The ECJ was prepared to disapprove of the

---

[49] *Deutsche Grammophon GmbH v Metro-SB-Grossmärkte GmbH & Co KG* [1971] ECR 487.
[50] *Centrafarm BV and Adriaan De Peijper v Winthrop BV* [1974] ECR 1183.
[51] *Van Zuylen Frères v Hag Ag* [1974] ECR 731.
[52] *Terrapin (Overseas) Ltd v Terranova Industrie CA Kapferer & Co* [1976] ECR 1039.
[53] *Deutsche Renault AG v Audi AG* [1993] ECR I-6227, [1993] 1 CMLR 461.
[54] *Pharmon BV v Hoechst AG* [1985] ECR 2281.

decision in *Hag I*,[55] and, in *CNL-Sucal NV v HAG GFAG (Hag II)*,[56] reached a different decision to *Hag I* although factually the cases could not be distinguished. In *Hag II*, there was a reverse set of facts whereby the Belgium company sought to sell into the German market. The ECJ stated:

> Trade mark rights are, it should be noted, an essential element in the system of undistorted competition which the Treaty seeks to establish and maintain. Under such a system, an undertaking must be in a position to keep its customers by virtue of the quality of its products and services, something which is possible only if there are distinctive marks which enable customers to identify those products and services. For the trade mark to be able to fulfil this role, it must offer a guarantee that all goods bearing it have been produced under the control of a single undertaking which is accountable for their quality.

The ECJ emphasised the determining factor to be the absence of any consent on the part of the proprietor of the trade mark protected by national legislation in a situation where the first marketing is by an undertaking that is economically and legally independent. The ECJ also pointed out that the essential function of the trade mark would be jeopardised because of possible confusion by the public. In *IHT Internazionale Heiztechnick GmbH v Ideal Standard GmbH*,[57] the ECJ had to consider the situation of trade marks of common origin and a voluntary assignment to an unconnected assignee. It was held that the consent implicit in any assignment is not the consent required for application of the doctrine of exhaustion of rights. For that, the owner of the right in the importing State must, directly or indirectly, be able to determine the products to which the trade mark may be affixed in the exporting State and to control their quality. That power was held to be lost if, by assignment, control over the trade mark was surrendered to a third party having no economic link with the assignor.

[33.23] The consent required under art 7(1) of the Harmonisation Directive[58] must be a consent relating to each individual item of the product in respect of which exhaustion is pleaded.[59] The ECJ ruled that a consent can be implied.[60] However, given the statements on when an implied consent cannot be inferred, it is an unusual set of circumstances, such as in *Mastercigars Direct v Hunters & Frankau Ltd*,[61] where implied consent would arise. It is not inferred, for example, from the fact that the goods carry no warning of a prohibition of their being placed on the market within the EEA. However, where the proprietor imports into the EEA with a view to sale but where no sale has actually taken

---

55 *Van Zuylen Frères v Hag AG* [1974] ECR 731.

56 *CNL-Sucal NVSA v HAG GFAG* [1990] ECR I-3711.

57 *IHT Internationale Heiztechnik GmbH and Danziger v Ideal-Standard GmbH and Wabco Standard GmbH* [1994] ECR I-2789; see also *Doncaster Pharmaceuticals v Bolton Pharmaceutical Co* [2006] ETMR 65.

58 Council Directive 2008/95/EC ([2008] OJ L 299/25), which repealed and replaced Directive 89/104/EEC ([1989] OJ L40/1).

59 *Sebago Inc v GB-UNIC SA* [1999] ETMR 681.

60 *Zino Davidoff SA v A&G Imports and Levi Strauss & Co v Tesco Stores* [2002] ETMR 9; see *Adidas-Salomon AG v Microhaven Ltd* [2003] ETMR 94; *Makro Zelfbedieningsgroothandel CV v Diesel SpA* [2010] ETMR 2.

61 *Mastercigars Direct v Hunters & Frankau Ltd* [2007] ETMR 44.

place, this does not amount to exhaustion.[62] Also, tester or demonstration products distinguishable from the products normally sold may be precluded from the principle of exhaustion.[63] In *Roche Products Ltd v Kent Pharmaceuticals*,[64] the use of an EU recognised symbol on packaging was held to be a sign of quality assurance and could not be viewed as an indication that the trade mark proprietor had consented to placement within the EEA.

[33.24] It is no defence to a claim of exhaustion to show that first marketing was in a Member State where there was, in fact, no protection[65] or that there was a divergence between the laws of the EU Member States concerned.[66]

[33.25] The wording in s 16(1) of TMA 1996 specifies that the trade mark proprietor should put the product on sale in the EEA. In *EMI Records Ltd v CBS*,[67] the ECJ held that the former art 28 of the EC Treaty (now art 34 of the Treaty) did not apply to goods coming from outside the EU. The trade mark owner could rely on a national registration to prevent importation from the US. In the UK, under the former Trade Marks Act 1938, corresponding to the Irish TMA 1963, the Court of Appeal did not support international exhaustion in *Revlon Inc v Cripps & Lee Ltd*,[68] but this was distinguished in *Colgate-Palmolive v Markwell Finance Ltd*;[69] but in that case, the quality of the product first sold in Brazil did not correspond to those on sale under the trade mark in the UK.[70] The ECJ, in *Silhouette International v Hartlauer*,[71] held that Member States do not have any discretion on the issue of whether or not to allow for international exhaustion. National laws which provide for exhaustion in respect of products put on the market outside the EEA are contrary to art 7(1) of the Trade Mark Harmonisation Directive.[72]

[33.26] In *Van Doren v Lifestyle Sports*[73] the ECJ had to consider whether a defendant who pleaded a defence of exhaustion has the evidential burden of proving first marketing in the EEA with the proprietor's consent. The ECJ held that such a burden of proof could, in certain circumstances, result in a partitioning of national markets and that consequently the burden of proving initial sale outside the EEA may be placed on the trade mark proprietor. Such circumstances include a situation where the trade mark proprietor markets its products in the EEA using an exclusive distribution system.

---

[62] *Peak Holding AB v Axolin-Elinor AB* [2005] ETMR 28.
[63] *Coty Prestige Lancaster Group GmbH v Simex Trading AG* [2010] ETMR 41.
[64] *Roche Products Ltd v Kent Pharmaceuticals* [2006] ETMR 81, [2007] ETMR 27.
[65] *Merck & Co Inc v Stephar BV and Petrus Stephanus Exler* [1981] ECR 2063.
[66] *Keurkoop BV v Nancy Kean Gifts BV* [1982] ECR 2853.
[67] *EMI Records Ltd v CBS United Kingdom Ltd* [1976] ECR 811.
[68] *Revlon Inc v Cripps & Lee Ltd* [1980] FSR 85.
[69] *Colgate-Palmolive v Markwell Finance Ltd* [1989] RPC 497.
[70] See also *Castrol Ltd v Automotive Oil Supplies Ltd* [1983] RPC 315.
[71] *Silhouette International Schmied GmbH & Co KG v Hartlauer Handelsgesellschaft mbH* [1998] ETMR 539; see also *Sebago Inc v GB-UNIC SA* [1999] ETMR 681.
[72] Council Directive 2008/95/EC ([2008] OJ L 299/25), which repealed and replaced Directive 89/104/EEC ([1989] OJ L40/1).
[73] *Van Doren v Lifestyle Sports* [2003] ETMR 75.

[33.27] Exhaustion of rights does not take effect where the goods have been changed or impaired after they have been put onto the market, and consequently, under s 16(2) of TMA 1996, there exist legitimate reasons for the proprietor of the trade mark to oppose further dealings in the goods. The question of repackaging and relabelling of trade marked goods has been considered by the ECJ in a number of cases. In *Hoffmann La Roche & Co v Centrafarm,*[74] the importer purchased VALIUM in the UK, repacking it in different quantities for the German market, adding the trade mark with its own name and address. The ECJ held that it was permissible to oppose the importation and sale. The essential function of a trade mark was to guarantee to consumers the original identity of the trade marked product. This requires that the goods have not been tampered with. The ECJ has set out guidelines under which an importer may avoid infringement. Thus, in *Pfizer Inc v Eurim-Pharm GmbH,*[75] repackaging took place but the packaging clearly indicated that the goods were repackaged and imported and consumers were not misled as to origin, hence there was no infringement.

[33.28] In *Bristol-Myers Squibb v Paranova,*[76] the ECJ emphasised that the parallel importer should engage in the least amount of tampering with the original packaging necessary to market in the Member State of importation and stated:

> The owner may oppose the repackaging of the product in the new external packaging where the importer is able to achieve packaging which may be marketed in the Member State of importation by, for example, affixing to the original external or inner packaging new labels in the language of the Member State of importation, or by adding new user instructions or information in the language of the Member State of importation, or by replacing an additional article not capable of gaining approval in the Member State of importation with a similar article that has obtained such approval.

In a series of cases,[77] the ECJ listed stringent requirements with which a parallel importer must comply when repackaging goods, or, for example, applying an external overstickering label,[78] particularly pharmaceutical products, namely:

(a) he must indicate on the external packaging who repackaged the product and who manufactured the product, printed in such a way as to be understood by a person with normal eyesight exercising a normal degree of attentiveness;

(b) if the parallel importer has added an extra article to the package, he must ensure that its origin is indicated in such a way as to dispel any impression that the trade mark owner is responsible for it;

---

74 *Hoffmann-La Roche & Co AG v Centrafarm Vertriebsgesellschaft Pharmazeutischer Erzeugnisse mbH* [1978] ECR 1139.
75 *Pfizer Inc v Eurim-Pharm GmbH* [1981] ECR 2913.
76 *Bristol-Myers Squibb v Paranova* [1997] FSR 102.
77 *Bristol-Myers Squibb v Paranova; Eurim-Pharm v Beiersdorf; MPA Pharma v Rhône-Poulenc* [1997] FSR 102.
78 *Boehringer Ingelheim KG v Swingward Ltd* [2007] ETMR 71.

(c)   he must give the trade mark owner advance notice of the product being put on sale.[79] The trade mark owner may also require the parallel importer to supply him with a specimen of the repackaged product before it goes on sale;

(d)   the presentation of the repackaged product must not be such as to damage the reputation of the trade mark and of the proprietor; thus, the repackaging must not be defective, of poor quality or untidy.[80]

It is not necessary for the parallel importer to state that the repackaging was carried out without the authorisation of the trade mark owner. The ECJ has accepted that replacement packaging of pharmaceutical products is objectively necessary because of strong resistance from a significant proportion of consumers to relabelled pharmaceutical products.[81] However, compliance with regulatory requirements may impose limitations on repackaging[82] and the presentation of the packaging should be assessed against the condition that it should not be such as to be liable to damage the reputation of the trade mark or that of its proprietor.[83]

[33.29] In *Centrafarm v American Home Products*,[84] the ECJ considered the question of re-affixing a trade mark. American Home Products sold tranquillisers under the trade marks SERENID in the UK and SERESTA in the Netherlands, which were considered to be identical products. The parallel importer imported SERENID into the Netherlands and applied the trade mark SERESTA. It was held that there was infringement but the ECJ cautioned that if a trade mark proprietor had deliberately pursued a policy of using different trade marks in EU countries in order to partition the market, then the exercise of the right may constitute a disguised restriction on trade within the meaning of the former art 30 of the EC Treaty (now art 36 of the Treaty). In *Pharmacia & Upjohn v Paranova*,[85] the importer repackaged under the trade mark recognised in the importing country because of differing trade marks used by the manufacturer in various EU countries. The ECJ ruled that it is necessary to assess the circumstances prevailing at the time of marketing in the Member State of import to establish whether it is objectively necessary to replace the original mark in order that the product may be marketed by the parallel importer.

[33.30] In *Frits Loendersloot v George Ballantine & Son Ltd*,[86] the ECJ was asked to consider the activities of a Dutch company, who removed identification numbers from the labels of Scotch whisky producers and in some instances replaced labels with similar

---

[79]   *Boehringer Ingelheim KG v Swingward Ltd* [2002] ETMR 78.

[80]   *Boehringer Ingelheim KG v Swingward Ltd* [2007] ETMR 71.

[81]   *Merck, Sharp, Dohme v Paranova* [2002] ETMR 80; see also *Boehringer Ingelheim v Swingward Ltd* [2004] ETMR 65.

[82]   *Aventis Pharma v Kohlpharma* [2003] ETMR 11.

[83]   *Wellcome Foundation Ltd v Paranova Pharmazeutika Handels GmbH* [2009] ETMR 20.

[84]   *Centrafarm BV v American Home Products Corpn* [1978] ECR 1823; see also *Dr Karl Thomae v EC Commission* [2003] ETMR 95.

[85]   *Pharmacia & Upjohn v Paranova* [1999] ETMR 937.

[86]   *Frits Loendersloot v George Ballantine & Son Ltd* [1998] ETMR 10, see also *Microsoft v Computer Future Distribution Ltd* [1998] ETMR 597.

labels removing reference to the word '*PURE*' and the importer's name on the labels. It was held that even if it constituted a barrier to intra-EU trade, the owner of the trade mark rights could prevent the removal and reaffixing or replacing of labels bearing the trade mark unless:

- it is established that the use of the trade mark rights by the owner to oppose the marketing of its relabelled products under the trade mark would contribute to artificial partitioning of the markets between Member States;
- it is shown that the relabelling cannot affect the original condition of the product;
- the presentation of the relabelled product is not such as to be liable to damage the reputation of the trade mark and its owner; and
- the person who relabels the products informs the trade mark owner of the relabelling before the relabelled products are put on sale.

[33.31] In *Parfums Christian Dior v Evora*,[87] the ECJ held that the principle of exhaustion allows the reseller to advertise under the trade mark in the further commercialisation of the goods. However, the ECJ went on to consider whether or not under art 7(2) of the Trade Mark Harmonisation Directive,[88] there were legitimate reasons for opposing further commercialisation. It had to try and strike a balance between the legitimate interest of the trade mark owner in being protected against resellers using its trade mark for advertising in a manner which could damage the reputation of the trade mark and the reseller's legitimate interest in being able to resell the goods in question by using advertising methods which are customary in its section of trade. In general, the interests of the reseller are to prevail unless there are special circumstances where the use would seriously damage the reputation of the trade mark.

[33.32] In *CHEETAH Trade Mark*,[89] the defendant purchased a herbicide in Belgium and sold it in the UK without altering the packaging. However, the defendant did use the plaintiff's different UK trade mark on delivery notes and invoices. Infringement was held to have occurred. The use of different marks in different countries, in the absence of other evidence, was held not to be a disguised restriction on trade.

[33.33] In *Copad SA v Christian Dior Couture SA*,[90] the ECJ had to consider sales by a licensee in breach of the licence agreement and concluded that if the breach fell within the provisions of art 8(2) of the Harmonisation Directive, then the goods had been put on the market without the consent of the trade mark proprietor.

---

87 *Parfums Christian Dior v Evora* [1998] ETMR 26.
88 Council Directive 2008/95/EC ([2008] OJ L 299/25), which repealed and replaced Directive 89/104/EEC ([1989] OJ L40/1).
89 *CHEETAH Trade Mark* [1993] FSR 263.
90 *Copad SA v Christian Dior Couture SA* [2009] ETMR 40.

DISCLAIMERS OR LIMITATIONS

[33.34] Section 17 of TMA 1996 provides for both voluntary and mandatory disclaimers, the latter being introduced during the passage of the Trade Marks Bill through the Dáil. Irish law differs from UK law in this regard. The purpose of a disclaimer was well stated in the Trade Marks Rules 1963[91] as being 'in order that the public generally may understand what the applicant's rights, if his mark is registered, will be'.

[33.35] The imposition of a disclaimer requirement on an applicant under s 22 of TMA 1963 was a common occurrence. A disclaimer statement would read 'registration of this trade mark shall give no right to the exclusive use of ...'. Thus, on examination, it might be considered that the overall trade mark was sufficiently distinctive but contained certain elements which, in isolation, might be considered non-distinctive. By use of a disclaimer condition, the Controller is able to grant exclusivity in the overall mark but, at the same time, to ensure to the public that the scope of such exclusivity does not extend to prevent third-party use in respect of a particular part of the trade mark. In *VIRGINIA SLIMS Trade Mark*,[92] Costello J considered the circumstances under which the Controller could exercise his discretion to impose a disclaimer condition under s 22 of TMA 1963 and accepted that just because a feature of a mark is of a non-distinctive character, it does not follow that a disclaimer should be entered as a matter of course. The court should bear in mind the disadvantages that the applicant will suffer if the disclaimer is required and weigh them against the public's interest in having the applicant's rights clarified by means of a disclaimer. The danger of the absence of a disclaimer is unjustifiable claims to a monopoly right. However, even where a disclaimer entry does not exist, it does not mean that rights extend to the non-distinctive element. It depends, amongst other things, on the nature of the element and the prominence of that element in the overall mark. There are many instances in which it would be self-evident that, despite the absence of a disclaimer, no exclusivity could extend to a particular element. Although there is no provision providing for disclaimers under the Trade Mark Harmonisation Directive,[93] it is to be noted that provision for disclaimers exists under the CTM Regulation[94] and s 17(2) of TMA 1996 is clearly modelled on art 37(2) of the CTM Regulation.

[33.36] A registration with a disclaimer does not affect the proprietor's rights under the law of passing off and it is true that a disclaimer entry is, in effect, a snapshot at the date of registration and that the disclaimed element may subsequently have become distinctive through usage. It is always possible for a trade mark proprietor to re-apply for registration and to argue against a disclaimer condition subsequently, once the trade mark has been used for a number of years. Although a disclaimer means that infringement proceedings will be precluded, there are advantages of owning a

---

[91] SI 268/1963.

[92] *VIRGINIA SLIMS Trade Mark* (7 October 1980, unreported), HC.

[93] 89/104/EEC.

[94] 207/2009/EC, which repealed and replaced Council Regulation 40/94/EC.

registration even with a disclaimed element. When carrying out examination, the Controller can still cite, under s 10 of TMA 1996, an earlier trade mark where the similarity resides in the disclaimed element. In *GRANADA Trade Mark*,[95] it was held that in opposition proceedings, regard was to be had to a disclaimed element since a disclaimer does not affect the significance that a mark conveys to others.[96] A disclaimed element is entered on the Register and should be picked up by third-party searching and may thus serve as a deterrent by giving notice as to possible common law rights and citation and/or opposition to an application, even though use of the disclaimed element will not amount to infringement.

[33.37] A limitation may be entered on a voluntary basis, and s 17(1)(b) of TMA 1996 specifically refers to the example of a territorial limitation, whereby it would be agreed only to use the mark in a particular part of the State or for export use. A limitation as to a particular colour or colours may be self-imposed by an applicant in an attempt to show distinctiveness as, for example, in colour schemes for tablet capsules.[97]

[33.38] Under the transitional provisions of TMA 1996, a disclaimer or limitation entered previously on the Register was transferred to the new register under TMA 1996,[98] but conditions ceased to have any effect.[99]

TRANSITIONAL PROVISIONS

[33.39] In respect of acts committed prior to 1 July 1996, which is the commencement date of TMA 1996, it is TMA 1963 that determines whether or not there is infringement.[100] This means that the scope of protection is limited to unauthorised third-party use in the course of trade in relation to the goods covered by the registration. If the registration is in Part B of the Register, then for acts committed prior to 1 July 1996, the defence under s 13(2) of TMA 1963 is available to a defendant who can show that the use of which the plaintiff complains is not likely to deceive or cause confusion or indicate a connection in the course of trade with the trade mark proprietor.

[33.40] It is also not an infringement to continue to use a mark after 1 July 1996, which did not amount to an infringement under TMA 1963.[101]

[33.41] As from 1 July 1996 and for acts committed after that date, the distinction between Parts A and B of the Register, as far as the scope of protection is concerned, is removed.

---

[95] *GRANADA Trade Mark* [1979] RPC 303.
[96] See also *L'AMY Trade Mark* [1983] RPC 137.
[97] *Parke Davis Application* [1976] FSR 195.
[98] TMA 1996, Sch 3, para 2(5).
[99] TMA 1996, Sch 3, para 2(4).
[100] TMA 1996, Sch 3, para 3(2).
[101] TMA 1996, Sch 3, para 3(3).

Chapter 34

Trade Marks Act 1996: Registration Procedure and Ownership

REGISTRATION PROCEDURE

Searches

[34.01] Prior to making an application to register a trade mark with the Patents Office, it is normal to carry out a search to establish what registrations/applications of a conflicting nature already exist. The search must embrace not only trade marks on the Irish register but also the Community trade mark (CTM) register. It is also necessary to search against international trade marks registered under the Madrid Agreement extending to Ireland.[1] The searches in the various trade mark registers should be in the international class covering the goods/services for which the mark is to be used and cross-referencing to further classes covering similar goods/services. Despite these searches, it should be borne in mind that, in some cases, a trade mark application can be refused even in the case of dissimilar goods/services under s 10(3) of the Trade Marks Act 1996 (TMA 1996). This arises where use of the mark would take unfair advantage of, or be detrimental to, the distinctive character or reputation of the earlier mark on the Register. Since the requirement is that the earlier mark has a reputation, it would almost certainly be known to an applicant, but as a precautionary measure, it is normal for a search to identify at least an identical mark in all classes. More difficult to identify are common law rights, which are unregistered, and well-known marks under s 61 of TMA 1996. In general, the test of ownership in a mark is that ownership vests in the party first using it in this jurisdiction.[2] Searches can be made in trade and telephone directories, company and business name registers, etc. However, this will not necessarily disclose the prior mark because there is no requirement for there to be trading under the prior mark in the State. A search of the design registers (Irish and Community) can also be advisable depending on the nature of the mark because an industrial design can also be a basis for refusal of a trade mark application.[3]

---

[1]   Protocol Relating to the Madrid Agreement Concerning the International Registration of Marks 1989. See para **[27.50]**.
[2]   *Montex Holdings v Diesel SpA* [2000] ETMR 658.
[3]   TMA 1996, s 10(4)(b).

Application

[34.02] When filing an Irish trade mark application, there are certain minimum formalities required in order to secure a filing date and, unless subsequently lost, this will be the eventual date of registration for all purposes under TMA 1996.[4] Once registration takes place, an infringement action can claim damages from the filing date since the rights have effect from that date.[5] In order to secure this date, documents must be filed:

(a)   indicating that registration of a trade mark is sought and containing the name and address of the person requesting registration;

(b)   containing a representation of the mark for which registration is sought; and

(c)   in which the goods or services are stated.[6]

If not filed at the date of application, then subsequently an applicant must lodge the prescribed Form 1 which is scheduled to the Trade Marks Rules 1996.[7] This form includes the statement in s 37(2) of TMA 1996 that the trade mark is being used by the applicant or with their consent or that the applicant has a *bona fide* intention that it should be so used. It is also not clear whether use or intention to use relates to the position in the State. Although there are no specific statements as to the consequences of making a false statement, it would arguably be considered to be an application made in bad faith.[8] However, the Irish Patents Office generally requires some evidence to be presented to support the allegation of lack of *bona fide* intention to use.[9] The statement also pertains to the entire goods and/or services so the practice of including specifications that are actually broader than the intended use may also constitute an application made in bad faith.[10] In reality the Irish Patents Office is very reluctant to uphold bad faith merely because of broad specifications. In relation to invalidity, under s 52(5) of TMA 1996 the trade mark should only be declared invalid in so far as it relates to those goods or services for which no intention to use existed.

[34.03] Under TMA 1996, there is no longer a requirement that the applicant be the actual or intended user or that such a user be identified by way of a simultaneously filed registered user application.

[34.04] When filing, it is necessary to identify the goods and/or services in the application. There is an international classification of goods/services[11] (Nice Classification) and goods and services should be classified accordingly. Under the Trade

---

4   TMA 1996, s 45(3).
5   TMA 1996, s 13(3).
6   Trade Marks Rules 1996 (SI 199/1996), r 12.
7   Trade Marks Rules 1996, Sch 2, as amended by the Trade Marks (Amendment) Rules 2010.
8   TMA 1996, s 8(4)(b).
9   *McDermott Laboratories Ltd's application; Opposition of May & Baker Ltd* [2006] ETMR 17.
10   Contrast with position before *OHIM – TRILLIUM* [2000] ETMR 1054. See paras **[30.51]**–**[30.55]**.
11   Nice Classification for dividing goods into 34 Classes (1–34) and services into a further 11 Classes (35–45).

Marks Act 1963 (TMA 1963), a separate application was required in each class. Under the Trade Marks Rules 1996,[12] a multi-class application is possible with an additional official fee required for each class. Ultimately, the Controller is the final arbiter as to the appropriate class and a decision of the Controller in this regard is final.[13] Classification is not usually a problem given that most goods/services are indexed in the Nice Classification. If in doubt, a procedure exists whereby WIPO can be asked to adjudicate on a matter of classification. Classification is a significant aid to searching. There is a tendency to use broad specifications and, in some instances, even the international class heading. It cannot be presumed that the goods and/or services although falling into a given class also fall within the class heading and it is important for an applicant to try and be product/service-specific and not to rely on the class heading or on broad terms. In *Avenet Inc v Isoact Ltd*,[14] Jacob J observed in relation to the phrase 'advertising and promotional services':

> In my view, specifications for services should be scrutinised carefully and they should not be given a wide construction covering a vast range of activities. They should be confined to the substance, as it were, the core of the possible meanings attributable to the rather general phrase.

OHIM has issued a communication No 4/03, which states that 'all the general indications listed in the class heading of a particular class constitute a claim to all the goods or services falling within the particular class'. This statement, which is one of administrative convenience, is legally questionable because in many instances, goods falling in a particular class are absent from the class heading. Thus, for example, the class 15 heading is 'musical instruments' and this would not include music stands or musical instrument cases, which also fall into class 15. This issue is currently the subject of a referral to the ECJ from the UK Intellectual Property Office involving an application for IP TRANSLATOR No 2528977.[15]

[34.05] If official application fees are not paid at the date of application, then they must be paid within one month of the filing date, otherwise the application will be deemed abandoned.[16]

[34.06] It is possible to file what is called a series of trade marks under one application. This is defined in s 46(2) of TMA 1996 to mean a number of trade marks which resemble each other as to their material particulars and differ only in respect of matter of a non-distinctive character which does not substantially affect the identity of the trade mark. The most common examples would be trade marks in upper/lower case lettering or trade marks in black and white or colour. The Trade Marks (Amendment) Rules 2010 introduced a limit on the number of marks which may appear in a series, with the

---

[12] Trade Marks Rules 1996, r 14.

[13] TMA 1996, s 39(2).

[14] *Avenet Inc v Isoact Ltd* [1997] ETMR 562.

[15] Reference for a preliminary ruling from the Appointed Person by the Lord Chancellor (UK) made on 28 June 2010 – *The Chartered Institute of Patent Attorneys v Registrar of Trade Marks,* Case C-307/10, OJ C 246, p 23 of 11 September 2010.

[16] Trade Marks Rules 1996, r 12(5).

maximum being six marks.[17] Where a series application contains three or more marks, an additional fee is required for the third and each subsequent mark.[18]

Priority

[34.07] If priority is to be claimed under the Paris Convention,[19] then such an application must be filed within six months from the date of filing of the first Convention application.[20] The application can cover some or all of the goods/services of the application from which priority is claimed. What is not clear from the Trade Marks Rules 1996 is whether or not a claim to priority can be made subsequent to the filing date but still within the six-month period allowed under the Paris Convention. Rule 12(2)(b) simply states that where a right to priority is claimed, the information required by Form No 1 concerning claims to priority shall be furnished in the form. Since Form No 1 does not have to be filed in order to secure a filing date, it would seem that a claim to priority can be delayed until the filing of the form, and provided this is still within the six-month period. There is a three-month period from the filing date within which to file the priority document by way of evidence of the first Convention application from the competent authority,[21] which is usually the national trade marks office in that country.

[34.08] It is a requirement that the first application be what is termed a regular national filing, which means that it must be possible to determine the date of filing. It is not necessary that such an application itself proceeds to registration.[22] The application from which priority is claimed must be the first one in any Convention country for that trade mark. Section 40(4) of TMA 1996 contains a limited exception, where at the time of the subsequent application from which priority is being claimed:

(a)   the previous application has been withdrawn, abandoned or refused, without having been laid open to public inspection and without leaving any rights outstanding; and

(b)   it has not yet served as a basis for claiming a right of priority.

It is not clear how this provision can ever have application because a trade mark is open to public inspection within a very short space of time after filing.

[34.09] A merging of applications is possible[23] but only under very limited circumstances, which are prescribed in the Trade Marks Rules 1996.[24] The merger must

---

[17]   Trade Marks Rules 1996, r 30(1), as substituted by the Trade Marks (Amendment) Rules 2010, effective from 4 October 2010.

[18]   The prescribed fee was not set in the Trade Marks (Amendment) Rules 2010 and the imposition of the fee for the third to sixth marks in a series should not come into effect until that fee is set.

[19]   Paris Convention for the Protection of Industrial Property 1883 (Paris Convention). See para **[27.03]**.

[20]   TMA 1996, s 40(1).

[21]   SI 199/1996, r 13.

[22]   TMA 1996, s 40(3).

[23]   TMA 1996, s 46(1)(b).

[24]   Trade Marks Rules 1996, r 29, as amended by the Trade Marks (Amendment) Rules 2010.

take place before a notice of acceptance has been issued in relation to any of the applications. This could arise when the first official action is issued from the Patents Office or when advertisement takes place in the Patents Office Journal. All the applications must bear the same date and be in respect of the same trade mark. This means that there were very few instances of merger except in the early days of TMA 1996. Prior to 1 July 1996, over 7,000 service mark applications had been filed under a system that required separate applications in each class. An applicant who had a number of simultaneously filed applications for the same mark in different service classes had an advantage in a merger because of reduced registration fees and future renewal fees.

[34.10] It is also possible to merge registrations. Again, the registrations must be for the same mark and have the same date. Any registrable transaction must be recorded against all of the marks being merged and each mark must have the same disclaimer or limitation, if any. It is not possible to merge collective or certification mark registrations.

[34.11] It is also possible to divide an application into several applications, each containing some of the goods/services contained in the original application and each of which will have the same filing date as the original application.[25] Division is limited under the Trade Marks Rules to applications in relation to which a notice of acceptance has not yet been issued[26] or which has been opposed. In practice, it is the latter that will cover almost every situation in which an applicant is likely to wish to divide an application. In particular, in the case of a multi-class application which has been opposed and where the opposition relates only to some but not to all of the classes, an applicant is able to divide the application and allow the remaining classes to proceed. If the opposition is defeated, then merger can take place subsequently. What is unfortunate is that if an application is advertised and threatened with opposition, it is not possible to divide until the actual notice of opposition has been lodged.

Formalities

[34.12] Once a trade mark application is filed, a receipt issues from the Patents Office. This receipt allocates a number to the application and acknowledges the date upon which the application was received. The numbering system is the year followed by a number which is the next number in respect of applications filed that year, eg 2010/02090 would be the two thousand and ninetieth application filed in 2010. The details of the application by way of the trade mark, number, date and applicant's name, together with classes and goods/services, are entered onto a database for searching purposes.

[34.13] There is no statutory time period within which the trade mark application must be examined by the Patents Office. Examination takes place to establish whether or not the requirements of TMA 1996[27] and the Trade Marks Rules 1996 have been met. This means that there is examination both as to formalities and to substantive matters. It is extremely important for an applicant to fulfil the minimum requirements to establish a

---

[25]   TMA 1996, s 46(1)(a).
[26]   Trade Marks Rules 1996, r 28.
[27]   TMA 1996, s 42(1).

filing date[28] because although formality irregularities in this regard may be remedied, the filing date will be the date when all such formalities are complete. Similarly, it is also important to pay all class fees within one month of the filing date. The Controller, on examination of formalities, will identify the absence of correct fees but such examination may well take place more than one month after filing. If an application fee is not submitted within the prescribed one-month period, the application is deemed abandoned. It is uncertain as to what will happen in the case of a wrong calculation in the official fee payable, for example, on a multi-class application. Presumably, at a minimum, the entire application will not be deemed abandoned and the Controller will allow the filing date in so far as it relates to the number of classes in respect of which the official application fee has been paid. The remaining formal requirement over which there is a statutory time limit is the filing of the priority document where priority is claimed.[29] Failure to file this document within the prescribed three-month period means that an applicant must relinquish the claim to priority. However, this particular time period is extendible, provided that such extension request is made before the expiry of the normal period.[30]

[34.14] The most common formality requirements raised by a Controller relate to the specification of goods/services. A specification which reads 'all goods in class ...' will not be accepted by the Controller. An applicant will be asked to specify the exact goods/services in the particular class. It is possible to register in respect of a class heading in Ireland. If the Controller is unsure whether the goods/services fall into the class indicated by an applicant, then clarification will be sought and, if necessary, amendment made to the specification. The Controller, who ultimately decides on all matters of classification, may insist on deletion of certain goods/services or on additional class fees being paid.[31]

[34.15] If colour is claimed as part of a trade mark, it is necessary to furnish coloured representations. An application in respect of a three-dimensional mark requires representations by way of a photographic reproduction or a graphic representation showing different perspectives, not exceeding six in total.[32]

Substantive requirements

[34.16] The Controller also carries out a substantive examination of the application, which will relate to the following:

    (a)   whether the mark is a trade mark within the definition in s 6(1) of TMA 1996, which requires the mark to be capable of being represented graphically and of distinguishing the applicant's goods/services from those of other undertakings;

---

[28] TMA 1996, s 38; Trade Marks Rules 1996, r 12(1).
[29] Trade Marks Rules 1996, r 13.
[30] Trade Marks Rules 1996, r 63(3).
[31] Trade Marks Rules 1996, r 14(3).
[32] Trade Marks Rules 1996, r 12(3)(c).

(b)   the absolute grounds of refusal in s 8, which includes an examination as to distinctiveness and whether or not the mark is deceptive or contrary to law or public policy;

(c)   whether, under s 9, the mark includes a specially protected emblem of the State or the national flag;

(d)   whether, under ss 62 or 63, the mark includes national flags or State emblems or other emblems, which have been notified under art 6*ter* of the Paris Convention;[33] and

(e)   the relative grounds of refusal under s 10 of TMA 1996 in so far as they relate to earlier trade marks.

This necessitates the Controller carrying out searches of the Irish, CTM and International registers but the Trade Marks Rules 1996 simply state the scope and methodology of such a search shall be as determined by the Controller.[34] In practice, the search is not limited to identical conflicting earlier trade marks and there is also cross-searching to related classes in order to assess the position as regards similarity of goods/services.

[34.17] If the examination of either the formalities or the substantive requirements results in the Controller taking the view that the requirements have not been met, then an official action issues to the applicant or its authorised agent, providing an opportunity to make representations or to amend the application. There is no specific statutory time period within which to respond to an official action and the time period allowed is stated by the Controller[35] in the official communication, and is extendible.[36] The Controller issued guidelines, which came into effect on 1 May 2010, regarding extensions of time.[37] In practice, there are often a number of exchanges of communication between an applicant or its agent and the Controller dealing with the official action. If the applicant fails to respond or satisfy the Controller that the requirements for registration have been met, or to amend the application to the Controller's satisfaction, then the application is refused.[38] This is subject to the right to request a hearing before the Controller,[39] which requires payment of an official fee.[40]

[34.18] If the requirements of registration are met, then the application is accepted[41] and allowed to proceed to publication (advertisement). This should be contrasted with the position under TMA 1963 where it was possible for the Controller to advertise a trade

---

[33]   See para **[32.76]**.

[34]   Trade Marks Rules 1996, r 16.

[35]   TMA 1996, s 42(2).

[36]   Trade Marks Rules 1996 (SI 199/1996), r 63, as amended by the Trade Marks (Amendment) Rules 2010.

[37]   'Patents Office Guidelines For Dealing With "Applications For Extensions Of Time" In Respect Of Trade Marks', available at www.patentsoffice.ie.

[38]   TMA 1996, s 42(3).

[39]   TMA 1996, s 71.

[40]   Trade Marks Rules 1996, r 61, as amended by the Trade Marks (Amendment) Rules 2010.

[41]   TMA 1996, s 42(4).

mark prior to acceptance and then, if necessary, to re-advertise. This does not appear to be an option open to the Controller under TMA 1996. The combined effect of ss 42(3) and (4) of TMA 1996 is to eliminate the discretion that the Controller previously had under TMA 1963 and requires the Controller to decide as to registrability prior to advertisement.[42]

Publication/advertisement

[34.19] Advertisement takes place in the Patents Office Journal, which is published fortnightly. The purpose of advertisement is to give third parties an opportunity to oppose an application before it is allowed to proceed to registration. Under TMA 1963, the opposition period was one month from the date of advertisement but this period was extendible upon request for extension being received within the one-month period. The TMA 1996 introduced a new regime of a three-month opposition period, which is not extendible.[43] The three-month period runs to a day prior to the actual three-month anniversary date of the advertisement.[44]

[34.20] There is no specific listing of the grounds of opposition and, therefore, the grounds that exist must be the same as those which form the basis for a trade mark application to be refused generally. In *Yell Ltd's Application*,[45] the Controller ruled that an amendment of a notice of opposition may be allowed pursuant to r 75, even though the effect of the amendment may be to introduce new grounds of opposition after the expiry of the three month statutory opposition period. There is no restriction on who can lodge an opposition but it must be by way of a written statement of the grounds of opposition accompanied by an official fee.[46] In practice, the opposition, including the statement of grounds in broad terms, simply identifies the sections of TMA 1996 upon which the opposition is to be based. It is sent in duplicate to the Controller who sends a copy to the applicant or its agent.[47] Within three months, the applicant must file with the Controller, in duplicate, a counter-statement.[48] The counter-statement is a denial or admittance of any of the grounds of opposition. This period of three months is also non-extendible.[49] If the counter-statement is not filed, the application is deemed to have been withdrawn.[50] The Controller sends a copy of the counter-statement to the opponent. There subsequently follows three-month time periods, which are extendible, and within which the opponent, and subsequently the applicant, must file with the Controller their

---

[42] *EUROLAMB Trade Mark* [1997] ETMR 420.
[43] Trade Marks Rules 1996, r 18(1).
[44] *Nolan's Application* [2000] ETMR 208.
[45] *Yell Ltd's Application* [2009] ETMR 25.
[46] TMA 1996, s 43(2); Trade Marks Rules 1996, r 18(2).
[47] Trade Marks Rules 1996, r 18(3).
[48] Trade Marks Rules 1996, r 19(1); amended by Trade Marks Act 1996 (Community Trade Mark) Regulation 2000 (SI 229/2000), r 13(a).
[49] Trade Marks Rules 1996, r 63(2), as amended by the Trade Marks (Amendment) Rules 2010.
[50] Trade Marks Rules 1996, r 19(2).

evidence by way of statutory declaration[51] and furnish the other side with a copy. Statutory declaration evidence should contain factual matters only and not lay opinion or legal argument.[52]

[34.21] When the applicant furnishes its evidence, a further two-month extendible period is given to the opponent to file further statutory declarations if desired, but which must be confined to matters strictly in reply.[53] The Controller has a discretion to accept further evidence.[54] When the evidence is complete, the Controller invites the parties to attend at a hearing. It is normal practice for parties to attend such a hearing, at which they are usually represented by their trade mark agent or counsel.

[34.22] The Trade Marks (Amendment) Rules 2010 introduced a new procedure whereby parties to an opposition have the option to file written submissions in lieu of attending at a hearing.[55] The purpose behind this change is to allow parties who do not wish to attend at a hearing an opportunity to file legal arguments and statements of opinion, which are not appropriate for statutory declaration evidence. The parties are asked to elect between a hearing or filing written submissions, assuming that they do not wish to have the matter decided exclusively on the basis of their statutory declaration evidence filed. The Controller will notify the parties when the evidence is complete and the parties then have a period of two months to make this election.[56] If a party elects to file written submissions in lieu of attending at the hearing, that party has a non-extendible period of four months from the original request to file the written submissions. [57] If both parties elect to file written submissions, each party will have a further period of one month from receipt of the other party's written submissions to file further written submissions confined strictly to matters in reply. Any written submissions filed must be copied to the other party. After the initial two month election period, if either party has elected to attend at a hearing, the Controller will notify the parties of the hearing date. The parties must be given at least 30 days notice of a hearing date and have 14 days from receipt of notice of the hearing date to indicate whether they will attend at the hearing.[58] A party who does not elect to attend at the hearing shall not be heard at the hearing without leave of the Controller.

---

[51] Trade Marks Rules 1996, rr 20 and 21; Rule 20(1) amended by Trade Marks Act 1996 (Community Trade Mark) Regulation 2000 (SI 229/2000), r 13(b).

[52] *Bus Éireann/Irish Bus v Controller of Patents Designs and Trademarks* [2007] IEHC 221 (HC), Laffoy J.

[53] Trade Marks Rules 1996, r 22.

[54] Trade Marks Rules 1996, r 23.

[55] Trade Marks Rules 1996, r 25(1) to (5), as substituted by the Trade Marks (Amendment) Rules 2010; see also r 25(2) of the Trade Marks Rules 1996 as inserted by the Trade Marks (Amendment) Rules 2010 for the transitional provisions.

[56] Trade Marks Rules 1996, r 25(2), as substituted by the Trade Marks (Amendment) Rules 2010.

[57] Trade Marks Rules 1996, r 25(3), as substituted by the Trade Marks (Amendment) Rules 2010, and r 63(2), as amended by the Trade Marks (Amendment) Rules 2010.

[58] Trade Marks Rules 1996, r 25(6) and (7), as substituted by the Trade Marks (Amendment) Rules 2010.

[34.23] Following a hearing and/or consideration of any written submissions, the Controller notifies the decision to the parties, who have a one-month extendible period within which to request the written grounds of the decision.[59] This decision can be appealed to the High Court,[60] and, in exceptional circumstances, it may be possible to produce additional evidence at the appeal.[61] Section 79 stated that unless provided otherwise by the rules of the court, the appeal must be lodged within three months from the date of the Controller's decision. This meant that it was sometimes necessary to lodge an appeal before actually being in receipt of the written grounds. In *Procter and Gamble v Controller of Patents*,[62] Finnegan J had to consider a situation where a special summons issued outside of the three months from the decision of the Controller but within the period of three months computed from the handing down of the written grounds of the decision. It was held that having to decide on an appeal and to formulate the same in advance of the receipt of the statement of grounds could not have been the intention of the legislature. On an application under O 122, r 7 of the Rules of the Superior Courts 1986, the plaintiff was allowed to bring an application for enlargement of time. Finnegan J also stated that if compelled to do so, the Controller's letter refusing the application would not be regarded as a final decision until such date as the statement of grounds is handed down. This anomaly has been rectified by s 44 of the Patents (Amendment) Act 2006, which replaced s 79 of the TMA 1996 with the following provision:

> 79(1)(a)Save as otherwise provided by this Act and subject to paragraph (*b*), except by leave of the Court, an appeal shall lie to the Court from a decision of the Controller under this Act within three months from the date of the decision.
>
> (b) Where a written statement of the grounds of the decision of the Controller, in the exercise of his discretionary power, has been requested in the prescribed manner and within the prescribed period by a party to the proceedings, the period of three months shall begin on the date on which the written statement is furnished to the party requesting it.

[34.24] Under the general principle of procedural law known as the prohibition on *reformatio in pejus*, a higher court competent to rule on appeal cannot vary a contested decision of the lower court to the appellant's detriment, if the appellant is the only party to have sought that remedy. The worst outcome of the remedy applied for by the appellant must be the dismissal of the appeal and the simple upholding of the contested decision.[63]

[34.25] Once the application is advertised, it is also possible for any person to make written observations to the Controller as to why they consider that an application should be refused.[64] The applicant is notified of such observations and, although not stated,

---

59 Trade Marks Rules 1996, r 27.

60 TMA 1996, s 79.

61 *ETAT Française v Bernard Matthews plc* [2002] ETMR 90.

62 *Procter and Gamble v Controller of Patents* [2001] ETMR 112.

63 *Les Editions Albert Rene v OHIM* [2009] ETMR 21.

64 TMA 1996, s 43(3).

presumably of the identity of the party making the observations. A person who simply makes observations does not become a party to proceedings.[65]

[34.26] The purpose of making observations is to try and persuade the Controller to withdraw acceptance, without the need to engage in the expense of opposition. Section 45 of TMA 1996 allows for an acceptance to be withdrawn on the grounds that such acceptance was erroneous having regard to matters subsequently coming to the attention of the Controller. The observations do not have to be made within the three-month opposition period but it is advisable to do so if seeking withdrawal of acceptance as an alternative to opposition. However, in reality, potential opponents are always obliged to lodge an opposition to preserve their position since a decision from the Controller may not issue within the three months or may be again reversed in favour of an applicant following further submissions.

[34.27] It is possible to withdraw or amend a trade mark application. A common amendment is to restrict the specification of goods/services. It is not possible to broaden a specification. If the application has already been advertised, any withdrawal or restriction is also subsequently advertised in the Patents Office Journal. If the restriction occurs subsequent to any opposition, then an opponent is given an opportunity to withdraw the opposition or to amend such if desired.[66] Any withdrawal of the application is irrevocable after the expiry of three months from the date of notice of the withdrawal.[67]

[34.28] Unlike the position under the CTM Regulation[68] and the corresponding UK provision, it is also possible to make any other amendment that does not substantially affect the identity of the trade mark.[69] This includes, but is not limited to, correction of the name or address of the applicant, errors of wording or of copying, or obvious mistakes. If the application has not yet been advertised, it is only the amended mark that is published in the Patents Office Journal.[70]

TRANSITIONAL PROVISIONS

[34.29] All applications filed prior to 1 July 1996 are examined and oppositions determined under the criteria of TMA 1963.[71] No additional rules were prescribed to deal with opposition periods for such marks. This means that for applications filed prior to 1 July 1996, a one-month opposition period applies, which is extendible, but for applications filed as and from 1 July 1996, a three-month non-extendible opposition

---

65 TMA 1996, s 43(4).
66 Trade Marks Rules 1996, r 26.
67 TMA 1996, s 44(2).
68 Council Regulation 207/2009/EC ([2009] OJ L78/1), which repealed and replaced Council Regulation 40/94/EC ([1994] OJ L11/1).
69 TMA 1996, s 44(3).
70 Trade Marks Rules 1996, r 26(3).
71 TMA 1996, Sch 3, para 8(2).

period applies. The procedure for applications filed prior to 1 July 1996 will be determined by the Trade Marks Rules 1963.[72]

[34.30] In relation to any application filed prior to 1 July 1996, which had not yet been advertised, it was possible to convert such an application so that it was examined and opposition determined under the criteria of TMA 1996.[73] This conversion was irrevocable and the request must have been made prior to 1 January 1997. Any such conversion means that the application loses its filing date and instead receives the commencement date for TMA 1996, ie 1 July 1996. Thus, prior to any conversion, it was advisable to carry out searches to establish the position as regards conflicting marks between the filing date and 1 July 1996. If there were any conflicting marks, then conversion was a last resort.

[34.31] All applications for service marks filed prior to 1 July 1996 did not require any conversion and were automatically given a filing date of 1 July 1996 and dealt with under TMA 1996.[74] Over 7,000 service mark applications had been filed prior to 1 July 1996.

REGISTRATION

[34.32] If there is no opposition or if any opposition has been withdrawn or decided in favour of the applicant, then upon payment of the final registration fee, a certificate of registration issues. An exception arises where, having regard to matters coming to the Controller's notice since acceptance, it is believed that the acceptance was made in error.[75] This would normally arise following written observations[76] by a third party.

[34.33] The registration fee must be paid within two months of the request for such by the Controller[77] and the fact of registration is published in the Patents Office Journal.[78] This date of publication is important because it determines the date of completion of the registration procedure[79] which is the date from which the five-year period runs for revocation on the grounds of non-use[80] and from which infringement proceedings can commence.[81] However, the date of registration is the date of filing of the application[82] and this is the effective date from which rights accrue to a trade mark proprietor.[83]

---

72 SI 268/1963.
73 TMA 1996, Sch 3, para 9.
74 TMA 1996, Sch 3, para 15.
75 TMA 1996, s 45(1).
76 TMA 1996, s 43(2).
77 Trade Marks Rules 1996, r 73.
78 TMA 1996, s 45(4).
79 TMA 1996, s 45(5).
80 TMA 1996, s 51(1).
81 TMA 1996, s 13(4).
82 TMA 1996, s 45(3).
83 TMA 1996, s 13(3).

Duration and renewal

[34.34] Under s 47 of TMA 1996, the duration of a trade mark registration is 10 years from the date of registration (filing date) and is renewable for successive 10-year periods. Unlike other forms of intellectual property, a trade mark registration can remain in force indefinitely upon payment of the requisite renewal fees. The TMA 1963 provided for an initial registration period of seven years and then renewal periods every 14 years. To determine the renewal date of a registration, it is necessary to establish the registration date. If such date is 1 July 1996 or after that date, then the renewal date is due on each 10-year anniversary date. If the registration date is prior to 1 July 1996, then the next renewal date is determined under TMA 1963, ie 7 or 14 years but subsequently every 10 years.[84] A term of renewal takes effect from the expiry date of the registration and not from the date of payment of a renewal fee.[85] It is not possible to pay a renewal fee more than six months before the anniversary date[86] and the Controller is obliged to send a renewal notice at least one month before the anniversary date.[87] It is possible to make late payment of a renewal fee provided such is within six months of the anniversary date and the requisite fees including a late renewal fee are paid.[88]

[34.35] Even where a trade mark is removed from the Register for non-payment of a renewal fee, it is still taken into account in determining the registrability of a later mark for a period of one year from the anniversary date. A removed trade mark can remain as a citation and thus a basis for refusal of an application during this period unless the Controller is satisfied that there was no *bona fide* use of the mark in the two years immediately preceding expiry.[89]

[34.36] Restoration is provided for in r 40 of the Trade Marks Rules 1996 but is limited to six months from the date of publication of removal of the mark in the Patents Office Journal. This time period is non-extendible.[90] It is also necessary to show to the satisfaction of the Controller that having regard to all the circumstances, it is just to restore the registration. This obviously requires an explanation to the Controller as to the reason for failure to renew and could, for example, include the failure of the Patents Office to send out the renewal reminder.[91] Unlike the position under the Patents Act 1992, there is no provision dealing with the effect of late renewal or restoration on third parties. In relation to the six-month grace period for late renewal, the trade mark must still be considered as a registered trade mark.[92]

---

[84] TMA 1996, Sch 3, para 10.
[85] TMA 1996, s 48(5).
[86] Trade Marks Rules 1996, r 38.
[87] Trade Marks Rules 1996, r 37.
[88] Trade Marks Rules 1996, r 39(1).
[89] TMA 1996, s 11(3).
[90] Trade Marks Rules 1996, r 63(2), as amended by the Trade Marks (Amendment) Rules 2010.
[91] *Ling's Patent* [1981] RPC 85.
[92] TMA 1996, s 48(4).

[34.37] It is possible for the proprietor of a registered trade mark to add to or alter the registration in any manner not substantially affecting the identity of the registered mark.[93] This provision corresponds to s 43 of TMA 1963 but differs from the position under both Council Regulation 207/2009/EC and the UK Trade Marks Act 1994 where alteration is limited to the name or address of a proprietor, which may appear in the mark.

[34.38] The practice under TMA 1963 and the former UK Trade Marks Act 1938 was to view a change as being substantial even though it affected only one letter in the mark, if either the pronunciation or the appearance of the mark altered. Hence, the change from OTRIVIN[94] to OTRIVINE was not allowed. However, in the case of a non-invented word, there was a tendency to be more liberal and the change from PELICAN[95] to PELIKAN was allowed. An important factor taken into account was the effect of the alteration on the position of other parties as to possible infringement. This is the reason why the altered mark is advertised and open to opposition.[96]

[34.39] Under s 50 of TMA 1996, it is also possible for a trade mark proprietor to surrender a registration in respect of some or all of the goods or services for which it is registered. There are also provisions in the Trade Marks Rules 1996, r 36 for protecting the interests of other persons having a right in the registered trade mark. The Controller is obliged not to act upon a notice of surrender unless the proprietor certifies that it is not precluded by contract or other agreement from surrendering the mark. In addition, the proprietor must specify the name and address of each person entered in the Register as having an interest. Each of these persons must have been given three months' notice and not objected to the surrender. Notice of the surrender or partial surrender is published in the Patents Office Journal and is effective from this date. However, no action for infringement lies in respect of any act carried out before that date.

PROPERTY RIGHTS IN TRADE MARKS

[34.40] Both a registered trade mark and a trade mark application are personal property rights.[97] A director, by registering a trade mark in his own name and for his own benefit, can be in breach of his fiduciary duty to the company.[98]

Jointly owned marks

[34.41] Section 27 of TMA 1996 provides:

(1) Where the relations between two or more persons interested in a trade mark are such that no one of them is entitled, as between himself and the other or others, to use it except—

---

[93] TMA 1996, s 49.
[94] *OTRIVIN Trade Mark* [1967] RPC 613.
[95] *PELICAN Trade Mark* [1978] RPC 424.
[96] TMA 1996, s 49; Trade Marks Rules 1996, r 35.
[97] *Val Marks* (1923) 40 RPC 103; *Tarantela* (1910) 27 RPC 573 at 584.
[98] TMA 1996, ss 26 and 31(1).

(a)   on behalf of both or all of them, or

(b)   in relation to an article with which both or all of them are connected in the course of trade,

those persons may be registered as joint proprietors of the trade mark.

The same rights apply as if the trade mark had been vested in a single person.[99] Section 27(4) states that the rights of any person registered as a joint owner shall be deemed to be infringed by any of the other joint owners who uses the trade mark in physical or other relation to goods or services in respect of which the trade mark is registered but with which all of the joint owners are not, and have not been, connected in the course of trade.[100] If there are joint applicants, the Controller may call for confirmation either that none of the applicants will use the mark except on behalf of all or both of the joint applicants or alternatively, that the mark will be used in relation only to goods or services with which all joint applicants are connected in the course of trade.[101] An example of such a connection would be where one joint owner is a manufacturer and the other is a distributor. Section 27(2) precludes the registration of a mark to two or more persons who use or propose to use the mark independently of one another.

Assignments and registrable transactions

[34.42] Under s 28 of TMA 1996, a registered trade mark or an application[102] can be assigned in the same way as other personal property either in connection with the goodwill of a business or independently. The TMA 1963, as interpreted by the Irish courts, had not allowed the assignment of a pending trade mark application.[103] The TMA 1963 also contained restrictions on assignments, which were designed to protect the public from being misled. This included an association requirement whereby the Controller could compel the owner of an identical or similar mark when assigning the trade marks to do so *en bloc* so that confusingly similar marks would not be held separately. Associations have been dispensed with under TMA 1996 and even for trade marks, which were associated under TMA 1963, such associations no longer have any effect.[104] However, an assignment which renders the subsequent use of the trade mark likely to mislead the public, may lead to revocation of a registration under s 51(1)(d) of TMA 1996. In *Elizabeth Emanuel v Continental Shelf 128 Ltd,*[105] the ECJ considered the effect of an assignment of a name trade mark from a designer and whether as a result, the public would be misled. The ECJ concluded that the fact of such assignment alone could not lead to a conclusion that the public would be misled, in particular where the goodwill associated with the mark had been assigned together with the business producing the goods to which the mark related.

---

[99]   *Ball v Eden Project Ltd* [2001] ETMR 87.

[100]   TMA 1996, s 27(3).

[101]   TMA 1996, s 27(4).

[102]   TMA 1996, s 31(1).

[103]   *Western States Bank Card Association v Controller* (1975, unreported), HC.

[104]   TMA 1996, Sch 3, para 2(3) (transitional provision).

[105]   *Elizabeth Emanuel v Continental Shelf 128 Ltd* [2006] ETMR 56.

[34.43] There was also a requirement under s 30(7) of TMA 1963, that an assignment of a used trade mark other than in connection with the goodwill of the business in which it was being used, was required to be advertised. This is no longer a requirement under TMA 1996. The statutory provision that allows assignment separately from the goodwill of a business was required to abrogate the common law rule whereby a trade mark could not be assigned separately from its owner's business[106] because otherwise, a trade mark would become deceptive.[107] The common law principle still applies in relation to an unregistered mark, which can only be assigned as part of the goodwill of a business.[108] The courts have shied away from giving any definition of what is meant by goodwill, but it has been described as:

> the benefit and advantage of the good name, reputation and connection of a business. It is the attractive force which brings in custom. It is the one thing which distinguishes an old established business from a new business at its start.[109]

[34.44] Section 28(2) of TMA 1996 allows for partial assignment in respect of some but not all of the goods[110] or services relating to use of the trade mark in a particular manner or a particular locality. There is no discretion on behalf of the Controller to refuse to accept such an assignment and it is up to the trade mark proprietor to determine if it runs the risk of revocation on the grounds that the trade mark is now deceptive.[111] In *Dasema Trading Ltd,*[112] although an assignment recordal had taken place, the Register was amended in circumstances where in fact the purported assignor had no authority to assign. Under art 17(4) of the CTM Regulation,[113] it is possible for OHIM to refuse to record a transfer where such is likely to mislead the public as to the nature, quality or geographical origin of the goods or services. An assignment of a CTM must be for the whole of the EU.

[34.45] Where there is a licence under a registered trade mark, which is subsequently assigned, then, unless the licence states otherwise, it is binding on the successor in title.[114] In order to be effective, an assignment of a registered trade mark must be in writing.[115] A registered trade mark may be the subject of a charge in the same way as other personal property[116] and may be assigned by way of security.[117] The TMA 1963 continues to apply in relation to assignments which took place prior to 1 July 1996.[118]

---

[106] *Bowden Wire Co Ltd v Bowden Brake Co Ltd* (1914) 31 RPC 385.

[107] *Pinto v Badman* (1891) 8 RPC 181.

[108] TMA 1996, s 28(6).

[109] *IRC v Muller's & Co's Margarine Ltd* [1901] AC 217.

[110] *Sunbeam Motor Car Co* (1916) 33 RPC 389.

[111] TMA 1996, s 51(1)(d).

[112] *Dasema Trading Ltd* [2007] ETMR 15.

[113] Council Regulation 207/2009/EC.

[114] TMA 1996, s 32(4).

[115] TMA 1996, s 28(3).

[116] TMA 1996, s 28(5).

[117] TMA 1996, s 28(4).

[118] TMA 1996, Sch 3, para 6(1).

Section 30 of TMA 1963 contained certain prohibitions on partial assignments likely to deceive or cause confusion.

[34.46] Provision is made in s 29 of TMA 1996 for recordal in the trade mark register of certain interests, which are termed registrable transactions. These are assignments, licences, grants of security, assents, matters arising by operation of law, such as a merger of the proprietor,[119] and court orders or an order of any other competent authority transferring a registered trade mark or any right in or under it. Until an application has been made to record a registrable transaction, it is ineffective as against a person acquiring a competing interest in ignorance of the transaction. This would suggest that if an application has been made but not yet been entered on the Register, a party is still nevertheless affixed with notice despite the fact that there may well be a lengthy period of time between application and recordal. There is no requirement that a trade mark proprietor be actually entered on the Register before taking an infringement action but a licensee in a position to take such an action must have at least applied to record such a licence on the Register.[120]

[34.47] The penalties for not making application to record a registrable transaction do not arise unless six months have elapsed from the transaction date. Even then, the courts may excuse this upon being satisfied that it was not practical to make an application earlier and steps were taken as soon as practically possible.[121] The penalties are a denial of any entitlement to damages or an account of profits for infringement between the date of the transaction and the application for recordal.

[34.48] Section 99 of the Companies Act 1963, as amended by s 122 of the Companies (Amendment) Act 1990, requires that a company register with the Registrar of Companies certain charges including a charge on goodwill or on a trade mark. Once the requisite application being made, the Registrar enters the relevant particulars on the Register including the date of creation of the charge, the amount secured, particulars of the property charged and particulars of the person entitled to the charge.

[34.49] The formalities for recordal of a registrable transaction are set out in r 45 of the Trade Marks Rules 1996[122] and require submission of a certified copy of the instrument or document upon which the claim is based. If the instrument is chargeable with stamp duty, evidence that such has been paid is required. The Controller must be satisfied that the document provided authenticates the claim of the applicant for recordal.[123] Although s 28(3) of TMA 1996 indicates that an assignment executed by the assignor alone is sufficient, r 45(1)(a) as originally enacted suggested that the assignment must be signed by or on behalf of both parties to the assignment before recordal can take place. The rule

---

119 TMA 1996, s 29(2)(ca), as inserted by the Patents (Amendment) Act 2006, which came into effect on 4 October 2010 pursuant to the Patents (Amendment) Act 2006 (Section 41) (Commencement) Order 2010 (SI 432/2010).
120 TMA 1996, s 29(3)(b).
121 TMA 1996, s 29(4)(a) and (b).
122 As amended by the Trade Marks (Amendment) Rules, 2010.
123 Trade Marks Rules 1996, r 45(3) as inserted by the Trade Marks (Amendment) Rules 2010.

in this regard appeared to be *ultra vires* the Act and this additional requirement of the signature of the assignee was removed by the Trade Marks (Amendment) Rules 2010. Even though a registrable transaction may be dated prior to 1 July 1996, provided application for recordal is subsequent to or still pending on this date, the provisions and thus procedures under s 29 of TMA 1996 apply.[124]

[34.50] An equitable interest in a trade mark, such as an agreement to grant a licence, is enforceable but not recordable on the Register.[125] The position as regards recordal of registrable transactions against a pending trade mark application is essentially the same as that of a registration.[126]

LICENSING OF TRADE MARKS

[34.51] Article 8 of the Trade Mark Harmonisation Directive[127] states as follows:

1. A trade mark may be licensed for some or all of the goods or services for which it is registered and for the whole or part of the Member State concerned. A licence may be exclusive or non-exclusive.

2. The proprietor of a trade mark may invoke the rights conferred by that trade mark against a licensee who contravenes any provision in his licensing contract with regard to:

   (a)   its duration;

   (b)   the form covered by the registration in which the trade mark may be used;

   (c)   the scope of the goods or services for which the licence is granted;

   (d)   the territory in which the trade mark may be affixed; or

   (e)   the quality of the goods manufactured or of the services provided by the licensee.

Under art 10(3), use of a trade mark with consent is deemed to constitute use by the proprietor. These statements are not repeated in TMA 1996 and, to some limited extent, can be extracted primarily from the licensing provisions in ss 32 and 33 of TMA 1996. However, there is no express provision corresponding to art 8(2) and the normal remedy for a trade mark owner would be for breach of contract.

[34.52] In *Copad SA v Christian Dior Couture SA*,[128] the ECJ ruled that a licensee in breach of art 8(2) effectively put goods on the market without the consent of the proprietor of the trade mark.

[34.53] Although licensing was also provided for under TMA 1963, it necessitated recordal on the Register by way of a registered user entry, which required proof of a prescribed control relationship between the parties. Only use by a registered user could be attributed to the proprietor and, for example, a trade mark in use by a licensee was

---

[124] TMA 1996, Sch 3, para 6(2) and (4).
[125] TMA 1996, s 30.
[126] TMA 1996, s 31(1).
[127] Council Directive 2008/95/EC ([2008] OJ L 299/25), which repealed and replaced Directive 89/104/EEC ([1989] OJ L40/1).
[128] *Copad SA v Christian Dior Couture SA* [2009] ETMR 40.

vulnerable to cancellation on the grounds of non-use if the licensee was not registered. The regime under TMA 1996 is to leave the contractual relationship between parties at their discretion in recognition of the fact that a trade mark proprietor will exercise due control over a licensee's use because it is in the proprietor's interest to maintain the integrity of the trade mark.

[34.54] Section 32(2) of TMA 1996 gives examples of certain limited licences, namely a licence in respect of some but not all of the goods and services and for the use of a trade mark in a particular manner or a particular locality.

[34.55] A licence of a registered trade mark is not effective unless it is in writing signed by or on behalf of the grantor.[129] It is thus in the interest of both parties to conclude a written agreement because, in the absence of such, a purported licensee is in fact an infringer. A licence is also a registrable transaction under s 29(2)(c) of TMA 1996, which means that non-recordal results in a number of disadvantages, in particular for a licensee. Firstly, the licence is ineffective as against a person acquiring a conflicting interest.[130] Secondly, a licensee will be unable to recover damages or an account of profits,[131] and thirdly, a licensee will be unable to bring an infringement action in its own name.[132] In *Leofelis SA v Lonsdale Sports Ltd,*[133] the Court of Appeal did not consider that acceptance of royalties, with knowledge of a sub-licence for which consent had not been sought or given, made the sub-licence one to which consent has been given, rather than waiving any right to terminate the agreement on the grounds of the breach involved. A sub-licence is permissible but is a matter for the licence agreement itself.[134] Section 32(4) of TMA 1996 states that unless a licence provides otherwise, it is binding on a successor in title to the grantor's interest but s 29(3)(a) requires an application to record a licence on the Register, otherwise the 'transaction' is stated to be ineffective as against a person acquiring a conflicting interest in or under the registered trade mark in ignorance of such an interest. This would suggest that a distinction must be drawn between acquiring ownership by virtue of succession and an acquisition through purchase. In the case of inheritance subject to a specific provision to the contrary in the licence itself, the owner is bound by the licence. In the case of a purchase, the purchaser is not bound by the terms of the licence unless such has been recorded and the purchaser is on notice. It will therefore be common for a licensee to insist on recordal and for a vendor to warrant, by way of disclosure, any licences which may exist under the trade mark.

[34.56] Article 10(2) of the Trade Mark Harmonisation Directive[135] states that use of the trade mark with the consent of the proprietor, shall be deemed to constitute use by the

---

[129] TMA 1996, s 32(3).
[130] TMA 1996, s 29(3)(a).
[131] TMA 1996, s 29(4).
[132] TMA 1996, s 29(3)(b); TMA 1996, s 34.
[133] *Leofelis SA v Lonsdale Sports Ltd* [2008] ETMR 63.
[134] TMA 1996, s 32(5).
[135] Council Directive 2008/95/EC ([2008] OJ L 299/25), which repealed and replaced Directive 89/104/EEC ([1989] OJ L40/1).

proprietor. TMA 1963 had a very similar provision[136] but, quite ironically, there is no statement to this effect in TMA 1996 except in s 51(1)(a) dealing with revocation on the grounds of non-use. During the course of the debates on the UK Trade Marks Bill, it was stated that all use of the mark by the proprietor or with his consent is genuine use and that there was no need to spell it out. However, this is not so apparent and s 51(1)(c) and (d) of TMA 1996 suggest that use by a licensee may lead to the trade mark becoming a common name or misleading. Although this could also arise by virtue of the manner of use made by the proprietor, it could arise by virtue of the licensee generating their own goodwill under the mark. Therefore, in addition to quality control provisions, a trade mark owner would normally insist that a licensee indicate in their use that the trade mark is so used under the authority of the trade mark owner. A licence agreement also normally provides that the goodwill will belong to the trade mark owner.

[34.57] Section 36(6) of TMA 1963 allowed the Controller to refuse to register a user where it appeared that this would tend to facilitate trafficking in a trade mark. This provision was never interpreted by the Irish courts nor was it raised by the Controller in refusing applications under TMA 1963. In the UK, the House of Lords in *American Greetings Corpn's Application*,[137] held that the HOLLY HOBBIE trade mark could not be registered because the owner intended to grant licences in such a way that the mark was being dealt with primarily as a commodity in its own right and that there would be no real trade connection between the owner of the mark and the goods to which the mark would be applied. Thus, trade mark owners engaging in character merchandising sometimes found it difficult to register their marks in the UK. Although neither the UK Trade Marks Act 1994 nor the Irish TMA 1996 contains this prohibition, it is still a matter which could arise in the Irish courts. This is because of the transitional provisions, whereby applications filed prior to 1 July 1996 and not converted will be determined under TMA 1963.[138] In addition, TMA 1963 also applies in relation to licences granted prior to 1 July 1996.[139] The validity of existing registrations is also determined under TMA 1963.[140]

Exclusive, sole and non-exclusive licences

[34.58] An exclusive licence is specifically defined in s 33 of TMA 1996 and is essentially a licence excluding all other parties including the licensor. In a sole licence, although there are no other licensees, the licensor is not precluded from exploiting the trade mark. Sole licence is a term which is not defined in the legislation but this meaning is well-recognised and is in common use. In a non-exclusive licence, the licensor may grant further licences and also exploit the mark personally. An exclusive licence may be limited, for example, as to certain but not all of the goods or services covered by a registration or confined to a specific location.

---

[136] TMA 1963, s 36(2).
[137] *American Greetings Corpn's Application* [1984] FSR 199.
[138] TMA 1996, Sch 3, paras 8, 7(3) and (4).
[139] TMA 1996, Sch 3, para 7(1).
[140] TMA 1996, Sch 3, para 13.

[34.59] The reason why an exclusive licence is specifically defined is that an exclusive licensee is granted certain rights and remedies under TMA 1996, which do not exist for a sole or non-exclusive licensee.

[34.60] Section 33(2) of TMA 1996 states that an exclusive licensee has the same rights against a successor in title, who is bound by the licence, as the exclusive licensee has against the person granting the licence. A successor in title will not be bound if the licence provides otherwise.[141]

Licensee's right to take infringement proceedings

[34.61] Section 34 of TMA 1996 provides that a licensee can bring infringement proceedings in its own name but this particular provision does not apply to exclusive licensees who have a right to bring proceedings in their own name under different statutory provisions in s 35. Under s 34(2), if the terms of a licence do not provide otherwise, then a licensee is entitled to call on the proprietor of the registered trade mark to take infringement proceedings in respect of any matter which affects the licensee's interests. This would obviously include any infringement of the mark covered by the licence. If the goods of the infringer's use fall outside the scope of the licence agreement, it is still arguable that a licensee's interests might be affected, for example, because of inferior quality goods similar to those of the licence agreement.

[34.62] The licensee must call upon the trade mark proprietor to institute proceedings and the proprietor must refuse or fail to do so within two months of receiving the request, for the licensee to be entitled to take action in its own name.[142] A licensee cannot avail of the provisions of ss 34 or 35 of TMA 1996 until application has been made to record the licence on the Register.[143]

[34.63] If the requirements are met, then the licensee may bring the proceedings in its own name as if it was the proprietor. The proprietor must be joined as a party to the proceedings unless the licensee obtains leave of the court to do otherwise. An exception is made in the case of interlocutory relief where relief may be sought by a licensee alone.[144] A proprietor who is added as a defendant shall not be liable for any costs unless it takes part in the proceedings.[145] A court is directed to take into account any loss suffered or likely to be suffered by a licensee even where proceedings are brought in the name of the trade mark proprietor and may direct the extent to which the proceeds of any pecuniary remedy are held on behalf of a licensee.[146]

[34.64] The default position of an exclusive licensee is covered by s 35 of TMA 1996 except to the extent that a licence provides otherwise. A licence may give an exclusive licensee the same rights and remedies as if the licence had been an assignment.[147] An

---

[141] TMA 1996, s 32(4).
[142] TMA 1996, s 34(3).
[143] TMA 1996, s 29(3)(b).
[144] TMA 1996, s 34(4).
[145] TMA 1996, s 34(5).
[146] TMA 1996, s 34(6).
[147] TMA 1996, s 35.

exclusive licensee in such a position may bring proceedings in its own name without, for example, putting the proprietor on notice and awaiting the two-month period under s 34. An exclusive licensee may institute proceedings immediately in such circumstances and, for example, may avail of additional remedies such as delivery up.

[34.65] An exclusive licensee under s 35 of TMA 1996 is deemed to have rights and remedies concurrent with those of the trade mark proprietor.[148] This means that both the trade mark proprietor and exclusive licensee must, unless they have the leave of the court to do otherwise, join the other party to the proceedings. An exception is made in the case of interlocutory relief. Where a proprietor or licensee is added to the proceedings as a defendant, then they will not be liable for costs unless they take part in the proceedings.[149] Because an exclusive licensee is essentially put in the same position as the trade mark proprietor, s 35(4) allows a defendant to avail of any defence that would have been available if the action had been brought by the trade mark proprietor. The position as regards damages and an account of profits is also dealt with in such a way as to ensure that an infringer is not held doubly liable and that there is apportionment between the concurrent rights holders.[150] The trade mark proprietor must notify an exclusive licensee with a concurrent right before applying for an order of delivery up[151] and a court may, upon application, order delivery up to the licensee as opposed to the trade mark proprietor. The whole of s 35 dealing with the concurrent rights of certain exclusive licensees is subject to any contractual rights to the contrary[152] and also to recordal of the licence agreement.[153]

COMPETITION LAW ASPECTS OF ASSIGNMENTS/LICENSING

[34.66] Any assignment or a licence agreement must be considered in the context of EU competition law and the domestic equivalent, namely the Competition Acts 2002 and 2006. Article 34[154] of the Treaty on the Functioning of the European Union (the Treaty) states that:

> Quantitative restrictions on imports and all measures having equivalent effect shall, without prejudice to the following provisions, be prohibited between Member States.

National intellectual property rights fall within art 34 but art 36[155] recognises as an exception intellectual property rights where they are necessary to achieve the reasonable

---

[148] TMA 1996, s 35(3).
[149] TMA 1996, s 36(2).
[150] TMA 1996, s 36(3) and (4).
[151] TMA 1996, s 36(5).
[152] TMA 1996, s 36(6).
[153] TMA 1996, s 29(3)(b).
[154] Formerly EC Treaty, art 28; *Commission v Germany* Case 325/00 [2003] ETMR 33; *Commission v Italy* Case C-14/00 [2003] ETMR 73.
[155] Formerly EC Treaty, art 30.

purposes for which they were introduced.[156] Trade mark rights cannot serve as a means of arbitrary discrimination or as a disguised restriction on trade.

[34.67] In the case of a trade mark licence, the rules on exhaustion of rights apply in relation to the licensee. Under art 7 of the Trade Mark Harmonisation Directive,[157] a trade mark shall not entitle the proprietor to prohibit use in relation to goods which have been put on the market in the Community under that trade mark by the proprietor or with its consent. Consent is the key word in relation to a licensee and the ECJ has in this context viewed all entities within a corporate group as operating under consent from the trade mark proprietor.[158]

[34.68] Assignments are viewed differently with regard to the operation of the principle of exhaustion of rights.[159] In *IHT Internazionale Heiztechnick GmbH v Ideal-Standard GmbH*,[160] it was held that a national trade mark right which had been voluntarily assigned, could be used to prevent importation by a successor in title to the assignee. However, as stated by the ECJ, where undertakings independent of each other enter into trade mark assignments following a market sharing agreement, the prohibition against anti-competitive agreements under art 101 of the Treaty[161] applies. In determining whether a trade mark assignment can be treated as giving effect to an agreement prohibited under art 101, it is necessary to analyse the context, the commitments underlying the assignment, the intention of the parties and the consideration for the assignment.

Block exemptions

[34.69] Article 101 of the Treaty prohibits agreements between undertakings, decisions by associations of undertakings and concerted practices, which may affect trade between Member States and which have as their objective or effect the prevention, restriction or distortion of competition within the internal market. Agreements which infringe art 101 are void. Article 101(3) allows the European Commission to exempt certain agreements provided that they satisfy the criteria set out in art 101(3), whereby there are positive attributes of the agreement which outweigh the anti-competitive provisions. The agreement must contribute to the improvement of the production or distribution of goods, or promote technical or economic progress. Also, a fair share of the resultant benefit must be passed to consumers.

[34.70] The European Commission has issued a number of block exemption regulations. If an agreement is not covered by a block exemption, it is potentially anti-competitive and the parties must assess the potential effects on the agreement. Until May 2004,

---

[156] *Officier Van Justitie v De Peijper* [1976] ECR 613.

[157] Council Directive 2008/95/EC ([2008] OJ L 299/25), which repealed and replaced Directive 89/104/EEC ([1989] OJ L40/1).

[158] *Centrafarm BV v Winthrop BV* [1974] ECR 1183.

[159] See paras **[33.18]–[33.33]**.

[160] *IHT Internazionale Heiztechnik GmbH v Ideal-Standard GmbH* [1994] ECR I-2789.

[161] Formerly EC Treaty, art 81.

agreements that were not covered by a block exemption could be individually notified to the European Commission for a ruling on whether they were anti-competitive. Alternatively, any agreements to which the block exemption did not apply but which did not contain any prohibited clauses could be notified to the European Commission and deemed automatically exempt if the European Commission took no action within a specified four-month period. These notification systems were removed in May 2004.

[34.71] The relevant block exemptions for trade marks are primarily:

- Commission Regulation 330/2010/EC on the application of art 101(3) of the Treaty on the Functioning of the European Union to categories of vertical agreements and concerted practices[162]
- Commission Regulation 772/2004/EC, the Technology Transfer Agreements Block Exemption.[163]

Commission Regulation 330/2010/EC[164] is a block exemption regulation relating to vertical agreements, namely those between undertakings which operate at a different level of the production or distribution chain (for example, distribution or franchise arrangements) and relating to conditions under which the parties may purchase, sell or resell certain goods or services. It became effective on 1 June 2010 and is due to expire on 31 May 2022.

[34.72] The relevance of competition law to vertical agreements has long been recognised. In *Consten and Grundig v Commission*,[165] it was argued that the prohibition in art 101(1)[166] of the Treaty only applied to so-called 'horizontal agreements', namely agreements made by undertakings that would otherwise compete with each other at the same level of trade or industry, eg between manufacturers or between retailers of competing products. This was not accepted by the ECJ who held that it applied equally to 'vertical agreements', namely between firms at different levels of trade or industry such as a supplier and customer or licensor and licensee. In this case, a distribution agreement infringed art 101 on a number of fronts including a provision whereby the distributor was allowed to register the manufacturer's trade mark so as to keep out goods from other distributors in a crude attempt to avoid the principle of exhaustion of rights.

[34.73] Regulation 330/2010/EC applies to agreements that relate to assignments or use of intellectual property rights provided that those provisions do not constitute the primary object of those agreements and that those provisions are directly related to the use, sale or resale of goods or services.[167] Therefore, pure intellectual property assignments or licences are not covered by Regulation 330/2010/EC as the intellectual property provisions are the primary object of those agreements. This was also the case

---

[162] Commission Regulation 330/2010/EC ([2010] OJ L102/1).

[163] See paras **[6.41]**–**[6.45]**.

[164] Which replaced its predecessor, Commission Regulation 2790/1999/EC.

[165] *Etablissements Consten SARL and Grundig-Verkaufs-GmbH v European Commission* [1966] CMLR 418.

[166] Formerly the EC Treaty, art 81(1).

[167] Regulation 330/2010/EC, art 2(3).

under earlier block exemptions. In *Moosehead Breweries Ltd v Whitbread & Co's Agreement*,[168] it was held that the principal interest of the parties lay in the exploitation of the trade mark rather than the know-how. In the circumstances, the provision of the agreement relating to trade marks was not ancillary and therefore, Regulation 556/89/EC (a now-repealed know-how licence agreement block exemption) did not apply. In *Davide Campari-Milano SpA*,[169] it was held that an exclusive trade mark licence agreement automatically falls within art 101(1)[170] although it is sometimes acceptable for a limited degree of territorial exclusivity to be conferred on a trade mark licensee. Regulation 330/2010/EC is more permissive of internet sales than previous block exemptions, although limitations on internet sales are still envisaged in certain circumstances by the Guidelines which accompany the Regulation.[171]

[34.74] The following types of agreements are automatically covered by Regulation 330/2010/EC and are not anti-competitive, provided that they do not contain any of the black-listed clauses referred to below:

1. Any agreements between associations of undertakings and their members or between an association and its suppliers, where the members of the association are retailers and provided that no individual member has a total annual turnover exceeding €50 million.[172]

2. Any non-reciprocal vertical agreements between competing undertakings[173] where (i) the supplier is a manufacturer and distributor and the buyer is a distributor and is not competing at the manufacturing level or (ii) the supplier is a provider of services at several levels of trade and the buyer provides its goods and services at the retail level and is not competing at the level of trade where it purchases the services.[174]

3. Any agreement between parties where they each have a market share of the relevant market which does not exceed 30 per cent.

The relevant market is usually narrowly defined and as a consequence an exclusive trade mark licence agreement will rarely fall within this *de minimis* exemption. In *Hilti v Commission*,[175] the ECJ defined the relevant market as being nails designed for use in a specific nail gun.

[34.75] The effect of the Regulation is to indicate guidelines by way of clauses which are prohibited (black-listed clauses) in certain types of agreements. If the type of agreement falls within the Regulation and it does not include any of the prohibited clauses, then it

---

[168] *Moosehead Breweries Ltd v Whitbread & Co's Agreement* [1991] 4 CMLR 391.
[169] *Davide Campari-Milano SpA* [1978] 2 CMLR 397.
[170] Formerly EC Treaty, art 81(1).
[171] Commission Notice, Guidelines on Vertical Restraints, Patents Office Journal ([2010] C 130/1).
[172] Regulation 330/2010/EC, art 2(2).
[173] As defined in Regulation 330/2010/EC, art 1(c).
[174] Regulation 330/2010/EC, art 2(4).
[175] *Hilti AG v European Commission* [1994] ECR I-667.

may be exempted from art 101 of the Treaty. The black-listed clauses under Regulation 330/2010/EC are as follows:

(1) Any obligations which directly or indirectly, in isolation or in combination with other facts under the control of the parties, have as their object:[176]

(i) Resale price maintenance, although the imposition of maximum sales prices or recommended sales prices is permitted so long as it does not amount to a fixed or minimum sales price as a result of pressure or incentives;

(ii) Restrictions on sales to territories or customers except the following permitted clauses:

(a) Restrictions on active sales into exclusive territories or customers reserved for the licensor;

(b) Restrictions on sales to end users by a buyer who is a wholesaler;

(c) Restrictions on sales to unauthorised distributors by members of a selective distribution system;[177]

(d) Restrictions on sales of components supplied for the purposes of incorporation to customers who would use them for manufacture of the same type of goods.

(iii) Restrictions on active or passive sales to end-users by members of a selective distribution system, without prejudice to the possibility of preventing a member from operating out of an unauthorised place of establishment.

(iv) Restrictions on cross-supplies between distributors within a selective distribution system.

(v) Restrictions between a supplier of components and a buyer, who incorporates those components, on the supplier's ability to sell the components as spare parts to end users or to repairers or other service providers, which the buyer does not entrust with repair or servicing of the products.

(2) Any direct or indirect obligations which:

(i) Contain non-compete obligations of indefinite term or which exceed five years, including those which are tacitly renewable. However, the five-year limit does not apply where the goods or services are sold by the buyer from premises and land owned by the supplier or leased by the supplier, provided that the duration of the non-compete obligation does not exceed the period of occupancy of the premises and land by the buyer.

(ii) Cause the buyer after termination not to manufacture, purchase, sell or resell goods or services. However, there is an exception for obligations relating to competing goods and services, which are limited to the premises and land from which the buyer operated, which are indispensable to protect the know-how transferred and which are limited to a period of one year after termination. In

---

[176] Regulation 330/2010/EC, art 4.

[177] Regulation 330/2010/EC, art 1(e), for example the distribution systems of luxury consumer brands, which can only be sold through certain prestigious outlets and not through discount stores, etc.

addition, restrictions of unlimited duration can be imposed on use and disclosure of know-how which has not entered the public domain.

(iii) Cause members of a selective distribution system not to sell the brands of a competing system.[178]

[34.76] In *Nungesser v Commission (Maize Seed Case)*,[179] the ECJ held that an open exclusive licence is not itself contrary to art 101(1)[180] of the Treaty. An open exclusive licence is described by the ECJ as an agreement whereby the owner merely undertakes not to grant other licences in respect of the same territory and not to compete itself with the licensee in that territory. Such a licence allows parallel imports of the protected product into the designated territory.

[34.77] The ECJ has recognised in a number of cases that quality control provisions in a licence agreement may be necessary to protect the essential or specific subject matter of the trade mark. In *DDD Ltd and Delta Chemie's Agreement*,[181] strict requirements imposed by a licensor on the manner in which stain removers were to be manufactured and packaged were considered not to fall within art 101(1)[182] of the Treaty.

[34.78] In *World Wide Fund for Nature v World Wrestling Federation*,[183] the defendant argued that an agreement which had been concluded between the parties was unenforceable as an unreasonable restraint of trade. The Court of Appeal refused to set aside the agreement, Carnwath LJ stating:

> The protection of the intellectual property rights of one business inevitably implies some restriction on the rights of others with potentially conflicting interests. The laws governing those rights are designed to set reasonable limits to the restrictions, but the limits are not always clear cut. Where there are disputes, it is in the interests of everyone, including the public, for those disputes to be settled by agreement, rather than litigation, and for such agreements to be respected.

[34.79] In *Pronuptia*,[184] the ECJ considered what it termed 'distribution franchising' whereby the franchisee operated as an independent business while, at the same time, using the name and know-how of the franchisor. The ECJ viewed such franchises favourably as a means by which an undertaking can derive financial benefit from another's expertise without investing its own capital. It was held that provisions strictly necessary in order to ensure that know-how and assistance provided by the franchisor did not benefit competitors did not constitute restrictions of competition for the purposes of art 101(1).[185] Examples of such were clauses prohibiting the franchisee, during the period of the validity of the contract and for a reasonable period after its expiry, from opening a shop of the same or a similar nature in an area whereby it may

---

[178] Regulation 330/2010/EC, art 5.
[179] *Nungesser (L C) KG and Kurt Eisele v European Commission* [1982] ECR 2015.
[180] Formerly EC Treaty, art 81(1).
[181] *Re Delta Chemie/DDD (EC Commission Decision 88/563)* [1989] 4 CMLR 535.
[182] Formerly EC Treaty, art 81(1).
[183] *World Wide Fund for Nature v World Wrestling Federation* [2002] ETMR 53.
[184] *Pronuptia de Paris GmbH v Pronuptia de Paris Irmgard Schilgalis* [1986] ECR 353.
[185] Formerly EC Treaty, art 81(1).

compete with a member of the franchise network. The same may be said of the franchisee's obligation not to transfer its shop to another party without the prior approval of the franchisor. The franchisor is also entitled to take measures necessary for maintaining the identity and reputation of the network bearing its business name or symbol. Examples are obligations to apply certain business methods, to sell goods only in premises at particular locations with certain layouts and for all advertising to be approved by the franchisor. In some cases, there is also no practical solution other than for a franchisor to insist that the franchisee sell only products that have been supplied by the franchisor or by suppliers selected by the franchisor. Such a provision may not have the effect of preventing the franchisee from obtaining those products from other franchisees.

Abuse of a dominant position

[34.80] Article 102 of the Treaty[186] states that any abuse by one or more undertaking(s) of a dominant position within the internal market or in a substantial part of it, shall be prohibited as incompatible with the internal market in so far as it may affect trade between Member States. In *United Brands*,[187] it was stated that:

> The dominant position referred to in this Article relates to a position of economic strength enjoyed by an undertaking which enables it to prevent effective competition being maintained on the relevant market by giving it the power to behave to an appreciable extent independently of its competitors, customers and ultimately of its consumers.

The existence of an intellectual property right, such as a trade mark, is not evidence in its own right that the owner has a dominant position.[188] However in combination with other factors, an abuse of a dominant position can occur. An example would be for an undertaking in a dominant position to register a mark knowing it to be in use by a competitor. An undertaking in a dominant position which cashes in on the reputation of a brand name known and valued by customers, cannot stop supplying a long-standing customer who abides by regular commercial practice, if the orders placed by this customer are in no way out of the ordinary.[189] In a case involving the acquisition of the trade mark WILKINSON SWORD, the European Commission held that the transfer and certain delimitation of trade mark rights infringed art 102[190] and ordered a divestiture of the mark.[191] For an abuse to occur the following principles apply: (a) the dominated market and the market affected by the abuse must be the same; (b) to extend the concept of abuse to another market requires a close link between the two markets; (c) any extension to related markets must be circumscribed so as to ensure that it is extended only where an undertaking had a responsibility under art 102[192] with regard to its

---

[186] Formerly EC Treaty, art 82.
[187] *United Brands Co v European Commission* [1978] ECR 207.
[188] *Deutsche Grammophon GmbH v Metro-SB-Grossmärkte GmbH & Co KG* [1971] ECR 487.
[189] *United Brands Co v European Commission* [1978] ECR 207.
[190] Formerly EC Treaty, art 82.
[191] *Warner Lambert and Bic SA v Gillette and Eemland NV* [1993] 5 CMLR 559.
[192] Formerly EC Treaty, art 82.

conduct in those other markets.[193] In *Der Grune Punkt-Duales System Deutschland GmbH v Commission of the European Communities*,[194] the ECJ, in consideration of an application to annul a Commission Decision of abuse of a dominant position, had to consider an argument that the decision was disproportionate as it prevented the trade mark owner from levying a fee on each package bearing its logo. The ECJ upheld the European Commission Decision finding that the function of the trade mark was not in fact adversely affected.

[34.81] In *Sot Lelos kai Sia EE v GlaxoSmithKline*,[195] the ECJ had to consider whether the actions of a pharmaceutical company in limiting supplies to the Greek market, thus avoiding parallel imports from Greece, amounted to an abuse of a dominant position. The ECJ held that the refusal to meet ordinary orders from wholesalers did amount to such an abuse but that it was for a national court to ascertain whether the orders are ordinary, in light of the size of the orders in relation to the wholesaler's requirements and their previous business relations.

THE REGISTER

[34.82] The Controller is obliged to maintain a register of trade marks.[196] This is now kept in computer form[197] and is open to public inspection.[198] Rule 43 of the Trade Marks Rules 1996 prescribes the information which must be available on the Register upon registration, namely:

(a) the name and address of the proprietor and the address for service. Although r 10 of the Trade Marks Rules 1996 states that the address for service must be in the State, regard must be had to the European Communities (Provision of Services Concerning Trade Marks and Industrial Designs) Regulations 2007,[199] which provide that a person established in another Member State of the EU and suitably qualified under the law of that State is entitled to represent trade mark owners before the Controller. The Trade Marks (Amendment) Rules 2010 broadened this to Member States of the EEA;[200]

(b) the goods or services in respect of which the mark is registered and their class or classes;

---

[193] *Claritas (UK) Ltd v Post Office* [2001] ETMR 63; *Tetra Pak International SA v European Commission* [1996] ECR I-595 1.
[194] *Der Grune Punkt-Duales System Deutschland GmbH v Commission of the European Communities* [2007] ETMR 66.
[195] *Sot Lelos kai Sia EE v GlaxoSmithKline* [2009] ETMR 4.
[196] TMA 1996, s 66(1).
[197] Trade Marks Rules 1996, r 42.
[198] TMA 1996, s 66(3)(a).
[199] SI 622/2007.
[200] SI 410/2010.

(c)   the date of filing, being the date of registration.[201] The importance of this lies in s 13(3) of TMA 1996, which provides that the rights of the proprietor of a registered trade mark have effect from this date;

(d)   details of any priority date claimed under ss 40 or 41 of TMA 1996. This date is sometimes necessary to determine which rights take precedence;

(e)   the date of publication of the registration,[202] which is the date from which the five-year non-use provision is calculated and consequently required for a determination whether a registration is subject to revocation on the grounds of non-use under s 51(1)(a) of TMA 1996;

(f)   if the mark is a series, collective or certification mark;

(g)   any disclaimer or limitation subject to which the mark is registered. Such entries made under TMA 1963 are transferred to the Register and maintained by the Controller under TMA 1996;[203] and

(h)   details of any consent furnished by the proprietor of an earlier trade mark or right.[204]

[34.83] Information regarding registrations granted prior to TMA 1996 are transferred to the Register and maintained under TMA 1996.[205] This is important because the distinction between Part A and B registrations as regards invalidity has been maintained.[206] It is no longer necessary to maintain details of associations because these no longer have any effect.[207] Conditions entered on the former register are also not carried forward.[208]

[34.84] Also entered on the Register are details of assignments,[209] licences including information on whether they are exclusive or non-exclusive and their duration,[210] security interests,[211] vesting assents by a personal representative,[212] matters arising by operation of law such as a merger of a proprietor[213] and any order, including a court order transferring any rights in or under the mark.[214]

[34.85] It is also possible to obtain limited details of pending applications, which is imperative to enable proper searching of prior rights. The practice is for applications to be entered onto the database shortly after filing and, thereafter, details of the trade mark

---

[201] TMA 1996, s 45(3).

[202] TMA 1996, s 45(5).

[203] TMA 1996, Sch 3, para 2(5).

[204] TMA 1996, s 10(6).

[205] TMA 1996, Sch 3, para 2(1).

[206] TMA 1996, Sch 3, para 13.

[207] TMA 1996, Sch 3, para 2(3).

[208] TMA 1996, Sch 3, para 2(4).

[209] Trade Marks Rules 1996, r 44(a).

[210] Trade Marks Rules 1996, r 44(b).

[211] Trade Marks Rules 1996, r 44(c).

[212] Trade Marks Rules 1996, r 44(d).

[213] Trade Marks Rules 1996, r 44(f) as inserted by the Trade Marks (Amendment) Rules 2010.

[214] Trade Marks Rules 1996, r 44(e).

applicant, date of application and goods/services together with their classes is made available. Rule 60(2) of the Trade Marks Rules 1996 states the information made available on pending applications should in fact be that contained in the prescribed form of application (Form 1) and any certificate from the national authority in any country from which priority is claimed. Although the prescribed Form 1 is a requirement, it is not necessary in order to obtain a filing date but it is not the practice of the Controller to delay entry of the application onto the database until the prescribed form has been filed.

[34.86] Once a trade mark has been approved and advertised for opposition purposes, a number of documents on the file become open to public inspection,[215] namely:[216]

(a) the prescribed application Form 1 and priority certificate, if any. Form 1 requires an applicant to state at the time of application whether or not a trade mark is being used or whether there is a *bona fide* intention to use;

(b) written grounds of the Controller's decisions in any *inter partes* proceedings;

(c) notices of opposition to a trade mark application;

(d) an application to alter a registered trade mark, including the reasons and any evidence filed in support thereof;[217]

(e) notifications of surrender of a registered trade mark;[218]

(f) applications for revocation,[219] invalidity[220] or rectification of an error or omission in the Register;[221]

(g) details of applications made to amend an application prior to advertisement and the Controller's decision;[222] and

(h) any instrument or document submitted as a registrable transaction and which has been retained by the Patents Office. Inspection of such an instrument or document is only possible with the consent of the party who submitted the instrument or document.

Prior to publication, the above information is not available without the consent of the applicant[223] unless the applicant has warned that, upon registration, it will bring proceedings against that person in respect of acts done after publication of the application.[224] Regrettably, public access to files is far more limited than that provided for under the corresponding UK provisions. It is possible for an applicant to file a statutory declaration as evidence of the extent to which they have used a mark in the State in order to show distinctiveness. A copy of such evidence is not available to an opponent in opposition proceedings unless divulged during the course of such

---

215 TMA 1996, s 70(1).
216 Trade Marks Rules 1996, r 60(3).
217 TMA 1996, s 49(1); Trade Marks Rules 1996, r 35(1).
218 Trade Marks Rules 1996, r 36(1).
219 TMA 1996, s 51.
220 TMA 1996, s 52.
221 TMA 1996, s 67.
222 TMA 1996, s 44.
223 TMA 1996, s 70(3).
224 TMA 1996, s 70(4).

proceedings. It may therefore be difficult for a potential opponent to assess the likelihood of successful opposition. The Freedom of Information Act 1997 may form a basis upon which further documents could be made available.

[34.87] The proprietor of a registered trade mark can make an application to record a change in their name or address.[225] It is also possible for the proprietor to amend a specification of goods, provided that it is limiting and does not extend the rights.[226] The failure to provide for amendment of a specification in respect of services appears to be an oversight. The proprietor may also enter a disclaimer or memorandum, provided such does not extend the rights granted by the registration.[227]

[34.88] Under s 67(1) of TMA 1996, any person having a sufficient interest may apply for the rectification of an error or omission in the Register. Rectification under s 67 does not relate to matters affecting the validity of a registration. The application can be made to the High Court or to the Controller except where proceedings concerning the trade mark are already in the High Court, in which case the application for rectification must be made to the High Court. Where the application is made by a person other than the proprietor, the Controller will send a copy of the application and the statement of grounds to the proprietor[228] who may, within three months, oppose the application.[229] Unless otherwise directed, the effect of any rectification is that the error or omission in question is deemed never to have been made.[230]

[34.89] The Controller has the power to reclassify goods or services and to require a proprietor to amend a specification, failing which the Controller may cancel or refuse to renew the registration.[231]

---

[225] TMA 1996, s 67(5)(a).
[226] TMA 1996, s 67(5)(b).
[227] TMA 1996, s 67(5)(c).
[228] Trade Marks Rules 1996, r 41(2).
[229] Trade Marks Rules 1996, r 41(3).
[230] TMA 1996, s 67(3).
[231] TMA 1996, s 68.

Chapter 35

Trade Marks Act 1996: Revocation and Invalidity

REVOCATION OF REGISTRATION

[35.01] Because of the scope of protection granted by a registration and the more liberal regime under the Trade Marks Act 1996 (TMA 1996) as to what can be registered, there is an ever-increasing number of registrations. A large percentage are Community trade mark (CTM) registrations[1] and international registrations under the Madrid Protocol.[2] The clearance of a new mark is increasingly problematic. Apart from earning revenue, one of the reasons behind the renewal fees charged by the State is to clear at least a certain amount of dead wood from the Register. Another way is to require that a trade mark be used. As stated in the preamble to the Trade Mark Harmonisation Directive:[3]

> In order to reduce the total number of trade marks registered and protected in the Community and, consequently, the number of conflicts which arise between them, it is essential to require that registered trade marks must actually be used or, if not used, be subject to revocation.

[35.02] In some countries, such as the US, a proprietor must provide evidence of use at a specified stage during the lifetime of a registration in order to maintain the registration in force. Certain countries have elected for a system requiring evidence of use at the time of renewal. Neither of these are a requirement under Irish law, where non-use only leads to revocation where action is taken by a third party. Section 51(1) of TMA 1996 identifies the two instances where a registration can be revoked on the grounds of non-use, as follows:

(a) if the mark has not been put to genuine use in the State in relation to the goods/ services embraced by the registration within five years from when the trade mark was actually registered;[4] and

(b) where, after registration, genuine use in relation to the goods/services is suspended for an uninterrupted period of five years.[5]

In both instances, there is an exception where there are proper reasons for non-use.

---

[1] See Ch 28.
[2] Protocol Relating to the Madrid Agreement Concerning the International Registration of Marks 1989. See para **[27.50]**.
[3] Council Directive 2008/95/EC ([2008] OJ L 299/25), which repealed and replaced Directive 89/104/EEC ([1989] OJ L40/1).
[4] TMA 1996, s 51(1)(a).
[5] TMA 1996, s 51(1)(b).

[35.03] These non-use provisions implement art 10(1) of the Harmonisation Directive[6] and similar provisions also existed under the Trade Marks Act 1963 (TMA 1963).[7] However, TMA 1963 did provide for revocation in the case of a registration less than five years old on the grounds that the applicant had no *bona fide* intention to use and there had in fact been no *bona fide* use. Under TMA 1996, it is necessary in such circumstances to rely on s 52(1) and claim invalidity on the grounds of bad faith because of a failure to comply with s 37(2) requiring a *bona fide* intention to use.

[35.04] Under TMA 1963, the onus to show non-use lay on the party seeking revocation.[8] Section 99 of TMA 1996 shifts the onus of proving use onto the trade mark proprietor. This increases the number of speculative revocation actions because the expense of investigation into non-use can now be avoided. It is important for a party seeking revocation to plead partial revocation in the event that the proprietor can provide use in respect of some only of the goods/services.[9]

[35.05] The five-year non-use period runs from completion of the registration procedure,[10] which s 51(1) of TMA 1996 describes as the date of publication of the registration, which should correspond to the time that the certificate of registration issues but may be earlier.[11]

[35.06] It is possible to commence or recommence use and thereby remedy a position whereby the registration was previously vulnerable to revocation on the grounds of non-use. However, use during the three-month period immediately preceding the application for revocation is disregarded unless preparations for the commencement or resumption of use began before the proprietor became aware that the application for revocation might be made.[12] This means that it is possible to write to a trade mark proprietor seeking voluntary cancellation on the grounds of non-use. The proprietor may be prompted to commence use upon receiving such a communication but use for the first three months will be disregarded. It is therefore important for a third party not receiving a positive response within three months to preserve its position by filing an application for revocation. Under TMA 1963, the use period disregarded was one month. In *Omega SA v Omega Engineering Inc*,[13] Jacob J held that the date of application for revocation should be taken to be the relevant date for revocation in the absence of any clearly formulated request for revocation from an earlier date.

---

[6]   Council Directive 2008/95/EC ([2008] OJ L 299/25), which repealed and replaced Directive 89/104/EEC ([1989] OJ L40/1).

[7]   TMA 1963, s 34.

[8]   *Cheseborough Manufacturing Co's Trade Mark* [1902] 2 Ch 1, 19 RPC 342; *Anheuser-Busch Inc v Budweiser Budvar* [1997] ETMR 171.

[9]   *Stefcom SpA* [2005] ETMR 82.

[10] Council Directive 2008/95/EC ([2008] OJ L 299/25), which repealed and replaced Directive 89/104/EEC ([1989] OJ L40/1), art 10(1).

[11] TMA 1996, s 45(4). See Ch 34.

[12] TMA 1996, s 51(3); *Philosophy Inc v Ferretti Studio Srl* [2003] ETMR 8.

[13] *Omega SA v Omega Engineering Inc* [2003] FSR 49.

[35.07] In *Ansul BV v Ajax Brandbeveiliging BV*,[14] the ECJ was asked by the Dutch courts to interpret the words 'genuine use' in the context of a trade mark, MINIMAX, registered in respect of fire extinguishers and associated products. Use in respect of fire extinguishers had ceased but continued in respect of component parts and extinguishing substances for fire extinguishers as well as maintenance and repair services. The ECJ ruled that genuine use arises:

> where the mark is used in accordance with its essential function, which is to guarantee the identity of the origin of the goods or services for which it is registered, in order to create or preserve an outlet for those goods or services; genuine use does not include token use for the sole purpose of preserving the rights conferred by the mark. When assessing whether use of the trade mark is genuine, regard must be had to all the facts and circumstances relevant to establishing whether the commercial exploitation of the mark is real, particularly whether such use is viewed as warranted in the economic sector concerned to maintain or create a share in the market for the goods or services protected by the mark, the nature of the goods or services, the characteristics of the market and the scale and frequency of use of the mark. The fact that a mark is not used for goods newly available on the market but for goods that were sold in the past does not mean that its use is not genuine, if the proprietor makes actual use of the same mark for the component parts that are integral to the make-up or structure of such goods, or for goods or services directly connected with the goods previously sold and intended to meet the needs of customers of those goods.

[35.08] The General Court, in *La Mer Technology Inc v OHIM*,[15] stated:

> it is not possible to determine a priori and in the abstract what quantitative threshold should be chosen in order to determine whether use is genuine or not. A de minimis rule, which would not allow OHIM or, on appeal, the [General Court], to appraise all the circumstances of the dispute before it, cannot therefore be laid down. Thus, the Court has held that, when it serves a real commercial purpose, even minimal use can be sufficient to establish genuine use.

[35.09] In *Compagnie Gervais Danone v Glanbia Foods Society Ltd*,[16] the Supreme Court had to consider whether or not there was genuine use of a trade mark ESSENSIS which was registered in respect of goods, including yoghurt, but where use was in conjunction with the word 'Bifidus' as the name of an ingredient of the yoghurt, namely a pro-biotic culture. In the Supreme Court, Macken J upheld an appeal from a decision of the High Court, which had held that since use had been unequivocally confined to referring to an identified ingredient of the yoghurt as distinct from the yoghurt itself, the trade mark did not serve as a guarantee of origin in relation to the goods of registration. Macken J, in reversing the High Court decision, equated the use with that of a spare part for a product and thus falling within the parameters of what constituted genuine use as

---

[14] *Ansul BV v Ajax Brandbeveiliging BV* [2003] ETMR 85; see also *La Mer Technology v Laboratoires Goemar SA* [2004] ETMR 47.

[15] *La Mer Technology Inc v OHIM* [2008] ETMR 9.

[16] *Compagnie Gervais Danone v Glanbia Foods Society Ltd* Decision of 19 May, 2010, [2010] IESC 36.

set out by the ECJ in the *Ansul* decision,[17] finding the use to be integral to the make-up or structure of the goods.

[35.10] The onus is on the trade mark proprietor to show genuine use. Under TMA 1963, the use had to be *bona fide*. There is likely to be very little difference, if any, between the court's interpretation of the word 'genuine' as opposed to the words '*bona fide*'. The Irish courts followed the Court of Appeal decision in *Electrolux Ltd v Electrix Ltd*,[18] in which *bona fide* use was held to mean substantial and genuine use of the mark judged by ordinary commercial standards. The words do not imply that there has to be a particular volume or duration of use.

[35.11] The General Court, in *HI WATT*,[19] stated that:

> genuine use implies real use of the mark on the market concerned for the purpose of identifying goods or services. Genuine use is therefore to be regarded as excluding minimal or insufficient use for the purpose of determining that a mark is being put to real, effective use on a given market. In that regard, even if it is the owner's intention to make real use of his trade mark, if the trade mark is not objectively present on the market in a manner that is effective, consistent over time and stable in terms of the configuration of the sign, so that it cannot be perceived by consumers as an indication of the goods or services in question, there is no genuine use of the trade mark.

The mere act of sponsorship does not establish genuine use[20] but the threshold of use required may be lower in respect of a non-profit-making organisation.[21]

[35.12] The provision in s 51(3) of TMA 1996, which allows the proprietor to rely upon preparations to commence or resume use, although not in TMA 1963, was a factor considered by the Controller in *Re Frisk*.[22] In that case, the only use of the trade mark had been in relation to a consignment of imported goods, which had not cleared customs. It was held that this use was *bona fide* and the Controller refused to expunge the trade mark from the Register.

[35.13] In *CONCORD Trade Mark*,[23] the English courts applied more stringent criteria and seemed to require that the use had to be for the purposes of establishing goodwill in the mark so as to make trading under that mark profitable in itself.[24] In doing so, the emphasis was placed more on the requirement that the use be substantial rather than genuine. The use of the name of a cartoon character in a book was not regarded as

---

[17] *Ansul Decision* [2003] ETMR 85.
[18] *Electrolux Ltd v Electrix Ltd* (1954) 71 RPC 23; see also *Gerber Products Co v Gerber Foods International Ltd* [2002] ETMR 77.
[19] *Kabushiki Kaisha Fernandes v OHIM* [2002] ECR II-5233.
[20] *ILG Ltd v Crunch Fitness* [2008] ETMR 17.
[21] *Verein Radetsky-Orden v BKFR* [2009] ETMR 14.
[22] *Carnation Co v Ocean Harvest Ltd* (1970) Supp OJ111 p 17.
[23] *CONCORD Trade Mark* [1987] FSR 209. See also *HERMES* [1982] RPC 425.
[24] See also *Imperial Group Ltd v Philip Morris & Co Ltd* [1982] FSR 72.

indicating trade source in respect of entertainment services.[25] A similar position was adopted in relation to the use of the name of a band on a CD.[26]

[35.14] In *Harold Radford & Austin Motor Co's Applications*,[27] it was held that advertisements for sale, and orders resulting from such advertisements, did not constitute use of the trade mark. It was not, however, necessary that the goods exist concurrently with the advertisement. What was required was that the proprietor had, at the time of advertisement, taken positive steps to trade in goods marked with the trade mark. Advertising would usually be sufficient to at least fulfil the requirement that preparations for the commencement or resumption of the trade mark had begun.[28]

[35.15] Section 51(2) of TMA 1996, in implementing art 10(1) of the Trade Mark Harmonisation Directive,[29] allows the following to constitute use:

(a)   use of the trade mark in a form differing in elements from the registration but which does not alter the distinctive character of the mark in the form in which it was registered; and

(b)   affixing of the trade mark to goods or to the packaging thereof in the State solely for export purposes.

[35.16] In relation to use of a trade mark in a form differing in element from the registration as set out in (a) above, a similar provision existed under s 38 of TMA 1963. There has always been a tendency to register word trade marks in block capital letters on the basis that most stylisation or different casing of letters will be viewed as a difference from the registered mark, which does not alter the distinctive character.[30] This provision is a recognition that over time, the format in which a trade mark is used may alter but the substantial identity remains intact.[31] Where possible, a proprietor can register a series mark providing for different formats in the registration itself.[32] However, in *Safeway Stores v Hachette Filipacchi Presse*,[33] Lloyd J observed that in determining whether use of a trade mark other than as registered constitutes use, it was not helpful to draw an analogy with provisions of TMA 1996 dealing with the registration of a series of different but related marks. It was held that by the omission of a device and by conversion of the four letters of the word ELLE from lower to upper case, the distinctive character of the registered form was altered. An example where the courts refused to accept use of a trade mark with just a one letter difference is *HUGGARS Trade Mark*,[34]

---

[25]   *Animated Music Ltd's Application 'NELLIE THE ELEPHANT'* [2004] ETMR 79.

[26]   *R v Johnstone* [2004] ETMR 2.

[27]   *Harold Radford & Austin Motor Co's Applications* (1951) 68 RPC 221; see also *REVUE Trade Mark* [1979] RPC 27.

[28]   TMA 1996, s 51(3).

[29]   Council Directive 2008/95/EC ([2008] OJ L 299/25), which repealed and replaced Directive 89/104/EEC ([1989] OJ L40/1).

[30]   TMA 1963, s 38: 'Not substantially affecting its identity'.

[31]   See *GFK AG v OHIM* [2006] ETMR 58.

[32]   TMA 1996, s 46(2). See para **[34.06]**.

[33]   *Safeway Stores v Hachette Filipacchi Presse* [1997] ETMR 552.

[34]   *HUGGARS Trade Mark* [1979] FSR 310.

where use was made of HUGGERS. The court was heavily influenced by the fact that although HUGGARS was meaningless, the word HUGGERS was descriptive in relation to the goods being clothing. Decisions made under s 49(1) of TMA 1996 in relation to permissible alterations to a trade mark registration are likely to be of guidance. In *Seaforth Maritime Ltd's Application*,[35] an amendment was refused on the basis that the change in visual impression created by the alteration was substantial. It was held that what is important are 'the features by which the mark will be recognised either by its meaning, phonetically or visually and which serve to distinguish the goods of the proprietor of the mark from the similar goods of other traders'.[36] In *Spillers Ltd v Quaker Oats Ltd*,[37] it was held that use of a non-hyphenated word trade mark could be taken as equivalent to use of the registered hyphenated version.

[35.17] The provision allowing for export use to be taken into account also existed under TMA 1963. It is limited to the affixing of the trade mark to goods or their packaging and there is no inclusion of a service mark for export trade. No such use of a service mark will defeat an action for revocation.

[35.18] A revocation action can be defeated where it can be shown that there were proper reasons for non-use. There is no definition of what is meant by the words 'proper reasons'. Under TMA 1963, a similar defence to revocation also arose if the registered proprietor could show that non-use was due to special circumstances in the trade and was not due to any intention not to use or to abandon the mark.[38] In *Haupl v Lidl Stiftung*,[39] the ECJ stated that:

> obstacles having a sufficiently direct relationship with a trade mark making its use impossible or unreasonable, and which arise independently of the will of the proprietor of that mark, may be described as 'proper reasons for non-use' of that mark.

[35.19] An example of proper reasons would be the need to secure regulatory approval before the launch of a pharmaceutical product. In *Manus AB v RJ Fulwood & Bland Ltd*,[40] a number of external restrictions on trade due to the Second World War were deemed sufficient reasons to justify non-use. An intention to use the mark as soon as the technical problems have been overcome has been held not to be sufficient reason for non-use.[41] It is possible that a similar decision would be reached under TMA 1996 and proper reasons are still likely to be external reasons common to the trade as a whole, as opposed to business difficulties experienced by a particular trader. In *Invermont Trade Mark*,[42] it was held that the term 'proper' was not intended to cover normal situations or routine difficulties. It could, however, extend to technical difficulties surrounding

---

35 *Seaforth Maritime Ltd's Application* [1993] RPC 72.
36 See also *OTRIVIN Trade Mark* [1967] RPC 613 and *PELICAN Trade Mark* [1978] RPC 424.
37 *Spillers Ltd v Quaker Oats Ltd* [1969] FSR 510.
38 TMA 1963, s 34(3).
39 *Haupl v Lidl Stiftung* [2007] ETMR 61.
40 *Manus AB v RJ Fulwood & Bland Ltd* (1949) 66 RPC 71.
41 *Thermax* [1985] RPC 403.
42 *Invermont Trade Mark* [1997] RPC 125.

manufacture.[43] In *Glen Catrine Bonded Warehouse Ltd's Application*[44] Tuck LJ considered that the word 'proper' may be more liberally interpreted and a 'tribunal may, therefore perhaps be able to find that disruptive situations in which the registered proprietor's business alone is affected are, nonetheless proper' and that the word 'proper' in the context of s 51 of TMA 1996 means 'acceptable, reasonable, justifiable in all the circumstances'. It was also held that there is a statutory discretion in s 51 and that revocation is not automatic where there is non-use.

[35.20] A common occurrence is where there may be partial use, ie use on some but not all of the goods/services covered by a registration. This is dealt with in s 51(5) of TMA 1996, which provides that 'where grounds for revocation exist in respect of only some of the goods or services for which the trade mark is registered, revocation shall relate to those goods or services only'.[45] It is common practice to hold registrations with specifications for a broad range of goods/services. In any application for revocation, it is important to identify the exact goods/services against which revocation is sought. The revocation action should properly define the scope of the relief sought, ie the extent to which revocation is sought. However, in view of broad specifications, a court may be prepared to limit the specification in such a way as to have proper regard to the use that the proprietor has in fact made. In *Decon Laboratories v Fred Baker Scientific,*[46] the court qualified the specification by the words 'all for non-domestic use'. In *Pomaco Ltd's Application,*[47] Jacob J held that in restricting the specification of goods, the court was not limited to the deletion of items, but could also exclude a subset of a wide general description. In *West v Fuller Smith and Turner plc,*[48] a specification in respect of beer was revoked except in so far as it related to bitter, being the only beer in respect of which use had been proved. TMA 1963 contained a discretion to allow goods to remain in the specification despite non-use where there was use on goods of the same description in the specification; this discretion may also exist under TMA 1996.[49] In the *ALADIN* decision,[50] the General Court held that the principle of partial use was a limitation on the rights of the proprietor and should not be interpreted too broadly, stating:

> if a trade mark has been registered for goods or services defined so precisely and narrowly that it is not possible to make any significant sub-divisions within the category concerned, then the proof of genuine use of the mark for the goods or services necessarily covers the entire category.

[35.21] The definition of a trade mark in s 6(1) of TMA 1996 is also of critical importance in the context of revocation on the grounds of non-use because s 51(1)

[43] *MAGIC BALL* [2000] ETMR 226.

[44] *Glen Catrine Bonded Warehouse Ltd's Application* [1996] ETMR 56.

[45] *Premier Brands UK Ltd v Typhoon Ltd* [2000] ETMR 1071 and *Minerva* [2000] FSR 734.

[46] *Decon Laboratories v Fred Baker Scientific* [2001] ETMR 46.

[47] *Pomaco Ltd's Application* [2001] ETMR 92.

[48] *West v Fuller Smith and Turner plc* [2003] ETMR 30.

[49] *Glen Catrine Bonded Warehouse Ltd's Application* [1996] ETMR 56.

[50] *Reckitt Benckiser v OHIM* [2006] ETMR 50.

requires use as a trade mark. In *KODAK Trade Mark*,[51] revocation was sought against the KODAK registration in respect of clothing. Kodak Ltd did use their mark on t-shirts but it was held that this was not trade mark use and was simply advertising so as to encourage people to buy their photographic products. This decision was decided under the UK Trade Marks Act 1938, corresponding to the Irish TMA 1963. The definition of a trade mark under TMA 1963 was limited to the function of a trade mark as an indication of origin. Whether or not the *KODAK* case will be followed under TMA 1996 depends on the extent to which the role of the trade mark is seen as a vehicle for advertising and promotion. As stated by Pumfrey J in *Daimler Chrysler AG v Javid Alavi*:[52]

> There is no rule that t-shirt use of a mark primarily used in relation to some other kind of goods altogether, say computers, does not confer on the user a goodwill in relation to t-shirts. It is a question of fact in every case, but one should not blindly accept that this kind of advertising use necessarily gives rise to a protected goodwill in respect of the substrate which carries the advertisement.

However, in *Silberquelle GmbH v Maselli-Strickmode GmbH*,[53] the ECJ held that genuine use does not occur where the proprietor applies the trade mark to goods that it gives away free of charge by way of a promotion.

[35.22] Article 10(2) of the Harmonisation Directive[54] provides that use of the trade mark with the consent of the proprietor shall be deemed to constitute use by the proprietor. This consent is likely to be interpreted as meaning use by a party who is in the position of a licensee. A proprietor should ensure that there is proper control over a licensee as a matter of principle. In *JOB Trade Mark*,[55] it was held that insufficient control of the licensee's activities was maintained and therefore use by the licensee could not be relied on. This decision was made under the UK Trade Marks Act 1938 but it could still be followed because uncontrolled licensing can be viewed as tantamount to an assignment of the trade mark. Uncontrolled use can also lead to a trade mark being considered misleading and subject to revocation under s 51(1)(d).

[35.23] It is not stated that the use must be by the registered proprietor and this would suggest that an assignee who has not recorded its ownership on the Register may nevertheless rely on its use.[56]

Generic use

[35.24] A further ground for revocation exists under s 51(1)(c) of TMA 1996 and arises where, as a consequence of the acts or inactivity of the proprietor, the trade mark has become the common name in the trade for a product or service for which the trade mark

---

51 *KODAK Trade Mark* [1990] FSR 49.
52 *Daimler Chrysler AG v Javid Alavi* [2001] ETMR 98.
53 *Silberquelle GmbH v Maselli-Strickmode GmbH* [2009] ETMR 28.
54 Council Directive 2008/95/EC ([2008] OJ L 299/25), which repealed and replaced Directive 89/104/EEC ([1989] OJ L40/1).
55 *JOB Trade Mark* [1993] FSR 118.
56 *TROOPER Trade Mark* [1994] RPC 26.

is registered. It is important for a trade mark owner to ensure that it properly polices its trade mark so that it does not become generic or descriptive. The relevant trade has been interpreted by the ECJ to include intermediaries.[57] The trade comprises all consumers and end users and, depending on the features of the market concerned, all those in the trade who deal with that product commercially. Examples of trade marks that have become generic through trade use are ASPRIN and FORMICA.

[35.25] In *JERYL LYNN*,[58] Laddie J considered the sign to be overwhelmingly generic having regard to its incapacity to distinguish. Particular emphasis was placed on the question of whether the sign could be used without misdescription on other products.

[35.26] A similar provision existed under s 23 of TMA 1963 but with one particularly important difference. TMA 1963 allowed for revocation in the case of generic use by the trade in relation to goods not covered by the registration, ie where the generic use is in respect of goods of the same description. This was somewhat ironic, given that the proprietor under TMA 1963 could not in fact take an infringement action against unauthorised use on goods not embraced by the registration, and consequently may not have been in a position to prevent the generic use. In *Daiquiri Rum*,[59] the trade mark registered in respect of rum was removed from the Register on evidence of generic use by the trade in respect of a rum cocktail. This would not be the position under TMA 1996, given that the generic use must be in respect of a product or service embraced by the registration. Also, under TMA 1996, the proprietor can take an infringement action where goods or services are similar[60] and even in some cases dissimilar.[61]

[35.27] The trade mark must become the common name in the trade due to acts or inactivity of the proprietor. Such inactivity would typically be the failure to properly control use by a licensee or to continually allow the mark to be infringed. In *RFU and Nike v Cotton Traders Ltd*,[62] Lloyd J accepted evidence of sales over a long number of years without licence as showing that it had become customary in the trade to use a rose by way of association with the English rugby team and declared the registration invalid. Acts of the proprietor would involve use the trade mark in a descriptive manner, for example, as a noun, verb or in plural form. Although there is no legal requirement to indicate a trade mark as being registered by use of the symbol ® or otherwise, apart from serving as a deterrent, it helps to indicate that the trade mark is not a product description but the subject of proprietary rights. Even if a trade mark is not registered, it is possible to use the initials TM.

---

[57] *Björnekulla Fruktindustrier AB and Procordia Food AB* [2004] ETMR 69.

[58] *JERYL LYNN* [2000] ETMR 75.

[59] *Daiquiri Rum* [1969] RPC 600; see also *BSS* [2000] ETMR 217.

[60] TMA 1996, s 14(2).

[61] TMA 1996, s 14(3).

[62] *RFU and Nike v Cotton Traders Ltd* [2002] ETMR 76; see also *SA Bardinet v Ego-Fruits SCP* [2002] ETMR 85.

[35.28] A CTM grants broader protection under art 10 of the CTM Regulation.[63] If use of a CTM in a dictionary, encyclopaedia or similar reference work gives the impression that it constitutes the generic name of the goods or services for which the trade mark is registered, the publisher of the work shall, at the request of the proprietor of the CTM, ensure that the reproduction of the trade mark, at the latest in the next edition of the publication, is accompanied by an indication that it is a registered trade mark. A word may be generic in a particular country but not in another.[64]

Misleading use

[35.29] Under s 51(1)(d) of TMA 1996, revocation can arise due to use which is liable to mislead the public. Examples given of the type of deception envisaged refer to the nature, quality or geographical origin of goods or services. This is not an exhaustive list and another example would be misleading use as to mode of manufacture. The position was similar under TMA 1963, but in *GE Trade Mark*,[65] the House of Lords ruled that if the likelihood of confusion did not exist at the time of registration but arose subsequently, then revocation was only possible due to some blameworthy act of the registered proprietor. While TMA 1996 requires that the misleading use must be as a consequence of use by or with the consent of the proprietor, there is no requirement of any culpability and it could be inadvertent use. It is possible that a deceptive trade mark may be viewed as misleading in Ireland even if lawfully marketed in another Member State of the EU.[66]

[35.30] An example of misleading use would be to use a trade mark on a product of a particular origin and then, without sufficient notice, which would otherwise avoid public confusion, subsequently to use the trade mark on a product of a different origin.[67] It is important for a trade mark owner to exercise proper quality control provisions amongst its licensees. If the quality of a product varies between different licensees selling under the same trade mark, there is certainly a strong argument that the public will be misled.

[35.31] Under TMA 1963, it was possible for the court or Controller to impose a condition on registration in an attempt to avoid any subsequent confusion. Thus, if the trade mark was a geographical location, a condition would typically read:

> It is a condition of registration that the trade mark will only be used on goods manufactured in [that location].[68]

If this condition was breached, then the registration was liable to cancellation. The imposition of such a condition is no longer possible under TMA 1996 and the transitional provisions[69] also caused existing conditions to cease to have effect. The onus

---

63 Council Regulation 207/2009/EC.

64 *House of Donuts International v OHIM* [2007] ETMR 53.

65 *GE Trade Mark* [1973] RPC 297.

66 *Frateli Graffione SNC v Ditta Fransa* [1997] ETMR 71.

67 See *Thorne & Sons Ltd v Pimms Ltd* (1909) 26 RPC 221.

68 See *WATERFORD* Registration No 110772.

69 TMA 1996, Sch 3, para 2(4).

has shifted from protecting against public confusion, under TMA 1963, to the owner who may otherwise suffer the consequence of revocation under s 51(1)(d) of TMA 1996.

[35.32] Under Council Regulation 510/2006/EC on the protection of geographical indications and designations of origin for agricultural products and foodstuffs,[70] it is possible to register certain geographical and, in some cases, even non-geographical names, which identify origin.[71] Such a registration prevents unauthorised use in any way liable to mislead the public as to the true origin of the product. It is necessary to use the protected name in accordance with the product specification, which must be furnished under Regulation 510/2006/EC, otherwise the name is likely to be viewed as misleading.

[35.33] Section 51(5) of TMA 1996 deals with the position as regards partial revocation: where grounds for revocation exist in respect of only some of the goods or services for which the trade mark is registered, revocation relates to those goods or services only.

Application for revocation

[35.34] An application for revocation can be made by any person[72] and unlike TMA 1963, does not require *locus standi* by way of being a person aggrieved.[73] The most common instances are by way of a counterclaim in infringement proceedings, in response to opposition proceedings or where the Controller has raised an earlier mark by way of a citation under the relative grounds for refusal. The applicant for revocation can elect to take the action before either the High Court or the Controller. The vast majority of revocation actions take place before the Controller. If proceedings concerning the trade mark in question are pending in the High Court in, for example, an infringement suit, then the application for revocation must be made to the High Court.[74] If the application is made to the Controller, then he or she may at any stage refer the application to the High Court.[75]

[35.35] The procedure before the Controller is governed by rule 41 of the Trade Marks Rules 1996.[76] An application for revocation requires a statement of the grounds and when this is filed, a copy is sent by the Controller to the proprietor of the registered mark. The proprietor has three months within which to lodge a notice of opposition (similar to the counter-statement in an opposition action) by way of defence. If the revocation action claims non-use under s 51(1)(a) or (b) of TMA 1996, then the proprietor must file evidence of the use upon which it is intended to rely. Failure to file such evidence means that the Controller has a discretion to dismiss the defence and grant the revocation. Subsequent procedures will be determined by the Controller but parties have a right to be heard. In proceedings before the High Court, the Controller is entitled

---

70 Which repealed and replaced Council Directive 2081/92/EC.
71 See para **[37.12]**.
72 TMA 1996, s 51(4).
73 TMA 1963, ss 34 and 40.
74 TMA 1996, s 51(4)(a).
75 TMA 1996, s 51(4)(b).
76 SI 199/1996.

to appeal and be heard.[77] Unless otherwise directed by the High Court, the Controller may submit evidence by way of written statement.[78] An appeal from the Controller's decision lies to the High Court[79] and, on appeal, fresh evidence may be admissible in special circumstances.[80] The Controller may award costs[81] and it is usual for costs to follow the successful party. Awards made by the Controller tend to be nominal and do not compensate the successful party for the actual costs incurred.

Effective date of revocation

[35.36] The effective date of revocation is dealt with in s 51(6) of TMA 1996. Where the registration of a trade mark is revoked to any extent, the rights of the proprietor shall be deemed to have ceased to that extent as from:

(a)   the date of the application for revocation; or

(b)   if the Controller or the court is satisfied that the grounds for revocation existed at an earlier date, that date.

If the revocation is by way of counterclaim in infringement proceedings, then it would be expected that an order be sought claiming that revocation should take effect from a date immediately prior to the alleged acts of infringement. If a party wants revocation to take effect from a date earlier than the date of application for revocation, it should set out what date it wants and explicitly allege that the grounds for revocation existed at an appropriate earlier date.[82]

[35.37] Under the transitional provisions, applications for revocation on the grounds of non-use under s 51(1)(a) or (b) apply to all registrations including those registered under TMA 1963.[83]

[35.38] It is unclear, however, whether the grounds under s 51(1)(c) or (d) of TMA 1996 apply to trade marks dated prior to 1 July 1996, ie the commencement date of TMA 1996. The uncertainty arises because of the division in TMA 1996 between grounds for revocation (s 51) and grounds for invalidity (s 52).

[35.39] It is only the validity of existing registrations, which the transitional provisions state will be determined under TMA 1963. No objection to the validity of registrations under TMA 1963 may be taken on the grounds of failure to satisfy the requirements of TMA 1996.[84] The fact that the transitional provisions are silent on s 51(1)(c) and (d) of TMA 1996 might suggest that these grounds will not be available against trade marks

---

77   TMA 1996, s 78(1).
78   TMA 1996, s 78(2).
79   TMA 1996, s 79(1).
80   *ETAT Française v Bernard Matthews plc* [2002] ETMR 90.
81   TMA 1996, s 72(1).
82   *Omega SA v Omega Engineering Inc* [2003] FSR 893.
83   TMA 1996, Sch 3, para 11(2).
84   TMA 1996, Sch 3, para 13.

dated prior to 1 July 1996. However, art 12 of the Trade Mark Harmonisation Directive[85] does not allow States to derogate from the provisions in s 51(1)(c) and (d) in relation to existing registrations and, therefore, it is likely that these grounds will also be held to exist against all registrations irrespective of their date. No application for revocation on grounds of non-use could be made in relation to a defensive trade mark until 1 July 2001, ie five years from the commencement date of TMA 1996.[86]

INVALIDITY OF REGISTRATION

[35.40] The main grounds for challenging the validity of a trade mark registration are set out in s 52 of TMA 1996, which implements arts 3 and 4 of the Harmonisation Directive[87] and provides that both the absolute and relative grounds for refusal also arise post-registration by way of an action for invalidity. Essentially, the action is available against trade marks which, although registered, should not have been.[88] However, a situation may arise where a trade mark, although invalidly registered, has acquired distinctiveness through use and can therefore remain on the Register.[89] This arises in the context of the absolute grounds in s 8 of TMA 1996. These grounds, which form a basis on which the Controller can refuse an application and on which an application can be opposed following advertisement, are also grounds for invalidity. If, however, it is claimed that the trade mark is devoid of distinctive character,[90] is purely descriptive[91] or is a trade use,[92] then the proprietor can rely on post-registration use to show that even if these grounds existed earlier, they no longer apply.[93] In addition, a mark which might once have been able to denote trade origin can lose its capacity to denote it as a result of use by third parties, and indeed from other factors.[94]

[35.41] A common ground for seeking invalidity under TMA 1963 was a lack of a *bona fide* intention to use the trade mark on the goods of application. Under s 37(2) of TMA 1996, it is also a requirement that there be use or, at a minimum, a *bona fide* intention to use. Therefore, failure to comply with this requirement could also be considered a ground for invalidity by virtue of s 8(4)(b) of TMA 1996 as being an application made in bad faith.[95] Post-registration use cannot subsequently remedy this position. The grounds for invalidity must exist at the time of registration and a trade mark cannot be declared

---

85   Council Directive 2008/95/EC ([2008] OJ L 299/25), which repealed and replaced Directive 89/104/EEC ([1989] OJ L40/1).
86   TMA 1996, Sch 3, para 11(3).
87   Council Directive 2008/95/EC ([2008] OJ L 299/25), which repealed and replaced Directive 89/104/EEC ([1989] OJ L40/1).
88   *Alcon v OHIM* [2004] ETMR 6.
89   *MINILITE* [2000] ETMR 256.
90   TMA 1996, s 8(1)(b).
91   TMA 1996, s 8(1)(c).
92   TMA 1996, s 8(1)(d).
93   TMA 1996, s 52(1); *BP Amoco plc v John Kelly Ltd* [2001] ETMR CN14, [2002] FSR 5.
94   *Score Draw Ltd v Finch* [2007] ETMR 54.
95   *SCIP r NOSCO* [2005] ETMR CN2.

invalid on the grounds that it has subsequently ceased to be distinctive. In such a case, it is necessary to consider whether the grounds for revocation under s 51(1)(c) or (d) are available.

[35.42] The transitional provisions contained in TMA 1996, Sch 3, para 13 state that TMA 1963 continues to apply as regards the validity of existing registrations, ie trade marks dated prior to 1 July 1996. This creates a number of problems. A trade mark registered under TMA 1963 may be declared invalid even though the grounds for invalidity do not exist under TMA 1996. A proprietor cannot rely on post-registration use under TMA 1963. It is necessary to consider both the grounds for invalidity under TMA 1963 and also whether or not the trade mark was registered under Part A or Part B of the Register. This is because under s 21 of TMA 1963, a Part A registration after seven years is taken to be valid in all respects unless the registration was obtained fraudulently or was contrary to s 19 of TMA 1963, ie trade marks likely to deceive or cause confusion or otherwise disentitled to protection in a court of law. In the case of a Part B registration or a Part A registration of less than seven years duration, it is necessary to give consideration to invalidity on grounds including ss 2 and 25 of TMA 1963 and, in particular, the definition of a trade mark. In the absence of service mark registrations prior to TMA 1996, trade mark owners sought to obtain a footing on the Register by registering in respect of certain goods, although the trade mark owner's activities were purely in the services sector. For example, it was quite common for entities in the services industry to register marks in respect of printed publications (class 16) and the validity of a number of these registrations is questionable. The Supreme Court in *ITT World Directories Inc v Controller*,[96] although accepting that it was not necessary to sell goods under the trade mark, still required a commercial activity under the mark. This does not arise if use of a trade mark on the goods is simply as a means of advertising services.

[35.43] The relative grounds for refusal of an application in s 10 of TMA 1996 form the basis for an action for invalidity under s 52(2) unless the proprietor of the earlier trade mark or earlier right has consented to the registration. It is not clear whether this ground is to be determined by reference to the position at the date of the application for invalidity or at the date of registration. The effect of a successful action which declares a registration invalid is that the registration is deemed never to have existed.[97] Together with the fact that the grounds for refusal and invalidity are dealt with together in art 4 of the Harmonisation Directive,[98] this suggests that the question should be determined by the position at the date of registration.

[35.44] Because of the transitional provisions, which provide that the validity of registrations dated prior to 1 July 1996 must be determined under TMA 1963, it is necessary to consider the grounds which exist under both TMA 1963 and TMA 1996.[99]

---

[96] *ITT World Directories Inc v Controller* [1985] ILRM 30 (GOLDEN PAGES Trade Mark).

[97] TMA 1996, s 52(6).

[98] Council Directive 2008/95/EC ([2008] OJ L 299/25), which repealed and replaced Directive 89/104/EEC ([1989] OJ L40/1).

[99] TMA 1996, Sch 3, para 13.

[35.45] If the trade mark being challenged is dated after 1 July 1996 and the earlier trade mark is an identical registration in respect of identical goods/services, then no proofs by way of a likelihood of confusion are required. Under s 12(4)(b) of TMA 1996, no defence by way of honest concurrent use is available. If invalidity is sought against a registration dated prior to 1 July 1996, then it is necessary to establish if it is registered in Part A or B of the Register, and the date of registration. If the registration is in Part A of the Register and more than seven years old, then the grounds for invalidity under s 20 of TMA 1963 are not available, and it is necessary to rely on s 19 of TMA 1963. Section 19 requires proof that the trade mark is likely to deceive or cause confusion because of the use of the earlier trade mark.

[35.46] In a case involving one of the following:

(a)   identical marks and similar goods/services;
(b)   similar marks and identical goods/services; and
(c)   similar marks and similar goods/services,

then TMA 1996 requires a likelihood of confusion which includes the likelihood of association.[100]

[35.47] The relative grounds that exist for dissimilar goods/services are new to Irish trade mark law and TMA 1963 did not include a provision corresponding to s 10(3) of TMA 1996. Under TMA 1963, it was necessary to rely on s 19. In *Gallaher (Dublin) Ltd v Health Education Bureau*,[101] Costello J stated:

> It seems to me that if it can be shown that a person used another's trade mark in a way which means that the registered proprietor cannot use it again on the goods for which he obtained registration, then it is highly likely the use complained of must have been in relation to the goods in respect of which it was registered as otherwise, no damage would have been done to his mark. If there is a dispute as to whether or not the user of the mark complained of was 'in relation to' goods, the fact that the goodwill in the mark has been injured does lend consider-able support to a plaintiff's claim that there has been use of the mark in relation to the goods for which the mark was registered.

This is certainly supportive of the view that there are circumstances where a conflicting mark for dissimilar goods may be declared invalid because of possible damage to the proprietor's goodwill under an earlier trade mark.

[35.48] The grounds for invalidity based on unregistered trade mark rights under TMA 1996 are narrower than those that existed under TMA 1963. Therefore, a trade mark registered under TMA 1996 is less susceptible to invalidity on this ground than trade marks registered under TMA 1963. Section 52(2)(b) of TMA 1996 allows for invalidity on the basis of unregistered earlier rights identified in s 10(4) (a) and (b) of TMA 1996. This requires the proprietor of an earlier right to have enforceable intellectual property rights such as copyright, registered designs or grounds to sustain an action for passing off. On the other hand, the grounds for invalidity in s 19 of TMA 1963, although requiring a need to show a likelihood of confusion or deception, did not require the same

---

[100] See paras **[31.37]**–**[31.43]**.
[101] *Gallaher (Dublin) Ltd v Health Education Bureau* [1982] ILRM 240.

proofs as an action for passing off.[102] Section 19 was also interpreted to include grounds existing by virtue of unregistered rights in the form of other intellectual property rights, such as copyright, and registrations conflicting with such rights were viewed as 'contrary to law'.[103]

[35.49] The definition of 'earlier trade mark' in s 11(1) of TMA 1996 includes well-known trade marks under art 6*bis* of the Paris Convention.[104] Therefore, such a trade mark, even though unregistered, may form a basis for seeking invalidity of a later trade mark.

Application for invalidity

[35.50] Similar to the position as regards revocation, an application for invalidity under s 52 of TMA 1996 can be made by any person and need not necessarily be made by a person aggrieved, and can be made to the High Court or the Controller. Section 52(4) allows the Controller to seek a declaration of invalidity in the case of bad faith in the registration of a trade mark.

[35.51] Where the grounds for invalidity exist in respect of only some of the goods or services for which the trade mark is registered, the trade mark is declared invalid as regards those goods or services only.[105] Where the registration of a trade mark is declared invalid to any extent, the registration shall, to that extent, be deemed never to have been made, with the exception of transactions past and closed.[106]

[35.52] A person may be estopped from taking invalidity proceedings. In *Hormel Foods Corp v Antilles Landscape Investments NV*,[107] a distinction was drawn between invalidity proceedings and revocation proceedings. Having unsuccessfully attacked the validity of the defendant's mark in Registry proceedings, the claimant was barred from doing so in the High Court due to estoppel, notwithstanding the fact that there was now reliance upon different grounds. However, this decision can be contrasted with the Court of Appeal decision in *Special Effects v L'Oreal*,[108] where it was held that estoppel does not apply and there was no legislative bar to a party, having failed in opposition, from launching a declaration of invalidity.

[35.53] The legislation will have to be read alongside the equitable doctrine of estoppel, an example of which can be seen in *JOB Trade Mark*,[109] where a licensee was estopped from taking an action for invalidity. Section 53 of TMA 1996 requires acquiescence for a continuous period of five years in the use of a registered trade mark in the State, while being aware of such use. The effect of such acquiescence is to deny a right to seek a

---

[102] *BALI* [1969] RPC 472.

[103] *KARO STEP* [1977] RPC 255.

[104] Paris Convention for the Protection of Industrial Property 1883 (Paris Convention).

[105] TMA 1996, s 52(5).

[106] TMA 1996, s 52(6).

[107] *Hormel Foods Corp v Antilles Landscape Investments NV* [2005] ETMR 54.

[108] *Special Effects v L'Oreal* [2007] ETMR 51.

[109] *JOB Trade Mark* [1993] FSR 118.

declaration of invalidity but, in keeping with the Trade Mark Harmonisation Directive,[110] there is no such exclusion in relation to revocation proceedings.

[35.54] Section 65(3) of TMA 1996, which implements art 6*septies* of the Paris Convention, allows the proprietor of a mark to apply for a declaration of invalidity against an unauthorised registration taken out by an agent or representative. In an Italian decision, *Hifonics Europe v Denico Srl*,[111] it was held that art 6*septies* of the Paris Convention does not apply to mere distributors. Under s 25 of TMA 1963, it is also possible to claim invalidity by virtue of the fact that such an agent or representative falsely claimed to be the trade mark proprietor, or that under s 19 of TMA 1963, use would be likely to deceive or cause confusion.[112]

[35.55] The procedures for an application for a declaration of invalidity ('invalidity action') are set out in r 41 of the Trade Marks Rules 1996, which was substantially amended by the Trade Marks (Amendment) Rules 2010 to align the procedures to those of an opposition action, which an invalidity action closely resembles. Rule 41(3)(c) of the Trade Marks Rules 1996[113] provides that rr 19 to 25 apply to invalidity actions, with appropriate changes. These rules apply to:

- filing a notice of opposition or counter-statement by way of defence (which, in the case of an invalidity action, is not mandatory);
- filing evidence in support of the action by the applicant for invalidity;
- filing evidence by the proprietor of the contested mark;
- filing evidence in reply by the applicant for invalidity;
- filing further evidence with the leave of the Controller;
- access to exhibits; and
- attendance at a hearing or filing written submissions in lieu thereof.

These changes apply to invalidity actions filed on or after 4 October 2010.[114]

---

[110] Council Directive 2008/95/EC ([2008] OJ L 299/25), which repealed and replaced Directive 89/104/EEC ([1989] OJ L40/1).

[111] *Hifonics Europe v Denico Srl* (9 February 1995, unreported), Court of Milan.

[112] *KSabatier* [1993] RPC 97.

[113] As inserted by the Trade Marks (Amendment) Rules 2010.

[114] Trade Marks (Amendment) Rules 2010, r 9(2).

Chapter 36

Certification and Collective Marks

CERTIFICATION MARKS

[36.01] A certification mark is defined in s 55 of the Trade Marks Act 1996 (TMA 1996) to mean a mark indicating that the goods or services in connection with which it is used are certified by the proprietor of the mark in respect of origin, material, mode or manufacture of goods or performance of services, quality, accuracy or other characteristics. The provisions dealing with certification marks are contained in Sch 2 to TMA 1996. The Trade Marks Act 1963 (TMA 1963) also provided for certification marks but only in respect of goods.

[36.02] A certification mark acts as a warranty that goods or services have particular characteristics. The owner can be an individual, but is more normally a trade association or other organised body who, although not trading in the goods or services, can by way of registration protect against traders using the mark and thereby falsely claiming certain attributes. An example of a certification mark is STILTON, which is owned by the Stilton Cheese Makers Association and denotes cheese originating from a particular region and with certain characteristics as to quality. It is quite common for a certification mark to be used alongside a trade mark; the former identifies the individual trader, while the certification mark is a statement that such a trader produces goods or provides services, which have certain characteristics with which any other user of the certification mark also complies. An example would be a group of traders in a particular location grouping together with a shared interest by way of a certification mark that can only be used on goods originating from that particular location; but at the same time, each individual member would promote their own particular product. While there would be competition between individual members, there would be a common objective to prevent use of any false geographical indicator.

[36.03] The characteristics of a certification mark demand that the proprietor cannot carry on a business involving the supply of goods or services of the kind certified.[1] It must be owned by a proprietor not engaged in trade in the goods or services in relation to which the mark is used.

[36.04] The definition of a trade mark in s 6(1) of TMA 1996 is equally applicable to a certification mark,[2] except that the capacity to distinguish is between goods or services that are certified from those that are not certified. Under TMA 1963, it was necessary

---

[1] TMA 1996, Sch 2, para 4.
[2] TMA 1996, Sch 2, para 2.

for a certification mark to be adapted to distinguish and therefore fulfil the requirements for registration in Part A of the Register. This is no longer a requirement under TMA 1996 and, for example, in keeping with other marks, it is possible to register as a certification mark the shape of goods or their packaging, which are capable of distinguishing. It is also necessary that the mark is capable of being represented graphically.

[36.05] Article 15(2) of the Trade Mark Harmonisation Directive[3] allowed Member States the option of allowing registration of certification marks that consist of signs or indications that designate geographical origin. This option has been implemented in TMA 1996[4] and therefore nullifies the position that would have otherwise applied under s 8(1)(c) of TMA 1996. There is a proviso that the proprietor of such a certification mark cannot restrain use in accordance with honest practices and, in particular, use by a person who is entitled to use a geographical name.

[36.06] A certification mark must be refused registration if it is liable to mislead the public as to the character or significance of the mark, in particular, if it is likely to be taken to be something other than a certification mark.[5] The Controller may require the mark to include an indication that it is a certification mark, and an application can be amended in this regard if necessary.[6] In practice, such a requirement is now rarely imposed.

[36.07] It is necessary for the applicant for registration of a certification mark to file with the Controller regulations governing the use of the mark. These regulations must indicate at a minimum: [7]

- who is authorised to use the mark;
- the characteristics to be certified by the mark;
- how the certifying body is to test the characteristics and to supervise use;
- the fees (if any) to be paid in connection with the operation of the mark; and
- the procedures for resolving disputes.

The Minister must approve the regulations and, in addition to the minimum requirements, it is necessary that the regulations are not contrary to public policy or to accepted principles of morality.[8] Public policy would include an obligation to allow any party who meets the characteristics and complies with the regulations to use the mark. It is also usual for there to be a right of appeal to an independent body in the event of refusal to permit use or if such permission is withdrawn. Regulations also usually provide for a register of users and for the issue of a certificate to an authorised user. The Minister must also be satisfied with the competence of the applicant to certify

---

3   Council Directive 2008/95/EC ([2008] OJ L 299/25), which repealed and replaced Directive 89/104/EEC ([1989] OJ L40/1).

4   TMA 1996, Sch 2, para 3.

5   TMA 1996, Sch 2, para 5(1).

6   TMA 1996, Sch 2, para 5(2).

7   TMA 1996, Sch 2, para 6(2).

8   TMA 1996, Sch 2, para 7(1)(a).

the goods or services.[9] This does not mean that the applicant is actually bound to inspect the goods.

[36.08] The regulations do not have to be filed at the date of application but must be lodged within six months of the Controller's initial decision to allow an applicant to proceed.[10] The regulations are open to public inspection from the date of advertisement in the Patents Office Journal[11] and may be amended with the consent of the Minister.[12]

[36.09] Once advertised in the Patents Office Journal, the normal three-month period for opposition and/or observations applies. A notice of opposition must be filed with the Minister and a copy sent to the Controller.[13] The grounds for opposition include that the regulations do not comply with the requirements for registration.

[36.10] A certification mark cannot be effectively assigned or transmitted without the consent of the Minister.[14]

[36.11] Generally, the normal infringement provisions apply in respect of a certification mark. However, the proprietor of a certification mark designating geographical origin is not entitled to restrain use in accordance with honest practices in industrial or commercial matters.[15] Unless there is an agreement to the contrary, an authorised user can call on the proprietor to take infringement proceedings in respect of any matter which affects the authorised user's interests.[16] If the proprietor refuses, then after two months, the authorised user may bring proceedings in their own name.[17] The proprietor must be joined as a plaintiff or added as a defendant, unless the authorised user has the leave of the High Court to do otherwise.[18] If added as a defendant, the proprietor is not liable for costs unless they take part in the proceedings.[19] Where infringement proceedings are brought by the proprietor of a certification mark, the High Court must take into account any loss suffered or likely to be suffered by authorised users. The court may further direct that any award be held on behalf of such user(s).[20]

[36.12] The normal grounds for revocation contained in s 51 of TMA 1996 equally apply in relation to certification marks. However, there are additional grounds as follows:

---

9 TMA 1996, Sch 2, para 7(1)(b); *UNIS & UNIS FRANCE TM* (1922) 39 RPC 346.
10 Trade Marks Rules 1996 (SI 199/1996), r 33(1); TMA 1996, Sch 2, para 7(2) and (3).
11 Trade Marks Rules 1996, r 33(4)(a).
12 TMA 1996, Sch 2, para 11; Trade Marks Rules 1996, r 34.
13 Trade Marks Rules 1996, r 33(4)(c).
14 TMA 1996, Sch 2, para 12.
15 TMA 1996, Sch 2, para 3.
16 TMA 1996, Sch 2, para 13(2).
17 TMA 1996, Sch 2, para 13(3).
18 TMA 1996, Sch 2, para 13(4)(a).
19 TMA 1996, Sch 2, para 13(4)(b).
20 TMA 1996, Sch 2, para 13(6).

(a)   the proprietor has begun to trade in the goods or services certified, thus not complying with para 4 of Sch 2;[21]

(b)   the manner in which the mark has been used has made it misleading to the public as regards the character or significance of the mark; in particular, if it is likely to be taken to be something other than a certification mark;[22]

(c)   the proprietor has failed to observe or secure observance of the regulations governing the use of the mark;[23]

(d)   there has been an amendment to the regulations as a consequence of which they no longer comply with the statutorily prescribed contents or are contrary to public policy or accepted principles of morality;[24] and

(e)   the proprietor is no longer competent to certify the goods or services for which the mark is registered.[25]

This latter ground was the subject of revocation proceedings in *SEA ISLAND COTTON Certification Trade Mark*[26] where it was held that there was no obligation to carry out any examination or investigation but the proprietor must have the legal and practical ability to certify. One must take into account the constitution of the certifying body and whether, in practice, it could and did carry out the duty of certification.

[36.13] Revocation on the grounds identified at (a), (b) and (e) above must be made to the Minister. The grounds for invalidity in s 52 of TMA 1996 also apply to certification marks. Also included as grounds for invalidity are regulations which are contrary to public policy, or to accepted principles of morality or which do not fulfil the requirements stated in para 7(1) (Sch 2) as being a prerequisite to Ministerial approval.[27] Invalidity can arise through use liable to mislead the public as to the character or signification of the mark. A certification mark may also be declared invalid if the proprietor commences business involving the supply of goods or services of the kind certified.

[36.14] In *ChocoSuisse Union v Cadbury*[28] the Court of Appeal held that a trade association did not have the requisite *locus standi* to pursue an action for passing off.[29] This enhances the importance of registration of a certification mark as a protector of goodwill in circumstances where the trade association is not itself a manufacturer or vendor.

---

21   TMA 1996, Sch 2, para 14(1)(a).
22   TMA 1996, Sch 2, para 14(1)(b).
23   TMA 1996, Sch 2, para 14(1)(c).
24   TMA 1996, Sch 2, para 14(1)(d).
25   TMA 1996, Sch 2, para 14(1)(e).
26   *SEA ISLAND COTTON Certification Trade Mark* [1989] RPC 87.
27   TMA 1996, Sch 2, para 15.
28   *ChocoSuisse Union v Cadbury* [1999] ETMR 1020.
29   A decision that might be decided the other way today after the further development of extended passing off in *Diageo North America Inc v Intercontinental Brands (ICB) Ltd* [2010] ETMR 17; see Tumbridge, '*Diageo North America Inc v Intercontinental Brands (ICB) Ltd*: vodka is special: the VODKAT case' (2010) EIPR 32(6), 290–294.

COLLECTIVE MARKS

[36.15] Collective marks, which are provided for under the EU Trade Mark Harmonisation Directive,[30] were introduced to Irish law by TMA 1996.[31] No provision for such marks existed under TMA 1963 or earlier legislation. A collective mark is defined in s 54 to mean:

> A mark distinguishing the goods or services of members of the association which is the proprietor of the mark from those of other undertakings.

[36.16] The TMA 1996 contains no definition of what is meant by association. However, art 66 of the Community Trade Mark Regulation[32] refers to an association as:

> Associations of manufacturers, producers, suppliers of services, or traders which, under the terms of the law governing them, have the capacity in their own name to have rights and obligations of all kinds, to make contracts or accomplish other legal acts and sue and be sued, as well as legal persons governed by public law.

The same provisions governing the registration of marks generally also apply in relation to collective marks, but the capacity to distinguish is as between the goods or services of the members of the particular association that is the proprietor of the mark from those of other undertakings that are not members of the association.[33]

[36.17] A geographical name may be registered as a collective mark even if such serves in the trade to designate the geographical origin of the goods or services.[34] Such a registration does not entitle the proprietor to prevent use by a third party, provided that the use is in accordance with honest practices in industrial or commercial matters.[35]

[36.18] As well as the normal absolute grounds for refusal, a collective mark cannot be registered if the public is liable to be misled in relation to the character or significance of the mark.[36] This includes a belief that the mark is other than a collective mark. The Controller can call upon an applicant to amend a mark to include an indication that it is a collective mark.[37]

[36.19] An applicant for registration of a collective mark must file regulations governing the use of the mark[38] within six months of the date of application.[39] The regulations are required at a minimum to address the following:[40]

---

30 Council Directive 2008/95/EC ([2008] OJ L 299/25), which repealed and replaced Directive 89/104/EEC ([1989] OJ L40/1).
31 TMA 1996, s 54 and Sch 1.
32 Council Regulation 207/2009/EC.
33 TMA 1996, Sch 1, para 2.
34 TMA 1996, Sch 1, para 3(1).
35 TMA 1996, Sch 1, para 3(2).
36 TMA 1996, Sch 1, para 4(1).
37 TMA 1996, Sch 1, para 4(2).
38 TMA 1996, Sch 1, para 5(1).
39 SI 199/1996, r 31(1).
40 TMA 1996, Sch 1, para 5(2).

(a)   the persons who are authorised to use the collective mark;

(b)   the conditions of membership of the association; and

(c)   where they exist, the conditions of use of the collective mark, including any sanctions against misuse.

Unlike certification marks, approval of regulations governing collective marks rests with the Controller,[41] who must also be satisfied that such regulations are not contrary to public policy or to accepted principles of morality.[42]

[36.20] If the Controller accepts the application, then it is advertised for opposition purposes in the Patents Office Journal and the regulations are open to public inspection.[43] There is a three-month period for opposition or the making of observations.[44] The regulations may be amended but if amended are not effective until filed with, and accepted by, the Controller.[45]

[36.21] Unless there is an agreement to the contrary, an authorised user can call on the proprietor to take infringement proceedings in respect of any matter that affects the authorised user's interests.[46] If, after a period of two months, the proprietor refuses or fails to take proceedings, the authorised user may bring the proceedings in his or her own name.[47] The proprietor must be either joined as a plaintiff or added as a defendant, unless the authorised user has the leave of the High Court to do otherwise.[48] A proprietor added as a defendant is not liable for costs unless they take part in the proceedings.[49] This does not affect the ability of an authorised user to seek interlocutory relief in their own right.[50]

INFRINGEMENT PROCEEDINGS TAKEN BY THE PROPRIETOR

[36.22] Any loss or potential loss suffered by authorised users will be taken into account by the High Court. The High Court may give directions regarding the extent to which the plaintiff shall hold the proceeds of any pecuniary remedy on behalf of such authorised users.[51]

[36.23] The normal grounds for revocation exist as set out in s 51 of TMA 1996, but additional grounds also apply in relation to collective marks, namely:

---

[41]   TMA 1996, Sch 1, para 6(1)(a).

[42]   TMA 1996, Sch 1, para 6(1)(b).

[43]   TMA 1996, Sch 1, paras 8(1) and 9.

[44]   SI 199/1996, r 31(3).

[45]   TMA 1996, Sch 1, para 10.

[46]   TMA 1996, Sch 1, para 11(2).

[47]   TMA 1996, Sch 1, para 11(3).

[48]   TMA 1996, Sch 1, para 11(4)(a).

[49]   TMA 1996, Sch 1, para 11(4)(b).

[50]   TMA 1996, Sch 1, para 11(5).

[51]   TMA 1996, Sch 1, para 11(6).

(a) the manner of use by the proprietor has made the mark misleading to the public as to its character or significance; in particular, if it is likely to be taken as something other than a collective mark;[52]

(b) the proprietor has failed to observe or to secure the observance of the regulations governing the use of the mark;[53] and

(c) the regulations have been amended and no longer comply with the statutory requirements[54] or are contrary to public policy or to accepted principles of morality.[55]

[36.24] The grounds for invalidity contained in s 52 of TMA 1996 apply to collective marks but further grounds arise where at the time of registration:

(a) the mark was liable to mislead the public as regards its character or significance; in particular, if it is likely to be taken to be something other than a collective mark;[56] or

(b) the regulations governing use fail to comply with the prescribed requirements or are contrary to public policy or accepted principles of morality.[57]

[36.25] The minutes of the Council meeting at which the earlier CTM Regulation[58] was adopted state that it is considered that a collective mark, which is available for use only by a member of an association which owns the mark, is liable to mislead if it gives the impression that it is available for use by anyone who is able to meet certain objective standards.

---

[52] TMA 1996, Sch 1, para 12(a).

[53] TMA 1996, Sch 1, para 12(b).

[54] TMA 1996, Sch 1, para 5(2).

[55] TMA 1996, Sch 1, para 12(c).

[56] TMA 1996, Sch 1, paras 13 and 4(1).

[57] TMA 1996, Sch 1, paras 13 and 6(1).

[58] Council Regulation 40/94/EC.

Chapter 37

Geographical Indications and Appellations of Origin

INTRODUCTION

[37.01] A geographical indication can have many facets. As an indication of source, it can be perceived by the public as indicating the origin of particular goods or services. There are, however, generic geographical indications that are merely descriptors for goods or services such as, for example, BERMUDA for a certain type of shorts. An appellation of origin is, however, a geographical indication used to designate goods or services that originate from the region or place in question and whose qualities and characteristics are due exclusively or essentially to the geographical environment.[1] It is this type of geographical indication for which there are different avenues of protection designed to prevent misuse and hence public confusion.

[37.02] Council Regulation 510/2006/EC[2] on the protection of geographical indications and designations of origin for agricultural products and foodstuffs is only a more recent attempt at creating a protective right. There are already in existence four multilateral treaties, namely:

- the Madrid Agreement for the Repression of False or Deceptive Indications of Source of Goods 1891 (Madrid Agreement);[3]
- the Paris Convention for the Protection of Industrial Property 1883 (Paris Convention);
- the Lisbon Agreement for the Protection of Appellations of Origin and their International Registration 1958 (Lisbon Agreement); and
- the TRIPS Agreement;

as well as EU Wine Regulations and the Stresa Convention on the Use of Appellations of Origin and Designations of Cheeses 1951.[4] In addition, under art 1 of Protocol No 1 of the European Convention on Human Rights, the right of peaceful enjoyment of possessions is applicable to intellectual property.[5]

---

[1] Agreement on Trade-Related Aspects of Intellectual Property Rights (TRIPS), art 22.

[2] Which repealed and replaced Council Regulation 2081/92/EEC ([1992] OJ L208/1).

[3] Not to be confused with the unrelated 'Madrid Agreement Concerning the International Registration of Marks'.

[4] Ireland is not a member. Austria, Denmark, France, Italy, Norway, Sweden, Switzerland and the Netherlands have ratified this Convention.

[5] *Anheuser-Busch Inc v Portugal* [2007] ETMR 24.

[37.03] In addition to these, there are laws at national level, in countries such as Ireland, which address such issues as consumer protection guarding against unfair or misleading commercial practices,[6] as well as general trade mark law including the registration of certification and collective marks and the law of passing off/unfair competition. At EU level, there are a number of regulations that define certain terms by reference to specific product characteristics and definitive properties.[7] In some instances there is mandatory information, which must appear on labelling.[8]

[37.04] French law provides that a geographical denomination, which constitutes an appellation of origin, or any other mention conjuring up this denomination, may not be used in connection either with a similar product or with another product or service, whenever this use is likely to divest or weaken the renown of the appellation of origin.[9] The ECJ initially ruled that the earlier Regulation 2081/92/EEC did not conflict with the enforcement of a national law.[10] An example of such a national law is the French law that sets the conditions of use for the name 'MONTAGNE' in respect of agricultural products and foodstuffs. However, French law, which reserved the use of the name 'MONTAGNE' only for those products produced on home territory and developed from home-produced raw materials, was held to conflict with art 36 of the Treaty on the Functioning of the European Union (the Treaty).[11] The ECJ later changed its position,[12] and held that the Regulation provides a uniform and exhaustive system of protection so it is exhaustive in nature and precludes any national protection in EU Member States or protection under bilateral instruments between EU Member States.

[37.05] There are also a number of bilateral agreements between France/Germany, France/Italy, Germany/Switzerland, Germany/Spain, France/Spain and France/Switzerland. The agreement between France and Spain[13] has already come under scrutiny by the ECJ in a decision on 10 November 1992.[14] The effect of the agreement was to prohibit Spanish undertakings from using protected Spanish designations in France if they were denied the right to use them by Spanish law, and to prohibit French undertakings from using protected French designations in Spain, if they were

---

6   Consumer Protection Act 2007.

7   Council Regulation 110/2008/EC ([2008] OJ L39/16), which repealed and replaced 1576/89/EEC, defining use of 'whisky' or 'whiskey': see *Scotch Whisky Association v Glen Kella Distillers Ltd* [1997] ETMR 470; *Matthew Gloag & Son Ltd v Welsh Distillers Ltd* [1998] ETMR 504 and *Scotch Whisky Association v Cofepp and Casal* [1998] ETMR 629.

8   Council Regulation 2333/92/EEC ([1992] OJ L231/9) concerning sparkling wines; *VERBRAUCHERSCHUTZVEREIN EV* [1999] ETMR 269.

9   *Champagne Perfume by Yves Saint Laurent* (15 December 1993), Court of Appeal of Paris.

10 *Budejovicky Budvar v Rudolf Ammersin* [2004] ETMR 21.

11 Formerly EC Treaty, art 30; *PISTRE, BARTHES, MILHAU & OBERTI v FRANCE* [1997] ETMR 457.

12 *Budjovický Budvar National Corporation v Rudolf Ammersin GmbH* [2009] ETMR 65, which dealt with Regulation 510/2006/EC ([2006] OJ L93/12), but also held that this applied to Regulation 2081/92/EEC.

13 27 June 1973.

14 *Exportur SA v Lor SA* [1992] ECR I-5529.

denied the right to use them by French law. This agreement provided that certain names including 'Turron De Alicante' and 'Turron De Jijona' were reserved exclusively on French territory to Spanish goods and products and could only be used on the conditions provided for by Spanish legislation. It was held that even if the denomination in question was accompanied by terms such as 'type', 'kind' or 'style', arts 34 and 36 of the Treaty[15] would not preclude the application of rules laid down by a bilateral convention between Member States on the protection of indications of provenance and appellations of origin, provided that the protected designations have not acquired, either at the time of the entry into force of the agreement or subsequently from that time, a generic connotation in the country of origin. The ECJ also upheld a provision in Spanish law which required that wine from the Rioja region, which was intended for export, had to be bottled only in authorised cellars in the region of production.[16] The bilateral agreements which involve EU Member States must be regarded as of doubtful validity in light of the decision of the ECJ on the exhaustive nature of the Regulation.[17]

[37.06] There are a number of limitations to the various multilateral agreements. Ireland is not a member of the Madrid Agreement for the Repression of False or Deceptive Indications of Source of Goods 1891. This Agreement does not provide for the repression of false or deceptive indications used in translation or together with correct qualifying terms such as 'kind', 'type', etc. Also, it does not protect indications of source against transformation into a generic name except for regional appellations concerning the source of products of the vine. Sanctions provided under the Agreement are also very limited.

[37.07] Article 1(2) of the Paris Convention specifically contains a reference to 'indications of source' and 'appellations of origin' in the list of objects of industrial property. There is an obligation to protect 'indications of source' contained in art 10. Article 10(1) provides that the sanctions (art 9) also apply to a 'false indication or source'. The effect is that no indication of source may be used that refers to a geographical area from which the products in question do not originate. Use includes indirect use such as in advertising.

[37.08] Article 10*bis* of the Paris Convention provides protection against unfair competition, which includes misleading indications, and countries are obliged to ensure effective protection against such unfair competition. Article 10*ter* requires appropriate legal remedies in favour of federations and associations representing producers or merchants. A problem which arises is that art 10(1) does not protect against uses which, although not false, may still be misleading. An example of this arises in situations where the same geographical name may exist in different countries or indeed within a country itself.

[37.09] Only 26 countries are party to the Lisbon Agreement and only six are from within the EU: France, Italy, Hungary, Slovakia, Czech Republic and Portugal. The

---

15 Formerly EC Treaty, arts 28 and 30.
16 *Belgium v Spain* Case C-388/95 [2000] ECR I-3121, [2000] ETMR 999.
17 *Budjovický Budvar National Corporation v Rudolf Ammersin GmbH* [2009] ETMR 65.

Agreement provides for the registration of appellations of origin. Unlike the Madrid Agreement, the use of corrective or qualifying terms are not allowed (art 3) and the Lisbon Agreement prevents a registered appellation of origin from becoming a general name in the country of origin (art 6). The problem with the Lisbon Agreement is the very narrow definition of 'Appellation of Origin' (art 2(a)). There is a requirement of prior recognition and protection under a specific official act in the country of origin. This is all very well in countries such as France where there is a strong legislative tradition for enacting laws protecting specifically identified appellations of origin but this is not the case in Ireland and the UK, where protection arises under the common law by way of an action for passing off.

[37.10] Article 22(2) of TRIPS provides that States must allow for remedies to prevent the public being misled as to the geographical origin of goods or use that constitutes unfair competition under art 10*bis* of the Paris Convention. The remedies include opposition to or invalidation of marks if use of the indication in the trade mark for such goods in that Member State is of such a nature as to mislead the public as to the true place of origin. This arises even if the indication is literally true as to the territory, region or locality in which the goods originate, but, nevertheless, falsely represents to the public that the goods originate in another territory.[18]

[37.11] Despite the varying forms of protection already in existence, DG Agriculture and Rural Development,[19] the part of the EU Commission that deals with agriculture, formed a view that there was a requirement for protective provisions for agricultural products or foodstuffs given the growing demand for such products and foodstuffs with an identifiable geographical origin; hence Regulation 2081/92/EEC on the protection of geographical indications and designations of origin for agricultural products and foodstuffs and its successor, Regulation 510/2006/EC.

PGIs AND PDOs

[37.12] Regulation 2081/92/EEC entered into force on 26 July 1993 and within it, as the preamble states, a distinction is drawn between 'protected geographical indications' (PGI) and 'protected designations of origin' (PDO). This distinction was maintained in Regulation 510/2006/EC, which entered into force on 31 March 2006. These terms are defined in art 2.1 of Regulation 510/2006/EC. A PDO is the name of a region or place (even, in exceptional cases, a country) used to describe an agricultural product or foodstuff originating there. The quality and other characteristics of the product must be 'essentially or exclusively due to a particular geographical environment with its inherent natural and human factors, and the production, processing and preparation of which take place in the defined geographical area'. The definition suggests that it is equivalent to the pre-existing term 'appellation of origin' as defined in art 2 of the Lisbon Agreement.

---

[18] TRIPS, art 22(4).
[19] Formerly known as DG VI.

[37.13] The definition of a PGI begins in the same way but the differences are that:

(a)   the product only needs to possess a specific quality, reputation or other characteristic attributable to the location. This contrasts with the essential or exclusive connection of the PDO; and

(b)   it is the production *and/or* processing *and/or* preparation taking place at the location which is required for a PGI. The PDO requires production, processing *and* preparation.

A PDO applies to products which have characteristic qualities that are due to conditions existing in the geographical area, whereas, a PGI applies to any products originating in the geographical area to which the indication refers. In the wine industry, this would be termed as '*indication de provenance*'. Thus, for example, 'French wine' is an *indication de provenance* indicating simply the source of the product, whereas, 'Champagne' and 'Burgundy' would be '*appellations d'origine*' because of their characteristics, in addition to the fact that they are also French wines. In other words, all appellations of origin (PDOs) are PGIs but not all PGIs are PDOs. It can also be noted that under art 2(2) of Regulation 510/2006/EC, 'certain traditional geographical or non-geographical names' can be considered a PDO provided that other conditions are fulfilled. Perhaps the best known example would be FETA cheese. FETA is not a geographical location but is the Greek word for a slice. A PDO may require certain operations such as slicing, grating or packaging to also take place in the region of production.[20]

[37.14] Regulation 510/2006/EC provides in substance for Community protection of designations of origin and of geographical indications of agricultural products and foodstuffs. Specifically excluded are wine products and spirit drinks. Specifically included are beer, beverages made from plant extracts, bread, pastry, cakes, confectionery and other baker's wares, natural gums and resins, mustard paste and pasta. A wide variety of other products are also covered, including meat, fish and dairy products.[21] The protection is secured by way of a registration.

DISENTITLEMENT TO REGISTRATION

[37.15] Article 3(1) of Regulation 510/2006/EC states that 'names that have become generic may not be registered', ie if it has become the common name for such goods. This may be a difficult question to answer because account may be taken of the meaning of the name throughout the EU. It has also been stated in a European Commission paper that 'responsibility for proving that a name is generic, rests with the party who claims that it is such'.[22] The German and Danish Governments failed in their arguments that the word 'FETA'[23] was a generic term despite its use for some considerable time in certain

---

[20] *GRANA PADANO* [2004] ETMR 22; *PARMA HAM* [2004] ETMR 23.

[21] Annex 1 to the Treaty on the Functioning of the European Union.

[22] *PILSEN URQUELL v Industrie Poretti* [1998] ETMR 169.

[23] *FETA* [2006] ETMR 16.

EU countries apart from Greece. The General Court has also cautioned on the strict criteria to be applied even in reaching a conclusion that a part of a PDO is generic.[24]

[37.16] Under art 3(3) of the predecessor to Regulation 510/2006/EC, namely Regulation 2081/92/EEC, a non-exhaustive list of generic names was meant to be published in the EU Patents Office Journal prior to entry into force of the Regulation. This did not happen, but the European Commission did adopt a proposal that included as generic names, BRIE, CAMEMBERT, CHEDDAR, EDAM, EMMENTALE and GOUDA. The Greek Government sought and obtained PDO registration in respect of FETA. The European Commission reaching the conclusion that FETA was not generic. The Danish, French and German Governments challenged the validity of the registration on the grounds that use in their respective countries had taken place for a considerable number of years. The ECJ annulled the PDO registration on the basis that the European Commission had failed to take into account the extent to which FETA was manufactured in countries other than Greece[25] but upon further reconsideration the PDO registration was allowed because it was not proven to be generic. As regards a PGI, a name becomes generic only if the direct link between, on the one hand, the geographical origin of the product and, on the other hand, a specific quality of that product, its reputation or another characteristic of the product, attributable to that origin, has disappeared, and the name does no more than describe a style or type of product.[26]

[37.17] Furthermore, under art 3(2) of Regulation 510/2006/EC, a name may not be registered where it conflicts with the name of a plant variety or an animal breed *and* as a result, is likely to mislead the public as to the true origin of the product. In art 3(4), there is a provision which states that a designation of origin or geographical indication shall not be registered where, in the light of a trade mark's reputation and renown and the length of time it has been used, registration is liable to mislead the consumer as to the true identity of the product. This is a ground for objecting to an application under art 7(3).

[37.18] After Regulation 2081/92/EC came into force, the French government enacted legislation that allowed for a limited duration of eight years of continued use of certain specified labels bearing a geographical indication of origin. The French government was held to have failed to fulfil its obligations under art 34 of the Treaty.[27]

REGISTRATION PROCEDURE

[37.19] There is a normal registration procedure under Regulation 510/2006/EC, arts 5, 6 and 7; and for a period of time after the enactment of its predecessor, Regulation 2081/92/EEC, there existed a simplified or fast track procedure (art 17 of Regulation 2081/92/

---

[24] *Biraghi's Application* [2008] ETMR 3.

[25] *FETA* [1999] ETMR 478.

[26] *Bavaria NV and Bavaria Italia SRL v Bayerischer Brauerbund* EV [2009] ETMR 61.

[27] Formerly EC Treaty, art 28; *Commission v France* Case C-6/02 [2003] ECR I-2389, [2003] ETMR 86.

EEC).[28] Both procedures require specifications to be presented. Article 4 lays down what the specifications are to include. Under Regulation 2081/92/EEC, this commenced with the words 'to be eligible to *use* [a PDO or PGI] ... the agricultural product or foodstuff must comply with a specification'. It was recognised that the word 'use' is incorrect and this should be a reference to registration. The relevant sentence of Regulation 510/2006/EC commences with 'to be eligible for' a PDO or PGI, an agricultural product or foodstuff shall comply with a product specification. The specification is more than simply the name of goods, and includes evidence of the link between the quality or characteristics of the product and the geographical environment (PDO) or the specific quality, reputation or other characteristic of the product and the geographical origin (PGI) as well as a description of the method of obtaining the product and verification of compliance structures.[29]

[37.20] An application is made by a group as defined in art 5 of Regulation 510/2006/EC, which states that an applicant can be an association or a natural or legal person 'where the person concerned is the only producer in the defined geographical area willing to submit an application'. The application may be accepted only where the geographical area defined possesses characteristics that differ appreciably from those of neighbouring areas and/or the characteristics of the product are different.[30]

[37.21] The application is sent to the Member State in which the geographical area is located. If Member States believe the 'application is justified', and satisfies the requirements of Regulation 510/2006/EC, it is then sent to the European Commission.[31] Member States must grant to any person who has a legitimate interest in a favourable decision a means of appeal.[32]

[37.22] The earlier Regulation 2081/92/EEC had a vague reference to the fact that if an application concerned a name also situate in another Member State, that other State should be consulted before any decision is taken. There was no reference to what is meant by 'consultation' or the effect of failure to do so. This was replaced by art 5(4) of Regulation 510/2006/EC, which states that where the registration application relates to a geographical area in a given Member State, the application shall be addressed to that Member State.

[37.23] Upon receipt of an application, the European Commission has 12 months in which to advise a Member State as to whether the specification requirements have been met.[33] This follows a scrutiny procedure. The question that immediately arises is whether or not the European Commission can refuse to allow the application to proceed

---

[28] Commission Regulations 1107/96/EC ([1996] OJ L148/1), 1263/96/EC ([1996] OJ L163/19) and 123/97/EC ([1997] OJ L22/19) annexed registrations achieved under the fast track procedure (art 17); *Spreewalder Gurken* [2002] ETMR 8 and [2003] ETMR 3.

[29] Regulation 510/2006/EC, art 4(2).

[30] Regulation 1898/2006/EC ([2006] OJ L369/1), art 2 laying down detailed rules for the implementation of Regulation 510/2006/EC.

[31] *Northern Foods plc v DEFRA* [2006] ETMR 31.

[32] Regulation 510/2006/EC, art 5(6).

[33] Regulation 510/2006/EC, art 6(1).

to publication if it does not make such a decision within 12 months, as the Regulation merely states that the scrutiny 'should not' exceed 12 months. The European Commission was certainly of the view that a similar provision of the predecessor, Regulation 2081/92/EEC, was only for examination as to formalities and not a substantive examination, so that the specified period, in the European Commission's view, was not mandatory. If the European Commission concludes that the name qualifies for protection, details are published in the EU Patents Office Journal,[34] and if no objections are notified, registration is automatic.[35]

[37.24] The existence of Regulation 510/2006/EC does not preclude a national law from prohibiting the misleading use of a geographical indication of source,[36] provided such does not have an actual or potential effect on trade between Member States by prohibiting use where it was not liable to mislead a reasonably well-informed and reasonably observant and circumspect consumer.

Procedure for lodging objections

[37.25] Objection must be taken within six months of publication and must be made by a Member State or third country.[37] A legitimately-concerned objector must send a statement of objection to the authority in the Member State where they reside or are established. Under art 7 of Regulation 510/2006/EC, the objection must state that the application is:

    (a)   outside the definition of a PDO or PGI; or

    (b)   contrary to art 3, paras 2, 3 and 4;[38] or

    (c)   would jeopardise the existence of an entirely or partly identical name or trade mark or the existence of products that are legally on the market for at least five years preceding the date of publication;[39] or

    (d)   generic in nature.

If the objection is deemed admissible, then it is for Member States to reach agreement, failing which the European Commission will determine the issue 'having regard to fair and traditional usage and of the actual likelihood of confusion'.[40]

---

[34] See, by way of example, Commission Regulations 1107/96/EC and 1263/96/EC although these applications were under the simplified/fast track procedure (art 17).

[35] Regulation 510/2006/EC, art 7(4).

[36] *Warsteiner* [2000] ETMR 734 and [2003] ETMR 6.

[37] Regulation 510/2006/EC, art 7(1).

[38] It is strongly suggested by the authors that this must logically be read as 'paras 2, 3 or 4', as the same name would not generally be contrary to all three paragraphs, so the conditions should be alternatives, not cumulative.

[39] The date of publication of Regulation 2081/92/EEC.

[40] Regulation 510/2006/EC, art 7(5).

Simplified or fast track procedure

[37.26] The time period for availing of this procedure expired on 26 January 1994 and there were no Irish applications filed under this procedure. In order to avail of this procedure it was required that the name must have been protected in the Member State in accordance with national law. This included a system of protection based on case law. The big advantage for applicants who availed of the fast track procedure was that there was no opposition procedure.[41]

Verification of compliance structures

[37.27] Under art 10 of Regulation 510/2006/EC, each Member State must designate competent authorities[42] to ensure that the requirements laid down to verify compliance with the specifications are met.[43] Ultimately, a registration can be cancelled if the product specification is not being met.[44]

Protection afforded to registered names

[37.28] The protection afforded to registered names is set out in art 13 of Regulation 510/2006/EC and, apart from preventing direct or indirect commercial usage of the name in respect of the products registered, it extends to any practice liable to mislead the public as to the trade origin. It also extends to 'comparable' products if the use exploits the reputation of the protected name. The use of expressions such as 'style', 'type', 'method', 'as produced in', 'imitation', is no defence. Registered names are protected against any misuse, imitation or evocation, even if the true origin of the product is indicated.[45] The ECJ has ruled that it is possible for a PDO to be evoked even where there is no likelihood of confusion between the products concerned and even where no EU protection extends to the parts of that designation which are echoed in the term or terms at issue. Thus, 'PARMESAN' was regarded as an evocation of the PDO 'PARMIGIANO REGGIANO'.[46] Article 13(3) allows terms to be used for up to five years if products have been marketed legally using such expressions for at least five years preceding the date of publication of the PDO/PGI. This is, however, a matter for national law and the exception does not allow the marketing of products freely in the territory of a Member State where such expressions are prohibited. However, since entry into force of Regulation 510/2006/EC and its predecessor Regulation 2081/92/EEC, it is not possible for Member States to alter a designation of origin that has been registered under the Regulation by adopting

---

[41] Regulation 2081/92/EEC, art 7; *Altenburger Ziegenkase* [2002] ETMR 55.

[42] Which operate under Regulation 882/2004/EC on official controls performed to ensure the verification of compliance with feed and food law, animal health and animal welfare rules.

[43] Regulation 510/2006/EC, art 11.1; European Communities (Protection of Geographical Indications and Designations of Origin for Agricultural Products and Foodstuffs) Regulations 2007 (SI 704/2007).

[44] Regulation 510/2006/EC, art 12.

[45] *FORMAGGIO GORGONZOLA v KASEREI CHAMPIGNON* [1999] ETMR 454.

[46] *Commission v Germany* [2008] ETMR 32.

conflicting provisions of national law.[47] In *Dante Bigi*,[48] the ECJ ruled that the derogation did not apply to goods originating in the state of the protected designation of origin even though intended for export.

[37.29] The term 'PARMA HAM' is a protected designation of origin under Regulation 510/2006/EC. In *Consorzio del Proscuitto di Parma v ASDA Stores Ltd*,[49] the defendant sold genuine Parma ham but which was sliced and packed in England. It was held that the product specification defining the quality or characteristics did not include a requirement that the ham be sliced or packed in Parma despite such a requirement under national Italian law. The Court of Appeal further held that the predecessor to Regulation 510/2006/EC, Regulation 2081/92/EEC, did not have direct effect under national law stating that 'it is not sufficiently clear and precise and also does not provide an appropriate source of information as to the right sought to be enforced'.

CONFLICT WITH TRADE MARKS

[37.30] Practitioners will have to be aware of PDO and PGI registrations under Regulation 510/2006/EC and to search against these in order to advise their clients fully. Under art 14, an application to register a trade mark, which would be considered as prohibited from use under art 13, must be refused registration where it relates to 'the same class of product'.[50] This provision applies to trade mark applications that have been filed after the advertisement/publication of the PDO or PGI application in the Patents Office Journal and also in cases of prior trade mark applications that are still pending at the time of advertisement/publication.

[37.31] Article 14 of Regulation 510/2006/EC goes on to deal with trade marks 'registered in good faith' before the date that the PDO or PGI application was lodged. In such a case, the trade mark use may continue, provided that the trade mark registration would not be vulnerable to revocation or invalidity on any grounds set out in Council Directive 2008/95/EEC to approximate the laws of the Member States relating to trade marks or Council Regulation 207/2009/EC on the Community trade mark (which repealed and replaced Council Regulation 40/94/EC).

[37.32] In *FORMAGGIO GORGONZOLA v KASEREI CHAMPIGNON*,[51] the ECJ had to consider a question raised by the Austrian courts in relation to the use of a trade mark CAMBOZOLA, which was registered prior to registration of the PDO, GORGONZOLA. It was held that it was up to a national court to determine the issue of good faith and therefore whether use of the earlier trade mark could continue

47 *EPOISSES DE BOURGOGNE* [1998] ETMR 550.
48 *Dante Bigi* [2002] ECR I-5917, [2003] ETMR 55.
49 *Consorzio del Proscuitto di Parma v ASDA Stores Ltd* [1998] ETMR 481 and [1999] ETMR 319.
50 Presumably not class in the sense of the Nice Classification.
51 *FORMAGGIO GORGONZOLA v KASEREI CHAMPIGNON* [1999] ETMR 454.

in face of the PDO on the basis that use of the name CAMBOZOLA did not *per se* constitute an attempt to deceive the consumer.

USE OF REGULATION 510/2006/EC

[37.33] A wide variety of products have been covered including cheese, fresh meats, meat-based products, fruit and vegetables, oils and fats, mineral and spring waters, honey and confectionery products. Regulations 1107/96/EC,[52] 1263/96/EC,[53] 123/97/EC,[54] 813/2000/EC,[55] 1347/2001/EC [56] and 1778/2001/EC [57] contain lists of applications that have been approved for registration under the fast track procedure in art 17 of Regulation 2081/92/EC. There have also been numerous applications approved following the normal opposition procedure.[58] Some of the more well-known names on the list include WHITE AND BLUE STILTON CHEESE as PDOs; NEWCASTLE BROWN ALE[59] as a PGI and FETA as a PDO. When it can be seen that also on the list of registrations are SCOTTISH BEEF and SCOTTISH LAMB, as PGIs, it is surprising that steps have not been taken to register IRISH BEEF and IRISH LAMB or indeed, for example, WICKLOW LAMB given further precedents of registrability for SHETLAND LAMB and ORKNEY LAMB[60] as PDOs. In instances of a compound term such as *'CAMEMBERT DE NORMANDIE'* and *'CHABICHOU DE POITOU'*, the words *'CAMEMBERT'* and *'CHABICHOU'* are expressly stated not to be protected.[61] However, the fact of an absence of such a limitation (disclaimer) does not necessarily mean that each of its constituent parts is protected.[62] The following Irish names have been registered: IMOKILLY REGATO[63] as a PDO and CLARE ISLAND SALMON,[64] TIMOLEAGUE BROWN PUDDING[65] and CONNEMARA HILL LAMB/UAIN SLÉIBHE CHONAMARA[66] as PGIs.

---

[52] Commission Regulation 1107/96/EC.
[53] Commission Regulation 1263/96/EC ([1996] OJ L163/19).
[54] Commission Regulation 123/97/EC ([1997] OJ L22/19).
[55] Council Regulation 813/2000/EC ([2000] OJ L100/5).
[56] Council Regulation 1347/2001/EC ([2001] OJ L182/3)
[57] Council Regulation 1778/2001/EC ([2001] OJ L240/6).
[58] Commission Regulation 2400/96/EC ([1996] OJ L327/11).
[59] Subsequently revoked; see Rangnekar, 'The intellectual properties of geography'(2009) EIPR 31(11), 537–539.
[60] And CONNEMARA HILL LAMB, referred to below.
[61] Commission Regulation 1107/96/EC.
[62] *EPOISSES DE BOURGOGNE* [1998] ETMR 550.
[63] Commission Regulation 2107/1999/EC ([1999] OJ L272/26); ([1998] OJ C343/5).
[64] Commission Regulation 2107/1999/EC; ([1999] OJ C4/5).
[65] Commission Regulation 2446/2000/EC ([2000] OJ L281/12); ([2000] OJ C21/20).
[66] Commission Regulation 148/2007/EC ([2007] OJ L46/14).

REGULATION 509/2006/EC ON CERTIFICATES OF SPECIFIC CHARACTER FOR AGRICULTURAL PRODUCTS AND FOODS[67]

[37.34] Under Council Regulation 509/2006/EC,[68] producers can identify specific characteristics to which their agricultural product or foodstuff adheres and obtain a Community certificate of specific character. The specific character is defined to mean 'the characteristic or set of characteristics which distinguishes an agricultural product or foodstuffs clearly from other similar products or foodstuffs belonging to the same category'.[69] This does not include presentation but is not restricted to qualitative, quantitative composition or to a mode of production.

[37.35] Registration is not permitted if the specific character is due to the product's provenance or geographical origin.[70] A product specification must be filed that includes, as part of the requirements of registration, a description of the method of production, including the nature and characteristics of the raw material and/or ingredients used and/or the method of preparation of the agricultural product or foodstuff referring to its specific character.[71] Protection by way of registration, subject to certain limitations, affords protection in respect of the name enjoying the specific character. Registration also enables the producers to use a 'Community symbol', details of which are set out in Regulation 1216/2007/EC [72] and which symbol includes the words in English, 'TRADITIONAL SPECIALITY GUARANTEED'.

---

[67] Which repealed and replaced Regulation 2082/92/EEC.
[68] Council Regulation 509/2006/EC ([2006] OJ L93/1) on agricultural products and foodstuffs as traditional specialities guaranteed.
[69] Regulation 509/2006/EC, art 2(1).
[70] Regulation 509/2006/EC, art 4(1).
[71] Regulation 509/2006/EC, art 6.2(c).
[72] Commission Regulation 1216/2007/EC ([2007] OJ L275/3) of 18 October 2007 laying down detailed rules for the implementation of Council Regulation 509/2006/EC on agricultural products and foodstuffs as traditional specialities guaranteed.

Chapter 38

Taxation and Intellectual Property Rights

STAMP DUTY[1]

[38.01] Intellectual property rights are a form of personal property, which can be licensed or assigned. Section 79 of the Patents Act 1992 states that the rules of law applicable to the ownership and devolution of personal property shall apply in relation to patent applications and patents as they apply in relation to other choses in action. Similarly, s 120 of the Copyright and Related Rights Act 2000 also specifically identifies copyright transmissible by assignment as personal property and, furthermore, provides that no assignment (whether total or partial) can have effect unless it is in writing signed by or on behalf of the assignor. Section 26 of the Trade Marks Act 1996 states that a registered trade mark is personal property and goes on to provide in s 28 that a registered trade mark is transmissible by assignment either in connection with the goodwill of a business or independently. These provisions also apply in respect of a trade mark application.[2] An assignment is not effective unless it is in writing.[3] A registered design under the Industrial Designs Act 2001 is also referred to as a property right. Section 17(1) of the Plant Varieties (Proprietary Rights) Act 1980 also provides for assignment of such as a property right. In relation to topography rights in semiconductor products, although not specifically identified as property rights, by implication, they must be treated as such, given the rights that are conferred by statute.[4] The only form of intellectual property which it has been held does not constitute property for the purpose of stamp duty is 'know-how',[5] a form of unregistered right under the common law.

[38.02] Since stamp duty arises primarily on instruments that convey or transfer property, for many years intellectual property rights fell within the ambit of the stamp duty provisions of finance legislation. Given the huge values that can be attributed to certain intellectual property rights, and a top rate of nine per cent, the stamp duty on

---

[1] On stamp duty generally, see Donegan and Friel, *Irish Stamp Duty Law* (5th edn, Bloomsbury Professional, 2009).

[2] Trade Marks Act 1996, s 31.

[3] Trade Marks Act 1996, s 28(3).

[4] European Communities (Protection of Topographies of Semiconductor Products) Regulations 1988 (SI 101/1988).

[5] *Musker v English Electric Co Ltd* (1964) 41 TC 556; *John and E Strange Ltd v Hessel* (1975) 5 TC 573.

a transfer could be immense. Also, the granting of an exclusive and irrevocable licence may be considered as equivalent to a conveyance of property.[6]

[38.03] The Finance Act 2004 abolished stamp duty on the sale, transfer or other disposition of intellectual property in Ireland. Section 74(1), which added a new s 101 to the Stamp Duties Consolidation Act 1999, abolished stamp duty for the following intellectual property:

(a) trade marks (whether registered or unregistered), patents, registered designs, design rights, inventions or domain names;

(b) copyright or related rights within the meaning of the Copyright and Related Rights Act 2000;

(c) supplementary protection certificates provided for under Council Regulation 1768/92/EEC[7] (medicinal products) or Council Regulation 1610/96/EC[8] (plant protection products);

(d) plant breeders' rights within the meaning of s 4 of the Plant Varieties (Proprietary Rights) Act 1980, as amended by the Plant Varieties (Proprietary Rights) (Amendment) Act 1998;

(e) applications for the grant or registration of any of the above;

(f) licences or other rights in respect of any of the above;

(g) rights granted under the law of any country, territory, State or area other than Ireland, or under any international treaty, convention or agreement to which Ireland is a party, that correspond to or are similar to any of the above; and

(h) goodwill to the extent that it is directly attributable to any of the above.

If the property being transferred is made up both of intellectual property and other types of property, the consideration must be apportioned between the two types of property on a just and reasonable basis, and stamp duty may be charged on the consideration applicable to the non-intellectual property. The abolition only applies to transfers that have taken place after 1 April 2004.[9] For transfers that took place prior to that date, stamp duty will still apply, subject to possible reliefs and exemptions.

[38.04] The abolition of stamp duty means that agreements for the transfer of non-Irish intellectual property are no longer liable for stamp duty where the transfer documents are executed in Ireland. It is likely that the abolition will be widely construed to include, for example, charges and database rights.

[38.05] If copyright is created in Ireland, then, on the face of it, the right has its *situs* in the State and an instrument of transfer will not attract stamp duty in Ireland. Article 9 of the Trade-Related Aspects of Intellectual Property Rights (TRIPS) Agreement requires compliance with arts 1–21 and the Appendix of the Berne Copyright Convention (1971). Article 5(2) of the Berne Convention states that the rights granted shall be

---

6   *Smelting Co of Australia Ltd v IRC* [1897] 1 QB 175.

7   Council Regulation 1768/92/EEC ([1992] OJ L182/1).

8   Council Regulation 1610/96/EC ([1996] OJ L198/21).

9   Finance Act 2004 (Section 74) (Commencement) Order 2004 (SI 140/2004).

independent of the existence of protection in the country of origin. It is also quite legitimate to transfer copyright in so far as it arises in different jurisdictions and, for example, retain copyright just in Ireland while transferring rights to the rest of the world. Consequently, it can certainly be strongly argued that separate assignments can be executed, one for Ireland and a further assignment in respect of the independent right to copyright that exists in a country where such stamp duty is still applicable, if this is advantageous as regards the liability to stamp duty in that other country. In the English courts, there is already judicial authority that copyright can have a *situs* other than in the country of origin of the copyright work.[10]

[38.06] One issue that may still arise, particularly in relation to assignments of patent or trade mark rights which occurred before the abolition of stamp duty, is the necessity to ensure that the correct document is used to record the assignment with the Irish Patents Office. The British case of *Brown and Root McDermott Fabricators Ltd v Coflexip Stena Offshore Ltd*[11] addressed the issue of replacing an existing formal assignment with a new one, which identifies the value of the patent rights being transferred so that the appropriate stamp duty could then be paid. In this case, the original patentee contracted, by way of a single agreement, to transfer to the respondent a ship, a large number of other assets and a number of patents, some of which were UK patents. The total purchase price was US$31.5m. The patent agent prepared a short form of assignment (A1) of the patents, which was duly executed. Upon learning that the original contract to assign was not stamped, it became apparent that the short form assignment needed a valuation for stamping before recordal on the Register could take place. A fresh assignment (A2) was then executed, which contained a valuation. A2 was stamped and then used as a basis for recording the change in ownership on the UK Patent Register. It was argued that A2 was void because A1 complied with the Patents Act in all respects and it was consequently A1 which vested the change in ownership and the Register should be rectified by the removal of any reference to A2. This would mean that the Register would then still show the original patentee as the owner. The importance of this to the applicant was that when A1 was subsequently stamped and recorded on the Register, it would be too late for the respondent to claim damages or an account of profits given the provisions of s 68 of the UK Patents Act 1977 (of which there is no corresponding provision in the Irish Patents Act 1992 but there is under s 29(4) of the Trade Marks Act 1996). Jacob J accepted the somewhat circular argument that, given that under s 14(4) of the Stamp Act 1891 an unstamped instrument cannot be given in evidence or made available for any purposes whatsoever, the first assignment (A1) could not be used to invalidate the second assignment (A2). This had the effect that it could not then be established that A2 was void since this could only be proved by reference to A1. Thus, on the admissible evidence, A2 had been properly registered. In conclusion, Jacob J stated:

---

[10] *Novello & Co Ltd v Hinrichsen Edition Ltd* [1951] 1 All ER 779.
[11] *Brown and Root McDermott Fabricators Ltd v Coflexip Stena Offshore Ltd* [1996] STC 483.

I reach my conclusion without intellectual satisfaction. But there is some rough justice. It was an attempt to comply with the Stamp Act 1891 which caused the trouble and it is the Stamp Act 1891 which saves the position.

[38.07] Section 29(4) of the Trade Marks Act 1996 (TMA 1996) provides that late application for recordal[12] of the change in ownership on the Register means that damages or an account of profits will be denied. This means that practitioners must be cautious in their use of a short form assignment following a much longer agreement that is expressed to be an assignment.

[38.08] The complexity of stamp duty legislation in the context of intellectual property rights, which are extremely hard to value and where assignments are often concluded on a global basis without reference to Irish taxation provisions, has resulted in extreme difficulties for practitioners in ensuring both their client's compliance and also their personal obligations under the Stamp Duties Consolidation Act 1999. After much lobbying, including several submissions by the Association of Patent and Trade Mark Agents to the Department of Finance, the archaic and punitive stamp duty provisions were finally removed.[13]

PATENT ROYALTIES[14]

[38.09] An exemption from corporation tax or income tax arising from patents for inventions devised within the State was created in the Finance Act 1973 and is set out in its current form in s 234 of the Taxes Consolidation Act 1997. The rationale is to encourage research and development in Ireland and to stimulate innovation. The exemption is only available to residents of the State, which is defined to mean any person who is resident in the State for the purposes of income tax and who is not resident elsewhere. A company is regarded as resident in the State if it is controlled and managed in the State.

[38.10] To avail of this exemption it is necessary to possess a 'qualifying patent' which is stated in s 234 to mean:

A patent in relation to which the research, planning, processing, experimenting, testing, devising, designing, developing or similar activity leading to the invention which is the subject of the patent was carried out in an EEA state.[15]

[38.11] It is necessary that all of these activities took place within the EEA, but the Revenue Commissioners recognise that in some instances difficulties can arise in establishing whether the work concerned was wholly carried out in the EEA (for example, study and research may have to be carried out in libraries abroad into works of reference not available in the EEA or tests may have to be made in other countries in

---

12 More than six months from date of transaction.
13 For an excellent summary of stamp duty on intellectual property rights in Ireland, see Hackett (1995) Commercial Law Practitioner (March).
14 See *Irish Income Tax* 2010 (Bloomsbury Professional).
15 As amended by the Finance Act 2007, s 45.

particular climatic or other circumstances). The Revenue Commissioners accept that the exemption may still apply where the spirit of the section is fulfilled, namely that the exemption arises out of genuine inventions researched and developed in the EEA.[16]

[38.12] An individual claiming the exemption must have been involved, solely or jointly, in the research, planning, processing, experimenting, testing, devising, designing, developing or similar activity, leading to the patented invention.[17] The limitation that the claimant must have been involved in these activities does not apply to a company and it is possible for an Irish company to acquire a qualifying patent and then claim the relief on foot of this. A granted patent (rather than an application) is required to claim the exemption, although the Revenue Commissioners have on occasion permitted exemption of royalties made retrospectively in respect of periods after the complete specification for the patent was filed, provided that the patent was subsequently granted. No distinction is drawn by the legislation between a short-term patent and a normal or long-term patent for this purpose.

[38.13] The income from a qualifying patent, which is exempt from tax, is comprised of any royalty or other sum paid in respect of the user of the invention to which the qualifying patent relates and includes any sum paid for the grant of a licence to exercise rights under such a patent. The royalty or other sum must be paid for the purpose of activities that:

(a) are regarded as the manufacture of goods for the purposes of the relief under Pt 14 of the Taxes Consolidation Act 1997[18] (often called 'manufacturing relief'). This excludes international financial services carried on from the International Financial Services Centre and Shannon Zone services activities;[19] or

(b) would fall within the definition of activities to which manufacturing relief applies if they were carried out in the State by a company, which the Revenue Commissioners Manual interprets as covering circumstances where the activities are carried out by an entity which is not a company (eg an unincorporated association or a partnership) or carried out outside the State.[20]

Manufacturing relief under Pt 14 of the Taxes Consolidation Act 1997 is due to expire on 31 December 2010. However, the patent royalty exemption is not reliant on Pt 14 but

---

[16] See Revenue Commissioners Tax & Duty Manuals, Income Tax, Capital Gains Tax and Corporation Tax, Part 6.4.1 (as of 1 July 2010).

[17] Taxes Consolidation Act 1997, s 234(3).

[18] See Revenue Commissioners Notes for Guidance – Taxes Consolidation Act 1997 – 2008 Edition, Part 14, 'Taxation of Companies Engaged in Manufacturing Trades, Certain Trading Operations Carried on in Shannon Airport and Certain Trading Operations Carried on in The Custom House Docks Area'.

[19] Repair and maintenance of aircraft in the Shannon Zone are not excluded from the relief, as per the Revenue Commissioners Tax & Duty Manuals, Income Tax, Capital Gains Tax and Corporation Tax, Part 6.4.1 (as of 1 July 2010).

[20] See Revenue Commissioners Tax & Duty Manuals, Income Tax, Capital Gains Tax and Corporation Tax, Part 6.4.1 (as of 1 July 2010).

merely uses the definition of manufacture of goods contained therein as one of the criteria for claiming the patent royalty exemption. Therefore, the expiry of manufacturing relief under Pt 14 should not affect the patent royalty exemption.[21]

There is an exception to this: if a royalty or other sum paid meets the criteria relating to connected persons referred to below, relief can be claimed even where the payments are for activities to which manufacturing relief does not apply.

[38.14] As regards royalties or other sums paid after 23 April 1996, any royalty or other sum paid to the holder of a patent, which exceeds an amount which would be paid between persons acting at arm's length, is not treated as income from a qualifying patent. This covers licence agreements already in existence on that date. No criteria are included as to what factors will be taken into account in determining whether the payments are equivalent to those of an arm's length agreement. This is likely to involve consideration of the strength of the patent itself and also the cost of the research and development leading to the patent, together with the terms of the licence on issues such as exclusivity and territoriality.

[38.15] Royalties or other sums are also treated as income from a qualifying patent:

(a)   where the payer is not connected[22] with the beneficial recipient of the royalty or other sum; and

(b)   where no arrangements exist that have as a main purpose the satisfying of the condition that the royalty or other sum must be received from a unconnected person. In other words, if third parties are included in order to take advantage of the exemption, the royalties or other sums are not exempt.

[38.16] Up until the mid-1980s the exemption was not widely used, but as other tax exemptions were closed off an increased awareness of the exemption arose. The first inroad into the exemption arose under s 28 of the Finance Act 1994, which amended the definition of 'income from a qualifying patent' so that if the licensor and licensee are connected then the income must be paid in respect of activities to which manufacturing relief applies. The Finance Act 2007 introduced a cap on the amount of income from patent royalties upon which exemption can be claimed to €5m *per annum*.[23] This cap applies cumulatively to connected persons such as groups of companies.

[38.17] Under s 141 of the Taxes Consolidation Act 1997, dividends and other distributions paid by a company from patent income qualifying for exemption under s 234 of the Taxes Consolidation Act 1997, are exempt from tax in the hands of the shareholders. This also covers situations where a company receives the distribution from another company. The effect of this is that the distribution to the recipient paid out of disregarded income is also exempt from tax in the hands of the recipient. The distribution should in so far as possible be made out of income from that accounting

---

21   See Revenue Commissions Tax Briefing TB53, August 2003, p 16.

22   'Connected' means connected for the purposes of capital gains tax as defined in the Taxes Consolidation Act 1997, s 10.

23   Applies to work carried out on or after 1 January 2008.

period but it is possible to apply any amounts by which the distribution exceeds the income for that period against income from preceding accounting periods. The recipient is deemed to have 'disregarded income'. The Finance Act 1992 imposed restrictions on this exemption by providing that only distributions to a holder of 'eligible shares'[24] in the company or to a person directly involved in the research and development activity leading to the invention[25] are exempt from tax.

[38.18] A further restriction was introduced in 1996[26] in situations where the royalty income arises as a result of an agreement with a connected person in respect of use of the patented invention for the purpose of activities to which manufacturing relief applies. This is referred to as 'specified income'. Any distribution out of 'specified income' can only be exempt from tax if it is in respect of a qualifying patent for an invention that:

(a)   involved radical innovation, and

(b)   was patented for *bona fide* commercial reasons and not primarily for the purpose of avoiding liability to taxation.[27]

There is no definition of the words 'radical innovation'. It is no longer enough for there to be a patent in place and some inventions which fulfil the criteria of patentability in being new and involving an inventive step will not be a substantial enough advance to secure the tax exemption. The Minister for Finance, Ruairí Quinn, made the following statement during the passage of the Bill through Committee Stage in the Dáil:

> The term 'radical innovation' means the creation of something which is fundamentally novel. The degree of novelty cannot be other than a subjective judgement. However, there is an OECD precedent for classifying innovations as 'completely new', 'modestly improved' and merely a differentiation of an existing product or process. In viewing the foregoing categories in the context of radical innovation some-thing completely new would come within its scope but a mere differentiation would not. The modestly improved product which is not a mere differentiation is more likely to be considered radical innovation than a modestly improved process ... A body of precedents exists to which inspectors can refer and the interpretation of 'radical' or 'innovative' can be reasonably adduced. This matter will be clarified with the taxation administration committee and guidelines will be given to domestic tax practitioners.[28]

[38.19] The Revenue Commissioners will consider any evidence submitted as to the radically innovative nature of the invention and *bona fides* of the patent, and the Revenue Commissioners Manual[29] states that the Revenue, in making this determination, may consult appropriate experts, and that a determination can be appealed to the Appeal Commissioners and subsequently to the courts.

---

24   Taxes Consolidation Act 1997, s 141(1).
25   See the Taxes Consolidation Act 1997, s 141(4)(a)(ii).
26   Finance Act 1996, s 32(2), replaced by the Taxes Consolidation Act 1997, s 141(1).
27   See the Taxes Consolidation Act 1997, s 141(5)(d).
28   Select Committee on Finance and General Affairs, 24 April 1996, Col 199.
29   See Revenue Commissioners Tax & Duty Manuals, Income Tax, Capital Gains Tax and Corporation Tax, Part 6.4.1 (as of 1 July 2010).

[38.20] Distributions from specified income are limited by reference to the research and development expenditure incurred by the company and its group companies over a three-year period,[30] unless the patent involves 'radical innovation' and the patent was registered for *bona fide* commercial purposes and not primarily for the purposes of avoiding liability to taxation. The Finance Act 2006[31] provided that even where this three-year specified income limit applies, the company is still required to show that the patent was patented for *bona fide* commercial reasons and not primarily for the purpose of tax avoidance before any distributions made by the company out of exempt patent royalties would be exempt from tax in the hands of the recipient.

[38.21] The Finance Act 2006 also provided for a further restriction, which applies to arrangements involving intellectual property rights such as franchising, trade mark or copyright licensing or similar fees between unconnected parties, where the amounts attributed as patent royalty payments in respect of those arrangements could be insufficient in the case of payments received by the company or excessive in the case of payments made by the company. Tax exemption for such distributions in the hands of the recipient out of such income is limited by reference to research and development expenditure incurred by the company and its group companies over a three-year period (the same as the limitation which applies to connected persons). The company is also still required to show that the patent was patented for *bona fide* commercial reasons and not primarily for the purpose of tax avoidance before any distributions made by the company out of exempt patent royalties would themselves be tax free in the hands of the recipient. [32]

[38.22] The patent royalty exemption has been retained after conflicting recommendations for and against its proposed removal issued from the European Commission on Taxation Report in 2009 and the Innovation Taskforce in 2010. However, the exemption available is subject to increased tax rates by means of the high earners' cap, for which the income threshold was reduced in the Finance Act 2010 to €125,000 with increasing rates of tax for income up to €400,000, as well as the income levy of up to six per cent.

ARTISTS' EXEMPTION FROM INCOME TAX

[38.23] An exemption from tax for income from certain works of writers, composers and artists was introduced in 1969[33] and is set out in its current form in s 195 of the Taxes Consolidation Act 1997. The individual claiming the exemption must be: (i) resident in the State and not elsewhere; or (ii) ordinarily resident and domiciled in the State (and not resident elsewhere) and have written, composed or executed either solely or jointly a qualifying work. The work must be determined by the Revenue Commissioners as being

---

30 Taxes Consolidation Act 1997, s 141(5), as amended by the Finance Act 2004.
31 See Revenue Commissioners Tax & Duty Manuals, Income Tax, Capital Gains Tax and Corporation Tax, Part 6.4.1 (as of 1 July 2010).
32 Taxes Consolidation Act 1997, s 141(5A) as inserted by the Finance Act 2006.
33 Finance Act 1969, s 2. See *Irish Income Tax 2010* (Bloomsbury Professional).

generally recognised as having cultural or artistic merit. Section 195(1) provides that a work must be an original and creative work falling under one of the following categories:

(a)   a book or other writing;

(b)   a play;

(c)   a musical composition;

(d)   a painting or like picture;

(e)   a sculpture.

[38.24] An Comhairle Ealaíon (the Arts Council) and the Minister for Arts, Culture, Sport and Tourism drew up a set of guidelines as an aid to determination on whether or not works are original and creative and whether they have, or are generally recognised as having, cultural or artistic merit. The following guidelines have been issued:

Cultural or artistic merit

A work has cultural merit if its contemplation enhances the quality of individual or social life by virtue of that work's intellectual, spiritual or aesthetic form and content.

A work has artistic merit when its combined form and content enhance or intensify the aesthetic apprehension of those who experience or contemplate it.

Original and creative

For the purpose of a determination under Section 2 of the Finance Act 1969, the term original and creative encompasses any unique work which is brought into existence for the first time as an independent entity by the exercise of its creator's imagination.

A non-fiction work in category (a), a book or other writing will be considered original and creative only if:

(i)   it comes within one of the following categories:

–   The following categories of literature (and any combination thereof) coming fully within the terms of reference of the Arts Council encompassing the subjects of fiction writing, drama, music, film, dance, mime or visual arts, and related commentaries by *bona fide* artists:

Arts criticism;
Arts history;
Arts subject works;
Arts diaries;
Autobiography;
Belles-lettres essays;
Cultural dictionaries;
Literary translation;
Literary criticism;
Literary history;
Literary diaries.

–   The following category of works coming fully within the terms of reference of the Heritage Council including works which, in their entirety, comprise one or more of the these categories:

Archaeology;

Publications associated with items or areas of significant heritage value.

– The following categories of works coming fully within the terms of reference of the National Archives Advisory Council:

Publications which relate to archives which are more than 30 years old concerning Ireland, and are based largely on research from such archives.

– Categories of works which in their entirety comprise one or more of the categories cited in the above paragraphs.

(ii) the essence of the work is the presentation of the author's own ideas or insights in relation to the subject matter, and the ideas or insights are of such significance that the work would be regarded as a pioneering work casting new light on its subject matter or changing the generally accepted understanding of the subject matter.

Exclusions from the ambit of 'original and creative'

The following types of work in the categories set out in Section 2 of the [Finance Act 1969] … will not be regarded as coming within the ambit of original and creative:

(a) **A book or other writing (excluding those at (i) and (ii) above)**

A book or other writing published primarily for, or which is or will be used primarily by students pursuing a course of study or persons engaged in any trade, profession, vocation or branch of learning as an aid to professional or other practice in connection with the trade, profession, vocation or branch of learning.

An article or series of articles published in a newspaper, magazine, book or elsewhere – except a book consisting of a series of articles by the same author connected by a common theme and therefore capable of existing independently in its own right.

(b) **A play**

Types or kinds of plays written for advertising purposes which do not exist independently in their own right by reason of quality or duration.

(c) **A musical composition**

Types or kinds of musical compositions written for advertising purposes which do not exist independently in their own right by reason of quality or duration.

Arrangements, adaptations and versions of musical compositions by a person other than a *bona fide* composer who is also actively engaged in musical composition.

(d) **A painting or like picture**

Types or kinds of photographs or drawings (other than a set or sets of photographs or drawings that are collectively created for an artistic purpose) which are mainly of record, or which serve a utilitarian function, or which would not exist independently in their own right by reason of quality or by reference to their potentiality for inclusion as part of an art exhibition.

(e) **A sculpture**

Types or kinds of objects which are primarily functional in nature, objects produced by processes other than by hand, objects produced by persons other than those actively engaged as *bona fide* artists in the field of the visual arts.

[38.25] In *IRC v Colm O'Loinsigh*,[34] the respondent was a school teacher who wrote a series of four books entitled *Pathways to History*, which were intended primarily for the education of school children. Murphy J in the High Court upheld the decision of the Appeal Commissioner that the books were original and creative within s 2 of the Finance Act 1969.[35]

[38.26] In reaching a determination as to cultural or artistic merit, the Revenue Commissioners may consult any person or body of persons as may provide authoritative assistance to them in establishing whether a work is a qualifying work and will consider any evidence in relation to the matter, which the individual submits. The exemption applies to both an individual who is engaged generally in producing cultural or artistic works and to an individual who produces a particular cultural or artistic work. As regards a claim relating to a particular work, the Revenue Commissioners will only make the determination after the publication, production or sale of that work.

[38.27] If the claim is successful, the profits or gains accruing to the individual arising from the publication, production or sale, as the case may be, of the work or works will be exempt from income tax.

[38.28] The artists' exemption has been retained despite the recommendation of the European Commission on Taxation Report in 2009 that it should be removed. However, the exemption available is subject to increased tax rates by means of the high earners' cap, for which the income threshold was reduced in the Finance Act 2010 to €125,000 with increasing rates of tax for income up to €400,000, as well as the income levy of up to six per cent.

TAX ALLOWANCES FOR ACQUISITION OF PATENTS AND OTHER RIGHTS

[38.29] A wide-ranging scheme of tax allowances was introduced in 2009 for capital expenditure incurred on the acquisition of intellectual property rights and in particular on 'managing, developing or exploiting' those rights (s 291A of the Taxes Consolidation Act 1997 as inserted by the Finance Act 2009). The rights covered by the scheme, termed 'intangible assets', include trade marks, copyright and related rights, design rights, patents and know-how related to manufacturing or processing and domain names, product and medical authorisations as well as licences and goodwill deriving its value from any of these categories. The Finance Act 2010 specifically included applications for and registrations of the applicable rights and computer software acquired for commercial exploitation for the purposes of receiving a royalty or other sum from third parties. It also extended the types of know-how to industrial, commercial or scientific

---

[34]   *IRC v Colm O'Loinsigh* [1994] ITR 1994 (HC), Murphy J.
[35]   See also *Mara v Hummingbird Ltd* [1982] ILRM 421; *Healy v Breathnach (Inspector of Taxes)* [1986] IR 105.

know-how such as secret processes, formulae or information. These provisions are not limited to Irish rights but extend to rights in any country. The ability to benefit from these provisions is not limited to Irish companies but extends to any companies that trade in Ireland, and the concept of trade is broadly interpreted.

[38.30] There is no definition of what is meant by provision, management, development or exploitation of rights. The important issue is that the allowances are only available where the intellectual property is used for trading activities and not held as an investment. The Revenue Commissioners have indicated that the criteria set out in *Noddy Subsidiary Rights Company Ltd v IRC*[36] are important in determining whether or not an activity constitutes a trade.

[38.31] The tax allowances can be set against 80 per cent of the annual trading income arising from that part of the activities which consists of the management, development or exploitation of intellectual property or the sale of goods or services deriving the greater part of their value from the intellectual property rights. The Finance Act 2010 expanded the qualifying income to *the whole* of any such activities rather than *that part* which is attributable to the intellectual property rights.

[38.32] Where the asset is not the type that depreciates, for example, a trade mark which has a potentially unlimited lifespan, the value of the expenditure can be written off over 15 years. In all other cases, the value is written off in line with standard accounting procedure in the same manner as plant and machinery, unless the intellectual property owner opts for the 15-year write-off.

[38.33] The scheme also includes the usual types of anti-avoidance provisions concerning arm's length transactions, *bona fide* commercial reasons and transactions with related companies, including a limited ability to claim tax relief on interest on intra-company loans for the provision of intellectual property. There is also a claw-back period for sale of the rights, reduced by the Finance Act 2010 from 15 years to 10 years. The legislation does not allow a double deduction to be claimed on the same expenditure, so the intellectual property owner must make a choice between writing the expenditure off over the life of the asset or taking the cost as a deduction in the year in which it is incurred, for example, in the case of trade mark registration and renewal costs.

OTHER TAX PROVISIONS RELEVANT TO INTELLECTUAL PROPERTY

[38.34] Expenses incurred in obtaining, for the purpose of a trade, the grant or renewal of a patent[37] or trade mark[38] are deductible as a trading expense, as is the cost of

---

[36] *Noddy Subsidiary Rights Company Ltd v IRC* [1966] 43 TC 458.
[37] Taxes Consolidation Act 1997, s 758; this deduction is being phased out because of the introduction of the intangible assets scheme but the deduction can be claimed for expenditure incurred up to the 7 May 2011.
[38] Taxes Consolidation Act 1997, s 86.

acquiring know-how.[39] However, this deduction cannot be claimed if relief is also being claimed under the capital allowances provisions and *vice versa*.

[38.35] The Finance Act 2010 also (i) extended the credit for foreign intellectual property royalty income received from non-EU and non-tax treaty countries to cover all trading companies, and (ii) abolished Irish withholding taxes on payment of patent royalties and 'pure income' royalties (earned without incurring any expense) paid to entities in the EU or tax treaty countries.

[38.36] These changes, in conjunction with the low corporate tax rate of 12.5 per cent, the tax credits for research and development and the abolition of stamp duty on intellectual property transactions, ensure that Ireland remains attractive to intellectual property owners as a location for trade and for intellectual property centralisation.[40]

---

[39] Taxes Consolidation Act 1997, s 768.

[40] For further discussion on the deductions and reliefs available for intellectual property expenditure, including R&D relief, see 'Read My Lips: No IP Taxes!' Niamh Hall & Derek Andrews, *IIPLQ*, issue 1 (2010).

Appendices

Appendix I

Berne Convention for the Protection of
Literary and Artistic Works

Paris Act 24 June 1971 as amended on 28 September 1979

The countries of the Union, being equally animated by the desire to protect, in as effective and uniform a manner as possible, the rights of authors in their literary and artistic works,

Recognizing the importance of the work of the Revision Conference held at Stockholm in 1967,

Have resolved to revise the Act adopted by the Stockholm Conference, while maintaining without change Articles 1 to 20 and 22 to 26 of that Act.

Consequently, the undersigned Plenipotentiaries, having presented their full powers, recognized as in good and due form, have agreed as follows:

Article 1

The countries to which this Convention applies constitute a Union for the protection of the rights of authors in their literary and artistic works.

Article 2

(1) The expression "literary and artistic works" shall include every production in the literary, scientific and artistic domain, whatever may be the mode or form of its expression, such as books, pamphlets and other writings; lectures, addresses, sermons and other works of the same nature; dramatic or dramaticomusical works; choreographic works and entertainments in dumb show; musical compositions with or without words; cinematographic works to which are assimilated works expressed by a process analogous to cinematography; works of drawing, painting, architecture, sculpture, engraving and lithography; photographic works to which are assimilated works expressed by a process analogous to photography; works of applied art; illustrations, maps, plans, sketches and three-dimensional works relative to geography, topography, architecture or science.

(2) It shall, however, be a matter for legislation in the countries of the Union to prescribe that works in general or any specified categories of works shall not be protected unless they have been fixed in some material form.

(3) Translations, adaptations, arrangements of music and other alterations of a literary or artistic work shall be protected as original works without prejudice to the copyright in the original work.

(4) It shall be a matter for legislation in the countries of the Union to determine the protection to be granted to official texts of a legislative, administrative and legal nature, and to official translations of such texts.

(5) Collections of literary or artistic works such as encyclopaedias and anthologies which, by reason of the selection and arrangement of their contents, constitute intellectual creations shall be protected as such, without prejudice to the copyright in each of the works forming part of such collections.

(6) The works mentioned in this Article shall enjoy protection in all countries of the Union. This protection shall operate for the benefit of the author and his successors in title.

(7) Subject to the provisions of Article 7(4) of this Convention, it shall be a matter for legislation in the countries of the Union to determine the extent of the application of their laws to works of applied art and industrial designs and models, as well as the conditions under which such works, designs and models shall be protected. Works protected in the country of origin solely as designs and models shall be entitled in another country of the Union only to such special protection as is granted in that country to designs and models; however, if no such special protection is granted in that country, such works shall be protected as artistic works.

(8) The protection of this Convention shall not apply to news of the day or to miscellaneous facts having the character of mere items of press information.

Article 2*bis*

(1) It shall be a matter for legislation in the countries of the Union to exclude, wholly or in part, from the protection provided by the preceding Article political speeches and speeches delivered in the course of legal proceedings.

(2) It shall also be a matter for legislation in the countries of the Union to determine the conditions under which lectures, addresses and other works of the same nature which are delivered in public may be reproduced by the press, broadcast, communicated to the public by wire and made the subject of public communication as envisaged in Article 11bis(1) of this Convention, when such use is justified by the informatory purpose.

(3) Nevertheless, the author shall enjoy the exclusive right of making a collection of his works mentioned in the preceding paragraphs.

Article 3

(1) The protection of this Convention shall apply to:

   (a) authors who are nationals of one of the countries of the Union, for their works, whether published or not;

   (b) authors who are not nationals of one of the countries of the Union, for their works first published in one of those countries, or simultaneously in a country outside the Union and in a country of the Union.

(2) Authors who are not nationals of one of the countries of the Union but who have their habitual residence in one of them shall, for the purposes of this Convention, be assimilated to nationals of that country.

(3) The expression "published works" means works published with the consent of their authors, whatever may be the means of manufacture of the copies, provided that the availability of such copies has been such as to satisfy the reasonable requirements of

the public, having regard to the nature of the work. The performance of a dramatic, dramatico-musical, cinematographic or musical work, the public recitation of a literary work, the communication by wire or the broadcasting of literary or artistic works, the exhibition of a work of art and the construction of a work of architecture shall not constitute publication.

(4) A work shall be considered as having been published simultaneously in several countries if it has been published in two or more countries within thirty days of its first publication.

Article 4

The protection of this Convention shall apply, even if the conditions of Article 3 are not fulfilled, to:

(a) authors of cinematographic works the maker of which has his headquarters or habitual residence in one of the countries of the Union;

(b) authors of works of architecture erected in a country of the Union or of other artistic works incorporated in a building or other structure located in a country of the Union.

Article 5

(1) Authors shall enjoy, in respect of works for which they are protected under this Convention, in countries of the Union other than the country of origin, the rights which their respective laws do now or may hereafter grant to their nationals, as well as the rights specially granted by this Convention.

(2) The enjoyment and the exercise of these rights shall not be subject to any formality; such enjoyment and such exercise shall be independent of the existence of protection in the country of origin of the work. Consequently, apart from the provisions of this Convention, the extent of protection, as well as the means of redress afforded to the author to protect his rights, shall be governed exclusively by the laws of the country where protection is claimed.

(3) Protection in the country of origin is governed by domestic law. However, when the author is not a national of the country of origin of the work for which he is protected under this Convention, he shall enjoy in that country the same rights as national authors.

(4) The country of origin shall be considered to be:

(a) in the case of works first published in a country of the Union, that country; in the case of works published simultaneously in several countries of the Union which grant different terms of protection, the country whose legislation grants the shortest term of protection;

(b) in the case of works published simultaneously in a country outside the Union and in a country of the Union, the latter country;

(c) in the case of unpublished works or of works first published in a country outside the Union, without simultaneous publication in a country of the Union, the country of the Union of which the author is a national, provided that:

(i)   when these are cinematographic works the maker of which has his headquarters or his habitual residence in a country of the Union, the country of origin shall be that country, and

(ii) when these are works of architecture erected in a country of the Union or other artistic works incorporated in a building or other structure located in a country of the Union, the country of origin shall be that country.

Article 6

(1) Where any country outside the Union fails to protect in an adequate manner the works of authors who are nationals of one of the countries of the Union, the latter country may restrict the protection given to the works of authors who are, at the date of the first publication thereof, nationals of the other country and are not habitually resident in one of the countries of the Union. If the country of first publication avails itself of this right, the other countries of the Union shall not be required to grant to works thus subjected to special treatment a wider protection than that granted to them in the country of first publication.

(2) No restrictions introduced by virtue of the preceding paragraph shall affect the rights which an author may have acquired in respect of a work published in a country of the Union before such restrictions were put into force.

(3) The countries of the Union which restrict the grant of copyright in accordance with this Article shall give notice thereof to the Director General of the World Intellectual Property Organization (hereinafter designated as "the Director General") by a written declaration specifying the countries in regard to which protection is restricted, and the restrictions to which rights of authors who are nationals of those countries are subjected. The Director General shall immediately communicate this declaration to all the countries of the Union.

Article 6*bis*

(1) Independently of the author's economic rights, and even after the transfer of the said rights, the author shall have the right to claim authorship of the work and to object to any distortion, mutilation or other modification of, or other derogatory action in relation to, the said work, which would be prejudicial to his honor or reputation.

(2) The rights granted to the author in accordance with the preceding paragraph shall, after his death, be maintained, at least until the expiry of the economic rights, and shall be exercisable by the persons or institutions authorized by the legislation of the country where protection is claimed. However, those countries whose legislation, at the moment of their ratification of or accession to this Act, does not provide for the protection after the death of the author of all the rights set out in the preceding paragraph may provide that some of these rights may, after his death, cease to be maintained.

(3) The means of redress for safeguarding the rights granted by this Article shall be governed by the legislation of the country where protection is claimed.

Article 7

(1) The term of protection granted by this Convention shall be the life of the author and fifty years after his death.

(2) However, in the case of cinematographic works, the countries of the Union may provide that the term of protection shall expire fifty years after the work has been made available to the public with the consent of the author, or, failing such an event within fifty years from the making of such a work, fifty years after the making.

(3) In the case of anonymous or pseudonymous works, the term of protection granted by this Convention shall expire fifty years after the work has been lawfully made available to the public. However, when the pseudonym adopted by the author leaves no doubt as to his identity, the term of protection shall be that provided in paragraph (1). If the author of an anonymous or pseudonymous work discloses his identity during the above-mentioned period, the term of protection applicable shall be that provided in paragraph (1). The countries of the Union shall not be required to protect anonymous or pseudonymous works in respect of which it is reasonable to presume that their author has been dead for fifty years.

(4) It shall be a matter for legislation in the countries of the Union to determine the term of protection of photographic works and that of works of applied art in so far as they are protected as artistic works; however, this term shall last at least until the end of a period of twenty-five years from the making of such a work.

(5) The term of protection subsequent to the death of the author and the terms provided by paragraphs (2), (3) and (4) shall run from the date of death or of the event referred to in those paragraphs, but such terms shall always be deemed to begin on the first of January of the year following the death or such event.

(6) The countries of the Union may grant a term of protection in excess of those provided by the preceding paragraphs.

(7) Those countries of the Union bound by the Rome Act of this Convention which grant, in their national legislation in force at the time of signature of the present Act, shorter terms of protection than those provided for in the preceding paragraphs shall have the right to maintain such terms when ratifying or acceding to the present Act.

(8) In any case, the term shall be governed by the legislation of the country where protection is claimed; however, unless the legislation of that country otherwise provides, the term shall not exceed the term fixed in the country of origin of the work.

Article 7*bis*

The provisions of the preceding Article shall also apply in the case of a work of joint authorship, provided that the terms measured from the death of the author shall be calculated from the death of the last surviving author.

Article 8

Authors of literary and artistic works protected by this Convention shall enjoy the exclusive right of making and of authorizing the translation of their works throughout the term of protection of their rights in the original works.

Article 9

(1) Authors of literary and artistic works protected by this Convention shall have the exclusive right of authorizing the reproduction of these works, in any manner or form.

(2) It shall be a matter for legislation in the countries of the Union to permit the reproduction of such works in certain special cases, provided that such reproduction does not conflict with a normal exploitation of the work and does not unreasonably prejudice the legitimate interests of the author.

(3) Any sound or visual recording shall be considered as a reproduction for the purposes of this Convention.

Article 10

(1) It shall be permissible to make quotations from a work which has already been lawfully made available to the public, provided that their making is compatible with fair practice, and their extent does not exceed that justified by the purpose, including quotations from newspaper articles and periodicals in the form of press summaries.

(2) It shall be a matter for legislation in the countries of the Union, and for special agreements existing or to be concluded between them, to permit the utilization, to the extent justified by the purpose, of literary or artistic works by way of illustration in publications, broadcasts or sound or visual recordings for teaching, provided such utilization is compatible with fair practice.

(3) Where use is made of works in accordance with the preceding paragraphs of this Article, mention shall be made of the source, and of the name of the author if it appears thereon.

Article 10*bis*

(1) It shall be a matter for legislation in the countries of the Union to permit the reproduction by the press, the broadcasting or the communication to the public by wire of articles published in newspapers or periodicals on current economic, political or religious topics, and of broadcast works of the same character, in cases in which the reproduction, broadcasting or such communication thereof is not expressly reserved. Nevertheless, the source must always be clearly indicated; the legal consequences of a breach of this obligation shall be determined by the legislation of the country where protection is claimed.

(2) It shall also be a matter for legislation in the countries of the Union to determine the conditions under which, for the purpose of reporting current events by means of photography, cinematography, broadcasting or communication to the public by wire, literary or artistic works seen or heard in the course of the event may, to the extent justified by the informatory purpose, be reproduced and made available to the public.

Article 11

(1) Authors of dramatic, dramatico-musical and musical works shall enjoy the exclusive right of authorizing:

    (i) the public performance of their works, including such public performance by any means or process;

    (ii) any communication to the public of the performance of their works.

(2)   Authors of dramatic or dramatico-musical works shall enjoy, during the full term of their rights in the original works, the same rights with respect to translations thereof.

Article 11*bis*

(1)   Authors of literary and artistic works shall enjoy the exclusive right of authorizing:

    (i)   the broadcasting of their works or the communication thereof to the public by any other means of wireless diffusion of signs, sounds or images;

    (ii)   any communication to the public by wire or by rebroadcasting of the broadcast of the work, when this communication is made by an organization other than the original one;

    (iii)   the public communication by loudspeaker or any other analogous instrument transmitting, by signs, sounds or images, the broadcast of the work.

(2)   It shall be a matter for legislation in the countries of the Union to determine the conditions under which the rights mentioned in the preceding paragraph may be exercised, but these conditions shall apply only in the countries where they have been prescribed. They shall not in any circumstances be prejudicial to the moral rights of the author, nor to his right to obtain equitable remuneration which, in the absence of agreement, shall be fixed by competent authority.

(3)   In the absence of any contrary stipulation, permission granted in accordance with paragraph (1) of this Article shall not imply permission to record, by means of instruments recording sounds or images, the work broadcast. It shall, however, be a matter for legislation in the countries of the Union to determine the regulations for ephemeral recordings made by a broadcasting organization by means of its own facilities and used for its own broadcasts. The preservation of these recordings in official archives may, on the ground of their exceptional documentary character, be authorized by such legislation.

Article 11*ter*

(1)   Authors of literary works shall enjoy the exclusive right of authorizing:

    (i)   the public recitation of their works, including such public recitation by any means or process;

    (ii)   any communication to the public of the recitation of their works.

(2)   Authors of literary works shall enjoy, during the full term of their rights in the original works, the same rights with respect to translations thereof.

Article 12

Authors of literary or artistic works shall enjoy the exclusive right of authorizing adaptations, arrangements and other alterations of their works.

Article 13

(1)   Each country of the Union may impose for itself reservations and conditions on the exclusive right granted to the author of a musical work and to the author of any words, the recording of which together with the musical work has already been authorized by the latter, to authorize the sound recording of that musical work, together with such

words, if any; but all such reservations and conditions shall apply only in the countries which have imposed them and shall not, in any circumstances, be prejudicial to the rights of these authors to obtain equitable remuneration which, in the absence of agreement, shall be fixed by competent authority.

(2) Recordings of musical works made in a country of the Union in accordance with Article 13(3) of the Conventions signed at Rome on June 2, 1928, and at Brussels on June 26, 1948, may be reproduced in that country without the permission of the author of the musical work until a date two years after that country becomes bound by this Act.

(3) Recordings made in accordance with paragraphs (1) and (2) of this Article and imported without permission from the parties concerned into a country where they are treated as infringing recordings shall be liable to seizure.

Article 14

(1) Authors of literary or artistic works shall have the exclusive right of authorizing:

   (i) the cinematographic adaptation and reproduction of these works, and the distribution of the works thus adapted or reproduced;

   (ii) the public performance and communication to the public by wire of the works thus adapted or reproduced.

(2) The adaptation into any other artistic form of a cinematographic production derived from literary or artistic works shall, without prejudice to the authorization of the author of the cinematographic production, remain subject to the authorization of the authors of the original works.

(3) The provisions of Article 13(1) shall not apply.

Article 14*bis*

(1) Without prejudice to the copyright in any work which may have been adapted or reproduced, a cinematographic work shall be protected as an original work. The owner of copyright in a cinematographic work shall enjoy the same rights as the author of an original work, including the rights referred to in the preceding Article.

(2) (a) Ownership of copyright in a cinematographic work shall be a matter for legislation in the country where protection is claimed.

   (b) However, in the countries of the Union which, by legislation, include among the owners of copyright in a cinematographic work authors who have brought contributions to the making of the work, such authors, if they have undertaken to bring such contributions, may not, in the absence of any contrary or special stipulation, object to the reproduction, distribution, public performance, communication to the public by wire, broadcasting or any other communication to the public, or to the subtitling or dubbing of texts, of the work.

   (c) The question whether or not the form of the undertaking referred to above should, for the application of the preceding subparagraph *(b)*, be in a written agreement or a written act of the same effect shall be a matter for the legislation of the country where the maker of the cinematographic work has his headquarters or habitual residence. However, it shall be a matter for the legislation of the country of the Union where protection is claimed to provide that the said undertaking shall be in a written agreement or a written act of the same effect. The countries whose legislation so provides shall notify the Director General by means of a written declaration, which will be immediately communicated by him to all the other countries of the Union.

(d) By "contrary or special stipulation" is meant any restrictive condition which is relevant to the aforesaid undertaking.

(3) Unless the national legislation provides to the contrary, the provisions of paragraph (2)(b) above shall not be applicable to authors of scenarios, dialogues and musical works created for the making of the cinematographic work, or to the principal director thereof. However, those countries of the Union whose legislation does not contain rules providing for the application of the said paragraph (2)(b) to such director shall notify the Director General by means of a written declaration, which will be immediately communicated by him to all the other countries of the Union.

Article 14*ter*

(1) The author, or after his death the persons or institutions authorized by national legislation, shall, with respect to original works of art and original manuscripts of writers and composers, enjoy the inalienable right to an interest in any sale of the work subsequent to the first transfer by the author of the work.

(2) The protection provided by the preceding paragraph may be claimed in a country of the Union only if legislation in the country to which the author belongs so permits, and to the extent permitted by the country where this protection is claimed.

(3) The procedure for collection and the amounts shall be matters for determination by national legislation.

Article 15

(1) In order that the author of a literary or artistic work protected by this Convention shall, in the absence of proof to the contrary, be regarded as such, and consequently be entitled to institute infringement proceedings in the countries of the Union, it shall be sufficient for his name to appear on the work in the usual manner. This paragraph shall be applicable even if this name is a pseudonym, where the pseudonym adopted by the author leaves no doubt as to his identity.

(2) The person or body corporate whose name appears on a cinematographic work in the usual manner shall, in the absence of proof to the contrary, be presumed to be the maker of the said work.

(3) In the case of anonymous and pseudonymous works, other than those referred to in paragraph (1) above, the publisher whose name appears on the work shall, in the absence of proof to the contrary, be deemed to represent the author, and in this capacity he shall be entitled to protect and enforce the author's rights. The provisions of this paragraph shall cease to apply when the author reveals his identity and establishes his claim to authorship of the work.

(4) (a) In the case of unpublished works where the identity of the author is unknown, but where there is every ground to presume that he is a national of a country of the

Union, it shall be a matter for legislation in that country to designate the competent authority which shall represent the author and shall be entitled to protect and enforce his rights in the countries of the Union.

(b) Countries of the Union which make such designation under the terms of this provision shall notify the Director General by means of a written declaration giving full information concerning the authority thus designated. The Director General shall at once communicate this declaration to all other countries of the Union.

Article 16

(1) Infringing copies of a work shall be liable to seizure in any country of the Union where the work enjoys legal protection.

(2) The provisions of the preceding paragraph shall also apply to reproductions coming from a country where the work is not protected, or has ceased to be protected.

(3) The seizure shall take place in accordance with the legislation of each country.

Article 17

The provisions of this Convention cannot in any way affect the right of the Government of each country of the Union to permit, to control, or to prohibit, by legislation or regulation, the circulation, presentation, or exhibition of any work or production in regard to which the competent authority may find it necessary to exercise that right.

Article 18

(1) This Convention shall apply to all works which, at the moment of its coming into force, have not yet fallen into the public domain in the country of origin through the expiry of the term of protection.

(2) If, however, through the expiry of the term of protection which was previously granted, a work has fallen into the public domain of the country where protection is claimed, that work shall not be protected anew.

(3) The application of this principle shall be subject to any provisions contained in special conventions to that effect existing or to be concluded between countries of the Union. In the absence of such provisions, the respective countries shall determine, each in so far as it is concerned, the conditions of application of this principle.

(4) The preceding provisions shall also apply in the case of new accessions to the Union and to cases in which protection is extended by the application of Article 7 or by the abandonment of reservations.

Article 19

The provisions of this Convention shall not preclude the making of a claim to the benefit of any greater protection which may be granted by legislation in a country of the Union.

Article 20

The Governments of the countries of the Union reserve the right to enter into special agreements among themselves, in so far as such agreements grant to authors more extensive rights than those granted by the Convention, or contain other provisions not contrary to this

Convention. The provisions of existing agreements which satisfy these conditions shall remain applicable.

Article 21

(1) Special provisions regarding developing countries are included in the Appendix.

(2) Subject to the provisions of Article 28(1)(b), the Appendix forms an integral part of this Act.

Article 22

(1) (a) The Union shall have an Assembly consisting of those countries of the Union which are bound by Articles 22 to 26.

(b) The Government of each country shall be represented by one delegate, who may be assisted by alternate delegates, advisors, and experts.

(c) The expenses of each delegation shall be borne by the Government which has appointed it.

(2) (a) The Assembly shall:

    (i) deal with all matters concerning the maintenance and development of the Union and the implementation of this Convention;

    (ii) give directions concerning the preparation for conferences of revision to the International Bureau of Intellectual Property (hereinafter designated as "the International Bureau") referred to in the Convention Establishing the World Intellectual Property Organization (hereinafter designated as "the Organization"), due account being taken of any comments made by those countries of the Union which are not bound by Articles 22 to 26;

    (iii) review and approve the reports and activities of the Director General of the Organization concerning the Union, and give him all necessary instructions concerning matters within the competence of the Union;

    (iv) elect the members of the Executive Committee of the Assembly;

    (v) review and approve the reports and activities of its Executive Committee, and give instructions to such Committee;

    (vi) determine the program and adopt the biennial budget of the Union, and approve its final accounts;

    (vii) adopt the financial regulations of the Union;

    (viii) establish such committees of experts and working groups as may be necessary for the work of the Union;

    (ix) determine which countries not members of the Union and which intergovernmental and international non-governmental organizations shall be admitted to its meetings as observers;

    (x) adopt amendments to Articles 22 to 26;

    (xi) take any other appropriate action designed to further the objectives of the Union;

(xii) exercise such other functions as are appropriate under this Convention;

(xiii) subject to its acceptance, exercise such rights as are given to it in the Convention establishing the Organization.

(b) With respect to matters which are of interest also to other Unions administered by the Organization, the Assembly shall make its decisions after having heard the advice of the Coordination Committee of the Organization.

(3) (a) Each country member of the Assembly shall have one vote.

(b) One-half of the countries members of the Assembly shall constitute a quorum.

(c) Notwithstanding the provisions of subparagraph *(b)*, if, in any session, the number of countries represented is less than one-half but equal to or more than one-third of the countries members of the Assembly, the Assembly may make decisions but, with the exception of decisions concerning its own procedure, all such decisions shall take effect only if the following conditions are fulfilled. The International Bureau shall communicate the said decisions to the countries members of the Assembly which were not represented and shall invite them to express in writing their vote or abstention within a period of three months from the date of the communication. If, at the expiration of this period, the number of countries having thus expressed their vote or abstention attains the number of countries which was lacking for attaining the quorum in the session itself, such decisions shall take effect provided that at the same time the required majority still obtains.

(d) Subject to the provisions of Article 26(2), the decisions of the Assembly shall require two-thirds of the votes cast.

(e) Abstentions shall not be considered as votes.

(f) A delegate may represent, and vote in the name of, one country only.

(g) Countries of the Union not members of the Assembly shall be admitted to its meetings as observers.

(4) (a) The Assembly shall meet once in every second calendar year in ordinary session upon convocation by the Director General and, in the absence of exceptional circumstances, during the same period and at the same place as the General Assembly of the Organization.

(b) The Assembly shall meet in extraordinary session upon convocation by the Director General, at the request of the Executive Committee or at the request of one-fourth of the countries members of the Assembly.

(5) The Assembly shall adopt its own rules of procedure.

Article 23

(1) The Assembly shall have an Executive Committee.

(2) (a) The Executive Committee shall consist of countries elected by the Assembly from among countries members of the Assembly. Furthermore, the country on whose

territory the Organization has its headquarters shall, subject to the provisions of Article 25(7)(b), have an ex officio seat on the Committee.

(b) The Government of each country member of the Executive Committee shall be represented by one delegate, who may be assisted by alternate delegates, advisors, and experts.

(c) The expenses of each delegation shall be borne by the Government which has appointed it.

(3) The number of countries members of the Executive Committee shall correspond to one-fourth of the number of countries members of the Assembly. In establishing the number of seats to be filled, remainders after division by four shall be disregarded.

(4) In electing the members of the Executive Committee, the Assembly shall have due regard to an equitable geographical distribution and to the need for countries party to the Special Agreements which might be established in relation with the Union to be among the countries constituting the Executive Committee.

(5) (a) Each member of the Executive Committee shall serve from the close of the session of the Assembly which elected it to the close of the next ordinary session of the Assembly.

(b) Members of the Executive Committee may be re-elected, but not more than two-thirds of them.

(c) The Assembly shall establish the details of the rules governing the election and possible reelection of the members of the Executive Committee.

(6) (a) The Executive Committee shall:

   (i) prepare the draft agenda of the Assembly;

   (ii) submit proposals to the Assembly respecting the draft program and biennial budget of the Union prepared by the Director General;

   (iii) [*deleted*]

   (iv) submit, with appropriate comments, to the Assembly the periodical reports of the Director General and the yearly audit reports on the accounts;

   (v) in accordance with the decisions of the Assembly and having regard to circumstances arising between two ordinary sessions of the Assembly, take all necessary measures to ensure the execution of the program of the Union by the Director General;

   (vi) perform such other functions as are allocated to it under this Convention.

(b) With respect to matters which are of interest also to other Unions administered by the Organization, the Executive Committee shall make its decisions after having heard the advice of the Coordination Committee of the Organization.

(7) (a) The Executive Committee shall meet once a year in ordinary session upon convocation by the Director General, preferably during the same period and at the same place as the Coordination Committee of the Organization.

(b) The Executive Committee shall meet in extraordinary session upon convocation by the Director General, either on his own initiative, or at the request of its Chairman or one-fourth of its members.

(8) (a) Each country member of the Executive Committee shall have one vote.

(b) One-half of the members of the Executive Committee shall constitute a quorum.

(c) Decisions shall be made by a simple majority of the votes cast.

(d) Abstentions shall not be considered as votes.

(e) A delegate may represent, and vote in the name of, one country only.

(9) Countries of the Union not members of the Executive Committee shall be admitted to its meetings as observers.

(10) The Executive Committee shall adopt its own rules of procedure.

Article 24

(1) (a) The administrative tasks with respect to the Union shall be performed by the International Bureau, which is a continuation of the Bureau of the Union united with the Bureau of the Union established by the International Convention for the Protection of Industrial Property.

(b) In particular, the International Bureau shall provide the secretariat of the various organs of the Union.

(c) The Director General of the Organization shall be the chief executive of the Union and shall represent the Union.

(2) The International Bureau shall assemble and publish information concerning the protection of copyright. Each country of the Union shall promptly communicate to the International Bureau all new laws and official texts concerning the protection of copyright.

(3) The International Bureau shall publish a monthly periodical.

(4) The International Bureau shall, on request, furnish information to any country of the Union on matters concerning the protection of copyright.

(5) The International Bureau shall conduct studies, and shall provide services, designed to facilitate the protection of copyright.

(6) The Director General and any staff member designated by him shall participate, without the right to vote, in all meetings of the Assembly, the Executive Committee and any other committee of experts or working group. The Director General, or a staff member designated by him, shall be ex officio secretary of these bodies.

(7) (a) The International Bureau shall, in accordance with the directions of the Assembly and in cooperation with the Executive Committee, make the preparations for the conferences of revision of the provisions of the Convention other than Articles 22 to 26.

(b) The International Bureau may consult with intergovernmental and international non-governmental organizations concerning preparations for conferences of revision.

(c) The Director General and persons designated by him shall take part, without the right to vote, in the discussions at these conferences.

(8) The International Bureau shall carry out any other tasks assigned to it.

Article 25

(1) (a) The Union shall have a budget.

(b) The budget of the Union shall include the income and expenses proper to the Union, its contribution to the budget of expenses common to the Unions, and, where applicable, the sum made available to the budget of the Conference of the Organization.

(c) Expenses not attributable exclusively to the Union but also to one or more other Unions administered by the Organization shall be considered as expenses common to the Unions. The share of the Union in such common expenses shall be in proportion to the interest the Union has in them.

(2) The budget of the Union shall be established with due regard to the requirements of coordination with the budgets of the other Unions administered by the Organization.

(3) The budget of the Union shall be financed from the following sources:

(i) contributions of the countries of the Union;

(ii) fees and charges due for services performed by the International Bureau in relation to the Union;

(iii) sale of, or royalties on, the publications of the International Bureau concerning the Union;

(iv) gifts, bequests, and subventions;

(v) rents, interests, and other miscellaneous income.

(4) (a) For the purpose of establishing its contribution towards the budget, each country of the Union shall belong to a class, and shall pay its annual contributions on the basis of a number of units fixed as follows:

Class I	25
Class II	20
Class III	15
Class IV	10
Class V	5
Class VI	3
Class VII	1

(b) Unless it has already done so, each country shall indicate, concurrently with depositing its instrument of ratification or accession, the class to which it wishes to belong. Any country may change class. If it chooses a lower class, the country must announce it to the Assembly at one of its ordinary sessions. Any such change shall take effect at the beginning of the calendar year following the session.

(c) The annual contribution of each country shall be an amount in the same proportion to the total sum to be contributed to the annual budget of the Union by all countries as the number of its units is to the total of the units of all contributing countries.

(d) Contributions shall become due on the first of January of each year.

(e) A country which is in arrears in the payment of its contributions shall have no vote in any of the organs of the Union of which it is a member if the amount of its arrears equals or exceeds the amount of the contributions due from it for the preceding two full years. However, any organ of the Union may allow such a country to continue to exercise its vote in that organ if, and as long as, it is satisfied that the delay in payment is due to exceptional and unavoidable circumstances.

(f) If the budget is not adopted before the beginning of a new financial period, it shall be at the same level as the budget of the previous year, in accordance with the financial regulations.

(5) The amount of the fees and charges due for services rendered by the International Bureau in relation to the Union shall be established, and shall be reported to the Assembly and the Executive Committee, by the Director General.

(6) (a) The Union shall have a working capital fund which shall be constituted by a single payment made by each country of the Union. If the fund becomes insufficient, an increase shall be decided by the Assembly.

(b) The amount of the initial payment of each country to the said fund or of its participation in the increase thereof shall be a proportion of the contribution of that country for the year in which the fund is established or the increase decided.

(c) The proportion and the terms of payment shall be fixed by the Assembly on the proposal of the Director General and after it has heard the advice of the Coordination Committee of the Organization.

(7) (a) In the headquarters agreement concluded with the country on the territory of which the Organization has its headquarters, it shall be provided that, whenever the working capital fund is insufficient, such country shall grant advances. The amount of these advances and the conditions on which they are granted shall be the subject of separate agreements, in each case, between such country and the Organization. As long as it remains under the obligation to grant advances, such country shall have an ex officio seat on the Executive Committee.

(b) The country referred to in subparagraph *(a)* and the Organization shall each have the right to denounce the obligation to grant advances, by written notification. Denunciation shall take effect three years after the end of the year in which it has been notified.

(8) The auditing of the accounts shall be effected by one or more of the countries of the Union or by external auditors, as provided in the financial regulations. They shall be designated, with their agreement, by the Assembly.

Article 26

(1) Proposals for the amendment of Articles 22, 23, 24, 25, and the present Article, may be initiated by any country member of the Assembly, by the Executive Committee, or by the Director General. Such proposals shall be communicated by the Director General to the member countries of the Assembly at least six months in advance of their consideration by the Assembly.

(2) Amendments to the Articles referred to in paragraph (1) shall be adopted by the Assembly. Adoption shall require three-fourths of the votes cast, provided that any amendment of Article 22, and of the present paragraph, shall require four-fifths of the votes cast.

(3) Any amendment to the Articles referred to in paragraph (1) shall enter into force one month after written notifications of acceptance, effected in accordance with their respective constitutional processes, have been received by the Director General from three-fourths of the countries members of the Assembly at the time it adopted the amendment. Any amendment to the said Articles thus accepted shall bind all the countries which are members of the Assembly at the time the amendment enters into force, or which become members thereof at a subsequent date, provided that any amendment increasing the financial obligations of countries of the Union shall bind only those countries which have notified their acceptance of such amendment.

Article 27

(1) This Convention shall be submitted to revision with a view to the introduction of amendments designed to improve the system of the Union.

(2) For this purpose, conferences shall be held successively in one of the countries of the Union among the delegates of the said countries.

(3) Subject to the provisions of Article 26 which apply to the amendment of Articles 22 to 26, any revision of this Act, including the Appendix, shall require the unanimity of the votes cast.

Article 28

(1) (a) Any country of the Union which has signed this Act may ratify it, and, if it has not signed it, may accede to it. Instruments of ratification or accession shall be deposited with the Director General.

(b) Any country of the Union may declare in its instrument of ratification or accession that its ratification or accession shall not apply to Articles 1 to 21 and the Appendix, provided that, if such country has previously made a declaration under Article VI(1) of the Appendix, then it may declare in the said instrument only that its ratification or accession shall not apply to Articles 1 to 20.

(c) Any country of the Union which, in accordance with subparagraph (b), has excluded provisions therein referred to from the effects of its ratification or accession may at any later time declare that it extends the effects of its ratification or accession to those provisions. Such declaration shall be deposited with the Director General.

(2) (a) Articles 1 to 21 and the Appendix shall enter into force three months after both of the following two conditions are fulfilled:

    (i) at least five countries of the Union have ratified or acceded to this Act without making a declaration under paragraph (1)(b),

    (ii) France, Spain, the United Kingdom of Great Britain and Northern Ireland, and the United States of America, have become bound by the Universal Copyright Convention as revised at Paris on July 24, 1971.

  (b) The entry into force referred to in subparagraph (a) shall apply to those countries of the Union which, at least three months before the said entry into force, have deposited instruments of ratification or accession not containing a declaration under paragraph (1)(b).

  (c) With respect to any country of the Union not covered by subparagraph (b) and which ratifies or accedes to this Act without making a declaration under paragraph (1)(b), Articles 1 to 21 and the Appendix shall enter into force three months after the date on which the Director General has notified the deposit of the relevant instrument of ratification or accession, unless a subsequent date has been indicated in the instrument deposited. In the latter case, Articles 1 to 21 and the Appendix shall enter into force with respect to that country on the date thus indicated.

  (d) The provisions of subparagraphs (a) to (c) do not affect the application of Article VI of the Appendix.

(3) With respect to any country of the Union which ratifies or accedes to this Act with or without a declaration made under paragraph (1)(b), Articles 22 to 38 shall enter into force three months after the date on which the Director General has notified the deposit of the relevant instrument of ratification or accession, unless a subsequent date has been indicated in the instrument deposited. In the latter case, Articles 22 to 38 shall enter into force with respect to that country on the date thus indicated.

Article 29

(1) Any country outside the Union may accede to this Act and thereby become party to this Convention and a member of the Union. Instruments of accession shall be deposited with the Director General.

(2) (a) Subject to subparagraph (b), this Convention shall enter into force with respect to any country outside the Union three months after the date on which the Director General has notified the deposit of its instrument of accession, unless a subsequent date has been indicated in the instrument deposited. In the latter case, this Convention shall enter into force with respect to that country on the date thus indicated.

  (b) If the entry into force according to subparagraph (a) precedes the entry into force of Articles 1 to 21 and the Appendix according to Article 28(2)(a), the said country shall, in the meantime, be bound, instead of by Articles 1 to 21 and the Appendix, by Articles 1 to 20 of the Brussels Act of this Convention.

Article 29*bis*

Ratification of or accession to this Act by any country not bound by Articles 22 to 38 of the Stockholm Act of this Convention shall, for the sole purposes of Article 14(2) of the Convention establishing the Organization, amount to ratification of or accession to the said Stockholm Act with the limitation set forth in Article 28(1)(b)(i) thereof.

Article 30

(1) Subject to the exceptions permitted by paragraph (2) of this Article, by Article 28(1)(b), by Article 33(2), and by the Appendix, ratification or accession shall automatically entail acceptance of all the provisions and admission to all the advantages of this Convention.

(2) (a) Any country of the Union ratifying or acceding to this Act may, subject to Article V(2) of the Appendix, retain the benefit of the reservations it has previously formulated on condition that it makes a declaration to that effect at the time of the deposit of its instrument of ratification or accession.

(b) Any country outside the Union may declare, in acceding to this Convention and subject to Article V(2) of the Appendix, that it intends to substitute, temporarily at least, for Article 8 of this Act concerning the right of translation, the provisions of Article 5 of the Union Convention of 1886, as completed at Paris in 1896, on the clear understanding that the said provisions are applicable only to translations into a language in general use in the said country. Subject to Article I(6)(b) of the Appendix, any country has the right to apply, in relation to the right of translation of works whose country of origin is a country availing itself of such a reservation, a protection which is equivalent to the protection granted by the latter country.

(c) Any country may withdraw such reservations at any time by notification addressed to the Director General.

Article 31

(1) Any country may declare in its instrument of ratification or accession, or may inform the Director General by written notification at any time thereafter, that this Convention shall be applicable to all or part of those territories, designated in the declaration or notification, for the external relations of which it is responsible.

(2) Any country which has made such a declaration or given such a notification may, at any time, notify the Director General that this Convention shall cease to be applicable to all or part of such territories.

(3) (a) Any declaration made under paragraph (1) shall take effect on the same date as the ratification or accession in which it was included, and any notification given under that paragraph shall take effect three months after its notification by the Director General.

(b) Any notification given under paragraph (2) shall take effect twelve months after its receipt by the Director General.

(4)   This Article shall in no way be understood as implying the recognition or tacit acceptance by a country of the Union of the factual situation concerning a territory to which this Convention is made applicable by another country of the Union by virtue of a declaration under paragraph (1).

Article 32

(1)   This Act shall, as regards relations between the countries of the Union, and to the extent that it applies, replace the Berne Convention of September 9, 1886, and the subsequent Acts of revision. The Acts previously in force shall continue to be applicable, in their entirety or to the extent that this Act does not replace them by virtue of the preceding sentence, in relations with countries of the Union which do not ratify or accede to this Act.

(2)   Countries outside the Union which become party to this Act shall, subject to paragraph (3), apply it with respect to any country of the Union not bound by this Act or which, although bound by this Act, has made a declaration pursuant to Article 28(1)(b). Such countries recognize that the said country of the Union, in its relations with them:

   (i)   may apply the provisions of the most recent Act by which it is bound, and

   (ii)   subject to Article I(6) of the Appendix, has the right to adapt the protection to the level provided for by this Act.

(3)   Any country which has availed itself of any of the faculties provided for in the Appendix may apply the provisions of the Appendix relating to the faculty or faculties of which it has availed itself in its relations with any other country of the Union which is not bound by this Act, provided that the latter country has accepted the application of the said provisions.

Article 33

(1)   Any dispute between two or more countries of the Union concerning the interpretation or application of this Convention, not settled by negotiation, may, by any one of the countries concerned, be brought before the International Court of Justice by application in conformity with the Statute of the Court, unless the countries concerned agree on some other method of settlement. The country bringing the dispute before the Court shall inform the International Bureau; the International Bureau shall bring the matter to the attention of the other countries of the Union.

(2)   Each country may, at the time it signs this Act or deposits its instrument of ratification or accession, declare that it does not consider itself bound by the provisions of paragraph (1). With regard to any dispute between such country and any other country of the Union, the provisions of paragraph (1) shall not apply.

(3)   Any country having made a declaration in accordance with the provisions of paragraph (2) may, at any time, withdraw its declaration by notification addressed to the Director General.

Article 34

(1) Subject to Article 29*bis* no country may ratify or accede to earlier Acts of this Convention once Articles 1 to 21 and the Appendix have entered into force.

(2) Once Articles 1 to 21 and the Appendix have entered into force, no country may make a declaration under Article 5 of the Protocol Regarding Developing Countries attached to the Stockholm Act.

Article 35

(1) This Convention shall remain in force without limitation as to time.

(2) Any country may denounce this Act by notification addressed to the Director General. Such denunciation shall constitute also denunciation of all earlier Acts and shall affect only the country making it, the Convention remaining in full force and effect as regards the other countries of the Union.

(3) Denunciation shall take effect one year after the day on which the Director General has received the notification.

(4) The right of denunciation provided by this Article shall not be exercised by any country before the expiration of five years from the date upon which it becomes a member of the Union.

Article 36

(1) Any country party to this Convention undertakes to adopt, in accordance with its constitution, the measures necessary to ensure the application of this Convention.

(2) It is understood that, at the time a country becomes bound by this Convention, it will be in a position under its domestic law to give effect to the provisions of this Convention.

Article 37

(1) (a) This Act shall be signed in a single copy in the French and English languages and, subject to paragraph (2), shall be deposited with the Director General.

    (b) Official texts shall be established by the Director General, after consultation with the interested Governments, in the Arabic, German, Italian, Portuguese and Spanish languages, and such other languages as the Assembly may designate.

    (c) In case of differences of opinion on the interpretation of the various texts, the French text shall prevail.

(2) This Act shall remain open for signature until January 31, 1972. Until that date, the copy referred to in paragraph (1)*(a)* shall be deposited with the Government of the French Republic.

(3) The Director General shall certify and transmit two copies of the signed text of this Act to the Governments of all countries of the Union and, on request, to the Government of any other country.

(4) The Director General shall register this Act with the Secretariat of the United Nations.

(5) The Director General shall notify the Governments of all countries of the Union of signatures, deposits of instruments of ratification or accession and any declarations

included in such instruments or made pursuant to Articles 28(1)*(c)*, 30(2)*(a)* and *(b)*, and 33(2), entry into force of any provisions of this Act, notifications of denunciation, and notifications pursuant to Articles 30(2)*(c)*, 31(1) and (2), 33(3), and 38(1), as well as the Appendix.

Article 38

(1) Countries of the Union which have not ratified or acceded to this Act and which are not bound by Articles 22 to 26 of the Stockholm Act of this Convention may, until April 26, 1975, exercise, if they so desire, the rights provided under the said Articles as if they were bound by them. Any country desiring to exercise such rights shall give written notification to this effect to the Director General; this notification shall be effective on the date of its receipt. Such countries shall be deemed to be members of the Assembly until the said date.

(2) As long as all the countries of the Union have not become Members of the Organization, the International Bureau of the Organization shall also function as the Bureau of the Union, and the Director General as the Director of the said Bureau.

(3) Once all the countries of the Union have become Members of the Organization, the rights, obligations, and property, of the Bureau of the Union shall devolve on the International Bureau of the Organization.

APPENDIX

Article I

(1) Any country regarded as a developing country in conformity with the established practice of the General Assembly of the United Nations which ratifies or accedes to this Act, of which this Appendix forms an integral part, and which, having regard to its economic situation and its social or cultural needs, does not consider itself immediately in a position to make provision for the protection of all the rights as provided for in this Act, may, by a notification deposited with the Director General at the time of depositing its instrument of ratification or accession or, subject to Article V(1)*(c)*, at any time thereafter, declare that it will avail itself of the faculty provided for in Article II, or of the faculty provided for in Article III, or of both of those faculties. It may, instead of availing itself of the faculty provided for in Article II, make a declaration according to Article V(1)*(a)*.

(2) (a) Any declaration under paragraph (1) notified before the expiration of the period of ten years from the entry into force of Articles 1 to 21 and this Appendix according to Article 28(2) shall be effective until the expiration of the said period. Any such declaration may be renewed in whole or in part for periods of ten years each by a notification deposited with the Director General not more than fifteen months and not less than three months before the expiration of the ten-year period then running.

(b) Any declaration under paragraph (1) notified after the expiration of the period of ten years from the entry into force of Articles 1 to 21 and this Appendix according to Article 28(2) shall be effective until the expiration of the ten-year period then running. Any such declaration may be renewed as provided for in the second sentence of subparagraph *(a)*.

(3) Any country of the Union which has ceased to be regarded as a developing country as referred to in paragraph (1) shall no longer be entitled to renew its declaration as provided in paragraph (2), and, whether or not it formally withdraws its declaration, such country shall be precluded from availing itself of the faculties referred to in paragraph (1) from the expiration of the ten-year period then running or from the expiration of a period of three years after it has ceased to be regarded as a developing country, whichever period expires later.

(4) Where, at the time when the declaration made under paragraph (1) or (2) ceases to be effective, there are copies in stock which were made under a license granted by virtue of this Appendix, such copies may continue to be distributed until their stock is exhausted.

(5) Any country which is bound by the provisions of this Act and which has deposited a declaration or a notification in accordance with Article 31(1) with respect to the application of this Act to a particular territory, the situation of which can be regarded as analogous to that of the countries referred to in paragraph (1), may, in respect of such territory, make the declaration referred to in paragraph (1) and the notification of renewal referred to in paragraph (2). As long as such declaration or notification remains in effect, the provisions of this Appendix shall be applicable to the territory in respect of which it was made.

(6) (a) The fact that a country avails itself of any of the faculties referred to in paragraph (1) does not permit another country to give less protection to works of which the country of origin is the former country than it is obliged to grant under Articles 1 to 20.

(b) The right to apply reciprocal treatment provided for in Article 30(2)(b), second sentence, shall not, until the date on which the period applicable under Article I(3) expires, be exercised in respect of works the country of origin of which is a country which has made a declaration according to Article V(1)(a).

Article II

(1) Any country which has declared that it will avail itself of the faculty provided for in this Article shall be entitled, so far as works published in printed or analogous forms of reproduction are concerned, to substitute for the exclusive right of translation provided for in Article 8 a system of non-exclusive and nontransferable licenses, granted by the competent authority under the following conditions and subject to Article IV.

(2) (a) Subject to paragraph (3), if, after the expiration of a period of three years, or of any longer period determined by the national legislation of the said country, commencing on the date of the first publication of the work, a translation of such work has not been published in a language in general use in that country by the owner of the right of translation, or with his authorization, any national of such country may obtain a license to make a translation of the work in the said language and publish the translation in printed or analogous forms of reproduction.

(b)   A license under the conditions provided for in this Article may also be granted if all the editions of the translation published in the language concerned are out of print.

(3) (a)   In the case of translations into a language which is not in general use in one or more developed countries which are members of the Union, a period of one year shall be substituted for the period of three years referred to in paragraph (2)*(a)*.

(b)   Any country referred to in paragraph (1) may, with the unanimous agreement of the developed countries which are members of the Union and in which the same language is in general use, substitute, in the case of translations into that language, for the period of three years referred to in paragraph (2)*(a)* a shorter period as determined by such agreement but not less than one year. However, the provisions of the foregoing sentence shall not apply where the language in question is English, French or Spanish. The Director General shall be notified of any such agreement by the Governments which have concluded it.

(4) (a)   No license obtainable after three years shall be granted under this Article until a further period of six months has elapsed, and no license obtainable after one year shall be granted under this Article until a further period of nine months has elapsed

(i)   from the date on which the applicant complies with the requirements mentioned in Article IV(1), or

(ii)   where the identity or the address of the owner of the right of translation is unknown, from the date on which the applicant sends, as provided for in Article IV(2), copies of his application submitted to the authority competent to grant the license.

(b)   If, during the said period of six or nine months, a translation in the language in respect of which the application was made is published by the owner of the right of translation or with his authorization, no license under this Article shall be granted.

(5)   Any license under this Article shall be granted only for the purpose of teaching, scholarship or research.

(6)   If a translation of a work is published by the owner of the right of translation or with his authorization at a price reasonably related to that normally charged in the country for comparable works, any license granted under this Article shall terminate if such translation is in the same language and with substantially the same content as the translation published under the license. Any copies already made before the license terminates may continue to be distributed until their stock is exhausted.

(7)   For works which are composed mainly of illustrations, a license to make and publish a translation of the text and to reproduce and publish the illustrations may be granted only if the conditions of Article III are also fulfilled.

(8)   No license shall be granted under this Article when the author has withdrawn from circulation all copies of his work.

(9) (a)   A license to make a translation of a work which has been published in printed or analogous forms of reproduction may also be granted to any broadcasting

organization having its headquarters in a country referred to in paragraph (1), upon an application made to the competent authority of that country by the said organization, provided that all of the following conditions are met:

  (i)   the translation is made from a copy made and acquired in accordance with the laws of the said country;

  (ii) the translation is only for use in broadcasts intended exclusively for teaching or for the dissemination of the results of specialized technical or scientific research to experts in a particular profession;

  (iii) the translation is used exclusively for the purposes referred to in condition (ii) through broadcasts made lawfully and intended for recipients on the territory of the said country, including broadcasts made through the medium of sound or visual recordings lawfully and exclusively made for the purpose of such broadcasts;

  (iv) all uses made of the translation are without any commercial purpose.

(b) Sound or visual recordings of a translation which was made by a broadcasting organization under a license granted by virtue of this paragraph may, for the purposes and subject to the conditions referred to in subparagraph (a) and with the agreement of that organization, also be used by any other broadcasting organization having its headquarters in the country whose competent authority granted the license in question.

(c) Provided that all of the criteria and conditions set out in subparagraph (a) are met, a license may also be granted to a broadcasting organization to translate any text incorporated in an audio-visual fixation where such fixation was itself prepared and published for the sole purpose of being used in connection with systematic instructional activities.

(d) Subject to subparagraphs (a) to (c), the provisions of the preceding paragraphs shall apply to the grant and exercise of any license granted under this paragraph.

Article III

(1) Any country which has declared that it will avail itself of the faculty provided for in this Article shall be entitled to substitute for the exclusive right of reproduction provided for in Article 9 a system of nonexclusive and non-transferable licenses, granted by the competent authority under the following conditions and subject to Article IV.

(2) (a) If, in relation to a work to which this Article applies by virtue of paragraph (7), after the expiration of

  (i)   the relevant period specified in paragraph (3), commencing on the date of first publication of a particular edition of the work, or

  (ii) any longer period determined by national legislation of the country referred to in paragraph (1), commencing on the same date,

copies of such edition have not been distributed in that country to the general public or in connection with systematic instructional activities, by the owner of the right of reproduction or with his authorization, at a price reasonably related to

905

that normally charged in the country for comparable works, any national of such country may obtain a license to reproduce and publish such edition at that or a lower price for use in connection with systematic instructional activities.

(b) A license to reproduce and publish an edition which has been distributed as described in subparagraph *(a)* may also be granted under the conditions provided for in this Article if, after the expiration of the applicable period, no authorized copies of that edition have been on sale for a period of six months in he country concerned to the general public or in connection with systematic instructional activities at a price reasonably related to that normally charged in the country for comparable works.

(3) The period referred to in paragraph (2)(a)(i) shall be five years, except that

(i) for works of the natural and physical sciences, including mathematics, and of technology, the period shall be three years;

(ii) for works of fiction, poetry, drama and music, and for art books, the period shall be seven years.

(4) (a) No license obtainable after three years shall be granted under this Article until a period of six months has elapsed

(i) from the date on which the applicant complies with the requirements mentioned in Article IV(1), or

(ii) where the identity or the address of the owner of the right of reproduction is unknown, from the date on which the applicant sends, as provided for in Article IV(2), copies of his application submitted to the authority competent to grant the license.

(b) Where licenses are obtainable after other periods and Article IV(2) is applicable, no license shall be granted until a period of three months has elapsed from the date of the dispatch of the copies of the application.

(c) If, during the period of six or three months referred to in subparagraphs (a) and (b), a distribution as described in paragraph (2)(a) has taken place, no license shall be granted under this Article.

(d) No license shall be granted if the author has withdrawn from circulation all copies of the edition for the reproduction and publication of which the license has been applied for.

(5) A license to reproduce and publish a translation of a work shall not be granted under this Article in the following cases:

(i) where the translation was not published by the owner of the right of translation or with his authorization, or

(ii) where the translation is not in a language in general use in the country in which the license is applied for.

(6) If copies of an edition of a work are distributed in the country referred to in paragraph (1) to the general public or in connection with systematic instructional activities, by the owner of the right of reproduction or with his authorization, at a

price reasonably related to that normally charged in the country for comparable works, any license granted under this Article shall terminate if such edition is in the same language and with substantially the same content as the edition which was published under the said license. Any copies already made before the license terminates may continue to be distributed until their stock is exhausted.

(7) (a) Subject to subparagraph (b), the works to which this Article applies shall be limited to works published in printed or analogous forms of reproduction.

(b) This Article shall also apply to the reproduction in audio-visual form of lawfully made audiovisual fixations including any protected works incorporated therein and to the translation of any incorporated text into a language in general use in the country in which the license is applied for, always provided that the audio-visual fixations in question were prepared and published for the sole purpose of being used in connection with systematic instructional activities.

Article IV

(1) A license under Article II or Article III may be granted only if the applicant, in accordance with the procedure of the country concerned, establishes either that he has requested, and has been denied, authorization by the owner of the right to make and publish the translation or to reproduce and publish the edition, as the case may be, or that, after due diligence on his part, he was unable to find the owner of the right. At the same time as making the request, the applicant shall inform any national or international information center referred to in paragraph (2).

(2) If the owner of the right cannot be found, the applicant for a license shall send, by registered airmail, copies of his application, submitted to the authority competent to grant the license, to the publisher whose name appears on the work and to any national or international information center which may have been designated, in a notification to that effect deposited with the Director General, by the Government of the country in which the publisher is believed to have his principal place of business.

(3) The name of the author shall be indicated on all copies of the translation or reproduction published under a license granted under Article II or Article III. The title of the work shall appear on all such copies. In the case of a translation, the original title of the work shall appear in any case on all the said copies.

(4) (a) No license granted under Article II or Article III shall extend to the export of copies, and any such license shall be valid only for publication of the translation or of the reproduction, as the case may be, in the territory of the country in which it has been applied for.

(b) For the purposes of subparagraph *(a)*, the notion of export shall include the sending of copies from any territory to the country which, in respect of that territory, has made a declaration under Article I(5).

(c) Where a governmental or other public entity of a country which has granted a license to make a translation under Article II into a language other than English, French or Spanish sends copies of a translation published under such license to another country, such sending of copies shall not, for the purposes of subparagraph *(a)*, be considered to constitute export if all of the following conditions are met:

    (i)   the recipients are individuals who are nationals of the country whose competent authority has granted the license, or organizations grouping such individuals;

    (ii)   the copies are to be used only for the purpose of teaching, scholarship or research;

    (iii)   the sending of the copies and their subsequent distribution to recipients is without any commercial purpose; and

    (iv)   the country to which the copies have been sent has agreed with the country whose competent authority has granted the license to allow the receipt, or distribution, or both, and the Director General has been notified of the agreement by the Government of the country in which the license has been granted.

(5)   All copies published under a license granted by virtue of Article II or Article III shall bear a notice in the appropriate language stating that the copies are available for distribution only in the country or territory to which the said license applies.

(6)   (a)   Due provision shall be made at the national level to ensure

    (i)   that the license provides, in favour of the owner of the right of translation or of reproduction, as the case may be, for just compensation that is consistent with standards of royalties normally operating on licenses freely negotiated between persons in the two countries concerned, and

    (ii)   payment and transmittal of the compensation: should national currency regulations intervene, the competent authority shall make all efforts, by the use of international machinery, to ensure transmittal in internationally convertible currency or its equivalent.

    (b)   Due provision shall be made by national legislation to ensure a correct translation of the work, or an accurate reproduction of the particular edition, as the case may be.

Article V

(1)   (a)   Any country entitled to make a declaration that it will avail itself of the faculty provided for in Article II may, instead, at the time of ratifying or acceding to this Act:

    (i)   if it is a country to which Article 30(2)(a) applies, make a declaration under that provision as far as the right of translation is concerned;

    (ii)   if it is a country to which Article 30(2)(a) does not apply, and even if it is not a country outside the Union, make a declaration as provided for in Article 30(2)(b), first sentence.

    (b)   In the case of a country which ceases to be regarded as a developing country as referred to in Article I(1), a declaration made according to this paragraph shall be effective until the date on which the period applicable under Article I(3) expires.

(c) Any country which has made a declaration according to this paragraph may not subsequently avail itself of the faculty provided for in Article II even if it withdraws the said declaration.

(2) Subject to paragraph (3), any country which has availed itself of the faculty provided for in Article II may not subsequently make a declaration according to paragraph (1).

(3) Any country which has ceased to be regarded as a developing country as referred to in Article I(1) may, not later than two years prior to the expiration of the period applicable under Article I(3), make a declaration to the effect provided for in Article 30(2)(b), first sentence, notwithstanding the fact that it is not a country outside the Union. Such declaration shall take effect at the date on which the period applicable under Article I(3) expires.

Article VI

(1) Any country of the Union may declare, as from the date of this Act, and at any time before becoming bound by Articles 1 to 21 and this Appendix:

   (i) if it is a country which, were it bound by Articles 1 to 21 and this Appendix, would be entitled to avail itself of the faculties referred to in Article I(1), that it will apply the provisions of Article II or of Article III or of both to works whose country of origin is a country which, pursuant to (ii) below, admits the application of those Articles to such works, or which is bound by Articles 1 to 21 and this Appendix; such declaration may, instead of referring to Article II, refer to Article V;

   (ii) that it admits the application of this Appendix to works of which it is the country of origin by countries which have made a declaration under (i) above or a notification under Article I.

(2) Any declaration made under paragraph (1) shall be in writing and shall be deposited with the Director General. The declaration shall become effective from the date of its deposit.

Appendix II

Paris Convention for the Protection of Industrial Property of 20 March 1883

(As revised at Brussels on 14 December 1900, at Washington on 2 June 1911, at the Hague on 6 November 1925, at London on 2 June 1934, at Lisbon on 31 October 1958, and at Stockholm on 14 July 1967, and as amended on 2 October 1979.)

Article 1

[Establishment of the Union; Scope of Industrial Property]')

(1)   The countries to which this Convention applies constitute a Union for the protection of industrial property.

(2)   The protection of industrial property has as its object patents, utility models, industrial designs, trademarks, service marks, trade names, indications of source or appellations of origin, and the repression of unfair competition.

(3)   Industrial property shall be understood in the broadest sense and shall apply not only to industry and commerce proper, but likewise to agricultural and extractive industries and to all manufactured or natural products, for example, wines, grain, tobacco leaf, fruit, cattle, minerals, mineral waters, beer, flowers, and flour.

(4)   Patents shall include the various kinds of industrial patents recognized by the laws of the countries of the Union, such as patents of importation, patents of improvement, patents and certificates of addition, etc.

Article 2

[National Treatment for Nationals of Countries of the Union]

(1)   Nationals of any country of the Union shall, as regards the protection of industrial property, enjoy in all the other countries of the Union the advantages that their respective laws now grant, or may hereafter grant, to nationals; all without prejudice to the rights specially provided for by this Convention. Consequently, they shall have the same protection as the latter, and the same legal remedy against any infringement of their rights, provided that the conditions and formalities imposed upon nationals are complied with.

(2)   However, no requirement as to domicile or establishment in the country where protection is claimed may be imposed upon nationals of countries of the Union for the enjoyment of any industrial property rights.

(3)   The provisions of the laws of each of the countries of the Union relating to judicial and administrative procedure and to jurisdiction, and to the designation of an address for service or the appointment of an agent, which may be required by the laws on industrial property are expressly reserved.

911

Article 3

[Same Treatment for Certain Categories of Persons as for Nationals of Countries of the Union]

Nationals of countries outside the Union who are domiciled or who have real and effective industrial or commercial establishments in the territory of one of the countries of the Union shall be treated in the same manner as nationals of the countries of the Union.

Article 4

[A to I. Patents, Utility Models, Industrial Designs, Marks, Inventors' Certificates: Right of Priority. – G. Patents: Division of the Application]

A.—

(1) Any person who has duly filed an application for a patent, or for the registration of a utility model, or of an industrial design, or of a trademark, in one of the countries of the Union, or his successor in title, shall enjoy, for the purpose of filing in the other countries, a right of priority during the periods hereinafter fixed.

(2) Any filing that is equivalent to a regular national filing under the domestic legislation of any country of the Union or under bilateral or multilateral treaties concluded between countries of the Union shall be recognized as giving rise to the right of priority.

(3) By a regular national filing is meant any filing that is adequate to establish the date on which the application was filed in the country concerned, whatever may be the subsequent fate of the application.

B.—

Consequently, any subsequent filing in any of the other countries of the Union before the expiration of the periods referred to above shall not be invalidated by reason of any acts accomplished in the interval, in particular, another filing, the publication or exploitation of the invention, the putting on sale of copies of the design, or the use of the mark, and such acts cannot give rise to any third–party right or any right of personal possession. Rights acquired by third parties before the date of the first application that serves as the basis for the right of priority are reserved in accordance with the domestic legislation of each country of the Union

C.—

(1) The periods of priority referred to above shall be twelve months for patents and utility models, and six months for industrial designs and trademarks.

(2) These periods shall start from the date of filing of the first application; the day of filing shall not be included in the period.

(3) If the last day of the period is an official holiday, or a day when the Office is not open for the filing of applications in the country where protection is claimed, the period shall be extended until the first following working day.

(4) A subsequent application concerning the same subject as a previous first application within the meaning of paragraph (2), above, filed in the same country of the Union shall

be considered as the first application, of which the filing date shall be the starting point of the period of priority, if, at the time of filing the subsequent application, the said previous application has been withdrawn, abandoned, or refused, without having been laid open to public inspection and without leaving any rights outstanding, and if it has not yet served as a basis for claiming a right of priority. The previous application may not thereafter serve as a basis for claiming a right of priority.

D.—

(1)   Any person desiring to take advantage of the priority of a previous filing shall be required to make a declaration indicating the date of such filing and the country in which it was made. Each country shall determine the latest date on which such declaration must be made.

(2)   These particulars shall be mentioned in the publications issued by the competent authority, and in particular in the patents and the specifications relating thereto.

(3)   The countries of the Union may require any person making a declaration of priority to produce a copy of the application (description, drawings, etc.) previously filed. The copy, certified as correct by the authority which received such application, shall not require any authentication, and may in any case be filed, without fee, at any time within three months of the filing of the subsequent application. They may require it to be accompanied by a certificate from the same authority showing the date of filing, and by a translation.

(4)   No other formalities may be required for the declaration of priority at the time of filing the application. Each country of the Union shall determine the consequences of failure to comply with the formalities prescribed by this Article, but such consequences shall in no case go beyond the loss of the right of priority.

(5)   Subsequently, further proof may be required.

Any person who avails himself of the priority of a previous application shall be required to specify the number of that application; this number shall be published as provided for by paragraph (2), above.

E.—

(1)   Where an industrial design is filed in a country by virtue of a right of priority based on the filing of a utility model, the period of priority shall be the same as that fixed for industrial designs

(2)   Furthermore, it is permissible to file a utility model in a country by virtue of a right of priority based on the filing of a patent application, and vice versa.

F.—

No country of the Union may refuse a priority or a patent application on the ground that the applicant claims multiple priorities, even if they originate in different countries, or on the ground that an application claiming one or more priorities contains one or more elements that were not included in the application or applications whose priority is claimed, provided that, in both cases, there is unity of invention within the meaning of the law of the country.

With respect to the elements not included in the application or applications whose priority is claimed, the filing of the subsequent application shall give rise to a right of priority under ordinary conditions.

G.—

(1) If the examination reveals that an application for a patent contains more than one invention, the applicant may divide the application into a certain number of divisional applications and preserve as the date of each the date of the initial application and the benefit of the right of priority, if any.

(2) The applicant may also, on his own initiative, divide a patent application and preserve as the date of each divisional application the date of the initial application and the benefit of the right of priority, if any. Each country of the Union shall have the right to determine the conditions under which such division shall be authorized.

H. —

Priority may not be refused on the ground that certain elements of the invention for which priority is claimed do not appear among the claims formulated in the application in the country of origin, provided that the application documents as a whole specifically disclose such elements.

I.—

(1) Applications for inventors' certificates filed in a country in which applicants have the right to apply at their own option either for a patent or for an inventor's certificate shall give rise to the right of priority provided for by this Article, under the same conditions and with the same effects as applications for patents.

(2) In a country in which applicants have the right to apply at their own option either for a patent or for an inventor's certificate, an applicant for an inventor's certificate shall, in accordance with the provisions of this Article relating to patent applications, enjoy a right of priority based on an application for a patent, a utility model, or an inventor's certificate.

Article 4*bis*

[Patents: Independence of Patents Obtained for the Same Invention in Different Countries]

(1) Patents applied for in the various countries of the Union by nationals of countries of the Union shall be independent of patents obtained for the same invention in other countries, whether members of the Union or not.

(2) The foregoing provision is to be understood in an unrestricted sense, in particular, in the sense that patents applied for during the period of priority are independent, both as regards the grounds for nullity and forfeiture, and as regards their normal duration.

(3) The provision shall apply to all patents existing at the time when it comes into effect.

(4) Similarly, it shall apply, in the case of the accession of new countries, to patents in existence on either side at the time of accession.

(5)   Patents obtained with the benefit of priority shall, in the various countries of the Union, have a duration equal to that which they would have, had they been applied for or granted without the benefit of priority.

Article 4*ter*

[Patents: Mention of the Inventor in the Patent]

The inventor shall have the right to be mentioned as such in the patent.

Article 4*quater*

[Patents: Patentability in Case of Restrictions of Sale by Law]

The grant of a patent shall not be refused and a patent shall not be invalidated on the ground that the sale of the patented product or of a product obtained by means of a patented process is subject to restrictions or limitations resulting from the domestic law.

Article 5

[A. Patents: Importation of Articles; Failure to Work or Insufficient Working; Compulsory Licenses. —

B. Industrial Designs: Failure to Work; Importation of Articles. —

C. Marks: Failure to Use; Different Forms; Use by Co–proprietors. —

D. Patents, Utility Models, Marks, Industrial Designs: Marking]

A.—

(1)   Importation by the patentee into the country where the patent has been granted of articles manufactured in any of the countries of the Union shall not entail forfeiture of the patent.

(2)   Each country of the Union shall have the right to take legislative measures providing for the grant of compulsory licenses to prevent the abuses which might result from the exercise of the exclusive rights conferred by the patent, for example, failure to work.

(3)   Forfeiture of the patent shall not be provided for except in cases where the grant of compulsory licenses would not have been sufficient to prevent the said abuses. No proceedings for the forfeiture or revocation of a patent may be instituted before the expiration of two years from the grant of the first compulsory license.

(4)   A compulsory license may not be applied for on the ground of failure to work or insufficient working before the expiration of a period of four years from the date of filing of the patent application or three years from the date of the grant of the patent, whichever period expires last; it shall be refused if the patentee justifies his inaction by legitimate reasons. Such a compulsory license shall be non–exclusive and shall not be transferable, even in the form of the grant of a sub–license, except with that part of the enterprise or goodwill which exploits such license.

(5)   The foregoing provisions shall be applicable, mutatis mutandis, to utility models.

B. —

The protection of industrial designs shall not, under any circumstance, be subject to any forfeiture, either by reason of failure to work or by reason of the importation of articles corresponding to those which are protected.

C.—

(1) If, in any country, use of the registered mark is compulsory, the registration may be cancelled only after a reasonable period, and then only if the person concerned does not justify his inaction.

(2) Use of a trademark by the proprietor in a form differing in elements which do not alter the distinctive character of the mark in the form in which it was registered in one of the countries of the Union shall not entail invalidation of the registration and shall not diminish the protection granted to the mark.

(3) Concurrent use of the same mark on identical or similar goods by industrial or commercial establishments considered as co–proprietors of the mark according to the provisions of the domestic law of the country where protection is claimed shall not prevent registration or diminish in any way the protection granted to the said mark in any country of the Union, provided that such use does not result in misleading the public and is not contrary to the public interest.

D. —

No indication or mention of the patent, of the utility model, of the registration of the trademark, or of the deposit of the industrial design, shall be required upon the goods as a condition of recognition of the right to protection.

Article 5*bis*

[All Industrial Property Rights: Period of Grace for the Payment of Fees for the Maintenance of Rights; Patents: Restoration]

(1) A period of grace of not less than six months shall be allowed for the payment of the fees prescribed for the maintenance of industrial property rights, subject, if the domestic legislation so provides, to the payment of a surcharge.

(2) The countries of the Union shall have the right to provide for the restoration of patents which have lapsed by reason of non–payment of fees.

Article 5*ter*

[Patents: Patented Devices Forming Part of Vessels, Aircraft, or Land Vehicles]

In any country of the Union the following shall not be considered as infringements of the rights of a patentee:

1. the use on board vessels of other countries of the Union of devices forming the subject of his patent in the body of the vessel, in the machinery, tackle, gear and other accessories, when such vessels temporarily or accidentally enter the waters of the said country, provided that such devices are used there exclusively for the needs of the vessel;

2. the use of devices forming the subject of the patent in the construction or operation of aircraft or land vehicles of other countries of the Union, or of accessories of such aircraft or land vehicles, when those aircraft or land vehicles temporarily or accidentally enter the said country.

Article 5*quater*

[Patents: Importation of Products Manufactured by a Process Patented in the Importing Country]

When a product is imported into a country of the Union where there exists a patent protecting a process of manufacture of the said product, the patentee shall have all the rights, with regard to the imported product, that are accorded to him by the legislation of the country of importation, on the basis of the process patent, with respect to products manufactured in that country.

Article 5*quinquies*

[Industrial Designs]

Industrial designs shall be protected in all the countries of the Union.

Article 6

[Marks: Conditions of Registration; Independence of Protection of Same Mark in Different Countries]

(1) The conditions for the filing and registration of trademarks shall be determined in each country of the Union by its domestic legislation.

(2) However, an application for the registration of a mark filed by a national of a country of the Union in any country of the Union may not be refused, nor may a registration be invalidated, on the ground that filing, registration, or renewal, has not been effected in the country of origin.

(3) A mark duly registered in a country of the Union shall be regarded as independent of marks registered in the other countries of the Union, including the country of origin.

Article 6*bis*

[Marks: Well–Known Marks]

(1) The countries of the Union undertake, ex officio if their legislation so permits, or at the request of an interested party, to refuse or to cancel the registration, and to prohibit the use, of a trademark which constitutes a reproduction, an imitation, or a translation, liable to create confusion, of a mark considered by the competent authority of the country of registration or use to be well known in that country as being already the mark of a person entitled to the benefits of this Convention and used for identical or similar goods. These provisions shall also apply when the essential part of the mark constitutes a reproduction of any such well–known mark or an imitation liable to create confusion therewith.

(2) A period of at least five years from the date of registration shall be allowed for requesting the cancellation of such a mark. The countries of the Union may provide for a period within which the prohibition of use must be requested.

(3) No time limit shall be fixed for requesting the cancellation or the prohibition of the use of marks registered or used in bad faith.

Article 6*ter*

[Marks: Prohibitions concerning State Emblems, Official Hallmarks, and Emblems of Intergovernmental Organizations]

(1) (a) The countries of the Union agree to refuse or to invalidate the registration, and to prohibit by appropriate measures the use, without authorization by the competent authorities, either as trademarks or as elements of trademarks, of armorial bearings, flags, and other State emblems, of the countries of the Union, official signs and hallmarks indicating control and warranty adopted by them, and any imitation from a heraldic point of view.

(b) The provisions of subparagraph (a), above, shall apply equally to armorial bearings, flags, other emblems, abbreviations, and names, of international intergovernmental organizations of which one or more countries of the Union are members, with the exception of armorial bearings, flags, other emblems, abbreviations, and names, that are already the subject of international agreements in force, intended to ensure their protection.

(c) No country of the Union shall be required to apply the provisions of subparagraph (b), above, to the prejudice of the owners of rights acquired in good faith before the entry into force, in that country, of this Convention. The countries of the Union shall not be required to apply the said provisions when the use or registration referred to in subparagraph (a), above, is not of such a nature as to suggest to the public that a connection exists between the organization concerned and the armorial bearings, flags, emblems, abbreviations, and names, or if such use or registration is probably not of such a nature as to mislead the public as to the existence of a connection between the user and the organization.

(2) Prohibition of the use of official signs and hallmarks indicating control and warranty shall apply solely in cases where the marks in which they are incorporated are intended to be used on goods of the same or a similar kind.

(3) (a) For the application of these provisions, the countries of the Union agree to communicate reciprocally, through the intermediary of the International Bureau, the list of State emblems, and official signs and hallmarks indicating control and warranty, which they desire, or may hereafter desire, to place wholly or within certain limits under the protection of this Article, and all subsequent modifications of such list. Each country of the Union shall in due course make available to the public the lists so communicated. Nevertheless such communication is not obligatory in respect of flags of States.

(b) The provisions of subparagraph (b) of paragraph (1) of this Article shall apply only to such armorial bearings, flags, other emblems, abbreviations, and names, of international intergovernmental organizations as the latter have communicated to the countries of the Union through the intermediary of the International Bureau.

(4)   Any country of the Union may, within a period of twelve months from the receipt of the notification, transmit its objections, if any, through the intermediary of the International Bureau, to the country or international intergovernmental organization concerned.

(5)   In the case of State flags, the measures prescribed by paragraph (1), above, shall apply solely to marks registered after November 6, 1925.

(6)   In the case of State emblems other than flags, and of official signs and hallmarks of the countries of the Union, and in the case of armorial bearings, flags, other emblems, abbreviations, and names, of international intergovernmental organizations, these provisions shall apply only to marks registered more than two months after receipt of the communication provided for in paragraph (3), above.

(7)   In cases of bad faith, the countries shall have the right to cancel even those marks incorporating State emblems, signs, and hallmarks, which were registered before November 6, 1925.

(8)   Nationals of any country who are authorized to make use of the State emblems, signs, and hallmarks, of their country may use them even if they are similar to those of another country.

(9)   The countries of the Union undertake to prohibit the unauthorized use in trade of the State armorial bearings of the other countries of the Union, when the use is of such a nature as to be misleading as to the origin of the goods.

(10)   The above provisions shall not prevent the countries from exercising the right given in paragraph (3) of Article 6*quinquies*, Section B, to refuse or to invalidate the registration of marks incorporating, without authorization, armorial bearings, flags, other State emblems, or official signs and hallmarks adopted by a country of the Union, as well as the distinctive signs of international intergovernmental organizations referred to in paragraph (1), above.

Article 6*quater*

[Marks: Assignment of Marks]

(1)   When, in accordance with the law of a country of the Union, the assignment of a mark is valid only if it takes place at the same time as the transfer of the business or goodwill to which the mark belongs, it shall suffice for the recognition of such validity that the portion of the business or goodwill located in that country be transferred to the assignee, together with the exclusive right to manufacture in the said country, or to sell therein, the goods bearing the mark assigned.

(2)   The foregoing provision does not impose upon the countries of the Union any obligation to regard as valid the assignment of any mark the use of which by the assignee would, in fact, be of such a nature as to mislead the public, particularly as regards the origin, nature, or essential qualities, of the goods to which the mark is applied.

Article 6*quinquies*

*[Marks: Protection of Marks Registered in One Country of
the Union in the Other Countries of the Union]*

A.—

(1)　Every trademark duly registered in the country of origin shall be accepted for filing and protected as is in the other countries of the Union, subject to the reservations indicated in this Article. Such countries may, before proceeding to final registration, require the production of a certificate of registration in the country of origin, issued by the competent authority. No authentication shall be required for this certificate.

(2)　Shall be considered the country of origin the country of the Union where the applicant has a real and effective industrial or commercial establishment, or, if he has no such establishment within the Union, the country of the Union where he has his domicile, or, if he has no domicile within the Union but is a national of a country of the Union, the country of which he is a national.

B. —

Trademarks covered by this Article may be neither denied registration nor invalidated except in the following cases:

1.　when they are of such a nature as to infringe rights acquired by third parties in the country where protection is claimed;

2.　when they are devoid of any distinctive character, or consist exclusively of signs or indications which may serve, in trade, to designate the kind, quality, quantity, intended purpose, value, place of origin, of the goods, or the time of production, or have become customary in the current language or in the bona fide and established practices of the trade of the country where protection is claimed;

3.　when they are contrary to morality or public order and, in particular, of such a nature as to deceive the public. It is understood that a mark may not be considered contrary to public order for the sole reason that it does not conform to a provision of the legislation on marks, except if such provision itself relates to public order.

This provision is subject, however, to the application of Article 10*bis*.

C.—

(1)　In determining whether a mark is eligible for protection, all the factual circumstances must be taken into consideration, particularly the length of time the mark has been in use.

(2)　No trademark shall be refused in the other countries of the Union for the sole reason that it differs from the mark protected in the country of origin only in respect of elements that do not alter its distinctive character and do not affect its identity in the form in which it has been registered in the said country of origin.

D. —

No person may benefit from the provisions of this Article if the mark for which he claims protection is not registered in the country of origin.

E. —

However, in no case shall the renewal of the registration of the mark in the country of origin involve an obligation to renew the registration in the other countries of the Union in which the mark has been registered.

F. —

The benefit of priority shall remain unaffected for applications for the registration of marks filed within the period fixed by Article 4, even if registration in the country of origin is effected after the expiration of such period.

Article 6*sexies*

[Marks: Service Marks]

The countries of the Union undertake to protect service marks. They shall not be required to provide for the registration of such marks.

Article 6*septies*

[Marks: Registration in the Name of the Agent or Representative of the Proprietor Without the Latter's Authorization]

(1)   If the agent or representative of the person who is the proprietor of a mark in one of the countries of the Union applies, without such proprietor's authorization, for the registration of the mark in his own name, in one or more countries of the Union, the proprietor shall be entitled to oppose the registration applied for or demand its cancellation or, if the law of the country so allows, the assignment in his favor of the said registration, unless such agent or representative justifies his action.

(2)   The proprietor of the mark shall, subject to the provisions of paragraph (1), above, be entitled to oppose the use of his mark by his agent or representative if he has not authorized such use.

(3)   Domestic legislation may provide an equitable time limit within which the proprietor of a mark must exercise the rights provided for in this Article.

Article 7

[Marks: Nature of the Goods to which the Mark is Applied]

The nature of the goods to which a trademark is to be applied shall in no case form an obstacle to the registration of the mark.

Article 7*bis*

[Marks: Collective Marks]

(1)   The countries of the Union undertake to accept for filing and to protect collective marks belonging to associations the existence of which is not contrary to the law of the

country of origin, even if such associations do not possess an industrial or commercial establishment.

(2)   Each country shall be the judge of the particular conditions under which a collective mark shall be protected and may refuse protection if the mark is contrary to the public interest.

(3)   Nevertheless, the protection of these marks shall not be refused to any association the existence of which is not contrary to the law of the country of origin, on the ground that such association is not established in the country where protection is sought or is not constituted according to the law of the latter country.

Article 8

[Trade Names]

A trade name shall be protected in all the countries of the Union without the obligation of filing or registration, whether or not it forms part of a trademark.

Article 9

[Marks, Trade Names: Seizure, on Importation, etc., of Goods Unlawfully Bearing a Mark or Trade Name]

(1)   All goods unlawfully bearing a trademark or trade name shall be seized on importation into those countries of the Union where such mark or trade name is entitled to legal protection.

(2)   Seizure shall likewise be effected in the country where the unlawful affixation occurred or in the country into which the goods were imported.

(3)   Seizure shall take place at the request of the public prosecutor, or any other competent authority, or any interested party, whether a natural person or a legal entity, in conformity with the domestic legislation of each country.

(4)   The authorities shall not be bound to effect seizure of goods in transit.

(5)   If the legislation of a country does not permit seizure on importation, seizure shall be replaced by prohibition of importation or by seizure inside the country.

(6)   If the legislation of a country permits neither seizure on importation nor prohibition of importation nor seizure inside the country, then, until such time as the legislation is modified accordingly, these measures shall be replaced by the actions and remedies available in such cases to nationals under the law of such country.

Article 10

[False Indications: Seizure, on Importation, etc., of Goods Bearing False Indications as to their Source or the Identity of the Producer]

(1)   The provisions of the preceding Article shall apply in cases of direct or indirect use of a false indication of the source of the goods or the identity of the producer, manufacturer, or merchant.

(2)   Any producer, manufacturer, or merchant, whether a natural person or a legal entity, engaged in the production or manufacture of or trade in such goods and established either in the locality falsely indicated as the source, or in the region where such

locality is situated, or in the country falsely indicated, or in the country where the false indication of source is used, shall in any case be deemed an interested party.

Article 10*bis*

[Unfair Competition]

(1) The countries of the Union are bound to assure to nationals of such countries effective protection against unfair competition.

(2) Any act of competition contrary to honest practices in industrial or commercial matters constitutes an act of unfair competition.

(3) The following in particular shall be prohibited:

1. all acts of such a nature as to create confusion by any means whatever with the establishment, the goods, or the industrial or commercial activities, of a competitor;

2. false allegations in the course of trade of such a nature as to discredit the establishment, the goods, or the industrial or commercial activities, of a competitor;

3. indications or allegations the use of which in the course of trade is liable to mislead the public as to the nature, the manufacturing process, the characteristics, the suitability for their purpose, or the quantity, of the goods.

Article 10*ter*

[Marks, Trade Names, False Indications, Unfair Competition: Remedies, Right to Sue]

(1) The countries of the Union undertake to assure to nationals of the other countries of the Union appropriate legal remedies effectively to repress all the acts referred to in Articles 9, 10, and 10[bis].

(2) They undertake, further, to provide measures to permit federations and associations representing interested industrialists, producers, or merchants, provided that the existence of such federations and associations is not contrary to the laws of their countries, to take action in the courts or before the administrative authorities, with a view to the repression of the acts referred to in Articles 9, 10, and 10[bis], in so far as the law of the country in which protection is claimed allows such action by federations and associations of that country.

Article 11

[Inventions, Utility Models, Industrial Designs, Marks: Temporary Protection at Certain International Exhibitions]

(1) The countries of the Union shall, in conformity with their domestic legislation, grant temporary protection to patentable inventions, utility models, industrial designs, and trademarks, in respect of goods exhibited at official or officially recognized international exhibitions held in the territory of any of them.

(2) Such temporary protection shall not extend the periods provided by Article 4. If, later, the right of priority is invoked, the authorities of any country may provide that the period shall start from the date of introduction of the goods into the exhibition.

(3)   Each country may require, as proof of the identity of the article exhibited and of the date of its introduction, such documentary evidence as it considers necessary.

Article 12

[Special National Industrial Property Services]

(1)   Each country of the Union undertakes to establish a special industrial property service and a central office for the communication to the public of patents, utility models, industrial designs, and trademarks.

(2)   This service shall publish an official periodical journal. It shall publish regularly:

(a)   the names of the proprietors of patents granted, with a brief designation of the inventions patented;

(b)   the reproductions of registered trademarks.

Article 13

[Assembly of the Union]

(1)   (a)   The Union shall have an Assembly consisting of those countries of the Union which are bound by Articles 13 to 17.

(b)   The Government of each country shall be represented by one delegate, who may be assisted by alternate delegates, advisors, and experts.

(c)   The expenses of each delegation shall be borne by the Government which has appointed it.

(2)   (a)   The Assembly shall:

(i)   deal with all matters concerning the maintenance and development of the Union and the implementation of this Convention;

(ii)   give directions concerning the preparation for conferences of revision to the International Bureau of Intellectual Property (hereinafter designated as "the International Bureau") referred to in the Convention establishing the World Intellectual Property Organization (hereinafter designated as "the Organization"), due account being taken of any comments made by those countries of the Union which are not hound by Articles 13 to 17;

(iii)   review and approve the reports and activities of the Director General of the Organization concerning the Union, and give him all necessary instructions concerning matters within the competence of the Union;

(iv)   elect the members of the Executive Committee of the Assembly;

(v)   review and approve the reports and activities of its Executive Committee, and give instructions to such Committee;

(vi)   determine the program and adopt the biennial budget of the Union, and approve its final accounts;

(vii)   adopt the financial regulations of the Union;

(viii)　establish such committees of experts and working groups as it deems appropriate to achieve the objectives of the Union;

(ix)　determine which countries not members of the Union and which intergovernmental and international nongovernmental organizations shall be admitted to its meetings as observers;

(x)　adopt amendments to Articles 13 to 17;

(xi)　take any other appropriate action designed to further the objectives of the Union;

(xii)　perform such other functions as are appropriate under this Convention;

(xiii)　subject to its acceptance, exercise such rights as are given to it in the Convention establishing the Organization.

(b)　With respect to matters which are of interest also to other Unions administered by the Organization, the Assembly shall make its decisions after having heard the advice of the Coordination Committee of the Organization.

(3)　(a)　Subject to the provisions of subparagraph (b), a delegate may represent one country only.

(b)　Countries of the Union grouped under the terms of a special agreement in a common office possessing for each of them the character of a special national service of industrial property as referred to in Article 12 may be jointly represented during discussions by one of their number.

(4)　(a)　Each country member of the Assembly shall have one vote.

(b)　One–half of the countries members of the Assembly shall constitute a quorum.

(c)　Notwithstanding the provisions of subparagraph (b), if, in any session, the number of countries represented is less than one–half but equal to or more than one–third of the countries members of the Assembly, the Assembly may make decisions but, with the exception of decisions concerning its own procedure, all such decisions shall take effect only if the conditions, set forth hereinafter are fulfilled. The International Bureau shall communicate the said decisions to the countries members of the Assembly which were not represented and shall invite them to express in writing their vote or abstention within a period of three months from the date of the communication. If, at the expiration of this period, the number of countries having thus expressed their vote or abstention attains the number of countries which was lacking for attaining the quorum in the session itself, such decisions shall take effect provided that at the same time the required majority still obtains.

(d)　Subject to the provisions of Article 17(2), the decisions of the Assembly shall require two– thirds of the votes cast.

(e)　Abstentions shall not be considered as votes.

(5)　(a)　Subject to the provisions of subparagraph (b), a delegate may vote in the name of one country only.

(b) The countries of the Union referred to in paragraph (3)(b) shall, as a general rule, endeavor to send their own delegations to the sessions of the Assembly. If, however, for exceptional reasons, any such country cannot send its own delegation, it may give to the delegation of another such country the power to vote in its name, provided that each delegation may vote by proxy for one country only. Such power to vote shall be granted in a document signed by the Head of State or the competent Minister.

(6) Countries of the Union not members of the Assembly shall be admitted to the meetings of the latter as observers.

(7) (a) The Assembly shall meet once in every second calendar year in ordinary session upon convocation by the Director General and, in the absence of exceptional circumstances, during the same period and at the same place as the General Assembly of the Organization.

(b) The Assembly shall meet in extraordinary session upon convocation by the Director General, at the request of the Executive Committee or at the request of one–fourth of the countries members of the Assembly.

(8) The Assembly shall adopt its own rules of procedure.

Article 14

[Executive Committee]

(1) The Assembly shall have an Executive Committee.

(2) (a) The Executive Committee shall consist of countries elected by the Assembly from among countries members of the Assembly. Furthermore, the country on whose territory the Organization has its headquarters shall, subject to the provisions of Article 16(7)(b), have an ex officio seat on the Committee.

(b) The Government of each country member of the Executive Committee shall be represented by one delegate, who may be assisted by alternate delegates, advisors, and experts.

(c) The expenses of each delegation shall be borne by the Government which has appointed it.

(3) The number of countries members of the Executive Committee shall correspond to one–fourth of the number of countries members of the Assembly. In establishing the number of seats to be filled, remainders after division by four shall be disregarded.

(4) In electing the members of the Executive Committee, the Assembly shall have due regard to an equitable geographical distribution and to the need for countries party to the Special Agreements established in relation with the Union to be among the countries constituting the Executive Committee.

(5) (a) Each member of the Executive Committee shall serve from the close of the session of the Assembly which elected it to the close of the next ordinary session of the Assembly.

(b) Members of the Executive Committee may be re–elected, but only up to a maximum of two–thirds of such members.

(c) The Assembly shall establish the details of the rules governing the election and possible re– election of the members of the Executive Committee.

(6) (a) The Executive Committee shall:

    (i) prepare the draft agenda of the Assembly;

    (ii) submit proposals to the Assembly in respect of the draft program and biennial budget of the Union prepared by the Director General;

    (iii) [deleted]

    (iv) submit, with appropriate comments, to the Assembly the periodical reports of the Director General and the yearly audit reports on the accounts;

    (v) take all necessary measures to ensure the execution of the program of the Union by the Director General, in accordance with the decisions of the Assembly and having regard to circumstances arising between two ordinary sessions of the Assembly;

    (vi) perform such other functions as are allocated to it under this Convention.

(b) With respect to matters which are of interest also to other Unions administered by the Organization, the Executive Committee shall make its decisions after having heard the advice of the Coordination Committee of the Organization.

(7) (a) The Executive Committee shall meet once a year in ordinary session upon convocation by the Director General, preferably during the same period and at the same place as the Coordination Committee of the Organization.

(b) The Executive Committee shall meet in extraordinary session upon convocation by the Director General, either on his own initiative, or at the request of its Chairman or one–fourth of its members.

(8) (a) Each country member of the Executive Committee shall have one vote.

(b) One–half of the members of the Executive Committee shall constitute a quorum.

(c) Decisions shall be made by a simple majority of the votes cast.

(d) Abstentions shall not be considered as votes.

(e) A delegate may represent, and vote in the name of, one country only.

(9) Countries of the Union not members of the Executive Committee shall be admitted to its meetings as observers.

(10) The Executive Committee shall adopt its own rules of procedure.

Article 15

[International Bureau]

(1) (a) Administrative tasks concerning the Union shall be performed by the International Bureau, which is a continuation of the Bureau of the Union united with the Bureau of the Union established by the International Convention for the Protection of Literary and Artistic Works.

(b) In particular, the International Bureau shall provide the secretariat of the various organs of the Union.

(c) The Director General of the Organization shall be the chief executive of the Union and shall represent the Union.

(2) The International Bureau shall assemble and publish information concerning the protection of industrial property. Each country of the Union shall promptly communicate to the International Bureau all new laws and official texts concerning the protection of industrial property. Furthermore, it shall furnish the International Bureau with all the publications of its industrial property service of direct concern to the protection of industrial property which the International Bureau may find useful in its work.

(3) The International Bureau shall publish a monthly periodical.

(4) The International Bureau shall, on request, furnish any country of the Union with information on matters concerning the protection of industrial property.

(5) The International Bureau shall conduct Studies, and shall provide services, designed to facilitate the protection of industrial property.

(6) The Director General and any staff member designated by him shall participate, without the right to vote, in all meetings of the Assembly, the Executive Committee, and any other committee of experts or working group. The Director General, or a staff member designated by him, shall be ex officio secretary of these bodies.

(7) (a) The International Bureau shall, in accordance with the directions of the Assembly and in cooperation with the Executive Committee, make the preparations for the conferences of revision of the provisions of the Convention other than Articles 13 to 17.

(b) The International Bureau may consult with intergovernmental and international non–governmental organizations concerning preparations for conferences of revision.

(c) The Director General and persons designated by him shall take part, without the right to vote, in the discussions at these conferences.

(8) The International Bureau shall carry out any other tasks assigned to it.

Article 16

[Finances]

(1) (a) The Union shall have a budget.

(b) The budget of the Union shall include the income and expenses proper to the Union, its contribution to the budget of expenses common to the Unions, and, where applicable, the sum made available to the budget of the Conference of the Organization.

(c) Expenses not attributable exclusively to the Union but also to one or more other Unions administered by the Organization shall be considered as expenses common to the Unions. The share of the Union in such common expenses shall be in proportion to the interest the Union has in them.

(2)   The budget of the Union shall be established with due regard to the requirements of coordination with the budgets of the other Unions administered by the Organization.

(3)   The budget of the Union shall be financed from the following sources:

    (i)   contributions of the countries of the Union;

    (ii)   fees and charges due for services rendered by the International Bureau in relation to the Union;

    (iii)   sale of, or royalties on, the publications of the International Bureau concerning the Union;

    (iv)   gifts, bequests, and subventions;

    (v)   rents, interests, and other miscellaneous income.

(4)   (a)   For the purpose of establishing its contribution towards the budget, each country of the Union shall belong to a class, and shall pay its annual contributions on the basis of a number of units fixed as follows:

Class I	25
Class II	20
Class III	15
Class IV	10
Class V	5
Class VI	3
Class VII	1

    (b)   Unless it has already done so, each country shall indicate, concurrently with depositing its instrument of ratification or accession, the class to which it wishes to belong. Any country may change class. If it chooses a lower class, the country must announce such change to the Assembly at one of its ordinary sessions. Any such change shall take effect at the beginning of the calendar year following the said session.

    (c)   The annual contribution of each country shall be an amount in the same proportion to the total sum to be contributed to the budget of the Union by all countries as the number of its units is to the total of the units of all contributing countries.

    (d)   Contributions shall become due on the first of January of each year.

    (e)   A country which is in arrears in the payment of its contributions may not exercise its right to vote in any of the organs of the Union of which it is a member if the amount of its arrears equals or exceeds the amount of the contributions due from it for the preceding two full years. However, any organ of the Union may allow such a country to continue to exercise its right to vote in that organ if, and as long as, it is satisfied that the delay in payment is due to exceptional and unavoidable circumstances.

(f) If the budget is not adopted before the beginning of a new financial period, it shall be at the same level as the budget of the previous year, as provided in the financial regulations.

(5) The amount of the fees and charges due for services rendered by the International Bureau in relation to the Union shall be established, and shall be reported to the Assembly and the Executive Committee, by the Director General.

(6) (a) The Union shall have a working capital fund which shall be constituted by a single payment made by each country of the Union. If the fund becomes insufficient, the Assembly shall decide to increase it.

(b) The amount of the initial payment of each country to the said fund or of its participation in the increase thereof shall be a proportion of the contribution of that country for the year in which the fund is established or the decision to increase it is made.

(c) The proportion and the terms of payment shall be fixed by the Assembly on the proposal of the Director General and after it has heard the advice of the Coordination Committee of the Organization.

(7) (a) In the headquarters agreement concluded with the country on the territory of which the Organization has its headquarters, it shall be provided that, whenever the working capital fund is insufficient, such country shall grant advances. The amount of these advances and the conditions on which they are granted shall be the subject of separate agreements, in each case, between such country and the Organization. As long as it remains under the obligation to grant advances, such country shall have an ex officio seat on the Executive Committee.

(b) The country referred to in subparagraph (a) and the Organization shall each have the right to denounce the obligation to grant advances, by written notification. Denunciation shall take effect three years after the end of the year in which it has been notified.

(8) The auditing of the accounts shall be effected by one or more of the countries of the Union or by external auditors, as provided in the financial regulations. They shall be designated, with their agreement, by the Assembly.

Article 17

[Amendment of Articles 13 to 17]

(1) Proposals for the amendment of Articles 13, 14, 15, 16, and the present Article, may be initiated by any country member of the Assembly, by the Executive Committee, or by the Director General. Such proposals shall be communicated by the Director General to the member countries of the Assembly at least six months in advance of their consideration by the Assembly.

(2) Amendments to the Articles referred to in paragraph (1) shall be adopted by the Assembly. Adoption shall require three–fourths of the votes cast, provided that any amendment to Article 13, and to the present paragraph, shall require four–fifths of the votes cast.

(3) Any amendment to the Articles referred to in paragraph (1) shall enter into force one month after written notifications of acceptance, effected in accordance with their respective constitutional processes, have been received by the Director General from three–fourths of the countries members of the Assembly at the time it adopted the amendment. Any amendment to the said Articles thus accepted shall bind all the countries which are members of the Assembly at the time the amendment enters into force, or which become members thereof at a subsequent date, provided that any amendment increasing the financial obligations of countries of the Union shall bind only those countries which have notified their acceptance of such amendment.

Article 18

[Revision of Articles 1 to 12 and 18 to 30]

(1) This Convention shall be submitted to revision with a view to the introduction of amendments designed to improve the system of the Union.

(2) For that purpose, conferences shall be held successively in one of the countries of the Union among the delegates of the said countries.

(3) Amendments to Articles 13 to 17 are governed by the provisions of Article 17.

Article 19

[Special Agreements]

It is understood that the countries of the Union reserve the right to make separately between themselves special agreements for the protection of industrial property, in so far as these agreements do not contravene the provisions of this Convention.

Article 20

[Ratification or Accession by Countries of the Union; Entry Into Force]

(1) (a) Any country of the Union which has signed this Act may ratify it, and, if it has not signed it, may accede to it. Instruments of ratification and accession shall be deposited with the Director General.

   (b) Any country of the Union may declare in its instrument of ratification or accession that its ratification or accession shall not apply:

   (i)   to Articles 1 to 12, or

   (ii) to Articles 13 to 17.

   (c) Any country of the Union which, in accordance with subparagraph (b), has excluded from the effects of its ratification or accession one of the two groups of Articles referred to in that subparagraph may at any later time declare that it extends the effects of its ratification or accession to that group of Articles. Such declaration shall be deposited with the Director General.

(2) (a) Articles 1 to 12 shall enter into force, with respect to the first ten countries of the Union which have deposited instruments of ratification or accession without making the declaration permitted under paragraph (1)(b)(i), three months after the deposit of the tenth such instrument of ratification or accession.

(b) Articles 13 to 17 shall enter into force, with respect to the first ten countries of the Union which have deposited instruments of ratification or accession without making the declaration permitted under paragraph (1)(b)(ii), three months after the deposit of the tenth such instrument of ratification or accession.

(c) Subject to the initial entry into force, pursuant to the provisions of subparagraphs (a) and (b), of each of the two groups of Articles referred to in paragraph (1)(b)(i) and (ii), and subject to the provisions of paragraph (1)(b), Articles 1 to 17 shall, with respect to any country of the Union, other than those referred to in subparagraphs (a) and (b), which deposits an instrument of ratification or accession or any country of the Union which deposits a declaration pursuant to paragraph (1)(c), enter into force three months after the date of notification by the Director General of such deposit, unless a subsequent date has been indicated in the instrument or declaration deposited. In the latter case, this Act shall enter into force with respect to that country on the date thus indicated.

(3) With respect to any country of the Union which deposits an instrument of ratification or accession, Articles 18 to 30 shall enter into force on the earlier of the dates on which any of the groups of Articles referred to in paragraph (1)(b) enters into force with respect to that country pursuant to paragraph (2)(a), (b), or (c).

Article 21

Accession by Countries Outside the Union; Entry Into Force]

(1) Any country outside the Union may accede to this Act and thereby become a member of the Union. Instruments of accession shall be deposited with the Director General.

(2) (a) With respect to any country outside the Union which deposits its instrument of accession one month or more before the date of entry into force of any provisions of the present Act, this Act shall enter into force, unless a subsequent date has been indicated in the instrument of accession, on the date upon which provisions first enter into force pursuant to Article 20(2)(a) or (b); provided that:

(i) if Articles 1 to 12 do not enter into force on that date, such country shall, during the interim period before the entry into force of such provisions, and in substitution therefor, be bound by Articles 1 to 12 of the Lisbon Act,

(ii) if Articles 13 to 17 do not enter into force on that date, such country shall, during the interim period before the entry into force of such provisions, and in substitution therefor, be bound by Articles 13 and 14(3), (4), and (5), of the Lisbon Act.

If a country indicates a subsequent date in its instrument of accession, this Act shall enter into force with respect to that country on the date thus indicated.

(b) With respect to any country outside the Union which deposits its instrument of accession on a date which is subsequent to, or precedes by less than one month, the entry into force of one group of Articles of the present Act, this Act shall, subject to the proviso of subparagraph (a), enter into force three months after the date on which its accession has been notified by the Director General, unless a subsequent date has been indicated in the instrument of accession. In the latter case, this Act shall enter into force with respect to that country on the date thus indicated.

(3) With respect to any country outside the Union which deposits its instrument of accession after the date of entry into force of the present Act in its entirety, or less than one month before such date, this Act shall enter into force three months after the date on which its accession has been notified by the Director General, unless a subsequent date has been indicated in the instrument of accession. In the latter case, this Act shall enter into force with respect to that country on the date thus indicated.

Article 22

[Consequences of Ratification or Accession]

Subject to the possibilities of exceptions provided for in Articles 20(1)(b) and 28(2), ratification or accession shall automatically entail acceptance of all the clauses and admission to all the advantages of this Act.

Article 23

[Accession to Earlier Acts]

After the entry into force of this Act in its entirety, a country may not accede to earlier Acts of this Convention.

Article 24

[Territories]

(1) Any country may declare in its instrument of ratification or accession, or may inform the Director General by written notification any time thereafter, that this Convention shall be applicable to all or part of those territories, designated in the declaration or notification, for the external relations of which it is responsible.

(2) Any country which has made such a declaration or given such a notification may, at any time, notify the Director General that this Convention shall cease to be applicable to all or part of such territories.

(3) (a) Any declaration made under paragraph (1) shall take effect on the same date as the ratification or accession in the instrument of which it was included, and any notification given under such paragraph shall take effect three months after its notification by the Director General.

     (b) Any notification given under paragraph (2) shall take effect twelve months after its receipt by the Director General.

Article 25

[Implementation of the Convention on the Domestic Level]

(1) Any country party to this Convention undertakes to adopt, in accordance with its constitution, the measures necessary to ensure the application of this Convention.

(2)　It is understood that, at the time a country deposits its instrument of ratification or accession, it will be in a position under its domestic law to give effect to the provisions of this Convention.

Article 26

[Denunciation]

(1)　This Convention shall remain in force without limitation as to time.

(2)　Any country may denounce this Act by notification addressed to the Director General. Such denunciation shall constitute also denunciation of all earlier Acts and shall affect only the country making it, the Convention remaining in full force and effect as regards the other countries of the Union.

(3)　Denunciation shall take effect one year after the day on which the Director General has received the notification.

(4)　The right of denunciation provided by this Article shall not be exercised by any country before the expiration of five years from the date upon which it becomes a member of the Union.

Article 27

[Application of Earlier Acts]

(1)　The present Act shall, as regards the relations between the countries to which it applies, and to the extent that it applies, replace the Convention of Paris of March 20, 1883 and the subsequent Acts of revision.

(2)　(a)　As regards the countries to which the present Act does not apply, or does not apply in its entirety, but to which the Lisbon Act of October 31, 1958, applies, the latter shall remain in force in its entirety or to the extent that the present Act does not replace it by virtue of paragraph (1).

　　(b)　Similarly, as regards the countries to which neither the present Act, nor portions thereof, nor the Lisbon Act applies, the London Act of June 2, 1934, shall remain in force in its entirety or to the extent that the present Act does not replace it by virtue of paragraph (1).

　　(c)　Similarly, as regards the countries to which neither the present Act, nor portions thereof, nor the Lisbon Act, nor the London Act applies, the Hague Act of November 6, 1925, shall remain in force in its entirety or to the extent that the present Act does not replace it by virtue of paragraph (1).

(3)　Countries outside the Union which become party to this Act shall apply it with respect to any country of the Union not party to this Act or which, although party to this Act, has made a declaration pursuant to Article 20(1)(b)(i). Such countries recognize that the said country of the Union may apply, in its relations with them, the provisions of the most recent Act to which it is party.

Article 28

[Disputes]

(1) Any dispute between two or more countries of the Union concerning the interpretation or application of this Convention, not settled by negotiation, may, by any one of the countries concerned, he brought before the International Court of Justice by application in conformity with the Statute of the Court, unless the countries concerned agree on some other method of settlement. The country bringing the dispute before the Court shall inform the International Bureau; the International Bureau shall bring the matter to the attention of the other countries of the Union.

(2) Each country may, at the time it signs this Act or deposits its instrument of ratification or accession, declare that it does not consider itself bound by the provisions of paragraph (1). With regard to any dispute between such country and any other country of the Union, the provisions of paragraph (1) shall not apply.

(3) Any country having made a declaration in accordance with the provisions of paragraph (2) may, at any time, withdraw its declaration by notification addressed to the Director General.

Article 29

[Signature, Languages, Depositary Functions]

(1) (a) This Act shall be signed in a single copy in the French language and shall be deposited with the Government of Sweden.

(b) Official texts shall be established by the Director General, after consultation with the interested Governments, in the English, German, Italian, Portuguese, Russian and Spanish languages, and such other languages as the Assembly may designate.

(c) In case of differences of opinion on the interpretation of the various texts, the French text shall prevail.

(2) This Act shall remain open for signature at Stockholm until January 13, 1968.

(3) The Director General shall transmit two copies, certified by the Government of Sweden, of the signed text of this Act to the Governments of all countries of the Union and, on request, to the Government of any other country.

(4) The Director General shall register this Act with the Secretariat of the United Nations.

(5) The Director General shall notify the Governments of all countries of the Union of signatures, deposits of instruments of ratification or accession and any declarations included in such instruments or made pursuant to Article 20(1)(c), entry into force of any provisions of this Act, notifications of denunciation, and notifications pursuant to Article 24.

Article 30

[Transitional Provisions]

(1)   Until the first Director General assumes office, references in this Act to the International Bureau of the Organization or to the Director General shall be deemed to be references to the Bureau of the Union or its Director, respectively.

(2)   Countries of the Union not bound by Articles 13 to 17 may, until five years after the entry into force of the Convention establishing the Organization, exercise, if they so desire, the rights provided under Articles 13 to 17 of this Act as if they were bound by those Articles. Any country desiring to exercise such rights shall give written notification to that effect to the Director General; such notification shall be effective from the date of its receipt. Such countries shall be deemed to be members of the Assembly until the expiration of the said period.

(3)   As long as all the countries of the Union have not become Members of the Organization, the International Bureau of the Organization shall also function as the Bureau of the Union, and the Director General as the Director of the said Bureau.

(4)   Once all the countries of the Union have become Members of the Organization, the rights, obligations, and property, of the Bureau of the Union shall devolve on the International Bureau of the Organization.

Appendix III

Nice Classification (9th edition)

Class Headings

Goods

Class 1	Chemicals used in industry, science and photography, as well as in agriculture, horticulture and forestry; unprocessed artificial resins, unprocessed plastics; manures; fire extinguishing compositions; tempering and soldering preparations; chemical substances for preserving foodstuffs; tanning substances; adhesives used in industry.
Class 2	Paints, varnishes, lacquers; preservatives against rust and against deterioration of wood; colorants; mordants; raw natural resins; metals in foil and powder form for painters, decorators, printers and artists.
Class 3	Bleaching preparations and other substances for laundry use; cleaning, polishing, scouring and abrasive preparations; soaps; perfumery, essential oils, cosmetics, hair lotions; dentifrices.
Class 4	Industrial oils and greases; lubricants; dust absorbing, wetting and binding compositions; fuels (including motor spirit) and illuminants; candles and wicks for lighting.
Class 5	Pharmaceutical and veterinary preparations; sanitary preparations for medical purposes; dietetic substances adapted for medical use, food for babies; plasters, materials for dressings; material for stopping teeth, dental wax; disinfectants; preparations for destroying vermin; fungicides, herbicides.
Class 6	Common metals and their alloys; metal building materials; transportable buildings of metal; materials of metal for railway tracks; non-electric cables and wires of common metal; ironmongery, small items of metal hardware; pipes and tubes of metal; safes; goods of common metal not included in other classes; ores.
Class 7	Machines and machine tools; motors and engines (except for land vehicles); machine coupling and transmission components (except for land vehicles); agricultural implements other than hand-operated; incubators for eggs.
Class 8	Hand tools and implements (hand-operated); cutlery; side arms; razors.

Goods

Class 9	Scientific, nautical, surveying, photographic, cinematographic, optical, weighing, measuring, signalling, checking (supervision), life-saving and teaching apparatus and instruments; apparatus and instruments for conducting, switching, transforming, accumulating, regulating or controlling electricity; apparatus for recording, transmission or reproduction of sound or images; magnetic data carriers, recording discs; automatic vending machines and mechanisms for coin-operated apparatus; cash registers, calculating machines, data processing equipment and computers; fire-extinguishing apparatus.
Class 10	Surgical, medical, dental and veterinary apparatus and instruments, artificial limbs, eyes and teeth; orthopedic articles; suture materials.
Class 11	Apparatus for lighting, heating, steam generating, cooking, refrigerating, drying, ventilating, water supply and sanitary purposes.
Class 12	Vehicles; apparatus for locomotion by land, air or water.
Class 13	Firearms; ammunition and projectiles; explosives; fireworks.
Class 14	Precious metals and their alloys and goods in precious metals or coated therewith, not included in other classes; jewellery, precious stones; horological and chronometric instruments.
Class 15	Musical instruments.
Class 16	Paper, cardboard and goods made from these materials, not included in other classes; printed matter; bookbinding material; photographs; stationery; adhesives for stationery or household purposes; artists' materials; paint brushes; typewriters and office requisites (except furniture); instructional and teaching material (except apparatus); plastic materials for packaging (not included in other classes); printers' type; printing blocks.
Class 17	Rubber, gutta-percha, gum, asbestos, mica and goods made from these materials and not included in other classes; plastics in extruded form for use in manufacture; packing, stopping and insulating materials; flexible pipes, not of metal.
Class 18	Leather and imitations of leather, and goods made of these materials and not included in other classes; animal skins, hides; trunks and travelling bags; umbrellas, parasols and walking sticks; whips, harness and saddlery.

Goods

Class 19	Building materials (non-metallic); non-metallic rigid pipes for building; asphalt, pitch and bitumen; non-metallic transportable buildings; monuments, not of metal.
Class 20	Furniture, mirrors, picture frames; goods (not included in other classes) of wood, cork, reed, cane, wicker, horn, bone, ivory, whalebone, shell, amber, mother-of-pearl, meerschaum and substitutes for all these materials, or of plastics.
Class 21	Household or kitchen utensils and containers; combs and sponges; brushes (except paint brushes); brush-making materials; articles for cleaning purposes; steelwool; unworked or semi-worked glass (except glass used in building); glassware, porcelain and earthenware not included in other classes.
Class 22	Ropes, string, nets, tents, awnings, tarpaulins, sails, sacks and bags (not included in other classes); padding and stuffing materials (except of rubber or plastics); raw fibrous textile materials.
Class 23	Yarns and threads, for textile use.
Class 24	Textiles and textile goods, not included in other classes; bed and table covers.
Class 25	Clothing, footwear, headgear.
Class 26	Lace and embroidery, ribbons and braid; buttons, hooks and eyes, pins and needles; artificial flowers.
Class 27	Carpets, rugs, mats and matting, linoleum and other materials for covering existing floors; wall hangings (non-textile).
Class 28	Games and playthings; gymnastic and sporting articles not included in other classes; decorations for Christmas trees.
Class 29	Meat, fish, poultry and game; meat extracts; preserved, frozen, dried and cooked fruits and vegetables; jellies, jams, compotes; eggs, milk and milk products; edible oils and fats.
Class 30	Coffee, tea, cocoa, sugar, rice, tapioca, sago, artificial coffee; flour and preparations made from cereals, bread, pastry and confectionery, ices; honey, treacle; yeast, baking-powder; salt, mustard; vinegar, sauces (condiments); spices; ice.
Class 31	Agricultural, horticultural and forestry products and grains not included in other classes; live animals; fresh fruits and vegetables; seeds, natural plants and flowers; foodstuffs for animals, malt.

Goods

Class 32	Beers; mineral and aerated waters and other non-alcoholic drinks; fruit drinks and fruit juices; syrups and other preparations for making beverages.
Class 33	Alcoholic beverages (except beers).
Class 34	Tobacco; smokers' articles; matches.

Services

Class 35	Advertising; business management; business administration; office functions.
Class 36	Insurance; financial affairs; monetary affairs; real estate affairs.
Class 37	Building construction; repair; installation services.
Class 38	Telecommunications.
Class 39	Transport; packaging and storage of goods; travel arrangement.
Class 40	Treatment of materials.
Class 41	Education; providing of training; entertainment; sporting and cultural activities.
Class 42	Scientific and technological services and research and design relating thereto; industrial analysis and research services; design and development of computer hardware and software.
Class 43	Services for providing food and drink; temporary accommodation.
Class 44	Medical services; veterinary services; hygienic and beauty care for human beings or animals; agriculture, horticulture and forestry services.
Class 45	Legal services; security services for the protection of property and individuals; personal and social services rendered by others to meet the needs of individuals.

Appendix IV

States Party to the Madrid Agreement

Status on September 17, 2010

State/IGO	Date on which State became party to the Madrid Agreement[2]	Date on which State/IGO became party to the Madrid Protocol (1989)
Albania	October 4, 1995	July 30, 2003
Algeria	July 5, 1972	–
Antigua and Barbuda	–	March 17, 2000
Armenia	December 25, 1991	October 19, 2000[6,10]
Australia	–	July 11, 2001[5,6]
Austria	January 1, 1909	April 13, 1999
Azerbaijan	December 25, 1995	April 15, 2007
Bahrain	–	December 15, 2005[10]
Belarus	December 25, 1991	January 18, 2002[6,10]
Belgium	July 15, 1892[3]	April 1, 1998[3,6]
Bhutan	August 4, 2000	August 4, 2000
Bosnia and Herzegovina	March 1, 1992	January 27, 2009
Botswana	–	December 5, 2006
Bulgaria	August 1, 1985	October 2, 2001[6,10]
China	October 4, 1989[4]	December 1, 1995[4,5,6]
Croatia	October 8, 1991	January 23, 2004
Cuba	December 6, 1989	December 26, 1995
Cyprus	November 4, 2003	November 4, 2003[5]
Czech Republic	January 1, 1993	September 25, 1996
Democratic People's Republic of Korea	June 10, 1980	October 3, 1996
Denmark	–	February 13, 1996[5,6,7]
Egypt	July 1, 1952	September 3, 2009

State/IGO	Date on which State became party to the Madrid Agreement[2]	Date on which State/IGO became party to the Madrid Protocol (1989)
Estonia	–	November 18, 1998[5,6,8]
European Union	–	October 1, 2004[6,10]
Finland	–	April 1, 1996[5,6]
France	July 15, 1892[9]	November 7, 1997[9]
Georgia	–	August 20, 1998[6,10]
Germany	December 1, 1922	March 20, 1996
Ghana	–	September 16, 2008[5,6]
Greece	–	August 10, 2000[5,6]
Hungary	January 1, 1909	October 3, 1997
Iceland	–	April 15, 1997[6,10]
Iran (Islamic Republic of)	December 25, 2003	December 25, 2003[5]
Ireland	–	October 19, 2001[5,6]
Israel	-	September 1, 2010[5,6]
Italy	October 15, 1894	April 17, 2000[5,6]
Japan	–	March 14, 2000[6,10]
Kazakhstan	December 25, 1991	December 8, 2010
Kenya	June 26, 1998	June 26, 1998[5]
Kyrgyzstan	December 25, 1991	June 17, 2004[6]
Latvia	January 1, 1995	January 5, 2000
Lesotho	February 12, 1999	February 12, 1999
Liberia	December 25, 1995	December 11, 2009
Liechtenstein	July 14, 1933	March 17, 1998
Lithuania	–	November 15, 1997[5]
Luxembourg	September 1, 1924[3]	April 1, 1998[3,6]
Madagascar	–	April 28, 2008[10]
Monaco	April 29, 1956	September 27, 1996
Mongolia	April 21, 1985	June 16, 2001
Montenegro	June 3, 2006	June 3, 2006
Morocco	July 30, 1917	October 8, 1999

State/IGO	Date on which State became party to the Madrid Agreement[2]	Date on which State/ IGO became party to the Madrid Protocol (1989)
Mozambique	October 7, 1998	October 7, 1998
Namibia	June 30, 2004	June 30, 2004[8]
Netherlands	March 1, 1893[3,11]	April 1, 1998[3,6,11]
Norway	–	March 29, 1996[5,6]
Oman	–	October 16, 2007[10]
Poland	March 18, 1991	March 4, 1997[10]
Portugal	October 31, 1893	March 20, 1997
Republic of Korea	–	April 10, 2003[5,6]
Republic of Moldova	December 25, 1991	December 1, 1997[6]
Romania	October 6, 1920	July 28, 1998
Russian Federation	July 1, 1976[12]	June 10, 1997
San Marino	September 25, 1960	September 12, 2007[6,10]
Sao Tome and Principe	-	December 8, 2008
Serbia[13]	April 27, 1992	February 17, 1998
Sierra Leone	June 17, 1997	December 28, 1999
Singapore	–	October 31, 2000[5,6]
Slovakia	January 1, 1993	September 13, 1997[10]
Slovenia	June 25, 1991	March 12, 1998
Spain	July 15, 1892	December 1, 1995
Sudan	May 16, 1984	February 16, 2010
Swaziland	December 14, 1998	December 14, 1998
Sweden	–	December 1, 1995[5,6]
Switzerland	July 15, 1892	May 1, 1997[6,10]
Syrian Arab Republic	August 5, 2004	August 5, 2004[5]
Tajikistan	December 25, 1991	–
The former Yugoslav Republic of Macedonia	September 8, 1991	August 30, 2002
Turkey	–	January 1, 1999[5,6,8]
Turkmenistan	–	September 28, 1999[6,10]
Ukraine	December 25, 1991	December 29, 2000[5,6]

State/IGO	Date on which State became party to the Madrid Agreement[2]	Date on which State/IGO became party to the Madrid Protocol (1989)
United Kingdom	–	December 1, 1995[5,6,14]
United States of America	–	November 2, 2003[5,6]
Uzbekistan	–	December 27, 2006[6,10]
Viet Nam	March 8, 1949	July 11, 2006[6]
Zambia	–	November 15, 2001
Total: (85)	(56)	(83)

1   The Madrid Union is composed of the States party to the Madrid Agreement and the Contracting Parties to the Madrid Protocol.

2   All the States party to the Madrid Agreement have declared, under Article 3*bis* of the Nice or Stockholm Act, that the protection arising from international registration shall not extend to them unless the proprietor of the mark so requests.

3   The territories of Belgium, Luxembourg and the Kingdom of the Netherlands in Europe are to be deemed a single country, for the application of the Madrid Agreement as from January 1, 1971, and for the application of the Protocol as from April 1, 1998.

4   Not applicable to either the Hong Kong Special Administrative Region or the Macau Special Administrative Region.

5   In accordance with Article 5(2)(b) and (c) of the Protocol, this Contracting Party has declared that the time limit to notify a refusal of protection shall be 18 months and that, where a refusal of protection results from an opposition to the granting of protection, such refusal may be notified after the expiry of the 18–month time limit.

6   In accordance with Article 8(7)(a) of the Protocol, this Contracting Party has declared that, in connection with each request for territorial extension to it of the protection of an international registration and the renewal of any such international registration, it wants to receive an individual fee, instead of a share in the revenue produced by the supplementary and complementary fee.

7   Not applicable to the Faroe Islands and to Greenland.

8   In accordance with Article 14(5) of the Protocol, this Contracting Party has declared that the protection resulting from any international registration effected under this Protocol before the date of entry into force of this Protocol with respect to it cannot be extended to it.

9   Including all Overseas Departments and Territories.

10   In accordance with Article 5(2)(b) of the Protocol, this Contracting Party has declared that the time limit to notify a refusal of protection shall be 18 months.

11   The instrument of ratification of the Stockholm Act and the instrument of acceptance of the Protocol were deposited for the Kingdom in Europe. The Netherlands extended the application of the Madrid Protocol to the Netherlands Antilles with effect from April 28, 2003.

12   Date of accession by the Soviet Union, continued by the Russian Federation as from December 25, 1991.

13   Serbia is the continuing State from Serbia and Montenegro as from June 3, 2006.

14   Ratification in respect of the United Kingdom and the Isle of Man.

Appendix V

Council Directive 2008/95/EC of the European Parliament and of the Council of 22 October 2008 to Approximate the Laws of the Member States Relating to Trade Marks

(Codified version)
(Text with EEA relevance)

THE EUROPEAN PARLIAMENT AND THE COUNCIL OF THE EUROPEAN UNION,

Having regard to the Treaty establishing the European Community, and in particular Article 95 thereof,

Having regard to the proposal from the Commission,

may afford to undertakings wishing to acquire trade marks.

Having regard to the opinion of the European Economic and Social Committee,[1]

Acting in accordance with the procedure laid down in Article 251 of the Treaty,[2]

Whereas:

(1) The content of Council Directive 89/104/EEC of 21 December 1988 to approximate the laws of the Member States relating to trade marks[3] has been amended.[4] In the interests of clarity and rationality the said Directive should be codified.

(2) The trade mark laws applicable in the Member States before the entry into force of Directive 89/104/EEC contained disparities which may have impeded the free movement of goods and freedom to provide services and may have distorted competition within the common market. It was therefore necessary to approximate the laws of the Member States in order to ensure the proper functioning of the internal market.

(3) It is important not to disregard the solutions and advantages which the Community trade mark system

(4) It does not appear to be necessary to undertake full-scale approximation of the trade mark laws of the Member States. It will be sufficient if approximation is limited to those national provisions of law which most directly affect the functioning of the internal market.

---

[1] OJ C 161, 13.7.2007, p. 44.
[2] Opinion of the European Parliament of 19 June 2007 (OJ C 146 E, 12.6.2008, p. 76) and Council Decision of 25 September 2008.
[3] OJ L 40, 11.2.1989, p. 1.
[4] See Annex I, Part A.

(5) This Directive should not deprive the Member States of the right to continue to protect trade marks acquired through use but should take them into account only in regard to the relationship between them and trade marks acquired by registration.

(6) Member States should also remain free to fix the provisions of procedure concerning the registration, the revocation and the invalidity of trade marks acquired by registration. They can, for example, determine the form of trade mark registration and invalidity procedures, decide whether earlier rights should be invoked either in the registration procedure or in the invalidity procedure or in both and, if they allow earlier rights to be invoked in the registration procedure, have an opposition procedure or an *ex officio* examination procedure or both. Member States should remain free to determine the effects of revocation or invalidity of trade marks.

(7) This Directive should not exclude the application to trade marks of provisions of law of the Member States other than trade mark law, such as the provisions relating to unfair competition, civil liability or consumer protection.

(8) Attainment of the objectives at which this approximation of laws is aiming requires that the conditions for obtaining and continuing to hold a registered trade mark be, in general, identical in all Member States. To this end, it is necessary to list examples of signs which may constitute a trade mark, provided that such signs are capable of distinguishing the goods or services of one undertaking from those of other undertakings. The grounds for refusal or invalidity concerning the trade mark itself, for example, the absence of any distinctive character, or concerning conflicts between the trade mark and earlier rights, should be listed in an exhaustive manner, even if some of these grounds are listed as an option for the Member States which should therefore be able to maintain or introduce those grounds in their legislation. Member States should be able to maintain or introduce into their legislation grounds of refusal or invalidity linked to conditions for obtaining and continuing to hold a trade mark for which there is no provision of approximation, concerning, for example, the eligibility for the grant of a trade mark, the renewal of the trade mark or rules on fees, or related to the noncompliance with procedural rules.

(9) In order to reduce the total number of trade marks registered and protected in the Community and, consequently, the number of conflicts which arise between them, it is essential to require that registered trade marks must actually be used or, if not used, be subject to revocation. It is necessary to provide that a trade mark cannot be invalidated on the basis of the existence of a non-used earlier trade mark, while the Member States should remain free to apply the same principle in respect of the registration of a trade mark or to provide that a trade mark may not be successfully invoked in infringement proceedings if it is established as a result of a plea that the trade mark could be revoked. In all these cases it is up to the Member States to establish the applicable rules of procedure.

(10) It is fundamental, in order to facilitate the free movement of goods and services, to ensure that registered trade marks enjoy the same protection under the legal systems of all the Member States. This should not, however, prevent the Member States from granting at their option extensive protection to those trade marks which have a reputation.

(11) The protection afforded by the registered trade mark, the function of which is in particular to guarantee the trade mark as an indication of origin, should be absolute in the case of identity between the mark and the sign and the goods or services. The protection should apply also in the case of similarity between the mark and the sign and the goods or services. It is indispensable to give an interpretation of the concept of similarity in relation to the likelihood of confusion. The likelihood of confusion, the appreciation of which depends on numerous elements and, in particular, on the recognition of the trade mark on the market, the association which can be made with the used or registered sign, the degree of similarity between the trade mark and the sign and between the goods or services identified, should constitute the specific condition for such protection. The ways in which likelihood of confusion may be established, and in particular the onus of proof, should be a matter for national procedural rules which should not be prejudiced by this Directive.

(12) It is important, for reasons of legal certainty and without inequitably prejudicing the interests of a proprietor of an earlier trade mark, to provide that the latter may no longer request a declaration of invalidity nor may he oppose the use of a trade mark subsequent to his own of which he has knowingly tolerated the use for a substantial length of time, unless the application for the subsequent trade mark was made in bad faith.

(13) All Member States are bound by the Paris Convention for the Protection of Industrial Property. It is necessary that the provisions of this Directive should be entirely consistent with those of the said Convention. The obligations of the Member States resulting from that Convention should not be affected by this Directive. Where appropriate, the second paragraph of Article 307 of the Treaty should apply.

(14) This Directive should be without prejudice to the obligations of the Member States relating to the time limit for transposition into national law of Directive 89/104/EEC set out in Annex I, Part B,

HAVE ADOPTED THIS DIRECTIVE:

Article 1

Scope

This Directive shall apply to every trade mark in respect of goods or services which is the subject of registration or of an application in a Member State for registration as an individual trade mark, a collective mark or a guarantee or certification mark, or which is the subject of a registration or an application for registration in the Benelux Office for Intellectual Property or of an international registration having effect in a Member State.

Article 2

Signs of which a trade mark may consist

A trade mark may consist of any signs capable of being represented graphically, particularly words, including personal names, designs, letters, numerals, the shape of goods or of their packaging, provided that such signs are capable of distinguishing the goods or services of one undertaking from those of other undertakings.

Article 3

Grounds for refusal or invalidity

1. The following shall not be registered or, if registered, shall be liable to be declared invalid:

    (a) signs which cannot constitute a trade mark;

    (b) trade marks which are devoid of any distinctive character;

    (c) trade marks which consist exclusively of signs or indications which may serve, in trade, to designate the kind, quality, quantity, intended purpose, value, geographical origin, or the time of production of the goods or of rendering of the service, or other characteristics of the goods or services;

    (d) trade marks which consist exclusively of signs or indications which have become customary in the current language or in the bona fide and established practices of the trade;

    (e) signs which consist exclusively of:

         (i)   the shape which results from the nature of the goods themselves;

         (ii) the shape of goods which is necessary to obtain a technical result;

         (iii) the shape which gives substantial value to the goods;

    (f) trade marks which are contrary to public policy or to accepted principles of morality;

    (g) trade marks which are of such a nature as to deceive the public, for instance as to the nature, quality or geographical origin of the goods or service;

    (h) trade marks which have not been authorised by the competent authorities and are to be refused or invalidated pursuant to Article *6ter* of the Paris Convention for the Protection of Industrial Property, hereinafter referred to as the 'Paris Convention'.

2. Any Member State may provide that a trade mark shall not be registered or, if registered, shall be liable to be declared invalid where and to the extent that:

    (a) the use of that trade mark may be prohibited pursuant to provisions of law other than trade mark law of the Member State concerned or of the Community;

    (b) the trade mark covers a sign of high symbolic value, in particular a religious symbol;

    (c) the trade mark includes badges, emblems and escutcheons other than those covered by Article 6 *ter* of the Paris Convention and which are of public interest, unless the consent of the competent authority to their registration has been given in conformity with the legislation of the Member State;

    (d) the application for registration of the trade mark in bad faith by the applicant.

3. A trade mark shall not be refused registration or be declared invalid in accordance with paragraph 1(b), (c) or (d) if, before the date of application for registration and following the use which has been made of it, it has acquired a distinctive character. Any Member State may in addition provide that this provision shall also apply where the distinctive character was acquired after the date of application for registration or after the date of registration.

4. Any Member State may provide that, by derogation from paragraphs 1, 2 and 3, the grounds of refusal of registration or invalidity in force in that State prior to the date of entry into force of the provisions necessary to comply with Directive 89/104/EEC, shall apply to trade marks for which application has been made prior to that date.

Article 4

Further grounds for refusal or invalidity concerning conflicts with earlier rights

1. A trade mark shall not be registered or, if registered, shall be liable to be declared invalid:

   (a) if it is identical with an earlier trade mark, and the goods or services for which the trade mark is applied for or is registered are identical with the goods or services for which the earlier trade mark is protected;

   (b) if because of its identity with, or similarity to, the earlier trade mark and the identity or similarity of the goods or services covered by the trade marks, there exists a likelihood of confusion on the part of the public; the likelihood of confusion includes the likelihood of association with the earlier trade mark.

2. Earlier trade marks' within the meaning of paragraph 1 means:

   (a) trade marks of the following kinds with a date of application for registration which is earlier than the date of application for registration of the trade mark, taking account, where appropriate, of the priorities claimed in respect of those trade marks;

      (i) Community trade marks;

      (ii) trade marks registered in the Member State or, in the case of Belgium, Luxembourg or the Netherlands, at the Benelux Office for Intellectual Property;

      (iii) trade marks registered under international arrangements which have effect in the Member State;

   (b) Community trade marks which validly claim seniority, in accordance with Council Regulation (EC) No 40/94[5] (1) of 20 December 1993 on the Community trade mark, from a trade mark referred to in (a)(ii) and (iii), even when the latter trade mark has been surrendered or allowed to lapse;

   (c) applications for the trade marks referred to in points (a) and (b), subject to their registration;

---

5. OJ L 11, 14.1.1994, p. 1.

(d) trade marks which, on the date of application for registration of the trade mark, or, where appropriate, of the priority claimed in respect of the application for registration of the trade mark, are well known in a Member State, in the sense in which the words 'well known' are used in Article 6 *bis* of the Paris Convention.

3. A trade mark shall furthermore not be registered or, if registered, shall be liable to be declared invalid if it is identical with, or similar to, an earlier Community trade mark within the meaning of paragraph 2 and is to be, or has been, registered for goods or services which are not similar to those for which the earlier Community trade mark is registered, where the earlier Community trade mark has a reputation in the Community and where the use of the later trade mark without due cause would take unfair advantage of, or be detrimental to, the distinctive character or the repute of the earlier Community trade mark.

4. Any Member State may, in addition, provide that a trade mark shall not be registered or, if registered, shall be liable to be declared invalid where, and to the extent that:

(a) the trade mark is identical with, or similar to, an earlier national trade mark within the meaning of paragraph 2 and is to be, or has been, registered for goods or services which are not similar to those for which the earlier trade mark is registered, where the earlier trade mark has a reputation in the Member State concerned and where the use of the later trade mark without due cause would take unfair advantage of, or be detrimental to, the distinctive character or the repute of the earlier trade mark;

(b) rights to a non-registered trade mark or to another sign used in the course of trade were acquired prior to the date of application for registration of the subsequent trade mark, or the date of the priority claimed for the application for registration of the subsequent trade mark, and that nonregistered trade mark or other sign confers on its proprietor the right to prohibit the use of a subsequent trade mark;

(c) the use of the trade mark may be prohibited by virtue of an earlier right other than the rights referred to in paragraph 2 and point (b) of this paragraph and in particular:

(i) a right to a name;

(ii) a right of personal portrayal;

(iii) a copyright;

(iv) an industrial property right;

(d) the trade mark is identical with, or similar to, an earlier collective trade mark conferring a right which expired within a period of a maximum of three years preceding application;

(e) the trade mark is identical with, or similar to, an earlier guarantee or certification mark conferring a right which expired within a period preceding application the length of which is fixed by the Member State;

(f) the trade mark is identical with, or similar to, an earlier trade mark which was registered for identical or similar goods or services and conferred on them a right which has expired for failure to renew within a period of a maximum of two years preceding application, unless the proprietor of the earlier trade mark gave his agreement for the registration of the later mark or did not use his trade mark;

(g) the trade mark is liable to be confused with a mark which was in use abroad on the filing date of the application and which is still in use there, provided that at the date of the application the applicant was acting in bad faith.

5. The Member States may permit that in appropriate circumstances registration need not be refused or the trade mark need not be declared invalid where the proprietor of the earlier trade mark or other earlier right consents to the registration of the later trade mark.

6. Any Member State may provide that, by derogation from paragraphs 1 to 5, the grounds for refusal of registration or invalidity in force in that State prior to the date of the entry into force of the provisions necessary to comply with Directive 89/104/EEC, shall apply to trade marks for which application has been made prior to that date.

Article 5

Rights conferred by a trade mark

1. The registered trade mark shall confer on the proprietor exclusive rights therein. The proprietor shall be entitled to prevent all third parties not having his consent from using in the course of trade:

(a) any sign which is identical with the trade mark in relation to goods or services which are identical with those for which the trade mark is registered;

(b) any sign where, because of its identity with, or similarity to, the trade mark and the identity or similarity of the goods or services covered by the trade mark and the sign, there exists a likelihood of confusion on the part of the public; the likelihood of confusion includes the likelihood of association between the sign and the trade mark.

2. Any Member State may also provide that the proprietor shall be entitled to prevent all third parties not having his consent from using in the course of trade any sign which is identical with, or similar to, the trade mark in relation to goods or services which are not similar to those for which the trade mark is registered, where the latter has a reputation in the Member State and where use of that sign without due cause takes unfair advantage of, or is detrimental to, the distinctive character or the repute of the trade mark.

3. The following, *inter alia*, may be prohibited under paragraphs 1 and 2:

(a) affixing the sign to the goods or to the packaging thereof;

(b) offering the goods, or putting them on the market or stocking them for these purposes under that sign, or offering or supplying services thereunder;

(c) importing or exporting the goods under the sign;

(d) using the sign on business papers and in advertising.

4. Where, under the law of the Member State, the use of a sign under the conditions referred to in paragraph 1(b) or paragraph 2 could not be prohibited before the date of entry into force of the provisions necessary to comply with Directive 89/104/EEC in the Member State concerned, the rights conferred by the trade mark may not be relied on to prevent the continued use of the sign.

5. Paragraphs 1 to 4 shall not affect provisions in any Member State relating to the protection against the use of a sign other than for the purposes of distinguishing goods or services, where use of that sign without due cause takes unfair advantage of, or is detrimental to, the distinctive character or the repute of the trade mark.

Article 6

Limitation of the effects of a trade mark

1. The trade mark shall not entitle the proprietor to prohibit a third party from using, in the course of trade:

(a) his own name or address;

(b) indications concerning the kind, quality, quantity, intended purpose, value, geographical origin, the time of production of goods or of rendering of the service, or other characteristics of goods or services;

(c) the trade mark where it is necessary to indicate the intended purpose of a product or service, in particular as accessories or spare parts;

provided he uses them in accordance with honest practices in industrial or commercial matters.

2. The trade mark shall not entitle the proprietor to prohibit a third party from using, in the course of trade, an earlier right which only applies in a particular locality if that right is recognised by the laws of the Member State in question and within the limits of the territory in which it is recognised.

Article 7

Exhaustion of the rights conferred by a trade mark

1. The trade mark shall not entitle the proprietor to prohibit its use in relation to goods which have been put on the market in the Community under that trade mark by the proprietor or with his consent.

2. Paragraph 1 shall not apply where there exist legitimate reasons for the proprietor to oppose further commercialisation of the goods, especially where the condition of the goods is changed or impaired after they have been put on the market.

Article 8

Licensing

1. A trade mark may be licensed for some or all of the goods or services for which it is registered and for the whole or part of the Member State concerned. A licence may be exclusive or non-exclusive.

2. The proprietor of a trade mark may invoke the rights conferred by that trade mark against a licensee who contravenes any provision in his licensing contract with regard to:

    (a) its duration;

    (b) the form covered by the registration in which the trade mark may be used;

    (c) the scope of the goods or services for which the licence is granted;

    (d) the territory in which the trade mark may be affixed; or

    (e) the quality of the goods manufactured or of the services provided by the licensee.

Article 9

Limitation in consequence of acquiescence

1. Where, in a Member State, the proprietor of an earlier trade mark as referred to in Article 4(2) has acquiesced, for a period of five successive years, in the use of a later trade mark registered in that Member State while being aware of such use, he shall no longer be entitled on the basis of the earlier trade mark either to apply for a declaration that the later trade mark is invalid or to oppose the use of the later trade mark in respect of the goods or services for which the later trade mark has been used, unless registration of the later trade mark was applied for in bad faith.

2. Any Member State may provide that paragraph 1 shall apply *mutatis mutandis* to the proprietor of an earlier trade mark referred to in Article 4(4)(a) or an other earlier right referred to in Article 4(4)(b) or (c).

3. In the cases referred to in paragraphs 1 and 2, the proprietor of a later registered trade mark shall not be entitled to oppose the use of the earlier right, even though that right may no longer be invoked against the later trade mark.

Article 10

Use of trade marks

1. If, within a period of five years following the date of the completion of the registration procedure, the proprietor has not put the trade mark to genuine use in the Member State in connection with the goods or services in respect of which it is registered, or if such use has been suspended during an uninterrupted period of five years, the trade mark shall be subject to the sanctions provided for in this Directive, unless there are proper reasons for non-use.

(a) where a provision in force prior to that date attached sanctions to non-use of a trade mark during an uninterrupted period, the relevant period of five years mentioned in the first subparagraph of paragraph 1 shall be deemed to have begun to run at the same time as any period of nonuse which is already running at that date;

(b) where there was no use provision in force prior to that date, the periods of five years mentioned in the first subparagraph of paragraph 1 shall be deemed to run from that date at the earliest.

The following shall also constitute use within the meaning of the first subparagraph:

(a) use of the trade mark in a form differing in elements which do not alter the distinctive character of the mark in the form in which it was registered;

(b) affixing of the trade mark to goods or to the packaging thereof in the Member State concerned solely for export purposes.

2.   Use of the trade mark with the consent of the proprietor or by any person who has authority to use a collective mark or a guarantee or certification mark shall be deemed to constitute use by the proprietor.

3.   In relation to trade marks registered before the date of entry into force in the Member State concerned of the provisions necessary to comply with Directive 89/104/EEC:

(a) where a provision in force prior to that date attached sanctions to non-use of a trade mark during an uninterrupted period, the relevant period of five years mentioned in the first subparagraph of paragraph 1 shall be deemed to have begun to run at the same time as any period of non use which is already running at that date;

(b) where there was no use provision in force prior to that date, the periods of five years mentioned in the first subparagraph of paragraph 1 shall be deemed to run from that date at the earliest.

Article 11

Sanctions for non-use of a trade mark in legal or administrative proceedings

1.   A trade mark may not be declared invalid on the ground that there is an earlier conflicting trade mark if the latter does not fulfil the requirements of use set out in Article 10(1) and (2), or in Article 10(3), as the case may be.

2.   Any Member State may provide that registration of a trade mark may not be refused on the ground that there is an earlier conflicting trade mark if the latter does not fulfil the requirements of use set out in Article 10(1) and (2) or in Article 10(3), as the case may be.

3.   Without prejudice to the application of Article 12, where a counter-claim for revocation is made, any Member State may provide that a trade mark may not be successfully invoked in infringement proceedings if it is established as a result of a plea that the trade mark could be revoked pursuant to Article 12(1).

4.   If the earlier trade mark has been used in relation to part only of the goods or services for which it is registered, it shall, for purposes of applying paragraphs 1, 2 and 3, be deemed to be registered in respect only of that part of the goods or services.

Article 12

Grounds for revocation

1.   A trade mark shall be liable to revocation if, within acontinuous period of five years, it has not been put to genuine use in the Member State in connection with the goods or services in respect of which it is registered, and there are no proper reasons for non-use.

However, no person may claim that the proprietor's rights in a trade mark should be revoked where, during the interval between expiry of the five-year period and filing of the application for revocation, genuine use of the trade mark has been started or resumed.

The commencement or resumption of use within a period of three months preceding the filing of the application for revocation which began at the earliest on expiry of the continuous period of five years of non-use shall be disregarded where preparations for the commencement or resumption occur only after the proprietor becomes aware that the application for revocation may be filed.

2.   Without prejudice to paragraph 1, a trade mark shall be liable to revocation if, after the date on which it was registered:

  (a)   in consequence of acts or inactivity of the proprietor, it has become the common name in the trade for a product or service in respect of which it is registered;

  (b)   in consequence of the use made of it by the proprietor of the trade mark or with his consent in respect of the goods or services for which it is registered, it is liable to mislead the public, particularly as to the nature, quality or geographical origin of those goods or services.

Article 13

Grounds for refusal or revocation or invalidity relating to only some of the goods or services

Where grounds for refusal of registration or for revocation or invalidity of a trade mark exist in respect of only some of the goods or services for which that trade mark has been applied for or registered, refusal of registration or revocation or invalidity shall cover those goods or services only.

Article 14

Establishment a posteriori of invalidity or revocation of a trade mark

Where the seniority of an earlier trade mark which has been surrendered or allowed to lapse is claimed for a Community trade mark, the invalidity or revocation of the earlier trade mark may be established *a posteriori*.

Article 15

Special provisions in respect of collective marks, guarantee marks and certification marks

1. Without prejudice to Article 4, Member States whose laws authorise the registration of collective marks or of guarantee or certification marks may provide that such marks shall not be registered, or shall be revoked or declared invalid, on grounds additional to those specified in Articles 3 and 12 where the function of those marks so requires.

2. By way of derogation from Article 3(1)(c), Member States may provide that signs or indications which may serve, in trade, to designate the geographical origin of the goods or services may constitute collective, guarantee or certification marks. Such a mark does not entitle the proprietor to prohibit a third party from using in the course of trade such signs or indications, provided he uses them in accordance with honest practices in industrial or commercial matters; in particular, such a mark may not be invoked against a third party who is entitled to use a geographical name.

Article 16

Communication

Member States shall communicate to the Commission the text of the main provisions of national law adopted in the field governed by this Directive.

Article 17

Repeal

Directive 89/104/EEC, as amended by the Decision listed in Annex I, Part A, is repealed, without prejudice to the obligations of the Member States relating to the time limit for transposition into national law of that Directive, set out in Annex I, Part B.

References to the repealed Directive shall be construed as references to this Directive and shall be read in accordance with the correlation table in Annex II.

Article 18

Entry into force

This Directive shall enter into force on the 20th day following its publication in the Official Journal of the European Union.

Article 19

Addressees

This Directive is addressed to the Member States.

Done at Strasbourg, 22 October 2008.

Appendix VI

Council Regulation (EC) No 510/2006 of 20 March 2006 on the Protection of geographical indications and Designations of Origin for Agricultural Products and Foodstuffs

THE COUNCIL OF THE EUROPEAN UNION,

Having regard to the Treaty establishing the European Community, and in particular Article 37 thereof,

Having regard to the proposal from the Commission, Having regard to the opinion of the European Parliament,[1]

Whereas:

(1) The production, manufacture and distribution of agricultural products and foodstuffs play an important role in the Community economy.

(2) The diversification of agricultural production should be encouraged so as to achieve a better balance between supply and demand on the markets. The promotion of products having certain characteristics can be of considerable benefit to the rural economy, particularly in less-favoured or remote areas, by improving the incomes of farmers and by retaining the rural population in these areas.

(3) A constantly increasing number of consumers attach greater importance to the quality of foodstuffs in their diet rather than to quantity. This quest for specific products generates a demand for agricultural products or foodstuffs with an identifiable geographical origin.

(4) In view of the wide variety of products marketed and the abundance of product information provided, the consumer should, in order to be able to make the best choices, be given clear and succinct information regarding the product origin.

(5) The labelling of agricultural products and foodstuffs is subject to the general rules laid down in Directive 2000/13/EC of the European Parliament and of the Council of 20 March 2000 on the approximation of the laws of the Member States relating to the labelling, presentation and advertising of foodstuffs.[2] In view of their specific nature, additional special provisions should be adopted for agricultural products and foodstuffs from a defined geographical area requiring producers to use the appropriate Community symbols or indications on packaging. The use of such symbols or indications should be made obligatory in the case of Community designations, on the one hand, to make this category of products and the guarantees attached to them better known to consumers and, on the other, to permit easier identification of these products on the market so as to facilitate checks. A

---

[1] Not yet published in the Official Journal.

[2] OJ L 109, 6.5.2000, p. 29. Directive as last amended by Directive 2003/89/ EC (OJ L 308, 25.11.2003, p. 15).

reasonable length of time should be allowed for operators to adjust to this obligation.

(6) Provision should be made for a Community approach to designations of origin and geographical indications. A framework of Community rules on a system of protection permits the development of geographical indications and designations of origin since, by providing a more uniform approach, such a framework ensures fair competition between the producers of products bearing such indications and enhances the credibility of the products in the consumer's eyes.

(7) The rules provided for should apply without interfering with existing Community legislation on wines and spirit drinks.

(8) The scope of this Regulation should be limited to certain agricultural products and foodstuffs for which a link exists between product or foodstuff characteristics and geographical origin. However, its scope could be enlarged to encompass other agricultural products or foodstuffs.

(9) In the light of existing practices, two different types of geographical description should be defined, namely protected geographical indications and protected designations of origin.

(10) An agricultural product or foodstuff bearing such a description should meet certain conditions set out in a specification.

(11) To qualify for protection in the Member States, geographical indications and designations of origin should be registered at Community level. Entry in a register should also provide information to those involved in the trade and to consumers. To ensure that Community-registered names meet the conditions laid down by this Regulation, applications should be examined by the national authorities of the Member State concerned, subject to compliance with minimum common provisions, including a national objection procedure. The Commission should subsequently be involved in a scrutiny procedure to ensure that applications satisfy the conditions laid down by this Regulation and that the approach is uniform across the Member States.

(12) The Agreement on Trade-Related Aspects of Intellectual Property Rights (TRIPS Agreement 1994, contained in Annex 1C to the Agreement establishing the World Trade Organisation) contains detailed provisions on the availability, acquisition, scope, maintenance and enforcement of intellectual property rights.

(13) The protection afforded by this Regulation, subject to registration, should be open to the geographical indications of third countries where these are protected in their country of origin.

(14) The registration procedure should enable any natural or legal person having a legitimate interest in a Member State or a third country to exercise their rights by notifying their objections.

(15) There should be procedures to permit amendment of specifications on request of groups having a legitimate interest, after registration, in the light of technological progress and cancellation of the geographical indication or designation of origin for an agricultural product or foodstuff, in particular if that product or foodstuff

ceases to conform to the specification on the basis of which the geographical indication or designation of origin was granted.

(16) The designations of origin and geographical indications protected on Community territory should be subject to a monitoring system of official controls, based on a system of checks in line with Regulation (EC) No 882/2004 of the European Parliament and of the Council of 29 April 2004 on official controls performed to ensure the verification of compliance with feed and food law, animal health and animal welfare rules (1), including a system of checks to ensure compliance with the specification of the agricultural products and foodstuffs concerned.

(17) Member States should be authorised to charge a fee to cover the costs incurred.

(18) The measures necessary for the implementation of this Regulation should be adopted in accordance with Council Decision 1999/468/EC of 28 June 1999 laying down the procedures for the exercise of implementing powers conferred on the Commission.[3]

(19) The names already registered under Council Regulation (EEC) No 2081/92 of 14 July 1992 on the protection of geographical indications and designations of origin for agricultural products and foodstuffs[4] on the date of entry into force of this Regulation should continue to be protected under this Regulation and automatically included in the register. Provision should also be made for transitional measures applicable to registration applications received by the Commission before the entry into force of this Regulation.

(20) In the interests of clarity and transparency, Regulation (EEC) No 2081/92 should be repealed and replaced by this Regulation,

HAS ADOPTED THIS REGULATION:

Article 1

Scope

1. This Regulation lays down the rules on the protection of designations of origin and geographical indications for agricultural products intended for human consumption listed in Annex I to the Treaty and for foodstuffs listed in Annex I to this Regulation and for agricultural products listed in Annex II to this Regulation.

It shall not, however, apply to wine-sector products, except wine vinegars, or to spirit drinks. This paragraph shall be without prejudice to the application of Council Regulation (EC) No 1493/1999 of 17 May 1999 on the common organisation of the market in wine.[5]

Annexes I and II to this Regulation may be amended in accordance with the procedure referred to in Article 15(2).

---

[3] OJ L 184, 17.7.1999, p. 23.

[4] OJ L 208, 24.7.1992, p. 1. Regulation as last amended by Regulation (EC) No 806/2003 (OJ L 122, 16.5.2003, p. 1).

[5] OJ L 179, 14.7.1999, p. 1.

2.   This Regulation shall apply without prejudice to other specific Community provisions.

3.   Directive 98/34/EC of the European Parliament and of the Council of 22 June 1998 laying down a procedure for the provision of information in the field of technical standards and regulations and of rules on Information Society Services[6] shall not apply to the designations of origin and geographical indications covered by this Regulation.

Article 2

Designation of origin and geographical indication

1.   For the purpose of this Regulation:

(a)   'designation of origin' means the name of a region, a specific place or, in exceptional cases, a country, used to describe an agricultural product or a foodstuff:

—   originating in that region, specific place or country,

—   the quality or characteristics of which are essentially or exclusively due to a particular geographical environment with its inherent natural and human factors, and

—   the production, processing and preparation of which take place in the defined geographical area;

(b)   'geographical indication' means the name of a region, a specific place or, in exceptional cases, a country, used to describe an agricultural product or a foodstuff:

—   originating in that region, specific place or country, and

—   which possesses a specific quality, reputation or other characteristics attributable to that geographical origin, and

—   the production and/or processing and/or preparation of which take place in the defined geographical area.

2.   Traditional geographical or non-geographical names designating an agricultural product or a foodstuff which fulfil the conditions referred to in paragraph 1 shall also be considered as designations of origin or geographical indications.

3.   Notwithstanding paragraph 1(a), certain geographical designations shall be treated as designations of origin where the raw materials for the products concerned come from a geographical area larger than, or different from, the processing area, provided that:

(a)   the production area of the raw materials is defined;

(b)   special conditions for the production of the raw materials exist; and

(c)   there are inspection arrangements to ensure that the conditions referred to in point (b) are adhered to.

---

6.   OJ L 204, 21.7.1998, p. 37.

The designations in question must have been recognised as designations of origin in the country of origin before 1 May 2004.

Article 3

Generic nature, conflicts with names of plant varieties, animal breeds, homonyms and trademarks

1. Names that have become generic may not be registered.

    For the purposes of this Regulation, a 'name that has become generic' means the name of an agricultural product or a foodstuff which, although it relates to the place or the region where this product or foodstuff was originally produced or marketed, has become the common name of an agricultural product or a foodstuff in the Community.

    To establish whether or not a name has become generic, account shall be taken of all factors, in particular:

    (a) the existing situation in the Member States and in areas of consumption;

    (b) the relevant national or Community laws.

2. A name may not be registered as a designation of origin or a geographical indication where it conflicts with the name of a plant variety or an animal breed and as a result is likely to mislead the consumer as to the true origin of the product.

3. A name wholly or partially homonymous with that of a name already registered under this Regulation shall be registered with due regard for local and traditional usage and the actual risk of confusion. In particular:

    (a) a homonymous name which misleads the consumer into believing that products come from another territory shall not be registered even if the name is accurate as far as the actual territory, region or place of origin of the agricultural products or foodstuffs in question is concerned;

    (b) the use of a registered homonymous name shall be subject to there being a sufficient distinction in practice between the homonym registered subsequently and the name already on the register, having regard to the need to treat the producers concerned in an equitable manner and not to mislead the consumer.

4. A designation of origin or geographical indication shall not be registered where, in the light of a trademark's reputation and renown and the length of time it has been used, registration is liable to mislead the consumer as to the true identity of the product.

Article 4

Product specification

1. To be eligible for a protected designation of origin (PDO) or a protected geographical indication (PGI), an agricultural product or foodstuff shall comply with a product specification.

2.   The product specification shall include at least:

(a) the name of the agricultural product or foodstuff comprising the designation of origin or the geographical indication;

(b) a description of the agricultural product or foodstuff, including the raw materials, if appropriate, and principal physical, chemical, microbiological or organoleptic characteristics of the product or the foodstuff;

(c) the definition of the geographical area and, where appropriate, details indicating compliance with the requirements of Article 2(3);

(d) evidence that the agricultural product or the foodstuff originates in the defined geographical area referred to in Article 2(1)(a) or (b), as the case may be;

(e) a description of the method of obtaining the agricultural product or foodstuff and, if appropriate, the authentic and unvarying local methods as well as information concerning packaging, if the applicant group within the meaning of Article 5(1) so determines and gives reasons why the packaging must take place in the defined geographical area to safeguard quality or ensure the origin or ensure control;

(f) details bearing out the following:

    (i) the link between the quality or characteristics of the agricultural product or foodstuff and the geographical environment referred to in Article 2(1)(a) or, as the case may be,

    (ii) the link between a specific quality, the reputation or other characteristic of the agricultural product or foodstuff and the geographical origin referred to in Article 2(1)(b);

(g) the name and address of the authorities or bodies verifying compliance with the provisions of the specification and their specific tasks;

(h) any specific labelling rule for the agricultural product or foodstuff in question;

Article 5

Application for registration

1.   Only a group shall be entitled to apply for registration.

For the purposes of this Regulation, 'group' means any association, irrespective of its legal form or composition, of producers or processors working with the same agricultural product or foodstuff. Other interested parties may participate in the group. A natural or legal person may be treated as a group in accordance with the detailed rules referred to in Article 16(c).

In the case of a name designating a trans-border geographical area or a traditional name connected to a trans-border geographical area, several groups may lodge a joint application in accordance with the detailed rules referred to in Article 16(d).

2.   A group may lodge a registration application only for the agricultural products or foodstuffs which it produces or obtains.

3.   The application for registration shall include at least:

(a)   the name and address of the applicant group;

(b)   the specification provided for in Article 4;

(c)   a single document setting out the following:

(i)   the main points of the specification: the name, a description of the product, including, where appropriate, specific rules concerning packaging and labelling, and a concise definition of the geographical area,

(ii)   a description of the link between the product and the geographical environment or geographical origin referred to in Article 2(1)(a) or (b), as the case may be, including, where appropriate, the specific elements of the product description or production method justifying the link.

4.   Where the registration application relates to a geographical area in a given Member State, the application shall be addressed to that Member State.

The Member State shall scrutinise the application by appropriate means to check that it is justified and meets the conditions of this Regulation.

5.   As part of the scrutiny referred to in the second subparagraph of paragraph 4, the Member State shall initiate a national objection procedure ensuring adequate publication of the application and providing for a reasonable period within which any natural or legal person having a legitimate interest and established or resident on its territory may lodge an objection to the application.

The Member State shall consider the admissibility of objections received in the light of the criteria referred to in the first subparagraph of Article 7(3).

If the Member State considers that the requirements of this Regulation are met, it shall take a favourable decision and forward to the Commission the documents referred to in paragraph 7 for a final decision. If not, the Member State shall decide to reject the application.

The Member State shall ensure that its favourable decision is made public and that any natural or legal person having a legitimate interest has means of appeal.

The Member State shall ensure that the version of the specification on which its favourable decision is based is published, and assure electronic access to the specification.

6.   The Member State may, on a transitional basis only, grant protection under this Regulation at national level to the name, and, where appropriate, an adjustment period, with effect from the date on which the application is lodged with the Commission.

The adjustment period provided for in the first subparagraph may be granted only on condition that the undertakings concerned have legally marketed the products in question, using the names concerned continuously for at least the past five years and have made that point in the national objection procedure referred to in the first subparagraph of paragraph 5.

Such transitional national protection shall cease on the date on which a decision on registration under this Regulation is taken.

The consequences of such transitional national protection, where a name is not registered under this Regulation, shall be the sole responsibility of the Member State concerned.

The measures taken by Member States under the first subparagraph shall produce effects at national level only, and they shall have no effect on intra-Community or international trade.

7.   In respect of any favourable decision as referred to in the third subparagraph of paragraph 5, the Member State concerned shall forward to the Commission:

(a)   the name and address of the applicant group;

(b)   the single document referred to in paragraph 3(c);

(c)   a declaration by the Member State that it considers that the application lodged by the group and qualifying for the favourable decision meets the conditions of this Regulation and the provisions adopted for its implementation;

(d)   the publication reference of the specification referred to in the fifth subparagraph of paragraph 5.

8.   Member States shall introduce the laws, regulations or administrative provisions necessary to comply with paragraphs 4 to 7 not later than 31 March 2007.

Bulgaria and Romania shall introduce the said laws, regulations or administrative provisions not later than one year after the date of accession.

9.   Where the registration application concerns a geographical area situated in a third country, it shall comprise the elements provided for in paragraph 3 and also proof that the name in question is protected in its country of origin.

The application shall be sent to the Commission, either directly or via the authorities of the third country concerned.

10.   The documents referred to in this Article sent to the Commission shall be in one of the official languages of the institutions of the European Union or accompanied by a certified translation in one of those languages.

11.   In the case of Bulgaria and Romania, the national protection of geographical indications and designations of origin existing on the date of their accession may continue for twelve months from the date of their accession.

Where an application for registration under this Regulation is forwarded to the Commission by the end of the abovementioned period such protection shall cease on the date on which a decision on registration under this Regulation is taken.

The consequences of such national protection, where a name is not registered under this Regulation, shall be the sole responsibility of the Member State concerned.

Article 6

Scrutiny by the Commission

1. The Commission shall scrutinise by appropriate means the application received pursuant to Article 5 to check that it is justified and meets the conditions laid down in this Regulation. This scrutiny should not exceed a period of 12 months.

    The Commission shall, each month, make public the list of names for which registration applications have been submitted to it, as well as their date of submission to the Commission.

2. Where, based on the scrutiny carried out pursuant to the first subparagraph of paragraph 1, the Commission considers that the conditions laid down in this Regulation are met, it shall publish in the Official Journal of the European Union the single document and the reference to the publication of the specification referred to in the fifth subparagraph of Article 5(5).

    Where this is not the case, the Commission shall decide, to reject the application, following the procedure referred to in Article 15(2).

Article 7

Objection/decision on registration

1. Within six months from the date of publication in the Official Journal of the European Union provided for in the first subparagraph of Article 6(2), any Member State or third country may object to the registration proposed, by lodging a duly substantiated statement with the Commission.

2. Any natural or legal person having a legitimate interest, established or resident in a Member State other than that applying for the registration or in a third country, may also object to the proposed registration by lodging a duly substantiated statement.

    In the case of natural or legal persons established or resident in a Member State, such statement shall be lodged with that Member State within a time-limit permitting an objection in accordance with paragraph 1.

    In the case of natural or legal persons established or resident in a third country, such statement shall be lodged with the Commission, either directly or via the authorities of the third country concerned, within the time limit-set in paragraph 1.

3. Statements of objection shall be admissible only if they are received by the Commission within the time-limit set in paragraph 1 and if they:

    (a) show non-compliance with the conditions referred to in Article 2; or

    (b) show that the registration of the name proposed would be contrary to paragraphs 2, 3 and 4 of Article 3; or

    (c) show that the registration of the name proposed would jeopardise the existence of an entirely or partly identical name or of a trademark or the existence of products which have been legally on the market for at least five years preceding the date of the publication provided for in Article 6(2); or

967

(d) give details from which it can be concluded that the name for which registration is requested is generic within the meaning of Article 3 (1).

The Commission shall check the admissibility of objections.

The criteria referred to in points (b), (c) and (d) of the first subparagraph shall be evaluated in relation to the territory of the Community, which in the case of intellectual property rights refers only to the territory or territories where the said rights are protected.

4.   If the Commission receives no admissible objection under paragraph 3, it shall register the name.

The registration shall be published in the Official Journal of the European Union.

5.   If an objection is admissible under paragraph 3, the Commission shall invite the interested parties to engage in appropriate consultations.

If the interested parties reach an agreement within six months, they shall notify the Commission of all the factors which enabled that agreement to be reached, including the applicant's and the objector's opinions. If the details published in accordance with Article 6(2) have not been amended or have been amended in only a minor way, to be defined in accordance with Article 16(h), the Commission shall proceed in accordance with paragraph 4 of this Article. The Commission shall otherwise repeat the scrutiny referred to in Article 6(1).

If no agreement is reached, the Commission shall take a decision in accordance with the procedure referred to in Article 15(2), having regard to fair and traditional usage and the actual likelihood of confusion.

The decision shall be published in the Official Journal of the European Union.

6.   The Commission shall maintain updated a register of protected designations of origin and protected geographical indications.

7.   The documents referred to in this Article sent to the Commission shall be drafted in an official language of the institutions of the European Union or accompanied by a certified translation into one of those languages.

Article 8

Names, indications and symbols

1.   A name registered under this Regulation may be used by any operator marketing agricultural product or foodstuffs conforming to the corresponding specification.

2.   In the case of the agricultural products and foodstuffs originating in the Community marketed under a name registered in accordance with this Regulation, the indications 'protected designation of origin' and 'protected geographical indication' or the Community symbols associated with them shall appear on the labelling.

3.   In the case of agricultural products and foodstuffs originating in third countries marketed under a name registered in accordance with this Regulation the indications referred to in paragraph 2 and the Community symbols associated with them may equally appear on the labelling.

Article 9

Approval of changes to specifications

1. A group satisfying the conditions of Article 5(1) and (2) and having a legitimate interest may apply for approval of an amendment to a specification, in particular to take account of developments in scientific and technical knowledge or to redefine the geographical area referred to in Article 4(2)(c).

   Applications shall describe and give reasons for the amendments requested.

2. Where the amendment involves one or more amendments to the single document, the amendment application shall be covered by the procedure laid down in Articles 5, 6 and 7. However, if the proposed amendments are only minor, the Commission shall decide whether to approve the application without following the procedure laid down in Article 6(2) and Article 7 and in the case of approval shall proceed to publication of the elements referred to in Article 6(2).

3. Where the amendment does not involve any change to the single document, the following rules shall apply:

   (i) where the geographical area is in a given Member State, that Member State shall express its position on the approval of the amendment and, if it is in favour, shall publish the amended specification and inform the Commission of the amendments approved and the reasons for them;

   (ii) where the geographical area is in a third country, the Commission shall determine whether to approve the proposed amendment.

4. Where the amendment concerns a temporary change in the specification resulting from the imposition of obligatory sanitary or phytosanitary measures by the public authorities, the procedures set out in paragraph 3 shall apply.

Article 10

Official controls

1. Member States shall designate the competent authority or authorities responsible for controls in respect of the obligations established by this Regulation in conformity with Regulation (EC) No 882/2004.

2. Member States shall ensure that any operator complying with this Regulation is entitled to be covered by a system of official controls.

3. The Commission shall make public the name and address of the authorities and bodies referred to in paragraph 1 or in Article 11 and update it periodically.

Article 11

Verification of compliance with specifications

1. In respect of geographical indications and designations of origin relating to a geographical area within the Community, verification of compliance with the specifications, before placing the product on the market, shall be ensured by:

   — one or more competent authorities referred to in Article 10 and/or

— one or more control bodies within the meaning of Article 2 of Regulation (EC) No 882/2004 operating as a product certification body.

The costs of such verification of compliance with the specifications shall be borne by the operators subject to those controls.

2.   In respect of the geographical indications and designations of origin relating to a geographical area in a third country, verification of compliance with the specifications, before placing the product on the market, shall be ensured by:

— one or more public authorities designated by the third country and/or

— one or more product certification bodies.

3.   The product certification bodies referred to in paragraphs 1 and 2 shall comply with and, from 1 May 2010 be accredited in accordance with European standard EN 45011 or ISO/IEC Guide 65 (General requirements for bodies operating product certification systems).

4.   Where, the authorities referred to in paragraphs 1 and 2, have chosen to verify compliance with the specifications, they shall offer adequate guarantees of objectivity and impartiality, and have at their disposal the qualified staff and resources necessary to carry out their functions.

Article 12

Cancellation

1.   Where the Commission, in accordance with the detailed rules referred to in Article 16(k), takes the view that compliance with the conditions of the specification for an agricultural product or foodstuff covered by a protected name is no longer ensured, it shall initiate the procedure referred to in Article 15(2) for the cancellation of the registration, which shall be published in the Official Journal of the European Union.

2.   Any natural or legal person having a legitimate interest, may request cancellation of the registration, giving reasons for the request.

The procedure provided for in Articles 5, 6 and 7 shall apply mutatis mutandis.

Article 13

Protection

1.   Registered names shall be protected against:

(a) any direct or indirect commercial use of a registered name in respect of products not covered by the registration in so far as those products are comparable to the products registered under that name or in so far as using the name exploits the reputation of the protected name;

(b) any misuse, imitation or evocation, even if the true origin of the product is indicated or if the protected name is translated or accompanied by an expression such as 'style', 'type', 'method', 'as produced in', 'imitation' or similar;

(c) any other false or misleading indication as to the provenance, origin, nature or essential qualities of the product, on the inner or outer packaging, advertising material or documents relating to the product concerned, and the packing of the product in a container liable to convey a false impression as to its origin;

(d) any other practice liable to mislead the consumer as to the true origin of the product.

Where a registered name on the appropriate agricultural product or foodstuff shall not be considered to be contrary to points (a) or (b) in the first subparagraph.

2. Protected names may not become generic.

3. In the case of names for which registration is applied for under Article 5, provision may be made for a transitional period of up to five years under Article 7(5), solely where a statement of objection has been declared admissible on the grounds that registration of the proposed name would jeopardise the existence of an entirely or partly identical name or the existence of products which have been legally on the market for at least five years preceding the date of the publication provided for in Article 6(2).

A transitional period may also be set for undertakings established in the Member State or third country in which the geographical area is located, provided that the undertakings concerned have legally marketed the products in question, using the names concerned continuously for at least five years preceding the date of the publication referred to in Article 6(2) and have noted that point in the national objection procedure referred to in the first and second subparagraphs of Article 5(5) or the Community objection procedure referred to in Article 7(2). The combined total of the transitional period referred to in this subparagraph and the adjustment period referred to in Article 5 (6) may not exceed five years. Where the adjustment period referred to in Article 5(6) exceeds five years, no transitional period shall be granted.

4. Without prejudice to Article 14, the Commission may decide to allow, under the procedure provided for in Article 15(2), the coexistence of a registered name and an unregistered name designating a place in a Member State or in a third country where that name is identical to the registered name, provided that all the following conditions are met:

(a) the identical unregistered name has been in legal use consistently and equitably for at least 25 years before 24 July 1993;

(b) it is shown that the purpose of its use has not at any time been to profit from the reputation of the registered name and that the consumer has not been nor could be misled as to the true origin of the product;

(c) the problem resulting from the identical names was raised before registration of the name.

The registered name and the identical unregistered name concerned may co-exist for a period not exceeding a maximum of 15 years, after which the unregistered name shall cease to be used.

Use of the unregistered geographical name concerned shall be authorised only where the country of origin is clearly and visibly indicated on the label.

Article 14

Relations between trademarks, designations of origin and geographical indications

1. Where a designation of origin or a geographical indication is registered under this Regulation, the application for registration of a trademark corresponding to one of the situations referred to in Article 13 and relating to the same class of product shall be refused if the application for registration of the trademark is submitted after the date of submission of the registration application to the Commission.

   Trademarks registered in breach of the first subparagraph shall be invalidated.

2. With due regard to Community law, a trademark the use of which corresponds to one of the situations referred to in Article 13 which has been applied for, registered, or established by use, if that possibility is provided for by the legislation concerned, in good faith within the territory of the Community, before either the date of protection of the designation of origin or geographical indication in the country of origin or before 1 January 1996, may continue to be used notwithstanding the registration of a designation of origin or geographical indication, provided that no grounds for its invalidity or revocation exist as specified by First Council Directive 89/104/EEC of 21 December 1988 to approximate the laws of the Member States relating to trade marks[7] or Council Regulation (EC) No 40/94 of 20 December 1993 on the Community trade mark.[8]

Article 15

Committee procedure

1. The Commission shall be assisted by the Standing Committee on Protected Geographical Indications and Protected Designations of Origin.

2. Where reference is made to this paragraph, Articles 5 and 7 of Decision 1999/468/EC shall apply.

   The period laid down in Article 5(6) of Decision 1999/468/EC shall be set at three months.

3. The Committee shall adopt its own Rules of Procedure. Article 16 Implementing rules

   In accordance with the procedure referred to in Article 15(2), detailed rules shall be adopted for the implementation of this Regulation. They shall cover in particular:

   (a) a list of the raw materials referred to in Article 2(3);

   (b) the information that must be included in the product specification referred to in Article 4(2);

---

[7] OJ L 40, 11.2.1989, p. 1.
[8] OJ L 11, 14.1.1994, p. 1.

(c)   the conditions under which a natural or legal person may be treated as a group;

(d)   the submission of a registration application for a name designating a trans-border geographical area as referred to in the third subparagraph of Article 5(1);

(e)   the content and method of transmission to the Commission of the documents referred to in Articles 5(7) and (9);

(f)   objections referred to in Article 7, including rules on appropriate consultations between the interested parties;

(g)   the indications and symbols referred to in Article 8;

(h)   a definition of minor amendments as referred to in the second subparagraph of Article 7(5) and in Article 9(2), bearing in mind that a minor amendment cannot relate to the essential characteristics of the product or alter the link;

(i)   the register of designations of origin and geographical indications provided for in Article 7(6);

(j)   the conditions for checking compliance with the product specifications;

(k)   the conditions for cancellation of registration.

Article 17

Transitional provisions

1.   The names that, on the date of entry into force of this Regulation, are listed in the Annex of Commission Regulation (EC) No 1107/96[9] and those listed in the Annex of Commission on Regulation (EC) No 2400/96[10] shall be automatically entered in the register referred to in Article 7(6) of this Regulation. The corresponding specifications shall be deemed to be the specifications referred to in Article 4(1). Any specific transitional provisions associated with such registrations shall continue to apply.

2.   In respect of pending applications, statements and requests received by the Commission before the date of entry into force of this Regulation:

(a)   the procedures in Article 5 shall not apply, without prejudice to Article 13(3); and

---

[9].   Commission Regulation (EC) No 1107/96 of 12 June 1996 on the registration of geographical indications and designations of origin under the procedure laid down in Article 17 of Council Regulation (EEC) No 2081/92 (OJ L 148, 21.6.1996, p. 1). Regulation as last amended by Regulation (EC) No 704/2005 (OJ L 118, 5.5.2005, p. 14).

[10].   Commission Regulation (EC) No 2400/96 of 17 December 1996 on the entry of certain names in the 'Register of protected designation of origin and protected geographical indications' provided for in Council Regulation (EEC) No 2081/92 on the protection of geographical indications and designations of origin for agricultural products and foodstuffs (OJ L 327, 18.12.1996, p. 11). Regulation as last amended by Regulation (EC) No 417/2006 (OJ L 72, 11.3.2006, p. 8).

(b) the summary of the specification drawn up in conformity with Commission Regulation (EC) No 383/2004[11] (3) shall replace the single document referred to in Article 5(3)(c).

3. The Commission may adopt, if necessary, other transitional provisions in accordance with the procedure referred to in Article 15(2).

Article 18

Fees

Member States may charge a fee to cover their costs, including those incurred in scrutinising applications for registration, statements of objection, applications for amendments and requests for cancellations under this Regulation.

Article 19

Repeal

Regulation (EEC) No 2081/92 is hereby repealed.

References made to the repealed Regulation shall be construed as being made to this Regulation and should be read in accordance with the correlation table in Annex III.

Article 20

Entry into force

This Regulation shall enter into force on the day of its publication in the Official Journal of the European Union.

However, Article 8(2) shall apply with effect from 1 May 2009, without prejudice to products already placed on the market before that date.

This Regulation shall be binding in its entirety and directly applicable in all Member States.

ANNEX I

Foodstuffs referred to in Article 1(1)

— beers,

— beverages made from plant extracts,

— bread, pastry, cakes, confectionery and other baker's wares,

— natural gums and resins,

— mustard paste,

— pasta,

— salt.

[11.] Commission Regulation (EC) No 383/2004 of 1 March 2004 laying down detailed rules for applying Council Regulation (EEC) No 2081/92 as regards the summary of the main points of the product specifications (OJ L 64, 2.3.2004, p. 16).

ANNEX II

Agricultural products referred to in Article 1(1)

— hay,

— essential oils,

— cork,

— cochineal (raw product of animal origin),

— flowers and ornamental plants,

— wool,

— wicker,

— scutched flax,

— cotton.

ANNEX III

Correlation Table

Regulation (EEC) No 2081/92	This Regulation
Article 1	Article 1
Article 2(1)	—
Article 2(2)	Article 2(1)
Article 2(3)	Article 2(2)
Article 2(4)	Article 2(3), first subparagraph
Article 2(5)	—
Article 2(6)	Article 2(3), second subparagraph
Article 2(7)	—
First, second and third subparagraphs of Article 3(1)	First, second and third subparagraphs of Article 3(1)
Article 3(1), fourth subparagraph	—
Article 3(2)	Article 3(2)
Article 3(3)	—
Article 4	Article 4
Article 5(1), (2) and (3)	Article 5(1), (2) and (3)
Article 5(4)	Article 5(4), first subparagraph
Article 5(5), first subparagraph	Article 5(4), second subparagraph
—	Article 5(5)
Article 5(5), second subparagraph	Article 5(6), first subparagraph
—	Article 5(6), second subparagraph
Article 5(5), third subparagraph	Article 5(6), third subparagraph

Regulation (EEC) No 2081/92	This Regulation
Article 5(5), fourth and fifth subparagraphs	Article 5(6), fourth and fifth subparagraphs
Article 5(5) sixth, seventh and eighth subparagraphs	—
—	Article 5(7)
Article 5(6)	Article 5(8)
—	Article 5(9) and (10)
Article 6(1), first subparagraph	Article 6(1), first subparagraph
Article 6(1), second subparagraph	—
Article 6(1), third subparagraph	Article 6(1), second subparagraph
Article 6(2)	Article 6(2), first subparagraph
Article 6(3) and (4)	Article 7(4)
Article 6(5), first subparagraph	Article 6(2), second subparagraph
Article 6(5), second subparagraph	—
Article 6(6), first subparagraph	—
Article 6(6), second subparagraph	Article 3(3)
Article 7(1)	Article 7(1)
Article 7(2)	—
Article 7(3)	Article 7(2), first subparagraph
—	Article 7(2), second and third subparagraph
Article 7(4)	Article 7(3)
Article 7(5)	Article 7(5)
—	Article 7(6) and (7)
—	Article 8(1)
Article 8	Article 8(2)
—	Article 8(3)
Article 9, first subparagraph	Article 9(1)
Article 9, second and third subparagraphs	Article 9(2)
—	Article 9(3) and (4)
—	Article 10(1)
Article 10(1)	—
Article 10(2)	Article 11(1)
—	Article 11(2)
Article 10(3)	Article 11(3) and (4)
Article 10(4)	—

Regulation (EEC) No 2081/92	This Regulation
Article 10(5)	Article 10(3)
Article 10(6)	Article 10(2)
Article 10(7)	Article 11(1), second subparagraph
Article 11(1) to (3)	—
Article 11(4)	Article 12(1)
Article 11a(a)	Article 12(2)
Article 11a(b)	—
Articles 12 to 12d	—
Article 13(1)	Article 13(1)
Article 13(3)	Article 13(2)
Article 13(4)	Article 13(3), first subparagraph
—	Article 13(3), second subparagraph
Article 13(5)	Article 13(4)
Article 14(1) and (2)	Article 14(1) and (2)
Article 14(3)	Article 3(4)
Article 15	Article 15
Article 16	Article 16
—	Articles 17 to 19
Article 18	Article 20
Annex I	Annex I
Annex II	Annex II

Appendix VII

Council Directive 2001/84/EC of the European Parliament and of the Council of 27 September 2001 on the resale right for the benefit of the author of an original work of art

THE EUROPEAN PARLIAMENT AND THE COUNCIL OF THE EUROPEAN UNION,

Having regard to the Treaty establishing the European Community, and in particular Article 95 thereof,

Having regard to the proposal from the Commission(1),

Having regard to the opinion of the Economic and Social Committee(2),

Acting in accordance with the procedure laid down in Article 251 of the Treaty(3), and in the light of the joint text approved by the Conciliation Committee on 6 June 2001,

Whereas:

(1) In the field of copyright, the resale right is an unassignable and inalienable right, enjoyed by the author of an original work of graphic or plastic art, to an economic interest in successive sales of the work concerned.

(2) The resale right is a right of a productive character which enables the author/artist to receive consideration for successive transfers of the work. The subject-matter of the resale right is the physical work, namely the medium in which the protected work is incorporated.

(3) The resale right is intended to ensure that authors of graphic and plastic works of art share in the economic success of their original works of art. It helps to redress the balance between the economic situation of authors of graphic and plastic works of art and that of other creators who benefit from successive exploitations of their works.

(4) The resale right forms an integral part of copyright and is an essential prerogative for authors. The imposition of such a right in all Member States meets the need for providing creators with an adequate and standard level of protection.

(5) Under Article 151(4) of the Treaty the Community is to take cultural aspects into account in its action under other provisions of the Treaty.

(6) The Berne Convention for the Protection of Literary and Artistic Works provides that the resale right is available only if legislation in the country to which the author belongs so permits. The right is therefore optional and subject to the rule of reciprocity. It follows from the case-law of the Court of Justice of the European Communities on the application of the principle of non-discrimination laid down in Article 12 of the Treaty, as shown in the judgment of 20 October 1993 in Joined Cases C-92/92 and C-326/92 Phil Collins and Others(4), that domestic provisions containing reciprocity clauses cannot be relied upon in order to deny nationals of other Member States rights conferred on national authors. The application of such clauses in the Community context runs

counter to the principle of equal treatment resulting from the prohibition of any discrimination on grounds of nationality.

(7) The process of internationalisation of the Community market in modern and contemporary art, which is now being speeded up by the effects of the new economy, in a regulatory context in which few States outside the EU recognise the resale right, makes it essential for the European Community, in the external sphere, to open negotiations with a view to making Article 14b of the Berne Convention compulsory.

(8) The fact that this international market exists, combined with the lack of a resale right in several Member States and the current disparity as regards national systems which recognise that right, make it essential to lay down transitional provisions as regards both entry into force and the substantive regulation of the right, which will preserve the competitiveness of the European market.

(9) The resale right is currently provided for by the domestic legislation of a majority of Member States. Such laws, where they exist, display certain differences, notably as regards the works covered, those entitled to receive royalties, the rate applied, the transactions subject to payment of a royalty, and the basis on which these are calculated. The application or non-application of such a right has a significant impact on the competitive environment within the internal market, since the existence or absence of an obligation to pay on the basis of the resale right is an element which must be taken into account by each individual wishing to sell a work of art. This right is therefore a factor which contributes to the creation of distortions of competition as well as displacement of sales within the Community.

(10) Such disparities with regard to the existence of the resale right and its application by the Member States have a direct negative impact on the proper functioning of the internal market in works of art as provided for by Article 14 of the Treaty. In such a situation Article 95 of the Treaty constitutes the appropriate legal basis.

(11) The objectives of the Community as set out in the Treaty include laying the foundations of an ever closer union among the peoples of Europe, promoting closer relations between the Member States belonging to the Community, and ensuring their economic and social progress by common action to eliminate the barriers which divide Europe. To that end the Treaty provides for the establishment of an internal market which presupposes the abolition of obstacles to the free movement of goods, freedom to provide services and freedom of establishment, and for the introduction of a system ensuring that competition in the common market is not distorted. Harmonisation of Member States' laws on the resale right contributes to the attainment of these objectives.

(12) The Sixth Council Directive (77/388/EEC) of 17 May 1977 on the harmonisation of the laws of the Member States relating to turnover taxes – common system of value added tax: uniform basis of assessment(5), progressively introduces a Community system of taxation applicable inter alia to works of art. Measures confined to the tax field are not sufficient to guarantee the harmonious functioning of the art market. This objective cannot be attained without harmonisation in the field of the resale right.

(13) Existing differences between laws should be eliminated where they have a distorting effect on the functioning of the internal market, and the emergence of any new differences of that kind should be prevented. There is no need to eliminate, or prevent

the emergence of, differences which cannot be expected to affect the functioning of the internal market.

(14) A precondition of the proper functioning of the internal market is the existence of conditions of competition which are not distorted. The existence of differences between national provisions on the resale right creates distortions of competition and displacement of sales within the Community and leads to unequal treatment between artists depending on where their works are sold. The issue under consideration has therefore transnational aspects which cannot be satisfactorily regulated by action by Member States. A lack of Community action would conflict with the requirement of the Treaty to correct distortions of competition and unequal treatment.

(15) In view of the scale of divergences between national provisions it is therefore necessary to adopt harmonising measures to deal with disparities between the laws of the Member States in areas where such disparities are liable to create or maintain distorted conditions of competition. It is not however necessary to harmonise every provision of the Member States' laws on the resale right and, in order to leave as much scope for national decision as possible, it is sufficient to limit the harmonisation exercise to those domestic provisions that have the most direct impact on the functioning of the internal market.

(16) This Directive complies therefore, in its entirety, with the principles of subsidiarity and proportionality as laid down in Article 5 of the Treaty.

(17) Pursuant to Council Directive 93/98/EEC of 29 October 1993 harmonising the term of protection of copyright and certain related rights(6), the term of copyright runs for 70 years after the author's death. The same period should be laid down for the resale right. Consequently, only the originals of works of modern and contemporary art may fall within the scope of the resale right. However, in order to allow the legal systems of Member States which do not, at the time of the adoption of this Directive, apply a resale right for the benefit of artists to incorporate this right into their respective legal systems and, moreover, to enable the economic operators in those Member States to adapt gradually to the aforementioned right whilst maintaining their economic viability, the Member States concerned should be allowed a limited transitional period during which they may choose not to apply the resale right for the benefit of those entitled under the artist after his death.

(18) The scope of the resale right should be extended to all acts of resale, with the exception of those effected directly between persons acting in their private capacity without the participation of an art market professional. This right should not extend to acts of resale by persons acting in their private capacity to museums which are not for profit and which are open to the public. With regard to the particular situation of art galleries which acquire works directly from the author, Member States should be allowed the option of exempting from the resale right acts of resale of those works which take place within three years of that acquisition. The interests of the artist should also be taken into account by limiting this exemption to such acts of resale where the resale price does not exceed €10,000.

(19) It should be made clear that the harmonisation brought about by this Directive does not apply to original manuscripts of writers and composers.

(20) Effective rules should be laid down based on experience already gained at national level with the resale right. It is appropriate to calculate the royalty as a percentage of the sale price and not of the increase in value of works whose original value has increased.

(21) The categories of works of art subject to the resale right should be harmonised.

(22) The non-application of royalties below the minimum threshold may help to avoid disproportionately high collection and administration costs compared with the profit for the artist. However, in accordance with the principle of subsidiarity, the Member States should be allowed to establish national thresholds lower than the Community threshold, so as to promote the interests of new artists. Given the small amounts involved, this derogation is not likely to have a significant effect on the proper functioning of the internal market.

(23) The rates set by the different Member States for the application of the resale right vary considerably at present. The effective functioning of the internal market in works of modern and contemporary art requires the fixing of uniform rates to the widest possible extent.

(24) It is desirable to establish, with the intention of reconciling the various interests involved in the market for original works of art, a system consisting of a tapering scale of rates for several price bands. It is important to reduce the risk of sales relocating and of the circumvention of the Community rules on the resale right.

(25) The person by whom the royalty is payable should, in principle, be the seller. Member States should be given the option to provide for derogations from this principle in respect of liability for payment. The seller is the person or undertaking on whose behalf the sale is concluded.

(26) Provision should be made for the possibility of periodic adjustment of the threshold and rates. To this end, it is appropriate to entrust to the Commission the task of drawing up periodic reports on the actual application of the resale right in the Member States and on the impact on the art market in the Community and, where appropriate, of making proposals relating to the amendment of this Directive.

(27) The persons entitled to receive royalties must be specified, due regard being had to the principle of subsidiarity. It is not appropriate to take action through this Directive in relation to Member States' laws of succession. However, those entitled under the author must be able to benefit fully from the resale right after his death, at least following the expiry of the transitional period referred to above.

(28) The Member States are responsible for regulating the exercise of the resale right, particularly with regard to the way this is managed. In this respect management by a collecting society is one possibility. Member States should ensure that collecting societies operate in a transparent and efficient manner. Member States must also ensure that amounts intended for authors who are nationals of other Member States are in fact collected and distributed. This Directive is without prejudice to arrangements in Member States for collection and distribution.

(29) Enjoyment of the resale right should be restricted to Community nationals as well as to foreign authors whose countries afford such protection to authors who are nationals of Member States. A Member State should have the option of extending enjoyment of this right to foreign authors who have their habitual residence in that Member State.

(30) Appropriate procedures for monitoring transactions should be introduced so as to ensure by practical means that the resale right is effectively applied by Member States. This implies also a right on the part of the author or his authorised representative to obtain any necessary information from the natural or legal person liable for payment of royalties. Member States which provide for collective management of the resale right may also provide that the bodies responsible for that collective management should alone be entitled to obtain information,

HAVE ADOPTED THIS DIRECTIVE:

Chapter I
Scope

Article 1

Subject matter of the resale right

1. Member States shall provide, for the benefit of the author of an original work of art, a resale right, to be defined as an inalienable right, which cannot be waived, even in advance, to receive a royalty based on the sale price obtained for any resale of the work, subsequent to the first transfer of the work by the author.

2. The right referred to in paragraph 1 shall apply to all acts of resale involving as sellers, buyers or intermediaries art market professionals, such as salesrooms, art galleries and, in general, any dealers in works of art.

3. Member States may provide that the right referred to in paragraph 1 shall not apply to acts of resale where the seller has acquired the work directly from the author less than three years before that resale and where the resale price does not exceed €10,000.

4. The royalty shall be payable by the seller. Member States may provide that one of the natural or legal persons referred to in paragraph 2 other than the seller shall alone be liable or shall share liability with the seller for payment of the royalty.

Article 2

Works of art to which the resale right relates

1. For the purposes of this Directive, "original work of art" means works of graphic or plastic art such as pictures, collages, paintings, drawings, engravings, prints, lithographs, sculptures, tapestries, ceramics, glassware and photographs, provided they are made by the artist himself or are copies considered to be original works of art.

2. Copies of works of art covered by this Directive, which have been made in limited numbers by the artist himself or under his authority, shall be considered to be original works of art for the purposes of this Directive. Such copies will normally have been numbered, signed or otherwise duly authorised by the artist.

Chapter II
Particular Provisions

Article 3

Threshold

1. It shall be for the Member States to set a minimum sale price from which the sales referred to in Article 1 shall be subject to resale right.

2. This minimum sale price may not under any circumstances exceed EUR 3000.

Article 4

Rates

1. The royalty provided for in Article 1 shall be set at the following rates:

    (a) 4 % for the portion of the sale price up to €50,000;

    (b) 3 % for the portion of the sale price from €50,000.01 to €200,000;

    (c) 1 % for the portion of the sale price from €200,000,01 to €350,000;

    (d) 0.5 % for the portion of the sale price from €350,000,01 to €500,000;

    (e) 0.25 % for the portion of the sale price exceeding €500,000.
    However, the total amount of the royalty may not exceed €12,500.

2. By way of derogation from paragraph 1, Member States may apply a rate of 5 % for the portion of the sale price referred to in paragraph 1(a).

3. If the minimum sale price set should be lower than €3,000, the Member State shall also determine the rate applicable to the portion of the sale price up to €3,000; this rate may not be lower than 4 %.

Article 5

Calculation basis

The sale prices referred to in Articles 3 and 4 are net of tax.

Article 6

Persons entitled to receive royalties

1. The royalty provided for under Article 1 shall be payable to the author of the work and, subject to Article 8(2), after his death to those entitled under him/her.

2. Member States may provide for compulsory or optional collective management of the royalty provided for under Article 1.

Article 7

Third-country nationals entitled to receive royalties

1. Member States shall provide that authors who are nationals of third countries and, subject to Article 8(2), their successors in title shall enjoy the resale right in accordance with this Directive and the legislation of the Member State concerned only if legislation in the country of which the author or his/her successor in title is

a national permits resale right protection in that country for authors from the Member States and their successors in title.

2. On the basis of information provided by the Member States, the Commission shall publish as soon as possible an indicative list of those third countries which fulfil the condition set out in paragraph 1. This list shall be kept up to date.

3. Any Member State may treat authors who are not nationals of a Member State but who have their habitual residence in that Member State in the same way as its own nationals for the purpose of resale right protection.

Article 8

Term of protection of the resale right

1. The term of protection of the resale right shall correspond to that laid down in Article 1 of Directive 93/98/EEC.

2. By way of derogation from paragraph 1, those Member States which do not apply the resale right on (the entry into force date referred to in Article 13), shall not be required, for a period expiring not later than 1 January 2010, to apply the resale right for the benefit of those entitled under the artist after his/her death.

3. A Member State to which paragraph 2 applies may have up to two more years, if necessary to enable the economic operators in that Member State to adapt gradually to the resale right system while maintaining their economic viability, before it is required to apply the resale right for the benefit of those entitled under the artist after his/her death. At least 12 months before the end of the period referred to in paragraph 2, the Member State concerned shall inform the Commission giving its reasons, so that the Commission can give an opinion, after appropriate consultations, within three months following the receipt of such information. If the Member State does not follow the opinion of the Commission, it shall within one month inform the Commission and justify its decision. The notification and justification of the Member State and the opinion of the Commission shall be published in the Official Journal of the European Communities and forwarded to the European Parliament.

4. In the event of the successful conclusion, within the periods referred to in Article 8(2) and (3), of international negotiations aimed at extending the resale right at international level, the Commission shall submit appropriate proposals.

Article 9

Right to obtain information

The Member States shall provide that for a period of three years after the resale, the persons entitled under Article 6 may require from any art market professional mentioned in Article 1(2) to furnish any information that may be necessary in order to secure payment of royalties in respect of the resale.

Chapter III
Final Provisions

Article 10

Application in time

This Directive shall apply in respect of all original works of art as defined in Article 2 which, on 1 January 2006, are still protected by the legislation of the Member States in the field of copyright or meet the criteria for protection under the provisions of this Directive at that date.

Article 11

Revision clause

1. The Commission shall submit to the European Parliament, the Council and the Economic and Social Committee not later than 1 January 2009 and every four years thereafter a report on the implementation and the effect of this Directive, paying particular attention to the competitiveness of the market in modern and contemporary art in the Community, especially as regards the position of the Community in relation to relevant markets that do not apply the resale right and the fostering of artistic creativity and the management procedures in the Member States. It shall examine in particular its impact on the internal market and the effect of the introduction of the resale right in those Member States that did not apply the right in national law prior to the entry into force of this Directive. Where appropriate, the Commission shall submit proposals for adapting the minimum threshold and the rates of royalty to take account of changes in the sector, proposals relating to the maximum amount laid down in Article 4(1) and any other proposal it may deem necessary in order to enhance the effectiveness of this Directive.

2. A Contact Committee is hereby established. It shall be composed of representatives of the competent authorities of the Member States. It shall be chaired by a representative of the Commission and shall meet either on the initiative of the Chairman or at the request of the delegation of a Member State.

3. The task of the Committee shall be as follows:

    –   to organise consultations on all questions deriving from application of this Directive,

    –   to facilitate the exchange of information between the Commission and the Member States on relevant developments in the art market in the Community.

Article 12

Implementation

1. Member States shall bring into force the laws, regulations and administrative provisions necessary to comply with this Directive before 1 January 2006. They shall forthwith inform the Commission thereof.

When Member States adopt these measures, they shall contain a reference to this Directive or shall be accompanied by such reference on the occasion of their official publication. The methods of making such a reference shall be laid down by the Member States.

2.   Member States shall communicate to the Commission the provisions of national law which they adopt in the field covered by this Directive.

Article 13

Entry into force

This Directive shall enter into force on the day of its publication in the Official Journal of the European Communities.

Article 14

Addressees

This Directive is addressed to the Member States.

Done at Brussels, 27 September 2001.

Appendix VIII

WIPO Copyright Treaty

(adopted in Geneva on December 20, 1996)

Preamble

The Contracting Parties,

Desiring to develop and maintain the protection of the rights of authors in their literary and artistic works in a manner as effective and uniform as possible,

Recognizing the need to introduce new international rules and clarify the interpretation of certain existing rules in order to provide adequate solutions to the questions raised by new economic, social, cultural and technological developments,

Recognizing the profound impact of the development and convergence of information and communication technologies on the creation and use of literary and artistic works,

Emphasizing the outstanding significance of copyright protection as an incentive for literary and artistic creation,

Recognizing the need to maintain a balance between the rights of authors and the larger public interest, particularly education, research and access to information, as reflected in the Berne Convention,

Have agreed as follows:

Article 1

Relation to the Berne Convention

(1) This Treaty is a special agreement within the meaning of Article 20 of the Berne Convention for the Protection of Literary and Artistic Works, as regards Contracting Parties that are countries of the Union established by that Convention. This Treaty shall not have any connection with treaties other than the Berne Convention, nor shall it prejudice any rights and obligations under any other treaties.

(2) Nothing in this Treaty shall derogate from existing obligations that Contracting Parties have to each other under the Berne Convention for the Protection of Literary and Artistic Works.

(3) Hereinafter, "Berne Convention" shall refer to the Paris Act of July 24, 1971, of the Berne Convention for the Protection of Literary and Artistic Works.

(4) Contracting Parties shall comply with Articles 1 to 21 and the Appendix of the Berne Convention.[1]

Article 2

Scope of Copyright Protection

Copyright protection extends to expressions and not to ideas, procedures, methods of operation or mathematical concepts as such.

Article 3

Application of Articles 2 to 6 of the Berne Convention

Contracting Parties shall apply *mutatis mutandis* the provisions of Articles 2 to 6 of the Berne Convention in respect of the protection provided for in this Treaty.[2]

Article 4

Computer Programs

Computer programs are protected as literary works within the meaning of Article 2 of the Berne Convention. Such protection applies to computer programs, whatever may be the mode or form of their expression.[3]

Article 5

Compilations of Data (Databases)

Compilations of data or other material, in any form, which by reason of the selection or arrangement of their contents constitute intellectual creations, are protected as such. This protection does not extend to the data or the material itself and is without prejudice to any copyright subsisting in the data or material contained in the compilation.[4]

Article 6

Right of Distribution

(1) Authors of literary and artistic works shall enjoy the exclusive right of authorizing the making available to the public of the original and copies of their works through sale or other transfer of ownership.

(2) Nothing in this Treaty shall affect the freedom of Contracting Parties to determine the conditions, if any, under which the exhaustion of the right in paragraph (1) applies after the first sale or other transfer of ownership of the original or a copy of the work with the authorization of the author.[5]

Article 7

Right of Rental

(1) Authors of

   (i) computer programs;

   (ii) cinematographic works; and

   (iii) works embodied in phonograms, as determined in the national law of Contracting Parties,

   shall enjoy the exclusive right of authorizing commercial rental to the public of the originals or copies of their works.

(2)   Paragraph (1) shall not apply

   (i)   in the case of computer programs, where the program itself is not the essential object of the rental; and

   (ii)   in the case of cinematographic works, unless such commercial rental has led to widespread copying of such works materially impairing the exclusive right of reproduction.

(3)   Notwithstanding the provisions of paragraph (1), a Contracting Party that, on April 15, 1994, had and continues to have in force a system of equitable remuneration of authors for the rental of copies of their works embodied in phonograms may maintain that system provided that the commercial rental of works embodied in phonograms is not giving rise to the material impairment of the exclusive right of reproduction of authors.[6,7]

Article 8

Right of Communication to the Public

Without prejudice to the provisions of Articles 11(1)(ii), 11*bis*(1)(i) and (ii), 11*ter*(1)(ii), 14(1)(ii) and 14*bis*(1) of the Berne Convention, authors of literary and artistic works shall enjoy the exclusive right of authorizing any communication to the public of their works, by wire or wireless means, including the making available to the public of their works in such a way that members of the public may access these works from a place and at a time individually chosen by them.[8]

Article 9

Duration of the Protection of Photographic Works

In respect of photographic works, the Contracting Parties shall not apply the provisions of Article 7(4) of the Berne Convention.

Article 10

Limitations and Exceptions

(1)   Contracting Parties may, in their national legislation, provide for limitations of or exceptions to the rights granted to authors of literary and artistic works under this Treaty in certain special cases that do not conflict with a normal exploitation of the work and do not unreasonably prejudice the legitimate interests of the author.

(2)   Contracting Parties shall, when applying the Berne Convention, confine any limitations of or exceptions to rights provided for therein to certain special cases that do not conflict with a normal exploitation of the work and do not unreasonably prejudice the legitimate interests of the author.[9]

Article 11

Obligations concerning Technological Measures

Contracting Parties shall provide adequate legal protection and effective legal remedies against the circumvention of effective technological measures that are used by authors in connection with the exercise of their rights under this Treaty or the Berne Convention and that restrict acts, in respect of their works, which are not authorized by the authors concerned or permitted by law.

Article 12

Obligations concerning Rights Management Information

(1) Contracting Parties shall provide adequate and effective legal remedies against any person knowingly performing any of the following acts knowing, or with respect to civil remedies having reasonable grounds to know, that it will induce, enable, facilitate or conceal an infringement of any right covered by this Treaty or the Berne Convention:

    (i) to remove or alter any electronic rights management information without authority;

    (ii) to distribute, import for distribution, broadcast or communicate to the public, without authority, works or copies of works knowing that electronic rights management information has been removed or altered without authority.

(2) As used in this Article, "rights management information" means information which identifies the work, the author of the work, the owner of any right in the work, or information about the terms and conditions of use of the work, and any numbers or codes that represent such information, when any of these items of information is attached to a copy of a work or appears in connection with the communication of a work to the public.[10]

Article 13

Application in Time

Contracting Parties shall apply the provisions of Article 18 of the Berne Convention to all protection provided for in this Treaty.

Article 14

Provisions on Enforcement of Rights

(1) Contracting Parties undertake to adopt, in accordance with their legal systems, the measures necessary to ensure the application of this Treaty.

(2) Contracting Parties shall ensure that enforcement procedures are available under their law so as to permit effective action against any act of infringement of rights covered by this Treaty, including expeditious remedies to prevent infringements and remedies which constitute a deterrent to further infringements.

Article 15

Assembly

(1) (a) The Contracting Parties shall have an Assembly.

    (b) Each Contracting Party shall be represented by one delegate who may be assisted by alternate delegates, advisors and experts.

    (c) The expenses of each delegation shall be borne by the Contracting Party that has appointed the delegation. The Assembly may ask the World Intellectual

Property Organization (hereinafter referred to as "WIPO") to grant financial assistance to facilitate the participation of delegations of Contracting Parties that are regarded as developing countries in conformity with the established practice of the General Assembly of the United Nations or that are countries in transition to a market economy.

(2) (a) The Assembly shall deal with matters concerning the maintenance and development of this Treaty and the application and operation of this Treaty.

(b) The Assembly shall perform the function allocated to it under Article 17(2) in respect of the admission of certain intergovernmental organizations to become party to this Treaty.

(c) The Assembly shall decide the convocation of any diplomatic conference for the revision of this Treaty and give the necessary instructions to the Director General of WIPO for the preparation of such diplomatic conference.

(3) (a) Each Contracting Party that is a State shall have one vote and shall vote only in its own name.

(b) Any Contracting Party that is an intergovernmental organization may participate in the vote, in place of its Member States, with a number of votes equal to the number of its Member States which are party to this Treaty. No such intergovernmental organization shall participate in the vote if any one of its Member States exercises its right to vote and *vice versa*.

(4) The Assembly shall meet in ordinary session once every two years upon convocation by the Director General of WIPO.

(5) The Assembly shall establish its own rules of procedure, including the convocation of extraordinary sessions, the requirements of a quorum and, subject to the provisions of this Treaty, the required majority for various kinds of decisions.

Article 16

International Bureau

The International Bureau of WIPO shall perform the administrative tasks concerning the Treaty.

Article 17

Eligibility for Becoming Party to the Treaty

(1) Any Member State of WIPO may become party to this Treaty.

(2) The Assembly may decide to admit any intergovernmental organization to become party to this Treaty which declares that it is competent in respect of, and has its own legislation binding on all its Member States on, matters covered by this Treaty and that it has been duly authorized, in accordance with its internal procedures, to become party to this Treaty.

(3) The European Community, having made the declaration referred to in the preceding paragraph in the Diplomatic Conference that has adopted this Treaty, may become party to this Treaty.

Article 18

Rights and Obligations under the Treaty

Subject to any specific provisions to the contrary in this Treaty, each Contracting Party shall enjoy all of the rights and assume all of the obligations under this Treaty.

Article 19

Signature of the Treaty

This Treaty shall be open for signature until December 31, 1997, by any Member State of WIPO and by the European Community.

Article 20

Entry into Force of the Treaty

This Treaty shall enter into force three months after 30 instruments of ratification or accession by States have been deposited with the Director General of WIPO.

Article 21

Effective Date of Becoming Party to the Treaty

This Treaty shall bind:

(i)   the 30 States referred to in Article 20, from the date on which this Treaty has entered into force;

(ii) each other State, from the expiration of three months from the date on which the State has deposited its instrument with the Director General of WIPO;

(iii) the European Community, from the expiration of three months after the deposit of its instrument of ratification or accession if such instrument has been deposited after the entry into force of this Treaty according to Article 20, or, three months after the entry into force of this Treaty if such instrument has been deposited before the entry into force of this Treaty;

(iv) any other intergovernmental organization that is admitted to become party to this Treaty, from the expiration of three months after the deposit of its instrument of accession.

Article 22

No Reservations to the Treaty

No reservation to this Treaty shall be admitted.

Article 23

Denunciation of the Treaty

This Treaty may be denounced by any Contracting Party by notification addressed to the Director General of WIPO. Any denunciation shall take effect one year from the date on which the Director General of WIPO received the notification.

Article 24

Languages of the Treaty

(1)   This Treaty is signed in a single original in English, Arabic, Chinese, French, Russian and Spanish languages, the versions in all these languages being equally authentic.

(2)   An official text in any language other than those referred to in paragraph (1) shall be established by the Director General of WIPO on the request of an interested party, after consultation with all the interested parties. For the purposes of this paragraph, "interested party" means any Member State of WIPO whose official language, or one of whose official languages, is involved and the European Community, and any other intergovernmental organization that may become party to this Treaty, if one of its official languages is involved.

Article 25

Depositary

The Director General of WIPO is the depositary of this Treaty.

* Entry into force: March 6, 2002.

Source: International Bureau of WIPO.

Note: The agreed statements of the Diplomatic Conference that adopted the Treaty (WIPO Diplomatic Conference on Certain Copyright and Neighboring Rights Questions) concerning certain provisions of the WCT are reproduced in endnotes below.

1 Agreed statement concerning Article 1(4):

The reproduction right, as set out in Article 9 of the Berne Convention, and the exceptions permitted thereunder, fully apply in the digital environment, in particular to the use of works in digital form. It is understood that the storage of a protected work in digital form in an electronic medium constitutes a reproduction within the meaning of Article 9 of the Berne Convention.

2 Agreed statement concerning Article 3:

It is understood that, in applying Article 3 of this Treaty, the expression "country of the Union" in Articles 2 to 6 of the Berne Convention will be read as if it were a reference to a Contracting Party to this Treaty, in the application of those Berne Articles in respect of protection provided for in this Treaty. It is also understood that the expression "country outside the Union" in those Articles in the Berne Convention will, in the same circumstances, be read as if it were a reference to a country that is not a Contracting

Party to this Treaty, and that "this Convention" in Articles 2(8), 2bis(2), 3, 4 and 5 of the Berne Convention will be read as if it were a reference to the Berne Convention and this Treaty. Finally, it is understood that a reference in Articles 3 to 6 of the Berne Convention to a "national of one of the countries of the Union" will, when these Articles are applied to this Treaty, mean, in regard to an intergovernmental organization that is a Contracting Party to this Treaty, a national of one of the countries that is member of that organization.

3 Agreed statement concerning Article 4:

The scope of protection for computer programs under Article 4 of this Treaty, read with Article 2, is consistent with Article 2 of the Berne Convention and on a par with the relevant provisions of the TRIPS Agreement.

4 Agreed statement concerning Article 5:

The scope of protection for compilations of data (databases) under Article 5 of this Treaty, read with Article 2, is consistent with Article 2 of the Berne Convention and on a par with the relevant provisions of the TRIPS Agreement.

5 Agreed statement concerning Articles 6 and 7:

As used in these Articles, the expressions "copies" and "original and copies," being subject to the right of distribution and the right of rental under the said Articles, refer exclusively to fixed copies that can be put into circulation as tangible objects.

6 Agreed statement concerning Articles 6 and 7:

As used in these Articles, the expressions "copies" and "original and copies," being subject to the right of distribution and the right of rental under the said Articles, refer exclusively to fixed copies that can be put into circulation as tangible objects.

7 Agreed statement concerning Article 7:

It is understood that the obligation under Article 7(1) does not require a Contracting Party to provide an exclusive right of commercial rental to authors who, under that Contracting Party's law, are not granted rights in respect of phonograms. It is understood that this obligation is consistent with Article 14(4) of the TRIPS Agreement.

8 Agreed statement concerning Article 8:

It is understood that the mere provision of physical facilities for enabling or making a communication does not in itself amount to communication within the meaning of this Treaty or the Berne Convention. It is further understood that nothing in Article 8 precludes a Contracting Party from applying Article 11bis(2).

9 Agreed statement concerning Article 10:

It is understood that the provisions of Article 10 permit Contracting Parties to carry forward and appropriately extend into the digital environment limitations and exceptions in their national laws which have been considered acceptable under the Berne Convention. Similarly, these provisions should be understood to permit Contracting

Parties to devise new exceptions and limitations that are appropriate in the digital network environment.

It is also understood that Article 10(2) neither reduces nor extends the scope of applicability of the limitations and exceptions permitted by the Berne Convention.

10 Agreed statement concerning Article 12:

It is understood that the reference to "infringement of any right covered by this Treaty or the Berne Convention" includes both exclusive rights and rights of remuneration.

It is further understood that Contracting Parties will not rely on this Article to devise or implement rights management systems that would have the effect of imposing formalities which are not permitted under the Berne Convention or this Treaty, prohibiting the free movement of goods or impeding the enjoyment of rights under this Treaty.

Appendix IX

WIPO Performances and Phonograms Treaty (WPPT)

Preamble

The Contracting Parties,

Desiring to develop and maintain the protection of the rights of performers and producers of phonograms in a manner as effective and uniform as possible,

Recognizing the need to introduce new international rules in order to provide adequate solutions to the questions raised by economic, social, cultural and technological developments,

Recognizing the profound impact of the development and convergence of information and communication technologies on the production and use of performances and phonograms,

Recognizing the need to maintain a balance between the rights of performers and producers of phonograms and the larger public interest, particularly education, research and access to information,

Have agreed as follows:

Chapter I
General Provisions

Article 1

Relation to Other Conventions

(1) Nothing in this Treaty shall derogate from existing obligations that Contracting Parties have to each other under the International Convention for the Protection of Performers, Producers of Phonograms and Broadcasting Organizations done in Rome, October 26, 1961 (hereinafter the "Rome Convention").

(2) Protection granted under this Treaty shall leave intact and shall in no way affect the protection of copyright in literary and artistic works. Consequently, no provision of this Treaty may be interpreted as prejudicing such protection.[1]

(3) This Treaty shall not have any connection with, nor shall it prejudice any rights and obligations under, any other treaties.

Article 2

Definitions

For the purposes of this Treaty:

(a) "performers" are actors, singers, musicians, dancers, and other persons who act, sing, deliver, declaim, play in, interpret, or otherwise perform literary or artistic works or expressions of folklore;

999

(b) "phonogram" means the fixation of the sounds of a performance or of other sounds, or of a representation of sounds, other than in the form of a fixation incorporated in a cinematographic or other audiovisual work;[2]

(c) "fixation" means the embodiment of sounds, or of the representations thereof, from which they can be perceived, reproduced or communicated through a device;

(d) "producer of a phonogram" means the person, or the legal entity, who or which takes the initiative and has the responsibility for the first fixation of the sounds of a performance or other sounds, or the representations of sounds;

(e) "publication" of a fixed performance or a phonogram means the offering of copies of the fixed performance or the phonogram to the public, with the consent of the rightholder, and provided that copies are offered to the public in reasonable quantity;[3]

(f) "broadcasting" means the transmission by wireless means for public reception of sounds or of images and sounds or of the representations thereof; such transmission by satellite is also "broadcasting"; transmission of encrypted signals is "broadcasting" where the means for decrypting are provided to the public by the broadcasting organization or with its consent;

(g) "communication to the public" of a performance or a phonogram means the transmission to the public by any medium, otherwise than by broadcasting, of sounds of a performance or the sounds or the representations of sounds fixed in a phonogram. For the purposes of Article 15, "communication to the public" includes making the sounds or representations of sounds fixed in a phonogram audible to the public.

Article 3

Beneficiaries of Protection under this Treaty

(1) Contracting Parties shall accord the protection provided under this Treaty to the performers and producers of phonograms who are nationals of other Contracting Parties.

(2) The nationals of other Contracting Parties shall be understood to be those performers or producers of phonograms who would meet the criteria for eligibility for protection provided under the Rome Convention, were all the Contracting Parties to this Treaty Contracting States of that Convention. In respect of these criteria of eligibility, Contracting Parties shall apply the relevant definitions in Article 2 of this Treaty.[4]

(3) Any Contracting Party availing itself of the possibilities provided in Article 5(3) of the Rome Convention or, for the purposes of Article 5 of the same Convention, Article 17 thereof shall make a notification as foreseen in those provisions to the Director General of the World Intellectual Property Organization (WIPO).[5]

Article 4

National Treatment

(1) Each Contracting Party shall accord to nationals of other Contracting Parties, as defined in Article 3(2), the treatment it accords to its own nationals with regard to the exclusive rights specifically granted in this Treaty, and to the right to equitable remuneration provided for in Article 15 of this Treaty.

(2) The obligation provided for in paragraph (1) does not apply to the extent that another Contracting Party makes use of the reservations permitted by Article 15(3) of this Treaty.

Chapter II
Rights of Performers

Article 5

Moral Rights of Performers

(1) Independently of a performer's economic rights, and even after the transfer of those rights, the performer shall, as regards his live aural performances or performances fixed in phonograms, have the right to claim to be identified as the performer of his performances, except where omission is dictated by the manner of the use of the performance, and to object to any distortion, mutilation or other modification of his performances that would be prejudicial to his reputation.

(2) The rights granted to a performer in accordance with paragraph (1) shall, after his death, be maintained, at least until the expiry of the economic rights, and shall be exercisable by the persons or institutions authorized by the legislation of the Contracting Party where protection is claimed. However, those Contracting Parties whose legislation, at the moment of their ratification of or accession to this Treaty, does not provide for protection after the death of the performer of all rights set out in the preceding paragraph may provide that some of these rights will, after his death, cease to be maintained.

(3) The means of redress for safeguarding the rights granted under this Article shall be governed by the legislation of the Contracting Party where protection is claimed.

Article 6

Economic Rights of Performers in their Unfixed Performances

Performers shall enjoy the exclusive right of authorizing, as regards their performances:

(i) the broadcasting and communication to the public of their unfixed performances except where the performance is already a broadcast performance; and

(ii) the fixation of their unfixed performances.

Article 7

Right of Reproduction

Performers shall enjoy the exclusive right of authorizing the direct or indirect reproduction of their performances fixed in phonograms, in any manner or form.[6]

Article 8

Right of Distribution

(1) Performers shall enjoy the exclusive right of authorizing the making available to the public of the original and copies of their performances fixed in phonograms through sale or other transfer of ownership.

(2) Nothing in this Treaty shall affect the freedom of Contracting Parties to determine the conditions, if any, under which the exhaustion of the right in paragraph (1) applies after the first sale or other transfer of ownership of the original or a copy of the fixed performance with the authorization of the performer.[7]

Article 9

Right of Rental

(1) Performers shall enjoy the exclusive right of authorizing the commercial rental to the public of the original and copies of their performances fixed in phonograms as determined in the national law of Contracting Parties, even after distribution of them by, or pursuant to, authorization by the performer.

(2) Notwithstanding the provisions of paragraph (1), a Contracting Party that, on April 15, 1994, had and continues to have in force a system of equitable remuneration of performers for the rental of copies of their performances fixed in phonograms, may maintain that system provided that the commercial rental of phonograms is not giving rise to the material impairment of the exclusive right of reproduction of performers.[8]

Article 10

Right of Making Available of Fixed Performances

Performers shall enjoy the exclusive right of authorizing the making available to the public of their performances fixed in phonograms, by wire or wireless means, in such a way that members of the public may access them from a place and at a time individually chosen by them.

Chapter III
Rights of Producers of Phonograms

Article 11

Right of Reproduction

Producers of phonograms shall enjoy the exclusive right of authorizing the direct or indirect reproduction of their phonograms, in any manner or form.[9]

Article 12

Right of Distribution

(1) Producers of phonograms shall enjoy the exclusive right of authorizing the making available to the public of the original and copies of their phonograms through sale or other transfer of ownership.

(2) Nothing in this Treaty shall affect the freedom of Contracting Parties to determine the conditions, if any, under which the exhaustion of the right in paragraph (1) applies after the first sale or other transfer of ownership of the original or a copy of the phonogram with the authorization of the producer of the phonogram.[10]

Article 13

Right of Rental

(1) Producers of phonograms shall enjoy the exclusive right of authorizing the commercial rental to the public of the original and copies of their phonograms, even after distribution of them, by or pursuant to, authorization by the producer.

(2) Notwithstanding the provisions of paragraph (1), a Contracting Party that, on April 15, 1994, had and continues to have in force a system of equitable remuneration of producers of phonograms for the rental of copies of their phonograms, may maintain that system provided that the commercial rental of phonograms is not giving rise to the material impairment of the exclusive rights of reproduction of producers of phonograms.[11]

Article 14

Right of Making Available of Phonograms

Producers of phonograms shall enjoy the exclusive right of authorizing the making available to the public of their phonograms, by wire or wireless means, in such a way that members of the public may access them from a place and at a time individually chosen by them.

Chapter IV
Common Provisions

Article 15

Right to Remuneration for Broadcasting and Communication to the Public

(1) Performers and producers of phonograms shall enjoy the right to a single equitable remuneration for the direct or indirect use of phonograms published for commercial purposes for broadcasting or for any communication to the public.

(2) Contracting Parties may establish in their national legislation that the single equitable remuneration shall be claimed from the user by the performer or by the producer of a phonogram or by both. Contracting Parties may enact national legislation that, in the absence of an agreement between the performer and the producer of a phonogram, sets the terms according to which performers and producers of phonograms shall share the single equitable remuneration.

(3)   Any Contracting Party may, in a notification deposited with the Director General of WIPO, declare that it will apply the provisions of paragraph (1) only in respect of certain uses, or that it will limit their application in some other way, or that it will not apply these provisions at all.

(4)   For the purposes of this Article, phonograms made available to the public by wire or wireless means in such a way that members of the public may access them from a place and at a time individually chosen by them shall be considered as if they had been published for commercial purposes.[12,13]

Article 16

Limitations and Exceptions

(1)   Contracting Parties may, in their national legislation, provide for the same kinds of limitations or exceptions with regard to the protection of performers and producers of phonograms as they provide for, in their national legislation, in connection with the protection of copyright in literary and artistic works.

(2)   Contracting Parties shall confine any limitations of or exceptions to rights provided for in this Treaty to certain special cases which do not conflict with a normal exploitation of the performance or phonogram and do not unreasonably prejudice the legitimate interests of the performer or of the producer of the phonogram.[14,15]

Article 17

Term of Protection

(1)   The term of protection to be granted to performers under this Treaty shall last, at least, until the end of a period of 50 years computed from the end of the year in which the performance was fixed in a phonogram.

(2)   The term of protection to be granted to producers of phonograms under this Treaty shall last, at least, until the end of a period of 50 years computed from the end of the year in which the phonogram was published, or failing such publication within 50 years from fixation of the phonogram, 50 years from the end of the year in which the fixation was made.

Article 18

Obligations concerning Technological Measures

Contracting Parties shall provide adequate legal protection and effective legal remedies against the circumvention of effective technological measures that are used by performers or producers of phonograms in connection with the exercise of their rights under this Treaty and that restrict acts, in respect of their performances or phonograms, which are not authorized by the performers or the producers of phonograms concerned or permitted by law.

Article 19

Obligations concerning Rights Management Information

(1)   Contracting Parties shall provide adequate and effective legal remedies against any person knowingly performing any of the following acts knowing, or with respect to civil remedies having reasonable grounds to know, that it will induce, enable, facilitate or conceal an infringement of any right covered by this Treaty:

   (i)   to remove or alter any electronic rights management information without authority;

   (ii) to distribute, import for distribution, broadcast, communicate or make available to the public, without authority, performances, copies of fixed performances or phonograms knowing that electronic rights management information has been removed or altered without authority.

(2)   As used in this Article, "rights management information" means information which identifies the performer, the performance of the performer, the producer of the phonogram, the phonogram, the owner of any right in the performance or phonogram, or information about the terms and conditions of use of the performance or phonogram, and any numbers or codes that represent such information, when any of these items of information is attached to a copy of a fixed performance or a phonogram or appears in connection with the communication or making available of a fixed performance or a phonogram to the public.[16]

Article 20

Formalities

The enjoyment and exercise of the rights provided for in this Treaty shall not be subject to any formality.

Article 21

Reservations

Subject to the provisions of Article 15(3), no reservations to this Treaty shall be permitted.

Article 22

Application in Time

(1)   Contracting Parties shall apply the provisions of Article 18 of the Berne Convention, *mutatis mutandis*, to the rights of performers and producers of phonograms provided for in this Treaty.

(2)   Notwithstanding paragraph (1), a Contracting Party may limit the application of Article 5 of this Treaty to performances which occurred after the entry into force of this Treaty for that Party.

Article 23

Provisions on Enforcement of Rights

(1)   Contracting Parties undertake to adopt, in accordance with their legal systems, the measures necessary to ensure the application of this Treaty.

(2)   Contracting Parties shall ensure that enforcement procedures are available under their law so as to permit effective action against any act of infringement of rights covered by this Treaty, including expeditious remedies to prevent infringements and remedies which constitute a deterrent to further infringements.

Chapter V
Administrative and Final Clauses

Article 24

Assembly

(1)   (a)   The Contracting Parties shall have an Assembly.

    (b)   Each Contracting Party shall be represented by one delegate who may be assisted by alternate delegates, advisors and experts.

    (c)   The expenses of each delegation shall be borne by the Contracting Party that has appointed the delegation. The Assembly may ask WIPO to grant financial assistance to facilitate the participation of delegations of Contracting Parties that are regarded as developing countries in conformity with the established practice of the General Assembly of the United Nations or that are countries in transition to a market economy.

(2)   (a)   The Assembly shall deal with matters concerning the maintenance and development of this Treaty and the application and operation of this Treaty.

    (b)   The Assembly shall perform the function allocated to it under Article 26(2) in respect of the admission of certain intergovernmental organizations to become party to this Treaty.

    (c)   The Assembly shall decide the convocation of any diplomatic conference for the revision of this Treaty and give the necessary instructions to the Director General of WIPO for the preparation of such diplomatic conference.

(3)   (a)   Each Contracting Party that is a State shall have one vote and shall vote only in its own name.

    (b)   Any Contracting Party that is an intergovernmental organization may participate in the vote, in place of its Member States, with a number of votes equal to the number of its Member States which are party to this Treaty. No such intergovernmental organization shall participate in the vote if any one of its Member States exercises its right to vote and vice versa.

(4)   The Assembly shall meet in ordinary session once every two years upon convocation by the Director General of WIPO.

(5)   The Assembly shall establish its own rules of procedure, including the convocation of extraordinary sessions, the requirements of a quorum and, subject

to the provisions of this Treaty, the required majority for various kinds of decisions.

Article 25

International Bureau

The International Bureau of WIPO shall perform the administrative tasks concerning the Treaty.

Article 26

Eligibility for Becoming Party to the Treaty

(1)   Any Member State of WIPO may become party to this Treaty.

(2)   The Assembly may decide to admit any intergovernmental organization to become party to this Treaty which declares that it is competent in respect of, and has its own legislation binding on all its Member States on, matters covered by this Treaty and that it has been duly authorized, in accordance with its internal procedures, to become party to this Treaty.

(3)   The European Community, having made the declaration referred to in the preceding paragraph in the Diplomatic Conference that has adopted this Treaty, may become party to this Treaty.

Article 27

Rights and Obligations under the Treaty

Subject to any specific provisions to the contrary in this Treaty, each Contracting Party shall enjoy all of the rights and assume all of the obligations under this Treaty.

Article 28

Signature of the Treaty

This Treaty shall be open for signature until December 31, 1997, by any Member State of WIPO and by the European Community.

Article 29

Entry into Force of the Treaty

This Treaty shall enter into force three months after 30 instruments of ratification or accession by States have been deposited with the Director General of WIPO.

Article 30

Effective Date of Becoming Party to the Treaty

This Treaty shall bind

(i)   the 30 States referred to in Article 29, from the date on which this Treaty has entered into force;

(ii)   each other State from the expiration of three months from the date on which the State has deposited its instrument with the Director General of WIPO;

(iii) the European Community, from the expiration of three months after the deposit of its instrument of ratification or accession if such instrument has been deposited after the entry into force of this Treaty according to Article 29, or, three months after the entry into force of this Treaty if such instrument has been deposited before the entry into force of this Treaty;

(iv) any other intergovernmental organization that is admitted to become party to this Treaty, from the expiration of three months after the deposit of its instrument of accession.

Article 31

Denunciation of the Treaty

This Treaty may be denounced by any Contracting Party by notification addressed to the Director General of WIPO. Any denunciation shall take effect one year from the date on which the Director General of WIPO received the notification.

Article 32

Languages of the Treaty

(1) This Treaty is signed in a single original in English, Arabic, Chinese, French, Russian and Spanish languages, the versions in all these languages being equally authentic.

(2) An official text in any language other than those referred to in paragraph (1) shall be established by the Director General of WIPO on the request of an interested party, after consultation with all the interested parties. For the purposes of this paragraph, "interested party" means any Member State of WIPO whose official language, or one of whose official languages, is involved and the European Community, and any other intergovernmental organization that may become party to this Treaty, if one of its official languages is involved.

Article 33

Depositary

The Director General of WIPO is the depositary of this Treaty.

* Entry into force: May 20, 2002.

Source: International Bureau of WIPO.

Note: The agreed statements of the Diplomatic Conference that adopted the Treaty (WIPO Diplomatic Conference on Certain Copyright and Neighboring Rights Questions) concerning certain provisions of the WPPT, are reproduced in endnotes below.

1 Agreed statement concerning Article 1(2):

It is understood that Article 1(2) clarifies the relationship between rights in phonograms under this Treaty and copyright in works embodied in the phonograms. In cases where authorization is needed from both the author of a work embodied in the phonogram and a performer or producer owning rights in the phonogram, the need for the authorization of the author does not cease to exist because the authorization of the performer or producer is also required, and vice versa.

It is further understood that nothing in Article 1(2) precludes a Contracting Party from providing exclusive rights to a performer or producer of phonograms beyond those required to be provided under this Treaty.

2 Agreed statement concerning Article 2(b):

It is understood that the definition of phonogram provided in Article 2(b) does not suggest that rights in the phonogram are in any way affected through their incorporation into a cinematographic or other audiovisual work.

3 Agreed statement concerning Articles 2(e), 8, 9, 12, and 13:

As used in these Articles, the expressions "copies" and "original and copies," being subject to the right of distribution and the right of rental under the said Articles, refer exclusively to fixed copies that can be put into circulation as tangible objects.

4 Agreed statement concerning Article 3(2):

For the application of Article 3(2), it is understood that fixation means the finalization of the master tape ("bande-mère").

5 Agreed statement concerning Article 3:

It is understood that the reference in Articles 5(a) and 16(a) (iv) of the Rome Convention to "national of another Contracting State" will, when applied to this Treaty, mean, in regard to an intergovernmental organization that is a Contracting Party to this Treaty, a national of one of the countries that is a member of that organization.

6 Agreed statement concerning Articles 7, 11 and 16:

The reproduction right, as set out in Articles 7 and 11, and the exceptions permitted thereunder through Article 16, fully apply in the digital environment, in particular to the use of performances and phonograms in digital form. It is understood that the storage of a protected performance or phonogram in digital form in an electronic medium constitutes a reproduction within the meaning of these Articles.

7 Agreed statement concerning Articles 2(e), 8, 9, 12, and 13:

As used in these Articles, the expressions "copies" and "original and copies," being subject to the right of distribution and the right of rental under the said Articles, refer exclusively to fixed copies that can be put into circulation as tangible objects.

8 Agreed statement concerning Articles 2(e), 8, 9, 12, and 13:

As used in these Articles, the expressions "copies" and "original and copies," being subject to the right of distribution and the right of rental under the said Articles, refer exclusively to fixed copies that can be put into circulation as tangible objects.

9 Agreed statement concerning Articles 7, 11 and 16:

The reproduction right, as set out in Articles 7 and 11, and the exceptions permitted thereunder through Article 16, fully apply in the digital environment, in particular to the use of performances and phonograms in digital form. It is understood that the storage of a protected performance or phonogram in digital form in an electronic medium constitutes a reproduction within the meaning of these Articles.

10 Agreed statement concerning Articles 2(e), 8, 9, 12, and 13:

As used in these Articles, the expressions "copies" and "original and copies," being subject to the right of distribution and the right of rental under the said Articles, refer exclusively to fixed copies that can be put into circulation as tangible objects.

11 Agreed statement concerning Articles 2(e), 8, 9, 12, and 13:

As used in these Articles, the expressions "copies" and "original and copies," being subject to the right of distribution and the right of rental under the said Articles, refer exclusively to fixed copies that can be put into circulation as tangible objects.

12 Agreed statement concerning Article 15:

It is understood that Article 15 does not represent a complete resolution of the level of rights of broadcasting and communication to the public that should be enjoyed by performers and phonogram producers in the digital age. Delegations were unable to achieve consensus on differing proposals for aspects of exclusivity to be provided in certain circumstances or for rights to be provided without the possibility of reservations, and have therefore left the issue to future resolution.

13 Agreed statement concerning Article 15:

It is understood that Article 15 does not prevent the granting of the right conferred by this Article to performers of folklore and producers of phonograms recording folklore where such phonograms have not been published for commercial gain.

14 Agreed statement concerning Articles 7, 11 and 16:

The reproduction right, as set out in Articles 7 and 11, and the exceptions permitted thereunder through Article 16, fully apply in the digital environment, in particular to the use of performances and phonograms in digital form. It is understood that the storage of a protected performance or phonogram in digital form in an electronic medium constitutes a reproduction within the meaning of these Articles.

15 Agreed statement concerning Article 16:

The agreed statement concerning Article 10 (on Limitations and Exceptions) of the WIPO Copyright Treaty is applicable mutatis mutandis also to Article 16 (on Limitations and Exceptions) of the WIPO Performances and Phonograms Treaty. [The text of the agreed statement concerning Article 10 of the WCT reads as follows: "It is understood that the provisions of Article 10 permit Contracting Parties to carry forward and appropriately extend into the digital environment limitations and exceptions in their national laws which have been considered acceptable under the Berne Convention. Similarly, these provisions should be understood to permit Contracting Parties to devise new exceptions and limitations that are appropriate in the digital network environment.

"It is also understood that Article 10(2) neither reduces nor extends the scope of applicability of the limitations and exceptions permitted by the Berne Convention."]

16 Agreed statement concerning Article 19:

The agreed statement concerning Article 12 (on Obligations concerning Rights Management Information) of the WIPO Copyright Treaty is applicable mutatis mutandis also to Article 19 (on Obligations concerning Rights Management Information) of the WIPO Performances and Phonograms Treaty. [The text of the agreed statement concerning Article 12 of the WCT reads as follows: "It is understood that the reference to 'infringement of any right covered by this Treaty or the Berne Convention' includes both exclusive rights and rights of remuneration.

"It is further understood that Contracting Parties will not rely on this Article to devise or implement rights management systems that would have the effect of imposing formalities which are not permitted under the Berne Convention or this Treaty, prohibiting the free morvement of goods or impeding the enjoyment of rights under this Treaty."]

Index

All references are to *paragraph* numbers.